PROCEEDINGS OF THE INTERNATIONAL CONGRESS OF MATHEMATICIANS

ICM

VANCOUVER

1974

Volume 1

The Proceedings of the International Congress of Mathematicians held in Vancouver, August 21—29, 1974, is in two volumes. Volume 1 contains an account of the organization of the Congress, the list of members, the work of the Fields medalists, the expository addresses, and the addresses in Sections 1—7. Volume 2 contains the addresses in Sections 8—20 and the list of short communications.

Canadian Shared Cataloguing in Publication Data

International Congress of Mathematicians,
Vancouver, B.C., 1974.
Proceedings of the International Congress
of Mathematicians / [editor, Ralph D. James].—
1. Mathematics—Congresses. I. James, Ralph Duncan, ed.
QA1.I8 1974 510.631
ISBN 0-919558-04-6

Library of Congress Catalog Card No. 74-34533

Printed in the United States of America

International Congresses of Mathematicians

Congrès Internationaux des Mathematiciens

1897 / Zürich

1900 / Paris

1904 / Heidelberg

1908 / Rome

1912 / Cambridge, U.K.

1920 / Strasbourg

1924 / Toronto

1928 / Bologna

1932 / Zürich

1936 / Oslo

1950 / Cambridge, U.S.A.

1954 / Amsterdam

1958 / Edinburgh

1962 / Stockholm

1966 / Moscow

1970 / Nice

1974 / Vancouver

Recipients of Fields Medals

Recipients des Medailles Fields

1936 / Lars Ahlfors
Jesse Douglas

1950 / Atle Selberg
Laurent Schwartz

1954 / Kunihiko Kodaira
Jean-Pierre Serre

1958 / Klaus Roth
René Thom

1962 / Lars Hörmander
John Milnor

1966 / Michael Atiyah
Paul J. Cohen
Alexander Grothendieck
Stephen Smale

1970 / Alan Baker
Heisuke Hironaka
Sergei Novikov
John G. Thompson

1974 / Enrico Bombieri
David Mumford

Patron

His Excellency, The Right Honourable
Jules Leger, C.C., C.M.M., Governor-General of Canada
Son Excellence, le Très Honorable
Jules Leger, C.C., C.M.M., *Gouverneur Général du Canada*

Honorary Committee of Welcome

Comité Honoraire d'Accueil

The Honourable David Barrett	Premier of British Columbia *Premier Ministre de la Colombie Britannique*
The Honourable Eileen Dailly	Minister of Education of British Columbia *Ministre de l'Education de la Colombie Britannique*
His Worship Mayor Art Phillips	Mayor of Vancouver *Maire de Vancouver*
Dr. W. G. Schneider	President of National Research Council of Canada *Président du Conseil National des Recherches du Canada*
Mr. John G. Prentice	Chairman of Canada Council *Président du Conseil des Arts du Canada*
Mr. Kenneth P. Caple	Chancellor, Simon Fraser University *Chancellier, Université Simon Fraser*
Dr. Hugh Keenleyside	Chancellor, Notre Dame University *Chancellier, Université Notre Dame*
The Honourable Mr. Justice N. T. Nemetz	Chancellor, University of British Columbia *Chancellier, Université de la Colombie Britannique*
Dr. Robert Wallace	Chancellor, University of Victoria *Chancellier, Université de Victoria*

Donors

Canada, Department of the Secretary of State

Canada Council
National Science Foundation (U.S.A.)
National Research Council of Canada
Province of British Columbia

University of British Columbia
Simon Fraser University
University of Victoria

American Mathematical Society
Canadian Mathematical Congress
International Mathematical Union

British Columbia Forest Products Ltd.
House of Seagrams Ltd.
British Columbia Telephone Company
Shell Canada Ltd.
Gulf Oil Canada Ltd.
Standard Oil Co. of British Columbia Ltd.
IBM Canada Ltd.
Trans Mountain Pipe Line Company Ltd.
Imperial Oil Ltd.
Hiram Walker & Sons Ltd.
Warnock Hersey International Ltd.

Contents

Section 1—Mathematical Logic and the Foundations of Mathematics

Section 2—Algebra

Section 3—Number Theory

Section 4—Algebraic Geometry

Section 5—Algebraic Groups and Discrete Subgroups

Section 6—Geometry

Section 7—Algebraic and Differential Topology

Photo courtesy of UBC Archives

International Congress of Mathematicians, Vancouver, 197

PROFESSORS ▶
K. Chandrasekharan
and M. Sion

Photo
by John Coury

The University of British Columbia

◀ ACADEMICIAN
L. S. Pontrjagin

▼ PROFESSOR
Rolf Nevanlinna

*Photos by
John Coury*

▼ Frederick Wood Theatre

Organization of the Congress

The 1974 International Congress of Mathematicians was held in Vancouver, Canada, at the invitation of the Canadian Mathematical Congress, representing the Canadian mathematical community, and with the approval of the International Mathematical Union, representing the international mathematical community. As official hosts the Canadian Mathematical Congress assumed the responsibility for all the arrangements and appointed the Organizing Committee whose members were A. H. Cayford, Aubert Daigneault, T. E. Hull, R. D. James (Chairman), Maurice Sion (Deputy Chairman). The International Mathematical Union maintained control over the scientific program and appointed, in consultation with the Canadian Mathematical Congress, the Consultative Committee whose members were G. A. Gratzer, H. A. Heilbronn, F. E. P. Hirzebruch, L. Hörmander (Chairman), T. E. Hull, T. Husain, S. V. Jablonskiĭ, N. Jacobson, L. Schwartz.

The main organizer of the Congress at the practical level was Maurice Sion who, as Chairman of the Local Arrangements Committee, took direct responsibility for all aspects of the Congress with the exception of the list of invited speakers. The other members of the Local Arrangements Committee were G. W. Bluman, A. H. Cayford, Armin Frei, S. S. Page, J. V. Zidek. Nominally the Local Arrangements Committee was under the supervision of the Organizing Committee. In fact the composition and the responsibilities of the two committees overlapped to a considerable extent. Special subcommittees were established as the time of the opening of the Congress approached. Notable assistance on these subcommittees was given by G. W. Bluman, James Carrell, A. H. Cayford, John Coury, T. E. Cramer, Armin Frei, Virginia Green, Lorne Halabisky, Ronald Harrop, Rene Held, Erhard Luft, George Maxwell, L. A. Mysak, S. S. Page, L. G. Roberts, Dennis Sjerve, Keith Wales, J. V. Zidek, and the graduate students in the Department of Mathematics, University of British Columbia.

The publication of the Proceedings of the Congress is the responsibility of the Publications Committee whose members are Aubert Daigneault, G. A. Gratzer, H. A. Heilbronn, R. D. James (Chairman), Erhard Luft, W. O. J. Moser. The committee gratefully acknowledges the advice and assistance given by A. H. Cayford, who acted as Managing Editor, and Gordon L. Walker (Executive Director) and Margaret Reynolds (Editorial Assistant) of the American Mathematical Society.

Opening Ceremonies

The inaugural session of the Vancouver Congress took place in the Queen Elizabeth Theatre on the morning of August 21, 1974. Professor K. Chandrasekharan opened the proceedings by proposing that Professor H. S. M. Coxeter be elected President of the Congress by acclamation. Following his election, Professor Coxeter announced that a telegram would be sent to His Excellency, the Right Honourable Jules Leger, C. C., C.M.M., Governor General of Canada, Patron of the Congress. The text of the telegram is as follows:

> We much appreciate your agreeing to serve as Patron of the first meeting in Vancouver of the International Congress of Mathematicians. We regret your inability to be present and we convey our warmest wishes for a complete recovery.

Professor Coxeter then called on His Honour, the Honourable Walter S. Owen, Lieutenant Governor of British Columbia who welcomed members of the Congress to Canada and to British Columbia.

Professor Coxeter then gave his presidential address to the Congress.

> The last congress meeting in Canada was in August 1924, almost exactly fifty years ago. That was when the Fields Medals were established. Professor Fields was the president, and gave a long address on *A foundation for the theory of ideals*. He was editor of the PROCEEDINGS, which contained a nice photograph of La Vallée Poisson presenting a commemorative wreath to the University of Toronto. There was also a map of Canada showing the route of the Transcontinental Excursion, which included a stop in Vancouver. Perhaps one or two of you can still remember that occasion.
>
> In opening the 1954 congress in Amsterdam, Professor Schouten declared that "The place of mathematics in the world has changed entirely after the second war." What he meant was that, whereas formerly mathematics was studied by exceptional people, in ivory towers, the subject had become immensely popular. Even sport was affected: footballs (for soccer) began to be made to look like truncated icosahedra, electronic computers were springing up everywhere, and departments of mathematics in all universities were expanding to accommodate crowds of eager students. As soon as they graduated, the best students were urged to write original papers. The slogan was "publish or perish." Although some of the resulting work was second-rate, much of it was excellent. In fact, the accumulation of mathematical knowledge has been so rapid that, as Professor Nevanlinna remarked at Stockholm in 1962, no one of us can appreciate all its branches.
>
> Why, then, do we now come together from all the countries on earth? What do we have in common? Perhaps it is our appreciation of patterns of abstract ideas, our striv-

ing for order and truth and beauty in a world full of confusion and deceit and pollution. We understand, with William Wordsworth, that mathematics is "An independent world created out of pure intelligence" or, as Alfred North Whitehead put it, "The science of Pure Mathematics, in its modern developments, may claim to be the most original creation of the human spirit."

To see the extent of the feverish activity mentioned by Schouten and Nevanlinna, we merely have to measure the volumes of *Mathematical Reviews* on our shelves. (This is reasonable because it is usually the most important books and papers that deserve the longest reviews.) The volumes from 1941 to '51 measure 21 inches, 1952 to '62 45 inches, and 1963 to '73, 87 inches. Thus each period of eleven years produces twice as much as the preceding period. Such a proliferation of mathematical research, if continued in the future, would make the number of writers surpass the number of readers, the same discoveries would be made over and over again, and all the libraries in the world would not suffice to accommodate the mass of material.

However, such a calamity may now have been averted in an unexpected manner. The present generation has been engulfed by a wave of anti-intellectualism, with the result that most universities are short of students. Young people find that the problem of looking for a job is not facilitated by a university education. The idea of "art for art's sake" is less prevalent than it used to be, and pure mathematics is abandoned in favour of applied mathematics, statistics, or computing. Thus the editors of pure mathematical journals may soon be able to relax and get rid of their terrifying backlog of papers waiting to be assessed for possible publication.

What, then, should be our advice to a student who is wondering whether to specialize in mathematics? In view of the present scarcity of suitable jobs, I would advise him to take up some other subject, unless his love for mathematics is so intense that he finds himself doing it in almost all his spare time, even thinking about it while sleeping, or between dreams. For such a person, as Hermann Minkowski declared, "The purpose of life is to behold the truth, to understand it well, and to expound it perfectly."

Some of the mathematicians who attended the Congress in Nice are no longer with us. I think especially of Abraham Robinson, who died so tragically a few months ago, at the height of his powers. He made contributions to applied mathematics as well as to algebra and logic, on which he spoke at Nice. Since that time, his nonstandard analysis has opened up new vistas in both research and pedagogy. When I was a boy, I was introduced to calculus the "easy" way, using infinitesimals. At college I was told to put away childish things and become rigorous. How wonderful it is that the name "infinitesimal calculus" has been restored to respectability!

Before sitting down, I wish to propose a vote of thanks to the Consultative Committee, appointed by IMU to plan the academic program, namely Professors L. Hörmander, F. Hirzebruch, S. V. Jablonskiĭ, N. Jacobson, L. Schwarz, G. A. Gratzer, T. Husain, T. E. Hull, H. Heilbronn.

And now it is my pleasure to call upon Professor Chandrasekharan, the president of IMU to make an important announcement.

Professor Chandrasekharan, chairman of the Fields Medals Committee, then presented the following report:

The proposal to institute two gold medals, to be awarded "for outstanding discoveries in mathematics," at successive International Congresses of Mathematicians, was first mooted by Professor J. C. Fields, President of the International Congress of Mathematicians held in Toronto in 1924. The fund for the founding of the medals was constituted by a balance left over after financing the Toronto Congress. That proposal was accepted with thanks, after the death of Professor Fields, by the International Congress of

Mathematicians which met in Zürich in 1932. The first two such medals were presented at the Oslo Congress in 1936. After an interruption, caused by the war, two medals were presented at each of the following Congresses: at Harvard in 1950, Amsterdam 1954, Edinburgh 1958, and Stockholm 1962; while four medals were presented at the Moscow Congress in 1966, and at the Nice Congress in 1970. Each medal carries with it a cash prize of 1500 Canadian dollars. The medals are struck at the Royal Canadian Mint. It is expressly provided that there should not be attached to them, in any way, the name of any country or institution. Although, in common parlance, they are known as the Fields medals, the name of Fields does not appear on them.

Following established practice, the Executive Committee of the International Mathematical Union appointed, about two years ago, an international committee to adjudicate the award of the medals at this congress. The Committee consists of Professors J. F. Adams, K. Kodaira, L. S. Pontrjagin, B. Malgrange, A. Mostowski, J. Tate, A. Zygmund, and myself, as Chairman. May I take this opportunity to convey to all the members of the Committee the appreciation and thanks of the Union for the service they have rendered. The Committee, in turn, is indebted to many individual mathematicians whose expert knowledge provided valuable assistance.

The Committee decided, at the outset, and not without discussion, to confine the award to mathematicians under forty, as in the past. The names of some who have done brilliant work in recent years, but who are now on the wrong side of forty, have had regrettably to be omitted. Even so, more than a score of names figured on our first list. The task of reducing that number was by no means easy. There was a great deal of consultation, deliberation, and reflection. The Committee elected finally to select two names for the award. That decision was reached as unanimously as one could reasonably expect. We are aware of the very strong claims of many of those not selected, some of them so young that many Congresses will meet before they are forty. Nevertheless, we are convinced that the two selected are mathematicians of exceptional merit, whose work has advanced the development of important branches of our science. May I offer them our warmest congratulations, and invite them to come forward to receive the medals from the hands of His Honour, the Lieutenant Governor of British Columbia. They are, in alphabetical order, ENRICO BOMBIERI and DAVID MUMFORD.

His Worship, Mayor Art Phillips of Vancouver gave a short address in which he welcomed members of the Congress to the City of Vancouver.

Professor Coxeter announced that reports of the work of the Fields medalists would be given in the evening. Professor Chandrasekharan would report on the work of Enrico Bombieri and Professor J. Tate on the work of David Mumford.

The inaugural session was then declared closed.

Closing Ceremonies

The closing session of the Vancouver Congress took place in the Frederick Wood Theatre, University of British Columbia, on the afternoon of August 29, 1974. Professor H. S. M. Coxeter, President of the Congress, was in the chair.

Professor Coxeter read a message from His Excellency the Governor General of Canada expressing his thanks for the telegram sent on behalf of the Congress at the inaugural session. He then called on Professor K. Chandrasekharan, President of the International Mathematical Union, to present the following report:

It is my pleasant duty to announce that the Seventh General Assembly of the International Mathematical Union, which met at Harrison Hot Springs, from August 17 to 19, 1974, elected the following Executive Committee for a term of four years beginning January 1, 1975.

President:	Professor Deane Montgomery (Princeton, N.J., U.S.A.)
Vice Presidents:	Professor J.W.S. Cassels (Cambridge, U.K.)
	Academician M. Nicolescu (Bucharest)
Secretary:	Professor J.-L. Lions (Paris)
Members:	Professor E. Bombieri (Pisa)
	Professor M. Kneser (Göttingen)
	Professor O. Lehto (Helsinki)
	Professor M. Nagata (Kyoto)
	Academician L.S. Pontrjagin (Moscow)

I am sure you will join me in wishing the new Committee every success in the work ahead.

The main object of the International Mathematical Union is "to promote international co-operation in mathematics," and, in particular, "to support and assist the International Congress of Mathematicians." May I, on behalf of the Union, express our gratitude to the Canadian Mathematical Congress for having played host to this International Congress in such a beautiful place as Vancouver. Our warmest thanks go to the members and staff of the Organizing Committee headed by Professor R.D. James, and to the members and staff of the Local Arrangements Committee headed by Professor M. Sion, for having ministered to our needs unobtrusively and efficiently, both at Harrison Hot Springs and at Vancouver.

The Congress has brought together mathematicians from many lands, united in a friendship which stems from a common devotion to mathematics, transcending the stresses of politics, and happily free from the strains of competitive sport. We trust that the next Congress in 1978 will be a worthy successor. May I, as Chairman of the

Committee to select a site for the next Congress, request you, Mr. President, to invite Professor Rolf Nevanlinna to speak on behalf of the National Committee for mathematics in Finland.

Professor Coxeter called on Professor Nevanlinna who spoke as follows:

On behalf of the Finnish National Committee of Mathematics, I have the honor to invite you to the next International Congress of Mathematicians in Helsinki.

Finland is a small country and it may seem risky to undertake the organization of such big meeting, the more so as many previous congresses have been so splendidly run like this fine meeting in Vancouver. But we know that the International Mathematical Union will help us, and support has also been promised to us by the Finnish Government and by the University of Helsinki. Therefore we feel confident that we shall be able to organize the Congress in a satisfactory manner.

Ladies and Gentlemen: Hoping that you will accept our invitation, I welcome you all to the next International Congress of Mathematicians to be held in August 1978 in Helsinki.

The invitation was accepted by acclamation.

Speaking on behalf of the members of the Congress, Professors J. Tits and B. Szökefalvi-Nagy expressed their thanks to those who had participated in the arrangements for the Congress. Professors R. D. James and Maurice Sion replied for all concerned.

Professor Coxeter then declared the Vancouver Congress closed.

Invited Speakers

Note: An asterisk indicates that no manuscript has been received from the author for publication.

Expository Addresses

V. I. Arnold
H. Bauer
E. Bombieri
G. Debreu
P. Deligne
G. F. D. Duff
C. Fefferman
J. G. Glimm
H.-O. Kreiss
J. L. Lions
E. C. Milner
D. G. Quillen
W. Schmidt
I. M. Singer
D. P. Sullivan
J. Tits
A. G. Vitushkin

1. Mathematical Logic and the Foundations of Mathematics

K. J. Barwise
H. Friedman
A. V. Kuznetsov
Y. N. Moschovakis
S. Shelah
J. H. Silver
C. E. M. Yates

2. Algebra

H. Bass
G. M. Bergman
A. H. Clifford
D. Eisenbud
P. Gabriel*
S. M. Gersten
G. Higman*
B. Jónsson
V. Mazurov
K. M. McCrimmon
W. Scharlau
M. Sweedler
V. E. Voskresenskii

3. Number Theory

A. Frohlich
C. Hooley
A. A. Karatsuba
A. F. Lavrik*
B. Mazur
H. L. Montgomery
S. A. Stepanov

4. Algebraic Geometry

N. A'Campo
S. J. Arakelov
W. Barth
C. H. Clemens
M. Inoue
W. Schmid*
A. N. Varchenko

5. Algebraic Groups and Discrete Subgroups

A. Borel
E. Freitag
H. Garland
R. Howe
H. M. Jacquet
D. A. Kazdan*
G. Lusztig
V. P. Platonov

6. Geometry

W. J. Firey
V. L. Klee
P. McMullen
C. A. Rogers
S. S. Ryskov

7. Algebraic and Differential Topology

V. M. Bukhstaber*
T. A. Chapman
A. T. Fomenko
W. Hsiang
R. J. Milgram
T. Petrie
P. Schweitzer
W. Thurston

8. Differential Geometry and Analysis on Manifolds

J. Cheeger
B. Lawson
J. Lelong-Ferrand
G. A. Margulis
J. N. Mather
V. K. Patodi
J. Simons*

9. General Topology, Real and Functional Analysis

Z. Ciesielski
P. Enflo
V. V. Filippov
A. Hajnal
H. Herrlich
N. P. Korneichuk
B. Maurey
M. E. Rudin

10. Operator Algebras, Harmonic Analysis and Representation of Groups

A. Connes
M. Duflo
K. Knapp
J. R. Ringrose
E. Størmer
J. L. Taylor
V. S. Varadarajan
D. Zelobenko

11. Probability and Mathematical Statistics, Potential, Measure and Integration

R. V. Ambartzumian
R. M. Dudley
J. Faraut
P. J. Huber
J. Neveu
C. R. Rao
F. L. Spitzer
V. Statulevicius
J. B. Walsh
B. Walsh

12. Complex Analysis

M. M. Džrbašjan
F. Gehring
A. F. Leontiev
B. Maskit
H. L. Royden
K. Strebel

13. Partial Differential Equations

W. K. Allard
C. Baiocchi
M. S. Baouendi
M. S. Birman*
H. Brezis
M. G. Crandall
J. J. Duistermaat
D. Kinderlehrer
L. Nirenberg
M. I. Visik

14. Ordinary Differential Equations and Dynamic Systems

D. V. Anosov
R. Bowen
W. Krieger
M. N. Nehoroshev
M. M. Peixoto
A. M. Vershik*
B. Weiss

15. Control Theory and Related Optimization Problems

A. Bensoussan
V. F. Demyanov
A. Friedman
H. G. Hermes
H. J. Kushner
L. Markus
A. F. Subbotin

16. Mathematical Physics and Mechanics

J. M. Combes
R. L. Dobrushin*
O. Lanford
E. H. Lieb
A. Martin
C. W. Misner*
E. Nelson
B. Simon
A. A. Slavnov*
V. E. Zakharov*

17. Numerical Mathematics

J. Bramble
E. W. Cheney
A. A. Samarskii
H. J. Stetter
G. Strang
A. G. Sveshnikov
J. H. Wilkinson
P. Wolfe

18. Discrete Mathematics and Theory of Computation

J. M. Barzdin
A. J. Hoffman
D. J. Kleitman
R. Lindner
A. R. Meyer
M. S. Paterson
R. Rado
V. Strassen
E. Szemeredi
J. L. Vasiljev*

19. Applied Statistics, Mathematics in the Social and Biological Sciences

K. J. Arrow*
N. Buslenko*
E. B. Dynkin
S. Karlin*
P. A. P. Moran
J. W. Tukey
E. C. Zeeman

20. History and Education

B. V. Gnedenko
Th. Hawkins
G. Matthews
C. Truesdell

Members of the Congress*

*Not all members attended the Congress in person.

A'CAMPO, Norbert (France)
AARNES, Johan (Norway)
AARTS, Johannes (Netherlands)
ABBOTT, Harvey (Canada)
ABDELMALEK, Nabih (Canada)
ABDI, Wazir (Australia)
ABE, Kinetsu (U. S. A.)
ABE, Michio (Japan)
ABE, Shingo (Japan)
ABELES, Francine (U. S. A.)
ABIKOFF, William (U. S. A.)
ABIODUN, Rufus (Nigeria)
ABOFF, Neil (U. S. A.)
ABRHAM, Jaromir (Canada)
ABSAR, Ilyas (Canada)
ABUBAKAR, Iya (Nigeria)
ACHACHE, A. (France)
ACKERMANS, Stan (Netherlands)
ACZEL, Janos (Canada)
ADAMS, J. Frank (England)
ADAMS, Michael (Canada)
ADAMS, Robert (Canada)
ADAMSON, Alan (Canada)
ADAMSON, Iain (Scotland)
ADLER, Roy (U. S. A.)
ADYAN, Sergey (U. S. S. R.)
AFGHAHI, Mohammad (Iran)
AGOSTON, Max (U. S. A.)
AHSAN, Javed (Pakistan)
AIRAULT, Helene (France)
AISSEN, Michael (U. S. A.)
AITCHISON, Peter (Canada)
AKEMANN, Charles (U. S. A.)
AKUTOWICZ, Edwin (France)
AL-DHAHIR, M. Wassel (Kuwait)
AL-DHAHIR, Nawar (England)
AL-GWAIZ, Mohammed (Saudi Arabia)
AL-HUSSAINI, Ata N (Canada)
ALAMIRI, Hassoon (U. S. A.)
ALAOGLU, Leonidas (U. S. A.)
ALBERS, Donald (U. S. A.)
ALBERT, Jeffrey (U. S. A.)
ALBRIGHT, Hugh (U. S. A.)
ALCORN, David (New Zealand)
ALDER, Henry (U. S. A.)
ALEXANDER, David (Canada)
ALEXANDERSON, Gerald (U. S. A.)
ALFRED, Auslender (France)
ALLARD, William (U. S. A.)
ALLAWAY, William (Canada)
ALLEGRETTO, Walter (Canada)
ALLENBY, Reginald (England)
ALLING, Norman (U. S. A.)
ALLISON, Bruce (Canada)
ALMGREN, Frederick (U. S. A.)
ALMGREN, Jean Taylor (U. S. A.)
ALPERIN, Jonathan (U. S. A.)
ALPERIN, Roger (U. S. A.)
ALPERT, Seth (U. S. A.)
ALSPACH, Brian (Canada)
ALTMAN, Allen (U. S. A.)
ALVAREZ-SHERER, Ma De La Paz (Mexico)
AMANOV, Tuleobai (U. S. S. R.)
AMARA, Mohamed (Tunisia)
AMBARTZUMIAN, Rouben (U. S. S. R.)
AMELIN, Charles (U. S. A.)
AMICE, Yvette (France)
AMIDI, Ali (France)
AMIYA, Masanobu (Japan)
ANDERSEN, Kenneth (Canada)
ANDERSON, Barbara (U. S. A.)
ANDERSON, Bernard (U. S. A.)
ANDERSON, Claude (U. S. A.)
ANDERSON, Donald (U. S. A.)
ANDERSON, Joel (U. S. A.)
ANDERSON, Karl (Sweden)
ANDERSON, Michael (U. S. A.)
ANDERSON, Norman (England)
ANDERSON, Richard (U. S. A.)
ANDERSON, Robert (Canada)
ANDERSON, Tim (Canada)
ANDLER, Daniel (France)
ANDLER, Martin (France)
ANDRUSHKIW, Joseph (U. S. A.)
ANDRUSHKIW, Roman (U. S. A.)
ANOSOV, Dmitriy (U. S. S. R.)

ANSELONE, Philip (U. S. A.)
ANSORGE, Rainer (Fed. Rep. Germany)
ANTIBI, Andre (France)
ANTONIUS, Rachad (Egypt)
ANVARI, Morteza (Iran)
ANYANWU, Donatus (Nigeria)
AOKI, Norihiro (Japan)
ARAKELOV, Suren (U. S. S. R.)
ARAKI, Huzihiro (Japan)
ARANAKE, Ramkrishna (India)
ARCHER, David (U. S. A.)
ARENS, Richard (U. S. A.)
AREZMENDI, Hugo (Mexico)
ARGYRAKOS, John (Greece)
ARKIN, Joseph (U. S. A.)
ARMENDARIZ, Armando (U. S. A.)
ARMINJON, Paul (Canada)
ARNOLD, V. I. (U. S. S. R.)
AROCA, Jose (Spain)
ARON, Richard (U. S. A.)
ARROW, K. J. (U. S. A.)
ARSCOTT, Felix (Canada)
ARTZNER, Philippe (France)
ARYA, Shashi (England)
ASCHE, David (England)
ASH, J. Marshall (U. S. A.)
ASSMUS, Edward (U. S. A.)
ASTIE, Annie (France)
ATIYAH, Michael (England)
ATKINSON, Graham (England)
ATKINSON, Harold (Canada)
AU-YEUNG, Yik-Hoi (Hong Kong)
AUGE, Juan (Spain)
AULL, Charles (U. S. A.)
AULT, John (England)
AUSLANDER, Bernice (U. S. A.)
AUSLANDER, Maurice (U. S. A.)
AVILA-MURILLO Fernando (Mexico)
AXLER, Sheldon (U. S. A.)
AYALAZ, Ignacio (Mexico)
AYOUB, Raymond (U. S. A.)
BA, Boubakar (Niger)
BAAS, Nils Andreas (Norway)
BAAYEN, P. C. (Netherlands)
BACLAWSKI, Kenneth (U. S. A.)
BACOPOULOS, Alexis (Canada)
BADJI, Cherif (Senegal)
BAGGS, Ivan (Canada)
BAILEY, G. H. (England)
BAILEY, Paul (U. S. A.)
BAILLETTE, Aimee (France)
BAIOCCHI, Claudio (Italy)
BAKER, Alan (England)
BAKER, John (U. S. A.)
BAKER, Kirby (U. S. A.)
BAKTAVATSALOU, (Ivory Coast)
BALASKO, Yves (France)
BALDWIN, John (U. S. A.)
BAMBAH, R. P. (India)
BANDLE, Catherine (Switzerland)
BANKS, Dallas (U. S. A.)
BAOUENDI, Mohamed Salah (U. S. A.)
BAREISS, Erwin (U. S. A.)
BARGE, Jean (France)
BARKER, William (U. S. A.)
BARLOTTI, Adriano (Italy)
BARNER, Martin (Fed. Rep. Germany)
BARNES, Earl (U. S. A.)
BARNES, Frank (England)
BARNHART, Richard (U. S. A.)
BARR, Dennis (Puerto Rico)
BARRAR, Richard (U. S. A.)
BARRAT, Pierre (France)
BARRUCAND, Pierre (France)
BARSHAY, Jacob (U. S. A.)
BART, Harm (Netherlands)
BARTH, Karl (U. S. A.)
BARTH, Wolf (Netherlands)
BARTLOW, Thomas (U. S. A.)
BARTON, Norman (Canada)
BARWISE, K. Jon (U. S. A.)
BARZDIN, Jan (U. S. S. R.)
BASKERVILLE, Jon (Canada)
BASS, Hyman (U. S. A.)
BASSOTTI, Lucilla (Italy)
BASU, Sudhamay (Canada)
BATES, Susan (Canada)
BAUER, Heinz (Fed. Rep. Germany)
BAUM, Leonard (U. S. A.)
BAUR, Walter (U. S. A.)
BAUSSET, Max (France)
BAVINCK, Herman (Netherlands)
BAXTER, Kathleen (U. S. A.)
BEALS, Richard (U. S. A.)
BEAMER, James (Canada)
BEAN, Donald (Canada)
BEAUVILLE, Arnaud (France)
BEAUZAMY, Bernard (France)
BECK, Anatole (England)
BECK, Robert (U. S. A.)
BECKENBACH, Edwin (U. S. A.)
BECKER, Alexander (U. S. A.)
BECKER, Gerhard (Fed. Rep. Germany)
BECKER, Ilse (Fed. Rep. Germany)
BECKER, Ronald (South Africa)
BECKMANN, Philip (Canada)
BECUKER, Helmut (Fed. Rep. Germany)
BEEKMAN, John (U. S. A.)
BEEKMANN, Wolfgang (Fed. Rep. Germany)
BEESACK, Paul (Canada)
BEGUERI, Lucile (France)
BEHBOODIAN, Javad (Iran)
BEHNCKE, Horst (Fed. Rep. Germany)
BEITER, Marion (U. S. A.)
BELAGE, Abel (France)
BELENOT, Steven (U. S. A.)
BELINSKI, Pavel (U. S. S. R.)
BELL, Howard (Canada)
BELL, Raymond (U. S. A)
BELLAICHE Andre (France)

BELLOT-ROSADO Francisco (Spain)
BELOUSOR, Nicolay (U. S. S. R.)
BEN-GHANDOUR, Addi (Israel)
BENES, Vaclav (U. S. A.)
BENILAN, Philippe (France)
BENKOSKI, Stanley (U. S. A.)
BENNEWITZ, Christer (Sweden)
BENSOUSSAN, Alain (France)
BENTLEY, Herschel (U. S. A.)
BERARD-BERGERY, Lionel (France)
BERCOV, Ronald (Canada)
BERENSTEIN, Carlos (U. S. A.)
BERESTYCKI, Henri (France)
BERG, Christian (Denmark)
BERGER, Thomas (U. S. A.)
BERGGREN, John (Canada)
BERGMAN, George (U. S. A.)
BERGMAN, Stefan (U. S. A.)
BERLING, Chantal (France)
BERMAN, Elizabeth (U. S. A.)
BERMAN, Joel (U. S. A.)
BERMAN, Stephen (Canada)
BERQUIER, Francoise (France)
BERRICK, Jon (England)
BERRY, John (Canada)
BERS, Lipman (U. S. A.)
BERTHIAUME, Pierre (Canada)
BERTOLINI, Fernando (Italy)
BERTRAND, Daniel (France)
BESCHLER, Edwin (U. S. A.)
BEYER, William (U. S. A.)
BEZUSZKA, Stanley (U. S. A.)
BHATNAGAR, P. (India)
BICHTELER, Klaus (U. S. A.)
BIERI, Robert (Switzerland)
BIERSTEDT, Klaus (Fed. Rep. Germany)
BIERSTONE, Edward (Canada)
BIGARD, Alain (France)
BIGGS, Richard (Canada)
BILLERA, Louis (U. S. A.)
BIRD, Carol (Canada)
BIRKHOFF, Garrett (U. S. A.)
BIRMAN, M. S. (U. S. S. R.)
BIRNBAUM, Z. William (U. S. A.)
BJORK, Jan-Erik (Sweden)
BLACKMORE, Denis (U. S. A.)
BLAIR, David (U. S. A.)
BLAKLEY, G. (U. S. A.)
BLANKE, Ulrich (Fed. Rep. Germany)
BLANTON, John (U. S. A.)
BLASS, Andreas (U. S. A)
BLOCK, Richard (U. S. A.)
BLOOM, Thomas (Canada)
BLUM, Lenore (U. S. A)
BLUM, Peter (U. S. A.)
BLUM, Richard (Canada)
BLUMAN, G. W. (Canada)
BLUMENTHAL, Leonard (U. S. A.)
BOBROWSKI, Dobiestaw (Poland)
BODY, Richard (Canada)
BOEHME, Reinhold (Fed. Rep. Germany)
BOEHMER, Klaus (Fed. Rep. Germany)
BOENECKE, Ernst (Fed. Rep. Germany)
BOERS, Arie (Netherlands)
BOFFI, Vinicio (Italy)
BOGO, Jacki (Belgium)
BOGUE, Neil (U. S. A)
BOHUN-CHUDYNIV, Boris (U. S. A.)
BOHUN-CHUDYNIV, Volodymyr (U. S. A)
BOILEAU, Andre (Canada)
BOJADZIEV, George (Canada)
BOKOWSKI, Jurgen (Fed. Rep. Germany)
BOLKER, Ethan (U. S. A)
BOLLOBAS, Bela (England)
BOLTON, John (England)
BOMBIERI, Enrico (Italy)
BONAR, Daniel (U. S. A.)
BONY, Jean-Michel (France)
BOONE, William (U. S. A.)
BOORMAN, Evelyn (U. S. A.)
BOOSS, Bernhelm (Fed. Rep. Germany)
BOOTHBY, William (U. S. A.)
BORDEN, Stephen (Canada)
BOREL, Armand (U. S. A.)
BORON, Leo (U. S. A.)
BORRELLI, Robert (U. S. A.)
BORWEIN, David (Canada)
BOTTO-MURA, Roberta (Canada)
BOTTS, Truman (U. S. A.)
BOUCHET, Andre (France)
BOURGIN, David (U. S. A.)
BOUTOT, Jean-Francois (France)
BOUVIER, Alain (France)
BOWDEN, Leon (Canada)
BOWEN, Rufus (U. S. A.)
BOWERS, John (England)
BOWTELL, Graham (England)
BOYD, David (Canada)
BOYDRON, Yves (France)
BOZOVIC, Ivan (Yugoslavia)
BOZOVIC, Natasa (Yugoslavia)
BRADSHAW, Jack (Canada)
BRAKKE, Kenneth (U. S. A.)
BRAMBLE, James (U. S. A.)
BRANDENBURG, Willem (Netherlands)
BRANNAN, David (England)
BRAUER, Alfred (U. S. A.)
BRAUER, George (U. S. A.)
BRAUN, Hel (Fed. Rep. Germany)

BRAUN, Robert (Fed. Rep. Germany)
BREEN, Lawrence (France)
BRELOT, Marcel (France)
BREMNER, Andrew (England)
BRENNER, David (Canada)
BRENNER, Sheila (England)
BREWSTER, Douglas (England)
BREZINSKI, Claude (France)
BREZIS, Haim (France)
BRIESKORN, Egbert (Fed. Rep. Germany)
BRILLHART, John (U. S. A.)
BRISCHLE, Till (Fed. Rep. Germany)
BRITTEN, Daniel (Canada)
BRITTON, John (England)
BROERE, Izak (Rep. South Africa)
BROMAN, Arne (Sweden)
BROOKS, Foster (U. S. A.)
BROUE, Michel (France)
BROVERMAN, Samuel (Canada)
BROWDER, Felix (U. S. A)
BROWDER, William (U. S. A.)
BROWN, Edgar (U. S. A.)
BROWN, Gavin (England)
BROWN, Gordon (U. S. A.)
BROWN, James (U. S. A.)
BROWN, Julia (Canada)
BROWN, Lawrence (U. S. A.)
BROWN, Leon (U. S. A.)
BROWN, Margaret (England)
BROWN, Richard (Canada)
BROWN, Robert (U. S. A.)
BROWN, Tom (Canada)
BROWNELL, Frank (U. S. A.)
BRUEHLMANN, Heinz (German Dem. Rep.)
BRUENING, Jochen (Fed. Rep. Germany)
BRUMFIEL, Gregory (U. S. A.)
BRUNK, Hugh (U. S. A.)
BRUNO, Vincent (U. S. A.)
BRUNSWICK, Natascha (U. S. A.)
BRYAN, Robert (Canada)
BRYANT, John (U. S. A.)
BRYLINSKI, Jean-Luc (France)
BUCHNER, Michael (Rep. South Africa)
BUCK, R. Creighton (U. S. A.)
BUCY, Richard (U. S. A)
BUDACH, Lothar (German Dem. Rep.)
BUI, An-Ton (Canada)
BUKHSTABER, V. M. (U. S. S. R.)
BULL, Everett (U. S. A.)
BULLEN, Peter (Canada)
BUNGE, Marta (Canada)
BUNTINAS, Martin (U. S. A.)
BURDE, Gerhard (Fed. Rep. Germany)
BURDE, Klaus (Fed. Rep. Germany)
BURDEN, Charles (New Zealand)
BUREAU, Florent (Belgium)
BURES, Donald (Canada)
BURGESS, C. E. (U. S. A.)
BURGHELEA Dan (Rumania)
BURKHOLDER, Donald (U. S. A.)
BURLAK J. (U. S. A.)
BURNS, Robert (Canada)
BURR, Stefan (U. S. A.)
BURRIS, Stanley (Canada)
BURRY, John (Canada)
BUSHAW, D. (U. S. A.)
BUSLENKO, N. (U. S. S. R.)
BUTLER, Geoffrey (Canada)
BUTLER, Jean (Canada)
BUTLER, Michael (England)
BUTTON, Lilian (England)
BUYUKYENEREL, Gultekin (Turkey)
BYATT-SMITH, John Graham (Scotland)
BYERS, Victor (Canada)

CALLAHAN, Thomas (Canada)
CALLOWAY, Jean (U. S. A.)
CALVO, Adina (France)
CALVO, Bernard (France)
CAMBERN, Michael (U. S. A.)
CAMERON, Norman (Canada)
CAMPBELL, Colin (Scotland)
CAMPOS, Alberto (Columbia)
CANDIOTTI, Alan (U. S. A.)
CANFELL, Michael (Australia)
CANNON, John (U. S. A.)
CANTOR, David (U. S. A)
CANTOR, Murray (U. S. A.)
CARADUS, Selwyn (Canada)
CAREY, Richard (U. S. A)
CARLSSON, Renate (Fed. Rep. Germany)
CARLTON, Eloise (U. S. A.)
CARR, Donna (England)
CARRELL, James (Canada)
CARSON, Andrew (Canada)
CARSWELL, James (Canada)
CARTAN, Henri (France)
CARTER, David (U. S. A.)
CARTER, Roger (England)
CASS, Frank (Canada)
CASSELS, J. W. S. (England)
CASSIDY, Phyllis (U. S. A.)
CASTI, John (U. S. A.)
CATES, Marshall (U. S. A.)
CATHELINEAU, Jean Louis (France)
CATTANEO, Carlo (Italy)
CATTANEO, Ida (Italy)
CAUBET, Jean-Pierre (France)
CAYFORD, Afton (Canada)
CECIL, Thomas (U. S. A.)
CEDER, Jack (U. S. A.)
CEJALVO, Flor (Philippines)
CENKL, Bohumil (U. S. A.)
CERQUEIRA, L.P. de Maria Helena (Brazil)
CHADEMAN, Arsalan (Iran)

CHAKRAVARTTY, Iswar (Canada)
CHAMBERS, Graham (Canada)
CHAN, Gin-Hor (Singapore)
CHAN, Nai Ng (Hong Kong)
CHANDNA, C. M. (Canada)
CHANDRA, Jagdish (U. S. A.)
CHANDRASEKHARAN, Komaravolu (Switzerland)
CHANG, John (U. S. A.)
CHANG, Pang-Liang (Rep. China)
CHANG, Shao-Chien (Canada)
CHAPMAN, Gerald (Canada)
CHAPMAN, Thomas (U. S. A.)
CHAPTAL, Nicole (France)
CHASE, Stephen (U. S. A.)
CHASTENET-DEGERY, Jerome (France)
CHATELET, Gilles (France)
CHATTERJI, Srishti (Switzerland)
CHAVES, Manuel (Portugal)
CHAYE, Jacques (France)
CHEBLI, Houcine (France)
CHEEGER, Jeff (U. S. A.)
CHEHIL, Dalip (Canada)
CHELLEVOLD, John (U. S. A.)
CHEN, Bang-Yen (U. S. A.)
CHEN, Kuang-Ho (U. S. A.)
CHEN, Yi (Canada)
CHEN, Yu-Why (U. S. A.)
CHENEY, Ward (U. S. A.)
CHENON, Rene (France)
CHERLIN, Gregory (U. S. A.)
CHERN, Shiing (U. S. A.)
CHERNOFF, William (Canada)
CHETIVAUX, Francoise (France)
CHEUNG, Alan (Canada)
CHEVALIER, Michel (France)
CHING, Wai-Mee (U. S. A.)
CHOI, Chang (U. S. A.)
CHOI, Man-Duen (U. S. A.)
CHOLLET, Anne Marie (France)
CHOU, Chin-Cheng (France)
CHRESTENSON, Hubert (U. S. A.)
CHRISTIAN, Robert (Canada)
CHRISTIANSEN, Bent (Denmark)
CHUNG, Kai-Lai (U. S. A.)
CHURCH, Alonzo (U. S. A.)
CHVATAL, Vaclav (Canada)
CIESIELSKI, Zbigniew (Poland)
CIGNETTI, Alberto (Italy)
CLAPP, Robert (U. S. A.)
CLARK, Colin (Canada)
CLARK, Douglas (Scotland)
CLARK, Ronald (England)
CLARKE, A. Bruce (U. S. A.)
CLAUS, Heinz Jorg (Fed. Rep. Germany)
CLAUSING, Achim (Fed. Rep. Germany)
CLEMENS, Herbert (U. S. A.)
CLEMENTS, John (Canada)
CLEMONS, Arthur (U. S. A.)
CLIFFORD, Alfred (U. S. A.)
COGHLAN, Francis (England)
COHEN, Alexandra (France)
COHEN, Arjeh (Netherlands)
COHEN, Daniel (England)
COHEN, Elie (Canada)
COHEN, Fred (U. S. A.)
COHEN, Joel (U. S. A.)
COHEN, Maurice (Canada)
COHN, Harvey (U. S. A.)
COHN, J. H. E. (England)
COHN, Paul (England)
COLE, Nancy (U. S. A.)
COLEBROOK, Merle (Canada)
COLEMAN, A. John (Canada)
COLEMAN, Courtney (U. S. A.)
COLLATZ, Lothar (Germany)
COLLINO, Alberto (Italy)
COLLINS, Donald (England)
COLLINS, Michael (England)
COLLINS, Peter (England)
COLVIN, Burton (U. S. A.)
COLWELL, Peter (U. S. A.)
COMBES, Jean (France)
COMBES, Jean Michel (France)
COMERFORD, Jonell (U. S. A.)
COMERFORD, Leo (U. S. A.)
COMFORT, W. Wistar (U. S. A.)
COMPOS, Ramon (Mexico)
COMSTOCK, Craig (U. S. A.)
CONCUS, Paul (U. S. A.)
CONDE, Antonio (Brazil)
CONDUCHE, Daniel (France)
CONLAN, James (Canada)
CONLON, Lawrence (U. S. A.)
CONLON, Samuel (Australia)
CONNELL, Ian (Canada)
CONNES, Alain (France)
CONNETT, William (U. S. A.)
CONNOLLY, Dennis (Canada)
CONTI, Roberto (Italy)
COOK, Lyle (U. S. A.)
COOKE, Kenneth (U. S. A.)
COOPER, J. Lionel (England)
COPPEL, Andrew (Australia)
COPPINI, Mario (Italy)
CORAY, Daniel (Switzerland)
CORMACK, Sheila (Scotland)
COT, Norbert (France)
COUDRAIS, Jacques (France)
COUGHLIN, Mary (U. S. A.)

COULOMB, Genevieve (France)
COURY, John (Canada)
COWEN, Carl (U. S. A.)
COWLES, John (U. S. A.)
COWLES, Mary Jane (U. S. A.)
COX, David (U. S. A.)
COX, Samuel (U. S. A.)
COXETER, H. S. Mac Donald (Canada)
CRAGGS, Robert (U. S. A.)
CRAMER, T. E. (Canada)
CRANDALL, Michael (U. S. A.)
CRAPO, Henry (Canada)
CRAVEN, Bruce (Australia)
CRAWFORTH, Denis (England)
CREE, George (Canada)
CREPEL, Pierre (France)
CRITTENDEN, Richard (U. S. A.)
CROFT, Hallard (England)
CROOM, Frederick (U. S. A.)
CROSS, George (Canada)
CROSS, James (Australia)
CROWE, David (England)
CROWELL, Richard (U. S. A.)
CROWNOVER, Richard (U. S. A.)
CRUMEYROLLE, Albert (France)
CSASZAR, Akos (Hungary)
CULL, Paul (U. S. A.)
CULLEN, Helen (U. S. A.)
CUMMINGS, Larry (Canada)
CUNNINGHAM, Barry (Canada)
CUPONA, Gorgi (Yugoslavia)
CURRAN, Peter (U. S. A.)
CURRY, Haskell (U. S. A.)
CURTIS, Edward (U. S. A.)
CUSICK, Thomas (U. S. A.)
CUTTLE, Yvonne (Canada)
CZERNIAKIEWICZ, Anastasia (U. S. A.)

D'AMBROSIO, Ubiratan (Brazil)
D'HOMBRES, Jean Guy (France)
DACUNHA-CASTELLE, Didier (France)
DAI, Taen-Yu (U. S. A.)
DAIGNEAULT, Aubert (Canada)
DALES, H. Garth (England)
DALLA, Ronald (U. S. A.)
DALSIN, Gordon (Canada)
DAMLAMIAN, Alain (France)
DAMUOHLER, Wilhelm (Argentina)
DANCIS, Jerome (U. S. A.)
DANG-NGOC, Nghiem (France)
DANKERT, Gabriele (Canada)
DARCHEN, Jean Claude (France)
DARST, Richard (U. S. A.)
DASHIELL, Fred (U. S. A.)
DAUBISSE, Jean-Claude (France)
DAUNS, John (U. S. A.)
DAVEY, Brian (Canada)
DAVIES, Roy (England)
DAVIS, Anthony (England)
DAVIS, Chandler (Canada)
DAVIS, Gary (Australia)
DAVIS, Martin (U. S. A.)
DAVIS, Michael (U. S. A.)
DAVISON, John (Canada)
DAWES, Alexander (Canada)
DAWSON, Donald (Canada)
DAWSON, John (U. S. A.)
DAY, Alan (Canada)
DAZORD, Jean (U. S. A.)
DE CARVALHO, Carlos (Brazil)
DE GUZMAN, Miguel (Spain)
DE HOYOS, Arnoldo (Mexico)
DE ROBERT, Etienne (France)
DE SOCIO, Luciano (Italy)
DEAKIN, Michael (Australia)
DEAN, David (U. S. A.)
DEB, Susanta (Canada)
DEBNATH, Lokenath (U. S. A.)
DEBREU, Gerard (U. S. A.)
DEDECKER, Paul (Belgium)
DELANEY, Matthew (U. S. A.)
DELANGE, Hubert (France)
DELEON, M. J. (U. S. A.)
DELIGNE, Pierre (Belgium)
DELKIN, Jay (Canada)
DELURY, Daniel (Canada)
DEMARR, Ralph (U. S. A.)
DEMPSTER M. A. H. (England)
DEMYANOV, V. F. (U. S. S. R.)
DENNIS, Keith (U. S. A.)
DENZEL, Gene (Canada)
DEPAIX, Michel (France)
DESOLNEUX-MOULIS, Nicole (France)
DESQ, Roger (France)
DETTMAN, John (U. S. A.)
DETWILER, Bettie (U. S. A.)
DEYO, Roderic (U. S. A.)
DI LIBERTO, Francesco (France)
DIANTONIO, G. (U. S. A.)
DIAS-AGUDO, Fernando (Portugal)
DIAZ, Joaquin (U. S. A.)
DICKEY, Leroy (Canada)
DIERKER, Egbert (Germany)
DIERKER, Hildegard (Germany)
DINOLT, George (U. S. A.)
DION, Jean-Pierre (Canada)
DIONNE, Philippe (New Zealand)
DIPERNA, Ronald (U. S. A.)
DIXMIER, Suzanne (France)
DIXON, John (Canada)
DJEDOUR, Mohamed (Algeria)
DJOKOVIC, Dragomir (Canada)
DJRBACHIAN, Mkhitar (U. S. S. R.)
DLAB, Vlastimil (Canada)
DO, Claude (France)
DOBBER, Eelkje (Netherlands)

DOBBS, David (U. S. A.)
DOBRUSHIN, R. L. (U. S. S. R.)
DOLBEAULT, Pierre (France)
DOLBEAULT-LEMOIN, Simone (France)
DOLD, Albrecht (Fed. Rep. Germany)
DOLD-SAMPLONIUS, Yvonne (Germany)
DOLECKI, Szymon (Poland)
DONALDSON, James (U. S. A.)
DONIG, Joerg (Fed. Rep. Germany)
DONOGHUE, William, Jr. (U. S. A.)
DOOB, Joseph (U. S. A.)
DOOB, Michael (Canada)
DORS, George (U. S. A.)
DOSTAL, Milos (France)
DOU, Alberto (Spain)
DOU, Jordi (Spain)
DOUDOU-SAKIR, Thiam (France)
DOUGLAS, Allan (Canada)
DOUGLAS, Roy Rene (Canada)
DOWKER, Clifford (England)
DOWLING, Ivan (Canada)
DOWLING, Thomas (U. S. A.)
DRAPER, James (U. S. A.)
DROBOT, Stefan (U. S. A.)
DROBOT, Vladimir (U. S. A.)
DRUCKER, Daniel (U. S. A.)
DU PLESSIS, Andrew (England)
DUBIEL, Makgorzata (Poland)
DUBINS, Lester (U. S. A.)
DUBINSKY, Ed (U. S. A.)
DUBISCH, Roy (U. S. A.)
DUBOIS, Eugene (France)
DUBOIS, Jacques (Canada)
DUBROVSKY, Diana (Canada)
DUBUC, Eduardo (Canada)
DUDLEY, Richard (U. S. A.)
DUFF, George (Canada)
DUFFIN, Richard (U. S. A.)
DUFLO, Michel (France)
DUGGAL, Krishan (Canada)
DUISTERMAAT, Johannes (Netherlands)
DUKE, Richard (U. S. A.)
DULMAGE, A. Lloyd (Canada)
DUNHAM, Charles (Canada)
DUNWOODY, Martin (England)
DURFEE, Alan (U. S. A.)
DUVAUT, Georges (France)
DWIVEDI, Tryambkeshwar (Canada)
DWORIC, Bernard (U. S. A.)
DWYER, Thomas (U. S. A.)
DWYER, William (U. S. A.)
DYE, Henry (U. S. A.)
DYNKIN, E. B. (U. S. S. R.)

EAGLE, Ruth (England)
EAMES, William (Canada)
EARLE, Clifford (U. S. A.)
EBERLEIN, Ernst (Fed. Rep. Germany)
EBERLEIN, Patrick (U. S. A.)
EBERLEIN, William (U. S. A.)
ECKHOFF, Jurgen (Fed. Rep. Germany)
ECKLUND, Earl (U. S. A.)
ECKMANN, Beno (Switzerland)
EDELSTEIN, Michael (Canada)
EDMUNDS, Charles (Canada)
EDWARDS, Harold (U. S. A.)
EDWARDS, Martin (England)
EDWARDS, Robert (U. S. A.)
EELLS, James (England)
EFROYMSON, Gus (U. S. A.)
EGGAN, Lawrence (U. S. A.)
EGGLETON, Roger (Israel)
EGUCHI, Kazuo (Japan)
EHLE, Byron (Canada)
EICHHORN, Wolfgang (Fed. Rep. Germany)
EILENBERG, Samuel (U. S. A.)
EINSELE, Charles (Switzerland)
EISENBUD, David (U. S. A.)
EKLOF, Paul (U. S. A.)
ELGOT, Calvin (U. S. A.)
ELIE, Laure (France)
ELIE, Richard (France)
ELJOSEPH, Nathan (Israel)
ELLERS, Eric (Canada)
ELLIOTT, George (Denmark)
ELLIOTT, Peter (England)
ELLIS, Alan (Wales)
ELLIS, Hubert (Canada)
ELLIS, Richard (U. S. A.)
ELWORTHY, Kenneth (England)
ELZEIN, Fouad (France)
EMA, Emmanuel (Nigeria)
EMAMI-RAD, Hassan Ali (Iran)
EMBRY, Mary (U. S. A.)
EMERSON, John (U. S. A.)
EMSALEM, Jacques (France)
ENDERTON, Herbert (U. S. A.)
ENFLO, Per (U. S. A.)
ENGBER, Michael (U. S. A.)
ENGQUIST, Michael (U. S. A.)
ENGUEHARD, Michel (France)
ENRIGHT, T. J. (U. S. A.)
EPHRAIM, Robert (U. S. A.)
ERBACH, David (England)
ERDAHL, Robert (Canada)
ERDOS, John (England)
ERDOS, Paul (Hungary)
ERIKSSON, Folke (Sweden)
ERKAMA, Timo (Finland)
ERNEST, John (U. S. A.)
ERSHOV, Youri (U. S. S. R.)

ESPELIE, Solveig (U. S. A.)
ESTRADA, Mario (Cuba)
EVANS, Arwel (Canada)
EVANS, Buell (U. S. A.)
EVANS, Edward (U. S. A.)
EVERITT, William (Scotland)
EWELL, John (U. S. A.)
EYMARD, Gerald (France)
EYMARD, Pierre (France)
EZEILO, James (Nigeria)

FADELL, Edward (U. S. A.)
FAIRCHILD, William (U. S. A.)
FAIRES, Douglas (U. S. A.)
FAIRWEATHER, Graeme (U. S. A.)
FAKIR, Sabah (France)
FALBO, Clement (U. S. A.)
FARAHAT, Hanafi (Canada)
FARAUT, Jacques (France)
FARKAS, Miklos (Hungary)
FARY, Istvan (U. S. A.)
FASANO, Antonio (Italy)
FEFFERMAN, Charles (U. S. A.)
FEICHTINGER, Oskar (U. S. A.)
FEIN, Burton (U. S. A.)
FEJES-TOTH, Laszlo (Hungary)
FELDMAN, Chester (U. S. A.)
FELDMAN, Jacob (U. S. A.)
FENCHEL, Werner (Denmark)
FENN, Roger (England)
FERGUSON, Le Baron (U. S. A.)
FERNANDEZ, Delvis (U. S. A.)
FERNANDEZ, Patricia (U. S. A.)
FERRIER, Jean-Pierre (France)
FERRIS, Ian (U. S. A.)
FIGIEL, Tadeusz (Poland)
FILIPPOV, Vladimir (U. S. S. R.)
FILLMORE, Peter (Canada)
FINKELSTEIN, Leib (Israel)
FINLAYSON, Henry (Canada)
FINN, Robert (U. S. A.)
FIREY, William (U. S. A.)
FISCHER, Wolfgang (Fed. Rep. Germany)
FISCHER, Herbert (Fed. Rep. Germany)
FISHBACK, William (U. S. A.)
FISHER-PALMQUIST, Janet (U. S. A.)
FISK, Donald (U. S. A.)
FLAHERTY, Frank (U. S. A.)
FLANCHEC, Annick (France)
FLATH, Daniel (U. S. A.)
FLEISHMAN, Bernard (U. S. A.)
FLETCHER, Beryl (England)
FLETCHER, Trevor (England)
FLEURY, Patrick (U. S. A.)
FLORES-ESPINOZA, Ruben (Mexico)
FLYNN, Thomas (U. S. A.)
FOGLIO, Susana (Argentina)
FOLLAND, Gerald (U. S. A.)
FOLLMER, Hans (Germany)
FOMENKO, A. (U. S. S. R.)
FONG, Jeffrey (U. S. A.)
FONTAINE, Jean Marc (France)
FORBES, Douglas (Canada)
FORD, James (England)
FORMAN, William (U. S. A.)
FORNAESS, John (Norway)
FORRESTER, Herbert (U. S. A.)
FORSEY, Hal (U. S. A.)
FORSTER, Otto (Fed. Rep. Germany)
FOURNIER, John (Canada)
FOX, Charles (Canada)
FOX, Leslie (England)
FOX, Ralph (New Zealand)
FRAGA, Robert (Lebanon)
FRAKER, Ross (U. S. A.)
FRAME, J. Sutherland (U. S. A.)
FRANCO, Ernesto (Puerto Rico)
FRANK, Evelyn (U. S. A.)
FRANK, Leonid (Israel)
FRANKEL, Robert (U. S. A.)
FRANKENA, Jan (Netherlands)
FRANKS, John (U. S. A.)
FRASER, David (U. S. A.)
FRASER, Grant (U. S. A.)
FRASER, Wallace (Canada)
FREDMAN, Michael (U. S. A.)
FREEDMAN, Michael (U. S. A.)
FREI, Armin (Canada)
FREITAG, Eberhard (Fed. Rep. Germany)
FREMLIN, David (England)
FRIED, Ervin (Hungary)
FRIEDLANDER, Eric (U. S. A.)
FRIEDLANDER, John (Canada)
FRIEDLANDER, Susan (U. S. A)
FRIEDMAN, Avner (U. S. A.)
FRIEDMAN, Harvey (U. S. A)
FRIEDMAN, Nathaniel (U. S. A.)
FRIEDMAN, Sy (U. S. A.)
FRIEDRICHS, Kurt (U. S. A.)
FRIEL, James (U. S. A.)
FRISTEDT, Bert (U. S. A.)
FRITSCH, Rudolf (Fed. Rep. Germany)
FROHLICH, Albrecht (England)
FROMM, Jens (Fed. Rep. Germany)
FROSTMAN, Otto (Sweden)
FUCH, Gerard (France)
FUCHS, Laszlo (U. S. A.)
FUCHS, Wolfgang (U. S. A.)
FUCHSSTEINER, Benno (Fed. Rep. Germany)
FUENTE, Maria (Mexico)

FUJIWARA, Masahiko (Japan)
GAAL, Lisl (U. S. A.)
GAAL, Steven (U. S. A.)
GABRIEL, Peter (Switzerland)
GAETA, Federico (U. S. A.)
GAFFNEY, Matthew (U. S. A.)
GALAMBOS, Janos (U. S. A.)
GALAYE, Dia (Senegal)
GALBRAITH, Alan (U. S. A.)
GALE, Deborah (U. S. A.)
GALLETTO, Dionigi (Italy)
GAL'PERIN, E. A. (Israel)
GAMLEN, John (New Zealand)
GANDHI, J. M. (U. S. A.)
GANELIUS, Tord (Sweden)
GAPAILLARD, Christiane (France)
GAPAILLARD, Jacques (France)
GARANCON, Maurice (Canada)
GARCIA, O. C. (Mexico)
GARDNER, Barry (Australia)
GARDNER, L. Terrell (Canada)
GARDNER, Robert (U. S. A.)
GARG, Krishna (Canada)
GARLAND, Howard (U. S. A.)
GARLAND, Roy (U. S. A.)
GARNER, Cyril (Canada)
GARNETT, John (U. S. A.)
GAROLA, Claudio (Italy)
GARRISON, Betty (U. S. A.)
GARWIN, Charles (U. S. A.)
GASPER, George (U. S. A.)
GASYMOV, Mirrubbus (U. S. S. R.)
GATTESCHI, Luigi (Italy)
GAUDRY, Garth (Australia)
GAUGER, Michael (U. S. A.)
GAUTHERON, Veronique (France)
GAVURIN, Lester (U. S. A.)
GEHRING, Frederick (U. S. A.)
GEIVAERTS, Marcel (Belgium)
GENOT, Marie-Luce (Canada)
GEORGE, Keith (England)
GERAMITA, Anthony (Canada)
GERAMITA, Joan (Canada)
GERARD, Dubois (France)
GERBER, Porter (U. S. A.)
GERHARD, Arthur (Canada)
GERHARDS, Leonhard (Fed. Rep. Germany)
GERLACH, Eberhard (Canada)
GERMAY, Noel (Belgium)
GERSTEIN, Larry (U. S. A.)
GERSTEN, Stephen (U. S. A.)
GHAFFARI, Abolghassem (U. S. A.)
GHALIB, Mudhafar (Iraq)
GHISLAIN, Morin (Canada)
GIBB, Glenadine (U. S. A.)
GIFFEN, Charles (U. S. A.)
GILANI, Muntaz Shah (Canada)
GILBARG, David (U. S. A.)
GILBERT, William (Canada)
GILES, John (Australia)
GILLAM, Basil (U. S. A.)
GILLESPIE, T. Alastair (Scotland)
GILLIGAN, Bruce (Canada)
GILLIS, Joseph (Israel)
GILLMAN, Leonard (U. S. A.)
GILMAN, Jane (U. S. A.)
GILMAN, Robert (U. S. A.)
GILMORE, Lynnette (New Zealand)
GINE, Evarist (Venezuela)
GINSBURG, John (Canada)
GIRARD, Jean Yves (France)
GIRI, Narayan (Canada)
GITLER, Samuel (Mexico)
GITTLEMAN, Arthur (U. S. A.)
GIUSTI, Marc (France)
GLASNER, Moses (U. S. A.)
GLAUBERMAN, George (U. S. A.)
GLICKSBERG, Irving (U. S. A.)
GLIMM, James (U. S. A.)
GNEDENKO, Boris (U. S. S. R.)
GOBLOT, Remi (France)
GODBILLON, Claude (France)
GODDARD, Laurence (England)
GODET-THOBIE, Christiane (France)
GODFREY, Colin (U. S. A.)
GOELMAN, Don (U. S. A.)
GOETZE, Ernst (Canada)
GOLDBERG, Donald (U. S. A.)
GOLDBERG, Michael (U. S. A.)
GOLUBITSKY, Martin (U. S. A.)
GONDARD, Danielle (France)
GOOD, Anton (Switzerland)
GOODAIRE, Edgar (Canada)
GOODMAN, Adolph (U. S. A.)
GOODMAN, Gerald (Italy)
GOODMAN, Jacob Eli (U. S. A.)
GOODRICK, Richard (U. S. A.)
GORDON, Cameron (England)
GOTO, Morikuni (U. S. A.)
GOULD, Sydney (Rep. China)
GOULLET DE RUGY, Alain (France)
GOURSAUD, Jean-Marie (France)
GOW, Roderick (Canada)
GRABINER, Sandy (U. S. A.)
GRAHAM, Ian (Canada)
GRAHAM, R. L. (U. S. A.)
GRANGER, Jean-Michel (France)
GRANT, Douglass (Canada)
GRANT, John (England)
GRATZER, George (Canada)
GRAY, Alfred (U. S. A.)
GRAY, Ayton (U.S.A.)

GRAY, Jack (Australia)
GRAY, Mary (U. S. A.)
GREEN, Judy (U. S. A.)
GREEN, Leon (U. S. A.)
GREENE, Curtis, (U. S. A.)
GREENLEAF, Frederick (U. S. A.)
GREEVER, John (U. S. A.)
GREGORY, David (Canada)
GREGORY, John (U. S. A.)
GREIG, Margaret (England)
GREIG, William (England)
GREINER, Peter (Canada)
GRELAUD, Gerard (France)
GREVILLE, Thomas (U. S. A.)
GRIFFIN, Ernest (U. S. A.)
GRIFFIN, Malcolm (Canada)
GRIGELIONIS, Bronius (U. S. S. R.)
GRIOLI, Guiseppe (Italy)
GROEMER, Helmut (U. S. A.)
GROSSMAN, Edna (U. S. A.)
GROSSMAN, Edward (U. S. A.)
GROSSWALD, Emil (U. S. A.)
GROVE, Karsten (Denmark)
GRUBB, Anthea (England)
GRUENBERG, Karl (England)
GRUNBAUM, A. Alberto (U. S. A.)
GRUNBAUM, Branka (U. S. A.)
GUCKENHEIMER, John (U. S. A.)
GUERASIMOV, Ivan (U. S. S. R.)
GUERINDON, Jean (France)
GUICHARDET, Alain (France)
GUILLOTTE, Guy (Canada)
GUINAND, Andrew (Canada)
GUIRO, Abdoulaye (Senegal)
GULLIVER, Robert (U. S. A.)
GUNDLACH, Karl-Bernhard (Fed. Rep. Germany)
GUNSON, J. M. (Canada)
GUNTHER, Claus (Fed. Rep. Germany)
GUNTHER, Georg (Canada)
GUPTA, Hansraj (India)
GUPTA, Kanta (Canada)
GUPTA, Narain (Canada)
GUSTAFSON, Karl (U. S. A.)
GUY, Roland (Canada)
GYIRES, Bela (Hungary)

HAFF, Charles (Canada)
HAG, Kari (Norway)
HAG, Per (Norway)
HAGEDORN, Peter (Fed. Rep. Germany)
HAHN, Alexander (U. S. A.)
HAHN, Marjorie (U. S. A.)
HAHN, Peter (U. S. A.)
HAIMO, Deborah (U. S. A.)
HAIMO, Franklin (U. S. A.)
HAJNAL, András (Hungary)
HALABISKY, Lorne (Canada)
HALBERG, Charles (U. S. A.)
HALE, Victor (England)
HALES, Alfred (U. S. A.)
HALES, Stanton (U. S. A.)
HALL, Gaineford (U. S. A.)
HALL, William (U. S. A.)
HALLETT, Richard (Canada)
HALMOS, P. R. (U. S. A.)
HALPERIN, Israel (Canada)
HALPERIN, Miriam (U. S. A.)
HALPERN, Herbert (U. S. A.)
HAMADA, Noboru (Japan)
HAMBLETON, Ian (Canada)
HAMEL, Ray (U. S. A.)
HAMERNIK, Wolfgang (Fed. Rep. Germany)
HAMET, Seydi (Senegal)
HAMMOND, William (U. S. A.)
HAMMOND-SMITH, David (England)
HANDELMAN, David (Canada)
HANES, Kit (U. S. A.)
HANSEN, Idar (Norway)
HANSEN, Vagn (Denmark)
HANSON, Denis (Canada)
HARARI, Sami (France)
HARARY, Frank (U. S. A.)
HARASE, Takashi (Japan)
HARBORTH, Heiko (Fed. Rep. Germany)
HARDIE, K. (Rep. South Africa)
HARDT, Robert (U. S. A.)
HARGRAVE, Barry (Scotland)
HARIS, Stephen (U. S. A.)
HARLOW, Donald (England)
HARPER, John (New Zealand)
HARRINGTON, Leo (U. S. A.)
HARRIS, Bruno (U. S. A.)
HARRIS, L. Frank (Canada)
HARRIS, Michael (U. S. A).
HARRISON, David (U. S.A.)
HARRISON, Jenny (U. S. A.)
HARRISON, Kenneth (Australia)
HARRISON, Wei-Jen (U. S. A.)
HARROLD, Orville (U. S. A.)
HARROP, Ronald (Canada)
HART, Neal (U. S. A.)
HARTSHORNE, Robin (U. S. A.)
HARUKI, Hiroshi (Canada)
HARZALLAH, Khelifa (Tunisia)
HARZHEIM, Egbert (Fed. Rep. Germany)
HASSANI, Nouredine (Algeria)
HASUMI, Moris Uke (Japan)
HATCHER, Allen (U. S. A.)
HATCHER, Theodore (U. S. A.)
HATORI, Tsukasa (Japan)
HATTORI, Akio (Japan)
HAUPTMANN, Wolfgang (Fed. Rep. Germany)
HAUSMANN, Jean-Claude (Switzerland)
HAUSRATH, Alan (U. S. A.)
HAUSSMANN, Ulrich (Canada)

HAUSSMANN, Werner (Fed. Rep. Germany)
HAVNEN, Johan (Norway)
HAWKINS, Thomas (U. S. A.)
HAYASHI, Hiroshi (Japan)
HAYDEN, T. (U. S. A.)
HAYES, Lois (U. S. A.)
HAYMAN, Walter (England)
HAZELL, John (Canada)
HAZEWINKEL, Michiel (Netherlands)
HEADLEY, Velmer (Canada)
HEARD, Melvin (U. S. A.)
HEBLE, Madhav (Canada)
HECHLER, Stephen (U. S. A.)
HEDBERG, Lars Inge (Sweden)
HEIDEMA, Clare (U. S. A.)
HEIL, Erhard (Fed. Rep. Germany)
HEILBRONN, Hans (Canada)
HEINEKEN, Hermann (Fed. Rep. Germany)
HEINICKE, Allan (Canada)
HEINIG, Hans (Canada)
HELD, Rene (Canada)
HELFFER, Bernard (France)
HELLING, Heinz (Fed. Rep. Germany)
HEMERNIK, Wolfgang (Fed. Rep. Germany)
HEMSTEAD, Polly (U. S. A.)
HEMSTEAD, Robert (U. S. A.)
HENDERSON, James (Canada)
HENGARTNER, Walter (Canada)
HENRICH, Christopher (U. S. A.)
HENRIKSEN, Melvin (U. S. A.)
HENRY, Jean-Pierre (France)
HENTZEL, Irvin (U. S. A.)
HERING, Franz (Fed. Rep. Germany)
HERING, Heinrich (Fed. Rep. Germany)
HERMAN, Michael (France)
HERMES, Henry (U. S. A.)
HERN, Thomas (U. S. A.)
HERRIOT, John (U. S. A.)
HERRIOT, Sarah (U. S. A.)
HERRLICH, Horst (Fed. Rep. Germany)
HERSH, Reuben, (U. S. A.)
HERSZBERG, Jerzy (England)
HERZBERGER, Jurgen (Fed. Rep. Germany)
HESPEL, Christiane (France)
HEUZE, Daniele (France)
HEWER, Gary (U. S. A.)
HEYWOOD, John (Canada)
HEYWOOD, Philip (Scotland)
HICKERSON, Dean (U. S. A.)
HIGASHIYAMA, Teiko (Japan)
HIGGINSON, William (Canada)
HIGGS, Denis (Canada)
HIGMAN, Graham (England)
HILBERT, Stephen (U. S. A.)
HILL, Joe (U. S. A.)
HILL, Lee (U. S. A.)
HINDMAN, Neil (U. S. A.)
HIRSCHFELD, James (England)
HIRZEBRUCH, Friedrich (Fed. Rep. Germany)
HISCOCKS, Jack (Canada)
HITOTSUMATSU, Shin (Japan)
HO, Shung-pun (Canada)
HOANG, Xuan (Dem. Rep. Viet-Nam)
HOBBS, Arthur (U. S. A.)
HOCQUENGHEM, Alexis (France)
HOCQUENGHEM, Serge (France)
HODGES, Wilfrid (England)
HODGKIN, Luke (England)
HOEHN, Erwin (Canada)
HOFFMAN, Alan (U. S. A.)
HOFFMAN, Frederick (U. S. A.)
HOFFMAN, Peter (Canada)
HOFFMAN, William (U. S. A.)
HOGARTH, Pauline (Australia)
HOGARTH, William (Australia)
HOGBE-NLEND, Henri (France)
HOHN, Franz (U. S. A.)
HOITSMA, David (U. S. A.)
HOLLAND, Anthony (Canada)
HOLMAN, Derek (U. S. A.)
HOLME, A. Berit (Norway)
HOLME, Audun (Norway)
HOLMES, Charles (U. S. A.)
HOLROYD, Frederick (England)
HONG, Im-Sik (Japan)
HONG, Sung Sa (Canada)
HOO, Cheong (Canada)
HOOBLER, Raymond (U. S. A.)
HOOLEY, C. (England)
HOOPER, R. (U. S. A.)
HORIKAWA, Eiji (Japan)
HORMANDER, Lars (Sweden)
HORN, Andreas (Fed. Rep. Germany)
HORVATH, John (U. S. A.)
HOSCHEK, Josef (Fed. Rep. Germany)
HOSKINS, William (Canada)
HOSTINSKY, Aileen (U. S. A.)
HOUH, Chorng Shi (U. S. A.)
HOUSEHAM, Keith (Rep. South Africa)
HOWE, Algy (Australia)
HOWE, Roger (U. S. A.)
HOWROYD, Terry (Canada)
HRYCAY, Rudolph (Canada)
HSIA, John (U. S. A.)
HSIANG, Wu-Yi (U. S. A.)
HSIEH, Po-Fang (U. S. A.)
HSIEH, Tsu-Teh (Canada)
HSIUNG, Chuan-Chih (U. S. A.)
HUBBARD, John (U. S. A.)
HUBER, Catherine (France)
HUBER, Peter (Switzerland)
HUET, Denise (France)
HUET, Patrick (France)

HUFF, Melvyn (U. S. A.)
HUFF, Robert (U. S. A.)
HUGELSHOFER, Rene (Switzerland)
HUGHART, Stanley (U. S. A.)
HUGHES, Edward (Canada)
HUGHES, Ian (Canada)
HUGHES, Kenneth (Rep. South Africa)
HUIGE, Gustavos (Canada)
HUMKE, Paul (U. S. A.)
HUMPHREYS, Gweneth (U. S. A.)
HUNT, Alice (U. S. A.)
HUNT, Burrowes (U. S. A.)
HUNT, Fern (U. S. A.)
HUNT, John (Mexico)
HUNT, Louis (U. S. A.)
HUNTER, David (England)
HURD, Albert (Canada)
HURLEY, James (U. S. A.)
HURRELBRINK, Jurgen (Fed. Rep. Germany)
HURTEVENT, Jacques (France)
HUSAIN, Taqdir (Canada)
HUSSAIN, Mansour (Kuwait)
HUTCHINSON, Joan (U. S. A.)
HYERS, Donald (U. S. A.)

IARROBINO, Anthony (U. S. A.)
IBISCH, Horst (France)
ICHIJO, Yoshihiro (Japan)
IGLEHART, Donald (U. S. A.)
ILLMAN, Soren (Finland)
ILLUSIE, Luc (France)
IMAI, Chuichi (Japan)
IMRICH, Wilfried (Austria)
INDELLI, Paola (U. S. A.)
INFANTOZZI, Carlos (Uruguay)
INOUE, Atsushi (Japan)
INOUE, Masahisa (Japan)
INSLEY, Robin (Canada)
ION, Patrick (England)
ISHAQ, Mohammad (Canada)
ISHIHARA, Shigeru (Japan)
ISMAIL, Mourad (Canada)
ISOBE, Kiro (Japan)
ISRAEL, Robert (Canada)
ITANO, Mitsuyuki (Japan)
ITO, Nozono (U. S. A.)
ITO, Takashi (Japan)
ITO, Takashi (U. S. A.)
ITO, Yoshihiko (Japan)
IVANOFF, Vladimir (U. S. A.)
IVANOV, George (Australia)
IVERSEN, Birger (Denmark)
IWANAGA, Yasuo (Japan)
IWANOWSKI, Peter (Fed. Rep. Germany)
IYAHEN, Sunday (Nigeria)
IYANAGA, Shokichi (Japan)

JABLONSKII, Sergei (U. S. S. R.)
JACKSON, Howard (Canada)
JACKSON, Lynn (U. S. A.)
JACKSON, Terence (England)
JACOB, Genevieve (France)
JACOB, Gerard (France)
JACOBSON, David (Canada)
JACOBSON, Florence (U. S. A.)
JACOBSON, Nathan (U. S. A.)
JACQUET, Herve (U. S. A.)
JAFFE, Arthur (U. S. A.)
JAFFE, Norman (Canada)
JAIN, Darshan Lal (U. S. A.)
JAIN, Naresh (U. S. A.)
JAIN, Rajendra (India)
JAIN, S.K. (U. S. A.)
JAMBU, Michel (France)
JAMES, Donald (U. S. A.)
JAMES, Ioan (England)
JAMES, R.D. (Canada)
JAMES, Robert (U. S. A.)
JAVANSHIR, Mohamadgholi (Iran)
JEANQUARTIER, Pierre (Switzerland)
JECH, Thomas (U. S. A.)
JEFFERIES, Clark (Canada)
JEFFERY, Ralph (Canada)
JENNER, W.E. (U. S. A.)
JERISON, Meyer (U. S. A.)
JEWETT, Robert (U. S. A.)
JIMOURIAN, James (Canada)
JOFFE, Anatole (Canada)
JOHANNSON, Klaus (Fed. Rep. Germany)
JOHANSON, Arnold (U. S. A.)
JOHNSEN, Eugene (U.S.A.)
JOHNSON, Charles (U.S.A.)
JOHNSON, David (England)
JOHNSON, David (U. S. A.)
JOHNSON, Emma (U. S. A.)
JOHNSON, James (U. S. A.)
JOHNSON, Jerry (U. S. A.)
JOHNSON, Joseph (U.S.A.)
JOHNSON, Ronald (Canada)
JOHNSON, Roy (U. S. A.)
JOHNSON, Wells (U. S. A.)
JOHNSTON, Laurence (Canada)
JOHNSTONE, Peter (England)
JOLLENSTEN, Ralph (U. S. A.)
JONES, Burton (U. S. A.)
JONES, F.B. (U. S. A.)
JONES, James (Canada)
JONES, Phillip (U. S. A.)
JONES, Wayne (U. S. A.)
JONKER, Leo (Canada)
JONSSON, Bjarni (U. S. A.)
JORGENSEN, Palle (Denmark)
JOSEPH, Gerard (Australia)
JOSEPHY, Michael (Canada)
JUCOVIC, Ernest (Czechoslovakia)
JUDGE, David (Ireland)
JUHASZ, Istvan (Hungary)
JUSTICE, James (U. S. A.)

KAAPKE, Juergen (Fed.Rep. Germany)
KAASHOEK, Marinus (Netherlands)
KABIR, Abm Lutful (Canada)
KADISON, Richard (U. S. A.)

KAHANE, Jean-Pierre (France)
KAKEHASHI, Tetsujiro (Japan)
KAKUTANI, Shizuo (U. S. A.)
KALFAIAN, Jean-Paul (France)
KALLAHER, Michael (U. S. A.)
KALLSTROM, Anders (Sweden)
KALMAN, John (New Zealand)
KALNINS, Ernest (Canada)
KALONI, Purna (Canada)
KAMBAYASHI, Tatsuji (U. S. A.)
KAMBER, Franz (U. S. A.)
KAMOWITZ, Herbert (U. S. A.)
KAMPE DE FERIET, Joseph (France)
KANEYUKI, Soji (Japan)
KANNAPPAN, P. (Canada)
KAPER, Hans (U. S. A.)
KAPPOS, Demetrios (Greece)
KARATSUBA, A. A. (U. S. S. R.)
KAREL, Martin (U. S. A.)
KARGAPOLOV, Mikhail (U. S. S. R.)
KARLIN, Samuel (U. S. A.)
KAROUBI, Max (France)
KARRASS, Abe (Canada)
KARREMAN, Herman (U. S. A.)
KARUSH, William (U. S. A.)
KATZ, Jerome (U. S. A.)
KATZ, Leo (U. S. A.)
KATZ, Nicholas (U. S. A.)
KATZ, Richard (U. S. A.)
KAUP, Ludger (Fed. Rep. Germany)
KAUTSKY, Jaroslav (Australia)
KAWADA, Yukiyoshi (Japan)
KAWAI, Takahiro (Japan)
KAWASAKI, Tetsuro (Japan)
KAWAZU, Kiyoshi (Japan)
KAZDAN, Jerry (U. S. A.)
KAZI, Asifali (Pakistan)
KEARSLEY, Elliot (U. S. A.)
KEARSLEY, Mary (England)
KEARTON, Cherry (England)
KEEN, Linda (U. S. A.)
KEENER, Lee (Canada)
KEEPING, Anthony (England)
KEGEL, Otto (England)
KELLER, Heinrich (Switzerland)
KELLOGG, Frank (U. S. A.)
KELLY, David (Canada)
KELLY, David (U. S. A.)
KELLY, John (U. S. A.)
KEMPERMAN, Johan (U. S. A.)
KENNEY, Margaret (U. S. A.)
KENT, Clement (Canada)
KEOGH, Frank (U. S. A.)
KERBY, William (Fed. Rep. Germany)
KERKYACHARIAN, Gerard (France)
KERR, Charles (U. S. A.)
KERR-LAWSON, Angus (Canada)
KERWIN, Carolyn (U. S. A.)
KERZMAN, Norberto (U. S. A.)
KEYFITZ, Barbara (U. S. A.)
KHOSROSHAHI, Golamreza (Iran)
KIBBEY, Donald (U. S. A.)
KIBBLEWHITE, Kenneth (Canada)
KIBLER, Robert (U. S. A.)
KIELY, John (England)
KIJIMA, Yoichi (Japan)
KILLGROVE, Raymond (U. S. A.)
KILTINEN, John (U. S. A.)
KIM, C.W. (Canada)
KIM, Churl (U. S. A.)
KIM, Hong (U. S. A.)
KIMENYEMBO, Mafinge (France)
KINDERLEHRER, David (U. S. A.)
KINDRED, Jerold (U. S. A.)
KING, Henry (U. S. A.)
KING. James (U. S. A.)
KING, Paul (U. S. A.)
KIPNIS, Claude (France)
KIRBY, Robion (U. S. A.)
KIREMIDJIAN, Garo (U. S. A.)
KIRK, Ronald (U. S. A.)
KIRWAN, William (U. S. A.)
KISILEVSKY, Hershy (U. S. A.)
KITAMURA, Taiichi (Japan)
KITT, Larry (Canada)
KLASA, Stan (Canada)
KLEE, Victor (U. S. A.)
KLEIMAN, Steven L. (U.S.A.)
KLEIN, Abel (U. S. A.)
KLEIN, Larisse (U. S. A.)
KLEINFELD, Erwin (U. S. A.)
KLEISLI, Heinrich (Switzerland)
KLEITMAN, Daniel (U. S. A.)
KLEMOLA, Tapio (Canada)
KLEPPNER, Adam (U. S. A.)
KLOESGEN, Willy (Fed. Rep. Germany)
KLUGE, Reinhard (German Dem. Rep.)
KLUVANEK, Igor (Australia)
KNAPP, Anthony (U. S. A.)
KNAUER, Ulrich (Fed. Rep. Germany)
KNIGHT, Dorothy (U. S. A.)
KNIGHT, Julia (U. S. A.)
KNIGHT, Lyman (U. S. A.)
KNIGHT, William (U. S. A.)
KNILL, Ronald (U. S. A.)
KNOEBEL, R. Arthur (U. S. A.)
KNOPFMACHER, John (Rep. South Africa)
KNOWLES, Robert (U. S. A.)
KOBAYASHI, Shoshichi (U. S. A.)
KOBLITZ, Neal (U. S. A.)
KOCAK, Cevdet (Turkey)
KOCH, Helmut (German Dem. Rep.)

KOCHER, Frank (U. S. A.)
KOEHLER, Don (U .S. A.)
KOGISO, Yukio (Japan)
KOHN, Joseph (U. S. A.)
KOIZUMI, Shoji (Japan)
KOLCHIN, Ellis (U.S.A.)
KOLMAN, Bernard (U. S. A.)
KOLMER, Shirley (U. S. A.)
KOLODNER, Ignace (U. S. A.)
KOMATSU, Gen (Japan)
KOMATSU, Yusaku (Japan)
KOMHOFF, Magelone (Fed. Rep. Germany)
KOMLOS, Janos (Hungary)
KOMORNICKI, Wojciech (U. S. A.)
KORENBLUM, Boris (Israel)
KORNEICHUK, Nikolai (U. S. S. R.)
KORTRAM, Ronald (Netherlands)
KOSACHEVSKAYA, Helen (U. S. S. R.)
KOSCHORKE, Ulrich (U. S. A.)
KOSMAN, Yvette (France)
KOSTINSKY, Alan (U. S. A.)
KOTA, Osamu (Japan)
KOTTWITZ, Robert (U. S. A.)
KOTZIG, Anton (Canada)
KOUTROUFIOTIS, Dimitri (U. S. A.)
KOVACS, Laszlo (Australia)
KOVARI, Thomas (England)
KOVHCIC, Jerald (U. S. A.)
KOZMA, Ilan (Israel)
KRAEMER, Helmut (Germany)
KRAFT, Hanspeter (Switzerland)
KRAFT, Richard (U. S. A.)
KRAMER, Thomas (U. S. A.)
KRANTZ, Steven (U. S. A.)
KRASNER, Marc (France)
KREISS, Heinz (Sweden)
KRENER, Arthur (U. S. A.)
KREYSZIG, Erwin (Canada)
KRIEGER, Wolfgang (Fed. Rep. Germany)
KRISHNAMURTHY, Visvanatha (India)
KRISTENSEN, Leif (Denmark)
KRIZANCIC, Ignace (Canada)
KRNANOVA-PROULX, Viera (U. S. A.)
KRONSTADT, Eric (U. S. A.)
KRONSTEIN, Karl (U. S. A.)
KROONENBERG, Nelly (U. S. A.)
KRUGMAN, Edward (U.S.A.)
KRUSE, Arthur (U. S. A.)
KRUSE, Robert (U. S. A.)
KRUSEMEYER, Mark (Netherlands)
KRUSKAL, Martin (U. S. A.)
KUDRYAVTSEV, Lev (U. S. S. R.)
KUEKER, David (U. S. A.)
KUIPER, Nicolaas (France)
KUIPERS, Jack (U. S. A.)
KUIPERS, Lauwerens (U. S. A.)
KUMAR, Arunod (U. S. A.)
KUMMER, Hans (Canada)
KUNUGI, Kinjiro (Japan)
KUNZE, Ray (U. S. A.)
KURAN, Ulku (England)
KUREPA, Djuro (Yugoslavia)
KURSS, Herbert (U. S. A.)
KURTZ, Thomas (U. S. A.)
KUSHNER, Harold (U. S. A.)
KUYK, Willem (Belgium)
KUZNETSOV, A. V. (U. S. S. R.)
KYNCH, George (England)

L'ABBE, Marcel (Canada)
LABELLE, Gilbert (Canada)
LACHER, R. Christopher (U. S. A.)
LACHLAN, Alistair (Canada)
LACOMBA, Ernesto (Mexico)
LACROIX, Norbert (Canada)
LADDE, Gangaram (U. S. A.)
LADY, Lee (U. S. A.)
LAFON, Jean-Pierre (France)
LAFON, Monique (France)
LAHA, Radha (U. S. A.)
LAI, Hang-Chin (Rep. China)
LAI, Hon-Fei (U. S. A.)
LAINE, Ilpo (Finland)
LAKSHMIKANTHAM, Vangipuram (U. S. A.)
LALLI, Bikkar (Canada)
LAM, Kee (Canada)
LAMBERT, Jack (Scotland)
LAMBERT, Joseph (U. S. A.)
LAMOUREUX, Claude (France)
LAMPE, William (U. S. A.)
LANCASTER, G. Maurice (Canada)
LANCE, Christopher (England)
LANCHON, Helene (France)
LANDMAN, Alan (U. S. A.)
LANDROCK, Peter (Denmark)
LANDSTAD, Magnus (Norway)
LANFORD, Oscar (U.S.A.)
LANG, George (U. S. A.)
LAPRESTE, Jean-Thierry (France)
LARA, Miguel (Mexico)
LARMORE, Lawrence (U. S. A.)
LASCARIDES, Constantine (Greece)
LASHOF, Richard (U. S. A.)
LASRY, Jean-Michel (France)
LASSEZ, Jean-Louis (Canada)
LATORRE, Donald (U. S. A.)
LAU, Anthony (Canada)
LAUGWITZ, Detlef (Fed. Rep. Germany)
LAUMON, Gerard (France)
LAURENT, Pierre (France)
LAURSEN, Kjeld (Denmark)
LAVINE, Richard (U. S. A.)
LAVOIE, Jean L. (Canada)
LAVRENTEV, Mikhaie (U. S. S. R.)

LAVRIENTIEV, Mikail (U. S. S. R.)
LAVRIK, A.F. (U. S. S. R.)
LAW, Alan (Canada)
LAWRENCE, John (Canada)
LAWRUK, Bohdan (Canada)
LAWSON, H. Blaine (U. S. A.)
LAWSON, Terry (U. S. A.)
LAX, Peter (U. S. A.)
LAX, Robert (U. S. A.)
LAXTON, Ronald (England)
LAY, David (U. S. A.)
LAZARUS, Michel (France)
LE, Dung Trang (Dem. Rep. Vietnam)
LE DIMET, Jean-Yves (France)
LE VAN, Thiem (Dem. Rep. Vietnam)
LEADER, Solomon (U. S. A.)
LEAHEY, William (U. S. A.)
LEARY, Kevin (U. S. A.)
LEAVITT, William (U. S. A.)
LEBAUD, Colette (France)
LEBAUD, Georges (France)
LEBORGNE, Daniel (France)
LEDRAPPIER, Francois (France)
LEE, Seng-Luan (Malaysia)
LEE, Shing-Meng (Rep. China)
LEE, Sung (Canada)
LEEB, Klaus (Germany)
LEECH, Jonathan (U. S. A.)
LEEDHAM-GREEN, Charles (England)
LEELA, Srinivasa (U. S. A.)
LEES, Paul (England)
LEESE, Stephen (England)
LEGGETT, Anne (U. S. A.)
LEGRAND, Denise (France)
LEGRAND, Solange (France)
LEHMAN, Alfred (Canada)
LEHMAN, Eugene (Canada)
LEHMAN, R. Sherman (U. S. A.)
LEHMER, Derrick (U. S. A.)
LEHNER, Guydo (U. S. A.)
LEHTO, Olli (Finland)
LEICHT, Johann (German Dem. Rep.)
LEIMANIS, Eugene (Canada)
LEINDLER, Laszlo (Hungary)
LEIPNIK, Roy (U. S. A.)
LEISENRING, Albert (U. S. A.)
LEKKERKERKER, Cornelis (Netherlands)
LELONG, Pierre (France)
LELONG-FERRAND, Jacqueline (France)
LEMAIRE, Claude (Canada)
LEMIRE, Francis (Canada)
LEONARD, I. Edward (U. S. A.)
LEONOR, Concepcion (Phillipines)
LEONTIEV, Aleyei (U. S. S. R.)
LEPOWSKY, James (U. S. A.)
LERMAN, Manuel (U. S. A.)
LERUSTE, Christian (France)
LESLIE, Robert (U. S. A.)
LEUNG, Dominic (U. S. A.)
LEVEQUE, William (U. S. A.)
LEVINSON, Henry (U. S. A.)
LEVKO, John (U. S. A.)
LEWAND, Robert (U. S. A.)
LEWIS, Clayton (Canada)
LEWIS, D. (U. S. A.)
LEWIS, Harly (U. S. A.)
LICKORISH, W.B. Raymond (England)
LIDDELL, Gerrard (Canada)
LIEB, Elliott (U. S. A.)
LIEBECK, Hans (England)
LIGGETT, Thomas (U. S. A.)
LIGHTHILL, James (England)
LIGOZAT, Gerard (France)
LIM, Chong-Keang (Malaysia)
LIM, Rudolf (U. S. A.)
LIN, Tsad-Young (U.S.A.)
LIND, Douglas (U. S. A.)
LINDENBERG, Wolfgang (Fed. Rep. Germany)
LINDNER, Rolf (German Dem. Rep.)
LING, William (U. S. A.)
LINIS, Viktors (Canada)
LIONS, Jacques (France)
LIPINSKI, Jan (Poland)
LIPSCHUTZ-YEVICK, Miriam (U. S. A.)
LIPSICH, H. David (U. S. A.)
LIPSMAN, Ronald (U. S. A.)
LIU, Chamond (U. S. A.)
LIULEVICIUS, Arunas (U. S. A.)
LIVERPOOL, Lennox (Sierra Leone)
LLUIS, Emilio (Mexico)
LODAY, Jean-Louis (France)
LOEB, Henry (U. S. A.)
LOEB, Peter (U. S. A.)
LOEBL, Richard (U. S. A.)
LOESCH, Friedrich (Fed. Rep. Germany)
LOFQUIST, George (U. S. A.)
LOJASIEWICZ, Stanislaw (Poland)
LONGYEAR, Judith (U. S. A.)
LOPEZ DE MEDRANO, Santiago (Mexico)
LORCH, Lee (Canada)
LORD, Graham (New Zealand)
LORD, Harriet (U. S. A.)
LOSEY, Gerald (Canada)
LOUHIVAARA, Ilppo Simo (Finland)
LOVASZ, Laszlo (Hungary)
LUCHINS, Edith (U. S. A.)
LUEHR, Charles (U. S. A.)
LUFT, Erhard (Canada)
LUHAHI, Lahi (Rep. of Zaire)
LUKACS, Eugene (U. S. A.)
LUNA, George (U. S. A.)
LUNBECK, Rudolf (Netherlands)
LUND, Bruce (Canada)
LUNDELL, Albert (U. S. A.)
LUSZTIG, George (England)
LUTHAR, Indar (India)
LUTZ, Elisabeth (France)
LUXEMBURG, Wilhelmus (U. S. A.)

MAC DONNELL, John (U. S. A.)
MACK, John (Australia)
MACKEY, George (U. S. A.)
MAC LANE, Saunders (U. S. A.)

MAC PHAIL, Moray (Canada)
MADAN, Manohar (U. S. A.)
MADDEROM, Peter (Canada)
MADDUX, Roger (U. S. A.)
MADLENER, Klaus (Fed. Rep. Germany)
MADSEN, I. B. Henning (Denmark)
MAGATTE, Thiam (Senegal)
MAGENES, Enrico (Italy)
MAGID, Andy (U. S. A.)
MAGLIO, Rodolfo (U. S. A.)
MAGNUS, Wilhelm (U. S. A.)
MAH, Peter (Canada)
MAHJOUB, Bechir (Tunisia)
MAHONY, Lowis (U. S. A.)
MAHROUS, Mohamed (U. S. A.)
MAILHOS, Line (France)
MAJEED, Abdul (Pakistan)
MAJUMDAR, Samir (Canada)
MAKAR, Boshra (U. S. A.)
MAKINEN, Jukka (Finland)
MAKKAI, Michael (Canada)
MAKKY, Sadia Murad (Iraq)
MAKOWSKI, Gary (U. S. A.)
MAKOWSKY, Johann (Switzerland)
MALIK, M. A. (Canada)
MALLIAVIN, Marie (France)
MALLIAVIN, Paul (France)
MALM, Donald (U. S. A.)
MANASTER, Alfred (U. S. A.)
MANN, Larry (U. S. A.)
MANNING, Anthony (England)
MANSFIELD, Lois (U. S. A.)
MANWELL, Alfred (Rhodesia)
MARATHE, Kishore (U. S. A.)
MARCEL, Bassene (Senegal)
MARCHIONNA, Cesarina (Italy)
MARCHIONNA, Ermanno (Italy)
MARCHUK, Guriy (U. S. S. R.)
MARCJA, Annalisa (Italy)
MARCUARD, Jean Claude (France)
MARCUS, Brian (U. S. A.)
MARCUS, Robert (U. S. A.)
MARDEN, Morris (U. S. A.)
MARDESIC, Sibe (Yugoslavia)
MARECHAL, Odile (France)
MARGULIS, G. A. (U. S. S. R.)
MARINO, Ricardo (Spain)
MARKEL, Frank (Canada)
MARKUS, Lawrence (U. S. A.)
MAROWITZ, Michael (U. S. A.)
MARQUETTY, Antoine (France)
MARRY, Pierre (France)
MARSDEN, Jerrold (Canada)
MARSHALL, Charles (Fed. Rep. Germany)
MARSHALL, Donald (U. S. A.)
MARSHALL, Murray (Canada)
MARTENS, Henrik (Norway)
MARTENS, Phillip (U. S. A.)
MARTIN, André (France)
MARTIN, Donald (U. S. A.)
MARTIN, George (U. S. A.)
MARTIN, John (Canada)
MARTINEAU, Patrick (England)
MARTIO, Olli (Finland)
MARUYAMA, Gishiro (Japan)
MARVILLE, Jean Pierre (Switzerland)
MASANI, Pesi (U. S. A.)
MASCART, Henri (France)
MASIH, Samuel (U. S. A.)
MASKIT, Bernard (U. S. A.)
MASLEY, John (U. S. A.)
MASON, David (England)
MASON, Gordon (Canada)
MASSER, David (England)
MASSEY, William (U. S. A.)
MATE, Attila (Hungary)
MATHER, Bertha (U. S. A.)
MATHER, John (U. S. A.)
MATHIAS, Adrian (England)
MATSUMOTO, Kozi (Japan)
MATSUMOTO, Makoto (Japan)
MATSUMOTO, Shigenori (Japan)
MATSUMOTO, Yukio (Japan)
MATTHES, Klaus (German Dem. Rep.)
MATTHEWS, Geoffrey (England)
MAU QUAN, Pham (France)
MAULDIN, Daniel (U. S. A.)
MAUREY, Bernard (France)
MAUS, Eckart (Fed. Rep. Germany)
MAXFIELD, John (U. S. A.)
MAXWELL, Edwin (England)
MAXWELL, George (Canada)
MAY, Everette (U. S. A.)
MAY, Robert (U. S. A.)
MAYER, Meinhard (U. S. A.)
MAYLAND, Edward (Canada)
MAZEN, Henrietta (U. S. A.)
MAZUR, Barry (U. S. A.)
MAZUROW, Victor (U. S. S. R.)
MC ALISTER, Donald (U. S. A.)
MC ARTHUR, Charles (U. S. A.)
MC AULEY, Louis (U. S. A.)
MC BRIEN, Vincent (U. S. A.)
MC CABE, John (Scotland)
MC CARTNEY, James (Scotland)

MC COLLUM, Gerald (U. S. A.)
MC CONNELL, James (Ireland)
MC COOL, James (Canada)
MC COY, Peter (U. S. A.)
MC COY, Robert (U. S. A.)
MC CREA, Michael (U. S. A.)
MC CRIMMON, K. M. (U. S. A.)
MC CRORY, Clint (U. S. A.)
MC CULLOH, Leon (U. S. A.)
MC DONALD, Ian (Canada)
MC DONALD, John (U. S. A.)
MC DONOUGH, Thomas (Wales)
MC ELWAIN, Sean (Australia)
MC GEHEE, Richard (U. S. A.)
MC GREGOR, James (U. S. A.)
MC GREGOR, Malcolm (England)
MC INTOSH, Alan (Australia)
MC KAY, John (Canada)
MC KEEHAN, James (U. S. A.)
MC KENNA, James (U. S. A.)
MC KEVEY, Robert (U. S. A.)
MC LEOD, Bryce (England)
MC LEOD, Edward (U. S. A.)
MC LEOD, John (England)
MC MULLEN, Peter (England)
MC NULTY, George (U. S. A.)
MC PEEK, L. Joseph (Canada)
MC PHAIL, Gerard (Canada)
MC QUEEN, Paul (Canada)
MC RAE, George (U. S. A.)
MC SHANE, Edward (U. S. A.)
MEACHAM, Robert (U. S. A.)
MEAD, Ernest (Canada)
MEAKIN, John (Australia)
MEEK, Dereck (Canada)
MEIR, Amram (Canada)
MELAMED, Samuel (Canada)
MELCHIOR, Ulrich (Fed. Rep. Germany)
MELDRUM, John (Scotland)
MELZAK, Zdzislaw (Canada)
MENDELSOHN, Eric (Canada)
MENDELSOHN, Nathan (Canada)
MENY, Georges (France)
MERLE, Michel (France)
MERUCCI, Claude (France)
MESSING, William (U. S. A.)
METAKIDES, George (U. S. A.)
MEYER, Albert (U. S. A.)
MEYER, Burnett (U. S. A.)
MEYER, Christian (U. S. A.)
MEYERS, Leroy (U. S. A.)
MIAMEE, Abolghassen (Iran)
MICHAEL, David (England)
MICHAEL, Ernest (U. S. A.)
MICHAELIS, Walter (U. S. A.)
MICHEL, Emsalem (France)
MICHEL, Philippe (France)
MICHELETTI, Anwa Maria (Italy)
MICHELOW, Jaime (Chile)
MIERS, Bob (Canada)
MIKOLAS, Miklos (Hungary)
MIKUSINSKI, Jan (Poland)
MILES, E. P., Jr. (U. S. A.)
MILGRAM, Richard (U. S. A.)
MILLER, B. Arthur (Canada)
MILLER, C. Brandt (Canada)
MILLER, Carman (Canada)
MILLER, D. D. (U. S. A.)
MILLER, Donald (U. S. A.)
MILLER, Edward (U. S. A.)
MILLER, Hugh (Canada)
MILLER, Sanford (U. S. A.)
MILLER, Victor (U. S. A.)
MILLETT, Kenneth (U. S. A.)
MILLMAN, Richard (U. S. A.)
MILLSON, John (Canada)
MILMAN, Pier (Israel)
MILNER, Eric (Canada)
MILNES, Paul (Canada)
MILOSLAVSKY, George (U. S. A.)
MILTON, E. (U. S. A.)
MIMURA, Yukio (Japan)
MINDA, Carl (U. S. A.)
MING, Ronald (U. S. A.)
MINSKER, Steven (U. S. A.)
MIRANDA, Edward (U. S. A.)
MISHRA, Ratan Shanker (India)
MISNER, Charles (U. S. A.)
MITCHELL, Andrew (Scotland)
MITCHELL, Josephine (U. S. A.)
MITCHELL, Rae (England)
MITCHELL, Theodore (U. S. A.)
MITCHELL, William (U. S. A.)
MITROPOLSKI, Iouri (U. S. S. R.)
MITSUI, Takayoshi (Japan)
MIURA, Robert (U. S. A.)
MIYAKE, Toshi-Tsune (Japan)
MIYATAKE, Osamu (Japan)
MIYAZAKI, Toshi-Hiro (Japan)
MIZUMURA, Hideo (Japan)
MIZUTANI, Tadayoshi (Japan)
MOELLER, Regina (Fed. Rep. Germany)
MOH, Tzuong-Tsieng (U. S. A.)
MOKOBODZKI, Gabriel (France)

MOLINARO, Annick (France)
MOLLIN, Richard (Canada)
MONG, Shaw (U. S. A.)
MONTGOMERY, Deane (U. S. A.)
MONTGOMERY, Hugh (U. S. A.)
MONTGOMERY, Peter (U. S. A.)
MONTGOMERY, Richard (U. S. A.)
MONTZINGO, Lloyd (U. S. A.)
MOODY, Robert (Canada)
MOORE, Berrien (U. S. A.)
MOORE, John (U. S. A.)
MOORE, Michael (Canada)
MOORE, Robert (U. S. A.)
MOORE LEE, Carolyn (Canada)
MORALES, Bernardo (Guatemala)
MORALES-CASTRO, Jorge A. (Mexico)
MORALES-MARTINEZ, Rodolfo, (Mexico)
MORAN, Patrick (Australia)
MOREAU, Jean-Jacques (France)
MOREL, Anne (U. S. A.)
MORGAN, Christopher (U. S. A.)
MORGAN, J. W. (U. S. A.)
MORGAN, Kathryn (U. S. A.)
MORREY, Charles (U. S. A.)
MORRIS, Alun (Wales)
MORRIS, Grainger (Australia)
MORRIS, Peter (U. S. A.)
MORRIS, Robert (U. S. A.)
MORRIS, Rosa (England)
MORRISON, Barbara (U. S. A.)
MORRISON, John (U. S. A.)
MORROW, James (U. S. A.)
MORTELL, Michael (Ireland)
MOSAK, Richard (U. S. A.)
MOSCHOVAKIS, Joan Rand (U. S. A.)
MOSCHOVAKIS, Yiannis (U. S. A.)
MOSER, Jurgen (U. S. A.)
MOSER, Louise (U. S. A.)
MOSER, William (Canada)
MOSEVICH, Jack (Canada)
MOSTOW, George (U. S. A.)
MOSTOWSKI, Tadeusz (Poland)
MOYER, Robert (U. S. A.)
MOYLS, Ben (Canada)
MUELLER, Helmut (Fed. Rep. Germany)
MUELLER, Thomas (U. S. A.)
MUKHERJEE, Some (India)
MULDOON, Martin (Canada)
MULDOWNEY, James (Canada)
MULLA, Fuad (Kuwait)
MULLIKIN, Harry (U. S. A.)
MULLIS, Robert (Canada)
MULVEY, Christopher (England)
MUMFORD, David (U. S. A.)
MUNKHOLM, Hans (Denmark)
MUNN, Douglas (Scotland)
MUNOZ, Edgar (Guatemala)
MURASE, Ichiro (Japan)
MURASUGI, Kunio (Canada)
MURDOCH, David (Canada)
MURPHY, Noel (Canada)
MURRE, Jacob (Netherlands)
MURTY, U. S. R. (Canada)
MUTO, Yoshio (Japan)
MYCIELSKI, Jan (U. S. A.)
MYUNG, Hyo (U. S. A.)
MYSAK, L. A. (Canada)

NAATANEN, Marjatta (Finland)
NADUM, Adil (Iraq)
NAGANO, Tadashi (U. S. A.)
NAHOUM, Albert (France)
NAIMPALLY, Som (Canada)
NAKAMURA, Michiko (Japan)
NAKAMURA, Yatsuka (Japan)
NAKANISHI, Kazuhiro (Japan)
NAKANO, Kazumi (U. S. A.)
NAKAZAWA, Hideaki (Japan)
NAKKI, Raimo (Finland)
NAMIOKA, Isaac (U. S. A.)
NARASIMHAN, M. S. (India)
NARASIMHAN, Mysore (U. S. A.)
NARAYANASWAMI, Pallasena (Canada)
NARCOWICH, Francis (U. S. A.)
NARUSHIMA, Hiroshi (Japan)
NASH-WILLIAMS, Crispin (Scotland)
NASSIF, Maher (Nigeria)
NATHANSON, Melvyn (U. S. A.)
NEFTIDJI, Phedre (Greece)
NEGREPONTIS, Stylianos (Canada)
NEHOROSHEV, Nicolai (U. S. S. R.)
NEL, Louis (Canada)
NELIUS, Christian (Fed. Rep. Germany)
NELSEN, Roger (U. S. A.)
NELSON, Edward (U. S. A.)
NERON, Andre (France)
NESBITT, Cecil (U. S. A.)
NESS, Linda (U. S. A.)
NESTELL, Merlynd (U. S. A.)
NEUBERGER, John (U. S. A.)
NEUMANN, Bernhard (Australia)
NEVANLINNA, Rolf (Finland)
NEVEU, Jacques (France)
NEWBERGER, Edward (U. S. A.)
NEWBERGER, Stuart (U. S. A.)

NEWMAN, Michael (Australia)
NEWMAN, Morris (U. S. A.)
NEYMAN, Jerzy (U. S. A.)
NI CHUIV, Nora (Canada)
NICHOLS, Nancy (England)
NICHOLSON, William (Canada)
NICKEL, Karl (Fed. Rep. Germany)
NICO, William (U. S. A.)
NICOLACOPOULOU Ioanna (Greece)
NICOLAS, Jean-Louis (France)
NICOLESCU, Miron (Romania)
NIELSEN, Ole (Canada)
NIETO, Jose (Canada)
NIIRO, Fumio (Japan)
NIJENHUIS, Albert (U. S. A.)
NIKOLSKII, Serguei (U. S. S. R.)
NILSSON, Nils (Sweden)
NIMAN, John (U. S. A.)
NINOMIYA, Nobuyuki (Japan)
NIRENBERG, Louis (U. S. A.)
NISHIMIYA, Han (Japan)
NISHIURA, Togo (U. S. A.)
NITSCHE, Johannes (U. S. A.)
NIVEN, Ivan (U. S. A.)
NORI, Madhav (India)
NORIYUKI, Hirose (Japan)
NORMAND, Gerard (Canada)
NORTON, Karl (U. S. A.)
NOSAL, Miloslav (Canada)
NOTTROT, Roelof (Netherlands)
NOVAK, Josef (Czechoslovakia)
NOZAKI, Yasuo (Japan)

OBA, Sachio (Japan)
OBERAI, Kirti (Canada)
OBI, Chike (Nigeria)
O'BRIAN, Nigel (England)
O'BRIEN, Richard (Canada)
O'BRIEN, Thomas (U. S. A.)
O'CALLAGHAN, Liam (U. S. A.)
O'CONNOR, Thomas (U. S. A.)
ODA, Tadao (Japan)
O'DONOVAN, Donal (Ireland)
OEHMKE, Robert (U. S. A.)
O'FARRELL, Anthony (Ireland)
OGIUE, Koichi (U. S. A.)
OHKUMA, Tadashi (Japan)
OHWAKI, Shin-Ichi (Japan)
OKAWA, Sachiko (Japan)
OKEE, Jeker (Uganda)
OKOH, Frank (Canada)
OKUBO, Tanjiro (Canada)
OLAOFE, G. Oluremi (Nigeria)
OLECH, Czeslaw (Poland)
OLEINIK, Olga (U. S. S. R.)
OLIN, Philip (Canada)
OLIVER, Robert (U. S. A.)
OLSEN, Catherine (U. S. A.)
OLSON, Andrew (Chile)
OLSSON, Jorn (Denmark)
OLVER, Peter (U. S. A.)
O'MALLEY, Sister Mary (U. S. A.)
O'NEIL, Richard (U. S. A.)
O'NEILL, Anne (U. S. A.)
O'NEILL, Michael (Canada)
ONG, Boon (Canada)
ONO, Tamio (Japan)
OORT, Frans (Netherlands)
OPFER, Gerhard (Fed. Rep. Germany)
ORIHARA, Masae (Japan)
ORLIK, Peter (U. S. A.)
ORMELL, Christopher (England)
ORNSTEIN, Avraham (Israel)
OSBORN, J. Marshall (U. S. A.)
OSBORNE, Mason (U. S. A.)
OSGOOD, Charles (U. S. A.)
OSHIO, Shigeru (Japan)
OSHOBI, Emmanuel (Nigeria)
OSNER, Henry (U. S. A.)
OSOFSKY, Barbara (U. S. A.)
OSSERMAN, Robert (U. S. A.)
OSTIANU, Natalia (U. S. S. R.)
OTSUKA, Kayo (Japan)
OTSUKI, Tominosuke (Japan)
OZOLS, Vilnis (U. S. A.)

PAALMAN-DEMIRAND, Aida (Netherlands)
PABST, Gunther (Canada)
PACIOREK, Joseph (U. S. A.)
PACKEL, Edward (U. S. A.)
PADMANABHAN, Ranganathan (Canada)
PAGANI, Carlo (Italy)
PAGE, S. S. (Canada)
PAHLINGS, Herbert (Fed. Rep. Germany)
PAINE, Christine (Australia)
PAL, Edward (Canada)
PAL, Laszlo (Nigeria)
PALAIS, Richard (U. S. A.)
PALMER, John (U. S. A.)
PAN, Ting (U. S. A.)
PANDEY, Nagendra (U. S. A.)
PAPADOPOULOS, M. (U. S. A.)
PAPAKYRIAKOPOULOS, Christos (U. S. A.)
PAPP, F. J. (Canada)
PAREEK, Chandra Mohan (Kuwait)
PARKER, Phil (U. S. A.)
PARKS, Harold (U. S. A.)
PARMENTER, Michael (Canada)
PARSHALL, Brian (U. S. A.)
PARTIS, Michael (Scotland)
PASCAUD, Jean-Louis (France)
PASSI, Inder (India)
PASSOW, Eli (U. S. A.)
PASTIJN, Francis (Belgium)
PATERA, Jiri (Canada)
PATERSON, Michael (England)
PATODI, Vijay (India)
PATTON, Ralph (U. S. A.)

PAULSON, Edward (U. S. A.)
PAYSANT-LE ROUX, Roger (France)
PEARSON, Lennart (U. S. A.)
PEDERSEN, Erik (Denmark)
PEDERSEN, Gert (Denmark)
PEDOE, Daniel (U. S. A.)
PEEL, Michael (England)
PEETRE, Jaak (Sweden)
PEIXOTO, Mauricio (Brazil)
PELCZYNSKI, Aleksander (Poland)
PELL, William (U. S. A.)
PELLES, Donald (U. S. A.)
PELLETIER, Donald (Canada)
PELLETIER, Joan (Canada)
PENICO, Anthony, (U. S. A.)
PENOT, J. P. (France)
PERSSON, Jan (Norway)
PERSSON, Ulf (Sweden)
PESCHL, Ernst (Fed. Rep. Germany)
PETERSEN, Bent (U. S. A.)
PETERSEN, Gordon (New Zealand)
PETERSON, Dale (U. S. A.)
PETERSON, Franklin (U. S. A.)
PETERSON, Leroy (U. S. A.)
PETRICH, Mario (U. S. A.)
PETRIDIS, Nicholas (U. S. A.)
PETRIE, Ted (U. S. A.)
PETTET, Martin (Canada)
PETTY, Clinton (U. S. A.)
PEYRIERE, Jacques (France)
PFEFFER, Washek (U. S. A.)
PHELPS, Robert (U. S. A.)
PHILLIPS, John (Canada)
PHILLIPS, Ralph (U. S. A.)
PHYTHIAN, John (England)
PICARD, Colette (France)
PICARDELLO, Angelo (Italy)
PICCARD, Sophie (Switzerland)
PICCININI, Livio (Italy)
PICKEL, Paul (U. S. A.)
PIERART, Philippe (France)
PIERCE, Stephen (Canada)
PIETROWSKI, Alfred (Canada)
PIETSCH, Albrecht (German Dem. Rep.)
PIGER, Jean (Chile)
PIGOZZI, Don (U. S. A.)
PILAR, Martin (Spain)
PINCUS, Joel (U. S. A.)
PINKHAM, Henry (U. S. A.)
PIRANIAN, George (U. S. A.)
PISIER, Gilles (France)
PITCHER, Everett (U. S. A.)
PITMAN, Jane (Australia)
PITT, David (England)
PITT, Loren (U. S. A.)
PITTENGER, Arthur (U. S. A.)
PIZER, Arnold (U. S. A.)
PLACENTINI, Giuliamaria (Italy)
PLATONOV, Vladimir (U. S. S. R.)
PLATT, Craig (Canada)
PLEASANTS, Peter (England)
PLEIJEL, Ake (Sweden)
PLESKEN, Wilhelm (Fed. Rep. Germany)
POGUNTKE, Detlev (Fed. Rep. Germany)
POLLAK, Barth (U. S. A.)
POLLAK, Henry (U. S. A.)
POMAREDA, Rolando Jorge (Chile)
PONNAPALL, R. (Canada)
PONTRJAGIN, Lev (U. S. S. R.)
POPOV, Blagoj (Yugoslavia)
PORRU, Giovanni (Italy)
PORST, Hans (Fed. Rep. Germany)
PORTE, Daniel (France)
PORTEOUS, Hugh (England)
PORTEOUS, Ian (England)
POSTMAN, Robert (U. S. A.)
POTOCZNY, Henry (U. S. A.)
POTTER, Anthony (Scotland)
POTTER, Ronda (Australia)
POZNIAK, Edoupo (U. S. S. R.)
PRAKASH, Nirmala (India)
PRESSMAN, Irwin (Canada)
PRESTON, Christopher (England)
PRETZEL, Oliver (England)
PRICE, David (U. S. A.)
PRICE, Kenneth (U. S. A.)
PRIKRY, Karel (U. S. A.)
PRILEPKO, Alexei (U. S. S. R.)
PRIMROSE, Eric (England)
PRINDLE, Paul (U. S. A.)
PRINTIS, R. (U. S. A.)
PROMISLOW, David (Canada)
PROPPE, Harold (Canada)
PROTOMASTRO, Gerard (U. S. A.)
PROULX, Ronald (U. S. A.)
PUCCI, Carlo (Italy)
PURI, Pratap (U. S. A.)
PURZITSKY, Norman (Canada)
PUTERMAN, Martin (U. S. A.)
PUTNAM, Alfred (U. S. A.)
PUTTASWAMAIAH, Bannikuppe (Canada)
PUTTASWAMY, Tumkur (U. S. A.)

QUILLEN, Daniel (U. S. A.)

RACINE, Ly (Sengal)
RACINE, Michel (Canada)
RADER, Cary (U. S. A.)
RADO, Richard (England)
RAGGETT, Graham (England)
RAGOZIN, David (U. S. A.)
RAIMI, Ralph (U. S. A.)
RAJAGOPALAN, Minakshisundar (India)
RAMALHO, Roberto (Brazil)
RAMSAY, Arlan (U. S. A.)
RANICKI, Andrew (England)
RANKIN, Robert (Scotland)
RANKIN, Stuart (Canada)
RAO, C. R. (India)
RAO, D. Ramakrishna (Iran)
RAO, Kulkarni Kish (India)
RAO, Veldanda (Canada)

RATNER, Lawrence (U. S. A.)
RAUZY, Gerard (France)
RAY, Ajit (Canada)
RAY-CHAUDHURI, Diljen (U. S. A.)
RAZZAGHI, Mohsen (Iran)
REA, Claudio (Italy)
READE, Maxwell (U. S. A.)
RECILLAS-JUAREX, Felix (Mexico)
REDHEFFER, Raymond (U. S. A.)
REE, Rimhak (Canada)
REED, Michael (U. S. A.)
REES, David (England)
REICHERT, Marianne (Fed. Rep. Germany)
REID, Aenea (Scotland)
REID, Brooks (U. S. A.)
REID, Miles (England)
REID, Stephen (Canada)
REILLY, Ivan (New Zealand)
REILLY, Norman (Canada)
REILLY, Robert (U. S. A.)
REINGOLD, Haim (U. S. A.)
REINHART, Bruce (U. S. A.)
REISSIG, Gisela (Fed. Rep. Germany)
REISSIG, Rolf (Fed. Rep. Germany)
REITEN, Idun (Norway)
REJTO, Peter (U. S. A.)
REMPFER, Robert (U. S. A.)
RENZ, Peter (Canada)
REYNOLDS, Robert (Fed. Rep. Germany)
RHEMTULLA, Akbar (Canada)
RHIN, Georges (France)
RIBENBOIM, Paulo (Canada)
RIBES, Luis (Canada)
RIBET, Kenneth (U. S. A.)
RICE, Thelma, (U. S. A.)
RICHARDSON, Roger (England)
RICHERT, Arthur (U. S. A.)
RICHMOND, Bruce (Canada)
RICHTER, Guenther (Fed. Rep. Germany)
RICKARD, John (Australia)
RICHART, Charles (U. S. A.)
RICKEY, V. Frederick (U. S. A.)
RIDDELL, James (Canada)
RIDEOUT, Donald (Canada)
RIEGER, Georg (Germany)
RIEHM, Carl (Canada)
RIEMANSCHNEIDER, Sherman (Canada)
RIEMER, Rolf-Ingraban (Fed. Rep. Germany)
RIGBY, John (Wales)
RILES, James (U. S. A.)
RILEY, Geoffrey (Australia)
RINGEL, Claus (Fed. Rep. Germany)
RINGROSE, John (England)
RISCH, Robert (U. S. A.)
RIVAL, Ivan (Canada)
RIVET, Roger (France)
RIVLIN, Theodore (U. S. A.)
RIZV, S. Jawaid (Pakistan)
RIZZA, Glovanni Batt. (Italy)
RIZZI, Alfredo (Italy)
ROBERT, Didier (France)
ROBERTS, Joel (U. S. A.)
ROBERTS, L. G. (Canada)
ROBERTS, Leslie (Canada)
ROBERTSON, Alexander (Australia)
ROBERTSON, Malcolm (Canada)
ROBERTSON, Mark (England)
ROBERTSON, Neil (Canada)
ROBINSON, Donald (U. S. A.)
ROBINSON, Gilbert (Canada)
ROBINSON, Raphael (U. S. A.)
ROBINSON, Stanley (U. S. A.)
ROCKAFELLAR, Tyrrell (U. S. A.)
RODGERS, Richard (U. S. A.)
RODIER, Francois (France)
RODRIGUEZ SANCHEZ, Oscar-Mario (Mexico)
ROEDER, David (U. S. A.)
ROGER, Claude (France)
ROGERS, Claude Ambrose (England)
ROGGENKAMP, Klaus (Fed. Rep. Germany)
ROGOSINSKI, Peter (Wales)
ROHRL, Helmut (U. S. A.)
ROITMAN, Judith (U. S. A.)
RONVEAUX, Andre (Belgium)
ROONEY, Paul (Canada)
ROSA, Alexander (Canada)
ROSATI, Mario (Italy)
ROSEN, Kenneth (U. S. A.)
ROSENBERG, Harold (France)
ROSENBERG, Ivo (Canada)
ROSENBERGER, Gerhard (Fed. Rep. Germany)
ROSENBLATT-ROTH, Millu (U. S. A.)
ROSENBLOOM, Paul (U. S. A.)
ROSENBLUM, Marvin (U. S. A.)
ROSENLICHT, Maxwell (U. S. A.)
ROSENSTEIN, Joseph G. (U. S. A.)
ROSENTHAL, John (U. S. A.)
ROSENTHAL, Peter (Canada)
ROSKES, Gerald (U. S. A.)
ROSS, Roderick (Canada)
ROTHAUS, Oscar (U. S. A.)
ROTHSCHILD, Linda (U. S. A.)
ROW, Don (Australia)
ROWLEY, Christopher (England)
ROWLEY, Rosemary (England)
ROWLINSON, Peter (Scotland)
ROY, Ashoke (India)
ROYDEN, Halsey (U. S. A.)
ROYSTER, Wimberly (U. S. A.)
RUBIN, Joel (U. S. A.)
RUBINSTEIN, Joachim (Australia)
RUBIO, Jose Luis (Spain)
RUCHTI, Rene (Switzerland)

RUCKLE, William (U. S. A.)
RUDIN, Mary Ellen (U. S. A.)
RUDIN, Walter (U. S. A.)
RUSKAI, Mary Beth (U. S. A.)
RUSSELL, Dennis (Canada)
RUSTON, Anthony (Wales)
RUTTER, John (England)
RYCHKOV, Serzgei (U. S. S. R.)
RYEBURN, David (Canada)

SAAVEDRA, Neantro (Chile)
SABBAGH, Gabriel (France)
SABININ, Larissa (Nigeria)
SABININ, Leo (Nigeria)
SACERDOTE, George (U. S. A.)
SADOWSKY, John (U. S. A.)
SAEKI, Sadahiro (Japan)
SAGEEV, Gershon (U. S. A.)
SAHNEY, Badri (Canada)
SAINT-DONAT, Bernard (France)
SAITOTI, George (Kenya)
SAKAI, Yoshiko (Japan)
SAKS, Victor (Costa Rica)
SAKUMA, Motohoshi (Japan)
SALLES, Danielle (France)
SALZBERG, Pablo (Chile)
SALZER, Herbert (U. S. A.)
SALZMANN, Helmut (Fed. Rep. Germany)
SAMARSKII, A. A. (U. S. S. R.)
SAMELSON, Hans (U. S. A.)
SANCHO, Neville (Canada)
SANDS, Arthur (Scotland)
SANDS, Bill (Canada)
SANKARAN, Subramanian (England)
SAPKAREV, Ilija (Yugoslavia)
SARASON, Leonard (U. S. A.)
SARASWATHI, Kalpakam (India)
SARD, Arthur (U. S. A.)
SARIO, Leo (U. S. A.)
SASAKI, Usa (Japan)
SATAKE, Ichiro (U. S. A.)
SATO, Daihachiro (Canada)
SATO, Isuke (Japan)
SATYANARAYANA, Upadhyayula (India)
SAUER, Norbert (Canada)
SAVOLAINEN, Onerva (Finland)
SAWAKI, Sumio (Japan)
SAWASHIMA, Ikuko (Japan)
SAWYER, Stanley (U. S. A.)
SAYEKI, Hidemitsu (Canada)
SCHAFER, Alice (U. S. A.)
SCHAFER, James (U. S. A.)
SCHAFFER, Juan (U. S. A.)
SCHARLAU, Winfried (Fed. Rep. Germany)
SCHARLEMANN, Martin (U. S. A.)
SCHATZ, Alfred (U. S. A.)
SCHAUFELE, Ronald (Canada)
SCHEFFER, Carel (Netherlands)
SCHEFFER, Vladimir (U. S. A.)
SCHEIBLICH, Herman (U. S. A.)
SCHIFF, Joel (New Zealand)
SCHIFFER, Menahem (U. S. A.)
SCHIRMER, Helga (Canada)
SCHLIPF, John (U. S. A.)
SCHMERL, James (U. S. A.)
SCHMID, Wilfried (U. S.A .)
SCHMIDT, Asmus (Denmark)
SCHMIDT, Wolfgang (U. S. A.)
SCHNEIDER, Joel (U. S. A.)
SCHNEIDER, Manfred (Fed. Rep. Germany)
SCHNEIDER, Rolf (Fed. Rep. Germany)
SCHNITZPAN, Daniel (France)
SCHOBER, Glenn (U. S. A.)
SCHOCHETMAN, Irwin (U. S. A.)
SCHOENEBERG, Bruno (Fed. Rep. Germany)
SCHOENFELD, Lowell (U. S. A.)
SCHONBEK, Tomas (U. S. A.)
SCHORI, Richard (U. S. A.)
SCHRAMM, Ruben (Israel)
SCHREIBER, Bertram (U. S. A.)
SCHREIBER, Michel (France)
SCHROECK, Franklin (U. S. A.)
SCHUBERT, Cedric (Canada)
SCHULTZ, Reinhard (U. S. A.)
SCHUMACHER, Barbara (Fed. Rep. Germany)
SCHUPP, Paul (U. S. A.)
SCHUTTE, Hendrik (Rep. South Africa)
SCHWARTZ, Alan (U. S. A.)
SCHWARTZ, Harley (Canada)
SCHWARTZ, Jean-Marie (France)
SCHWARZ, Gerald (U. S. A.)
SCHWARZ, Stefan (Czechoslovakia)
SCHWEIGERT, Dietmar (Fed. Rep. Germany)
SCHWEITZER, Paul (Brazil)
SCOTT, Elizabeth (U. S. A.)
SCOTT, Ridgway (U. S. A.)
SCOTT, William (U. S. A.)
SCOTT-THOMAS, John (Canada)
SCRIBA, Christoph (Fed. Rep. Germany).
SEALY, Robert (Canada)
SEAMAN, Donna (U. S. A.)
SEELEY, Robert (U. S. A.)
SEGAL, Jack (U. S. A.)
SEIBERT, Peter (Chile)
SEIDEL, J. J. (Netherlands)
SEIDEN, Esther (U. S. A.)
SELIGMAN, George (U. S. A.)
SEMANDENI, Zbigniew (Poland)
SEMMENS, Edmund (Canada)
SENEZ, John (Canada)
SEREWO, Edgel (U. S. A.)

SERRIN, James (U. S. A.)
SERVIEN, Claude (France)
SETH, Bhojraj (India)
SEYDI, Hamet (Senegal)
SHAFFER, Dorothy (U. S. A.)
SHAH, Swarupchand (U. S. A.)
SHANHOLT, Gerald (U. S. A.)
SHAPIRO, Harold (U. S. A.)
SHAPIRO, Victor L. (U. S. A.)
SHARMA, Ambikeshwar (Canada)
SHARPE, Richard (U. S. A.)
SHATZ, Stephen (U. S. A.)
SHEIL-SMALL, Terence (England)
SHEKOURY, Raymond (Iraq)
SHELAH, Saharon (Israel)
SHEPHARD, Geoffrey (England)
SHERMAN, Malcolm (U. S. A.)
SHIBAGAKI, Wasao (Japan)
SHIFFMAN, Bernard (U. S. A.)
SHIFFMAN, Max (U. S. A.)
SHIFRIN, David (U. S. A.)
SHIH, Kung-Sing (Rep. China)
SHIH, Weishu (France)
SHIMA, Kazuhisa (Japan)
SHIMRAT, Moshe (Canada)
SHINBROT, Marvin (Canada)
SHIODA, Tetsuji (Japan)
SHIU, Sai-Wan (Rep. China)
SHIUE, Jau-Shyong (Rep. China)
SHORE, Richard (U. S. A.)
SHORROCK, Richard (Canada)
SHUARD, Hilary (England)
SHUCK, John (U. S. A.)
SHULMAN, Herbert (U. S. A.)
SHULTZ, Frederic (U. S. A.)
SHUM, Kar-Ping (Rep. China)
SIBIRSKI, Constantin (U. S. S. R.)
SIBONY, Nessim (France)
SICHLER, Jiri (Canada)
SIDDIQI, Jamil (Canada)
SIEBENMANN, Laurence (France)
SIGRIST, Francois (Switzerland)
SIKORSKI, Roman (Poland)
SILK, Jean-Marie (U. S. A.)
SILVER, Jack (U. S. A.)
SILVERMAN, Ruth (U. S. A.)
SILVIA, Evelyn (U. S. A.)
SIMMONS, Gustavus (U. S. A.)
SIMON, Arthur (U. S. A.)
SIMON, Barry (U. S. A.)
SIMON, Leon (U. S. A.)
SIMON, Martha (U. S. A.)
SIMON, Udo (Fed. Rep. Germany)
SIMONS, J. (U. S. A.)
SIMONS, Stephen (U. S. A.)
SIMPSON, R. Justin (Canada)
SIMS, Benjamin (U. S. A.)
SINCLAIR, Roy (Canada)
SINE, Robert (U. S. A.)
SINGAL, Mahendra (India)
SINGER, I. M. (U. S. A.)
SINGER, Ivan (Romania)
SINGH, Kuldip (Canada)
SINGH, Vijendra (U. S. A.)
SINGLEY, Donald (U. S. A.)
SINGMASTER, David (England)
SION, Maurice (Canada)
SIRAJDINOV, Sagdy (U. S. S. R.)
SIU, Yum-Tong (U. S. A.)
SJERVE, Denis (Canada)
SJOLIN, Per (Sweden)
SKARDA, Vencil (U. S. A.)
SKLAR, Abe (U. S. A.)
SKOF, Fulvia (Italy)
SKOVGAARD, Helge (Denmark)
SLATER, Morton (U. S. A.)
SLAVNOV, A. A. (U. S. S. R.)
SLEATOR, Frederick (U. S. A.)
SLEFMAN, Brian (Scotland)
SLOAN, Alan (U. S. A.)
SLOYAN, Stephanie (U. S. A.)
SMALE, Stephen (U. S. A.)
SMALL, Charles (Canada)
SMALL, Ken (Canada)
SMART, Peter (Canada)
SMELKIN, Alfred (U. S. S. R.)
SMILEY, Malcolm (U. S. A.)
SMILEY, Patrick (U. S. A.)
SMITH, Arthur (Canada)
SMITH, David (New Zealand)
SMITH, Edwin (England)
SMITH, Frank (U. S. A.)
SMITH, Harry (U. S. A.)
SMITH, James (U. S. A.)
SMITH, Martha (U. S. A.)
SMITH, Robert (Canada)
SMITH, Stephen (U. S. A.)
SMITH, Stoddart (U. S. A.)
SMOKE, William (U. S. A.)
SMOLOWITZ, Lawrence (U. S. A.)
SMORODINSKY, Meir (Israel)
SMYTHE, Neville (Australia)
SNAITH, Victor (England)
SNAPPER, Ernst (U. S. A.)
SNEDDON, Ian (Scotland)
SNELL, Laurie (U. S. A.)
SNELL, Roy C. (Canada)
SNIATYCKI, Jedrzej (Canada)
SNIDER, Robert (Canada)
SNOW, Donald (U. S. A.)
SOARES, Rui (Portugal)
SOCOLESCU, Dan (Fed. Rep. Germany)
SOCOLESCU, Rodica (Fed. Rep. Germany)
SOETENS, Edward (Belgium)
SOLITAR, Donald (Canada)
SOLOMON, Ronald (U. S. A.)
SOMMESE, Andrew (U. S. A.)
SONIS, Michael (Israel)

SORNBERGER, G. Clinton (U. S. A.)
SOTO-ANDRADE, Jorge (Chile)
SOULE, Christophe (France)
SOUNDALGEKAR, Vyenkatesh (India)
SOUROUR, Ahmed (Egypt)
SPANIER, Edwin (U. S. A.)
SPANIER, Jerome (U. S. A.)
SPECHT, Edward (U. S. A.)
SPENCER, Donald (U. S. A.)
SPERNER, Emanuel (Fed. Rep. Germany)
SPIEGEL, Wolfgang (Fed. Rep. Germany)
SPIELBERG, Stephen (U. S. A.)
SPINELLI, Giancarlo (Italy)
SPISELMAN, Toby (U. S. A.)
SPITZER, Frank (U. S. A.)
SPRECHER, David (U. S. A.)
SPRINDZUK, Vladimir (U. S. S. R.)
SPRINGER, George (U. S. A.)
SPRINGER, Tonny (Netherlands)
SPRUCK, Joel (U. S. A.)
SRINIVASACHARYULU, Kilambi (Canada)
SRINIVASAN, Bhama (U. S. A.)
ST.-JEAN PAULIN, Jeannine (France)
STAAL, Ralph (Canada)
STALLMANN, Friedemann (U. S. A.)
STANLEY, Richard (U. S. A.)
STANOJEVIC, Caslav (U. S. A.)
STANTON, Ralph (Canada)
STARBIRD, Mike (U. S. A.)
STARBIRD, Thomas (U. S. A.)
STARK, David (U. S. A.)
STARK, Harold (U. S. A.)
STARR, Norton (U. S. A.)
STASHEFF, James (U. S. A.)
STATE, Emile (Canada)
STATULEVICIUS, Vytautas (U. S. S. R.)
STECHER, Michael (U. S. A.)
STEEN, Lunn (U. S. A.)
STEFFEN, Klaus (Fed. Rep. Germany)
STEGEMAN, Jan (Netherlands)
STEGER, William (U. S. A.)
STEHNEY, Ann (U. S. A.)
STEIN, Charles (U. S. A.)
STEIN, Elias (U. S. A.)
STEIN, Elise (England)
STEIN, Junior (U. S. A.)
STEIN, Michael (U. S. A.)
STEIN, Sherman (U. S. A.)
STEINBERG, Robert (U. S. A.)
STEINLAGE, Ralph (U. S. A.)
STELLMACHER, Bernd (Fed. Rep. Germany)
STEPANOV, Serguei (U. S. S. R.)
STERN, Jacques (France)
STERN, Ronald (U. S. A.)
STETTER, Hans (Austria)
STEWART, Cameron (Canada)
STEWART, Ian (England)
STEWART, James (Canada)
STIEGLITZ, Andreas (Fed. Rep. Germany)
STILL, Harold (Canada)
STOCKS, Douglas (U. S. A.)
STOLTENBERG, Ronald (U. S. A.)
STOLTZEUS, Neal (U. S. A.)
STONE, Arthur (Canada)
STONE, Marshall (U. S. A.)
STONE, Michael (Canada)
STONE, Norman (U. S. A.)
STONE, Wesley (U. S. A.)
STONE, William (U. S. A.)
STØRMER, Erling (Norway)
STOUT, Edgar (U. S. A.)
STOY, Gabrielle (England)
STRADE, Helmut (Fed. Rep. Germany)
STRAFFIN, Philip (U. S. A.)
STRALEY, William (U. S. A.)
STRALKA, Albert (U. S. A.)
STRANG, Gilbert (U. S. A.)
STRASSEN, Volker (Switzerland)
STRASSER, Elvira (U. S. A.)
STRATTON, Anthony (England)
STRAUS, Ernst (U. S. A.)
STRAUS, Sandor (U. S. A.)
STRAUSS, Monty (U. S. A.)
STRAY, Arne (Norway)
STREAT, Janet (Canada)
STREBEL, Kurt (Switzerland)
STREDDER, Peter (England)
STRELITZ, Shlomo (Israel)
STROMBECK, Peter (Sweden)
STROOKER, Jan (Netherlands)
STRUIK, Rebekka (U. S. A.)
SU, Jin-Chen (U. S. A.)
SU, Li Pi (U. S. A.)
SUBBARAO, Dore (Canada)
SUBBARAO, Mathukumalli (Canada)
SUBBOTIN, A. F. (U. S. S. R.)
SUCCI, Francesco (Italy)
SUCHESTON, Louis (U. S. A.)
SUDA, Hiroshi (Japan)
SULLIVAN, Dennis (U. S. A.)
SULLIVAN, John (U. S. A.)
SUMMERS, W. H. (Brazil)
SUN, Hugo (U. S. A.)
SUNDARESAM, Kondagunta (U. S. A.)
SUNDAY, Dan (Canada)
SUNDAY, J. G. (Canada)
SUNG, Chen-Han (Rep. China)
SUNOUCHI, Haruo (Japan)
SURANYI, Janos (Hungary)
SUSSMANN, Hector (U. S. A.)
SUTHERLAND, Colin (Canada)

SUTHERLAND, William (Canada)
SUTTI NODARI, Carla (Italy)
SUVAK, John (Canada)
SUWA, Tatsuo (U. S. A.)
SUZUKI, Haruo (Japan)
SUZUKI, Komei (Japan)
SUZUKI, Noboru (U. S. A.)
SUZUKI, Tosio (Japan)
SVANES, Torgny (Denmark)
SWAMINATHAN, Srinivasa (Canada)
SWARTZ, Charles (U.S.A.)
SWEEDLER, Moss (U. S. A.)
SWEENEY, William (U. S. A.)
SWEET, Lowell (Canada)
SWETT, Allan (Canada)
SWIATAK, Halina (Canada)
SWITZER, Robert (Fed. Rep. Germany)
SYNOWIEC, John (U. S. A.)
SZABADOS, Jozsef (Hungary)
SZABO, Manfred (Canada)
SZEKERES, George (Australia)
SZEMEKEPI, Endre (Hungary)
SZENDREI, Janos (Hungary)
SZENTHE, Janos (Hungary)
SZIGETI, Ferenc (Hungary)
SZOKEFALVI-NAGY, Bela (Hungary)

TAAM, Choy-Tak (U. S. A.)
TACHIKAWA, Hiroyuki (Japan)
TAFARIAN, Ali Akbar (Iran)
TAFT, Earl (U. S. A.)
TAKAHASHI, Masayuki (Japan)
TAKAHASHI, Motoo (Japan)
TAKAHASHI, Reiji (France)
TAKAHASHI, Shuichi (Canada)
TAKENOUCHI, Osamu (Japan)
TAKESAK, Masamichi (U. S. A.)
TAKUSHIRO, Ochiai (Japan)
TALL, Franklin (Canada)
TAMASCHKE, Rosalie (U. S. A.)
TAMURA, Ichiro (Japan)
TAMURA, Takayuki (U. S. A.)
TAN, Henry (U. S. A.)
TAN, Sie-Keng (Rep. Singapore)
TANG, C. (Canada)
TANG, Victor (U. S. A.)
TANGORA, Martin (U. S. A.)
TANIMOTO, Taffee (U. S. A.)
TAPE, Walter (U. S. A.)
TARTAR, Luc (France)
TATE, John (U.S.A.)
TAUSSKY-TODD, Olga (U. S. A.)
TAYLOR, Clare (U. S. A.)
TAYLOR, Donald (Australia)
TAYLOR, Gerald (U. S. A.)
TAYLOR, Joseph (U. S. A.)
TAYLOR, Laurence (U. S. A.)
TAYLOR, Peter (Canada)
TAYLOR, Samuel (England)
TEISSIER, B. (France)
TERRAS, Audrey (U. S. A.)
THALER, Alvin (U. S. A.)
THEDY, Armin (Fed. Rep. Germany)
THICKSTUN, Thomas (U. S. A.)
THIELE, Ernst (Fed. Rep. Germany)
THIELE, Helmut (German Dem. Rep.)
THIELEKER, Ernest (U. S. A.)
THIERAUF, Georg (Fed. Rep. Germany)
THIERRIN, Gabriel (Canada)
THOM, Rene (France)
THOMAS, Charles (England)
THOMAS, Emery (U. S. A.)
THOMAS, Garth (Canada)
THOMAS, Robert (Canada)
THOMASON, Steven (Canada)
THOMEIER, Siegfried (Canada)
THOMPSON, Anthony (Canada)
THOMPSON, Robert (U. S. A.)
THOMSON, Brian (Canada)
THORP, Edward (U. S. A.)
THORPE, Brian (England)
THOUVENOT, Jean-Paul (France)
THURSTON, William (U. S. A.)
TILLIER, André (France)
TILSON, Bret (U. S. A.)
TIMM, Juergen (Fed. Rep. Germany)
TIMMESFELD, Franz-Georg (Fed. Rep. Germany)
TIMOURIAN, James (Canada)
TINGLEY, Arnold (Canada)
TITS, Jacques (Belgium)
TITUS, Charles (U. S. A.)
TOBIN, Sean (Ireland)
TODA, Hiroshi (Japan)
TODD, John (U. S. A.)
TOERNIG, Willi (Fed. Rep. Germany)
TOFFIN, Philippe (France)
TOGNOLI, Alberto (Italy)
TOMIDA, Masamichi (Japan)
TOMIYAMA, Jun (Japan)
TOMTER, Per (Norway)
TONDRA, Richard (U. S. A.)
TONTI, Enzo (Italy)
TORALBALLA, Leopoldo (U. S. A.)
TORUNCZYK, Henryk (Poland)

TOTTEN, Jim (Canada)
TOURE, Saliou (Ivory Coast)
TRANSUE, William (U. S. A.)
TRAORE, Sekou (Congo)
TRAUBER, Philip (U. S. A.)
TRAYNOR, Tim (Canada)
TRETKOFF, Marvin (U. S. A.)
TROJAN, Allan (Canada)
TRONEL, Gerard (France)
TROTMAN, David (England)
TRUDINGER, Neil (Australia)
TRUESDELL, Clifford (U. S. A.)
TRUFFAULT, Bernard (France)
TRUMAN, Aubrey (Scotland)
TSAGAS, Grigorios (Greece)
TSUBOTA, Etsuko (Japan)
TUCHINSKY, Philip (U. S. A.)
TUKEY, John W. (U. S. A.)
TULCEA, C. (U. S. A.)
TULLY, Edward (U. S. A.)
TUNNELL, Jerrold (U. S. A.)
TURQUETTE, Atwell (U. S. A.)
TWEDDLE, Ian (Scotland)
TYMCHATYN, Edward (Canada)

UAVANTAGGIATI, Antonio (Italy)
UCHIYAMA, Saburo (Japan)
UENO, Kenji (Japan)
UETAKE, Tsuneo (Japan)
UHL, Jerry (U. S. A.)
UHLENBECK, Karen (U. S. A.)
UHLENBROCK, Dietrich (Fed. Rep. Germany)
ULLMAN, Joseph (U. S. A.)
ULMER, Friedrich (Switzerland)
UMMEL, Brian (U. S. A.)
UNGAR, Gerald (U. S. A.)
URBANIK, Kazimierz (Poland)
URWIN, Ross (New Zealand)
USTINA, Fred (Canada)
UTZ, W.R. (U. S. A.)

VAILLANCOURT, Remi (Canada)
VAILLANT, Jean (France)
VALLE-FLORES, Enrique (Mexico)
VALLEE, Robert (France)
VAN ASCH, Abraham (Netherlands)
VAN DELM, Denise (Belgium)
VAN DER HOUT, Reinier (Netherlands)
VAN DER KALLEN, Wilberd (Netherlands)
VAN DER MARK, Johannes (Rep. South Africa)
VAN DER PUT, Marius (Netherlands)
VANDULST, Dick (Netherlands)
VAN DYK, Gerrit (Netherlands)
VAN LINT, Jacobus (Netherlands)
VAN METER, Robert (U. S. A.)
VAN OYSTAEYEN, Freddy (Belgium)
VAN PRAAG, Paul (Belgium)
VAN ROSSUM, Herman (Netherlands)
VANSTONE, James (Canada)
VAN ZWALENBERG George (U. S. A.)
VARADARAJAN, Verravalli (U. S. A.)
VARADHAN, Srinivasa (U. S. A.)
VARAH, James (Canada)
VARCHENKO, A. N. (U. S. S. R.)
VASIC, Petar (Yugoslavia)
VASILACH, Serge (Canada)
VASILAKY, Walter (U. S. A.)
VASILJEV, Yuri (U. S. S. R.)
VAUGHAN, Jerry (U. S. A.)
VAUGHAN, Robert (England)
VAUGHAN, Theresa (U. S. A.)
VAUTHIER, Jacques (France)
VELU, Jacque (France)
VENKATARAMAN, Rangachari (Canada)
VENZKE, Paul (U. S. A.)
VERDIER, Jean-Louis (France)
VERGNE, Michele (France)
VERKHOVSKY, Boris (U. S. A.)
VERMA, B.G. (India)
VERNER, Robert (Canada)
VERNON, Ralph (Canada)
VERON, Laurent (France)
VERSHIK, A.M. (U. S. S. R.)
VIENNOT, Gerard (France)
VIJAYAN, Kulakkatt (Germany)
VILOIAUSKAS, Al R. (Canada)
VINCENT, Georges (Switzerland)
VINCENT-SMITH, Graham (England)
VINUESA, Jaime (Spain)
VISIK, M.I. (U. S. S. R.)
VITTER, Albert (U. S. A.)
VITUSHKIN, Anatoli (U. S. S. R.)
VIVIENTE, Jose (Spain)
VLADIMIROV, Vasilii (U. S. S. R.)
VOGEL, Pierre (France)
VON LIENEN, Horst (Fed. Rep. Germany)
VON RENTELN, Michael (Fed. Rep. Germany)
VOSKRESENSKII, V. E. (U. S. S. R.)
VOUGHT, Eldon (U. S. A.)
VRANCH, John (Canada)

WADE, William (U. S. A.)
WAGNER, Diane (U. S. A.)
WAGON, Stanley (Canada)
WAGONER, J. (Switzerland)

WALES, David (U. S. A.)
WALKER, Andrew (England)
WALKER, Gordon (U. S. A.)
WALLACH, Nolan (U. S. A.)
WALLEN, Lawrence (U. S. A.)
WALLIS, Walter (Australia)
WALSH, Bertram (U. S. A.)
WALSH, John (Canada)
WALTERS, Peter (England)
WANG, E.S.C. (U. S. A.)
WANG, Hsien-Chung (U. S. A.)
WANG, Shu-Ping (U. S. A.)
WARD, Augustus (England)
WARD, Martin (Australia)
WARFIELD, Robert (U. S. A.)
WARGA, Jack (U. S. A.)
WARNER, Frank (U. S. A.)
WARREN, Richard (U. S. A.)
WASHINGTON, Lawrence (U. S. A.)
WASOW, Wolfgang (U. S. A.)
WASSERMAN, Robert (U. S. A.)
WASSERMANN, Simon (England)
WATANABE, Junzo (Japan)
WATANABE, Michiaki (Japan)
WATANABE, Toitsu (Japan)
WATKINS, Murray (Canada)
WATSON, Martha (U. S. A.)
WATTERS, John (England)
WATTON, Mary E. (Canada)
WEBER, William (U. S. A.)
WEFELSCHEID, Heinrich (Fed. Rep. Germany)
WEGNER, Gerd (Fed. Rep. Germany)
WEHRHAHN, Karl (Canada)
WEIL, Wolfgang (Fed. Rep. Germany)
WEINBERGER, Hans (U. S. A.)
WEINERT, Hanns (Fed. Rep. Germany)
WEINSTEIN, Alan (U. S. A.)
WEINSTEIN, Joseph (U. S. A.)
WEINTRAUB, Steven (U. S. A.)
WEINZWEIG, Avrum Israel (Canada)
WEISFELD, Morris (U. S. A.)
WEISS, Benjamin (Israel)
WELLAND, Grant (U. S. A.)
WELLS, John (U. S. A.)
WELLS, R. O. (U. S. A.)
WELSH, Wayne (Canada)
WENDEL, James (U. S. A.)
WERMER, John (U. S. A.)
WERTHEIM, Douglas (Canada)
WESSFLIUS, Willem (Netherlands)
WEST, Trevor (Ireland)
WESTBROOK, David (Canada)
WESTMAN, Joel (U. S. A.)
WESTON, Kenneth (U. S. A.)
WESTWICK, Roy (Canada)
WETS, Roger (U. S. A.)
WEYL, F. Joachim (U. S. A.)
WHITE, Alvin (U. S. A.)
WHITE, David (England)
WHITE, James (U. S. A.)
WHITE, Robert (U. S. A.)
WHITFIELD, John (Canada)
WHITMAN, Andrew (U. S. A.)
WHITNEY, Stephen (Canada)
WHITTAKER, James (Canada)
WICK, Brian (U. S. A.)
WICKE, Howard (U. S. A.)
WICKER, Fletcher (U. S. A.)
WIDLUND, Olof (U. S. A.)
WIDOM, Harold (U. S. A.)
WIGLEY, Neil (Canada)
WILANSKY, Albert (U. S. A.)
WILCOX, Calvin (U. S. A.)
WILKENS, David (England)
WILKER, John (Canada)
WILKERSON, Clarence (Canada)
WILKINSON, James (England)
WILLANS, Joseph (Canada)
WILLIAMS, Beryl (U. S. A.)
WILLIAMS, Bruce (U. S. A.)
WILLIAMS, Hugh (Canada)
WILLIAMS, James (U. S. A.)
WILLIAMS, Kenneth (Canada)
WILLIAMS, Robert (U. S. A.)
WILLIAMS, Scott (U. S. A.)
WILLIAMS, Vincent (U. S. A.)
WILLIAMSON, John (England)
WILLIAMSON, Robert (U. S. A.)
WILLIS, Patricia (U. S. A.)
WILLIS, Paul (U. S. A.)
WILLS, Goerg (Fed. Rep. Germany)
WILMUT, Michael (Canada)
WILSON, Douglas (Canada)
WILSON, Edward (U. S. A.)
WILSON, John (England)
WILSON, Leslie (U. S. A.)
WILSON, Richard (U. S. A.)
WILSON, Robert (U. S. A.)
WILSON, Robin (England)
WILSON, Stephen (U. S. A.)
WIMMER, Harald (Austria)
WINKELNKEMPER, Horst Eimar (Fed. Rep. Germany)
WINKLER, Wolfgang (German Dem. Rep.)
WINNINK, Marinus (Netherlands)
WINTER, Paul (England)
WINTHROP, Joel (U. S. A.)
WIRTH, Andrew (Australia)
WISCHNEWSKY, Manfred (Fed. Rep. Germany)
WITHALM, Claudio (Austria)
WITTER, George (U. S. A.)
WLODARSKI, Lech (Poland)
WLOKA, Joseph (Fed. Rep. Germany)
WOLF, Joseph (U. S. A.)
WOLFE, John (Canada)
WOLFE, Philip (U. S. A.)
WOLFE, Warren (Canada)
WOLFF, Karl (Fed. Rep. Germany)
WONENBURGER, Maria (U. S. A.)
WONG, Chi Song (Canada)
WONG, James (Canada)
WONG, Pui-Kei (U. S. A.)
WONG, Raymond (U. S. A.)
WONG, Roderick (Canada)

WONG, Shau-King (Canada)
WONG, Ship-Fah (Canada)
WONG, Yung-Chow (Hong Kong)
WOO, Joseph (Rep. China)
WOO, Kai Yuen (Canada)
WOOD, Alastair (England)
WOOD, Geoffrey (England)
WOODROW, Robert (Canada)
WOODS, E. James (Canada)
WOODS, R. Grant (Canada)
WOODS, Sheila (Canada)
WOODSIDE, William (Canada)
WOOLFSON, Richard (England)
WORTMAN, Dennis (U. S. A.)
WOUK, Arthur (Canada)
WRAY, Thomas (Canada)
WRIGHT, Christopher (Northern Ireland)
WRONA, Wloozimierz (U. S. A.)
WULBERT, Daniel (U. S. A.)
WULFSOHN, Aubrey (Israel)
WURSTER, Marie (U. S. A.)
WYMAN, Bostwick (U. S. A.)
WYNN, Peter (Canada)
YAGI, Akiko (Japan)
YAHYA, Syed Mohammad (Pakistan)
YAJIMA, Takeshi (Japan)
YAMABI, Masakatsu (Japan)
YAMASHITA, Michinori (Japan)
YANG, Chung-Chun (U. S. A.)
YANO, Kentaro (Japan)
YAQUB, Adil (U. S. A.)
YAQZAN, Matin (Canada)
YATES, C. E. M. (England)
YAZAKI, Keiko (Japan)
YOOD, Bertram (U. S. A.)
YOSHII, Tensho (Japan)
YOSHIZAWA, Taro (Japan)
YOUNGER, Daniel (Canada)
YUI, Noriko (U. S. A.)
YUNG-CHEN, Lu (Rep. China)
YUS, Nicolas (Chile)

ZAGIER, Don (U. S. A.)
ZAHAR, Ray (England)
ZAJTA, Aurel (Kenya)
ZAKHAROV, V. E. (U. S. S. R.)
ZALC, Anne (U. S. A.)
ZALCMAN, Lawrence (U. S. A.)
ZALCSTEIN, Yechezkel (U. S. A.)
ZAME, William (U. S. A.)
ZEDEK, Mishael (U. S. A.)
ZEEMAN, Erik (England)
ZEHNDER, Edward (Switzerland)
ZELAZKO, Wieslaw (Poland)
ZELOBENKO, D. (U. S. S. R.)
ZENOR, Phillip (U. S. A.)
ZIDEK, James (Canada)
ZIELEZNY, Zbigniew (U. S. A.)
ZIEMBA, William (Canada)
ZIESCHANG, Heiner (Fed. Rep. Germany)
ZIRILLI, Francesco (Italy)
ZISKIND, Steven (U. S. A.)
ZIZCENKO, Alexei (U. S. S. R.)
ZOUGDANI, Hassan (Libya)
ZULAUF, Achim (New Zealand)
ZWAHLEN, Bruno (Switzerland)
ZWIER, Paul (U. S. A.)

Membership by Countries

Algeria	2	Kuwait	4
Argentina	3	Lebanon	1
Australia	44	Libya	1
Austria	4	Malaysia	2
Belgium	14	Mexico	20
Brazil	8	Netherlands	39
Bulgaria	5	New Zealand	15
Canada	514	Niger	1
Chile	9	Nigeria	16
China, Republic of	11	Norway	16
Columbia	1	Pakistan	7
Congo	1	Philippines	2
Costa Rica	1	Poland	18
Cuba	1	Portugal	3
Czechoslovakia	4	Puerto Rico	2
Denmark	19	Rhodesia	1
Egypt	2	Romania	5
England	181	Saudi Arabia	1
Finland	11	Scotland	27
France	245	Senegal	10
Germany, Democratic Republic of	11	Sierra Leone	1
		Singapore	2
Germany, Federal Republic of	146	South Africa, Republic of	9
Greece	7	Spain	11
Guatemala	2	Sweden	17
Hong Kong	3	Switzerland	28
Hungary	24	Tunisia	3
India	26	Turkey	2
Iran	11	Uganda	1
Iraq	4	Uruguay	1
Ireland, Northern	1	U. S. A.	1274
Ireland, Republic of	7	U. S. S. R.	50
Israel	20	Venezuela	2
Italy	45	Vietnam, Democratic Republic	4
Ivory Coast	2	Wales	6
Japan	114	Yugoslavia	10
Kenya	3	Zaire, Republic of	3

Professor
J. L. Lions
lecturing

Photo by John Coury

SOME
VIEWS
of the Congress

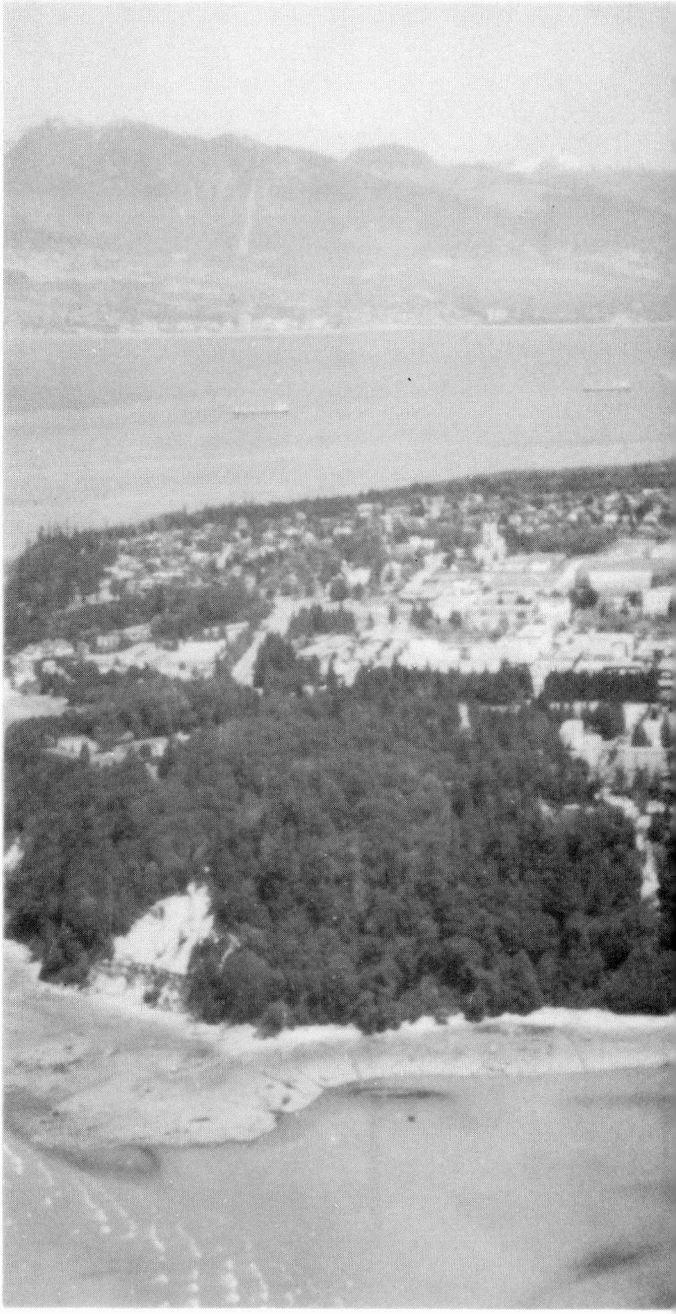

AERIAL VIEW OF THE SITE

Photo courtesy UBC Information Services

CLOSE-UPS

BOOK
EXHIBIT

Photo by John Coury

Photo by John Coury

CLOSED-CIRCUIT TELEVISION

PORTRAITS OF MATHEMATICIANS

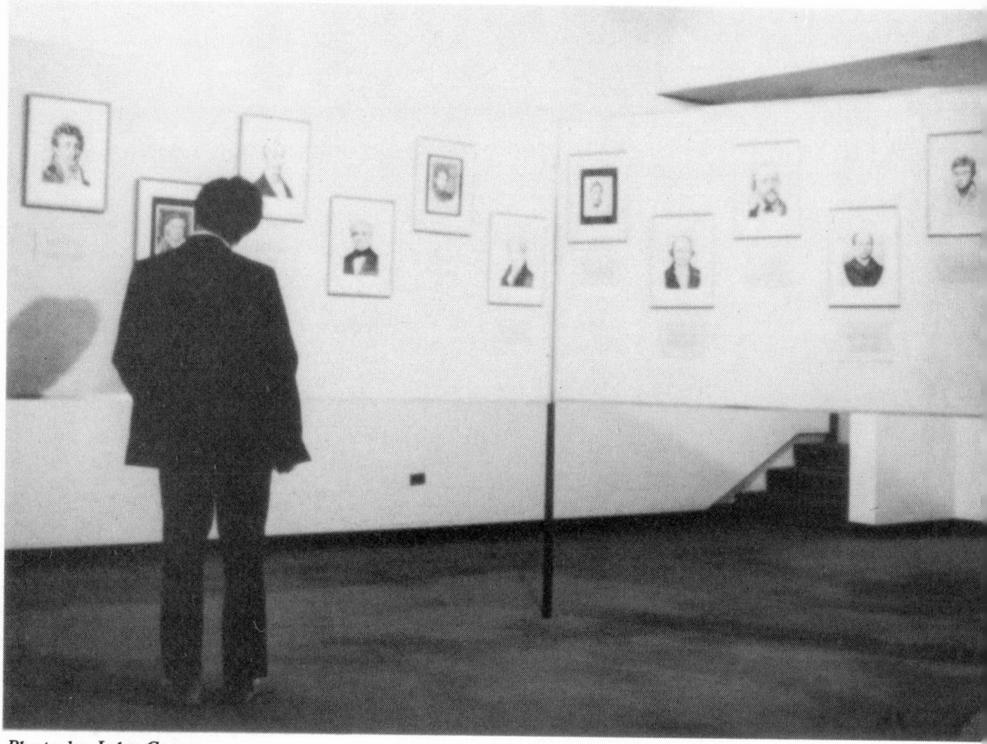

Photo by John Coury

Dave Roels photo

Professor Enrico Bombieri

Professor David Mumford

FIELDS MEDAL WINNERS 1974

Fields Medalists

Proceedings of the International Congress of Mathematicians
Vancouver, 1974

The Work of Enrico Bombieri

K. Chandrasekharan

Bombieri's work ranges over many fields: number theory, univalent functions, several complex variables, partial differential equations, algebraic geometry. I do not seek to describe it all. I shall not touch upon his work in algebraic geometry, nor shall I anticipate his article in these PROCEEDINGS on partial differential equations. I shall speak only about three of his contributions. They should give some idea of the variety and depth of his work.

1. The distribution of primes. First among Bombieri's achievements is his remarkable theorem on the distribution of primes in arithmetical progressions, which he obtained by an application of the method of the *large sieve* (Mathematika **12** (1965), 201—225).

The prime number theorem for the arithmetical progression $a + mq$, where a and q are integers, $q > 0$, $(a, q) = 1$, $0 \leqq a < q$, and $m = 1, 2, \cdots$, is equivalent to the assertion that

$$\psi(x; q, a) \sim x/\varphi(q),$$

as $x \to \infty$, where φ stands for Euler's function, and

$$\psi(x; q, a) = \sum_{n \leqq x;\, n \equiv a \,(\mathrm{mod}\, q)} \Lambda(n),$$

where $\Lambda(n) = \log p$ if is n a power of a prime p, and $\Lambda(n) = 0$ otherwise.

Bombieri's theorem is concerned with an estimate of the error term $E(x; q, a) = \psi(x; q, a) - x/\varphi(q)$, *not* for an individual q, but *on the average* over q, up to a certain bound. It states that given a positive constant A, there exists a positive constant $B = B(A)$, such that

(1) $$\sum_{q \leqq Q} \max_{y \leqq x} \max_{a, (a, q)=1} \left| E(y; q, a) \right| \ll x(\log x)^{-A},$$

if $Q = x^{1/2}(\log x)^{-B}$.

A slightly weaker result, which is less widely applicable, was obtained independently by A. I. Vinogradov (also in 1965) by a different method.

The significance of Bombieri's theorem becomes clear, if we note that, for any *fixed* q (that is, fixed relative to x), the best result so far known is that

$$E(x; q, a) = O(x \exp(-c(\log x)^{\theta})),$$

with $c > 0$, $\frac{1}{2} \leqq \theta < 1$. If q is a function of x, the main term $x/\varphi(q)$ in the asymptotic formula for ψ decreases as q increases. Therefore estimates uniform in q are required. But an estimate which is *uniform* in q requires a strong restriction on the range of q (in the present state of knowledge). Such an estimate was first deduced by Arnold Walfisz (1936) from a theorem of C. L. Siegel (1935) on the location of the real zeros of Dirichlet's L-functions with real, nonprincipal, characters. It is as follows:

$$E(x; q, a) = O(x \exp(-c_0(\log x)^{1/2}))$$

where c_0 is a positive constant, *uniformly* for $q \leqq \log^{\alpha} x$, where α is a given positive number however large.

If, on the other hand, one *assumes* the "extended Riemann hypothesis", that not only the Riemann zeta-function but all the L-functions, modulo q, of Dirichlet, have all their zeros in the critical strip *on* the critical line, one would get the much stronger estimate: $E(x; q, a) = O(x^{1/2} \log^2 x)$, *uniformly* for $q \leqq x$. This would, if used on the left-hand side of (1), give a result comparable to Bombieri's, with $B = A + 2$, but even this, it is to be noted, is *not* significant if q *exceeds* $x^{1/2}$.

Bombieri's theorem may therefore, and *does* sometimes, serve as a substitute for the assumption of the extended Riemann hypothesis, which has far-reaching implications in number theory. His proof is as remarkable as his result. To explain it one might perhaps cast a glance backwards.

A *sieve*, in simple terms, is a combination of (i) a finite sequence $\mathscr{N}$ of integers, (ii) a finite set of distinct primes $\mathscr{P}$, and (iii) corresponding to each prime $p \in \mathscr{P}$, a subset Ω_p of residue classes modulo p. If one *sieves out*, or deletes, from the given sequence $\mathscr{N}$, all those integers whose residue class modulo p belongs to Ω_p for some $p \in \mathscr{P}$, the problem is to estimate, from above and from below, the number of integers left over in $\mathscr{N}$ after the *sieving* (or deletion).

A sieve is called *large* or *small*, according as $|\Omega_p|$, the number of residue classes in Ω_p, is, on the average, large or small.

If we take $\mathscr{N}$ to be the sequence of consecutive integers $1, 2, \cdots, N$; $\mathscr{P}$ to be the set of *all* primes $p \leqq N^{1/2}$; and Ω_p to consist of the single residue class $0 \pmod p$ for each $p \leqq N^{1/2}$, we get the (ancient) sieve of Eratosthenes, which is obviously a *small* sieve. The elements left over in $\mathscr{N}$ after the sieving are the integer 1, together with all primes p, such that $N^{1/2} < p \leqq N$.

Viggo Brun was the first to introduce, in 1920, an ingenious sieve method to prove that every sufficiently large even integer is a sum of two integers, each of which has not more than nine prime factors. Improvements of Brun's method were made in later years by H. Rademacher, T. Estermann, G. Ricci, and A. A. Buchstab; until Atle Selberg, during the years 1946—1951, developed a sieve method more general and more powerful than Brun's and its improved versions.

We are here concerned, however, with the method of the *large sieve*, which is different from the small sieves of Brun and of Selberg, and which, when *combined* with analytical arguments, yields results that are beyond the reach of the other sieves.

The idea of the *large sieve* originated with Yu. V. Linnik in 1941, in his attempt to tackle I. M. Vinogradov's hypothesis (which is yet to be proved or disproved) on $h_2(p)$, the least quadratic nonresidue modulo p. The hypothesis is that given $\varepsilon > 0$, there exists a constant $c = c(\varepsilon)$ such that $h_2(p) < cp^{\varepsilon}$. Linnik sought to estimate the number of primes $p \leqq x$, say, for which $h_2(p) > p^{\varepsilon}$, for any given $\varepsilon > 0$.

Let $n_1, n_2, \cdots, n_Z$ be Z integers, such that $M + 1 \leqq n_1 < n_2 < \cdots < n_Z \leqq M + N$. Let the prime p be called *exceptional*, if the number of residue classes *not* represented by the numbers (n_j), $j = 1, 2, \cdots, Z$, is *greater than* τp, where τ is a fixed number such that $0 < \tau < 1$. Linnik proved that for *any* such sequence (n_j), the number of exceptional primes $p \leqq N^{1/2}$ does not exceed $c_1 N/\tau^2 Z$, where c_1 is an *absolute* constant. As an application, he proved the striking theorem that the number of primes $p \leqq N$ for which the least quadratic nonresidue is greater than N^{ε}, for a fixed number $\varepsilon > 0$, is bounded. It follows that the number of primes $p \leqq X$ for which the least quadratic nonresidue is greater than p^{ε} is $\ll \log\log X$.

In the context of the definition of a sieve, the sequence (n_j), $j = 1, 2, \cdots, Z$, may be looked upon as the sequence of elements *left over* in the interval $[M + 1, M + N]$, *after* a sieving has been effected (*on* the sequence of all integers in that interval, for example), with a *sieving set* $\{\Omega_p\}$ of residue classes modulo p, $p \leqq N^{1/2}$, which has the property that for each *exceptional* $p \leqq N^{1/2}$, the corresponding Ω_p has *more than* τp elements. Hence the name large sieve.

The next important step was taken by A. Rényi. If $Z(p, a)$ denotes the number of elements in the given sequence (n_j) such that $n_j = a \pmod p$, Linnik's result takes the form: The number of primes $p \leqq N^{1/2}$ such that $Z(p, a) = 0$ for *at least* τp values of a, where $0 < \tau < 1$, does *not exceed*

$$c_1 N/\tau^2 Z.$$

Rényi considered instead the sum

$$S_X = \sum_{p \leqq X} p \sum_{a=0}^{p-1} (Z(p, a) - Z/p)^2,$$

and proved in 1950 that

$$S_X \leqq 2NZ, \quad \text{for } X = (N/12)^{1/3}. \tag{2}$$

Again, in the context of the definition of a sieve, we have $Z(p, a) = 0$ if $a \in \Omega_p$, so that

$$S_X \geqq \sum_{p \leqq X} \frac{|\Omega_p|}{p} Z^2,$$

which, when combined with (2), gives an upper bound for Z—and also Linnik's result *provided that* $X = N^{1/2}$.

As an application of his inequality, Rényi proved the striking theorem that every sufficiently large *even* integer is the sum of a prime and an almost prime (that is, an integer which is the product of a bounded number of prime factors).

Though Rényi's inequality yields more precise information than Linnik's result for the range of primes $p \ll N^{1/3}$, it does not work for the wider range $p \ll N^{1/2}$ of Linnik, which is more appropriate in the context of arithmetical applications. This defect was sought to be repaired by many mathematicians. It was not until 1965, however, that important further progress was made by K. F. Roth (Mathematika **12** (1965), 1–9) and, independently, by Bombieri (Mathematika **12** (1965), 201–225). Roth proved that Rényi's inequality (2) holds for $X = (N/\log N)^{1/2}$, and Bombieri that it holds for $X = N^{1/2}$ (with $\ll$ in place of $\leqq$).

Bombieri proceeded to place Rényi's inequality in a more general setting and proved, by a simple and ingenious argument, an inequality for trigonometrical double sums, which is as follows: Let $x_1, x_2, \cdots, x_R$ be real numbers which are δ-well-spaced, in the sense that $\|x_k - x_l\| \geqq \delta > 0$ for $k \neq l$ (where $\|\theta\|$, for any real θ, denotes the distance of θ from the nearest integer). Let $T(x) = \sum_{n=M+1}^{M+N} a_n\, e^{2\pi inx}$, where the (a_n) are complex numbers. Then

$$\sum_{k=1}^{R} |T(x_k)|^2 \leqq \left(N + \frac{2}{\delta}\right) \sum_{n=M+1}^{M+N} |a_n|^2 \tag{3}$$

(Acta Arith. **18** (1971), 401–404; Proc. Internat. Conf. Number Theory, Moscow, 1971). This corresponds, as Bombieri has shown, to something like Bessel's inequality in a Hilbert space.

If we take x_k to be rational, $x_k = a/q$, say, where $(a, q) = 1, q \leqq Q$, with $a_n = 1$ for $n = n_j$ and $a_n = 0$ for $n \neq n_j$, we get (more than) Rényi's inequality (2) in case q is a prime, and something similar to the inequality given by Selberg's upper-bound sieve, in case q is composite.

Thus many results previously obtained by Selberg's method can now be proved by using (3).

Bombieri then considered the analogue of his *large-sieve inequality* (3) for sums of Dirichlet characters χ modulo q instead of trigonometrical sums. The connecting link is the Gaussian sum

$$G(\chi) = \sum_{a=1}^{q} \chi(a) \exp(2\pi ia/q),$$

since

$$\begin{aligned} \sum_{\chi} |G(\chi)|^2\, \chi(m)\overline{\chi(n)} &= \varphi(q)\, S_{m-n,q}, \quad && \text{if } (mn, q) = 0, \\ &= 0, && \text{if } (mn, q) > 1, \end{aligned}$$

where

$$S_{m,q} = \sum_{a=1;\,(a,q)=1}^{q} \exp(2\pi iam/q)$$

is the well-known Ramanujan sum (*not* to be confused with S_X in (2)).

Vital for Bombieri's proof of his theorem on arithmetical progressions is the following inequality: Let Q be *any* finite set of positive integers, (a_n) *any* complex numbers. Then

$$(4)\qquad \sum_{q\in Q}\frac{1}{\varphi(q)}\sum_{\chi}|G(\chi)|^2\cdot\Big|\sum_{X<n\leqq Y}\chi(n)a_n\Big|^2 \leqq 7D\max(Y-X, M^2)\sum_{X<n\leqq Y}d(n)|a_n|^2.$$

Here $\sum_\chi$ denotes summation over *all* characters χ modulo q, $d(n)$ denotes the divisor function, $D = D(q) = \max_{q\in Q} d(q)$, $M = M(Q) = \max_{q\in Q} q$.

By skilful and *repeated* application of this inequality, with different choices of X, Y, and a_n, Bombieri deduced a *new* type of *density theorem* for the zeros of L-functions. The theorem gives an estimate for the sum

$$\sum_{q\in Q}\frac{1}{\varphi(q)}\sum_{\chi}|G(\chi)|^2 N(\alpha, T; \chi),$$

which is *uniform* with respect to Q, for $\frac{1}{2} \leqq \alpha \leqq 1$, $T \geqq 2$. Here $N(\alpha, T; \chi)$ denotes the number of zeros of Dirichlet's function $L(s, \chi)$ in the rectangle $\alpha \leqq \operatorname{Re} s \leqq 1$, $\frac{1}{2} \leqq \alpha \leqq 1$, $|\operatorname{Im} s| \leqq T$, in the complex s-plane.

From his density theorem Bombieri deduced his theorem on primes in arithmetical progressions, by an appeal to classical arguments in the theory of L-functions, combined with an application of the Siegel-Walfisz theorem (stated at the beginning).

Bombieri's work has given rise to a general method for treating problems that were previously solved either on the assumption of the extended Riemann hypothesis, or by Linnik's 'dispersion method', or by highly complicated, ad hoc methods. It thus furnishes a new approach to such important results as I. M. Vinogradov's theorem (1937) that every sufficiently large *odd* integer is a sum of three primes, or Linnik's theorem (1961) that *every* sufficiently large integer is a sum of a prime and two squares, or Chen's result (1967) that every sufficiently large *even* integer is a sum of a prime and an integer with at most two prime factors. Bombieri's theorem represents a deep synthesis of the most important modern methods in prime number theory. It has not put an end to any one question; rather it has led to many new ones.

His inequality for sums of Dirichlet characters has been extended to general multiplicative characters of the form $\chi(n)n^{it}$ which are "δ-well-spaced". In consequence, the *best* bounds *so far* known have been obtained for $N(\alpha, T; \chi)$, yielding as special cases such results as the following: The difference between the consecutive primes p_{n+1}, p_n has the estimate $p_{n+1} - p_n \ll p_n^{7/12+\varepsilon}$, for every $\varepsilon > 0$. (It is known that the Riemann hypothesis implies this with the exponent 1/2 in place of 7/12.) The "density hypothesis" $N(\alpha, T; \chi_0) \ll T^{2(1-\alpha)+\varepsilon}$ holds for $\alpha > 13/16$. (Here χ_0 is the principal character, so that the zeros are those of Riemann's zeta-function.) Bombieri's method has also been generalized to algebraic number fields. Many mathematicians have played a part in the development of his method—H. Davenport, H. Halberstam, P. X. Gallagher, H. L. Montgomery,

G. Halász, M. N. Huxley, M. Jutila and, more recently, M. Forti and C. Viola, to mention but a few. There is little doubt that Bombieri's theorems have inspired that development.

2. Univalent functions and the local Bieberbach conjecture. Bombieri's work on the local validity of the Bieberbach conjecture is an impressive achievement in an altogether different branch of mathematics. It shows his power and ingenuity in attacking problems of 'hard analysis'.

Let $\mathcal{S}$ denote the family of functions $f(z) = z + a_2z^2 + a_3z^3 + \cdots$ which are (normalized) holomorphic and univalent in the unit disc $|z| < 1$. Bieberbach's conjecture is that if $f(z) \in \mathcal{S}$, then $\operatorname{Re} a_n \leqq n$, with the equality holding only if $f(z) = z/(1 - \rho z)^2$, and $\rho^{n-1} = 1$. The conjecture has so far been proved for $2 \leqq n \leqq 6$ on the one hand, and for a large number of subfamilies of $\mathcal{S}$ on the other.

In 1965 P. R. Garabedian and M. Schiffer raised the question of the *local* validity of that conjecture, that is: If $2 - \operatorname{Re} a_2$ is small enough, is it true that $n - \operatorname{Re} a_n$ is non-negative? They answered it in the affirmative if n is *even*. They proved the existence of a positive constant ε_{2m}, say, such that if $|2 - a_2| < \varepsilon_{2m}$, then $\operatorname{Re} a_{2m} \leqq 2m$, with the equality holding if and only if $f(z) = z(1 - z)^{-2} = \sum_{n=1}^{\infty} nz^n$, the Koebe function.

Bombieri proved this in 1967 for *all n*, odd as well as even, the case of n odd being the more difficult (Invent. Math. **4** (1967), 26–67). To be precise, he proved that

$$\liminf_{a_2 \to 2} \frac{n - \operatorname{Re} a_n}{2 - \operatorname{Re} a_2} > 0, \quad \text{if } n \text{ is even,}$$

and

$$\liminf_{a_3 \to 3} \frac{n - \operatorname{Re} a_n}{3 - \operatorname{Re} a_3} > 0, \quad \text{if } n \text{ is odd,}$$

where the 'lim inf' is taken over all functions of the family $\mathcal{S}$.

An independent, though less direct, proof of this has since been published by Garabedian and Schiffer (Arch. Rational Mech. Anal. **26** (1967), 1–32).

Bombieri's proof is based on an ingenious combination of K. Löwner's 'parametric method' with the theory of the 'second variation' developed by P. L. Duren and M. Schiffer. He uses the results of A. C. Schaefer and D. C. Spencer on Löwner curves, as well as an earlier result of his own concerning a set of quadratic forms (Q_n), in an infinite number of variables, which had been encountered by Duren and Schiffer in their theory of the second variation. These quadratic forms Q_n have the property that: (a) if Q_n is an indefinite form, then Bieberbach's conjecture is false for that n; (b) if Q_n is positive definite, then every analytic variation of the Koebe function decreases $\operatorname{Re} a_n$. Duren and Schiffer proved (1962/63) that Q_n is positive definite for $n = 2, 3, \cdots, 9$, and the same was checked with a computer for all $n \leqq 100$. Bombieri proved that Q_n is positive definite for *all n* (Boll. Un. Mat. Ital. (3) **22** (1967), 25–32).

3. Several complex variables. Bombieri's theorem concerning algebraic values of meromorphic maps (Invent. Math. **10** (1970), 267–287; **11** (1970), 163–166), motivated though it is by the theory of transcendental numbers, is an incursion of geometric integration theory in the analysis of functions of several complex variables. The theorem is as follows:

THEOREM. *Let K be an algebraic number field. Let $f_1, f_2, \cdots, f_N$ be meromorphic functions of finite order in C^n. Suppose that at least $n + 1$ of them are algebraically independent over K, and that for any j with $1 \leqq j \leqq N$ and ν with $1 \leqq \nu \leqq n$, the partial derivative $\partial f_j/\partial z_\nu$ is a polynomial in $f_1, f_2, \cdots, f_N$ with coefficients in K. Then, the set of points in C^n at which all the f_j are defined, and have values in K, is contained in an algebraic hypersurface in C^n. (If the given functions are of order $\leqq \rho$, then the degree of the hypersurface $\leqq n(n + 1)\rho[K: Q] + n$.)*

The case $n = 1$ was proved by S. Lang after previous work by Th. Schneider. It unifies divers results due to A. O. Gelfond and to Schneider, and contains, in particular, the transcendency of e^α for $\alpha \neq 0$, α algebraic, and of α^β for $\alpha \neq 0, 1$, α and β algebraic and β irrational. While Bombieri's extension does not seem immediately to lead to new theorems on transcendency, variants of it are applicable to the study of n-parameter subgroups of algebraic groups (Invent. Math. **11** (1970), 1–14).

But the real interest of the paper, once again, arises from the proof which contains an existence theorem and a structure theorem. The existence theorem, which generalizes previous work of L. Hörmander and of A. Martineau, states that for any pluri-subharmonic function p on C^n, $p \not\equiv -\infty$, there exists a nonzero entire function f on C^n, with

$$\int_{C^n} |f(z)|^2 e^{-p(z)} (1 + |z|^2)^{-3n} \, dz < +\infty.$$

The structure theorem, on the other hand, gives a sufficient condition for a current of degree (1,1) to be integration on an analytic set of codimension 1. Several authors had previously attempted, without success, to produce workable conditions of that type. Bombieri's result has since been used by F. Reese Harvey and James King (Invent. Math. **15** (1972), 47–52) to characterize those currents of degree (k, k), $k \geqq 1$, on a complex manifold that correspond to integration over (linear combinations of) complex subvarieties, thus settling a conjecture of P. Lelong which had been open for several years that those are precisely the positive currents that are d-closed and whose densities (or Lelong numbers) are locally bounded away from zero. For his proof, Bombieri makes use of Hörmander's work on L^2-estimates and existence theorems for solutions of the $\bar{\partial}$-Neumann problem, besides ideas from H. Federer's work in geometric measure theory. It bears the hallmark of a highly original analyst.

4. I have not spoken about Bombieri's contributions to the theory of partial differential equations and minimal surfaces—in particular, to the solution of Bernstein's problem in higher dimensions. Nor have I spoken about the fact that he was among the first to give effective applications of Dwork's method in the p-adic approach to André Weil's zeta-function. But I hope I have said enough to show that Bombieri's *versatility* and *strength* have combined to create many original patterns of ideas which are both rich and inspiring. It is in recognition of these qualities that he has been awarded a Fields Medal. To him mathematics is a private garden; may it bring forth many new blooms.

Eidg. Technische Hochschule
Zürich, Switzerland

Proceedings of the International Congress of Mathematicians
Vancouver, 1974

The Work of David Mumford

J. Tate

It is a great pleasure for me to report on Mumford's work. However I feel there are many people more qualified than I to do this. I have consulted with some of them and would like to thank them all for their help, especially Oscar Zariski.

Mumford's major work has been a tremendously successful multi-pronged attack on problems of the existence and structure of varieties of moduli, that is, varieties whose points parametrize isomorphism classes of some type of geometric object. Besides this he has made several important contributions to the theory of algebraic surfaces. I shall begin by mentioning briefly some of the latter and then will devote most of this talk to a discussion of his work on moduli.

Mumford has carried forward, after Zariski, the project of making algebraic and rigorous the work of the Italian school on algebraic surfaces. He has done much to extend Enriques' theory of classification to characteristic $p > 0$, where many new difficulties appear. This work is impossible to describe in a few words and I shall say no more about it except to remark that our other Field's Medalist, Bombieri, has also made important contributions in this area, and that he and Mumford have recently been continuing their work in collaboration.

We have a good understanding of divisors on an algebraic variety, but our knowledge about algebraic cycles of codimension > 1 is still very meager. The first case is that of 0-cycles on an algebraic surface. In particular, what is the structure of the group of 0-cycles of degree 0 modulo the subgroup of cycles rationally equivalent to zero, i.e., which can be deformed to 0 by a deformation which is parametrized by a line. This group maps onto the Albanese variety of the surface, but what about the kernel of this map? Is it "finite-dimensional"? Severi thought so; but Mumford proved it is not, if the geometric genus of the surface is ≥ 1. Mumford's proof uses methods of Severi, and he remarks that in this case the techniques of the classical Italian algebraic geometers seem superior to their vaunted intuition. However, in other cases Mumford has used modern techniques to justify Italian intuition, as in the construction by him and M. Artin of examples of unirational varieties X which are not rational, based on 2-torsion in $H^3(X, \boldsymbol{Z})$.

Probably Mumford's most famous result on surfaces is his topological characterization of nonsingularity. Let P be a normal point on an algebraic surface V in a complex projective space. Mumford showed that if V is topologically a manifold at P, then it is algebraically nonsingular there. Indeed, consider the intersection K of V with a small sphere about P. This intersection K is 3-dimensional and if V is a manifold at P, then K is a sphere and its fundamental group is trivial. Mumford showed how to compute this fundamental group $\pi_1(K)$ in terms of the diagram of the resolution of the singularity of V at P, and then he showed that $\pi_1(K)$ is not trivial unless the diagram is, i.e., unless V is nonsingular at P. A by-product of this proof is the fact that the Poincaré conjecture holds for the 3-manifolds which occur as K's. Mumford's paper was a critical step between the early work on singularities of branches of plane curves (where K is a torus knot) and fascinating later developments. Brieskorn showed that the analogs of Mumford's results are false in general for V of higher dimension. Consideration of the corresponding problem there led to the discovery of some beautiful relations between algebraic geometry and differential topology, including simple explicit equations for exotic spheres.

Let me now turn to Mumford's main interest, the theory of varieties of moduli. This is a central topic in algebraic geometry having its origins in the theory of elliptic integrals. The development of the algebraic and global aspects of this subject in recent years is due mainly to Mumford, who attacked it with a brilliant combination of classical, almost computational, methods and Grothendieck's new scheme-theoretic techniques.

Mumford's first approach was by the 19th century theory of invariants. In fact, he revived this moribund theory by considering its geometric significance. In pursuing an idea of Hilbert, Mumford was led to the crucial notion of "stable" objects in a moduli problem. The abstract setting behind this notion is the following: Suppose G is a reductive algebraic group acting on a variety V in projective space $\boldsymbol{P}_N$ by projective transformations. Then the action of G is induced by a linear and unimodular representation of some finite covering G^* of G on the affine cone $\boldsymbol{A}^{N+1}$ over the ambient $\boldsymbol{P}_N$. Mumford defines a point $x \in V$ to be *stable* for the action of G on V, relative to the embedding $V \subset \boldsymbol{P}_N$, if for one (and hence every) point $x^* \in \boldsymbol{A}^{N+1}$ over x, the orbit of x^* under G^* is closed in $\boldsymbol{A}^{N+1}$, and the stabilizer of x^* is a finite subgroup of G^*. His fundamental theorem is then that the set of stable points is an open set V_s in V, and V_s/G is a quasi-projective variety.

For example, suppose $V = (\boldsymbol{P}_n)^m$ is the variety of ordered m-tuples of points in projective n-space and G is PGL_n acting diagonally on V via the Segre embedding. Then a point $x = (x_1, x_2, \cdots, x_m) \in V$ is stable if and only if for each proper linear subspace $L \subset \boldsymbol{P}_n$, the number of points $x_i \in L$ is strictly less than $m(\dim L + 1)/(n + 1)$. In case $n = 1$, for example, this means that an m-tuple of points on the projective line is unstable if more than half the points coalesce. The reason such

m-tuples must be excluded is the following: Let $P_t = (tx_1, tx_2, \cdots, tx_r, x_{r+1}, \cdots, x_m)$ and $Q_t = (x_1, \cdots, x_r, t^{-1}x_{r+1}, \cdots, t^{-1}x_m)$, where the x_i are pairwise distinct. Then P_t is in the same orbit as Q_t, for $t \neq 0, \infty$, but $P_0 = (0, \cdots, 0, x_{r+1}, \cdots, x_m)$ is not in the same orbit as $Q_0 = (x_1, \cdots, x_r, \infty, \cdots, \infty)$ unless $m = 2r$, and even then is not in general. Thus if we want a separated orbit space in which $\lim_{t \to 0}$ (Orbit P_t) is unique, we must exclude P_0 or Q_0; and it is natural to exclude the one with more than half its components equal.

Using the existence of the orbit spaces V_s/G, Mumford was able to construct a moduli scheme over the ring of integers for polarized abelian varieties, relative Picard schemes (following a suggestion of Grothendieck), and also moduli varieties for "stable" vector bundles on a curve in characteristic 0. The meaning of stability for a vector bundle is that all proper subbundles are less ample than the bundle itself, if we measure the ampleness of a bundle by the ratio of its degree to its rank. In the special example $V = (\boldsymbol{P}_n)^m$ mentioned above, the results can be proved by explicit computations which work in any characteristic and even over the ring of integers. But in its general abstract form Mumford's theory was limited to characteristic 0 because his proofs used the semisimplicity of linear representations. He conjectures that in characteristic p, linear representations of the classical semisimple groups have the property that complementary to a stable line in such a representation there is always a stable hypersurface (though not necessarily a stable hyperplane which would exist if the representation were semisimple). If this conjecture is true[1] then Mumford's treatment of geometric invariant theory would work in characteristic p. Seshadri has proved the conjecture in case of SL_2. He has also shown recently that the conjecture can be circumvented, by giving different more complicated proofs for the main results of the theory which work in any characteristic.

For moduli of abelian varieties and curves, Mumford has given more refined constructions than those furnished by geometric invariant theory. In three long papers in *Inventiones Mathematicae* he has developed an algebraic theory of theta functions. Classically, over the complex numbers, a theta function for an abelian variety A can be thought of as a complex function on the universal covering space $H_1(A, \boldsymbol{R})$ which transforms in a certain way under the action of $H_1(A, \boldsymbol{Z})$. For Mumford, over any algebraically closed field k, a theta function is a k-valued function on $\prod_{l \in S} H_1(A, \boldsymbol{Q}_l)$ (étale homology) which transforms in a certain way under $\prod_{l \in S} H_1(A, \boldsymbol{Z}_l)$. Here S is any finite set of primes $l \neq \operatorname{char}(k)$, though in treating some of the deeper aspects of the theory Mumford assumed $2 \in S$. In order to get an idea of what these theta functions accomplish let us consider a classical special case. Let A be an elliptic curve over $\boldsymbol{C}$ with its points of order 4 marked. Then we get a canonical embedding $A \subsetneq \boldsymbol{P}^3$ via the theta functions $\theta[{}^a_b]$; $a, b = 0, 1$. Let 0_A be the origin on A, whose coordinates in $\boldsymbol{P}_3$ are the "theta Nullwerte". Then A is the intersection of all quadric surfaces in $\boldsymbol{P}_3$ which pass through the orbit of 0_A under a certain action of $(\boldsymbol{Z}/4\boldsymbol{Z}) \times (\boldsymbol{Z}/4\boldsymbol{Z})$ on $\boldsymbol{P}_3$. Thus 0_A determines A and

[1](ADDED DURING CORRECTION OF PROOFS). The conjecture is true; shortly after the Congress, it was proved by W. Haboush in general and by E. Formanek and C. Procesi for $GL(n)$ and $SL(n)$.

can be viewed as a "modulus". Moreover, 0_A lies on the quartic curve $\theta\left[{0 \atop 0}\right]^4 = \theta\left[{0 \atop 1}\right]^4 + \theta\left[{1 \atop 0}\right]^4$ in the plane $\theta\left[{1 \atop 1}\right] = 0$, and that curve minus a finite set of points is a variety of moduli for elliptic curves with their points of order 4 marked. Mumford's theory generalizes this construction to abelian varieties of any dimension, with points of any order $\geqq 3$ marked, in any characteristic $\neq 2$. The moduli varieties so obtained have a natural projective embedding, and their closure in that embedding is, essentially, an algebraic version of Satake's topological compactification of Siegel's moduli spaces. Besides these applications to moduli, the theory gives new tools for the study of a single abelian variety by furnishing canonical bases for all linear systems on it.

Next I want to mention briefly p-adic uniformization. Motivated by the study of the boundary of moduli varieties for curves, i.e., of how nonsingular curves can degenerate, Mumford was led to introduce p-adic Schottky groups, and to show how one can obtain certain p-adic curves of genus $\geqq 2$ transcendentally as the quotient by such groups of the p-adic projective line minus a Cantor set. The corresponding theory for genus 1 was discovered by the author, but the generalization to higher genus was far from obvious. Besides its significance for moduli, Mumford's construction is of interest in itself as a highly nontrivial example of "rigid" p-adic analysis.

The theta functions and p-adic uniformization give some insight into what happens on the boundary of the varieties of moduli of curves and abelian varieties, but a much more detailed picture can now be obtained by Mumford's theory of toroidal embeddings. This theory, which unifies ideas that had appeared earlier in the works of several investigators, reduces the study of certain types of varieties and singularities to combinatorial problems in a space of "exponents". The local model for a toroidal embedding is called a torus embedding. This is a compactification $\bar{V}$ of a torus V such that the action of V on itself by translation extends to an action of V on $\bar{V}$. The coordinate ring of V is linearly spanned by the monomials $x^a = x_1^{a_1} x_2^{a_2} \cdots x_n^{a_n}$, $n = \dim V$, with positive or negative integer exponents a_i. Viewing the exponent vectors a as integral points in Euclidean n-space, define a *rational cone* in that space to be a set consisting of r's such that $(r, a) \geqq 0$ for $a \in S$, where S is some finite set of exponent vectors. For each rational cone σ, the monomials x^a such that $(r, a) \geqq 0$ for all $r \in \sigma$ span the coordinate ring of an affine variety $V(\sigma)$ which contains V as an open dense subvariety, if σ contains no nonzero linear subspace of $\boldsymbol{R}^n$. Now if we decompose $\boldsymbol{R}^n$ into the union of a finite number of rational cones σ_α in such a way that each intersection $\sigma_\alpha \cap \sigma_\beta$ is a face of σ_α and σ_β, then the union of the $V(\sigma_\alpha)$ is a compactification of V of the type desired. All such compactifications $\bar{V}$ of V can be obtained in this way and the invariant sheaves of ideals on them can be described in terms of the decomposition into cones. One can also read off whether $\bar{V}$ is nonsingular, and if it is not one can desingularize it by suitably subdividing the decomposition. In short, there is a whole dictionary for translating questions about the algebraic geometry of V and $\bar{V}$ into combinatorial questions about decompositions of $\boldsymbol{R}^n$ into rational cones.

Mumford with the help of his coworkers has used these techniques to prove the following semistable reduction theorem. If a family of varieties X_t over $\boldsymbol{C}$, in general nonsingular, is parametrized by a parameter t on a curve C, and if X_{t_0} is singular, then one can pull back the family to a ramified covering of C in a neighborhood of t_0 and blow it up over t_0 in such a way that the new singular fiber is of the stablest possible kind, i.e., is a divisor whose components have multiplicities 1 and cross transversally. The corresponding problem in characteristic p is open. For curves in characteristic p the result was proved by Mumford and Deligne and was a crucial step in their proof of the irreducibility of the moduli variety for curves of given genus.

Toroidal embeddings can also be used to construct explicit resolutions of the singularities of the projective varieties $\overline{D/\Gamma}$, where D is a bounded symmetric domain, Γ is an arithmetic group, and the bar denotes the "minimal" compactification of Baily and Borel. The construction of these resolutions is a big step forward. With them one has a powerful tool to analyse the behavior of functions at the "boundary", compute numerical invariants, and, generally, study the finer structure of these varieties.

I hope this report, incomplete as it is, gives some idea of Mumford's achievements and their importance. I heartily congratulate him on them and wish him well for the future!

Harvard University
Cambridge, Massachusetts 02138, U.S.A.

Section 0

Expository Addresses

Proceedings of the International Congress of Mathematicians
Vancouver, 1974

Critical Points of Smooth Functions*

V. I. Arnold

The *critical points* of a smooth function are the points where the differential vanishes. A critical point is *nondegenerate* if the second differential is a nondegenerate quadratic form. In some neighbourhood of a nondegenerate critical point the function can be represented in the Morse normal form

$$f = \pm x_1^2 \pm \cdots \pm x_n^2 + \text{const}$$

using suitable local coordinates.

Every degenerate critical point bifurcates into some nondegenerate points after an arbitrarily small deformation ("morsification"). So generically, functions have no degenerate critical points.

Degenerate critical points appear naturally when the function depends upon parameters. For example, the function $f(x) = x^3 - tx$ has a degenerate critical point for the value $t = 0$ of the parameter. Every family of functions close enough to this one-parameter family has a similar degenerate critical point for some small value of the parameter.

When the parameters are few, only the simplest degeneracies appear generically, and one can explicitly list them, giving normal forms for functions and families. When the number of parameters increases, more complicated degeneracies appear, and their classification seems hopeless. In recent years it has been found, however, that at least the initial part of the hierarchy of singularities is remarkably simple, as is described below.

Families of functions appear in all branches of analysis and mathematical physics. In this report three applications will be discussed: Lagrange singularities (or caustics), Legendre singularities (or wavefronts), and oscillating integrals (or stationary phase method).

*Delivered by E. Brieskorn.

Unexpectedly enough, the classification of the simplest singularities in all these problems turns out to be related to the Lie, Coxeter, and Weyl groups A_k, D_k, E_k, to Artin's and Brieskorn's braid groups, and to the classification of the platonics in Euclidean three space.

The occurrence of the diagrams A, D, E and of Coxeter groups in such different situations as the simple Lie algebra theory, the classification of simple categories of linear spaces (Gabriel, Gel′fand-Ponomarev, Roiter-Nasarova), the Kodaira classification of elliptic curves degenerations, the theory of platonics, and the theory of simple singularities gives an impression of a wonderful chain of coincidences of the results of independent classifications (certain relations between some of them being known, others suspected). As we will now see, the classification of more complex singularities provides new wonderful coincidences, where Lobatchevski triangles and automorphic functions take part.

1. Classification of critical points. Let f be a germ of a holomorphic function at a critical point O. The *multiplicity* (or the *Milnor number*) μ of the critical point is defined as the number of nondegenerate critical points to which O bifurcates after a morsification.

Two germs of functions are *equivalent* if one of them can be transformed into the other by a local diffeomorphism of the domain space. The jet (the Taylor polynomial) of a function at O is *sufficient* if it determines the germ up to equivalence.

Every germ of a smooth function at a critical point of finite multiplicity is equivalent to a germ of a polynomial (namely, of its Taylor polynomial), and its jet of sufficiently high order is sufficient (see Tougeron **[76]**, M. Artin **[14]**, Mather **[53]**, and also [3], for four different proofs).

So, the classification problem for critical points with finite μ is reduced to a sequence of algebraic problems dealing with linear actions of Lie groups on finite dimensional spaces of jets. The first steps in solving these algebraic problems were taken by Thom **[70]**, Mather **[53]**, and Siersma **[66]**.

The classification of the first degeneracies is discrete, but the further types of critical points depend upon parameters (moduli). One finds that it is the classification of singularities with a small number of moduli that is nice while the classification of classes with small μ or small codimension is not.

Let us call *modality* (or number of moduli) of a point $x \in X$ under the action of a Lie group G on X the minimum number m such that some neighbourhood of x is covered by a finite number of m-parameter families of orbits of the group G. The point x is called *simple* if its modality is 0, that is, if some neighbourhood of x intersects only a finite number of orbits.

The *modality of the germ* of a function at a critical point is the modality of its sufficient jet in the space of jets of functions with critical point O and critical value 0.

Two germs of holomorphic functions with different numbers of arguments are called *stably equivalent* if they become equivalent after the direct addition of a nondegenerate quadratic form of the suitable number of variables.

THEOREM 1 (SEE [6]). *Up to stable equivalence, simple germs of holomorphic functions are exactly the following germs*:

$$A_k : f(x) = x^{k+1}, \qquad D_k : f(x, y) = x^2y + y^{k-1},$$
$$E_6 : f(x, y) = x^3 + y^4, \qquad E_7 : f(x, y) = x^3 + xy^3,$$
$$E_8 : f(x, y) = x^3 + y^5.$$

(See Figure 1.)

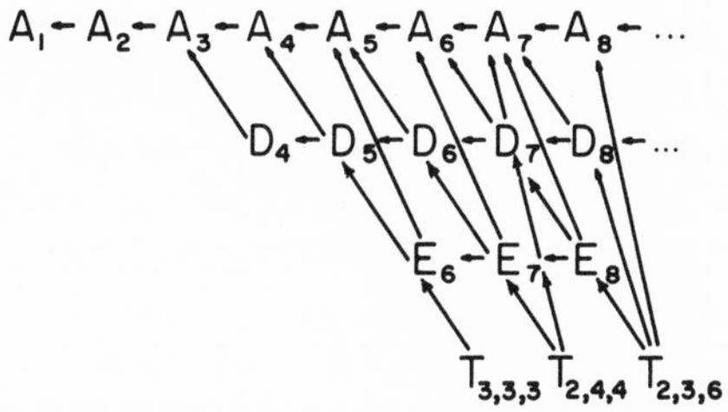

FIGURE 1. All the adherences of simple and parabolic singularities.

THEOREM 2 (SEE [7]). *Unimodular germs* (*that is, germs of modality* $m = 1$) *of holomorphic functions belong* (*up to stable equivalence*) *either to the following series of one-parameter families of functions*:

$$T_{p,q,r} : f(x, y, z) = axyz + x^p + y^q + z^r, \qquad \frac{1}{p} + \frac{1}{q} + \frac{1}{r} < 1, a \neq 0,$$

or to one of the following three families:

$$T_{3,3,3} : f(x, y, z) = x^3 + y^3 + z^3 + axyz, \qquad a^3 + 27 \neq 0,$$
$$T_{2,4,4} : f(x, y, z) = x^4 + y^4 + z^2 + ax^2y^2, \qquad a^2 \neq 4,$$
$$T_{2,3,6} : f(x, y, z) = x^3 + y^6 + z^2 + ax^2y^2, \qquad 4a^3 + 27 \neq 0,$$

or to one of the fourteen "exceptional" one-parameter families, given by the table below (*whose columns* 3—7 *will be explained later*).

There also exist tables of normal forms for all functions of two variables with nontrivial 3-jets [9] or nontrivial 4-jets, and tables of real normal forms.

THEOREM 3 (SEE [6], [7]). *The set of all nonsimple germs of functions of* $n \geqq 3$ *variables has codimension* 6, *and the set of germs with modality* $m > 1$ *has codimension* 10 *in the space of all germs of functions with critical value* 0.

Therefore every s-parameter family of functions can be made generic by a small variation, so that all germs of functions for all values of parameters will be stably equivalent to the germs of Theorem 1 (+ const) if $s < 6$, or to the germs of Theorems 1 and 2, if $s < 10$.

2. Factor singularities. The group $SU(2)$ acts linearly on C^2. Discrete subgroups of $SU(2)$ are known as binary groups of a polygon, a dihedron, a tetrahedron, a cube, or of an icosahedron (because they define the corresponding subgroups of the

TABLE

Notation	Normal form	Weights	Coxeter number	Dolgatchev numbers	Gabrielov numbers	Dual class
Q_{10}	$x^2z+y^3+z^4+ayz^3$	8 9 6	−24	2 3 9	3 3 4	K_{14}
Q_{11}	$x^2z+y^3+yz^3+az^5$	7 6 4	−18	2 4 7	3 3 5	Z_{13}
Q_{12}	$x^2z+y^3+z^5+ayz^4$	6 5 3	−15	3 3 6	3 3 6	Q_{12}
S_{11}	$x^2z+yz^2+y^4+ay^3z$	6 5 4	−16	2 5 6	3 4 4	W_{13}
S_{12}	$x^2z+yz^2+xy^3+ay^5$	5 4 3	−13	3 4 5	3 4 5	S_{12}
U_{12}	$x^3+y^3+z^4+axyz^2$	4 4 3	−12	4 4 4	4 4 4	U_{12}
Z_{11}	$x^3y+y^5+z^2+axy^4$	15 8 6	−30	2 3 8	2 4 5	K_{13}
Z_{12}	$x^3y+xy^4+z^2+ay^6$	11 6 4	−22	2 4 6	2 4 6	Z_{12}
Z_{13}	$x^3y+y^6+z^2+axy^5$	9 5 3	−18	3 3 5	2 4 7	Q_{11}
W_{12}	$x^4+y^5+z^2+ax^2y^3$	10 5 4	−20	2 5 5	2 5 5	W_{12}
W_{13}	$x^4+xy^4+z^2+ay^6$	8 4 3	−16	3 4 4	2 5 6	S_{11}
K_{12}	$x^3+y^7+z^2+axy^5$	21 14 6	−42	2 3 7	2 3 7	K_{12}
K_{13}	$x^3+xy^5+z^2+ay^8$	15 10 4	−30	2 4 5	2 3 8	Z_{11}
K_{14}	$x^3+y^8+z^2+axy^6$	12 8 3	−24	3 3 4	2 3 9	Q_{10}

rotation group of the sphere $\boldsymbol{C}P^1$ after factoring $SU(2)$ by its center $\pm E$).

The quotient space $\boldsymbol{C}^2/\Gamma$, for a binary group Γ, is an algebraic surface with one singular point.

The algebra of polynomials in two variables invariant under Γ possesses three generators. The relation (syzygy) between these generators is exactly the equation of the quotient variety $\boldsymbol{C}^2/\Gamma$, embedded in $\boldsymbol{C}^3$. The following theorem has been known since the time of H. A. Schwarz.

THEOREM 4 (SEE **[43]**, **[41]**, **[56]**, **[18]**). *All the surfaces* $\boldsymbol{C}^2/\Gamma$ *for binary groups* Γ *have simple singularities of types* A_k (*for polygons*), D_k (*for dihedrons*), E_6 (*for the tetrahedron*), E_7 (*for the cube*), *or* E_8 (*for the icosahedron*).

Now let us consider the group $SU(1,1)$ of 2×2 matrices with determinant one preserving the quadratic form $|Z_1|^2 - |Z_2|^2$. This group acts on the set P of vectors in $\boldsymbol{C}^2$ with positive value on this form. A discrete group of motions of the Lobatchevski plane with compact fundamental domain defines a "binary subgroup" $\Gamma \subset SU(1, 1)$ and an algebraic surface $M = (P/\Gamma) \cup O$ with singular point O. The coordinate ring of M is isomorphic to the ring of integer Γ_0-automorphic forms.

Let Δ be a Lobatchevski triangle with angles π/p, π/q, π/r. The reflections in its sides define a discrete group, and motions form a subgroup of index two in it. Thus for every such triangle Δ there is a binary group of the triangle in $SU(1,1)$.

The study of the 14 exceptional singularities led I. V. Dolgatchev to the following result.

THEOREM 5 (SEE DOLGATCHEV **[27]**). *There exist exactly* 14 *Lobatchevski triangles for which the surfaces* $M = (P/\Gamma) \cup O$, Γ *the binary group of the triangle, allow embeddings in* $\boldsymbol{C}^3$ (*in other words, for exactly* 14 *triangles the algebra of integer automorphic forms allows three generators*). *These* 14 *quotient surfaces have at* O *exactly* (*the* 14) *exceptional quasi-homogeneous unimodular singularities* (*see Theorem* 2 *above*). *The values of* p, q, r *are given in the column under "Dolgatchev numbers" in the table.*

The binary group for E_8 is $\mathrm{PSL}(2, F_5)$; and for K_{12} it is $\mathrm{PSL}(2, F_7)$ (Klein **[43]**). This example was the starting point of Dolgatchev's work.

3. Quadratic forms of singularities. To each isolated critical point of a holomorphic function f in n variables one can associate a manifold V with boundary ∂V. V is the *local nonsingular level manifold* of real dimension $2n - 2$. Let us consider a small ball with its centre at the critical point. Then V is the part of a level set $f^{-1}(z)$ inside the ball (for a z sufficiently close to the critical value) (Figure 2).

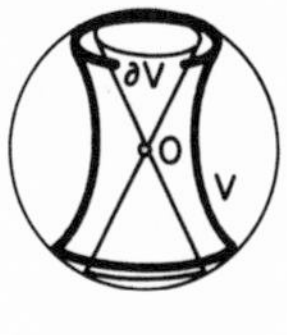

FIGURE 2. The local nonsingular level manifold.

[The boundary ∂V provides standard examples in differential topology, e.g., for the simple critical point E_8 in five variables, ∂V is one of the exotic 7-dimensional spheres of Milnor, which is homeomorphic but not diffemorphic to S^7. By attaching a disc to ∂V for E_8 in seven variables, one obtains a nonsmoothable 12-manifold (see Hirzebruch [**42**], Brieskorn [**19**], Milnor [**56**], Kuiper [**44**]).]

Milnor has proved that the local level manifold V^{2n-2} is homotopically equivalent to a bouquet of μ spheres S^{n-1}, so $H_{n-1}(V, Z) = Z^{\mu}$ (Milnor [**56**], Brieskorn [**24**]). The intersection index defines on H_{n-1} an integral bilinear form.

The *quadratic form of a singularity* is the self-intersection form on the homology of the nonsingular level manifold of a function in $n \equiv 3 \bmod 4$ variables, stably equivalent to the given function. [It is convenient to add squares to the function to obtain a symmetric intersection form. The effect of adding squares (or other direct summands) is described by the Sebastiani-Thom theorem [**64**]; see also [**32**].]

A singularity of a hypersurface is called *elliptic* (resp. *parabolic* or *hyperbolic*), if its quadratic form is negative definite (resp. nonpositive, or has 1 positive square).

Elliptic singularities have been classified by Tjurina [**73**].

THEOREM 6 (SEE [**73**], [**6**], [**71**]). *Elliptic singularities of hypersurfaces are exactly the simple singularities A, D, E of Theorem* 1. *The parabolic singularities are exactly* $T_{3,3,3}$, $T_{2,4,4}$ *and* $T_{2,3,6}$ *of Theorem* 2. *The hyperbolic singularities are exactly* $T_{p,q,r}$, *with* $1/p + 1/q + 1/r < 1$.

The assertion on parabolic singularities has been formulated as a conjecture by Milnor, inspired by Wagreich's work [**80**].

It is convenient to describe quadratic forms of singularities using Dynkin (or Coxeter) diagrams. Such a diagram is a graph, whose points correspond to "vanishing cycles" (basis vectors with square -2 in H_{n-1}). Two points are connected by k lines if the scalar product of corresponding vectors is equal to k, e.g. ·—· is a diagram for $-2x_1^2 + 2x_1x_2 - 2x_2^2$.

Very effective methods for determining diagrams of singularities have been elaborated by A. M. Gabrielov [**32**], [**33**] and S. M. Guseĭn-Zade [**37**], [**38**]. The method of the latter gives the diagrams for all functions in two variables directly from the picture of level curves of a convenient real morsification. Recently A'Campo has independently rediscovered the Guseĭn-Zade method.

The quadratic forms of simple singularities A, D, E are given by standard diagrams (Hirzebruch [**42**]):

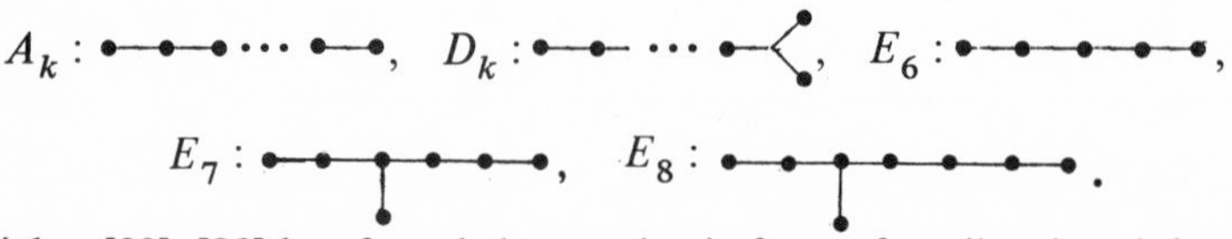

Gabrielov [**32**], [**33**] has found the quadratic forms for all unimodular singularities. Let τ_{p_1,p_2,p_3} denote the quadratic form, defined by a diagram having the shape of a letter T, with p_1, p_2, p_3, points on its three closed segments (e.g., $E_7 = \tau_{2,3,4}$).

THEOREM 7 (SEE [7], [32], [33]). *The quadratic form of every hyperbolic* (*parabolic*) *singularity* $T_{p,q,r}$ *is a direct sum* $\tau_{p,q,r} \oplus 0$ (*where* 0 *is a* 0-*form in one variable*). *The quadratic forms of the* 14 *exceptional singularities are of the form* $\tau_{p,q,r} \oplus \begin{pmatrix} 0 & 1 \\ 1 & 0 \end{pmatrix}$, *where the* 14 *triples* (p,q,r) *are given by the column "Gabrielov numbers" of the table above.*

4. The strange duality. The comparison of Dolgatchev and Gabrielov numbers of the 14 exceptional singularities leads to the following.

THEOREM 8. *Gabrielov numbers of every exceptional singularity are Dolgatchev numbers of another one; the Gabrielov numbers of the latter are the Dolgatchev numbers of the former.*

So there is an involution which transposes the eight singularities $Q_{10} \leftrightarrow K_{14}$, $Q_{11} \leftrightarrow Z_{13}$, $Z_{11} \leftrightarrow K_{13}$, $S_{11} \leftrightarrow W_{13}$ and leaves invariant all the six other (having multiplicity $\mu = 12$) (Figure 3).

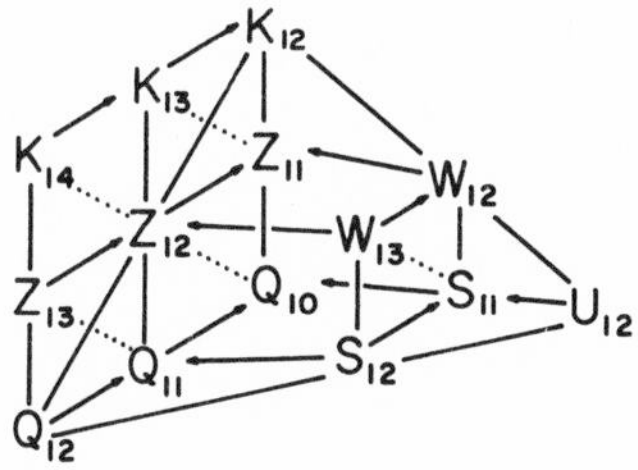

FIGURE 3. The pyramid of the 14 exceptional singularities.

There is no evident relation between singularities dual to each other (or between their Lobatchevski triangles, or quadratic forms), nor between Gabrielov and Dolgatchev numbers of the same singularity.

When Dolgatchev first reported his theorem, D. B. Fuks remarked that the sum of the multiplicity μ with the three Dolgatchev numbers is 24 for all the exceptional singularities but one (where Dolgatchev made some mistake).

This remark of Fuks joined to Theorem 8 implies that the sum of all the six Dolgatchev and Gabrielov numbers is 24 for any of the 14 exceptional singularities. One can also see that dual singularities are exactly the singularities with the same Coxeter number (defined below). There is no explanation for all these empirical facts. Singularity theory is, in its present state, an experimental science.

5. Versal deformation and the level bifurcation set. The *deformations* of a function f are the germs at O of smooth mappings from finite-dimensional "base spaces" to the function space which map O to f. A deformation is called *versal* if this mapping is transversal (in an understandable sense) to the orbit of f under the action of the pseudo-group of diffeomorphisms of the argument space. If the dimension of the base space has the minimal possible value (equal to the codimension of the orbit), the deformation is called *miniversal*.

One can define versal deformations for germs of functions. A germ of a function at a critical point of finite multiplicity μ allows a μ-parameter miniversal deformation; all other deformations are equivalent to deformations induced from this one by mappings of base spaces (for the proof see Tjurina **[74]**, Mather **[53]**, Latour **[46]**, Zakaljukin **[84]**).

The *local algebra* of the germ of a function f at a point O is the factor algebra of the algebra of (formal or convergent) series at O by the ideal generated by the partial derivatives of f. The dimension of this algebra as a module over the constant functions ($\boldsymbol{C}$ or $\boldsymbol{R}$) is exactly the multiplicity μ of f (see Palamodov **[59]**).

One can choose as a miniversal deformation of the germ of f at O the deformation $\lambda \to f + \lambda_1 e_1 + \cdots + \lambda_\mu e_\mu$ where the functions e_i define the generators of the local algebra as a module over the constants.

Let us fix some miniversal deformation of the germ of f at the origin. The *level bifurcation* set for f is the germ at O of the hypersurface in the base space, formed by all the values of the parameter λ such that 0 is a critical value for the corresponding function near the origin.

The complement to this bifurcation set is the base space of the fibration, whose typical fibre is a nonsingular level set of f. The action of the fundamental group of this complement on the homology of the fibre is called the *monodromy* of the singularity, and its image is called *monodromy group*.

THEOREM 9 (SEE **[6]**). *The complement of the level bifurcation set of a simple singularity is a $K(\pi, 1)$ space, where π is the corresponding braid group (defined by E. Artin for the case A, and by E. Brieskorn in the general case;* see **[21]**, **[22]**, **[23]**). *This complement is the space of regular orbits of the action of the corresponding Coxeter group on the complexification of the Euclidean space $\boldsymbol{R}^\mu$. The monodromy group of a simple singularity is the natural representation of the braid group on the Coxeter group.*

In case E the proof uses one theorem of Deligne **[26]** and one of Brieskorn **[20]**.

The topology of the complement to the bifurcation subsets seems to be very interesting, and might bring some algebraic structure to the amorphous set of singularity classes. The few results known on the homology (see **[4]**, **[22]**) show promising relations to loop spaces of the sphere (G. Segal **[65]**, Fuks **[30]**, **[31]**); there exist also some relations to pseudo-isotopies (Cerf **[25]**, Thom **[71]**) and to the algebraic K-theory (Volodin **[79]**, Wagoner **[81]**, Hatcher **[39]**).

Returning to the level bifurcation set for a function at a critical point of multiplicity μ, let us consider a straight line $\boldsymbol{C}^1$ near the origin of the base space $\boldsymbol{C}^\mu$ of the miniversal deformation. A generic $\boldsymbol{C}^1$ intersects the bifurcation set at μ different points near O. Let us fix such a $\boldsymbol{C}^1$ and call these μ points *distinguished points.*

Fix a base point in $\boldsymbol{C}^1$ (different from the μ distinguished points), and let V be the fibre of our fibration over the base point (V is the nonsingular local level manifold). Let us choose μ *distinguished paths,* coming from the base point to the μ distinguished points and having no intersections outside the base point. The fibre over a point near the distinguished one has a *vanishing cycle* of Picard-Lefshetz (that is, an embedded sphere S^{n-1} which generates the homology of the local level manifold at the distinguished point) (Figure 4).

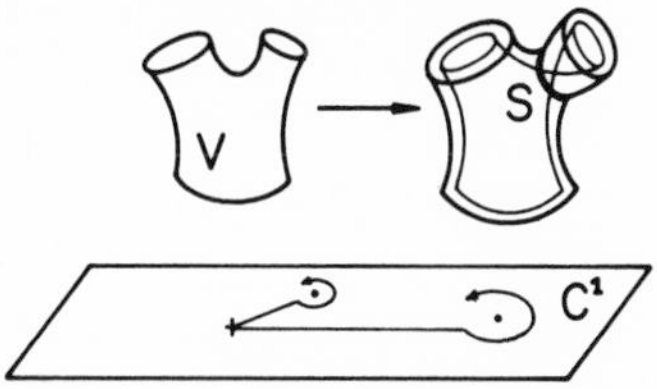

FIGURE 4. A distinguisted vanishing cycle.

Returning to the base point along the distinguished path, one defines a *distinguished vanishing cycle* in $H_{n-1}(V)$. The μ distinguished cycles thus obtained form the *distinguished basis* of H_{n-1} (Lamotke **[45]**, Gabrielov **[32]**). The fundamental group of the complement to the level bifurcation set is generated by the μ *distinguished loops* on $\boldsymbol{C}^1$; one obtains these loops from the distinguished paths, turning around the distinguished points (the fundamental group theorem of Zariski **[85]**, see also **[77]**, **[48]**).

Now let us suppose that n is odd (n is the number of variables). In this case the action of every distinguished generator of the fundamental group on the homology of V is the reflection in the orthogonal complement to the distinguished vanishing cycle (the Picard-Lefshetz theorem).

So, to calculate the monodromy group of a singularity it is sufficient to find the Dynkin diagram *for the base formed by the* μ *distinguished vanished cycles*. The first important examples of this were given by Pham (see Pham **[60]**, Brieskorn **[19]**): The Pham basis is in fact a distinguished one. Articles of Gabrielov **[32]**, **[33]** and of Guseĭn-Zade **[37]**, **[38]** include many examples of such diagrams (e.g., **[33]** includes all the unimodular singularities and **[38]** all the singularities stably equivalent to functions of two variables).

The Dynkin diagram for a distinguished basis is always connected (Lazzeri **[47]**, see also **[34]**). It follows that the critical point cannot bifurcate if the critical value does not.

The *classical monodromy* of a function germ f is the action on $H_{n-1}(V)$ of the product of all distinguished generators. This operator is related to the asymptotics of different integrals containing f, and it is important to calculate it (see, e.g., Milnor and Orlik **[57]**, Brieskorn **[24]**, A'Campo **[1]**, Malgrange **[51]**). If the diagram for a distinguished basis is known, the calculation of the classical monodromy is reduced to a multiplication of matrices.

For simple singularities, the classical monodromy operator is the Coxeter element of the Coxeter group. Its order N is the Coxeter number $N(A_k) = k + 1$, $N(D_k) = 2k - 2$, $N(E_6) = 12$, $N(E_7) = 18$, $N(E_8) = 30$.

A'Campo **[2]** has proved that the classical monodromy operator for degenerate singularities is never the identity.

6. The function bifurcation set. Let $\mathfrak{m}^2$ be the space of germs of functions with critical value 0 of the critical point $O \in \boldsymbol{C}^n$. The group of germs of diffeomorphisms of $\boldsymbol{C}^n$ preserving O acts on $\mathfrak{m}^2$. A germ T of a manifold of minimal dimension, transversal to the orbit of f in $\mathfrak{m}^2$, has dimension $\mu - 1$. One can consider the embedding of T as a $(\mu - 1)$-parameter deformation of the germ f. This deformation, as any other deformation, is induced from the miniversal deformation by some mapping of the base spaces $\tau: T \to \boldsymbol{C}^\mu$.

The level bifurcation set Σ is the image of T under τ. Σ is irreducible and has a nonsingular normalisation T (see Teissier [**68**], Gabrielov [**34**]).

Let $\mathfrak{m}$ be the space of germs at O of functions with value 0 at O (O not necessarily being a critical point). The deformation inside this class will be called *restricted deformations*. A miniversal restricted deformation has $\mu - 1$ parameters. We obtain an *extended miniversal deformation* with μ parameters from the restricted one by adding an arbitrary constant at the μth parameter.

Let us fix the representative of a miniversal restricted deformation of a germ f. One calls the points in the base space $\boldsymbol{C}^{\mu-1}$ for which the associated function has less than μ different critical values near O the *function bifurcation points*. The set of all such points is the *function bifuracation subset* for f; this is a hypersurface Δ in $\boldsymbol{C}^{\mu-1}$ (more precisely, we will consider the germ of Δ at O) (Figure 5).

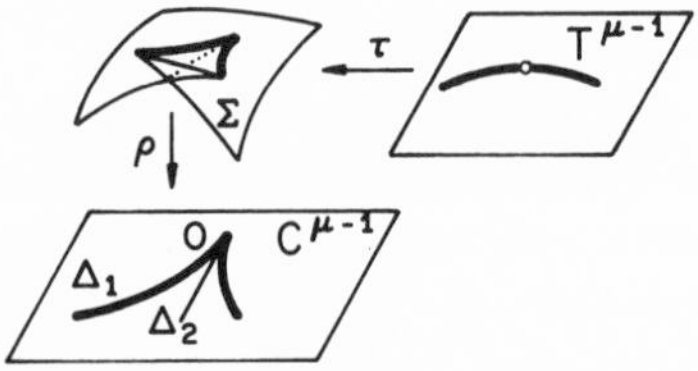

FIGURE 5. The level bifurcation set Σ and the function bifurcation set Δ for A_3.

THEOREM 10 (SEE [**67**], [**34**]). *The restriction to the level bifurcation set Σ of the natural mapping $\rho: \boldsymbol{C}^\mu \to \boldsymbol{C}^{\mu-1}$ from the base space of the extended miniversal deformation to that of the restricted one defines a μ-fold covering over the complement to Δ in $\boldsymbol{C}^{\mu-1}$ (in some neighbourhood of O). The group of this covering is the whole symmetric group, S_μ.*

THEOREM 11 (LOOIJENGA [**50**], LIASCHKO [**9**]). *For simple germs of functions the complement of the function bifurcation set (in some neighbourhood of O in $\boldsymbol{C}^{\mu-1}$) is a $K(\pi, 1)$ space, where π is a subgroup of finite index $\nu = \mu! N^\mu W^{-1}$ (N = Coxeter number, W = order of the Weyl group) in the Artin braid group with μ strings.*

The function bifurcation set Δ is the union of two hypersurfaces Δ_1 and *Δ_2*; Δ_1 corresponds to functions having degenerate critical points, and Δ_2 to functions having coincident critical values.

The smooth mapping $\rho \circ \tau: T^{\mu-1} \to \boldsymbol{C}^{\mu-1}$ from the transversal space to the base space of the restricted deformation has Δ_1 as the critical value set and defines a μ-fold covering over the complement to Δ_1.

The hypersurface Δ_1 is called the *caustic*, and Δ_2 the *cut locus* (or the Maxwell stratum).

7. Lagrange singularities and caustic classification. One can see caustics on a wall lit up by sun rays reflected by some curved surface (e.g., by the inside surface of a cup). Moving the cup, one can see that generic caustics allow only standard singularities, while more complicated singularities bifurcate into standard ones under small perturbation.

The study of caustics is a part of the theory of *Lagrange singularities* (see [6] and articles of J. Guckenheimer [36], A. Weinstein [82], Hörmander [40]) similar to the usual theory of singularities of smooth mappings of Whitney, Thom, and Mather ([83], [69], [53]).

The *symplectic structure* on a manifold M^{2n} is a closed 2-form ω, nondegenerate at every point of M.

A *Lagrange submanifold* of a symplectic manifold (M^{2n}, ω) is a submanifold of the greatest possible dimension where ω vanishes (that is, of dimension n). The fibration $p: M^{2n} \to B^n$ is a *Lagrange fibration* if all its fibres are Lagrange submanifolds. A typical example is the cotangent fibration $T^*B \to B$ (the "phase space" of classical mechanics).

Let $i : L \to M$ be the embedding from a Largrange submanifold to the total space of a Lagrange fibration $p : M \to B$. Then $p \circ i : L \to B$ is called a *Lagrange mapping*, and one calls its set of critical value *caustics*.

A *Lagrange equivalence* is a mapping between two Lagrange fibrations respecting the symplectic structure. Two Lagrange mappings are *equivalent* iff there exists a Lagrange equivalence which maps the first of the corresponding Lagrange submanifolds on the second. Caustics of equivalent mappings are diffeomorphic.

A Lagrange mapping is *stable* at a point O iff every Lagrange mapping, close enough to the given one, has, at some point near O, a germ equivalent to the given germ at O.

The germ of a Lagrange mapping is *simple* iff all nearby germs belong to a finite number of equivalence classes. A simple germ can be nonstable and a stable germ can be nonsimple.

THEOREM 12 (SEE [6]). *Simple stable germs of Lagrange mappings are classified by the A, D, and E singularities. Iff $n \leqq 5$ every Lagrange mapping of L^n can be approximated by a mapping whose germ at every point is stable and simple.*

We give below an explicit description of Lagrange germs of the types A, D, and E, listing coordinate normal forms. It follows from the list, for example, that generic caustics in three-space have besides normal crossings only Lagrange singularities A_3 (cuspidal edges), discrete point singularities A_4 (swallow tails) and $D_4^{\pm}$ (points of contact of three cuspidal edges, two of which may be complex) (Figure 6).

8. Legendre singularities and classification of wavefronts. To obtain an example of a wavefront one can start from an ellipse, construct inside normals, and choose

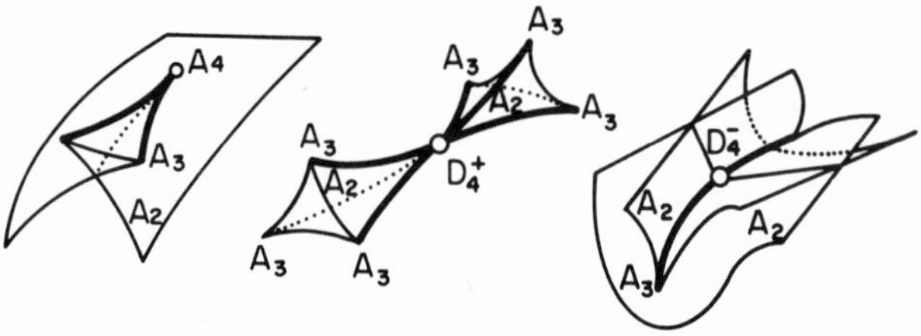

FIGURE 6. Generic singularities of the caustics in the 3-space.

points at the distance t from the ellipse points on the normals (Figure 7). The curve so obtained may have singularities which cannot be removed by a small variation of the initial ellipse. The study of front singularities is a part of the theory of Legendre singularities (see **[10]**, **[11]**; the name comes from classical "Legendre transformation", which provides typical examples of Legendre singularities).

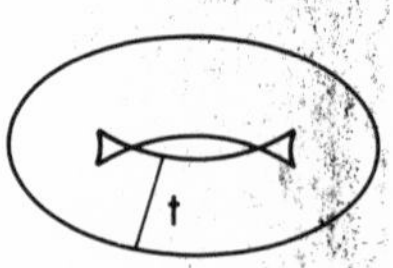

FIGURE 7. The singularities of a wavefront.

The theory of Legendre singularities is parallel to the theory of Lagrange singularities, with the following differences: One has to replace the symplectic structure with the contact one, the affine structure with the projective one, gradients with Legendre transformations, functions with hypersurfaces, and so on.

The parallelism between the two theories is the real origin of the Hamilton "optical-mechanical analogy".

The *contact structure* on a manifold M^{2n+1} is a field of tangent hyperplanes (called *contact planes*), verifying the "maximum nonintegrability" condition (if α is the 1-form defining contact planes, $\alpha \wedge (d\alpha)^n$ is nondegenerate). Standard examples of contact manifolds are the total space of the projective cotangent bundle PT^*V^{n+1} and the manifold of 1-jets of functions $J^1(W^n, \boldsymbol{R})$ with their natural contact structures (defined by the integrability conditions).

The *Legendre submanifold* of a contact manifold M^{2n+1} is an integral submanifold of maximal dimension (that is, of dimension n). The fibration $p : M^{2n+1} \to B^{n+1}$ is a *Legendre fibration* if all its fibres are Legendre submanifolds.

A typical example is the projective cotangent fibration $p\colon PT^*B \to B$. All Legendre fibrations of the same dimension are locally equivalent (locally = near every point of the total space). Fibres of a Legendre fibration locally have the structure of a projective space defined intrinsically by the Legendre fibration.

Let $i : L^n \to M^{2n+1}$ be an embedding of a Legendre submanifold in the total space of a Legendre fibration $p : M^{2n+1} \to B^{n+1}$. The mapping $p \circ i : L^n \to B^{n+1}$ is then the *Legendre mapping*, and its image the *front*.

Legendre equivalence, stability, and simplicity of germs are defined in the same way as in the Lagrange case.

THEOREM 13 (SEE **[10]**, **[11]**). *Simple stable germs of Legendre mappings are classified by the A, D, and E singularities. Iff $n \leqq 5$, every Legendre mapping of L^n can be approximated by a mapping whose germs at all points are stable and simple.*

We give the list of explicit normal forms for simple stable Legendre germs in the next section. It follows from the list, e.g., that generic fronts in three-space have (besides normal crossings) only Legendre singularities A_2 (cuspidal edges) and A_3 (swallow tails). The singularity of the moving front slips along the caustic, and at some discrete moment may change its shape under some standard "catastrophe" of the types A_4 or $D_4^{\pm}$ (compare the pictures in the book of Thom **[70]**) (Figure 8).

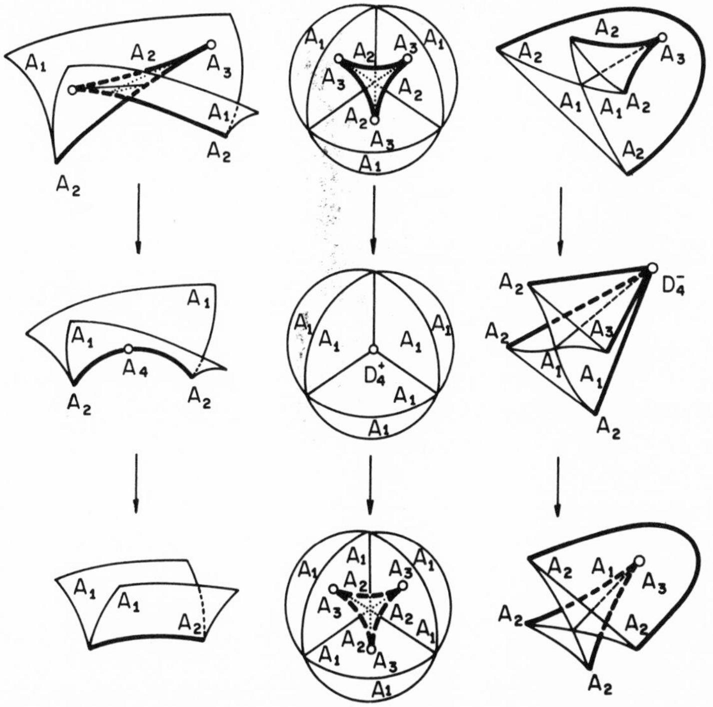

FIGURE 8. The modifications of the wavefronts near the catastrophes A_4 and $D_4^{\pm}$.

There exists a *symplectisation functor* associating to a contact M^{2n+1} a symplectic E^{2n+2}. However, the symplectisations of generic Legendre singularities are very special (conical) Lagrange singularities. The right way to deal with the Legendre case is rather the *contactisation functor*, associating to a symplectic M^{2n} a contact E^{2n+1} (defined, in fact, either for germs or for symplectic structures defining an integer class in $H_2(M^{2n})$).

9. Normal forms for caustics and fronts. I shall use here the old-fashioned coordinate notations: Let $F(x, \lambda)$ be a deformation of a function $f(x)$ in k variables, $x \in \boldsymbol{R}^k$ and one parameter, $\lambda \in \boldsymbol{R}^l$. Let $n = k + l$, and let us consider a symplectic space $\boldsymbol{R}^{2n}$ with coordinates $x \in \boldsymbol{R}^k$, $y \in \boldsymbol{R}^{k*}$, $\lambda \in \boldsymbol{R}^l$, $\kappa \in \boldsymbol{R}^{l*}$, with a symplectic structure $\omega = dx \wedge dy + d\kappa \wedge d\lambda$ and with a Lagrange fibration structure $(x, y, \lambda, \kappa) \mapsto (y, \lambda)$. The equations

$$(1) \qquad y = \partial F/\partial x, \qquad \kappa = -\partial F/\partial \lambda$$

define a Lagrange submanifold, and we denote by $\mathscr{L}$ the Lagrange mapping so obtained.

Let us construct two more families of functions in the variable x

$$\Phi(x; \lambda, y, z) = F(x, \lambda) - z - xy$$

(parameters are $\lambda \in \boldsymbol{R}^l$, $y \in \boldsymbol{R}^{k*}$, $z \in \boldsymbol{R}$);

$$G(x; a, \lambda) = F(a + x, \lambda) - F(a, \lambda) - xF'_a(a, \lambda)$$

(parameters are $a \in \boldsymbol{R}^k$, $\lambda \in \boldsymbol{R}^l$). Let $G(x, O, O)$ be $g(x)$.

THEOREM 14. *The following conditions are equivalent*:
(i) *The germ of* $\mathscr{L}$ *at the point* $x = 0$, $\lambda = 0$ *is Lagrange stable.*
(ii) *The deformation* G *is transversal to the orbit of* g *in* $\mathfrak{m}^2$.
If $f \in \mathfrak{m}^2$, *each of the conditions* (i), (ii) *is equivalent to*:
(iii) *The deformation* Φ *is a versal deformation of* f *at* O.

THEOREM 15 (SEE [**6**]). *Simple stable germs of Lagrange mappings are equivalent to the germs* $\mathscr{L}$ *defined by* (1), *where* F *is a deformation of a simple germ of* f *such that the deformation* Φ *is versal.*

For example, if $f = x^4$ (the A_3 case), one can choose $F = x^4 + \lambda x^2$ (the complete list of F for all the cases A, D, E can be found in [**6**]).

Turning now to the Legendre case, let us extend $\boldsymbol{R}^{2n}$ to $\boldsymbol{R}^{2n+1} = \boldsymbol{R}^{2n} \times \boldsymbol{R}^1$ and let z be the coordinate in $\boldsymbol{R}^1$. Let us define the contact structure of $\boldsymbol{R}^{2n+1}$ by the form $\alpha = xdy + \kappa d\lambda + dz$ and the Legendre fibration by $(x, y, \lambda, \kappa; z) \mapsto (y, \lambda; z)$. The equations

$$(2) \qquad y = \partial F/\partial x, \qquad \kappa = -\partial F/\partial\lambda, \qquad z = F - x\partial F/\partial x$$

define a Legendre submanifold, and we denote by $\mathscr{L}'$ the Legendre mapping so obtained.

[Every Lagrange (resp. Legendre) submanifold or mapping in the standard coordinate symplectic (contact) manifold is locally defined by at least one of the 2^n formulae (1) (resp. (2)), corresponding to the 2^n choices of a coordinate "x-subspace" $\boldsymbol{R}^k \subset \boldsymbol{R}^n$.]

THEOREM 16 (SEE [**10**], [**11**]). *Simple stable germs of Legendre mappings are equivalent to the germs* $\mathscr{L}$, *defined by* (2), *F being the same as in the previous theorem.*

Besides the argument change group, there are the multiplications by the group of nonvanishing functions acting on the function space. The direct product of those two groups acts on the function space too. One calls the deformation of a function f *versal for levels*, if it is transversal to the orbit of this group.

As a versal for level deformation of a germ of f at O one can choose the deformation $\lambda \mapsto f + \lambda_1 e_1 + \cdots + \lambda_r e_r$, the e_s defining generators over $\boldsymbol{R}$ of the factor algebra of power series at O by the ideal $(f, \partial f/\partial x)$.

The product of the group of multiplications by nonvanishing germs at O with the group of diffeomorphisms leaving O fixed acts on $\mathfrak{m}^2$.

THEOREM 17. *The following conditions are equivalent:*

(i′) *The germ of* $\mathscr{L}'$ *at the point* $x = 0$, $\lambda = 0$ *is Legendre stable.*

(ii′) *The deformation* G *is transversal to the orbit of* g *under the action of the product group on* $\mathfrak{m}^2$.

If $f \in \mathfrak{m}^2$, *each of the conditions* (i′), (ii′) *is equivalent to:*

(iii′) *The deformation* Φ *is versal for levels.*

Comparing these results with those of previous sections, we can formulate

THEOREM 18. *The mapping* τ *from the transversal space* $T^{\mu-1}$ *to the base space of the miniversal deformation is a Legendre mapping, the level bifurcation set being its front. The mapping* $\rho \circ \tau$ *from the transversal space* T *to the restricted miniversal deformation space is a Lagrange mapping, the function bifurcation set being its caustic.*

[The above theorems may become more clear if we introduce the germ of the restricted critical set C of the deformation $F(x, \cdot)$ defined as $C = \{(x, \lambda): \partial F/\partial \lambda = 0, F(x, \lambda) = 0\}$.

If the deformation F is miniversal, C is a germ of a smooth $(\mu - 1)$-manifold. The canonical projection $(x, \lambda) \mapsto \lambda$ defines a mapping $\pi: C \to \Sigma$. The coordinate system defines a diffeomorphism $j: C \to T$ to the transversal to the orbit (j is defined by the translations of the critical points to the origin). The diagram

$$\begin{array}{ccc} T & \xleftarrow{\;j\;} & C \\ & {\scriptstyle\tau}\searrow \quad \swarrow{\scriptstyle\pi} & \\ & \Sigma & \end{array}$$

commutes; therefore π as τ, normalizes Σ; $\rho \circ \pi$ has the properties of $\rho \circ \tau$ and so on.]

10. Oscillating integrals. The study of the intensity of light near the caustic leads to the problem of asymptotics for an "oscillating integral"

$$I(h, \lambda) = \int e^{iF(x, \lambda)/h} \phi \, dx, \qquad x \in \boldsymbol{R}^k, \lambda \in \boldsymbol{R}^l,$$

depending on a parameter λ, for $h \to 0$. Here the parameter λ represents the point of observation, ϕ has compact support, F is a real smooth "phase function", and h defines the wave length.

Of course, one meets such integrals in all branches of mathematics and physics —e.g., in number theory and P.D.E. theory (see **[78]**, **[54]**, **[40]**).

If the light is intense enough to destroy the medium, the destruction will begin at the singular points of the caustics, where I is maximal. Thus arises the problem of defining asymptotics for $h \to 0$ of the maximum of I in λ, which can be met for generic F. The classification of simple singularities was found as a byproduct when this problem, communicated to me by Maslov [**55**], was being solved for $l = 3$ (see [**5**]).

The stationary phase principle is the assertion that the main part of the oscillating integral is given by the integration over the neighbourhoods of the critical points of F (for fixed λ). For a generic function all these points are nondegenerate, and the integral decreases for $h \to 0$ as $h^{k/2}$ (Fresnel [**29**]). However, degenerate critical points appear for some "caustic value" of the parameter λ even for a generic $F(x, \lambda)$. So at some points λ the integral decreases more slowly (as $h^{(k/2)-\beta}$).

The number β so defined is called the *degree of singularity* [**5**] of the corresponding critical point.

To be more precise, let us consider a critical point of finite multiplicity μ. The integral I allows then an asymptotic expansion

$$I \sim \sum_{\alpha, \kappa} C_{\alpha, \kappa}\, h^{(k/2)-\alpha} \ln^{\kappa} h,$$

where $0 \leqq \kappa \leqq k - 1$ and α belongs to the union of a finite number of rational arithmetical progressions (see I. Bernstein and S. Gel′fand [**16**], Atiyah [**15**], I. Bernštein [**17**], B. Malgrange [**51**] and [**52**]). Now β is the minimum of α such that there exists $C_{\alpha, \kappa} \neq 0$ for some ϕ with arbitrarily small support containing the critical point.

THEOREM 19 (SEE [**5**], [**6**], [**7**]). *For simple critical points, $\beta = 1/2 - 1/N$, where N is the Coxeter number. For parabolic and hyperbolic singularities $\beta = 1/2$.*

Probably, for all other critical points, $\beta > 1/2$. We define the *Coxeter number N of any singularity* by the formula $\beta = 1/2 - 1/N$, where β is the degree of singularity.

THEOREM 20 (SEE [**7**]). *The maximum of the degrees of singularities inevitable in generic families of functions in $k \geqq 3$ variables depending on $l \leqq 10$ parameters is $\beta = 1/2 - 1/N$, where N is given by the table*

l	0	1	2	3	4	5	6	7	8	9	10, $k=3$	11, $k=3$	10, $k>3$
N	+2	+3	+4	+6	+8	+12	∞	∞	−24	−16	−12	−8	−6

All the numbers $\beta_l(k)$ are rational, and do not depend on k when k is large enough; β_l, the limit for $k \to \infty$, increases probably as $\sqrt{2l}/6$ with l.

Probably, β is semicontinuous and even more, for every λ near λ_0,

$$\left|I(h, \lambda)\right| \leqq C(\varepsilon, \phi) h^{(k/2)-\beta(\lambda_0)-\varepsilon} \quad \text{for all } \varepsilon > 0.$$

Such an "uniform estimation" has been proved by I. M. Vinogradov [**78**] for the singularities of the type A and by Duistermaat [**28**] for all simple and parabolic singularities.

11. Semi-quasi-homogeneous functions and the Newton diagram. The first proofs of the classification theorems [6], [7] need long calculations, which can be replaced with some geometrical arguments, based upon the Newton diagrams.

A function $f(x_1, \cdots, x_n)$ is quasi-homogeneous of degree d with weights $(\alpha_1, \cdots, \alpha_n)$, if $f(t^{\alpha_1}x_1, \cdots, t^{\alpha_n}x_n) = t^d f(x_1, \cdots, x_n)$ identically in $t \in \boldsymbol{C}^*$. Here $0 \leqq \alpha_i \leqq \frac{1}{2}$ are rational numbers (see Saito [62], Milnor and Orlik [57], Orlik and Wagreich [58], Saito [63]).

The function f is semi-quasi-homogeneous, if $f = f_0 + f'$, where f_0 is quasi-homogeneous of degree 1, and has an isolated critical point at o, while the degrees of all the monomials of f' are higher than 1.

THEOREM 21 (SEE [8]). *Every semi-quasi-homogeneous function is equivalent to a "normal form" $f \sim f_0 + c_1e_1 + \cdots + c_re_r$ where c_s are numbers and the monomials e_s are the elements of a monomial basis of the local algebra of f_0 at O, whose degrees are more than* 1.

The Newton diagram of $f(x_1, \cdots, x_n)$ is a convex polyhedron in $\boldsymbol{R}^n$ constructed from the exponents of the monomials having nonzero coefficients in the Taylor series; it contains a lot of information on the singularity, but I shall formulate here only one result of A. G. Kushnirenko.

Let us suppose the the Newton diagram contains points on all coordinate axes (that is not a restriction, see the theorem of Tougeron [76]).

THEOREM 22 (KUSHNIRENKO). *Let us denote by V the volume of the positive orthant of $\boldsymbol{R}^n$ under the Newton diagram, by V_i the $(n-1)$-dimensional volume under the diagram on the ith coordinate hyperplane, by V_{ij} the $(n-2)$-dimensional volume on the coordinate plane orthogonal to the ith and the jth coordinate lines, and so on.*

Then for all functions f having a given Newton diagram

$$\mu(f) \geqq n!V - (n-1)! \sum V_i + (n-2)! \sum V_{ij} - \cdots \pm 1,$$

and for almost all functions f having this diagram, the equality holds.

For instance, for almost all functions in two variables with a given Newton diagram, we have $\mu = 2S - a - b + 1$, where S is the area under the diagram, a and b the coordinates of the diagram points on the axis (Figure 9).

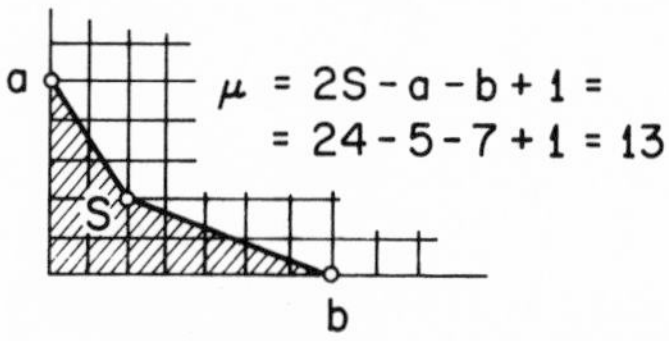

FIGURE 9. The calculation of the Milnor number.

12. Concluding remarks. It is not known whether the μ = const stratum (that is, the subvariety of the versal deformation base space, formed by points corresponding to functions with a critical point of multiplicity μ) is smooth. It was proved by Le Dung Trang and Ramanujan [49] that, for $n \neq 3$, neither the topology of the singular level set nor the topology of the Milnor fibration change along μ = const stratum. Probably, neither the topology of the function nor the β changes (for n = 3, as for other n).

The topology of bifurcation sets may change (Pham [**60**]). The dimension of the μ = const stratum is semicontinuous and so equal to the modality m of the critical point (Gabrielov [**34**]). Using some results of Teissier [**68**], Kushnirenko and Gabrielov [**35**] were able to prove that the modality of semihomogeneuos singularities is equal to the number of generators of a monomial basis of the local algebra above and on the Newton diagram.

The same is probably true for all semi-quasi-homogeneous singularities. The modality m of functions of two variables is probably equal to the number of integer points between the coordinate rays passing through the point (2, 2) and the Newton diagram (for almost all functions with a given diagram, see [**8**]).

In this article I did not even mention many important sides of the theory of critical points of functions, especially the algebraic ones (see, e.g., [**65**]). I like to stress the importance and power of transcendental, topological methods, based upon the study of the hierarchy of singularities (first for the cases of small codimension), of the adherence of different classes of singularities to others, upon semicontinuity and general position arguments, arguments which go back to the bifurcation theory of Poincaré (see [**12**]) and were formalised by Thom's transversality theorems. G. M. Tjurina was the first to apply these ideas to the study of singular points of hypersurfaces (see [**13**], [**73**], [**74**], [**75**].)

References

1. N. A'Campo, *Sur la monodromie des singularités isolées d'hypersurfaces complexes*, Invent. Math. **20** (1973), 147–170.

2. ———, *Le nombre de Lefschetz d'une monodromie*, Indag. Math. (1973).

3. V. I. Arnold, *Singularities of smooth mappings*, Uspehi Mat. Nauk **23** (1968), no. 1 (139), 3-44 = Russian Math. Surveys **23** (1968), no. 1, 1–43. MR **37** #2243.

4. ———, *On some topological invariants of algebraic functions*, Trudy Moskov. Mat. Obšč. **21** (1970), 27–46 = Trans. Moscow Math. Soc. **21** (1970), 30–52. MR **43** #225.

5. ———, *Integrals of rapidly oscillating functions and singularities of projections of Lagrangian manifolds*, Funkcional. Anal. i Priložen. **6** (1972), no. 3, 61–62=Functional Anal. Appl. **6** (1972), 222–224.

6. ———, *Normal forms for functions near degenerate critical points, the Weyl groups A_k, D_k, E_k and Lagrangian singularities,* Funkcional. Anal. i Priložen. **6** (1972), no. 4, 3–25 = Functional Anal. Appl. **6** (1972), 254–272.

7. ———, *Some remarks on the stationary phase method and Coxeter numbers*, Uspehi Mat. Nauk **28** (1973), no. 5 (173), 17–44 = Russian Math. Surveys **28** (1973), no. 5, 19–48.

8. ———, *Normal forms of functions near degenerate critical points*, Uspehi Mat. Nauk **29** (1974), no. 2 (176), 11–49. (Russian)

9. ———, *Critical points of functions and the classification of caustics*, Séminaire I. G. Petrovski, Sept. 1973, Uspehi Mat. Nauk **29** (1974), no. 3 (177), 243–244. (Russian)

10. ———, *Mathematical methods of classical mechanics,* "Nauka," Moscow, 1974.

11. ———, *Contact manifolds, Legendrian mappings and singularities of wavefronts*, Moscow Math. Soc., 12. III, 1974; Uspehi Mat. Nauk **29** (1974), no. 4 (178), 153–154.

12. ———, *Lectures on bifurcations and versal families*, Uspehi Mat. Nauk **27** (1972), no. 5 (167), 119–184 = Russian Math. Surveys **27** (1972), no. 5, 54–123.

13. V. I. Arnold, I. M. Gel'fand, Ju. I. Manin, B. G. Moĭshezon, S. P. Novikov and I. R. Šafarevič, *Galina Nikolaevna Tjurina obituary*, Uspehi Mat. Nauk **26** (1971), no. 1 (157), 207–211. (Russian) MR **44** #6430.

14. M. Artin, *On the solutions of analytic equations*, Invent. Math. **5** (1968), 277–291. MR **38** #344.

15. M. F. Atiyah, *Resolution of singularities and division of distributions*, Comm. Pure Appl. Math. **23** (1970), 145–150. MR **41** #815.

16. I. N. Bernšteĭn and S. I. Gel'fand, *The function P^λ is meromorphic*, Funkcional. Anal. i Priložen. **3** (1969), no. 1, 84–86. (Russian)

17. I. N. Bernšteĭn, *The analytic continuation of generalized functions with respect to a parameter*, Funkcional. Anal. i Priložen. **6** (1972), no. 4, 26–40 = Functional Anal. Appl. **6** (1972), 273–285. MR **47** #9269.

18. E. V. Brieskorn, *Rationale Singularitäten komplexer Flächen*, Invent. Math. **4** (1967–68), 336–358. MR **36** #5136.

19. ———, *Beispiele zur Differentialtopologie von Singularitäten*, Invent. Math. **2** (1966), 1–14. MR **34** #6788.

20. ———, *Singular elements of semi-simple algebraic groups*, Proc. Internat. Congress Math. (Nice, 1970), vol. 2, Gauthier-Villars, Paris, 1971, pp. 279–284.

21. ———, *Die Fundamentalgruppe des Raumes der regularen Orbits einer endlichen komplexen Spiegelungsgruppe*, Invent. Math. **12** (1971), 57–61. MR **45** #2692.

22. ———, *Sur les groupes des tresses* (*d' après V. I. Arnold*), Séminaire N. Bourbaki **24** (1971/72), no. 401.

23. E. V. Brieskorn and K. Saito, *Artin-Gruppen und Coxeter-Gruppen*, Invent. Math. **17** (1972), 245–271. MR **48** #2263.

24. E. V. Brieskorn, *Die Monodromie der isolierten Singularitäten von Hyperflächen*, Manuscripta Math. **2** (1970), 103–161. MR **42** #2509.

25. J. Cerf, *La stratification naturelle des espaces de fonctions différentiables réeles et le théorème de la pseudo-isotopie*, Inst. Hautes Études Sci. Publ. Math. No. 39 (1970), 5–173. MR **45** #1176.

26. P. Deligne, *Les immeubles des groupes des tresses generalises*, Invent. Math. **17** (1972), 273–302.

27. I. V. Dolgačev, *Factor-conical singularities of complex surfaces*, Funkcional. Anal. i Priložen. **8** (1974), no. 2, 75–76. (Russian)

28. J. J. Duistermaat, *Oscillatory integrals, Lagrange immersions and unfoldings of singularities*, 1973 (preprint).

29. A. Fresnel, *Mémoire sur la diffraction de la lumière*, Mém. Acad. Sci. Paris **5** (1818), 339–353.

30. D. B. Fuks, *Cohomology of braid group* mod 2, Funkcional. Anal. i Priložen. **4** (1970), no. 2, 62–73 = Functional Anal. Appl. **4** (1970), 143–151. MR **43** #226.

31. ———, *Quillenisation and bordisms*, Funkcional. Anal. i Priložen. **8** (1974), no. 1, 43–54. (Russian)

32. A. M. Gabrielov, *Intersection matrixes of some singularities*, Funkcional. Anal. i Priložen. **7** (1973), no. 3, 18–32 = Functional Anal. Appl. **7** (1973), 182–193 (1974). MR **48** #2418.

33. ———, *Dynkin diagrams of unimodular singularities*, Funkcional. Anal. i Priložen. **8** (1974), no. 3. (Russian)

34. ———, *Bifurcations, Dynkin diagrams and number of modules of isolated singularities*, Funkcional. Anal. i Priložen. **8** (1974), no. 2, 7–12. (Russian)

35. A. M. Gabrielov and A. G. Kušnirenko, *Deformations with constant Milnor number for homogeneous functions*, Funkcional. Anal. i Priložen. **9** (1975), no. 3. (Russian)

36. J. Guckenheimer, *Catastrophes and partial derivative equations*, Ann. Inst. Fourier (Grenoble) **23** (1973), fasc. 2, 31–59.

37. S. M. Guseĭn-Zade, *Intersection matrixes of some singularities of functions of two variables*, Funkcional. Anal. i Priložen. **8** (1974), no. 1, 11–15. (Russian)

38. ———, *Dynkin diagrams for singularities of functions of two variables*, Funkcional. Anal. i Priložen. **8** (1974), no. 4. (Russian)

39. A. E. Hatcher, *Parametrized h-cobordism theory*, Ann. Inst. Fourier (Grenoble) **23** (1973), fasc. 2, 61–74.

40. L. Hörmander, *Fourier integral operators*, I, Acta Math. **127** (1971), 71–183.

41. F. Hirzebruch, *The topology of normal singularities of an algebraic surface* (*d'après Mumford*), Séminaire N. Bourbaki **15** (1962/63), no. 250.

42. F. Hirzebruch and K. H. Mayer, *O(n)-Mannigfaltigkeiten, exotische Sphären und Singularitäten*, Lecture Notes in Math., no. 57, Springer-Verlag, Berlin and New York, 1968. MR **37** #4825.

43. F. Klein, *Vorlesungen über die Entwicklung der Mathematik im* 19 *Jahrhundert*, Berlin, 1926.

44. N. H. Kuiper, *Algebraic equations for nonsmoothable* 8-*manifolds*, Inst. Hautes Études Sci. Publ. Math. No. 33 (1967), 139–155. MR **39** #3494.

45. K. Lamotke, *Isolated critical points and monodromy*, Liverpool Singularity Symposium, I, 1970.

46. F. Latour, *Stabilité des champs d'applications différentiables: Généralisation d'un théoreme de J. Mather*, C. R. Acad. Sci. Paris Sér. A-B **268** (1969), A1331-A1334. MR **39** #7617.

47. F. Lazzeri, *A theorem on the monodromy of isolated singularities*, Singularites a Cargese, Asterisque **7/8** (1973), 269–276.

48. Lê Dũng Tráng, *Les théorèmes de Zarisky de type de Lefschetz*, Centre Math. École Polytechnique, Paris, 1971.

49. Lê Dũng Tráng and C. P. Ramanujan, *The invariance of Milnor's number implies the invariance of the topological type*, École Polytechnique, Paris, 1973.

50. E. Looijenga, *The complement of the bifurcation variety of a simple singularity*, Invent. Math. **32** (1974), 105–116.

51. B. Malgrange, *Intégrales asymptotiques et monodromie*, Séminaire Leray, 1972–73.

52. ———, *Sur les polynomes de I. N. Bernstein*, Uspehi Mat. Nauk **29** (1974), no. 4 (178).

53. J. N. Mather, *Stability of C^∞ mappings*. I. *The division theorem*, Ann. of Math. (2) **87** (1968), 89–104. MR **38** #726.

———, II. *Infinitesimal stability implies stability*, Ann. of Math. (2) **89** (1969), 254–292. MR **41** #4582.

———, III. *Finitely determined map germs*, Inst. Hautes Études Sci. Publ. Math. No. 35 (1968), 279–308. MR **43** #1215a.

———, IV. *Classification of stable germs by R-algebras*, Inst. Hautes Études Sci. Publ. Math No. 37 (1969), 223–248. MR **43** #1215b.

———, V. *Transversality*, Advances in Math. **4** (1970), 301–336. MR **43** #1215c.

———, VI, Lecture Notes in Math., no. 192, Springer-Verlag, New York, 1971, pp. 207–253.

54. V. P. Maslov, *Asymptotical methods and perturbation theory*, Moscow University, 1965.

55. ———, *On the concentration of energy in a crystal lattice*, Uspehi Mat. Nauk **27** (1972), no. 6 (168), 224. (Russian)

56. J. Milnor, *Singular points of complex hypersurfaces*, Ann. of Math. Studies, no. 61, Princeton Univ. Press, Princeton, N. J.; Univ. of Tokyo Press, Tokyo, 1968. MR **39** #969.

57. J. Milnor and P. Orlik, *Isolated singularities defined by weighted homogeneous polynomials*, Topology **9** (1970), 385–393. MR **45** #2757.

58. P. Orlik and P. Wagreich, *Isolated singularities of algebraic surfaces with C* action*, Ann. of Math. (2) **93** (1971), 205–228. MR **44** #1662.

59. V. P. Palamodov, *The multiplicity of a homolorphic mapping*, Funkcional. Anal. i Priložen. **1** (1967), no. 3, 54–65 = Functional Anal. Appl. **1** (1967), 218–226. MR **38** #4720.

60. F. Pham, *Formules de Picard-Lefschetz généralisées et ramification des intégrales*, Bull. Soc. Math. France **93** (1965), 333–367. MR **33** #4064.

61. ———, *Remarque sur l'équisingularité universelle*, Faculté des Sciences, Nice, 1970, 1–24.

62. K. Saito, *Quasihomogene isolierte Singularitäten von Hyperflächen*, Invent. Math. **14** (1971), 123–142. MR **45** #3767.

63. ———, *Einfach-elliptische Singularitäten*, Invent. Math. **23** (1974), 289–325.

64. M. Sebastiani and R. Thom, *Un résultat sur la monodromie*, Invent. Math. **13** (1971), 90–96. MR **45** #2201.

65. G. Segal, *Configuration-spaces and iterated loop-spaces*, Invent. Math. **21** (1973), 213–222.

66. D. Siersma, *The singularities of C^∞-functions of right-codimension smaller than or equal to eight*, Indag. Math. **35** (1973), 31–37.

67. *Singularités à Cargèse*, Astérisque **7/8** (1973).

68. B. Teissier, *Cycles evanescents, sections planes et conditions de Whitney*, Astérisque **7/8** (1973), 285–362.

69. R. Thom and H. Levine, *Stability of differentiable mappings*, I, Bonner mathematische Schriften **6** Bonn, 1959.

70. R. Thom, *Stabilité structurelle et morphogenèse*, 1969.

71. ———, *The bifurcation subset of a space of maps*, Manifolds-Amsterdam 1970 (Proc. Nuffic Summer School), Lecture Notes in Math., vol. 197, Springer-Verlag, Berlin, 202–208. MR **43** #6941.

72. ———, *Ensembles et morphismes stratifiés*, Bull. Amer. Math. Soc. **75** (1969), 240–284. MR **39** #970.

73. G. N. Tjurina, *The topological properties of isolated singularities of complex spaces of codimension one*, Izv. Akad. Nauk SSSR Ser. Mat. **32** (1968), 605–620 = Math. USSR Izv. **2** (1968), 557–572. MR **37** #3053.

74. ———, *Locally semi-universal flat deformation of isolated singularities of complex spaces*, Izv. Akad. Nauk SSSR Ser. Mat. **33** (1969), 1026–1058 = Math. USSR Izv. **3** (1969), 967–1000. MR **40** #5903.

75. ———, *Resolution of singularities of flat deformations of double rational points*, Funkcional. Anal. i Priložen. **4** (1970), no. 1, 77–83 = Functional Anal. Appl. **4** (1970), 68–73. MR **42** #2031.

76. J. C. Tougeron, *Idéaux de fonctions différentiables*. I, Ann. Inst. Fourier (Grenoble) **18** (1968), fasc. 1, 177–240. MR **39** #2171.

77. A. N. Varčenko, *Theorems of topological equisingularity of families of algebraic varieties and families of polynomial mappings*, Izv. Akad. Nauk SSSR Ser. Mat. **36** (1972), 957–1019 = Math. USSR Izv. **6** (1972), 949–1008.

78. I. M. Vinogradov, *The method of trigonometrical sums in the theory of numbers*, rev. ed., "Nauka", Moscow, 1971; English transl. of 1st ed., Interscience, New York, 1964. MR **15**, 941.

79. I. A. Volodin, *Generalised Whitehead group and pseudo-isotopies*, Uspehi Mat. Nauk **27** (1972) no. 5 (167), 229–230. (Russian)

80. P. Wagreich, *Singularities of complex surfaces with solvable local fundamental group*, Topology **11** (1972), 51–72. MR **44** #2754.

81. J. B. Wagoner, *Algebraic invariants for pseudo-isotopies*, Proc. Liverpool Singularities Sympos. II, Lecture Notes in Math., no. 209, Springer-Verlag, New York, 1971, pp. 164–190.

82. A. Weinstein, *Singularities of families of functions*, Differentialgeometrie in Grossen Oberwolfach, **4** (1971).

83. H. Whitney, *On singularities of mappings of euclidean spaces*. I. *Mappings of the plane into the plane*, Ann. of Math. (2) **62** (1955), 374–410. MR **17**, 518.

84. V. M. Zakaljukin, *A theoreme on versality*, Funkcional. Anal. i Priložen. **7** (1973), no. 2, 28–31 = Functional Anal. Appl. **7** (1973), 110–112. MR **47** #9670.

85. O. Zariski, *On the Poincaré group of a projective hypersurface*, Ann. of Math. **38** (1937), 131–141.

MOSCOW UNIVERSITY
MOSCOW, U.S.S.R.

Proceedings of the International Congress of Mathematicians
Vancouver, 1974

Aspects of Modern Potential Theory

Heinz Bauer

Dedicated to Professor Marcel Brelot on the occasion of his 70th birthday

In 1964 Pierre Jacquinot opened a colloquium on potential theory in Orsay, France, by comparing potential theory with a road intersection in mathematics.[1] This was ten years ago. Meanwhile traffic has increased, and crossroads had to be converted into interchanges of highways—also in potential theory.

This article should be considered as an attempt to describe the interchange 'Potential Theory' not by a precise map revealing the structure of the interchange in all its complications but by a sketch making evident at least some major aspects of the construction.

We shall start by describing three classical approaches to the former intersection. Then the interchange will be roughly sketched. Finally, and this will be the main part of the article, we shall drive along a recently constructed new highway which had to be inserted in the system of flyovers.

1. Three aspects of classical potential theory. In the following we restrict the discussion to Euclidean n-space $\boldsymbol{R}^n$ of dimension $n \geqq 3$. Results without particular reference can be found in [5], [19], [24], [29].

1.1. *Superharmonic functions.* For every open ball $B \subset \boldsymbol{R}^n$ and every point $x \in B$ we denote by μ_x^B the *harmonic measure* of x with respect to B. This is the measure

$$\mu_x^B := P(x, \cdot)\sigma_B \tag{1.1}$$

(concentrated on the boundary B^* of B) where σ_B denotes the normalized Lebesgue measure on B^* and where $P: B \times B^* \to \boldsymbol{R}_+$ is the Poisson kernel

[1]'La théorie du potentiel est un véritable carrefour de la Mathématique'. Cf. du Plessis [29, p. vii].

$$(1.2) \qquad P(x, z) := r^{n-2} \frac{r^2 - \|x - x_0\|^2}{\|x - z\|^n}$$

(x_0 = center of B, r = radius of B, $\| \ \|$ = Euclidean norm).

A function $u: U \to]-\infty, +\infty]$ on an open set $U \subset \mathbf{R}^n$ is called *hyperharmonic* if it is lower semicontinuous and if, for all open balls $B \mathrel{\dot{\subset}} \bar{B} \subset U$ and all $x \in B$,

$$(1.3) \qquad \int u \, d\mu_x^B \leqq u(x)$$

holds. Since the Dirichlet problem for a continuous boundary function $f: B^* \to \mathbf{R}$ is solved by the harmonic function

$$x \mapsto H_f(x) := \int f(z) \, \mu_x^B(dz)$$

on B, formula (1.3) amounts to saying: For every continuous real boundary function f satisfying $f \leqq u$ on B^* the corresponding Dirichlet solution H_f is majorized by u on B. In this sense hyperharmonic functions generalize harmonic functions, the solutions of the Laplace equation $\Delta h = 0$.

A hyperharmonic function on a domain in $\mathbf{R}^n$ is either the constant $+\infty$ or finite on a dense subset. Hyperharmonic functions on an open set U satisfying this latter condition are called *superharmonic*. We denote by $\mathscr{S}_+$, resp. $\mathscr{S}_+^c$, the set of all nonnegative, resp. nonnegative, real-valued, continuous, superharmonic functions defined on $\mathbf{R}^n$.

One of the basic potential theoretic constructions is based on the richness of the cone $\mathscr{S}_+$. It leads to the heart of the theory, namely to *balayage theory*. Given an arbitrary set $E \subset \mathbf{R}^n$ and a function $u \in \mathscr{S}_+$ one tries to find the smallest function $v \in \mathscr{S}_+$ satisfying $v = u$ on E. The obvious candidate is the *presweep* (or réduite function)

$$(1.4) \qquad R_u^E := \inf\{v \in \mathscr{S}_+ \mid v = u \text{ on } E\}.$$

Since R_u^E is not lower semicontinuous in general, one replaces R_u^E by the greatest lower semicontinuous function $\leqq R_u^E$. This is the *sweep* (or balayée function) of u relative to E:

$$(1.5) \qquad \hat{R}_u^E(x) := \liminf_{y \to x} R_u^E(y) \qquad (x \in \mathbf{R}^n).$$

We have $\hat{R}_u^E \in \mathscr{S}_+$ and obviously

$$(1.6) \qquad 0 \leqq \hat{R}_u^E \leqq R_u^E \leqq u.$$

The initial interest leads then to the study of the *base* of E:

$$(1.7) \qquad b(E) := \bigcap_{u \in \mathscr{S}_+} \{x \in \mathbf{R}^n \mid \hat{R}_u^E(x) = u(x)\}.$$

It has the following fundamental properties:

$$(1.8) \qquad \mathring{E} \subset b(E) \subset \bar{E};$$

$$(1.9) \qquad b(E) = \{x \in \mathbf{R}^n \mid \hat{R}_{u_0}^E(x) = u_0(x)\} \quad \text{for some } u_0 \in \mathscr{S}_+^c,$$

consequently $b(E)$ is *a* G_δ-set;

$$(1.10) \qquad E \backslash b(E) \text{ is } \textit{polar},$$

i.e., a subset of $u^{-1}(+\infty)$ for some $u \in \mathcal{S}_+$. For nice closed sets E one has $b(E) = E$. What 'nice' means will become clear in §3.

Up to now we were sweeping, i.e., minimizing superharmonic functions. But this is intimately connected with sweeping masses, hence with the original ideas of H. Poincaré [**30**]. In fact (at least) for every Radon measure $\mu \geqq 0$ on $\boldsymbol{R}^n$ with compact support we have

THEOREM 1. *There exists a unique Radon measure $\mu^E \geqq 0$ on $\boldsymbol{R}^n$ satisfying*

$$\int u \, d\mu^E = \int \hat{R}_u^E \, d\mu \quad \textit{for all } u \in \mathcal{S}_+. \tag{1.11}$$

The measure μ^E is called the *swept-out* of μ on E. It is carried by the base $b(E)$.

By choosing for μ unit masses ε_x at points $x \in \boldsymbol{R}^n$, it follows that

$$b(E) = \{x \in \boldsymbol{R}^n \mid \varepsilon_x^E = \varepsilon_x\}. \tag{1.12}$$

For open balls $B \subset \boldsymbol{R}^n$ and points $x \in B$ the harmonic measure μ_x^B is an important example of a swept-out measure:

$$\mu_x^B = \varepsilon_x^{\complement B}. \tag{1.13}$$

This is due to the fact that in this case the two functions $R_u^{\complement B}$ and $\hat{R}_u^{\complement B}$ coincide with

$$x \mapsto \begin{cases} u(x), & x \in \complement B, \\ \int u \, d\mu_x^B, & x \in B, \end{cases} \qquad (u \in \mathcal{S}_+).$$

1.2. *Newtonian kernel and potentials*. In the preceding paragraph functions were predominant; measures appeared only at the end. The situation is quite different if we introduce potentials with respect to the *Newtonian kernel function* $G : \boldsymbol{R}^n \to]0, +\infty]$ defined by

$$G(x) := 1/\|x\|^{n-2}. \tag{1.14}$$

For every Radon measure $\mu \geqq 0$ on $\boldsymbol{R}^n$,

$$G^\mu(x) := \int G(x - y)\mu(dy) = G * \mu(x) \tag{1.15}$$

defines a hyperharmonic function $\geqq 0$ since $x \mapsto G(x-y)$ is superharmonic for all $y \in \boldsymbol{R}^n$. G^μ is called a *potential* (generated by μ) if G^μ is superharmonic. μ will then be called a potential generating measure. All measures $\mu \geqq 0$ with compact support are of this type.

From potentials the set of nonnegative hyperharmonic functions can be recovered by a simple limit procedure: A function $u : \boldsymbol{R}^n \to [0, +\infty]$ is hyperharmonic if and only if it is the supremum of an increasing sequence of potentials. Conversely, a function $p \in \mathcal{S}_+$ is a potential if and only if $h = 0$ is the only harmonic function satisfying $0 \leqq h \leqq p$.

Balayage of measures appears now in a much more direct way by means of

THEOREM 2. *For every Radon measure $\mu \geqq 0$ on $\boldsymbol{R}^n$ with compact support and every set $E \subset \boldsymbol{R}^n$ the swept-out μ^E is the only potential generating measure with the following two properties.*

$$\mu^E \textit{ is carried by } b(E); \tag{1.16}$$

(1.17) $$G^{\mu^E} = G^\mu \text{ quasi-everywhere on } E,$$

i.e., everywhere on E with the exception of a polar set $P \subset E$.

The connection with the approach of 1.1 is given by the formula

(1.18) $$\hat{R}^E_{G^\mu} = G^{\mu^E},$$

valid for (at least) all measures $\mu \geqq 0$ with compact support.

The predominance of measures in the kernel approach becomes even more evident by the appearance of energy, that is by the introduction of

(1.19) $$\langle \mu, \nu \rangle : = \int G^\mu \, d\nu = \int G^\nu \, d\mu$$

for positive measures μ, ν on $\boldsymbol{R}^n$. If we denote by $\mathscr{E}_+$ the set of all measures $\mu \geqq 0$ on $\boldsymbol{R}^n$ of *finite energy* $\langle \mu, \mu \rangle^{1/2} < +\infty$, the map $(\mu, \nu) \mapsto \langle \mu, \nu \rangle$ extends in a unique way to a positive symmetric form $\langle \cdot, \cdot \rangle$ on the linear space $\mathscr{E} : = \mathscr{E}_+ - \mathscr{E}_+$ generated by $\mathscr{E}_+$. Then $\mathscr{E}$ becomes a (Hausdorff) pre-Hilbert space with norm $\langle \mu, \mu \rangle^{1/2}$. In this space $\mathscr{E}_+$ is complete. Hence for every closed convex set $\mathscr{F} \subset \mathscr{E}_+$ and every $\mu \in \mathscr{E}$ the projection $\mathrm{proj}_{\mathscr{F}}\, \mu$ of μ onto $\mathscr{F}$ is defined.

For compact $K \subset \boldsymbol{R}^n$ the set $\mathscr{E}_K$ of all measures $\lambda \in \mathscr{E}_+$ carried by K is such a set $\mathscr{F}$. A classical result of H. Cartan then states

(1.20) $$\mu^K = \mathrm{proj}_{\mathscr{E}_K}\, \mu$$

for every $\mu \in \mathscr{E}_+$ with compact support.

1.3. *Brownian motion.* Brownian motion is the probabilistic version of a simple analytic object, namely the *Gaussian semigroup* $(\mu_t)_{t>0}$ on $\boldsymbol{R}^n$: μ_t is the measure $g_t\lambda^n$ with the function

(1.21) $$g_t(x) : = (2\pi t)^{-n/2} \exp(-\|x\|^2/2t) \qquad (x \in \boldsymbol{R}^n, t > 0)$$

as density with respect to n-dimensional Lebesgue measure λ^n. All μ_t are probability measures, $t \mapsto \mu_t$ is vaguely continuous, and $\mu_{s+t} = \mu_s * \mu_t$ holds for all $s,t > 0$.

Each μ_t can be viewed as a *kernel* P_t on $\boldsymbol{R}^n$, i.e., as a function P_t defined on the product $\boldsymbol{R}^n \times \mathscr{B}$ of $\boldsymbol{R}^n$ with the σ-algebra $\mathscr{B}$ of its Borel sets such that $x \mapsto P_t(x, B)$ is $\mathscr{B}$-measurable for all $B \in \mathscr{B}$ and such that $B \mapsto P_t(x, B)$ is a positive measure on $\mathscr{B}$ for all $x \in \boldsymbol{R}^n$. We just have to define

(1.22) $$P_t(x, B) : = (\mu_t * 1_B)(x)$$

or, equivalently,

(1.23) $$P_t f(x) : = (\mu_t * f)(x) = \int f(y) P_t(x, dy)$$

for $\mathscr{B}$-measurable functions $f \geqq 0$ on $\boldsymbol{R}^n$. Then P_t appears as an operator and $(P_t)_{t>0}$ is a semigroup of such operators.

Brownian motion can be considered as a quadruple

$$X = (\Omega, \mathscr{A}, (P^x)_{x \in \boldsymbol{R}^n}, (X_t)_{t \geqq 0})$$

where $(\Omega, \mathscr{A})$ is a measurable space, $(P^x)_{x \in \boldsymbol{R}^n}$ a family of probability measures on $\mathscr{A}$ and where $(X_t)_{t \geqq 0}$ is a stochastic process of random variables $X_t : \Omega \to \boldsymbol{R}^n$ with continuous paths $t \mapsto X_t(\omega)$, $\omega \in \Omega$. X can be chosen in such a way that

(1.24) $$P^x\{X_t \in B\} = P_t(x, B)$$

holds for all $x \in \boldsymbol{R}^n$, $t \geqq 0$ and $B \in \mathscr{B}$ and that the so-called Markov property is present. P_0 is by definition the unit kernel $P_0(x, B) := 1_B(x)$.

The Gaussian semigroup $(\mu_t)_{t>0}$ is connected with potential theory, namely with the Newtonian kernel function G, by a simple analytic fact: A change of variables yields

(1.25) $$G = c_n \int_0^\infty g_t \, dt$$

with some real constant $c_n > 0$.[2] We thus have $G\lambda^n = c_n \int_0^\infty \mu_t \, dt$ or, equivalently,

(1.26) $$G^{f\lambda^n} = c_n \int_0^\infty P_t f \, dt$$

for all $\mathscr{B}$-measurable functions $f \geqq 0$ on $\boldsymbol{R}^n$.

Since G governs potential theory as we have seen in 1.2 it is natural to ask which potential theoretic facts can be expressed in terms of the Gaussian semigroup or of Brownian motion. It is well known now (cf. **[23]**) that all important potential theoretic notions and results have a probabilistic interpretation by means of Brownian motion. The key to all this is due to Doob **[11]** and Hunt **[21]**:

THEOREM 3. *A Borel measurable function* $u : \boldsymbol{R}^n \to [0, +\infty]$ *is hyperharmonic if and only if it is excessive with respect to the semigroup* $(P_t)_{t>0}$, *i.e.,*

(1.27) $$\sup_{t>0} P_t u = u.$$

As an example of the many consequences we mention the probabilistic interpretation of balayage. The *first hitting time* of a Borel set $E \subset \boldsymbol{R}^n$ is $T_E(\omega) := \inf\{t > 0 : X_t(\omega) \in E\}$ $(\omega \in \Omega)$ with the convention $\inf \varnothing = +\infty$. Then $\omega \mapsto X_{T_E(\omega)}(\omega)$ (after a suitable completion of $\mathscr{A}$) is a random variable on $\{T_E < +\infty\}$. Its distribution is the kernel

(1.28) $$P_E(x, B) := P^x(\{X_{T_E} \in B\} \cap \{T_E < +\infty\}).$$

A famous result of Hunt **[21]** states that

(1.29) $$P_E u = \hat{R}_u^E \quad \text{for all } u \in \mathscr{S}_+.$$

In particular, we obtain the swept-out of ε_x on E:

(1.30) $$P_E(x, \cdot) = \varepsilon_x^E.$$

2. Aspects of present-day potential theory. We have seen that the notion of a nonnegative hyperharmonic function and the central results of balayage can be approached from different initial objects: from harmonic functions, from the Newtonian kernel function, from the Gaussian semigroup or from Brownian motion. It is typical for the present situation of potential theory that each of these objects appears suitably generalized in applications and that each of these generalized

[2] $1/c_n = \Gamma((n-2)/2)/2\pi^{n/2}$.

objects leads to a branch of potential theory of its own importance. Let us try to make this statement more evident by a few examples without making the attempt of being systematic.[3]

2.1. *Harmonic spaces.* The fundamental properties of harmonic functions like the sheaf property, the existence of a base of open relatively compact sets for which the Dirichlet problem has a unique solution for each continuous real boundary function, and weakened versions of Harnack's convergence theorem are available for extended classes of second order elliptic and also parabolic differential equations—like the heat equation. These properties suitably formulated for a complete presheaf of linear spaces of real-valued continuous functions on a locally compact space with countable base lead to the notion of a *harmonic space*. For example, each Riemann surface is such a space. The potential theory on these spaces has been developed quite extensively in recent years. The theory is particularly rich on strong harmonic spaces. These are harmonic spaces on which the nonnegative superharmonic functions separate points linearly. For example, a Riemann surface, viewed as a harmonic space, has this property if and only if it is hyperbolic. The main reference is the book of Constantinescu and Cornea **[7]**.

2.2. *Markov processes.* Brownian motion is just one example of a large class of Markov processes for which potential theoretic notions can be studied successfully in order to investigate the structure of the process. For example, the probabilistic balayage operator P_E of (1.28) can be introduced for the important classes of standard and Hunt processes on locally compact spaces with countable base. The main refences are Blumenthal and Getoor **[4]** and Meyer **[26]**.

2.3. *Excessive functions.* Theorem 3 suggests considering a semigroup $(P_t)_{t>0}$ of kernels on a locally compact space as initial object. The corresponding potential theory concerns the study of the excessive function of such a semigroup. Closely related is the corresponding problem for resolvents $(V_\lambda)_{\lambda>0}$ of kernels which often appear as the Laplace transform $V_\lambda = \int_0^\infty e^{-\lambda t} P_t \, dt$ of such a semigroup. In particular, (1.26) leads to the problem of deciding whether a given kernel V is the zero element V_0 of such a resolvent. Problems of this type connect potential theory with functional analysis. The main reference is Meyer **[25]** and the recent work of Mokobodzki on cones of potentials (cf. **[27]**).

There are many other aspects which we must leave aside. For example: All the above theories neglect the group structure of $\boldsymbol{R}^n$ and translation invariance of classical potential theory. For locally compact (mainly abelian) groups compatibility of the above sketched theories with the group structure leads to important branches of potential theory, such as harmonic groups **[3]**, transient convolution semigroups of measures **[2]** and the theory of infinitely divisible processes **[31]**. We also leave aside the role of martingale theory **[11]**, **[25]** and the theory of Dirichlet spaces **[10]**; the latter is in closest connection with the classical Dirichlet integral and the notion of energy.

However, one important phenomenon should be underlined. It is the unifying role

[3] A more systematic and more complete survey on potential theory has been given by Brelot **[6]**.

of probability theory. An illuminating result in this direction is a theorem of Meyer-Constantinescu-Cornea-Hansen [1]. According to it there exists a Markov process with continuous paths on any strong harmonic space E on which the constant function 1 is superharmonic such that the interplay between the process and the potential theory on E is formally the same as the one between Brownian motion and classical potential theory on $\boldsymbol{R}^n$. More precisely, if one takes (1.24) as definition for $(P_t)_{t>0}$ Theorem 3 and the subsequent results on balayage remain valid.

The importance of probabilistic arguments will become clear also from the third part of the article. There we shall see that even potential theory on $\boldsymbol{R}^n$ is still full of surprises.

3. Fine potential theory. Again $\boldsymbol{R}^n$ is considered for dimensions $n \geqq 3$, at least at the beginning. In (1.12) we have characterized the base $b(E)$ of a set $E \subset \boldsymbol{R}^n$. E is called *thin* at a point $x \in \boldsymbol{R}^n$ if $x \notin b(E)$, that is if $\varepsilon_x^E \neq \varepsilon_x$. A set $G \subset \boldsymbol{R}^n$ is called *finely open* if $\complement G$ is thin at all points $x \in G$. In particular, every open set G is finely open since $\varepsilon_x^{\complement G}$ is carried by $b(\complement G) \subset \complement G$. The system $\mathscr{T}_f$ of all finely open sets is a topology on $\boldsymbol{R}^n$; the preceding example shows that $\mathscr{T}_f$ is finer than the Euclidean topology. $\mathscr{T}_f$ is called the *fine topology* on $\boldsymbol{R}^n$. The prefix f in connection with a topological notion (closed, boundary, etc.) will always refer to this topology.

$\mathscr{T}_f$ is the coarsest topology on $\boldsymbol{R}^n$ making all functions in $\mathscr{S}_+$ continuous. Even every hyperharmonic function defined on an open set $U \subset \boldsymbol{R}^n$ is f-continuous. This is due to the fact that thinness of a set E at $x \notin E$ is a local property; it is in fact equivalent to the existence of a superharmonic function u defined in a neighborhood of x such that

$$\liminf_{y \to x,\, y \in E} u(y) > u(x).^4 \tag{3.1}$$

Fine topology was introduced in 1940 by H. Cartan as an interpretation of Brelot's notion of thinness. It is an extremely useful tool. But as a topology it has been considered pathological. There are good reasons for this opinion, e.g., the only f-compact sets are the finite subsets and there is no countable base of f-open sets. Doob [12] pointed out the first positive and interesting result about this topology, the quasi-Lindelöf property. But Fuglede [14] did the essential step by showing that $\mathscr{T}_f$ not only has remarkable topological properties but that $\mathscr{T}_f$ leads to an extension of classical potential theory, namely to fine potential theory. Its fundamental notion is that of a finely hyperharmonic function. The definition is suggested by the fact that the harmonic measures μ_x^B for balls B are the swept-out measures $\varepsilon_x^{\complement B}$ and that for every f-open set V the measure

$$\mu_x^V := \varepsilon_x^{\complement V} \tag{3.2}$$

is carried by the f-boundary $\partial_f V$ of V.

A function $u: U \to]-\infty, +\infty]$ defined on an f-open set $U \subset \boldsymbol{R}^n$ is called *f-hyperharmonic* if it is f-lower semicontinuous and if there exists a base $\mathfrak{B}$ of f-open subsets V of U such that, for all $V \in \mathfrak{B}$,

[4] According to the convention $\inf \emptyset = +\infty$ we have $\liminf_{y \to x; y \in E} u(y) = +\infty$ if $x \notin \bar{E}$.

$$\bar{V}^f = (f\text{-closure of } V) \subset U, \tag{3.3}$$
$$\int^* u \, d\mu_x^V \leqq u(x) \quad \text{for all } x \in V. \tag{3.4}$$

u is called *f-harmonic* if it is f-continuous, real-valued, μ_x^V-integrable for all $V \in \mathfrak{B}$ and $x \in V$, and if equality holds in (3.4).

This extends the notion of a hyperharmonic function. On every f-open, nonopen set U there are f-harmonic functions which are not restrictions of harmonic functions on a larger open set. A potential G^μ is f-harmonic on an f-open set U provided that $\mu^*(U) = 0$ and G^μ is finite on U.

f-hyperharmonic functions are the origin of a rich theory. Many properties of hyperharmonic functions remain valid; but even the very first results are far from being trivial: f-hyperharmonicity is a local notion, f-harmonic functions are those functions u for which $\pm u$ are f-hyperharmonic, for every increasingly directed family of f-harmonic functions the upper envelope is f-harmonic provided that it is finite.

Of particular interest is the comparison between classical and fine hyperharmonicity.

THEOREM 4. *A numerical function u defined on an open set $U \subset \boldsymbol{R}^n$ is hyperharmonic (resp. harmonic) if and only if it is f-hyperharmonic and locally bounded from below (resp. f-harmonic and locally bounded from one side).*

Before we discuss an important consequence of this we consider the case $n = 2$ of the plane, so far excluded. On $\boldsymbol{R}^2$ all functions in $\mathscr{S}_+$ are constant. Therefore, the original definition of the fine topology is not appropriate. But thinness of a set at a point as well as hyperharmonicity are local notions. Furthermore, on bounded open sets of $\boldsymbol{R}^2$ nonnegative superharmonic functions separate points as they do on $\boldsymbol{R}^n$ for $n \geqq 3$. Consequently, by using the preceding definitions of thinness and swept-out measures only with respect to open bounded subsets of $\boldsymbol{R}^2$, one can define the fine topology and the fine potential theoretic notions also for the plane. $\mathscr{T}_f$ is then the coarsest topology making all superharmonic functions (defined on arbitrary open sets) continuous. With these definitions the preceding properties of $\mathscr{T}_f$ and of f-hyperharmonic functions remain valid. However, because of the peculiarities of the plane, there is one result without analogue in higher dimensions **[15]**:

THEOREM 5. *On every open set $U \subset \boldsymbol{R}^2$ all f-hyperharmonic (resp. f-harmonic) functions are hyperharmonic (resp. harmonic).*

For the further discussion we assume $n \geqq 2$. We have seen above that for increasingly directed families of f-harmonic functions with finite supremum this supremum is again f-harmonic. This property leads directly to a result which historically was at the beginning of the fine theory **[13]**:

THEOREM 6. *The fine topology $\mathscr{T}_f$ is locally connected.*

Together with Theorem 4 this leads (via indicator functions) to the fact that an *open* set $U \subset \boldsymbol{R}^n$ is *connected if and only if it is finely connected.* Hence every f-

connected open set is arcwise connected. It is highly remarkable that this remains valid for all f-domains:

THEOREM 7. *Every f-domain is pathwise (even arcwise) connected (with respect to Euclidean topology).*

The proof of this is given by means of a probabilistic interpretation of f-domains due to Nguyen Xuan-Loc and Watanabe **[28]**: An f-open set U is f-connected if and only if for every $x \in U$ and every f-open set $V \subset U$, $V \neq \emptyset$, the probability that Brownian motion starting at x reaches V before leaving U is strictly positive. Hence every pair of points in U can be connected by a path in U which is obtained by gluing together a sequence of pieces of Brownian paths. A classical topological result allows then the reduction of such a path to an arc.

The method of using Brownian paths in order to connect points in f-domains as well as fine potential theory finds illuminating applications in the field of access theorems **[17]**. The classical representative of such a theorem is a result of Iversen **[22]**: Given an entire nonconstant holomorphic function f, then there exists a (continuous) path Υ in $\boldsymbol{C}$ tending to infinity such that $|f(z)|$ tends to infinity along Υ. Since $|f|$ is a subharmonic function, it is natural to ask whether corresponding results hold for general subharmonic functions on $\boldsymbol{R}^n$ with a certain behavior at infinity. Partial results for continuous subharmonic functions and extensions to discontinuous ones for the case of the plane (obtained by deep analytical results) are known **[18]**. The instruments of fine potential theory and of Brownian paths lead to far-reaching general results of which we mention two typical ones:

THEOREM 8. *Let $s > 0$ be a superharmonic and u a subharmonic function on $\boldsymbol{R}^n$, $n \geqq 2$, satisfying*

$$\limsup_{\|x\| \to +\infty} \frac{u(x)}{s(x)} = +\infty.$$

Then there exists a path Υ in $\boldsymbol{R}^n$ converging to the point at infinity such that u/s tends to $+\infty$ along Υ.[5]

For $s = 1$ and $u = |f|$ this yields Iversen's theorem.[6]

THEOREM 9. *Let u be subharmonic and let $h > 0$ be harmonic in an open set $U \subset \boldsymbol{R}^n$, $n \geqq 2$. For any $x_0 \in U$ and any number $\alpha < u(x_0)/h(x_0)$ there exists a path Υ in U,*[5] *starting at x_0 and approaching the boundary of U (in the one-point compactification of $\boldsymbol{R}^n$) such that $\alpha < u/h$ on Υ and u/h has a limit (in $\bar{\boldsymbol{R}}$) along Υ.*

For $n = 2$ this generalizes a recent result of Hornblower and Thomas **[20]**. The crucial step of the proofs is the analysis of the f-components of the f-open sets $\{u/s > \lambda\}$ or $\{u/h > \lambda\}$ together with Theorem 7 or the idea of its proof. We leave aside several other results of this type and refer the reader to **[17]**.

[5] γ may be chosen to be even injective.

[6] For $s = 1$ a nonprobabilistic proof of Theorem 8 has been given recently by L. Carleson (Institut Mittag-Leffler, Report 1, 1974); γ can then be chosen even as a polygonal path.

We also leave aside the interesting application of fine potential theory to function algebras and to finely holomorphic functions due to Debiard and Gaveau [**8**], [**9**].

We close with the remark that the tool of fine potential theory is available also for certain strong harmonic spaces, namely those satisfying the 'domination axiom'. The power of the new tool is above all due to the fact that the set of f-hyperharmonic functions and the underlying fine topology are connected in a natural way. The connection is so natural that f-continuous numerical functions turn out to be of the *first* (Euclidean) *Baire class* and that f-hyperharmonic functions are *f-continuous* [**16**], [**14**]. Consequently, there is no fine-fine topology.

Bibliography

1. H. Bauer, *Harmonic spaces and associated Markov processes*, Potential Theory (C.I.M.E., I Ciclo, Stresa, 1969), Edizioni Cremonese, Rome, 1970, pp. 23–67. MR **43** #8123.

2. Chr. Berg and G. Forst, *Potential theory on locally compact abelian groups*, Ergebnisse der Mathematik und ihrer Grenzgebiete, Springer-Verlag, Berlin and New York (to appear).

3. J. Bliedtner, *Harmonische Gruppen und Huntsche Faltungskerne*, Seminar über Potentialtheorie, Lecture Notes in Math., vol. 69, Springer-Verlag, Berlin and New York, 1968, pp. 69–102. MR **41** #500.

4. R. M. Blumenthal and R. K. Getoor, *Markov processes and potential theory*, Pure and Appl. Math., vol. 29, Academic Press, New York and London, 1968. MR **41** #9348.

5. M. Brelot, *Éléments de la théorie classique du potentiel*, 4e éd., Centre de Documentation Universitaire, Paris, 1969.

6. ———, *Les étapes et les aspects multiples de la théorie du potentiel*, Enseignement Math. **18** (1972), 1–36.

7. C. Constantinescu and A. Cornea, *Potential theory on harmonic spaces*, Die Grundlehren der math. Wissenschaften, Band 158, Springer-Verlag, Berlin and New York, 1972.

8. A. Debiard and B. Gaveau, *Potentiel fin et algèbres de fonctions analytiques*. I, J. Functional Analysis **16** (1974), 289–304.

9. ———, *Potentiel fin et algèbres de fonctions analytiques*. II, Inst. H. Poincaré, Paris (preprint).

10. J. Deny, *Méthodes hilbertiennes en théorie du potentiel*, Potential Theory (C.I.M.E., I Ciclo, Stresa, 1969), Edizioni Cremonese, Rome, 1970, pp. 121–201. MR **44** #1833.

11. J. L. Doob, *Semimartingales and subharmonic functions*, Trans. Amer. Math. Soc. **77** (1954), 86–121. MR **16**, 269.

12. ———, *Applications to analysis of a topological definition of smallness of a set*, Bull. Amer. Math. Soc. **72** (1966), 579–600. MR **34** #3514.

13. B. Fuglede, *Connexion en topologie fine et balayage des mesures*, Ann. Inst. Fourier (Grenoble) **21** (1971), fasc. 3, 227–244.

14. ———, *Finely harmonic functions*, Lecture Notes in Math., vol. 289, Springer-Verlag, Berlin and New York, 1972.

15. ———, *Fonctions harmoniques et fonctions finement harmoniques*, Ann. Inst. Fourier (Grenoble) (to appear).

16. ———, *Remarks on fine continuity and the base operation in potential theory*, Math. Ann. **210** (1974), 207–212.

17. ———, *Asymptotic paths for subharmonic functions*, Math. Ann. **213** (1975), 261–274.

18. W. K. Hayman, *Einige Verallgemeinerungen des Iversenschen Satzes auf subharmonische Funktionen*, Jber. Deutsch. Math. Verein. **71** (1969), Heft 3, Abt. 1, 115–122. MR **41** #8697.

19. L. L. Helms, *Introduction to potential theory*, Pure and Appl. Math., vol. 22, Wiley, New York and London, 1969. MR **41** #5638.

20. R. Hornblower and E. S. Thomas, Jr., *The access theorem for subharmonic functions*, Trans. Amer. Math. Soc. **172** (1972), 287–297. MR **46** #7534.

21. G. A. Hunt, *Markoff processes and potentials*. I, Illinois J. Math. **1** (1957), 44–93. MR **19,** 951.

22. F. Iversen, *Recherches sur les fonctions inverses des fonctions méromorphes*, Thèse, Helsingfors, 1914.

23. A. W. Knapp, *Connection between Brownian motion and potential theory*, J. Math. Anal. Appl. **12** (1965), 328–349. MR **34** #5173.

24. N. S. Landkof, *Foundations of modern potential theory*, Die Grundlehren der math. Wissenschaften, Band 180, Springer-Verlag, Berlin and New York, 1972.

25. P. -A. Meyer, *Probability and potentials*, Blaisdell, Waltham, Mass., 1966. MR **34** #5119.

26. ———, *Processus de Markov*, Lecture Notes in Math., vol. 26, Springer-Verlag, Berlin and New York, 1967. MR **36** #2219.

27. G. Mokobodzki, *Cônes de potentiels et noyaux subordonnés*, Potential Theory (C.I.M.E., I Ciclo, Stresa, 1969), Edizioni Cremonese, Rome, 1970, pp. 207–248. MR **43** #551.

28. Nguyen Xuan-Loc and T. Watanabe, *A characterization of fine domains for a certain class of Markov processes with applications to Brelot harmonic spaces*, Z. Wahrscheinlichkeitstheorie und verw. Gebiete **21** (1972), 167–178. MR **47** #1136.

29. N. du Plessis, *An introduction to potential theory*, Oliver & Boyd, Edinburgh, England, 1970.

30. H. Poincaré, *Théorie du potentiel newtonien*, Caré et Naud, Paris, 1899.

31. S. C. Port and C. J. Stone, *Infinitely divisible processes and their potential theory*, Ann. Inst. Fourier (Grenoble) **21** (1971), fasc. 2, 157–275; fasc. 4, 179–265.

Mathematisches Institut, Universität Erlangen-Nürnberg
Erlangen, Federal Republic of Germany

Proceedings of the International Congress of Mathematicians
Vancouver, 1974

Variational Problems and Elliptic Equations

Enrico Bombieri

I. Variational problems. In this expository article I will be concerned with second-order, nonlinear, elliptic equations arising from variational problems. Perhaps the simplest example is the

Dirichlet problem. Find a function $u(x)$ harmonic in a given bounded open set Ω and taking given boundary values on $\partial\Omega$.

The variational formulation of Dirichlet's problem is expressed through the

Dirichlet principle. The function $u(x)$ is the unique solution of the variational problem

$$\int_\Omega |Du|^2 \, dx = \min, \qquad u = f \text{ on } \partial\Omega,$$

where Du denotes the gradient of u.

The approach to the Dirichlet problem through the Dirichlet principle was soon criticized because the existence of a minimum for the Dirichlet integral was not obvious; in particular, some conditions are needed in order to have a finite Dirichlet integral. This is not unnatural to assume a priori, since, for example, in physical models the Dirichlet integral represents the energy of a system, which should be finite to start with. Once these limitations of the variational approach were understood, its usefulness became clear and the Dirichlet principle became again a respectable tool in mathematics.

More generally, one may ask to minimize the functional

$$J[u] = \int_\Omega f(x, u, Du) \, dx$$

under appropriate boundary conditions for the competing functions u. Actually

$u(x)$ may be a vector-valued function. If $J[u] = \min$, then $J[u] \leqq J[u + \varepsilon v]$ for every v with compact support in Ω and, expanding $J[u + \varepsilon v]$ in a Taylor series in ε,

$$J[u + \varepsilon v] = J[u] + \varepsilon\delta J[u] + \varepsilon^2\delta^2 J[u] + \cdots,$$

we see that we need $\delta J[u] = 0$ and $\delta^2 J[u] \geqq 0$ for all such v, i.e. (writing $p = (p_1, \cdots, p_n)$ for Du),

$$\begin{aligned}\delta J[u] &= \int_\Omega \left(\sum_i \frac{\partial f}{\partial p_i} \frac{\partial v}{\partial x_i} + \frac{\partial f}{\partial u} v \right) dx \\ &= \int_\Omega \left(- \sum_i \frac{\partial}{\partial x_i} \left(\frac{\partial f}{\partial p_i} \right) + \frac{\partial f}{\partial u} \right) v \, dx = 0,\end{aligned}$$

and we obtain the well-known Euler equation

$$\sum_i \frac{\partial}{\partial x_i} \left(\frac{\partial f}{\partial p_i} \right) = \frac{\partial f}{\partial u}.$$

A simple condition, which implies $\delta^2 J \geqq 0$, is

$$\sum_{ij} \frac{\partial^2 f}{\partial p_i \partial p_j} \xi_i \xi_j > 0, \qquad \xi \in \boldsymbol{R}^n, \xi \neq 0,$$

which expresses a kind of convexity condition for the functional $J[u]$. If this condition is satisfied, one says that the integrand $f(x, u, p)$ is regular elliptic. In case one considers vector-valued solutions $u = (u^1, \cdots, u^\lambda, \cdots, u^N)$, the regularity condition imposed on $f = f(x, u^\lambda, p^\lambda)$ is

$$\sum_{ij} \sum_{\lambda\mu} \frac{\partial^2 f}{\partial p_i^\lambda \partial p_j^\mu} \eta^\lambda \eta^\mu \xi_i \xi_j > 0$$

at every point $(x, u^\lambda, p^\lambda)$ and all $\eta \in \boldsymbol{R}^N$, $\xi \in \boldsymbol{R}^n$, $\eta, \xi \neq 0$.

In his 19th problem of his address at the International Congress of Mathematicians in 1900, Hilbert raised the question whether solutions of regular elliptic, analytic variational problems are necessarily analytic. This problem of regularlity, together with the problem of existence of solutions, form two central questions in the theory of variational problems.

II. Elliptic equations: the early work. In his celebrated thesis of 1904, S. Bernstein proved the remarkable result that C^3 solutions of a single elliptic, nonlinear, analytic equation in two variables are necessarily analytic; this was considered at the time a solution to Hilbert's 19th problem. Having thus attacked the problem of regularity, he went on with the existence problem in an important series of papers, between 1906 and 1912. We owe to him the basic idea (and the name) of an "a priori estimate", which still has a central role in the theory: If we have the right majorizations for all solutions (and their derivatives) of an elliptic equation, then existence and regularity of solutions of the Dirichlet problem will follow. Since in obtaining these estimates we assume "a priori" that we are dealing with smooth solutions, we have the name "a priori estimates". Bernstein himself showed how to prove such estimates in some important cases, using the maximum principle and what is known today as the method of barriers.

Bernstein's work was rather involved and relied heavily on analyticity, and was later improved and generalized to several variables and elliptic systems by the work of several authors, among which are Gevrey, Giraud, Lichtenstein, H. Lewy, E. Hopf, T. Rado, I. Petrowsky and Bernstein himself. However, one had to wait until the years between 1932 and 1937 before the basic reasons for the importance of the "a priori estimates" in the existence problem were fully understood and clarified through the work of Schauder, Leray and Caccioppoli and in particular the classical paper of Leray and Schauder of 1934.

Consider for example a quasi-linear equation

$$\begin{aligned} \sum a_{ij}(x, u, Du)D_iD_ju &= 0 \quad \text{in } \Omega, \\ u &= f \quad \text{on } \partial\Omega. \end{aligned}$$

We denote by T the operator which to a function u associates the unique solution v of the linear Dirichlet problem

$$\begin{aligned} \sum a_{ij}(x, u, Du)D_iD_jv &= 0 \quad \text{in } \Omega, \\ v &= f \quad \text{on } \partial\Omega. \end{aligned}$$

Since the latter problem is linear, it is much easier to solve, and the question is reduced to finding a fixed point $u = Tu$ for the operator T. The main point is that very general fixed point theorems are available if we have the right "a priori estimates" for the solutions of the original equation and of the linearized equation. The advantage of this procedure over an iteration scheme $u_{n+1} = Tu_n$ (used by Bernstein) is obvious: If uniqueness is not satisfied, the iteration need not converge.

The fundamental "a priori estimates" for the linearized equation were found by Schauder; the search for such estimates in the nonlinear case is still today more of an art than of a method.

III. Direct methods and weak solutions. Another approach to the existence problem in the variational case is provided by the so-called "direct methods in the calculus of variations". Roughly speaking, one wants to show

(A) the integrand $J[u]$ is lower semicontinuous and bounded below, with respect to a suitable notion of convergence in some admissible class of competing functions u;

(B) a minimizing sequence $\{u_n\}$, i.e., $J[u_n] \to \operatorname{Inf} J[u]$ converges to an admissible u; hence $J[u] = \min$ by (A).

This idea was used perhaps for the first time by Zaremba and also by Hilbert in his investigations on the Dirichlet principle. It became a standard approach to variational problems in the hands of Lebesgue, Courant, Fréchet and especially Tonelli. If the integrand $J[u]$ satisfies an inequality $f(x, u, p) \geqq m_1|p|^r - m_2$, $m_1 > 0$, with $1 \leqq r < +\infty$, then Tonelli's method, using absolutely continuous functions and uniform convergence, works provided $r \geqq n = \dim \Omega$, which is a too strong condition if $n \geqq 3$. A notable success of this method was however Haar's work of 1927 on functionals of the type $J[u] = \int_\Omega f(Du)\,dx$, for the case of $n = 2$ variables. Here one assumes that Ω is a smooth convex domain, and the boundary values are also smooth, satisfying a certain "three-point condition". The class of competing functions used by Haar is a class of functions satisfying a uniformly bounded Lipschitz condition.

The deep reason for the limitation of Tonelli's approach was found only later, through the fundamental work of Sobolev and Morrey in 1938. The Sobolev spaces $H^{k,p}(\Omega)$ are the Banach spaces of functions on Ω whose derivatives of order $\leqq k$ are in L^p. Sobolev discovered the fundamental embedding theorems for these spaces, the simplest being (one assumes Ω bounded and $\partial\Omega$ smooth):

(i) if $f \in H^{1,p}(\Omega)$, $1 \leqq p < n$, then $f \in L^s(\Omega)$ with $s = np/(n-p)$, and

$$\| f \|_{L^s} \leqq C(\Omega) \| f \|_{H^{1,p}};$$

(ii) if $f \in H^{1,p}(\Omega)$, $p > n$, then f satisfies a Hölder condition in Ω.

The new approach to the existence problem could now be summarized as follows:

(A) the integrand $J[u]$ determines naturally a function space $\mathscr{F}$ (usually a Sobolev space), in which the lower semicontinuity becomes a natural statement;

(B) by means of "a priori estimates" one shows that there exists a convergent minimizing sequence (here the Sobolev embedding theorems are often crucial).

From (A) and (B) one deduces the existence of a solution in the function space $\mathscr{F}$. However, one expects the solution so obtained to be very smooth. In some cases, e.g., those in which Tonelli's method works, the smoothness of solutions is automatic (compare (ii) of Sobolev's embedding theorem); in general, there remains the difficult problem of "regularization":

(C) the "weak solutions" so obtained are in fact differentiable solutions.

The necessary results about lower semicontinuity have been obtained by Serrin; stages (B) and (C) require an extensive use of "a priori estimates", the regularization part being often difficult if not intractable.

This approach led to remarkable results especially in two cases: nonlinear second-order equations in $n = 2$ variables, where one could also use tools from quasi-conformal mapping (Morrey, Bers, Nirenberg), and linear equations and systems with smooth coefficients (we may mention the work of Ladyzenskaya and Caccioppoli of 1951 for second-order equations, and the general theory of Friedrichs, F. John, Agmon-Douglis-Nirenberg of 1959, who also considered higher-order systems and the problem of boundary regularity).

The first breakthrough in the nonlinear case came in 1957—1958 when De Giorgi and independently Nash for parabolic equations succeeded in proving Hölder continuity of weak solutions of uniformly elliptic equations

$$\sum D_i(a_{ij}(x) D_j u) = 0$$

with measurable coefficients a_{ij} and with the ellipticity condition

$$m|\xi|^2 \leqq \sum a_{ij}(x)\, \xi_i\, \xi_j \leqq M|\xi|^2,$$

where m, M are positive constants independent of x.

This result has some striking applications to nonlinear problems. De Giorgi himself showed how his theorem implied that weak extremals of uniformly elliptic analytic integrands of the type $\int_\Omega f(Du)\,dx = \min$ are indeed analytic in Ω. Stampacchia and Gilbarg found another application, namely the extension of Haar's theorem to the case of $n > 2$ variables; further important applications and generalizations have been given by Morrey, Ladyzenskaya and Uraltseva, Oleinik and many others, in particular to the study of second-order quasi-linear equations which are quadratic in the first-order derivatives.

Of great importance was also a new proof of De Giorgi's theorem, found by Moser in 1960, using the Sobolev inequalities rather than the isoperimetric inequalities of De Giorgi. This also led to a proof of the Harnack inequality: If $\Omega' \Subset \Omega$ and if u is a positive solution in Ω of a uniformly elliptic equation $\sum D_i(a_{ij}(x)D_j u) = 0$, then $\max_{\Omega'} u \leqq C \min_{\Omega'} u$, where C depends only on Ω', Ω and the ellipticity constant $L = M/m$. Hence one obtains a Liouville theorem: A bounded solution over $\boldsymbol{R}^n$ of such an equation is necessarily a constant.

IV. Weak solutions of elliptic systems. The problem of the extension of De Giorgi's regularization to systems of equations or to higher-order equations remained outstanding for awhile, until in 1968 De Giorgi found an example of a uniformly elliptic linear system of variational type with bounded measurable coefficients, with the discontinuous solution $x/|x|$. By adapting De Giorgi's example, in 1969 Giusti and Miranda showed that if $n > 2$ the integrand

$$\int |D\boldsymbol{u}|^2 + \left[\sum_{ij}\left(\delta_{ij} + \frac{4}{n-2}\,\frac{u^i u^j}{1+|\boldsymbol{u}|^2}\right) D_j u^i\right]^2 dx$$

with $\boldsymbol{u} = (u^1, \cdots, u^n)$ is a regular uniformly elliptic analytic integrand, while $u = x/|x|$ is an extremal which is not real analytic at $x = 0$. These examples pointed out the great importance of the results obtained by Morrey in 1968 on the regularity problem for systems in $n > 2$ variables.

Here the breakthrough came with the introduction of new powerful compactness methods, originally introduced by De Giorgi and especially Almgren in 1960—1966, in the study of minimal surfaces.

In rather crude terms, the idea behind the use of compactness methods may be described as follows. Suppose we want to prove an "a priori estimate" of local nature for solutions of a class of variational problems which is invariant by linear changes of the coordinates. If the estimate we want fails in every neighborhood of a point x_0, this means that we can find a sequence of elliptic equations or systems over a fixed domain Ω, and a sequence of solutions, for which the desired estimate fails in smaller and smaller neighborhoods of x_0. By performing a linear change of coordinates, we can expand these neighborhoods to a fixed neighborhood of x_0, and in doing so we have to replace our equations by new equations still in the same class and defined over larger and larger domains. Using the appropriate compactness theorems then one shows that this sequence of equations and solutions converges in some sense to a limiting equation, now defined over $\boldsymbol{R}^n$, and to a limiting solution for which the desired "a priori estimate" still fails. The main point however is that, in doing so, we have replaced an elliptic operator by its "tangent operator" at x_0, and thus the limiting equation is often of a very simple type, for example linear with constant coefficients, and, for it, it may be easy to check that the "a priori estimate" we want does in fact hold. This gives a contradiction and establishes the local estimate we were looking for. In the nonlinear case, convergence to a limiting equation is usually obtained by assuming certain mild conditions about the local behaviour of solutions at a point. If these conditions are valid almost everywhere, which is often the case because of measure theoretic arguments, one ends up with estimates which are valid only near almost every point, and in turn one establishes only regularity almost everywhere.

In this way it was proved by Morrey in 1968 that weak solutions of a large class of nonuniformly elliptic analytic variational problems of the type

$$\int f(x, \boldsymbol{Du})\, dx = \min,$$

and also of uniformly elliptic analytic variational problems of the type

$$\int f(x, \boldsymbol{u}, \boldsymbol{Du})\, dx = \min$$

are in fact analytic almost everywhere. Giusti and Miranda, in 1970—1972, extended and substantially simplified this work, and they have also been able to obtain good estimates for the Hausdorff dimension of the exceptional set in which the solutions are not analytic.

The outstanding problem here is to determine the structure of the singular set; for example, is it semi-analytic? In special cases, one can even prove that solutions are everywhere analytic, and it is an interesting open question to find good conditions which imply regularity everywhere.

V. The minimal surface equation. A well-known variational problem is the *Problem of Plateau.* Find a surface of least area among all surfaces having a prescribed boundary.

This is not a regular variational problem, if taken in this generality, and it is not possible for me to explain in this article all the new fundamental results obtained between 1960 and 1974 by Federer, Fleming, Reifenberg, De Giorgi, Almgren, Allard and many others. I will restrict my attention instead to the case of minimal graphs (the nonparametric Plateau problem) and to some special questions about the parametric Plateau problem in codimension one.

If the graph $y = u(x)$ of a function $u(x)$, $x \in \Omega \subset \boldsymbol{R}^n$, is a solution of Plateau's problem, then it minimizes the area functional $\int_\Omega (1 + |Du|^2)^{1/2}\, dx$, and the associated Euler equation is

$$\sum D_i(D_i u/W) = 0, \qquad W = (1 + |Du|^2)^{1/2},$$

which expresses the fact that the graph has mean curvature 0 at every point.

The strong nonlinearity of this equation gives rise to unexpected phenomena, which have no counterpart in the theory of linear equations. For $n = 2$ variables:

(i) the Dirichlet boundary value problem is soluble for arbitrary continuous data if and only if Ω is convex (Bernstein, Finn);

(ii) a solution defined over a disk minus the centre extends to a solution over the disk, i.e., isolated singularities are removable (Bers);

(iii) if $u > 0$ is a solution over $|x| < R$ then

$$(1 + |Du(0)|^2)^{1/2} \leqq \exp(\pi u(0)/2R)$$

and this estimate is sharp (Finn, Serrin);

(iv) a solution defined over $\boldsymbol{R}^2$ is linear (Bernstein).

The solution of the analogous problems for $n > 2$ variables has been obtained only recently. We have:

(i) the Dirichlet boundary value problem is soluble for arbitrary continuous data if and only if $\partial\Omega$ has positive mean curvature at every point (Serrin, Bombieri, De Giorgi and Miranda, 1968);

(ii) a solution defined over Ω minus K, where K is a compact subset of Ω with $(n - 1)$-dimensional Hausdorff measure 0, extends to the whole of Ω (De Giorgi and Stampacchia, 1965);

(iii) if $u > 0$ is a solution over $|x| < R$ then

$$|Du(0)| < c_1 \exp(c_2 u(0)/R)$$

(Bombieri, De Giorgi and Miranda, 1968);

(iv) if $n \leqq 7$, a solution defined over $\boldsymbol{R}^n$ is linear (Fleming's new proof in 1962 for the case $n=2$, De Giorgi for $n=3$ in 1964, Almgren for $n=4$ in 1966, Simons for $n \leqq 7$ in 1968); on the other hand, if $n \geqq 8$, there are solutions defined over $\boldsymbol{R}^n$ which are not linear (Bombieri, De Giorgi and Giusti, 1969).

What about the methods of proof? In his talk at the International Congress of Mathematicians in 1962, L. Nirenberg made the statement that "most results for nonlinear problems are still obtained via linear ones, i.e. despite the fact that the problems are nonlinear not because of it". The minimal surface equation is no exception to this statement; but since the linearization procedure is rather unusual, it is worthwhile to describe it.

Let us define a vector $\boldsymbol{\nu}$ with components

$$\nu_i = -(D_i u)/W, \qquad i = 1, \cdots, n,$$
$$\nu_{n+1} = 1/W,$$

and differential operators

$$\delta_i = D_i - \nu_i \sum_{j=1}^{n+1} \nu_j D_j, \qquad i = 1, \cdots, n+1,$$

in $\boldsymbol{R}^{n+1}$.

If we denote by S the graph of $x_{n+1} = u(x)$ in $\boldsymbol{R}^{n+1}$, then the vector $\boldsymbol{\nu}$ is the normal unit vector to S at the point $P = (x,u(x))$ and the operators are δ_i the projections of the operators D_i on the tangent space to S at the point P. The "Laplacian" $\mathscr{D} = \sum \delta_i\delta_i$ is actually the Laplace-Beltrami operator on S, and the fact that S has mean curvature 0 at every point is nicely expressed by the fact that the coordinate functions x_i are harmonic on S for the Laplace-Beltrami operator. Moreover it can be shown that the normal vector $\boldsymbol{\nu}$ satisfies the nonlinear elliptic system $\mathscr{D}\boldsymbol{\nu} + c^2(x)\boldsymbol{\nu} = 0$ on S where $c^2(x) = \sum_{ij} (\delta_i\nu_j)^2$ is the sum of the squares of the principal curvatures of S at P. In particular since $\nu_{n+1} > 0$ it follows that $\mathscr{D}\nu_{n+1} \leqq 0$, i.e., ν_{n+1} is superharmonic on S.

Now we have two main facts (Miranda, 1967):

(a) if f has compact support and S is minimal, then

$$\int \delta_i f \, d\|S\| = 0, \quad \text{all } i,$$

or in other words the operators δ_i can be integrated by parts on the surface S;

(b) if f has compact support, S is minimal and $1 \leqq p < n$ then

$$\left(\int |f|^{np/(n-p)} \, d\|S\|\right)^{(n-p)/n} \leqq c(p, n) \int |\delta f|^p \, d\|S\|,$$

or in other words we have a uniform Sobolev inequality on S for the differential operators δ_i.

We can use (a) and (b) together with De Giorgi's regularization technique (which is highly nonlinear) to investigate the differential inequality $\mathscr{D}\nu_{n+1} \leqq 0$, and eventually one arrives at the "a priori estimate" (iii). The solubility of the Dirichlet problem, and also the analyticity of weak solutions, depends on this "a priori estimate".

More generally, one may investigate uniformly elliptic equations of the type $\sum \delta_i(a_{ij}(x)\delta_j u) = 0$ on an absolutely minimizing surface S of codimension one (Bombieri and Giusti, 1972). Thus one obtains the extension of the Moser-Harnack theorem to these equations, and as an application one gets that if u is a positive harmonic function on a minimal surface in $\boldsymbol{R}^{n+1}$ without boundary, then u is constant. Since the coordinate functions x_i are harmonic on S, one gets as a corollary a theorem of Miranda that a minimal surface without boundary contained in a half-space is a hyperplane. Also, a minimal surface without boundary is connected (Bombieri and Giusti, 1972).

The extension of Bernstein's theorem up to dimension 7, and the construction of a counterexample in dimension $n \geqq 8$, depends on different ideas. It was Fleming in 1962 who used compactness techniques to show that the failure of Bernstein's theorem in dimension n implied the existence of a singular minimal cone in $\boldsymbol{R}^{n+1}$. De Giorgi later proved that in fact one would get the existence of such a cone in $\boldsymbol{R}^n$, and in this way extended Bernstein's theorem through dimension $n = 3$. Then the question centered about the existence of minimal cones, and eventually Simons succeeded in proving the nonexistence of singular minimal cones in $\boldsymbol{R}^n$, $n \leqq 7$. Moreover, Simons proved that the cone in $\boldsymbol{R}^8$ given by $x_1^2 + x_2^2 + x_3^2 + x_4^2 = x_5^2 + x_6^2 + x_7^2 + x_8^2$ was at least a locally minimal cone, i.e., area would increase with every sufficiently small deformation. Making use of the invariance of this cone by SO(3) $\times$ SO(3), Bombieri, De Giorgi and Giusti proved that this cone was in fact minimal in the large, by reducing the problem to a question about a system of first-order ordinary differential equations. It was natural to see whether this cone was associated with the failure of Bernstein's theorem in dimension 8, and this was obtained by constructing explicitly a subsolution u^-, and a supersolution u^+, of the minimal surface equation in $\boldsymbol{R}^8$, with the property that $u^- \leqq u^+$ everywhere and that no function between u^- and u^+ could be linear. Now an application of the maximum principle and also of the "a priori estimate" for the gradient obtained before showed the existence of a solution u defined everywhere comprised between u^- and u^+. It should be noted that the choice of u^- and u^+ was in fact suggested by the results obtained in the investigation of Simons' cone.

VI. Further results. I will end this article by mentioning some results and directions of research which I could not treat more explicitly, but which seem to me of great importance.

First of all, the facts which I have stated about the minimal surface equation are not limited to that special case. A whole class of elliptic equations can be treated with similar methods, among which are the equations of surfaces with prescribed mean curvature, the equation of capillarity phenomena, and many others. Here much recent work has been done by Ladyzenskaya and Uraltseva, Bombieri and Giusti, Trudinger, Finn, Serrin and many others.

Second, and more importantly, I have limited myself in this article to variational problems of a nonparametric nature. The parametric point of view, in which one considers functionals on geometrical objects rather than on functions, has led to the modern geometric measure theory, the theory of integral currents and varifolds and of parametric elliptic integrands. Here the work of Federer, Fleming and especially Almgren is outstanding. Also, among more recent developments, I may mention the work of Allard on the first variation of a varifold and that of Jean Taylor on the structure of the singular set of soap films and soap bubbles.

Another fruitful idea which I could not treat in this article is that of variational problems in which the solutions have to satisfy additional constraints. Here one may ask for solutions satisfying inequalities, thus obtaining classical problems with obstacles, or asking for solutions with gradient not exceeding certain bounds (an example is the potential equation for a subsonic gas flow), or one may impose convexity, as for the Monge-Ampère equations, and so on. Here the theory of variational inequalities begins to give a general foundation for many problems of this type. Fortunately many of these questions will receive special attention in these PROCEEDINGS, and I have to refer to the more specialized articles for further illustrations of the directions in which the theory of variational problems and of elliptic equations is moving.

References

Section II

S. Bernstein, *Sur la nature analytique des solutions des équations aux derivées partielles du second ordre*, Math. Ann. **59** (1904), 20–76.

J. Leray and J. Schauder, *Topologie et équations fonctionnelles*, Ann. Sci. Ecol. Norm. Sup. (3), **51** (1934), 45–78.

Section III

C. B. Morrey, Jr., *Multiple integrals in the calculus of variations*, Die Grundlehren der math. Wissenschaften, Band 130, Springer-Verlag, New York, 1966. MR **34** #2380.

L. Nirenberg, *Some aspects of linear and nonlinear partial differential equations*, Proc. Internat.

Congress Math. (Stockholm, 1962), Inst. Mittag-Leffler, Djursholm, 1963, pp. 147–162. MR **31** #471.

O. A. Ladyženskaya and N. N. Uraltseva, *Linear and quasi-linear equations of elliptic type*, "Nauka", Moscow, 1964; English transl., Academic Press, New York, 1968. MR **35** #1955; **39** #5941.

S. Agmon, A. Douglis and L. Nirenberg, *Estimates near the boundary for solutions of elliptic partial differential equations satisfying general boundary conditions*. I, II, Comm. Pure Appl. Math. **12** (1959), 623–727; ibid. **17** (1964), 35–92. MR **23** #A2610; **28** #5252.

E. De Giorgi, *Sulla differenziabilità e l'analiticità delle estremali degli integrali multipli regolari*, Mem. Accad. Sci. Torino Cl. Sci. Fis. Mat. Nat. (3) **3** (1957), 25–43. MR **20** #172.

J. Moser, *On Harnack's theorem for elliptic differential equations*, Comm. Pure Appl. Math. **14** (1961), 577–591. MR **28** #2356.

Section IV

E. De Giorgi, *Un esempio di estremali discontinue per un problema variazionale di tipo ellittico*, Boll. Un. Mat. Ital. (4) **1** (1968), 135–147. MR **37** #3411.

E. Giusti and M. Miranda, *Un esempio di soluzioni discontinue per un problema di minimo relativo ad un integrale regolare del calcolo delle variazioni*, Boll. Un. Mat. Ital. (4) **1** (1968), 219–226. MR **38** #591.

C. B. Morrey, Jr., *Partial regularity results for non-linear elliptic systems*, J. Math. Mech. **17** (1967/68), 649–670. MR **38** #6224.

E. Giusti, *Regolarità parziale delle soluzioni di sistemi ellittici quasi-lineari di ordine arbitrario*, Ann. Scuola Norm. Sup. Pisa (3) **23** (1969), 115–141. MR **40** #527.

Section V

R. Finn, *On equations of minimal surface type*, Ann. of Math. (2) **60** (1954), 397–416. MR **16,** 592.

S. Bernstein, *Über eine geometrisches Theorem und seine Anwendung auf die partiellen Differentialgleichungen vom elliptischen Typus*, Math. Z. **26** (1927), 551–558.

J. Serrin, *The problem of Dirichlet for quasilinear elliptic differential equations with many independent variables*, Philos. Trans. Roy. Soc. London Ser. A **264** (1969), 413–496. MR **43** #7772.

E. Bombieri, E. De Giorgi and M. Miranda, *Una maggiorazione a priori relativa alle ipersuperfici minimali non parametriche*, Arch. Rational Mech. Anal. **32** (1969), 255–267. MR **40** #1898.

J. Simons, *Minimal varieties in Riemannian manifolds*, Ann. of Math. (2) **88** (1968), 62–105. MR **38** #1617.

E. De Giorgi and G. Stampacchia, *Sulle singolarità eliminabili delle ipersuperficie minimali*, Atti Accad. Naz. Lincei Rend. Cl. Sci. Fis. Mat. Natur. (8) **38** (1965), 352–357. MR **32** #4612.

E. Bombieri, E. De Giorgi and E. Giusti, *Minimal cones and the Bernstein problem*, Invent. Math. **7** (1969), 243–268. MR **40** #3445.

E. Bombieri and E. Giusti, *Harnack's inequality for elliptic differential equations on minimal surfaces*, Invent. Math. **15** (1972), 24–46. MR **46** #8057.

Section VI

O. A. Ladyženskaya, and N. N. Uraltseva, *Local estimates for gradients of solutions of non-uniformly elliptic and parabolic equations*, Comm. Pure Appl. Math. **23** (1970), 677–703. MR **42** #654.

E. Bombieri and E. Giusti, *Local estimates for the gradient of non-parametric surfaces of prescribed mean curvature*, Comm. Pure Appl. Math. **26** (1973), 381–394.

N. Trudinger, *Gradient estimates and mean curvature* (to appear).

R. Finn, *Capillarity phenomena*, Uspehi Mat. Nauk (to appear).

H. Federer, *Geometric measure theory*, Die Grundlehren der math. Wissenschaften, Band 153, Springer-Verlag, New York, 1969. MR **41** #1976.

F. J. Almgren, Jr., *Existence and regularity almost everywhere of solutions to elliptic variational problems among surfaces of varying topological type and singularity structure*, Ann. of Math. (2) **87** (1968), 321–391. MR **37** #837.

W. K. Allard, *On the first variation of a varifold*, Ann. of Math. (2) **95** (1972), 417–491. MR **46** #6136.

J. E. Taylor, *Regularity of the singular sets of two-dimensional area-minimizing flat chains modulo* 3 *in* R^3, Invent. Math. **22** (1973), 119–160.

F. J. Almgren, Jr., *Existence and regularity almost everywhere of solutions to elliptic variational problems with constraints* (to appear).

SCUOLA NORMALE SUPERIORE
PISA, ITALY

Proceedings of the International Congress of Mathematicians
Vancouver, 1974

Four Aspects of the Mathematical Theory of Economic Equilibrium

Gerard Debreu*

The observed state of an economy can be viewed as an equilibrium resulting from the interaction of a large number of agents with partially conflicting interests. Taking this viewpoint, exactly one hundred years ago, Léon Walras presented in his *Eléments d'Economie Politique Pure* the first general mathematical analysis of this equilibrium problem. During the last four decades, Walrasian theory has given rise to several developments that required the use of basic concepts and results borrowed from diverse branches of mathematics. In this article, I propose to review four of them.

1. The existence of economic equilibria. As soon as an equilibrium state is defined for a model of an economy, the fundamental question of its existence is raised. The first solution of this problem was provided by A. Wald [**1933–1935**], and after a twenty-year interruption, research by a large number of authors has steadily extended the framework in which the existence of an equilibrium can be established. Although no work was done on the problem of existence of a Walrasian equilibrium from the early thirties to the early fifties, several contributions, which, later on, were to play a major role in the study of that problem, were made in related areas during that period. One of them was a lemma proved by J. von Neumann [**1937**] in connection with his model of economic growth. This lemma was reformulated by S. Kakutani [**1941**] as a fixed-point theorem which became the most powerful tool for proofs of existence in economics. Another contribution, due to J. Nash [**1950**], was the first use of that tool in the solution of a problem of socia

*The author gratefully acknowledges the support of the Miller Institute of the University of California, Berkeley, and of the National Science Foundation, and the comments of Birgit Grodal, Werner Hildenbrand, Andreu Mas-Colell, and Herbert Scarf.

equilibrium. For later reference we state Kakutani's theorem. Given two sets U and V, a *correspondence* ρ from U to V associates with every element $u \in U$, a nonempty subset $\rho(u)$ of V.

THEOREM. *If D is a nonempty, compact, convex subset of a Euclidean space, and ρ is a convex-valued, closed-graph correspondence from D to D, then there is d^* such that $d^* \in \rho(d^*)$.*

As a simple prototype of a Walrasian equilibrium problem, we now consider an exchange economy with l commodities, and a finite set A of consumers. The consumption of consumer $a \in A$ is described by a point x_a in R^l_+; the ith coordinate x^i_a of x_a being the quantity of the ith commodity that he consumes. A price system p is an l-list of strictly positive numbers, i.e., a point in $P = \text{Int } R^l_+$; the ith coordinate of p being the amount to be paid for one unit of the ith commodity. Thus the value of x_a relative to p is the inner product $p \cdot x_a$. Given the price vector $p \in P$, and his wealth $w \in L$, the set of strictly positive numbers, consumer a is constrained to satisfy the budget inequality $p \cdot x_a \leqq w$. Since multiplication of p and w by a strictly positive number has no effect on the behavior of consumers, we can normalize p, restricting it to the strictly positive part of the unit sphere $S = \{p \in P \mid \|p\| = 1\}$. We postulate that, presented with the pair $(p, w) \in S \times L$, consumer a demands the consumption vector $f_a(p, w)$ in R^l_+, and that the demand function f_a is continuous. If that consumer is insatiable, f_a also satisfies

(1) *for every* $(p, w) \in S \times L, \quad p \cdot f_a(p, w) = w.$

To complete the description of the economy $\mathscr{E}$, we specify for consumer a an initial endowment vector $e_a \in P$. Thus the characteristics of consumer a are the pair (f_a, e_a), and $\mathscr{E}$ is the list $((f_a, e_a))_{a \in A}$ of those pairs for $a \in A$. Consider now a price vector $p \in S$. The corresponding wealth of consumer a is $p \cdot e_a$; his demand is $f_a(p, p \cdot e_a)$. Therefore the excess demand of the economy is

$$F(p) = \textstyle\sum_{a \in A} [f_a(p, p \cdot e_a) - e_a].$$

And p is an equilibrium price vector if and only if $F(p) = 0$. Because of (1), the function F from S to R^l satisfies

Walras' law. $p \cdot F(p) = 0$.

Consequently, F is a continuous vector field on S, all of whose coordinates are bounded below. Finally, we make an assumption about the behavior of F near ∂S.

Boundary condition. If p_n in S tends to p_0 in ∂S, then $\{F(p_n)\}$ is unbounded.

This condition expresses that every commodity is collectively desired. Here and below I freely make unnecessarily strong assumptions when they facilitate the exposition. Of the many variants of the existence theorem that have been proposed, I select the following statement by E. Dierker [**1974**, §8], some of whose antecedents were L. McKenzie [**1954**], D. Gale [**1955**], H. Nikaido [**1956**], and K. Arrow and F. Hahn [**1971**].

THEOREM. *If F is continuous, bounded below, and satisfies Walras' law and the boundary condition, then there is an equilibrium.*

We indicate the main ideas of a proof because they will recur in this section and in the next. Here it is most convenient to normalize the price vector so that it belongs to the simplex $\Pi = \{p \in R^l_+ \mid \sum_{i=1}^l p^i = 1\}$.

Consider a price vector $p \notin \partial\Pi$ yielding an excess demand $F(p) \neq 0$. According to a commonly held view of the role of prices, a natural reaction of a price-setting agency to this disequilibrium situation would be to select a new price vector so as to make the excess demand $F(p)$ as expensive as possible, i.e., to select (K. Arrow and G. Debreu **[1954]**) a price vector in the set

$$\mu(p) = \left\{\pi \in \Pi \mid \pi \cdot F(p) = \operatorname*{Max}_{q \in \Pi} q \cdot F(p)\right\}.$$

When $p \in \partial\Pi$, the excess demand is not defined. In this case, we let $\mu(p) = \{\pi \in \Pi \mid \pi \cdot p = 0\}$.

By Kakutani's theorem, the correspondence μ from Π to Π has a fixed point p^*. Obviously, $p^* \notin \partial\Pi$. But then $p^* \in \mu(p^*)$ implies $F(p^*) = 0$.

From the fact that $\mu(p)$ is always a face of Π one suspects (rightly as we will see in the next section) that Kakutani's theorem is too powerful a tool for this result. But such is not the case in the general situation to which we will turn after having pointed out the broad interpretation that the concept of commodity must be given. In contemporary Walrasian theory, a commodity is defined as a good or a service with specified physical characteristics, to be delivered at a specified date, at a specified location, if (K. Arrow **[1953]**) a specified event occurs. Aside from this mere question of interpretation of a concept, the model can be expanded so as to include a finite set B of producers. Producer $b \in B$ chooses a production vector y_b (whose positive coordinates correspond to outputs, and negative coordinates to inputs) in his production set Y_b, a nonempty subset of R^l, interpreted as the set of feasible production vectors. When the price vector p is given, producer b actually chooses his production vector in a nonempty subset $\psi_b(p)$ of Y_b. It is essential here, as it was not in the case of consumers, to provide for situations in which p does not uniquely determine the reaction of every producer, which may arise for instance if producer b maximizes his profit $p \cdot y_b$ in a cone Y_b with vertex 0 (constant returns to scale technology). In an economy with production, consumer a not only demands goods and services, but also supplies certain quantities of certain types of labor, which will appear as negative coordinates of his consumption vector x_a; this vector x_a is constrained to belong to his consumption set X_a, a given nonempty subset of R^l. A suitable extension of the concept of demand function covers this case. However, the wealth of a consumer is now the sum of the value of his endowment vector and of his shares of the profits of producers. In this manner, an integrated model of consumption and production is obtained, in which a state of the economy is a list $((x_a)_{a \in A}, (y_b)_{b \in B}, p)$ of vectors of R^l, where, for every $a \in A$, $x_a \in X_a$; for every $b \in B$, $y_b \in Y_b$; and $p \in \Pi$. The problem of existence of an equilibrium for such an economy has often been reduced to a situation similar to that of the last theorem, the continuous excess demand function being replaced by an excess demand correspondence with a closed graph. Alternatively, it can be formulated in the following general terms, in the spirit of J. Nash **[1950]**. The social system is composed of a finite set C of agents. For each $c \in C$, a set D_c of possible actions is given. Consequently, a state of the system is an element d of the product $D = \times_{c \in C} D_c$. We denote by $d_{C \setminus c}$ the list of actions obtained by deleting d_c from d. Given $d_{C \setminus c}$, i.e., the actions chosen by all the other agents, agent c reacts by choosing his own action in the set $\rho_c(d_{C \setminus c})$. The state d^* is an equilibrium if and only if, for every $c \in C$, $d_c^* \in \rho_c(d_{C \setminus c}^*)$. Thus, the reaction correspondence ρ from D to D being defined by $\rho(d) = \times_{c \in C} \rho_c(d_{C/c})$, the state d^* is an equilibrium if and only if it is a fixed point of ρ. In the integrated economic model of consumption and production that we discussed, one of the agents is the impersonal market to which we assign the reaction correspondence μ introduced in the proof of the existence theorem.

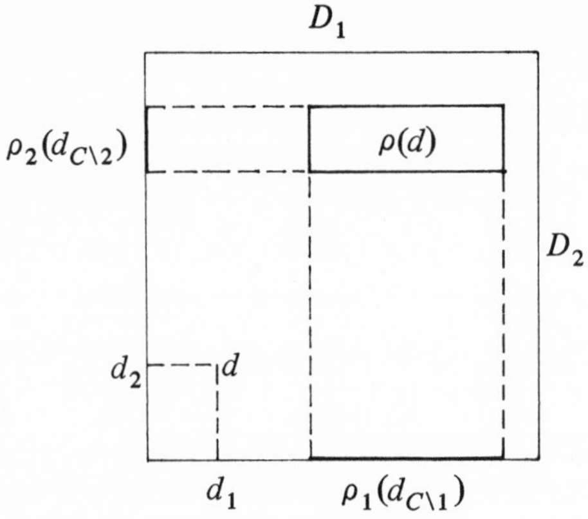

FIGURE 1

Still broader interpretations and further extensions of the preceding model have been proposed. They include negative or zero prices, preference relations with weak properties instead of demand functions for consumers, measure spaces of agents, infinite-dimensional commodity spaces, monopolistic competition, public goods, redistribution of income, indivisible commodities, transaction costs, money, the use of nonstandard analysis,.... Since this extensive, and still rapidly growing, literature cannot be surveyed in detail here, I refer to the excellent account by K. Arrow and F. Hahn [**1971**], to the books mentioned in the next sections, and to recent volumes of Econometrica, Journal of Economic Theory, and Journal of Mathematical Economics.

2. The computation of economic equilibria. While the first proof of existence is forty years old, decisive steps towards an efficient algorithm for the computation of Walras equilibria were taken only during the last decade. In 1964, C. Lemke and J. Howson gave an effective procedure for the computation of an equilibrium of a non-zero-sum two-person game. H. Scarf [**1967**], [**1973**] then showed how a technique similar to that of C. Lemke and J. Howson could be used to compute an approximate Walras equilibrium, and proposed a general algorithm for the calculation of an approximate fixed point of a correspondence. This algorithm, which has revealed itself to be surprisingly efficient, had the drawback of not permitting a gradual improvement of the degree of approximation of the solution. An essential extension due to C. Eaves **[1972]**, **[1974]**, stimulated by a fixed-point theorem of F. Browder **[1960]**, overcame this difficulty.

Before presenting a version of the algorithm based on H. Scarf **[1973]**, and C. Eaves **[1974]**, we note that in the preceding proof of existence, we have actually associated with every point $p \in \Pi$ a set $\Lambda(p)$ of integers in $I = \{1, \cdots, l\}$, as follows.

$$\begin{aligned} \Lambda(p) &= \{i \mid F^i(p) = \mathrm{Max}_j F^j(p)\} \quad \text{if } p \notin \partial\Pi, \\ &= \{i \mid p^i = 0\} \qquad\qquad\qquad\quad \text{if } p \in \partial\Pi. \end{aligned}$$

The point p^* is an equilibrium if and only if $\Lambda(p^*) = I$, in other words, if and only if it is in the intersection of the closed sets $E_i = \{p \mid i \in \Lambda(p)\}$. Showing that this intersection is not empty would yield an existence proof in the manner of D. Gale **[1955]**.

We specify our terminology. By a simplex, we always mean a closed simplex, and, of course, similarly for a face of a simplex. *A facet* of an n-simplex is an $(n-1)$-face. For each $p \in \Pi$, select now a label $\lambda(p)$ in $\Lambda(p)$. A set M of points is said to be *completely labeled*, abbreviated to *c.l.*, if the set $\lambda(M)$ of its labels is I. The labeling λ is chosen so as to satisfy the following restrictions on $\partial\Pi$:

(α) the set of vertices of Π is c.l.,

(β) no facet of Π is c.l.[1]

The algorithm will yield a c.l. set of l points of Π whose diameter can be made arbitrarily small, and consequently a point of Π at which the value of F can be made arbitrarily small.

Let T be the part of R^l_+ that is above Π, and $\mathscr{T}$ be a standard regular triangulation

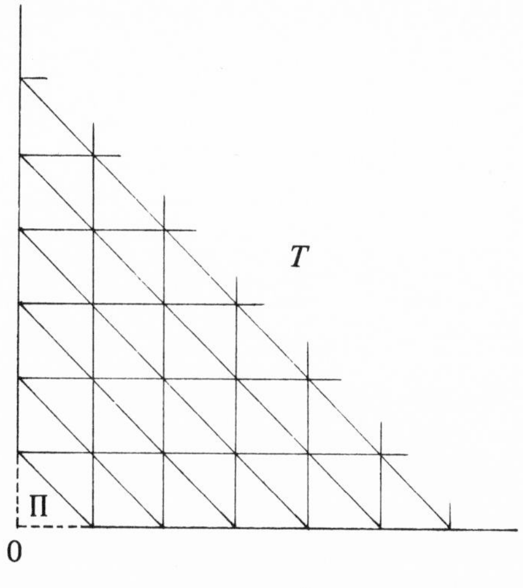

FIGURE 2

[1]Here is a simple example of a labeling of $\partial\Pi$ satisfying those restrictions. Given $p \in \partial\Pi$, select any $\lambda(p)$ in $\Lambda(p)$ such that $\lambda(p) - 1 \pmod{l}$ is not in $\Lambda(p)$.

of T having for vertices the points of T with integral coordinates, used by H. Kuhn **[1960]**, **[1968]**, T. Hansen **[1968]**, and C. Eaves **[1972]**, and illustrated by the figure. (Other considerably more efficient triangulations of, or more appropriately pseudo-manifold structures on, T have been used, C. Eaves **[1972]**, **[1974]**.) Give any point in T the same label as its projection from 0 into Π; and say that two $(l-1)$-simplexes of $\mathscr{T}$ are *adjacent* if there is an l-simplex of $\mathscr{T}$ of which they are facets. Consider now an $(l-1)$-simplex s of $\mathscr{T}$ with c.l. vertices.

(i) If $s = \Pi$, s is a facet of exactly one l-simplex of $\mathscr{T}$; hence there is exactly one $(l-1)$-simplex of $\mathscr{T}$ with c.l. vertices adjacent to s.

(ii) If $s \neq \Pi$, because of (β), s is not in the boundary of T; therefore s is a facet of exactly two l-simplexes of $\mathscr{T}$; hence there are exactly two $(l-1)$-simplexes of $\mathscr{T}$ with c.l. vertices adjacent to s.

The algorithm starts from $s^0 = \Pi$. Take s^1 to be the unique $(l-1)$-simplex of $\mathscr{T}$ with c.l. vertices adjacent to s^0. For $k > 0$, take s^{k+1} to be the unique $(l-1)$-simplex of $\mathscr{T}$ with c.l. vertices adjacent to s^k, and other than s^{k-1}. Clearly this algorithm never returns to a previously used $(l-1)$-simplex and never terminates. Given any integer n, after a finite number of steps, one obtains an $(l-1)$-simplex with c.l. vertices above the hyperplane $\{p \in R^l \mid \sum_{i=1}^{l} p^i = n\}$. Projecting from 0 into Π, one obtains a sequence of c.l. sets of l points of Π whose diameter tends to 0 as n tends to $+\infty$.

An approximate fixed point (i.e., a point close to its image) of a continuous function from a finite-dimensional, nonempty, compact, convex set to itself can be obtained by a direct application of this algorithm. But in order to solve the analogous problem for a fixed point of a correspondence, and consequently, for a Walras equilibrium of an economy with production, H. Scarf and C. Eaves have used vector labels rather than the preceding integer labels. With every point p of Π, one now associates a suitably chosen vector $\lambda(p)$ in R^{l-1}, and one says that a set M of points of Π is c.l. if the origin of R^{l-1} belongs to the convex hull of $\lambda(M)$. As before, the labeling λ of Π is restricted to satify (α) and (β). The last two paragraphs can then be repeated word for word with the following single exception. Let σ be an l-simplex of $\mathscr{T}$, and s be a facet of σ with c.l. vertices. Denote by V_σ (resp. V_s) the set of vertices of σ (resp. of s). If $\lambda(V_\sigma)$ is in general position in R^{l-1}, then 0 is interior to the convex hull of $\lambda(V_s)$, and there is exactly one other facet of σ with c.l. vertices. However, if $\lambda(V_\sigma)$ is not in general position, a degenerate case where there are several other facets of σ with c.l. vertices may arise. An appropriate use of the lexic refinement of linear programming resolves this degeneracy. In this general form, the algorithm can indeed be directly applied to the computation of approximate Kakutani fixed points.

The simplicity of this algorithm is very appealing, but its most remarkable feature is its efficiency. Experience with several thousand examples has been reported, in particular in H. Scarf **[1973]** and R. Wilmuth **[1973]**. As a typical case of the version of the integer-labeling algorithm presented above (which uses an inefficient triangulation of T), let $l = 10$. To reach an elevation $n = 100$ in T, i.e., a triangulation of Π for which every edge is divided into 100 equal intervals, the number of iterations required rarely exceeds 2,000, and the computing time on an IBM 370 is usually less than 15 seconds. The number of vertices that are examined in the computation is therefore a small fraction of the number of vertices of the triangulation of Π at elevation 100.

The best general reference on the problem discussed in this section is H. Scarf [**1973**]. *Mathematical Programming* is a good bibliographical source for more recent developments.

3. Regular differentiable economies. The model $\mathscr{E} = ((f_a, e_a))_{a\in A}$ of an exchange economy presented at the beginning of § 1 would provide a complete explanation of the observed state of that economy in the Walrasian framework if the set $E(\mathscr{E})$ of its equilibrium price vectors had exactly one element. However, this global uniqueness requirement has revealed itself to be excessively strong, and was replaced, in the last five years, by that of local uniqueness. Not only does one wish $E(\mathscr{E})$ to be discrete, one would also like the correspondence E to be continuous. Otherwise, the slightest error of observation on the data of the economy might lead to an entirely different set of predicted equilibria. This consideration, which is common in the study of physical systems, applies with even greater force to the study of social systems. Basic differential topology has provided simple and satisfactory answers to the two questions of discreteness of $E(\mathscr{E})$, and of continuity of E.

At first, we keep the list $f = (f_a)_{a\in A}$ of demand functions fixed, and we assume that each one of them is of class C^r $(r \geqq 1)$. Thus an economy is identified with the point $e = (e_a)_{a\in A}$ in P^A. We denote by E the set of $(e, p) \in P^A \times S$ such that p is an equilibrium price vector for the economy e, and by $E(e)$ the set of equilibrium price vectors associated with a given e. The central importance of the manifold E, or of a related manifold of S. Smale [**1974**], has been recognized by S. Smale [**1974**] and Y. Balasko [**1974a**]. Recently, Y. Balasko [**1974b**] has noticed the property of C^r-isomorphism to P^A.

THEOREM. *E is a C^r-submanifold of $P^A \times S$ of the same dimension as P^A. If for every $a \in A$ the range of f_a is contained in P, then E is C^r-isomorphic to P^A.*

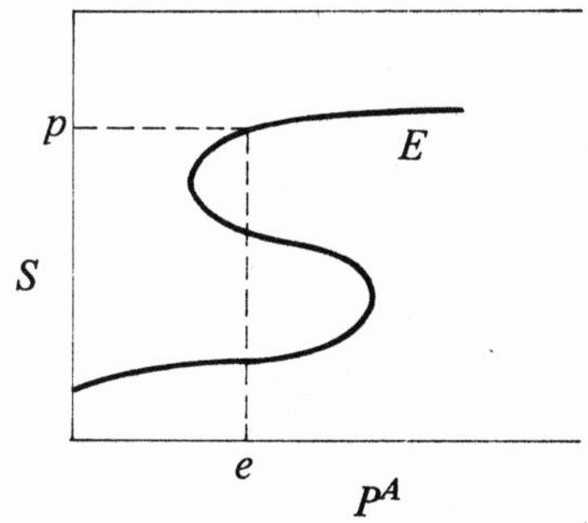

FIGURE 3

Now let π be the projection $P^A \times S \to P^A$, and $\tilde{\pi}$ be its restriction to the manifold E.

Definition. The economy $\mathscr{E} = (f, e)$ is *regular* if e is a regular value of $\tilde{\pi}$. It is *critical* if it is not regular.

By Sard's theorem, the set of critical e has Lebesgue measure zero. Suppose in addition we assume that every demand function f_a satisfies the

Strong boundary condition. If (p_n, w_n) in $S \times L$ tends to (p_0, w_0) in $\partial S \times L$, then $\{f_a(p_n, w_n)\}$ is unbounded.

Then we readily obtain that $\tilde{\pi}$ is proper (Y. Balasko [**1974b**]). In this case the critical set is closed (relative to P^A). It is therefore negligible in a strong sense. As for economies in the regular set $\mathscr{R}$, the complement of the critical set, they are well behaved in the following sense. At $e \in \mathscr{R}$, the compact set $E(e) = \tilde{\pi}^{-1}(e)$ is discrete, therefore finite, and $\tilde{\pi}^{-1}$ is locally a C^r-diffeomorphism.

In order to prepare for the discussion of regular economies in the context of the next section, we note an equivalent definition (E. and H. Dierker [**1972**]) of a critical point of the manifold E for $\tilde{\pi}$. Given e, let $F(p)$ be the excess demand associated with p, and denote by $\hat{F}(p)$ the projection of $F(p)$ into some fixed $(l-1)$-dimensional coordinate subspace of R^l. Because of Walras' law, and because p is strictly positive, $F(p) = 0$ is equivalent to $\hat{F}(p) = 0$. Let then $J[\hat{F}(p)]$ be the Jacobian determinant of $\hat{F}$ at p. As Y. Balasko [**1974b**] shows, (e, p) is a critical point of $\tilde{\pi}$ if and only if $J[\hat{F}(p)] = 0$.

Since it is desirable to let demand functions vary as well as initial endowments (F. Delbaen [**1971**], E. and H. Dierker [**1972**]), we endow the set D of C^r demand functions ($r \geqq 1$) satisfying the strong boundary condition with the topology of uniform C^r-convergence.

An economy $\mathscr{E}$ is now defined as an element of $(D \times P)^A$, a regular element of the latter space being a pair (f, e) for which the Jacobian determinant introduced in the last paragraph is different from zero for every equilibrium price vector associated with (f, e). The regular set is then shown to be open and dense in $(D \times P)^A$. Another extension, by S. Smale [**1974**], established the same two properties of the regular set in the context of utility functions with weak properties, rather than in the context of demand functions.

Still further generalizations, for instance, to cases where production is possible, have been obtained. E. Dierker [**1974**] surveys a large part of the area covered in this section more leisurely than I did. Recent volumes of the three journals listed at the end of §1 are also relevant here.

4. The core of a large economy. So far the discussion of consumer behavior has been in terms of demand functions. We now introduce for consumer a the more basic concept of a binary preference relation $\precsim_a$ on R^l_+, for which we read "$x \precsim_a y$" as "for agent a, commodity vector y is at least as desired as commodity vector x." The relation of strict preference "$x \prec_a y$" is defined by "$x \precsim_a y$ and not $y \precsim_a x$," and of indifference "$x \sim_a y$" by "$x \precsim_a y$ and $y \precsim_a x$." Similary for two vectors x, y in R^l we denote by "$x \leqq y$" the relation "$y - x \in R^l_+$," by "$x < y$" the relation "$x \leqq y$ and not $y \leqq x$," and by "$x \ll y$" the relation "$y - x \in P$."

We assume that $\precsim_a$ is a complete preorder with a closed graph, and that it satisfies the monotony condition, $x < y$ implies $x \prec_a y$, expressing the desirability of all commodities for consumer a. The set of preference relations satisfying these assumptions is denoted by $\mathscr{P}$, and viewing an element of $\mathscr{P}$ as a closed subset of R^{2l}, we endow $\mathscr{P}$ with Hausdorff's **[1957]** topology of closed convergence (Y. Kannai **[1970]**).

The characteristics of consumer $a \in A$ are now a pair $(\precsim_a, e_a)$ of a preference relation in $\mathscr{P}$, and an endowment vector in R^l_+. Thus an exchange *economy* $\mathscr{E}$ is a function from A to $\mathscr{P} \times R^l_+$. The result of any exchange process in this economy is an *allocation*, i.e., a function x from A to R^l_+, that is *attainable* in the sense that $\sum_{a \in A} x_a = \sum_{a \in A} e_a$.

A proposed allocation x is *blocked* by a coalition E of consumers if

(i) $E \neq \varnothing$,

and the members of E can reallocate their own endowments among themselves so as to make every member of E better off, i.e., if

(ii) there is an allocation y such that $\sum_{a \in E} y_a = \sum_{a \in E} e_a$ and, for every $a \in E$, $x_a \prec_a y_a$.

From this viewpoint, first taken by F. Edgeworth **[1881]**, only the unblocked attainable allocations are viable. The set of those allocations is the *core* $C(\mathscr{E})$ of the economy. The goal of this section is to relate the core to the equilibrium concept that underlies the analysis of the first three sections. Formally, we define a *Walras allocation* as an attainable allocation x for which there is a price system $p \in \Pi$ such that, for every $a \in A$, x_a is a greatest element for $\precsim_a$ of the budget set $\{z \in R^l_+ \mid p \cdot z \leqq p \cdot e_a\}$.

The set of Walras allocations of $\mathscr{E}$ is denoted by $W(\mathscr{E})$. It satisfies the mathematically trivial but economically important relation $W(\mathscr{E}) \subset C(\mathscr{E})$.

Simple examples show that for small economies the second set is much larger than the first. However, F. Edgeworth **[1881]** perceived that as the number of agents tends to $+\infty$ in such a way that each one of them becomes insignificant relative to their totality, the two sets tend to coincide. The conditions under which F. Edgeworth proved his limit theorem were very special. The first generalization was obtained by H. Scarf **[1962]**, after M. Shubik **[1959]** had called attention to the connection between F. Edgeworth's "contract curve" and the game-theoretical concept of the core. The problem was then placed in its natural setting by R. Aumann **[1964]**. The agents now form a positive measure space $(A, \mathscr{A}, \nu)$ such that $\nu(A) = 1$. The elements of $\mathscr{A}$ are the *coalitions*, and for $E \in \mathscr{A}$, $\nu(E)$ is interpreted as the fraction of the totality of agents in coalition E. Since the characteristics of an agent $a \in A$ are the pair $(\precsim_a, e_a)$, an *economy* $\mathscr{E}$ is defined (W. Hildenbrand **[1974]**), as a measurable function from A to $\mathscr{P} \times R^l_+$ such that e is integrable. The definitions of an unblocked attainable allocation and of a Walras allocation are extended in an obvious fashion. As trivially as before $W(\mathscr{E}) \subset C(\mathscr{E})$. But in the case in which the space of agents is atomless, i.e., in which every agent is negligible, R. Aumann **[1964]** has proved the

THEOREM. *If the economy $\mathscr{E}$ is atomless and $\int_A e\, d\nu \gg 0$, then $W(\mathscr{E}) = C(\mathscr{E})$.*

This remarkable result reconciles two fundamental and a priori very different equilibrium concepts. Its proof can be based (K. Vind [**1964**]) on Lyapunov's theorem on the convexity of the range of an atomless finite-dimensional vector measure.

There remains to determine the extent to which the equality of the core and of the set of Walras allocations holds approximately for a finite economy with a large number of nearly insignificant agents. This program is the object of W. Hildenbrand [**1974**], one of whose main results we now present.

Letting $K = \mathscr{P} \times R^l_+$ be the set of agents' characteristics, we introduce the basic concepts associated with the economy $\mathscr{E}$ that we need. The image measure $\mu = \nu \circ \mathscr{E}^{-1}$ of ν via $\mathscr{E}$ is a probability on K called the *characteristic distribution* of $\mathscr{E}$. Given an allocation x for $\mathscr{E}$ (i.e., an integrable function from A to R^l_+), consider the function γ_x from A to $K \times R^l_+$ defined by $\gamma_x(a) = (\mathscr{E}(a), x(a))$. The image measure $\nu \circ \gamma_x^{-1}$ of ν via γ_x is a probability on $K \times R^l_+$ called the *characteristic-consumption distribution* of x. We denote by $\mathscr{D}_W(\mathscr{E})$ the set of characteristic-consumption distributions of the Walras allocations of $\mathscr{E}$, and similarly by $\mathscr{D}_C(\mathscr{E})$ the set of characteristic-consumption distributions of the core allocations of $\mathscr{E}$. Finally, we formalize the idea of a competitive sequence of finite economies. $\# A_n$ will denote the number of agents of $\mathscr{E}_n$, μ_n the characteristic distribution of $\mathscr{E}_n$, and pr_2 the projection from K into R^l_+. The sequence $(\mathscr{E}_n)$ is *competitive* if

(i) $\# A_n \to +\infty$,

(ii) μ_n converges weakly to a limit μ,

(iii) $\int pr_2\, d\mu_n \to \int pr_2\, d\mu \gg 0$.

We denote by $\mathscr{E}^\mu$ the economy defined as the identity map from K, endowed with its Borel σ-field $\mathscr{B}(K)$, and the measure μ, to K. Then, endowing the set of probability measures on $K \times R^l_+$ with the topology of weak convergence, we obtain the theorem of W. Hildenbrand [**1974**, Chapter 3].

THEOREM. *If the sequence $(\mathscr{E}_n)$ is competitive, and U is a neighborhood of $\overline{\mathscr{D}_W(\mathscr{E}^\mu)}$, then, for n large enough, $\mathscr{D}_C(\mathscr{E}_n) \subset U$.*

To go further, and to obtain full continuity results, as well as results on the rate of convergence of the core of $\mathscr{E}_n$, we need an extension (F. Delbaen [**1971**], K. Hildenbrand [**1974**], and H. Dierker [**1974**]) of the concepts and of the propositions of § 3 to the present context of a measure space of agents. Specifically, we place ourselves in the framework of H. Dierker [**1974**]. In addition to being in $\mathscr{P}$, the preference relations of consumers are now assumed to satisfy the following conditions. For every point $x \in P$, the preference-or-indifference set $\{y \in P \mid x \precsim y\}$ is convex, and the indifference set $I(x) = \{y \in P \mid y \sim x\}$ is a C^2-hypersurface of P whose Gaussian curvature is everywhere nonzero, and whose closure relative to R^l is contained in P. Finally denoting by $g(x)$ the positive unit normal of $I(x)$ at the point x, we assume that g is C^1 on P. These conditions make it possible to identify the preference relation $\precsim$ with the C^1 vector field g on P.

The set G of these vector fields is endowed with the topology of uniform C^1 convergence on compact subsets. $\mathcal{M}$ then denotes the set of characteristic distributions on $G \times P$ with compact support. The assumptions that we have made imply that every agent has a C^1 demand function. Therefore it is possible to define a *regular* element μ of $\mathcal{M}$ as a characteristic distribution μ in $\mathcal{M}$ such that the Jacobian determinant introduced in §3 is different from zero for every equilibrium price vector associated with μ. Having suitably topologized the set $\mathcal{M}$, one can give, in the manner of H. Dierker [**1974**], general conditions under which the regular set is open and dense in $\mathcal{M}$.

In this framework, the following result on the rate of convergence of the core of an economy has recently been obtained (B. Grodal [**1974**]) for the case in which the agents' characteristics belong to a compact subset Q of $G \times P$. For a finite set A, d^A denotes the metric defined on the set of functions from A to R^l by $d^A(x, y) = \operatorname{Max}_{a \in A} \| x(a) - y(a) \|$, and $\delta^A(X, Y)$ denotes the associated Hausdorff distance of two compact sets X, Y of functions from A to R^l. In the statement of the theorem, $\mathcal{M}_Q$ denotes the set of characteristic distributions on Q with the topology of weak convergence.

THEOREM. *If Q is a compact subset of $G \times P$, and μ is a regular characteristic distribution on Q, then there are a neighborhood V of μ in $\mathcal{M}_Q$, and a real number k such that for every economy $\mathcal{E}$ with a finite set A of agents, and whose characteristic distribution belongs to V,*

$$\delta^A [C(\mathcal{E}), W(\mathcal{E})] \leqq k/\#A.$$

Thus if $(\mathcal{E}_n)$ is a competitive sequence of economies on Q, and if the limit characteristic distribution is regular, then $\delta^{A_n} [C(\mathcal{E}_n), W(\mathcal{E}_n)]$ tends to 0 at least as fast as the inverse of the number of agents.

The basic reference for this section is W. Hildenbrand [**1974**].

The analysis of Walras equilibria, of the core, and of their relationship has yielded valuable insights into the role of prices in an economy. But possibly of greater importance has been the recognition that the techniques used in that analysis are indispensable for the mathematical study of social systems: algebraic topology for the test of existence that mathematical models of social equilibrium must pass; differential topology for the more demanding tests of discreteness, and of continuity for the set of equilibria; combinatorial techniques for the computation of equilibria; and measure theory for the study of large sets of small agents.

References

K. J. Arrow (1953), *Le rôle des valeurs boursières pour la répartition la meilleure des risques*, Econométrie, pp. 41–47; discussion, pp. 47–48, Colloq. Internat. Centre National de la Recherche Scientifique, no. 40 (Paris, 1952), Centre de la Recherche Scientifique, Paris, 1953; Translated in Review of Economic Studies **31** (1964), 91–96. MR **16**, 943.

K. J. Arrow and G. Debreu (1954), *Existence of an equilibrium for a competitive economy*, Econometrica **22**, 265–290. MR **17**, 985.

K. J. Arrow and F. H. Hahn (1971), *General competitive analysis*, Holden-Day, San Francisco, Calif.

R. J. Aumann (1964), *Markets with a continuum of traders*, Econometrica **32**, 39–50. MR **30** #2908.

Y. Balasko (1974a), *On the graph of the Walras correspondence*, Econometrica (to appear).

——— (1974b), *Some results on uniqueness and on stability of equilibrium in general equilibrium theory*, J. Math. Economics (to appear).

F. E. Browder (1960), *On continuity of fixed points under deformations of continuous mappings*, Summa Brasil. Mat. **4**, 183–191. MR **24** #A543.

F. Delbaen (1971), *Lower and upper semi-continuity of the Walras correspondence*, Doctoral Dissertation, Free University of Brussels.

E. Dierker (1974), *Topological methods in Walrasian economics*, Lecture Notes in Economics and Mathematical Systems, **92**, Springer-Verlag, Berlin.

E. and H. Dierker (1972), *On the local uniqueness of equilibria*, Econometrica **40**, 867–881.

H. Dierker (1974), *Smooth preferences and the regularity of equilibria*, J. Math. Economics (to appear).

B. C. Eaves (1972), *Homotopies for computation of fixed points*, Math. Programming **3**, 1–22. MR **46** #3089.

——— (1974), *Properly labeled simplexes*, Studies in Optimization, MAA Studies in Mathematics, 10, G. B. Dantzig and B. C. Eaves, eds., Mathematical Association of America.

F. Y. Edgeworth (1881), *Mathematical Psychics*, Paul Kegan, London.

D. Gale (1955), *The law of supply and demand*, Math. Scand. **3**, 155–169. MR **17**, 985.

B. Grodal (1974), *The rate of convergence of the core for a purely competitive sequence of economies*, J. Math. Economics (to appear).

T. Hansen (1968), *On the approximation of a competitive equilibrium*, Ph.D. Dissertation, Yale University, New Haven, Conn.

F. Hausdorff (1957), *Set theory*, Chelsea, New York. MR **19**, 111.

K. Hildenbrand (1974), *Finiteness of $\Pi(\mathscr{E})$ and continuity of Π*, Appendix to Chapter 2 in W. Hildenbrand (1974).

W. Hildenbrand (1974), *Core and equilibria of a large economy*, Princeton Univ. Press, Princeton, N.J.

S. Kakutani (1941), *A generalization of Brouwer's fixed point theorem*, Duke Math. J. **8**, 457–459. MR **3**, 60.

Y. Kannai (1970), *Continuity properties of the core of a market*, Econometrica **38**, 791–815.

H. W. Kuhn (1960), *Some combinatorial lemmas in topology*, IBM J. Res. Develop. **4**, 518–524. MR **23** #A1358.

——— (1968), *Simplicial approximation of fixed points*, Proc. Nat. Acad. Sci. U.S.A. **61**, 1238–1242.

C. E. Lemke and J. T. Howson, Jr. (1964), *Equilibrium points of bimatrix games*, J. Soc. Indust. Appl. Math. **12**, 413–423. MR **30** #3769.

L. W. McKenzie (1954), *On equilibrium in Graham's model of world trade and other competitive systems*, Econometrica **22**, 147–161.

J. Nash (1950), *Equilibrium points in n-person games*, Proc. Nat. Acad. Sci. U.S.A. **36**, 48–49. MR **11**, 192.

J. von Neumann (1937), *Über ein ökonomisches Gleichungssystem und eine Verallgemeinerung des Brouwerschen Fixpunktsatzes*, Ergebnisse eines mathematischen Kolloquiums, no. 8, 83–73; Translated in Review of Economic Studies **13** (1945), 1–9.

H. Nikaidô (1956), *On the classical multilateral exchange problem*, Metroecon. **8**, 135–145. MR **18**, 266.

H. Scarf (1962), *An analysis of markets with a large number of participants*, Recent Advances in Game Theory, Princeton University Conference Report.

——— (1967), *The approximation of fixed points of a continuous mapping*, SIAM J. Appl. Math. **15**, 1328–1343. MR **39** #3814.

——— (1973), (with the collaboration of T. Hansen) *The computation of economic equilibria*, Yale Univ. Press, New Haven, Conn.

M. Shubik (1959), *Edgeworth market games*, Contributions to the Theory of Games, vol. IV, Ann. of Math. Studies, no. 40, Princeton Univ. Press, Princeton, N. J. MR **21** #2538.

S. Smale (1974), *Global analysis and economics*. IIA, J. Math. Economics **1**, 1–14.

K. Vind (1964), *Edgeworth-allocations in an exchange economy with many traders*, Internat. Economic Rev. **5**, 165–177.

A. Wald (1935), *Über die eindeutige positive Lösbarkeit der neuen Produktionsgleichungen*, Ergebnisse eines mathematischen Kolloquiums, no. 6, 12–20.

——— (1936), *Über die Produktionsgleichungen der ökonomischen Wertlehre*, Ergebnisse eines mathematischen Kolloquiums, no. 7, 1–6.

——— (1936), *Über einige Gleichungssysteme der mathematischen Ökonomie*, Z. Nationalökonomie **7**, 637–670; Translated as *On some systems of equations of mathematical economics*, Econometrica **19** (1951), 368–503. MR **13**, 370.

L. Walras (1874–1877), *Eléments d'économie politique pure*, Lausanne, Corbaz; Translated as *Elements of pure economics*, Irwin, Homewood, Ill., 1954.

R. J. Wilmuth (1973), *The computation of fixed points*, Ph.D. Disseration, Stanford University, Stanford, Calif.

UNIVERSITY OF CALIFORNIA
BERKELEY, CALIFORNIA 94720, U.S.A.

Actes du Congrès International des Mathématiciens
Vancouver, 1974

Poids dans la Cohomologie des Variétés Algébriques

Pierre Deligne

1. Soit X une variété algébrique complexe (i.e., un schéma séparé de type fini sur $\boldsymbol{C}$). On note encore X l'espace topologique usuel $X(\boldsymbol{C})$ sous-jacent à X. Dans cet exposé, nous décrivons une filtration remarquable des groupes de cohomologie rationnelle de X, la *filtration par le poids*, et nous donnons un fascicule de résultats de ses propriétés. Sa définition sera donnée au §12. Pour les démonstrations, nous renvoyons aux travaux cités dans la bibliographie où les théorèmes sont souvent prouvés dans des cadres plus généraux; travailler sur $\boldsymbol{C}$ nous permet de disposer simultanément de la théorie de Hodge, d'action de groupes de Galois, et de la résolution des singularités.

La filtration par le poids est une filtration finie croissante. Nous la noterons W. Elle est également définie dans des situations relatives (ou en cohomologie à support propres). Elle dépend non seulement de l'espace topologique X, mais encore de la façon dont il est réalisé comme variété algébrique. Elle est compatible aux isomorphismes de Künneth (i.e., via l'isomorphisme $H^*(X \times Y) = H^*(X) \otimes H^*(Y)$, on a

$$W_j(H^*(X \times Y)) = \sum_{j'+j''=j} W_{j'}(H^*(X)) \otimes W_{j''}(H^*(Y))$$

et est fonctorielle pour les morphismes algébriques. Plus précisément, si $f\colon X \to Y$ est algébrique, alors $f^*\colon H^*(Y) \to H^*(X)$ est *strictement* compatible aux filtrations par le poids de $H^*(Y)$ et $H^*(X)$: Si la classe $x \in H^i(X)$ est dans l'image de f^*, elle est de filtration $\leqq i$ si et seulement si elle est l'image d'une classe de filtration $\leqq i$. Plus généralement, toute application naturelle est *strictement* compatible aux filtrations par le poids.

La filtration par le poids est un invariant discret; elle est invariante par déformation de la structure algébrique de X. Plus précisément, on a le théorème suivant.

2. Théorème. *Soit $f:X \to S$ un morphisme. Pour $t \in S$, soit $X_t = f^{-1}(t)$. Si le faisceau $R^i f\mathbf{Q}_*$ est localement constant (un système local), il existe une filtration par le poids W de $R^i f_* \mathbf{Q}$ par des sous-systèmes locaux, telles que les flèches r_t: $(R^i f_* \mathbf{Q})_t \to H^i(X_t)$ soient strictement compatibles aux filtrations par le poids, et qu'en particulier là où r_t est un isomorphisme, W induise la filtration par le poids de $H^i(X_t)$.*

3. En gros, la filtration par le poids exprime comment la cohomologie de X peut se bâtir en terme de la cohomologie de variétés projectives non singulières. Voici quelques exemples.

Exemple 3.1. Si X est propre (=compacte, par exemple projective) et lisse (=non singulière), alors $H^i(X) =_{\text{dfn}} H^i(X, \mathbf{Q})$ est purement de poids i: $\text{Gr}_j^W(H^i(X)) = 0$ pour $i \neq j$. En d'autres termes, $W_{i-1}(H^i(X)) = 0$ et $W_i(H^i(X)) = H^i(X)$.

Exemple 3.2. Soient X propre, lisse, connexe, de dimension d et P un point de X. Des groupes de cohomologie à support $H^i_{\{P\}}(X) = H^i(X \operatorname{mod}(X - \{P\}))$, seul celui d'indice $2d$ est non nul, et

$$H^{2d}_{\{P\}}(X) \xrightarrow{\sim} H^{2d}(X) = \mathbf{Q}. \tag{3.2.1}$$

D'après nos principes, $H^{2d}_{\{P\}}(X)$ est donc purement de poids $2d$. L'inverse de l'isomorphisme (3.2.1) peut être vu comme un isomorphisme de Thom-Gysin

$$\mathbf{Q} = H^0(P) \xrightarrow{\sim} H^{2d}_{\{P\}}(X);$$

on constate qu'il ne respecte pas les poids. La situation générale est la suivante: pour Y une sous-variété lisse purement de codimension d dans une variété lisse X, l'isomorphisme de Thom-Gysin $H^i(Y) \xrightarrow{\sim} H^{i+2d}_Y(X)$ transforme W^k en W^{k+2d}. Notant (n) un décalage de $2n$ pour W $(W(n)_k = W_{k-2n})$, ceci s'écrit comme un isomorphisme filtré

$$H^i(Y)(-d) \xrightarrow{\sim} H^{i+2d}_Y(X).$$

Exemple 3.3. Soient X propre et lisse, et Y une sous-variété lisse (fermée) purement de codimension d. On dispose d'une suite exacte

$$\cdots \to H^i(X) \to H^i(X - Y) \xrightarrow{\delta} H^{i+1}_Y(X) \to \cdots.$$

D'après 3.1 et 3.2, on a donc $\text{Gr}_j^W(H^i(X - Y)) = 0$ pour $j \neq i, i + 1$; W_i est l'image de $H^i(X)$.

Exemple 3.4. Soit X propre, et lisse sauf pour un point singulier isolé P. Supposons que la variété $\tilde{X}$ déduite de X en éclatant P soit lisse, et que le diviseur exceptionnel D image inverse de P soit lisse: X se déduit de $\tilde{X}$ (propre et lisse) en contractant en un point D (propre et lisse). L'espace X a le type d'homotopie de $[\tilde{X} \cup$ (un cône de base D)], dont la cohomologie se calcule par Mayer-Vietoris; on trouve une suite exacte

$$\cdots \to H^{i-1}(D) \xrightarrow{\delta} H^i(X) \to H^i(\tilde{X}) \oplus H^i(P) \to \cdots$$

qui montre que $\text{Gr}_j^W(H^i(X)) = 0$ pour $j \neq i - 1, i$; W_{i-1} est l'image de δ. Pour

$i \neq 0$, c'est encore le noyau de $H^i(X) \to H^i(\tilde{X})$, et $\mathrm{Gr}_i^W(H^i(X))$ est l'image de $H^i(X)$ dans $H^i(\tilde{X})$.

Exemple 3.5. Les variétés de drapeaux sont des variétés propres et lisses. La filtration par le poids de leur cohomologie est donc donnée par 3.1. Si G est un groupe réductif connexe, le même resultat vaut pour la cohomologie de BG [**1**, III]. Ceci permet de calculer la filtration par le poids de la cohomologie de G, liée à celle de BG par transgression. On trouve que $W_i H^i(G) = 0$, et que $W_{i+1}H^i(G)$, nul pour i pair, est égal à la partie primitive de la cohomologie de degré i de G [**1**, III]. Si $f:G \to H$ est une application algébrique entre variétés de groupes réductifs, l'image réciproque d'une classe de cohomologie rationnelle primitive de H est donc encore primitive. Pour d'autres corollaires, voir [**1**, III].

4. La filtration par le poids est graduable en un sens très fort. Il existe des graduations $\underline{W}$ des $H^i(X)$, qui décomposent W:

$$W_n(H^i(X)) = \bigoplus_{j \leq n} \underline{W}_j(H^i(X)) \tag{4.1}$$

et qui soient compatibles au cup-produit et aux opérations supérieures dérivées du cup-produit (produits de Massey $\cdots$). Ces dernières n'étant pas partout définies, le sens de "compatible à une graduation" doit être précisé. Le plus simple est de voir une graduation comme une action du groupe $\boldsymbol{G}_m$, i.e., une action de $\boldsymbol{Q}^*$ donnée par des formules algébriques: à une graduation $\underline{W}$ on associe l'action où $\lambda \in \boldsymbol{Q}^*$ agit sur $\underline{W}_j$ par multiplication par λ^j. La "compatibilité" est que $\boldsymbol{Q}^*$ agit par des automorphismes de $H^*(X)$ muni de sa graduation par le degré, du cup-produit, et des opérations supérieures dérivées du cup-produit.

5. Supposons pour simplifier X connexe, et soit $\mathscr{M}$ le modèle minimal du type d'homotopie rationnel de X, au sens de Sullivan [7]. C'est une algèbre différentielle graduée à degrés ≥ 0, connexe ($\mathscr{M}^0 = \boldsymbol{Q}$), (anti) commutative libre en tant qu'algèbre graduée, et engendrée par ses éléments indécomposables (i.e., $d\mathscr{M} \subset (\mathscr{M}^{>0})^2$). On a $H^*(\mathscr{M}) = H^*(X)$, et si X est simplement connexe, $\mathscr{M}^{>0}/(\mathscr{M}^{>0})^2 = (\pi_*(X) \otimes \boldsymbol{Q})^\vee$.

Un énoncé plus précis, et plus commode, que celui donné en § 4 est qu'il existe une graduation $\underline{W}$ vérifiant (4.1) déduite d'une graduation $\underline{W}$ de $\mathscr{M}$ (à degrés ≥ 0, somme de graduations des $\mathscr{M}^i$, telle que d et le produit soient homogènes de degré 0; en d'autres termes, $\boldsymbol{Q}^*$ agit par automorphismes de $\mathscr{M}$).

6. La seule existence de W et $\underline{W}$ n'impose aucune restriction au type d'homotopie de X: On peut toujours prétendre que $\mathscr{M}$ est tout entière de poids 0. N'importe quel polyèdre fini a d'ailleurs le même type d'homotopie qu'une variété algébrique. Soit en effet S un ensemble fini, muni d'un ensemble $\mathscr{S}$ de parties (les simplexes). On suppose que toute partie d'un élément de $\mathscr{S}$ est encore dans $\mathscr{S}$. Identifions S à l'ensemble des vecteurs de base de $\boldsymbol{R}^S$, et pour $\sigma \subset S$, soit $|\sigma|$ le simplexe tendu par les $s \in \sigma$. Montrons que $|S| = \bigcup_{\sigma \in \mathscr{S}} |\sigma|$ a le type d'homotopie d'une variété algébrique X. Si on pose $|\sigma|_C$ = espace affine complexe tendu par $\sigma \subset \boldsymbol{C}^S$, il suffit de prendre $X = \bigcup_{\sigma \in \mathscr{S}} |\sigma|_C$, dont $|S|$ est un rétracte par déformation. On peut vérifier que dans cet exemple $H^*(X)$ est purement de filtration par le poids 0.

Toutefois, dès que les poids sont non nuls, des contraintes apparaissent sur le type d'homotopie de X (cf. §10.). Les règles suivantes aident à localiser les poids.

7. Pour un groupe de cohomologie H de type donné, chaque règle consistera à décrire une partie $\mathscr{E}$ de $\mathbf{Z} \times \mathbf{Z}$. Les poids seront *contrôlés* par $\mathscr{E}$ au sens suivant: Si $\mathrm{Gr}_n^W(H) \neq 0$, il existe $(p, q) \in \mathscr{E}$, avec $p + q = n$. Cette façon de s'exprimer, qui ici parait artificielle, ne l'est pas: D'autres informations que les poids possibles sont contrôlées par la même région $\mathscr{E}$, cf. §15.

(7.1) $H^n(X)$ est contrôlé par le carré $[0, n] \times [0, n]$.

(7.2) Si X est propre, $H^n(X)$ est contrôlé par la partie de ce carré en-dessous de la seconde diagonale, soit $\{(p, q) \in [0, n] \times [0, n] \mid p + q \leqq n\}$. Si X est lisse, $H^n(X)$ est contrôlé par la partie de ce carré au-dessus de cette diagonale, soit $\{(p, q) \in [0, n] \times [0, n] \mid p + q \geqq n\}$.

(7.3) Si $N = \dim X \leqq n$, le carré $[0, n] \times [0, n]$ peut être remplacé par le carré $[n - N, N] \times [n - N, N]$.

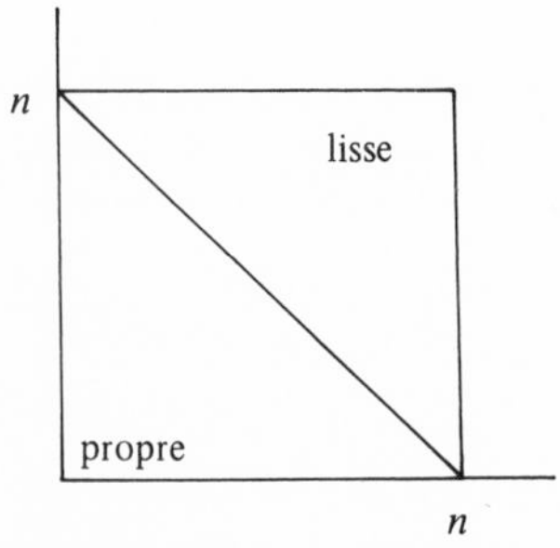

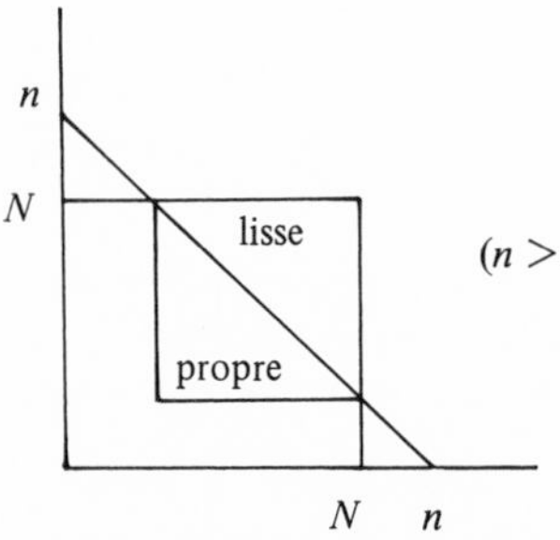

$(n > N)$

8. Variantes. (8.1) Le groupe de cohomologie à support propre $H_c^n(X)$ est contrôlé par la partie du carré $[0, n] \times [0, n]$ en-dessous de la seconde diagonale. Pour $N = \dim X \leqq n$, on peut encore remplacer ce carré par $[n - N, N] \times [n - N, N]$. En particulier, $H_c^{2N}(X)$ est purement de poids $2N$.

(8.2) La "dualité" entre les cas propres et lisses peut se déduire de la dualité de Poincaré: pour X lisse purement de dimension N,

$$H^n(X) = \mathrm{Hom}(H_c^{2N-n}(X), H_c^{2N}(X)) = (H_c^{2N-n}(X)^{\mathrm{dual}})(-N).$$

Cet argument permet d'étendre les résultats donnés pour X lisse au cas où X est une "rational homology manifold". Pour un tel X, l'image de $H_c^n(X)$ dans $H^n(X)$ est purement de poids n.

(8.3) Pour X seulement supposé normal, il reste vrai que $H^1(X)$ est contrôlé par $\{(0, 1), (1, 0), (1, 1)\}$.

9. Soient X une variété connexe, $x \in X$, et $\Pi^{(n)}$ le plus grand quotient nilpotent de longueur n et sans torsion de $\pi_1(X, x)$. On sait que les groupes H d'indice fini dans $\Pi^{(n)}$ et assez petits ont la propriété suivante.

($*$) Il existe une algèbre de Lie nilpotente de longueur n, $(\mathscr{H}, [\ \ ])$, avec $\mathscr{H}$ un

$\mathbf{Z}$-module libre, telle que la formule de Campbell-Hausdorff

$$x \circ y = x + y + [x, y]/2 + [x, [x, y]]/12 + [y, [y, x]]/12 + \cdots$$

fasse de $\mathscr{H}$ un groupe, isomorphe à H.

De plus, l'algèbre de Lie $\mathscr{L}^{(n)} = \mathscr{H} \otimes \mathbf{Q}$ ne dépend que de $\Pi^{(n)}$, non de H.

10. Théorème (Morgan). *Si X est normale, $\mathscr{L}^{(n)}$ admet une graduation W, à degrés < 0, telle que $\mathscr{L}^{(n)}$ soit engendrée par des éléments de degré -1 et -2, ceux ci n'étant soumis qu'à des relations de degré -2, -3 et -4, plus la nullité des commutateurs n fois itérés.*

Il est plus commode de travailler avec le système projectif $\mathscr{L}^{(\infty)}$ des $\mathscr{L}^{(n)}$. Définissant $H^i(\mathscr{L}^{(\infty)}) = \text{inj lim } H^i(\mathscr{L}^{(n)})$, on a

$$H^1(\mathscr{L}^{(\infty)}) = H^1(X), \qquad H^2(\mathscr{L}^{\infty}) \subsetneq H^2(X).$$

De plus, une graduation $\underline{W}$ de $\mathscr{M}$ comme au §5 définit des graduations compatibles de $\mathscr{L}^{(\infty)}$, de sa cohomologie, et de celle de X. D'après (8.3), (resp. (7.1)), $H^1(X)$ est de poids 1 et 2 et $H^2(X)$ de poids $\leqq 4$. Dès lors, $H^1(\mathscr{L}^{(\infty)})$ (le dual du groupe $\mathscr{L}^{\infty}/[\mathscr{L}^{\infty}, \mathscr{L}^{\infty}]$ des générateurs de $\mathscr{L}^{\infty}$) est de poids 1 et 2, et $H^2(\mathscr{L}^{(\infty)})$, le dual du groupe des relations entre générateurs, est de poids $\leqq 4$. Ceci vérifie le théorème.

11. Pour une variété propre et lisse la filtration par le poids se réduit à peu de chose (3.1). Le fait qu'elle soit graduable au sens §4 implique la nullité de tous les produits de Massey. Qu'elle le soit au sens §5 implique même que le type d'homotopie rationnel de X peut se lire sur son algèbre de cohomologie—voir [**3**].

12. Théorie de Hodge. Le groupe de cohomologie $H^i(X)$ de toute variété algébrique complexe est munie d'une structure de Hodge mixte (W, F) (W est une filtration de $H^i(X)$, et F une filtration de $H^i(X) \otimes \mathbf{C} = H^i(X, \mathbf{C})$, W et F vérifiant des axiomes convenables—voir [**1**]). La filtration par le poids est par définition la filtration W.

13. Théorie l-adique. Une variété algébrique X se définit en terme d'un nombre fini d'équations polynômes. Les coefficients de ces équations engendrent un sous-anneau de type fini R de $\mathbf{C}$, de corps des fractions K, et X se déduit par extension des scalaires à $\mathbf{C}$ d'un schéma sur K, voire sur R. Les énoncés qui suivent deviennent vrai lorsqu'on remplace R par $R[1/f]$ avec $f \in R$ assez divisible.

(13.1) Soit l un nombre premier. Le groupe $H^i(X) \otimes \mathbf{Q}_l$ s'identifie au groupe de cohomologie l-adique $H^i(X, \mathbf{Q}_l)$. Ce dernier est défini de façon purement algébrique, donc est muni par transport de structure d'une action de $\text{Aut}(\mathbf{C}/K)$.

(13.2) Soit $\bar{K}$ la clôture algébrique de K dans $\mathbf{C}$. L'action se factorise par $\text{Gal}(\bar{K}/K)$. Elle est non ramifiée sur $R[1/l]$, i.e., se factorise par le groupe de Galois de la plus grande extension $K_{\text{nr}}^{(l)} \subset \bar{K}$ de K non ramifiée sur $R[1/l]$.

(13.3) Soit m un idéal maximal de $R[1/l]$, et $N(m) = \#R/m$ (R/m est un corps fini). A m correspond une classe de conjugaison de substitutions de Frobenius $\phi_m \in \text{Gal}(K_{\text{nr}}/K)$, d'inverses les Frobenius géométriques $F_m = \phi_m^{-1}$.

14. Théorème. *Pour f assez divisible, on a*

(i) *Pour tout l et m, les valeurs propres* α *de* F_m *(dans une extension finie convenable de* $\boldsymbol{Q}_l$*) sont des entiers algébriques. Pour chaque* α*, il existe un entier* $w(\alpha)$ *tels que tous les conjugués complexes de* α *soient de valeur absolue* $N(m)^{w(\alpha)/2}$.

(ii) *Choisissons un Frobenius géométrique* F_m*, et soit* ${}_mW_j$*. la somme des sous-espaces propres généralisés correspondant aux valeurs propres* α *de* F_m *telles que* $w(\alpha) = j$*. La filtration par les* $\bigoplus_{j\leqq i}{}_mW_j$ *est indépendante de m et du choix de* F_m*; elle est rationnelle et sa trace sur* $H^i(X)$ *est indépendante de l; c'est la filtration par le poids.*

Principe de Démonstration. On exprime (via une suite spectrale) la cohomologie de X en terme de la cohomologie de variétés propres et lisses, comme en **[1]**. La suite spectrale aboutit à une filtration W de $H^*(X)$, qui est par définition la filtration par le poids de la théorie de Hodge. Cette suite spectrale a un analogue l-adique; le l-adifié W_l de W est donc stable par un groupe de Galois. On déduit de la conjecture de Weil que les valeurs propres de F_m sur $\mathrm{Gr}_j^{W_l}$ sont des entiers algébriques de valeurs absolues complexes $N(m)^{j/2}$, et le théorème en résulte.

15. Dans les cas considérés en (7.1), (7.2) et (7.3), la région $\mathscr{E}$ décrite contrôle non seulement les poids, mais encore les nombres de Hodge et la divisibilitié des valeurs propres des F_m: dans (7.1), (7.2) et (7.3), une région $\mathscr{E}$ a été assignée à un groupe H, et

(a) Les nombres de Hodge h^{pq} non nuls des structure de Hodge $\mathrm{Gr}_j^W(H)$ vérifient $(p, q) \in \mathscr{E}$.

(b) (Utile seulement dans le cas (7.3).) Si les $(p, q) \in \mathscr{E}$ avec $p + q = j$ vérifient $p, q \geqq k$, alors (toujours pour f assez divisible), les valeurs propres de F_m de valeurs absolues complexes $N(m)^{j/2}$ sont divisibles par $N(m)^k$.

On espère que ceci est un cas particulier d'un principe général, cf. **[4]**.

16. Le résultat suivant est clair du point de vue de la théorie de Hodge.

(16.1) Pour j impair dim $\mathrm{Gr}_j^W H^i(X)$ est pair.

Par contre, je ne sais démontrer jusqu'ici §§ 2 et 5 que par voie 1-adique. Pour § 5, la méthode de § 14 permet d'obtenir une graduation 1-adique; une astuce de Sullivan permet d'en déduire l'existence de graduations rationnelles du type voulu.

Les propriétés de fonctorialité de la filtration par le poids sont évidentes du point de vue l-adique (car Galois commute à tout ce qui se peut définir). Il est toutefois utile de les prouver du point de vue de la théorie de Hodge, pour obtenir des propriétés analogues pour la filtration F. Morgan a obtenu de nombreux résultats dans cette direction—assez pour prouver un résultat un peu plus faible que §10 par théorie de Hodge.

17. Ainsi que § 5 le suggère, une filtration par le poids existe aussi sur les groupes d'homotopie (tensorisés par $\boldsymbol{Q}$) sous des hypothèses de simple connexité.

Elle existe aussi sur les groupes de cycles évanescents (cf. **[6]**), et j'espère qu'elles nous aideront à mieux comprendre ces derniers.

Bibliographie

1. P. Deligne, *Théorie de Hodge*. I, Proc. Internat. Congress Math. (Nice, 1970), vol. I, Gauthier-

Villars, Paris, 1971, pp. 425–430; II, Inst. Hautes Études Sci. Publ. Math. No. 40 (1972), 5–58; III, Inst. Hautes Études Sci. Publ. Math. No. 44 (à paraître).

2. ———, *La conjecture de Weil.* I, II, Inst. Hautes Études Sci. Publ. Math. Nos. 43 et 44 (á paraître).

3. P. Deligne, P. A. Griffiths, J. Morgan and D. Sullivan. *Real homotopy theory of Kähler manifolds* (à paraître).

4. B. Mazur, *Frobenius and the Hodge filtration* (*estimates*), Ann. of Math. (2) **98** (1973), 58–95. MR **48** #297.

5. J. Morgan.

6. J. H. M. Steenbrink, *Limits of Hodge structures and intermediate jacobians*, Thèse, Amsterdam, 1974.

7. D. Sullivan, *Differential forms and the topology of manifolds*, Proc. Japan Conference on Manifolds, 1973.

Institut des Hautes Etudes Scientifiques
91440 Bures-sur-Yvette, France

Proceedings of the International Congress of Mathematicians
Vancouver, 1974

Mathematical Problems of Tidal Energy

G. F. D. Duff

1. Tidal energy. Recent studies of alternative energy sources have embraced a number of "exotic" forms such as solar, wind, geothermal or tidal energy. Here we shall examine recent developments in the mathematical understanding of tides and tidal power, with particular reference to the Bay of Fundy in eastern Canada which has the highest tides and may be the test site for further development of this mode of electrical energy production.

From the observed increase in length of the day [**21**] and the observed lunar acceleration, the total rate of all tidal energy dissipation is known to be about 3×10^{19} ergs per second—a rate comparable to mankind's present consumption of energy. Much of this energy is dissipated in certain oceanic high tide regions where shallow continental shelf areas create large amplitudes by resonance, shallowing and convergence. Thus the English Channel and Irish Sea absorb perhaps 4% of the overall total while the Bay of Fundy and Gulf of Maine account for about 1%, an energy flow equal to the present capacity of the Canadian electricity network.

Recent engineering studies have shown [**2**] that recommended sites at Economy Point, Nova Scotia, and Cape Maringouin, New Brunswick, would be feasible but probably not yet economical. Tidal energy is renewable, but not conservable, predictable but intermittent, and large yet limited (at these sites perhaps 8,000 megawatts capacity could be installed). An interesting recent suggestion for excess power at peak generating periods is compressed air storage in salt caverns, with subsequent coal burning.

The applied mathematical problems discussed here are of two types. First is the description and calculation of oceanic and estuarial tidal wave motion and the modifications that would be induced by the construction of a tidal barrier with sluice gates and turbines. The second problem is the optimal control of sluice and turbine operations in which the tidal wave motions and energy generation processes interact.

2. Equations of motion. Let (θ, ϕ) be latitude and longitude, and (u, v) components of fluid velocity to the east and north, respectively. Let z denote sea level above equilibrium, and $\bar{z}$ the formal "equilibrium tide". The equations of motion introduced by Laplace in 1775 **[15]** are, with vertical acceleration neglected,

$$\begin{aligned} &\frac{\partial u}{\partial t} - (2\Omega \sin \theta) v = \frac{-g}{a \cos \theta} \frac{\partial}{\partial \phi}(z - \bar{z}), \\ (2.1) \qquad &\frac{\partial v}{\partial t} + (2\Omega \sin \theta) u = \frac{-g}{a} \frac{\partial}{\partial \theta}(z - \bar{z}), \\ &\frac{\partial z}{\partial t} + \frac{1}{a \cos \theta}\left(\frac{\partial (Hu)}{\partial \phi} + \frac{\partial (Hv \cos \theta)}{\partial \theta}\right) = 0, \end{aligned}$$

where also g denotes gravity, a earth's radius, Ω angular velocity of earth's daily rotation and $H = D + z$ where $D = D(\theta, \phi)$ is the ocean depth. In the late nineteenth century, these oceanographic equations were studied by Poincaré, Darwin, and others, and various particular solutions and special cases were solved. Many recent theoretical and numerical studies of these equations in various geometries and geographies have now been made, including Hendershott **[14]**, Longuet-Higgins **[17]**, Pekeris **[23]**.

It is apparent that accuracy of numerical solutions is difficult to achieve because of the sensitivity of nearly resonant motions to erorrs of discretization.

For smaller basins or gulfs the earth's curvature can be neglected, and in Cartesian coordinates (x, y) the equations become, with quadratic friction terms (**[29]**, **[30]**),

$$\begin{aligned} &\frac{\partial u}{\partial t} - fv = -g \frac{\partial (z - \bar{z})}{\partial x} + r\frac{u|u|}{H}, \\ (2.2) \qquad &\frac{\partial v}{\partial t} + fu = -g \frac{\partial (z - \bar{z})}{\partial y} + r\frac{v|u|}{H}, \\ &\frac{\partial z}{\partial t} + \frac{\partial (Hu)}{\partial x} + \frac{\partial (Hv)}{\partial y} = 0. \end{aligned}$$

This is a symmetric hyperbolic system with monotone nonlinearity, of a type treated generally by Lions **[16]**. Boundary conditions at a coastline with normal $\boldsymbol{n}$ are $\boldsymbol{u} \cdot \boldsymbol{n} = 0$ and at a sea boundary may take the form of given values for z, or $\boldsymbol{u} \cdot \boldsymbol{n}$ or of a radiation condition on z.

The tide raising forces, represented by the $\bar{z}$ terms in (2.2), are almost periodic in time because of the various combinations (Godin **[12]**) of the several astronomical constants of the moon and sun. For convenience in finding analytic or numerical solutions it is customary to model the harmonic constituents separately, and thus to neglect certain nonlinear convective and frictional interactions which however are almost always very small.

When depth H and Coriolis parameter f are assumed constant, various plane wave solutions of the Poincaré or Kelvin types are easily derived and have been extensively used in the qualitative discussion of real problems (Hendershott and Munk [**14**], Platzman [**24**], [**25**]). Along the western shore of Nova Scotia and the southern flank of the Bay of Fundy, the M_2 and other semidiurnal tidal components take the form of a Kelvin wave following a right-handed coastline.

3. The wave equation. If the Coriolis and frictional forces are neglected, the system (2.2) becomes equivalent to the classical wave equation

$$(3.1)\quad L\Phi \equiv \frac{\partial^2\Phi}{\partial t^2} - \frac{\partial}{\partial x}\left(gH\frac{\partial\Phi}{\partial x}\right) - \frac{\partial}{\partial y}\left(gH\frac{\partial\Phi}{\partial y}\right)=0 \text{ for a potential } \Phi=\Phi(x,y,t)$$

where $\Phi_x = u$, $\Phi_y = v$, $\Phi_t = z$. The local wave propogation velocity is c, where $c^2 = gH(x,y)$, and its variability plays a significant role in the refractive generation of topographical waves (Meyer [**19**]).

Actual problems will involve a nonhomogeneous boundary condition of the first or second kind, or a forcing term, which is almost periodic with respect to the time variable because of the incommensurability of the various orbital constants of the sun and moon. Thus the theory of almost periodic solutions of the wave equation of Amerio and Prouse [**1**], Lions and Strauss [**16**], Zaidman [**32**], and others applies directly to this model of tidal motions. The nonlinear wave equation with friction term $r\Phi_t|\Phi_t|$ treated by Amerio and Prouse is of the same type but is not directly equivalent.

At a vertical coastline the position of the boundary does not depend on sea level z. At sloping beaches in high tidal areas, the boundary position may vary as much as several kilometres depending on sea level. This is expressible as a "unilateral" condition (Brezis [**4**]) $\partial\Phi/\partial t = z > -D(x,y)$, and an existence theorem covering this case has been established by Brezis for the wave equation although the more general case of the Eulerian equations (2.2) remains to be treated.

4. Resonant alteration of amplitudes. Tidal power plants would be sited in bays where high amplitudes occur in part because of resonant amplification due to a near coincidence of the imposed period (usually lunar semidiurnal M_2) and the natural period of the bay or gulf. As major construction changes the geometry and dynamics of the tidal motion, the amplitude will change in response. Calculations made for barrier sites at the tip of Cape Chignecto have suggested that a substantial decrease may occur, with the new natural period well removed from the 12^h25^m forcing period (Duff [**5**]). To make such calculations, however, it is necessary to fix an outer sea boundary beyond which no change is assumed, and here a succession of complexities has emerged. In early work for the Bay of Fundy region the sea boundary was taken at the geographic limits of the bay, but this did not even permit an explanation of the existing resonant amplification (Yuen [**30**]). Subsequent extension of the sea boundary to the continental shelf edge gave an indication of resonant natural periods (Duff [**5**], Garrett [**9**]), but still did not include in the model the interaction or impedance relationship between the deep outer ocean and the shallow high tide area of energy dissipation.

Significant grounds for supposing that inclusion of extensive deep ocean areas would be necessary in a realistic tidal model arise from recent work of Garrett [**8**], who applied the theory of harbour resonance (Miles and Munk [**20**]) to the Bay of Fundy and Gulf of Maine and showed that their response to harmonic forcing at three semidiurnal frequencies indicated a fundamental natural period of approximately 13.3 hours. This suggests that tidal barrier construction at the head of the Bay of Fundy would actually increase amplitudes rather than reducing them as had earlier been supposed. A similar calculation using twelve stations at the head of the Bay of Fundy gave a period of 12.85 hours (Duff [**7**]).

Following a method adapted by Platzman [**25**], Garrett [**9**] has also calculated the first three natural periods (eigenvalues) and normal modes (vector eigenfunctions) of the oceanographic equations for the Bay of Fundy and Gulf of Maine. The natural period of the lowest mode is calculated in the range of 12.5 to 13 hours depending on the precise location of the lateral sea boundaries and the open or closed boundary conditions assumed at certain places. The second and third modes have periods of 9.5 and 5.7 hours, and it is apparent that the first mode carries nearly all the observed tidal oscillations in the Bay of Fundy.

The first three natural periods and modes for the North Atlantic have been calculated by Platzman [**26**]; the periods turn out to be 21.2, 14.0 and 11.5 hours, with some uncertainty about the third of these values. Thus it appears that the semidiurnal tidal periods M_2 of 12.42 hours, S_2 of 12.0 hours, N_2 of 12.66 hours, and others, lie between closely spaced second and third natural periods. This may help explain the unusually high semidiurnal amplitudes in the North Atlantic, but many detailed aspects of the resonant response to this array of semidiurnal frequencies remain unexplained.

The magnitude of Fundy tides may be seen as having been reached by a balance between a dissipative mechanism, with assumed quadratic frictional forces, and an energy imparting mechanism in the deep ocean where work done by the tide raising force is proportional to distance travelled and hence to the first power of amplitude. Further, it now appears that the second and third North Atlantic modes are those primarily stimulated by the Fundian resonance. To represent these processes within one model both the continental shelf shallows and oceanic areas must be included, as well as their zone of interaction across the continental shelf.

5. Numerical models of oceanic tides. Large-scale numerical calculations of global oceanic M_2 tides have been undertaken by Bogdanov and Magarik [**3**], Pekeris and Accad [**23**], Zahel [**31**] and Hendershott [**14**], the continental shelf shallows being omitted and treated as coastlines with various assumptions of permeability or impedance. Fairly good qualitative agreement for the North Atlantic has been obtained. However the substantial energy flows into the Gulf of Maine, Baffin Bay, or the English Channel-Irish Sea region suggest that accurate representation of these resonant sea motions will require detailed modelling of the dissipative regions. As deep sea tidal observations have been possible only recently and at limited numbers of stations, a detailed reconciliation of theory and observation will take many years, but it is now regarded as feasible two hundred years after Laplace [**15**] and nearly three hundred after Newton [**22**].

Such oceanic tidal models involve large-scale numerical computation (Heaps [**13**]), as thousands of grid points and depth measurements are needed to begin to represent the far from smooth topography of coastlines and ocean depths. To represent one harmonic tidal constituent such as M_2 a periodic solution is required, and this is found by calculating a sufficient number of tidal cycles to obtain convergence to a periodic solution for large times. Whereas in shallow waters with comparatively strong bottom friction a few cycles may suffice, a hundred cycles may be required for a deep ocean model, even with devices for acceleration of convergence. For problems of this scale the older explicit methods of numerical solution of partial differential equations are giving way to the more stable implicit and alternating direction methods that permit much longer time steps [**18**].

A brief description will now be given of an attempt made by the author to model the combined shallow dissipative region, in this case the Bay of Fundy and Gulf of Maine, and the deep sea region, in this case the North Atlantic. To obtain a detailed representation of the Bay of Fundy and at the same time a uniform coordinate grid suitable for implicit methods, a transformed system of spherical coordinates with pole about 3° inland from the New Brunswick coast was adopted. The system can thus be plotted on a Mercator projection with this point as North Pole. The oceanic region comprises the North Atlantic from Newfoundland to the Azores, thence to the African and South American coasts and then on a line through the West Indies to the coast of North America. The local conformal condition for a first-order square grid leads to the use of equal intervals of the longitude ϕ and of $y = \log \tan[\theta/2 + \pi/4]$, where θ represents latitude in the transformed system. Of 2,000 grid points in total, 32 lie in the Bay of Fundy and 200 in the Gulf of Maine.

The finite difference equations in this model are formulated with a splitting of z into two components $z = z_1 + z_2$ where the time rates of change of z_1 and z_2 are obtained as the x and y terms of the continuity equation. In each momentum equation, the corresponding z term is treated implicitly while the other term is included explicitly and the time steps for the two implicit systems are staggered to avoid extrapolation of explicit terms. In effect, the model treats two implicit systems of one-dimensional channels, each with explicit crossover terms. Tide raising forcing terms based on zero lunar declination and boundary data based on the oceanic tidal models described above are used.

Preliminary results from this model indicate that tidal barrier construction at the three preferred sites will increase the M_2 amplitude at Economy Point, Nova Scotia, and decrease the amplitude at the New Brunswick sites.

Further refinement of such models will be necessary if reliable forecasts for large-scale projects are ultimately required. Features such as self-gravitation, crustal reaction, and the effect of solid earth tides present themselves for consideration, and for the latter two more observational studies are needed.

6. The control problem for tidal energy generation. Let a one-dimensional channel have headwater at a, barrier position b and open sea boundary c on the x-axis; let $Z(x, t)$ denote sea level above equilibrium at point x, $Q(x, t)$ the flow at x, $Q = A(x, t)u(x, t)$ where $A(x,t)$ is cross section and $u(x, t)$ current. Let $b(x,t)$ denote surface breadth of the channel, and $k = 0.003$ the dimensionless quadratic friction constant. The equations of motion in this channel take the form (Proudman **[29]**, Yuen **[30]**)

$$Z_t = -\frac{1}{b(x)} Q_x, \qquad Q_t = -AgZ_x - \frac{kQ|Q|}{A(x)H}, \tag{6.1}$$

where $H = D + Z$ again denotes total depth and g gravity.

Boundary conditions are $Q(a, t) = 0$ and $Z(c, t) = Z_0(c) \cos(\omega t - \Upsilon)$, while at the barrier position b, Z is in general discontinuous, and $Q(b,t)$ is regulated by sluice and turbine controls (Duff **[6]**). Thus $Q_b = Q(b,t) = \lambda q + \mu \bar{V}$ where λ $(-1 \leqq \lambda \leqq 1)$ is the "double effect" two-way turbine control with maximum flow q, and μ $(0 \leqq \mu \leqq 1)$ is the sluice control with maximum permitted flow $\bar{V}$ which for simplicity may be assumed to have the Torricellian form

$$\bar{V} = g^{1/2} A \left| Z_+ - Z_- \right|^{1/2} \operatorname{sgn}(Z_+ - Z_-)$$

in terms of the limiting values Z_+, Z_- of sea level on either side of the barrier.

Let $N(q, h)$ denote the power derived from turbines operating at head $h = |Z_+ - Z_-|$ and flow q, and let $p(t)$ denote the unit value of power at time t. Assuming the conservation of total water mass rather than (6.1), Gibrat formulated the problem of maximizing returns from a tidal power plant as a problem in the calculus of variations (Gibrat **[10]**, Godin **[11]**), and these results are effectively in use at the 240 megawatt Rance tidal power station at St. Malo. Integration by parts of the first variation of J yields initial terminal and boundary conditions for ϕ, Φ, a barrier condition for ϕ, as well as conditions for the variations of λ and μ, namely for λ

$$p(t)\,(\partial N/\partial q_1)(q, h) - [\phi/b]_-^+ \begin{cases} > 0, & \lambda = +1, \\ = 0, & -1 < \lambda < +1, \\ < 0, & \lambda = -1, \end{cases} \tag{6.2}$$

and for μ,

$$[\phi/b]_-^+ \bar{V} \begin{cases} > 0, & \mu = 0, \\ < 0, & \mu = 1. \end{cases} \tag{6.3}$$

The dual partial differential equations for ϕ, Φ take the following forms (with certain additional minor simplifications)

$$\phi_t + \frac{\partial}{\partial x}(Ag\,\Phi) = 0, \qquad \Phi_t + \frac{\partial}{\partial x}\left(\frac{\phi}{b}\right) - 2k\frac{|Q|\Phi}{AH} = 0. \tag{6.4}$$

The combined Hamiltonian system (6.1), (6.2), (6.3), (6.4) gives optimal (or at least, extremal) solutions to the control problem (Pontryagin **[28]**). Because terminal conditions for Φ, ϕ are required, the usual complexities of a time horizon appear. However for periodic solutions these difficulties can be avoided and numerical solutions obtained for single semidiurnal periods or fortnightly or monthly cycles involving two or more frequencies and corresponding to spring and neap tidal cycles (Duff [7]).

Such a system in operation can be regarded as having limited artificial intelligence directed toward the extraction of energy from the tidal sea motions. The apparent strategy such a system will follow involves the maximizing at certain times of operating head h by the timing of internal surges in the enclosed basin, and the operation of sluice gates to maximize the extraction of energy from the sea in accordance with the change of resonance created by the barrier itself. A complete synthesis of these considerations will require a combination of the most extensive tidal models with such a control system.

References

1. L. Amerio and G. Prouse, *Almost periodic functions and functional equations*, Van Nostrand Reinhold, New York, 1971. MR **43** #819.

2. Atlantic Tidal Power Programming Board "Fundy Tidal Power", Report and 11 appendices, Ottawa and Halifax, 1969.

3. K. I. Bogdanov and V. Magarik, *Numerical solutions to the problem of distribution of semidiurnal tides M_2 and S_2 in the world oceans*, Dokl. Acad. Nauk. SSSR **172** (1967), 1315–1317. (Russian)

4. H. Brezis, *Problèmes unilateraux*, Thesis, Paris, 1970.

5. G. F. D. Duff, *Tidal resonance and tidal barriers in the Bay of Fundy system*, J. Fish. Res. Bd. Canada **27** (1970), 1701–1728.

6. ———, *A note on hydrodynamic optimization for tidal barriers*, Proc. 25th Canad. Math. Congress, 1971, pp. 337–348.

7. ———, *Mathematical problems of Tidal Energy*, Séminaires IRIA, Analyse et Controle des Systèmes, 1973, pp. 97–174.

8. C. J. R. Garrett, *Tidal resonance in the Bay of Fundy and Gulf of Maine*, Nature **238** (1972), 441.

9. ———, *Normal modes of the Bay of Fundy and Gulf of Maine*, Canad. J. Earth Sciences **11** (1974), 549–556.

10. R. Gibrat, *L'energie des Marées*, Presses Universitaires de France, 1966.

11. G. Godin, *Theory of the exploitation of tidal energy and its application to the Bay of Fundy*, J. Fish. Res. Bd. Canada **26** (1969), 2887–2957.

12. ———, *The analysis of tides*, University of Toronto Press, 1972.

13. N. S. Heaps, *A two dimensional numerical sea model*, Philos. Trans. Roy. Soc. A **265** (1969), 93–137.

14. M. Hendershott and W. H. Munk, *Tides*, Ann. Rev. Fluid Mech. **2** (1970), 205–224.

15. P. S. de Laplace, *Recherches sur quelques points du système du monde*, Mém. Acad. Roy. Sci., 1775; *Oeuvres complètes* (9), 88, 187.

16. J.-L. Lions and W. A. Strauss, *Some non-linear evolution equations*, Bull. Soc. Math. France **93** (1965), 43–96. MR **33** #7663.

17. M. S. Longuet-Higgins and G. S. Pond, *The forced oscillations of fluid on a hemisphere bounded by meridians of longitude*, Philos. Trans. Roy. Soc. A **266** (1970), 193–233.

18. G. I. Marchuk, R. D. Gordeev, V. Ya. Rivkind and B. A. Kagan, *A numerical method for the solution of tidal dynamics equations and the results of its application*, J. Computational Physics **13** (1973), 15–34.

19. R. E. Meyer, *Resonance of unbounded water bodies*, Lectures in Appl. Math., vol. 14, Amer. Math. Soc., Providence, R. I., 1971, pp. 189–228.

20. J.W. Miles and W. H. Munk, *Harbor paradox,* J. Waterways Harb., Div. Am. Soc. Civ. Eng. **87** (1961), 111–129.

21. W. H. Munk and G. J. F. MacDonald, *The rotation of the earth: A geophysical discussion*, Cambridge Monographs on Mechanics and Appl. Math., Cambridge Univ. Press, New York, 1960. MR **22** #9277.

22. Isaac Newton, *Principia.* Books II, III, London, 1687.

23. C. L. Pekeris and Y. Accad, *Solution of Laplace's equation for the M_2 tide in the world oceans*, Philos. Trans. Roy. Soc. A **265** (1969), 413–436.

24. G. W. Platzman, *Ocean tides and related waves*, Lectures in Appl. Math., vol. 14, Amer. Math. Soc., Providence, R. I., 1971, pp. 239–292.

25. ———, *Two dimensional free oscillations in natural basins*, J. Phys. Ocean. **2** (1972), 117–138.

26. ———, *North Atlantic Ocean, preliminary description of normal modes*, Science **178** (1972), 156–157.

27. H. Poincaré, *Sur l'equilibre et les mouvements des mers*, Liouville **5** (1896), 57–217.

28. L. S. Pontrjagin, V. G. Boltjanskiĭ, R. V. Gamkrelidze and E. F. Miščenko, *The mathematical theory of optimal processes*, Fizmatgiz, Moscow, 1961; English transl., Wiley, New York, 1962. MR **29** #3316b.

29. J. Proudman, *Dynamical oceanography*, Methuen, London, 1953.

30. K. B. Yuen, *Effect of tidal barriers on the M_2 tide in the Bay of Fundy*, J. Fish. Res. Bd. Canada **26** (1969), 2477–2492.

31. W. Zahel, *Die Reproduktion Gezeitenbedingter Bewegungsvorgänge in Weltozean mittels des hydrodynamische-numerische Verfahrens*, Mitt. Inst. Meereskunde der Univ. Hamburg **17** (1970).

32. S. Zaidman, *Sur la presque-périodicité des solutions de l'équation des ondes non-homogéne*, J. Math. Mech. **8** (1959), 369–382. MR **21** #2812

University of Toronto
Toronto, Ontario, Canada M5S 1A1

Proceedings of the International Congress of Mathematicians
Vancouver, 1974

Recent Progress in Classical Fourier Analysis

Charles Fefferman*

In what sense does $\int_{R^n} e^{ix\cdot\xi}\hat{f}(\xi)\,d\xi$ converge to a given function f on R^n? How do properties such as the size and smoothness of f influence the behavior of its Fourier transform $\hat{f}$? These simple questions lie at the heart of much of classical analysis. Their deeper study leads naturally to certain basic auxiliary operators defined on functions on R^n; and Fourier analysts seek to understand these operators and their generalizations, and to apply them to various branches of analysis. In this paper I shall describe some basic results and applications of Fourier analysis and speculate briefly on the future. I have left out many topics of great importance, and emphasized merely those subjects I know something about.

Let me begin by sketching the state of the art as of about 1950. At that time, the field was well developed only in the one-dimensional case. Since it had long been known that the Fourier series of a continuous function on $[0, 2\pi]$ need not converge at every point, Lebesgue measure (and in particular L^p) was clearly recognized as a basic tool. The Plancherel theorem $\int_0^{2\pi}|f(x)|^2\,dx = 2\pi\sum_{-\infty}^{\infty}|a_k|^2$ with $f(x) \sim \sum_{-\infty}^{\infty} a_k e^{ikx}$ gave a complete characterization of L^2 functions in terms of their Fourier coefficients and established norm convergence of Fourier series. However, the study of L^p $(p \neq 2)$ was known to be much harder. As an indication of the difficulty of the problems of L^p, take a function $f(x) \sim \sum_{-\infty}^{\infty} a_k e^{ikx}$ belonging to L^p $(p < 2)$ but not to L^2, and modify its Fourier series by writing $g(x) \sim \sum_{-\infty}^{\infty} \pm a_k e^{ikx}$ with each $\pm$ sign picked independently by flipping a coin. Then with probability one, g does not belong to L^p (or even to L^1) but is merely a distribution with nasty singularities. Consequently, the assertion $f \sim \sum_{-\infty}^{\infty} a_k e^{ikx} \in L^p$ depends not only on the sizes $|a_k|$ of the Fourier coefficients, but also on subtle relationships among the phases $\arg(a_k)$.

*I could not have prepared this article without very generous help by Mrs. Yit-Sin Choo and Dr. K. G. Choo.

Despite the difficulty of the problem, a fair amount was known by 1940 about the relationship between the size of a function and the nature of its Fourier series, thanks to pioneering efforts by Hardy and Littlewood, M. Riesz, Paley, Zygmund, Marcinkiewicz and others. A result typical of the deepest work is as follows (see **[95]**):

THEOREM 1 (LITTLEWOOD-PALEY). *Let* $\{S_k\}_{k=-\infty}^{+\infty}$ *be a sequence of* $\pm$ *signs which stays constant on each dyadic block. (A dyadic block is an interval of the form* $[2^N, 2^{N+1})$ *or* $(-2^{N+1}, -2^N]$*; the collection of all dyadic blocks will be denoted by* Δ.) *Then if* $f(x) \sim \sum_{\infty}^{-\infty} a_k e^{ikx}$ *belongs to* L^p $(1 < p < \infty)$, *it follows that* $\sum_{-\infty}^{\infty} S_k a_k e^{ikx}$ *also belongs to* L^p.

Thus, although the phases $\arg(a_k)$ play a decisive role in determining the size of $\sum_{-\infty}^{\infty} a_k e^{ikx}$, only the relationship of $\arg(a_k)$ to relatively "nearby" $\arg(a_{k'})$ really matters.

Although the original techniques used to prove this and related theorems are very complicated, the underlying strategy is simple. The starting point is to rewrite Dirichlet's formula for the Nth partial sum of a Fourier series as

$$\begin{aligned} S_N f(x) &= e^{-iNx} \int_{R^1} e^{iN(x-y)} f(x-y) \frac{dy}{y} - e^{iNx} \int_{R^1} e^{-iN(x-y)} (x-y) \frac{dy}{y} \\ &= e^{-iNx} H(e^{iNy} f(y)) - e^{+iNx} H(e^{-iNy} f(y)) \end{aligned}$$

with $Hf(x) \equiv \int_{R^1} (f(x-y)/y)\, dy$, the integral being interpreted in the principal-value sense. (Hf is called the Hilbert transform of f.) This is a bold step, since for $C_0^\infty(R^1)$ (say), the integral in Dirichlet's formula converges absolutely, while that defining the Hilbert transform does not.

Now the Hilbert transform also arises in complex analysis, for if $F = u + iv$ is a well-behaved analytic function on the upper half-plane R_+^2, then on the boundary R^1, v is the Hilbert transform of u. Therefore we may hope to prove theorems on the Hilbert transform and related operators via complex analysis (e.g., Cauchy's theorem, Jensen's formula and Blaschke products, conformal mapping) and then translate the results into information on Fourier series. To illustrate the "complex method", let us prove a simple case of M. Riesz's famous theorem that the Fourier series of an L^p function on $[0, 2\pi]$ converges in norm $(1 < p < \infty)$. This comes down to proving that the Hilbert transform is bounded on $L^p(R^1)$, and we give the argument for the easiest nontrivial case $p = 4$. Given a well-behaved analytic function $F = u + iv$ on R_+^2, we have to show that $\int_{R^1} v^4\, dx \leqq C \int_{R^1} u^4\, dx$ with C independent of F. However, Cauchy's theorem for $F^4 = u^4 + 4iu^3v - 6u^2v^2 - 4iuv^3 + v^4$ yields $\int_{R^1} F^4\, dx = 0$ so that $0 = \int_{R^1} \mathrm{Re}(F^4)\, dx = \int_{R^1} (u^4 - 6u^2 v^2 + v^4)\, dx$. Hence $\int_{R^1} v^4\, dx \leqq 6 \int_{R^1} u^2v^2\, dx \leqq 6 (\int_{R^1} u^4\, dx)^{1/2} (\int_{R^1} v^4\, dx)^{1/2}$ by Cauchy-Schwarz. Dividing both sides by $(\int_{R^1} v^4 dx)^{1/2}$ and squaring gives the desired inequality $\int_{R^1} v^4\, dx \leqq 36 \int_{R^1} u^4 dx$. The general case $(p \neq 4)$ is similar, though not so easy.[1]

[1]See the ingenious paper of S. Pichorides **[72]** for the exact norm of the Hilbert transform on L^p and other related constants.

Now I can give a vague idea of the proof of the Littlewood-Paley theorem. The idea is to relate an auxiliary operator S arising from complex analysis with an operator G arising from Fourier series. Specifically, given $f \sim \sum_k a_k e^{ikx}$ on $[0, 2\pi]$ (say $a_0 = 0$), we break up the Fourier series into dyadic blocks

$$f \sim \sum_k a_k e^{ikx} = \sum_{I \in \Delta} \left(\sum_{k \in I} a_k e^{ikx} \right) \equiv \sum_{I \in \Delta} f_I(x)$$

and define $G(f)$ as $G(f)(x) = (\sum_{I \in \Delta} |f_I(x)|^2)^{1/2}$. The function $S(f)$ is defined in terms of the Poisson integral $u(r, \theta)$ of f by the equation

$$S(f)(x) = \left(\iint_{(r,\theta) \in \Gamma(x)} |\nabla u(r, \theta)|^2 \, r \, dr \, d\theta \right)^{1/2}$$

where $\Gamma(x)$ is the Stoltz domain $\{(r, \theta) | \, |x - \theta| < 1 - r < \frac{1}{2}\}$ in the unit disc. $S^2(f)$ has a natural interpretation as the area of the image of $\Gamma(x)$ under the analytic function $u + iv$ whose real part is u. For our purposes, the basic facts concerning S and G are:

(a) $\|S(f)\|_p \sim \|f\|_p$ $(1 < p < \infty)$. In other words, $\|S(f)\|_p / \|f\|_p$ is bounded above and below. This can be proved by complex methods. Note that already (a) contains the L^p-boundedness of the Hilbert transform, since for $F = u + iv$ analytic we have $|\nabla u| = |\nabla v|$ by the Cauchy-Riemann equations, and hence $S(u) = S(v)$.

(b) $\|S(f)\|_p \sim \|G(f)\|_p$ $(1 < p < \infty)$. Limitations of space prevent even a vague description of the proof, but the basic tool here is the L^p-boundedness of the Hilbert transform acting on functions which take their values in a Hilbert space.

Once we know (a) and (b), the Littlewood-Paley theorem follows at once, since evidently $f = \sum_{I \in \Delta} f_I$ and $g = \sum_{I \in \Delta} \pm f_I$ always have the same G-function. An extensive discussion of the Littlewood-Paley theorem and of complex methods in general may be found in Zygmund [**95**]. It must be admitted that the ingenious complex-variable proofs of classical Fourier analysis leave the researcher in the unhappy position of accepting the main theorems of the subject without any real intuitive explanation of why they are true.

Now I want to speak of the profound changes which took place in classical Fourier analysis, starting with the fundamental paper of Calderón and Zygmund [**17**] in 1952.[2] We shall be concerned here with efforts to generalize the basic operators, especially the Hilbert transform, from R^1 to R^n. These generalizations are anything but routine, because Blaschke products do not generalize to functions of several complex variables, and consequently (for this and other reasons) the whole complex method has to be abandoned and the results reproved by real-variable techniques. Moreover, the real-variable methods and the n-variable analogues of the Hilbert transform, S-function, etc., play an important role in partial differential equations, several complex variables, probability and potential theory, and will probably continue to find further applications as time goes on.

The operators. Let us begin with the Laplace equation $\Delta u = f$ in R^n $(n > 2)$

[2]In retrospect we can see many of the ideas anticipated in the work of Titchmarsh, Besicovitch, and Marcinkiewicz. (See [**95**].)

which one solves with the standard Newtonian potential

$$u(x) = c_n \int_{R^n} \frac{f(y)\,dy}{|x-y|^{n-2}}. \tag{1}$$

If f belongs to some function space (L^p, Lip(α), $C(R^n)$, etc.) does it follow that the second derivatives of u all belong to the same function space? Differentiating the right-hand side of (1) (carefully) under the integral sign, we obtain for the second derivatives of u the formula

$$u_{jk}(x) = \frac{\partial^2 u(x)}{\partial x_j \partial x_k} = c_{jk} f(x) + \int_{R^n} \frac{\Omega_{jk}(x-y)}{|x-y|^n} f(y)\,dy, \tag{2}$$

where Ω_{jk} is homogeneous of degree zero, and smooth away from the origin. Note that the integral in (2) diverges absolutely, but at least for "nice" functions f we may define that integral as

$$\lim_{\varepsilon\to 0+} \int_{|x-y|>\varepsilon} \frac{\Omega_{jk}(x-y)}{|x-y|^n} f(y)\,dy,$$

and the limit exists by virtue of the essential cancellation $\int_{S^{n-1}} \Omega_{jk}(y)\,dy = 0$. In general, a *singular integral operator* is defined on functions on R^n by

$$Tf(x) = \lim_{\varepsilon\to 0} \int_{|x-y|>\varepsilon} \frac{\Omega(x-y)}{|x-y|^n} f(y)\,dy, \tag{3}$$

where Ω is reasonably smooth and homogeneous of degree zero, and $\int_{S^{n-1}} \Omega(y)dy = 0$. For example, if we set $\Omega(y) = \operatorname{sgn}(y)$ on R^1, then (3) becomes $Tf(x) = \int_{R^1} (f(y)\,dy/(x-y))$, i.e., T is the Hilbert transform. Thus regularity properties of solutions to the Laplace equation come down to boundedness on various function spaces of a few specific singular integral operators; that is, certain n-variable generalizations of the Hilbert transform.

More generally, the theory of singular integral operators plays an essential role in a host of problems of partial differential equations. To see why, start with a pure mth order differential operator

$$L = \sum_{|\alpha|=m} a_\alpha(x) \left(\frac{\partial}{\partial x_1}\right)^{\alpha_1} \cdots \left(\frac{\partial}{\partial x_n}\right)^{\alpha_n},$$

and write

$$L = \left(\sum_{|\alpha|=m} a_\alpha(x) R_1^{\alpha_1} \cdots R_n^{\alpha_n}\right)\cdot(-\Delta)^{-m/2},$$

where $R_j = (\partial/\partial x_j)(-\Delta)^{-1/2}$. Now R_j is called the jth Riesz transform, and is given as a singular integral operator by the formula

$$R_j f(x) = c\int_{R^n} \frac{x_j - y_j}{|x-y|^{n+1}} f(y)\,dy.$$ [3]

(Note that in one dimension, the single Riesz transform is just the Hilbert trans-

[3] See Horváth **[52]** and Stein **[85]**.

form.) Therefore, L factors as $L = T(-\Delta)^{m/2}$, where T is a *variable-coefficient singular integral operator*, i.e., an operator of the form

(4) $$Tf(x) = c(x)f(x) + \int_{R^n} \frac{\Omega(x, (x-y)/|x-y|)}{|x-y|} f(y)\, dy,$$

with $c(\cdot) \in C^\infty(R^n)$, $\Omega \in C(R^n \times S^{n-1})$, and $\int_{S^{n-1}} \Omega(x, \omega)\, d\omega = 0$ for all x. In other words, modulo the factor $(-\Delta)^{m/2}$ a partial differential operator is merely a special type of singular integral operator.

As a substitute for the Fourier transform, we associate to the operator T of (4) its *symbol* $\sigma(T)$ defined by

(5) $$\sigma(x, \xi) = c(x) + \int_{R^n} \frac{\Omega(x, \omega/|\omega|)}{|\omega|^n} e^{i\xi\cdot\omega}\, d\omega.$$

Clearly, $\sigma(x, \xi)$ is homogeneous of degree zero in ξ and smooth on $R^n \times (R^n \backslash 0)$. In the special case $T = (\sum_{|\alpha|=m} a_\alpha(x)(\partial/\partial x)^\alpha)(-\Delta)^{-m/2}$ the symbol is just $\sigma(x, \xi) = \sum_{|\alpha|=m} a_\alpha(x)(i\xi)^\alpha/|\xi|^m$. Moreover,

(6) Every smooth homogeneous $\sigma(x, \xi)$ on R^{2n} arises as the symbol of a unique singular integral operator, which we denote by $\sigma(x, D)$.

(7) The class of all symbols forms an algebra of functions. The mapping $\sigma(x, \xi) \to \sigma(x, D)$ is an approximate homomorphism from functions to operators. That is, $\sigma_1(x, D) \circ \sigma_2(x, D) = (\sigma_1 \cdot \sigma_2)(x, D) +$ a "negligible" error.

(8) The adjoint of $\sigma(x, D)$ is given approximately by the complex-conjugate symbol: $(\sigma(x, D))^* = \bar{\sigma}(x, D) +$ a "negligible" error.

By virtue of (6)—(8) we may construct useful operators merely by making elementary manipulations with symbols. For instance, an elliptic singular integral operator $\sigma(x, D)$ (i.e., an operator with nonvanishing symbol) evidently has an approximate inverse—we simply take $(1/\sigma)(x, D)$—and the standard interior regularity results on elliptic partial differential equations follow easily from these observations.

So far we have described the theory as it first appeared in the pioneering work of Calderón [**12**] on uniqueness of solutions to Cauchy problems. (Calderón used singular integrals to diagonalize a matrix of differential operators. See also earlier work of Giraud [**43**] and Mihlin [**66**].) Nowadays it is more common to work with the closely related theory of pseudodifferential operators, invented by Kohn and Nirenberg [**60**] and developed by Seeley [**75**], Hörmander [**48**], [**49**], Calderón and Vaillancourt [**16**] and others. To arrive at the notion of pseudodifferential operators[4] one uses (5) and the Fourier inversion formula in (4) to obtain

(9) $$Tf(x) = \int_{R^n} e^{ix\cdot\xi}\sigma(x, \xi)\hat{f}(\xi)\, d\xi.$$

Now we take (9) as the definition of $\sigma(x, D)$, broaden the class of symbols to include all functions satisfying suitable estimates, say

(10) $$|(\partial/\partial x)^\alpha (\partial/\partial \xi)^\beta \sigma| \leqq C_{\alpha\beta}|\xi|^{-|\beta|} \quad \text{for all } \alpha, \beta,$$

[4]Actually Kohn and Nirenberg were led to pseudodifferential operators by their work on the $\bar{\partial}$-Neumann problem of several complex variables.

and prove refinements of (7) and (8) directly from (9). Pseudodifferential operators have the advantage of making it relatively easy to refine (7) and (8) to "Leibniz' rules"

(11) $a(x, D)\circ b(x, D) = (a\circ b)(x, D)$ with $(a\circ b)(x, \xi) \sim \sum_\alpha (1/\alpha)\, [\partial/\partial\xi]^\alpha\, a\cdot[i^{-1}\partial/\partial x]^\alpha b$

and

$$(a(x, D))^* = a\#(x, D) \text{ with } a\# \sim \sum_\alpha \frac{1}{\alpha!}\left[\frac{1}{i}\frac{\partial}{\partial x}\right]^\alpha\left[\frac{\partial}{\partial\xi}\right]^\alpha \bar{a}. \quad (12)$$

Later on, we shall see problems in which singular integrals have advantages over pseudodifferential operators. However, for many purposes the two theories are equivalent.

The applications of pseudodifferential operators to index problems in topology and geometry are so well known that it is enough for me to pay them lip service. But I would like to take a few paragraphs to explain two recent developments in partial differential equations in which pseudodifferential operators and singular integrals played a crucial rôle. Both developments have their roots in a basic phenomenon of several complex variables, namely that the restriction of an analytic function F to a hypersurface $V \subseteq C^n$ satisfies a system of partial differential equations. To see this, we start with the n Cauchy-Riemann equations $\partial F/\partial\bar{z}_j = 0$ in C^n. From the restriction of F to the hypersurface V, we know only the $2n - 1$ tangential derivatives of F, and thus we must solve one of the Cauchy-Riemann equations for the remaining (normal) derivative. Consequently, the restriction of F to V must satisfy $n - 1$ first-order partial differential equations, called the *tangential Cauchy-Riemann equations* on V.

Our first topic in partial differential equations arises from the case $V =$ the unit sphere in C^2, where are we dealing with one equation in one unknown. In a suitable coordinate system on the sphere, that equation takes the form

$$[\partial/\partial t + i(\partial/\partial x + t\partial/\partial y)]F = 0.$$

Therefore it is natural to try to "correct" functions which are "close to to analytic" by solving

$$[\partial/\partial t + i(\partial/\partial x + t\partial/\partial y)]u = f, \quad (13)$$

with $f \in C^\infty$ (say). Such "correction" procedures are common practice in complex variables. Thus, the discovery, by H. Lewy in 1957 **[63]** that equation (13) cannot be solved, even if we require $f \in C^\infty$ and demand only that u be a distribution defined in some neighborhood of a point, came as a great shock to researchers in partial differential equations. Prior to Lewy's discovery, it was universally assumed that all nondegenerate linear partial differential equations (and certainly those arising from "real life") could be solved. After Lewy's paper, intensive research began on the problem of deciding which equations admit local solutions. At the moment, systematic results are available only for equations of principal type, i.e., roughly equations in which all lower-order terms may be regarded as trivial perturbations of the highest-order terms. These include the Laplace and wave equations, but not the heat equation or the Schrödinger equation. For equations $\sum_{|\alpha|=m} a_\alpha(x)(i^{-1}\partial/\partial x)^\alpha u = f$ of principal type, Nirenberg and Trèves **[70]**, **[71]** formulated the following condition and amassed overwhelming evidence to show that it is necessary and sufficient for existence of local solutions:

(P) Let $a(x, \xi)$ and $b(x, \xi)$ be the real and imaginary parts of $\sum_{|\alpha|=m} a_\alpha(x)\xi^\alpha$. Then for any point $(x_0, \xi_0) \in R^n \times (R^n\backslash 0)$ with $a(x_0, \xi_0) = b(x_0, \xi_0) = 0$, the function b has constant sign when restricted to the "bicharacteristic curve" $(x(t), \xi(t))$ obtained by solving the ordinary differential equations $\dot{x}_j = \partial a/\partial \xi_j$, $\dot{\xi}_j = -\partial a/\partial x_j$, $(x(0), \xi(0)) = (x_0, \xi_0)$.

In fact condition (P) is now known to imply local solvability (see Beals and Fefferman **[4]**, **[5]** as well as Hörmander **[50]**, Egorov **[26]**, **[27]**, and Trèves **[92]**, **[93]**). There is no space here to discuss the ideas in any detail. Let me just mention two of the main techniques, namely the use of canonical transformations in (x, ξ)-space to "straighten out" the zero sets of symbols of pseudodifferential operators via conjugation with Fourier integral operators (discussion of which would take us too far afield), and "microlocalization", i.e., the use of suitable partitions of unity $1 = \sum_j \phi_j(x, \xi)$ in (x, ξ)-space to define approximate projection operators $\phi_j(x, D)$ and thus split $L^2(R^n)$ into a big direct sum of subspaces $H_j =$ image of $\phi_j(x, D)$. By microlocalizing, we hope to split up one hard problem into many easy ones, and then patch the easy results together. In patching together, one has to use a calculus of pseudodifferential operators with "exotic" symbols Ω satisfying merely

$$|(\partial/\partial x)^\alpha (\partial/\partial \xi)^\beta \sigma| \leqq C_{\alpha\beta} |\xi|^{|\alpha|/2-|\beta|/2}$$

instead of the usual estimates (10). We shall say more about exotic symbols later on.

Now let us return to the tangential Cauchy-Riemann equations on the sphere $S^{2n-1} \subseteq C^n$, and this time suppose $n > 2$. A linear fractional transformation maps the sphere to the hypersurface $H = \{(z', z^n) \in C^{n-1} \times C^1 \,|\, \mathrm{Re}(z^n) = |z'|^2\}$, which has the structure of a nilpotent Lie group under the multiplication law $(z', z^n)\cdot(w', w^n) = (z'+w', z^n+w^n+2z'\cdot\bar{w}')$. By analogy with the R^n theory sketched above, one expects that very sharp results on existence and regularity of solutions of the tangential Cauchy-Riemann equations on H can be proved by using "singular integrals" of the form $Tf(x) = \int_H K(xy^{-1}) f(y)\, dy$, where K has appropriate properties of cancellation and homogeneity with respect to the natural "dilations" $\delta \circ (z', z^n) = (\delta z', \delta^2 z^n)$ on H. Moreover, once the results are known for H, one can build a "variable-coefficient" theory of "singular integrals" on (say) the boundary of a strongly pseudoconvex domain in C^n, by osculating the domain with biholomorphic images of H. Thus, a natural analogue of singular integrals provides a powerful machine to study the tangential Cauchy-Riemann equations. (Note that we cannot use the pseudodifferential operators viewpoint here, because the non-abelian Fourier transform on H is [so far] too cumbersome even to deal with the constant-coefficient case.) The ideas explained here come from Folland and Stein **[41]**, although singular integrals on nilpotent Lie groups have already appeared in Knapp and Stein **[59]** in connection with irreducibility of the principal series. See also Folland and Kohn [**40**] for the initial work of Kohn on tangential Cauchy-Riemann equations, as well as Folland [**39**] and Stein [**87**].[5]

I have attempted to show by a few examples how n-dimensional analogues of the Hilbert transform enter naturally into various branches of analysis. Let us now review some techniques which have been used to study such operators, and then see what insights we can gain into the Fourier transform in R^n.

The techniques. The first step in analyzing operators that generalize the Hilbert transform is to prove L^2-boundedness. Fortunately, this is often an easy consequence of the Plancherel theorem, as in the case of a constant-coefficient singular integral operator

$$Tf(x) = \int_{R^n} \frac{\Omega(x-y)}{|x-y|^n} f(y)\,dy$$

where one has $(\hat{T}f)(\xi) = \sigma(\xi)\hat{f}(\xi)$ with $\sigma \in L^\infty$. The S-function falls into this category —it is not hard to show that $\|S(f)\|_2 = (\text{const})\|f\|_2$. However, when an operator cannot be diagonalized by the Fourier transform or its variants, there are remarkably few L^2-techniques available to deal with it. Sometimes in a lucky case we may be able to reduce matters back to constant-coefficient questions. For instance, let

$$Tf(x) = \int_{R^2} \frac{\Omega(x, (x-y)/|x-y|)}{|x-y|^2} f(y)\,dy$$

be a variable-coefficient singular integral operator on R^2. For each fixed x we expand $\Omega(x, \cdot)$ in a Fourier series on the unit circle, obtaining $\Omega(x, \omega) = \sum_{k=-\infty}^{\infty} c_k(x)\Omega_k(\omega)$ with $\Omega_k(\omega) = e^{ik\theta}$ for $\omega = (r, \theta)$, and $c_0(x) \equiv 0$. Now our operator T may be expanded in a series of constant-coefficient operators $Tf(x) = \sum_{k=-\infty}^{\infty} c_k(x)T_k f(x)$, with

$$T_k f(x) = \int_{R^2} \frac{\Omega_k(x-y)}{|x-y|^2} f(y)\,dy.$$

Since $\Omega(x, \omega) \in C^\infty$, it follows that $|c_k(x)| \leqq C/(k^2+1)$ (say); moreover, the T_k $(k \neq 0)$ are uniformly bounded on L^2, as one sees from Plancherel. Therefore,

$$\|Tf\|_2 \leqq \sum_{k\neq 0} \frac{C}{k^2+1} \|T_k f\|_2 \leqq C\|f\|_2,$$

and our L^2-result is proved. In R^n $(n > 2)$ the same trick works, with Fourier series replaced by spherical harmonics.

A promising idea which has begun to find applications recently is Cotlar's lemma on "almost orthogonal operators".

LEMMA. *Suppose that the operators $T_1, T_2, \cdots, T_N$ on a Hilbert space H satisfy the "orthogonality conditions"*

---

[5]Compare with the theory of "parabolic" singular integrals devised by Jones [**58**], Fabes and Rivière [**28**], Lizorkin [**64**], Krée [**62**] and others; and in connection with parabolic singular integrals, see the recent striking results of Negel, Rivière and Wainger [**69**].

(14) $$\| T_i^* T_j \| \leqq C(i-j),$$

(15) $$\| T_i T_j^* \| \leqq C(i-j),$$

where $\|\cdot\|$ *denotes the operator norm, and* $\sum_{k=-\infty}^{\infty}(C(k))^{1/2} \leqq A$. *Then* $\|\sum_{k=1}^{N} T_k\| \leqq A$.

The simplest special case says merely that a direct sum $\sum_i \oplus T_i : \sum_i \oplus H_i \to \sum_i \oplus H_i$ of operators $T_i : H_i \to H_i$ has norm $\sup_i \|T_i\|$. The lemma was first given by Cotlar [**24**] in the case of commuting operators, and then extended by Knapp and Stein [**59**] to the general case. See also Calderón and Vaillancourt [**16**].

The proof of Cotlar's lemma is so simple that I can give it here. We start with the formulas

$$\left\|\sum_{i=1}^{N} T_i\right\| = \left\|\left(\sum_{i=1}^{N} T_i\right)\left(\sum_{i=1}^{N} T_i^*\right)\right\|^{1/2} = \left\|\left[\left(\sum_{i=1}^{N} T_i\right)\left(\sum_{i=1}^{N} T_i^*\right)\right]^k\right\|^{1/2k},$$

which imply

$$\left\|\sum_{i=1}^{N} T_i\right\|^{2k} \leqq \sum_{i_1, i_2 \cdots, i_{2k}=1}^{N} \| T_{i_1} T_{i_2}^* T_{i_3} \cdots T_{i_{2k-1}} T_{i_{2k}}^* \|.$$

Hypotheses (14) and (15) show that each summand on the right is dominated both by

$$\begin{aligned} \Lambda &= \|T_{i_1}\| \cdot \|T_{i_2}^* T_{i_3}\| \cdot \cdots \cdot \|T_{i_{2k-2}}^* T_{i_{2k-1}}\| \cdot \|T_{i_{2k}}^*\| \\ &\leqq C^{1/2}(0) C(i_2 - i_3) C(i_4 - i_5) \cdots C(i_{2k-2} - i_{2k-1}) C^{1/2}(0) \end{aligned}$$

and by

$$P = \|T_{i_1} T_{i_2}^*\| \cdot \|T_{i_3} T_{i_4}^*\| \cdot \cdots \cdot \|T_{i_{2k-1}} T_{i_{2k}}^*\| \leqq C(i_1 - i_2) C(i_3 - i_4) \cdots C(i_{2k-1} - i_{2k})$$

and hence also by the geometric mean $\Lambda^{1/2} P^{1/2} \leqq C^{1/2}(0) C^{1/2}(i_1 - i_2) C^{1/2}(i_2 - i_3) \cdots C^{1/2}(i_{2k-1} - i_{2k})$. Consequently,

$$\begin{aligned} \left\|\sum_{i=1}^{N} T_i\right\|^{2k} &\leqq \sum_{i_1, \cdots, i_{2k}=1}^{N} C^{1/2}(0) C^{1/2}(i_1 - i_2) C^{1/2}(i_2 - i_3) \cdots C^{1/2}(i_{2k-1} - i_{2k}) \\ &\leqq C^{1/2}(0) N A^{2k-1}, \end{aligned}$$

so that $\|\sum_{i=1}^{N} T_i\| \leqq (C^{1/2}(0)N)^{1/2k} A^{(2k-1)/2k}$. Now just let k tend to infinity, and Cotlar's lemma is proved.

To see how Cotlar's lemma applies to the operators we have been discussing, let us reprove the L^2-boundedness of the Hilbert transform without using the Plancherel theorem. The idea is simply to write

$$Hf(x) = \int_{R^1} \frac{f(x-y)\,dy}{y} = \sum_{j=-\infty}^{\infty} \int_{2^j \leqq |y| < 2^{j+1}} \frac{f(x-y)\,dy}{y} \equiv \sum_{j=-\infty}^{\infty} H_j f(x).$$

Each H_j is a convolution operator whose convolution kernel

$$\begin{aligned} K_j(y) &= y^{-1} \quad \text{if } 2^j \leqq |y| < 2^{j+1}, \\ &= 0 \quad \text{if not,} \end{aligned}$$

has L^1 norm dominated by a constant independent of j. Moreover, $H_i^* H_j = H_i H_j^*$ is the convolution operator with kernel $-K_i * K_j$, and elementary estimates using

$\int_{R^1} K_i(y)\,dy = \int_{R^1} K_j(y)\,dy = 0$ show that $\|K_i * K_j\|_1 \leqq C\cdot 2^{-|i-j|}$. Thus, $\|H_i^* H_j\| \leqq C\cdot 2^{-|i-j|}$ and $\|H_i H_j^*\| \leqq C^{-|i-j|}$, and the L^2-boundedness of $H = \sum_{i=-\infty}^{\infty} H_i$ is immediate from Cotlar's lemma.

Of course the L^2-boundedness of the Hilbert transform is nothing new. However, the proof sketched above applies also to the Knapp-Stein singular integrals on nilpotent groups—in fact it is the only method known to handle those operators, since as we pointed out earlier, the nonabelian Fourier transform does not help. Details are in **[59]**.

A second application of Cotlar's lemma is the theorem of Calderón and Vaillancourt **[16]** on L^2-boundedness of pseudodifferential operators with exotic symbols. (See also Hörmander **[49]** for earlier work on the subject, and Beals **[2]**, **[3]** for extensions and applications.) The basic special case of their result which one uses in microlocalization arguments for equations of principal type is the following.

THEOREM 2. *Assume that $\sigma(x, \xi)$ satisfies the estimates*

$$|(\partial/\partial x)^\alpha (\partial/\partial \xi)^\beta \sigma(x, \xi)| \leqq C_{\alpha\beta}(1 + |\xi|)^{|\alpha|/2-|\beta|/2}$$

for all multi-indices α, β. Then the corresponding pseduodifferential operator $\sigma(x, D)$ is bounded on L^2.

The main idea in the proof of the Calderón-Vaillancourt theorem is to apply Cotlar's lemma to the decomposition $\sigma(x, D) = \sum_{j=1}(\phi_j\sigma)(x, D)$, where $\sum_j \phi_j(x,\xi) = 1$ is a smooth partition of unity in (x, ξ)-space, constructed so that each ϕ_j is supported in a region of the form $\{(x, \xi)|\ |x - x_0| \leqq |\xi_0|^{-1/2},\ |\xi - \xi_0| \leqq |\xi_0|^{+1/2}\}$.

When neither the Plancherel theorem nor Cotlar's lemma applies, L^2-boundedness of singular operators presents very hard problems, each of which must (so far) be dealt with on its own terms. I shall mention two outstanding L^2-results of the last decade, and say a few words about their proofs and implications.

Commutator integrals. Let $D \subseteq \boldsymbol{C}^1$ be a domain bounded by a C^1 curve Γ. Just as in the case of the unit disc, there is a "Hilbert transform" T defined on functions on Γ which sends the real part $u|_\Gamma$ of an analytic function $F = u + iv$ to its imaginary part $v|_\Gamma$, and it is natural to ask whether T is bounded on $L^2(\Gamma)$ with respect to the arclength measure on Γ. This question is closely connected to the problem of understanding harmonic measure on Γ, i.e., the probability distribution of the place where a particle undergoing Brownian motion starting at a fixed point $P_0 \in D$ first hits Γ.

In effect, T is an integral operator on functions on $\boldsymbol{R}^1$, given by the formula

$$Tf(x) = \int_{-\infty}^{\infty} \frac{f(y)\,dy}{(x - y) + i(A(x) - A(y))}$$

with $A \in C^1(R^1)$. Expanding the denominator of the integrand in a geometric series we obtain T as an infinite sum of operators

$$T_k f(x) = \int_{-\infty}^{\infty} \frac{(A(x) - A(y))^k}{(x - y)^{k+1}} f(y)\,dy.$$

T_k is called the kth commutator integral corresponding to $A(x)$.

Commutator integrals also arise naturally when one tries to construct a calculus of singular integral operators to handle differential equations with nonsmooth coefficients. T_0 is just the Hilbert transform, but already the following two results are deep.

THEOREM 3. *Let A be a C^1 function on the line. Then*
(A) (*Calderón* [**14**], 1965) *T_1 is bounded on L^2.*
(B) (*Coifman and Y. Meyer* 1974, *still unpublished*) *T_2 is bounded on L^2.*

See also Calixto Calderón [**18**]. To prove (A), Calderón used special contour integration arguments which unforunately do not apply to higher T_k's. Coifman and Meyer modified and built on Calderón's ideas to produce a far more flexible proof, which can probably be pushed further in the near future to cover all the T_k's and possibly T itself. We shall return to commutators in a moment.

Pointwise convergence of Fourier series. No discussion of Fourier analysis can be complete without mentioning the fundamental theorem of Carleson [**19**] to the effect that the Fourier series of an L^2 function on $[0, 2\pi]$ converges almost everywhere. Carleson's theorem provides the sharpest and most satisfactory answer to the historic problem of representation of an "arbitrary" function as the sum of a Fourier series. The result came as a surprise for several reasons. First of all, most specialists thought that pointwise convergence would turn out to be false even for continuous functions, the supporting evidence being an old example of Kolmogoroff (see [**95**]) of an L^1 function with everywhere divergent Fourier series, and the fact that for thirty years no one had succeeded in improving the classical result of Kolmogoroff-Seliverstoff-Plessner which said that the nth partial sum of an L^2 Fourier series is $o((\log n)^{1/2})$ almost everywhere. Moreover, it was widely assumed that some radical new techniques would be needed to crack the pointwise convergence problem, while Carleson succeeded by pushing the known techniques very far and very hard.

Unfortunately, Carleson's proof is so technical that it is impossible in so little space to give even the vaguest idea of its inner workings. I will only point out that the problem reduces immediately to showing that

$$f \to Mf(x) = \sup_n \left| \int_{R^1} \frac{e^{iny} f(y)\, dy}{x - y} \right|$$

is bounded on L^2, so that pointwise convergence is really a problem about the Hilbert transform. R. Hunt extended Carleson's result to L^p $(p > 1)$ in [**54**], and his paper also gives the best presentation of Carleson's proof. P. Sjölin [**76**] proved the sharpest known result near L^1 (the Fourier series of f converges a.e. if $f \log^+ |f| \log^+ \log^+ |f| \in L^1$), and Sjölin [**77**], Tevzadze [**90**], and Fefferman [**30**], [**31**] discovered some extensions to functions of n variables. See also the alternate proof of Carleson's theorem [**33**] (based partly on Cotlar's lemma) whose relationship with Carleson's proof is not well understood.

Both Carleson's convergence theorem and the Calderón-Coifman-Meyer results are stated purely in terms of L^2, but, at least as far as we know today, purely L^2 methods are not strong enough for the proofs. In fact, the known proofs of the pointwise convergence and commutator theorems in one form or another involve the full force of the "Calderón-Zygmund" machinery described below, whose usual purpose is to pass from L^2 to L^p. I am not the only analyst who suspects a strong hidden connection between commutators and pointwise convergence. In any event, our understanding of L^2 boundedness of variable-coefficient operators is still rudimentary.

The "Calderón-Zygmund" techniques used to prove L^p boundedness of singular integrals contain the deepest ideas of the theory. In the next two sections, I hope to convey more than a superficial notion of how the proofs go, even though this necessitates a more technical discussion than is customary in a survey article.[6] We begin with a seeming digression on a topic in real variables.

The maximal function. As preparation for the L^p-theory of singular integrals, we shall discuss the following basic result of Hardy and Littlewood **[44]** and Wiener **[94]**.

THEOREM 4 (THE MAXIMAL THEOREM). *Define the maximal function Mf of a locally integrable function f on R^n by the equation*

$$Mf(x) = \sup_{Q \ni x} |Q|^{-1} \int_Q |f(y)|\, dy.$$

(Here Q denotes a cube in R^n with sides parallel to the coordinate axes.) Then we have the inequalities

$$\text{(A)} \qquad \|Mf\|_p \leqq C_p \|f\|_p \; (1 < p \leqq \infty),$$

$$\text{(B)} \qquad |\{Mf > \alpha\}| \leqq C\|f\|_1/\alpha.$$

The technical-looking result (B) is the heart of the matter—it is the natural conjecture that comes to mind upon staring at the simple example $f = \delta^{-1} \chi_{[-\delta, \delta]}$ on the line. (In that case, $Mf(x) \sim (\delta + x)^{-1}$.)

The maximal theorem is really a sharp form of Lebesgue's theorem on differentiability of the integral. For, one knows trivially that $|Q|^{-1}\int_Q f(y)\, dy \to f(x)$ as Q shrinks to x, whenever f belongs to the dense subspace $C_0^\infty \subseteq L^1$. To pass from the dense subspace to all of L^1 one needs an a priori inequality, and part (B) of the maximal theorem exactly does the job.

One set of applications of the maximal theorem concerns stronger theorems than Lebesgue's on differentiation of multiple integrals. In the plane R^2, for example, let $\boldsymbol{R}_0, \boldsymbol{R}_1, \boldsymbol{R}_2$ be respectively the family of all squares, the family of all rectangles with sides parallel to the coordinate axes, and the family of all rectangles with arbitrary direction. The standard Lebesgue theorem in R^2 says that $|R|^{-1} \int_R f(y_1, y_2)\, dy_1\, dy_2 \to f(x_1, x_2)$ a. e. for $f \in L^1(R^2)$, when $R \in \boldsymbol{R}_0$ shrinks to (x_1, x_2). What happens if we allow R to belong to the larger familes $\boldsymbol{R}_1$ and $\boldsymbol{R}_2$? The answer is contained in the following list of results:

[6]Much has been deleted from an original version of this article.

(16) $|R|^{-1} \int_R f(y_1, y_2)\, dy_1\, dy_2 \to f(x_1, x_2)$ a.e. as $R \in \boldsymbol{R}_1$ shrinks to (x_1, x_2), provided $f \in L^p(R^2)$ with $p > 1$.

(17) The result (16) may be sharpened—instead of $f \in L^p$ $(p > 1)$, it is enough to assume that $f \log^+|f|$ is integrable on R^2.

(18) However, there exist L^1 functions f for which $|R|^{-1} \int_R f(y_1, y_2)\, dy_1\, dy_2$ does not tend to a finite limit as $R \in \boldsymbol{R}_1$ shrinks to any point $(x_1, x_2) \in R^2$.

(19) The family $\boldsymbol{R}_2$ is even worse. Even for bounded functions f it may happen that $|R|^{-1} \int_R f(y_1, y_2)\, dy_1\, dy_2$ tends to $f(x_1, x_2)$ almost nowhere, as $R \in \boldsymbol{R}_2$ shrinks to (x_1, x_2).

The positive results (16) and (17) cannot be established by the usual textbook proof of Lebesgue's theorem, because the Vitali covering lemma is false if we use $\boldsymbol{R}_1$ in place of $\boldsymbol{R}_0$. However, with the aid of the maximal theorem (16) is a triviality. Since $|R|^{-1} \int_R f(y_1, y_2)\, dy_1\, dy_2 \to f(x_1, x_2)$ for f in the dense subspace $C_0^\infty \subseteq L^p$ $(1 < p < \infty)$, it is enough to prove the maximal inequality

$$(\mathrm{A}^+) \qquad \begin{gathered} \| M^+ f \|_p \leqq C_p \| f \|_p \ (1 < p < \infty) \text{ with} \\ M^+ f(x_1, x_2) = \sup_{R \ni (x_1, x_2);\, R \in \boldsymbol{R}_1} |R|^{-1} \int_R |f(y_1, y_2)|\, dy_1\, dy_2, \end{gathered}$$

just as in the familiar case of Lebesgue's theorem. Now set

$$M_1 f(x_1, x_2) = \sup_{Q \ni x_1;\, Q \subseteq R^1} |Q|^{-1} \int_Q |f(y_1, x_2)|\, dy_1$$

and

$$M_2 f(x_1, x_2) = \sup_{Q \ni x_2;\, Q \subseteq R^1} |Q|^{-1} \int_Q |f(x_1, y_2)|\, dy_2.$$

The ordinary one-dimensional maximal theorem shows that M_1 and M_2 are bounded operators on L^p. On the other hand, it is trivial to show that $M^+ f \leqq M_1(M_2 f)$ pointwise, so that $\| M^+ f \|_p \leqq \| M_1(M_2 f) \|_p \leqq C_p \| M_2 f \|_p \leqq C_p^2 \| f \|_p$ and (A^+) is proved. Thus, the maximal theorem implies statement (16), the "strong differentiability" of the integral. The refined positive result (17) again follows from $M^+ f \leqq M_1(M_2 f)$, using a more detailed version of the maximal theorem. Limitations of space prevent adequate discussion of the negative results (18) and (19), but I want to point out that they are intimately connected with the failure of the conjectures

(B^+) $|\{M^+ f > \alpha\}| \leqq C \|f\|_1/\alpha$, and

(A^{++}) $\|\sup_{R \ni (x_1, x_2);\, R \in \boldsymbol{R}_2} |R|^{-1} \int_R |f(y_1, y_2)|\, dy_1\, dy_2 \|_p \leqq C_p \|f\|_p$.

In particular (19) and (A^{++}) are strongly related to the Kakeya needle problem. (See Busemann and Feller [**10**].)

Let us now try to understand why the maximal theorem is true. To simplify the discussion, I shall weaken the result slightly by restricting attention from all cubes to the special family of *dyadic* cubes. We start with the unit cube $Q_0 \subseteq R^n$, "bisect" Q_0 into 2^n subcubes of side $\frac{1}{2}$, "bisect" each of these cubes into 2^n subcubes with side $\frac{1}{4}$, "bisect" each of these cubes, etc., etc., and continue forever. The family $\mathscr{D}$ of all cubes so obtained is called the family of dyadic cubes. From now on, we shall look only at dyadic cubes—in particular we change the definition of the maximal function so that the "sup" is taken only over dyadic cubes. This restriction is not severe, for given any cube $Q \subseteq Q_0$ we can find a dyadic cube $\tilde{Q}$ of about the same size, at about the same place; so dyadic cubes are almost as "general" as arbitrary cubes. However, for dyadic cubes we have the very convenient observation

(20) Two dyadic cubes are always disjoint, unless one is contained in the other.

The easiest way to become convinced of the dyadic inequality (B) is to vent one's probabilistic intuition on the following game of chance, constructed from the set-up for the maximal theorem. Let $f \geqq 0$ be a fixed L^1 function on the unit cube Q_0. Our fortune at time $t = 0$ is $|Q_0|^{-1} \int_{Q_0} f(y)\, dy$, and we can either rest content or take a chance. If we decide to gamble, the dealer picks a cube Q_1 at random from among the 2^n dyadic subcubes of Q_0 of side $\frac{1}{2}$ (all possible Q_1's have equal probability), and our fortune at time $t = 1$ is $|Q_1|^{-1} \int_{Q_1} f(y)\, dy$. Again we may rest content or take a chance. If we again decide to gamble, the dealer picks a cube Q_2 at random from among the 2^n dyadic subcubes of Q_1 of side $\frac{1}{4}$ (all possible Q_2's have equal probability), and our fortune at time $t = 2$ is $|Q_2|^{-1} \int_{Q_2} f(y)\, dy$. The game continues in this way, either forever or until we decide to quit.

The most important feature of our game of chance is that it is absolutely fair (i.e., it is a "martingale"). More precisely, suppose we find ourselves at time $t = k$ at the cube Q_k so that our fortune is $|Q_k|^{-1} \int_{Q_k} f(y)\, dy$. If we gamble once more, we may win or lose money, but our average fortune at time $t = k + 1$ will be

$$\sum_{\substack{Q_{k+1} \subseteq Q_k;\\ \text{side}(Q_{k+1}) = 2^{-(k+1)}}} \frac{1}{2^n} \cdot \frac{1}{|Q_{k+1}|} \int_{Q_{k+1}} f(y)\, dy = \frac{1}{|Q_k|} \int_{Q_k} f(y)\, dy,$$

i.e., exactly the same as our present fortune. Thus, the game is fair.

Now consider the strategy "quit while you're ahead". We pick in advance a large number $\alpha > \int_{Q_0} f(y)\, dy$, and we stop playing the first time our fortune exceeds α—if our fortune never exceeds α, we keep playing forever. In the lucky case (one of our fortunes exceeds α), we shall have fortune at least α at the end of the game; and even in the unlucky case we shall have at least zero, since $f \geqq 0$. Therefore our average (or expected) fortune at the end of the game is at least $\alpha \times$ Probability of the lucky case $= \alpha \times$ Probability$\{\sup_k |Q_k|^{-1} \int_{Q_k} f(y)\, dy > \alpha\}$, and a few moments' thought shows that this is the same as $\alpha \cdot |\{Mf > \alpha\}|$. On the other hand, since the game is fair, our average fortune at the end of the game is merely our initial fortune $\int_{Q_0} f(y)\, dy$, no matter which clever strategy we use. Therefore, $\alpha \cdot |\{Mf > \alpha\}| \leqq \int_{Q_0} f(y)\, dy$, which is exactly the estimate (B). Part (A) of the maximal theorem follows from part (B) by a useful "interpolation" theorem which we state only in a basic special case. (For more general results, see Zygmund **[95]** and Hunt **[53]**.)

THEOREM 5 (MARCINKIEWICZ INTERPOLATION THEOREM). *Let T be a linear or sublinear operator defined on functions on some measure space, and suppose that $p_0 < p < p_1 \leqq \infty$. If T is bounded on L^{p_1}, and if the "weak-type (p_0, p_0) inequality" $|\{|Tf| > \alpha\}| \leqq C\|f\|_{p_0}^{p_0}/\alpha^{p_0}$ holds, then it follows that T is bounded on L^p.*

To deduce the maximal theorem, we take $p_0 = 1$, $p_1 = \infty$.

L^p-estimates for singular integrals. The techniques we have just discussed for the maximal function apply also to a wide class of singular integral operators. For simplicity, we will start with a constant-coefficient operator $T: f \to K * f$ on R^n, where K is a distribution locally integrable away from the origin. Thus, K might be x^{-1} on the line, or $\Omega(x)/|x|^n$ in R^n.

Our assumptions on K are

(21) T is bounded on $L^2(R^n)$, and

(22) $\int_{|x|>2|y|} |K(x) - K(x-y)|\,dx \leqq C < \infty$ for all $y \in R^n$.

Condition (22) is always satisfied if $|\text{grad } K(x)| \leqq C/|x|^{n+1}$, so (a) and (b) hold for all the usual singular integral operators.

THEOREM 6 (CALDERÓN-ZYGMUND INEQUALITY). *Let T be a convolution operator satisfying hypotheses* (21) *and* (22). *Then*

(A) *T is bounded on L^p* $(1 < p < \infty)$,

(B) $|\{|Tf| > \alpha\}| \leqq C\|f\|_1/\alpha$.

The proof of Theorem 6 is based on further careful study of the game of chance used to prove the maximal theorem. See Stein [**85**].

Although for simplicity we stated the Calderón-Zygmund inequality only for convolution operators, its proof applies to virtually all the variable-coefficient singular integral operators mentioned above. In particular, the following operators are bounded on L^p $(1 < p < \infty)$:

(A) A singular integral

$$Tf(x) = c(x)f(x) + \int_{R^n} \frac{\Omega(x, (x-y)/|x-y|)}{|x-y|^n} f(y)\,dy$$

with c and Ω as described above. (Actually, one can weaken considerably the assumptions on Ω.)

(B) A "classical" pseudodifferential operator

$$Tf(x) = \int_{R^n} e^{ix\cdot\xi}\sigma(x, \xi)\hat{f}(\xi)\,d\xi,$$

where $|(\partial/\partial x)^\alpha(\partial/\partial\xi)^\beta\sigma(x, \xi)| \leqq C_{\alpha\beta}|\xi|^{-|\beta|}$ for all multi-indices α, β.

(C) The commutator integrals

$$T_1f(x) = \int_{R^1} \frac{A(x) - A(y)}{(x-y)^2} f(y)\,dy, \quad T_2f(x) = \int_{R^1} \frac{(A(x) - A(y))^2}{(x-y)^3} f(y)\,dy$$

on R^1, with $A' \in L^\infty$.

(D) The Knapp-Stein singular integrals on nilpotent Lie groups. (See Korányi and Vági [**61**].)

Moreover, the Calderón-Zygmund inequality turns out to be exactly the right tool to prove the classical results of Fourier analysis on the S-function and the G-function, which we discussed briefly at the beginning of this paper in connection with complex methods. (See Stein [**81**], [**83**], J. Schwartz [**74**], Hörmander [**47**], Benedek, Calderón and Panzone [**6**].) Typical results are

(E) $\|S(f)\|_p \sim \|f\|_p \,(1 < p < \infty)$.

(F) Let $\psi_k(\xi) = \psi_0(2^{-k}\xi)$ on R^1, with ψ_0 a fixed smooth function supported in $\{\frac{1}{2} \leqq |\xi| \leqq 2\}$, chosen so that $\sum_{k=-\infty}^{\infty} |\psi_k(\xi)|^2 \equiv 1$. Define $\mathscr{G}(f)(x) = (\sum_{k=-\infty}^{\infty} |A_k f(x)|^2)^{1/2}$, where $(A_k f(\xi))^\wedge = \psi_k(\xi)\hat{f}(\xi)$. Then $\|G(f)\|_p \sim \|f\|_p$ $(1 < p < \infty)$.

(G) $\|G(f)\|_p \sim \|f\|_p \,(1 < p < \infty)$. Recall that (in effect) $G(f)(x) = (\sum_{k=-\infty}^{\infty} |B_k f(x)|^2)^{1/2}$, where $(B_k f(\xi))^\wedge = \chi_{\{2^k \leqq |\xi| < 2^{k+1}\}}(\xi) \cdot \hat{f}(\xi)$.

The main idea in proving (E), (F), (G) is to regard S, $\mathscr{G}$ and G as convolution operators mapping ordinary scalar-valued functions to functions with values in a Hilbert space, and then apply the Calderón-Zygmund inequality.

Actually, the connections between the maximal function, the Hilbert transform, and the S-function are now known to be far closer even than had been suggested by the Calderón-Zygmund inequality and its applications (A)—(G). The main ideas here were developed by Burkholder, Gundy and Silverstein **[8]**, **[9]** and Fefferman and Stein **[38]** in the context of the H^p spaces. The key to the new results is the game of chance introduced above in connection with the maximal function. We consider a fair game of chance (e.g., matching pennies) in which the gambler is allowed to vary the size of his bets depending on past history. (For example: Bet \$1.00 the first time. If you win, bet 2^{-k} dollars at time k $(k \geqq 2)$; if you lose, bet 2^{+k} dollars at time k $(k \geqq 2)$.) Then the following three events are equivalent, except on a set with probability zero. (See Burkholder and Gundy **[8]**.)

(a) The gambler's fortune remainds bounded as time tends to ∞.

(b) The gambler's fortune approaches a finite limit as time tends to ∞.

(c) The sum of the squares of the bets is finite.

The simplest special case is the old "three series" theorem, which says that a series $\sum_n \pm c_n$ with random $\pm$ signs converges with probability one if $\sum_n |c_n|^2 < \infty$ and diverges with probability one if $\sum_n |c_n|^2 = \infty$.

By analogy, one hopes that for an arbitrary harmonic function u on the upper half-plane (not necessarily a Poisson integral), the following conditions on a boundary point x are equivalent outside a set of measure zero:

(a′) u is nontangentially bounded at x, i.e., $\sup_{z \in \Gamma(x)} |u(z)| < \infty$.

(b′) u has a nontangential limit at x, i.e., $\lim_{z \to x;\, z \in \Gamma(x)} u(z)$ exists.

(c′) $S(u)(x) = (\iint_{\Gamma(x)} |\nabla u(z)|^2 \, dz \, d\bar{z})^{1/2} < \infty$.

See Privalov **[73]**, Marcinkiewicz and Zygmund **[65]**, and Spencer **[79]** for the case of the upper half-plane, and Calderón **[11]** and Stein **[82]** for extensions to harmonic functions of several variables. Note that since $S(u) \equiv S(v)$ for conjugate harmonic functions, the equivalence of (b′) and (c′) shows that u and v have nontangential limits at essentially the same set of boundary points. Thus, we obtain a "local" analogue of M. Riesz's theorem on the Hilbert transform.

So far, the analogy with gambling had done nothing but clarify the known results (a′) $\Leftrightarrow$ (b′) $\Leftrightarrow$ (c′) and the maximal theorem. However, further work of Burkholder, Gundy and Silverstein **[9]** and Fefferman and Stein **[38]** uses probabilistic methods in recasting the theory of H^p-spaces into a "Calderón-Zygmund" real-variable framework. Unfortunately, I have not the space here to say anything about H^p, and I must simply refer the interested reader to a relevant survey paper [1].

Up to now we have seen how singular integrals act on L^p $(1 < p < \infty)$ and on L^1. I want to close this section with a brief discussion of L^∞. Surprisingly, one can write down explicitly the essential characterizing property of the Hilbert transform of a bounded function. The basic example to keep in mind is $H(\operatorname{sgn}(x)) = (2/\pi) \log |x|^{-1}$.

THEOREM 7 (SPANNE [78], STEIN [84]). *Let $g \in L^\infty$ and let K be a convolution kernel satisfying the hypotheses of the Calderón-Zygmund inequality. Then $K * g$ is a function of bounded mean oscillation.*

A function $f \in L^1_{\text{loc}}(R^n)$ is said to be of bounded mean oscillation (BMO) if it satisfies the condition

$$(23) \qquad \sup_Q |Q|^{-1} \int_Q |f(x) - f_Q| \, dx < \infty, \quad \text{with } f_Q = |Q|^{-1} \int_Q f(y) \, dy.$$

Thus on R^1, $L^\infty \subseteq$ BMO, $|x|^{-\delta} \notin$ BMO, $\log |x|^{-1} \in$ BMO, but $\operatorname{sgn}(x) \log |x|^{-1} \notin$ BMO. Functions of bounded mean oscillation were introduced by John and Nirenberg [57], who proved the following result in connection with partial differential equations.

THEOREM 8. *The condition* (23) *is equivalent to the seemingly far stronger statement*

$$(24) \qquad \sup_Q |Q|^{-1} \int_Q \exp(\lambda |f(x) - f_Q|) \, dx < \infty \quad \textit{for some } \lambda > 0.$$

In particular, functions of bounded mean oscillation are (*locally*) *exponentially integrable.*

The claim that (23) and (24) are the basic properties of $K * g$ with $g \in L^\infty$ is supported by the following converse result in the case of Riesz transforms:

THEOREM 9. *Every function f of bounded mean oscillation may be written in the form $f = g_0 + \sum_{j=1}^n R_j g_j$ with $g_0, g_1, \cdots, g_n \in L^\infty$.*

This is equivalent to the duality of H^1 and BMO [38]. In the one-dimensional case of the Hilbert transform H, we can say even more.

THEOREM 10. *A function $f \in L^1_{\text{loc}}(R^1)$ may be written in the form $f = g_0 + Hg_1$ with $g_0 \in L^\infty$ and $\|g_1\|_\infty < 1$ if and only if* (24) *holds with $\lambda = \pi/2$.*

The proof of Theorem 10 is truly remarkable. One starts with the following question, which seemingly has nothing to do with bounded mean oscillation: Given a positive measure $d\mu = \omega(x)dx$ on R^1, is the Hilbert transform H a bounded operator on $L^p(d\mu)$? Clearly, various partial results could be proved without much trouble, but a complete solution seems too much to expect. However, at least for L^2, one has not merely one necessary and sufficient condition, but two.

THEOREM 11 (HELSON AND SZEGÖ [45]). *H is bounded on $L^2(d\mu)$ if and only if $\log \omega(x)$ may be written in the form $g_0 + Hg_1$, with $g_0 \in L^\infty$ and $\|g_1\|_\infty < \pi/2$.*

THEOREM 12 (HUNT, MUCKENHOUPT AND WHEEDEN [55]). *H is bounded on* $L^p(d\mu)$ *if and only if*

$$(A_p) \qquad \sup_Q \left(|Q|^{-1} \int_Q \omega(x)\, dx\right)\left(|Q|^{-1} \int_Q \omega^{-1/(p-1)}\, dx\right)^{p-1} < \infty$$

holds.

The Helson-Szegö theorem is proved by a simple but ingenious application of the Hahn-Banach theorem, while the proof of the Hunt-Muckenhoupt-Wheeden theorem uses Calderón-Zygmund methods, and builds on Muckenhoupt's solution of the corresponding problem for the maximal function [68]. (See also Coifman and Fefferman [22].) Since the Helson-Szegö condition and (A_2) are necessary and sufficient conditions for the same thing, they must be equivalent. That is the proof of Theorem 10.

Various applications of BMO are presented in John [56], Moser [67], Fefferman and Stein [38], and [34].

Multiple Fourier transforms. After all the progress of Fourier analysis in the last twenty years, we still know almost nothing about the Fourier transform in R^n. We can use the techniques of singular integrals to prove theorems like the following (see [85]).

THEOREM 13 (LITTLEWOOD-PALEY THEOREM IN R^n). *Let* $f \sim \sum_{k \in Z^n} a_k e^{ik\cdot x}$ *be the multiple Fourier series of a function* $f \in L^p([0, 2\pi]^n)$ $(1 < p < \infty)$, *and let* $\{S_k\}_{k\in Z^n}$ *be a sequence of* $\pm$ *signs. Suppose that* $\{S_k\}$ *is constant on each parallelopiped of the form* $I_1 \times I_2 \times \cdots \times I_n$, *where each* I_j *is a dyadic block* (*see Theorem* 1). *Then* $Tf \sim \sum_k S_k a_k e^{ik\cdot x}$ *also belongs to* L^p, *and* $\|Tf\|_p \leqq C_p \|f\|_p$.

But in many respects, R^n is fundamentally different from R^1, so that merely proving R^n analogues of R^1-theorems misses a great deal. For example, given $f \in L^p(R^n)$ with $1 < p < 2$, what can we say about the size of the Fourier transform $\hat{f}$? The familiar Hausdorff-Young theorem $\|\hat{f}\|_{p'} \leqq \|f\|_p$ $(1/p' + 1/p = 1)$ is virtually all we can say in R^1.[7] (There are further results, but they are in the nature of refinements.) Already in R^2, however, we can go much further. Here is an elementary "restriction theorem" to drive home the point.

THEOREM 14 [29]. *For* $f \in L^p(R^2) \cap L^1(R^2)$ $(1 \leqq p < 4/3)$ *we have a priori inequality*

$$(25) \qquad \|\hat{f}\|_{L^1(S^1)} \leqq C_p \|f\|_{L^p(R^2)}$$

where S^1 *denotes the unit circle.*

It follows that $\hat{f}|_{S^1}$ is well defined for $f \in L^p$ $(p < 4/3)$ even though in principle the Fourier transform is defined only up to sets of measure zero.[8] The correspond-

[7]However, recent work of Babenko and Beckner shows that the norm of the Fourier transform as an operator from L^p to $L^{p'}$ is strictly less than one and can be computed. See Stein's lecture in [1].

[8]Actually, the sharp estimate is $\|\hat{f}\|_{L^{p/3}(S^1)} \leqq C_p \|f\|_{L^p(R^2)}$ for $p < 4/3$. The example $f = \hat{\chi}_B$ with $B=$ unit disc ($f \in L^p$ for $p > 4/3$) shows that we cannot expect to define $\hat{f}|_{S^1}$ for $f \in L^p$ $(p > 4/3)$.

ing statement for a straight line (replacing S^1) is utter nonsense. The first theorem of this kind is due to Stein (see [**29**]).

The proof of the restriction theorem takes only a paragraph. We have to show that the operator $T : f \to \hat{f}\,|_{S^1}$ is bounded from $L^p(R^2)$ to $L^1(S^1)$; to do so, we prove that the adjoint T^* maps $L^\infty(S^1)$ to $L^{p'}(R^2)$ for $p' > 4$. This comes down to showing that

$$\|(f\,d\theta)^\wedge\|^2_{L^{p'}(R^2)} \in C_p \|f\|_{L^\infty(S^1)},$$

where $d\theta$ denotes uniform measure on the circle. Now we write

$$\begin{aligned}\|(f\,d\theta)^\wedge\|^2_{L^{p'}(R^2)} &= \|((f\,d\theta)^\wedge)^2\|_{L^{p'/2}(R^2)} \\ &= \|((f\,d\theta) * (f\,d\theta))^\wedge\|_{L^{p'/2}(R)^2} \leqq \|(f\,d\theta) * (f\,d\theta)\|_{L^r(R^2)}\end{aligned}$$

with $1/r + 1/(p'/2) = 1$ (the last step follows from Hausdorff-Young, since $1 \leqq r < 2$ for $p' > 4$), and the obvious pointwise inequality $|(f\,d\theta) * (f\,d\theta)| \leqq \|f\|^2_\infty \cdot (d\theta * d\theta)$ yields $\|f\,d\theta\|^2_{L^{p'}(R^2)} \leqq \|f\|^2_{L^\infty(S^1)} \cdot \|(d\theta * d\theta)\|_{L^r(R^2)}$. Thus, our restriction theorem comes down to checking that $d\theta * d\theta \in L^r(R^2)$ for $r < 2$. We omit the details, but we note that it is here that the difference between circles and straight lines shows up in the proof. A closely related idea appears in Zygmund [**97**].

In some ways, the Fourier transform is more intractable in R^n than in R^1. For instance, for many problems on partial sums of multiple Fourier series, the natural analogue of the Hilbert transform is an operator T_0 defined on $L^2(R^n)$ by $(T_0 f)^\wedge(\xi) = \chi_B(\xi)\hat{f}(\xi)$, where χ_B is the characteristic function of the unit ball. T_0 behaves far worse than the usual singular integrals, for its convolution kernel looks like $e^{i|x|}/x^{(n+1)/2}$ at infinity, compared to which $\Omega(x)/|x|^n$ is very tame. As a "Hilbert transform", T_0 is intimately connected to a certain maximal function, but it is not the usual maximal function. Rather (in R^2, say) the right maximal function is $M_2 f(x) = \sup_{R \ni x} |R|^{-1} \int_R |f(y)|\,dy$, where R is a rectangle of arbitrary size, shape, and direction. We have already noted that M_2 is not bounded on L^p ($p < \infty$), by virtue of the Besicovitch-Perron constructions for the Kakeya needle problem, and consequently T_0 is unbounded on L^p ($p \neq 2$). (See [**32**], [**46**].) Thus, a basic analogue of the Hilbert transform is a "bad" operator, and so, in dealing with multiple Fourier series, we expect trouble.

This is not to imply that nothing positive can be said about T_0. We define the Bochner-Riesz operators T_δ ($\delta > 0$) on L^2 by

$$(T_\delta f)^\wedge(\xi) = (1 - |\xi|^2)^\delta \chi_B(\xi)\hat{f}(\xi);$$

T_δ is related to T_0 just as Cesaró summation of Fourier series on $[0, 2\pi]$ is related to ordinary convergence (see Bochner [**7**]). By analogy between the Bochner-Riesz operators and restriction theorems on Fourier transforms, Carleson and Sjölin [**21**] proved the following result in the two-dimensional case. (See also [**35**] and Hörmander [**51**].)

THEOREM 15. *T_δ ($\delta > 0$) is bounded on $L^p(R^2)$ for $4/3 \leqq p \leqq 4$.*

The result is essentially sharp (Herz [**46**]).

A. Cordoba **[23]** has recently shown that the Carleson-Sjölin theorem can be related to a positive result for a maximal function closely connected to M_2. In fact, setting $M^N f(x) = \sup_{R \ni x} |R|^{-1} \int_R |f(y)|\, dy$ where R is a rectangle of arbitrary direction with (Longer side of R)/(Shorter side of R) $< N$, we have:

THEOREM 16 (CORDOBA MAXIMAL THEOREM). $\|M^N f\|_2 \leqq C(\log N)^3 \|f\|_2$.

The three basic Theorems 14, 15 and 16 suggest a program to force us to come to grips with some genuinely n-dimensional Fourier analysis. First of all, the known results should be extended from the two-dimensional case (where they are really too easy) to R^n. The natural conjectures are

(26) $\|\hat{f}\|_{L^{2n/(n+1)}(S^{n-1})} \leqq C_p \|f\|_{L^p(R^n)}$ if $1 \leqq p < 2n/(n+1)$.

(27) T_δ is bounded on $L^p(R^n)$ if $|1/p - 1/2| < (\delta + \frac{1}{2})/n$ and $\delta > 0$.

(28) Let $M^N f(x) = \sup_{R \ni x} |R|^{-1} \int_R |f(y)|\, dy$ where R is any rectangular parallelopiped of arbitrary direction, and sides $\delta_1 \times \delta_1 \times \cdots \times \delta_1 \times \delta_2$ with $1 \leqq \delta_2/\delta_1 \leqq N$. Then

$$\|M^N f\|_{L^n(R^n)} \leqq C(\log N)^A \|f\|_{L^n(R^n)}.$$

So far, the best partial result known is a clever theorem of P. Tomas **[91]**:

THEOREM 17. *The following inequalities hold.*

$$\|\hat{f}\|_{L^2(S^{n-1})} \leqq C\|f\|_{L^{[(2n+2)/(n+3)]-\varepsilon}(R^n)}, \tag{29}$$

and

$$\|T_\delta f\|_{L^p(R^n)} \leqq C\|f\|_{L^p(R^n)} \tag{30}$$

for $|1/p - 1/2| < (\delta + \frac{1}{2})/n$ *and* $\delta > (n-1)/(2n+2) + \varepsilon$ (*cf.* **[29]** *and* **[35]**).

See Carleson and Sjölin **[21]** for the three-dimensional case.[9]

It seems that we are still far from complete solutions. Even after our conjectures have been settled, we shall only have barely started to grasp the real situation. It is as if we had just proved Cesaró summability of Fourier series on $[0, 2\pi]$ but still knew nothing about the Hilbert transform. One natural problem is to relate the geometry of the maximal function M_2 to the behavior of the "Hilbert transform" T_0 in R^n.[10] The only result known in this direction is Cordoba's Theorem 16. We still know so little that we cannot answer intelligently the question "How big is the Fourier transform of a function in $L^p(R^2)$?" Perhaps $\{|\hat{f}| > \alpha\}$ for large α can be covered efficiently by rectangles (of no fixed direction). If true, this would explain why $\hat{f}$ can be restricted to circles but not to straight lines, for a circle is harder to cover by thin rectangles than a straight line. Coverings by rectangles play a major role in the study of T_0, where the "Kakeya" set of Besicovitch exerts an influence all out of proportion to its small area. A recent counterexample of Carleson **[20]** to various conjectures on the polydisc related to Theorems 9 and 10 has a similar flavor. Perhaps in dealing with the Fourier transform in R^n, we must abandon our fixation on Lebesgue measure, and search for new quantities (defined

[9] E. M. Stein has modified Tomas' argument to handle $\varepsilon = 0$ in (29) and (30).

[10] There is also an analogue of the S-function for T_0, which we have not mentioned.

possibly in terms of coverings by thin rectangles) to express the size or importance of a set of points. This is easier said than done, but we have seen evidence suggesting that it is forced on us by the phenomena we seek to understand. I do not know where—if anywhere—these ideas lead.

References[11]

1. J. Marshall Ash, Proceedings of a Conference on Fourier Analysis held at DePaul University (to appear).

2. R. Beals, *Spatially inhomogeneous pseudodifferential operators*. II, Comm. Pure Appl. Math. (to appear).

3. ———, *A general calculus of pseudodiffererential operators* (to appear).

4. R. Beals and C. Fefferman, *On local solvability of linear partial differential equations*, Ann. of Math. (2) **97** (1970), 552–571.

5. ———, *Spatially inhomogeneous pseudodifferential operators*, Comm. Pure Appl. Math. **27** (1974), 1–24.

6. A. Benedek, A. P. Calderón and R. Panzone, *Convolution operators on Banach space valued functions*, Proc. Nat. Acad. Sci. U.S.A. **48** (1962), 356–365. MR **24** #A3479.

7. S. Bochner, *Summation of multiple Fourier series by spherical means*, Trans. Amer. Math. Soc. **40** (1936), 175–207.

8. D. Burkholder and R. Gundy, *Extrapolation and interpolation of quasilinear operators on martingales*, Acta Math. **124** (1970), 249–304.

9. D. Burkholder, R. Gundy and M. Silverstein, *A maximal function characterization of the class H^p*, Trans. Amer. Math. Soc. **157** (1971), 137–153. MR **43** #527.

10. H. Busemann and W. Feller, *Zur Differentiation des Lebesguesche Integrale*, Fund. Math. **22** (1934), 226–256.

11. A. P. Calderón, *On the behavior of harmonic functions at the boundary*, Trans. Amer. Math. Soc. **68** (1950), 47–54. MR **11**, 357.

12. ———, *Uniqueness in the Cauchy problem for partial differential equations*, Amer. J. Math. **80** (1958), 16–36. MR **21** #3675.

13. ———, *Singular integrals and their applications to hyperbolic differential equations*, Curos y Seminarios de Matemática, fasc. 3, Universidad de Buenos Aires, Buenos Aires, 1960. MR **23** #A1156.

14. ———, *Commutators of singular integral operators*, Proc. Nat. Acad. Sci. U.S.A. **53** (1965), 1092–1099. MR **31** #1575.

15. ———, *Singular integrals*, Bull. Amer. Math. Soc. **72** (1966), 427–465. MR **35** #813.

16. A. P. Calderón and R. Vaillancourt, *A class of bounded pseudo-differential operators*, Proc. Nat. Acad. Sci. U.S.A. **69** (1972), 1185–1187. MR **45** #7532.

17. A. P. Calderón and A. Zygmund, *On the existence of certain singular integrals*, Acta Math. **88** (1952), 85–139. MR **14**, 637.

18. C. Calderón, (preprint).

19. L. Carleson, *On convergence and growth of partial sums of Fourier series*, Acta Math. **116** (1966) 135–157. MR **33** #7774.

20. ———, *A counterexample for measures bounded on H^p for the polydisc*, 1974 (mimeographed notes).

21. L. Carleson and P. Sjölin, *Oscillatory integrals and a multiplier problem for the disc*, Studia Math. **44** (1972), 287–299.

22. R. Coifman and C. Fefferman, Studia Math. (to appear).

23. A. Cordoba, *The Kakeya maximal function and the spherical summation operators*, Amer. J. Math. (to appear).

[11]I am grateful to B. Cohn for helping me with the bibliography.

24. M. Cotlar, *A unified theory of Hilbert transforms and ergodic theory*, Rev. Math. Cuyana **1** (1955), 105–167 (1956). MR **18**, 893.

25. J. J. Duistermaat and L. Hörmander, *Fourier integral operators*. II, Acta Math. **128** (1971), 183–269.

26. Ju. V. Egorov, *Hypoelliptic pseudodifferential operators*, Trudy Moskov. Mat. Obšč. **16** (1967), 99–108 = Trans. Moscow Math. Soc. 1967, 107–116. MR **36** #6985.

27. ———, *The canonical transformations of pseudodifferential operators*, Uspehi Mat. Nauk **24** (1969), no. 5 (149), 235–236. (Russian) MR **42** #657.

28. E. B. Fabes and N. M. Rivière, *Singular integrals with mixed homogeneity*, Studia Math. **27** (1966), 19–38. MR **35** #683.

29. C. Fefferman, *Inequalities for strongly singular convolution operators*, Acta Math. **124** (1970), 9–36. MR **41** #2468.

30. ———, *On the divergence of multiple Fourier series*, Bull. Amer. Math. Soc. **77** (1971), 191–195. MR **43** #5251.

31. ———, *On the convergence of multiple Fourier series*, Bull. Amer. Math. Soc. **77** (1971), 744–745.

32. ———, *The multiplier problem for the ball*, Ann. of Math. (2) **94** (1971), 330–336. MR **45** #5661.

33. ———, *Pointwise convergence of Fourier series*, Ann. of Math (2) **98** (1973), 551–572.

34. ———, *L^p bounds for pseudodifferential operators*, Israel J. Math. **14** (1973), 413–417.

35. ———, *A note on spherical summation multipliers*, Israel J. Math. **15** (1973), 44–52. MR **47** #9160.

36. ———, *The Bergman kernel and biholomorphic mappings of pseudoconvex domains*, Invent. Math. (to appear).

37. C. Fefferman, J. P. Kahane and E. M. Stein, *A partial survey of A. Zygmund's mathematical work* (to appear).

38. C. Fefferman and E. M. Stein, *H^p-spaces of several variables*, Acta Math. **129** (1972), 137–193.

39. G. B. Folland, *The tangential Cauchy-Riemann complex on spheres*, Trans. Amer. Math. Soc. **171** (1972), 83–133. MR **46** #8266.

40. G. B. Folland and J. J. Kohn, *The Neumann problem for the Cauchy-Riemann complex*, Ann. of Math. Studies, no. 75, Princeton Univ. Press, Princeton, N. J., 1972.

41. G. B. Folland and E. M. Stein, *Estimates for the $\bar{\partial}_b$-complex and analysis on the Heisenberg group*, Comm. Pure Appl. Math. **27** (1974), 429–522.

42. A. Garsia, *Martingale inequalities-seminar notes on recent progress*, Benjamin, New York, 1973.

43. G. Giraud, Ann. Sci. École Norm. Sup. **51** (1934), 251–372.

44. G. Hardy and J. Littlewood, *A maximal function with function-theoretic applications*, Acta Math. **54** (1930), 81–116.

45. H. Helson and G. Szegö, *A problem in prediction theory*, Ann. Mat. Pura Appl. (4) **51** (1960), 107–138. MR **22** #12343.

46. C. S. Herz, *On the mean inversion of Fourier and Hankel transforms*, Proc. Nat. Acad. Sci. U.S.A. **40** (1954), 996–999. MR **16**, 127.

47. L. Hörmander, *Estimates for translation invariant operators in L^p spaces*, Acta Math. **104** (1960), 93–140. MR **22** #12389.

48. ———, *Pseudo-differential operators and non-elliptic boundary problems*, Ann. of Math. (2) **83** (1966), 129–209. MR **38** #1387.

49. ———, *Pseudodifferential operators and hypoelliptic equations*, Proc. Sympos. Pure Math., vol. 10, Amer. Math. Soc., Providence, R. I., 1967, pp. 138–183.

50. ———, *Fourier integral operators*. I, Acta Math. **127** (1971), 79–183.

51. ———, *Oscillatory integrals and multipliers on FL^p* (preprint).

52. J. I. Horváth, *Sur les fonctions conjuguées à plusieurs variables*, Nederl. Akad. Wetensch. Proc. Ser. A **56** = Indag. Math. **15** (1953), 17–29. MR **14**, 747.

53. R. Hunt, *An extension of the Marcinkiewicz interpolation theorem to Lorentz spaces*, Bull. Amer. Math. Soc. **70** (1964), 803–807; erratum, ibid. **71** (1965), 396. MR **29** #6292; **30** #2331.

54. ———, *On the convergence of Fourier series*, Orthogonal Expansions and Their Continuous Analogues (Proc. Conf., Edwardsville, Ill., 1967), Southern Illinois Univ. Press, Carbondale, Ill., 1968, pp. 235–255. MR **38** #6296.

55. R. Hunt, B. Muckenhoupt and R. Wheeden, *Weighted norm inequalities for the conjugate function and Hilbert transform*, Trans. Amer. Math. Soc. **176** (1973), 227–251. MR **47** #710.

56. F. John, *Rotation and strain*, Comm. Pure Appl. Math. **14** (1961), 391–413. MR **25** #1672.

57. F. John and L. Nirenberg, *On functions of bounded mean oscillation*, Comm. Pure Appl. Math. **14** (1961), 415–426. MR **24** #A1348.

58. B. F. Jones, Jr., *A class of singular integrals*, Amer. J. Math. **86** (1964), 441–462. MR **28** #4308.

59. A. W. Knapp and E. M. Stein, *Intertwining operators on semisimple Lie groups*, Ann. of Math. (2) **93** (1971), 489–578.

60. J. J. Kohn and L. Nirenberg, *An algebra of pseudo-differential operators*, Comm. Pure Appl. Math. **18** (1965), 269–305. MR **31** #636.

61. A. Korányi and S. Vági, *Intégrales singulières sur certains espaces homogènes*, C. R. Acad. Sci. Paris Sér. A-B **268** (1969), A765–A768. MR **44** #4151; erratum, **44**, p. 1633.

62. P. Krée, *Sur les multiplicateurs dans FL^p*, Ann. Inst. Fourier (Grenoble) **16** (1966), fasc. 2, 31–89. MR **35** #7079.

63. H. Lewy, *An example of a smooth linear partial differential equation without solution*, Ann. of Math. (2) **66** (1957), 155–158. MR **19**, 551.

64. P. I. Lizorkin, *(L_p, L_q)-multipliers of Fourier integrals*, Dokl. Akad. Nauk SSSR **152** (1963), 808–811 = Soviet Math. Dokl. **4** (1963), 1420–1424. MR **27** #4016.

65. J. Marcinkiewicz and A. Zygmund, *A theorem of Lusin*, Duke J. Math. **4** (1938), 473–485.

66. S. G. Mihlin, *Singular integral equations*, Uspehi Mat. Nauk **3** (1948), no. 3 (25), 29–112; English transl., Amer. Math. Soc. Transl. (1) **10** (1962), 84–198. MR **10**, 305.

67. J. Moser, *On Harnack's theorem for elliptic differential equations*, Comm. Pure. Appl. Math. **14** (1961), 577–591. MR **28** #2356.

68. B. Muckenhoupt, *Weighted norm inequalities for the Hardy maximal function*, Trans. Amer. Math. Soc. **165** (1972), 207–226. MR **45** #2461.

69. A. Negel, N. Rivière and S. Wainger, Studia Math. (to appear).

70. L. Nirenberg and F. Trèves, *Solvability of a first-order linear partial differential equation*, Comm. Pure Appl. Math. **16** (1963), 331–351. MR **29** #348.

71. ———, *On local solvability of linear partial differential equations.* I. *Necessary conditions;* II. *Sufficient conditions*, Comm. Pure Appl. Math **23** (1970), 1–38, 459–509. MR **41** #9064a, b.

72. S. Pichorides, *On the best values of the constants in the theorems of M. Riesz, Zygmund and Kolmogoroff*, Studia Math. **44** (1972), 165–179. MR **47** #702.

73. I. Privalov, *Intégrale de Cauchy*, Saratov, 1919, pp. 1–104.

74. J. Schwartz, *A remark on inequalities of Calderón-Zygmund type for vector-valued functions*, Comm. Pure Appl. Math. **14** (1961), 785–799. MR **26** #597.

75. R. T. Seeley, *Singular integrals on compact manifolds*, Amer. J. Math. **81** (1959), 658–690. MR **22** #905.

76. P. Sjölin, *An inequality of Paley and convergence a.e. of Walsh-Fourier series*, Ark. Math. **7** (1969) 551–570. MR **38** #3222.

77. ———, *On convergence a.e. of certain singular integrals and multiple Fourier series*, Ark. Math. **9** (1971), 65–90.

78. S. Spanne, *Sur l'interpolation entre les espaces $\mathscr{L}_k^{p\Phi}$*, Ann. Scuola Norm. Sup. Pisa (3) **20** (1966), 625–648. MR **35** #728.

79. D. C. Spencer, *A function-theoretic identity*, Amer. J. Math. **65** (1943), 147–160. MR **4**, 137.

80. E. M. Stein, *Interpolation of linear operators*, Trans. Amer. Math. Soc. **83** (1956), 482–492. MR **18**, 575.

81. ———, *On the functions of Littlewood-Paley, Lusin and Marcinkiewicz*, Trans. Amer. Math. Soc. **88** (1958), 430–466; correction, ibid. **98** (1961), 186. MR **22** #3778; **22**, p. 2546.

82. ———, *On the theory of harmonic functions of several variables.* II. *Behavior near the boundary*, Acta Math. **106** (1961), 137–174. MR **30** #3234.

83. ———, *On some functions of Littlewood-Paley and Zygmund*, Bull. Amer. Math. Soc. **67** (1961), 99–101. MR **23** #A1194.

84. ———, *Singular integrals, harmonic functions, and differentiability properties of functions of several variables*, Proc. Sympos. Pure Math., vol. 10, Amer. Math. Soc., Providence, R. I., 1967, pp. 316–335.

85. ———, *Singular integrals and differentiability properties of functions*, Princeton Math. Ser., no. 30, Princeton Univ. Press, Princeton, N. J., 1970. MR **44** #7280.

86. ———, *Topics in harmonic analysis related to the Littlewood-Paley theory*, Ann. of Math. Studies, no. 63, Princeton Univ. Press, Princeton, N. J.; Univ. of Tokyo Press, Tokyo, 1970. MR **40** #6176.

87. ———, *Boundary behavior of holomorphic functions of several complex variables*, Princeton Univ. Press, Princeton, N. J., 1972.

88. E. M. Stein and G. Weiss, *On the theory of harmonic functions of several variables.* I. *The theory of H^p-spaces*, Acta Math. **103** (1960), 25–62. MR **22** #12315.

89. ———, *Introduction to Fourier analysis on Euclidean spaces*, Princeton Math. Ser., no. 32, Princeton Univ. Press, Princeton, N. J., 1971. MR **46** #4102.

90. N. R. Tevzadze, *The convergence of the double Fourier series of a square summable function*, Sakharth. SSR Mecn. Akad. Moambe **58** (1970), 277–279. (Russian) MR **45** #7390.

91. P. Tomas, *A restriction theorem for Fourier transforms* (to appear).

92. F. Trèves, *On the local solvability of linear partial differential equations in two independent variables*, Amer. J. Math. **92** (1970), 174–204. MR **41** #3974.

93. ———, *On local solvability of linear partial differential equations*, Bull. Amer. Math. Soc. **76** (1970), 552–571. MR **41** #2200.

94. N. Wiener, *The ergodic theorem*, Duke Math. J. **5** (1939), 1–18.

95. A. Zygmund, *Trigonometric series.* Vols. I, II, 2nd ed., Cambridge Univ. Press, New York, 1959. MR **21** #6498.

96. ———, *Intégrales singulières*, Lecture notes in Math., vol. 204, Springer-Verlag, New York, 1971, pp. 1–52.

97. ———, *A Cantor-Lebesgue theorem for double trigonometric series*, Studia Math. **43** (1972), 173–178. MR **47** #711.

UNIVERSITY OF CHICAGO
CHICAGO, ILLINOIS 60637, U.S.A.

PRINCETON UNIVERSITY
PRINCETON, NEW JERSEY 08540, U.S.A.

Proceedings of the International Congress of Mathematicians
Vancouver, 1974

Analysis over Infinite-Dimensional Spaces and Applications to Quantum Field Theory

James Glimm

Analysis is the study of functions and operators. The functions f customarily depend on a finite-dimensional variable x, in a Euclidean space R^n, or a finite-dimensional manifold $\mathscr{M}_n$. However, there are examples where it is natural, and even necessary, to analyze functions of an infinite-dimensional variable. Thus x belongs to a Banach space X, or to some more general space. Typically x is itself a function defined on R^n and f is a function of a function.

To demonstrate that analysis over infinite-dimensional spaces is not an exercise in abstraction, we show that it is required in five examples drawn from mathematical physics. Before doing this, we consider separately the two simple components of these examples: *first*, functions as labels of position (continuum mechanics) and *second*, functions as probability densities of position (statistical and quantum mechanics). In quantum field theory and continuum (or infinite volume) statistical mechanics, both components occur. We are forced to consider functions of functions, that is, analysis over infinite-dimensional spaces.

Continuum mechanics. A fluid, governed for example by the Navier-Stokes equation

$$v_t + (v \cdot \nabla)v + \nabla p = \Delta v, \qquad \nabla \cdot v = 0, \tag{1}$$

is described at fixed time $t = 0$ by its velocity field $\boldsymbol{v}$,

$$\boldsymbol{v}(\boldsymbol{x}, 0) = \boldsymbol{v}(\boldsymbol{x}) = (v_1(\boldsymbol{x}), v_2(\boldsymbol{x}), v_3(\boldsymbol{x})), \tag{1'}$$

namely a function $\boldsymbol{v}: R^3 \to R^3$. The state of an elastic solid or vibrating string is also given by a function. The dynamics is then specified by some linear or nonlinear equation, for example,

(2) $$\phi_{tt} - \phi_{xx} + m_0^2\phi + \lambda_0\phi^3 = 0,$$

with time zero Cauchy data

(3) $$\phi(x, 0),\ \phi_t(x, 0) = \text{given functions.}$$

The same statement applies to discrete but infinite systems, such as an infinite gas or crystal; the initial state is a function $\{r_i, v_i\}_{i=1}^{\infty}$ specifying the initial positions and velocities of the gas molecules.

Statistical and quantum mechanics. In statistical and quantum mechanics, the positions and velocities no longer assume definite values. Rather, probability densities are the fundamental objects. For a gas of N particles, a statistical mechanics state is a function (probability density) ρ of the N positions r_i and N velocities v_i. ρ satisfies

(4) $$\rho(r, v) \geqq 0, \qquad \int \rho\, dr\, dv = 1.$$

In quantum mechanics, the state is a function

(5) $$f = f(r_1, \cdots, r_N) \in L_2(R^{3N}), \qquad \|f\|_{L_2} = 1,$$

of the particle positions, and

(6) $$\rho(r) = |f(r)|^2$$

is a probability density as in (4) above.

Combining the ideas in the two paragraphs above, we find that *the quantum or statical mechanics of continuum or infinite discrete systems leads to analysis over infinite-dimensional spaces*. In these problems, the analysis occurs for example in $L_2(X, dx)$, where X is some Banach space.

Five examples. The simplest and best known problem of this nature is Brownian motion: the motion of a small particle suspended in a fluid, caused by random collisions with the fluid molecules. The random nature of the collisions makes the problem statistical, while the absence of a deterministic equation of motion, as in (2), (3), makes the time evolution a continuum problem. The mathematical framework for this problem is given by the Wiener integral, an integral on the space $C(R)$ of continuous functions (= Wiener paths = Brownian trajectories) on the real line R. Turbulence may also be a problem of this nature. When turbulence is treated statistically, it involves an integral over a Banach space X of velocity vector fields v; see (1′).

The quantum statistical mechanics of an infinite gas or crystal falls into the framework we are considering, as does the quantum mechanics of a relativistic field. The simplest relativisitic field is a solution ϕ of the Klein-Gordon equation (2)—(3). The coupled Maxwell-Dirac equations arise in the interaction of electrons with light (quantum electrodynamics).

The heat equation solves quantum field theory. The linear Klein-Gordon equation, with $\lambda_0 = 0$ in (2), is called a free field. The substitution $t \to it$ transforms this hyperbolic equation into an elliptic equation

(7) $$(-\Delta + m_0^2)\phi = 0.$$

The substition $t \to it$ also transforms the quantum mechanical Schrödinger equation into an associated heat equation. Skipping over some details, we jump to a probabilistic or Wiener integral solution of the heat equation (see **[6]** for a survey of the central ideas). The Wiener integral we are interested in is a Gaussian measure dW on $S'(R^d)$. Here d is the space-time dimension, $\phi \in S'$, and for each $f \in S(R^d)$, we consider the linear coordinate function

(8) $$S' \ni \phi \to \langle \phi, f \rangle \equiv \phi(f)$$

defined on S'. dW is then characterized by the formula

(9) $$\int \exp(i\phi(f))\, dW(\phi) = \exp(-\langle f, Cf \rangle/2),$$

where

(10) $$C = (-\Delta + m_0^2)^{-1}$$

and $\langle \cdot, \cdot \rangle$ denotes the L_2 inner product,

(11) $$\langle f, Cf \rangle = \int f(x)^{-} C(x-y) f(y)\, dx\, dy.$$

C is the covariance of this measure, so that

(12) $$\int \phi(f)\phi(g)\, dW(\phi) = \langle f, Cg \rangle.$$

The case $d = 1$, $m_0 = 0$, is the conventional Wiener integral.

For the interacting field, $\lambda_0 \not\equiv 0$ in (2), the Feynman-Kac formula for solutions of heat equations with potential leads us to replace dW by a measure

(13) $$d\phi = \exp\left(-\frac{1}{4}\lambda_0 \int_{R^d} \phi(x)^4\, dx\right) dW.$$

THEOREM 1 (**[16]** FOR $d \leqq 3$; **[18]**, **[19]** FOR $d \leqq 4$). *Assuming existence and certain properties ("axioms") of the measure $d\phi$, analytic continuation $it \to t$ back to real time is possible and yields a quantum field theory satisfying Wightman's axioms.*

For $d = 2$, quantum fields were first constructed in **[7]**, **[20]** using different methods. Various constructions based on the function space measure (13) are found in **[1]**, **[2]**, **[4]**, **[5]**, **[13]**, **[14]**, **[16]**. In addition to the work of Jaffe and the author on the problem of constructing quantum fields, Nelson, Segal, Rosen, Guerra, Simon, Osterwalder, Schrader, Spencer and many others have made important contributions, as surveyed for example in **[6]**, **[8]**, **[9]**, **[12]**.

Structure of quantum fields I. Particles. A typical reaction time for elementary particles is $\sim 10^{-17}$ sec. Thus one observes primarily the $t \to \pm\infty$ asymptotes of any interaction process. In the $t \to \pm\infty$ asymptotes, the particles separate and move independently.

In any quantum mechanical problem, the time evolution is given by a unitary group $U(t) = e^{-itH}$; H is by definition the Hamiltonian or energy operator. By elementary spectral theory, the $t \to \pm\infty$ asymptotes are described by the eigenfunctions and eigenvalues of H. Thus particles provide a set of labels for the energy eigenfunctions and eigenvalues. This idea lies at the heart of the Haag-Ruelle scattering theory **[15]**, which we reformulate loosely as follows:

The joint spectrum of the energy and momentum operators is a Lorentz invariant semigroup contained in the interior of the dual light cone $H = P_0 \geqq 0$, $P_0^2 - \boldsymbol{P}^2 \geqq 0$ in $(R^d)^\wedge$. The generators of this semigroup lie on Lorentz invariant orbits and, excluding the trivial orbit at the origin, these orbits describe the elementary particles and bound states of the theory.

From the point of view of the measure (13), a particle of mass m is associated with an exponential decay rate

$$\langle \phi(x), \phi(y) \rangle = \lim_{|x-y| \to \infty} \langle \phi(x)\phi(y) \rangle + O(e^{-m|x-y|}) \tag{14}$$

in the two-point correlation function. In general, the leading (slowest) decay rate is associated with the lightest particle, and for a $P(\phi)$ interaction, as in (2), any higher decay rates remaining after this leading decay rate is subtracted are expected to be due to:

(a) bound states of mass m_b, formed from pairs or triples of elementary particles, and moving as a single particle as $t \to \pm\infty$,

(b) pairs, triples, $\cdots$ of elementary particles, moving independently with large space separation as $t \to \pm\infty$. The associated decay rate is at least $2m$.

THEOREM 2 (**[12]**, **[13]**). *The* $P(\phi)_2$ *quantum field theory, for weak coupling* $\lambda_0/m_0^2 \ll 1$, *has particles of mass* m. $m = m_0 + o(1)$ *as* $\lambda_0/m_0^2 \to 0$. *There is no mass spectrum in the intervals* $(0, m)$ *and* $(m, 2m - o(1))$.

THEOREM 3 **[12]**. *The* $(\phi^6 - \phi^4)_2$ *quantum field model for weak coupling has mass spectrum in the bound state interval* $m_b \in (2m - o(1), 2m)$.

THEOREM 4 (**[13]**, **[21]**). *The* ϕ_2^4 *quantum field theory, in the single phase region, has no even bound states.*

The last two results express the idea that ϕ^4 leads to repulsive forces while $-\phi^4$ leads to attractive forces. A more complete analysis of the particle structure for weak coupling is based on a study of the decay rate of the Bethe-Salpeter equation by T. Spencer.

High temperature expansions. The proof of these weak coupling results is based on a convergent perturbation expansion similar to the high temperature expansions of statistical mechanics. Let L be the set of lattice line segments joining nearest neighbor lattice points $i, i' \in Z^2$. Let Δ_L be the Laplacian with Dirichlet data on all line segments $l \in L$. Let

$$C_L = (-\Delta_L + m_0^2)^{-1}, \tag{15}$$

let dW_L be the Gaussian measure with covariance C_L, and let

$$d\phi_L = \exp\left(-\int_{R^2} \phi^4(x)\, dx\right) dW_L, \tag{16}$$

as in (13). Then

(17) $$\langle\phi(x)\phi(y)\rangle_L = \int \phi(x)\phi(y)\, d\phi_L = 0,$$

if x and y belong to disjoint lattice squares. Thus $d\phi_L$ has an exponential decay rate $m_L = \infty$. We take $d\phi_L$ as the zeroth order or unperturbed measure in the cluster expansion, and remove the Dirichlet data on line segments $l \in L$ as a perturbation, to obtain $d\phi$.

The main idea behind the expansion can be formulated roughly as follows. We are not interested in removing the nonlinear coupling between distinct normal modes of the free field (a nonconvergent expansion in powers of λ_0). Rather we group the degrees of freedom into blocks (associated with $\phi(x)$, x in a singel lattice square) and then remove as a perturbation the (linear) coupling between these distinct blocks. The success of this method rests on the fact that the coupling between distinct lattice squares is sufficiently small.

Structure of quantum fields II. Critical points and phase transitions. The critical points of quantum field theory are related to the critical points of Morse theory. We start with an interaction potential $V(\phi(x))$ in the exponent in (13). For $V(\xi) = \xi^4 + \sigma\xi^2$, V has a critical point at $\sigma = 0$, a single minimum for $\sigma > 0$ and double minima for $\sigma < 0$; see Figure 1.

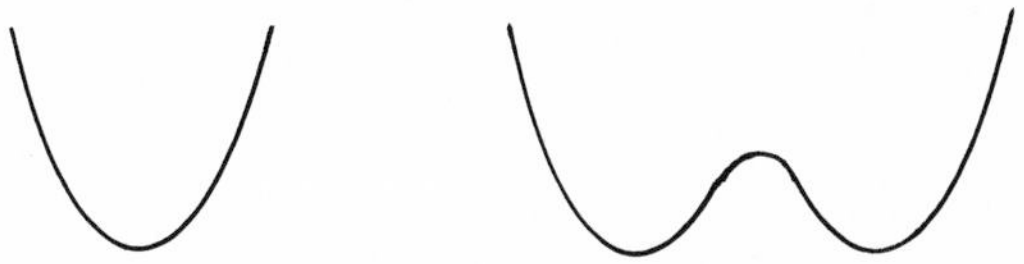

$\sigma > 0$ $\sigma < 0$

FIGURE 1. $V(\xi) = \xi^4 + \sigma\xi^2$.

In the case of two minima, the quantum field is expected to decompose into the direct sum of exactly two distinct (pure phase) quantum field theories; see **[1]**, **[5]**. For $\sigma \gg 1$, it is known that no such decomposition is possible **[13]**. Heuristically, this picture is based on the idea that most of the measure $dq = \exp(-\int V)\, dW$ is concentrated near minima of V. A further analysis (linearizing the equations of motion about this minimum or, equivalently, replacing V by its Taylor's expansion up to second order) leads to the idea that the mass (exponential decay rate) should be identified with $V''^{1/2}$, evaluated at the minimum. In case $\boldsymbol{\phi} = (\phi_1, \cdots, \phi_n)$ is a vector-valued field, there are n masses identified with the square roots of the eigenvalues of the Hessian $\partial^2 V/\partial\xi^2$. References including the older literature are given in **[12]**, **[22]**.

At the transition between the one- and two-phase regions in Figure 1, there is a critical point of V where the Jacobian vanishes:

(18) $$\operatorname{Det} \partial^2 V/\partial\xi^2\big|_{\sigma=0} = 0.$$

We expect the following critical phenomena for some critical value $\sigma = \sigma_c$ in quantum field theory:

(i) No exponential decay of correlations.
(ii) No particles, at least for $d = 2, 3$.
(iii) Critical singularities, as $\sigma \to \sigma_c$, for example,

$$\int \langle \phi(x)\phi(y) \rangle \, dx \sim (\sigma - \sigma_c)^{-\gamma}, \qquad \sigma \downarrow \sigma_c. \tag{19}$$

The γ above is an example of what is known as a critical exponent. There are several simple ("classical") theories (van der Waals, mean field, Landau) in which one can calculate these exponents [**22**]. For example $\gamma_{\text{classical}} = 1$.

For a ϕ^4 quantum field theory, the inequality mean field $\leqq$ quantum field has been proved in the sense of the following theorem.

THEOREM [**11**]. *Assume the existence of critical behavior for a ϕ_2^4 quantum field. Then*

$$1 = \gamma_{\text{classical}} \leqq \gamma, \quad \tfrac{1}{2} = \nu_{\text{classical}} \leqq \nu, \quad 0 = \eta_{\text{classical}} \leqq \eta.$$

Bibliography

1. R. Dobrušin and R. Minlos, *Construction of a one dimensional quantum field via a continuous Markov field*, Funkcional. Anal. i Priložen. **7** (1973) = Functional Anal. Appl. **7** (1973), 324–325.

2. J.-P. Eckmann, J. Magnen and R. Seneor, *Decay properties and Borel summability for the Schwinger functions in $P(\Phi)_2$ theories*, Comm. Math. Phys. **39** (1975), 251–271.

3. J. Feldman, *On the absence of bound states in the ϕ^4 quantum field model without symmetry breaking*, Canad. J. Phys. **52** (1974), 1583–1587.

4. J. Fröhlich, *Verification of axioms for Euclidean and relativistic fields and Haag's theorem in a class of $P(\phi)_2$ models*, Ann. Inst. H. Poincaré **21** (1974).

5. ———, *Schwinger functions and their generating functionals*. II, Harvard (preprint).

6. J. Glimm, *The mathematics of quantum field theory*, Advances in Math. (to appear).

7. J. Glimm and A. Jaffe, *The $\lambda(\phi_2^4)$ quantum field theory without cutoffs*. III. *The physical vacuum*, Acta Math. **125** (1970), 203–267. MR **42** #4130.

8. ———, *Quantum field models*, Statistical Mechanics and Quantum Field Theory, ed. by C. de Witt and R. Stora, Gordon and Breach, New York, 1971.

9. ———, *Boson quantum field models*, Mathematics of Contemporary Physics, ed. by R. Streater, Academic Press, New York, 1972.

10. ———, *Two and three body equations in quantum field theory*, Comm. Math. Phys. (to appear).

11. ———, *ϕ^4 quantum field model in the single phase region: Differentiability of the mass and bounds on critical exponents*, Phys. Rev. **D10** (1974), 536–539.

12. J. Glimm, A. Jaffe and T. Spencer, *The particle structure of the weakly coupled $P(\phi)_2$ model and other applications of high temperature expansions*, Constructive Quantum Field Theory, ed. by G. Velo and A. Wightman, Springer, New York, 1973.

13. ———, *The Wightman axioms and particle structure in the $P(\phi)_2$ quantum field model*, Ann. of Math. (2) **100** (1974), 585–632.

14. F. Guerra, L. Rosen and B. Simon, *The $P(\phi)_2$ Euclidean quantum field theory as classical statistical mechanics*, Ann. of Math. (2) **101** (1975), 111.

15. R. Jost, *The general theory of quantized fields*, Lectures in Appl. Math., vol. 4, Amer. Math. Soc., Providence, R.I., 1965. MR **31** #1929.

16. E. Nelson, *Construction of quantum fields from Markoff fields*, J. Functional Analysis **12** (1973), 97–112.

17. ———, *Probability theory and Euclidean field theory*, Constructive Quantum Field Theory, ed. by G. Velo and A. Wightman, Springer, New York, 1973.

18. K. Osterwalder and R. Schrader, *Axioms for Euclidean Green's functions*, Comm. Math. Phys. **31** (1973), 83–112.

19. ———, *Axioms for Euclidean Green's functions*. II (to appear).

20. R. Schrader, *Yukawa quantum field theory in two space-time dimensions without cutoffs*, Ann. Physics **70** (1972), 412–457. MR **46** #1241.

21. T. Spencer, *The absence of even bound states in* ϕ_4^2, Comm. Math. Phys. **39** (1974), 77–79.

22. E. Stanley, *Introduction to phase transitions and critical phenomena*, Oxford, New York, 1971.

ROCKEFELLER UNIVERSITY
NEW YORK, NEW YORK 10021, U.S.A.

Proceedings of the International Congress of Mathematicians
Vancouver, 1974

Initial Boundary Value Problems for Hyperbolic Partial Differential Equations

Heinz-Otto Kreiss

1. Differential equations in one space dimension. The simplest hyperbolic differential equation is given by

$$\partial u/\partial t = c\partial u/\partial x, \tag{1.1}$$

where c is a constant. Its general solution is $u(x, t) = F(x + ct)$, i.e., it is constant along the "characteristic lines" $x + ct = \text{const}$ (see Figure 1). Therefore, if we

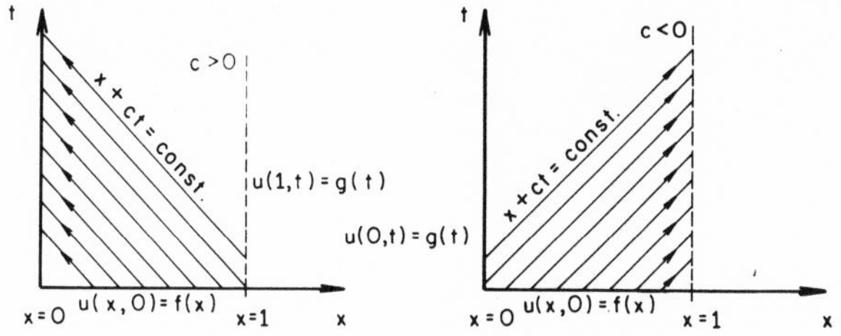

FIGURE 1

want to determine the solution of (1.1) in the region $0 \leqq x \leqq 1$, $t \geqq 0$, we have to describe initial conditions

$$u(x, 0) = f(x), \tag{1.2}$$

for $t = 0$ and boundary conditions

$$\begin{aligned} u(1, t) &= g(t) \quad \text{if } c > 0, \\ u(0, t) &= g(t) \quad \text{if } c < 0, \end{aligned} \tag{1.3}$$

for $x = 1, 0$ respectively.

There is no difficulty in generalizing the above results to systems

$$\partial u/\partial t = A\partial u/\partial x. \tag{1.4}$$

Here $u(x,t) = (u^{(1)}(x, t), \cdots, u^{(n)}(x, t))'$ denotes a vector function and A a constant $n \times n$ matrix. Hyperbolicity implies that A can be transformed to real diagonal form, i.e., there is a nonsingular transformation S such that

$$SAS^{-1} = \begin{pmatrix} A^{\mathrm{I}} & 0 \\ 0 & A^{\mathrm{II}} \end{pmatrix} = \tilde{A} \tag{1.5}$$

where

$$A^{\mathrm{I}} = \begin{pmatrix} a_1 & \cdots\cdots\cdots & 0 \\ 0 & a_2 \cdots\cdots & 0 \\ \cdots & \cdots & \cdots \\ 0 & \cdots\cdots 0 & a_r \end{pmatrix} < 0, \qquad A^{\mathrm{II}} = \begin{pmatrix} a_{r+1} & 0 & \cdots\cdots & 0 \\ 0 & a_{r+2n} & \cdots\cdots & 0 \\ \cdots & \cdots & \cdots & \cdots \\ 0 & \cdots\cdots & 0 & a_n \end{pmatrix} > 0$$

are definite diagonal matrices. We can thus introduce new variables

$$v = Su \tag{1.6}$$

and get

$$\partial v/\partial t = \tilde{A}\partial v/\partial x. \tag{1.7}$$

The last equation can also be written in partitioned form

$$\partial v^{\mathrm{I}}/\partial t = A^{\mathrm{I}}\partial v^{\mathrm{I}}/\partial x, \qquad \partial v^{\mathrm{II}}/\partial t = A^{\mathrm{II}}\partial v^{\mathrm{II}}/\partial x, \tag{1.8}$$

where $v^{\mathrm{I}} = (v^{(1)}, \cdots, v^{(r)})'$, $v^{\mathrm{II}} = (v^{(r+1)}, \cdots, v^{(n)})'$. (1.5) represents n scalar equations. Therefore we can write down its general solution

$$v^{(j)}(x, t) = v^{(j)}(x + a_j t), \qquad j = 1, 2, \cdots, n, \tag{1.9}$$

which are constant along the characteristic lines $x + a_j t = \text{const}$. The solution is uniquely determined in the domain $0 \leqq x \leqq 1$, $t \geqq 0$, and can be computed explicitly if we specify initial conditions

$$v(x, 0) = f(x), \qquad 0 \leqq x \leqq 1, \tag{1.10}$$

and boundary conditions

$$v^{\mathrm{II}}(0, t) = R_0 v^{\mathrm{II}}(0, t) + g_0(t), \qquad v^{\mathrm{II}}(1, t) = R_1 v^{\mathrm{II}}(1, t) + g_1(t). \tag{1.11}$$

Here R_0, R_1 are rectangular matrices and g_0, g_1 are given vector functions. If we consider wave propagation, then the boundary conditions describe how the waves are reflected at the boundary.

Nothing essentially is changed if $A = A(x, t)$ and $R_j = R_j(t)$ are functions of x, t. Now the characteristics are not straight lines but the solutions of the ordinary differential equations $dx/dt = a_j(x, t)$. More general systems

$$\partial v/\partial t = \tilde{A}(x, t)\partial v/\partial x + B(x, t)v + F(x, t) \tag{1.12}$$

can be solved by the iteration

$$\partial v^{[n+1]}/\partial t = \tilde{A}(x, t)\partial v^{[n+1]}/\partial x + F^{[n]} \tag{1.13}$$

where $F^{[n]} = B(x, t)v^{[n]} + F$. Furthermore, it is no restriction to assume that $\tilde{A}$ has diagonal form. If not, we can, by a change of dependent variables, achieve the form (1.10).

We can therefore develop a rather complete theory for initial boundary value problems by using characteristics. This has of course been known for a long time. The only trouble is that this theory cannot be easily generalized to problems in more than one space dimension. For difference approximations it is already inadequate in one space dimension.

2. The energy method. The main tool for proving the existence of solutions in more than one space dimension consists of "a priori estimates". Once these estimates have been established the existence and uniqueness of solutions follow by standard functional analytic arguments. The estimates are of the following type.

Consider a system of partial differential equations

$$\partial u/\partial t = P(x, t, \partial/\partial x)u \tag{2.1}$$

in a domain Ω with initial conditions

$$u(x, t_1) = f(x) \tag{2.2}$$

at some time $t = t_1$, and boundary condition

$$R(x, t)u = 0 \quad \text{on } \partial\Omega. \tag{2.3}$$

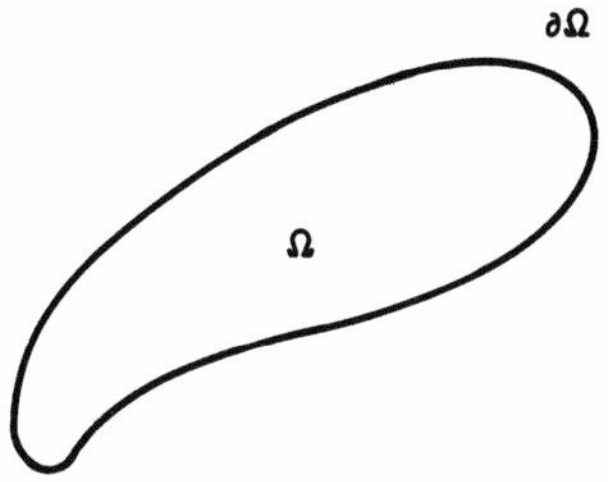

FIGURE 2

The problem is called weakly well posed if

$$\|u(x, t_2)\|_\Omega \leqq K \exp(\alpha(t_2 - t_1))\|u(x, t_2)\|_{\Omega, p}. \tag{2.4}$$

Here $\|\cdot\|_\Omega$ denotes the usual L_2-norm over Ω and $\|\cdot\|_{\Omega, p}$ the L_2-norm which also contains all space derivatives up to order p. If $p = 0$ then we call the problem strongly well posed.

There is a large class of problems for which the estimate (2.4) is immediate. This is the class of problems for which P is semibounded, i.e., for every fixed t and all sufficiently smooth w which fulfill the boundary conditions we have

$$(w, Pw) + (Pw, w)_\Omega \leqq 2\alpha\|w\|_\Omega^2. \tag{2.5}$$

Here α is some constant independent of w. (2.5) implies for all sufficiently smooth solutions

$$\partial \|u\|_\Omega^2 /\partial t = (\partial u/\partial t, u)_\Omega + (u \cdot \partial u/\partial t)_\Omega = (Pu, u)_\Omega + (u, Pu)_\Omega \leqq 2\alpha \|u\|_\Omega^2.$$

Therefore

$$\|u(x, t_2)\|_\Omega \leqq \exp(\alpha(t_2 - t_1)) \|u(x, t_2)\|_\Omega.$$

For symmetric hyperbolic systems this theory has been developed by K.O. Friedrichs [3]. As an example consider a first-order system

$$\partial u/\partial t = A\partial u/\partial x_1 + \sum_{j=2}^{m} B_j \partial u/\partial x_j = P(\partial/\partial x)u \tag{2.6}$$

with constant coefficients for $t \geqq 0$ and $x \in \Omega$. Here Ω denotes the half-space $0 \leqq x_1 < \infty$, $-\infty < x_j < \infty$, $j = 2, \cdots, m$. Furthermore A has the diagonal form (1.5) and the B_j are symmetric matrices.

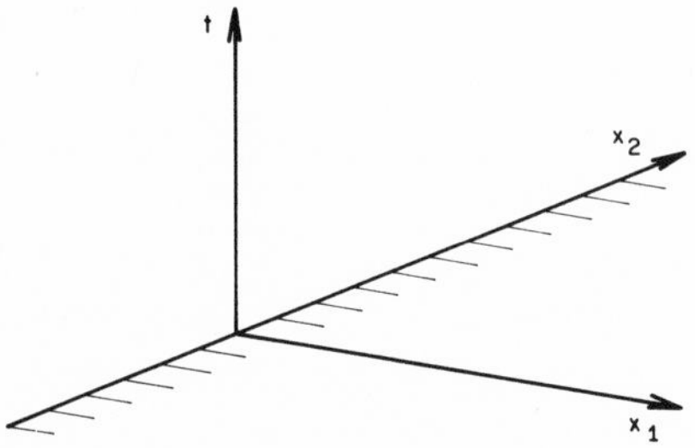

FIGURE 3

For $t = 0$ initial values

$$u(x, 0) = f(x), \qquad \|f\|_\Omega < \infty, \tag{2.7}$$

and for $x_1 = 0$ boundary conditions

$$u^{\mathrm{I}}(0, x_-, t) = R_0 u^{\mathrm{II}}(0, x_-, t), \quad x_- = (x_2, \cdots, x_m), \tag{2.8}$$

are given.

Partial integration gives for all sufficiently smooth $w \in L_2(\Omega)$ which fulfill the boundary conditions

$$\begin{aligned}(w, Pw)_\Omega + (Pw, w)_\Omega &= -\int_{\partial\Omega} w^* A w|_{x_1=0}\, dx_- \\ &= -\int_{\partial\Omega} (w^{\mathrm{II}})^*(A^{\mathrm{II}} + R_0^* A^{\mathrm{I}} R_0) w^{\mathrm{II}}|_{x_1=0}\, dx_-.\end{aligned}$$

Therefore the operator P is semibounded if R_0 is such that $A^{\mathrm{II}} + R_0^* A^{\mathrm{I}} R_0 \geqq 0$. This is for example the case if $|R_0|$ is sufficiently small. The disadvantage of the energy method is that it is a trick. When it works it is the most simple method to derive existence theorems. But it does not give necessary and sufficient conditions.

We shall now discuss another technique based on the Laplace transform which gives necessary and sufficient conditions.

3. Laplace transform. We consider again the problem (2.6)—(2.8) and assume now that the system is either symmetric or strictly hyperbolic, i.e., the matrices A and B_j are symmetric or the eigenvalues of the symbol

$$P(i\omega) = i\Big(A\omega_1 + \sum_{j=2}^{m} \omega_j B_j\Big), \quad \omega_\nu \text{ real}, \ \sum |\omega_\nu|^2 \neq 0,$$

are all distinct and purely imaginary. Furthermore the matrix A has the form (1.5) which is obviously no restriction.

In one space dimension the initial boundary value problem is always well posed. This is not true in higher dimensions. Already S. Agmon **[2]** has observed

LEMMA 3.1 *Assume that the problem* (2.6)—(2.8) *has a solution of the form*

$$w(x, t) = \phi(x) \exp(st + i\langle\omega_-, x_-\rangle), \qquad \langle\omega_-, x_-\rangle = \sum_{j=2}^{m} \omega_j x_j, \ \omega_j \text{ real}, \tag{3.1}$$

where real $s > 0$ *and* $\|\phi(x_1)\|^2 = \int_0^\infty |\phi|^2 \, dx_1 < \infty$.

Then the problem is ill posed.

PROOF. If $w(x, t)$ is a solution then the same is true for

$$w_\tau(x, t) = \exp\left(\tau(st + i\langle\omega_-, x_-\rangle)\right) \phi(\tau x_1)$$

for all real numbers $\tau > 0$. Thus there are solutions which grow arbitrarily fast with time.

We shall now derive algebraic conditions such that there are solutions of the above form. Introducing (3.1) into (2.6) gives us

LEMMA 3.2. *There is a solution of type* (3.1) *if and only if the eigenvalue problem*

$$s\phi = A\, d\phi/dx_1 + iB(\omega_-)\phi, \qquad B(\omega_-) = \sum B_j\omega_j, \ \|\phi\| < \infty, \ \phi^{\mathrm{I}}(0) = R_0\phi^{\mathrm{II}}(0), \tag{3.2}$$

has an eigenvalue with real $s > 0$.

(3.2) is a system of ordinary differential equations which can also be written in the form

$$d\phi/dx_1 = M\phi, \qquad M = A^{-1}(s - iB(\omega_-)). \tag{3.3}$$

For M we have

LEMMA 3.3. *For real* $s > 0$ *the matrix* M *has no eigenvalues* κ *with real* $\kappa = 0$. *The number of eigenvalues with real* $\kappa < 0$ *is equal to r, the number of boundary conditions.*

Therefore the general solutions of (3.2) belonging to L_2 can be written as

$$\sum_{j=1}^{r} \lambda_j \phi_j(x). \tag{3.4}$$

Introducing (3.4) into the boundary conditions gives us a system of linear equations

$$C(s)\lambda = 0, \qquad \lambda = (\lambda_1, \cdots, \lambda_r)'.$$

Thus we can express our results also in the following form:

LEMMA 3.4. *The problem* (2.6)—(2.8) *is not well posed if* $\text{Det}|C(s)| = 0$ *for some s with real* $s > 0$.

The main result of this section is (see **[7]**, **[14]**, **[13]**):

THEOREM 3.1. *Assume that* $\text{Det}|C(s)| \neq 0$ *for real* $s \geqq 0$. *Then the problem is strongly well posed.*

There is still the boundary case that $\text{Det}|C(s)| = 0$ for some $s = i\xi$, ξ real. As R. Hersh **[5]** has shown these are weakly well-posed problems. The main trouble is that the generalization of these boundary cases to variable coefficients is very difficult.

4. Problems with variable coefficients in general domains. Now we consider systems (2.6)—(2.8) with variable coefficients in a general domain $\Omega \times (0 \leqq t \leqq T)$.

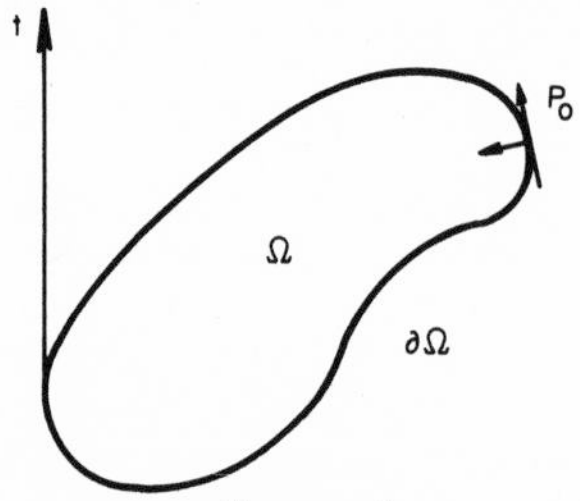

FIGURE 4

Here we assume that the coefficients and the boundary $\partial\Omega$ are sufficiently smooth. Connected with this problem there is a set of half-plane problems which we get in the following way: Let $P_0 = (x_0, t_0)$, $\partial\Omega \times (0 \leqq t \leqq T)$, be a boundary point and let $\tilde{x} = S(x)$, $\tilde{t} = t - t_0$ with $S(x_0) = 0$ be a smooth transformation which locally transforms the boundary into the half-plane $\tilde{x}_1 = 0$. Apply this transformation to the differential equations and the boundary conditions, freeze the coefficients at $\tilde{x} = \tilde{t} = 0$ and consider the half-plane problem with constant coefficients. Then we have

THEOREM 4.1. *Assume that for all the half-plane problems the conditions of* § 2 *hold, i.e., that all the operators connected with the half-plane problems are semibounded. Then the original problem is strongly well posed* (*see* **[3]**).

THEOREM 4.2. *If the system* (2.6) *is strictly hyperbolic and if for all the half-plane problems with frozen coefficients the determinant condition of Theorem* 3.1 *is fulfilled then the original problem is strongly well posed* (*see* **[7]**, **[14]**, **[13]**).

REMARKS. (1) It is not known whether the determinant condition guarantees well-posedness for symmetric systems which are not strictly hyperbolic. This is a rather disturbing gap in the theory.

(2) Quite a lot of progress has been made for the boundary case that $\text{Det}|C(s)|$

$= 0$ for some $s = i\xi$, ξ real. The key is to consider not only the half-plane problem for $\partial u/\partial t = Pu$ but also all perturbed problems $\partial u/\partial t = Pu + Bu$ where B is a constant matrix.

(3) It is assumed that A is nonsingular. However, progress has been made also for the singular case (see **[12]**).

(4) If the boundary is not smooth then new serious problems arise. See for example **[10]**, **[11]**.

5. Difference approximations in one space dimension. We start with an example which explains most of our difficulties. Consider the differential equation

$$\partial u/\partial t = \partial u/\partial x \tag{5.1}$$

in the quarter-plane $x \geqq 0$, $t \geqq 0$, with initial values

$$u(x, 0) = f(x). \tag{5.2}$$

From § 1 we know that no boundary conditions need to be specified for $x = 0$, $t \geqq 0$. We want to solve the above problem using the leap-frog scheme. For that reason we introduce a time step $\Delta t > 0$ and a mesh with $\Delta x > 0$ and divide the x-axis into intervals of length Δx. Using the notation $v_\nu(t) = v(x_\nu, t)$, $x_\nu = \nu\Delta x$, $t = t_\mu = \mu\Delta t$, we approximate (5.1), (5.2) by

$$v_\nu(t + \Delta t) = v_\nu(t - \Delta t) + 2\Delta t D_0 v_\nu(t), \qquad \nu = 1, 2, \cdots, \tag{5.3}$$

with initial values

$$v_\nu(0) = f(x_\nu), \quad v_\nu(\Delta t) = f(x_\nu) + \Delta t f(x_\nu)/\partial x. \tag{5.4}$$

Here $D_0 v_\nu = (v_{\nu+1} - v_{\nu-1})/2\Delta x$ denotes the usual centered difference operator. We assume that (5.3) is stable for the Cauchy problem, i.e., $0 < \Delta t/\Delta x \leqq 1$.

It is obvious that the solution of (5.3), (5.4) is not yet uniquely determined. We must give an additional equation for v_0. For example

$$v_0 = 0. \tag{5.5}$$

This relation is obviously not consistent. In general it will destroy the convergence. Let $f(x) \equiv 1$. Then $u(x, t) \equiv 0$ and $v_\nu(t) = 1 + (-1)^\nu y_\nu(t)$, where $y_\nu(t)$ is the solution of

$$\begin{aligned} y_\nu(t + \Delta t) &= y_\nu(t - \Delta t) - 2\Delta t D_0 y_\nu(t), \qquad \nu = 1, 2, \cdots, \\ y_\nu(0) &= y_\nu(\Delta t) = 0, \end{aligned} \tag{5.6}$$

with boundary conditions

$$y_0(t) = -1. \tag{5.7}$$

(5.6) and (5.7) is an approximation to the problem $\partial w/\partial t = -\partial w/\partial x$, $w(x, 0) = 0$, $w(0, t) = -1$, i.e.,

$$\begin{aligned} w(x, t) &= 0 \quad \text{for } t < x, \\ &= -1 \quad \text{for } t \geqq x. \end{aligned}$$

Therefore

$$\begin{aligned} v_\nu(t) &\sim 1 && \text{for } t < x, \\ &\sim 1 - (-1)^\nu && \text{for } t \geqq x. \end{aligned}$$

This behaviour is typical for all nondissipative centered schemes. Therefore one needs to be very careful when overspecifying boundary conditions. The oscillation decays if the approximation is dissipative. However, near the boundary the error is as bad and, for systems, it can be propagated into the interior via the ingoing characteristics.

Now we replace (5.5) by an extrapolation rule

$$v_0(t) - 2v_1(t) + v_2(t) = 0, \tag{5.8}$$

which is the same as using for $\nu = 1$ the one-sided difference formula

$$v_1(t + \Delta t) = v_1(t - \Delta t) + (2\Delta t/\Delta x)(v_2(t) - v_1(t)). \tag{5.9}$$

The approximation is only useful if it is stable. If we choose

$$\begin{aligned} v_\nu(0) &= 1 \quad \text{for } \nu = 0, \\ &= 0 \quad \text{for } \nu > 0, \end{aligned} \qquad v_\nu(\Delta t) \equiv 0 \quad \text{for all } \nu,$$

as initial values then an easy calculation shows that

$$\|v(t)\|_{\Delta x} = \text{const}(t/\Delta t), \qquad \|v\|_{\Delta x} = \sum |v_\nu|^2 \Delta x.$$

This growth rate is the worst possible and one might consider the approximation to be useful. However, if we consider (5.1) in a finite interval $0 \leqq x \leqq 1$ and add the boundary condition

$$u(1, t) = v_N(t) = 0, \qquad N\Delta x = 1, \tag{5.10}$$

for both the differential equation and the difference approximation, then there are solutions which grow like

$$\|v(t)\|_{\Delta x} = \text{const}(t/\Delta t)^t, \tag{5.11}$$

which is not tolerable. This behaviour can be explained as follows: At the boundary $x = 0$ a wave is created which grows like $t/\Delta t$. This wave is reflected at the boundary $x = 1$ and is increased by another factor $t/\Delta t$ when it hits the boundary $x = 0$ again, and so on.

All these difficulties can be avoided by using, instead of (5.9), the one-sided approximation $v_1(t + \Delta t) = v_1(t) + (\Delta t/\Delta x)(v_2(t) - v_1(t))$ or

$$v_1(t + \Delta t) = v_1(t - \Delta t) + (\Delta t/\Delta x)(v_2(t) - \tfrac{1}{2}(v_1(t + \Delta t) + v_1(t - \Delta t))).$$

One can also keep (5.8) if one replaces the leap-frog scheme by the Lax-Wendroff approximation or any other dissipative approximation.

Let us discuss the general theory. (For details see **[4]**, **[7]**, **[8]**.) We consider general difference approximations

$$v_{\nu+1}(t + \Delta t) = Qv_\nu(t) \tag{5.12}$$

with boundary conditions

(5.13) $$Bv_0 \doteq 0$$

such that the solution is uniquely determined by the initial values $v_\nu(0) = f_\nu$.

The approximation is useful only if it is

(1) consistent, i.e., it converges formally to the continuous problem,

(2) stable (weakly or strongly) which is the difference analog of well-posedness.

There is never any problem in deriving consistent approximations. It is the stability which causes the problem. Corresponding to the continuous problem there are two methods to decide whether a given method is stable: Laplace transform and energy method.

The theory based on Laplace transform is analogous to the theory for the continuous case. The stability is determined by the properties of the eigenvalue problem

(5.14) $$(z - Q)\phi_\nu = 0, \quad B\phi_0 = 0, \quad \|\phi\|^2_{\Delta x} = \sum |\phi_\nu|^2 \Delta x < \infty.$$

Corresponding to Lemma 3.2 we have, under reasonable assumptions for Q:

LEMMA 5.1. *Assume that* (5.14) *has an eigenvalue* $z = z_0$ *with* $|z_0| > 1$. *Then the approximation is not stable.*

This condition can also be expressed as a determinant condition $\mathrm{Det}|C(z_0)| = 0$ for some $z = z_0$ with $|z_0| > 1$. Then, corresponding to Theorem 3.1, we have

THEOREM 5.1. *The approximation is strongly stable if* $\mathrm{Det}|C(z)| \neq 0$ *for* $|z| \geqq 1$.

Now we turn to the energy method. Consider again the differential equation (5.1), (5.2). The problem is well posed because there is an energy equality

(5.15) $$(u, \partial u/\partial x) + (\partial u/\partial x, u) = -|u(0)|^2.$$

Therefore we want to construct approximations to $\partial/\partial x$ which have the corresponding property.

We define a discrete norm

(5.16) $$(u, v)_{\Delta x} = \tilde{u}^* A \tilde{v} \Delta x + \sum_{\nu=r}^{\infty} u_\nu^* v_\nu \Delta x.$$

Here $\tilde{u} = (u_0, \cdots, u_{r-1})'$, $\tilde{v} = (v_0, \cdots, v_{r-1})'$ denote the first r components of u, v and $A = A^*$ is a positive definite $r \times r$ matrix. In [9] we have shown that one can construct accurate approximations Q for which (5.16) holds. The main trouble is that the norm and the approximation near the boundary are very complicated. This makes its generalisation to approximations in more than one space dimension on general domains difficult. Furthermore, it is not known how to include dissipation in the construction. However, it should be pointed out that this construction also works in more than one space dimension provided the net follows the boundary.

6. Difference approximations in more than one space dimension. Nothing essentially new needs to be added to derive the theory of difference approximations for half-planes because Fourier transforms of the tangential variables x_- give us a set of one-dimensional problems. The situation becomes much more complicated if we consider general domains with smooth boundaries. Observe that this is not the case for the differential equations because we can always introduce a local coordinate system, thus reducing the problem to a set of half-plane problems. This is not possible for difference approximations. Once we have picked the net everything is fixed. D. Schaeffer [**15**] has tried to handle this situation and has developed a beautiful theory. However, its practical importance is somewhat doubtful. Let us consider a very simple example. We want to solve the differential equation

$$\partial u/\partial t = -\partial u/\partial x \tag{6.1}$$

in the two-dimensional domains $2y - x \leqq 0$. The initial values are

$$u(x, y, 0) = f(x, y) \quad \text{for } 2y - x \leqq 0,\ t = 0, \tag{6.2}$$

and the boundary conditions are given by

$$u(x, y, t) = g(x, y, t) \quad \text{for } 2y - x = 0,\ t \geqq 0. \tag{6.3}$$

We introduce gridpoints by $x_j = j\Delta x$, $y_i = i\Delta y$, $\Delta x = \Delta y$.

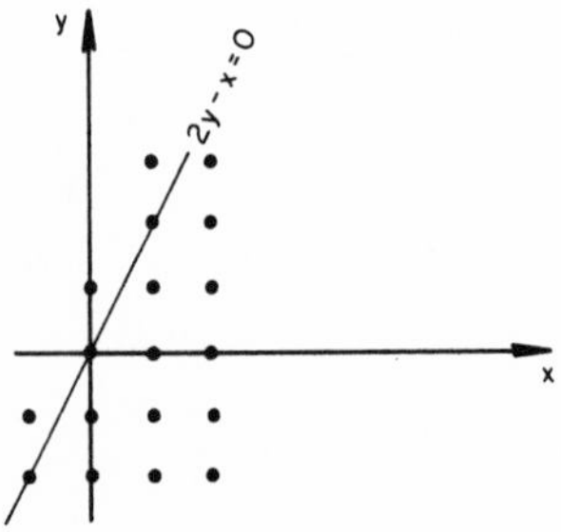

FIGURE 5

Thus, there is a gridpoint on the boundary only on every second row. Now we approximate (6.1) by the leap-frog scheme and the boundary conditions by

$$\begin{aligned} v_{i,j} &= g_{i,j} && \text{if } 2j = i, \\ v_{i,j} + v_{i+1,j} &= 2g_{i+1/2,j} && \text{if } 2j = i + 1. \end{aligned}$$

Here $v_{i,j} = v(i\Delta x, j\Delta y, t)$. Therefore we get two different solutions on two different meshes. As long as the solution of the differential equation is smooth the solutions of the difference equation on these different meshes fit together. However, if for example $f \equiv 0$ and $g \equiv 1$ then the solution of the differential equation is a discontinuous wave propagating into the interior. Now the solutions of the difference approximation on the different nets do not fit together.

We get oscillations in the tangential direction of the wave. There are two possible methods for remedying the situation: (1) Add dissipation to smooth out the tangential oscillations. (2) Introduce curved meshes which follow the boundary. The second procedure is much more accurate and should be preferred if possible. A lot of progress has been made in this direction. See for example [**1**].

References

1. A. A. Amsden and C. W. Hirt, *A simple scheme for generating general curvilinear grids*, J. Computational Physics **II** (1973).

2. S. Agmon, *Problèmes mixtes pour les équations hyperboliques d'ordre supérieur*, Les Équations aux Dérivées Partielles (Paris, 1962), Centre National de la Recherche Scientifique, Paris, 1963, pp. 13–18. MR **29** #6189.

3. K. O. Friedrichs, *Symmetric hyperbolic linear differential equations*, Comm. Pure Appl. Math. **7** (1954), 345–392. MR **16**, 44.

4. B. Gustafsson, H.-O. Kreiss and A. Sundström, *Stability theory of difference approximations for mixed initial boundary value problems*. II, Math. Comp. **26** (1972), 649–686.

5. R. Hersh, *Mixed problems in several variables*, J. Math. Mech. **12** (1963), 317–334. MR **26** #5304.

6. H.-O. Kreiss, *Initial boundary value problems for hyperbolic systems*, Comm. Pure. Appl. Math. **23** (1970), 277–298.

7. ———, *Stability theory for difference approximations of mixed initial boundary value problems*. I, Math. Comp. **22** (1968), 703–714. MR **39** #2355.

8. ———, *Difference approximations for initial boundary value problems*, Proc. Roy. Soc. London A **323** (1971).

9. H.-O. Kreiss and G. Scherer, *Difference and finite element methods for initial boundary value problems* (to appear).

10. S. Osher, *Initial-boundary value problems for hyperbolic systems in regions with corners*. I, Trans. Amer. Math. Soc. **176** (1973), 141–165. MR **47** #9076.

11. ———, *Initial boundary value problems for hyperbolic systems in regions with corners*. II, Report, Department of Computer Sciences, Uppsala University, Sweden, 1973.

12. ———, (to appear).

13. J. Rauch, *L_2 is a continuable initial condition for Kreiss' mixed problems*, Comm. Pure Appl. Math. **25** (1972), 265–285.

14. R. Sakamoto, *Mixed problems for hyperbolic equations*. I. *Energy inequalities*; II. *Existence theorems with zero initial data and energy inequalities with initial data*, J. Math. Kyoto Univ. **10** (1970), 349–373, 403–417. MR **44** #632a, b.

15. D. G. Schaeffer, *An application of von Neumann algebras to finite difference equations*, Ann. of Math. (2) **95** (1972), 117–129. MR **45** #5563.

UNIVERSITY OF UPPSALA
UPPSALA, SWEDEN

Actes du Congrès International des Mathématiciens
Vancouver, 1974

Sur la Théorie du Controle

J. L. Lions

1. Introduction. Soit un système dont *l'état* $y(s) = y(s; v)$ à l'instant s, lorsqu'on applique le controle v, est un vecteur de $\boldsymbol{R}^n$ donné par la solution de l'équation différentielle:

(1.1) $$dy/ds = g(y; v), \quad s > t, \quad y(t) = x, x \in \boldsymbol{R}^n,$$

où g est une fonction continue Lipschitzienne donnée pour $y \in \boldsymbol{R}^n$ et où v est une fonction à valeurs dans $\mathscr{U}_1 \subset \boldsymbol{R}^m$.

Admettant que l'on est dans une situation où (1.1) définit y de manière unique, on considère la *fonction coût* $J(v)$ donnée par:

(1.2) $J(v) = \int_t^T f(y(s; v), s, v(s))\, ds$, T donné fini ou non,

où f est donnée; on cherche

(1.3) $\inf J(v)$, $v \in$ ensemble $\mathscr{U}_{\text{ad}}$ des contrôles admissibles,

des fonctions à valeurs dans $\mathscr{U}_1$.

Une famille classique de problèmes de contrôle consiste en (1.3) avec $t = t_0$, $x = x_0$ fixés et en la recherche de v_0 (s'il existe) réalisant le minimum dans (1.3) (*le contrôle optimal*).

Dans le cas "sans contrainte" où $\mathscr{U}_1 = \boldsymbol{R}^m$, des conditions suffisantes ou nécessaires et suffisantes, sont données par le *système d'optimalité d'Euler*, étendu au cas avec contraintes par L. S. Pontryagin et son école (cf. Pontryagin, Boltjanskiĭ, Gamkrelidze et Mishenko [**1**]), dans le *Principe du maximum* (cf. aussi Hestenes [**1**]).

Une autre approche, en quelque sorte duale, consiste à considérer dans (1.3) x et t comme *variables* et donc à introduire

(1.4) $$u(x, t) = \inf J(v), \quad v \in \mathscr{U}_{\text{ad}},$$

et à essayer:

(i) de caractériser directement u,

(ii) d'en déduire, si possible, le contrôle optimal, s'il existe. C'est la méthode de Hamilton-Jacobi, étendue, de façon généralement formelle, par Bellman **[1]** aux cas stochastiques en particulier, et par Isaacs **[1]** au cas des jeux.

La fonction u satisfait *formellement* à une équation aux dérivées partielles non linéaire hyperbolique

$$(1.5) \qquad -\frac{\partial u}{\partial t} - \inf_{\lambda \in \mathscr{U}_1} \left[\sum_{i=1}^{n} g_i(x, \lambda) \frac{\partial u}{\partial x_i} + f(x, t, \lambda) \right] = 0,$$

avec la condition "initiale" (on intègre en t dans le sens rétrograde):

$$(1.6) \qquad u(x, T) = 0.$$

On doit rajouter des *conditions aux limites* lorsqu'on l'on introduit des contraintes sur l'état.

Lorsque l'on remplace (1.1) par une *équation différentielle stochastique*,

$$(1.7) \qquad dy = g(y; v)ds + \sigma\, dw(s)$$

où $\sigma > 0$, w = processus de Wiener standard dans $\boldsymbol{R}^n$, la fonction coût devient:

$$(1.8) \qquad J(v) = E[\textstyle\int_t^T f(y(s, v), s, v(s))\, ds], \qquad E = \text{espérance mathématique};$$

la fonction u, encore définie par (1.4), satisfait alors à l'équation non linéaire parabolique

$$(1.9) \qquad -\frac{\partial u}{\partial t} - \frac{\sigma^2}{2} \Delta u - \inf_{\lambda \in \mathscr{U}_1} \left[\sum g_i(x, \lambda) \frac{\partial u}{\partial x_i} + f(x, t, \lambda) \right] = 0$$

avec (1.6) et d'éventuelles conditions aux limites en cas de contraintes sur l'état.

S'appuyant alors, soit sur des méthodes probabilistes, soit sur des méthodes d'équations aux dérivées partielles et d'analyse fonctionnelle, on peut étudier—sous des hypothèses convenables—les problèmes (1.5), (1.9); nous renvoyons au livre de W. Fleming et R. Rishel **[1]** et à la bibliographie de cet ouvrage.

Notre objet est de donner quelques indications sur les situations suivantes:

(i) étude des cas où le contrôle dans (1.1) *n'est* plus une varabile continue, mais un *temps d'arrêt* ou un *contrôle impulsionnel;*

(ii) étude des cas où l'équation d'état (1.1) ou (1.7) n'est plus une équation différentielle, mais une *équation aux dérivées partielles déterministe ou stochastique.*

REMARQUE 1.1. Ces extensions sont motivées par de *nombreuses applications,* dont nous mentionnons *quelques-unes* (consulter aussi la bibliographie des travaux ci-après):

pour (i), problèmes d'économie et de gestion, cf. Bensoussan et Lions **[7]**;

pour (ii), problèmes de contrôle de processus physiques, cf. Butkowski **[1]**, P.K.C.Wang **[1]**, Boujot, Mercier et Temam **[1]**, Kuroda **[1]**, Yvon **[1]**;

problèmes chimiques ou biochimiques, cf. Kernevez et Thomas **[1]**,

usage de l'énergie des marées, cf. G. Duff **[1]**,

problèmes de mécanique (optimum design), cf. Pironneau **[1]**, problème de pollution, cf. W. Hullett [**1**], etc.

2. Temps d'arrêt et inéquations variationnelles.

2.1. *Le cas stationnaire.* Soit $\mathcal{O}$ un ouvert de $\boldsymbol{R}^n$, de frontière Γ; *l'état* est donné par l'équation de Ito:

$$dy = g(y)ds + \sigma dw(s), \quad y(0) = x, x \in \mathcal{O}, \tag{2.1}$$

dont la solution est notée $y_x(s)$. La *fonction coût* est:

$$J(\tau) = E\left(\textstyle\int_0^\tau e^{-\alpha s} f(y_x(s))\, ds\right), \quad \alpha > 0, \tag{2.2}$$

où τ = variable de contrôle = temps d'arrêt, $0 \leqq \tau \leqq \theta(x)$, où $\theta(x)$ est le temps d'atteinte (aléatoire) de $\mathcal{O}$.

Le problème de *temps d'arrêt optimal* consiste en la recherche de

$$u(x) = \inf J(\tau), \qquad 0 \leqq \tau \leqq \theta(x), \tag{2.3}$$

et de la fonction τ (si elle existe) réalisant le minimum dans (2.3).

On démontre que la fonction *u peut être caractérisée par l'ensemble des inégalités suivantes* (Bensoussan et Lions [**1**], Fleming [**1**]):

$$\begin{gathered} -\frac{\sigma^2}{2}\Delta u - \sum_{i=1}^n g_i(x)\frac{\partial u}{\partial x_i} + \alpha u - f \leqq 0, \quad u \leqq 0, \\ \left(-\frac{\sigma^2}{2}\Delta u - g_i(x)\frac{\partial u}{\partial_i x} + \alpha u - f\right)u = 0 \quad \text{dans } \mathcal{O}, \end{gathered} \tag{2.4}$$

avec la condition aux limites

$$u = 0 \quad \text{sur } \Gamma. \tag{2.5}$$

2.2. *Inéquations variationnelles* (*en abrégé I.V.*). La résolution directe du système (2.4), (2.5) repose sur la technique des I.V. (Lions et Stampacchia [**1**]); on suppose pour simplifier que $\mathcal{O}$ est borné (sinon, cf. Bensoussan et Lions [**1**]).

Soit $H^1(\mathcal{O})$ l'espace de Sobolev d'ordre 1 des fonctions v à valeurs réelles telles que $v, \partial v/\partial x_1, \cdots, \partial v/\partial x_n \in L^2(\mathcal{O})$; pour $u, v \in H^1(\mathcal{O})$, on pose

$$\begin{aligned} a(u, v) = {} & \frac{\sigma^2}{2}\int_{\mathcal{O}} \operatorname{grad} u \cdot \operatorname{grad} v\, dx \\ & - \sum \int_{\mathcal{O}} g_i(x)\frac{\partial u}{\partial x_i} v\, dx + \alpha \int_{\mathcal{O}} uv\, dx; \end{aligned} \tag{2.6}$$

soit K l'ensemble convexe fermé non vide de $H^1(\mathcal{O})$ formé des fonctions v telles que

$$v = 0 \quad \text{sur } \Gamma, \qquad v \leqq 0 \quad \text{p.p. dans } \mathcal{O}. \tag{2.7}$$

Alors (2.4), (2.5) peut être formulé sous la forme de 1' I.V.: trouver $u \in K$ telle que

$$a(u, v-u) \geqq (f, v-u) \qquad \forall\, v \in K, \text{ où } (f, v) = \int_{\mathcal{O}} fv\, dx. \tag{2.8}$$

Si l'on suppose que:[1]

[1]Hypothèse non indispensable.

$$\alpha + \frac{1}{2} \Sigma \frac{\partial g_i}{\partial x_i} \geqq 0 \quad \text{dans } \mathcal{O} \tag{2.9}$$

alors la forme $a(u, v)$ est coercive au sens:

$$a(v, v) \geqq c \| v \|^2_{H^1(\mathcal{O})}, \qquad c > 0, \forall\, v \in K, \tag{2.10}$$

et, d'après Lions et Stampacchia, loc. cit., (2.8) admet une *solution unique*.

On obtient ainsi une solution "*faible*" de (2.4); mais on peut passer de là à *des solutions "fortes"*: c'est le problème de la *régularité* des solutions des I.V., cf. H. Brezis et Stampacchia [**1**], H. Brezis [**1**].

2.3. *Cas d'évolution*. L'état est maintenant donné par:

$$dy = g(y)ds + \sigma dw(s), \qquad y(t) = x, x \in \mathcal{O}, s > t, \tag{2.11}$$

dont la solution est $y_{x,t}(s)$; la fonction coût est donnée par:

$$J(\tau) = E\left(\int_t^\tau e^{-\alpha(s-t)} f(y_{x,t}(s), s)\, ds\right) \tag{2.12}$$

et l'on cherche

$$u(x, t) = \inf J(v), \tag{2.13}$$

τ temps d'arrêt inférieur au temps d'atteinte de $\mathcal{O}$.

On démontre (Bensoussan et Lions [**1**]) que *u est caractérisée par l'ensemble des inégalités*

$$\begin{gathered} - \frac{\partial u}{\partial t} - \frac{\sigma^2}{2} \Delta u - \sum^n g_i \frac{\partial u}{\partial x_i} + \alpha u - f \leqq 0, \\ u \leqq 0, \qquad \left(- \frac{\partial u}{\partial t} - \frac{\sigma^2}{2} \Delta u - \sum^n g_i \frac{\partial u}{\partial x_i} + \alpha u - f\right) u = 0 \end{gathered} \tag{2.14}$$

dans $\mathcal{O} \times]t_0, +\infty[$ (t_0 choisi quelconque), avec la condition aux limites analogue à (2.5) et une condition "initiale" de type (cf. Bensoussan et Lions, loc.cit., pour des énoncés précis) "u ne croît pas trop vite lorsque $t \to +\infty$".

Par les *techniques des I.V. d'évolution*, on démontre *l'existence* et *l'unicité* de u solution de (2.14) satisfaisant aux conditions aux limites et initiales.

2.4. REMARQUES. (1) Pour l'extension de ce qui précède au cas *des jeux*, cf. Bensoussan et Friedman [**1**].

(2) Dans le cas "$\sigma = 0$", on aboutit à des *I.V. pour des opérateurs du* 1er *ordre* et en faisant $\sigma \to 0$, on obtient des résultats sur *les perturbations singulières dans les I.V.* (Bensoussan et Lions [**2**]).

(3) Pour des résultats supplémentaires, en particulier de régularité, cf. Friedman [**1**] et la bibliographie de ce travail.

3. Surfaces libres.

3.1. *Problème de Stefan*. Considérons un cas très particulier de (2.14): $n = 1$, $\sigma = \sqrt{2}$, $g_i = 0$, $\alpha = 0$, et inversons le sens du temps (ce qui est losible); le problème devient:

$$\frac{\partial u}{\partial t} - \frac{\partial^2 u}{\partial x^2} - f \leqq 0, \quad u \leqq 0, \quad u\left(\frac{\partial u}{\partial t} - \frac{\partial^2 u}{\partial x^2} - f\right) = 0, \tag{3.1}$$

avec les conditions aux limites et initiales.

Soit (formellement) $x = s(t)$ la courbe séparant la région $u < 0$ *de continuation* de la région $u = 0$ *de saturation*; dans la région $\mathscr{C}$ où $u < 0$, on a:

$$\partial u/\partial t - \partial^2 u/\partial x^2 = f, \tag{3.2}$$

et sur *la surface libre* $x = s(t)$, on a:

$$u(s(t), t) = 0, \tag{3.3}$$

$$\partial u(s(t), t)/\partial x = 0.^2 \tag{3.4}$$

Si l'on introduit alors la fonction

$$w = \partial u/\partial t \tag{3.5}$$

on voit que, dans $\mathscr{C}$:

$$\partial w/\partial t - \partial^2 w/\partial x^2 = \partial f/\partial t \tag{3.6}$$

avec sur la surface libre $x = s(t)$:

$$w(s(t), t) = 0, \tag{3.7}$$

$$\partial w(s(t), t)/\partial x = f s'.^3 \tag{3.8}$$

La recherche de w solution de (3.6), (3.7), (3.8) est un cas particulier du problème classique de Stefan.

La démarche suivie par, en particulier, McKean **[1]**, Grigelionis et Shiryaev **[1]**, van Moerbeke **[1]**, **[2]** est de *ramener les problèmes des inégalités aux dérivées partielles du type* (2.14) *au problème de Stefan.*

La technique des I.V. rend cette transformation inutile et *l'idée précédente peut au contraire être utilisée dans la direction inverse:* Si l'on a à résoudre le problème de Stefan (3.6), (3.7), (3.8) (et avec une condition initiale), on *introduit u* par (3.5), (3.3) et *on vérifie alors que u est caractérisé par une* I.V.; cf. G. Duvaut **[1]** pour une situation plus générale.

3.2. *Réduction de problèmes de surfaces libres à des I.V.* L'idée précédente de réduction, par changement de fonction inconnue, de problèmes de surfaces libres à des I.V. a été introduite (dans une situation plus délicate) par C. Baiocchi **[1]**, **[2]** à propos de *problèmes d'infiltration*. Par des adaptations convenables, cette méthode a été appliquée par H. Brezis et G. Stampacchia **[2]**, H. Brezis et G. Duvaut **[1]**, J. F. Bourgat et G. Duvaut **[1]**, à des problèmes d'hydrodynamique. Une question générale est alors:

Problème 1. Quels sont les problèmes de frontière libre que l'on peut réduire a des I.V.?

4. Contrôle impulsionnel et inéquations quasi-variationnelles.

4.1. *Cas stationnaire.* L'état est donné dans $\boldsymbol{R}^n$ par

[2]Cela utilise la "*régularite*" de u.

[3]$w_x = u_{tx}$; d'après (3.4) $u_{tx} + u_{xx}\, s' = 0$ et utilisant (3.2) $u_{tx} = (f - u_t)s' = fs'$ sur la courbe $x = s(t)$ d'où (3.8).

(4.1) $$dy = g(y)ds + \sigma dw(s) + \sum_{i=1}^{N} \zeta^i \delta(s - \theta^i)ds, \qquad y(0) = x,$$

où dans (4.1) les θ^i (instants d'impulsion) sont à notre disposition, ainsi que les ζ^i assujettis à

(4.2) $$\zeta^i \in \mathcal{U} \subset \boldsymbol{R}^n;$$

le nombre N est également à notre disposition; le contrôle v est donc

(4.3) $$v = \{\theta^1, \zeta^1; \theta^2, \zeta^2; \cdots ;\theta^N, \zeta^N; N\},$$
$$0 \leqq \theta^1 < \theta^2 < \cdots < \theta^N \leqq T \text{ (donné fini ou non)}, \ \zeta^i \in \mathcal{U}, N = N(v).$$

L'état est désigné par $y_x(v) = y_x(s, v)$ et la *fonction coût* est donnée par:

(4.4) $$J(v) = E\,\{\textstyle\int_0^T e^{-\alpha s} f(y_x(s; v))\, ds + kN(v)\},$$

où f est une fonction donnée $\geqq 0$ et k un nombre > 0.[4]

On démontre alors (Bensoussan et Lions [**1**], Bensoussan, Goursat et Lions [**1**]) que la fonction

(4.5) $$u(x) = \inf_v J(v),$$

est caractérisée *par l'ensemble d'inégalités* dans $\boldsymbol{R}^n$:

(4.6) $$-\frac{\sigma^2}{2}\Delta u - \sum g_i \frac{\partial u}{\partial x_i} + \alpha u - f \leqq 0,$$
$$u - M(u) \leqq 0, \qquad \left(-\frac{\sigma^2}{2}\Delta u - \sum g_i \frac{\partial u}{\partial x_i} + \alpha u - f\right)(u - M(u)) = 0,$$

où

(4.7) $$M(u)(x) = \inf_{\zeta \in \mathcal{U}} u(x + \zeta) + k.$$

Dans le cas de contraintes sur l'état, traduites par x, $y_x(s) \in \mathcal{O}$, $\mathcal{O}$ ouvert de $\boldsymbol{R}^n$, $M(u)$ est défini par (4.7) avec x et $x + \zeta \in \mathcal{O}$ et l'on ajoute à (4.6) les conditions aux limites

(4.8) $$u - M(u) \leqq 0, \quad \frac{\partial u}{\partial \nu} \leqq 0, \quad (u - M(u))\frac{\partial u}{\partial \nu} = 0 \text{ sur } \Gamma,$$

où $\partial/\partial\nu$ = dérivée normale dirigée vers l'extérieur de $\mathcal{O}$.

4.2. *Inequations quasi-variationnelles* (*en abrégé* (*I.Q.V.*)). Avec la notation (2.6) le problème (4.6), (4.8) peut se formuler: Trouver $u \in H^1(\mathcal{O})$ telle que,

(4.9) $$u \leqq M(u),$$

(4.10) $$a(u, v - u) \geqq (f, v - u) \qquad \forall\, v \in H^1(\mathcal{O}) \text{ avec } v \leqq M(u).$$

C'est une I.Q.V. *elliptique*, qui diffère des I.V. par le fait que les contraintes sur les fonctions v *dépendent de la fonction inconnue u.*

On démontre *l'existence et l'unicité* d'une solution de (4.10) (cf. Bensoussan et

[4] Cf. la conférence de A. Bensoussan [**1**] à ce Congrès sur l'interprétation de ce type de problème.

Lions, loc.cit., L. Tartar [**1**], une démonstration directe de l'unicité étant due à Th. Laetsch [**1**]; cf. également Joly et Mosco [**1**]). Nous renvoyons en particulier à l'exposé A. Bensoussan à ce Congrès.

4.3. *I.Q.V. d'évolution.* Si l'état est donné par (4.1) avec $y(t) = x$ et si dans (4.4), on intègre de t à T, on a:

$$\inf J(v) = u(x, t), \tag{4.11}$$

u étant alors caractérisée par une I.Q.V. d'*évolution.*

Voir Bensoussan et Lions [**4**] où l'on verra également comment l'on peut obtenir un contrôle optimal à partir de la connaissance de u.

4.4. *I.Q.V. et surfaces libres.* La solution u de (4.6) vérifie $u < M(u)$ dans une région de continuation séparée de la région de saturation $u = M(u)$ par une *surface libre* qui satisfait à des conditions de transmission *non locales* à cause du *caractère non local* de M.

Pour une transformation adéquate, C. Baiocchi [**3**] a réduit des problèmes de surface libre de l'hydrodynamique à certaines I.Q.V., d'où la question générale:

Problème 2. Quels sont les problèmes de surfaces libres qui peuvent se réduire à des I.Q.V.?

4.5. REMARQUES. (1) On peut étudier des problèmes où le contrôle comprend une partie impulsionnelle et une partie continue. Cf. Bensoussan et Lions [**5**].

(2) De nombreuses questions restent ouvertes dans ces directions. Citons:

Problème 3. Etude de la *régularité* des solutions des I.Q.V.[5]

Problème 4. Quelles sont les I.V. ou les I.Q.V. dont la solution peut s'exprimer par un problème d'optimisation sur des trajectoires caractéristiques convenables? Par exemple, est-ce possible pour certains problèmes d'élasto-plasticité (cf. Duvaut et Lions [**1**])?

5. Equations d'état de dimension infinie.

5.1. REMARQUES GÉNÉRALES. L'état est de dimension infinie dans les cas principaux suivants:

(i) l'équation d'état est une équation différentielle avec *retard*; cf. Banks et Jacobs [**1**], Delfour et Mitter [**1**] et la bibliographie de ces travaux;

(ii) l'équation d'état est une *équation aux dérivées partielles* déterministe ou stochastique. La donnée initiale, notée h au lieu de x (réservé aux variables géométriques), est alors un élément d'un espace H de dimension infinie; la fonction $u(h, t)$ définie sur $H \times]-\infty, T]$ par l'analogue de (1.4) satisfait formellement à une *équation aux dérivées partielles et fonctionnelles* ($\mathscr{E}$)—cela, lorsque le contrôle v est une fonction distribuée dans le domaine ou sur la frontière ou ponctuelle. Si le contrôle est un temps d'arrêt ou de nature impulsionnelle, on aboutit à l'étude (qui est en cours) des I.V. et des I.Q.V. en dimension infinie.

Nous allons examiner un cas très particulier où ($\mathscr{E}$) *se réduit à une équation aux dérivées partielles.*

REMARQUE. Les équations aux dérivées partielles et fonctionelles apparaissent

[5]Des résultats très partiels sont donnés dans Bensoussan et Lions et Joly, Mosco et Troianniello, à paraître.

également, dans un contexte différent mais pas indépendant, dans l'étude *des solutions statistiques des équations aux dérivées partielles*; cf. Visik et Furcikov [**1**], C. Foias, [**1**], C. Foias et G. Prodi [**1**], M. Viot [**1**].

5.2. *Le cas linéaire quadratique*. Soit Ω un ouvert de $\boldsymbol{R}^n$ de frontière Γ; dans Ω on se donne un opérateur elliptique du 2ème ordre A

$$A\varphi = -\sum \frac{\partial}{\partial x_i}\left(a_{ij}(x)\frac{\partial \varphi}{\partial x_j}\right),$$
(5.1)
$$a_{ij} \in L^\infty(\Omega),\ \sum a_{ij}(x)\zeta_i\zeta_j \geqq \alpha \sum \zeta_i^2,\ \alpha > 0,\ x \in \Omega.$$

On suppose que l'*état* est donné par

(5.2) $$\partial y/\partial s + Ay = v \quad \text{dans } Q = \Omega \times]\,t, T\,[,\ v \in L^2(Q),$$

avec la donnée initiale

(5.3) $$y(x, t) = h(x) \quad \text{dans } \Omega,\ h \in L^2(\Omega) = H,$$

et les conditions aux limites

(5.4) $$y = 0 \quad \text{sur } \Gamma \times]\,t, T\,[\,.$$

Soit la fonction coût donnée par

(5.5) $$J(v) = \textstyle\int_t^T |y(s)|^2\, ds + N \int_t^T |v(s)|^2\, ds,$$

T fini donné, $N > 0$ donné, où $|\ |$ = norme dans $L^2(\Omega)$, où dans (5.5) $y(s) = y(s; v)$ désigne *la* solution de (5.2), (5.3), (5.4). Soit alors

(5.6) $$u(h, t) = \inf J(v), \quad v \in L^2(Q).$$

On vérifie, *formellement,* que

(5.7) $$-\partial u(h, t)/\partial t + (u_h(h, t), Ah) - \inf_{\lambda \in H}[N|\lambda|^2 + (\lambda, u_h(h, t))] = |h|^2,$$ [6]

avec la condition "initiale"

(5.8) $$u(h, T) = 0.$$

Dans (5.7), on a posé $(u_h(h, t), k) = (d/d\xi)u_h(h + \xi k, t)|_{\xi=0}$. Explicitant le inf qui apparaît dans (5.7), on en déduit:

(5.9) $$-(\partial u/\partial t)(h, t) + (u_h(h, t), Ah) + |u_h(h, t)|^2/4N = |h|^2 \quad \forall\, h \in D(A).$$

Mais l'homogénéité de (5.9) montre que $u(h, t)$ est une forme quadratique en h; on peut écrire

(5.10) $$u(h,t) = (P(t)h, h) \quad \text{(produit scalaire dans } H),\ P(t)^* = P(t),$$

et, utilisant (5.10) dans (5.9), on en déduit que $P(t)$ considéré comme opérateur linéaire continu de H dans H vérifie (dans un sens convenable; cf. Lions [**1**]):

(5.11) $$-\partial P/\partial t + PA + A^*P + P \cdot P/N = I \quad \text{(identité dans } H)$$

avec la condition initiale (correspondante à (5.8)):

[6] Cela, pour tout h dans le domaine $D(A)$ de l'opérateur non borné A.

(5.12) $$P(T) = 0.$$

Mais, d'après le théorème des noyaux de L. Schwartz, l'opérateur $P(t)$ s'exprime par un noyau $P(x, \zeta, t)$:

(5.13) $$P(t)\varphi(x) = \int_\Omega P(x, \zeta, t)\, \varphi(\zeta)\, d\zeta,$$

et (5.11) correspond à l'*équation aux dérivées partielles* (*non linéaire*)

(5.14) $$-\frac{\partial P}{\partial t} + (A_x^* + A_\xi^*)\, P(x, \xi, t) + \frac{1}{N}\int_\Omega P(x, \xi, t)\, P(\zeta, \xi, t)\, d\zeta = \delta(x - \xi),^7$$

à quoi on ajoute les conditions aux limites (correspondant au fait que $P(t)$ applique H dans $D(A)$):

(5.15) $$P(x, \zeta, t) = 0 \quad \text{si } x \in \Gamma, \zeta \in \Omega \text{ ou si } x \in \Omega, \zeta \in \Gamma,$$

et évidemment $P(x, \zeta, T) = 0$.

Tout cela peut être justifié, dans des conditions plus générales. Cf. Lions **[1]**, **[2]**.

En résumé, dans le cas particulier présent, *l'équation aux dérivées partielles et fonctionnelles* (5.9) *se réduit à l'équation aux dérivées partielles non linéaire* (5.14).

5.3. Remarques. (1) Dans Lions, loc. cit., on a utilisé la théorie du contrôle pour résoudre (5.14), (5.15), (5.12). Une étude directe (sans usage de la théorie du contrôle) d'équations non linéaires à inconnus opérateurs—contenant en particulier (5.14)—est dûe à R. Temam **[1]**, Da Prato **[1]**, L. Tartar **[2]**.

Pour l'étude numérique de ces équations, cf. Nedelec **[1]** qui adapte les méthodes des pas fractionnaires, Marchouk **[1]**, Yanenko **[1]**.

(2) Pour les cas stochastiques, cf. Bensoussan **[2]**, Balakrishnan **[1]**, Bismut **[1]**.

6. Système d'optimalité.

6.1. *Cas linéaire quadratique.* Reprenons la situation du N° 5.2., avec des *contrain tes* v:

(6.1) $$v \in \mathcal{U}_{\text{ad}} = \text{ensemble convexe fermé non vide de } L^2(Q).$$

Alors les considérations du N° 5.2. conduisent à une équation du type (5.7) où le inf est pris pour $\lambda \in \mathcal{U}_1$ si $\mathcal{U}_{\text{ad}}$ consiste en les fonctions à valeurs dans $\mathcal{U}_1$. Mais une étude *directe* du problème est plus simple. On prend $t = 0$ et h *fixé* (donné). Le problème

(6.2) $$\inf J(v), \qquad v \in \mathcal{U}_{\text{ad}}$$

admet une solution v_0 unique, qui est donnée par les systèmes d'équations et d'inéquations aux dérivées partielles suivant:

(6.3) $$\begin{aligned} &\frac{\partial y}{\partial t} + Ay = v_0, \qquad y(x, 0) = h(x), y = 0 \text{ sur } \Gamma \times]0, T[, \\ &-\frac{\partial p}{\partial t} + A^*p = y, \qquad p(x, T) = 0, p = 0 \text{ sur } \Gamma \times]0, T[, \\ &\int_Q (p + Nv_0)(v - v_0)\, dx\, dt \geqq 0 \quad \forall\, v \in \mathcal{U}_{\text{ad}}, v_0 \in \mathcal{U}_{\text{ad}}. \end{aligned}$$

---

7 $\delta(x-\xi)$ est le noyau de I.

C'est *le système d'optimalité,* qui est d'usage essentiel pour l'obtention d'algorithemes numériques. Donnons quelques indications sur l'extension (éventuelle) du système d'optimalité à des situations plus compliquées.[8]

6.2. *Contrôle de surfaces libres.* Supposons l'état donné par la solution de l'I.V.[9]

$$a(y, \varphi - y) \geqq \int_\Omega f(\varphi - y)\, dx + \int_\Gamma v(\varphi - y)\, d\Gamma \qquad \forall\, \varphi \in K, y \in K, \tag{6.4}$$

où a est donné par (2.6), $K = \{\varphi \mid \varphi \in H^1(\Omega), \varphi \geqq 0 \text{ sur } \Gamma = \partial\Omega\}$, $f \in L^2(\Omega)$, et où le contrôle v parcourt $\mathcal{U} = L^2(\Gamma)$.

Soit $y = y(v)$ la solution de (6.4) et soit la fonction coût

$$J(v) = \int_\Gamma (y(v) + g)^2\, d\Gamma + N \int_\Gamma v^2\, d\Gamma, \qquad g \text{ donnée} \geqq 0. \tag{6.5}$$

Alors le problème

$$\operatorname{Inf} J(v), \qquad v \in L^2(\Gamma), \tag{6.6}$$

admet une solution unique v_0 qui est caractérisée par le système suivant (cf. F. Mignot [**1**]):

$$\begin{aligned} &a(y, \varphi - y) \geqq \int_\Omega f(\varphi - y)\, dx - \frac{1}{N} \int_\Gamma p(\varphi - y)\, d\Gamma \quad \forall\, \varphi \in K, y \in K, \\ &a^*(p, \psi) = \int_\Gamma (y + g)\psi\, d\Gamma \end{aligned} \tag{6.7}$$

$\forall\, \psi$ tel que $\psi = 0$ sur l'ensemble $Z(y)$ de Γ où y s'annule, $p = 0$ sur $Z(y)$, puis,

$$v_0 = -\, p/N. \tag{6.8}$$

L'ensemble (6.7) *est une I.Q.V.*

Notons que dans (6.4) l'application $v \to y(v)$ de $L^2(\Gamma) \to H^1(\Omega)$ est Lipschitzienne, donc (Aronszajn [**1**]) dérivable "presque partout". Par des raisonnements ad hoc, Mignot [**1**] a pu *expliciter une* dérivée et en déduire, dans le cas présent, le système d'optimalité (6.7). Une question générale est:

Problème 5. Comment obtenir des systèmes d'optimalité dans les problèmes où l'état est Lipschitzien, non partout différentiable, en le contrôle?[10]

6.3. *Le contrôle est le domaine géométrique.* Dans de nombreux problèmes des mécanique ou de physique, la variable de contrôle est un *domaine géométrique.* Par exemple, l'état est donné par l'équation de Stokes[11]

$$-\, \nu\Delta y = -\, \operatorname{grad} \cdot p, \qquad \operatorname{div} y = 0, \text{ dans } \Omega, \tag{6.9}$$

y donné sur le bord de Ω, l'ouvert Ω étant à choisir (avec certaines contraintes géométriques et par exemple un volume donné) de manière à minimiser la trainée

[8]Cf. d'autres situations dans Barbu [**1**], Brauner et Penel [**1**], Kernevez [**1**], Slemrod [**1**], Yvon [**1**], etc. Pour le cas, essentiel, des contrôles frontières, on utilise la méthode de Lions et Magenes [**1**].

[9]Correspondant à un problème de mécanique unilatérale.

[10]Cette question est liée aux recherches de L. Neustadt, Halkin et Neustadt [**1**], Rockafellar, Clarke.

[11]Cf. Pironneau, dont on ne considère ici qu'un cas particulier.

(6.10) $$J(\Omega) = \frac{2}{\nu} \int_\Omega \sum \sigma_{ij}^2 \, dx, \qquad \sigma_{ij} = \frac{\nu}{2}\left(\frac{\partial y_i}{\partial x_j} + \frac{\partial x_j}{\partial x_i}\right).$$

Cela conduit à l'étude de la "dérivée en Ω"[12] de la fonction $\Omega \to y(\Omega)$. Il s'agit là d'un problème classique (Hadamard [**1**], P. Levy [**1**])[13] donnant lieu à des développements récents: Pironneau, loc. cit., J. Cea et son groupe [**1**], Murat et Simon [**1**]. Pour un théorème d'existence, par usage du théorème des fonctions implicites, cf. D. G. S. Schaeffer [**1**].

Des questions de conception optimale de matériaux élasto-plastiques conduisent au:

Problème 6. Comment étendre les formules de Hadamard sur la dérivée de $y(\Omega)$ en Ω aux solutions d'I.V.?

Une question liée à la précédente est:

Problème 7. Comment dépendent les surfaces libres de "variations" du domaine géométrique?

6.4. Remarques. (1) Par des changements de variables (possibles avec des hypothèses ad hoc sur la classe des ouverts Ω considérés), on peut ramener les problèmes de 6.3. à des problèmes *de contrôle dans les coefficients* de l'opérateur différentiel (ou encore "*le contrôle est l'opérateur*"); pour ce type de problèmes, cf. Spagnolo [**1**], Murat et Tartar [**1**], Zolezzi [**1**].

(2) *La nature du système d'optimalité* peut être quelque peu modifiée par usage de la théorie de *la dualité* au sens de Rockafellar [**1**], Ekeland et Temam [**1**]. C'est, entre autres, le cas (Mossino [**1**]) où l'on a des contraintes sur l'état. Cf. aussi Lions [**4**]. La théorie de la dualité permet aussi d'obtenir des solutions *relaxées* (ou généralisées); cf. Ekeland et Temam, loc.cit.

(3) Le système d'optimalité pour les problèmes *de temps optimal* a été étudié par Fattorini [**1**], [**2**] en vue de l'obtention de résultats du type "Bang-Bang".

(4) Les questions de temps optimal sont, comme dans la théorie classique des systèmes gouvernés par des équations différentielles (cf. R. Conti [**1**] et la bibliographie de ce livre), liées à la question de la structure de l'ensemble E des états à un instant donné lorsque le contrôle v varie, question étudiée par Fattorini et Russell [**1**], Russell [**1**], Fattorini [**3**].

(5) Les problèmes de (4) sont eux-mêmes liés à la question des *multiplicateurs de Lagrange en dimension infinie*. Dans cet ordre d'idées, notons que p dans (6.9) peut être considéré comme un multiplicateur de Lagrange. Peut-on généraliser ce résultat au problème suivant:[14] on cherche à minimiser:

(6.11) $$J(\varphi) = \frac{1}{2} \sum_{i,j=1}^{2} \int_\Omega \left(\frac{\partial \varphi_i}{\partial x_j}\right)^2 dx - \sum_{i=1}^{2} \int_\Omega f_i \varphi_i \, dx,$$

sur l'ensemble *non linéaire* des vecteurs $\varphi \in H^1(\varphi) \times H^1(\Omega)$, nuls au bord et tels que

[12]Pour Ω dans une classe convenable. Une tentative pour travailler "sans restrictions" sur Ω est faite dans Bensoussan et Lions [**6**].

[13]Qui introduit à ce sujet des équations aux dérivées fonctionnelles.

[14]Rencontré avec G. Duvaut dans un travail non publié.

(6.12) $$\operatorname{div} \varphi + \frac{\partial \varphi_1}{\partial x_1} \frac{\partial \varphi_2}{\partial x_2} - \frac{\partial \varphi_1}{\partial x_2} \frac{\partial \varphi_2}{\partial x_1} = 0 \text{ dans } \Omega.$$

Ce problème admet-il une solution y et existe-t-il un multiplicateur de Lagrange?

(6) L'écriture du système (ou d'un système) d'optimalité conduit également à des problèmes intéressants lorsque *l'état* est donné par une *valeur propre* ou une *fonction propre* (cf. F. Mignot [**2**]), lorsque l'on veut contrôler la stabilité de phénomènes pouvant devenir instables, (cf. J. Puel [**1**]).

(7) La simplification du système d'optimalité en présence de petits paramètres conduit à de nouveaux problèmes de perturbations singuliéres. (Cf. Lions [**5**], Jameson et O'Malley [**1**]).

(8) Pour les méthodes *numériques* correspondantes, nous renvoyons à Yvon [**1**], Lions et Yvon [**1**] et à la bibliographie de ces travaux.

Bibliographie

N. Aronszajn

[**1**] Cours de 3ème cycle, Paris, 1974.

C. Baiocchi

[**1**] *Sur un problème à frontière libre traduisant le filtrage de liquides à travers des milieux poreux*, C. R. Acad. Sci. Paris Sér. A-B **273** (1971), A1215–A1217. MR **45** #6265.

[**2**] *Free boundary problems in the theory of fluid flow through porous media*, these PROCEEDINGS.

[**3**] C. R. Acad. Sci. Paris Sér. A-B **278** (1974).

C. Baiocchi, V. Comincioli, E. Magenes and G. A. Pozzi

[**1**] Ann. Mat. Pura Appl. **97** (1973), 1–82.

A. V. Balakrishnan

[**1**] Appl. Math. and Optimisation Internat. J. **1** (1974).

H. T. Banks and M. Q. Jacobs

[**1**] J. Differential Equations **13** (1973), 127–149.

J. Baranger

[**1**] J. Math. Pures Appl. **52** (1973), 377–405.

V. Barbu

[**1**] SIAM J. Control 1974.

R. Bellman

[**1**] *Dynamic programming*, Princeton Univ. Press, Princeton, N.J., 1957. MR **19**, 820.

A. Bensoussan

[**1**] *Contrôle impulsionel et inéquations quasi variationelles*, these PROCEEDINGS.

A. Bensoussan et A. Friedaman

[**1**] Arch. Rational Mech. Anal. 1974.

A. Bensoussan et J.L. Lions

[**1**] *Inéquations variationnelles non linéaires du premier et du second ordre*, C. R. Acad. Sci. Paris Sér. A-B **276** (1973), A1411–A1415. MR **47** #5693; et article dans Appl. Anal. 1973, pp. 267–294.

[**2**] Colloque IRIA, Juin 1974.

[**3**] *Nouvelle formulation de problèmes de contrôle impulsionnel et applications*, C. R. Acad. Sci. Paris Sér. A-B **276** (1973), A1189–A1192. MR **47** #5690.

[**4**] *Contrôle impulsionnel et inéquations quasi-variationnelles d'évolution*, C. R. Acad. Sci. Paris Sér. A–B **276** (1973), A1333–A1338. MR **47** #5692.

[**5**] C. R. Acad. Sci. Paris Sér. A–B **278** (1974).

[**6**] Uspehi Mat. Nauk 1973.

[7] Livre en préparation.
A. Bensoussan, M. Goursat et J.L. Lions
[1] *Contrôle impulsionnel et inéquations quasi-variationnelles stationnaires*, C. R. Acad. Sci. Paris Sér. A–B **276** (1973), A1279–A1284. MR **47** #5691.
M. F. Bidaut
[1] Thèse, Paris, 1973.
J. M. Bismut
[1] Thèse, Paris, 1973.
C. Boujot, M. Mercier et R. Temam
[1] Appl. Math. and Optimization Int. J. (à paraître).
M. Bourgat et G. Duvaut
[1] Rapport Laboria, 1974.
C. M. Brauner et P. Penel
[1] (à paraître).
H. Brezis
[1] J. Math. Pures Appl. **51** (1972), 1–168.
H. Brezis et G. Duvaut
[1] *Écoulements avec sillages autour d'un profil symétrique sans incidence*, C. R. Acad. Sci. Paris Sér. A–B **276** (1973), A875–A878. MR **47** #4520.
H. Brezis et G. Stampacchia
[1] *Sur la régularité de la solution d'inéquations elliptiques*, Bull. Soc. Math. France **96** (1968), 153–180. MR **39** #659.
[2] *Une nouvelle méthode pour l'étude d'écoulements stationnaires*, C. R. Acad. Sci. Paris Sér. A–B **276** (1973), A129–A132. MR **47** #4521.
A. G. Butkovskiĭ
[1] *Theory of optimal control by systems with distributed parameters*, "Nauka", Moscow, 1965; English transl., Modern Analytic and Computational Methods in Sci. and Math., no. 11, American Elsevier, New York, 1969. MR **36** #759; **40** #6980.
J. Céa, D. Chesnais, A. Dervieux, M. Koenig, B. Palmerio et J. P. Zolesio
[1] Séminaire Université de Nice, 1973–1974.
R. Conti
[1] *Problemi di controllo et di controllo ottimale*, U.T.E.T., 1974.
G. Da Prato
[1] I, J. Math. Pures Appl. **48** (1969), 59–107; II, **49** (1970), 289–340; III, **52** (1973), 353–375.
M. Delfour et S. K. Mitter
[1] Conférences Delfour, Lecture Notes in Economics and Math. Systems, vol. 106, Springer-Verlag, New York, 1974.
G. Duff
[1] *Mathematical problems of tidal energy*, these PROCEEDINGS.
[2] Conférences IRIA, 1973.
G. Duvaut
[1] C. R. Acad. Sci. Paris Sér. A–B 1973.
G. Duvaut et J.L. Lions
[1] Livre, Dunod, Paris, 1972; Springer translation, 1976 (to appear).
H. Fattorini
[1] *Time-optimal control of solutions of operational differential equations*, J. Soc. Indust. Appl. Math. Ser. A Control **2** (1964), 54–59. MR **29** #6982.
[2] (à paraître).
[3] Local controllability. Report 1973.
H. Fattorini et D. L. Russell
[1] Report Madison, 1973.

W. H. Fleming
[1] *Optimal continuous-parameter stochastic control*, SIAM Rev. **11** (1969), 470–509. MR **41** #9633.
W. Fleming et R. Rishel
[1] Livre à paraître.
C. Foias
[1] *Un cadre fonctionnel pour la théorie de la turbulence* (à paraître).
G. Foias et G. Prodi
[1] Rend. Sem. Mat. Univ. Padova, 1972–1973.
A. Friedman
[1] *Stochastic differential games with stopping times and variational inequalities*, these PROCEEDINGS.
B. I. Grigelionis et A. N. Sirjaev
[1] *On the Stefan problem and optimal stopping rules for Markov processes*, Teor. Verojatnost. i Primenen. **11** (1966), 612–631 = Theor. Probability Appl. **11** (1966), 514–558. MR **35** #5738.
J. Hadamard
[1] *Leçons sur le calcul des variations*. Vol. 1, Hermann, Paris, 1910.
H. Halkin et L. W. Neustadt
[1] Livre à paraître.
M. R. Hestenes
[1] *Calculus of variations and optimal control theory*, Wiley, New York and London, 1966. MR **34** #3390.
W. Hullett
[1] Appl. Math. and Optimization Int. J. **1** (1974).
R. P. Isaacs
[1] *Differential games, a mathematical theory with applications to warfare and pursuit, control and optimization*, Wiley, New York and London, 1965. MR **35** #1362.
A. Jameson et R. O'Malley
[1] Appl. Math. and Optimization Int. J. (à paraître).
J. L. Joly et U. Mosco
[1] C. R. Acad. Sci. Paris Sér. A–B **278** (1974).
J. P. Kernevez et D. Thomas
[1] Appl. Math. and Optimization Int. J. 1975, 279-285.
Y. Kuroda
[1] (à paraître).
Th. Laetsch
[1] J. Functional Analysis 1974.
P. Lévy
[1] *Problèmes concrets d'analyse fonctionnelle*, 2ième éd., Gauthier-Villars, Paris, 1951. MR **12**, 834.
J. L. Lions
[1] *Contrôle optimal de systèmes gouvernés par des équations aux dérivées partielles*, Dunod; Gauthier-Villars, Paris, 1968; English transl., Die Grundlehren der math. Wissenschaften, Band 170, Springer-Verlag, New York, 1971. MR **39** #5920.
[2] Regional Conf. Series in Appl. Math., vol. 6, SIAM, 1972.
[3] Enseignement Math. **19** (1973), 125–166.
[4] Lecture Notes in Economics and Math. Systems, vol. 106, Springer-Verlag, New York, 1974, pp. 166–308.
[5] *Perturbations singulières dans les problèmes aux limites et en contrôle optimal*, Lecture Notes in Math., no. 323, Springer-Verlag, New York, 1973.
J. L. Lions et E. Magenes
[1] *Problèmes aux limites non homogènes et applications*. Vols. 1, 2, Travaux et Recherches

Mathématiques, nos. 17, 18, Dunod, Paris, 1968, 1970; English transl., Die Grundlehren der math. Wissenschaften, Band 181, 182, Springer-Verlag, New York, 1972. MR **40** #512.
J. L. Lions et G. Stampacchia
[1] *Variational inequalities*, Comm. Pure Appl. Math. **20** (1967), 493–519. MR **35** #7178.
J. L. Lions et J. P. Yvon
[1] Livre en préparation.
H. P. McKean, Jr.
[1] Ind. Manag. Review **6** (1965), 32–39.
G. I. Marčuk
[1] *Méthodes numériques de prévision météorologique*, A. Colin, Paris, 1969 (traduit du russe).
F. Mignot
[1] C. R. Acad. Sci. Paris Sér. A–B **278** (1974).
[2] (à paraître).
P. Van Moerbeke
[1] Arch. Rational Mech. Anal. 1974.
[2] Acta Math. (1974), 111–151.
J. Mossino
[1] (à paraître).
F. Murat et J. Simon
[1] Rapport Univ. Paris VI, 1974.
F. Murat et L. Tartar
[1] C. R. Acad. Sci. Paris Sér. A–B **278** (1974).
J. C. Nedelec
[1] Thèse, Paris, 1970.
O. Pironneau
[1] J. Fluid Mech. 1974.
L. S. Pontrjagin, V. G. Boltjanskiĭ, R. V. Gamkrelidze et E. F. Miščenko,
[1] *The mathematical theory of optimal processes*, Fizmatgiz, Moscow, 1961; English transl., Wiley, New York and London, 1962. MR **29** #3316a, b.
J. Puel
[1] (à paraître).
R. T. Rockafellar
[1] *Duality and stability in extremum problems involving convex functions*, Pacific J. Math. **21** (1967), 167–187. MR **35** #2636.
D. L. Russell
[1] *Control theory of hyperbolic equations related to certain questions in harmonic analysis and spectral theory*, J. Math. Anal. Appl. **40** (1972), 336–368. MR **48** #2580.
D. G. Schaeffer
[1] *The capacitor problem* (à paraître).
M. Slemrod
[1] (à paraître).
S. Spagnolo
[1] *Sulla convergenza di soluzioni di equazioni paraboliche ed ellittiche*, Ann. Scuola Norm. Sup. Pisa (3) **22** (1968), 571–597; errata, ibid. (3) **22** (1968), 673. MR **39** #1791.
L. Tartar
[1] C. R. Acad. Sci. Paris Sér. A–B **278** (1974).
[2] Arch. Rational Mech. Anal. 1973.
[3] Colloque IRIA, Juin 1974.
R. Teman
[1] *Sur l'équation de Riccati associée à des opérateurs non bornés, en dimension infinite*, J. Functional Analysis **7** (1971), 85–115. MR **43** #2564.

M. Viot
[1] (á paraître).
M. I. Višik et A. V. Furcikov
[1] *Analytic first integrals of nonlinear parabolic equations and their applications*, Mat. Sb. **92** (**134**) 347–377 = Math. USSR Sb. **21** (1973), 339–370.
P. K. C. Wang
[1] *Control of distributed parameter systems*, Advances in Control Systems, vol, 1. Academic Press, New York, 1964, pp. 75–172.
[2] Report UCLA, 1973.
N. N. Yanenko (Janenko)
[1] *The method of fractional steps, the solution of problems of mathematical physics in several variables*, Izdat. Sibirsk. Otdel. Akad. Nauk SSSR, Novosibirsk, 1966; French transl., A. Colin, Paris, 1968; English transl., Springer-Verlag, Berlin and New York, 1971. MR **36** #4815; **46** #6613.
J. P. Yvon
[1] Appl. Math. and Optimization Int. J. 1974.
[2] Survey Lecture, IFAC, 1975.
M. Zolezzi
[1] (à paraître).

Collège de France
Paris, France

Proceedings of the International Congress of Mathematicians
Vancouver, 1974

Transversal Theory

E. C. Milner

1. Introduction. Transversal theory is a branch of combinatorial mathematics which is only just beginning to emerge as a reasonably connected and coherent subject. Whether this is yet rich enough or mature enough to be called a 'theory' may be a matter for debate; indeed, it is by no means certain that this part of mathematics may not finally be classified under some broader, more comprehensive title. However, what is beyond dispute is the fact that during the last two decades a large number of papers have been published which include some reference to the so-called *marriage theorem* (Theorem 2.1), which is the starting point for transversal theory. These papers deal with surprisingly diverse problems and their only connecting link seems to be this common reference to the marriage theorem. The arguments employed have generally had an ad hoc flavour although some of these have been highly original. Transversal theory is a depository for developing those mathematical ideas of the marriage theorem type which frequently recur and which seem to belong to some more general framework.

Two books on the subject have been published recently by Crapo and Rota [**11**] and Mirsky [**44**] although these were written from rather differing viewpoints. The first part of this article will be expository and cover ground which is familiar to most combinatorial mathematicians. In the second part I shall describe some more recent work done on infinite transversals. The earlier bibliography, detailed proofs and a historical commentary can be found in Mirsky's book. Apart from the new result in set theory mentioned in § 6, I shall not dwell upon the applications of transversal theory to other branches of mathematics, but refer the reader interested in this aspect to the article by Harper and Rota [**31**]. Instead I shall try to give emphasis to those results which are either new or which have influenced the development of the subject.

2. Early results. The letter F will always denote the system $\langle F_i | i \in I \rangle$ of subsets of a set S having index set I. The sets F_i $(i \in I)$ are the *members* of the system but these are not necessarily different subsets of S. We write $|F| = |I|$ to denote the cardinality of F. If $F = \langle F_i | i \in I \rangle$ and $G = \langle G_j | j \in J \rangle$ are two systems, then we define $F = G$ and $F + G$ as follows: $F = G$ means that there is a bijection $f: I \to J$ such that $F_i = G_{f(i)}$ $(\forall\, i \in I)$; $F + G$ denotes the system $H = \langle H_\varepsilon | \varepsilon \in K \rangle$, where $K = (I \times \{0\}) \cup (J \times \{1\})$ and $H_{\langle i,0 \rangle} = F_i$ $(\forall\, i \in I)$, $H_{\langle j,1 \rangle} = G_j$ $(\forall\, j \in J)$.

A *transversal function* of F is an injective choice function for F, that is a function $\varphi: I \to S$ such that $\varphi(i) \neq \varphi(j)$ $(i \neq j)$ and $\varphi(i) \in F_i$ $(i \in I)$. The element $\varphi(i)$ is the *representative* of F_i in φ and $\langle \varphi(i) | i \in I \rangle$ is a *system of distinct representatives* for F. A *transversal* of F is the range $T = \{\varphi(i) | i \in I\}$ of a transversal function and a *partial transversal* is a transversal of some subsystem $F \restriction K = \langle F_i | i \in K \rangle$ $(K \subset I)$. We denote by TR(F) the set of all transversals of F and by PTR(F) the set of all partial transversals.

A system F has the *transversal property*, $F \in \mathscr{T}$, if and only if F has a transversal. Many problems in combinatorial mathematics reduce to the question of whether or not a certain system F has the transversal, or some similar type of property. Here I mention just two such related properties which will be considered in § 5 in the discussion of infinite systems. A system F has property $\mathscr{B}$, $F \in \mathscr{B}$, if and only if there is a set B such that $B \cap F_i \neq \emptyset \neq F_i \backslash B$ $(\forall\, i \in I)$. This property was first considered by Miller **[40]** (the letter $\mathscr{B}$ standing for Bernstein). F has property $\mathscr{B}_1$ (the selector property) if there is a set B such that $|F_i \cap B| = 1$ $(\forall\, i \in I)$. For other generalizations of these see **[19]**. The most primitive statement about transversals is the axiom of choice (which we assume): *If F is a system of nonempty pairwise disjoint sets, then $F \in \mathscr{T}$.*

An obvious *necessary* condition for F to have a transversal is that

$$|F(K)| \geqq |K| \qquad (\forall\, K \subset I) \tag{2.1}$$

where $F(K) = \bigcup_{i \in k} F_i$, and the marriage theorem states that this condition is also sufficient in the case of *finite* systems.

THEOREM 2.1. *If $|F| < \aleph_0$ then $F \in \mathscr{T}$ if and only if* (2.1) *holds.*

This was proved by P. Hall **[27]** and condition (2.1) is usually referred to as Hall's condition. König had earlier proved an equivalent result **[36]**, **[37]**, **[38]** which he expressed in the language of bipartite graphs. There is a natural representation for a set system F as a bipartite graph. We can assume without loss of generality that $I \cap S = \emptyset$ and then F defines a bipartite graph $G_F = (V, E)$ with vertex set $V = I \cup S$ and edge set $E = \{\{i, x\} | i \in I, x \in F_i\}$. A *matching* in a graph $G = (V,E)$ is a set of pairwise disjoint edges $W \subset E$; and, for $X \subset V$, an *X-matching* is a matching W such that every vertex of X is incident with some edge of W. It is easy to see that the set system F has a transversal if and only if the corresponding bipartite graph G_F has an I-matching. König showed that if $n < \aleph_0$ and G is any bipartite graph, then G has a matching of size n if and only if $|C| \geqq n$ whenever C is a *covering set* (i.e., a set of vertices incident with every edge of G). Since $(I \backslash K) \cup F(K)$ is a covering set of G_F ($K \subset I$), it follows from (2.1) that, if $|I| < \aleph_0$, then G_F has a matching of size $|I|$ and hence an I-matching.

This formulation of the transversal property in terms of matchings in bipartite graphs is frequently useful and gives proper emphasis to the dual roles played by the index set I and the ground set S. The terminology also suggests why Theorem 2.1 is sometimes called the marriage theorem. If I is a set of boys and F_i is the set of i's girl friends ($i \in I$), then a transversal of F (or a matching of G_F) corresponds to a marriage arrangement in which each boy marries one of his girl friends. While this might be considered satisfactory for the boys (I), it is most unlikely that it would be considered so by the girls in S left without husbands. Perhaps, therefore, we should instead seek criteria for the existence of a more socially satisfying *perfect matching*, that is a matching which is simultaneously an I-matching and an S-matching in G_F. But it is easily seen that a necessary and sufficient condition for this is that there should exist *some* I-matching (W) and *some* S-matching (W') (consider the graph with edge set $W \cup W'$). Therefore this reduces immediately to the one-sided problem of deciding which system $F \in \mathscr{T}$.

For those with more ambitious appetities, there is another natural generalization of Thereom 2.1 in which the ith boy demands a harem of size h_i [**30**].

THEOREM 2.2. *If* $|F| < \aleph_0$ *and* h_i *is a nonnegative integer* ($i \in I$), *then there are disjoint sets* $X_i \subset F_i$ ($i \in I$) *such that* $|X_i| = h_i$ *if and only if* $|F(K)| \geqq \sum_{i \in K} h_i$ ($\forall\, K \subset I$).

This follows immediately from Theorem 2.1 by considering an augmented system having h_i copies of F_i ($i \in I$). This is the simplest of a number of modifications that can be effected on a set system in order to exploit a self-strengthening characteristic of Theorem 2.1 (see [**44**, Chapter 3]).

A more important early extension of Theorem 2.1 was obtained by Marshall Hall [**28**] who showed that the condition (2.1) is also sufficient in the case when $|F|$ is arbitrary but each F_i ($i \in I$) is finite. The $2^{|I|} - 1$ conditions of (2.1) are mutually independent for a finite system of sets, but for an infinite system of *finite* sets (2.1) is equivalent to the smaller set of conditions

$$(2.1') \qquad |F(K)| \geqq |K| \qquad (\forall\, K \Subset I),$$

where $K \Subset I$ means that K is a finite subset of I. In view of this, Marshall Hall's theorem can be stated in the following way.

THEOREM 2.3. *Let F be a system of finite sets. Then* $F \in \mathscr{T}$ *if and only if* $F_0 \in \mathscr{T}$ ($\forall\, F_0 \Subset F$).

There are almost as many published proofs of this result as there are for Theorem 2.1. Algebraists use a variant of Zorn's lemma, topologists recognize it as a corollary of Tychonoff's theorem on the product of compact spaces, logicians employ Gödel's compactness theorem for the first order predicate calculus (see §5), while combinatorialists use Rado's selection lemma ([**23**], [**28**], [**30**], [**32**], [**44**]).

We do not know of any criteria analogous to Hall's condition (2.1) for the properties $\mathscr{B}$ or $\mathscr{B}_1$. Indeed we are extremely ignorant about these properties for finite system. For example, if $m(n)$ is the smallest number of sets of size n which do *not* have property $\mathscr{B}$, then $m(1) = 1$, $m(2) = 3$, $m(3) = 7$ and $m(4)$ is unknown. However, standard compactness arguments yield results for properties $\mathscr{B}$ and $\mathscr{B}_1$ similar to Theorem 2.3.

THEOREM 2.4. *If F is a system of finite sets and $\mathscr{C} \in \{\mathscr{B}, \mathscr{B}_1\}$, then $F \in \mathscr{C}$ if and only if $F_0 \in \mathscr{C}$ ($\forall F_0 \Subset F$).*

3. Abstract independence. Whitney was the first to study the abstract properties of linear independence and in his pioneering paper [**68**] he established the equivalence to different sets of axioms for this notion. The ones which most clearly reveal the underlying motivation of vectors in a vector space are the following. A *pre-independence structure* (Whitney used the term *matroid*) on a set S is a nonempty set $\mathscr{M} \subset \mathscr{P}(S) = \{X \mid X \subset S\}$ satisfying the conditions:

$I1$. $A \subset B \in \mathscr{M} \Rightarrow A \in \mathscr{M}$ (hereditary).

$I2$. $A, B \in \mathscr{M}, |B| = |A| + 1 < \aleph_0 \Rightarrow (\exists\, b \in B\backslash A)(A \cup \{b\} \in \mathscr{M})$ (exchange).

A set $X \subset S$ is *independent* or *dependent* according as $X \in \mathscr{M}$ or $X \in \mathscr{P}(S)\backslash\mathscr{M}$. Since Whitney's paper, quite a lot of work has been done on the notion of abstract independence and other axiom schemes have been given; in particular, the theory was greatly extended by Tutte ([**61**], [**62**]) who exploited various analogies and applications to graph theory.

Whitney only considered the case of finite $\mathscr{M}$, but many basic results can be extended to infinite structures if one assumes some additional finiteness type of condition. The most common of these is

$I3$. *$\mathscr{M}$ has finite character.*

If $\mathscr{M}$ satisfies $I1$—$I3$ we call it an *independence structure* on S; it is determined by its finite members. One of the first deductions to be made from $I1,2$ is that if $\mathscr{M}$ is a finite pre-independence structure, then the maximal independent sets (*bases*) all have the same (finite) cardinality. If $\mathscr{M}$ is infinite there need not be any maximal independent sets, and even when there are they need not have the same cardinality [**13**]. However, if $I3$ is assumed then it is easy to see that any independent set is contained in a basis and moreover the bases all have the same cardinality [**57**].

It follows from the above that if $\mathscr{M}$ is a pre-independence structure on S, then there is an associated rank function

$$\rho: \mathscr{P}(S) \to \{0, 1, 2, \cdots, \infty\} \tag{3.1}$$

which is defined by

$$\rho(A) = \sup\{|X| \mid X \in \mathscr{M} \cap P(A)\} \qquad (A \subset S).$$

The basic property of ρ, which follows easily from the definition, is that it satisfies

$$\rho(A) \leqq \rho(B) \qquad (A \subset B \subset S), \tag{3.2}$$

$$\rho(A \cup B) + \rho(A \cap B) \leqq \rho(A) + \rho(B) \qquad (A, B \subset S). \tag{3.3}$$

There is an intimate connection between increasing submodular functions and matroids ([**55**], [**18**]): *If* ρ *satisfies* (3.1)—(3.3), *then* $\mathscr{M}_\rho = \{X \subset S \mid \rho(X) \geqq |X|\}$ *satisfies* $I1$, $I2$ (although the rank function of $\mathscr{M}_\rho$ is not necessarily ρ).

It is natural to ask under what conditions a set system F should have a transversal which is independent in some independence structure on S. Rado ([**56**], [**57**]) was the first to consider this problem and he obtained the following extension of Theorems 2.1 and 2.3.

THEOREM 3.1. *Let F be a system of finite subsets of S and let $\mathscr{M}$ be an independence structure on S with rank function ρ. Then* $\mathscr{M} \cap \mathrm{TR}(F) \neq \varnothing$ *if and only if* $\rho(F(K)) \geqq |K|$ ($\forall\, K \Subset I$).

This theorem admits the same kind of extensions as Theorem 2.1 and has numerous applications (e.g., [**2**], [**3**], [**65**]).

We deduce immediately from Theorem 3.1 the following analogue of Marshall Hall's theorem (Theorem 2.3): *If F is a system of finite subsets of S and $\mathscr{M}$ is an independence structure on E, then the statements*

(3.4) $$\mathscr{M} \cap \mathrm{TR}(F) \neq \varnothing$$

and

(3.5) $$\mathscr{M} \cap \mathrm{TR}(F_0) \neq \varnothing \qquad (\forall\, F_0 \Subset F)$$

are equivalent. Rado [**57**] proved that this equivalence is actually a characterization of independence structures.

THEOREM 3.2. *The nonempty set $\mathscr{M} \subset \mathscr{P}(S)$ is an independence structure on E if and only if the statements* (3.4) *and* (3.5) *are equivalent for every system F of finite subsets of S.*

As we have already hinted, (pre-) independence structures abound in combinatorial mathematics apart from the more obvious algebraic ones, but for transversal theory the most important example is the following observation of Edmonds and Fulkerson [**17**].

THEOREM 3.3. *The set of partial transversals of F,* PTR(F), *is a pre-independence structure.*

This result is not difficult to prove, but it was important for the development of the subject since it initiated a new approach for subsequent research. In general, PTR(F) does not satisfy $I3$, but it does if F satisfies the local finiteness condition $|F^{-1}(x)| < \aleph_0$ ($\forall\, x \in S$), where $F^{-1}(x) = \{i \in I \mid x \in F_i\}$ [**46**]. Theorem 3.3 (and the fact that the bases of a finite matroid have equicardinality) immediately gives the following result for *finite* set systems ([**33**], [**39**]).

THEOREM 3.4. *If $F \in \mathscr{T}$ and $P \in$* PTR(F), *then there is $T \in$* TR(F) *such that $P \subset T$.*

For infinite systems this simple argument fails and the proof [**51**] depends upon an extension of the Banach mapping theorem due to Øre. There is an important practical consequence of Theorem 3.4. To check (2.1) for a large finite system would be both expensive and uninformative, but Theorem 3.4 shows that there is an efficient procedure for actually finding a maximal partial transversal of F which does not involve backtracking **[29]**.

We call a (pre-) independence structure $\mathcal{M}$ *transversal* if $\mathcal{M} = \mathrm{PTR}(F)$ for some F. Not all (pre-) independence structures are transversal, but the problem of deciding whether one is or not is not always easy (see **[6]**). However, transversal structures do arise in natural ways. For example, if $G = (V, E)$ is a graph, then the *matching matroid* of G, $\mathcal{M}_G = \{X \subset V \mid \exists$ *an X-matching in G*$\}$, is transversal **[17]**. While it is easily seen that $\mathcal{M}_G$ is a pre-independence structure, it is by no means obvious that it is transversal.

The *sum*

$$\mathcal{M} = \sum_{i \in I} \mathcal{M}_i = \left\{ \bigcup_{i \in I} X_i \,\middle|\, X_i \in M_i \right\}$$

of a system $\langle \mathcal{M}_i \mid i \in I \rangle$ of pre-independence structures on S is also a pre-independence structure (and if $|I| < \aleph_0$ and each $\mathcal{M}_i$ satisfies $I3$ then so does $\mathcal{M}$). The rank function for $\mathcal{M}$ is given by

$$\rho(A) = \min_{X \subset A} \left(\sum_{i \in I} \rho_i(X) + |A \backslash X| \right) \qquad (A \subset S), \tag{3.6}$$

where ρ_i is the rank function of $\mathcal{M}_i$. This important formula was first stated, for finite I, by Nash-Williams **[48]** (it is also implicit in Edmonds **[15]**); the infinite case is proved in **[3]**, **[55]**. While this result is not difficult to establish (e.g., see **[66]** for an elegant deduction of (3.6) from Theorem 3.1), it provides a useful general technique for solving a variety of problems (e.g., **[45]**).

As an illustration of the use of (3.6) we give an example due to Nash-Williams **[48]**. Consider the *cycle matroid* $\mathcal{M}_C = \{X \subset E \mid X$ is *acyclic*$\}$ on the edge set of a graph $G = (V, E)$. If G is finite, then the rank of a set $X \subset E$ is $|V| - t(X)$, where $t(X)$ is the number of connected components of the graph (V, X). The graph G contains k edge-disjoint spanning trees provided that E has rank $k(|V| - 1)$ in the matroid sum $\sum_{i=1}^{k} \mathcal{M}_i$, where $\mathcal{M}_i = \mathcal{M}_C$ $(1 \leqq i \leqq k)$. Thus, by (3.6), we see that a necessary and sufficient condition for this is that $k(|V| - 1) \leqq k(|V| - t(X)) + |E \backslash X|$ $(\forall\, X \subset E)$. Expressed differently, this condition states that

$$e(P) \geqq k(|P| - 1), \tag{3.7}$$

where $P = \{V_1, \cdots, V_t\}$ is any partition of V into disjoint, nonempty sets and $e(P)$ is the number of edges of G joining distinct V_j's. This result had earlier been proved by Tutte **[63]** and Nash-Williams **[47]** by more direct but very involved methods and this use of the rank formula is a good example of the elegance and insight which is sometimes gained through generalization. The argument just used fails for infinite graphs, although Nash-Williams **[50]** has conjectured that (3.7) is sufficient for the general case. A more general problem would be to find necessary and sufficient conditions for the existence of pairwise disjoint bases B_i of $\mathcal{M}_i$ $(i \in I)$, when the $\mathcal{M}_i$ are matroids on an infinite set S.

In this context it should be mentioned that Edmonds (see **[15]**) has suggested a more general setting for transversal theory by defining a 'transversal' for a system of independence structures $\langle \mathscr{M}_i | i \in I \rangle$ to be a set T which is the disjoint union of bases B_i of $\mathscr{M}_i$ $(i \in I)$. The original situation is regained when $\mathscr{M}_i$ is taken to be the *discrete matroid* $\{X \subset F_i \,|\, |X| \leqq 1\}$ on F_i $(i \in I)$. Many of the basic results of transversal theory extend to this more general setting provided the $\mathscr{M}_i$ are rank finite. For example, a generalization of Theorem 3.4 is that any partial transversal of a rank-finite system $\langle \mathscr{M}_i | i \in I \rangle$ can be extended to a complete transversal provided one exists. For a fuller discussion of this see Brualdi **[5]**.

So far we have only considered the existence of transversals of a single set system, but it is useful to consider the analogous problem when there are two or more systems. For example, Theorems 3.1 and 3.3 together immediately give the following extension of the marriage theorem (first proved in **[25]** in the context of flows in networks).

THEOREM 3.5. *The finite systems* $F = \langle F_1, \cdots, F_n \rangle$, $G = \langle G_1, \cdots, G_n \rangle$ *have a common transversal if and only if*

$$|F(K) \cap G(L)| \geqq |K| + |L| - n \qquad (K, L \subset \{1, 2, \cdots, n\}).$$

A transfinite analogue for Theorem 3.5 of the Schroeder-Bernstein type is the following theorem proved by Pym **[54]** and Brualdi **[4]**.

THEOREM 3.6. *The systems* $F = \langle F_i | i \in I \rangle$ *and* $G = \langle G_i | i \in I \rangle$ *have a common transversal if F has a common transversal with some subsystem of G and G has a common transversal with some subsystem of F.*

It would be useful to have a more quantitative type of condition for the existence of a common transversal of two infinite systems. More generally, when do two infinite matroids have a common basis? This is not known even for independence structures (for a partial solution see **[5]**).

Unfortunately, there is no result like Theorem 3.5 known which guarantees the existence of a common transversal for three or more systems. A more general problem is to find conditions for three pre-independence structures to have a common independent set of a given size. A solution to these problems would have several important consequences. For example, it would enable us to characterize those directed graphs having a Hamiltonian path **[67]**.

4. Systems with infinite members. The problem of extending Theorem 2.1 to arbitrary sytems remains as the central problem of transversal theory and is a prototype for similar questions in combinatorial set theory.

It is easily seen that Hall's condition (2.1) is not sufficient for $F \in \mathscr{T}$ even for systems having a single infinite member, e.g., consider $F = \langle \omega, \{0\}, \{1\}, \cdots \rangle$. Actually Rado and Jung **[58]** gave an extension of Theorem 2.1 to cover this case. Call a subsystem $F \restriction K$ of F *critical* if $\mathrm{TR}(F \restriction K) = \{F(K)\}$; for finite K this is equivalent to $F \restriction K \in \mathscr{T}$ and $|F(K)| = |K|$. Suppose F is a system of finite sets and A is an infinite set. Then the result of **[58]** is that $F + \langle A \rangle \in \mathscr{T}$ *if and only if* $F \in \mathscr{T}$ *and*

$$A \not\subset \bigcup_{F \restriction K \text{ critical}} F(K). \tag{4.1}$$

Extensions of this have been obtained by several authors ([**17**], [**24**], [**69**], [**12**], [**60**]) providing necessary and sufficient conditions for $F \in \mathscr{T}$ in the case when G has arbitrarily many finite sets and a finite number of infinite sets.

Recently, Damerell and I [**12**] settled a conjecture of Nash-Williams [**49**] giving necessary and sufficient conditions for any denumerable system of sets to have a transversal. For $X \subset S$, let $I(X) = \{i \in I \mid F_i \subset X\}$ and put

(4.2)
$$m_0(X) = |X| - |I(X)| \quad \text{if } |X| < \infty, \qquad = \infty \quad \text{if } |X| = \infty.$$

An obvious necessary condition (essentially (2.1)) for $F \in \mathscr{T}$ is that $m_0(X) \geqq 0$ ($\forall\, X \subset S$). In fact, for a finite set $X \subset S$, $m_0(X)$ measures the number of 'spare' elements in X which would be left over after choosing representatives for the sets $F_i \subset X$. For infinite X, $m_0(X)$ is simply a first approximation to this number of 'spare' elements in the sense that in this case there could *possibly* be infinitely many elements left over after choosing representatives for the sets $F_i \subset X$. Nash-Williams' idea was to find successively better and better estimates for the number of 'spare' elements in the following way. If $T = \langle T_n \mid n < \omega\rangle$ is an increasing sequence of subsets of X such that

(4.3)
$$T_0 \subset T_1 \subset \cdots \subset X = \bigcup_{n<\omega} T_n,$$

then put $D(T) = I(X) \setminus \bigcup_{n<\omega} I(T_n)$. A function $f : \mathscr{P}(S) \to \{0, \pm 1, \pm 2, \cdots, \pm \infty\}$ will be called a *valuation* on S. If f is a valuation on S, denote by $A(f, X)$ the set of all sequences $T = \langle T_n \mid n < \omega\rangle$ satisfying (4.3) and such that $f(T_n) = f(T_0) < \infty$ ($n < \omega$). For $T \in A(f, X)$ write $\bar{f}(T) = f(T_0)$. Now we define a transfinite sequence of valuations m_α ($\alpha \geqq 0$) by induction on α as follows. Suppose $\alpha > 0$ and that m_β has been defined for $\beta < \alpha$. For $X \subset S$ we put $m_\alpha(X) = \inf_{\beta<\alpha} m_\beta(X)$ if α is a limit ordinal, and for $\alpha = \beta + 1$ put

$$m_\alpha(X) = \inf_{T \in A(m_\beta, X)} (\bar{m}_\beta(T) - |D(T)|) \quad \text{if } A(m_\beta, X) \neq \varnothing, \qquad = \infty \quad \text{if } A(m_\beta, X) = \varnothing.$$

Then we have the following result [**12**].

THEOREM 4.1. *If* $|F| = \aleph_0$, *then* $F \in \mathscr{T}$ *if and only if*

(4.4)
$$m_{\omega_1}(X) \geqq 0 \qquad (\forall\, X \subset S).$$

Steffens [**60**] considered the following more qualitative type of condition which is somewhat similar to (4.1) and very easy to state:

(4.5)
$$F_i \not\subset F(K) \quad \textit{whenever } i \in I \setminus K \textit{ and } F \restriction K \textit{ is critical}.$$

Clearly (4.5) is necessary for $F \in \mathscr{T}$ and Podewsky and Steffens have recently proved the following theorem [**52**].

THEOREM 4.2. *If* $|F| = \aleph_0$, *then* $F \in \mathscr{T}$ *if and only if* (4.5) *holds.*

Theorem 4.1 and 4.2 both fail for nondenumerable systems. A good test case is the system $F' = \langle \alpha \mid \omega \leqq \alpha < \omega_1\rangle$ which has no transversal by an elementary theorem on regressive functions. However, both (4.4) and (4.5) are satisfied for this system.

On the other hand, both Theorems 4.1 and 4.2 can be extended to give necessary and sufficient conditions for the existence of transversals of denumerable systems in some independence structure $\mathcal{M}$ on S. For Theorem 4.1 the only change needed is to replace $|X|$ by $\rho(X)$ in (4.2), where ρ is the rank function. The proof of **[12]** carries over with only minor modifications. In order to state the appropriate generalization of Theorem 4.2, call a subsystem $F \restriction K$ *$\mathcal{M}$-critical* if $\mathcal{M} \cap \mathrm{TR}(F \restriction K) \neq \varnothing$ and if B is a maximal independent subset of $F(K)$ whenever $B \in \mathcal{M} \cap \mathrm{TR}(F \restriction K)$. Then it is easily shown **[42]** that, if $|F| \leqq \aleph_0$, then $\mathcal{M} \cap \mathrm{TR}(F) \neq \varnothing$ if and only if

(4.5′) *F_i does not depend upon $F(K)$ whenever $i \in I \setminus K$ and $F \restriction K$ is $\mathcal{M}$-critical.*

5. Compactness theorems. Let κ, λ, μ denote infinite cardinals. The cofinality cardinal of κ is cf κ and the succesor of κ is κ^+. We write $F \in S(\kappa, \lambda)$ if $|F| = \kappa$ and $|F_i| = \lambda$ ($\forall i \in \mathrm{I}$). Expressions like $S(\kappa, \leqq \lambda)$, $S(\kappa, < \lambda)$ have natural interpretations. We say F has property $\mathcal{T}(\mu)$ if $F' \in \mathcal{T}$ ($\forall\, F' \subset F, |F'| \leqq \mu$). Let $T(\kappa, \lambda, \mu)$ be an abbreviation for the assertion:

$$F \in S(\kappa, \lambda) \ \&\ F \in \mathcal{T}(\mu) \Rightarrow F \in \mathcal{T}.$$

Then Marshall Hall's theorem (Theorem 2.3) asserts that $T(\kappa, < \aleph_0, < \aleph_0)$ is true for every κ. It is natural to investigate if $T(\kappa, \lambda, \mu)$ holds for other triples and W. Gustin (see **[19]**, **[20]**) in the 1950's asked if

$$\neg T(\aleph_2, \aleph_0, \aleph_1) \tag{5.1}$$

is true. Erdös and Hajnal **[21]** noted that (5.1) holds in L. More generally, an easy consequence of a result of Jensen **[34]** is the following theorem **[43]**.

THEOREM 5.1. *If κ is regular and not weakly compact and if $\lambda < \kappa$, then $V = L \Rightarrow \neg T(\kappa, \lambda, < \kappa)$,*

The hypothesis $V = L$ is not needed to prove (5.1). For example, the system $F = \langle F_{\alpha\beta} | \omega \leqq \alpha < \omega_1 \leqq \beta < \omega_2 \rangle$, where $F_{\alpha\beta} = \alpha \times \{\alpha, \beta\} = \bigcup_{\nu<\alpha}\{(\nu, \alpha), (\nu, \beta)\}$, satisfies $F \in S(\aleph_2, \aleph_0) \cap T(\aleph_1)$ and $F \notin \mathcal{T}$. More generally, Shelah and I proved the following theorem **[43]**.

THEOREM 5.2. *If κ is regular, then*

$$\neg T(\kappa, \lambda, < \kappa) \Rightarrow \neg\, T(\kappa^+, \lambda, < \kappa^+).$$

Since $\neg T(\kappa^+, \kappa, \kappa)$ holds (consider κ^+ identical sets of size κ) we deduce from this that $\neg T(\aleph_{\alpha+n}, \aleph_\alpha, < \aleph_{\alpha+n})$ $(\alpha \geqq 0,\ 1 \leqq n < \omega)$. However, this leaves several questions unanswered. For example, we cannot deduce from Theorem 5.2 whether $\neg T(\kappa, \aleph_0, < \kappa)$ holds for $\kappa \geqq \aleph_\omega$. Theorem 5.1 shows that we cannot prove the falsity of this for $\kappa = \mu^+$, but (rather surprisingly) it is false for singular κ. Very recently Shelah (unpublished) has proved the following result.

THEOREM 5.3. *If* cf $\kappa < \kappa$ *and* $\lambda < \kappa$, *then* $T(\kappa, \lambda, < \kappa)$.

It is easily seen that this theorem of Shelah is best possible in the sense that λ cannot be replaced by $< \kappa$. More precisely, we have that cf $\kappa < \kappa \Rightarrow \neg T(\kappa, < \kappa, < \kappa)$.

To see this consider the system

$$F = \langle \{\alpha\} \mid \alpha \in \kappa \setminus C \rangle + \langle [\kappa_\rho, \kappa_{\rho+1}) \mid \rho < \mu \rangle + \langle C \rangle,$$

where $\mu = \mathrm{cf}\,\kappa < \kappa$, $C = \{\kappa_\rho \mid \rho < \mu\}$ is a closed, cofinal subset of κ and $[\kappa_\rho, \kappa_{\rho+1}) = \{\alpha \mid \kappa_\rho \leqq \alpha < \kappa_{\rho+1}\}$. It is easily seen that $F \notin \mathscr{T}$ whereas $F' \in \mathscr{T}$ for every proper subsystem $F' \subsetneqq F$.

Theorem 5.3 shows that the regularity of κ is an essential hypothesis in Theorem 5.1. So also is the condition that κ not be weakly compact. We have the following very simple theorem.

THEOREM 5.4. *If κ is weakly compact then $T(\kappa, < \kappa, < \kappa)$.*

This can be proved in the same manner that Henkin [**32**] proved Marshall Hall's theorem. One of the several equivalent characterizations for κ to be weakly compact is that the infinitary propositional calculus which permits the conjunction of $< \kappa$ formulae is κ-compact. Suppose $F \in \mathscr{S}(\kappa, < \kappa) \cap \mathscr{T}(< \kappa)$. We can assume that $F = \langle F_i \mid i < \kappa \rangle$ and that $F_i \subset \kappa$. Consider the set of κ sentences

$$S = \left\{ \bigvee_{x \in F_i} p_{xi} \,\middle|\, i < \kappa \right\} \cup \{\neg(p_{xi} \wedge p_{xj}) \mid x < \kappa,\ i \neq j < \kappa\},$$

where p_{xi} is a propositional variable (with intended meaning "$x \in F_i$"). The hypothesis ensures that any subcollection of $<\kappa$ sentences of S has a model, and hence S has a model if κ is weakly compact, i.e., $F \in \mathscr{T}$. In a similar way, as Jech remarked, one can prove a more exact analogue of Theorem 2.3 for large cardinals: *If λ is supercompact and $\kappa \geqq \lambda$, then $T(\kappa, < \lambda, < \lambda)$.* It should be possible to prove

$$T(\kappa, \ <\kappa, < \kappa) \Rightarrow \kappa \text{ weakly compact,} \tag{5.2}$$

but at present this is still open.

Theorems 5.1 and 5.2 show that one cannot, in general, decide if $F \in \mathscr{T}$ by examining all small subsystems of F. However, we do have the following compactness type of result [**43**].

THEOREM 5.5. *If $F_0 \in \mathscr{S}(\kappa, < \aleph_0)$, $F_1 \in \mathscr{S}(\lambda, \leqq \lambda)$ and $F = F_0 + F_1$, then*

$$F \in \mathscr{T} \Leftrightarrow F \in \mathscr{T}(\lambda). \tag{5.3}$$

For example, this enables us to extend Theorems 4.1 and 4.3 to the case where F contains countably many denumerable sets and an arbitrary number of finite sets. Čudnovskiĭ [**9**] has obtained the following more general theorem: *If $\mu, \lambda \geqq \nu \geqq \omega$ and the infinitary language $L_{\nu^+,\omega}$ is (μ, λ)-compact, then* (5.3) *holds if $F_0 \in \mathscr{S}(\kappa, < \aleph_0)$ and $F_1 \in \mathscr{S}(\mu, \leqq \nu)$.*

I conclude this section by mentioning some related results about the properties $\mathscr{B}$ and $\mathscr{B}_1$ introduced in § 2. First I state one of Miller's original results since there remains an interesting unsolved problem. Miller [**40**] proved that if $F \in \mathscr{S}(\kappa, \geqq \lambda)$ and $n < \aleph_0$, then

$$(\forall F' \subset F)\,(|F'| > \lambda \Rightarrow |\textstyle\bigcap F'| < n) \Rightarrow F \in \mathscr{B}.$$

This result is easily seen to be best possible in the sense that n cannot be replaced by $\aleph_0$. For example, let $A = \langle A_i | i < \omega \rangle$ be a system of $\aleph_0$ disjoint denumerable sets, let $\{T_\rho | \rho < 2^{\aleph_0}\}$ be all the transversals of A and let $\{C_\rho | \rho < 2^{\aleph_0}\}$ be any set of $2^{\aleph_0}$ *almost disjoint* (i.e., $|C_\rho \cap C_\sigma| < |C_\rho|$ for $\rho \neq \sigma$) infinite subsets of ω. Then the system $F = A + \langle T_\rho \upharpoonright C_\rho | \rho < 2^{\aleph_0} \rangle \in \mathscr{S}(2^{\aleph_0}, \aleph_0)$ and

(5.4) $$|F_i \cap F_j| < \aleph_0 \qquad (i \neq j),$$

but $F \notin \mathscr{B}$. One of the problems stated in **[19]** which still remains unsolved is whether (under the assumption that $2^{\aleph_0} > \aleph_1$) there is $F \in S(\aleph_1, \aleph_0)$ such that (5.4) holds and $F \notin \mathscr{B}$.

We say F has property $\mathscr{B}(\mu)$ if $F' \in \mathscr{B}$ ($\forall F' \subset F, |F'| \leqq \mu$). Let $\mathscr{B}(\kappa, \lambda, \mu)$ denote the assertion: $F \in \mathscr{S}(\kappa, \lambda)$ & $F \in \mathscr{B}(\mu) \Rightarrow F \in \mathscr{B}$. Similarly, we define $\mathscr{B}_1(\mu)$ and $\mathscr{B}_1(\kappa, \lambda, \mu)$. Essentially the same proof used to establish Theorem 5.4 above also gives that $B(\kappa, <\kappa, <\kappa)$ and $B_1(\kappa, <\kappa, <\kappa)$ are true if κ is weakly compact. Similar to Gustin's problem (5.1), Erdös and Hajnal **[19]** asked if the statements

(5.5) $$\neg B(\aleph_2, \aleph_0, \aleph_1),$$

(5.6) $$\neg B_1(\aleph_2, \aleph_0, \aleph_1)$$

are true. Węglorz **[64]** proved (5.6) assuming $2^{\aleph_0} = \aleph_2$ (i.e., (5.6) is consistent) and recently Čudnovskiĭ **[8]** proved this without any additional assumption. The same authors also proved (Węglorz assumed GCH, Čudnovskiĭ without GCH) the following theorem.

THEOREM 5.6. *$B_1(\kappa, <\kappa, <\kappa) \Leftrightarrow \kappa$ is weakly compact.*

The corresponding problems for property $\mathscr{B}$, like (5.2), remain open. In this connection, I should like to mention one additional new result due to Komjath and Hoffman **[35]** which gives a connection between the transversal property and property $\mathscr{B}$.

THEOREM 5.7. *If F is a system of infinite sets, then $F \in \mathscr{T} \Rightarrow F \in \mathscr{B}$.*

6. Almost disjoint transversals. In this final section I shall discuss some recent results in set theory which relate to questions of the form: "*how many almost disjoint transversals does a set system have?*" Such questions were first considered in **[22]** and **[41]**, and recently K. Prikry and J. Baumgartner used results of this kind to give elementary proofs of a remarkable new result (Theorem 6.1) of J. Silver **[59]**.

Let κ be a singular cardinal not cofinal with ω, i.e., $\omega < \lambda = \mathrm{cf}\,\kappa < \kappa$, and let $C = \{\kappa_\rho | \rho < \lambda\}$ be any closed cofinal set of cardinals in κ. In **[22]** Erdös, Hajnal and I proved the following result: *If $\mu^\lambda < \kappa$ ($\mu < \kappa$) and S is a stationary subset of λ, and if T is a set of almost disjoint transversals of the system $F = \langle \kappa_\rho | \rho \in S \rangle$, then $|T| \leqq \kappa$.* The elementary proofs given by Prikry and Baumgartner of Silver's theorem can be described in terms of the following extension of this result.

LEMMA 6.1. *If $\mu^\lambda < \kappa$ ($\mu < \kappa$) and S is stationary in λ, and if T is a set of almost disjoint transversals of the system $F = \langle \kappa_\rho^+ | \rho \in S \rangle$ then $|T| \leqq \kappa^+$.*

After Cohn **[10]** proved the independence of the continuum hypothesis, it was natural to investigate what possible values $2^{\aleph_\alpha}$ could assume. Easton [**14**] proved that if h is any ordinal valued function satisfying (i) $\alpha \leqq \beta \Rightarrow h(\alpha) \leqq h(\beta)$ and (ii) $\mathrm{cf}(\aleph_{h(\alpha)}) > \aleph_\alpha$, then it is consistent (with ZFC) that $2^{\aleph_\alpha} = \aleph_{h(\alpha)}$ ($\aleph_\alpha$ regular). In view of this arbitrariness for the possible values of 2^μ for regular μ, it was therefore very surprising when Silver [**59**] recently announced the following theorem.

THEOREM 6.2. *If* $\omega < \mathrm{cf}\,\kappa < \kappa$ *and* $A = \{\alpha < \kappa \mid \alpha$ *cardinal and* $2^\alpha = \alpha^+\}$ *is stationary in* κ, *then* $2^\kappa = \kappa^+$.

In particular, this shows that if GCH holds below $\aleph_{\omega_1}$ (i.e., $2^{\aleph_\alpha} = \aleph_{\alpha+1}$ $(\alpha < \omega_1)$), then $2^{\aleph_{\omega_1}} = \aleph_{\omega_1+1}$.

Silver's original proof uses sophisticated model theory but Prikry and Baumgartner gave an elementary combinatorial proof based upon Lemma 6.1. To obtain Silver's theorem from the lemma we argue as follows. If A is stationary in κ, then $\mu^\lambda < \kappa$ $(\mu < \kappa)$ and $A \cap C$ is stationary, i.e., $S = \{\rho < \lambda \mid 2^{\kappa_\rho} = \kappa_\rho^+\}$ is stationary in λ. Since $|\mathscr{P}(\kappa_\rho)| = \kappa_\rho^+$ for $\rho \in S$, we can write $\mathscr{P}(\kappa_\rho) = \{x_\nu^\rho \mid \nu < \kappa_\rho^+\}$ $(\rho \in S)$. Then, for each $X \subset \kappa$, there is a transversal function φ_X of $F = \langle \kappa_\rho^+ \mid \rho \in S\rangle$ defined by $\varphi_X(\rho) = \nu \Leftrightarrow X \cap \kappa_\rho = x_\nu^\rho$. Clearly φ_X, φ_Y have almost disjoint ranges if $X \neq Y \subset \kappa$ and therefore, by the lemma, $|\mathscr{P}(\kappa)| \leqq \kappa^+$.

PROOF OF LEMMA 6.1. We will assume that T is a set of κ^{++} almost disjoint transversal functions and deduce a contradiction.

Note that $S_0 = \{\rho \in S \mid \rho$ a limit ordinal$\}$ is also stationary in λ. For $\psi, \varphi \in T$ put $S(\psi, \varphi) = \{\rho \in S_0 \mid \psi(\rho) < \varphi(\rho)\}$, and let $G(\varphi) = \{\psi \in T \mid S(\psi, \varphi)$ *is stationary* in $\lambda\}$. G is a set mapping on T (i.e., $\varphi \notin G(\varphi)$) and

$$(\forall\, \psi, \varphi \in T)\ (\psi \neq \varphi \Rightarrow \psi \in G(\varphi) \text{ or } \varphi \in G(\psi))$$

since $S(\psi, \varphi) \cup S(\varphi, \psi)$ is a final section of S_0. Therefore, by a well-known theorem on set mappings (e.g., [**26**]), it follows that $|G(\varphi_0)| \geqq \kappa^+$ for some $\varphi_0 \in T$.

Since $\varphi_0(\rho) < \kappa_\rho^+$ $(\forall\, \rho \in S_0)$, there is an injective map $h_\rho : \varphi_0(\rho) \to \kappa_\rho$. Also, if $\psi \in G(\varphi_0)$ and $\rho \in S(\psi, \varphi_0)$, then there is $\sigma_\psi(\rho) < \rho$ such that $h(\psi(\rho)) < \kappa_{\sigma_\psi(\rho)}$ (since $\{\kappa_\rho \mid \rho < \lambda\}$ is closed and ρ is a limit ordinal). Now σ_ψ is regressive on the stationary set $S(\psi, \varphi_0)$ and hence there are $A_\psi \subset S$ and $\rho_\psi < \lambda$ such that $|A_\psi| = \lambda$ and $\sigma_\psi(\rho) < \rho_\psi$ $(\forall\, \rho \in A_\psi)$. There are only $2^\lambda \cdot \lambda < \kappa^+$ different pairs (A, ζ) with $A \subset \lambda$, $\zeta < \lambda$, and hence there is $G' \subset G(\varphi_0)$ such that $|G'| = \kappa^+$ and $(A_\psi, \rho_\psi) = (A, \zeta)$ $(\forall\, \psi \in G')$. Since $\kappa_\zeta^\lambda \leqq \kappa$ it follows that there are $\psi_1, \psi_2 \in G'$ such that $\psi_1(\rho) = \psi_2(\rho)$ $(\forall\, \rho \in A)$ and this is a contradiction since $|A| = \lambda$ and the members of T are pairwise disjoint.

It should be mentioned that Prikry has since obtained more general results than Lemma 6.1 and Theorem 6.2 by using refinements of the above argument. He also proved the following interesting companion result.

THEOREM 6.3. *Suppose that T is a set of almost disjoint transversals of the system* $F = \langle F_\rho \mid \rho < \kappa\rangle$, *where* $|F_\rho| < 2^{\aleph_0}$ $(\rho < \kappa)$ *and* $\omega < \mathrm{cf}\,\kappa \leqq \kappa < 2^{\aleph_0}$. *If* $2^{\aleph_0}$ *is real valued measurable, then* $|T| < 2^{\aleph_0}$.

Obviously, the condition that $\mathrm{cf}\,\kappa > \omega$ is essential.

Finally, I conclude by mentioning a strong result of the Silver type which was obtained (independently) by Hajnal and Galvin by using an extension of these ideas on almost disjoint transversals.

THEOREM 6.4. *If* $\omega < \operatorname{cf} \kappa < \kappa = \aleph_\alpha$ *and* $2^\mu < \kappa$ $(\forall \mu < \kappa)$, *then* $2^\kappa < \aleph_{(2^{|\alpha|})^+}$.

References

1. J. Baumgartner, Private communication.

2. R. A. Brualdi, *A general theorem concerning common transversals*, Combinatorial Mathematics and Its Applications (Proc. Conf., Oxford, 1969), Academic Press, London, 1971, pp. 39–60. MR **44** #6506.

3. ———, *Common transversals and strong exchange systems*, J. Combinatorial Theory **8** (1970), 307–329. MR **41** #1543.

4. ———, *On families of finite independence structures*, Proc. London Math. Soc. (3) **22** (1971), 265–293. MR **45** #5003.

5. ———, *Generalized transversal theory*, Théorie des Matroïdes, Springer-Verlag, Berlin, 1971, pp. 5–30.

6. R. A. Brualdi and G. W. Dinolt, *Characterisations of transversal matroids and their presentations*, J. Combinatorial Theory Ser. B. **12** (1972), 268–286. MR **46** #3345.

7. R. A. Brualdi and E. B. Scrimger, *Exchange systems, matchings and transversals*, J. Combinatorial Theory **5** (1968), 244–257. MR **38** #55.

8. G. V. Čudnovskiĭ, *Transversals and some properties of compactness type*, Dokl. Akad. Nauk SSSR **216** (1974), 748–750 = Soviet Math. Dokl. **15** (1974), 891–894.

9. ———, Private correspondence.

10. P. M. Cohn, *The independence of the continuum hypothesis*, Proc. Nat. Acad. Sci. U.S.A. **50** (1963), 1143–1148; ibid. **51** (1964), 105–110.

11. H. H. Crapo and G.-C. Rota, *On the foundations of combinatorial theory: Combinatorial geometries*, Preliminary edition, M.I.T. Press, Cambridge, Mass., 1970. MR **45** #74.

12. R. M. Damerell and E. C. Milner, *Necessary and sufficient conditions for transversals of countable set systems*, J. Combinatorial Theory **17** (1974), 350–374.

13. V. Dlab, *Axiomatic treatment of bases in arbitrary sets*, Czechoslovak Math. J. **15** **(90)** (1965), 554–564. MR **32** #4060; errata, **33**, p. 1601.

14. W. B. Easton, *Powers of regular cardinals*, Ph.D. Thesis, Princeton University, Princeton, N. J., 1964.

15. J. Edmonds, *Minimum partition of a matroid into independent subsets*, J. Res. Nat. Bur. Standards Sect. B **69B** (1965), 67–72. MR **32** #7441.

16. ———, *Lehman's switching game and a theorem of Tutte and Nash-Williams*, J. Res. Nat. Bur. Standards Sect. B **69B** (1965), 73–77. MR **32** #7442.

17. J. Edmonds and D. R. Fulkerson, *Transversals and matroid partition*, J. Res. Nat. Bur. Standards Sect. B **69B** (1965), 147–153. MR **32** #5531.

18. J. Edmonds and G.-C. Rota, (to appear).

19. P. Erdös and A. Hajnal, *On properties of families of sets*, Acta. Math. Acad. Sci. Hungar. **13** (1926), 223–226.

20. ———, *Unsolved problems in set theory*, Proc. Sympos. Pure Math., vol. 13, part I, Amer. Math. Soc., Providence, R.I., 1971, pp. 17–48. MR **43** #6101.

21. ———, *Solved and unsolved problems in set theory* (to appear).

22. P. Erdös, A. Hajnal and E. C. Milner, *On sets of almost disjoint subsets of a set*, Acta Math. Acad. Sci. Hungar. **19** (1968), 209–218. MR **37** #84.

23. C. J. Everett and G. Whaples, *Representations of sequences of sets*, Amer. J. Math. **71** (1949), 287–293. MR **10**, 517.

24. J. Folkman, *Transversals of infinite families with finitely many infinite members*, RAND Co. Mem. RM 5676-PR (1968); J. Combinatorial Theory **9** (1970), 200–220. MR **43** #1854.

25. L. R. Ford and D. R. Fulkerson, *Network flow and systems of representatives*, Canad. J. Math. **10** (1958), 78–84. MR **20** #4502.

26. A. Hajnal, *Proof of a conjecture of S. Ruziewicz*, Fund. Math. **50** (1961/62), 123–128. MR **24** #A1833.

27. P. Hall, *On representatives of subsets*, J. London Math. Soc. **10** (1935), 26–30.

28. M. Hall, Jr., *Distinct representatives of subsets*, Bull. Amer. Math. Soc. **54** (1948), 922–926. MR **10**, 238.

29. ———, *An algorithm for distinct representatives*, Amer. Math. Monthly **63** (1956), 716–717. MR **18**, 867.

30. P. R. Halmos and H. E. Vaughn, *The marriage problem*, Amer. J. Math. **72** (1950), 214–215. MR **11**, 423.

31. L. H. Harper and G.-C. Rota, *Matching theory, an introduction*, Advances in Probability and Related Topics, vol. 1, Dekker, New York, 1971, pp. 169–215. MR **44** #89.

32. L. Henkin, *Some interconnections between modern algebra and mathematical logic*, Trans. Amer. Math. Soc. **74** (1953), 410–427. MR **14**, 1052.

33. A. J. Hoffman and H. W. Kuhn, *Systems of distinct representatives and linear programming*, Amer. Math. Monthly **63** (1956), 455–460. MR **18**, 370.

34. R. Björn Jensen, *The fine structure of the constructible hierarchy*, Ann. Math. Logic **4** (1972), 229–308.

35. P. Komjath and G. Hoffman, (unpublished).

36. D. König, *Graphok és Matrixok*, Mat. Fiz. Lapok **38** (1932), 116–119. (Hungarian with German summary)

37. ———, *Über treuneude Knotenpunkte in Graphen*, Acta Lit. Sci. Sect. Sci. Math. (Szeged) **6** (1932–34), 155–179.

38. ———, *Theorie der endlichen und unendlichen Graphen, Kombinatorische Topologie der Stricken Komplexe*, Leipzig, 1936; photographic reproduction, Chelsea, Nwe York, 1950. MR **12**, 195.

39. N. S. Mendelsohn and A. L. Dulmage, *Some generalizations of the problem of distinct representatives*, Canad. J. Math. **10** (1958), 230–241. MR **20** #1635.

40. E. W. Miller, *On a property of families of sets*, C. R. Varsovie **30** (1937), 31–38.

41. E. C. Milner, *Transversals of disjoint sets*, J. London Math. Soc. **43** (1968), 495–500. MR **37** #3932.

42. ———, *Independent transversals for countable set systems*, J. Combinatorial Theory (to appear).

43. E. C. Milner and S. Shelah, *Some theorems on transversals*, Proc. Colloq. on Infinite and Finite Sets (Kesthély, 1973), Coll. Math. Soc. János Bolyai.

44. L. Mirsky, *Transversal theory. An account of some aspects of combinatorial mathematics*, Math. in Sci. and Engineering, vol. 75, Academic Press, New York and London, 1971. MR **44** #87

45. ———, *The rank formula of Nash-Williams as a source of covering and packing theorems* J. Math. Anal. Appl. **43** (1973), 328–347.

46. L. Mirsky and H. Perfect, *Applications of the notion of independence to problems of combinatorial analysis*, J. Combinatorial Theory **2** (1967), 327–357. MR **37** #1268.

47. C. St. J. A. Nash-Williams, *Edge-disjoint spanning trees of finite graphs*, J. London Math. Soc. **36** (1961), 445–450. MR **24** #A3087.

48. ———, *An application of matroids to graph theory*, Théorie des Graphes, Journées Internationales d'Études (Rome, 1966), Dunod, Paris, 1967, pp. 263–265.

49. ———, *Which infinite set systems have transversals? A possible approach*, Combinatorics Inst. of Math. Applications, 1972, pp. 237–253.

50. ———, *Infinite graphs—a survey*, J. Combinatorial Theory **3** (1967), 286–301. MR **35** #5351.

51. H. Perfect and J. S. Pym, *An extension of Banach's mapping theorem with applications to problems concerning common representatives*, Proc. Cambridge Philos. Soc. **62** (1966), 187–192. MR **33** #2553.

52. K. P. Podewsky and K. Steffens, *Injective choice functions for countable families*, J. Combinatorial Theory (submitted).

53. K. Prikry, Unpublished notes dated July, 1974.

54. J. S. Pym, *The linking of sets in graphs*, J. London Math. Soc. **44** (1969), 542–550. MR **38** #3172.

55. J. S. Pym and H. Perfect, *Submodular functions and independence structures*, J. Math. Anal. Appl. **30** (1970), 1–31. MR **41** #8269.

56. R. Rado, *A theorem on independence relations*, Quart. J. Math. Oxford Ser. **13** (1942), 83–89. MR **4**, 269.

57. ———, *Axiomatic treatment of rank in infinite sets*, Canad. J. Math. **1** (1949), 337–343. MR **11**, 238.

58. ———, *Note on the transfinite case of Hall's theorem on representatives*, J. London Math. Soc. **42** (1967), 321–324. MR **35** #2758.

59. J. Silver, An unpublished note dated June, 1974.

60. K. Steffens, *Injective choice functions*, J. Combinatorial Theory **17** (1974), 138–144.

61. W. T. Tutte, *Matroids and graphs*, Trans. Amer. Math. Soc. **90** (1959), 527–552. MR **21** #337.

62. ———, *Lectures on matroids*, J. Res. Nat. Bur. Standards Sect. B **69B** (1965), 1–47, 49–53. MR **31** #4023.

63. ———, *On the problem of decomposing a graph into n connected factors*, J. London Math. Soc. **36** (1961), 221–230. MR **25** #3858.

64. B. Węglorz, *Some remarks on selectors*. I, Fund. Math. **77** (1973), 295–304.

65. D. J. A. Welsh, *Some applications of a theorem of Rado*, Mathematika **15** (1968), 199–203. MR **39** #77.

66. ———, *On matroid theorems of Edmonds and Rado*, J. London Math. Soc. (2) **2** (1970), 251–256. MR **41** #3309.

67. ———, *Combinatorial problems in matroid theory*, Combinatorial Mathematics and Its Applications (Proc. Conf., Oxford, 1969), Academic Press, London, 1971, pp. 291–306. MR **43** #4701.

68. H. Whitney, *On the abstract properties of linear dependence*, Amer. J. Math. **57** (1935), 509–533.

69. D. R. Woodall, *Two results on infinite transversals*, Combinatorics, Inst. Math. Applications, 1972, pp. 341–350.

University of Calgary
Calgary, Alberta, Canada T2N 1N4

Proceedings of the International Congress of Mathematicians
Vancouver, 1974

Higher Algebraic K-Theory

Daniel Quillen

One of the problems discussed in Swan's talk on algebraic K-theory at the Nice Congress was to find the "good" generalization of the groups K_0A and K_1A of Bass to a sequence of groups K_nA, $n \in \mathbf{Z}$. This problem has since been solved, and considerable progress has been made toward understanding these higher K-groups. In this article I want to describe these developments and to discuss some of the problems in the theory awaiting solution.

1. K_0 and K_1. Let A be a ring (supposed always to be associative with identity) and let $\mathscr{P}_A$ be the category of finitely generated projective (left) A-modules. The group K_0A is defined to be the Grothendieck group of $\mathscr{P}_A$. It is the abelian group with one generator $[P]$ for each P in $\mathscr{P}_A$ and one relation $[P] = [P'] + [P'']$ for each short exact sequence $0 \to P' \to P \to P'' \to 0$.

Following Bass, one defines K_1A to be the group $\mathrm{GL}(A)/E(A)$ appearing in Whitehead's theory of simple homotopy types. Here $\mathrm{GL}(A) = \bigcup \mathrm{GL}_nA$ is the group of invertible infinite matrices over A equal to the identity matrix except for finitely many entries, and $E(A)$ is the subgroup generated by elementary matrices $e_{ij}^a = 1 + ae_{ij}$, $i \neq j$.

The book of Bass on algebraic K-theory demonstrates how rich the theory of the functors K_0 and K_1 is. The problem of higher K's consists in extending these functors to a sequence of functors K_n, $n \in \mathbf{Z}$, in such a way that the known results about K_0 and K_1 can be generalized insofar as possible. Examples due to Swan show that the excision property does not extend, but many results do, such as the following which shows that the functor K_0 is determined by K_1. Let $A[z, z^{-1}]$ be the ring of Laurent polynomials $\sum a_nz^n$ in the indeterminate z over A.

THEOREM 1. *There is a functorially-split exact sequence*

$$0 \to K_1A \to K_1A[z] \oplus K_1A[z^{-1}] \to K_1[z, z^{-1}] \to K_0A \to 0.$$

2. K_n for $n < 0$. Because of Theorem 1 it is natural to define K_n for $n < 0$ recursively using the formula

$$K_nA = \operatorname{Coker}\{K_nA[z] \oplus K_nA[z^{-1}] \to K_nA[z, z^{-1}]\}.$$

Bass showed this definition leads to a good theory of negative K-groups, and, in particular, that Theorem 1 continues to hold with K_0 and K_1 replaced by K_n and K_{n+1} for $n < 0$.

A simpler formula for these negative K-groups was found by Karoubi. Let CA be the ring of matrices (a_{ij}), $1 \leqq i, j < \infty$, over A which are finite A-linear combinations of matrices having entries 0 and 1, and at most a single 1 in each row and column. Karoubi defines the suspension of A, denoted SA, to be the quotient of CA by the ideal of matrices with finitely many nonzero entries. SA is a discrete analogue of the Calkin algebra of bounded operators modulo compact operators on Hilbert space. He has proved

THEOREM 2. $K_{-n}A = K_0(S^nA) = K_1(S^{n+1}A)$ *for* $n \leqq 0$.

Moreover he has characterized the negative K-groups axiomatically as derived functors of K_0 in a suitable sense.

For the simplest commutative rings such as fields and Dedekind domains, the negative K-groups are not very interesting, for Bass has proved quite generally that $K_nA = 0$ for $n < 0$ if A is regular noetherian.

3. Milnor's K_2. The group $E(A)$ is generated by elementary matrices e^a_{ij}, among which hold certain obvious relations. Milnor defines the Steinberg group $\mathrm{St}(A)$ to be the abstract group with generators x^a_{ij} subject to these obvious relations, and he defines K_2A to be the kernel of the canonical epimorphism $\mathrm{St}(A) \to E(A)$. Since $\mathrm{St}(A)$ turns out to be the universal central extension of $E(A)$, K_2A can also be described as the Schur multiplier of the perfect group $E(A)$.

When F is a field, a theorem of Matsumoto gives a presentation of K_2F which has been used by Tate and Bass to describe fairly completely the behavior of K_2 for fields, especially number fields. Matsumoto's theorem has been generalized to other classes of rings by Dennis, Stein, van der Kallen and others, giving one a hold on the K_2 of these rings.

4. K_n for $n \geqq 1$ as homotopy groups. To go beyond K_2 it seems necessary to use homotopy theory and define K_n as the nth homotopy group of a suitable space (or something essentially equivalent such as a semisimplicial group). Definitions of this type have been given by Swan, Gersten, Volodin, Wagoner, and myself. One of the achievements of the past four years has been the demonstration that these definitions are equivalent. The definition best suited to my purposes here is based on the following easy result of homotopy theory.

PROPOSITION. *Let X be a connected CW complex with basepoint, and let N be a normal subgroup of π_1X which is perfect, i.e., equal to its commutator subgroup*

Then there exist a CW complex Y and a map $f: X \to Y$ *such that*

(i) $\pi_1(f)$ *induces an isomorphism* $\pi_1 X/N \simeq \pi_1 Y$.

(ii) *For any* $\pi_1 Y$-*module L and integer q the map f induces an isomorphism* $H_q(X, f^{-1}L) \simeq H_q(Y, L)$.

Furthermore, the pair (Y, f) *is determined up to homotopy equivalence by these two properties.*

Applying this result to $X = \mathrm{BGL}(A)$, the classifying space of $\mathrm{GL}(A)$, and to $N = E(A) \subset \mathrm{GL}(A) = \pi_1 X$, we obtain a space which will be denoted $\mathrm{BGL}(A)^+$. We set $K_n A = \pi_n \mathrm{BGL}(A)^+$. It is easy to prove this agrees with the Bass K_1 and the Milnor K_2.

The space $\mathrm{BGL}(A)^+$ is an H-space, and, moreover, the canonical map $\mathrm{BGL}(A) \to \mathrm{BGL}(A)^+$ is universal among maps from $\mathrm{BGL}(A)$ to an H-space. Thus $\mathrm{BGL}(A)^+$ is obtained by altering $\mathrm{BGL}(A)$ in the least possible way so as to make it an H-space. One can think of $\mathrm{BGL}(A)^+$ as analogous to the infinite Grassmannian of the topological K-theory of Atiyah and Hirzebruch.

5. Some computations. Because $\mathrm{BGL}(A)^+$ is an H-space with the same homology as $\mathrm{BGL}(A)$, one approach to the computation of $K_n A$ for $n \geqq 1$ would be to compute the homology of $\mathrm{BGL}(A)$, and then try to use the known relations between homology and homotopy for H-spaces. For example, one has that $K_n A \otimes \mathbf{Q}$ is isomorphic to the subspace of primitive elements of $H_n(\mathrm{BGL}(A), \mathbf{Q})$. Borel, completing earlier work by Garland, has computed these homology groups by means of differential forms and Hodge theory on quotients of symmetric spaces by arithmetic groups. He obtains the following:

THEOREM 3. *Let A be the ring of integers in a number field having* r_1 *real and* r_2 *complex places. Then the dimension of* $K_n A \otimes \mathbf{Q}$ *is* 1 *for* $n = 0$, $r_1 + r_2 - 1$ *for* $n = 1$, *and for* $n \geqq 2$ *it is* 0, $r_1 + r_2$, 0, r_2 *if* $n \equiv 0, 1, 2, 3 \pmod 4$, *respectively.*

In the case of the finite field $\mathbf{F}_q$, I showed by homology computations that $\mathrm{BGL}(\mathbf{F}_q)^+$ is homotopy equivalent to the fibre of the map $\Psi^q - 1$ from BU to itself, where Ψ^q is the map corresponding to the qth Adams operation. From Bott's determination of $\pi_* BU$, one concludes:

THEOREM 4. $K_0 \mathbf{F}_q = \mathbf{Z}$ *and* $K_{2i} \mathbf{F}_q = 0$ *for* $i \geqq 1$. $K_{2i-1} \mathbf{F}_q$ *is cyclic of order* $q^i - 1$ *for* $i \geqq 1$.

6. The K-spectrum of a ring. Gersten and Wagoner have independently proved the following extension of Theorem 2.

THEOREM 5. *The space* $\Omega\, \mathrm{BGL}(SA)^+$ *is canonically homotopy equivalent to* $K_0 A \times \mathrm{BGL}(A)^+$. *Consequently* $K_{n+1}(SA) = K_n A$ *for all n.*

It follows that the sequence of spaces $K_0(S^n A) \times \mathrm{BGL}(S^n A)^+$ is an Ω-spectrum, whose nth homotopy group is $K_n A$. For A commutative, Loday has shown that the tensor product operation on $\mathscr{P}_A$ induces products in the generalized homology theory associated to this spectrum. In particular, there are products $K_i A \otimes K_j A \to K_{i+j} A$ in this case.

The generalization of Theorem 1 to positive K-groups has been established by Waldhausen and myself. Thus the exact sequence holds with K_0, K_1 replaced by K_n, K_{n+1} for all n.

7. K-groups of exact categories. Even if one is primarily interested in the K-theory of projective modules, it is necessary for technical reasons to work with the K-theory of other categories of modules. Hence one is led to define higher K-groups for additive categories equipped with a suitable notion of exact sequence which I call exact categories.

Let $\mathscr{A}$ be an abelian category, e.g., the category of modules over some ring. Let $\mathscr{M}$ be a full subcategory of $\mathscr{A}$ containing zero, which is closed under extensions in $\mathscr{A}$ in the sense that if $0 \to M' \to M \to M'' \to 0$ is a short exact sequence and if M' and M'' are in $\mathscr{M}$, then so is M. Call a sequence in $\mathscr{M}$ exact if it is exact in $\mathscr{A}$. Then $\mathscr{M}$ equipped with this notion of exact sequence is an example of an exact category, and every exact category is equivalent to such an $\mathscr{M}$.

To define the K-groups of $\mathscr{M}$, we introduce a new category $Q(\mathscr{M})$ having the same objects as $\mathscr{M}$ but with morphisms defined in the following manner. By an admissible layer in an object M of $\mathscr{M}$, we will mean a pair of subobjects M_1, M_2 of M such that M_1, M_2/M_1, M/M_2 are objects in $\mathscr{M}$. A $Q(\mathscr{M})$-morphism from M' to M is defined to be an isomorphism $M' \simeq M_2/M_1$ where (M_1, M_2) is an admissible layer of M.

Assuming $\mathscr{M}$ is a small category, $Q(\mathscr{M})$ has a classifying space $BQ(\mathscr{M})$; it is the geometric realization of the semisimplicial set whose p-simplices are chains $M_0 \to M_1 \to \cdots \to M_p$ of arrows in a small category equivalent to $Q(\mathscr{M})$. We put $K_n(\mathscr{M}) = \pi_{n+1}(BQ(\mathscr{M}))$, $n \geqq 0$.

It can be easily shown that this definition gives the usual Grothendieck of $\mathscr{M}$ when $n = 0$. Somewhat less trivial is the fact that $K_n(\mathscr{P}_A)$ coincides with K_nA for $n \geqq 0$. At the moment a theory of negative K-groups for exact categories has not been developed.

8. Localization. I shall illustrate some of the points of the higher K-theory of exact categories by outlining the proof of the following localization exact sequence. The overall form of the argument, incidentally, goes back to Grothendieck's work on Riemann-Roch.

THEOREM 6. *Let A be a Dedekind domain with field of fractions F. One has an exact sequence*

$$\to K_{n+1}F \to \bigoplus_m K_n(A/m) \to K_nA \to K_nF \to$$

where m runs over the nonzero maximal ideals of A.

To simplify, we suppose A has a single maximal ideal $m \neq 0$. Let $\mathscr{M}_A$ be the category of finitely generated A-modules, and let $\mathscr{T}_A$ be the full subcategory of torsion modules.

The first step of the proof consists in showing that the inclusion of $\mathscr{P}_A$ in $\mathscr{M}_A$

induces isomorphisms: $K_*A = K_*(\mathscr{P}_A) \simeq K_*(\mathscr{M}_A)$. This follows from the fact that every M in $\mathscr{M}_A$ has a finite resolution by objects of $\mathscr{P}_A$, using a general theorem about resolution which affirms that the map $BQ(\mathscr{P}_A) \to BQ(\mathscr{M}_A)$ is a homotopy equivalence under these circumstances.

We identify $\mathscr{P}_{A/m}$ with the full subcategory of $\mathscr{T}_A$ containing the modules killed by m. The second step is to show $K_*(A_m) = K_*(\mathscr{P}_{A/m})$ is isomorphic to $K_*(\mathscr{T}_A)$. This follows from the fact that every object of $\mathscr{T}_A$ has a finite filtration whose quotients are in $\mathscr{P}_{A/m}$, using a general result on dévissage.

The theorem now results from the exact sequence

$$\to K_{n+1}(\mathscr{P}_F) \to K_n(\mathscr{T}_A) \to K_n(\mathscr{M}_A) \to K_n(\mathscr{P}_F) \to$$

which follows from the homotopy exact sequence of a fibration, once it is proved that $BQ(\mathscr{T}_A) \to BQ(\mathscr{M}_A) \to BQ(\mathscr{P}_F)$ has the homotopy type of a fibration. This point is established by applying suitably the Dold-Thom theory of quasi-fibrations to the classifying spaces involved.

9. Problems. First, let me point out that many of the results known about K_0, K_1, K_2 can be formulated for all the K_n. In this way one can generate a huge list of interesting unsolved problems in higher algebraic K-theory.

Narrowing the field somewhat, I shall suppose A to be a regular noetherian commutative ring, because such rings have simpler K-theory, e.g., the negative groups are zero. The localization sequence (Theorem 6) can be generalized to a spectral sequence relating K_*A to the K-groups of the residue fields of the different prime ideals of A. Unfortunately, almost nothing is known about K_n of a field for $n > 2$.

Suppose in addition that A is finitely generated as an algebra over $\mathbf{Z}$. Bass has posed the question of whether K_nA is a finitely generated abelian group for all n. I showed this to be true if the Krull dimension of A is $\leqq 1$, but the general case is still open. At the moment the computation of K_n for rings of integers in number fields is stuck at $K_3\mathbf{Z}$; one knows this group is finite, and Karoubi has shown it has at least 48 elements, but it is not known whether there are any others.

The work of Tate on K_2 of global fields suggests that K_nA might be related to the étale cohomology of Spec(A). To be more precise, one might hope to have a spectral sequence, analogous to the Atiyah-Hirzebruch spectral sequence of topological K-theory, starting with the étale cohomology groups

$$\begin{aligned} E_2^{pq} = H^p(\text{Spec } A[l^{-1}]) &= 0, && q \text{ odd}, \\ &= \mathbf{Z}_l(i), && q = -2i, \end{aligned}$$

whose abutment would coincide with $K_{-p-q}A \otimes \mathbf{Z}_l$ at least in degrees $-p-q > 1 + d$, where d is the Krull dimension of A. If A is the ring of integers in a number field, and either l is odd or A is totally imaginary, this spectral sequence would degenerate, yielding cohomological formulas for the K-groups conjectured by Lichtenbaum.

Before one could expect to derive such a spectral sequence, it would be necessary to understand what happens for algebraically closed fields, which are points for the étale topology. In this case we have the following conjecture due to Lichtenbaum, which I like to think of as an analogue of Bott periodicity.

CONJECTURE. *Let F be an algebraically closed field of characteristic exponent p. Then for $i \geqq 1$, $K_{2i}F$ is a divisible torsion-free abelian group, and $K_{2i-1}F$ is a divisible group whose torsion subgroup is isomorphic to $\mathbf{Q}/\mathbf{Z}[p^{-1}]$.*

This conjecture is true for K_1 and K_2, the case of K_2 being a theorem of Tate. It is true if F is the algebraic closure of a finite field by passage to the limit in Theorem 4. One can also prove that when $p > 1$, the group K_iF is uniquely p-divisible for $i \geqq 1$, this being a general result about perfect rings. The conjecture is equivalent to the assertion that for each prime number $l \neq p$, the cohomology ring $H^*(\mathrm{BGL}(F), \mathbf{Z}/l\mathbf{Z})$ is a polynomial ring with generators of degrees 2, 4, 6, etc.

10. References. The basic reference for higher algebraic K-theory is Volume I of the Proceedings of the Conference on Algebraic K-theory held at Battelle, Springer Lecture Notes in Mathematics, No. 341. Nearly everthing treated in this article is covered in this book.

MASSACHUSETTS INSTITUTE OF TECHNOLOGY
CAMBRIDGE, MASSACHUSETTS 02139, U.S.A.

Proceedings of the International Congress of Mathematicians
Vancouver, 1974

Applications of Thue's Method in Various Branches of Number Theory

Wolfgang M. Schmidt*

1. Hermite's [1873][1] proof of the transcendency of e is roughly as follows. Construct polynomials $P_0(x), \cdots, P_d(x)$ such that

$$R(x) = P_0(x) + P_1(x)e^x + \cdots + P_d(x)e^{dx}$$

has a zero of high order at $x = 0$. Suppose each polynomial $P_i(x)$ is of degree $\leqq m$. Then each $P_i(x)$ has $m + 1$ coefficients at our disposal, and altogether there are $(d + 1)(m + 1)$ coefficients at our disposal. Now in $R(x) = c_0 + c_1x + \cdots$, each coefficient c_j is a linear combination of the coefficients of the polynomials $P_i(x)$. If we set $N = (d + 1)(m + 1) - 1$, then $c_0 = c_1 = \cdots = c_{N-1} = 0$ are N linear homogeneous equations in the coefficients of the $P_i(x)$, and since $N < (d + 1)(m + 1)$, we have fewer equations than unknown coefficients. Thus we can find nonzero polynomials $P_0(x), \cdots, P_d(x)$ such that $R(x)$ has a zero of order $\geqq N$.

Now Hermite did not rely on this existence argument. He actually *constructed* polynomials with the desired properties. In our present setting there is a unique function $R(x)$ with the desired properties such that the first nonvanishing coefficient is $c_N = 1$. It turns out that $R(1)$ is positive but quite small. The polynomials $P_i(x)$ have rational coefficients, the size of whose numerators and denominators can be estimated. Now if e were algebraic of degree d, then $R(1)$ would be algebraic of degree d and quite small. One could estimate the size of the conjugates of $R(1)$, with the result that for large m (which is still at our disposal) the norm of $R(1)$, i.e., the product of $R(1)$ and its conjugates, is quite small. But the norm of a nonzero

*The author was partially supported by NSF-GP-33026X.

[1]References are listed at the end. They are listed alphabetically by the name of the author, by the year, and finally by a,b, ⋯ if there are several works by the same author in the same year.

algebraic *integer* is at least 1 in absolute value, and $R(1)$ is in a sense not too far from being an algebraic integer, so that its norm should not be too small. Thus a contradiction is obtained.

2. Thue [**1909**] proved the famous theorem that if α is a real algebraic irrational, then there are only finitely many rationals p/q with

$$|\alpha - (p/q)| < q^{-\mu}, \tag{1}$$

provided that $\mu > \frac{1}{2}d + 1$ where d is the degree of α. For $d > 2$ this is an improvement over a theorem of Liouville [**1844**] which asserts that $|\alpha - (p/q)| \geqq c(\alpha)q^{-d}$.

Before discussing Thue's proof, let us remark that the denominators of two distinct good approximants p/q and p'/q' cannot be close together. For if, say, $|\alpha - (p/q)| < q^{-\mu}$, $|\alpha - (p'/q')| < q'^{-\nu}$, and if $q^\mu \leqq q'^\nu$, then

$$\frac{1}{qq'} \leqq \left|\frac{p}{q} - \frac{p'}{q'}\right| \leqq \left|\alpha - \frac{p}{q}\right| + \left|\alpha - \frac{p'}{q'}\right| < \frac{1}{q^\mu} + \frac{1}{q'^\nu} \leqq \frac{2}{q^\mu}.$$

Thus $q' \geqq \frac{1}{2}q^{\mu-1}$, i.e., q' is rather larger than q.

Thue's first step was to construct, for each n, polynomials $P(x)$, $Q(x)$, $P_0(x), \cdots, P_{d-1}(x)$ with rational coefficients, such that

$$P(x) - \alpha Q(x) = (x - \alpha)^n(P_0(x) + P_1(x)\alpha + \cdots + P_{d-1}(x)\alpha^{d-1}) \tag{2}$$

identically in x. This identity means that if we write the right-hand side as $R_0(x) + R_1(x)\alpha + \cdots + R_{d-1}(x)\alpha^{d-1}$ with polynomials $R_i(x)$ with rational coefficients, then $R_2(x), \cdots, R_{d-1}(x)$ are identically zero. The coefficients of $R_2(x), \cdots, R_{d-1}(x)$ are linear combinations of the coefficients of $P_0(x), \cdots, P_{d-1}(x)$. If we specify that $\deg P_j(x) \leqq m$ $(j = 0, 1, \cdots, d-1)$, then we have $d(m+1)$ coefficients at our disposal, and it may be seen that if, say, $m \geqq \frac{1}{2}dn$, then we have more unknown coefficients than linear conditions imposed on them. Thus there is a nontrivial solution of (2).

Now if p/q is a very good approximation to α, then with $x = p/q$ both sides of (2) become small, so that $P(p/q)/Q(p/q) = P_n/Q_n$, say (after all it depends on n), is again a good approximation to α. One thus obtains a sequence of good approximations with denominators $Q_1 < Q_2 < \cdots$ which do not grow too fast. Now if p'/q' were another very good approximation to α with large denominator q', the construction could be rigged so that the P_n/Q_n differ from p'/q'. The denominator q' would lie between some Q_n, Q_{n+1}. Thus we would have a very good approximation p'/q' and a good approximation (either P_n/Q_n or P_{n+1}/Q_{n+1}) whose denominators are close together, thus violating the principle stated above.

Thue's argument is ineffective. We need two very good approximants p/q and p'/q', where q is large and where q' is much larger than q. Thus a single good approximation gives no contradiction, and we cannot get a bound on the size of the denominator of a very good approximation. This noneffectiveness does *not* come from the fact that we have no *explicit* construction of the polynomials above.

This idea of asserting the existence of certain polynomials rather than explicitly constructing them is the essential new idea in Thue's work. As Siegel [**1970**] points out, a study of Thue's papers reveals that Thue at first tried hard to construct the polynomials explicitly, and he actually could do so when α is a dth root, i.e., when α^d is rational.

3. The two approximants p/q and p'/q' which occur in Thue's argument were put on a more equal footing by Siegel [**1921**], who constructed a polynomial $P(x, y)$ in two variables with a zero of high order at (α, α). Now if p_1/q_1 and p_2/q_2 were two very good approximants, then P would also have a zero of high order at the rational point $(p_1/q_1, p_2/q_2)$. The idea now is to show that this cannot happen for such a rational point. Here serious difficulties arise, and one can push the argument through only if q_1 is large and q_2 is much larger than q_1. In this way Siegel weakened Thue's condition $\mu > \frac{1}{2}d + 1$ to $\mu > 2\sqrt{d}$.

Finally Roth [**1955**] improved the condition to $\mu > 2$ by using a large number of approximants, say k approximants. He constructed a polynomial $P(x_1, \cdots, x_k)$ in k variables with a zero of high order at $(\alpha, \cdots, \alpha)$. If $p_1/q_1, \cdots, p_k/q_k$ were very good approximants to α, then P would also have a zero of high order at $(p_1/q_1, \cdots, p_k/q_k)$. The great difficulty now is to show that P *cannot* have a zero of high order at such a rational point. Roth surmounted this difficulty in a very ingenious way by proving a certain lemma, which is now called Roth's lemma.

The Siegel-Roth results use Thue's idea of constructing polynomials with certain properties by setting them up with undetermined coefficients, and by noting that the desired properties amount to linear conditions on the coefficients, which are fewer than the number of available coefficients. Thus the polynomials are not constructed explicitly. The transcendence results of Siegel [**1929**], Gelfond [**1934**], and Schneider [**1934**] also make use of this principle. Auxiliary functions are constructed which have certain zeros of high orders, and this is achieved by setting up polynomials with undetermined coefficients. The same is true of the transcendence results of Baker [**1966**], which also imply an effective but weaker version of Thue's theorem.

4. A few years ago (Schmidt [**1970**]; see also the survey paper [**1971**]) I generalized Roth's theorem to simultaneous approximation. It is becoming increasingly clear that the central theorem on simultaneous approximation is the following

SUBSPACE THEOREM (SCHMIDT [**1972**]). *Let $L_1(\boldsymbol{x}), \cdots, L_m(\boldsymbol{x})$ be m linearly independent linear forms with real or complex algebraic coefficients in vectors $\boldsymbol{x} = (x_1, \cdots, x_m)$. Write $\|\boldsymbol{x}\| = \max(|x_1|, \cdots, |x_m|)$. Given $\varepsilon > 0$, there are finitely many proper rational subspaces $S_1, \cdots, S_h$ of m-dimensional space, such that every solution $\boldsymbol{x} \neq \boldsymbol{0}$ with rational integer components of $|L_1(\boldsymbol{x}) \cdots L_m(\boldsymbol{x})| < \|\boldsymbol{x}\|^{-\varepsilon}$ lies in one of these subspaces.*

To deduce Roth's theorem, set

$$L_1(x_1, x_2) = \alpha x_1 - x_2, \qquad L_2(x_1, x_2) = x_1.$$

Now if $|\alpha - (p/q)| < q^{-2-\varepsilon}$, then $\boldsymbol{x} = (q, p)$ has $q \leqq \|\boldsymbol{x}\| \leqq cq$, whence

$$|L_1(\boldsymbol{x})L_2(\boldsymbol{x})| = |(\alpha q - p)q| < q^{-\varepsilon} < \|\boldsymbol{x}\|^{-\varepsilon/2}$$

if q is large. All the solutions lie in finitely many proper subspaces, i.e., 1-dimensional subspaces. In such a subspace p/q is fixed, and hence we get only finitely many rationals p/q.

A similar situation pertains with respect to simultaneous approximation. Suppose $1, \alpha_1, \cdots, \alpha_n$ are real, algebraic, and linearly independent over the rationals. Set $m = n + 1$ and $\boldsymbol{x} = (x_0, x_1, \cdots, x_n)$ and $L_0(\boldsymbol{x}) = x_0, L_i(\boldsymbol{x}) = \alpha_i x_0 - x_i$ $(i = 1, \cdots, n)$. Then if $p_1/q, \cdots, p_n/q$ is a simultaneous rational approximation to $\alpha_1, \cdots, \alpha_n$ with

$$|\alpha_1 - (p_1/q)| \cdots |\alpha_n - (p_n/q)| < q^{-n-1-\varepsilon}, \tag{3}$$

the m-tuple $\boldsymbol{x} = (q, p_1, \cdots, p_n)$ has $|L_0(\boldsymbol{x}) \cdots L_n(\boldsymbol{x})| < \|\boldsymbol{x}\|^{-\varepsilon/2}$. The solutions of this inequality lie in some proper subspaces. If such a subspace is given by an equation $c_0 q + c_1 p_1 + \cdots + c_n p_n = 0$ with rational coefficients $c_0, \cdots, c_n$, then

$$c_1(\alpha_1 - (p_1/q)) + \cdots + c_n(\alpha_n - (p_n/q)) = c_0 + c_1\alpha_1 + \cdots + c_n\alpha_n \neq 0$$

by the linear independence of $1, \alpha_1, \cdots, \alpha_n$ over the rationals. Hence there is some $|\alpha_i - (p_i/q)|$ which is not very small; say $|\alpha_n - (p_n/q)|$ is not very small. Then the product $|\alpha_1 - (p_1/q)| \cdots |\alpha_{n-1} - (p_{n-1}/q)|$ is small. Using induction on n, one sees in this way that (3) has only finitely many solutions.

5. Let K be a number field, let $|\ |_v$ be the valuations of K and let N_v be the usual exponents such that the product formula $\prod_v |\xi|_v^{N_v} = 1$ holds for $\xi \neq 0$ in K. Define the *height* of an n-tuple $\boldsymbol{\xi} = (\xi_1, \cdots, \xi_n)$ in K^n by

$$H(\boldsymbol{\xi}) = \prod_v \max(1, |\xi_1|_v^{N_v}, \cdots, |\xi_n|_v^{N_v}).$$

It can be shown that if $1, \alpha_1, \cdots, \alpha_n$ are algebraic and linearly independent over K, then there are only finitely many $\boldsymbol{\xi} \in K^n$ with

$$|\alpha_1 - \xi_1| \cdots |\alpha_n - \xi_n| < H(\boldsymbol{\xi})^{-n-1-\varepsilon}.$$

Since in the rational field

$$H(p_1/q, \cdots, p_n/q) = \max(|q|, |p_1|, \cdots, |p_n|) \approx |q|,$$

this is a generalization of (3). The case $n = 1$ is due to LeVeque [**1955**].

In fact, if K is of degree d, if the conjugates of an element ξ of K are $\xi^{(1)}, \cdots, \xi^{(d)}$, if the conjugate fields of K are $K^{(1)}, \cdots, K^{(d)}$, then the following holds (Schmidt, [**1975**]). Suppose that, for $1 \leqq i \leqq d$, the numbers $1, \alpha_{i1}, \cdots, \alpha_{in}$ are algebraic and linearly independent over $K^{(i)}$. Then there are only finitely many $\boldsymbol{\xi} \in K^n$ with

$$\prod_{i=1}^{d} \prod_{j=1}^{n} \min(1, |\alpha_{ij} - \xi_j^{(i)}|) < H(\boldsymbol{\xi})^{-n-1-\varepsilon}.$$

The case $n = 1$ was done by Mahler ([**1961**], [**1963**]). A p-adic version was given by Schlickewei (to appear).

One can show that if α is algebraic of degree $> d$, then there are only finitely many algebraic numbers ξ of degree d (in any field) with $|\alpha - \xi| < H(\xi)^{-d-1-\varepsilon}$. Similarly, if $P(x)$ is a polynomial with rational integer coefficients of degree $> d$, there are few polynomials $Q(x)$ with rational integer coefficients of degree d such that the resultant of P and Q is small.

6. Siegel [**1929**] used his results on approximation to algebraic numbers to classify all polynomial equations $F(x, y) = 0$ which have infinitely many solutions in rational integers x, y. Already Thue [**1909**] had observed that if $F(x, y)$ is an irreducible form of degree > 2 with integer coefficients, then an equation

$$F(x, y) = c \tag{4}$$

has only finitely many solutions. Now if $F(x, 1)$ has the root α, then $F(x, y)$ is, except for a constant factor, equal to $(x - \alpha^{(1)}y) \cdots (x - \alpha^{(d)}y)$, i.e., the norm of $x - \alpha y$. Thus Thue's equation is a special case of a *norm form* equation

$$\mathfrak{N}(\alpha_1 x_1 + \cdots + \alpha_n x_n) = c,$$

where $\alpha_1, \cdots, \alpha_n$ are linearly independent (over the rationals) elements of a number field K, and where $\mathfrak{N}$ denotes the norm. For a wide class of norm form equations, there are only finitely many solutions. But there are exceptions. For example, in $\mathfrak{N}(x + \sqrt{2}y + \sqrt{3}z) = c$ with the field $K = \boldsymbol{Q}(\sqrt{2}, \sqrt{3})$, it is clear that if $x + \sqrt{2}y$ is a particular solution, i.e., if $\mathfrak{N}(x + \sqrt{2}y) = c$, then if we multiply $x + \sqrt{2}y$ by a unit of $\boldsymbol{Q}(\sqrt{2}\ )$, we obtain again a solution. Thus we obtain certain well-defined "families of solutions". It can be shown (Schmidt [**1972**]) that there are only finitely many families of solutions. Baker's [**1968**] famous work gives an effective method to decide whether a Thue equation (4) has a solution. We have at present no such method for norm form equations in more than two variables. But by combining Baker's results with the theory of families of solutions one gets an effective method to decide if there are infinitely many solutions, provided the number of variables is at most five.

As a special application, Fujiwara [**1972**] showed that if $K = \boldsymbol{Q}(\alpha)$ is a number field of degree $d > 2n$, then the norm form equation

$$\mathfrak{N}(x_0 + \alpha x_1 + \cdots + \alpha^n x_n) = c$$

has only finitely many solutions.

Let K be a number field of degree d. It may or it may not have an integral basis of the type $1, \alpha, \cdots, \alpha^{d-1}$, i.e., a so-called *power base*. If α has this property, then so does β if $\alpha \equiv \beta \pmod 1$, i.e., if $\alpha - \beta$ is a rational integer. Dade and Taussky [**1964**] noted that such bases are connected with certain Thue equations if $d = 3$, and hence that in view of Thue's theorem, up to congruence modulo 1 there are only finitely many such elements α. Recently Knight (to appear) accomplished the same for $d = 4$ by using the general norm form results. But Györy [**1973**] had used Baker's method to prove this result in general.

7. Let $\mathfrak{K}$ be the field of formal power series $\alpha = a_k t^k + \cdots + a_0 + a_{-1}t^{-1} + \cdots$ with complex coefficients. Let $|\ |$ be the valuation with $|\alpha| = 2^k$ if the leading coefficient of α is $a_k \neq 0$. Almost all the results mentioned above have an analog in $\mathfrak{K}$. For example, Roth's theorem has such an analog, proved by Uchiyama [**1961**]:

If $\alpha \in \mathfrak{K}$ is algebraic over the subfield $\boldsymbol{C}(t)$ of rational functions $p(t)/q(t)$ with complex coefficients, then for $\varepsilon > 0$ there are only finitely many rational functions $p(t)/q(t)$ with

$$|\alpha - (p(t)/q(t))| < |q(t)|^{-2-\varepsilon}.$$

In $\mathfrak{K}$ we may also study differential equations. If the formal derivatives of α are $\alpha^{(0)} = \alpha, \alpha^{(1)}, \alpha^{(2)}, \cdots$, define the *denomination* of a "differential monomial" $(\alpha^{(0)})^{c_0}(\alpha^{(1)})^{c_1} \cdots (\alpha^{(k)})^{c_k}$ to be $c_0 + 2c_1 + \cdots + (k+1)c_k$. The denomination of a polynomial P in α and its derivatives is the maximum of the denominations of the monomials occurring in it. It was shown by Kolchin **[1959]** that if α satisfies a differential equation $P(\alpha, \alpha^{(1)}, \cdots, \alpha^{(k)}) = 0$ of denomination d with coefficients which lie in $\boldsymbol{C}(t)$, then

$$|\alpha - (p(t)/q(t))| \geqq c(\alpha)|q(t)|^{-d}.$$

This generalizes Liouville's theorem. But Osgood (**[1973]**, to appear) made the very interesting observation that an algebraic function α of degree d satisfies a differential equation of a denomination much smaller than d. He thus obtained for power series an effective improvement of Liouville's theorem stronger than the one obtained by Baker's method.

Suppose α satisfies a linear differential equation

$$\alpha^{(m)} + \beta_{m-1}\alpha^{(m-1)} + \cdots + \beta_1\alpha^{(1)} + \beta_0\alpha = \gamma$$

with coefficients $\beta_{m-1}, \cdots, \beta_0, \gamma$ which are algebraic over $\boldsymbol{C}(t)$. Then there are (Schmidt (to appear)) only finitely many rational functions $p(t)/q(t)$ with

$$|\alpha - (p(t)/q(t))| < |q(t)|^{-2-4m-\varepsilon}.$$

This is a consequence of a power series version of the subspace theorem. For $m = 0$ we get Uchiyama's result. It is likely that the exponent should really be $-2-\varepsilon$ for any m. The first step in this direction probably would be to show that the analog of Roth's theorem holds for integrals of algebraic functions.

8. We now turn to a rather different application of Thue's method. It was a great surprise when Stepanov (**[1969]**, **[1970]**, **[1971]**, **[1972a]**, **[1972b]**, **[1974]**) succeeded in proving in a new way special cases of Weil's **[1948]** celebrated theorem on the Riemann hypothesis for curves over finite fields. Let $F(x, y)$ be a polynomial with coefficients in the finite field with q elements which is absolutely irreducible, i.e., irreducible not only over the field with q elements but also over every algebraic extension of it. Then Weil's theorem says that the number N of solutions of the equation $F(x, y) = 0$ with x, y in the given field with q elements satisfies $|N - q| < cq^{1/2}$, where c is a constant which depends only on the degree of F.

Stepanov was at the 1974 International Congress and talked about his work. He first settled in a very simple way equations of the type $y^d = F(x)$, which include elliptic equations studied by Hasse **[1936a]**, **[1936b]**. He then dealt with equations $y^p - y = F(x)$ where p is the characteristic, and finally with more general equations $y^d + G_1(x)y^{d-1} + \cdots + G_d(x) = 0$. He imposed certain conditions on the degrees of the polynomials $G_i(x)$, which guarantee the absolute irreducibility of the equation. Then Bombieri [**1973**] and Schmidt [**1973**] independently extended Stepanov's results to the general absolutely irreducible equation.

The method of Stepanov consists in the construction of certain polynomials $P(x)$ with prescribed zeros of high order. These polynomials are set up with undetermined coefficients. Their having the prescribed zeros imposes linear conditions on the coefficients. It is then shown that the number of the linear conditions is smaller than the number of available coefficients, so that there exist the desired nonzero polynomials. Thus this is a new application of the method which was so successfully introduced by Thue to diophantine approximation and transcendental numbers. In fact before his work on equations over finite fields, Stepanov worked on diophantine approximation.

Stepanov's method is simplest for equations $y^d = F(x)$. We may suppose that d divides $q - 1$. The interesting solutions are those with $F(x) \neq 0$. Now $F(x)$ must be a dth power, and if this is the case, we obtain d solutions y. Thus if N' is the number of solutions with $F(x) \neq 0$, we have $N' = dL$, where L is the number of x for which $F(x)$ is a nonzero dth power, i.e., for which $F(x)^{(q-1)/d} = 1$.

Stepanov's idea was to construct a polynomial $P(x)$ which has a zero of order A for each x with $F(x)^{(q-1)/d} = 1$, and which is of a degree B which is not too large. This can be done such that $B/A \leqq (q/d) + c_1 q^{1/2}$. The total number of zeros of $P(x)$ counted with their multiplicities cannot exceed its degree, so that $LA \leqq B$, whence

$$N' = dL \leqq dB/A \leqq q + dc_1 q^{1/2} = q + c_2 q^{1/2}.$$

A lower bound is derived in a similar way.

This is not the occasion to go into the details of the construction of the polynomial $P(x)$. But I would like to point out some features which show that the present argument is not only a Thue-type argument, but that it has other similarities with the proof of the Thue-Siegel-Roth theorem. The polynomial $P(x)$ is set up in the form

$$P(x) = F(x)^A \sum_{i=0}^{d-1} \sum_{j=0}^{k} P_{ij}(x) F(x)^{i(q-1)/d} x^{q_j}.$$

Here the $P_{ij}(x)$ are polynomials of degrees $\leqq (q/d) - m$ with undetermined coefficients. In order to get the desired zeros one has to impose linear conditions on the coefficients of the P_{ij}'s. In other words, Thue's method.

It can be shown that one can choose the polynomials P_{ij}, not all zero, such that P has the desired zeros. But this does not quite finish the job! Even though the P_{ij}'s are not all zero, conceivably $P(x)$ could be zero! Now one *can* show that $P(x)$ is not zero. Here one either has to suppose, as Stepanov does, that d, deg F are relatively prime, or, more generally, that the equation $y^d = F(x)$ is absolutely irreducible. The showing of the nonvanishing of $P(x)$ is one of the more difficult parts of the proof. This situation is similar to the one of the Thue-Siegel-Roth theorem, where first a polynomial $P(x_1, \cdots, x_k)$ is constructed, and afterwards it is shown that P cannot have a zero of high order at certain rational points, which is achieved by the difficult Roth lemma.

The second similarity is perhaps more superficial, but is rather striking. To get zeros of high orders the natural thing to do would be to study the derivatives of

$P(x)$. But in the characteristic p case, always $P^{(p)}(x) = P^{(p+1)}(x) = \cdots = 0$, so that the higher derivatives are useless. Instead of the mth derivative with $D^m x^i = m!\binom{i}{m}x^{i-m}$, one has to use the operator ("Hasse derivative") $E^{(m)}$ with $E^{(m)}x^i = \binom{i}{m}x^{i-m}$. Now in Roth's theorem the characteristic is zero and the higher derivatives do not vanish identically. But one needs polynomials whose coefficients are not too large, and hence one also needs to replace mth derivatives by $E^{(m)}$. The reasons are different, but who knows if there is a deeper connection?

For general equations $F(x, y) = 0$ the argument is a little more complicated. Bombieri was able to avoid derivatives altogether, but had to use the zeta-function of the curve associated with the equation. Stark [**1973**] made a detailed study of hyperelliptic equations and obtained estimates for the number of solutions which sometimes go beyond those following from the Riemann hypothesis for curves over finite fields.

Not everybody would agree if I would say that the method of Thue-Stepanov is simpler or more elementary than Weil's proof which uses algebraic geometry. But the method is certainly different. It is simple and natural to mathematicians who are familiar with Thue's method. Thus it provides a bridge between diophantine approximation and transcendental numbers on the one hand, and equations over finite fields on the other hand. It is to be hoped that this new bridge will lead to new discoveries both in diophantine approximation and in equations over finite fields.

References

A. Baker (1966), *Linear forms in the logarithms of algebraic numbers*. I, II, III, Mathematika **13**, 204–216; ibid. **14** (1967), 102–107, 220–228. MR **36** #3732.

——— (1968), *Contributions to the theory of Diophantine equations*. II. *The Diophantine equation* $Y^2 = x^3 + k$, Philos. Trans. Roy. Soc. London Ser. A **263**, 193–208. MR **37** #4006.

E. Bombieri (1973), *Counting points on curves over finite fields (d'aprés S. A. Stepanov)*, Séminaire Bourbaki, 25e année 1972/73, no. 430, Juin 1973.

E. C. Dade and O. Taussky (1964), *On the different in orders in an algebraic number field and special units connected with it*, Acta Arith. **9**, 47–51. MR **29** #3460.

M. Fujiwara (1972), *Some applications of a theorem of W. M. Schmidt*, Michigan Math. J. **19**, 315–319. MR **47** #1743.

A. Gel'fond (1934), *Sur le septième problème de D. Hilbert*, Dokl. Akad. Nauk SSSR **II**, 1–3 (Russian), 4–6 (French).

——— (1934b), *Sur le septième problème de Hilbert*, Bull. Leningrad (7), 623–634.

K. Györy (1973), *Sur les polynômes à coefficients entiérs et de discriminant donné*, Acta Arith. **23**, 419–426.

H. Hasse (1936a), *Zur Theorie der abstrakten elliptischen Funktionenkörper*. II, J. Reine Angew. Math. **175**, 69–88.

——— (1936b), *Zur Theorie der abstrakten elliptischen Funktionenkörper*. III, J. Reine Angew. Math. **175**, 193–208.

Ch. Hermite (1873), *Sur la fonction exponentielle*, C. R. Acad. Sci. Paris **77**, 18–24, 74–79, 226–233, 285–293.

B. Knight, (to appear).

E. R. Kolchin (1959), *Rational approximation to solutions of algebraic differential equations*, Proc. Amer. Math. Soc. **10**, 238–244. MR **21** #6366.

W. J. LeVeque (1955), *Topics in number theory*, Addison-Wesley, Reading, Mass. MR **18**, 283.

J. Liouville (1844), *Sur des classes très étendues de quantités dont la valeur n^e est ni algébrique, ni même réductible à des irrationnelles algebriques*, C. R. Acad. Sci. Paris **18**, 883–885, 910–911.

K. Mahler (1961), *Lectures on diophantine approximations*. Part 1: *g-adic numbers and Roth's theorem*, Univ. of Notre Dame Press, Notre Dame, Ind. MR **26** #78.

——— (1963), *On the approximation of algebraic numbers by algebraic integers*, J. Austral. Math. Soc. **3**, 408–434. MR **29** #1182.

Ch. Osgood (1973), *An effective lower bound on the "diophantine approximation" of algebraic functions by rational functions*, Mathematika **20**, 4–15.

——— (to appear), *Effective bounds on the "diophantine approximation" of algebraic functions over fields of arbitrary characteristic and applications to differential equations.*

K. F. Roth (1955), *Rational approximations to algebraic numbers*, Mathematika **2**, 1–20, corrigendum, 168. MR **17**, 242.

H. P. Schlickewei (to appear), *Die p-adische Verallgemeinerung des Satzes von Thue-Siegel-Roth-Schmidt.*

W. M. Schmidt (1970), *Simultaneous approximation to algebraic numbers by rationals*, Acta Math. **125**, 189–201. MR **42** #3028.

——— (1971), *Approximation to algebraic numbers*, Enseignement Math. (2) **17**, 187–253.

——— (1972), *Norm form equations*, Ann. of Math. (2) **96**, 526–551.

——— (1973), *Zur methode von Stepanov*, Acta Arith. **24**, fasc. 4, 347–368. MR **48** #2034.

——— (to appear), *Rational approximation to solutions of linear differential equations with algebraic coefficients.*

——— (1975), *Simultaneous approximation to algebraic numbers by elements of a number field*, Monatsh. Math. **79**, 55–66.

Th. Schneider (1934), *Transzendenzuntersuchungen periodischer Funktionen*, J. Reine Angew. Math. **172**, 65–69, 70–74.

C. L. Siegel (1921), *Approximation algebraischer Zahlen*, Math Z. **10**, 173–213.

——— (1929), *Über einige Anwendungen diophantischer Approximationen*, Abh. Preuss. Akad. Wiss. Math. Phys. Kl., Nr. 1.

——— (1970), *Einige Erläuterungen zu Thues Untersuchungen über Annäherungswerte algebraischer Zahlen und diophantische Gleichungen*, Nachr. Akad. Wiss. Göttingen, Math. Phys. Kl., Nr. 8.

H. M. Stark (1973), *On the Riemann hypothesis in hyperelliptic function fields*, Proc. Sympos. Pure Math., vol. 24, Amer. Math. Soc., Providence, R. I., pp. 285–302.

S. A. Stepanov (1969), *On the number of points of a hyperelliptic curve over a finite prime field*, Izv. Akad. Nauk SSSR Ser. Mat. **33**, 1171–1181 = Math. USSR Izv. **3**, 1103–1114. MR **40** #5620.

——— (1970), *Elementary method in the theory of congruences for a prime modulus*, Acta Arith. **17**, 231–247. MR **42** #4552.

——— (1971), *On estimating rational trigonometric sums with prime denominator*, Trudy Mat. Inst. Steklov. **112**, 346–371 = Proc. Steklov Inst. Math. **112**, 358–385.

——— (1972a), *An elementary proof of the Hasse-Weil theorem for hyperelliptic curves*, J. Number Theory **4**, 118–143. MR **45** #3418.

——— (1972b), *Congruences in two unknowns*, Izv. Akad. Nauk SSSR Ser. Mat. **36**, 683–711 = Math. USSR Izv. **6**, 677–704. MR **47** #3398.

——— (1974), *Rational points on algebraic curves over finite fields*, Report of a 1972 Conference on Analytic Number Theory in Minsk, USSR, 223–243. (Russian)

A. Thue (1909), *Über Annäherungswerte algebraischer Zahlen*, J. Reine Angew. Math. **135**, 284–305.

S. Uchiyama (1961), *Rational approximations to algebraic functions*, J. Fac. Sci. Hokkaido Univ. Ser. I **15**, 173–192. MR **24** #A1882.

A. Weil (1948), *Sur les courbes algébriques et les variétés qui s'en déduisent*, Actualités Sci. Indust., no. 1041 = Publ. Inst. Math. Univ. Strasbourg 7, Hermann, Paris. MR **10**, 262.

UNIVERSITY OF COLORADO
BOULDER, COLORADO 80302, U.S.A.

Proceedings of the International Congress of Mathematicians
Vancouver, 1974

Eigenvalues of the Laplacian and Invariants of Manifolds

I. M. Singer

I. Introduction. Let M be a smooth oriented compact differentiable manifold and let d denote the exterior differential acting on the algebra of smooth differential forms. If a Riemannian metric is chosen on M, then d has a formal adjoint d^* and one can form the Laplacian $\Delta_p = dd^* + d^*d$ on p-forms. These are but some of the natural elliptic operators we can associate to the Riemannian manifold M. These operators have pure point spectrum and one can ask to what extent the spectrum of these operators determines the geometric, topological, or differential structure of M.

The celebrated antecedent of results of this type is due to H. Weyl who showed (for Ω a plane domain and the Dirichlet problem) that the spectrum of Δ_0 determines the volume as follows: Let $N(\lambda)$ denote the number of eigenvalues $\leqq \lambda$. Then $\lim_{\lambda \to \infty} N(\lambda)/\lambda = \text{area}(\Omega)/2\pi$. In his Gibbs lecture [**48**], after reviewing progress up to 1950, H. Weyl stated:

> I feel that these informations about the proper oscillations of a membrane, valuable as they are, are still very incomplete. I have certain conjectures of what a complete analysis of their asymptotic behavior should aim at; but since for more than 35 years I have made no serious effort to prove them, I think I had better keep them to myself.

There have been some interesting recent results on what the spectrum determines; the purpose of this article is to review some of them.

It is difficult to study the spectrum directly; instead one studies certain functions of the spectrum. The most useful to date come from the heat equation and the wave equation. Accordingly, let $e^{-t\Delta}$ denote the heat operator (our Laplacians are *positive* semidefinite), the solution to the heat equation $(\partial/\partial t + \Delta)u = 0$ with $u|_{t=0} = u_0$ being given by $e^{-t\Delta}(u_0)$. And let $e^{-it\Delta^{1/2}}$ be the wave operator corresponding to one factor of the wave equation

$$\partial^2/\partial t^2 + \Delta = (\partial/\partial t + i\Delta^{1/2})(\partial/\partial t - i\Delta^{1/2}) = 0.$$

If $0 \leqq \lambda_1 \leqq \lambda_2 \leqq \cdots$ is the spectrum of Δ, we study $\mathrm{tr}(e^{-t\Delta}) = \sum_j e^{-t\lambda_j}$ which converges for $t > 0$ and $\mathrm{tr}(e^{-it\Delta^{1/2}})$ which can be shown to be a tempered distribution on $\boldsymbol{R}^1$. Following Riemann, we can also form the zeta function $\zeta_\Delta(s) = \mathrm{tr}(\Delta^{-s}) = \sum \lambda_j^{-s}$ which by the Mellon transform equals $(1/\Gamma(s)) \int_0^\infty t^{s-1}\mathrm{tr}(e^{-t\Delta})\, dt$. For this, we must assume that there is no zero eigenvalue.

In [**36**], Minakshisundaram and Pleijel showed that if $p_0(t, x, y)$ denotes the kernel of the integral operator $e^{-t\Delta_0}$, then $p_0(t, x, x)$ has an asymptotic expansion as $t \to 0$ of the form $(4\pi t)^{-n/2} (\sum U_j(x)t^j)$, where $\dim(M) = n$. Integration over the manifold gives $\mathrm{tr}(e^{-t\Delta_0}) \sim (4\pi t)^{-n/2} (\sum c_j t^j)$. Weyl's theorem amounts to $c_0 = \mathrm{vol}(M)$ plus a Hardy-Littlewood Tauberian theorem. The Minakshisundaram-Pleijel technique can be extended to Δ_p (see [**9**], [**38**] for example) and in fact to any elliptic selfadjoint differential operator with scalar symbol. Using the Mellon transform, the asymptotic expansion implies that $\zeta_\Delta(s)$ is holomorphic for Real $s > n/m$ and has a meromorphic extension with simple poles at $(n - j)/m$; here m = order of Δ which for the moment is 2. The residues at $(n - j)/2$, $j < n$, are the c_j's; $\zeta_\Delta(s)$ has no pole at $s = 0$ because of the pole of $\Gamma(s)$ and $\zeta_\Delta(0) = c_{n/2}$. For a direct treatment of Δ^{-s} and the extension to pseudodifferential operators, see Seeley [**43**].

"How the spectrum determines M" was put most succinctly by M. Kac in his paper [**29**] entitled, *Can you hear the shape of a drum*? For the plane domain Ω, because of $\partial\Omega$, the asymptotic expansion of $\mathrm{tr}(e^{-t\Delta_0})$ involves $t^{1/2}$ and appears as $c_0/4\pi t + a_1/t^{1/2} + a_2 + O(t^{1/2})$. Pleijel showed in [**39**] that $a_1 = - L/4(2\pi)^{1/2}$ where L = length of $\partial\Omega$. Based on polygonal approximation of $\partial\Omega$, Kac conjectured that $a_2 = e(\Omega)/6$ where $e(\Omega)$ denotes the Euler characteristic of Ω. He concludes his article with:

> As our study of the polygonal drum shows, the structure of the constant term is quite complex since it combines metric and topological features. Whether these can be properly disentangled remains to be seen.

The past few years have seen considerable disentanglement. The $U_j(x)$'s are metric invariants. They turn out to be polynomials in the curvature and their covariant derivatives and are locally determined by the metric. Certain combinations are manifold invariants and via index theory give characteristic numbers. These are all local invariants, i.e., determined locally by the metric. This shows itself, for example, in the fact that the characteristic numbers of a k-fold covering of M are given by k times the corresponding characteristic numbers of M.

We shall first discuss the new local index theorem proved by heat equation methods. Then we shall discuss manifold invariants determined by the heat operator that are not local invariants, but have some interesting applications. And finally we shall turn to the wave operator and discuss what geometric information is contained in the distribution $\mathrm{tr}(e^{-it\Delta^{1/2}})$.

II. The local index theorem. (See Atiyah, Bott, and Patodi [**5**]). The index of an elliptic operator A can be obtained from the asymptotic behavior of associated Laplacians (Atiyah and Bott [**2**]) as follows: Note that the nonzero eigenvalues of A^*A and AA^* (with multiplicities) are equal, for if $A^*Au = \lambda u$, then $AA^*(Au) =$

λAu, and conversely. Suppose, then, f is a continuous function such that $f(A^*A)$ and $f(AA^*)$ are of trace class and $f(0) = 1$. Then index A = dim ker A − dim ker A^* = dim ker A^*A − dim ker AA^* = $\mathrm{tr}(f(A^*A) - f(AA^*))$. Choose $f(\lambda) = e^{-t\lambda}$ so that index $A = \mathrm{tr}(e^{-tA^*A} - e^{-tAA^*})$, for any t; in particular as $t \to 0$. Let $B^+ = A^*A$ and $B^- = AA^*$ and let $p^\pm(t, x, y)$ be the kernels for the integral operators $e^{-tB^\pm}$. Then $p^\pm(t, x, x) \sim (4\pi t)^{-n/2} (\sum U_j^\pm(x) t^j)$ when $B^\pm$ are Laplacians. Assume n is even, so that index $A = c_{n/2}^+ - c_{n/2}^-$ where $c_{n/2}^\pm = \int_M U_{n/2}^\pm (x)\, dx$.

For a general operator A, one cannot say much about $U_{n/2}^\pm(x)$; but for operators coming from the geometry of M, it turns out that the $U_j(x)$'s are determined by the curvature. Particular geometric operators are the Euler operator $E = d + d^*$: $\Lambda^{\text{even}} \to \Lambda^{\text{odd}}$, where Λ^{even} (Λ^{odd}) are the even (odd) forms, and the signature operator $S = d + d^*$: $\Lambda^+ \to \Lambda^-$, where $\Lambda^\pm$ are the forms which at each point of M are the ± 1 eigenvalues for τ with $\tau = (\sqrt{-1})^{p(p-1)+n/2} *$ on p-forms. Using the Hodge theorem and the fact that E^*E, EE^*, S^*S, and SS^* are Laplacians on appropriate subspaces of forms, it is easy to verify that index $E = e(M)$ and index S = sign(M), the signature of M. (There are two other basic geometric operators when M has additional structure: If M s a complex manifold, one has $\bar\partial^* + \bar\partial$; if M has a spin structure there is the Dirac operator D from $\mathscr{S}^+ \to \mathscr{S}^-$, where $\mathscr{S}^\pm$ are the smooth sections of vector bundles of $\pm$ spinors. See [3].)

The new, improved index theorem depends on a deeper understanding of the coefficient $U_{n/2}^+(x) - U_{n/2}^-(x)$. Following up Minakshisundaram and Pleijel, McKean and Singer [**32**] noted that the coefficients $U_j(x)$ were contractions of curvature tensors and their covariant derivatives. Yet the index theorem involves characteristic classes which depend only on the curvature tensor, not covariant derivatives. In particular, the Chern-Gauss-Bonnet theorem gives index E as an integral of the Euler form, a special polynomial in curvature, which implies that this polynomial equals $(U_{n/2}^+(x) - U_{n/2}^-(x))dx + du$. We asked whether $d\mu = 0$ and whether this could be shown directly to give a new proof of Chern-Gauss-Bonnet. Patodi [**38**] gave an affirmative answer by direct computation. (See his [**37**] for the Riemann-Roch case $A = \bar\partial^* + \bar\partial$.) Gilkey in his thesis [**21**] showed directly how the cancellation of the covariant derivatives of curvature takes place for all geometric operators so that $(U_{n/2}^+(x) - U_{n/2}^-(x))dx$ depends only on the curvature; in fact it is a characteristic polynomial in the curvature. This can be viewed as a generalization of Carleman's improvement of Weyl's theorem, i.e., $U_0(x) = 1$ [**11**].

The case $A = S$ gives Hirzebruch's signature theorem, sign $M = \int_M L$ where L is the L-polynomial in the curvature [**23**]. Extending these ideas to the case with coefficients in an arbitrary vector bundle leads to a new proof of the index theorem, as carried out by Atiyah, Bott, and Patodi. See their beautiful exposition [**5**]. One expects these methods will be extended to give the G-index theorem for a compact Lie group G.

We emphasize again that the invariants discussed so far are local, obtained by integrating polynomials in the curvature over M. But because one knows the integrands $U_{n/2}^+(x) - U_{n/2}^-(x)$ explicitly without an extra exact factor $d\mu$, the local index theorem has applications to nonlocal invariants, as we show in the next section.

Without taking differences, one may ask what the coefficients c_j determine. It depends on which Laplacians are allowed. Using the Laplacian on forms one can tell when M has constant curvature, when it is Einstein [**38**], when it is Einstein symmetric [**16**], when it is Kähler and when it is complex projective space [**22**]. But it is still unknown whether the spectrum of Δ_0 determines whether M is a sphere [**10**].

We end this discussion by observing that the spectrum directly gives nonlocal invariants. That is, the Hodge theorem states that the pth betti number is the multiplicity of the 0th eigenvalue of Δ_p, and betti numbers are *not* local invariants.

III. The η invariant. (See Atiyah, Patodi, Singer [**6**], [**7**] for details.) There are geometric selfadjoint elliptic operators A which are not positive semidefinite; their spectrum may have an infinite number of negative eigenvalues. An example is the special geometric operator A_0 on even forms given by $(-1)^{k+p+1}(*d - d*)$ on $2p$-forms where $\dim M = n = 4k - 1$. To take into account the negative spectrum, we pass from the zeta function to the analogue of the Dirichlet L-series and define

$$\eta_A(s) = \sum_{\lambda_j \neq 0} (\operatorname{sign} \lambda_j)|\lambda_j|^{-s}$$

where $\{\lambda_j\}$ is the spectrum of A. It is easy to verify that

$$\eta_A(s) = \operatorname{tr}((A^2)^{-(s+1)/2}A) = \frac{1}{\Gamma((s+1)/2)} \int_0^\infty t^{(s-1)/2} \operatorname{tr}(e^{-tA^2}A)\, dt$$

for $\operatorname{Re} s \gg 0$. This implies that $\eta_A(s)$ is homolorphic in a half-plane and has a meromorphic extension to the entire s-plane with simple poles. It turns out that $s = 0$ is not a pole for operators on odd-dimensional manifolds and for odd order operators on even-dimensional manifolds. The other cases remain an open problem. In fact, it would be interesting to find a direct analytic proof that $s = 0$ is not a pole. We now assume n is odd, and for simplicity, A is of order 1.

The map $A \to \eta_A(0)$ is not continuous on elliptic selfadjoint operators, $\tilde{\mathscr{F}}^1$, because we have ignored the 0 eigenvalue. This can contribute only an integer jump; it turns out that the map $\tilde{\mathscr{F}}^1 \to S^1$ given by $A \to \eta_A(0) \bmod Z$ is smooth, and gives a l-form on $\tilde{\mathscr{F}}^1$ in the usual way: $\dot{\eta}_A(B) = (d\eta_{A+tB}(0)/dt)\,|_{t=0}$. A computation shows $\dot{\eta}_A(B)$ equals the residue at $s = 0$ of $\operatorname{tr}((A^2)^{-(s+1)/2}B)$.

For the special geometric operator A_0 cited above, one can check that $\eta_{A_0}(0)$ is not local by looking at lens spaces. But because $\dot{\eta}$ is given by a residue, the derivative of η_{A_0} *is* local and leads to some interesting applications.

We now list some reasons for studying $\eta_A(0)$. First, Atiyah and Singer in [**4**] showed that $H^1(\mathscr{F}^1, Z) \simeq Z$ where $\mathscr{F}^1$ denotes the set of selfadjoint Fredholm operators. The 1-form $\dot{\eta}_A$ is the generator of this cohomology on what is a natural subset $\tilde{\mathscr{F}}^1$, once the order of the operators is accounted for. The generator of H^1 can be interpreted (Atiyah and Lusztig, unpublished) as the function which assigns to a family, $\theta \to A_\theta$ of selfadjoint operators parameterized by S^1, the net flow of the spectrum through the origin. This flow is $\int \dot{\eta}_{A_\theta}\, d\theta$.

For A_0, $\eta_{A_0}(0)$ can be viewed as defining the signature or inertial index of an infinite quadratic form: If $\alpha \in \Lambda^{2k-1}$, let $Q(\alpha) = -\int_M \alpha \wedge d\alpha$. The radical of the quadratic form Q is ker d, so that Q is really defined on $d\Lambda^{2k-1}$. A direct computation gives $Q(\alpha) = \langle d\alpha, A_0^{-1} d\alpha \rangle$. So the signature of Q should be the number of positive eigenvalues of A_0 minus the number of negative eigenvalues of A_0. But in fact $\eta_{A_0}(s)|_{s=0}$ is a convergence scheme for measuring this spectral asymmetry. (Note that the eigenvalues on the remaining even forms, aside from $d\Lambda^{2k-1}$, occur in opposite pairs so contribute nothing to $\eta_{A_0}(s)$.) The three-dimensional case is enlightening. There

$$A_0 = \begin{pmatrix} 0 & \text{div} \\ \text{grad} & \text{curl} \end{pmatrix}$$

on $\Lambda^{\text{even}} = \Lambda^0 \oplus \Lambda^2$, with $\eta_{A_0}(0)$ measuring the spectral asymmetry of curl.

The η-invariant $\eta_{A_0}(0)$ allows an extension of the Hirzebruch signature theorem to compact $4k$-manifolds X with smooth boundary $\partial X = M$. First consider the Chern-Gauss-Bonnet theorem for manifolds with boundary : $e(X) - \int_X K = \int_M \sigma$ where K is the Euler class in terms of curvature and σ is a polynomial in the curvature and the second fundamental form of M in X. For simplicity, we now assume the metric on X is a product near the boundary so that $\sigma = 0$ and $e(X) - \int_X K = 0$.

The Hirzebruch theorem for a $4k$-manifold X without boundary says sign $X - \int_X L = 0$. What happens when X has a boundary M? Using the Novikov additivity theorem for the signature it is easy to see that sign $X - \int_X L$ depends only on the Riemannian manifold M. We proved

$$\text{(I)} \qquad \text{sign } X - \int_X L = -\eta_{A_0}(0).$$

It is in the proof of this result that the local index theorem enters in a crucial way. Just as in the case without boundary where sign X = index S, one now sets up a boundary value problem $\tilde{S}$ whose index involves sign X. However, this boundary value problem [25], though elliptic, is not of a classical type involving local boundary conditions. One can nevertheless proceed in the usual way and compute index $\tilde{S}$ in terms of $\text{tr}(e^{-t\tilde{S}^*\tilde{S}} - e^{-t\tilde{S}\tilde{S}^*})$. There are two contributions to this trace, one at the boundary which is given by $\eta_{A_0}(0)$ and one from the interior given by $U_{2k}^+(x) - U_{2k}^-(x) = L|_X$ coming from the L-polynomial of the doubled manifold. It is important that there be no additional unidentified term $d\mu$, since $\int_X d\mu = \int_M \mu$, which would have given an additional unidentified contribution.

The proof works for other first-order operators besides A_0. But the operator must be geometric in order to identify the interior integration with characteristic classes in terms of curvature. And in general the index of the boundary value problem will not have a topological interpretation. So for example, for the Dirac operator D, one finds that the index of the appropriate boundary value problem equals

$$\text{(II)} \qquad \int_X \hat{A} - \frac{h + \eta_D(0)}{2}$$

where $\hat{A}$ is the Hirzebruch $\hat{A}$-polynomial in terms of curvature and h is the dimension of harmonic spinors on M.

This still turns out to be useful and gives a relation between the Adams e-invariant, the η-invariant $\eta_D(0)$, and Chern-Simons invariants, as follows. First, we note that we deal only with the special case of the Chern-Simons theory involving the top cohomology [13], [14]. And for simplicity, we assume M is a boundary ∂X of dimension $n = 8k - 1$. Chern and Simons assign to each connection $\mathcal{O}$ and each invariant integral polynomial f an element $\alpha(\mathcal{O}, f)$ of $\boldsymbol{R}/Z$: Extend $\mathcal{O}$ to a connection $\tilde{\mathcal{O}}$ on X which is a product connection near the boundary, and set $\alpha(\mathcal{O}, f) = \int_X f(\Omega_{\tilde{\mathcal{O}}})$ mod Z, where $\Omega_{\tilde{\mathcal{O}}}$ is the curvature of the connection. It is easy to see by gluing that this is independent of X. If f were a rational polynomial (as in L and $\hat{A}$), one gets an invariant in $\boldsymbol{R}/Q$. Formulas (I) and (II) show that $\alpha(\mathcal{O}, L) \equiv \eta_{A_0}(0)$ mod Q and $\alpha(\mathcal{O}, \hat{A}) \equiv \eta_D(0)/2$ mod Q when $\mathcal{O}$ is the Riemannian connection.

The Adams e-invariant $e(M, f)$ is defined when M has a given framing f and gives a cyclic element of π^s_{4k-1} which can be identified with an element of Q/Z [1]. Geometrically, it is $\int_X \hat{A}(\Omega\, \tilde{\mathcal{O}}_1)$ where $\mathcal{O}_1$ is the flat connection given by the framing. The framing also gives a Riemannian metric and comparing the Riemannian connection $\mathcal{O}$ with the flat one $\mathcal{O}_1$ gives

$$\text{(III)} \qquad e(M, f) = \tfrac{1}{2}(\eta_D(0) - h) - (\alpha(\mathcal{O}, \hat{A}) - \alpha(\mathcal{O}_1, \hat{A})) \text{ mod } Z.$$

The term $\alpha(\mathcal{O}, \hat{A}) - \alpha(\mathcal{O}_1, \hat{A})$ equals an integral $\int_M \omega$, for the difference is exact on X and one uses Stokes. The $8k - 1$ form ω is a Chern-Simons form associated to $\hat{A}$.

H. Donnelly has used these ideas to show that the spectrum of A_0 and D classifies seven and eleven spheres (unpublished). He uses the Eels-Kuiper invariant [19] which classifies these exotic spheres. This invariant is obtained by solving for the top Pontrjagin class as it occurs in L and in $\hat{A}$ and taking the difference. Thus the Eels-Kuiper invariant can be expressed in terms of $\eta_D(0)$, $\eta_{A_0}(0)$, and corresponding Chern-Simons invariants. Because these spheres can be immersed in Euclidean space so that the induced normal connection is trivial, the associated Chern-Simons invariants turn out to be zero and the Eels-Kuiper invariant depends only on $\eta_D(0)$ and $\eta_{A_0}(0)$.

Some interesting differential invariants stem from the fact that $\dot{\eta}$ is local. Let π_1 be the fundamental group of M and suppose $\chi: \pi_1 \to U(m)$ is a unitary representation of π_1 on $\boldsymbol{C}^m$. Let E_χ denote the associated flat unitary bundle and let A_χ be the associated selfadjoint first-order operator on even forms with values in E_χ. Then $\tilde{\eta}_\chi = \eta_{A_\chi}(0) - m\eta_{A_0}(0)$ is independent of the Riemannian metric because the difference of derivatives with respect to a metric is local, and locally E_χ is indistinguishable from the product bundle. When π_1 is finite, the differential invariant $\tilde{\eta}_\chi$ is the Fourier transform of the invariant $\sigma_g(\tilde{M})$ of [3] where $\tilde{M}$ is the simply connected covering of M on which π_1 acts freely as deck transformations. When π_1 is infinite, it would be interesting to find a nonspectral definition of this $\boldsymbol{R}$-valued invariant.

For other geometric operators like the Dirac operator D, one gets similar invariants. But now one must work mod Z because the 0 eigenvalue has no topological meaning and can vary. These $\boldsymbol{R}/Z$ invariants, $\eta_{D_\chi}(0) - m\eta_D(0)$, are cobordism invariants which for finite π_1 are the Q/Z invariants of [3]. More generally, for any selfadjoint elliptic operator $B: C^\infty(F) \to C^\infty(F)$, F a smooth vector bundle over M, one can define $B_\chi: C^\infty(F \otimes E_\chi) \to C^\infty(F \otimes E_\chi)$ with symbol B_χ = symbol $B \otimes I_{E_\chi}$. Because $\dot{\eta}$ is local, it turns out that $\eta_{B_\chi}(0) - m\eta_B(0) \bmod Z$ depends only on the homotopy type of the symbol of B. As a result, the character χ gives a homomorphism $K^1(TM) \to \boldsymbol{R}/Z$ which assigns to symbol B in $K^1(TM)$ the spectral invariant $\eta_{B_\chi}(0) - m\eta_B(0) \in \boldsymbol{R}/Z$. On the topological side, there is a natural map ind_χ: $K^1(TM) \to \boldsymbol{R}/Z$. The equality of these maps gives a refined index theorem which we will not go into here.

Is $\eta_{A_0}(0)$ computable? If M has an orientation reversing isometry, then $\eta_{A_0}(0) = 0$. This is the case, for example, if $M = S^{4k-1}$. When M is given explicitly as a boundary, formula (I) is effective. If π_1 is finite, η is computable via $\sigma_g(\tilde{M})$ as explained above. So, for a lens space $M = S^{2n-1}/G$ with G cyclic of order p and generator acting on $\sum \boldsymbol{C}$ by multiplication by $e^{i\Theta_j}$ on the jth factor,

$$\eta_{A_0}(0) = \frac{i^{-n}}{p} \sum_{l=1}^{p-1} \prod_{j=1}^{n} \cot \frac{l\Theta_j}{2}.$$

This formula can also be obtained by direct computation because the eigenvalues and their multiplicities are known **[34]**, **[40]**.

For M of constant negative curvature, J. Millson **[34]** has obtained a formula for η, by group representation methods, as the value at 0 of a new Selberg type zeta function. Here $M = \Gamma\backslash G/K$ with $G = \mathrm{SO}(4n-1, 1)$, $K = \mathrm{SO}(4n-1)$ and Γ a uniformizing discrete subgroup of G. (See §V for a discussion of Selberg trace formulas.)

Another case of interest is related to number theory. Suppose $T \in \mathrm{Sl}(2, Z)$ is hyperbolic. Let G be the three-dimensional solvable group with multiplication

$$\left(\begin{pmatrix} x \\ y \end{pmatrix}, t\right) \cdot \left(\begin{pmatrix} x_1 \\ y_1 \end{pmatrix}, t_1\right) = \left(\begin{pmatrix} x \\ y \end{pmatrix} + T^t \begin{pmatrix} x_1 \\ y_1 \end{pmatrix}, t + t_1\right) \quad \text{with } (x, y, t) \in \boldsymbol{R}^3.$$

Let Γ be the subgroup of integer entries, and let $M = G/\Gamma$ be the solvmanifold with left invariant metric which is the standard $\boldsymbol{R}^3$ metric at the identity coset. Then $\eta_{A_0}(0)$ turns out to be the value at 0 of a Hecke L-series for the real quadratic field which T defines. Explicitly, let $\mathfrak{A}$ denote the nonzero orbits of T on $Z \oplus Z$; then the Hecke L-series is $2 \sum_{a \in \mathfrak{A}} (\operatorname{sign} N_a) |N_a|^{-s}$ where N_a is the norm of the orbit, i.e., of the ideal the orbit determines. This computation can be done analytically (Atiyah-Singer, unpublished). It can also be obtained using (I) and Hirzebruch's work on the Hilbert modular group **[24]**. The connection occurs because G/Γ is the boundary of a cusp in the action of $\mathrm{Sl}(2, \mathcal{O})$ on $\mathscr{H} \times \mathscr{H}$ where $\mathcal{O}$ is the ring of integers of the real quadratic extension of the rationals. It will be interesting to see whether this formula holds for all totally real extensions.

IV. Torsion invariants [41], [42]. In the previous section we discussed the η invariant which is related to the signature and which, in a sense, is the inertial index of an infinite quadratic form. Now we discuss an invariant associated to the Euler characteristic and involving infinite determinants. Here, however, we have a known combinatorial invariant, Reidemeister-Franz torsion to guide us.

Briefly put, R-torsion τ can be defined as follows. Let M be a finite cell complex with fundamental group π_1 and let $\chi: \pi_1 \to O(M)$, the orthogonal group. Consider the chain complex $C(\chi) = C(\tilde{M}) \otimes_{\mathscr{L}} \boldsymbol{R}^m$ where $\mathscr{L}$ is the group algebra of π_1. It acts on $C(\tilde{M})$ via the linearization of the deck transformations and it acts on $\boldsymbol{R}^m$ via χ. The chains of $C(\chi)$ have an inner product stemming from the cells of M as an orthonormal base, so the boundary operator ∂ has an adjoint ∂^*. Suppose $C(\chi)$ is acyclic. Then define

$$\log \tau(M, \chi) = \Sigma(-1)^p p \log \det (\partial^*\partial + \partial\partial^*)\big|_{p\text{-chains}}.$$

$\partial^*\partial + \partial\partial^*$ is called the combinatorial Laplacian. This torsion turns out to be a combinatorial invariant, i.e., invariant under subdivisions. It was originally used to distinguish lens spaces of the same homotopy type which were combinatorially different.

When M is a smooth manifold the torsion for a smooth triangulation gives a manifold invariant. How can one obtain this analytically? Our candidate involves the notion of log det Δ, which we define as follows. Note that

$$\frac{d}{ds}\operatorname{tr}(\Delta^{-s}) = \frac{d}{ds}\Sigma\,\lambda_j^{-s} = \Sigma\,\lambda_j^{-s}\log\lambda_j.$$

Formally, at $s = 0$, this would be $\Sigma \log \lambda_j = \log\det \Delta$. Hence, we define

$$\log\det\Delta = \frac{d}{ds}\zeta_\Delta(s)\bigg|_{s=0},$$

and we define the analytic torsion $T(M, \chi)$ by

$$\log T(M, \chi) = \Sigma\,(-1)^p p \log\det \Delta_p^\chi$$

where Δ_p^χ is the Laplacian on p-forms with values in the flat bundle E_χ.

Here is what we know about analytic torsion. First, it is independent of the Riemannian metric on M used to define Δ_p^χ, so it gives a manifold invariant. Secondly, the differential of $\log T$ is a local invariant. Thirdly, $\tau = T$ in all known cases, i.e., lens spaces, where the zeta functions are computable [**40**]. Also T and τ satisfy the same functorial properties:

(i) multiplicative rule: If N is simply connected, then $\log T(M \times N, \tau) = e(N)\log T(M, \tau)$; and

(ii) induced representation rule: If M_1 is a covering of M with $\pi_1(M_1) \subsetneq \pi_1(M)$ and if χ_1 is an orthogonal representation of $\pi_1(M_1)$, then $\log T(M_1, \chi_1) = \log T(M, U_{\chi_1})$ where U_{χ_1} is the representation of $\pi_1(M)$ induced by χ_1.

Whether $\tau = T$ remains an open question. Some progress on this problem has been made by J. Dodziuk [**15**] and V. Patodi (see his report in these PROCEEDINGS). If one puts an inner product on the cochains of a smooth triangulation of M coming from the Whitney map of cochains into L_2 forms on M, then Dodziuk shows that for appropriate subdivisions of the triangulation the eigenvalues of the combinatorial Laplacian on 0-cochains converge to the eigenvalues of Δ_0. And Patodi can extend this result to p-cochains and Δ_p.

One can proceed analogously for a compact complex manifold using $\bar{\partial}$ and the $\bar{\partial}$ Laplacians. One obtains an invariant independent of the metric called holomorphic torsion which is a function of χ and the complex structure. We will not describe the details here, but wish to make several comments. First, this invariant distinguishes different complex structures when the period mapping is not available **[41]**, **[45]**. Certainly more work along these lines is in order. Secondly, this invariant has been calculated for Riemann surfaces. For $g = 1$, not surprisingly, it involves elliptic theta functions. For $g > 1$, it can be expressed as the value at $s = 0$ of an appropriate Selberg zeta function. Whether it can be expressed in terms of generalized theta functions of the Siegel upper half-plane, after viewing the moduli space of M as imbedded there via the period map, remains to be seen.

We close this section with a few remarks about the similarities of $\tilde{\eta}_\chi$ for the signature operator, $\tilde{\eta}_\chi$ for the Dirac operator, analytic torsion, and holomorphic torsion. They are associated in turn with signature, $\hat{A}$-genus, Euler characteristic, and arithmetic genus. They satisfy the multiplicative property relative to each of these classical invariants, respectively. They satisfy the inducedr epresentation rule. Their derivatives are local, but they are not. When appropriate, their values are given by Selberg-like, or number theoretic, zeta functions. Despite these similarities, we do not have a unified treatment of these nonlocal invariants. We have one for each geometric elliptic complex. Are there others?

V. The wave equation. We return to $N_P(\lambda)$, the number of eigenvalues less than or equal to λ, for P an elliptic positive semidefinite pseudodifferential operator of order m, acting on functions. Even when $P = \Delta_0$, the known Tauberian arguments are not strong enough to get much more than Weyl-Carleman from the knowledge of the asymptotic behavior of $\mathrm{tr}(e^{-t\Delta})$.

But wave equation methods have given very strong results, the definitive one that of L. Hörmander **[26]**. He showed, among other things, that

$$\text{(A)} \qquad N_P(\lambda) = \frac{\mathrm{vol}\, B_P}{(2\pi)^n} \lambda^{n/m} + O(\lambda^{(n-1)/m})$$

where $B_P = [\xi \in T^*(M),\ p(x, \xi) \leqq 1]$. This generalizes the second-order case of Levitan **[30]** and Avakumovic **[8]**. Hörmander studied the distribution $\mathrm{tr}(e^{-itP})$ near $t = 0$ for P first order using the propagation of singularities of hyperbolic equations, and the integral representation of e^{-itP} by what is now called a Fourier integral operator. Then a simple Tauberian argument gives formula (A) above from the behavior of $\mathrm{tr}(e^{-itP}) = \sum e^{-it\lambda_i} = \hat{\mu}(t)$ where μ is the spectral measure of P.

We do not give an exposition of the development here. However, the case $P = \Delta_0^{1/2}$ is of geometric interest and the techniques developed by Hörmander, Egorov, and Maslov **[20]**, **[33]** have been used by Duistermaat and Guillemin **[17]** to show, for example, that for a generic Riemannian metric the eigenvalues determine the lengths of closed geodesics. Some of their results have been obtained earlier by other methods (Colin de Verdiere **[46]** and Chazarain **[12]**, but the use of Fourier integral operators and wave front sets can be expected to go deeper. In particular, there appear to be connections with the Selberg trace formula that will no doubt be vigorously pursued. We close then with a brief discussion of these matters.

For M an n-torus $\mathbf{R}^n/L$, L a lattice subgroup of $\mathbf{R}^n$, the eigenfunctions of Δ_0 are $e^{2\pi i\langle x, l'\rangle}$, $l' \in L'$, the dual lattice. So the eigenvalues are $4\pi^2\|l'\|^2$, and $\operatorname{tr}(e^{-t\Delta_0}) = \sum_{\omega\in L'} e^{-4\pi^2 t\|\omega\|^2}$. The Jacobi identity (use the Poisson summation formula) states that this equals

$$\frac{\operatorname{vol}(M)}{(4\pi t)^{n/2}} \sum_{l\in L} e^{-\|l\|^2/4t}.$$

On the other hand, the closed geodesics on M lift to the line segments from 0 to l, $l \in L$ on $\mathbf{R}^n$. So the *length spectrum*, i.e., the lengths of closed geodesics, is $\{\|l\|\}_{l\in L}$. It is easy to see from the Jacobi identity that the eigenvalues of Δ_0 determine the length spectrum and vice versa. (Note that the Jacobi identity also shows that $\operatorname{tr}(e^{-t\Delta_0}) = \operatorname{vol}(M)/(4nt)^{d/2}$ + an exponentially small term.) Milnor's example **[35]** showing that the spectrum does not determine the Riemannian metric is given by two sixteen-dimensional tori with nonconjugate lattices but the same spectrum. If one allows the spectrum of Laplacians on flat bundles, then in these examples the geometry is determined by the spectrum.

The Selberg trace formula **[44]** can be viewed as a noncommutative generalization of the Poisson summation formula to the case where M is a Riemann surface of genus $g > 1$. Here $M = \Gamma\backslash H$, $\Gamma = \pi_1(M)$ a uniformizing discrete subgroup of $\mathrm{Sl}(2, R)$ and M with constant negative curvature inherited from its simply connected covering $H = \mathrm{Sl}(2, R)/\mathrm{SO}(2)$, the upper half-plane. On H, the kernel $p(t, x, y)$ of $e^{-t\Delta_0}$ is given by an explicit function $p(t, \cosh r(x, y))$ where r is the Poincaré distance. Averaging over the action of Γ on H eventually gives

$$\operatorname{tr}(e^{-t\Delta_0}) = \frac{e^{-t/4}}{(4\pi t)^{1/2}}\left\{\frac{\operatorname{vol}(M)}{(4\pi t)}\int_0^\infty \frac{ue^{-u^2/4t}}{\sinh u/2}\,du + \sum_{\tilde\gamma\in\tilde\Gamma} l(\tilde\gamma)\sum_{k=1}^\infty \frac{e^{-|l(\tilde\gamma^k)|^2/4t}}{2\sinh\frac{1}{2}l(\tilde\gamma^k)}\right\}.$$

Here the sum $\tilde\gamma \in \tilde\Gamma$ means sum over conjugacy classes of primitive elements of Γ. Also, $l(\tilde\gamma)$ is the length of a closed geodesic determined by $\tilde\gamma$. Explicitly, if $\gamma \in \Gamma \subset \mathrm{Sl}(2, R)$, then it is hyperbolic and is similar in $\mathrm{Sl}(2, R)$ to a diagonal matrix

$$\begin{pmatrix} e^\rho & 0 \\ 0 & e^{-\rho}\end{pmatrix}.$$

Then $l(\gamma) = 2\rho$. The term $2\sinh\frac{1}{2}l(\gamma) = e^\rho - e^{-\rho}$ can be interpreted as follows: On $S(M)$, we have geodesic flow φ_t. If $(x, \xi) \in S(M)$ is the origin and tangent vector of a closed geodesic γ starting at x with tangent ξ and of length L, then (x, ξ) is a fixed point of φ_L. So $d\varphi_L$: $T(S(M), (x, \xi)) \to T(S(M), (x, \xi))$. It preserves the geodesic flow vector field and hence induces a transformation, the Poincaré map, P_γ normal to that direction; i.e., P_γ is a linear transformation on a vector space of dimension 2 in the present case and of dimension $2n - 2$ if $\dim M = n$. For symmetric spaces P_γ can be computed using the Jacobi equation: For P_γ there is the map: $(V(0), V'(0)) \to (V(L), V'(L))$ where V is any Jacobi field along γ, normal to

ξ. It is easy to see that in the case above, $e^{\rho} - e^{-\rho} = 2|1 - \det P_\gamma|^{1/2}$. So we can write

$$\operatorname{tr}(e^{-t\Delta_0}) = \operatorname{vol}(M)/4\pi t\cdot f(t) + e^{-t/4}/(4\pi t)^{1/2} \sum_{\tilde\gamma\in\tilde\Gamma} l(\tilde\gamma) \sum_k \frac{e^{-l(\tilde\gamma^k)^2/4t}}{|\det(1 - P_{\tilde\gamma^k})|^{1/2}}$$

where $f(t)$ is independent of Γ.

From the right-hand side, one can read off the length spectrum. In fact, Selberg defines a zeta function $Z_M(s) = \prod_{\tilde\gamma\in\tilde\Gamma}\prod_k (1 - e^{-(s+k)l(\tilde\gamma)})$ whose nonreal zeros are $\frac{1}{2} \pm (\lambda_j + \frac{1}{4})^{1/2}$ so that the length spectrum also determines the spectrum of Δ_0.

In computing the η-invariant for hyperbolic spaces in terms of a Selberg-like zeta function, Millson found the intermediate formula

$$\operatorname{tr}(A_0 e^{-tA_0^2}) = 2^{2n-1} i^{2n} (2\pi)^{n+1} \Big(\sum_{\tilde\gamma\in\tilde\Gamma} \log|\mu_{\tilde\gamma}|^2$$
$$\cdot \sum_k \Big\{ \frac{\sin k\Theta_1 \cdots \sin k\Theta_{2n-1}}{|\mu_1^k - \mu_1^{-k}|^2 \cdots |\mu_{2n-1}^k - \mu_{2n-1}^{-k}|^2} \frac{e^{-\log(\mu_{\tilde\gamma})^{2k}/4t}}{(4\pi t)^{3/2}} \log|\mu_{\tilde\gamma}|^{2k} \Big\}\Big),$$

$\gamma \in \Gamma \subset SO(4n - 1, 1)$ has a normal form over the complexes as the diagonal matrix with entries $\mu_j^2 = \mu_\gamma^2 e^{2\pi i \Theta_j}$. It turns out that this formula can be rewritten as

$$\operatorname{tr}(A_0 e^{-tA_0^2}) = (-1)^n (2\pi)^{n+1} \cdot \sum_{\tilde\gamma\in\tilde\Gamma} l_{\tilde\gamma} \sum_k \frac{(\operatorname{tr}(\varphi_{\tilde\gamma}^+)^k - (\operatorname{tr}(\varphi_{\tilde\gamma}^-)^k)}{|\det I - P_{k\tilde\gamma}|^{1/2}} \frac{e^{-l_{k\tilde\gamma}^2/4t}}{(4\pi t)^{3/2}} l_{k\tilde\gamma}.$$

Here $\varphi_\gamma^\pm$ is parallel translation around γ on $\Lambda^\pm = \pm i$ eigenspace of $A_0(\dot\gamma)$.

We come now to the Duistermaat-Guillemin results. The distribution $\hat\mu = \operatorname{tr}(e^{-it\Delta_0^{1/2}})$ has its singular support in the length spectrum. When the metric is generic, i.e., when $\det(I - P_\gamma) \neq 0$ for all closed geodesics γ, then the length spectrum *is* the singular support. Moreover,

$$\text{(B)} \qquad \hat\mu = \sum_{\tilde\gamma} 2\pi l_{\tilde\gamma} \sum_{k>0} \frac{1}{|\det 1 - P_{k\tilde\gamma}|^{1/2}} \frac{e^{\pi/2\sigma_{k\tilde\gamma}}}{t - l_{k\tilde\gamma}} + f(t)$$

where $\tilde\gamma$ is a primitive geodesic and where $f(t)$ is locally integrable, $|f(t)| \leqq \log|t - l_{\tilde\gamma}|$ near $l_{\tilde\gamma}$, and $\sigma_{\tilde\gamma}$ is the Morse index of $\tilde\gamma$.

That the singular support of $\hat\mu$ is contained in the length spectrum is an easy consequence of the propagation of singularities. Suppose the Schwartz kernel distribution of $U_t = e^{-it\Delta_0^{1/2}}$ is $k_t(x, y)$. We want the singular support of $\int_M k_t(x,x)\,dx$. Since $U_0 = I$, the wave front set of $k_0(x, y)$ is the normal to the tangent bundle of the diagonal in $T^*(X \times X)$. Propagation of singularities states that the wave front set of $k_t(x, y)$ is obtained from that of $k_0(x, y)$ by the Hamiltonian flow of the vector field dual to the symbol of $\Delta_0^{1/2}$. In this simple case, it is geodesic flow. Now set $y = x$ and integrate; one can easily keep track of the wave front sets and determine the singular support of $\hat\mu$.

The deeper result on the nature of the singularities does not come so easily. One must use the integral representation of U_t as a Fourier integral operator with a precise form for the phase function, as Hörmander did in analyzing the singularity at $t = 0$. We cannot go into these matters here. But by such methods Duistermaat and Guillemin show that, though (A) is best possible (for spheres), if one assumes a generic metric one obtains

$$\text{(C)} \qquad N_P(\lambda) = \frac{\operatorname{vol} B_P}{(2\pi)^n} \lambda^{n/m} + O(\lambda^{n-1/m}).$$

In fact, they show that one can characterize Riemannian manifolds all of whose geodesics are closed of length L and of Morse index α by the property that the spectrum of Δ_0 clusters asymptotically about $(2\pi/L)(k - \alpha/4)^2$ for large k. In [**47**], Weinstein proves a finer clustering theorem when the symbol of Δ_0 is equivalent under the group of contact transformations to the symbol of the Laplacian on a sphere. Clustering occurs for all eigenvalues not just asymptotically.

What happens when Δ_0 is replaced by Δ_p on p-forms, and more generally for a Laplacian Δ on a vector bundle E over M? These operators have scalar symbol so that conjugation by $e^{-it\Delta^{1/2}}$ leaves the algebra of pseudodifferential operators invariant. Hence, $e^{-it\Delta^{1/2}}$ not only induces geodesic flow φ_t on $T(M)$ but also linear transformations ψ_t from $\pi^*(E)(m, \xi)$ to $\pi^*(E)(\varphi_t(m, \xi))$, covering φ_t, i.e., $\psi_t{:}\pi^*(E) \to \varphi_t{}^*(\pi^*(E))$. For Δ_p, ψ_t will be the map on p-forms induced by parallel translation. For a closed geodesic γ of length $l_\gamma = L$, (m, ξ) will be fixed under φ_L so that $\psi_L{:}\pi^*(E)(m, \xi) \to \pi^*(E)(m, \xi)$. One now can expect the factor $\operatorname{tr}(\psi_L)$ to appear in the singular support, by analogy with fixed point formulae.

We note that torsion and the η-invariant for constant negative curvature spaces are given by Selberg zeta functions determined by the length spectrum. There, explicit formulas for $\operatorname{tr}(e^{-t\Delta_0})$ and $\operatorname{tr}(A_0 e^{-tA_0^2})$ are given in terms of the length spectrum. The Duistermaat-Guillemin results show that generically $\hat{\mu}$ determines the length spectrum via the singular support of $\hat{\mu}$. Now

$$\operatorname{tr}(e^{-t\Delta_0}) = \mu(e^{-tx^2}) = \hat{\mu}(\widehat{e^{-tx^2}}) = \hat{\mu}\left(\frac{e^{-\xi^2/4t}}{(4\pi t)^{1/2}}\right).$$

Similarly if μ_1 is the spectral measure of A_0, then

$$\operatorname{tr}(Ae^{-tA^2}) = \mu_1(xe^{-tx^2}) = \hat{\mu}_1(\widehat{xe^{-tx^2}}) = \hat{\mu}_1\left(\frac{e^{-\xi^2/4t}}{(4\pi t)^{3/2}}\right).$$

If $\hat{\mu}$ is replaced by the first term in (B), and assuming a similar formula for $\hat{\mu}_1$, one obtains for constant negative curvature manifolds the results described above expressing torsion and η in terms of Selberg zeta functions. See [**42**, p. 170].

Do similar results hold for general compact spaces M of negative curvature? There $M = \boldsymbol{R}^n/\Gamma$, and the Poincaré maps P_γ are hyperbolic. In analogy with the Selberg zeta function, one can define

$$Z_\chi^\pm(s) = \prod_{\tilde{\gamma} \in \Gamma} \prod_{n_j:\text{ nonnegative integers}} \det\left(1 - \varphi^\pm(\tilde{\gamma})\chi(\tilde{\gamma})e^{-(sl_{\tilde{\gamma}} + \Sigma(n_j + 1/2)\log \tau_j(\tilde{\gamma}))}\right).$$

Here $\chi\colon \Gamma = \pi_1(M) \to O(M)$ is a representation of Γ. $\tilde{\gamma}$ is a primitive conjugacy class of Γ; and $\{\tau_j(\tilde{\gamma})\}$ is the set of absolute values > 1 of eigenvalues of P_γ. It is perhaps not too farfetched to hazard a guess that $\tilde{\eta}$ can be expressed as the value at $s = 0$ of ratios of such zeta functions. Such would be the case if only the first term in (B) were used.[1] We conjecture that the remainder terms cancel when

[1]This amounts to treating a primitive geodesic and its iteratives as the circle case $\{\hat{\mu}(\xi)\} = (1 + e^{2\pi i\xi/L})/(1 - e^{2\pi i\xi/L})$ with factors due to the action of A_0 on forms $\{\operatorname{tr}(\phi^+(\gamma^{\xi/L}) - \phi^-(\gamma^{\xi/L}))\}$ and the normal to the closed geodesic γ $\{|\det 1 - P_\gamma^{\xi/L}|^{-1/2}\}$.

taking ratios. Similarly, for torsion invariants.

In any case, the formula $\mathrm{tr}(e^{-t\Delta_0}) = \hat{\mu}(e^{-\xi^2/4t}/(4\pi t)^{1/2})$ shows that the heat asymptotic expansion and the residues of $\zeta_\Delta(s)$ are obtainable from $\hat{\mu}$, i.e., by wave equation methods. This program is being carried out by Duistermaat and Guillemin.

References

1. J. F. Adams, *On the groups J(x).* IV, Topology **5** (1966), 21–71; erratum, ibid. **7** (1968), 331. MR **33** #6628; **37** #5874.

2. M. F. Atiyah and R. Bott, *The Lefschetz fixed point theorem for elliptic complexes.* I, Ann. of Math. (2) **86** (1967), 374–407. MR **35** #3701.

3. M. F. Atiyah and I. M. Singer, *The index of elliptic operators.* III, Ann. of Math. (2) **87** (1968), 546–604. MR **38** #5245.

4. ———, *Index theory for skew-adjoint Fredholm operators*, Inst. Hautes Études Sci. Publ. Math. No. 37 (1969), 5–26. MR **44** #2257.

5. M. F. Atiyah, R. Bott and V. K. Patodi, *On the heat equation and the index theorem*, Invent. Math. **19** (1973), 279–330.

6. M. F. Atiyah, I. M. Singer and V. K. Patodi, *Spectral asymmetry and Riemannian geometry*, Bull. London Math. Soc. **5** (1973), 229–234.

7. ———, *Spectral asymmetry and Riemannian geometry.* I, Proc. Cambridge Philos. Soc. **77** (1975), 43–69.

8. V. G. Avakumović, *Über die Eigenfunktionen auf geschlossenen Riemannschen Mannigfaltigkeiten*, Math. Z. **65** (1956), 327–344. MR **18**, 316.

9. M. Berger, *Geometry of the spectrum*, Proc. Sympos. Pure Math., vol. 27, Part II, Amer. Math. Soc., Providence, R. I., 1975, pp. 129–152.

10. M. Berger, P. Gaudochon and E. Mazet, *Le spectre d'une variété riemannienne*, Lecture Notes in Math., vol. 194, Springer-Verlag, Berlin and New York, 1971. MR **43** #8025.

11. T. Carleman, *Propriétés asymptotiques des fonctions fondamentales des membranes vibranter*, C. R. Serre Congr. Math. Scand. Stockholm, 1934, pp. 34–44.

12. J. Chazarain, *Formula de Poisson pour les variétés Riemannienes*, Invent. Math. (to appear).

13. S. S. Chern and J. Simons, *Some cohomology classes in principal fiber bundles and their application to riemannian geometry*, Proc. Nat. Acad. Sci. U.S.A. **68** (1971), 791–794. MR **43** #5453.

14. ———, *Characteristic forms and geometric invariants*, Ann. of Math. (2) **99** (1974), 48–69.

15. J. Dodziuk, *Finite difference approach to the Hodge theory of harmonic forms* (submitted).

16. H. Donnelly, *Symmetric Einstein spaces and spectral geometry* (to appear).

17. J. J. Duistermaat and V. Guillemin, *The spectrum of positive elliptic operators and periodic geodesics*, Proc. Sympos. Pure Math., vol. 27, Part II, Amer. Math. Soc., Providence, R.I., 1975, pp. 205–210.

18. ———, *Oscillatory integrals, Lagrangian immersions, and unfoldings of singularities*, NYU, 1973 (mimeographed notes).

19. J. Eells and N. H. Kuiper, *An invariant for certain smooth manifolds*, Ann. Mat. Pura Appl. (4) **60** (1962), 93–110. MR **27** #6280.

20. Ju. V. Egorov, *The canonical transformations of pseudodifferential operators*, Uspehi Mat. Nauk **24** (1969), no. 5 (149), 235–236. (Russian) MR **42** #657.

21. P. Gilkey, *Curvature and the eigenvalues of the Laplacian for elliptic complexes*, Advances in Math. **10** (1973), 344–382.

22. ———, *The spectral geometry of real and complex manifolds*, Proc. Sympos. Pure Math., vol. 27, Amer. Math. Soc., Providence, R.I., 1975, pp. 265–280.

23. F. Hirzebruch, *Neue topologische Methoden in der algebraischen Geometrie*, Ergebnisse der Mathematik und ihrer Grenzbebiete, Heft 9, Springer-Verlag, Berlin and New York, 1956; English Transl., Die Grundlehren der math. Wissenschaften, Band 131, Springer-Verlag, New York, 1966. MR **18**, 509; **34** #2573.

24. ———, *Hilbert modular surfaces*, Enseignement Math. **19** (1973), 183–281.

25. L. Hörmander, *Pseudo-differential operators and nonelliptic boundary problems*, Ann. of Math. (2) **83** (1966), 129–209. MR **38** #1387.

26. ———, *The spectral function of an elliptic operator*, Acta. Math. **121** (1968), 193–217.

27. ———, *Fourier integral operators*. I, Acta. Math. **127** (1971), 79–183.

28. L. Hörmander and J. Duistermaat, *Fourier integral operators*. II, Acta. Math. **128** (1972), 183–269.

29. M. Kac, *Can one hear the shape of a drum*?, Amer. Math. Monthly **73** (1966), no. 4, part II, 1–23. MR **34** #1121.

30. B. M. Levitan, *On the asymptotic behavior of the spectral function of a self-adjoint differential equation of the second order*, Izv. Akad. Nauk SSSR Ser. Mat. **16** (1952), 325–352; English transl., Amer. Math. Soc. Transl. (2) **101** (1973), 192–221. MR **15**, 315.

31. ———, *On the asymptotic behavior of the spectral function of a self-adjoint differential equation of second order*. II, Izv. Akad. Nauk SSSR Ser. Mat. **19** (1955), 33–58. (Russian) MR **16**, 1027.

32. H. P. McKean, Jr. and I. M. Singer, *Curvature and the eigenvalues of the Laplacian*, J. Differential Geometry **1** (1967), 43–69. MR **36** #828.

33. V. P. Maslov, *Theory of perturbations and asymptotic methods*, Izdat. Moskov. Gos. Univ., Moscow, 1965; French transl., Dunod, Paris, 1972.

34. J. J. Millson, *η-invariants of constant curvature manifolds and a Selberg zeta function* (to appear).

35. J. W. Milnor, *Eigenvalues of the Laplace operator on certain manifolds*, Proc. Nat. Acad. Sci. U.S.A. **51** (1964), 542. MR **28** #5403.

36. S. Minakshisundaram and A. Pleijel, *Some properties of the eigenvalues of the Laplacian*, J. Differential Geometry **1** (1967), 43–69.

37. V. K. Patodi, *An analytic proof of Riemann-Roch-Hirzebruch theorem for Kaehler manifolds*, J. Differential Geometry **5** (1971), 251–283. MR **44** #7502.

38. ———, *Curvature and the eigenforms of the Laplace operator*, J. Differential Geometry **5** (1971), 233–249.

39. A. Pleijel, *A study of certain Green's functions with applications in the theory of vibrating membranes*, Ark. Mat. **2** (1954), 553–569. MR **15**, 798.

40. D. B. Ray, *Reidemeister torsion and the Laplacian on lens spaces*, Advances in Math. **4** (1970), 109–126. MR **41** #2709.

41. D. B. Ray and I. M. Singer, *R-torsion and the Laplacian on Riemannian manifolds*, Advances in Math. **7** (1971), 145–210. MR **45** #4447.

42. ———, *Analytic torsion for complex manifolds*, Ann. of Math. (2) **98** (1973), 154–177.

43. R. Seeley, *Complex powers of an elliptic operator*, Proc. Sympos. Pure Math., vol. 10, Amer. Math. Soc., Providence, R.I., 1971, pp. 288–307.

44. A. Selberg, *Harmonic analysis and discontinuous groups in weakly symmetric Riemannian spaces with applications to Dirichlet series*, J. Indian Math. Soc. **20** (1956), 47–87. MR **19**, 531.

45. N. K. Stanton, *Holomorphic R-torsion for Lie groups* (to appear).

46. Y. Colin de Verdiere, *Spectre du Laplacien et longueurs des geodesiques periodiques*, C. R. Acad. Sci. Paris Sér. A-B **275** (1972), A805–A808.

47. A. Weinstein, *Application des opérateurs intégreaux de Fourier aux spectres des variétés reimanniennes*, C.N.R.S. Colloq. Internat. sur les Opérateurs Intégrales de Fourier, Nice, May 1974.

48. H. Weyl, *Ramifications, old and new, of the eigenvalue problem*, Bull. Amer. Math. Soc. **56** (1950), 115–139. MR **11**, 666.

Massachusetts Institute of Technology
Cambridge, Massachusetts 02139, U.S.A.

Proceedings of the International Congress of Mathematicians
Vancouver, 1974

Inside and Outside Manifolds

D. Sullivan

Introduction. The classification theory of manifolds has evolved quite far. One theory fixes the homeomorphism or diffeomorphism type of a manifold in terms of the homotopy type and certain geometric invariants related to characteristic classes and the fundamental group (dimensions three and four excluded). In the simply connected case there is a further discussion which produces a purely algebraic invariant (the "homological configuration") determining the isomorphism class of the manifold and the group of automorphisms (isotopy classes) up to a finite ambiguity.

Further developments in this external theory of manifolds seems more and more algebraic. On the other hand, the study of geometrical objects inside one manifold is experiencing a resurgence which focuses attention on the classical goals and problems of "analysis situs". One organizing center for this activity is the qualitative study of dynamical systems which produces inside one manifold interesting compact subsets, families of intertwined noncompact submanifolds, geometrically defined measures and currents, with homological interpretations and relationships.

There are many problems concerning the structural stability, and a geometric description of the possible phenomena. These problems for flows generalize to higher dimensional foliations which are now known to exist abundantly.

For foliations of dimension greater than one there is a new ingredient, the Riemannian geometry of the leaves. The asymptotic properties of this geometry can be regarded as a *topological* invariant of the foliation.

Now we go into more detail. First we describe two classification theories for manifolds and then some topological problems concerning geometrical objects inside manifolds.

I. The two classification theorems. The invariants of manifolds we describe are interesting for all manifolds and classify completely for simply connected manifolds or other suitably restricted cases. Also the dimension of the manifolds must be larger than four.

The first theorem classifies the manifolds in a given homotopy type. The identification of the manifold homotopy type to a model homotopy type is part of the structure. We can picture all of our closed n-dimensional manifolds in one homotopy type as embedded in a nice domain of Euclidean space R^{2n+2} with smooth boundary. The domain will be isomorphic to a tubular neighborhood of each of these submanifolds (Figure 1). Two of these submanifolds will be considered equivalent if there is an isotopy of the domain carrying one onto another. For the first theorem we assume $\pi_1 = e$ and $n > 4$.

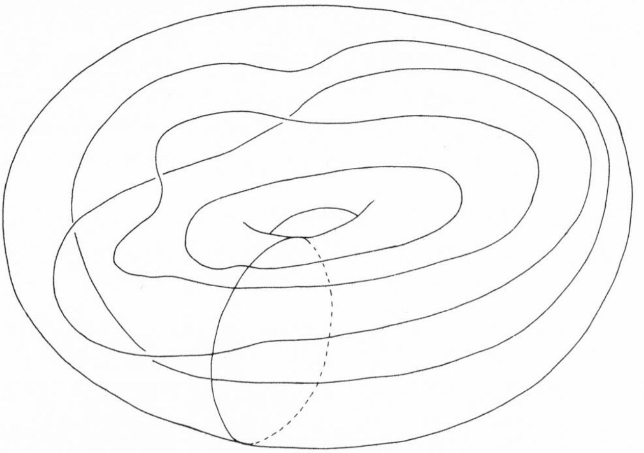

FIGURE 1. The manifolds in a homotopy type—pictured as a domain in Euclidean space.

THEOREM A. *The closed n-dimensional manifolds in a homotopy type X can be classified up to homeomorphism by the elements in a certain finitely generated abelian group h(X). h(X) is isomorphic modulo odd torsion to*

$$\bigoplus_i (H^{4i+2}(X, Z/2) \oplus H^{4i}(X, Z)), \qquad 0 < 4i,\ 4i + 2 < n.$$

The odd torsion in h(X) is the same as that in the real K-theory of X.

For more details see [**S1**] and [**S2**, Chapter 6].

We remark that the elements of $h(X)$ can be detected geometrically by spanning certain submanifolds or membranes across the domain representing X.

Each manifold in X is made transversal to these membranes, and numerical invariants are directly calculated from the intersections. The brunt of the information is carried by signatures of quadratic forms. Most of the theory for this is described in [**M-S**].

A nice example of this theorem is provided by complex projective n-space ($n \neq 2$). Here the homeomorphism types of manifolds having the same cohomology ring as CP^n are in one-to-one correspondence with

$$Z/2 \oplus Z \oplus Z/2 \oplus \cdots \oplus Z, \qquad n \text{ odd},$$
$$Z/2 \oplus Z \oplus Z/2 \oplus \cdots \oplus Z/2, \qquad n \text{ even},$$

where there are $(n - 1)$ summands. For any such manifold M the invariants can be read off from the sequence of submanifolds obtained by intersecting a homologically generating codimension 2 submanifold of M with itself.

To promote Theorem A to a classification up to diffeomorphism many more finite obstructions come in. For this most of the tools of algebraic topology can be utilized—K-theory, étale cohomology, localization, and specific calculations like the work of Milgram; see also [**S2**, Chapter 6]. The proof of Theorem A uses triangulations, transversality, and surgery. It depends heavily on the important work of Kirby and Siebenmann for topological manifolds. It was first proved in the piecewise linear context.

The next classification theorem will give one algebraic invariant which classifies the homeomorphism (or diffeomorphism) type up to a finite ambiguity. The new point here over Theorem A is homotopy theoretical and the homotopy problem is solved using differential forms. We will describe the "homological configuration" of a manifold. The idea is to build up a homological picture by starting with a basis of cycles in the extreme dimension (highest) and using intersections as much as possible as we work our way down through the homology. It is necessary to include

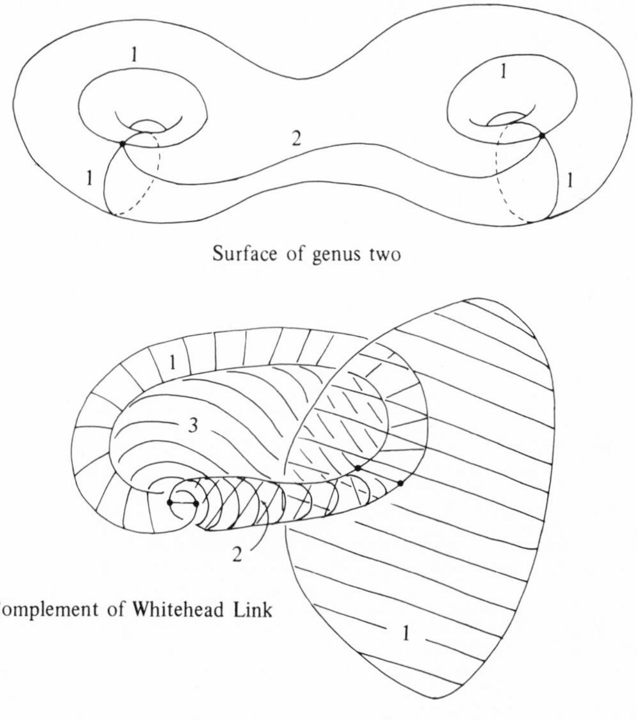

FIGURE 2. Examples of homology configurations with levels indicated.

chains or membranes to realize the homology relations among the pieces of the inductive configuration. (See Figure 2).

This construction is done rigorously using differential forms—starting in the extreme lowest dimension to build up a picture of the cohomology. One obtains a polynomial algebra tensor an exterior algebra with a differential (over Q) which determines the rational homotopy type.

The theory behind this is described in [S3] and [DGMS].

We can add to this Q-data

(a) the rational Pontryagin classes $p_1, p_2, \cdots$ with $p_i \in H^{4i}(M^n, Q)$,

(b) a certain lattice in the above algebra reflecting the integral structure,

(c) some information on the torsion in homology, for example, the order of the torsion subgroup.

If we refer to all this as the "integral homology configuration" of a manifold we have ($\pi_1 = e$, $n > 4$)

THEOREM B. *A manifold is determined up to a finite number of possibilities by its "integral homology configuration".*

A key step in the proof of Theorem B is the introduction of the arithmetic subgroups of Q-algebraic groups. A second part of the theorem says that the isotopy classes of automorphisms of the manifold are described up to a finite ambiguity (commensurability of groups) by automorphisms of the configuration. This shows these geometric automorphism groups are arithmetic groups [S4]. One can construct manifolds which realize any Q-homological configuration and characteristic classes subject to Poincaré duality and the Hirzebruch index theorem. Also, essentially all arithmetic groups occur as the group of components of Diff M, M simply connected.

An interesting sidelight is that the maximal normal nilpotent subgroup of all automorphisms contains those which are the identity on the spherical homology.

This theory of algebraic topology over Q based on differential forms can be used in more analytical questions, e.g., the topology of Kaehler manifolds, the study of closed geodesics, and Gel'fand-Fuks cohomology. See [S3], [DGMS], [H] and [S5].

II. Problems. Now we turn to more geometrical problems. The first question is the qualitative study of diffeomorphisms of manifolds under repeated iteration. One wants to describe as far as possible the orbit structure. Much has been done here but much is also unknown.

To illustrate these points consider a famous example (Figure 3) of Smale first on the solid torus and then on the 2-sphere. The solid torus is mapped into itself with degree 2, with half of it contracting into itself.

The nonwandering set $\{x\colon$ for all nghds U there exists n such that $f^n U \cap U \neq 0\}$ here is a structurally stable Cantor set plus one sink. The stable manifolds consisting of those points asymptotic (as $n \to +\infty$) to the Cantor set form a partial foliation of 2-manifolds coming out of the solid torus. The unstable manifolds of the Cantor set ($n \to -\infty$) form a dyadic solenoid running around the solid torus.

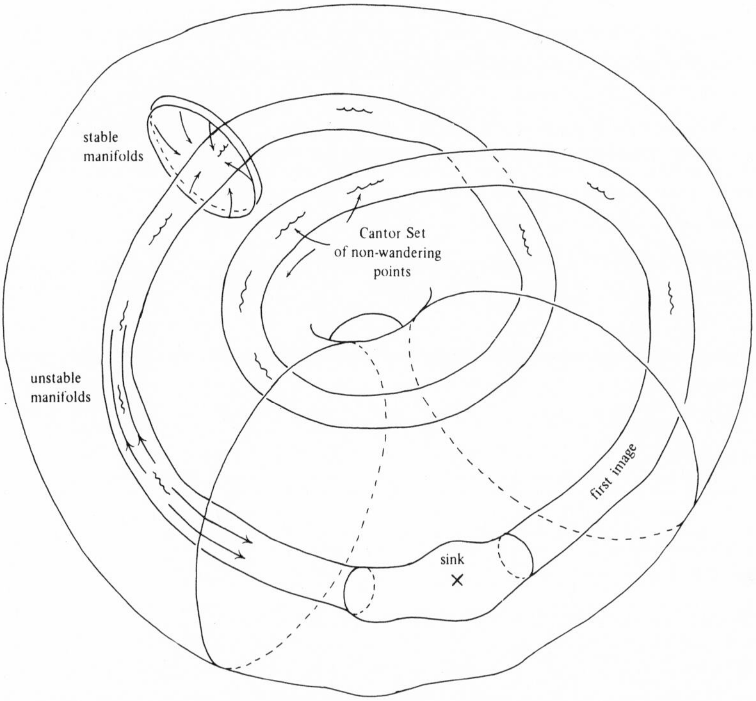

FIGURE 3. Smale's Axiom A of diffeomorphisms on the solid torus.

This picture is helpful for understanding Smale's general Axiom A diffeomorphisms. It is also not hard to see that handle preserving diffeomorphisms like these (always with zero-dimensional nonwandering set) form a C^0-dense set of all diffeomorphisms; see **[Sm]** and **[SS]**.

Problem 1. Try to understand the deformations between the various Axiom A structurally stable systems. See **[PN]**.

Problem 2. Try to construct and analyze the basic pieces of the nonwandering set having *positive* dimension. See **[B]** and **[W]** for the zero-dimensional and generalized solenoid cases respectively.

Now Smale originally studied this example on S^2. There are however many regions of Diff S^2 which are uncharted and do not contain Axiom A systems (see **[N]**). To begin to solve this problem one needs new notions of structurally stable descriptions. It is perhaps amusing to note that the counterexamples in this subject to the C^1 density of structurally stable *can be described*, so that their narrative description is at least structurally stable (**[Sm2]** and **[W2]**).

Problem 3. Describe more of the regions of Diff S^2 or Diff M outside the transversal Axiom A systems.

Problem 4. How much of Diff M can be described by perturbing transversal Axiom A systems to destroy carefully the transversality of stable and unstable manifolds? See **[Sm2]**, **[W]**, **[RW]**.

In another direction, we might recall Arnold's theorem [**A**] in Diff S^1 which states that for almost all irrational rotations the probability that a smooth perturbation is C^0 equivalent to an irrational rotation approaches 1 as the size of the perturbation approaches zero. This is a kind of structural stability which is of practical importance [**BK**] but is not included in the topological conjugacy idea.

Problem 5. Formulate a useful mixed notion of structural stability combining continuity and probability.

For practical application, attractors—closed invariant sets with invariant neighborhoods—are important (see [**T**]).

According to [**BR**] a measure one set of points in a no cycle Axiom A system goes to attractors. Thom asks the following:

Problem 6. Is it true, for a generic set (a countable intersection of dense opens) of Diff M, that almost all points in the manifold are asymptotic to attractors?

The questions of qualitative study are similar for flows. Here one uses especially the closed orbits, the Poincaré maps around them, and invariant measures. All the questions and concepts for nonsingular flows generalize to the qualitative study of foliations on a compact manifold. This generalization is quite challenging geometrically. Also understanding the qualitative behavior of foliations helps one understand the more classical problems for flows.

If we assume the ambient manifold has a Riemannian metric, each leaf of the foliation inherits a complete metric which is in a rough asymptotic sense independent of the ambient metric. For example, certain growth properties of volume $\{x \in \text{leaf}: \text{distance}(x, x_0) \leqq R\}$ are topological invariants of the foliation. It is easy to see this growth rate is at most exponential, and if it is subexponential, interesting homological arguments are possible [**P**]. One can form a limiting cycle using the chains 1/volume times $\{x \in \text{leaf}: \text{distance}(x, x_0) \geqq R\}$ and arrive at a "geometric current", roughly speaking a locally laminar submanifold with a transversal measure [**RS**].

More generally, we can ask what do leaves of foliations look like geometrically and topologically. See Figure 4 for examples of leaves in S^3.

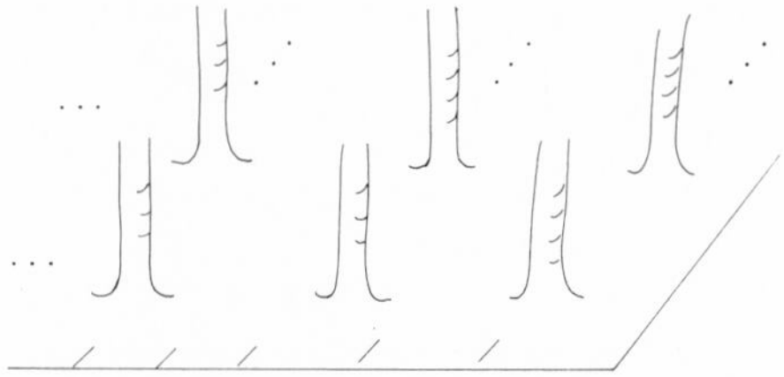

A leaf in S^3 of cubic growth

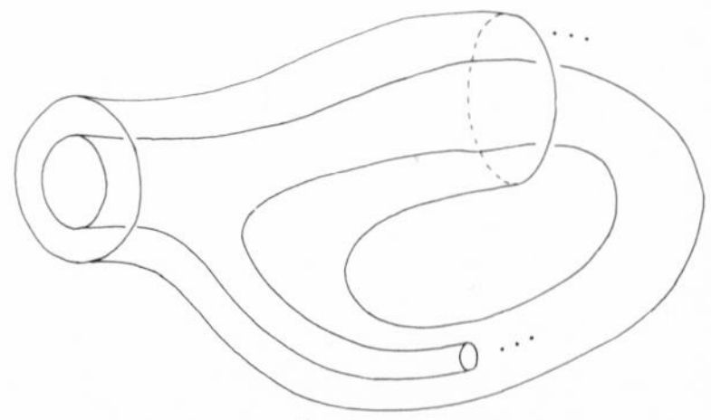

Part of a leaf in S^3, of exponential growth

FIGURE 4

Problem 7. Describe the nature of the equivalence relation on leaves induced by ambient diffeomorphisms.

Problem 8. What do 2-dimensional leaves in S^3 look like?

References

[A] V. I. Arnold, *Small denominators*. I: *Mappings of the circumference onto itself*, Izv. Akad. Nauk SSSR Ser. Mat. **25** (1961), 21–86; English transl., Amer. Math. Soc. Transl. (2) **46** (1965), 213–284. MR **25** #4113.

[B] R. Bowen, *Entropy versus homology for axiom A*, Topology **13** (1974), 61.

[BR] R. Bowen and D. Ruelle, *A measure associated to Axiom A attractors*, Inst. Hautes Études Sci., Paris (preprint).

[DGMS] P. Deligne, P. Griffiths, J. Morgan and D. Sullivan, *Topology of Kaehler manifolds*, Invent. Math. (to appear).

[H] A. Haefliger (to appear).

[BK] Bruce Knight, *Various papers on nerve cells in the horseshoe crab*, Rockefeller University, New York, N. Y.

[M-S] J. Morgan and D. Sullivan, *The transversality characteristic class and linking cycles in surgery theory*, Ann. of Math. (1974).

[N] S. Newhouse *Diffeomorphisms with infinitely many sinks*, Topology **13** (1974).

[P] J. Plante, *A generalization of Poincaré-Bendixson*, Topology (1972).

[PN] S. Newhouse and J. Palis, *Bifurcations of Morse-Smale dynamical systems*, Dynamical Systems (Proc. Sympos. Salvador, 1971), Academic Press, New York and London, 1973, pp. 303–366. MR **48** #1255.

[RS] D. Ruelle and D. Sullivan, *Currents, flows, and diffeomorphisms*, Inst. Hautes Études Sci., Paris, Topology, 1975 (preprint).

[S1] D. Sullivan, *Geometric periodicity and the invariants of manifolds*, Manifolds-Amsterdam, 1970 (Proc. Nuffic Summer School), Lecture Notes in Math., vol. 197, Springer-Verlag, Berlin, 1971, pp. 44–75. MR **44** #2236.

[S2] ———, *Geometric topology*. Part I. *Localization, periodicity, and Galois symmetry*, M.I.T., Cambridge, Mass., 1970 (preprint).

[S3] ———, *Differential forms and the topology of manifolds*, Proc. Japan Conference on Manifolds, 1973.

[S4] ———, *Algebraic topology is algebraic*, Bull. Amer. Math. Soc. (to appear).

[S5] ———, *A formula for the homology of function spaces*, Bull. Amer. Math. Soc. (to appear).

[Sm] S. Smale, *Stability and isotopy in discrete dynamical systems*, Dynamical Systems. (Proc. Sympos., Salvador, 1971), Academic Press, New York and London, 1973, pp. 527–530. MR **48** #1255.

[Sm2] ———, *Notes on differentiable dynamic systems*, Proc. Sympos. Pure Math., vol. 14, Amer. Math. Soc., Providence, R. I., 1970, pp. 277–287. MR **42** #1152.

[SS] M. Shub and D. Sullivan, *Homology theory and dynamical systems*, Topology (to appear).

[W] R. F. Williams, *Expanding attractors*, Inst. Hautes Études Sci. Publ. Math. (to appear).

[W2] ———, *The "DA" maps of Smale and structural stability*, Proc. Sympos. Pure Math., vol. 14, Amer. Math. Soc., Providence, R.I., 1970, pp. 329–334. MR **41** #9296.

[RW] C. Robinson and R. F. Williams, *Finite stability is not generic*, Dynamical Systems (Proc. Sympos., Salvador, 1971), Academic Press, New York and London, 1973, pp. 451–462. MR **48** #1255.

INSTITUT DES HAUTES ÉTUDES SCIENTIFIQUE
BURES-SUR-YVETTE, FRANCE

Proceedings of the International Congress of Mathematicians
Vancouver, 1974

On Buildings and their Applications

J. Tits

The buildings considered in this talk[1] are some particular simplicial complexes naturally associated to algebraic simple groups. The "real estate" terminology, due to N. Bourbaki [8], originated in the fact that the maximal simplices of these complexes are called "chambers" (in French, "chambre", that is, "room"), because of their close connection with the "Weyl chamber" in the theory of root systems.

1. A construction procedure. Let us first describe in rough terms a trivial but fruitful procedure to build up complicated geometrical objects from simpler ones. Take an object C, for instance a space of some kind or a simplicial complex, and a group G. To each "component" x of C (point of the space, simplex of the complex), attach a subgroup G_x of G. Then, there exists a unique minimal object extending C, on which G acts in such a way that no two components of G are equivalent under G and that G_x is the stability group of x in G, namely the quotient of the product $G \times C$ by the equivalence relation $(g, x) \sim (g', x') \Leftrightarrow x = x'$ and $g^{-1}g' \in G_x$. To make this description precise, one has of course to specify in which category, say, the product and the quotient are taken. In the sequel, C will most of the time be just a simplex, to each face σ of which a subgroup G_σ of G is attached; furthermore, the relation $G_{\sigma \vee \sigma'} = G_\sigma \cap G_{\sigma'}$ will always hold. Then, it is clear how $G \times C/\sim$, "defined" as above, is endowed with a structure of simplicial complex. Notice that, in view of the above equality, all G_σ are known as soon as the groups attached to the vertices of C are given.

[1]When preparing this report, I made much use of information received form A. Borel and J. B. Wagoner, and, most of all, from J.-P. Serre, who kindly took the trouble of reviewing for me the main applications of the theory of buildings known to him. To these acknowledgements, I wish to associate the Deutsche Forschungsgemeinschaft whose generous support made it possible for me to attend the Congress.

EXAMPLES. (1) Let the vertices of the simplex C be numbered from 1 to n. To each edge (ij), associate an integer $m_{ij} \geqq 2$ or the symbol ∞. Set

$$G = \langle r_1, \cdots, r_n \,|\, r_h^2 = (r_i r_j)^{m_{ij}} = 1 \text{ for } m_{ij} \neq \infty \rangle$$

and attach to the face σ of C the group $G_\sigma = \langle r_i \,|\, i \notin \bar{\sigma} \rangle$. The resulting complex Δ is called a *Coxeter complex* (cf. [**43**, §2]). For instance, if C is a one-simplex ($n = 2$) Δ is a closed chain of length $2m_{12}$ or a doubly infinite chain according as $m_{12} \neq$ or $= \infty$; if C is a triangle and if the three m_{ij}'s are ${}_3{}^2{}_5$ (resp. ${}_3{}^3{}_3$; resp. ${}_3{}^2{}_6$), Δ is the barycentric subdivision of an icosahedron (resp. the paving of the plane by equilateral triangles; resp. the barycentric subdivision of the paving of the plane by hexagonal honeycombs). When G is finite, Δ can be realized as a simplicial decomposition of a Euclidean $(n - 1)$-sphere on which G acts as a group of isometries. Δ is then called *spherical*. It is called *Euclidean* if it can be realized as a simplicial decomposition of a Euclidean space on which G operates by Euclidean isometries. The matrices $((m_{ij}))$ giving rise to spherical and Euclidean Coxeter complexes have been determined by H.S.M. Coxeter [**17**] and E. Witt [**48**].

(2) Let $G = \mathrm{SL}_3(\boldsymbol{F}_2)$ and let G_1 (resp. G_2) be the subgroup of all matrices $((g_{ij}))$ with $g_{21} = g_{31} = 0$ (resp. $g_{31} = g_{32} = 0$). If C is a one-simplex to the vertices of which we attach G_1 and G_2, the resulting complex is the graph of Figure 1, which is also obtained as follows: Its vertices are the points and lines of the projective plane over $\boldsymbol{F}_2$ and its edges join the pairs forming a flag (point + line through it).

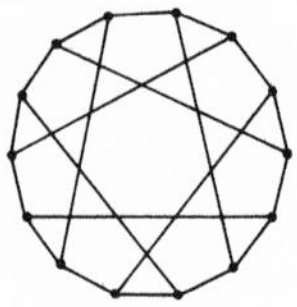

FIGURE 1

(3) More generally, let k be a division ring and $G = \mathrm{SL}_n(k)$. If we take for C an $(n - 1)$-simplex to the kth vertex of which we attach the group $\{((g_{ij})) \in G \,|\, g_{ij} = 0$ for $i > k \geqq j\}$, we get the "flag complex" of the $(n - 1)$-dimensional projective space Π over k, i.e., the complex whose vertices are the proper linear subspaces of Π and whose simplices are the flags of Π.

(4) Let k be a field with a discrete valuation whose residue field is $\boldsymbol{F}_2$, $\mathfrak{o}$ the ring of

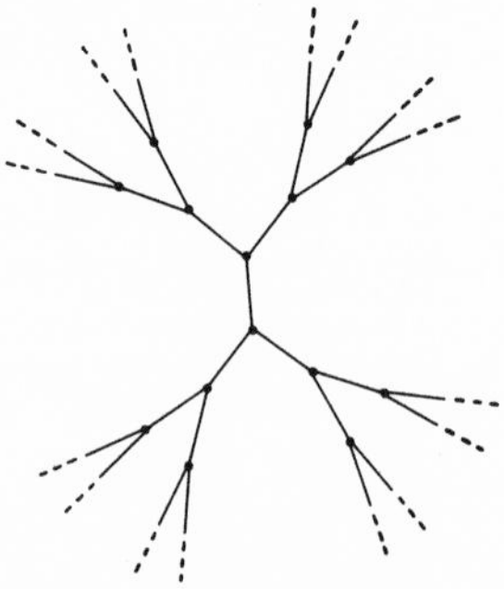

FIGURE 2

integers and π a uniformizing. Let $G = \mathrm{SL}_2(k)$. If we attach to the two vertices of a one-simplex C the subgroups $\mathrm{SL}_2(\mathfrak{o})$ and

$$G \cap \begin{pmatrix} \mathfrak{o} & \pi^{-1}\mathfrak{o} \\ \pi\mathfrak{o} & \mathfrak{o} \end{pmatrix}$$

we obtain a "homogeneous tree" whose vertices have order 3 (Figure 2).

(5) With k, $\mathfrak{o}$, π as above, let now $G = \mathrm{SL}_3(k)$ and let C be a two-simplex, to the vertices of which we attach the following subgroups:

$$\mathrm{SL}_3(\mathfrak{o}), \quad G \cap \begin{pmatrix} \mathfrak{o} & \pi^{-1}\mathfrak{o} & \pi^{-1}\mathfrak{o} \\ \pi\mathfrak{o} & \mathfrak{o} & \mathfrak{o} \\ \pi\mathfrak{o} & \mathfrak{o} & \mathfrak{o} \end{pmatrix}, \quad G \cap \begin{pmatrix} \mathfrak{o} & \mathfrak{o} & \pi^{-1}\mathfrak{o} \\ \mathfrak{o} & \mathfrak{o} & \pi^{-1}\mathfrak{o} \\ \pi\mathfrak{o} & \pi\mathfrak{o} & \mathfrak{o} \end{pmatrix}.$$

Then the resulting complex Δ is a kind of two-dimensional analogue of the tree of Figure 2: Every edge belongs to three two-simplices, the link of every vertex is the graph of Figure 1 and, in the same way as the tree contains "many" doubly infinite chains, so does Δ contain "many" subcomplexes isomorphic to the paving of a plane by equilateral triangles (cf. §3).

REMARKS. (a) In all examples given above, C was a simplex, but it may also be useful to start from other geometric objects. For instance, let G be the dihedral group of order 8, let us denote by U_2 its center, and by U_1, U_3 two other subgroups of order 2 such that $G = U_1U_2U_3$. Then, if one takes for C a hexagon to the vertices of which one attaches the groups G, U_1U_2, U_1, U_3, U_3U_2, G, the resulting complex is again the graph of Figure 1. Another instructive example is the following alternative construction of the tree of Figure 2: k, $\mathfrak{o}$ and π being defined as in Example (4), take for G the additive group of k, for C the "doubly infinite chain"

$$\begin{matrix} & -2 & & -1 & & 0 & & 1 & & 2 & \\ \cdots & | & \text{———} & | & \text{———} & | & \text{———} & | & \text{———} & | & \cdots \end{matrix}$$

and attach to the vertex i the subgroup $\pi^i\mathfrak{o}$ of G (this construction has an advantage over that of Example (4) in that it extends immediately to fields with non-discrete valuations; cf. [**11**, §7]).

(b) In this article, we are essentially interested in buildings, but the general procedure described above can also be used to construct other interesting complexes, for instance graphs related to some sporadic simple groups.

2. Buildings. Let G be a semisimple algebraic group defined over some field k. (By a common abuse of language, we shall often make no distinction between an algebraic group and the "abstract" group of its rational points over some ground field; thus, G will also denote the group of k-rational points of the algebraic group G.) There are two types of buildings which one associates to such pairs (G, k) and which we want to describe:

for arbitrary k, the *spherical building* constructed by means of the k-parabolic subgroups of G;

when k is local (i.e., endowed with a complete discrete valuation, whose residue field we assume to be perfect, for safety) the *Euclidean building* constructed by means of the parahoric subgroups of G.

To avoid technical complications, we shall assume that G is absolutely almost simple[2] (i.e., has over no field extension of k a proper normal subgroup of strictly positive dimension) and, when talking about the local case, that G is simply connected (this is a technical condition, satisfied for instance by the groups SL_n, $Spin_n$, Sp_n and their "twisted forms").

We recall that the *parabolic subgroups* of G are the algebraic subgroups P such that G/P is a complete (in fact, projective) variety (cf., e.g., **[2]**, **[5]**). There is no such simple characterization of the *parahoric subgroups*, a notion introduced by N. Iwahori and H. Matsumoto **[23]** in the case of Chevalley groups and successively extended by H. Hijikata **[21]** and by F. Bruhat and the author **[10]**; for a general definition, we refer the reader to **[10]** and **[11]**. Examples of parabolic and parahoric subgroups will be given in a moment, but we must first state a property of those subgroups which is essential for our purpose: There is a natural number l, called the *relative rank* of G, such that the following assertion holds:

($*$) All minimal k-parabolic (resp. parahoric) subgroups of G are conjugate; if B is one of them and if $P_1, \cdots, P_r$ denote the maximal proper subgroups of G containing B, one has $r = l$ (resp. $r = l + 1$), the 2^r subgroups $P_{i_1} \cap \cdots \cap P_{i_q}$ are all distinct, they are the only proper subgroups of G containing B and they form a complete system of representatives of the conjugacy classes of proper k-parabolic (resp. of parahoric) subgroups of G.

Thus, if we want to describe the parabolic or the parahoric subgroups of G, it suffices to exhibit *one* minimal such subgroup B. We start with some examples of parabolic subgroups:

If $G = SL_n(k)$, one can take for B the group of all upper triangular matrices.

If k is algebraically closed, B is any *Borel subgroup*, that is, any maximal connected (for the Zariski topology) solvable subgroup of G.

If k is perfect and if G is thought of as a group of matrices, one calls "unipotent subgroup" of G a subgroup consisting only of matrices all of whose eigenvalues are 1, and B is then the normalizer of any maximal unipotent subgroup (for instance, if char $k = p \neq 0$, B is the normalizer of any maximal p-subgroup of G: the "Sylow theorem" holds for such subgroups).

We now go over to the local case and denote by B a minimal parahoric subgroup of G. When k (and hence G) is locally compact, there is a characterization of B (essentially due to H. Matsumoto) similar to the characterization of minimal parabolic subgroups over perfect fields given above: B is the normalizer of any maximal pro-p-subgroup (projective limit of finite p-groups) of G, where p is the characteristic of the residue field. As a further example, let $G = SL_n(k)$ over any local field k whose ring of integers we again denote by $\mathfrak{o}$; then, one can take for B the group of all elements of $SL_n(\mathfrak{o})$ whose reduction modulo the prime ideal is upper triangular.

[2]In the sequel, the word "almost" will often be omitted when no confusion can arise.

The property (∗) makes the parabolic and parahoric subgroups well suited for applying the construction described in §1; one takes a simplex of dimension $r - 1 = l - 1$ (resp. l) whose vertices are numbered from 1 to r and one attaches to the face $(i_1, \cdots, i_q)$ the parabolic (resp. parahoric) subgroup $P_{i_1} \cap \cdots \cap P_{i_q}$ of G. The resulting complex is called the *spherical* (resp. *Euclidean*, or *affine*) *building* associated to G and k; simple examples are Examples (2) and (3) (resp. (4) and (5)) of §1. The first virtue of the geometric object thus attached to such pairs (G, k) is expressed by the

THEOREM. *If $l \geqq 2$, the building associated to (G, k) determines "canonically" the algebraic group G up to isogeny, the field k and, in the local case, the valuation of k.*

(For a more precise statement in the spherical case, cf. [**43**, 5.8].) In view of Example (3) of §1, that theorem can be regarded as a generalization of the "fundamental theorem of projective geometry"; it also includes the theorem of W. L. Chow and J. Dieudonné [**18**, III, §3] on the permutations of linear subspaces of quadrics which preserve the adjacency (at least for division rings which are finite dimensional over their center, but this restriction is not essential; cf. [**43**, §8]).

If $l = 0$ ("anisotropic group") the theory of buildings is of course empty (although, in the local case, buildings can also be used in the study of anisotropic groups; cf., e.g., [**10**, Proposition 6]). When $l = 1$, the Euclidean buildings are trees; they are quite useful (cf. for instance [**22**], [**32**], [**35**], [**36**], [**37**]) but do not have enough structure to give back G and k. The above theorem also suggests the following comment on Examples (4) and (5) of §1: If k and k' are two nonisomorphic totally ramified extensions of the field of dyadic numbers, the Euclidean buildings of $SL_2(k)$ and $SL_2(k')$ are isomorphic whereas those of $SL_3(k)$ and $SL_3(k')$ are not, though they look much alike "locally".

3. Apartments. The axiomatic approach. An important property of the buildings is that they contain "many" Coxeter subcomplexes. Indeed, every building Δ has a system $\mathscr{A}$ of Coxeter subcomplexes, called the *apartments* of Δ, such that:

(i) Every two simplices of Δ belong to an apartment.

(ii) If $\Sigma, \Sigma' \in \mathscr{A}$, there exists an isomorphism of Σ onto Σ' which fixes $\Sigma \cap \Sigma'$ (elementwise).

More precisely, Δ being associated to a group G (cf. §2):

(ii′) If $\Sigma, \Sigma' \in \mathscr{A}$, there exists an element of G which maps Σ onto Σ' and fixes $\Sigma \cap \Sigma'$.

For instance, in Examples (2), (3), (4), (5) of §1, the apartments are respectively hexagons (i.e., barycentric subdivisions of triangles), barycentric subdivisions of $(n - 1)$-simplices (the "coordinate frames" of the projective space in question), doubly infinite chains, and complexes isomorphic to the paving of a Euclidean plane by equilateral triangles. The terminology "spherical" and "Euclidean" introduced in §2 can now be motivated; the apartments of the buildings constructed by means of parabolic (resp. parahoric) subgroups are spherical (resp. Euclidean) Coxeter complexes.

Properties (i) and (ii) are responsible for many useful properties of the buildings. This suggests an axiomatic approach to the theory, in which these properties are taken as axioms. To avoid degeneracies, it is convenient to add the condition:

(iii) Every nonmaximal simplex of Δ is a face of at least three distinct simplices of Δ.

Thus, let us call "abstract building" a simplicial complex satisfying (iii) and having a system $\mathscr{A}$ of Coxeter subcomplexes such that (i) and (ii) hold. It can be shown that, if we require $\mathscr{A}$ to be maximal with these properties, it is unique. The question naturally arises to know how much more general this "abstract" notion is, compared to the "concrete" one introduced in §2. If the apartments are spherical of dimension $\geqq 2$ and "irreducible" (a Coxeter complex is irreducible if it is not the join of two nonempty Coxeter subcomplexes), or Euclidean of dimension $\geqq 3$, the answer is given by a classification theorem (for the spherical case, cf. [**43**]) which shows that the construction of §2 provides all such buildings if one extends the class of groups G considered so as to include the "classical groups" over arbitrary division rings and also some further "more exotic" groups. Thus, the notion of abstract building provides an elementary, "combinatorial", simultaneous approach to the algebraic semisimple groups and the classical groups of relative rank $\geqq 3$. For spherical abstract buildings of dimension one, a complete classification is out of the question but it is conjectured that a certain quite simple additional condition, the "Moufang property" (cf. [**43**, p. 274], and [**44**]), is sufficient to characterize among them the buildings associated to the classical groups, the algebraic simple groups and, again, some related "exotic" groups (e.g., the Ree groups of type ${}^2F_4$) of relative rank 2. Let us add here that the study of abstract buildings whose apartments are neither spherical nor Euclidean may be promising, as is suggested by the work of R. Moody and K. L. Teo [**29**] and R. Marcuson [**27**].

4. Metric. Topology. So far, we have only been interested in the "combinatorial" structure of the simplicial complexes we have considered. Now, it will be necessary to imagine the simplices "concretely" realized as spherical or Euclidean simplices. If Δ is the spherical (resp. Euclidean) building associated to a group G (cf. §2), its apartments are Euclidean spheres (resp. Euclidean spaces) endowed with a natural metric, well defined up to a scalar multiplication. It is easily seen that the distance functions in the various apartments can be chosen in such a way that for every $g \in G$ and every apartment Σ, g induces an isometry of Σ onto $g\Sigma$. Then, by property (ii′) of §2, the metrics on any two apartments agree on their intersection. Since, by (i), any two points belong to an apartment, Δ itself is endowed with a distance function d which can be shown to satisfy the triangular inequality. Thus, Δ is a metric space on which G acts as a group of isometries (*N.B.*: the metrics of Figures 1 and 2 are not induced by the natural metric of the underlying sheet of paper!). If Δ is spherical, its diameter is the common diameter of its apartments. We say that two points p, q of Δ are *opposite* if Δ is spherical, of diameter $d(p, q)$.

Let p, q be two nonopposite points of the building Δ. In any apartment Σ containing them, which is a Euclidean space or a sphere, they can be joined by a unique shortest geodesic, which turns out to be independent of Σ (cf. [**11**, 2.5.4] for the Euclidean case). From this, one deduces in the usual way that:

(i) *Euclidean buildings are contractible*;

(ii) *a spherical building minus the set of all points opposite to a given point is contractible.*

This last property readily implies that

(ii′) *a spherical building has the homotopy type of a bouquet of spheres.*

Furthermore, the number N of these spheres is easily determined; for instance, if the ground field k is finite of characteristic p, N is the p-contribution to the order of G.

The above properties are useful facts, as was first recognized by L. Solomon [**40**] who observed that, since G acts on Δ, it also operates on $\tilde{H}_{l-1}(\Delta) = \mathbf{Z}^N$ (l being, as before, the relative rank of G). One thus obtains a special G-module whose rank—in the finite case—is the order of the p-Sylow subgroups of G; as one may expect, this is nothing else but the *Steinberg module* of G. A similar idea was used by A. Borel and J.-P. Serre (unpublished, cf. however [**6**]) to define the "Steinberg module" of an algebraic simple group over a $\mathfrak{p}$-adic field: Here, one lets G operate on H^l_c (cohomology with compact support) of the Euclidean building of G, which is shown to be isomorphic with the Čech cohomology group H^{l-1} of the spherical building of G endowed with a nonstandard topology.

Further applications of the spherical buildings to the representation theory of finite simple groups "of Lie type" have been made by T. A. Springer (unpublished, except for some indications in [**41**]) and by G. Lusztig ([**25**], [**42**]) who considers moreover other complexes (e.g., the complex of "affine flags away from 0" in affine spaces) closely related to the buildings.

Properties (i) and (ii) are also used by D. Quillen in his proofs of various finiteness theorems in algebraic K-theory (cf. [**9**], [**34**] and other, unpublished results concerning the function field case). For further applications of buildings or "building-type constructions" to algebraic K-theory, we refer to [**1**], [**45**], [**46**] [**47**].

5. Euclidean buildings and symmetric spaces. In many respects, *the Euclidean buildings are the "ultrametric analogues" of the Riemannian symmetric spaces.* In other words, they play, in the study of $\mathfrak{p}$-adic simple groups, a role similar to that of the symmetric spaces in the theory of simple Lie groups. We shall illustrate this assertion by a few examples.

E. Cartan has shown that, in an irreducible, noncompact, simply connected symmetric space, every compact group of isometries has a fixed point (cf. [**12**, p. 19]). The same is true of a compact (and even a bounded) group of isometries of a Euclidean building [**11**, 3.2]. In fact, G. Prasad has observed that Cartan's proof itself can be carried over to Euclidean buildings: One just has to prove for the latter a certain metric inequality [**33**, 5.12] which, in the case of Riemannian spaces, characterizes the spaces with negative curvature. That the Euclidean buildings behave like spaces with negative curvature is further illustrated by other inequalities (e.g., [**11**, 3.2.1]) and by the unicity of the geodesic joining two points (cf. §4).

The fixed-point theorem mentioned above was used by Cartan to show the conjugacy of all maximal compact subgroups of a real simple Lie group. Its analogue for buildings enabled F. Bruhat and the author [**11**, §3] to show that, in a 𝔭-adic simple group (assumed to be simply connected, as previously agreed), the maximal compact subgroups are the maximal parahoric subgroups, and thus form $l + 1$ conjugacy classes ($l =$ the relative rank). The fixed-point theorem is also an essential tool in the process of extending the theory of Iwahori and Matsumoto to arbitrary 𝔭-adic simple groups (cf. [**10**, §6]): This is done by "Galois descent", and the compact group to which the theorem is applied is the Galois group of a "splitting field" of the 𝔭-adic group in question.

Another domain where Euclidean buildings are used as substitutes for the symmetric spaces is the cohomology of discrete subgroups. Let G be a real noncompact simple Lie group and Γ a discrete subgroup which, for simplicity, we shall assume without torsion. Then, Γ operates freely on the symmetric space X of G and, since X is contractible, $H^i(\Gamma) = H^i(X/\Gamma)$ for arbitrary coefficients. In particular, cd Γ is $\leqq \dim X$. Furthermore, using some differential operators on X related to the Riemannian curvature, Y. Matsushima was able to obtain more precise information on the groups $H^i(\Gamma,\boldsymbol{R})$; his results show, for instance, that for cocompact Γ and i "sufficiently small" $H^i(\Gamma, \boldsymbol{R})$ depends only on G and not on Γ. As J.-P. Serre pointed out, the Euclidean building X of a 𝔭-adic simple group G can be used similarly to investigate the cohomology of discrete subgroups Γ of G: The most obvious observation is that, since X is contractible (cf. §4), the above argument shows that if Γ is torsion-free, cd $\Gamma \leqq \dim X = l$ (relative rank of G); in [**38**] similar but more elaborate techniques are used to estimate—among other things—the cohomological dimension of S-arithmetic groups. (This dimension is *determined* in [**6**].) As for the result of Matsushima mentioned above, it can be compared with a conjecture of Serre proved by H. Garland [**19**] for "sufficiently large residue fields" (a restriction lifted by W. Casselman later on; cf. [**15**], [**20**]): If Γ is a torsion-free cocompact discrete subgroup of a 𝔭-adic simple group, then $H^i(\Gamma, \boldsymbol{R}) = 0$ for $0 < i < l$. The method of Garland bears striking formal similarities with that of Matsushima; the differential operators considered by the latter are here replaced by some "local combinatorial operators", regarded by Garland as the "𝔭-adic curvature" of the building X (cf. also [**3**]).

Mentioning those operators naturally leads us to another formal analogy between symmetric spaces and Euclidean buildings, namely the possibility of doing "harmonic analysis" on the latter as well as on the former. The simplest case is that of a locally finite tree T (remember Figure 2). If f is a complex-valued function on the set of vertices of T and if, for every vertex s, we denote by $\Lambda(f)(s)$ the average of the values of f in the vertices neighbouring s, it is well known that the operator $\Delta = \Lambda - 1$ is the "analogue" for T of the Laplace-Beltrami operator on a Riemannian manifold. The harmonic analysis on trees has been extensively studied by P. Cartier ([**13**], [**14**]). Instead of considering functions on vertices, i.e., 0-cochains, one may consider 1-cochains or, more generally, l-cochains on a locally finite Euclidean building X of dimension l, that is, functions defined on the set of all l-simplices. Such a function f is called *harmonic* if for every simplex σ of dimension $l - 1$, the sum of the values of f on all maximal simplices whose closure contains σ is zero. Taking for X the building of a $\mathfrak{p}$-adic simple group G and letting G operate on the Hilbert space of L^2 harmonic l-cochains on X, one obtains the so-called *special representation* of G which contains the Steinberg module (cf. §4) tensorized with $\boldsymbol{C}$ as a dense submodule, and which plays an important role in the theory of unitary representations of G. This representation was introduced by H. Matsumoto [**28**] and J. A. Shalika [**39**] (by I. M. Gelfand and M. I. Graev for GL_2); its interpretation as a representation on L^2 forms is due to A. Borel who also showed that the space of admissible vectors is the Steinberg module [**4**] and who constructed other, similar representations, using the Euclidean building [**4**]. (For related questions, cf. also [**26**] and its bibliography.)

6. Spherical buildings and symmetric spaces. We shall again introduce this section with a metamathematical statement, which will however be considerably vaguer than that of §5. Let G be a real or a $\mathfrak{p}$-adic simple group and let X be its symmetric space or Euclidean building. When studying various questions, one is sometimes led to add to G or X "points at infinity"; it turns out that

the "most natural choice" for the "space at infinity" of G or X is "often" closely related to the spherical building of G.

Restriction of space and competence forces me to be very brief in commenting on that sentence. With some good will however, the reader will grant that it is illustrated by the results enumerated below, and whose interconnections have perhaps not yet been fully investigated.

In [**6**], A. Borel and J.-P. Serre compactify the Euclidean building of a $\mathfrak{p}$-adic simple group G by adding to it the spherical building of G suitably retopologized (cf. also [**11**, 5.1.33]). In [**7**], considering an algebraic semisimple group G defined over a field $k \subset \boldsymbol{R}$ they enlarge the symmetric space X of the real Lie group $G(\boldsymbol{R})$ in a "manifold with corners" $\bar{X}$ and, if k is countable, $\bar{X} - X$ has the homotopy type of the spherical building of G over k. Both papers are primarily aimed at the study of arithmetic and S-arithmetic groups and, in particular, of their cohomology.

Let now G be an algebraic simple group over any field k. In [**31**, Chapter 2, §2], for the purpose of studying the "stability" in G-spaces, D. Mumford interprets the points of a certain dense subset $X_{\boldsymbol{Q}}$ of the spherical building of G over k as the equivalence classes of "one-parameter subgroups" (one-dimensional split tori) of G for a suitable equivalence relation. Intuitively, that relation describes a certain "asymptotic" behavior of the one-parameter subgroups, so that $X_{\boldsymbol{Q}}$ can be regarded as "lying at infinity" of G. A similar viewpoint is developed further in [**24**, IV, §2] (and in forthcoming continuations), where G is effectively enlarged into a scheme $\bar{G}$ by adding "at infinity" a scheme related with the spherical building of G on k (roughly speaking, $\bar{G} - G$ has a stratification whose "k-rational nerve" is the building).

Finally, it is appropriate to mention under the same heading the work of G.D.

Mostow [30] and G. Prasad [33] on the strong rigidity of cocompact discrete subgroups of real and $\mathfrak{p}$-adic simple groups, and perhaps also some aspects of the spectacular result of G. A. Margulis on the arithmeticity of lattices, which became known during this Congress. To conclude the article at a somewhat more "concrete" level, I shall try to give in a few words an extremely oversimplified idea of Mostow's proof of the following special but significant case of his result:

Let G, G' be two absolutely simple noncompact Lie groups of relative rank $\geqq 2$ and let $\Gamma \subset G$, $\Gamma' \subset G'$ be torsion-free, cocompact discrete subgroups; then, every isomorphism α: $\Gamma \to \Gamma'$ extends to an isomorphism of G onto G'.

Let X, X' be the symmetric spaces of G and G' and admit that the real spherical buildings Y and Y' of G and G' "lie at infinity" of X and X'. Because X, X' are topological cells, the manifolds X/Γ and X'/Γ' are $K(\Gamma, 1)$ and $K(\Gamma', 1)$, so that there exists a homotopy equivalence $X/\Gamma \to X'/\Gamma'$ which lifts to a mapping β: $X \to X'$ "compatible with α". Because X/Γ and X'/Γ' are compact, β "does not disturb much" the distance function in the large, from which one infers that it induces an isomorphism β': $Y \to Y'$ of the buildings at infinity. Finally, it follows from the canonicity assertion of the Theorem of §2 that β' is induced by an isomorphism of G onto G'.

Bibliography

1. D. W. Anderson, M. Karoubi and J. Wagoner, *Relations between higher algebraic K-theories* Algebraic *K*-Theory. I, Lecture Notes in Math., no. 341, Springer-Verlag, New York, 1973, pp. 73–84.

2. A. Borel, *Linear algebraic groups*, Benjamin, New York, 1969. MR **40** #4273.

3. ———, *Cohomologie de certains groupes discrets et laplacien p-adique (d'après H. Garland)* Sém. Bourbaki, Exposé 437, novembre 1973, Lecture Notes in Math., vol. 431, Springer-Verlag, Berlin and New York, 1975, pp. 12–35.

4. ———, *Admissible representations of a reductive p-adic group having vectors fixed under an Iwahori subgroup* (to appear).

5. A. Borel et J. Tits, *Groupes réductifs*, Inst. Hautes Études Sci. Publ. Math. No. 27 (1965), 55–150. MR **34** #7527.

6. A. Borel et J.-P. Serre, *Cohomologie à supports compacts des immeubles de Bruhat-Tits, applications à la cohomologie des groupes S-arithmétiques*, C. R. Acad. Sci. Paris Sér. A-B **272** (1971), A110–A113. MR **43** #221.

7. ———, *Corners and arithmetic groups*, Comment. Math. Helv. **48** (1973), 436–491.

8. N. Bourbaki, *Éléments de mathématique*. Fasc. XXXIV. *Groupes et algèbres de Lie*. Chaps 4, 5, 6, Actualités Sci. Indust., no. 1337, Hermann, Paris, 1968. MR **39** #1590.

9. L. Breen, *Un théorème de finitude en K-théorie (d'après D. Quillen)*, Sém. Bourbaki, Exposé 438, novembre 1973, Lecture Notes in Math., vol. 431, Springer-Verlag, Berlin and New York, 1975, pp. 36–57.

10. F. Bruhat et J. Tits, *Groupes algébriques simples sur un corps local*, Proc. Conf. Local Fields (Driebergen, 1966), Springer, Berlin, 1967, pp. 23–36. MR **37** #6396.

11. ———, *Groupes réductifs sur un corps local*. I. *Données radicielles valuées*, Inst. Hautes Études Sci. Publ. Math. No. 41 (1972), 5–251.

12. E. Cartan, *Groupes simples clos et ouverts et géométrie riemannienne*, J. Math. Pures Appl **8** (1929), 1–33.

13. P. Cartier, *Fonctions harmoniques sur les arbres*, Istituto Naz. di Alta Mat., Symposia Mathematica **9** (1971), 203–270. (Cf. also: *Harmonic analysis on trees*, Harmonic analysis on homogeneous spaces, Proc. Sympos. Pure Math., Vol. 26, Amer. Math. Soc., Providence, R.I., 1973, pp. 419–424.)

14. ———, *Géométrie et analyse sur les arbres*, Sém. Bourbaki, Exposé 407, février 1972, Lecture Notes in Math., no. 317, Springer-Verlag, Berlin and New York, 1973, pp. 123–140.

15. W. Casselman, *On a p-adic vanishing theorem of Garland's*, Vancouver, 1974 (preprint).

16. W. Casselman and D. Wigner, *Continuous cohomology and a conjecture of Serre's*, Invent. Math. **25** (1974), 199–211.

17. H. S. M. Coxeter, *The complete enumeration of finite groups of the form* $R_i^2 = (R_iR_j)^{k_{ij}} = 1$, J. London Math. Soc. **10** (1935), 21–25.

18. J. Dieudonné, *La géométrie des groupes classiques*, Ergebnisse der Math., N. F., Band 5, 2e éd., Springer-Verlag, Berlin, 1963. MR **28** #1239.

19. H. Garland, *p-adic curvature and the cohomology of discrete subgroups of p-adic groups*, Ann. of Math. (2) **97** (1973), 375–423. MR **47** #8719.

20. ———, *On the cohomology of arithmetic groups*, these PROCEEDINGS.

21. H. Hijikata, *On the arithmetic of p-adic Steinberg groups*, Yale University, New Haven, Conn., 1964 (mimeographed notes).

22. Y. Ihara, *On discrete subgroups of the two by two projective linear group over* $\mathfrak{p}$*-adic fields*, J. Math. Soc. Japan **18** (1966), 219–235. MR **36** #6511.

23. N. Iwahori and H. Matsumoto, *On some Bruhat decomposition and the structure of the Hecke ring of* $\mathfrak{p}$*-adic Chevalley groups*, Inst. Hautes Études Sci. Publ. Math. No. 25 (1965), 5–48. MR **32** #2486.

24. G. Kempf, F. Knudsen, D. Mumford and B. Saint-Donat, *Toroidal embeddings*. I, Lecture Notes in Math., no. 339, Springer-Verlag, New York, 1973.

25. G. Lusztig, *On the discrete series of* GL_n *over a finite field*, Ann. of Math. Studies, no. 81, Princeton Univ. Press, Princeton, N.J., 1974. (Cf. also similar title, Bull. Amer. Math. Soc. **79** (1973), 550–554. MR **47** #3559.)

26. I. G. Macdonald, *Spherical functions on a group of p-adic type*, Publ. Ramanujan Inst., no. 2, Madras, 1971.

27. R. Marcuson, *Tits' systems in generalized Steinberg groups*, J. Algebra (to appear).

28. H. Matsumoto, *Fonctions sphériques sur certains systèmes de Coxeter et de Tits*, Paris, 1974 (preprint).

29. R. V. Moody and K. L. Teo, *Tits' systems with crystallographic Weyl groups*, J. Algebra **21** (1972), 178–190. MR **47** #8705.

30. G. D. Mostow, *Strong rigidity of locally symmetric spaces*, Ann. of Math. Studies, no. 78, Princeton Univ. Press, Princeton, N. J., 1973.

31. D. Mumford, *Geometric invariant theory*, Ergebnisse der Math., N. F., Band 34, Springer-Verlag, Berlin and New York, 1965. MR **35** #5451.

32. ———, *An analytic construction of degenerating curves over complete local rings*, Compositio Math. **24** (1972), 129–174.

33. G. Prasad, *Lattices in semi-simple groups over local fields*, Institute for Advanced Study, Princeton, N. J., 1974 (preprint).

34. D. Quillen, *Finite generation of the groups* K_i *of algebraic integers*, Algebraic *K*-Theory. I, Lecture Notes in Math., no. 341, Springer-Verlag, New York, 1973, pp. 179–198.

35. M. Raynaud, *Construction analytique de courbes en géométrie non archimédienne (d'après D. Mumford)*, Sém. Bourbaki, Exposé 427, février 1973, Lecture Notes in Math., no. 383, Springer-Verlag, Berlin and New York, 1974, pp. 171–185.

36. J.-P. Serre, *Le problème des groupes de congruence pour* SL_2, Ann. of Math. (2) **92** (1970), 489–527. MR **42** #7671.

37. ———, *Arbres, amalgames et* SL_2, Collège de France, 1968/69, Lecture Notes in Math., Springer-Verlag, Berlin and New York (à paraître).

38. ———, *Cohomologie des groupes discrets*, Ann. of Math. Studies, no. 70, Princeton Univ. Press, Princeton, N. J., 1971, pp. 77–169.

39. J. A. Shalika, *On the space of cusp forms of a* $\mathfrak{p}$*-adic Chevalley group*, Ann. of Math. (2) **92** (1970), 262–278. MR **42** #423.

40. L. Solomon, *The Steinberg character of a finite group with BN-pair*, Theory of Finite Groups (Sympos., Harvard Univ., Cambridge, Mass., 1968), Benjamin, New York, 1969, pp. 213–221. MR **40** #220.

41. T. A. Springer, *Caractères de groupes de Chevalley finis*, Sém. Bourbaki, Exposé 429, février, 1973, Lecture Notes in Math., no. 383, Springer-Verlag, Berlin and New York, 1974, pp. 210–233.

42. ———, *Relèvement de Brauer et représentations paraboliques de* $\mathrm{GL}_n(\boldsymbol{F}_q)$ *(d'après G. Lusztig)*, Sém. Bourbaki, Exposé 441, novembre 1973, Lecture Notes in Math., no 431, Springer-Verlag, Berlin and New York, 1975, pp. 89–113.

43. J. Tits, *Buildings of spherical type and finite BN-pairs*, Lecture Notes in Math., no. 386, Springer-Verlag, Berlin and New York, 1974.

44. ———, *The classification of buildings of spherical types and Moufang polygons: a survey*, Proc. Conf. on Combinatorial Theories (Rome, 1973) (to appear).

45. I. A. Volodin, *Algebraic K-theory as an extraordinary homology theory on the category of associative rings with unit*, Izv. Akad. Nauk SSSR Ser. Mat. **35** (1971), 844–873 = Math. USSR Izv. **5** (1971), 859–887. MR **45** #5201.

46. J. B. Wagoner, *Buildings, stratifications and higher K-theory*, Algebraic *K*-Theory. I, Lecture Notes in Math., no. 341, Springer-Verlag, Berlin and New York, 1973, pp. 148–165.

47. ———, *Homotopy theory for the p-adic special linear group*, Univ. of California, Berkeley, 1974 (preprint).

48. E. Witt, *Spiegelungsgruppen und Aufzählung halbeinfacher Liescher Ringe*, Abh. Math. Sem. Hansischen Univ. Hamburg **14** (1941), 289–322. MR 3, 100.

Collège de France
Paris, France

Proceedings of the International Congress of Mathematicians
Vancouver, 1974

Coding of Signals with Finite Spectrum and Sound Recording Problems

A. G. Vitushkin

We will discuss one well-known problem of information theory, the problem which at present arises in various branches of radio engineering. We mean the problem of coding signals with finite spectrum. By way of an example, we consider how such problems arise, what comprises their mathematical content, and what conclusions can be drawn from results obtained. We will present an estimate of the length of codes for signals with finite spectrum and discuss it in connection with the problems of sound recording.

1. Raising of the question. Of the sound recording techniques the most widely used method is the so-called analogue method. When using this method a signal to be retained is recorded in its natural form without any preceding transformations. This system of recording is remarkable for its simplicity. The system's disadvantage is the impossibility of defending signals from interference. All defects of recording and reproducing devices, the inhomogeneity and aging of materials and the like lead to distortions in reproducing.

Another method of recording in which we are interested, the digital one, consists of the following: The signal is transformed into a discrete code, the code of the signal is recorded and, in order to be reproduced, it is again transformed into its natural continuous form. As far as this system is concerned, there are many ways of protecting signals from various sorts of noises. But in sound reproduction this system is not used because the existing schemes of coding still remain unacceptably complex.

Successful development of a digital recording system requires the construction of a handy mathematical model of sound signals and the discovery of simple schemes of coding. The first question arising is: How long must the codes be for the signals to be reproduced with a desirable accuracy? The qualitative estimate obtained seems encouraging.

2. The choice of the class of functions. The concept of signals with finite spectrum is usually associated with the Bernstein class of entire functions. We shall denote by B_σ the class of entire functions, real-valued on the real axis bounded in modulus by the constant 1 on the whole axis, and such that their Fourier transforms vanish outside the segment $[-\sigma, \sigma]$. We will call the functions of this class signals with spectrum σ.

By Kotelnikov's theorem [**1**] the informational content of a signal with spectrum σ is proportional to σ. Really, representing a function $f \in B_\sigma$ in the form

$$f(t) = \sum_{k=-\infty}^{\infty} f\left(K\frac{\pi}{\sigma'}\right) \frac{\sin \sigma'(t - K\pi/\sigma')}{\sigma'(t - K\pi/\sigma')}$$

(this representation is valid with any $\sigma' > \sigma$), we see that the number of parameters (per unit time) defining the function is proportional to σ.

Shannon [**2**] and Kolmogorov [**3**] have given more concrete forms of this assertion.

By the Kolmogorov-Tichomirov theorem [**3**] the entropy $H_\varepsilon(B_\sigma, T)$ of the class B_σ (the norm being the maximum of a function on the segment $[-T, T]$ satisfies the following inequality:

$$\frac{2\sigma T}{\pi} \log \frac{c_1}{\varepsilon} \leqq H_\varepsilon(B_\sigma, T) \leqq \frac{2\sigma T}{\pi} \log \frac{c_2}{\varepsilon}$$

where c_1 and c_2 are absolute constants.

It should be noted that this kind of theorem, formulated in terms of the uniform metric, has rather limited applications because in practice one has as a rule to deal with more complex forms of measurements.

3. The complexity of apparatus. Now we define the notion of an apparatus and the parameters characterizing its quality and complexity. An apparatus P is a pair of transformations P_1 and P_2 possessing the following properties.

A real-valued function $f(t)$ defined on the whole real axis is transformed by the operator P_1 into a function $\varphi = \varphi(K\tau, f)$ defined for all integers K. Here τ is a positive number constant for all input functions $f(t)$. The function φ may take only one of two values: either 1 or 0. In other words, the operator P_1 puts, in correspondence to the input function $f(t)$, the sequence of binary numbers $\varphi(K\tau, f)$ ($K = -\infty, \cdots, 0, \cdots, \infty$) uniformly distributed in time with the density τ^{-1} per unit time. This sequence is called a binary code of the function $f(t)$.

The second operator P_2 transforms the sequence $\varphi(K\tau, f)$ into a real-valued function $f^* = P(f)$ defined on the whole real axis and bounded in modulus by the constant 1.

It is assumed, moreover, that there exists a positive constant l such that for any function $f(t)$ and every integer K the value $\varphi(K\tau, f)$ depends only on the values of the function $f(t)$ at the segment $[K\tau - l, K\tau + l]$ and for every t the value $f^*(t)$ depends only on the values $P_1(K\tau)$ at the segment $t - l \leqq K\tau \leqq t + l$.

The constant l is called a delay of the apparatus and the number $h = \tau^{-1}$ is called a code density of the apparatus. If the condition of the boundedness of the apparatus delay were omitted from the definition, the notion of code density would not be strict. Really, by stretching the code sequence we can turn the code density into any desirable number.

The parameters h and l characterize, in a sense, the complexity of the apparatus.

4. The quality of apparatus. To describe the quality of reproduction we shall use three parameters: σ, ε and δ. But first of all we must say a few words about parameters used for the same purpose in engineering. The most essential of such parameters are the following. The first is σ. It is the maximal frequency which can be reproduced by the apparatus. The second is ε. This parameter characterises relative error of reproduction. The third is $\mathscr{D} = 20 \log_{10}(M/\delta)$. It is called the dynamic range of the apparatus. Here M is the maximum of the norm of output signals and δ is the norm of apparatus noise. The norm of a signal is defined as

$$\|f(t)\| = \max_t \left(\frac{1}{2\tau} \int_{t-r}^{t+r} f^2(x)\, dx\right)^{1/2}$$

where τ is a positive constant comparable to δ^{-1}.

DEFINITION. We fix positive constants σ, ε, δ and $r \geqq \sigma^{-1}$. Let $f(t)$ and $f^*(t)$ be two functions defined on the whole real axis. We will say that the function $f^*(t)$ is close to $f(t)$ if for any real t the following inequality is valid:

$$|f(t) - f^*(t)| \leqq \varepsilon \max_{t-r \leqq x \leqq t+r} |f(x)| + \delta.$$

We will say that the parameters of an apparatus are not worse than σ, ε, δ if for every function $f \in B_\sigma$ the corresponding function $f^* = P(f)$ is close to $f(t)$. To put it otherwise, the apparatus has parameters σ, ε and δ if it records and reproduces signals so precisely that for any signal with spectrum σ the corresponding output signal is close to the input one.

For an apparatus with parameters σ, ε, δ the number $\mathscr{D} = 20 \log_{10} \delta^{-1}$ is called the dynamic range of the apparatus. If an apparatus has a wide dynamic range, it means that both large and small signals can be reproduced with the same accuracy.

Thus all necessary definitions have been given and we can formulate the result.

5. Estimate of code density. For any positive numbers σ, ε and δ it is possible to construct an apparatus the parameters of which are not worse than σ, ε, δ, while the complexity of the apparatus is characterized by the following inequalities: $h \leqq (\sigma/\pi) \log (c/\varepsilon)$ and $l \leqq \max \{c/\varepsilon, c/\delta\}$, where c is an absolute constant.

It should be pointed out that the right-hand side of the first inequality does not contain the parameter δ. It means that it is possible to construct an apparatus with any desirable dynamic range, using codes with the density which is independent of dynamic range.

This is rather unexpected because in engineering another point of view prevails:

A sufficiently wide dynamic range is the most difficult thing to obtain when one constructs an apparatus with the analogue system of recording.

But we need not think that wide dynamic range can be obtained without any difficulties at all. In the digital system, obtaining wide dynamic range requires either long codes or complex schemes of coding.

It should be noted as well that it is impossible to construct an apparatus with infinite dynamic range using codes of finite density.

6. Entropy of the class B_σ. The estimate of code density consists, as usual, in counting the entropy of the corresponding functional class.

Let the numbers σ, ε, δ and r introduced above be fixed. Let B^* be a set of functions defined on a segment $[-T, T]$. This set is called a net of the class B_σ on the segment $[-T, T]$, if for any function $f \in B_\sigma$ there exists a function $f^* \in B^*$ close to f on the segment $[-T, T]$, i.e., such that for any $t \in [-T, T]$ the following inequality is valid:

$$|f(t) - f^*(t)| \leqq \varepsilon \max_{t-r \leqq x \leqq t+r} |f(x)| + \delta.$$

Denote by $N(T)$ the number of elements of the minimal net of the set B_σ on the segment $[-T, T]$. The number $H(T) = \log N(T)$ is called an (ε, δ)-entropy of the set B_σ on the segment $[-T, T]$.

THEOREM. *Let σ, $\varepsilon \leqq 1$, $\delta \leqq 1$ and $r \geqq \sigma^{-1}$ be positive numbers. Then for any sufficiently large T the entropy is*

$$H(T) = \frac{2\sigma T}{\pi} \log \frac{c}{\max\{\varepsilon, \delta\}},$$

where c is a positive function of σ, ε, δ, r which satisfies the inequality $c_1 \leqq c \leqq c_2$, where c_1 and c_2 are absolute positive constants [**4**].

Denote by $H = H(\sigma, \varepsilon, \delta)$ the minimum of code density $h = h(P)$ taken for all apparatuses with parameters σ, ε and δ. It can be easily shown that

$$H = \lim_{T\to\infty} \frac{1}{2T} H(T),$$

because for any T, on the one hand, any apparatus with parameters σ, ε and δ generates a net of the class B_σ on the segment $[-T, T]$ (this net is the set of all output signals when the input ones are all functions from the class B_σ) and, on the other hand, any net can be looked upon as an apparatus which puts, in correspondence to every function from B_σ, one of the nearest elements of the net.

So the theorem just formulated implies that

$$H = \frac{\sigma}{\pi} \log \frac{c}{\max\{\varepsilon, \delta\}},$$

i.e., the code density of the most economical apparatus with parameters σ, ε, δ is equal to $(\sigma/\pi) \log (c/\max\{\varepsilon, \delta\})$.

7. Estimate of polynomial derivatives. Now we present a result obtained while proving the above theorem. It seems to be interesting by itself.

Let $P(t)$ be a polynomial of degree K. Put $M = \max_{-1 \leqq t \leqq 1} |P(t)|$. By the Markov-Bernstein theorem the derivative $P'(0)$ at the point 0 satisfies the inequality $|P'(0)| \leqq MK$. It is well known that this estimate is the least upper bound. Buslayev has found another form of estimating derivatives.

If the polynomial $P(t)$ has real coefficients, then

$$|P'(0)| \leqq \lambda M\left(1 + q + \sum_{i=1}^{K-q} \frac{1}{|r_i|^2}\right),$$

λ is an absolute constant, q is the number of the roots of the polynomial located in the disk $|t| \leqq 1$ and $\{r_i\}$ are the roots of the polynomial located outside the disk.

Polynomials which arise as approximations of entire functions have widely scattered roots. For this kind of polynomial this estimate turns out to be much more effective than the Markov-Bernstein theorem. For polynomials with complex coefficients this estimate, generally speaking, is not valid. A counterexample is $P(t) = (1 + it/K^{1/2})^K$.

8. Some remarks. Returning to our main subject, the estimate of code density, we would like to make some remarks.

If we put $\delta = 0$ and take ε sufficiently small, then the constants $1/2^K$ (K running over all positive integers) are pairwise distant, i.e., none of these constants is close to another. Hence the entropy $H(T) = \infty$ and consequently $H = \infty$. It means that there is no apparatus with an infinite dynamic range.

It will be recalled that the definition of the closeness of signals includes the parameter r. We have been assuming all the time that $r \geqq \sigma^{-1}$. If we put $r = 0$, then the corresponding value H turns out to be equal to $(\sigma/\pi) \log (c/\min\{\varepsilon, \delta\})$. The symbol c is again understood as a positive function of all parameters separated from zero and infinity. We see that in the estimate of H the symbol $\min\{\varepsilon, \delta\}$ is substituted for $\max\{\varepsilon, \delta\}$, i.e., in the case when $r = 0$, $\delta < \varepsilon$, the code density H of the most economical apparatus turns out to be equal to $(\sigma/\pi) \log (c/\delta)$. We see that H turns out to be essentially dependent on the parameter δ.

This circumstance shows that the conclusion, that there exists an apparatus with a wide dynamic range and relatively small code density, is correct as much as the choice of metric is reasonable.

The notion of the closeness of signals has been defined to correspond to the system of measurements which at present is used in engineering. The condition $r \geqq \sigma^{-1}$ seems to be natural as well because errors of reproduction are usually related to the energy of the signal per some period of time and not to the momentary value of the signal. For sinusoidal signals, for example, the error is usually related to the energy per one period of the oscillation. So there is hope that our choice of metric is reasonable and our conclusion is correct.

Now, in conclusion, it should be noted that our article about coding has been centred around the sound recording problems only to make the discussion more concrete. The estimate presented relates to arbitrary signals with finite spectrum and therefore can be used in other applications. For example, the result may be looked upon as the estimate of the capacity of a communication channel.

Any radio communication channel uses signals with finite spectrum and hence can be interpreted as an apparatus. In this case we may use the parameters σ, ε and δ to characterise the frequency range of the channel, nonlinear distortions of the channel and the level of channel noise. The entropy $H(T)$ of the corresponding class B_σ characterises the information content of signals and the number $H(\sigma, \varepsilon, \delta)$ turns out to be equal to the channel capacity.

The fact that H does not essentially depend on the parameter δ when δ is sufficiently small with respect to ε means that the channel capacity does not depend in fact on the level of channel noise as soon as the noise is sufficiently small with respect to distortions.

Literature

1. V. A. Kotel'inkov, *Materials from the First All-Union Congress on questions of reconstruction of the connection and development of light industry*, Publishing House of the Workers' and Peasants' Red Army, 1933. (Russian)

2. C. E. Shannon, *A mathematical theory of communication*, Bell System Tech. J. **27** (1948), 379–423, 623–656. MR **10**, 133.

3. A. N. Kolmogorov and V. M. Tihomirov, *ε-entropy and ε-capacity of sets in functional spaces*, Uspehi Mat. Nauk **14** (1959), no. 2 (86), 3-86; English transl., Amer. Math. Soc. Transl. (2) **17** (1961), 277–364. MR **22** #2890; **23** #A2031.

4. V. I. Buslaev and A. G. Vituškin, *An estimate of the code length of signals with a finite spectrum in connection with sound recording problems*, Izv. Akad. Nauk SSSR Ser. Mat. **38** (1974), 867–895 = Math. USSR Izv. **8** (1974), 867–895.

Steklov Institute
Moscow, U.S.S.R.

Section 1

Mathematical Logic and the Foundations of Mathematics

Proceedings of the International Congress of Mathematicians
Vancouver, 1974

Admissible Sets and the Interaction of Model Theory, Recursion Theory and Set Theory

K. Jon Barwise

1. Introduction. The study of definability theory is usually considered the prerogative of the model theorist. This view tends to identify definability theory with generalizations of Beth's theorem and ignores the obvious relevance of set theoretic and recursion theoretic ideas (constructible sets, hyperarithmetic sets and inductive definability, to name three). It is time to abandon this restrictive outlook and search for a unified approach to the study of the way sets get defined, one which can take full advantage of the tools developed in all parts of mathematical logic.

I have no idea what the "ultimate" treatment of definability will contain. I do feel certain, though, that the study of *admissible sets with urelements* has an important role to play in developing a definitive theory. Here I would like to share with you some of the reasons for this belief.

This paper will contain no proofs or historical references. For these the reader is referred to my book *Admissible Sets and Structures* (to appear shortly in the Springer-Verlag series "Perspectives in Mathematical Logic"). I would like to mention some of the mathematicians who have made significant contributions to the theory described below. The order has, at most, psychological significance: Kripke, Platek, Kreisel, Moschovakis, Gandy, Ville, Aczel, Grilliot, Gordon, Makkai and Schlipf. Some of the most fundamental ideas of the subject go back to work of Gödel and Kleene.

2. Basic notions. Let L be a first order language with equality and a finite number of relation and function symbols. We use variables $p, q, p_1, \cdots$ for the variables of L. Let $\mathfrak{M} = \langle M, \cdots \rangle$ be a structure for L. To study definability over $\mathfrak{M}$ we want to work within the framework of admissible sets $\mathbf{A}_{\mathfrak{M}}$ having $\mathfrak{M}$ as a collection of urelements. Such admissible sets are transitive initial pieces of the universe $\mathbf{V}_M$ defined by

$$V_M(\alpha) = \bigcup_{\beta<\alpha} Power(M \cup V_M(\beta)),$$

$$\mathbf{V}_M = \bigcup_{\alpha} V_M(\alpha).$$

We use $\in_M$ to denote the membership relation on $\mathbf{V}_M$, dropping the subscript if no confusion can arise. A set $A \subseteq \mathbf{V}_M$ is transitive (in the sense of $\in_M$) if $x \in_M y \in A$ implies $x \in A$. A transitive set A containing M is *admissible over* $\mathfrak{M}$ if A is closed under pairs, union, Δ_0-separation and Δ_0-collection. To express the last two principles, we augment L with a $\in$-symbol and two new sorts of variables: $a, b, \cdots$ (to range over sets $\in \mathbf{V}_M$); $x, y, z, \cdots$ to range over $M \cup \mathbf{V}_M$. Let L* denote this new language. The Δ_0-formulas of L* are those in which all quantifiers are bounded. In particular, every atomic formula of the original language L is Δ_0. Δ_0-separation consists of all universal closures of formulas of the form

$$\exists b \forall x[x \in b \leftrightarrow x \in a \land \varphi(x)]$$

where φ is Δ_0 and b is not free in φ. Δ_0-collection consists of all universal closures of formulas of the form

$$\forall x \in a \exists y \varphi(x, y) \rightarrow \exists b \forall x \in a \exists y \in b \varphi(x, y),$$

with the same conditions on φ.

We use $\mathbf{A}_{\mathfrak{M}}$, $\mathbf{B}_{\mathfrak{M}}$ to denote admissible sets over $\mathfrak{M}$. We use $\mathbf{A}$, $\mathbf{B}$ to denote admissible sets with arbitrary urelement base $\mathfrak{M}$. The smallest admissible set over $\mathfrak{M}$ is $\mathbf{A}_{\mathfrak{M}} = HF_{\mathfrak{M}}$, where $a \in HF_{\mathfrak{M}}$ iff $TC(a)$, the transitive closure of a, is finite. This admissible set is too simple to be of much interest for definability theory.

An admissible set $\mathbf{A}_{\mathfrak{M}}$ is *admissible above* $\mathfrak{M}$ if $M \in \mathbf{A}_M$. Most of this paper is devoted to a discussion of the smallest admissible set above $\mathfrak{M}$, $HYP_{\mathfrak{M}}$.

All results from infinitary logic carry over to admissible sets with urelement more or less without change. In particular, the completeness, compactness and interpolation theorems hold for arbitrary countable admissible (in the extended sense used here) fragments $L_{\mathbf{A}}$ of $L_{\omega_1\omega}$. (The interpolation theorem itself could be the subject of an entire paper. It is especially relevant to the remarks made in §7. We will ignore it here, along with much related material.)

Our definition of admissible set is not (and cannot be) by means of a first-order theory. The closest we can come to axiomatizing admissible sets is by means of the theory KPU of L* whose axioms are: extensionality, pair, union, Δ_0-separation, Δ_0-collection and the scheme of foundation. KPU^+ is KPU plus the axiom $\exists a \forall x[x \in a \leftrightarrow \exists p(x = p)]$ which asserts that the collection of urelements forms a proper set.

The following simple fact is important for many results about admissible sets.

2.1. TRUNCATION LEMMA. *Let* $\mathfrak{B}_{\mathfrak{M}} = (\mathfrak{M}; B, E)$ *be any model of KPU and let* $\mathscr{W}\!\!\mathscr{f}(\mathfrak{B}_{\mathfrak{M}})$ *be the well-founded part of* $\mathfrak{B}_{\mathfrak{M}}$. *There is an admissible set* $\mathbf{A}_{\mathfrak{M}}$ *isomorphic to* $\mathscr{W}\!\!\mathscr{f}(\mathfrak{B}_{\mathfrak{M}})$. *The isomorphism* $c: \mathscr{W}\!\!\mathscr{f}(\mathfrak{B}_{\mathfrak{M}}) \cong \mathbf{A}_{\mathfrak{M}}$ *is given by* $c(p) = p$, *for* $p \in \mathfrak{M}$; $c(a) =$

$\{c(x) \mid xEa\}$, *for* $a \in \mathcal{W}\!\!/(\mathfrak{B}_{\mathfrak{M}})$.

It is only the word "admissible" that keeps the truncation lemma from degenerating into the collapsing lemma.

3. Elementary properties of $HYP_{\mathfrak{M}}$. Here I am going to discuss one special kind of admissible set almost exclusively. It shows how the simple addition of urelements greatly enriches the role of admissible set theory in definability theory.

3.1. DEFINITION. Let $\mathfrak{M}$ be a structure for L. $HYP_{\mathfrak{M}}$ is the intersection of all admissible sets $\mathbf{A}_{\mathfrak{M}}$ above $\mathfrak{M}$. $O(\mathfrak{M})$ is, by definition, the least ordinal not in $HYP_{\mathfrak{M}}$.

$HYP_{\mathfrak{M}}$ is admissible above $\mathfrak{M}$, but this is by no means obvious. The following, however, is obvious (by the truncation lemma).

3.2. COROLLARY. *$HYP_{\mathfrak{M}}$ is the intersection of all models of KPU^+ of the form $\mathfrak{A}_{\mathfrak{M}}$. More precisely, every model of KPU^+ of the form $\mathfrak{A}_{\mathfrak{M}}$ is (isomorphic to) an (end) extension of $HYP_{\mathfrak{M}}$.*

As an immediate consequence of 3.2 and the ordinary compactness theorem, we see that every structure has an elementary extension $\mathfrak{M}$ with $O(\mathfrak{M}) = \omega$. For such $\mathfrak{M}$, $HYP_{\mathfrak{M}}$ will contain infinite sets (say M itself) but no infinite ordinals. This possibility gives rise to some interesting applications of the theory, but it also demands that we take some care in developing the theory.

For example, in developing the theory of the *constructible sets over* $\mathfrak{M}$, we must not use the axiom of infinity, as we would if we thoughtlessly adapted the iterated first order definability approach. Let $\mathcal{F}_1, \cdots, \mathcal{F}_8, \cdots, \mathcal{F}_N$ be Gödel's basic operations with a few extra thrown in to handle the atomic relations of L (including =). Define

$$\mathcal{D}(b) = b \cup \{\mathcal{F}_i(x, y) \mid x, y \in b,\ 1 \leqq i \leqq N\}.$$

Using $\mathcal{D}$ as a slow approximation to defining sets in $\mathbf{V}_M$ (slow compared to iterated first-order definability), we can define the universe $L_{\mathfrak{M}}$ of constructible sets above $\mathfrak{M}$ as follows:

$$\begin{aligned} L(0)_{\mathfrak{M}} &= M; \\ L(\alpha + 1)_{\mathfrak{M}} &= \mathcal{D}(L(\alpha)_{\mathfrak{M}} \cup \{L(\alpha)_{\mathfrak{M}}\}); \\ L(\lambda)_{\mathfrak{M}} &= \textstyle\bigcup_{\alpha<\lambda} L(\alpha)_{\mathfrak{M}}, \text{ for limit } \lambda; \text{ and} \\ L_{\mathfrak{M}} &= \textstyle\bigcup_{\alpha} L(\alpha)_{\mathfrak{M}}. \end{aligned}$$

By defining this notion of constructibility within KPU^+ one can prove the following results.

3.3. THEOREM. *Let $\mathfrak{M}$ be a structure for* L *and let* $\alpha = O(\mathfrak{M})$.

(i) $HYP_{\mathfrak{M}} = L(\alpha)_{\mathfrak{M}}$.

(ii) *$HYP_{\mathfrak{M}}$ is admissible; hence it is the smallest admissible set above $\mathfrak{M}$.*

(iii) *Every $a \in HYP_{\mathfrak{M}}$ has a "good" Σ_1 definiton in $HYP_{\mathfrak{M}}$ with parameters from $M \cup \{M\}$, good in the sense that it works in every model of KPU^+ of the form $\mathfrak{A}_{\mathfrak{M}}$.*

(iv) *$HYP_{\mathfrak{M}}$ is projectible into $HF_{\mathfrak{M}}$. In other words, there is a $HYP_{\mathfrak{M}}$-recursive function π such that, for every $x, y \in HYP_{\mathfrak{M}}$, if $x \neq y$ then $\pi(x)$ and $\pi(y)$ are disjoint* *nonempty subsets of $HF_{\mathfrak{M}}$. If $\mathfrak{M}$ has a $HYP_{\mathfrak{M}}$-recursive pairing function, then $HYP_{\mathfrak{M}}$ is projectible into $\mathfrak{M}$ itself.*

If we take some care in defining $\mathcal{F}_1, \cdots, \mathcal{F}_N$ we can make sure that they are all (what Gandy calls) substitutable, that is, that the Δ_0-formulas are closed under substitutions by them. This gives us, for example, the following corollary.

3.4. COROLLARY. *If $O(\mathfrak{M}) = \omega$, then $S \in HYP_{\mathfrak{M}}$ iff S is first-order definable over M (with parameters from M), where S is a relation on $\mathfrak{M}$.*

Exploiting the substitutability of the $\mathcal{F}_i$, John Schlipf has proved the following result relating fundamental notions from model theory, recursion theory and set theory. The structure $\mathfrak{M}$ is *recursively saturated* if for every recursive set $\Phi(x, y_1 \cdots y_n)$ of formulas of $L_{\omega\omega}$, $\mathfrak{M}$ is a model of:

$$\forall y_1 \cdots y_n \left[\bigwedge_{\Phi_0 \in S_\omega(\Phi)} \exists x \bigwedge \Phi_0(x, \vec{y}) \rightarrow \exists x \bigwedge \Phi(x, \vec{y}) \right],$$

where $S_\omega(\Phi)$ is the set of finite subsets of Φ.

3.5. THEOREM. *A structure $\mathfrak{M}$ is recursively saturated if and only if $L(\omega)_{\mathfrak{M}}$ is admissible, i.e., iff $O(\mathfrak{M}) = \omega$.*

It is easy to see that every nonstandard model of Peano arithmetic which can be expanded to a model of analysis (Δ_1^1-comprehension) is recursively saturated.

In the next sections we discuss the relationship of $HYP_{\mathfrak{M}}$ with some other forms of definability.

4. On set existence. A set $a \in \mathbf{V}_{\mathfrak{M}}$ is $\mathfrak{M}$-*secured* by a set theory T if for every model $\mathfrak{A}_{\mathfrak{M}}$ of T, a is internal (in the usual sense of nonstandard analysis) to $\mathfrak{A}_{\mathfrak{M}}$. Corollary 3.2 shows that every $a \in HYP_{\mathfrak{M}}$ is $\mathfrak{M}$-secured by KPU^+. One would suspect that some stronger theory like ZFU^+ (ZF with M as a set of urelements) would $\mathfrak{M}$-secure a lot more sets. For countable structures $\mathfrak{M}$, this is just not the case. To us this suggests that $HYP_{\mathfrak{M}}$ is here to stay.

4.1. THEOREM. *Let $\mathfrak{M}$ be countable and let T be a recursive (or even Σ_1 on $HYP_{\mathfrak{M}}$) set theory true in some structure of the form $\mathfrak{A}_{\mathfrak{M}}$. Every set $a \in \mathbf{V}_{\mathfrak{M}}$, $\mathfrak{M}$-secured by T, is in $HYP_{\mathfrak{M}}$.*

5. A generalization of Kleene's theorem. Kleene's theorem (to the effect that a relation on the natural numbers is Δ_1^1 iff it is hyperarithmetic), and the analysis of Π_1^1 relations that goes into it, is probably the first real breakthrough into (applied) second-order logic. The following provides a similar analysis for any countable structure whatsoever.

5.1. THEOREM. *Let S be a relation on a countable structure $\mathfrak{M}$.*
(i) *S is Π_1^1 on $\mathfrak{M}$ if and only if S is Σ_1 on $HYP_{\mathfrak{M}}$.*
(ii) *S is Δ_1^1 on $\mathfrak{M}$ iff $S \in HYP_{\mathfrak{M}}$.*

(Part (ii) is immediate from (i). Part (i $\Rightarrow$) is proved by using the completeness theorem for the admissible fragment based on $HYP_{\mathfrak{M}}$. Part (i $\Leftarrow$) follows from

Corollary 3.2 and some rather tedious coding arguments.)

It came as a surprise (to me) that this theorem requires no coding assumption on $\mathfrak{M}$. For $\mathfrak{M}$ with a definable pairing function the proof is much like that given in Barwise-Gandy-Moschovakis for $\mathfrak{M} = \langle A, \in \rangle$, a countable transitive set closed under pairs.

5.2. COROLLARY. *A relation S on a countable structure $\mathfrak{M}$ is Δ_1^1 iff $S \in L(\alpha)_{\mathfrak{M}}$ for some $\alpha < O(\mathfrak{M})$.*

5.3. COROLLARY. *A relation S on a countable recursively saturated structure $\mathfrak{M}$ is Δ_1^1 iff it is first-order definable.*

The following generalization of an old result of Harrison for the natural numbers shows another direction for applications to definability theory.

5.4. THEOREM. *Let $\mathfrak{M}$ be countable and let $\boldsymbol{S}$ be a Σ_1^1 second-order relation over $\mathfrak{M}$:*

$$S \in \boldsymbol{S} \quad \textit{iff} \quad (\mathfrak{M}, S) \models \exists Q \varphi(Q, S).$$

Exactly one of the following holds:

(i) *There is an $\boldsymbol{S}' \in HYP_{\mathfrak{M}}$ such that $\boldsymbol{S} \subseteq \boldsymbol{S}'$ (in which case $\boldsymbol{S}$ is countable and a subset of $HYP_{\mathfrak{M}}$).*

(ii) *$\boldsymbol{S}$ contains a perfect subset (in which case $Card(\boldsymbol{S}) = 2^{\aleph_0}$).*

5.5. COROLLARY. *If $\mathfrak{M}$ is countable and recursively saturated and if $\boldsymbol{S}$ is a Σ_1^1 second-order relation over $\mathfrak{M}$ with $Card(\boldsymbol{S}) < 2^{\aleph_0}$ then every $S \in \boldsymbol{S}$ is first-order definable over $\mathfrak{M}$.*

For example, if $\mathfrak{M}$ is a countable recursively saturated elementary extension of $\langle \omega, +, \cdot \rangle$ then there are $2^{\aleph_0}$ distinct $\mathfrak{M}_0$ with $\mathfrak{M}_0 \prec \mathfrak{M}$ (for otherwise ω would be definable in $\mathfrak{M}$, by 5.5).

Actually, 5.4 is a special case of (a slight generalization of) a very powerful theorem of Makkai, a result which is especially useful in the present framework but too complicated to be stated here.

6. Inductive definitions. At about the same time that Kripke and Platek were developing the theory of (pure) admissible sets, Moschovakis was developing his notions of search computability and hyperelementary (*née* hyperprojective) relations over an arbitary structure $\mathfrak{M}$. We can incorporate these notions within admissible set theory by using the framework which admits urelements.

6.1. THEOREM. *Let $\mathfrak{M}$ be a structure for* L *and let S be a relation on M.*

(i) *S is semisearch computable on $\mathfrak{M}$ iff S is Σ_1 on $HF_{\mathfrak{M}}$.*

(ii) *S is search computable on $\mathfrak{M}$ iff S is Δ_1 on $HF_{\mathfrak{M}}$.*

6.2. THEOREM. *Let S be a relation on a structure $\mathfrak{M}$, where $\mathfrak{M}$ has an inductive pairing function.*

(i) *S is inductive on $\mathfrak{M}$ iff S is Σ_1 on $HYP_{\mathfrak{M}}$.*

(ii) *S is hyperelementary on $\mathfrak{M}$ iff $S \in HYP_{\mathfrak{M}}$.*

(iii) *$O(\mathfrak{M})$ is the closure ordinal of first-order positive inductive definitions over $\mathfrak{M}$.*

We can also use admissible sets to give an alternate characterization of the inductive and hyperelementary relations on M.

6.3. THEOREM. *Let S be a relation on a structure $\mathfrak{M}$, where $\mathfrak{M}$ has an inductive pairing function, and let $\alpha = O(\mathfrak{M})$.*

(i) *S is inductive on $\mathfrak{M}$ iff there is an α-r.e. set $\Phi(\vec{v}, \vec{w})$ of α-finite formulas such that, for some parameters $\vec{y} = y_1 \cdots y_k$, S is defined by*

$$S(\vec{x}) \quad \textit{if and only if} \quad \mathfrak{M} \models \bigvee \Phi(\vec{x}, \vec{y}).$$

(ii) *S is hyperelementary on $\mathfrak{M}$ iff there is an α-finite formula $\varphi(\vec{v}, \vec{w})$ such that, for some parameters $\vec{y} = y_1 \cdots y_k$, S is defined by $S(\vec{x})$ if and only if $\mathfrak{M} \models \varphi(\vec{x}, \vec{y})$.*

This theorem does not mention $HYP_{\mathfrak{M}}$, but $HYP_{\mathfrak{M}}$ plays an important role in its proof.

If we allow *extended* inductive definitions (inductive definitions which permit existential quantification over $HF_{\mathfrak{M}}$, arbitrary bounded quantifiers and arbitrary quantifiers over $\mathfrak{M}$), then the pairing function assumption may be dropped from 6.2 and 6.3.

7. Concluding remarks. At the 1960 International Congress for Logic, Methodology and Philosophy of Science, held at Stanford, John Addison predicted the existence of a *theory of hierarchies* which would unify mathematical logic and explain existing analogies from model theory, recursion theory and descriptive set theory. I hope that in the limited time and space available, I have been able to convey some of my reasons for believing that the theory of admissible sets with urelements is the realization of Addison's prediction.

UNIVERSITY OF WISCONSIN
MADISON, WISCONSIN 53706, U.S.A.

Proceedings of the International Congress of Mathematicians
Vancouver, 1974

Some Systems of Second Order Arithmetic and Their Use

Harvey Friedman

The questions underlying the work presented here on subsystems of second order arithmetic are the following. What are the proper axioms to use in carrying out proofs of particular theorems, or bodies of theorems, in mathematics? What are those formal systems which isolate the essential principles needed to prove them?

Ultimately, answers to these questions will require use of systems that are not subsystems of second order arithmetic, but have variables ranging over objects such as sets of sets of natural numbers. Such systems would be needed in order to formalize directly theorems about continuous functions on the reals, or measurable sets of reals. But the language of second order arithmetic is sufficient to formalize directly several fundamental theorems, and is basic among the possible languages relevant to the formalization of mathematics. Furthermore, our preliminary investigations reveal that the most important systems not formalized in the language of second order arithmetic are conservative extensions of those that are. In this way, the systematic study reported here of subsystems of second order arithmetic is a necessary and important step in answering the underlying questions.

In our work, two principal themes emerge. The first is as follows.

I. When the theorem is proved from the right axioms, the axioms can be proved from the theorem.

When this theme applies, we have a unique formalization of the theorem, up to provable equivalence. I occurs surprisingly often, but not always.

The second is more technical.

II. Much more is needed to define explicitly a hard-to-define set of integers than merely to prove their existence.

An example of this theme which we consider is that the natural axioms needed to define explicitly nonrecursive sets of natural numbers prove the consistency of the natural axioms needed to prove the existence of nonrecursive sets of natural numbers.

The language $\mathscr{L}$ of second order arithmetic has numerical variables n_i and set variables x_i, $0 \leqq i$, the constant 0, the unary successor function symbol N, the binary function symbols $+$, $\cdot$, and the binary relation symbols $<$, $=$, $\in$.

The terms of $\mathscr{L}$ are given by (a) 0, and each numerical variable is a term, and (b) $s + t$, $s \cdot t$, and $N(s)$ are terms if s, t are terms.

The atomic formulae of $\mathscr{L}$ are of the form $s = t$, $s < t$, or $s \in x$, for terms s, t, and set variables x.

The formulae of $\mathscr{L}$ are given by (a) atomic formulae are formulae, (b) if A, B are formulae, so are $(\sim A)$, $(A \,\&\, B)$, $(A \vee B)$, $(A \to B)$, and $(A \leftrightarrow B)$, and (c) if A is a formula, α a variable of $\mathscr{L}$, then $(\forall\alpha)(A)$, $(\exists\alpha)(A)$ are formulae.

The language $\mathscr{L}$ has the following interpretation. An $\mathscr{L}$-structure is a system $(D, n, a, m, \mathbf{0}, \prec, K)$, where $D \neq \emptyset$, n, a, m are unary, binary, and binary functions on D interpreting N, $+$, $\cdot$, $\mathbf{0} \in D$ interpreting 0, $\prec$ is a binary relation on D interpreting $<$, and $K \subset \mathscr{P}(D)$ is nonempty. We often write $\mathscr{A} = (M, K)$.

$\mathscr{A} \models A[f, g]$ is defined in the usual way, with $\mathscr{A} \models s = t[f, g]$ iff $\mathrm{Val}(\mathscr{A}, s, t) = \mathrm{Val}(\mathscr{A}, t, f)$, $\mathscr{A} \models s < t[f, g]$ iff $\mathrm{Val}(\mathscr{A}, s, f) \prec \mathrm{Val}(\mathscr{A}, t, f)$, $\mathscr{A} \models s \in x_i[f, g]$ iff $\mathrm{Val}(\mathscr{A}, s, f) \in g(i)$. Here $f(i) \in D$ is the interpretation of n_i, and $g(i) \in K$ is the interpretation of x_i.

We say that $\mathscr{A} = (M, K)$ is an ω-structure just in case M is the standard model of arithmetic. In this case, we identify $\mathscr{A}$ with $K \subset \mathscr{P}(\omega)$.

A formula is called arithmetic if it has no bound set variables, and a sentence is a formula with no free variables.

The Δ_0 formulae are given by (i) atomic formulae are Δ_0, (ii) propositional combinations of Δ_0 formulae are Δ_0, and (iii) if A is Δ_0, n is a numerical variable, t a term, then $(\exists n)(n < t \,\&\, A)$, $(\forall n)(n < t \to A)$ are Δ_0.

A formula is regular if it is of the form $(Q\alpha_1) \cdots (Q\alpha_n)(B)$, where B is a Δ_0 formula not beginning with a quantifier, $0 \leqq n$. The quantifiers $(Q\alpha_1), \cdots, (Q\alpha_n)$ are called the leading quantifiers.

The Σ_k^0 (Π_k^0) formulae are the regular arithmetic formulae with at most k leading quantifiers, beginning with an existential (universal) quantifier.

The Σ_k (Π_k) formulae are those regular formulae whose leading quantifiers begin with a block of at most k set quantifiers beginning with an existential (universal) one, followed by only arithmetic quantifiers.

The Σ (Π) formulae are the regular formulae with no universal (existential) set quantifiers.

I. Axioms for arithmetic sets. RCA (recursive comprehension axiom system) consists of

1. (successor axioms) $N(n) \neq 0$, $N(n) = N(m) \to n = m$.

2. (recursion axioms) $n + 0 = n$, $n + N(m) = N(n + m)$, $n \cdot 0 = 0$, $n \cdot N(m) = (n \cdot m) + n$, $n < m \leftrightarrow (\exists r)(r \neq 0 \,\&\, n + r = m)$.

3. (induction axioms) $(A(0) \,\&\, (\forall n)(A(n) \rightarrow A(N(n)))) \rightarrow (\forall n)(A(n))$, where A is arbitrary.

4. (recursive comprehension) $(\forall n)(A(n) \leftrightarrow B(n)) \rightarrow (\exists x)(\forall n)(n \in x \leftrightarrow A(n))$, where A is Σ_1^0, B is Π_1^0, x not free in A.

Note that the ω-models of RCA are just the collections of sets closed under join and relative recursivity. In RCA, we can define and prove the basic facts about coding. These include codes for finite sequences of natural numbers, for functions as sets, for finite and infinite sequences of sets and functions, for $\mathscr{L}$-structures, and for partial recursive functions and recursively enumerable sets (although not every index will provably define a p.r. function or an r.e. set, because of the weakness of the recursive comprehension axiom). In addition, the satisfaction relation for propositional calculus can be defined.

ACA (arithmetic comprehension axiom system) consists of RCA together with arithmetic comprehension: $(\exists x)(\forall n)(n \in x \leftrightarrow A(n))$, for arithmetic A in which x is not free. In ACA, we can define and prove the inductive clauses for the satisfaction relation for predicate calculus, which cannot be done in RCA. Note that the ω-models of ACA are just the collections of sets closed under join and relative arithmeticity.

In formalizing model theory in RCA, we use the following conventions. Given a structure $\mathscr{A}$, and a sentence A, we let $A^{(\mathscr{A})}$ be the formula that asserts that A holds in $\mathscr{A}$, obtained by relativizing the symbols in A to $\mathscr{A}$. Thus $A^{(\mathscr{A})}$ and A have the same complexity. For structures $\mathscr{A}$, set variables $y_1, \cdots, y_n$, set constants $c_1, \cdots, c_n$, we write $\mathrm{Rep}(\mathscr{A}, c_1, \cdots, c_n, y_1, \cdots, y_n)$ for the formula which asserts "$\mathscr{A}$ is a structure in the language $\mathscr{L}$ augmented with the set constants $c_1, \cdots, c_n$, and $\bar{n} \in c_i$ holds in $\mathscr{A}$ if and only if $n \in y_i$."

We now consider two important combinatorial principles. König's lemma asserts that every infinite finitely branching tree of finite sequences of natural numbers has an infinite path. Weak König's lemma asserts that every infinite tree of finite sequences of 0's and 1's has an infinite path.

Take KL (WKL) to be the system consisting of RCA together with König's lemma (weak König's lemma).

Let SHB (sequential Heine-Borel system) be the system consisting of RCA together with the axiom which asserts that every sequence of open intervals which covers [0, 1] has a finite initial segment which covers [0, 1]. In the formulation of SHB, reals are identified with the set of rationals less than them, and open intervals are identified with appropriate pairs of reals.

Let SLUB (sequential least upper bound system) be the system consisting of RCA together with the axiom which asserts that every bounded infinite sequence of reals has a least upper bound.

Let MLUB (monotone least upper bound system) be the system consisting of RCA together with the axiom which asserts that every bounded monotone increasing sequence has a least upper bound.

Let SBW (sequential Bolzano-Weierstrass system) consist of RCA together with the axiom which asserts that to every bounded sequence of distinct real numbers, there is a real number every neighborhood of which contains at least two terms.

By formalizing familar recursion theoretic constructions, we have

THEOREM 1.1. *ACA is equivalent to* (a) *KL,* (b) *SLUB,* (c) *MLUB, and* (d) *SBW.*

Theorem 1.1 is an illustration of our theme I. The following theorem is another illustration of theme I.

THEOREM 1.2. *WKL is equivalent to* (a) *the compactness theorem for propositional calculus,* (b) *the completeness theorem for sets of sentences in propositional calculus,* (c) *SHB, and* (d)

$$A(x_1, \cdots, x_k) \to (\exists \mathscr{A})(\mathrm{Rep}(\mathscr{A}, c_1, \cdots, c_k, x_1, \cdots, x_k) \;\&\; A(c_1, \cdots, c_k)^{(\mathscr{A})}),$$

where A has the free variables $x_1, \cdots, x_k$. *Other equivalents are* (e) *every consistent theory in predicate calculus has a complete consistent extension in the same language, and* (f) *every consistent theory in predicate calculus has a Henkin complete extension* (*with new Henkin constants added*).

Observe that (d) above is a reflection principle, asserting that if a statement is true, there is a structure in which it holds.

The ω-models of WKL have special significance. Let PA denote Peano arithmetic. A set $x \subset \omega$ is called binumerable in a complete consistent extension K of PA just in case $x = \{n : A(\bar{n}) \in K\}$, for some formula A with one free variable. A set $x \subset \omega$ is called representable in a model $\mathscr{A}$ of PA just in case $x = \{n : \mathscr{A} \models A(\bar{n})\}$, for some formula A with one free variable. The first half of the following theorem is due to Scott [7]. Our proof of the second half uses the continuum hypothesis, but it most likely is eliminable.

THEOREM 1.3. *The countable ω-models of WKL are precisely those collections of sets which, for some complete consistent extension K of PA, are the sets binumerable in K. The ω-models of WKL are precisely those collections of sets which, for some model $\mathscr{A}$ of PA, are the sets representable in $\mathscr{A}$.*

By taking a Δ_2^0 complete consistent extension of PA, we have an ω-model of WKL which is not an ω-model of ACA. It is also clear that the recursive sets do not form an ω-model of WKL.

Using formalized cut elimination, formalized recursion theory, and forcing, we obtain

THEOREM 1.4. *RCA and WKL prove the same Π formulae. However, they do not prove the same Σ_1 sentences.*

We now consider what recursion theory can be proved in WKL. WKL proves the existence of a plethora of incomparable Turing degrees. The best theorem we know along these lines is

THEOREM 1.5. *WKL proves that for any x_0 there is a sequence $\{x_n\}$, $0 \leqq n$, such that each x_n is nonrecursive, and the only sets recursive in more than one term are recursive.*

ACA would suffice to prove the existence of a perfect tree every two paths of which are of incomparable Turing degree, and we do not know if WKL is sufficient. ACA suffices to prove the existence of a set of minimal Turing degree, and again we do not know if WKL is sufficient.

ACA is obviously sufficient to explicitly define a nonrecursive set (e.g., the jump). WKL is not sufficient, and so the following theorem provides us with an illustration of our theme II. The proof uses forcing, symmetry arguments, and recursion theoretic diagonal arguments.

THEOREM 1.6. *There is an* ω*-model of* $WKL + (\exists ! x)(A(x)) \rightarrow (\exists x)(A(x)$ *& x is recursive), where* $A(x)$ *is an arbitrary formula with x as the only free set variable.*

The following concerns the corresponding rule.

THEOREM 1.7. *If WKL proves* $(\exists x)(A(x)$ *& x is not recursive) then WKL proves* $(\forall x)(\exists y)(A(y)$ *& y is not recursive and* $(\forall n)((x)_n \neq y))$*, where A is a* Σ *formula with x as the only free set variable.*

II. Axioms for hyperarithmetic sets. HCA (hyperarithmetic comprehension axiom system) consists of RCA together with $(\forall n)(A(n) \leftrightarrow B(n)) \rightarrow (\exists x)(\forall n)(n \in x \leftrightarrow A(n))$, where A is Σ_1, B is Π_1, and x is not free in A.

HAC (hyperarithmetic axiom of choice system) consists of RCA together with $(\forall n)(\exists x)(A(n, x)) \rightarrow (\exists y)(\forall n)(\exists x)(x = (y)_n \ \& \ A(n, x))$, where A is arithmetic, y not free in A.

HDC (hyperarithmetic axiom of dependent choice system) consists of RCA together with

$$(\forall x)(\exists y)(A(x, y)) \rightarrow (\forall w)(\exists z)(\forall n)(\exists x)(\exists y)\\ (x = (z)_n \ \& \ y = (z)_{n+1} \ \& \ A(x, y) \ \& \ w = (z)_0),$$

where A is arithmetic, n, z, w not free in A.

ABW (arithmetic Bolzano-Weierstrass) consists of RCA together with the axioms which assert that to every bounded arithmetic predicate of reals there is either a finite sequence of reals which includes all solutions, or a real, every neighborhood of which contains at least two solutions.

It is easy to see that HAC implies ABW, but we know very little about the consequences of ABW.

SL (sequential limit system) consists of RCA together with the axioms which assert that, whenever every neighborhood of x contains at least two solutions to an arithmetic predicate, x is the limit of some sequence of solutions from that predicate.

The following is an illustration of theme I.

THEOREM 2.1. *HAC is equivalent to SL.*

The first half of the following is due to Kreisel [5], and the second half is due to Feferman.

THEOREM 2.2. *The* ω*-models of HCA are closed under join and relative hyper-*

arithmeticity. Not every collection closed under join and relative hyperarithmeticity obeys HCA.

It is easy to see that HDC $\vdash$ HAC $\vdash$ HCA. The following is due to Friedman [1] and [3].

THEOREM 2.3. *HCA and HDC prove the same Π_2 formulae. There is a Σ_2 sentence provable in HDC but false in some ω-model of HAC.*

J. Steel has recently proved that HCA and HAC are not equivalent (in fact, there is an ω-model of HCA not satisfying HAC), solving a long outstanding problem. It is still open whether HCA proves each instance of HAC without parameters. Steel has also proved the independence of the relativized Kleene-Souslin theorem (every set Δ_1 in x is hyperarithmetic in x) from HDC. It is still open whether HDC (or HCA) proves the Kleene-Souslin theorem.

III. Axioms for arithmetic recursion. ATR (arithmetic transfinite recursion) consists of ACA together with axioms that assert that arithmetic recursion can be performed on any well ordering of natural numbers. (The H-sets on recursive well orderings are examples of the result of such transfinite recursions.)

The weak Π_1-AC consists of RCA together with $(\forall n)(\exists m)(A(n, m)) \rightarrow (\exists f)(\forall n)(A(n, f(n)))$, where A is Π_1, f not free in A.

CWO (comparability of well orderings system) consists of RCA together with the axiom which asserts that to each pair of well orderings of natural numbers, there is an isomorphism of one onto an initial segment of the other.

PST (perfect subtree theorem system) consists of RCA together with the axiom that asserts that every tree of finite sequences such that no infinite sequence of functions includes all infinite paths has a perfect subtree.

CDS (countability of discrete sets system) consists of ACA together with axioms which assert that to every arithmetic predicate of reals, every two distinct solutions of which are at least one unit apart, there is a sequence which includes all its solutions.

The following is an illustration of theme I.

THEOREM 3.1. *ATR is equivalent to* (a) *weak Π_1-AC,* (b) *PST,* (c) *CWO,* (d) *CDS, and* (e) *ACA + "to each pair of well orderings there is an isomorphism from one into the other."*

As far as comparisons with the axioms for hyperarithmetic sets, we have

THEOREM 3.2. *ATR proves HAC, but not HDC. ATR proves the existence of an ω-model of HDC. ATR + HDC proves the existence of an ω-model of ATR.*

The first part of the following theorem is due to Kreisel [6], and the second essentially due to Simpson [8].

THEOREM 3.3. *ATR proves the relativized Kleene-Souslin theorem. ATR proves the existence of a perfect tree, the paths of which are of distinct nonzero minimal hyperdegree.*

In the next section we will state that TI, a system which proves ATR, does not suffice to define explicitly a nonhyperarithmetic set. The next theorem concerns the corresponding rule.

THEOREM 3.4. *If ATR proves* $(\exists x)(A(x)$ & x *not hyperarithmetic), then ATR proves* $(\forall x)(\exists y)(A(y)$ & y *is not hyperarithmetic* & $(\forall n)((x)_n \neq y))$, *where A is a* Σ_2 *formula with x as the only free set variable.*

IV. Axioms for transfinite induction. TI (transfinite induction system) consists of RCA together with axioms which assert that transfinite induction can be applied to any well ordering of natural numbers with respect to any formula.

RFN (reflection system) consists of ACA together with the axioms

$$A(x_1, \cdots, x_k) \rightarrow (\exists \mathscr{A})(\text{Rep}(\mathscr{A}, c_1, \cdots, c_k, x_1, \cdots, x_k) \\ \& \ A(c_1, \cdots, c_k)^{(\mathscr{A})} \ \& \ \mathscr{A} \text{ is an } \omega \text{ structure}),$$

where A has only the free variables $x_1, \cdots, x_k$.

By formalizing the proof of the completeness of cut free rules for ω-logic, we obtain the following.

THEOREM 4.1. *TI and RFN are equivalent.*

Many questions arise in connection with systems obtained by restricting the complexity of the formulae to which the transfinite inductions are applied in TI. In the following theorem, which answers a few of the questions that arise, all systems are understood to include RCA.

THEOREM 4.2. *TI for* Σ_1 *formulae is equivalent to ATR. ATR does not prove TI for* Π_1 *formulae, but HDC does. TI for* Π *formulae proves HAC. TI for* Π_1 *formulae proves HCA. TI for* Σ_2 *formulae proves HDC.*

A β-structure is a $K \subset \mathscr{P}(\omega)$ such that if $P(x_1, \cdots, x_k)$ is true then $P(x_1, \cdots, x_k)$ holds in K, where $x_1, \cdots, x_k \in K$, and P is Σ_1 with only $x_1, \cdots, x_k$ free. Observe that any β-structure forms an ω-model of TI.

We now state the theorem mentioned previously about the failure of TI in explicitly defining a nonhyperarithmetic set. This is an illustration of theme II.

THEOREM 4.3. *There is an* ω*-model of TI (in fact, a* β*-structure) which satisfies* $(\exists! x)(A(x)) \rightarrow (\exists x)(A(x)$ & x *is hyperarithmetic), for arbitrary A whose only set variable is x.*

There is the corresponding rule:

THEOREM 4.4. *If TI proves* $(\exists x)(A(x)$ & x *is not hyperarithmetic), then TI proves* $(\forall x)(\exists y)(A(y)$ & y *is not hyperarithmetic* & $(\forall n)((x)_n \neq y))$, *for* Σ_2 *formulae A with x as its only free set variable.*

V. Axioms for the hyperjump. Π_1-CA consists of RCA together with $(\exists x)(\forall n)(n \in x \leftrightarrow A(n))$, for Π_1 formulae A without x free.

PKT (perfect kernel theorem system) consists of RCA together with the axiom which asserts that to every tree T of finite sequences with no infinite sequence of functions including all infinite paths, there is a perfect subtree S and a sequence of functions such that every infinite path through T is a path through S or a term in the sequence.

ALUB (arithmetic least upper bound system) consists of RCA together with the axioms which assert that if the solutions to a nonempty arithmetic predicate of real numbers have an upper bound, they have a least upper bound.

The following is an illustration of theme I.

THEOREM 5.1. *Π_1-CA, PKT, and ALUB are equivalent.*

The last part of the following theorem is proved in Friedman [**2**].

THEOREM 5.2. *Π_1-CA proves ATR + HDC. There is an ω-model of Π_1-CA that does not satisfy TI. Π_1-CA proves the existence of an ω-model of TI (in fact, the existence of a β-structure).*

The second clause in Theorem 5.2 can be generalized. Let T be any finite extension of RCA. Clearly RFN + T proves the existence of an ω-model of T. By the incompleteness theorem for ω-logic, not every ω-model of T satisfies RFN, or equivalently TI.

We have considered stronger systems of second order arithmetic, but our results to date do not provide significant illustrations of our themes. We have also considered systems with restricted induction (see Friedman [**4**]).

Bibliography

1. H. Friedman, *Subsystems of set theory and analysis*, Dissertation, M.I.T., Cambridge, Mass. 1967.

2. ———, *Bar induction and Π_1^1-CA*, J. Symbolic Logic **34** (1969), 353–362. MR **40** #4109.

3. ———, *Iterated inductive definitions and Σ_2^1-AC*, Intuitionism and Proof Theory (Proc. Conf. Buffalo, N.Y., 1968), North-Holland, Amsterdam, 1970, pp. 435–442. MR **44** #1555.

4. ———, *Systems of second order arithmetic with restricted induction*. I, II (abstract presented by-title, April 1975 meeting of the Association for Symbolic Logic), J. Symbolic Logic (to appear).

5. G. Kreisel, *The axiom of choice and the class of hyperarithmetic functions*, Nederl. Akad. Wetensch. Proc. Ser. A **65** = Indag. Math. **24** (1962), 307–319. MR **25** #3838.

6. ———, *A survey of proof theory*, J. Symbolic Logic **33** (1968), 321–388. MR **43** #7295.

7. D. S. Scott, *Algebras of sets binumerable in complete extensions of arithmetic*, Proc. Sympos. Pure. Math., vol. 5, Amer. Math. Soc., Providence, R.I., 1962, pp. 117–121. MR **25** #4993.

8. S. Simpson, *Minimal covers and hyperdegrees*, Trans. Amer. Math. Soc. **209** (1975), 45–64.

STATE UNIVERSITY OF NEW YORK AT BUFFALO
AMHERST, NEW YORK 14226, U.S.A.

Proceedings of the International Congress of Mathematicians
Vancouver, 1974

On Superintuitionistic Logics*

A. V. Kuznetsov

Since Brouwer has proclaimed in 1908 the untrustworthiness of classical logic by rejecting the law of the excluded middle, intuitionistic logic, managing without this law, began little by little to develop. As a calculus, it has been presented in a well-known paper of Heyting (1930), preceded by the interesting papers of A. N. Kolmogorov (1925) and V. I. Glivenko (1929). Soon after that, Kolmogorov (1932) proposed an interpretation of the intuitionistic logic as the logic of problems, which showed that it is valuable not only for intuitionists. This became quite clear after the appearance of the theory of algorithms and the constructive tendency in mathematics. Just the connection of the truth of the mathematical proposition with the problem of its demonstration, its falsity with the problem of its refutation, and the law of the excluded middle with the problem of construction of the algorithm allowing to prove or refute any proposition has generated ineradicable doubt in the validity of this law.

The papers of Tarski, Rasiowa, Curry and other mathematicians give the precise algebraic and topological interpretations of intuitionistic logic and its easy immersion into a modal logic $S4$ detected by Gödel. However in 1932 Gödel [**3**] proved that it is impossible to give exactly the intuitionistic logic by any finite truth matrix; though, as Jaśkowski [**22**] showed later on, it may be approximated by a sequence of such matrices. The attempts to give the exact pithy-semantical (meaningful) construction of the intuitionistic logic by means of, for example, precisely stating Kolmogorov's logic of problems have unexpectedly led to logics, slightly different from the intuitionistic—to the logic of recursive realizability of S. Kleene and G. Rose (see [**5**], [**14**]) and to the logic of finite problems of Ju. T. Medvedev [**10**] (as V. E. Plisko [**11**] has shown recently, these two logics are incomparable). The

*Delivered by Ju. L. Ershov.

complexity of the investigation of these logics has brought about an idea of approximatizing them by more simple logics, nearer to the classical. All these circumstances aroused interest in different logics, intermediate between the classical and intuitionistic, predetermining in such a way the idea of the general study of all such logics.

One might also criticize the laws of intuitionistic logic—either from the standpoint of refusing from the so-called "paradoxes of implication", which lead to different logics of rigorous implication; or from the point of view of accounting for the peculiarities of quantum-mechanical problems (in this case one axiom is doubtful, for the calculus without it see **[15]**); or in the light of immersion not in *S*4, but in weaker modal logic. Moreover, I am keeping to the view that none of fixed logic may be suitable in all the situations, for all cases of life; therefore a general investigation of different large classes of nonclassical logics is useful. However, being unable to embrace the nonembraceable, I shall here restrict myself only to the consideration of propositional logics, and from them only the superintuitionistic logics, i.e., classical, intuitionistic, intermediate (between them) and absolutely contradictory.

Systematic investigations of superintuitionistic (intermediate) logics started in 1955–1959 with papers of Umezawa (for example, **[17]**), are performed in the U.S.S.R., Japan (see the survey **[20b]**), Holland, Canada and U.S.A., and during the last years become active in Poland. In Kishinev (U.S.S.R.) my disciples and I have been studying these logics since 1963.

We proceed from the common concept of (propositional) formula—on the basis of the alphabet consisting of symbols of operations &, $\vee$, $\supset$ and $\neg$, variables p, q, r, s and t, perhaps with indices, and brackets. Every set of (such) formulae, containing all the axioms of the intuitionistic propositional calculus I and closed under rules of substitution and modus ponens, we call superintuitionistic (propositional) logic (SL). By each set of formulae $\{A, B, \cdots\}$ a logic $[A, B, \cdots]$ is generated—the smallest SL, containing this set.

Relative to $\subseteq$, the SL's form a lattice with zero (intuitionistic logic LI $= [(p \supset p)]$) and unity (absolutely contradictory logic $[p]$), without atoms, but with a single co-atom (classical logic $[(p \vee \neg p)]$). This lattice $\mathscr{L}$ is distributive and even implicative; hence it may be considered **[19]** as a pseudoboolean algebra. On the other hand to each pseudoboolean algebra $\mathfrak{A} = \langle E; \&, \vee, \supset, \neg\rangle$ (i.e., **[12]** to the lattice $\langle E; \&, \vee\rangle$ having pseudocomplement $\neg$ and relative pseudocomplement $\supset$, i.e., to implicative lattice with zero **[4]**), corresponds its logic $L\mathfrak{A}$—the set of all the formulae, valid on $\mathfrak{A}$, i.e., identically equal to its unity 1; we have $L\mathfrak{A} \in \mathscr{L}$. Considering the varieties of pseudoboolean algebras (i.e., classes of these algebras, given by the identities), take for each of them its free algebra $\mathfrak{A}$ with the countable number of generators and map this variety into $L\mathfrak{A}$; we get a dual isomorphism between the lattice of all these varieties (by $\subseteq$) and the lattice $\mathscr{L}$ (**[2a]**; the inverse mapping is the transition from logic $l \in \mathscr{L}$ to the variety Ml of all such pseudoboolean algebras, on which an identity $A = 1$ holds for each $A \in l$). This generates numerous connections with algebra.

The central place in the study of SL concerns the problems of its decidability (i.e., possibility of algorithmic recognition, for each formula, whether it belongs to the given SL). The hope that all the finitely axiomatizable SL (i.e., generated by a finite set of formulae) are decidable has been connected with the hypothesis about their finite approximability [**6a**]. In this, a logic l is called finitely approximable (f.a.) if it, say (for example, [**18**]), possesses the finite model property, i.e. it is approximable by finite (pseudoboolean) algebras in the following sense. We say that the logic l is approximable by algebras of class K if, for each formula A not contained in l, there exists an algebra $\mathfrak{A}$ in K separating A from l, i.e., such that on $\mathfrak{A}$ all the formulae of l are valid, whereas A is not valid. Every SL, for example, is approximable by finitely generated algebras (i.e., with a finite number of generators). The fact that logic l is f.a. is equivalent to the representation of l in the form $l_1 \cap l_2 \cap \cdots$, where each l_n $(n = 1, 2, \cdots)$ is tabular, i.e., is a logic of some finite algebra; this is equivalent to the fact that the free algebras of variety Ml are f.a. (an algebra is called finitely approximable [**9**], if for any different elements α and β of it there exists a homomorphism φ of it onto some finite algebra, such that $\alpha\varphi \neq \beta\varphi$); and also to the fact that Ml is generated by its finite algebras, i.e., it is the smallest variety containing all of them.

Troelstra [**16**], it seemed, had proved that all the SL are f.a. But his erroneous Theorem 3.4 was refuted in 1967 by V. A. Jankov [**21**], who constructed an example of an SL which is not f.a., and proved at the same time, that the cardinality of $\mathscr{L}$ is continual. The SL constructed by him is not finitely axiomatizable, though, but it is recursively enumerable (and it can be proved that every recursively enumerable SL is recursively axiomatizable, i.e., is generated by some recursive set of formulae). Later on the family of analogous examples was given by me in [**7**]. Also in [**7**] is indicated the refutation of the hypotheses from [**6a**] obtained by me in January of 1970 with the participation of V. Ja. Gerchiu—an example of a finitely axiomatizable SL which is not f.a.; this SL is generated by the formulae:

$$((p \supset q) \vee (q \supset r) \vee ((q \supset r) \supset r) \vee (r \supset (p \vee q))), \tag{1}$$

$$(p^9q \supset (r \vee (r \supset p^8q))), \tag{2}$$

$$(p^7 \supset (q \vee (q \supset p^6))) \tag{3}$$

(here $A^0B \leftrightharpoons (A \;\&\; B)$, $A^1B \leftrightharpoons (A \supset B)$, $A^2B \leftrightharpoons A$, $A^{2n+3}B \leftrightharpoons (A^{2n+1}B \supset A^{2n}B)$, $A^{2n+4}B \leftrightharpoons (A^{2n+1}B \vee A^{2n+2}B)$, $A^n \leftrightharpoons A^n(p \;\&\; \neg p)$, where $n = 0, 1, 2, \cdots$).

Then, V. Ja. Gerchiu in [**1**] simplified this example by discarding formula (3), and also constructed other examples; in particular, a segment (i.e., closed interval) in the lattice $\mathscr{L}$ which has the cardinality of continuum but does not contain f.a. logics—"the ends" of this segment are the logics [(1), $(s \vee (s \supset (2)))$] and [(1), $(s \vee (s \supset (2)))$, $(\neg p \vee \neg\neg p)$]. He also has proved there that among the SL containing (1) there exists a single logic possessing the property that it is not f.a., but every logic which is greater in $\mathscr{L}$ is f.a.—the logic of algebra $Z_2 + Z_\infty + Z_7 + Z_2$ (here Z_n is a pseudoboolean algebra with one generator, and the index shows its cardinality; $\mathfrak{A} + \mathfrak{B}$ denotes an algebra consisting of two sublattices, isomorphic to $\mathfrak{A}$ and $\mathfrak{B}$ respectively, having unique common element—the image of the unity from $\mathfrak{A}$ and of zero from $\mathfrak{B}$; see [**16**]).

It has been proved in [**16**] that, for any tabular SL, all greater SL are also tabular, and the number of them is finite. It has been stated there Theorem 3.5 which resulted in [**16**] from the erroneous Theorem 3.4, saying that every SL immediately smaller than the tabular is also tabular. I have succeeded in proving it (announced in [**6c**]). The proof is based upon the consideration of, first of all, pretabular SL's, i.e., such that they themselves are not tabular, but all the greater SL's are already tabular (every nontabular SL is included in some pretabular), and, secondly, the properties of finitely generated pseudoboolean algebras. L. L. Maximova [**8**] has proved (by using [**6c**]), that there exist just three pretabular SL's:

$$\mathrm{LC} = \bigcap_{n=1}^{\infty} L Ц_n, \quad \mathrm{LC}' = \bigcap_{n=1}^{\infty} L(Ц_2 + Ц_2^n + Ц_2), \quad \mathrm{LC}'' = \bigcap_{n=1}^{\infty} L(Ц_2^n + Ц_2),$$

where $Ц_n$ is the chain of cardinality n as the pseudoboolean algebra ($Ц_2 = Z_2$), and the powers are Cartesian; in this LC $= [((p \supset q) \vee (q \supset p))]$ (the logic of Dummett), LC$' = [(\neg p \vee \neg\neg p), (p \vee (p \supset (q \vee (q \supset (r \vee \neg r)))))]$ and LC$''$ $= [(p \vee (p \supset (q \vee \neg q)))]$ (these logics, defined otherwise, are studied in [**19**], [**20a**], whereas the latter was considered earlier by Jankov). A corollary is the existence of an algorithm for knowing for each formula A whether the logic $[A]$ is tabular.

The unpublished proof of my lemma, which was used in [**8**], stated that every pretabular SL is f.a. By using simplification and improving it, I have succeeded in proving a stronger proposition: Every SL which is not included in LC is f.a. (announced in [**6e**]). This is a part of my answer to the fifth and sixth problems from [**20b**]; another part of it shows that the cardinality of the set of SL, not included in LC, is continual. These problems are connected with the attempt of Hosoi [**19**] to survey the SL by means of partition of the lattice $\mathscr{L}$ into slices, at which the logic l belongs to one slice or the other depending on what logic is generated by $l \cup$ LC. The first slice contains only $LЦ_2$, i.e., classical logic; the second slice contains LC$''$, the logics of the form $L(Ц_2^n + Ц_2)$, where $n = 1, 2, 3, \cdots$, and only them [**20a**]. I succeeded in proving that the cardinality of the third slice (and all the following) is already continual, as well as that it contains SL, which is recursive enumerable and f.a., but not decidable. The proof is based upon the construction of an example of a sequence of algebras $\mathfrak{A}_1, \mathfrak{A}_2, \cdots, \mathfrak{A}_n, \cdots$, such that its subsequences generate pairwise different varieties, and the logic of each of these algebras belongs to the third slice. In this example $\mathfrak{A}_n$ ($n = 1, 2, \cdots$) is constructed by the help of defining its frame, i.e., the set of all its $\vee$-indecomposable elements; it is given as a (partially ordered) subset of the lattice $Ц_2^{n+2}$, consisting of its zero, unit, atoms and co-atoms. The most complicated is the limit (the ωth) slice consisting of logics which are included in LC.

In order to look better into the easily surveyed SL, as well as probably more complicated, we introduce the consideration of the following classes of logics:

(a) K_t—class of tabular SL;

(b) K_{fs}—class of finitely sliced SL, i.e., SL which are not included in LC;

(c) K_{tfs}—class of twice finitely sliced SL, i.e., such that they are not included either in LC or in LC′;

(d) K_{lt}—class of locally tabular SL, i.e., $l \in \mathscr{L}$ such that in the variety Ml all the finitely generated algebras are finite (compare **[2b]**, **[6d]**);

(e) K_{fa}—class of f.a. logics;

(f) K_{hfa}—class of hereditarily f.a. logics, i.e., $l \in \mathscr{L}$ for which all $l' \in \mathscr{L}, l \subseteq l'$, are f.a.;

(g) K_{top}—class of topologizable SL, i.e., $l \in \mathscr{L}$ such that l is the logic of some topological space, i.e., the logic of the pseudoboolean algebra of all its open sets **[12]**;

(h) K_m—class of modelable SL (in connection with Kripke's models), i.e., $l \in \mathscr{L}$ such that $l = L^*\mathfrak{M}$ for some partially ordered set $\mathfrak{M}$ (see **[20b]**), where $L^*\mathfrak{M}$ is the logic of the topological space obtained from $\mathfrak{M}$, when open sets are defined as subsets closed under increasing;

(i) K_1—class of SL which are approximable by the algebras of the form $\mathfrak{A}_1 + \mathfrak{A}_2 + \cdots + \mathfrak{A}_m$, where all terms are finite or isomorphic to Z_∞;

(j) K_2—class of SL which are approximable by algebras for each of which there exists a natural n such that it has no n pairwise incomparable elements;

(k) K_3—class of SL which are approximable by the algebras with the descending chain condition.

It may be proved that

$$K_t \subset K_{tfs} \subset K_{fs} \subset K_{lt} \subset K_{hfa} \subset K_{fa} \subset K_1 \subset K_2 \subset K_3 \subseteq K_m \subseteq K_{\text{top}} \subseteq \mathscr{L}.$$

There remain open the questions of coincidence of the last four classes of this chain. For the first nine classes of it the examples of their difference are respectively the logics LC″, LC′, LC, LZ_∞ (see **[1]**, **[7]**), LI, $L(Z_\infty + Z_7 + Z_2)$ (see **[7]**), $L((Z_\infty \times Z_2) + Z_2)$ ($\times$ denotes the Cartesian product) and $L(Z_\infty^2 + Z_7 + Z_2)$. The class K_{tfs} is interesting for the fact that it is countable (unlike K_{fs}); and K_1 for the fact that all its finitely axiomatizable logics are decidable.

We say that the given logic is elementarily decidable if there exists for it a decision algorithm, such that the period of its operation is upper estimated by some function of the length of tested formula which is a superposition of the exponential functions (elementarity by Kalmár); the elementary solvability of the algorithmic problem is defined similarly. In the case when the algorithm is not decided (solved), but reduced to another logic l and admits the mentioned estimation, at the possibility of sufficiently quick answers about the belonging of the formulae to it, we say that the given logic (problem) is elementarily reducible to logic l. And if the estimation is a polynom, we talk about polynomial reducibility. The logic $l \in \mathscr{L}$ is called elementarily (polynomially) f.a. if, for each formula not contained in l, there exists an algebra separating it from l, the cardinality of the frame of which is respectively estimated by the length of the formula. If the finitely axiomatizable logic is elementarily f.a. (polynomially f.a.), then it is elementarily decidable (respectively, polynomially reducible to classical). All the tabular logics and LC are polynomially f.a., but about the LC′, LC″ and LI the question is open. All the finitely sliced logics are elementarily f.a. Also every logic $[A]$ is elementarily f.a., where A can have negative occurrences of the variables only under the symbol $\neg$.

About the formula A and the list of formulae Σ we say that A is (functionally) expressible through Σ in logic l if A is equivalent in l to some formula, obtained from the formulae, belonging to Σ, and variables by superpositions (i.e., substitution of one into others). The list Σ is called functionally complete in l if all the formulae are expressible in l through Σ. Different questions of functional expressibility and completeness were considered by me in papers **[6b, d]**. Using them, as well as his own results from **[13a, b]**, relative to LZ_3 ($= L\text{Ц}_3$), M. F. Ratsa solved in June of 1970 the algorithmic problem of (recognizing) the functional completeness (f.c.) in the intuitionistic logic (later on he generalized it for an arbitrary SL; see **[13c]**). He proved that f.c. of the list Σ in LZ_5 and in $L(Z_2 + Z_5)$ is necessary and sufficient for it in LI and got also the more detailed criterion. Being guided by the latter, one can show that Σ is f.c. in LI if and only if every subset of the algebra $Z_3^3 + Z_2$, closed under the operations which are expressed by the formulae from Σ, is its subalgebra. As a corollary we get that the problem of f.c. in LI is polynomially reducible to classical logic.

References

1. В.Я. Герчиу, *О финитной аппроксимируемости суперинтуиционистских логик*, Мат. исследования **7**, вып. 1 (1972), 186–192; correction —also there, вып. 3, 278.

2. В.Я. Герчиу и А.В. Кузнецов, (a) *О многообразиях псевдобулевых алгебр, задаваемых тождеством ограниченной длины*, IX Всесоюзный алгебраический коллоквиум (резюме), Гомель, 1968, 54–56; (b) *О конечно аксиоматизируемых суперинтуиционистских логиках*, Доклады АН СССР **195** (1970), 1263–1266. MR **45** #4954

3. K. Gödel, *Zum intuitionistischen Aussagenkalkul*, Akad. Wiss. Anzeiger **69** (1932), 65–66.

4. Х. Карри, *Основания математической логики*, "МИР", Москва, 1969.

5. С.К. Клини, *Введение в метаматематику*, ИЛ, Москва, 1957.

6. А.В. Кузнецов, (a) *О неразрешимости общих проблем полноты, разрешения и эквивалентности для исчислений высказываний*, Алгебра и логика **2**, вып. 4 (1963), 47–66; (b) *Аналоги "штриха Шеффера" в конструктивной логике*, Доклады АН СССР **160** (1965), 274–277; (c) *Некоторые свойства структуры многообразий псевдобулевых алгебр*, XI Всесоюзный алгебраический коллоквиум (резюме), Кишинев, 1971, 255–256; (d) *О функциональной выразимости в суперинтуиционистских логиках*, Мат. исследования, **6**, вып. 4 (1971), 75–122; (e) *О конечнопорожденных псевдобулевых алгебрах и финитно аппроксимируемых многообразиях*, XII Всесоюзный алгебраический коллоквиум (тезисы), Свердловск, 1973, 281.

7. А.В. Кузнецов и В.Я. Герчиу, *О суперинтуиционистских логиках и финитной аппроксимируемости*, Доклады АН СССР **195** (1970), 1029–1032; correction of misprints also there, **199**, 1222. MR **45** # 4953.

8. Л.Л. Максимова, *Предтабличные суперинтуиционистские логики*, Алгебра и логика **11** (1972), 558–570.

9. А.И. Мальцев, *О гомоморфизмах на конечные группы*, Уч. зап. Ивановск. пед. ин-та **18** (1958), 49–60.

10. Ю.Т. Медведев, *Финитные задачи*, Доклады АН СССР **142** (1962), 1015–1018.

11. В.Е. Плиско, *О реализуемых предикатных формулах*, Доклады АН СССР **212** (1973), 553–556.

12. Е. Расёва и Р. Сикорский, *Математика метаматематики*, "Наука", Москва, 1972.

13. М.Ф. Раца, (a) *Критерий функциональной полноты в логике, соответствующей первой матрице Яськовского*, Доклады АН СССР **168** (1966), 524–527; (b) *О классе функций трехзначной логики, соответствующем первой матрице Яськовского*, Проблемы кибернетики, вып. 21, 1969, 185–214; (c) *Критерий функциональной полноты в интуиционистской логике высказываний*, Доклады АН СССР **201** (1971), 794–797.

14. G. F. Rose, *Propositional calculus and realizability*, Trans. Amer. Math. Soc. **75** (1953), 1–19. MR **15**, 1.

15. Ю.Н. Толстова, *О некотором ослаблении интуиционистской логики*, Записки научн. семинаров Ленинградского отд. МИАН СССР **20** (1971), 208–219. MR **45** #4951.

16. A. S. Troelstra, *On intermediate propositional logics*, Nederl. Akad. Wetensch. Proc. Ser. A **68** = Indag. Math. **27** (1965), 141–152. MR **30** #4674.

17. T. Umezawa, *On intermediate propositional logics*, J. Symbolic Logic **24** (1959), 20–36. MR **22** #4634.

18. R. Harrop, *Some structure results for propositional calculi*, J. Symbolic Logic **30** (1965), 271–292. MR **33** #2523.

19. T. Hosoi, *On intermediate logics*, J. Fac. Sci. Univ. Tokyo Sect. I **14** (1967), 293–312; ibid. **16** (1969), 1–12. MR **36** #4961.

20. T. Hosoi and H. Ono, (a) *The intermediate logics on the second slice*, J. Fac. Sci. Univ. Tokyo Sect. I **17** (1970), 457–461; (b) *Intermediate propositional logics* (*A survey*), J. Tsuda College **5** (1973), 67–82.

21. В.А. Янков, *Построение последовательности сильно независимых суперинтуиционистских пропозициональных исчислений*, Доклады АН СССР **181** (1968), 33–34. MR **38** #984.

22. S. Jaśkowski, *Recherches sur le système de la logique intuitioniste*, Internat. Congress Philos. Sci. **6** (1936), 58–61.

Institute of Mathematics and Computing Center
Academy of Sciences of the MSSR
Kishinev, U.S.S.R.

Proceedings of the International Congress of Mathematicians
Vancouver, 1974

New Methods and Results in Descriptive Set Theory

Yiannis N. Moschovakis*

For our purposes here, we define *descriptive set theory* as the study of the *continuum* and its subsets, particularly the *definable* sets of real numbers. Most of the significant classical results in this subject were obtained in the first third of the century and they were rightfully counted among the best contributions of the newly invented set theory to analysis and topology. The subject then went into decline and relatively little progress was made between 1940 and 1960.

There was good reason for this decline, as it turned out, since most of the central problems of the field were subsequently shown to be independent of the axioms of classical set theory. This realization prompted an attack on these old questions using powerful new set-theoretic hypotheses and techniques.

My aim in this article is to describe briefly some of the significant results that have been obtained in this direction. For the sake of brevity and clarity I will concentrate on just a few theorems and state these in their simplest and most concrete versions. A thorough study of recent developments in descriptive set theory will be given in Moschovakis (4).

1. Basic notions. Let $\mathscr{R}$ be the set of real numbers and for each $n = 1, 2, 3, \cdots$ let $\mathscr{R}^n$ be real n-space. By definition, a *pointset* is any subset of some $\mathscr{R}^n$, i.e., any n-ary relation on $\mathscr{R}$.

A pointset $P \subseteq \mathscr{R}^n$ is *Borel* if it belongs to the smallest collection of subsets of $\mathscr{R}^n$ which contains all open sets and is closed under complementation and countable unions. We say that $P \subseteq \mathscr{R}^n$ is Σ_1^1 (or *analytic*) if there is a Borel set $Q \subseteq \mathscr{R}^{n+1}$ whose projection in the last coordinate is P,

*During the preparation of this paper the author was partially supported by NSF grant GP-43906.

$$(*) \qquad P(x_1, \cdots, x_n) \Leftrightarrow (\exists y) Q(x_1, \cdots, x_n, y);$$

equivalently, P is Σ^1_1 if P is the continuous image of some Borel $S \subseteq \mathscr{R}^n$. A pointset $P \subseteq \mathscr{R}^n$ is Π^1_1 (or *co-analytic*) if its complement $\mathscr{R}^n - P$ is Σ^1_1. Proceeding inductively, P is Σ^1_{k+1} if it satisfies $(*)$ with some Π^1_k pointset Q and P is Π^1_{k+1} if $\mathscr{R}^n - P$ is Σ^1_{k+1}. Finally, P is Δ^1_k if it is both Σ^1_k and Π^1_k and P is *projective* if it is Σ^1_k for some k.

Thus the projective pointsets form the smallest collection of sets which contains the Borel sets and is closed under complementation and projection. These are also the relations on $\mathscr{R}$ which are *first-order definable* in the natural structure $\langle \mathscr{R}, \mathbf{Z}, +, \cdot, \leqq \rangle$ of the reals as an ordered field, where we take the integers $\mathbf{Z}$ as a distinguished subset and we allow parameters from $\mathscr{R}$ in the formulas.

The following diagram of proper inclusions holds for the classes Σ^1_k, Π^1_k, Δ^1_k:

$$\begin{array}{ccccccc}
 & \Sigma^1_1 & & & & \Sigma^1_2 & \cdots \\
\subsetneqq & & \supsetneqq & & \subsetneqq & & \\
\Delta^1_1 & & & \Delta^1_2 & & & \cdots \\
\supsetneqq & & \subsetneqq & & \supsetneqq & & \\
 & \Pi^1_1 & & & & \Pi^1_2 & \cdots
\end{array}$$

In particular,

$$\Sigma^1_1 \subsetneqq \Sigma^1_2 \subsetneqq \Sigma^1_3 \subsetneqq \cdots,$$

so the classes Σ^1_k impose a *hierarchy* on the projective sets.

2. Three important classical theorems. Gödel [**1939**] and Cohen [**1963**] showed that the continuum hypothesis ($2^{\aleph_0} = \aleph_1$) cannot be settled in the classical *Zermelo-Fraenkel set theory with the axiom of choice* (ZFC). On the other hand we would expect that the cardinality of simple, definable sets can be computed.

THEOREM A1. *Every uncountable* Σ^1_1 *set has a perfect subset and hence is equinumerous with* $\mathscr{R}$ (*Suslin, see Kuratowski* [**1966**, §39, I]).

In the same vein it can be shown that Σ^1_1 sets are Lebesgue measurable and have the property of Baire (see Kuratowski [**1966**, §11, VII]). Choquet [**1955**] shows that Σ^1_1 sets are also Newtonian capacitable. An optimist would hope that all projective sets are similarly "nice".

The next theorem gives a representation of Σ^1_2 sets in terms of (the much simpler) Borel sets.

THEOREM B1. *Every* Σ^1_2 *set is the union of* $\aleph_1$ *Borel sets* (*Sierpinski, see Kuratowski* [**1966**, §39, II]).

Of course, the result is trivial if the continuum hypothesis holds. On the other hand, if we think of $2^{\aleph_0}$ as a very large cardinal, then Theorem B1 can be viewed as a *construction principle* for Σ^1_2 sets.

Suppose $P \subseteq \mathscr{X} \times \mathscr{Y}$, where $\mathscr{X} = \mathscr{R}^n$ and $\mathscr{Y} = \mathscr{R}^m$. A subset $P^* \subseteq P$ *uniformizes* P if P^* is the graph of a *function* with domain $\{x: (\exists y)P(x, y)\}$. Intuitively, P^* *chooses* one point from each nonempty fiber $P_x = \{y: P(x, y)\}$.

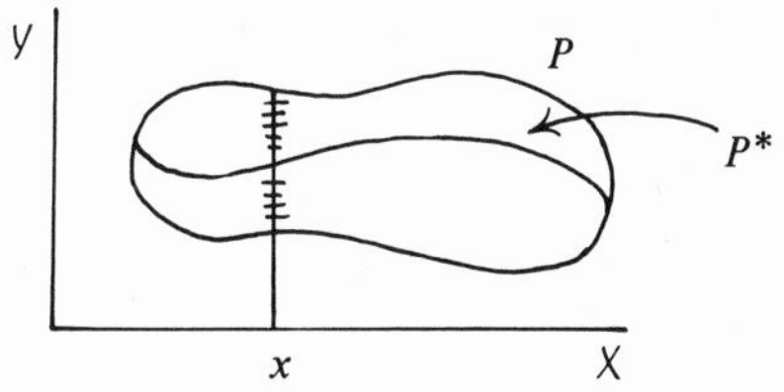

Every $P \subseteq \mathscr{X} \times \mathscr{Y}$ can be uniformized by some $P^* \subseteq P$, using the axiom of choice. The hope is that simple, definable sets can be uniformized definably.

THEOREM C1. *Every* $\boldsymbol{\Pi}^1_1$ *set can be uniformized by a* $\boldsymbol{\Pi}^1_1$ *set and every* $\boldsymbol{\Sigma}^1_2$ *set can be uniformized by a* $\boldsymbol{\Sigma}^1_2$ *set* (*Kondo* **[1938]**).

3. Independence results. The powerful metamathematical methods of Gödel **[1939]** and Cohen **[1963]** can be used to show that Theorems A1, B1 and C1 are best possible within ZFC. The next three results are proved on the hypothesis that ZFC is consistent.

THEOREM A2. *We cannot prove in ZFC that all uncountable* $\boldsymbol{\Sigma}^1_2$ *sets have cardinality* $2^{\aleph_0}$ (*implicit in Cohen* **[1963]**).

THEOREM B2. *We cannot prove in ZFC that every* $\boldsymbol{\Sigma}^1_3$ *set is the union of fewer than* $2^{\aleph_0}$ *Borel sets* (*Solovay, unpublished*).

THEOREM C2. *We cannot prove in ZFC that every* $\boldsymbol{\Sigma}^1_3$ *set can be uniformized by some projective set* (*Levy* **[1964]**).

4. Large cardinal hypotheses. Gödel **[1947]** suggested that the solution of natural and important questions about the continuum may depend on new set-theoretic hypotheses, specifically on axioms implying the existence of very large sets. The first significant applications of this idea to questions of descriptive set theory appeared in the fundamental paper of Solovay **[1969]**.

A *measurable cardinal* is the cardinal κ of a set X whose power set admits a κ-additive, two-valued measure μ such that $\mu(X) = 1$ and, for every singleton $\{x\}$, $\mu(\{x\}) = 0$.[1] It is known that if a measurable cardinal exists then it must be huge—bigger than the first strongly inaccessible cardinal, bigger than the first Mahlo cardinal, etc.

THEOREM A3. *If there exists a measurable cardinal, then every uncountable* $\boldsymbol{\Sigma}^1_2$ *set has a perfect subset and hence is equinumerous with* $\mathscr{R}$ (*Solovay* **[1969]**).

Similarly, if there exists a measurable cardinal, then $\boldsymbol{\Sigma}^1_2$ *sets are Lebesgue measurable and have the property of Baire* (*Solovay, unpublished*) *and they are Newtonian capacitable* (*Busch* **[1972]**, *Shochat* **[1972]**).

[1]We call μ κ-additive if for every $\lambda < \kappa$ and every sequence $\{A_\xi\}_{\xi<\lambda}$ of disjoint sets, $\mu(\bigcup_{\xi<\lambda} A_\xi) = \sum_{\xi<\lambda} \mu(A_\xi)$.

THEOREM B3. *If there exists a measurable cardinal, then every Σ_3^1 set is the union of $\aleph_2$ Borel sets* (*Martin* (3)).

THEOREM C3. *If there exists a measurable cardinal, then every Σ_3^1 set can be uniformized by a Σ_4^1 set* (*Martin-Solovay* [**1969**]).

Unfortunately, these results are best possible in the theory ZFC + (there exists a measurable cardinal)—for example we cannot prove from these hypotheses that every Σ_4^1 set can be projectively uniformized. It is still possible that stronger large cardinal hypotheses may settle these questions for all projective sets.

5. The hypothesis of projective determinacy. A new approach was suggested by Blackwell [**1967**] which gave a new proof of a basic fact about Σ_1^1 sets (the separation property) using a game-theoretic technique. Soon an almost complete structure theory for the projective sets was developed on the basis of the *hypothesis of projective determinacy* (PD); see Addison and Moschovakis [**1968**], Busch [**1972**], Kechris [**1973**], [**1974**], [**1975**], Kechris and Moschovakis [**1971**], [**1972**], Martin [**1968**], [**1970**], (3), Moschovakis [**1970**], [**1971**], [**1973**], Shochat [**1972**].

A brief summary of the key new results from PD is given in Moschovakis [**1973**]. One can also find in that paper a concise statement of the hypothesis PD—roughly speaking, this assumes that in every infinite, two-person game of perfect information which is projective, one of the two players has a winning strategy. Here we only put down the generalizations of Theorems A1, B1, C1 that follow from PD.

THEOREM A4. *If PD holds, then every uncountable projective set has a perfect subset and hence is equinumerous with $\mathscr{R}$.*

Actually, this is a simple consequence of older work in determinacy which also establishes (under PD) that all projective sets are Lebesgue measurable and have the property of Baire; see Gale and Stewart [**1953**], Davis [**1964**], Mycielski [**1964**] and Mycielski and Swierczkowski [**1964**]. Busch [**1972**] and Shochat [**1972**] prove that under PD projective sets are also Newtonian capacitable.

THEOREM B4. *If PD holds, then every Σ_4^1 set is the union of $\aleph_3$ Borel sets* (*Martin* (3)).

Martin has conjectured that the natural generalization of Theorem B4 also holds, i.e., under PD every Σ_{k+1}^1 is the union of $\aleph_k$ Borel sets. This would surely be a beautiful structure result.

THEOREM C4. *If PD holds, then every projective set can be uniformized by a projective set; in fact every Π_k^1 set* (*k odd*) *can be uniformized by a Π_k^1 set and every Σ_n^1 set* (*n even*) *can be uniformized by a Σ_n^1 set* (*Moschovakis* [**1971**]).

The precise statement in Theorem C4 is best possible, i.e., we can show under PD that, for even k, Π_k^1 sets cannot be uniformized by Π_k^1 sets. This reveals a very interesting *periodicity* phenomenon in the projective classes which we do not pursue here; see Addison and Moschovakis [**1968**], Martin [**1968**] and Moschovakis [**1971**], [**1973**].

6. Scales. Many of the results above depend on a *structure theorem* for projective sets which was established under PD in Moschovakis [**1971**]. We describe this briefly, as it gives some of the flavor of the subject.

A *semiscale* on a pointset P is a sequence $\bar{\varphi} = \{\varphi_n\}_{n=0}^{\infty}$ of functions $\varphi_n: P \to$ *ordinals* from P into the ordinals (*norms*), such that if $x_1, x_2, \cdots$ is a sequence of points in P, if $\lim_{i\to\infty} x_i = x$ and if for each n the sequence of ordinals $\varphi_n(x_1)$, $\varphi_n(x_2)$, $\varphi_n(x_3), \cdots$ is ultimately constant, then $x \in P$. If all the norms φ_n are into an ordinal κ, we call $\bar{\varphi}$ a κ-semiscale.

It is easy to check that a pointset P admits a κ-semiscale if and only if P is κ-*Suslin*, i.e., P is the continuous image of some closed set in the space ${}^{\omega}\kappa$ of all infinite sequences in κ. Suslin's discovery that the $\boldsymbol{\Sigma}_1^1$ sets are precisely the ω-Suslin sets is the key to most of the classical results in descriptive set theory. More recently topologists have studied κ-Suslin sets for arbitrary κ; see Stone [**1962**].

For the uniformization property we need a finer notion. A *scale* on P is a sequence of norms $\bar{\varphi} = \{\varphi_n\}_{n=0}^{\infty}$ such that if $x_1, x_2, \cdots$ is a sequence in P, if $\lim_{i\to\infty} x_i = x$ and if, for each n and all large i, $\varphi_n(x_i) = \lambda_n$, then $x \in P$ and, for all n, $\varphi_n(x) \leqq \lambda_n$. We say that $\bar{\varphi}$ is $\boldsymbol{\Sigma}_k^1$ (or $\boldsymbol{\Pi}_k^1$) if the following two relations are $\boldsymbol{\Sigma}_k^1$ (or $\boldsymbol{\Pi}_k^1$):

$$Q(n, x, y) \Leftrightarrow x \in P \,\&\, [y \notin P \vee \varphi_n(x) \leqq \varphi_n(y)],$$
$$R(n, x, y) \Leftrightarrow x \in P \,\&\, [y \notin P \vee \varphi_n(x) < \varphi_n(y)].$$

THEOREM. *If PD holds, then every $\boldsymbol{\Pi}_k^1$ set (k odd) admits a $\boldsymbol{\Pi}_k^1$-scale and every $\boldsymbol{\Sigma}_n^1$ set (n even) admits a $\boldsymbol{\Sigma}_n^1$-scale* (*Moschovakis* [**1971**]).

7. Generalizations. The results in this note extend easily from the reals to all separable, complete metric spaces.

8. Foundational questions. The work on which we are reporting here obviously poses some deep foundational problems. We are assuming hypotheses like the existence of measurable cardinals and PD which are by no means obvious on the basis of our present understanding of the notion of set. We may be able to replace them later with more plausible assumptions, but at present we have no inkling where to look for these. What are reasonable philosophical criteria for judging the credibility of interesting and fruitful hypotheses which are known to be independent of the currently accepted axioms of set theory?

It may be valuable to quote here directly from Gödel [**1947**] who anticipated precisely this problem. "There might exist axioms so abundant in their verifiable consequences, shedding so much light upon a whole discipline, and furnishing such powerful methods for solving given problems (and even solving them, as far as that is possible, in a constructivistic way) that quite irrespective of their intrinsic necessity they would have to be assumed at least in the same sense as any well established physical theory."

References

J. W. Addison and Y. N. Moschovakis, *Some consequences of the axiom of definable determinateness*, Proc. Nat. Acad. Sci. U.S.A. **59** (1968), 708–712. MR **36** #4979.

D. Blackwell, *Infinite games and analytic sets*, Proc. Nat. Acad. Sci. U.S.A. **58** (1967), 1836–1837. MR **36** #4518.

D. R. Busch, *Some problems connected with the axiom of determinacy*, Ph.D. Thesis, Rockefeller University, 1972.

G. Choquet, *Theory of capacities*, Ann. Inst. Fourier (Grenoble) **5** (1953/54), 131–295 (1955). MR **18**, 295.

P. J. Cohen, *The independence of the continuum hypothesis*. I, II, Proc. Nat. Acad. Sci. U.S.A. **50** (1963), 1143–1148; ibid. **51** (1964), 105–110. MR **28** #1118; #2962.

M. Davis, *Infinite games of perfect information*, Advances in Game Theory, Ann. of Math. Studies, no. 52, Princeton Univ. Press, Princeton, N.J., 1964, pp. 85–101. MR **30** #965.

D. Gale and F. M. Stewart, *Infinite games with perfect information*, Contributions to the Theory of Games, Ann. of Math. Studies, no. 28, Princeton Univ. Press, Princeton, N.J., 1953, pp. 245–266. MR **14**, 999.

K. Gödel, *Consistency proof for the generalized continuum hypothesis*, Proc. Nat. Acad. Sci. U.S.A. **25** (1939), 220–224.

———, *What is Cantor's continuum problem?*, Amer. Math. Monthly **54** (1947), 515–525. MR **9**, 403.

A. S. Kechris, *Measure and category in effective descriptive set theory*, Ann. Math. Logic **5** (1973), 337–384.

———, *On projective ordinals*, J. Symbolic Logic **39** (1974), 269–282.

———, *The theory of countable analytical sets*, Trans. Amer. Math. Soc. **202** (1975), 259–297.

A. S. Kechris and Y. N. Moschovakis, *Notes on the theory of scales*, multilithed circulated manuscript, 1971.

———, *Two theorems about projective sets*, Israel J. Math **12** (1972), 391–399. MR **48** #1900.

M. Kondo, *Sur l'uniformisation des complémentaires analytiques et les ensembles projectifs de la seconde classe*, Japan J. Math **15** (1938), 197–230.

K. Kuratowski, *Topology*. Vol. 1, new ed., rev. and aug., Academic Press, New York; PWN, Warsaw, 1966. MR **36** #840.

A. Lévy, *Definability in axiomatic set theory*. I, Logic, Methodology and Philosophy of Science (Proc. 1964 Internat. Congress), North-Holland, Amsterdam, 1965, pp. 127–151. MR **34** #5653.

D. A. Martin, *The axiom of determinateness and reduction principles in the analytical hierarchy*, Bull. Amer. Math. Soc. **74** (1968), 687–689. MR **37** #2607.

———, *Measurable cardinals and analytic games*, Fund. Math. **66** (1969/70), 287–291. MR **41** #3283.

———, *Projective sets and cardinal numbers* (to appear).

D. A. Martin and R. M. Solovay, *A basis theorem for Σ_3^1 sets*, Ann. of Math. (2) **89** (1969), 139–159. MR **41** # 53.

Y. N. Moschovakis, *Determinacy and prewellorderings of the continuum*, Math. Logic and Foundations of Set Theory (Proc. Internat. Colloq., Jerusalem, 1968), North-Holland, Amsterdam, 1970, pp. 24–62. MR **43** #6082.

———, *Uniformization in a playful universe*, Bull. Amer. Math. Soc. **77** (1971), 731–736. MR **44** #2609.

———, *Analytical definability in a playful universe*, Logic, Methodology and Philosophy of Science. IV, North-Holland, Amsterdam, 1973, pp. 77–85.

———, *Descriptive set theory* (in preparation).

J. Mycielski, *On the axiom of determinateness*, Fund. Math **53** (1963/64), 205–224. MR **28** #4991.

J. Mycielski and S. Swierczkowski, *On the Lebesgue measurability and the axiom of determinateness*, Fund. Math. **54** (1964), 67–71.

D. D. Shochat, *Capacitability of $\boldsymbol{\Sigma}^1_2$ sets*, Ph.D. Thesis, U.C.L.A., 1972.

R. M. Solovay, *On the cardinality of Σ^1_2 sets of reals*, Foundations of Math. (Sympos. Commemorating Kurt Gödel, Columbus, Ohio, 1966), Springer, New York, 1969, pp. 58–73. MR **43** #3115.

A. H. Stone, *Non-separable Borel sets*, Rozprawy Mat. **28** (1962), 41 pp. MR **27** #2435.

University of California
Los Angeles, California 90024, U.S.A.

Proceedings of the International Congress of Mathematicians
Vancouver, 1974

Why There Are Many Nonisomorphic Models for Unsuperstable Theories

Saharon Shelah*

We review here some theorems from **[S6]**, and try to show they are applicable in other contexts too.

1. Unsuperstable theories, in regular cardinalities. Let $PC(T_1, T)$ be the class of $L(T)$-reducts of models of T_1.

THEOREM 1.1. *If T is not superstable, $T \subseteq T_1$ (T complete), $\lambda > |T_1|$, λ regular, then in $PC(T_1, T)$ there are 2^λ models of cardinality λ, no one elementarily embeddable in another.*

This was mentioned in **[S4]**, and in fact in **[S2]**. We shall first sketch the proof and then point out some applications of the theorem and the method.

We generalize the notion of indiscernibility used in Ehrenfeucht-Mostowski models (from **[EM]**). Let I be an (index) model, M a model and, for each $s \in I$, $\bar{a}_s$ is a (finite) sequence from M. For $\bar{s} = \langle s(0), \cdots, s(n-1)\rangle$, $s(l) \in I$, let $\bar{a}_{\bar{s}} = \bar{a}_{s(0)} \wedge \cdots \wedge \bar{a}_{s(n-1)}$. The indexed set $\{\bar{a}_s \colon s \in I\}$ is called indiscernible if whenever $\bar{s}$, $\bar{t}$ are finite sequences from I realizing the same quantifier-free type, $\bar{a}_{\bar{s}}$ and $\bar{a}_{\bar{t}}$ realize the same type in M.

Now as T is not superstable, by **[S2]**, T has formulas $\varphi_n(\bar{x}, \bar{y}_n)$, a model M, and sequences $\bar{a}_\eta$, $\eta \in {}^{\omega \geqq}\lambda$ such that, for $\eta \in {}^{\omega}\lambda$, $\tau \in {}^{n}\lambda$, $M \models \varphi[\bar{a}_\eta, \bar{a}_\tau]$ iff τ is an initial segment of η. Clearly M has an elementary extension to a model M_1 of T_1. By using a generalization of Ramsey's theorem **[Rm]** to trees (a proof was in **[S3]**) and by compactness, we can assume $\{a_\eta \colon \eta \in I\}$ is indiscernible; where I is a model with universe ${}^{\omega \geqq}\lambda$, one place relations $P^I_\alpha = {}^{\alpha}\lambda$ ($\alpha \leqq \omega$), the lexicographical order $<_1$, and the function f, $f(\eta, \tau)$ = the lengthiest common initial segment.

*The author thanks NSF grant 43901 by which he was supported.

For each $\delta < \lambda$, cf $\delta = \omega$, choose an increasing sequence η_δ of ordinals converging to δ. For every set $w \subseteq \{\delta < \lambda : \text{cf } \delta = \omega\}$ let M^1_w be the Skolem hull of $\{\bar{a}_\eta : \eta \in {}^{\omega>}\lambda \text{ or } \eta = \eta_\delta,\ \delta \in w\}$, and let M_w be the $L(T)$-reduct of M^1_w. Now we can prove that if $M_{w(1)}$ can be elementarily embedded into $M_{w(2)}$ then $w(1) - w(2)$ is not stationary (using Fodor [**Fd**]). As every stationary subset of λ can be split to λ disjoint ones (see Solovay [**So**]), it is easy to finish.

We can apply this construction, e.g., to the theory of dense linear order. This was independently done by Baumgartner [**Ba**]. (Note that every unstable theory is unsuperstable, and T is unstable iff it has the order property, i.e., there is a formula $\varphi(\bar{x}, \bar{y})$ and sequences $\bar{a}_n$ is some model M of T such that $M \models \varphi[\bar{a}_n, \bar{a}_m] \Leftrightarrow n < m$.)

Fuchs [**Fu**] asked how many separable reduced p-groups of cardinality $\lambda > \aleph_0$ there are. The class of such groups is not elementary (we should omit the type $\{x \neq 0\} \cup \{(\exists y)(p^n y = x) : n < \omega\}$). However, we can find suitable $\bar{a}_\eta$, φ_n. Hence there are 2^λ nonisomorphic ones of cardinality $\lambda\ (> \aleph_0)$. For let G be a group generated freely by x_η ($\eta \in {}^{\omega\geqq}\lambda$) subject only to the conditions: If $\eta \in {}^n\lambda$, $p^{n+1} x_\eta = 0$; $x_\eta = \sum_{n<\omega} p^n x_{\eta \restriction n}$. (For λ singular, see §2; this solution appears in [**S5**].)

The first-order theory of any infinite Boolean algebra has the order property, hence is unstable and unsuperstable, so we can apply 1.1. Notice that, e.g., the theory of atomless Boolean algebras has elimination of quantifiers; hence "elementary embedding" can be replaced by embedding (the existence of 2^λ nonisomorphic Boolean algebras of cardinality λ was proved in [**S1**], [**X1**], [**X2**]).

The existence of a rigid model is somewhat more complex. Monk and McKenzie ask about the existence of rigid Boolean algebras of cardinality $\aleph_1$, when $2^{\aleph_0} > \aleph_1$ (in [**MM**], see there for references and results). Stepanek and Balcan [**SB**] show the consistency with ZFC of $2^{\aleph_0} > \aleph_1$ + there is a rigid Boolean algebra of cardinality $\aleph_1$ with rigid completion.

THEOREM 1.2. *For every $\lambda > \aleph_0$ there is a rigid Boolean algebra of power λ with a rigid completion. If λ is regular, the algebra satisfies the countable chain condition.*

PROOF. We prove it for regular λ (from that it is easy to prove for singular cardinalities). Let S_α $\{\alpha < \lambda\}$ be disjoint stationary subsets of $W^* = \{\delta < \lambda : \text{cf } \delta = \omega,\ \delta \text{ divisible by } |\delta|\}$. For each $\delta \in W^*$ choose an increasing sequence $\{\zeta(\delta, n) : n < \omega\}$ which converges to it, so that $\delta \in S_\alpha \Rightarrow \alpha < \zeta(\delta, 0)$, and $\zeta(\delta, n)$ is odd.

Let B' be the free Boolean algebra generated by $\{x_\alpha : \alpha < \lambda\} \cup \{y_\delta : \delta \in W^*\}$, and let h be a function from λ onto B' which maps δ onto the subalgebra generated by $\{x_i, y_j : i, j < \delta\}$ for $\delta \in W^*$. Let $B = B'/J$ where J is the ideal generated by $y_\delta - x_{\zeta(\delta,n)}$ ($\delta \in W^*$) and $y_\delta - h(\alpha)$ (for $\delta \in S_\alpha$).

Let B_α be the subalgebra generated by $\{x_i : i < \alpha\} \cup \{y_\delta : \delta < \alpha\}$. For any $a \in B$, B^* a subalgebra of B, let $F(a, B^*)$ be the filter $\{b \in B^* : b \geqq a\}$. Let $T_a = \{\alpha \in W^* :$ there is $b \leqq a$ such that $F(b, B_\alpha)$ is not principal$\}$. Clearly T_a is not uniquely determined by the isomorphism type of (B, a), but it is uniquely determined modulo D_λ. Also, $S_\alpha \subseteq T_a$, if $a = h(\alpha)/J$, and if $b = h(\beta)/J$ is disjoint to a, then $S_\beta \cap T_a = \emptyset$. Now for any automorphism F of B, $T_a = T_{F(a)} \bmod D_\lambda$, and, for some a, a, $F(a)$ are disjoint, except when F is the identity. Hence B is rigid. As B_λ is dense in its completion, it is not hard to prove that the completion is rigid. Also the proof of the c.c.c. is clear. Similarly we can prove

THEOREM 1.3. *For every* $\lambda > \aleph_0$ *there is a rigid order with a rigid completion of cardinality* $\leqq 2^{\aleph_0} + \lambda$. *This was well known for* $\lambda \geqq 2^{\aleph_0}$.

2. $I(\lambda, T_1, T)$ **for other cardinals.** Let $I(\lambda, T_1, T)$ be the number of nonisomorphic models in $PC(T_1, T)$ of cardinality λ.

THEOREM 2.1. *Let* $\lambda \geqq |T_1| + \aleph_1$, $T_1 \supseteq T$ *(T complete) and T unsuperstable. Then* $I(\lambda, T_1, T) = 2^\lambda$ *except possibly when all the following conditions hold.*

(1) $\lambda = |T_1|$;

(2) $T_1 \neq T$;

(3) *T is stable*;

(4) *for some* $\mu < \lambda$, $\mu^{\aleph_0} = 2^\lambda$.

We sketch the proof of the main cases. Of course for regular $\lambda > |T_1|$, the result follows by 1.1.

Case I. There is $\mu < \lambda \leqq \mu^{\aleph_0}$, $2^\mu < 2^\lambda$.

Let M_1, a_η ($\eta \in {}^{\omega\geqq}\mu$), φ_n be as in the proof of 1.1. For any $w \subseteq {}^\omega\mu$ let $M^1(w)$ be the Skolem hull of $\{a_\eta: \eta \in {}^{\omega>}\mu \text{ or } \eta \in w\}$, and $M(w)$ is the $L(T)$-reduct. Clearly $|w| = \lambda \Rightarrow \|M(w)\| = \lambda$, and $M(w_1) \simeq M(w_2)$ define an equivalence relation on $\{w: w \subseteq {}^\omega\mu, |w| = \lambda\}$. Each equivalence class has $\leqq 2^\mu$ members; hence there are 2^λ equivalence classes.

Case II. For some regular $\mu < \lambda$, $2^\mu = 2^\lambda$, and $\lambda > |T_1|$.

PROOF. Similar to 1.1.

Case III. $\lambda > |T_1|$, λ singular but not strong limit, and $\mu < \lambda \Rightarrow \mu^{\aleph_0} < \lambda$, $2^\mu < 2^\lambda$.

Choose regular $\mu < \lambda$ with $2^\mu \geqq \lambda$; and let M_1, $\bar{a}_\eta$ ($\eta \in {}^{\omega\geqq}\lambda$), φ_n be as in 1.1. For each sequence $\bar{w} = \langle w_i: i < \lambda\rangle$ of subsets of $\{\delta < \mu: \text{cf}\,\delta = \mu\}$, let $M^1(\bar{w})$ be the Skolem hull of

$$\{\bar{a}_\eta: \eta \in {}^{\omega>}\lambda, (\forall n > 0)\eta(n) > \mu\} \cup \{\eta \in {}^\omega\lambda: (\forall n)\eta(n+1) < \eta(n+2), \text{ and } \eta\text{'s limit} \in w_{\eta(0)}\}.$$

Let $M(\bar{w})$ be the $L(T)$-reduct of $M^1(\bar{w})$. Now we prove that if $M(\bar{w}^1)$, $M(\bar{w}^2)$ are isomorphic, where $\bar{w}^l = \langle \bar{w}^l_i: i < \lambda\rangle$ then for every $i < \lambda$ there are $n < \omega, j_1, \cdots, j_n < \lambda$ and closed unbounded $S \subseteq \lambda$ such that $w^1_i \subseteq S \cap \bigcap_{k=1}^n w_{j_k}$. (Again, variants of the Fodor theorem and downward Lowenheim-Skolem theorems are used.) The conclusion is now easy.

Case IV. $\lambda > |T_1|$, λ is a strong limit singular cardinal.

As the construction is somewhat complex, we describe a similar construction.

Let $\varphi_n(x, \bar{y}_n)$ be as in 1.1, let M, N be models of T, and we describe a game $G(M, N)$. In the nth move Player I chose a sequence $\bar{a}_n$ from M of the length of $\bar{y}_n$, and then Player II chose a sequence $\bar{b}_n$ from N of the length of $\bar{y}_n$. Player II wins if $\{\varphi_n(\bar{x}; \bar{a}_n): n < \omega\}$ is realized in M iff $\{\varphi_n(\bar{x}, \bar{b}_n): n < \omega\}$ is realized in N. Clearly if M, N are isomorphic, Player II has a winning strategy; hence if Player I has a winning strategy they are not isomorphic. Let M_i ($i < \alpha$) be models of T, and let

$\{\bar{b}_j: j < \kappa\}$ be an enumeration of the set of all sequences from some of the M_i's (so $\kappa = \sum_{i<\alpha}\|M_i\|$). Let M_1, $\bar{a}_\eta$ ($\eta \in {}^{\omega\geq}\kappa$), φ_n be as in 1.1, and let M^1_α be the Skolem hull of $\{\bar{a}_\eta: \eta \in {}^{\omega>}\kappa\} \cup \{\bar{a}_\eta: \eta \in {}^{\omega}\kappa$, and there is an i, such that $\bar{b}_{\eta(n)} \in M_i$ has length of $\bar{y}_n$ and M_i omits $\{\varphi_n(\bar{x}, \bar{b}_{\eta(n)}): n < \omega\}\}$. Let M_α be the $L(T)$-reduct of M^1_α. Now in the game $G(M_\alpha, M_i)$ Player I has a winning strategy: He will choose $\bar{a}_0 = \bar{a}_{\langle\,\rangle}$, and if in the nth move he has chosen $\bar{a}_\eta$ and Player II has chosen $\bar{b}_j$, he will choose in the $(n + 1)$th move $\bar{a}_{\eta\hat{}\langle j\rangle}$.

In this we can construct M_α, $\alpha < \lambda$, which are pairwise nonisomorphic, and $\|M_\alpha\| < \lambda$. With inessential changes we can have $\|M_\alpha\| = \lambda$. Now we can change the rules of the game so that each player chooses χ sequences each time; and then just as above we built one tower, we can build χ towers, and the place of each model in each of them is independent.

Case V. T unstable, $\lambda = |T_1|$.

The problem is more difficult for $\lambda = |T_1|$, because then it is harder to control the properties of the model. We can assume T is countable, and that $L(T_1)$ contains, except individual constants, only countably many nonlogical symbols. As T is unstable, there is a model M^1 of T_1, and an indiscernible sequence $\{\bar{a}_j: i < \mu\}$ in it (μ — a strong limit cardinal $> |T_1|$), such that $M_1 \models \varphi[a_i, a_j] \Leftrightarrow i < j$; $\varphi \in L(T)$. We expand M_1 by the one place predicate P^{M_1} = the set of individual constants in M_1, and Skolem functions, and we get M_2. So, by the Erdös-Rado theorem **[EHR]** and compactness we can have, for any ordered set I, a model $N_2(I)$ elementarily equivalent to M_2, and $\bar{a}_t \in M_2(I)$ for $t \in I$, and for $t, s \in I$,

$$M_2(I) \models \varphi[\bar{a}_s, \bar{a}_t] \Leftrightarrow s < t,$$

and $\{\bar{a}_s: s \in I\}$ is indiscernible over $P_I = \{a: M_2(I) \models P[a]\}$, and together they generate the model.

Let D be a good ultrafilter over μ (exists by Kunen **[Ku]**), $M_2'(I)$ be the elementary submodel of $M_2(I)^\mu/D$ with universe $\{f/D$: there are $n < \omega$, $s(1), \cdots, s(n) \in J$, such that, for every i, $f(i)$ belongs to the Skolem hull of $P_I \cup \bigcup_{s=1}^n \bar{a}_s(l)\}$. Now $M_2'(I)$ will be an elementary submodel of $M_2(I)$ of cardinality κ in a strong sense. (We chose κ so that $M_2'(I)$, T, $T_1\, \lambda \in H(\kappa)$ = the family of sets of hereditary power $< \kappa$ and takes an elementary submodel of $H(\kappa)$ to which i ($i \leqq \lambda$), T, T_1, $M_2'(I)$ belong and the cofinality of the ordinals in it is ω. We take the intersection of this submodel with $M_2'(I)$ as our model.) Let $M(I)$ be the $L(T)$-reduct of $M_2''(I)$, and the rest is in the line of **[S1]**.

References

[Ba] J. Baumgartner, *A new kind of order types*, Ann. Math. Logic.

[EHR] P. Erdös, A. Hajnal and R. Rado, *Partition relations for cardinal numbers*, Acta Math. Acad. Sci. Hungar. **16** (1965), 93–196. MR **34** #2475.

[EM] A. Ehrenfeucht and A. Mostowski, *Models of axiomatic theories admitting automorphisms*, Fund. Math. **43** (1956), 50–68. MR **18**, 863.

[Fd] G. Fodor, *Eine Bemerkung zur Theorie der regressiven Funktionen*, Acta Sci. Math. (Szeged) **17** (1956), 139–142. MR **18**, 551.

[Fu] L. Fuchs, *Infinite abelian groups*. Vol. II, Academic Press, New York and London, 1973.

[Ku] K. Kunen, *Good ultrafilters and independent families*, Trans. Amer. Math. Soc.

[MM] R. McKenzie and J. D. Monk, *On automorphism groups of Boolean algebras*.

[SB] P. Stepanek and B. Balcan, *Rigid Boolean algebras can exist independently of the continuum hypothesis*, Notices Amer. Math. Soc. **21** (1974), A-500. Abstract #74T–E57.

[S1] S. Shelah, *The number of non-isomorphic models of an unstable first-order theory*, Israel J. Math. **9** (1971), 473–487. MR **43** #4652.

[S2] ———, *Stability, the f.c.p., and superstability; model theoretic properties of formulas in first-order theory*, Ann. Math. Logic **3** (1971), no. 3, 271–362. MR **47** #6475.

[S3] ———, *Proof of Łos conjecture for uncountable theories*, Lecture notes by M. Brown, U.C.L.A., Fall 1970.

[S4] ———, *Categoricity of uncountable theories*, Proc. Sympos. Pure Math., vol. 25, Amer. Math. Soc., Providence, R.I., 1974, pp. 187–204.

[S5] ———, *Whitehead problem and construction of groups*, Israel J. Math. **18** (1974), 243–256.

[S6] ———, *Stability and number of non-isomorphic models*, North-Holland, Amsterdam (in preparation).

[SO] R. M. Solovay, *Real-valued measurable cardinals*, Proc. Sympos. Pure Math., vol. 13, part I, Amer. Math. Soc., Providence, R.I., 1971, pp. 397–428. MR **45** #55.

[X1] C. Tero, *The number of Boolean algebras of cardinality m*, Acta Salamenca, Univ. de Salamenca, 1971.

[X2] B. A. Efimov and V. M. Kuznecov, *On topological types of dyadic spaces*, Dokl. Akad. Nauk SSSR **195** (1970), 20–23 = Soviet Math. Dokl. **11** (1970), 1403–1407. MR **43** #3987.

THE HEBREW UNIVERSITY
JERUSALEM, ISRAEL

STANFORD UNIVERSITY
STANFORD, CALIFORNIA 94305, U.S.A.

Proceedings of the International Congress of Mathematicians
Vancouver, 1974

On the Singular Cardinals Problem*

Jack Silver

In this paper we show, for example, that if the GCH holds for every cardinal less than κ, a singular cardinal of uncountable cofinality, then the GCH holds at κ itself. This result is contrary to the previous expectations of nearly all set-theorists, including myself. Another consequence of Theorem 1.1 is that if the GCH holds for every singular cardinal cofinal with ω, then it holds for every singular cardinal.

The immediate stimulus for this result was some work of Kanamori and Magidor[1] concerning nonregular uniform ultrafilters over ω_1. The other principal influences were a result of Scott concerning the GCH at measurable cardinals, some work of Keisler on ultrapowers of the sort defined in 1.3, the two-cardinal theory developed by several model-theorists, some work of Prikry and Silver on indecomposable ultrafilters [3], [4], as well as Cohen's methods and work on nonstandard models of set theory [2].

Our terminology is mostly standard. If κ is a cardinal, S is called a *stationary subset of* κ if it intersects every closed cofinal subset of κ. A function $h: \lambda \to \kappa$ is *continuous* if, for every limit ordinal $\alpha \in \lambda$, $h(\alpha)$ is the least upper bound of $\{h(\beta): \beta \in \alpha\}$. If κ is a cardinal, κ^+ is the least cardinal greater than κ. Also, $\kappa^{(\beta)}$ is the βth cardinal greater than κ. Thus $\kappa^{(0)} = \kappa$, $\kappa^{(1)} = \kappa^+$, etc. The cofinality of κ is λ iff λ is the least cardinal such that κ can be written as a union of λ sets, each of cardinality $< \kappa$. κ is singular iff its cofinality is $< \kappa$.

1. Model-theoretic preliminaries. Suppose $\langle A, E\rangle$ is a model of ZFC, i.e., A is the universe of sets and E the membership relation for the model. If $a \in E$, let a_E be the

*This research was partially supported by NSF GP-24352 and a Sloan Foundation grant.

[1]The result of Magidor states, in particular: If there is a regular, nonuniform ultrafilter over ω_1 and $2^{\aleph_\alpha} = \aleph_{\alpha+1}$ for all $\alpha < \omega$, then $2^{\aleph_{\omega_1}} = \aleph_{\omega_1+1}$.

E-extension of a, i.e., $\{b \in A: b\ E\ a\}$. We sketch the proofs of two well-known lemmas, the first of which establishes a relation between the cardinalities of a_E and b_E where a is a cardinal in the sense of $\langle A, E\rangle$, and b is the successor cardinal in the sense of $\langle A, E\rangle$. Note that only Lemma 1.1 is needed for the GCH form of the main result.

LEMMA 1.1. *Suppose* $\langle A, E\rangle$ *is a model of ZFC, and* $a, b \in A$ *are such that* $\langle A, E\rangle \models$ *a is a cardinal, and* $\langle A, E\rangle \models b = a^+$ *(i.e.,* $\langle A, E\rangle \models$ *b is the successor cardinal of a). Then* card $b_E \leqq (\text{card } a_E)^+$.

PROOF. Let $\mu = \text{card } a_E$. We claim that E totally orders b_E in such a way that every member of b_E has at most μ predecessors. This will be sufficient since any ordered set whose every element has at most μ predecessors must itself have cardinality at most μ^+.

Clearly E totally orders b_E since $\langle A, E\rangle \models b$ is an ordinal, and E is the membership relation. It only remains to see that if $c \in b_E$, then c has at most μ E predecessors. Since $\langle A, E\rangle \models b = a^+ \wedge c \in b$, we have $\langle A, E\rangle \models \text{card } c \leqq b$, so there exists an element $g \in A$ such that $\langle A, E\rangle \models g$ is a 1-1 mapping of c into a. One easily verifies that $\{\langle u, v\rangle : \langle A, E\rangle \models g(u) = v\}$ is really a 1-1 mapping of c_E into a_E, whence card $c_E \leqq \text{card } a_E = \mu$. But c_E is just the set of E predecessors of c.

LEMMA 1.2. *Suppose* $\langle A, E\rangle$ *is a model of ZFC, and* $a, b, d \in A$ *are such that* $\langle A, E\rangle \models$ *a is a cardinal,* $\langle A, E\rangle \models b = a^{(d)}$*, and* d_E *has order type* δ*, an ordinal under E. Then* card $b_E \leqq (\text{card } a_E)^{(\delta)}$.

PROOF. Lemma 1.1 enables one to carry out an easy induction on δ.

We now sketch some methods used by Keisler in his first proof of the two-cardinal transfer theorems for ω-logic.

DEFINITION 1.3. Suppose M is a transitive model of ZFC and, for some ordinal Υ, D is an ultrafilter in $P\Upsilon \cap M$. We define Ult(M, D) and the canonical injection.

Let $S = \{f \in M: f: \Upsilon \to M\}$. Define an equivalence relation $\sim_D$ on S by $f \sim_D g$ if $\{i \in \Upsilon: f(i) = g(i)\} \in D$. If $f \in S$, let

$$\begin{aligned} f/D &= \text{the equivalence class of } f \text{ with respect to } \sim_D \\ &= \{g \in S: g \sim_D f, \text{ and nothing in } S \text{ of rank smaller than that of } g \text{ is } \sim_D f\}. \end{aligned}$$

Finally, Ult(M, D) is that structure $\langle A, E\rangle$ where $A = \{f/D: f \in S\}$ and $(f/D)E(g/D)$ iff $\{i \in \Upsilon: f(i) \in g(i)\} \in D$. The canonical injection j of M into Ult(M,D) is defined by $j(x) = c_x/D$ where $c_x: \Upsilon \to \{x\}$ is the constant function x.

LEMMA 1.4. *If M, D, and S are as in Definition* 1.3, *and* $f_1, \cdots, f_n \in S$, *then*

$$\text{Ult}(M, D) \models \varphi(f_1/D, \cdots, f_n/D) \text{ iff } \{i \in \Upsilon: \langle M, \varepsilon\rangle \models \varphi(f_1(i), \cdots, f_n(i))\} \in D,$$

φ any first-order formula. Hence the canonical injection j is an elementary monomorphism.

PROOF. One proceeds as usual by induction on formulas. In handling the existential quantifier step (the only nontrivial step), one uses the fact that the axiom of choice holds in M.

To avoid metamathematical complications, we systematically ignore the fact that satisfaction cannot be defined for the structure M and Ult(M, D) we will be using. There are well-known devices for handling this technical difficulty.

2. The main theorems.

THEOREM 2.1. *If κ is a singular cardinal of uncountable cofinality and $\{\nu < \kappa : 2^\nu = \nu^+\}$ is a stationary subset of κ, then $2^\kappa = \kappa^+$.*

PROOF. Let $T = \{\nu < \kappa : 2^\nu = \nu^+\}$ and let λ be the cofinality of κ. Suppose that h is a continuous, strictly-increasing map of λ onto a cofinal subset of κ. One easily shows that $\{\alpha < \lambda : h(\alpha) \in T\}$, which we call X, is a stationary subset of λ. Thus X is a stationary subset of λ such that, for all $\alpha \in X$, $2^{h(\alpha)} = h(\alpha)^+$.

Let $\mu = 2^\lambda$. Using either the method of Cohen or the method of Boolean-valued models, we can form an extension of the original universe in which μ is countable, but such that all cardinals greater than μ are preserved. Henceforth we work in that extension and call the original universe M. Thus, if ν is a cardinal of M and ν exceeds μ, then ν is really a cardinal. Moreover, if $U = {}^\lambda\lambda \cap M$ = set of functions from λ into λ which are members of M, then U is countable since it is in 1-1 correspondence with μ. It is our objective to show that, in M, $2^\kappa = \kappa^+$ holds.

A function $f: \lambda \to \lambda$ is called *regressive* if, for all $\alpha \neq 0, f(\alpha) < \alpha$. Since U is countable, there is an ultrafilter D in $P\lambda \cap M$ such that $X \in D$ and every regressive member of $U = {}^\lambda\lambda \cap M$ is constant on some member of D. To see this, let $\{f_i : i \in \omega, i > 0\}$ be the set of regressive members of U. Form a sequence $X_0 \supseteq X_1 \supseteq X_2 \supseteq \cdots$ of subsets of λ, each in M and stationary subsets of λ in the sense of M, such that $X_0 = X$ and f_i is constant on X_i. This is possible by a theorem of Fodor [**1**], which says that if X_i is stationary and f_{i+1} regressive, then there is a stationary subset of X_i on which f_{i+1} is constant (the regularity of λ is also used). Finally, let $D = \{B \in M : B \subseteq \lambda, B \text{ includes some } X_i\}$.

Form Ult(M, D) $= \langle A, E\rangle$ and let j be the canonical injection of M into Ult(M, D). Let e be the element of A represented by the identity function from λ into λ. The basic property of D implies that the set of E predecessors of e is precisely $\{j(\alpha) : \alpha < \lambda\}$. Since h is continuous, $j(h)$ is continuous in the sense of $\langle A, E\rangle$. Therefore, if $d = j(h)(e)$, then every predecessor of d is a predecessor of some $j(h)(j(\alpha)) = j(h(\alpha))$, $\alpha < \lambda$. But $j(h(\alpha))$ has fewer than κ predecessors, for each such predecessor is represented by some member of M which maps λ into $h(\alpha)$, and, κ being a strong limit cardinal in M, there are fewer than κ such functions. Hence d has exactly κ E predecessors.

Since $\{\alpha < \lambda : 2^{h(\alpha)} = h(\alpha)^+\} \in D$, Lemma 1.4 assures us that in Ult(M, D), $2^{j(h)(e)} = j(h)(e)^+$, i.e., Ult(M, D) $\models 2^d = d^+$. Let b be such that Ult(M, D) $\models d^+ = b$. Let $Q = \{Z : \text{Ult}(M, D) \models Z \subseteq d\}$. Since Ult($M$, D) $\models 2^d = b$, there is a 1-1 map of Q into b_E. By Lemma 1.1, there is a 1-1 map of b_E into κ^+. Hence there is a 1-1 map of Q into κ^+.

We complete the argument by showing that, if $2^\kappa = \kappa^+$ fails in M, then there is a 1-1 map of κ^{++} into Q, contradicting the preceding paragraph. By preservation of cardinals $> \mu$, $(\kappa^{++})^M = \kappa^{++}$. Hence, if $2^\kappa = \kappa^+$ fails in M, there is a 1-1 sequence $\langle C_\alpha : \alpha < \kappa^{++} \rangle$ of subsets of κ, each $C_\alpha \in M$. Set $k(\alpha) =$ that B such that $\mathrm{Ult}(M, D) \models B = d \cap j(C_\alpha)$. k is 1-1, for if $\gamma \in C_\alpha - C_\beta$, then $j(\gamma) E k(\alpha)$ while not $j(\gamma) E k(\beta)$.

THEOREM 2.2. *If κ is a singular cardinal of uncountable cofinality λ and β is an ordinal $< \lambda$ such that $\{\nu < \kappa : 2^\nu \leqq \nu^{(\beta)}\}$ is a stationary subset of κ, then $2^\kappa \leqq \kappa^{(\beta)}$.*

PROOF. One proceeds much as in the proof of Theorem 2.1, using Lemma 1.2 instead of 1.1.

Bibliography

1. G. Fodor, *Eine Bemerkung zur Theorie der regressiven Funktionen*, Acta Sci. Math. (Szeged) **17** (1956), 139–142. MR **18**, 551.

2. H. J. Keisler and J. Silver, *End extensions of models of set theory*, Proc. Sympos. Pure Math. vol. 13, part I, Amer. Math. Soc., Providence, R.I., 1971, pp. 177–187. MR **48** #96.

3. K. Prikry, *On descendingly complete ultrafilters*, Cambridge Summer School in Math. Logic, Lecture Notes in Math., vol. 377, Springer-Verlag, Berlin and New York, 1973, pp. 459–488.

4. J. Silver, *Indecomposable ultrafilters and* $0^\#$, Proc. Sympos. Pure Math., vol. 25, Amer. Math Soc., Providence, R.I., 1974, pp. 357–364.

UNIVERSITY OF CALIFORNIA
BERKELEY, CALIFORNIA 94720, U.S.A.

Proceedings of the International Congress of Mathematicians
Vancouver, 1974

A General Framework for Simple Δ_2^0 and Σ_1^0 Priority Arguments

C. E. M. Yates

In this paper an abstraction of simple priority arguments is presented in terms of what are called priorcomeager sets. To illustrate the versatility of the method, a number of different applications are described in §§ 4 and 5. Among them, for example, are the existence of minimal Δ_2^0 degrees and the nonexistence of minimal Σ_1^0 degrees.

Priorcomeager sets first appeared in our unpublished lecture notes [**11**], where separate but similar frameworks for Δ_2^0 and Σ_1^0 arguments were presented. Subsequently, in [**12**], we have described a framework for the Δ_2^0 theory in terms of what are called prioric games, connecting these with priorcomeager sets and deducing some additional corollaries. The present common framework for the Δ_2^0 and Σ_1^0 theories is a considerable improvement on these earlier rather inelegant versions. It possesses the additional merit of dealing with some simple priority arguments in the Σ_1^0 theory below a fixed nonzero Σ_1^0 degree; these previously needed separate treatment.

Finally, it should be mentioned that Lachlan [**2**] has presented some elegant ideas for a framework which is restricted to the Σ_1^0 theory but deals with two harder theorems in that theory: the existence of minimal pairs of Σ_1^0 degrees and the density of the Σ_1^0 degrees.

1. Preliminaries. The reader is referred to the bibliography, in particular to the earlier papers of the author, for most standard notation and terminology. However, the following are sufficiently nonstandard but basic to our presentation that they merit repetition. If T is a tree then

$$T \wedge \tau = \{\sigma\colon \sigma \in T \;\&\; \tau \leqq \sigma\},$$

$$\mathcal{N}(T) = \{B : B \in 2^N \;\&\; B = \lim X \text{ for some branch } X \text{ of } T\}.$$

If T is a basic tree of the form $\boldsymbol{S} \wedge \tau$ then $\mathcal{N}(\tau)$ will be used instead; in fact τ will then replace T throughout. A *tree system* is, for our purposes here, a set of Σ^0_1 trees containing $\boldsymbol{S}$ and closed under basic subtrees, i.e., if $T \in C$ and $\tau \in T$ then $T \wedge \tau \in C$. We follow [**13**] in writing $\mathbb{0}$ for the system of all basic trees and $\mathbb{1}$ for the system of all Σ^0_1 trees; note that $\mathbb{0} \subseteq \boldsymbol{C} \subseteq \mathbb{1}$ for all systems $\boldsymbol{C}$ as used here. (Different notation was used in [**12**].) It will help to motivate the present paper if we recall the definition of a $(\boldsymbol{C}, \boldsymbol{d})$-comeager set, introduced and used in [**13**] for perfect systems $\boldsymbol{C}$. A $\boldsymbol{C}$-probe is an operator Ω: $\boldsymbol{C} \to \boldsymbol{C}$ such that $T \supseteq \Omega(T)$ for all $T \in \boldsymbol{C}$. A sequence $(\mathscr{A}_e)$ of subsets of 2^N is $(\boldsymbol{C}, \boldsymbol{d})$*-dense* if there is a sequence (Ω_e) of $\boldsymbol{C}$-probes which is uniformly of degree $\leqq \boldsymbol{d}$ and such that, for all e and $T \in \boldsymbol{C}$, $\mathcal{N}(\Omega_e(T)) \subseteq \mathscr{A}_e$. 2^N is $(\boldsymbol{C}, \boldsymbol{d})$*-comeager* if $\mathscr{A} \supseteq \bigcap \mathscr{A}_e$ for some $(\boldsymbol{C}, \boldsymbol{d})$-dense sequence $(\mathscr{A}_e)$. The $(\boldsymbol{C}, \boldsymbol{d})$-comeager sets are easily seen to be closed under supersets and finite intersections (even some infinite intersections). The existence theorem for $(\boldsymbol{C}, \boldsymbol{d})$-comeager sets is trivial and just a generalised form of Baire's theorem. It asserts that if $\mathscr{A}$ is $(\boldsymbol{C}, \boldsymbol{d})$-comeager then $\mathscr{A}$ contains an element of degree $\leqq \boldsymbol{d}$. This abstracts the usual genericity and diagonal arguments. Our purpose below is to present a suitable generalisation which abstracts priority arguments of the simplest kind.

2. Some triples $(\boldsymbol{C}, \lesseqqgtr, \boldsymbol{d})$. Here $\boldsymbol{C}$ is a tree system (not necessarily perfect). $\lesseqqgtr$ is a recursive binary relation over $\boldsymbol{S}$ (most conveniently assumed to extend the relation $\leqq_1$ defined below) and $\boldsymbol{d}$ is some degree. The relations used in the most obvious applications are $\leqq$, $\leqq_1$, $\leqq^0$, $\leqq^0_1$, $\leqq^a$ and $\leqq^a_1$ all defined below. Although some results apply to all $\boldsymbol{C}$ we shall only specifically refer to $\mathbb{1}$ and $\mathbb{0}$. Also the usual values for $\boldsymbol{d}$ are $\boldsymbol{0}$ and $\boldsymbol{0}^{(1)}$:

$\sigma \leqq \tau \Leftrightarrow \tau$ is an extension of σ.

$\sigma \leqq_1 \tau \Leftrightarrow \sigma \leqq \tau \;\&\; |\tau| \leqq |\sigma| + 1$.

$\sigma \leqq^0 \tau \Leftrightarrow \forall x(\sigma(x) = 0 \Rightarrow \tau(x) = 0) \;\&\; |\sigma| \leqq |\tau|$.

$\sigma \leqq^0_1 \tau \Leftrightarrow \sigma \leqq^0 \tau \;\&\; |\tau| \leqq |\sigma| + 1$.

$\sigma \leqq^a \tau \Leftrightarrow \sigma \leqq^0 \tau \;\&\; (\sigma | \tau \Rightarrow a(|\tau|) \leqq n(\sigma, \tau))$,

where $n(\sigma, \tau) = \min x\, (\sigma(x) \neq \tau(x))$ and a is a 1-1 recursive function: $N \to N$.

$\sigma \leqq^a_1 \tau \Leftrightarrow \sigma \leqq^a \tau \;\&\; |\tau| \leqq |\sigma| + 1$.

2.1. Definition. A $(\boldsymbol{C}, \lesseqqgtr, \boldsymbol{d})$*-sequence* is a sequence $T_0, T_1, \cdots$ of elements of $\boldsymbol{C}$ which is of degree $\leqq \boldsymbol{d}$ (in the sense that the sequence of indices of $T_0, T_1, \cdots$ can be enumerated by a function of degree $\leqq \boldsymbol{d}$) and such that $\mu(T_0) \lesseqqgtr \mu(T_1) \lesseqqgtr \cdots$.

If $\boldsymbol{d}$ is irrelevant we shall just refer to $(\boldsymbol{C}, \lesseqqgtr)$-sequences. Our interest lies in the elements of 2^N to which $\mu(T_0) \lesseqqgtr \mu(T_1) \lesseqqgtr \cdots$ may converge, where a sequence $\tau_0, \tau_1, \cdots$ is said to converge to $B \in 2^N$ if for all $\sigma < B$ there is a K such that $\sigma \leqq \tau_k$ for all $k \geqq K$. The purpose of the binary relations listed above will be clearer once we have noted that

(i) if a $(\boldsymbol{C}, \leqq, \boldsymbol{0}^{(1)})$-sequence converges to $B \in 2^N$ then $B \in \Delta^0_2$, i.e., B represents a Δ^0_2 set,

(ii) if a $(\boldsymbol{C}, \leqq^0, \boldsymbol{0})$-sequence converges to $B \in 2^N$ then $B \in \Sigma^0_1$,

(iii) if a $(\boldsymbol{C}, \leqq^a, \boldsymbol{0})$-sequence converges to $B \in 2^N$ then $B \in \Sigma^0_1$ *and* B is of degree

$\leqq \boldsymbol{a}$ where $\boldsymbol{a}$ is the degree of the range of a.

(i) is obvious. To see (ii) just observe that if $\tau_k = \mu(T_k)$ for all k, where $T_0, T_1, \cdots$ is the sequence, then, for all x,

$$B(x) = 0 \Leftrightarrow \exists k(\tau_k(x) = 0).$$

To see (iii) for a similar sequence just observe that, for all x,

$$B(x) = 0 \Leftrightarrow \exists k(\tau_k(x) = 0 \,\&\, |\tau_k| \leqq M(x)),$$

where $M(x) = \max m\ (a(m) \leqq x)$, then remember that $|\tau_k|$ is monotonic.

Finally, the following definitions are important in the sequel. Let $\boldsymbol{C}^{<\omega}$ be the set of all nonempty finite sequences of elements of $\boldsymbol{C}$.

2.2. Definition. For any operator $\Omega\colon \boldsymbol{C}^{<\omega} \to \boldsymbol{C}$ we define its *trace* $\hat{\Omega}$ by setting

$$\begin{aligned}\hat{\Omega}(T^0, \cdots, T^n) &= \Omega(T^0, \cdots, T^m) && \text{for the largest } m < n \text{ for which this is defined if such an } m \text{ exists,}\\ &= T^0 && \text{otherwise.}\end{aligned}$$

2.3. Definition. A $(\boldsymbol{C}, \lessapprox)$-*probe* is an operator $\Omega\colon \boldsymbol{C}^{<\omega} \to \boldsymbol{C}$ satisfying

O: $\mu(T^n) \lessapprox \mu(\Omega(T^0, \cdots, T^n))$,

P: $T^0 \supseteq \Omega(T^0, \cdots, T^n)$,

R: if $\hat{\Omega}(T^0, \cdots, T^n) \wedge \mu(T^n)$ is trivial (i.e., a singleton) but $T^0 \wedge \mu(T^n)$ is not trivial then $\Omega(T^0, \cdots, T^n)$ is defined.

Note. The third condition **R** (for *remedial*) is redundant for perfect systems $\boldsymbol{C}$ such as $\mathbb{O}$. The purpose of **O** in producing $(\boldsymbol{C}, \lessapprox)$-sequences should be obvious enough. The purpose of **P** is more subtle, but it may be regarded simply as the appropriate generalisation of the definition of $\boldsymbol{C}$-probe.

3. $(\boldsymbol{C}, \lessapprox, \boldsymbol{d})$-priorcomeager sets. We begin with the most crucial concept in our framework.

3.1. Definition. Let Ω be a $(\boldsymbol{C}, \lessapprox)$-probe. A $(\boldsymbol{C}, \lessapprox)$-sequence $T^0, T^1, \cdots$ is Ω-*prioric* if, for all n,

(a) if $\Omega(T^0, \cdots, T^n)$ is defined then it is $= T^{n+1}$,

(b) $\hat{\Omega}(T^0, \cdots, T^n) \supseteq T^n$.

Note. It is immediate that $T^0 \supseteq T^n$ for all n, using 2.3**P**.

3.2. Definition. A sequence $(\mathscr{A}_e)$ of subsets of 2^N is $(\boldsymbol{C}, \lessapprox, \boldsymbol{d})$-*dense* if there is a sequence (Ω_e) of $(\boldsymbol{C}, \lessapprox)$-probes which is uniformly of degree $\leqq \boldsymbol{d}$ and such that, for each e and Ω_e-prioric $(\boldsymbol{C}, \lessapprox)$-sequence $T^0, T^1, \cdots$,

(I) $\lim_n \Omega_e(T^0, \cdots, T^n)$ exists ($= T^N$ say),

(II) $\mathscr{N}(T^N) \subseteq \mathscr{A}_e$.

3.3. Definition. A set $\mathscr{A} \subseteq 2^N$ is $(\boldsymbol{C}, \lessapprox, \boldsymbol{d})$-*priorcomeager* if $\mathscr{A} \supseteq \bigcap \mathscr{A}_e$ for some $(\boldsymbol{C}, \lessapprox, \boldsymbol{d})$-dense sequence $(\mathscr{A}_e)$.

Note. By 3.1(b) we have $T^N \supseteq T^n$ for all $n \geqq N$ in 3.2, so that if $\mu(T^0), \mu(T^1), \cdots$ converges to $B \in 2^N$ then $B \in \mathscr{A}_e$. This suggests two weaker notions described simultaneously below and of importance in the applications.

3.4. Defintion. A sequence $(\mathscr{A}_e)$ of subsets of 2^N is *weakly* $(\boldsymbol{C}, \lessapprox, \boldsymbol{d})$-*dense* (*under* $\boldsymbol{d}$) if there is a sequence (Ω_e) as in 3.2 such that, for each e and Ω_e-prioric $(\boldsymbol{C}, \lessapprox)$-

sequence $T^0, T^1, \cdots$ ($(C, \lesssim, d)$-sequence $T^0, T^1, \ldots$),

(I) as in 3.2,

(II) if $\mu(T^0), \mu(T^1), \cdots$ converges to $B \in 2^N$ then $B \in \mathscr{A}_e$.

3.5. DEFINITION. A set $\mathscr{A} \subseteq 2^N$ is *weakly* $(C, \lesssim, d)$-*priorcomeager* (*under* d) if $\mathscr{A} \supseteq \bigcap \mathscr{A}_e$ for some $(\mathscr{A}_e)$ which is weakly $(C, \lesssim, d)$-dense (under d). Each type of $(C, \lesssim, d)$-priorcomeager set is easily seen to be closed under supersets and finite intersections (even some infinite intersections).

An existence theorem for these concepts is not so trivial to prove. Nevertheless, it is not difficult and is the only point in the development at which a priority construction is needed.

3.6. EXISTENCE THEOREM. *If* $\mathscr{A}$ *is weakly* $(C, \lesssim, d)$-*priorcomeager under* d *then there is a* $(C, \lesssim, d)$-*sequence which converges to an element of* $\mathscr{A}$.

The direct proof of this theorem proceeds by defining a $(C, \lesssim, d)$-sequence which converges and is (Ω_e)-prioric, where (Ω_e) is as provided in 3.2. A $(C, \lesssim, d)$-sequence $T_0, T_1, \cdots$ is (Ω_e)-*prioric* if for each e there is a number $K(e)$ such that $(T_k)_{k \geqq K(e)}$ is Ω_e-prioric.

4. Applications to the Δ_2^0 theory. The principal classifications concerning the Δ_2^0 theory are of the sets $\mathscr{M}$, $\mathscr{I}$ and $\mathscr{J}$ where $\mathscr{M} = \{B: B \text{ is minimal}\}$, $\mathscr{I} = \{B: \boldsymbol{B} \text{ is incomparable with all nonzero, incomplete } \Sigma_1^0 \text{ degrees}\}$ and $\mathscr{J} = \{B: \boldsymbol{B}^{(1)} > \boldsymbol{B} \cup \boldsymbol{0}^{(1)}\}$. Namely, $\mathscr{M}$ is $(\mathbb{1}, \leqq, \boldsymbol{0}^{(1)})$-priorcomeager, $\mathscr{I}$ is $(C, \leqq_1, \boldsymbol{0}^{(1)})$-priorcomeager for any system C and $\mathscr{J}$ is weakly $(\mathbb{1}, \leqq, \boldsymbol{0}^{(1)})$-priorcomeager. It follows from the existence theorem that $\mathscr{M}$ and $\mathscr{I}$ both contain Δ_2^0 elements results first obtained by Sacks ([4] and [5]) and Yates [10] respectively.

By involving closure under finite intersections, we can deduce some further results. Using the theorem that every $(C, \leqq, \boldsymbol{0}^{(1)})$-priorcomeager set is $(C, \leqq_1, \boldsymbol{0}^{(1)})$-priorcomeager, it follows that $\mathscr{M} \cap \mathscr{I}$ is $(\mathbb{1}, \leqq_1, \boldsymbol{0}^{(1)})$-priorcomeager and so contains a Δ_2^0 element, a result first obtained by Sasso [6] and strengthening Shoenfield [9]. Also $\mathscr{M} \cap \mathscr{J}$ is weakly $(\mathbb{1}, \leqq, \boldsymbol{0}^{(1)})$-priorcomeager and so contains a Δ_2^0 element, a result first obtained by Sasso in collaboration with Cooper and Epstein and announced by Sasso [7].

The classification of $\mathscr{M}$ was first obtained in our unpublished lecture notes [11] and has since appeared in [12] along with the classification of $\mathscr{J}$. A classification of $\mathscr{I}$ was obtained in [11], but this involved an awkward modification of the notion of priorcomeager set and so was inferior to the result announced here. Another result obtained in [11] was Shoenfield's theorem [8] that if $\boldsymbol{0}^{(1)} \leqq \boldsymbol{c} \leqq \boldsymbol{0}^{(2)}$ and $\boldsymbol{c}$ is Σ_1^0 in $\boldsymbol{0}^{(1)}$ then there is a $\boldsymbol{b} \leqq \boldsymbol{0}^{(1)}$ such that $\boldsymbol{b}^{(1)} = \boldsymbol{c}$. This was the original application of the priority method to the Δ_2^0 theory (subsequently superseded by Sacks [5] where $\boldsymbol{b}$ was made Σ_1^0) and requires a notion of a $((C_e), \leqq, \boldsymbol{0}^{(1)})$-priorcomeager set for a sequence of systems (C_e) rather than a single system C.

5. Applications to the Σ_1^0 theory. The principal classifications concerning the Σ_1^0 theory are of the sets $\mathscr{P}$ and $\mathscr{S}(\boldsymbol{a})$ where $\mathscr{P} = \{B: (\boldsymbol{B})_0 | (\boldsymbol{B})_1\}$ and $\mathscr{S}(\boldsymbol{a}) = \{B: \boldsymbol{0} < \boldsymbol{B} \,\&\, \boldsymbol{a} \not\leqq \boldsymbol{B}\}$. (Here, $(B)_0(n) = B(2n)$ and $(B)_1(n) = B(2n+1)$ for all n; also $\boldsymbol{a}$

is a nonzero Σ_1^0 degree.) Namely, $\mathscr{P}$ is $(\mathbb{0}, \leqq^0, \mathbf{0})$-priorcomeager and $\mathscr{S}(\boldsymbol{a})$ is weakly $(\mathbb{0}, \leqq^0, \mathbf{0})$-priorcomeager under $\mathbf{0}$. Either of these results in combination with the existence theorem provides a Σ_1^0 set of degree strictly between $\mathbf{0}$ and $\mathbf{0}^{(1)}$; the first of course provides incomparable Σ_1^0 degrees. Of these, the first result abstracts the original solution to Post's problem (Friedberg [1] and Mučnic [3]); the second abstracts a technique first introduced by Sacks [4] (this was also abstracted by Lachlan in §2 of [2]).

Finally, it can be shown that both $\mathscr{P}$ and $\mathscr{S}(\boldsymbol{a})$ are weakly $(\mathbb{0}, \leqq^a, \mathbf{0})$-priorcomeager under $\mathbf{0}$, where a is a 1-1 recursive function ranging over a Σ_1^0 set of degree $\boldsymbol{a}$. This shows that there are no minimal Σ_1^0 degrees, a result first announced by Mučnic.

Bibliography

1. R. M. Friedberg, *Two recursively enumerable sets of incomparable degrees of unsolvability* (*solution of Post's problem,* 1944), Proc. Nat. Acad. Sci. U.S.A. **43** (1957), 236–238. MR **18**, 867.

2. A. H. Lachlan, *The priority method for the construction of recursively enumerable sets*, Proc. Conf. on Logic, Cambridge, 1971, pp. 299–310.

3. A. A. Mučnic, *On the unsolvability of the problem of reducibility in the theory of algorithms*, Dokl. Akad. Nauk SSSR **108** (1956), 194–197. (Russian) MR **18**, 457.

4. G. E. Sacks, *On the degrees less than* 0′, Ann. of Math. (2) **77** (1963), 211–231. MR **26** #3604.

5. ———, *Degrees of unsolvability*, Ann. of Math. Studies, no. 55, Princeton Univ. Press, Princeton, N. J., 1963; 2nd ed., 1966. MR **32** #4013.

6. L. P. Sasso, Jr., *A cornucopia of minimal degrees*, J. Symbolic Logic **35** (1970), 383–388. MR **44** #69.

7. ———, *A minimal degree not realising least possible jump*, J. Symbolic Logic **39** (1974), 571–574.

8. J. R. Shoenfield, *On degrees of unsolvability*, Ann. of Math. (2) **69** (1969), 644–653.

9. ———, *A theorem on minimal degrees*, J. Symbolic Logic **31** (1966), 539–544. MR **34** #5676.

10. C. E. M. Yates, *Recursively enumerable degrees and the degrees less than* $\mathbf{0}^{(1)}$, Sets Models and Recursion Theory (Proc. Summer School Math. Logic and Tenth Logic Colloq., Leicester, 1965), North-Holland, Amsterdam, 1967, pp. 264–271. MR **36** #2504.

11. ———, *Degrees of unsolvability*, mimeographed lecture notes, University of Colorado, Boulder, Col., 1971.

12. ———, *Prioric games and minimal degrees below* $\mathbf{0}^{(1)}$, Fund. Math. **82** (1974), 217–237.

13. ———, *Banach-Mazur games, comeager sets and degrees of unsolvability*, Proc. Cambridge Philos. Soc. (to appear).

THE UNIVERSITY
MANCHESTER, ENGLAND M13 9PL

Section 2

Algebra

Proceedings of the International Congress of Mathematicians
Vancouver, 1974

Algebraic *K*-Theory: A Historical Survey

Hyman Bass

Algebraic K-theory has been metamorphosed and given new focus by the recent work of Quillen (cf. [**30**], [**31**], [**32**]), discussed in his article in these PROCEEDINGS. I shall survey here some of the research themes with which the subject was inaugurated, and report on their current status.

1. In the beginning. Like the topological K-theory of Atiyah and Hirzebruch [**2**], algebraic K-theory started from Grothendieck's proof of his generalized Riemann-Roch theorem in 1957 [**12**]. There first appears the Grothendieck group $K(X)$ of vector bundles on a scheme X, which Grothendieck intended as a vehicle for the global intersection theory later developed in S.G.A. 6 [**21**]. Atiyah and Hirzebruch meanwhile took X to be a finite CW complex and defined $K^{-n}(X) = \tilde{K}(S^n X)$ for $n \geqq 1$, where S denotes suspension. If, in Grothendieck's case, $X = \operatorname{spec}(A)$ is affine, or, in the case of Atiyah-Hirzebruch, A is the ring $C(X)$ of continuous functions on X, then the category of vector bundles on X is equivalent to the category $\mathscr{P}(A)$ of finitely generated projective A-modules (cf. [**37**] and [**43**]). Whence a definition of $K(A)$ (or $K_0(A)$), as the Grothendieck group of $\mathscr{P}(A)$, which makes sense for an arbitrary ring A.

This $K_0(A)$ is, if nothing more, a useful tool for investigating the structure of projective A-modules P. Consider, for example, a problem that has greatly influenced our subject, posed by Serre in 1955 [**37**]: Is P free if $A = F[t_1, \cdots, t_n]$, a polynomial ring over a field F? Seshadri affirmed the first nontrivial case, $n = 2$ [**39**]. In 1958 Serre proved the following fundamental results [**38**]:

(1) $K_0(A) \to K_0(A[t])$ is an isomorphism for regular rings A.[1]

[1] In my book [**5**, Chapter 12], and elsewhere, I mistakenly attributed this theorem to Grothendieck, because of its appearance in [**12**].

(2) $P =$ (a free module) $\oplus$ (a module of rank $\leqq d$) if A is Noetherian and m-dim $(A) = d$.

Here m-dim (A) ($\leqq \dim(A)$) denotes dimension of the maximal ideal spectrum, and "regular" means all local rings $A_{\mathfrak{p}}$ are regular. Hilbert's syzygy theorem, in modern form, tells us that $A[t]$ is regular when A is. We thus conclude from (1), when $A = F[t_1, \cdots, t_n]$, that P is "stably free," i.e., that $P \oplus A^s \cong A^{r+s}$ for some s, and $r = \text{rank}(P)$. Assertion (2), coupled with the following "cancellation theorem" (see [**5**, Chapter IV]):

(3) $$P \oplus A \cong P' \oplus A \Rightarrow P \cong P' \quad \text{if rank } P > \text{m-dim } A,$$

then further implies that projective $F[t_1, \cdots, t_n]$-modules P of rank $> n$ are free (cf. [**4**]). This result has recently been significantly improved by Murthy and Towber [**28**], Swan [**46**], and Suslin and Vaserštein [**42**] (see [**7**] for a report on their work). We now know that P is free if rank $P > 1 + (n/2)$, if $n = 3$, if $n = 4$ and char$(F) \neq 2$, and if $n = 5$ and F is finite, char$(F) \neq 2$.

The theorems (1), (2), and (3) above can be viewed as algebraic analogues of homotopy invariance and stability properties of the functor $K(X)$ in topology. They suggested that a more systematic exploitation of the ideas and methods of topological K-theory might be profitable. A first step was to define relative groups $K(A, J)$, J an ideal; this was straightforward. The difficulty lay in finding a good analogue $K_n(A)$ for the topological $K^{-n}(X)$, lacking an obvious algebraic analogue of the suspension. This program, only recently consummated, is the subject of Quillen's address; it is also discussed in Swan's address [**45**] at the Nice Congress. At the outset however only a definition of $K_1(A)$, as the commutator quotient, $\text{GL}(A)/E(A)$, of $\text{GL}(A)$, was proposed, this definition being modeled on the description of bundles on SX by clutching functions. What made this definition also especially commendable was that, in case $A = Z\pi$, the integral group ring of a group π, a natural quotient of $K_1(Z\pi)$ had been introduced already in 1939 in J.H.C. Whitehead's theory of simple homotopy types [**54**]. The computation of such "Whitehead groups" $K_1(Z\pi)$ was thus a problem of interest to topologists, and for which algebraic techniques beyond those in the 1939 thesis [**22**] of Whitehead's student, G. Higman, seemed lacking.

The point of view of algebraic K-theory naturally suggested the first general theorems concerning Whitehead groups $K_1(A)$: stability theorems for Noetherian A and homotopy invariance for regular A. The stability theorems, proved by L. Vaserštein [**49**] and the author [**5**], yielded the finite generation of $K_1(Z\pi)$ and finiteness of $SK_1(Z\pi)$ when π is finite [**4**]. Examples with $SK_1(Z\pi) \neq 0$ were first exhibited only recently by Alperin, Dennis and Stein [**1**], applying the refined results of Dennis and Stein on K_2 of discrete valuation rings [**15**]. The stability theorems for K_1 were also a key step in the solution, by Milnor, Serre and the author [**9**], of the congruence subgroup problem for $\text{SL}_n(A)$, A the ring of integers in a number field F. This revealed a striking and unexpected connection between the relative groups $SK_1(A, J)$ and the explicit power reciprocity laws in F. Here was the origin of a persistent arithmetic theme in algebraic K-theory which has now become one of its most interesting aspects.

The homotopy invariance theorem for K_1 also had unexpected ramifications. Denoting the cokernel of $K_1(A) \to K_1(A[t])$ by $N(A)$, it was shown by Heller, Swan and the author ([**8**], see also [**5**, Chapter 12]) how to give explicit generators for $N(A)$, which vanish when A is regular, and that $K_1(A[t, t^{-1}]) = K_1(A) \oplus N(A) \oplus N(A) \oplus K_0(A)$. When $A = Z\pi$ this formula yields a description of $K_1(Z[\pi \times T])$ with T an infinite cyclic group, a formula generalized by Farrell and Hsiang [**17**] to semidirect products $\pi \rtimes_\alpha T$. Their interest arose from an obstruction in $K_1(Z[\pi \times T])$ constructed by Farrell [**16**] in connection with fiberings over a circle.

The above formula also showed that K_0 is an essential ingredient in the study of Whitehead groups. However geometric problems leading directly to obstructions in $K_0(Z\pi)$ had meanwhile been encountered, for example Wall's obstruction to finiteness of a CW complex [**53**], and Siebenmann's to capping an end of an open manifold [**41**].

2. Growing higher. Various approaches to constructing higher functors $K_n(A)$, $n = 0, 1, 2, 3, \cdots$, were developed independently by Milnor [**27**], Gersten [**18**], Swan [**44**], Karoubi and Villamayor [**24**], Anderson and Segal [**36**], Keune [**25**], Volodin [**51**], Wagoner [**52**], and Quillen [**30**] and [**31**]. But for the Karoubi-Villamayor theory, which satisfies an unrestricted homotopy axiom at the cost of discarding some interesting information, it is now known that the other theories give the same answer in the cases where they can be compared. These comparison theorems are described in [**29**, I, Part A]. They permit one to say with conviction, and without ambiguity, that higher K-theory "exists," a fact that was less apparent at the time of Swan's address [**45**] at the Nice Congress.

Quillen ([**30**], [**31**], [**33**], and unpublished lectures) has furnished the first effective tools for computing higher K-groups. He has proved homotopy invariance of $K_n(A)$ for regular A, and Waldhausen has derived the expected description of $K_n(A[t, t^{-1}])$. Quillen has given an approach to stability questions for K_n, giving so far only partial results. He has exactly calculated the groups $K_*(\boldsymbol{F}_q)$ and shown that there is a natural map from the stable homotopy of spheres into $K_*(Z)$ which is injective on the image of the J-homomorphism.

Much interest has been attached to the groups $K_n(A)$ when A is a ring of S-integers in a global field F. This was largely inspired by the work of Tate and others (see Tate's Nice Congress address [**47**]) on Milnor's $K_2(A)$ and $K_2(F)$, which were seen to be related to norm residue symbols and power reciprocity laws. Conjectures of Birch and Tate relating $K_2(A)$ to properties of the zeta function $\zeta_F(s)$ were one source of some spectacular conjectures of S. Lichtenbaum [**26**] relating all the groups $K_n(A)$ to $\zeta_F(s)$. Lichtenbaum's vision of the situation presupposes the groups $K_n(A)$ to be finitely generated. This was proved by Quillen in [**33**] when F is a number field, and very recently also in the function field case. Suppose now that F is a number field, A its ring of integers. Then, apart from $K_0(A) \cong \boldsymbol{Z} \oplus$

Pic(A) and $K_1(A) = A^*$ (units), which has rank $r_1 + r_2 - 1$, where $\boldsymbol{R} \otimes_{\boldsymbol{Q}} F \cong \boldsymbol{R}^{r_1} \times \boldsymbol{C}^{r_2}$, Lichtenbaum predicted that, for $m \geqq 1$, $K_{2m}(A)$ should be finite and $K_{2m+1}(A)$ should have rank r_2 for m odd and $r_1 + r_2$ for m even, the latter rank being in the respective cases, the order of the zero of $\zeta_F(s)$ at $s = -m$. This prediction was confirmed by Borel in **[10]**, without any knowledge of Lichtenbaum's ideas. Lichtenbaum further suggested the possibility of a formula of the type

$$(*) \qquad \lim_{s \to -m} (s + m)^{-t_m} \zeta_F(s) = \pm \frac{|K_{2m}(A)|}{|K_{2m+1}(A)_{\text{tors}}|} \cdot R_m(F)$$

where t_m is the order of the zero of ζ_F at $s = -m$, $|G|$ denotes the order of the finite group G, and $R_m(F)$ denotes a conjectural "regulator" whose relation to $K_{2m+1}(A)$ is analogous to that of the classical regulator to $K_1(A) = A^*$. Borel in his article in these PROCEEDINGS **[11]** has described reasonable candidates for these higher regulators for which he can verify the necessary rationality properties. The Lichtenbaum conjectures have been proved by Coates and Lichtenbaum **[14]** in special cases for some totally real fields and odd m (where the higher regulator question does not intervene because $K_{2m+1}(A)$ is then finite).

It now seems that Lichtenbaum's conjecture $(*)$ is not quite correct as stated. What might be called the most immediate problem in higher K-theory is the computation of the finite group $K_3(\boldsymbol{Z})$. Lichtenbaum predicted it has order 24, and Quillen's results give it a cyclic subgroup J of that order. However Karoubi, using results from his hermitian K-theory **[23**, pp. 381–383**]**, has shown that J has even index in $K_3(\boldsymbol{Z})$. Very recently R. Lee and R. Sczarba have announced further unpublished results, including the first known upper bound on the order of $K_3(\boldsymbol{Z})$.

The construction of the higher K-groups by Volodin and Wagoner **[52]** has two features that deserve comment. First it employs a generalization to rings of the "buildings" which have recently appeared in the theory of linear algebraic groups (see Tits' article in these PROCEEDINGS **[48]**) and which intervene also in Quillen's proof in **[33]** that the groups $K_n(A)$ are finitely generated in the arithmetic case. The other feature is that their groups $K_n(Z\pi)$ come equipped with a geometric interpretation, and hence potential application, in the theory of pseudo-isotopies.

Some possibly very interesting applications of algebraic K-theory to the theory of algebraic cycles in algebraic geometry are suggested by recent work of Quillen, Gersten, Bloch, and others. The main result in this direction is Quillen's proof in **[31]** of a beautiful conjecture of Gersten, made in **[19]**, which he discusses in these PROCEEDINGS.

3. Growing orthogonally. There is a so-called "hermitian K-theory" attached to each of the families of classical groups (orthogonal, symplectic, unitary), just as that above is to the general linear group. The main impulse behind hermitian K-theory came from surgery theory, and much of the subject has been developed by topologists, such as C. T. C. Wall, S. Novikov, W. C. Hsiang, S. Cappell, J. Shaneson, A. Ranicki, R. Sharpe, and many others.

Here the ring A is equipped with an involution $a \mapsto \bar{a}$ relative to which one can define ε-hermitian forms ($\varepsilon = \pm 1$) on an A-module P, $h(x, y) = \varepsilon\overline{h(y, x)}$. Such

(P, h)'s with P projective and h nonsingular, together with a related "quadratic form," constitute a category $Q_\varepsilon(A)$, whose study E. Artin might have called "geometric algebra over a ring." There is a "hyperbolic functor" $H: \mathscr{P}(A) \to Q_\varepsilon(A)$, and we can define "Witt groups" ${}_\varepsilon W_i(A)$ as the cokernels of the induced homomorphisms on K_i $(i = 0, 1)$. The cases $(\varepsilon, i) = (1, 0), (1, 1), (-1, 0), (-1, 1)$ yield essentially the groups $L_n(A)$, $n = 0, 1, 2, 3$ respectively, of surgery theory.

Stability theorems for the associated unitary groups, and hence for L_n with n odd, have been proved by Bak [3], Vaseršteĭn [50], and the author [6]. Fairly precise calculations of $L_n(Z\pi)$ with π a finite group, and especially finite abelian, have been made by Wall, R. Lee, T. Petrie, Bak-Scharlau, the author, and others. The general theory is now well enough developed so that such calculations, at least for π finite abelian, can be made with any desired degree of precision.

A general homotopy invariance theorem for the groups $L_n(A)$ was proved by Karoubi [23], without assuming regularity of A, but requiring instead that $\frac{1}{2} \in A$. This theorem, in the symplectic case, figures essentially in the work of Suslin and Vaseršteĭn on Serre's problem (see §1 above), and explains the restrictions "char $F \neq 2$" which appear there.

A Laurent polynomial formula of the type $L_n(A[t, t^{-1}]) = L_n(A) \oplus L_{n-1}(A)$ was proved by Shaneson [40] for $A = Z\pi$, using geometric methods. Algebraic proofs of this and various generalizations have been given by Ranicki (cf. [35]). In case $\pi = \pi_1 *_{\pi_0} \pi_2$, a free product with amalgamation, Cappell [13] has established the desired kind of Mayer-Vietoris sequence for the L-groups, provided that π_0 is "square root closed" in π.

Karoubi has recently applied Quillen's methods to the construction of higher hermitian K-groups. He conjectures that these groups enjoy certain periodicity properties analogous to real Bott periodicity. Some of these conjectures have been verified in special cases, and modulo 2-torsion.

References

1. R. C. Alperin, R. K. Dennis and M. R. Stein, *The non-triviality of $SK_1(Z\pi)$*, Proc. Conf. on Orders, Group Rings and Related Topics, Lecture Notes in Math., vol. 353, Springer-Verlag, Berlin and New York, 1973.

2. M. Atiyah and F. Hirzebruch, *Vector bundles and homogeneous spaces*, Proc. Sympos. Pure Math., vol. 3, Amer. Math. Soc., Providence, R.I., 1961, pp. 7–38. MR **25** #2617.

3. A. Bak, *The stable structure of quadratic modules*, Thesis, Columbia University, New York, 1969.

4. H. Bass, *K-theory and stable algebra*, Inst. Hautes Études Sci. Publ. Math. No. 22 (1964), 5–60. MR **30** #4805.

5. ———, *Algebraic K-theory*, Benjamin, New York, 1968. MR **40** #2736.

6. ———, *Unitary algebraic K-theory*, Proc. Battelle Conf. on Alg. K-theory. III, Lecture Notes in Math., vol. 343, Springer-Verlag, Berlin and New York, 1973, pp. 57–265.

7. ———, *Libération des modules projectifs sur certains anneaux de polynômes*, Sém. Bourbaki, Exposé 448, Juin 1974.

8. H. Bass, A. Heller and R. G. Swan, *The Whitehead group of a polynomial extension*, Inst. Hautes Études Sci. Publ. Math. No. 22 (1964), 61–79. MR **30** #4806.

9. H. Bass, J. Milnor and J.-P. Serre, *Solution of the congruence subgroup problem for SL_n $(n \geqq 3)$ and Sp_{2n} $(n \geqq 2)$*, Inst. Hautes Études Sci. Publ. Math. No. 33 (1967), 59–137. MR **39** #5574.

10. A. Borel, *Cohomologie réelle stable de groupes S-arithmétiques classiques*, C. R. Acad. Sci. Paris Sér. A-B **274** (1972), A1700–A1702. MR **46** #7400.

11. ———, *Cohomology of arithmetic groups*, these PROCEEDINGS.

12. A. Borel and J.-P. Serre, *Le théorème de Riemann-Roch*, Bull. Soc. Math. France **86** (1958), 97–136. MR **22** #6817.

13. S. Cappell, *Lecture notes on the splitting theorem*, Princeton University, Princeton, N.J.; See also: Bull. Amer. Math. Soc. **77** (1971), 281–286. MR **44** #2234.

14. J. Coates and S. Lichtenbaum, *On l-adic zeta functions*, Ann. of Math. (2) **98** (1973), 498–550.

15. K. Dennis and M. Stein, *K_2 of discrete valuation rings* (to appear).

16. F. T. Farrell, *The obstruction to fibering a manifold over a circle*, Thesis, Yale University, New Haven, Conn., 1967; See also: Bull. Amer. Math. Soc. **73** (1967), 737–740. MR **35** #6151.

17. F. T. Farrell and W. C. Hsiang, *Manifolds with $\pi_1 = G \times_\alpha T$*, Amer. J. Math. **95** (1973), 813–848.

18. S. M. Gersten, *On Mayer-Vietoris functors and algebraic K-theory*, J. Algebra **18** (1971), 51–88. MR **43** #6290.

19. ———, *Some exact sequences in the higher K-theory of rings*, Proc. Battelle Conf. on Alg. *K*-theory. I, Lecture Notes in Math., vol. 341, Springer-Verlag, Berlin and New York, 1973, pp. 211–243.

20. ———, *K-theory and algebraic cycle*, these PPOCEEDINGS.

21. A. Grothendieck, SGA 6, Lecture Notes in Math., vol. 225, Springer-Verlag, Berlin and New York, 1971.

22. G. Higman, *The units of group-rings*, Proc. London Math. Soc. (2) **46** (1940), 231–248. MR **2**, 5.

23. M. Karoubi, *Périodicité de la K-théorie hermitiènne*, Proc. Battelle Conf. on Alg. *K*-theory, III, Lecture Notes in Math., vol. 343, Springer-Verlag, Berlin and New York, 1973, pp. 301–411.

24. M. Karoubi and O. Villamayor, *K-théorie algébrique et K-théorie topologique*. I, Math. Scand. **28** (1971), 265–307. MR **47** #1915.

25. F. Keune, *Derived functors and algebraic K-theory*, Proc. Battelle Conf. on Alg. *K*-theory. I, Lecture Notes in Math., vol. 341, Springer-Verlag, Berlin and New York, 1973, pp. 166–176.

26. S. Lichtenbaum, *Values of zeta-functions, étale cohomology, and algebraic K-theory*. II, Proc. Battelle Conf. on Alg. *K*-theory. II, Lecture Notes in Math., vol. 342, Springer-Verlag, Berlin and New York, 1973, pp. 489–501.

27. J. Milnor, *Introduction to algebraic K-theory*, Ann. of Math. Studies, Princeton Univ. Press, Princeton, N.J., 1971.

28. M. P. Murthy and J. Towber, *Algebraic vector bundles over A^3 are trivial*, Invent. Math. **24** (1974), 173–189.

29. *Proceedings of the Battelle Conference on Algebraic K-theory*. I, *Higher K-theories;* II, *Classical algebraic K-theory and connections with arithmetic;* III, *Hermitian K-theory and geometric applications*, Lecture Notes in Math., vols. 341, 342, 343, Springer-Verlag, Berlin and New York, 1973.

30. D. Quillen, *On the cohomology and K-theory of the general linear groups over a finite field*, Ann. of Math. (2) **96** (1972), 552–586. MR **47** #3565.

31. ———, *Higher algebraic K-theory*. I, Proc. Battelle Conf. on Alg. *K*-theory. I, Lecture Notes in Math., vol. 341, Springer-Verlag, Berlin and New York, 1973.

32. ———, *Higher algebraic K-theory*. II (to appear).

33. ———, *Finite generation of the groups K_i of rings of algebraic integers*, Proc. Battelle Conf. on Alg. *K*-theory. I, Lecture Notes in Math., vol. 341, Springer-Verlag, Berlin and New York, 1973.

34. ———, *Higher algebraic K-theory*, these PROCEEDINGS.

35. A. Ranicki, *Algebraic L-theory*. III. *Twisted Laurent extensions*, Proc. Battelle Conf. on Alg. *K*-theory. III, Lecture Notes in Math., vol. 343, Springer-Verlag, Berlin and New York, 1973, pp. 412–463.

36. G. Segal, *Categories and cohomology theories*, Oxford University (preprint).
37. J.-P. Serre, *Faisceaux algébriques cohérents*, Ann. of Math. (2) **61** (1965), 197–278. MR **16**, 953.
38. ———, *Modules projectifs et espaces fibrés à fibre vectorielle*, Séminaire P. Dubreil, M. L. Dubreil-Jacotin et C. Pisot; lle année: 1957/58. Algèbre et théorie des nombres. 2 Vols., Secretariat mathématique, Paris, 1958. MR **21** #7222.
39. C. S. Seshadri, *Triviality of vector bundles over the affine space K^2*, Proc. Nat. Acad. Sci. U.S.A. **44** (1958), 456–458. MR **21** #1318.
40. J. L. Shaneson, *Wall's surgery obstruction groups for $Z \times G$*, Ann. of Math. (2) **90** (1969), 296–334. MR **39** #7614.
41. L. Siebenmann, *The structure of tame ends*, Notices Amer. Math. Soc. **13** (1966), 862. Abstract #66T-531.
42. A. Suslin and L. N. Vaseršteĭn, *Serre's problem on projective modules over polynomial rings and algebraic K-theory*, Funkcional. Anal. i Priložen. **8** (1974), 65–66. (Russian)
43. R. G. Swan, *Vector bundles and projective modules*, Trans. Amer. Math. Soc. **105** (1962), 264–277. MR **26** #785.
44. ———, *Nonabelian homological algebra and K-theory*, Proc. Sympos. Pure Math., vol. 17, Amer. Math. Soc., Providence, R.I., 1970, pp. 88–123. MR **41** #1839.
45. ———, *Algebraic K-theory*, Proc. Internat. Congress Math. (Nice, 1970), vol. 1, Gauthier-Villars, Paris, 1971, pp. 191–199.
46. ———, *A cancellation theorem for projective modules in the metastable range*, Invent. Math. (1975) (to appear).
47. J. Tate, *Symbols in arithmetic*, Proc. Internat. Congress Math. (Nice, 1970), vol. 1, Gauthier-Villars, Paris, 1971, pp. 201–211.
48. J. Tits, *On buildings and their applications*, these PROCEEDINGS.
49. L. N. Vaseršteĭn, *On the stabilization of the general linear group over a ring*, Mat. Sb. **79 (121)** (1969), 405–424 = Math. USSR Sb. **8** (1969), 383–400. MR **42** #1911.
50. ———, *Stabilization of unitary and orthogonal groups over a ring with involution*, Mat. Sb. **81 (123)** (1970), 328–351 = Math. USSR Sb. **10** (1970), 307–326. MR **42** #4617.
51. I. A. Volodin, *Algebraic K-theory as an extraordinary homology theory on the category of associative rings with unit*, Izv. Akad. Nauk SSSR Ser. Mat. **35** (1971), 844–873 = Math. USSR Izv. **5** (1971), 859–887. MR **45** #5201.
52. J. Wagoner, *Buildings, stratifications, and higher K-theory*, Proc. Battelle Conf. on Alg. K-theory. I, Lecture Notes in Math., vol. 341, Springer-Verlag, Berlin and New York, 1973, pp. 148–165.
53. C. T. C. Wall, *Finiteness conditions for CW-complexes*, Ann. of Math. (2) **81** (1965), 56–69. MR **30** #1515.
54. J. H. C. Whitehead, *Simplicial spaces, nuclei, and m-groups*, Proc. London Math. Soc. **45** (1939), 243–327.

COLUMBIA UNIVERSITY
NEW YORK, NEW YORK 10027, U.S.A.

Proceedings of the International Congress of Mathematicians
Vancouver, 1974

Some Category-Theoretic Ideas in Algebra (A Too-Brief Tour of Algebraic Structure, Monads, and the Adjoint Tower)

George M. Bergman

In recent years, categorists have come up with some very interesting ways of looking at algebraic constructions and algebraic objects. But most of what they write on this is technical and aimed at other categorists. I shall sketch some of these ideas here, emphasizing concrete examples, for the algebraist with a reasonable foundation in category theory (familiarity with adjoint functors and colimits). The unifying thread of the article will be the problem: What algebraic structure can be put on the values of a given set-valued functor?

1. Coalgebras, and representable functors [1]—review. Let $\mathscr{A}$ and $\mathscr{B}$ be varieties of algebras. ($\mathscr{A}$ may be, more generally, any category with colimits.) It is known that a functor $V: \mathscr{A} \to \mathscr{B}$ has a left adjoint if and only if at the set level it is representable; that is, if and only if, letting $U: \mathscr{B} \to \mathscr{E}ns$ denote the underlying-set functor of $\mathscr{B}$, one has $U \circ V \cong \mathrm{Hom}\,(R, —)$ for some object R of $\mathscr{B}$:

(1)

$$\begin{array}{ccc} & & \mathscr{B} \\ & \nearrow V & \downarrow U \\ \mathscr{A} & \xrightarrow{\quad\quad} & \mathscr{E}ns \\ & \mathrm{Hom}(R,—) & \end{array}$$

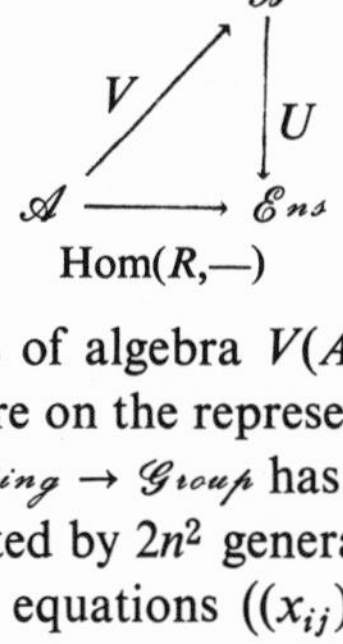

In this situation, the structures of algebra $V(A) \in \mathrm{Ob}(\mathscr{B})$ on the sets $\mathrm{Hom}\,(R, A)$ arise from a $\mathscr{B}$-coalgebra structure on the representing object R in $\mathscr{A}$.

EXAMPLE. The functor $\mathrm{GL}_n: \mathscr{R}ing \to \mathscr{G}roup$ has a left adjoint, because $U \circ \mathrm{GL}_n$ is represented by the ring R presented by $2n^2$ generators $x_{ij}, y_{ij}\ (i, j \leqq n)$ and the $2n^2$ relations comprising the matrix equations $((x_{ij}))((y_{ij})) = ((y_{ij}))((x_{ij})) = I_n$, i.e., the ring with a *universal* invertible $n \times n$ matrix, $x = ((x_{ij}))$. To study the multiplication of GL_n take the ring with *two* universal invertible $n \times n$ matrices, namely the coproduct of two copies of R, $R' \coprod R''$, and call these two matrices $x', x'' \in GL_n(R' \coprod R'')$; they correspond to the two coprojection maps, $R \to R' \coprod R''$. Form their product $x'x'' \in GL_n(R' \coprod R'')$, and represent it by a homomorphism $m: R \to R' \coprod R''$. The homomorphism m now "encodes" the multiplication of GL_n, just as the object R "encodes" the construction of GL_n as a set: Given any elements $a, b \in GL_n(A) = \operatorname{Hom}(R, A)$ (any ring A) one gets their product in $GL_n(A) = \operatorname{Hom}(R, A)$ as the composition:

$$R \xrightarrow{m} R' \coprod R'' \xrightarrow{(a,\, b)} A.$$

In the same way, the matrix-inverse operation of GL_n corresponds to a map $i: R \to R$ (namely, $x_{ij} \mapsto y_{ij}$, $y_{ij} \mapsto x_{ij}$); and the 0-ary operation giving the identity matrix $I_n \in GL_n(A)$ corresponds to a map of R into its 0-fold coproduct with itself, $\coprod_\varnothing R$, which is simply the initial object $\mathbf{Z}$ of $\mathcal{R}ing$ (namely, $x_{ij}, y_{ij} \mapsto \delta_{ij} \in \mathbf{Z}$). These maps, called *comultiplication, coinverse* and *counit*, comprise a structure of *cogroup* on the object R of $\mathcal{R}ing$.

For a very interesting exposition of coalgebras and related constructions, see P. Freyd [**1**]. Cf. also [**2**, §III.6] and [**4**].

(Warning to the ring-theorist: Do not confuse this use of the term "cogroup," and, more generally, of "coalgebra" with the deceptively similar meaning of the latter term in the theory of Hopf algebras! The relation between these concepts is discussed in [**4**, §8].)

2. Turnabout is fair play. Let us now reverse our viewpoint. Let $\mathcal{A}$ be a category with coproducts, and R be an object of $\mathcal{A}$. Suppose we form the representable functor $\operatorname{Hom}(R,—): \mathcal{A} \to \mathcal{E}ns$, and ask: What algebraic structure can we put on this functor? That is, what is the richest category of algebras $\mathcal{B}$ such that we can factor $\operatorname{Hom}(R,—)$ through the forgetful functor $U: \mathcal{B} \to \mathcal{E}ns$ as in (1)?

The remarks of the preceding section contain the answer: The n-ary *operations* we can put on $\mathcal{B}$ correspond precisely to the n-ary *cooperations* possessed by R in $\mathcal{A}$, i.e., to the set of all maps $R \to R \coprod \cdots \coprod R$. In general this will give a very big and unwieldy set of operations, but there may be some convenient subset which *generates* the rest.

The identities of $\mathcal{B}$ will come from "coidentities" of these co-operations of R.

EXAMPLE. What algebraic structure can we put, in a functorial manner, on the set of elements of exponent 2 in a group G?

The functor $G \mapsto \{x \in |G| \mid x^2 = e\}$ is represented by the object $\mathbf{Z}_2$ of $\mathcal{G}roup$. A description of all maps $\mathbf{Z}_2 \to \mathbf{Z}_2 \coprod \cdots \coprod \mathbf{Z}_2$, i.e., of all elements of exponent 2 in the group with presentation $\langle x_1, \cdots, x_n \mid x_1^2 = \cdots = x_n^2 = e\rangle$, may be obtained from classical results on the structure of coproducts of groups. (N.B. Not by "general nonsense"!) They are (as elements) precisely e, and all conjugates of the generators $x_1, \cdots, x_n$. From this it is not hard to deduce that the operations we get on $\operatorname{Hom}(\mathbf{Z}_2,—)$ are generated by the 0-ary operation e (induced by the trivial map

$\mathbf{Z}_2 \to \coprod_{\varnothing} \mathbf{Z}_2 = \{e\}$) and the binary operation of conjugation, $(x, y) \mapsto x^y = y^{-1}xy$ (induced by the map $\mathbf{Z}_2 = \langle t \mid t^2 = e\rangle \to \mathbf{Z}_2 \coprod \mathbf{Z}_2 = \langle x, y \mid x^2 = y^2 = e\rangle$ taking t to x^y).

A group-theoretic analysis of when iterated conjugates of generators in groups $\mathbf{Z}_2 \coprod \cdots \coprod \mathbf{Z}_2$ coincide leads to the result that all identities satisfied by these two operations follow from the following five:

$$e^x = e, \quad x^x = x, \quad x^{(y^z)} = ((x^z)^y)^z.$$
$$x^e = x, \quad (x^y)^y = x,$$

Hence let us call an algebra of type (0, 2) (i.e., a set with one zero-ary and one binary operation) satisfying these five identities an "involution algebra". Then the variety $\mathcal{I}nv$ of all involution algebras is the richest variety "$\mathcal{B}$" through which $\mathrm{Hom}(\mathbf{Z}_2, —): \mathcal{G}roup \to \mathcal{E}ns$ can be factored as in (1). This factorization corresponds to a structure of *involution coalgebra* on the representing object $\mathbf{Z}_2$ in $\mathcal{G}roup$.

For other examples see **[20]**.

3. Interpretation in terms of Lawvere's algebraic theories and algebraic structure. W. Lawvere introduced in his thesis [3] the idea of describing any variety $\mathcal{A}$ of algebras as the category $\mathcal{E}ns^\theta$ of all finite-direct-product preserving functors from a certain category θ, called the "theory" of $\mathcal{A}$, into the category $\mathcal{E}ns$ of sets. The category θ consists of an object 1, and finite products $1 \times \cdots \times 1$, and has for morphisms, in addition to maps constructible from projections, certain other maps corresponding to the *operations* of $\mathcal{A}$, with relations among their compositions corresponding to the *identities* of $\mathcal{A}$.

Actually, Lawvere defines the theory to be the opposite category, T, to the category θ I have described, so that he writes $\mathcal{A} = \mathcal{E}ns^{T^{\mathrm{op}}}$. This T is a little less natural to picture than θ, but has a formal advantage: The category *freely* generated by one object 1 under finite *coproducts* is (up to equivalence) the full subcategory of $\mathcal{E}ns$ with object-set $\omega = \{0, 1, 2, \cdots\}$; so Lawvere's algebraic theories T are precisely the coproduct-preserving and object-set-preserving extensions of that category.

The "theory" θ (respectively T) of a variety $\mathcal{A}$ can be looked at as the category with a universal $\mathcal{A}$-algebra object (respectively co-$\mathcal{A}$-algebra object) 1. Thus, in the category of all categories-with-finite-(co)products, and functors respecting these, θ (resp. T) *represents* the construction associating to a category $\mathcal{C}$ the category of all $\mathcal{A}$-(co)algebras in $\mathcal{C}$:

$$\mathcal{A}\text{-alg}(\mathcal{C}) \cong \mathcal{C}^\theta, \quad \text{respectively} \quad \mathcal{A}\text{-coalg}(\mathcal{C}) \cong \mathcal{C}^T.$$

One can also show that T is isomorphic to the full subcategory of $\mathcal{A}$ having for object-set the set of free algebras $\{F(0), F(1), \cdots\}$.

One may now check that the variety $\mathcal{B}$ we associated to any representable functor $\mathrm{Hom}(R, —): \mathcal{A} \to \mathcal{E}ns$ in the preceding section is described in Lawvere's terms as $\mathcal{E}ns^{T^{\mathrm{op}}}$ where T is the full subcategory of $\mathcal{A}$ with objects $\coprod_n R$ $(n = 0, 1, 2, \cdots)$!

Lawvere looked, too, at the question of what algebraic structure can be put on a functor $V: \mathcal{A} \to \mathcal{E}ns$, or more generally, $\mathcal{A} \to \mathcal{C}$ where $\mathcal{C}$ is any category with finite direct products. He observes that a functorial n-ary operation on the $V(A)$'s just means a morphism (natural transformation) of functors, $V^n \to V$. The full subcategory of the functor-category $\mathscr{C}^{\mathscr{A}}$, with object-set $\{V^0, V^1, V^2, \cdots\}$, will form an algebraic theory θ_V (unless V is trivial), which defines as above a variety $\mathscr{B}$ such that the values of V can be regarded as $\mathscr{B}$-objects in $\mathscr{C}$. Lawvere calls the theory θ_V, or rather its opposite, T_V, the "algebraic structure" of V.

If $V\colon \mathscr{A} \to \mathscr{E}\!ns$ is a representable functor, say $V = \operatorname{Hom}(R,—)$, we see from the Yoneda lemma that this category T_V will be isomorphic to the subcategory of $\mathscr{A}$ with objects $\{\coprod_n R \mid n = 0, 1, \cdots\}$ which we used to define the $\mathscr{B}$ of the preceding section. Thus, $\mathscr{B} = \mathscr{E}\!ns^{T_V}$, so the algebraic structure on V that we determined in the preceding section is indeed the algebraic structure of V in Lawvere's sense.

However, we shall see in §5 that there are in general also "higher" types of algebraic structure to be found in a functor V!

If T is an algebraic theory, Lawvere calls the associated variety $\mathscr{E}\!ns^T$ the "semantics" of T. Thinking of $\mathscr{E}\!ns^T$ as a category given with a (forgetful) functor U to $\mathscr{E}\!ns$, i.e., an object of $(\mathscr{C}\!at \mid \mathscr{E}\!ns)$, the *universality* of $\mathscr{B} = \mathscr{E}\!ns^{T_V}$ as a variety of algebras through which to factor $V\colon \mathscr{A} \to \mathscr{E}\!ns$ (an arbitrary member of $(\mathscr{C}\!at \mid \mathscr{E}\!ns)$) is expressed by Lawvere's celebrated result, "Structure is adjoint to semantics";

$$\mathscr{A}\!lgebraic\ \mathscr{T}\!heories \underset{\text{structure}}{\overset{\text{semantics}}{\rightleftarrows}} (\mathscr{C}\!at \mid \mathscr{E}\!ns)$$

4. Monads. (For more details see [**2**, Chapter VI], [**6**, Introduction], [**14**, Chapter 21].) We consider again a pair of adjoint functors,

$$\mathscr{A} \underset{F}{\overset{V}{\rightleftarrows}} \mathscr{C}, \text{ with unit } \eta\colon 1_{\mathscr{C}} \to VF, \text{ counit } \varepsilon\colon FV \to 1_{\mathscr{A}}.$$

If we forget the category $\mathscr{A}$, how much information about this adjunction can we "remember" in terms of the category $\mathscr{C}$?

The composite VF is an endofunctor $M\colon \mathscr{C} \to \mathscr{C}$, and the unit η is a morphism $1_{\mathscr{C}} \to M$ so these are already expressible in terms of $\mathscr{C}$.

The counit $\varepsilon\colon FV \to 1_{\mathscr{A}}$ cannot itself be described in $\mathscr{C}$, but $V\varepsilon F$ will be a morphism $\mu\colon MM \to M$ of endofunctors of $\mathscr{C}$.

Writing this "$\mathscr{C}$-data" on our adjunction as a 3-tuple $\mathscr{M} = (M, \eta, \mu)$, one finds that $\mathscr{M}$ will satisfy the identities indicated by the commuting diagrams:

$$\text{(2)} \qquad \begin{array}{ccc} M = 1_{\mathscr{C}}M & \xrightarrow{\eta\cdot 1_M} & MM \\ \| & & \\ M1_{\mathscr{C}} & 1_M & \downarrow \mu \\ 1_M\cdot\eta \downarrow & & \\ MM & \xrightarrow{\mu} & M \end{array} \qquad \begin{array}{ccc} MMM & \xrightarrow{\mu\cdot 1_M} & MM \\ 1_M\cdot\mu \downarrow & & \downarrow \mu \\ MM & \xrightarrow{\mu} & M \end{array}$$

An endofunctor M of a category $\mathscr{C}$ given with morphisms η and μ satisfying these identities is called a *monad* (because of the parallel with operations $e\colon 1 \to X$, $m\colon X \times X \to X$, and the corresponding identities, defining a *monoid* (X, e, m)! Another common term for monad is *triple*.)

As an example, consider the *underlying-set* functor $V\colon \mathcal{G}\mathit{roup} \to \mathcal{E}\mathit{ns}$, its left adjoint F, and the resulting monad $\mathcal{M} = (M, \eta, \mu)$. The functor $M = VF\colon \mathcal{E}\mathit{ns} \to \mathcal{E}\mathit{ns}$ takes a set S to the set of elements of the free group on S, which can be thought of as the set of all "abstract group-theoretic combinations of the elements of S". The description of η is clear. The morphism μ corresponds to the observation that an "abstract group-theoretic combination of abstract group-theoretic combinations of elements of S" can be "reduced", by composition of operations, to a single abstract combination of elements of S.

From this monad $\mathcal{M}$ on $\mathcal{E}\mathit{ns}$, can we reconstruct the original adjunction $\mathcal{G}\mathit{roup} \rightleftarrows \mathcal{E}\mathit{ns}$ and in particular recover the category $\mathcal{G}\mathit{roup}$? The answer is both a resounding "Yes!" and a definitive "No!"

To see the "yes", note that a group can be described as a set S, with "a way of evaluating within S all abstract group-theoretic combinations of its elements", i.e., a map $\alpha\colon M(S) \to S$. One finds that the conditions α must satisfy for such a formal evaluation procedure really to be a group structure are the commutativity of the diagrams:

(3)
$$\begin{array}{ccc} S & \xrightarrow{\eta(S)} & M(S) \\ & {\scriptstyle 1_S}\searrow & \downarrow{\scriptstyle \alpha} \\ & & S \end{array} \qquad\qquad \begin{array}{ccc} M(M(S)) & \xrightarrow{1_M \cdot \alpha} & M(S) \\ \downarrow{\scriptstyle \mu(S)} & & \downarrow{\scriptstyle \alpha} \\ M(S) & \xrightarrow{\alpha} & S \end{array}$$

To see the "no," let $t.f.\mathcal{G}p.$ denote the category of torsion-free groups, and note that the forgetful functor $t.f.\mathcal{G}p. \to \mathcal{E}\mathit{ns}$ also has the free group construction as left adjoint. This adjunction clearly yields the same monad on $\mathcal{E}\mathit{ns}$ that we have just considered; so the monad $\mathcal{M}$ does *not* uniquely determine the adjoint pair, and in particular, the other category of that pair.

The general situation is this: Given a monad $\mathcal{M} = (M, \eta, \mu)$ on a category $\mathcal{C}$, we may form a category whose objects are pairs (S, α), S an object of $\mathcal{C}$, α a morphism $M(S) \to S$ satisfying (3), and whose morphisms are object-maps making the obvious square commute. This is called the category of "algebras with respect to $\mathcal{M}$" and denoted $\mathcal{C}^{\mathcal{M}}$, and we get an adjunction

(4)
$$\mathcal{C}^{\mathcal{M}} \underset{(M(S),\, \mu(S)) \leftarrow\!\shortmid S}{\overset{(S,\, \alpha) \mapsto S}{\rightleftarrows}} \mathcal{C},$$

which is in an appropriate sense (§7 below) *universal* among adjoint pairs inducing $\mathcal{M}$ on $\mathcal{C}$. It is *not* the *unique* pair inducing $\mathcal{M}$; nonetheless many of the most important adjoint pairs are related to their monads in this manner.

In particular, any variety $\mathcal{A}$ of algebras is equivalent to $\mathcal{E}\mathit{ns}^{\mathcal{M}}$, where $\mathcal{M}$ is the monad on $\mathcal{E}\mathit{ns}$ induced by the underlying/free adjunction $\mathcal{A} \rightleftarrows \mathcal{E}\mathit{ns}$. In fact, there is a 1-1 correspondence between monads $\mathcal{M}$ on $\mathcal{E}\mathit{ns}$ and varieties of algebras! Given a monad $\mathcal{M}$, $\mathcal{E}\mathit{ns}^{\mathcal{M}}$ can be made a variety whose n-ary operations are the elements of $M(n)$, for each n. (Again, of course, in particular cases one may have much smaller *generating* sets of operations.) The identities, i.e., the rules for composing operations, are given by μ.

Actually, some set-theoretic qualifications are needed here. A precise statement is that monads on $\mathcal{E}ns$ correspond to varieties of algebras which *may* have infinitary operations (n must range through all cardinals, in the preceding statement) and whose operations may even form a proper class; but such that there are only a set of distinct derived operations of each arity. Varieties of "finitary" algebras correspond to those monads $\mathcal{M}$ such that for all $S \in \mathcal{E}ns$, $M(S) \cong \operatorname{colim}_{S_0 \text{ finite}, \subseteq S} M(S_0)$.

We can now give yet another view of our construction of the "structure" on a representable functor $V = \operatorname{Hom}(R, —)\colon \mathcal{A} \to \mathcal{E}ns$ ($\mathcal{A}$ a category with coproducts). The auxiliary variety $\mathcal{B}$ through which we factored V was precisely $\mathcal{E}ns^{\mathcal{M}}$, where $\mathcal{M}$ is the monad on $\mathcal{E}ns$ induced by V and its left adjoint F.

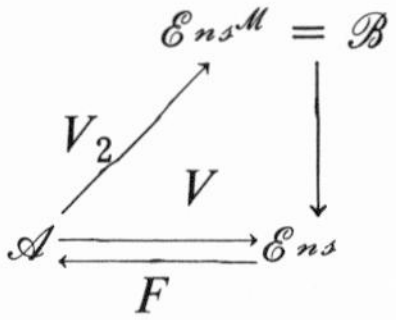

(This is imprecise because we only considered algebraic structure based on finitary operations in preceding sections. We may correct this by (a) allowing infinitary operations in our earlier discussions; or (b) replacing $\mathcal{M}$ by the submonad $\mathcal{M}_{\text{fin}}$, where $M_{\text{fin}}(S) = \operatorname{colim} M(S_0)$, thus discarding infinitary operations; or (c) if $\mathcal{A}$ is a variety, and the object R representing V is finitely generated, as was true for $\mathbf{Z}_2$ in groups, by noting that then $\mathcal{M} = \mathcal{M}_{\text{fin}}$, so in this case there is no problem.)

5. Higher structure. We have seen that the categories of algebras with respect to monads on $\mathcal{E}ns$ are varieties of algebras in the traditional sense. What, then, will we get if we *start* with a variety $\mathcal{C}$ of algebras and a monad $\mathcal{M}$ on $\mathcal{C}$, and form the category of algebras $\mathcal{C}^{\mathcal{M}}$?

It turns out that the objects of $\mathcal{C}^{\mathcal{M}}$ can be described as sets endowed with, *in addition* to the operations of $\mathcal{C}$, certain *partial* operations, and subject, in addition to the identities of $\mathcal{C}$, to certain "partial identities". Explicitly, if $A \in \operatorname{Ob}(\mathcal{C})$ is an object definable by generators $X_1, \ldots, X_n$ and a system of relations $r(X)$, then each element of $M(A)$ induces a partial operation on the objects $B \in \mathcal{C}^{\mathcal{M}}$, whose domain is the set of all n-tuples $(x_1, \ldots, x_n) \in |B|^n$ satisfying $r(x)$. (Thus the domains of these "second-stage" operations are defined with the help of the "first-stage" operations, those of $\mathcal{C}$.) Likewise, the map $\mu\colon M(M(A)) \to A$ gives identities in these partial (and total) operations which must be satisfied by all n-tuples satisfying r.

Again, for illustration consider the functor $V_1 = \operatorname{Hom}(\mathbf{Z}_2, —)\colon \mathcal{G}roup \to \mathcal{E}ns$, and its lifting $V_2\colon \mathcal{G}roup \to \mathcal{I}nv$ ($\mathcal{I}nv$ = the variety of involution algebras). V_2 has a left adjoint F_2, so this adjoint pair will induce a monad $\mathcal{M}_2$ on $\mathcal{I}nv \cdots$.

What does this mean concretely? An involution algebra A gives in a natural manner generators and relations for a certain group $F_2(A)$—exponent 2-generators, and conjugacy relations among these. This group can be characterized as having a universal map of involution algebras $A \xrightarrow{\eta_2(A)} V_2F_2(A)$. Now if our definition of "involution algebra" were a really complete picture of the structure of the sets of elements of exponent 2 in groups, we would expect the maps $\eta_2(A)$ to be isomorphisms. (Or if you don't buy that, let us just say it is natural, in studying elements of exponent 2 in groups, to ask whether this map will be an isomorphism.)

But η_2 is in general neither injective nor surjective. For example, let A be the involution algebra defined by two generators X, Y and one relation $X^Y = X$. One finds that A has underlying set $\{e, X, Y, Y^X\}$. $F_2(A)$ will be the group on generators X, Y and relations $X^2 = Y^2 = e$, $Y^{-1}XY = X$.

The latter relation says that X and Y commute, so $F_2(A)$ is the fours-group, with underlying set $\{e, X, Y, XY\}$, and all its elements have exponent 2. Hence the map $\eta_2(A)$ takes the form

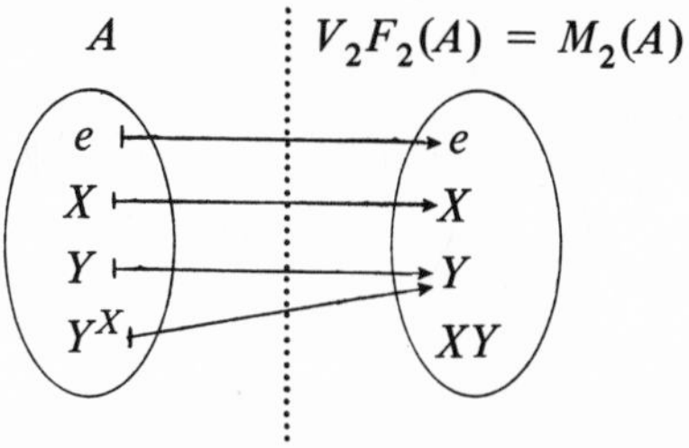

which is neither surjective nor injective. The "new" element XY in $M_2(A)$ leads to a partial binary operation on elements of exponent 2 in a group, associating to every pair (x, y) such that $x^y = x$ the element xy (which will have exponent 2 precisely because x and y commute). This operation is not definable in terms of conjugation.

The collapse of Y and Y^X in $M_2(A)$ likewise yields the "partial identity" (Horn sentence) holding in the involution algebra of any group, but not following from the full identities of involution algebras:

$$(\forall x, y)\ x^y = x \Rightarrow y^x = y.$$

If we gather together the partial operations and partial identities arising from the maps $\eta_2(A)$ for *all* $A \in \mathrm{Ob}(\mathcal{I}nv)$, and add these to our earlier list of operations and identities, we get axioms for what we may call a "second order involution algebra." In fact, the category $\mathcal{I}nv_2$ of second order involution algebras is precisely $\mathcal{I}nv_1^{\mathcal{M}_2} = (\mathcal{E}ns^{\mathcal{M}_1})^{\mathcal{M}_2}$. (I am now using the subscript 1 for "first order" involution algebras, i.e., what I previously just called involution algebras.) Since we get this additional structure on the objects $V_2(G)$ for any group G, we get a second factorization:

(5)

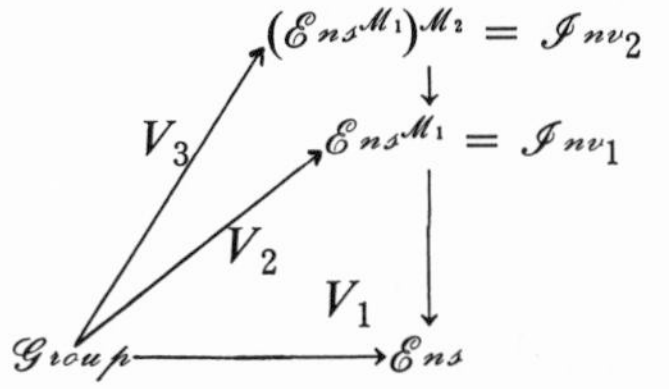

All this applies, mutatis mutandis to any representable set-valued functor V on a cocomplete category $\mathcal{A}$, in particular, on any variety $\mathcal{A}$ of algebras.

One can continue to iterate this process. At each step one obtains operations and identities whose *domains* are given by systems of equations in the previously constructed operations. The resulting diagram ((5) extended) is called the *adjoint tower* induced by the original functor V. The construction is due to Appelgate and Tierney; cf. [**12**].

Note that the problem of explicitly studying these classes of algebras is not one of general nonsense but, for instance, in the case $V_1 = \mathrm{Hom}(\mathbf{Z}_2, —)$, real group theory. I do not know, for example, whether $\mathscr{I}nv_2$ can be presented by finitely many partial operations and identities. I do not know whether at the *next* step one would find $\eta_3\colon A \to V_3F_3(A)$ always to be an isomorphism—in which case the tower would become constant after that point, and $\mathscr{I}nv_2$ would be equivalent to a full coreflective subcategory of $\mathscr{G}roup$, via F_3 and V_3—or not. Something positive that one *can* say in this case, because $\mathbf{Z}_2$ is finitely presented as a group, is that on the category $\mathscr{I}nv_\omega =_{\mathrm{def}} \lim_i) (\cdots \mathscr{E}ns^{\mathscr{M}_1})\cdots)^{\mathscr{M}_i}$ (the natural "ωth step of the adjoint tower")—sets with all the structure one gets at the finite steps, $\mathscr{I}nv_i$), the maps $\eta_\omega(A)$ will indeed be isomorphisms, and so $\mathscr{I}nv_\omega$ *is* equivalent to a full coreflective subcategory of $\mathscr{G}roup$. On the other hand, there *are* examples of adjoint towers of arbitrary transfinite height.

Let us note how Lawvere's approach to algebraic theories can be extended to these higher sorts of algebras. Given a category $\mathscr{A}$ with colimits, and an object R in $\mathscr{A}$, let $\mathscr{B}_i$ denote the category$((\cdots \mathscr{E}ns^{\mathscr{M}_1})\cdots)^{\mathscr{M}_i}$ arising at the ith level of the adjoint tower induced by Hom(R, —). We recall that $\mathscr{B}_1$, a variety, may be identified with the category of all product-respecting functors $T_1^{\mathrm{op}} \to \mathscr{E}ns$, where T_1 is the full subcategory of $\mathscr{A}$ having for object-set the coproducts of copies of R (in other words, the object-image of the adjoint $F_1\colon \mathscr{E}ns \to \mathscr{A}$. Again, if as in §2 we are interested only in finitary operations, we just use $\{F_1(n) \mid n < \omega\}$; and in fact if we make no such restriction at all there are set-theoretic worries; but we shall skip over these here). Likewise, to describe $\mathscr{B}_2$ let T_2 denote the full subcategory of all colimits in $\mathscr{A}$ of objects of T_1; then we find that $\mathscr{B}_2$ is equivalent to the category "$\mathscr{E}ns^{T_2^{\mathrm{op}}}$", where by this we mean all functors $T_2^{\mathrm{op}} \to \mathscr{E}ns$ respecting these (co)products and (co)limits. The object-set of $T_2 \subseteq \mathscr{A}$ can also be described as the image of $F_2\colon \mathscr{B}_1 \to \mathscr{A}$.

For instance, in our Z_2 example, T_2 contains not only the groups $\mathbf{Z}_2 \coprod \cdots \coprod \mathbf{Z}_2$ but also the difference-cokernel H:

$$\mathbf{Z}_2 \underset{t \mapsto x^y}{\overset{t \mapsto x}{\rightrightarrows}} \mathbf{Z}_2 \coprod \mathbf{Z}_2 \dashrightarrow H \text{ (the fours-group).}$$

Hence T_2 contains the map

$$\mathbf{Z}_2 \xrightarrow{t \mapsto xy} H$$

which induces in $\mathscr{B}_2$ the partial operation we discovered.

Note that given the "theory" of $\mathscr{I}nv_2$, either in the classical sense of a list of partial operations and identities, or in this Lawverian form, we can speak of "$\mathscr{I}nv_2$

-objects" in a general category. In particular, $\mathbf{Z}_2$ is now a co-$\mathcal{I}nv_2$-object in the category $\mathcal{G}roup$. (And in our general context, with $V_1 = \mathrm{Hom}(R, —)$, R will be a co-$\mathcal{B}_n$-object of $\mathcal{A}$ for all n.)

Lawvere's concept of the structure of a functor likewise generalizes naturally to this higher structure: In the formulation of that concept, where Lawvere took the full subcategory of the functor-category $\mathcal{C}^{\mathcal{A}}$ with object-set $\{V^n \mid n = 0, 1, \cdots\}$, one merely considers instead the full closure under (finite) limits of $\{V\}$ in $\mathcal{C}^{\mathcal{A}}$. For instance, our partial multiplication operation on $\mathrm{Hom}(\mathbf{Z}_2, —)$ now assumes the form of a morphism of functors $W \to V$, where $W \in \mathcal{E}ns^{\mathcal{G}roup}$ is the difference-kernel functor

$$W \dashrightarrow V^2 \underset{(x,\,y)\,\mapsto\, x^y}{\overset{(x,\,y)\,\mapsto\, x}{\rightrightarrows}} V.$$

6. Various examples and observations. The reader will find it instructive (and not too difficult) to describe completely the adjoint towers associated with the following functors: the underlying set functor of an arbitrary variety of algebras; the underlying set functor of the category (quasi-variety) of torsion-free groups; (example of A. Stone); the functor $\mathrm{Hom}(2, —)$: $\mathcal{P}oset \to \mathcal{E}ns$, where $2 \in \mathrm{Ob}(\mathcal{P}oset)$ is the chain of length 1, the same example with $\mathcal{C}at$, the category of small categories, in place of $\mathcal{P}oset$. (For 2 is also a category. Cf. [**13**, Q13].)

(From the torsion-free groups example one can generalize to get a characterization of quasi-varieties and semivarieties as certain categories of the form $(\mathcal{E}ns^{\mathcal{M}_1})^{\mathcal{M}_2}$.)

Suppose A, B, C are associative rings with 1, given with maps $A \to B$, $A \to C$. Then for any right B-module M and right C-module N, we can form $\mathrm{Hom}_A(M, N)$, getting a functor V: $(\mathcal{M}od\ B)^{\mathrm{op}} \times (\mathcal{M}od\ C) \to \mathcal{E}ns$ (not representable in the sense we have been considering). Through universal tricks, one can determine the structure of V in the sense of Lawvere: It is that of a $B \odot_A C$-module, where $B \odot_A C = \{x \in B \otimes_A C \mid \forall a \in A,\ ax = xa\}$, made a ring in a certain natural manner discovered by M. Sweedler. There can also be higher structure.

If we start with a *family* of objects $(R_i)_{i \in I}$ in a category $\mathcal{A}$, they induce a functor $(\mathrm{Hom}(R_i, —))_{i \in I}$: $\mathcal{A} \to \mathcal{E}ns^I$, which we can examine for structure of *many-sorted algebra.* In the category $\mathcal{H}\mathcal{T}op^{\cdot}$ of pointed topological spaces with homotopy classes of maps, the family of spheres, $(S^i)_{i \in N}$ induces the functor π_*: $\mathcal{H}\mathcal{T}op^{\cdot} \to \mathcal{E}ns^N$. The structure of this functor includes not only the group structures of each homotopy group π_n, but also operations between different degrees, e.g., the "Whitehead products" $\pi_m \times \pi_n \to \pi_{m+n-1}$, induced by maps $S^{m+n-1} \to S^m \coprod S^n$.

For applications of ideas related to those of this article to the foundations of algebraic geometry and differential geometry, see [**6**, pp. 146–244], [**9**], [**10**], [**11**]; for applications to measure theory, see [**17**].

By duality, one can apply the ideas we have discussed to representable contravariant functors. For instance, the (finitary) structure on the functor $\mathrm{Hom}(—, 2)$: $\mathcal{P}oset \to \mathcal{E}ns$ turns out to be precisely that of *distributive lattices.* (*Exercise.* Examine similarly $\mathrm{Hom}(—, 2)$: $\mathcal{E}ns \to \mathcal{E}ns$ and $\mathrm{Hom}(—, 2)$: $\mathcal{B}ool\mathcal{A}lg \to \mathcal{E}ns$.)

If one is interested in *relational* structure as well as *operations* on the values of a functor V, one should look not only at the morphisms among the V^n but also at their subfunctors. If V is the covariant (contravariant) representable functor determined by an object R, an important class of subfunctors of V^n are those induced by epimorphisms $R \coprod \dots \coprod R \to S$ (resp. by subobjects $S \subseteq R \times \dots \times R$).

EXAMPLES. If $\mathscr{DL}$ is the category of distributive lattices, the functor Hom(—, 2): $\mathscr{DL} \to \mathscr{E}\mathit{ns}$ has trivial finitary algebraic structure in the sense of Lawvere, but its finitary representable relational structure is precisely that of partially ordered sets, with "$\leqq$" induced by its graph, $3 \subseteq 2 \times 2$. The underlying set functor Hom(1, —): $\mathscr{P}\mathit{oset} \to \mathscr{E}\mathit{ns}$ likewise has no operations (so the adjoint tower construction will not get anywhere with it, in contrast to Hom(2, —)), but the relation "$\leqq$" is induced by the epimorphism $1 \coprod 1 \to 2$.

Exercise. The functor Hom($\mathbf{Z}_2$, —): $\mathscr{G}\mathit{roup} \to \mathscr{E}\mathit{ns}$ also has representable relational structure not induced by its operations. What does this say in elementary group-theoretic terms? If you are a group-theorist, find an example.

I mentioned that a monad on $\mathscr{E}\mathit{ns}$ could correspond to a variety of algebras with a proper *class* of operations, not generated by any *set* of them. An example, noted by Linton [**15**, p. 90], and studied by Manes [**6**, pp. 91–118], is the monad $\mathscr{M}$ arising from the adjunction

$$\mathscr{C}\mathit{pct}\mathscr{H}\mathit{aus} \underset{\text{Stone-Čech}}{\overset{\text{underlying set}}{\rightleftarrows}} \mathscr{E}\mathit{ns}$$

($\mathscr{C}\mathit{pct}\mathscr{H}\mathit{aus}$ = compact Hausdorff spaces). As Manes shows, the lifting functor V_2: $\mathscr{C}\mathit{pct}\mathscr{H}\mathit{aus} \to \mathscr{E}\mathit{ns}^{\mathscr{M}}$ is an equivalence of categories, so compact Hausdorff spaces may be regarded as a variety of (*very* infinitary) algebras.

A variety of infinitary algebras which does *not* correspond to a monad on $\mathscr{E}\mathit{ns}$ is that of complete Boolean algebras. For it has been shown [**5**], [**19**] that there is no free complete Boolean algebra on countably many generators. This is equivalent to saying that the $\aleph_0$-ary complete Boolean operations cannot be indexed by any set.

7. Mirror, mirror···. Let $\mathscr{A}\mathit{dj}$ denote the category of adjunctions $\mathscr{P} = (\mathscr{A}, \mathscr{C}; V, F; \eta, \varepsilon)$. Then the question with which we began §4, "Given an adjunction $\mathscr{P}$, if we forget the category $\mathscr{A}$ what can we 'remember' about $\mathscr{P}$ in terms of $\mathscr{C}$?" is really of the same nature as the question considered in §2. For it asks what "structure" can be put on the values of the forgetful functor:

$$\mathscr{A}\mathit{dj} \xrightarrow{\mathscr{V}_1:\ \mathscr{P} \mapsto \mathscr{C}} \mathscr{C}\mathit{at}.$$

The answer turned out to be: a structure of *monad*, giving a factorization:

(6)
$$\begin{array}{ccc} & & \mathscr{M}\mathit{on} \\ & \overset{\mathscr{V}_2}{\nearrow} & \downarrow \\ \mathscr{A}\mathit{dj} & \xrightarrow{\mathscr{V}_1} & \mathscr{C}\mathit{at} \end{array}$$

Of course, the definition of "algebraic structure" must be adjusted to the fact that we are working here with 2-categories, i.e., categories with morphisms between morphisms (e.g., natural transformations between functors, in $\mathcal{C}at$). Cf. Lawvere [**6**, pp. 141–155].

Let us think of the objects of $\mathcal{M}on$ as 4-tuples, $\mathcal{M} = (\mathcal{C}; M, \eta, \varepsilon)$. The construction from a monad $\mathcal{M}$ of the category of algebras $\mathcal{C}^{\mathcal{M}}$, and thence of the adjunction (4), is actually a right adjoint to the functor $\mathcal{V}_2$ of (6). One would expect, rather, a left adjoint here. This also exists; it is called the Kleisli construction; the new category involved is written $\mathcal{C}_{\mathcal{M}}$ [**2**, §VI.5], e.g., if $\mathcal{M}$ is a monad on $\mathcal{E}ns$, so that $\mathcal{E}ns^{\mathcal{M}}$ is a variety of algebras, $\mathcal{E}ns_{\mathcal{M}}$ turns out to be equivalent to the full subcategory of free algebras in $\mathcal{E}ns^{\mathcal{M}}$, that is, to the theory of this variety.

Both of these adjoints to $\mathcal{V}_2$ are left inverses to it as well; so it does not appear that (6) will also show higher structure.

8. Acknowledgements. I am in particular debt to Peter Freyd and Saunders Mac Lane, as authors of [**1**] and [**2**], for introducing me to coalgebra-representable functors and monads respectively; to Arthur Stone for his great assistance in bringing me up to date on the state of the art; to the audience and chairperson at my lecture for their patience with a poorly prepared talk, and finally, to Sammy Eilenberg for his colorful criticism afterwards:

> "You sounded like a neophyte who at the age of 30 has just discovered sex, and is so enthusiastic he doesn't know where to begin! You should have made that example at the end [structure on Hom($\mathbf{Z}_2$, —)] the whole talk⋯."

which I have followed to a large extent in this write-up.

Bibliography—items cited in the text, and some further reading

1. Peter Freyd, *Algebra-valued functors in general and tensor products in particular*, Colloq. Math. **14** (1966), 89–106. MR **33** #4116. (There is a minor lapse in this otherwise fascinating paper: the confused treatment of "constant operations". They should be regarded simply as 0-ary operations, remembering that the (co)product of the empty family in a category is the terminal (initial) object.)

2. Saunders Mac Lane, *Categories for the working mathematician*, Graduate Texts in Math., no. 5, Springer-Verlag, New York, 1971.

3. F. William Lawvere, *Functorial semantics of algebraic theories*, Ph.D. Thesis, Columbia University, New York, 1963 (unpublished, but xerox-propagated, iv+113 pp.)

4. W. Edwin Clark and George M. Bergman, *The automorphism class group of the category of rings*, J. Algebra **24** (1973), 80–99. MR **47** #210.

5. A. W. Hales, *On the non-existence of free complete Boolean algebras*, Fund. Math. **54** (1964), 45–66. MR **29** #1162.

6. *Seminar on triples and categorical homology theory*, B. Eckmann (editor), Lecture Notes in Math., vol. 80, Springer-Verlag, Berlin and New York, 1969.

7. John R. Isbell, *General functorial semantics*, Amer. J. Math. **94** (1972), 535–596.

8. P. J. Freyd and G. M. Kelly, *Categories of continuous functors*. I, J. Pure Appl. Algebra **2** (1972), 169–191. MR **48** #369.

9. F. Ulmer, *Locally α-presentable and locally α-generated categories*, Reports of the Midwest

Category Seminar. V(Zürich, 1970), Lecture Notes in Math., vol. 195, Springer-Verlag, Berlin and New York, 1971, pp. 230–247. MR **45** #1990.

10. P. Gabriel and F. Ulmer, *Lokal präsentierbare Kategorien*, Lecture Notes in Math., vol. 221, Springer-Verlag, Berlin and New York, 1971.

11. H. Appelgate and M. Tierney, *Categories with models*, Sem. on Triples and Categorical Homology Theory (E.T.H., Zürich, 1966/67), Springer, Berlin, 1969, pp. 156–244. MR **39** #4243.

12. ———, *Iterated cotriples*, Reports of the Midwest Category Seminar. IV, Lecture Notes in Math., vol. 137, Springer-Verlag, Berlin and New York, 1970, pp. 56–99. MR **42** #338.

13. Phreilambud, *Categorically, the final examination*, Lecture Notes in Math., vol. 137, Springer-Verlag, Berlin and New York, 1970, pp. 138–139.

14. H. Schubert, *Categories*, Springer-Verlag, Berlin and New York, 1972.

15. F. E. J. Linton, *Some aspects of equational categories*, Proc. Conf. Categorical Algebra (La Jolla, 1965), Springer-Verlag, Berlin and New York, 1966, pp. 84–94.

16. ———, *Applied functorial semantics*. I, Ann. di Mat. Pura Appl. (IV) **86** (1970), 1–14.

17. ———, *Functorial measure theory*, Proc. Conf. Funct. Analysis (Irvine, 1966), Thompson, Washington D.C., 1968, pp. 36–49.

18. Jean Bénabou, *Structures algébriques dans les catégories*, Thèse, Paris, 1966.

19. Haim Gaifman, *Infinite Boolean polynomials*. I, Fund. Math. **54** (1964), 229–250.

20. John Kennison and Dion Gildenhuys, *Equational completion, model-induced triples, and pro-objects*, J. Pure and Appl. Alg. **1** (1971), 317–346.

University of California
Berkeley, California 94720, U.S.A.

Proceedings of the International Congress of Mathematicians
Vancouver, 1974

Orthodox Semigroups Which Are Unions of Groups

A. H. Clifford

A semigroup S is called *orthodox* if it is regular ($a \in aSa$ for all a in S) and if the set E_S of idempotents of S is a subsemigroup of S. A semigroup S which is a union of groups is evidently regular, and hence is orthodox if and only if E_S is a subsemigroup; such a semigroup will be called an *orthogroup*. The purpose of this article is to present a structure theorem for orthogroups which I believe is an improvement over those of P.H.H. Fantham [4] and G. B. Preston (1961, unpublished). A full account of these two theorems was given in [1].

1. Introduction. For the theory (prior to 1960) of semigroups which are unions of groups, we refer to [3, §4.2]. Any such is a semilattice of completely simple semigroups, and, by the Rees theorem [3, §3.2], any completely simple semigroup is a rectangular band of groups.

As a first corollary, we have McLean's theorem [7] that any band (= idempotent semigroup) is a semilattice of rectangular bands.

As a second corollary, every inverse semigroup which is a union of groups is a semilattice of groups, and conversely. Any such can be constructed as follows. Let Y be a semilattice, and to each element α of Y assign a group G_α such that G_α and G_β are disjoint if $\alpha \neq \beta$. To each pair of elements α, β of Y such that $\alpha \geqq \beta$, assign a homomorphism $\phi_{\alpha,\beta}\colon G_\alpha \to G_\beta$ such that:

(1.1) $\alpha \geqq \beta \geqq \gamma$ implies $\phi_{\alpha,\beta}\,\phi_{\beta,\gamma} = \phi_{\alpha,\gamma}$;

(1.2) $\phi_{\alpha,\alpha}$ is the identity automorphism of G_α.

Let $S = \bigcup \{G_\alpha\colon \alpha \in Y\}$, and define the product ab of two elements a, b of S as follows: if $a \in G_\alpha$ and $b \in G_\beta$, then

(2) $$ab = (a\phi_{\alpha,\alpha\beta})(b\phi_{\beta,\alpha\beta}).$$

Here $\alpha\beta$ is the product (= meet) of α and β in Y. We call $\{\phi_{\alpha,\beta}\colon \alpha \geqq \beta\}$ the set of *connecting homomorphisms* of S.

Using the Rees theorem, it is easily seen that any orthodox completely simple semigroup is the direct product $G \times E$ of a group G and a rectangular band E; such will be called a *rectangular group*. Consequently as a third corollary, we have (M. Yamada [**12**], [**13**]): Any orthogroup S is a semilattice Y of rectangular groups $S_\alpha = G_\alpha \times E_\alpha$ ($\alpha \in Y$). Conversely (Petrich [**9**, Lemma 1]), any semilattice of rectangular groups is an orthogroup.

2. Preston's theorem. Let $S = \bigcup \{S_\alpha : \alpha \in Y\}$, $S_\alpha = G_\alpha \times E_\alpha$, be an orthogroup. $E_S = \{(1_\alpha, e) : \alpha \in Y, e \in E_\alpha\}$, where 1_α is the identity element of G_α. We can evidently define a product on the set $E = \bigcup \{E_\alpha : \alpha \in Y\}$ such that $(1_\alpha, e_\alpha)(1_\beta, f_\beta) = (1_{\alpha\beta}, e_\alpha f_\beta)$, and hence making E into a band isomorphic with E_S. We may identify e_α with $(1_\alpha, e_\alpha)$, and thus E with E_S.

If $\alpha > \beta$ in Y, then $S_\alpha \cup S_\beta$ is evidently a two-component suborthogroup of S. Its structure is described as follows.

LEMMA. *Let* $S_\alpha = G_\alpha \times E_\alpha$ *and* $S_\beta = G_\beta \times E_\beta = G_\beta \times I_\beta \times \Lambda_\beta$ *be disjoint rectangular groups. Assume that there exist:*

(a) *a representation* $t = t_{\alpha,\beta}$ *of* S_α *by left transformations of* I_β (*i.e., acting on the left*),

(b) *a representation* $\tau = \tau_{\alpha,\beta}$ *of* S_α *by right transformations of* Λ_β, *and*

(c) *a homomorphism* $\phi = \phi_{\alpha,\beta}$ *of* G_α *into* G_β.

For A *in* S_α *and* $B = (b; i, \lambda)$ *in* S_β, *define*

$$AB = (a\phi \cdot b; (tA)i, \lambda), \tag{3.1}$$

$$BA = (b \cdot a\phi; i, \lambda(A\tau)). \tag{3.2}$$

With products so defined, and keeping the given ones in S_α *and* S_β, $S_\alpha \cup S_\beta$ *becomes an orthogroup having* S_β *as ideal. Conversely, this procedure gives every possible way of making* $S_\alpha \cup S_\beta$ *into an orthogroup with* S_β *as ideal.*

If we know how products are formed in E and in each "vertical pair" $S_\alpha \cup S_\beta$ ($\alpha > \beta$), then we know all products in S. For suppose $\alpha, \beta \in Y$, $A = (a, e) \in S_\alpha$ and $B = (b, f) \in S_\beta$. Identifying e with $(1_\alpha, e)$, etc., $Ae = A$ and $fB = B$. Since $(ef)^2 = ef$,

$$AB = Aefb = A(ef)\cdot(ef)B. \tag{4}$$

Since $\alpha \geqq \alpha\beta$ and $\beta \geqq \alpha\beta$, and $ef \in E_{\alpha\beta}$, the products $A(ef)$ and $(ef)B$ are vertical, and both belong to $S_{\alpha\beta}$.

Preston's theorem [**1**, p. 288] essentially asserts that every orthogroup can be constructed in the following way. Let $E = \bigcup \{E_\alpha : \alpha \in Y\}$ be a band, expressed as a semilattice Y of rectangular bands E_α. To each α in Y assign a group G_α, and let $S_\alpha = G_\alpha \times E_\alpha$. Assume that for each pair $\alpha > \beta$ in Y there exist the items $t_{\alpha,\beta}$, $\tau_{\alpha,\beta}$, $\phi_{\alpha,\beta}$ of the lemma, so that "vertical products" AB and BA can be defined by (3.1) and (3.2). Assume furthermore that, for all α, β, γ in Y such that $\alpha > \beta > \gamma$,

$$\phi_{\alpha,\gamma} = \phi_{\alpha,\beta}\,\phi_{\beta,\gamma}, \tag{5}$$

(6.1) $$t_{\beta,\gamma}(AB) = (t_{\alpha,\gamma}A)(t_{\beta,\gamma}B),$$
(6.2) $$t_{\beta,\gamma}(BA) = (t_{\beta,\gamma}B)(t_{\alpha,\gamma}A),$$
(6.3) $$(AB)\tau_{\beta,\gamma} = (A\tau_{\alpha,\beta})(B\tau_{\beta,\gamma}),$$
(6.4) $$(BA)\tau_{\beta,\gamma} = (B\tau_{\beta,\gamma})(A\tau_{\alpha,\gamma}).$$

If we then define product for any two elements A, B of S by (4), $S = \bigcup \{S_\alpha : \alpha \in Y\}$ becomes an orthogroup.

On letting $\phi_{\alpha,\alpha}$ denote the identity automorphism of G_α, we see from (1.1), (1.2), and (5) that $Q = \bigcup \{G_\alpha : \alpha \in Y\}$ is a semilattice of groups if product is defined by (2). Clearly the mapping $(a, e) \mapsto a$ defines a surjective homomorphism of S onto Q. Moreover, $Q \cong S/\mathscr{Y}$, where, for any orthodox semigroup T, $\mathscr{Y}$ is the finest congruence on T such that $T/\mathscr{Y}$ is an inverse semigroup. It is convenient to regard S as an "orthodox extension" of the band E by the inverse orthogroup Q.

If we think of E and Q as given, they must have the same structure semilattice, but are otherwise arbitrary. M. Yamada [**12**], [**13**] defined the *spined product* Sp(Q, E) of Q and E to be the set $\bigcup \{G_\alpha \times E_\alpha : \alpha \in Y\}$ with product defined by $(a_\alpha, e_\alpha)(b_\beta, f_\beta) = (a_\alpha b_\beta, e_\alpha f_\beta)$, and showed that a semigroup is an orthodox band of groups if and only if it is the spined product of a semilattice of groups and a band.

In general, if $\phi_1 : S_1 \to T$ and $\phi_2 : S_2 \to T$ are homomorphisms, the spined product of S_1 and S_2 relative to ϕ_1 and ϕ_2 is defined to be the subsemigroup of their direct product $S_1 \times S_2$ consisting of all pairs (s_1, s_2) such that $s_1\phi_1 = s_2\phi_2$. Sp(Q, E) is the spined product of Q and E relative to the natural homomorphisms $Q \to Y$ and $E \to Y$.

If we regard Q, and hence the connecting homomorphisms $\phi_{\alpha,\beta}$, as given a priori, as well as E, then, by Preston's theorem all that remains is to find representations $t_{\alpha,\beta}$ and $\tau_{\alpha,\beta}$ satisfying (6). It is unfortunate that all vertical products AB must be defined before the conditions can be applied. Fantham's theorem [**4**], [**1**, p. 310] does not have this disadvantage, but it has others; for example, it does not bring out the semilattice of groups Q. (For further discussion, see [**1**, p. 336].)

3. The new theorem. Thanks to a remarkable structure theorem for orthodox semigroups due to T. E. Hall [**6**], I was able to find a structure theorem for othogroups which keeps the general form of Preston's theorem, reduces the four conditions (6) to a single condition (9), and expresses this condition on the basic materials before product is defined. Details will be given in [**2**]. The proof there, however, does not use Hall's theorem, but is based on the "theorem of vertical associativity" [**1**, p. 302]. A variant of the theorem is also given in [**2**] which has the general form of Fantham's theorem.

Let $E = \bigcup \{E_\alpha : \alpha \in Y\}$ be any band. Generalizing a well-known construction due to W. D. Munn [**8**], Hall [**6**] constructs a fundamental orthodox semigroup $W(E)$ such that $E_{W(E)} \cong E$. We may identify Y with the semilattice of idempotents of $\bar{W}(E) = W(E)/\mathscr{Y}$. Let Q be any inverse semigroup with $E_Q \cong Y$. Let $\phi : Q \to \bar{W}(E)$ be any homomorphism that induces an isomorphism of E_Q onto Y. Then Hall's theorem asserts that the spined product Sp(Q, $W(E)$, ϕ) of Q and

$W(E)$ relative to $\psi: Q \to \bar{W}(E)$ and $\mathscr{Y}^\natural: W(E) \to \bar{W}(E)$ is an orthodox semigroup; and, conversely, every orthodox semigroup S can be obtained in this way for some ψ, taking $E = E_S$ and $Q = S/\mathscr{Y}$.

Applied to orthogroups, $W(E)$ can be replaced by the greatest full suborthogroup $K(E)$ of $W(E)$, the existence of which was communicated to me by Dr. Hall. Q is now a semilattice of groups, and likewise $\bar{K}(E) = K(E)/\mathscr{Y}$.

Thanks to a reformulation of Hall's $W(E)$ due to P. A. Grillet [**5**], I was able to calculate explicitly the structure of $K(E)$ and $\bar{K}(E)$. For each e in E, let K_e be the group of all automorphisms of the band eEe which leave invariant the sets $E_\alpha \cap eEe$. For each α in Y, select and fix a representative element u_α of E_α, and write K_α for K_{u_α}. Then $\bar{K}(E)$ is isomorphic with the semilattice Y of groups K_α ($\alpha \in Y$) with set $\{\chi_{\alpha,\beta}: \alpha \geqq \beta\}$ of connecting homomorphisms defined as follows. For each σ in K_α and each x in $u_\beta E u_\beta$, define

(7) $$x(\sigma\chi_{\alpha,\beta}) = u_\beta\cdot(u_\alpha x u_\alpha)\sigma\cdot u_\beta.$$

Let $Q = \bigcup \{G_\alpha: \alpha \in Y\}$ be any semilattice of groups based on Y. By a remark made by Fantham [**4**], every homomorphism $\psi: Q \to \bar{K}(E)$ which respects Y is obtained from a set $\{\psi_\alpha: \alpha \in Y\}$ of homomorphisms $\psi_\alpha: G_\alpha \to K_\alpha$ such that

(8) $$\psi_\alpha\chi_{\alpha,\beta} = \phi_{\alpha,\beta}\psi_\beta \quad \text{for all } \alpha \geqq \beta \text{ in } Y.$$

(As Fantham observes, we may regard Y as a small category with a single morphism $\alpha \to \beta$ if $\alpha \geqq \beta$, and the systems $\{G_\alpha, \phi_{\alpha,\beta}\}$ and $\{K_\alpha, \chi_{\alpha,\beta}\}$ as functors from Y to the category of groups. Then (8) asserts that the system $\{\psi_\alpha\}$ is a natural transformation from the G-functor to the K-functor.)

We can combine (7) and (8) into the condition that

(9) $$x(a\phi_{\alpha,\beta}\psi_\beta) = u_\beta\cdot(u_\alpha x u_\alpha)(a\psi_\alpha)\cdot u_\beta$$

for all $\alpha \geqq \beta$ in Y, all a in G_α, and all x in $u_\beta E u_\beta$.

THEOREM. *With E and Q given as above, let $\psi_\alpha: G_\alpha \to K_\alpha$ be a homomorphism, for each α in Y, and assume that* (9) *holds. Let $S_\alpha = G_\alpha \times E_\alpha$ and $S = \bigcup \{S_\alpha: \alpha \in Y\}$. For α, β in Y, (a, e) in S_α and (b, f) in S_β, define $(a, e)(b, f) = (ab, \bar{e}\bar{f})$ where ab is the product* (2) *of a and b in Q,*

$$\bar{e} = e(u_\alpha efeu_\alpha)(a^{-1}\psi_\alpha)e, \qquad \bar{f} = f(u_\beta fefu_\beta)(b\psi_\beta)f,$$

and $\bar{e}\bar{f}$ is the product of $\bar{e}$ and $\bar{f}$ in $E_{\alpha\beta}$. Then S is an orthogroup which is an orthodox extension of E by Q, and every such can be obtained in this way.

Structure theorems for orthogroups have also been given recently by M. Yamada [**14**], R. J. Warne [**15**, Theorem 3.1] and M. Petrich [**11**, Theorem 5]. These are quite different from the foregoing, and from each other.

References

1. A. H. Clifford, *The structure of orthodox unions of groups*, Semigroup Forum **3** (1971/72), no. 4, 283–337. MR **46** #275.

2. ———, *A structure theorem for orthogroups*, J. Pure Appl. Algebra (to appear).

3. A. H. Clifford and G. B. Preston, *The algebraic theory of semigroups*. Vol. 1, Math. Surveys, no. 7, Amer. Math. Soc., Providence, R.I., 1961. MR **24** #A2627.

4. P. H. H. Fantham, *On the classification of a certain type of semigroup*, Proc. London Math. Soc. (3) **10** (1960), 409–427. MR **22** #12149.

5. P. A. Grillet, *An alternate construction of Hall's semigroup* $W(E)$, Semigroup Forum (to appear).

6. T. E. Hall, *Orthodox semigroups*, Pacific J. Math. **39** (1971), 677–686. MR **46** #5496.

7. D. McLean, *Idempotent semigroups*, Amer. Math. Monthly **61** (1954), 110–113. MR **15**, 681.

8. W. D. Munn, *Fundamental inverse semigroups*, Quart. J. Math. Oxford Ser. (2) **21** (1970), 157–170. MR **41** #7010.

9. M. Petrich, *Semigroups certain of whose subsemigroups have identities*, Czechoslovak Math. J. **16** **(91)** (1966), 186–198. MR **34** #266.

10. ———, *Topics in semigroups*, Lecture Notes, Pennsylvania State University, 1967.

11. ———, *The structure of completely regular semigroups*, Trans. Amer. Math. Soc. **189** (1974), 211–236.

12. M. Yamada, *Strictly inversive semigroups*, Bull. Shimane Univ. Nat. Sci. No. 13 (1963), 128–138.

13. ———, *Inversive semigroups*. I, Proc. Japan Acad. **39** (1963), 100–103. MR **27** #2573a.

14. ———, *Construction of inversive semigroups*, Mem. Fac. Lit. & Sci., Shimane Univ., Nat. Sci. **4** (1971), 1–9.

15. R. J. Warne, *On the structure of semigroups which are unions of groups*, Trans. Amer. Math. Soc. **186** (1973), 385–401; Semigroup Forum **5** (1972/73), 323–330. MR **48** #2286.

TULANE UNIVERSITY
NEW ORLEANS, LOUISIANA 70118, U.S.A.

Proceedings of the International Congress of Mathematicians
Vancouver, 1974

A Survey of Some Results on Free Resolutions*

David Eisenbud**

Consider the task of solving a system of linear homogeneous equations of rank r in n variables over a field K or, equivalently, of finding the kernel of a homomorphism of rank r of vector spaces: $K^n \to K^m$. As everyone knows, three facts make this process simple:

(0) There are $n - r$ linearly independent solutions which span the space of solutions.

(1) It is easy to tell whether a given set of solutions spans all the solutions: It does if and only if it spans a space of dimension $n - r$. Equivalently, if $\psi : K^p \to K^n$ is a map such that $\varphi\psi = 0$, then

$$K^p \xrightarrow{\psi} \psi K^n \xrightarrow{\varphi_0} K^m$$

is exact if and only if rank $\psi = n - r$.

(2) There is a "formula," in terms of the minors of φ, for a map ψ making the above sequence exact: For example, ψ can be taken as the map

$$\wedge^r K^{m*} \otimes \wedge^{r+1} K^n \xrightarrow{\psi_0} K^n$$

induced by φ. (Here * denotes $\mathrm{Hom}_K(—, K)$.)

In this note we will sketch some results from the theory of finite free resolutions which are analogues of (0), (1), (2) for rings more general than fields. We will also outline a technique for dealing with finite free resolutions that does not seem to have an interesting vector space analogue, and exhibit one of the interesting phenomena that arise when one works with infinite instead of with finite resolutions.

Throughout this paper, R will be a local Noetherian ring (the restrictions could

---

*This paper was prepared in collaboration with David A. Buchsbaum who was partially supported by the NSF.

**Partially supported by the Sloan Foundation and by the NSF.

be largely relaxed) and all modules will be finitely generated R-modules.

I. Some analogues. A map $F_1 \xrightarrow{\varphi_1} F_0$ of free R-modules (which may be considered as a system of homogeneous linear equations over R) will not in general have any of the nice properties (0), (1), (2). Because (0) may fail, a study of the solutions to the equations φ_1 must include a study of the dependence relations between the elements of a minimal set of solutions which spans all the solutions; that is, "solving" the equations must be taken to mean finding a whole free resolution

$$\boldsymbol{F}\colon \cdots F_3 \xrightarrow{\varphi_3} F_2 \xrightarrow{\varphi_2} F_1 \xrightarrow{\varphi_1} F_0$$

of coker φ_1. Once this has been said, there is an analogue of (0) holding for "nice" local rings.

THEOREM (AUSLANDER-BUCHSBAUM-SERRE). *If R is a regular local ring of dimension d, and $\boldsymbol{F}$ is a free resolution as above, with* rank $\varphi_i = r_i$, *then for all $i \geqq d - 1$,* ker φ_i *is spanned by* (rank F_i) $- r_i$ *linearly independent solutions; in other words* ker φ_i *is free. (Here as always the* rank *of φ_i is the largest integer r with $\wedge^r \varphi_i \neq 0$.)*

Since "solving a system of equations" means finding a free resolution, it is clear that the analogue of property (1) of the introduction should be a criterion for exactness of a complex of free modules:

$$\boldsymbol{G}\colon \cdots \xrightarrow{\varphi_3} G_2 \xrightarrow{\varphi_2} G_1 \xrightarrow{\varphi_1} G_0.$$

In general, no such criterion is known, but there is such a criterion if $\boldsymbol{G}$ is finite—that is, if $G_i = 0$ for $i \gg 0$. We need one more definition before we can state it: If $\varphi\colon F \to G$ is a map of free modules with rank $\varphi = r$, we define $I(\varphi)$ to be the ideal generated by the $r \times r$ minors of φ. Intrinsically put, $I(\varphi)$ is the image of the map

$$\wedge^r G^* \otimes \wedge^r F \to \wedge^0 G = R$$

induced by φ.

To state the theorem we must also recall that the *grade* of a proper ideal I of R is by definition the length of a maximal R-sequence in I. If $I = R$, we make the convention grade $I = \infty$. Or, simply define

$$\text{grade } I = \inf\{g \mid \operatorname{Ext}^g(R/I, R) \neq 0\}.$$

THEOREM [**B-E 1**]. *With the above notations, suppose that $G_i = 0$ for $i \gg 0$. Then G is exact if and only if for each $k \geqq 1$*

(1) $$\text{rank } \varphi_{k+1} + \text{rank } \varphi_k = \text{rank } G_k,$$

(2) $$\text{grade } I(\varphi_k) \geqq k.$$

The situation with regard to an analogue of property (2) of the introduction is both more complicated and less satisfactory. Given a map $\varphi\colon F \to G$ of rank r, we may still construct the map $\psi_0\colon \wedge^r G^* \otimes \wedge^{r+1} F \to F$, and we will still have $\varphi\psi_0 = 0$. It is easy to see, however, that

$$\wedge^r G^* \otimes \wedge^{r+1} F \xrightarrow{\psi_0} F \xrightarrow{\varphi} G$$

need not be exact. (If rank $G = r$, this sequence is exact if and only if grade $I(\varphi) =$ rank $F) - r + 1$, the largest possible value; see [**B-R**].) It is even easy to give examples of maps φ_i such that if $F_2 \xrightarrow{\varphi_2} F_1 \xrightarrow{\varphi_1} F_0$ is exact, then the ideal generated by the entries of a matrix for φ_2 is not contained in the ideal generated by the entries of a matrix for φ, so that φ_2 cannot be derived from φ_1 by a "formula" in any ordinary sense. To get an idea of what sort of thing might be true about the relation of φ_1 to φ_2, consider the following very useful theorem, which was proved in a special case by Hilbert, and extended to the general case by Burch [**Bur**]. This theorem has been a model for much of the work on finite free resolutions; it gives a sort of parametrization of ideals of projective dimension 1 which has been applied, for instance, to the study of deformations, residual complete intersections, factoriality, and the Zariski-Lipman conjecture.

THEOREM (HILBERT-BURCH). *Let*

$$\mathbf{F}: 0 \to R^{n-1} \xrightarrow{\varphi_2} R^n \xrightarrow{\varphi_1} R$$

be a complex. $\mathbf{F}$ *is exact if and only if* $\mathbf{F}$ *is isomorphic to a complex of the form*

$$0 \to R^{n-1} \xrightarrow{\varphi_2} R^n \xrightarrow{\varphi_1'} R$$

where φ_1' *is the composite map*

$$R^n \cong \wedge^{n-1} R^{n*} \xrightarrow{\wedge^{n-1}\varphi_2^*} \wedge^{n-1} R^{n-1*} \overset{can}{\cong} R \xrightarrow{a} R, \quad (\text{composite } \varphi_1')$$

where a is a non-zero-divisor, rank $\varphi_2 = n - 1$, *and* grade $I(\varphi_2) = 2$.

The essential point of this theorem is that if $\mathbf{F}$ is exact, there is a factorization of φ_1 through $\wedge^{n-1} \varphi_2^*$. Noting that rank $\varphi_1 = 1$, we see that the following theorem extends this result to a result for all finite free resolutions:

THEOREM ([**B-E 2**], [**E-N**]). *Let* $\mathbf{F}: 0 \to F_n \xrightarrow{\varphi_n} \cdots \xrightarrow{\varphi_1} F_0$ *be a finite free resolution, and set* $r_k =$ rank φ_k. *Then there are unique maps* $a_k: R \to \wedge^{r_k} F_{k-1}$ *such that the diagrams*

$$\begin{array}{ccc}
\wedge^{r_k} F_k & \xrightarrow{\wedge^{r_k}\varphi_k} & \wedge^{r_k} F_{k-1} \\
can \wr\| & & \\
\wedge^{r_{k+1}} F_k^* & & \nearrow a_k \\
 & \searrow a_{k+1}^* & \\
 & R &
\end{array}$$

commute. (The canonical isomorphisms exist because $r_k + r_{k+1} =$ *rank* F_k.) *Moreover,* a_n *is the composite*

$$R \cong \wedge^{r_n} F_n \xrightarrow{\wedge^{r_n}\varphi_n} \wedge^{r_n} F_{n-1},$$

and

$$\text{Rad } I(a_k) = \text{Rad } I(\varphi_k).$$

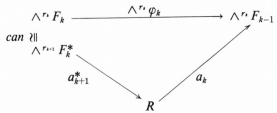

This extension of the Hilbert-Burch theorem is useful in several contexts; for example, it gives another proof of MacRae's strengthening of the theorem that a regular local ring is a unique factorization domain:

COROLLARY. *Let R be a local ring, I an ideal generated by 2 elements. If p.d. $R/I < \infty$, then p.d. $R/I \leqq 2$, and I is isomorphic to an ideal J generated by an R-sequence.*

PROOF [**B-E 2**]. Apply Theorem 2 to a finite free resolution

$$\cdots \to R^n \xrightarrow{\varphi_2} R^2 \xrightarrow{\varphi_1} R \to R/I \to 0,$$

obtaining a factorization

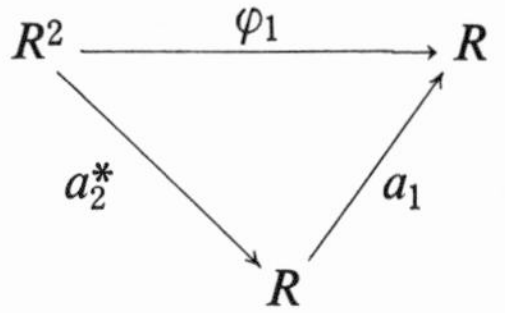

since a_2 also enters into a factorization of $\wedge^{r_2} \varphi_2$, $I(a_2^*) = J$ will be an ideal generated by an R-sequence x, y of length 2, and R/I will have a resolution of the form

$$0 \to R \xrightarrow{a_2} R^2 \xrightarrow{\varphi_1} R \to R/I \to 0. \quad \square$$

This theorem has recently been applied by Hochster [**Hoc**] to the construction of the "generic" free resolutions of length 2, which indicates that in a sense this theorem is a "complete" result for resolutions of length 2. However, for longer resolutions, or to achieve a direct generalization of the Hilbert-Burch theorem for ideals I with p.d. $I > 1$, more is needed. Since the "right" theorem of this type has not been found as yet, we content ourselves with an illustration of what may be done. See [**B-E 2**] for more results of this type.

THEOREM. *Let $0 \to F_n \xrightarrow{\varphi_n} F_{n-1} \xrightarrow{\varphi_{n-1}} F_{n-2} \to \cdots \to F_0$ be a free resolution, and set $r_k = \operatorname{rank} \varphi_k$. Then the map $\wedge^{r_{n-1}-i} \varphi_{n-1}$ can be factored through the dual of the map*

$$\wedge^i F_{n-1} \otimes \wedge^{r_n} F_n \xrightarrow{1 \otimes \wedge^{r_n} \varphi_n} \wedge^i F_{n-1} \otimes \wedge^{r_n} F_{n-1},$$

for $i \leqq n-2$.

II. Some new directions.

(A) *Algebra structures on free resolutions.* Let $\boldsymbol{F}$: $\cdots \to F_1 \to R$ be a free resolution of a cyclic module. The symmetric square $S_2(\boldsymbol{F})$ is a complex of free R-modules, and it agrees with $\boldsymbol{F}$ in degrees 0 and 1. There is thus a comparison map, unique up to homotopy, $S_2(\boldsymbol{F}) \xrightarrow{\nu} \boldsymbol{F}$, which may be regarded as equipping $\boldsymbol{F}$ with the structure of a (strictly skew-) commutative, homotopy-associative, differential graded algebra. We do not know whether ν may be chosen to make $\boldsymbol{F}$ associative as well, except in a few cases such as that of the minimal free resolution of the residue class field of R.

Using this idea, it is possible to obtain results like the Hilbert-Burch theorem for certain classes of resolutions of length 3. For example, suppose that

$$\begin{array}{cccccccc} F\colon 0 \longrightarrow & R & \longrightarrow & R^n & \xrightarrow{\varphi_1} & R^n & \xrightarrow{\varphi_2} & R \\ & \| & & \| & & \| & & \| \\ & F_3 & & F_2 & & F_1 & & F_0 \end{array}$$

is a minimal free resolution such that the complex $\boldsymbol{F}^* = \operatorname{Hom}(\boldsymbol{F}, R)$ is exact. (If R is a regular ring, and $\varphi_1\colon R^n \to R$, then coker φ_1 will have a minimal free resolution of this form if and only if coker φ_1 is a Gorenstein factor ring of R of codimension 3.) The algebra structure on $\boldsymbol{F}$ induces isomorphisms $F_i \to F^*_{3-i}$, and the commutativity of this algebra structure ensures that the composite map

$$F_1^* \longrightarrow F_2 \cong F_1 \quad (\text{composite } \varphi\colon F_1^* \to F_1)$$

is alternating. It turns out that n is odd and that im φ_1 is generated by the "principal $n-1 \times n-1$ pfaffians" of φ, from which one obtains a theorem parallel to the Hilbert-Burch theorem **[B-E 3]**.

It seems possible that this "multiplicative" technique, together, perhaps, with the idea of Liason of Peskine-Szpiro **[P-S]**, may eventually give structure theorems along the lines of the Hilbert-Burch theorem for all free resolutions of the form $\boldsymbol{F}\colon 0 \to F_3 \to F_2 \to F_1 \to R$ with $\boldsymbol{F}^*$ exact—that is, for all perfect ideals of grade 3. The first step in this program beyond the Gorenstein case is worked out in **[B-E 3]**.

(B) *A glimpse of the infinite case.* The only infinite free resolutions that have received much attention so far are the free resolutions of the residue class fields of (nonregular) local rings. As already remarked, these have the structure of associative algebras, and in fact they are free algebras, on generators of various degrees, about which much may be said (see **[G-L]** for an exposition). For our purposes we single out the following result:

THEOREM (BRAUER, GULLIKSEN). *Let R be a local ring, and let $\boldsymbol{F}\colon \cdots \to F_1 \to R \to k \to 0$ be a minimal free resolution of the residue class field k of R. Then the numbers $b_k =$* rank $\boldsymbol{F}$ *are bounded if and only if the maximal ideal of R is generated by at most $1 + \dim R$ elements. If this is so then $b_k = b$, a constant, for all $k \geqq 1 + \dim R$, and there are isomorphisms*

$$F_k \xrightarrow{\alpha_k} F_{k+2} \qquad (k \geqq 1 + \dim R)$$

such that

$$\varphi_{k+2} = \alpha_{k-1}\, \varphi_k\, \alpha_k^{-1} \qquad (k > 1 + \dim R).$$

In fact, something similar holds not only for the residue class field, but also for every module, and a little more is true. For the purpose of this theory we may harmlessly pass to the completion of R, after which, assuming that the maximal ideal of R can be generated by $1 + \dim R$ elements, we may write $R = S/(s)$, where S is a regular local ring and $s \in S$. We now have

THEOREM. *Let S be a regular local ring of dimension d, and let $s \in S$ be an element.*

Set $R = S/(s)$. *Let* $\boldsymbol{F}\colon \cdots \to F_1 \xrightarrow{\varphi_1} F_0$ *be a minimal free resolution over* R. *Then* rank F_k = rank F_{k+1} *for all* $k \geqq d$, *and there exist isomorphisms* $\alpha_k\colon F_k \to F_{k+2}$ $(k \geqq d)$ *such that* $\varphi_{k+2} = \alpha_{k-1}\varphi_k\alpha_k^{-1}$ $(k > d)$. *Moreover there are liftings of the maps*

$$F_{d+2} \xrightarrow{\varphi_{d+2}} F_{d+1} \xrightarrow{\alpha_d \varphi_{d+1}} F_{d+2}$$

to maps of free S-modules

$$\tilde{F}_{d+2} \xrightarrow{\tilde{\varphi}_{d+2}} \tilde{F}_{d+1} \xrightarrow{\tilde{\varphi}_{d+1}} \tilde{F}_{d+2}$$

such that $\tilde{\varphi}_{d+1}\tilde{\varphi}_{d+2} = s \cdot I = \tilde{\varphi}_{d+2}\tilde{\varphi}_{d+1}$, *where* I *is the identity map.*

This theorem may in fact be pushed a little farther to yield a one-to-one correspondence between Cohen-Macaulay R-modules of dimension $d - 1$, and factorizations in the matrix ring over S of the scalar matrix $s \cdot I$.

It seems reasonable to conjecture that some result of this type should hold for rings R which can be written as a quotient of a regular local ring S by an S-sequence: If

$$\boldsymbol{F}\colon \cdots \xrightarrow{\varphi_2} F_1 \xrightarrow{\varphi_1} F_0$$

is a free resolution over such a ring R, then for $k \gg 0$, there should be a formula for φ_k in terms of $\varphi_1, \cdots, \varphi_{k-1}$ as *is* the case for resolutions of the residue class fields.

References

[B-E 1] D. A. Buchsbaum and D. Eisenbud, *What makes a complex exact*? J. Algebra **25** (1973), 259–268. MR **47** #3369.

[B-E 2] ———, *Some structure theorems for finite free resolutions*, Advances in Math. **12** (1974), 84–139.

[B-E 3] ———, *Algebra structures for finite free resolutions, and some structure theorems for ideals of codimension* 3, Amer. J. Math. (to appear).

[B-R] D. A. Buchsbaum and D. S. Rim, *A generalized Koszul complex*. III, Proc. Amer. Math. Soc. **16** (1965), 555–558. MR **31** #1285.

[Bur] L. Burch, *On ideals of finite homological dimension in local rings*, Proc. Cambridge Philos. Soc. **64** (1968), 941–948. MR **37** #5208.

[E-N] J. Eagon, and D. G. Northcott, *On the Buchsbaum-Eisenbud theory of finite free resolutions*, J. Reine Angew. Math. **2621 263** (1973), 205–219.

[Hoc] M. Hochster, *Homological aspects of commutative ring theory*, Notes of the AMS regional conference at Lincoln, Nebraska, 1974.

[P-S] C. Peskine and L. Szpiro, *Liason des variétés algèbriques*, Invent. Math. (1974).

[G-L] T. H. Gulliksen and G. Levin, *Homology of local rings*, Queen's Paper in Pure and Appl. Math., no. 20, Queen's University, Kingston, Ont., 1969, MR **41** #6837.

Brandeis University
Waltham, Massachusetts 02154, U.S.A.

Proceedings of the International Congress of Mathematicians
Vancouver, 1974

K-Theory and Algebraic Cycles

S. M. Gersten

This is an expository lecture of work done in the past two years, much of which has appeared in the Proceedings of the Battelle Conference [2]. I refer the reader who desires further details to that volume, in particular to the papers of Quillen, Bloch, and myself.

1. Quillen K-theory. Quillen has associated functors $K_n(\mathscr{P})$, $n \geqq 0$, to a small category $\mathscr{P}$ with a notion of short exact sequence. In particular, this applies to a small (or skeletally small) abelian category. An important property of this theory is Quillen's localization theorem [2]: If $\mathscr{S} \subset \mathscr{A}$ is the inclusion of a thick subcategory $\mathscr{S}$ in the abelian category $\mathscr{A}$ (so $\mathscr{S}$ is closed under taking subobjects, quotient objects, and extensions in $\mathscr{A}$), then there is a long exact sequence

$$\cdots \to K_{n+1}(\mathscr{A}/\mathscr{S}) \to K_n(\mathscr{S}) \to K_n(\mathscr{A}) \to K_n(\mathscr{A}/\mathscr{S}) \to \cdots,$$

where $\mathscr{A}/\mathscr{S}$ is the quotient abelian category.

In general, if X is a scheme, one defines $K_n(X) = K_n(\mathscr{P}(X))$, where $\mathscr{P}(X)$ is the category of vector bundles on X. If X is a Noetherian scheme, one sets $K'_n(X) = K_n(\mathscr{M}(X))$, where $\mathscr{M}(X)$ is the abelian category of coherent sheaves of $\mathscr{O}_X$-modules. $K_n(X)$ is a contravariant functor whereas $K'_n(X)$ is contravariant for maps of finite Tor-dimension.

If X is Noetherian and regular (so $\mathscr{O}_{X,x}$ is a regular local ring for all $x \in X$) then the inclusion $\mathscr{P}(X) \subset \mathscr{M}(X)$ induces isomorphisms $K_n(X) \simeq K'_n(X)$. Also if R is a ring, one writes $K_n(R)$ for $K_n(\mathrm{Spec}\ R)$.

2. Filtration by codimension of supports. If X is a Noetherian scheme, then there is a filtration $\mathscr{M}(X) = \mathscr{M}^0 \supset \mathscr{M}^1 \supset \cdots \supset \mathscr{M}^p \supset \cdots$, where $\mathscr{M}^p$ is the full subcategory of $\mathscr{M}(X)$ consisting of sheaves $\mathscr{F}$ such that the codimension in X of the support of $\mathscr{F}$ is at least p. The category $\mathscr{M}^{p+1}$ is a thick subcategory of $\mathscr{M}^p$, and the quotient category $\mathcal{M}^p/\mathcal{M}^{p+1}$ is entirely ring theoretic in character; by a theorem of Gabriel, it is the sum of abelian categories,

$$\coprod_{x \in X^p} \text{Mod f.l.}(\mathcal{O}_{X,x}),$$

where $X^p = \{x \in X \mid \dim \mathcal{O}_{X,x} = p\}$, and "Mod f.l." denotes the category of modules of finite (Jordan-Hölder) length. From this description one deduces, via the localization theorem and further more elementary properties of K-groups, exact sequences:

$$\cdots \to K_q(\mathcal{M}^{p+1}) \to K_q(\mathcal{M}^p) \to \coprod_{x \in X^p} K_q(k(x)) \to K_{q-1}(\mathcal{M}^{p+1}) \to \cdots$$

where $k(x) = \mathcal{O}_{X,x}/m_x$, the residue class field at the point $x \in X$. These exact sequences fit together to form an exact couple, and hence a spectral sequence $\{E_r^{p,q}(X), r \geqq 1\}$,

$$E_1^{p,q}(X) = \coprod_{x \in X^p} K_{-p-q}(k(x)) \Rightarrow K'_{-p-q}(X).$$

The convention is that $K_n = 0$ if $n < 0$, so this spectral sequence is of cohomological type and concentrated in the fourth quadrant. Let me sketch a picture of it, including the row $y = -q$, for the E_1 term:

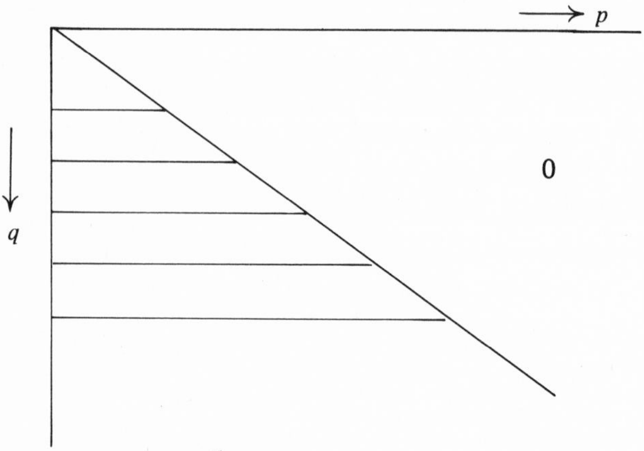

$$\coprod_{x \in X^0} K_q(k(x)) \xrightarrow{d^1} \coprod_{x \in X^1} K_{q-1}(k(x)) \to \cdots \to \coprod_{x \in X^q} K_0(k(x))$$

Since the qth row is functorial in X, one may sheafify it in the Zariski topology to get a complex of sheaves of abelian groups:

(2.1) $$0 \to \mathfrak{K}'_q \to \coprod_{x \in X^0} i_x K_q(k(x)) \to \cdots \to \coprod_{x \in X^{q-1}} i_x K_1(k(x)) \to \coprod_{x \in X^q} i_x K_0(k(x)) \to 0.$$

If A_x is an abelian group ($x \in X$), one has denoted here $i_x A_x$ the sheaf obtained from the simple sheaf A_x on $\overline{\{x\}}$ by extension by zero. Also, the sheaf $\mathfrak{K}'_q$ is the sheaf associated to the presheaf $U \to K'_q(U)$, while the map $\mathfrak{K}'_q \to \coprod_{x \in X^0} i_x K_q(k(x))$ selects the stalks at the generic points of irreducible components of X.

I should like to work an example of the first nontrivial case of (2.1). From now on in this section X will be assumed *regular*, so $\mathfrak{K}_q = \mathfrak{K}'_q$. If $q = 1$, there is a canonical map $\mathcal{O}_X^* \to \mathfrak{K}_1$ and a computation shows that this map is an isomorphism on stalks, so $\mathcal{O}_X^* \simeq \mathfrak{K}_1$. If I assume in addition that X is connected, then (using $K_1(k) = k^*$, $K_0(k) = \mathbf{Z}$ for k a field) (2.1) becomes

$$0 \to \mathcal{O}_X^* \to \underline{k(X)^*} \xrightarrow{d^1} \coprod_D i_D\mathbf{Z} \to 0 \tag{2.2}$$

where $\underline{k(X)^*}$ is the constant sheaf of rational functions on X and the sum is taken over all irreducible positive divisors D on X. The map d^1 assigns to a rational function f its divisor div f, and the sequence (2.2) is exact by the theorem of Auslander-Buchsbaum that regular local rings are factorial. From the exactness of (2.2) follow two consequences:

(a) a vanishing theorem, $H^p(X, \mathfrak{K}_1) = 0$ if $p > 1$, and

(b) $C^1(X)/C^1_{\text{rat}}(X) = H^1(X, \mathfrak{K}_1)$, where $C^1(X)$ denotes the group of codimension one cycles and $C^1_{\text{rat}}(X)$ denotes those cycles rationally equivalent to zero.

It was to generalize (a) and (b) that I proposed two years ago at Battelle.

CONJECTURE 2.3. The complex (2.1) is exact for regular schemes X.

At that time, I could establish exactness only when dim $X = 1$ and $k(x)$ is finite for $x \in X^1$ (for example, for Spec $\mathcal{O}_F$, the ring of integers in a number field F). However six months later Quillen settled the conjecture for schemes of geometric type.

THEOREM (QUILLEN [2]). *If X is a regular algebraic k-scheme where k is any field, then* (2.1) *is exact.*

I should point out that Conjecture 2.3 is still open for $X = \text{Spec}\,(\mathbf{Z}[x])$.

Since the schemes in (2.1) are all flabby except for $\mathfrak{K}'_q$, there follows the vanishing theorem:

COROLLARY. *If X is a regular algebraic k-scheme, then $H^p(X, \mathfrak{K}_q) = 0$ for $p > q$.*

One also has the analog of the relationship with algebraic cycles. To see this, observe that the flabby resolution of $\mathfrak{K}_q$ enables one to write

$$H^p(X, \mathfrak{K}_p) = C^p(X)/\text{Im}\, d^1 : \coprod_{x \in X^{p-1}} k(x)^* \to C^p(X).$$

Thus one must compute the map d^1.

Roughly, the answer is as follows. Let $y \in X^{p-1}$ and let $f \in k(y)^*$. Let $Y = \overline{\{y\}}$, so f may be viewed as a function $Y \xrightarrow{f} \mathbf{P}^1$. One may form, with some care, the divisor of f, div f, a codimension one cycle on Y, and hence a codimension p cycle on X. This cycle represents an element of Im d^1. However, this is precisely the description given by Samuel [3] for cycles rationally equivalent to zero. Hence there follows

COROLLARY. *If X is a smooth quasi-projective variety over a field k, then*

$$\text{Chow}^p(X) =_{\text{def}} C^p(X)/C^p_{\text{rat}}(X) \cong H^p(X, \mathfrak{K}_p).$$

Problem. There are pairings $\mathfrak{K}_p \otimes \mathfrak{K}_{p'} \to \mathfrak{K}_{p+p'}$ defined by the multiplicative structure on higher K-groups. Thus $\coprod_p H^p(X, \mathfrak{K}_p)$ is a graded ring with unit. It is natural to enquire whether the identification as the Chow group $\mathrm{Chow}(X) = \coprod_p \mathrm{Chow}^p(X)$ is a ring isomorphism.

A third consequence of Quillen's theorem is the computation of the $E_2^{p,q}$ term of the spectral sequence of codimension of supports.

COROLLARY. *If X is a regular algebraic k scheme, k a field, then $E_2^{p,-q} = H^p(X, \mathfrak{K}_q)$. Thus the picture of the E_2-terms is:*

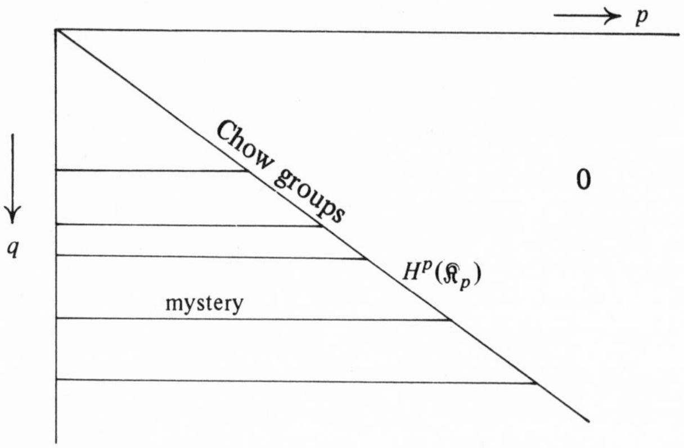

In general, the part of the E_2-term beneath the diagonal is a mystery. In addition a geometric interpretation for the global higher K-groups $K_n(X)$ is lacking. However in one case there is an interpretation.

3. Reciprocity laws. In this section X is a smooth connected curve over a field k.

DEFINITION. A reciprocity law (for $\boldsymbol{G}_m$) on X is a homomorphism

$$\coprod_{x \in X^1} k(x)^* \xrightarrow{\varphi} A,$$

A an abelian group, such that $\phi(\langle f, g \rangle) = 0$, $f, g \in k(X)^*$. Here $\langle f, g \rangle = \coprod_x \langle f, g \rangle_x$, where

$$\langle f, g \rangle_x = (-1)^{\mathrm{ord}_x(f)\mathrm{ord}_x(g)} \left(\frac{f^{\mathrm{ord}_x(g)}}{g^{\mathrm{ord}_x(f)}} \right)(x) \in k(x)^*.$$

It follows that there is a universal reciprocity law, namely the canonical map

$$\coprod_{x \in X^1} k(x)^* \to \coprod_{x \in X^1} k(x)^* / \underset{f, g \in k(X)^*}{\mathrm{subgroup}} \langle f, g \rangle.$$

Now the localization sequence for $\mathscr{M}^1 \subset \mathscr{M}^0$ contains the exact sequence

$$K_2(k(X)) \xrightarrow{d} \coprod_{x \in X^1} k(x)^* \to K_1(X),$$

and computation of the map d shows that $\coprod_{x \in X^1} k(x)^* \to \operatorname{coker} d$ is the universal reciprocity law. Since the spectral sequence $\{E_r^{p,q}(X)\}$ is degenerate at E_2 for a curve, it follows that

$$H^1(X, \mathfrak{K}_2) = \coprod_{x \in X^1} k(x)^* / \underset{f,g \in k(X)^*}{\text{subgroup}} \langle f, g, \rangle,$$

so the projection $\coprod_{x \in X^1} k(x)^* \to H^1(X, \mathfrak{K}_2)$ is the universal reciprocity law on X.

To show that these concepts are nonvacuous, let me exhibit a nontrivial reciprocity law. Suppose from now on that the curve X is complete. Define a map $\coprod_{x \in X^1} k(x)^* \xrightarrow{N} k^*$ whose x factor is the norm map $N_{k(x)/k}$.

THEOREM (WEIL). *The map N is a reciprocity law* (*see Bass* **[1]** *for a proof*).

One may enquire then when the Weil law N is universal. That is, when is the induced map N: $H^1(X, \mathfrak{K}_2) \to k^*$ an isomorphism? The following cases are known.

(a) If $k = \boldsymbol{F}_q$ or $\bar{\boldsymbol{F}}_q$, then N is an isomorphism. This is a restatement of a theorem of Bass, Milnor, and Serre.

(b) If k is arbitrary and $X = \boldsymbol{P}^1_k$ then N is an isomorphism. This follows from the computation of $K(\boldsymbol{P}^1)$.

(c) If $k = \boldsymbol{C}$ and genus $X = 1$, then N is never an isomorphism. This follows from arguments in the Harvard thesis of L. Roberts (unpublished).

Problem. Give a geometric interpretation for reciprocity laws. Since $K_1(X) = H^1(X, \mathfrak{K}_2) \oplus k^*$ for a complete curve X over k, this amounts to giving an interpretation for $K_1(X)$.

There is a situation analogous to that of reciprocity laws for $\boldsymbol{G}_m$ which has an adequate geometric interpretation. Recall that the universal reciprocity law is the same as the composition of two maps

$$K_2(k(X)) \xrightarrow{d} \coprod_{x \in X^1} k(x)^* \longrightarrow K_1(X)$$

in a K-theory exact sequence being zero.

We may pass from the curve X to the infinitesimal extension $X[\varepsilon]$ of X, $\varepsilon^2 = 0$,

$$X[\varepsilon] = X \times_{\operatorname{Spec} k} \operatorname{Spec}(k[\varepsilon]).$$

There is an analogous diagram

$$K_2(k(X)[\varepsilon]) \to \coprod_{x \in X^1} (k(x)[\varepsilon])^* \to K_1(X[\varepsilon])$$

in which the two arrows compose to zero **[4]**. (At the moment I have been unable to establish exactness in this diagram.) By a theorem of van der Kallen, there is a canonical surjection $K_2(k(X)[\varepsilon]) \twoheadrightarrow \Omega^1_{k(X)/k}$ and this map may be embedded in the commutative diagram

$$\begin{array}{ccccc} K_2(k(X)[\varepsilon]) & \to & \coprod_{x \in X^1} (k(x)[\varepsilon])^* & \to & K_1(X[\varepsilon]) \\ \downarrow & & \nwarrow & & \nearrow j \\ \Omega^1_{k(X)/k} & \xrightarrow{\coprod \operatorname{Res}_x} & & \coprod_{x \in X^1} k(x). & \end{array}$$

Here the map Res_x is the residue of a differential form ω at x, and the map j may be interpreted as summing the residues. The statement that $j(\coprod \operatorname{Res}_x) = 0$ is precisely the residue theorem for the curve X.

References

1. H. Bass, *Algebraic K-theory*, Benjamin, New York, 1968. MR **40** #2736.

2. ———, (editor), *Algebraic K-theory*. I, Lecture Notes in Math., vol. 341, Springer-Verlag, Berlin and New York, 1973.

3. *Séminaire C. Chevalley*. 2e année: 1958. *Anneaux de Chow et applications*, Secrétariat mathématique, Paris, 1958. MR **22** #1572.

4. S. Gersten, *The localization theorem for projective modules*, Comm. Algebra **2** (1974), 307–350.

University of Illinois at Urbana-Champaign
Urbana, Illinois 61801, U.S.A.

Proceedings of the International Congress of Mathematicians
Vancouver, 1974

Varieties of Algebras and their Congruence Varieties

Bjarni Jónsson

1. Congruence lattices. G. Birkhoff and O. Frink noted that the congruence lattice Con(A) of an algebra A (with operations of finite rank) is algebraic or compactly generated. The celebrated Grätzer-Schmidt theorem states that, conversely, every algebraic lattice is isomorphic to Con(A) for some algebra A. The importance of this is obvious, for it shows that unless something more is known about the algebra A, nothing can be said about Con(A) that does not follow from the fact that it is algebraic. This, however, leaves open the question of what happens when additional conditions are imposed on A. The most obvious question is for what similarity types τ, if any, it is true that every algebraic lattice is isomorphic to Con(A) for some τ-algebra A. It is easy to see that no preassigned number of unary operations will suffice, but other than that the problem is completely open. In particular, as several people have observed, it is not even known whether every algebraic lattice is isomorphic to the congruence lattice of some groupoid.

Little progress has also been made on the problem of characterizing the congruence lattices of the members of various familiar varieties, or equational classes, of algebras, e.g., it seems unlikely that every algebraic lattice is isomorphic to the congruence lattice of some semigroup, but no counterexample is known. (However, an unpublished example by R. N. McKenzie shows commutative semigroups will not suffice.) The congruence lattices of groups or, equivalently, the lattices of normal subgroups, are known to be modular and to satisfy certain even stronger identities, but there is little hope of characterizing these lattices. The congruence lattices of lattices are distributive (N. Funayama and T. Nakayama), but it is an open question whether every distributive algebraic lattice is isomorphic to the congruence lattice of some lattice. The situation is no better concerning most other varieties, e.g., various subvarieties of the above three. Among the exceptions are the variety of all Boolean algebras and the variety of all distributive lattices, for their congruence lattices are completely known.

2. Congruence varieties. It may well be that in many cases the problem of characterizing the congruence lattices of the members of a variety $\mathscr{V}$ is not just difficult, but that actually no useful characterization exists. A simpler problem might be to find a basis for the identities that hold in the congruence lattices, i.e., to find an equational basis for the variety Con($\mathscr{V}$) generated by the lattices Con(A) with $A \in \mathscr{V}$. For some varieties this is trivial, e.g., if $\mathscr{V}$ is a nontrivial variety of lattices, then Con($\mathscr{V}$) $= \mathscr{D}$, the variety of all distributive lattices. A big step toward the solution of this problem for varieties of semigroups was taken in Freese and Nation [**8**], where it is shown that Con($\mathscr{V}$) $= \mathscr{L}$, the variety of all lattices, except when $\mathscr{V}$ is a subvariety of the variety of all groups of some fixed exponent.

It is not hard to show that varieties of groups give rise to infinitely many different congruence varieties. In fact, let $\mathscr{G}_m$ ($\mathscr{A}_m$) be the variety of all groups (abelian groups) of exponent m, and in particular let $\mathscr{G} = \mathscr{G}_0$ ($\mathscr{A} = \mathscr{A}_0$) be the variety of all groups (abelian groups). Then $m \neq n$ implies that Con($\mathscr{G}_m$) $\neq$ Con($\mathscr{G}_n$) and Con($\mathscr{A}_m$) $\neq$ Con($\mathscr{A}_n$). On the other hand it is not known whether, for varieties of groups, $\mathscr{V} \neq \mathscr{V}'$ always implies Con($\mathscr{V}$) $\neq$ Con($\mathscr{V}'$). In fact, it is not even known whether Con($\mathscr{G}_m$) $\neq$ Con($\mathscr{A}_m$). It follows from a theorem in Herrmann and Poguntke [**10**] that if $\mathscr{A} \subseteq \mathscr{V} \subseteq \mathscr{G}$, then Con($\mathscr{V}$) is not finitely based, but for $\mathscr{G}_m$ and $\mathscr{A}_m$ with $m \neq 0$ the situation is not known. So far there is not a single nontrivial variety $\mathscr{V}$ of groups for which a basis for Con($\mathscr{V}$) is known, and in general the problem of finding such bases appears to be difficult.

3. Mal′cev conditions. Since the properties of the congruence lattice of an algebra are not first order properties of that algebra, the compactness theorem does not apply to such properties. One might call a property (P) compact if every variety whose members have this property is contained in a finitely based variety all of whose members have this property. Alternatively, (P) is compact just in case it is equivalent to a, possibly infinite, disjunction of finite conjunctions of identities. For congruence identities the nature of this disjunction can be further specified, for it follows from Taylor [**23**, Theorem 4.1] that a congruence identity is compact iff it is equivalent to a Mal′cev condition. It is not known whether every congruence identity is compact, but two important ones, congruence distributivity and congruence modularity, are. In fact, equivalent Mal′cev conditions are explicitly given in Jónsson [**12**] and Day [**6**].

4. Excluded varieties. We know that there are infinitely many congruence varieties, but we do not know infinitely many congruence varieties—not in the sense of being able to write down bases for their identities. In fact, apart from the trivial variety, the only known congruence varieties are $\mathscr{L}$ and $\mathscr{D}$, the variety of all lattices and the variety of all distributive lattices. It would be particularly interesting to know whether the variety $\mathscr{M}$ of all modular lattices is a congruence variety. On the other hand, many lattice varieties are known not to be congruence varieties. The first, and therefore the most important, result of this kind, in Nation [21], shows that if Con($\mathscr{V}$) satisfies a nontrivial inclusion of the form

$$\sigma_0 w \leqq \sum(\sigma_0\sigma_i, 1 \leqq i \leqq k)$$

where w is a lattice polynomial, $\sigma_0, \sigma_1, \cdots, \sigma_k$ are joins of variables, and the inclusion $w \leqq \sigma_0$ does not hold in every lattice, then $\mathscr{V}$ is congruence modular, and that if, further, σ_0 and w have no variable in common, then $\mathscr{V}$ is congruence distributive. This clearly excludes many varieties from being congruence varieties, e.g., a variety generated by a finite dimensional nondistributive lattice cannot be a congruence variety, because it satisfies the inclusion

$$x\sum(y_i, i \leqq m) \leqq \sum(x\sum(y_i, j \neq i \leqq m), j \leqq m)$$

for m sufficiently large. Also, if $\mathscr{V}$ is generated by a finite nonmodular lattice, then the lattice join $\mathscr{M} + \mathscr{V}$ is not a congruence variety because, for m large enough, it satisfies the inclusion

$$x\prod(xy_i + y_j, i < j \leqq m) \leqq \sum(xy_i, i \leqq m).$$

The question has been raised by R. N. McKenzie whether, for any variety $\mathscr{V}$ of algebras, either Con($\mathscr{V}$) $= \mathscr{L}$ or Con($\mathscr{V}$) $\subseteq \mathscr{M}$, and J. B. Nation formulated the more conservative conjecture that if $\mathscr{V}$ satisfies a nontrivial compact congruence identity, then Con($\mathscr{V}$) $\subseteq \mathscr{M}$. There is some further evidence in suppport of this conjecture, e.g., if Con($\mathscr{V}$) satisfies a nontrivial inclusion $\pi \leqq \sigma$ with π a meet of joins of variables and σ a join of meets of variables, then $\mathscr{V}$ is congruence distributive. Other examples of lattice inclusions that imply congruence modularity have been discovered by Nation and by A. Day and P. Mederly.

5. Applications. With three important exceptions, congruence identities have been investigated primarily for their intrinsic interest, and have not played a role in the study of other properties of the varieties and their members. These three exceptions are distributivity, modularity and the Arguesian identity, each of which has profound implications. The consequences of modularity and distributivity relating to direct and subdirect decompositions are classical and need not be stated. We also recall without going into details that the Arguesian identity has played a role in connection with certain imbedding problems. Congruence distributivity is particularly useful in the study of subvarieties of a given variety. The basic lemma here is the result in Jónsson [12] that if $\mathscr{K}$ is a subclass of a congruence distributive variety, then the variety $\mathscr{K}^v$ generated by $\mathscr{K}$ consists of algebras isomorphic to subdirect products of homomorphic images of subalgebras of ultraproducts of algebras in $\mathscr{K}$—in symbols $\mathscr{K}^v = P_sHSP_u(\mathscr{K})$. The advantage of this over Birkhoff's classical formula $\mathscr{K}^v = HSP(\mathscr{K})$, which holds for every class $\mathscr{K}$ of algebras, is that it shows that every subdirectly irreducible member of $\mathscr{K}^v$ belongs to $HSP_u(\mathscr{K})$. For an easy but important application take $\mathscr{K}$ to be a finite set of finite algebras (in a congruence distributive variety). Then $HSP_u(\mathscr{K}) = HS(\mathscr{K})$ has only finitely many nonisomorphic members, and the number of subvarieties of $\mathscr{K}^v$ is therefore finite. In fact, if the members of $\mathscr{K}$ are explicitly known, the subvarieties of $\mathscr{K}^v$

can be listed, and the subdirectly irreducible members of each given. A very difficult related result is K. Baker's elegant theorem that if, in addition, the similarity type of $\mathscr{K}$ is finite, then $\mathscr{K}^v$ is finitely based. (For the special case of finite lattices this was proved earlier in McKenzie [**17**].) This calls to mind Oates' and Powell's finite basis theorem for finite groups. It is tempting to ask for a common generalization of the two results, and the obvious common feature is congruence modularity. However, Baker's proof of his theorem in [**3**] and a shorter nonconstructive proof in Makkai [**16**] both make essential use of congruence distributivity, and it is hard to see how they could be modified to yield such a generalization.

Baker's finite basis theorem is part of a deep study in [**3**] and [**4**] of bases for varieties of the form $\mathscr{K}^v$ where $\mathscr{K}$ is a strictly elementary positive universal subclass of a congruence distributive variety. Most other studies, however, deal with some particular variety and its subvarieties, and naturally the variety $\mathscr{L}$ of all lattices has received the greatest attention. Many of the results can be formulated as theorems about the lattice Λ of all subvarieties of $\mathscr{L}$ or the lattice Λ_m of all subvarieties of $\mathscr{M}$. By Baker [**2**], Λ_m has an infinite, complete atomic Boolean algebra as a sublattice, and therefore has cardinality $2^{\aleph_0}$. (In McKenzie [**17**] the same result was proved for Λ.) It is an open question of long standing whether $\mathscr{M}$ is generated by its finite members, but in [**2**] it is shown that the variety generated by the rational projective plane is not generated by its finite members. Another example, the variety generated by all Fano planes, is given in Wille [**24**]. Considerable attention has been paid to covering relations in Λ and in Λ_m, and to small lattice varieties. Trivially, $\mathscr{D}$ is the only atom of Λ, and it is covered by just two members, $\mathscr{M}_3$ and $\mathscr{N}$, the varieties generated by the diamond and the pentagon. In Jónsson [**13**] an equational basis for $\mathscr{M}_3$ is given, and $\mathscr{M}_3$ is shown to be covered by just three members of Λ. The arguments make essential use of ideas from Grätzer [**9**]. The study of small lattice varieties is carried further in Hong [**11**], and McKenzie [**18**] is in part concerned with such problems. In [**18**] equational bases are found for several varieties, including $\mathscr{N}$, and sixteen varieties are listed that cover $\mathscr{N}$. It is not known whether that list is complete. It is easy to see that every member of Λ other than its unit $\mathscr{L}$ is covered by some member of Λ, but the corresponding problerm for Λ_m is open.

In [**18**], McKenzie resurrects P. M. Whitman's notion of a splitting of a lattice and applies it to Λ. (Actually he works with the dually isomorphic lattice of equational theories of lattices.) A splitting pair in Λ is an ordered pair $\langle \mathscr{U}, \mathscr{U}' \rangle$ of lattice varieties such that for every lattice variety $\mathscr{V}$, either $\mathscr{V} \subseteq \mathscr{U}$ or $\mathscr{U}' \subseteq \mathscr{V}$, but not both. Motivated by the familiar example $\langle \mathscr{M}, \mathscr{N} \rangle$, he shows that every splitting pair $\langle \mathscr{U}, \mathscr{U}' \rangle$ is induced by a finite, subdirectly irreducible lattice S, in the sense that $\mathscr{U}' = \{S\}^v$ and $\mathscr{U}$ is the class of all lattices L with $S \notin \{L\}^v$. Lattices S that induce splitting pairs, i.e., such that the class of all lattices L with $S \notin \{L\}^v$ is a variety, are called splitting lattices. Infinitely many splitting lattices are found, and an effective procedure is given for determining whether or not a given lattice is a splitting lattice. A noteworthy aspect of these investigations is that they yield new results about free lattices, e.g., procedures for determining whether a quotient in a free lattice is a prime quotient and whether a finite lattice is embeddable in a free lattice, and a theorem credited to A. Kostinsky to the effect that every finitely generated sublattice of a free lattice is projective.

Of other varieties, pseudocomplemented distributive lattices are best known; cf. Lakser [**14**] and Lee [**15**]. The subvarieties form a chain of type $\omega + 1$, and an explicit equational basis can be given for each. Others include Heyting algebras (Baker [**1**], Day [**7**]), polyadic algebras (Monk [**20**]), orthomodular lattices (Bruns and Kalmbach [**5**]), implicative semilattices (Nemitz and Whaley [**11**]), and implication algebras (Mitschke [**19**]).

This brief summary is obviously highly incomplete, and it does grave injustice to many of those who have contributed to these investigations. However, it does give some idea of the type of questions under consideration, and points out some of the numerous open problems. In conclusion I wish to thank Professors Alan Day, George Grätzer and J. B. Nation for valuable assistance in preparing this report.

Bibliography

1. K. A. Baker, *Equational bases for Heyting algebras* (preprint).

2. ———, *Equational classes of modular lattices*, Pacific J. Math. **28** (1969), 9–15. MR **39** #5435.

3. ———, *Finite equational bases for finite algebras in congruence-distributive varieties* (preprint).

4. ———, *Primitive satisfaction and equational problems for lattices and other algebras*, Trans. Amer. Math. Soc. **190** (1974), 125–150.

5. G. Bruns and G. Kalmbach, *Varieties of orthomodular lattices*. I, Canad. J. Math. **23** (1971), 802–810; II, ibid. **24** (1972), 328–337. MR **44** #6565; **45** #3267.

6. A. Day, *A characterization of modularity for congruence lattices of algebras*, Canad. Math. Bull. **12** (1969), 167–173. MR **40** #1317.

7. ———, *Varieties of Heyting algebras*. I, II (preprints).

8. R. S. Freese and J. B. Nation, *Congruence lattices of semilattices*, Pacific J. Math. **49** (1973), 51–58.

9. G. A. Grätzer, *Equational classes of lattices*, Duke Math. J. **33** (1966), 613–622. MR **33** #7278.

10. C. Herrmann and W. Poguntke, *The quasi-variety of normal subgroup lattices is not elementary*, Algebra Universalis **4** (1974), 280–286.

11. D. X. Hong, *Covering relations among lattice varieties*, Pacific J. Math. **40** (1972), 575–603. MR **46** #5195.

12. B. Jónsson, *Algebras whose congruence lattices are distributive*, Math. Scand. **21** (1967), 110–121. MR **38** #5689.

13. ———, *Equational classes of lattices*, Math. Scand. **22** (1968), 187–196. MR **40** #66.

14. H. Lakser, *The structure of pseudocomplemented distributive lattices*. I: *Subdirect decomposition*, Trans. Amer. Math. Soc. **156** (1971), 335–342. MR **43** #123.

15. K. B. Lee, *Equational classes of distributive pseudo-complemented lattices*, Canad. J. Math. **22** (1970), 881–891. MR **42** #151.

16. M. Makkai, *A proof of Baker's finite basis theorem on equational classes generated by finite elements of congruence distributive classes*, Algebra Universalis **3** (1973), 174–181.

17. R. N. McKenzie, *Equational bases for lattice theories*, Math. Scand. **27** (1970), 24–38. MR **43** #118.

18. ———, *Equational bases and nonmodular lattice varieties*, Trans. Amer. Math. Soc. **174** (1972), 1–43. MR **47** #1696.

19. A. Mitschke, *Implication algebras are 3-permutable and 3-distributive*, Algebra Universalis **1** (1971/72), 182–186. MR **46** #8933.

20. J. D. Monk, *On equational classes of algebraic versions of logic*. I, Math. Scand. **27** (1970), 53–71. MR **43** #6065.

21. J. B. Nation, *Varieties whose congruences satisfy certain lattice identities*, Algebra Universalis **4** (1974), 78–88.

22. W. Nemitz and T. Whaley, *Varieties of implicative semilattices*, Pacific J. Math. **37** (1971), 759–769; II, ibid. **45** (1973), 303–311. MR **47** #84.

23. W. Taylor, *Characterizing Mal'cev conditions*, Algebra Universalis **3** (1973), 351–397.

24. R. Wille, *Primitive Länge und primitive Weite bei modularen Verbänden*, Math. Z. **108** (1969), 129–136. MR **39** #2672.

VANDERBILT UNIVERSITY
NASHVILLE, TENNESSEE 37235, U.S.A.

Труды Международного Конгресса Математиков
Ванкувер, 1974

О Разрешимых Подгруппах Конечных Простых Групп

В. Д. Мазуров

Цель моего сообщения—рассказать о некоторых результатах, полученных в Новосибирске в последние 2 года. Они касаются конечных простых групп.

1. Насыщенные p-группы. Пусть G—конечная группа, p—простое число. Подгруппа D называется насыщенной в G, если D—силовская p-подгруппа в $O_{p',p}(N_G(D))$ и $N_G(D)$ p-скованная (p-constrained) группа.

Насыщенными являются, например, силовские p-подгруппы из G. Если в G нет других насыщенных подгрупп, то в G все разрешимые подгруппы имеют единичную p-длину. Строение таких групп при $p = 2$ хорошо изучено [**3**]. По теореме Алперина-Голдшмидта [**13**] в нормализаторах насыщенных правильных пересечений силовских p-подгрупп происходит слияние p-элементов группы.

В исследовании p-локальных подгрупп полезным оказывается следующий факт:

Лемма. *Верно одно из следующих двух утверждений:*
(а) *p-длина каждой разрешимой подгруппы из G не превосходит единицы,*
(б) *в G есть такая разрешимая подгруппа R p-длины 2, для которой $O_p(R)$—насыщенная в G подгруппа.*

С помощью этой леммы может быть получен такой результат [**7**].

Теорема. *Пусть G—конечная простая группа, в которой каждое насыщенное пересечение двух различных силовских 2-подгрупп имеет ранг $\leqq 2$. Тогда G изоморфна одной из следующих групп:*

$$L_2(q),\ L_3(q),\ U_3(q) \quad q \text{ нечетно},\ A_7,\ M_{11},$$
$$L_2(2^n),\ U_3(2^n),\ Sz(2^{2n-1}), \qquad n \geqq 2,$$

группе типа Янко-Ри.

Этот результат обобщает теоремы Судзуки [**18**], Мазурова [**2**], Герцога [**15**], Герцога-Шульта [**16**].

Из описания [**3**] и леммы легко получается следующий результат [**5**], [**6**].

Пусть T—силовская 2-подгруппа конечной простой группы G. Если T изоморфна S/Z, где S—силовская 2-подгруппа одной из групп $U_3(2^n)$, $Sz(2^n)$, $L_3(2^n)$, $n > 1$, а $Z < Z(S)$, то $Z = 1$ и G изоморфна $U_3(2^n)$, $Sz(2^n)$, $L_3(2^n)$.

Случай, когда $Z = 1$, рассматривался Сыскиным [**10**], Коллинзом [**11**], [**12**].

2. Силовские 2-подгруппы и централизаторы инволюций. Первый результат этого параграфа связан с таким вопросом:

Пусть для инволюции t простой группы G $C_G(t) = \langle t \rangle \times L$, где L—известная простая группа. Какова G?

Пусть $L = L_2(q)$. Если t—центральная инволюция, то результаты Харады [**14**], Уорда [**19**], Томпсона-Янко [**17**] показывают, что $q = 5$ или $q = 3^{2n+1}$ и G—группа типа Янко-Ри. Этот результат справедлив и без условия центральности инволюции t. Он получается без труда из следующих двух общих предложений:

Пусть G—простая группа, t—инволюция из G.

Предложение 1 [**4**]. *Пусть в $N_C(C_2)$, где $C = C_G(t)$, а C_2—силовская 2-подгруппа из C, есть циклическая подгруппа, транзитивно переставляющая при сопряжении неединичные элементы $C_2/\langle t \rangle$.*

Тогда G—группа типа Янко-Ри.

Предложение 2 [**4**], [**8**]. *Если в $\bar{C} = C_G(t)/\langle t \rangle 0(C_G(t))$ есть нормальная подгруппа $\bar{L}$ такая, что $C_{\bar{C}}(\bar{L}) = 1$, $\bar{L} \simeq L_2(q)$, q—нечетно, то G изоморфна группе Матье M_{12} или группе типа Янко-Ри.*

В теории конечных групп важное место занимает вопрос характеризации простых групп их силовскими 2-подгруппами. В следующей теореме дано описание простых групп, силовские 2-подгруппы которых содержат экстраспециальную подгруппу индекса 2.

Экстраспециальной называется p-группа H, у которой $|Z(H)| = |\phi(H)| = p$.

Теорема [**1**]. *Пусть G—простая группа с силовской 2-подгруппой T. Если в T есть экстраспециальная подгруппа индекса 2, то G изоморфна*

$$A_8,\ A_9,\ M_{11},\ M_{12},$$

$$L_2(q),\ L_3(q),\ U_3(q),\ G_2(q),\ D_4^2(q) \quad \text{или } PSp_4(q)$$

для подходящего нечетного q.

Здесь все сводится к нахождению возможных типов силовских 2-подгрупп группы G, после чего известные характеризационные теоремы дают этот список простых групп. Решающую роль играет изучение строения насыщенных пересечений силовских 2-подгрупп.

Продолжая свои исследования простых групп 2-ранга 3 [9], Сыскин получил такой результат:

Теорема. *Конечная простая группа 2-ранга 3 с нециклическими центрами силовских 2-подгрупп изоморфна* $L_2(8)$, $U_3(8)$, $Sz(8)$ *или группе типа Янко-Ри.*

Литература

1. В.В. Кабанов, В.Д. Мазуров, С.А. Сыскин, *Конечные простые группы, силовские 2-подгруппы которых обладают экстраспециальной подгруппой индекса* 2, Мат. заметки **14** (1973), 127–132.

2. В.Д. Мазуров, *Конечные простые группы с циклическими пересечениями силовских 2-подгрупп,* Алгебра и логика **10** (1971), 188–198.

3. ———, *Конечные простые группы, с единичной 2-длиной разрешимых подгрупп,* Алгебра и логика **11** (1972), 438–469.

4. ———, *О централизаторах инволюций в простых группах,* Мат. сборник **93** (1974), 530–540.

5. В.Д. Мазуров и С.А. Сыскин, *О конечных группах со специальными силовскими 2-подгруппами,* Мат. заметки **14** (1973), 217–222.

6. ———, *Характеризация* $L_3(2^n)$ *силовскими 2-подгруппами,* Известия АН СССР **38** (1974), 512–516.

7. ———, *Конечные группы с 2-силовскими пересечениями ранга* $\leqq 2$, Мат. заметки **16** (1974), 129–133.

8. В.М. Ситников, *О группе Матье* M_{12}, Мат. заметки **15** (1974), 651–660.

9. С.А. Сыскин, *Простые конечные группы 2-ранга 3 с разрешимыми централизаторами инволюций,* Алгебра и логика **10** (1971), 668–709.

10. ———, *О конечных группах с разрешимыми централизаторами инволюций,* Алгебра и логика **10** (1971), 329–347.

11. M. Collins, *The characterization of the unitary groups* $U_3(2^n)$ *by their Sylow 2-subgroups,* Bull. London Math. Soc. **4** (1972), 49–53.

12. ———, *The characterization of finite groups whose 2-Sylow subgroups are of type* $L_3(q)$, q *even,* J. Algebra **25** (1973), 490–512.

13. D. M. Goldschmidt, *A conjugation family for finite groups,* J. Algebra **16** (1970), 138–142.

14. K. Harada, *Groups with a certain type of Sylow 2-subgroups,* J. Math. Soc. Japan **19** (1967), 303–307.

15. M. Herzog, *Simple groups with cyclic central 2-Sylow intersections,* J. Algebra **25** (1973), 307–312.

16. M. Herzog and E. Shult, *Groups with central 2-Sylow intersections of rank at most one,* Proc. Amer. Math. Soc. **38** (1973), 465–470.

17. Z. Janko and J. G. Thompson, *On a class of finite simple groups of Ree,* J. Algebra **4** (1966), 274–292.

18. M. Suzuki, *Finite groups of even order in which Sylow 2-subgroups are independent,* Ann. of Math. (2) **80** (1964), 58–77.

19. H. N. Ward, *On Ree's series of simple groups,* Trans. Amer. Math. Soc. **121** (1966), 62–89.

Институт Математики СО АН СССР
Новосибирск, СССР

Proceedings of the International Congress of Mathematicians
Vancouver, 1974

Quadratic Methods in Nonassociative Algebras

Kevin McCrimmon

I want to convince you of the naturalness and utility of certain quadratic methods in nonassociative algebra. The prototype of the sort of quadratic product I have in mind is the composition xyx, where (say) x and y belong to some associative algebra. We can consider this as a "product" of x and y, linear in y but quadratic in x. Before abandoning the familiar bilinear products for the more complicated and unfamiliar quadratic products, I must convince you that the quadratic approach offers us important insights and perspectives.

1. Right Moufang planes. I begin with an example from geometry [**19**]. A *right Moufang plane* (relative to a line L) is a projective plane in which all translations (elations) with center on L (but arbitrary axis) exist. Dually, a *left Moufang plane* (relative to a point P) is one for which all possible translations exist having axis on P (but arbitrary centers). A *Moufang* (or little Desarguian) plane is one for which all possible translations exist.

Right Moufang

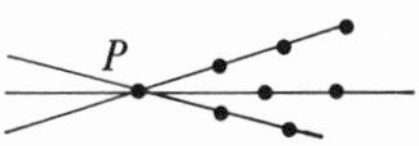

Left Moufang

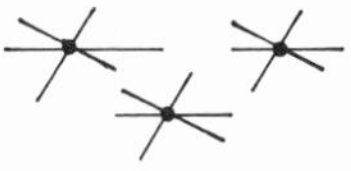

Moufang

Marshall Hall [**2**] showed how to introduce coordinates into an arbitrary projective plane once a coordinate system is chosen. Geometric properties of the plane are reflected in algebraic properties of the coordinate ring. In particular, a projective plane is

(1) right Moufang (rel. L) $\Leftrightarrow$ all coordinate rings (rel. coordinate systems with $L = L_\infty$) are nonassociative division rings (in which case they must in addition have the *right inverse property* RIP: $(yx)x^{-1} = y$);

(2) left Moufang (rel. P) $\Leftrightarrow$ all coordinate rings (rel. systems with $P = Y_\infty$) are nonassociative division rings (with *left inverse property* LIP: $x^{-1}(xy) = y$);
(3) Moufang $\Leftrightarrow$ all coordinate rings are nonassociative division rings (with *inverse property* IP: $x^{-1}(xy) = y = (yx)x^{-1}$).

Now the inverse properties correspond to algebraic identities:
(1) RIP $\Leftrightarrow$ right Moufang law $R_{(xy)x} = R_x R_y R_x$:
(2) LIP $\Leftrightarrow$ left Moufang law $L_{x(yx)} = L_x L_y L_x$:
(3) IP $\Leftrightarrow$ alternative laws $L_{x^2} = L_x^2$, $R_{x^2} = R_x^2$.

The reason for this is that the composition $U_x y = (xy)x$ in a RIP algebra can be built out of negatives and inverses:

$$\text{(Hua's identity)} \quad U_x y = x - \{x^{-1} - (x - y^{-1})^{-1}\}^{-1}.$$

Since the map $x \to R_x$ preserves negatives and inverses, $R_{x-y} = R_x - R_y$ (linearity) and $R_{x^{-1}} = R_x^{-1}$ (RIP), it must also preserve $U_x y$ and we have the right Moufang law $R_{(xy)x} = (R_x R_y) R_x$.

Thus RIP arises naturally out of geometry, and the right Moufang law out of the RIP. If we call an algebra satisfying the right Moufang law a *right Moufang algebra,* then a plane is right Moufang iff its coordinate rings are right Moufang. Dually for left Moufang.

In characteristic $\neq 2$ right Moufang equals right alternative, but in characteristic 2 Bruck **[13]** has constructed right alternative division rings which are not right Moufang (and so not RIP). Consequently it is the Moufang law involving the product $(xy)x$ which arises naturally, not the right alternative law.

2. Jordan algebras. The U-operator can be derived from the inverse not only via Hua's identity, but also via differentiation: $U_x = -\{dx^{-1}|_x\}^{-1}$. T. A. Springer **[18]** has based an entire theory of Jordan algebras directly on the inversion operation.

The more usual theory [3], **[6]** of *quadratic Jordan algebras* is based on the composition $U_x y$, where the U-operator satisfies the axioms

$$U_1 = \mathrm{Id}, \quad U_{U(x)y} = U_x U_y U_x, \quad U_x V_{y,x} = V_{x,y} U_x.$$

In contrast, *linear Jordan algebras* are based on a bilinear product $x \cdot y$ where the left multiplication operator satisfies $L_1 = \mathrm{Id}$, $L_x = R_x$, $L_x L_{x^2} = L_{x^2} L_x$. Just as right Moufang equals right alternative in characteristic $\neq 2$, so quadratic Jordan equals linear Jordan in characteristic $\neq 2$.

Even though the two theories are equivalent most of the time, the quadratic operator U_x is more natural than the linear multiplication operator L_x.

First, *it clarifies old concepts*:
(1) Inverses:
(a) x invertible $\Leftrightarrow$ U_x invertible;
(b) L_x not invertible—may have zero divisors $x \cdot y = 0$ in a division algebra.
(2) Isotopes:
(a) $U_x^{(u)} = U_x U_u$, $\{J^{(u)}\}^{(v)} = J^{(U_u v)}$;
(b) $L_x^{(u)} = L_{x \cdot u} + L_x L_u - L_u L_x$.

(3) Norms:
   (a) $N(U_x y) = N(x)^2 N(y)$;
   (b) $N(x \cdot y) \neq N(x)N(y)$.
(4) Peirce decompositions:
   (a) e idempotent $\Leftrightarrow U_e$ idempotent, $E_1 = U_e$, $E_{1/2} = U_{e,1-e}$, $E_0 = U_{1-e}$;
   (b) L_e not idempotent, $E_1 = 2L_e^2 - L_e$, $E_{1/2} = 4L_e - 4L_e^2$, $E_0 = 1 - 3L_e + 2L_e^2$.
(5) Ideals:
   (a) $B, C \lhd J \Rightarrow U_B C \lhd J$, Penico derived ideal is $U_B J$;
   (b) $B \cdot C \not\lhd J$, Penico derived ideal is $B^2 + B^2 \cdot J$ (not B^2).
(6) Associative algebras:
   (a) A simple or division ring $\Leftrightarrow A^+$ simple or division as a quadratic Jordan algebra;
   (b) A^+ need not be simple or division as linear Jordan algebra.

Second, *it leads to new concepts*:
(1) Inner ideals: subspaces $B \subset J$ with $U_B J \subset B$.
(2) Trivial elements (absolute zero divisors): elements z with $U_z = 0$.
(3) Structure group: transformations T with $U_{Tx} = TU_x T^*$.
(4) Inner structure group generated by U_x's, inner structure algebra generated by $V_{x,y}$'s.
(5) Jordan triple systems: $U_{U(x)y} = U_x U_y U_x$, $U_x V_{y,x} = V_{x,y} U_x$, $V_{U(x)y,y} = V_{x,U(y)x}$.

There is no right or left in a quadratic product xyx; instead, there is an inside and an outside. Just as a left ideal is a subspace invariant under left multiplication by the ambient algebra, so an inner ideal is a subspace invariant under inner multiplication by the ambient algebra. These inner ideals play the role that one-sided ideals do in the associative theory; in particular, the dcc on inner ideals is the analogue of the Artinian condition. Note that from the point of view of linear theory there can be no one-sided ideals, since by commutativity all one-sided ideals are two-sided.

A trivial ideal (one with all products zero) gives rise to a trivial element $U_z = 0$, though there is no reason why there should be an element with $L_z = 0$. Conversely, trivial elements almost generate trivial ideals, so the nonexistence of trivial elements (*strong semiprimeness*) is almost equivalent to nonexistence of trivial ideals (*semiprimeness*); since ideals are very hard to construct, describe, and relate to elements in nonassociative algebras, the strong semiprimeness condition on elements is very useful.

The structure group too involves the U-operators; the L's play no role.

Jordan algebras without regard to unit elements lead to Jordan triple systems and Jordan pairs studied recently by Meyberg [**12**] and Loos [**5**]. In many applications these are more natural than Jordan algebras because it is artificial to single out a distinguished element as unit.

In addition to clarifying old concepts and suggesting new ones, another advantage of the quadratic theory (and the main reason for its creation) is that *it handles all characteristics equally*. The standard kinds of Jordan algebras do not qualify as linear Jordan algebras unless there is a scalar $\frac{1}{2}$, and in characteristic 2 the simple linear Jordan algebras are pathological nodal algebras. On the other hand, the simple quadratic Jordan algebras are essentially the same in all characteristics:

STRUCTURE THEOREM. *A simple quadratic Jordan algebra with dcc on inner ideals is either*

(1) *a Jordan division algebra,*

(2) *a Jordan algebra of a nondegenerate quadratic form,*

(3) *the symmetric elements in a *-simple Artinian associative algebra with involution,*

(4) *an exceptional algebra of symmetric* 3×3 *matrices with entries in a Cayley algebra.*

In characteristic 2 there are also certain ample outer ideals in cases (2) and (3), so there is a slight variation on the basic theme.

The above theorem tacitly assumes a unit element; it is an open question whether a simple Jordan algebra with dcc has a unit, equivalently is semisimple. For finite dimensional algebras the Jacobson radical is nilpotent [**7**], but we would like this for all algebras with dcc:

Open Question. Is the radical nilpotent when the algebra has dcc?

Recently Slin'ko [**17**] has shown the absolute zero divisors in a *special* Jordan algebra generate a locally nilpotent ideal:

Open Question. Do absolute zero divisors generate locally nilpotent ideals?

Let me mention two other gaps where the Jordan theory is not as complete as the associative theory:

Open Problem. Develop a theory of Jordan rings of quotients and Jordan algebras with acc.

Open Problem. Develop a theory of Jordan rings with polynomial identities.

But the real reason the quadratic theory is the "right" one compared to the linear theory is *not* that the linear theory fails in characteristic 2, but that because it demands a scalar $\frac{1}{2}$ it fails to provide a theory of Jordan *rings*. The quadratic approach is a ring-theoretic approach; the scalars play almost no role.

3. Quadratic Jordan methods in nonassociative algebras.

(a) *Noncommutative Jordan algebras.* The passage from A to A^+ is a standard technique in nonassociative algebra; once the notion of Jordan algebra is freed from the necessity of $\frac{1}{2}$, this passage makes sense in general. If A is a noncommutative Jordan algebra then the algebra A^+ with U-operator

$$U_x y = x(xy + yx) - x^2 y = (xy + yx)x - yx^2$$

is a quadratic Jordan algebra [**8**]; in the case of left or right alternative algebras this reduces to the previously considered operators $U_x y = x(yx)$ or $U_x y = (xy)x$ With these operators we can carry the quadratic theory over to obtain a theory of noncommutative Jordan rings with dcc analogous to the theory for quadratic Jordan rings [**9**], [**10**].

(b) *Alternative rings.* In general the Jordan products x^2 and $U_x y$ are better behaved and easier to handle in an alternative ring than the product xy. For example, we have the Moufang identities $L_{U(x)y} = L_x L_y L_x$, $R_{U(x)y} = R_x R_y R_x$ and the identities $U_{xy} = L_x U_y R_x = R_y U_x L_y$.

By reducing an arbitrary polynomial identity to a Jordan polynomial identity and making use of these convenient relations for Jordan products, Shirshov **[14]** showed that a nil PI alternative algebra is locally nilpotent. Using just the essential parts of Shirshov's deep combinatorial methods, Slin'ko **[17]** showed the absolute zero divisors generate a locally nilpotent ideal. In characteristic $\neq 3$ we can do much better, for Kleinfeld **[4]** showed that an absolute zero divisor determines a nilpotent ideal, and this was used to show that a prime alternative ring of characteristic $\neq 3$ is associative or a Cayley order. By using Jordan methods and Slin'ko's result, Slater **[16]** has given a self-contained proof that a strongly prime (prime + no absolute zero divisors) alternative ring is associative or Cayley. This still leaves the general

Open Question. Are all prime alternative rings either associative or Cayley?

(c) *Right Moufang algebras.* Skornyakov **[15]** showed that a right Moufang division ring was alternative; this was extended by Albert **[1]** to simple right Moufang rings, under the assumption of finite-dimensionality and characteristic $\neq 2$. Using absolute zero divisors and U-operators, Thedy **[20]** has made progress on this classification problem: He showed that a strongly prime right Moufang ring with proper idempotent $e \neq 0, 1$ is alternative. But once again the general case is unsolved:

Open Question. Are all simple right Moufang rings alternative?

(d) *Associative rings with involution.* The archetypal Jordan algebra is the set of symmetric elements in an associative ring with involution. Indeed, Jordan algebras originated in an attempt to capture the "algebraic essence" of the Hermitian operators on Hilbert space. Thus it is not surprising that Jordan methods have played a role in rings with involution.

The property which makes the (Jordan) algebra of symmetric elements more tractable than the (Lie) algebra of skew elements is that while the latter is closed only under $xy - yx$, the former is closed both under $xy + yx$ and xyx. The additional operation $U_x y = xyx$ is the decisive factor.

4. Summary. In closing, let me summarize the advantages and insights to be gained from Jordan methods and emphasis upon the U-operators:

(1) these provide a *ring-theoretic approach* which avoids any restriction on the characteristic or a demand for $\frac{1}{2}$;

(2) they focus attention on *inner ideals*, which play the role in nonassociative algebras that one-sided ideals do in the associative case; in particular, they provide useful chain conditions;

(3) they focus attention on *absolute zero divisors*, giving a useful radical and semisimplicity criterion in terms of elements rather than elusive ideals;

(4) in the associative case they emphasize the basic symmetric product xyx in rings with involution;

(5) they play an important role in applications to analysis, as explained by Professor Koecher in his address to the 1970 International Congress.

Each nonassociative algebraist carries a bag of tricks, notions, and methods which he can apply to the variety of problems he meets. One example is linearization—faced with an identity one can linearize, substitute, interpret as operator relations, thus extracting much more information from the original identity. Another is Peirce decompositions—one can use an idempotent to break the algebra into pieces and recover much information from the way these pieces fit together. Yet another example involves multiplication algebras—translating problems from a nonassociative algebra to its associative algebra of multiplications. What I am urging is that nonassociative algebraists should add quadratic methods to their bag of tricks, as a powerful technique applicable in a wide variety of situations.

References

1. A. A. Albert, *The structure of right alternative algebras*, Ann. of Math. (2) **59** (1954), 408–417. MR **15**, 774.

2. M. Hall, *Projective planes*, Trans. Amer. Math. Soc. **54** (1943), 229–277. MR **5**, 72.

3. N. Jacobson, *Lectures on quadratic Jordan algebras*, Tata Institute Lecture Notes, Bombay, 1969.

4. E. Kleinfeld, *Alternative nil rings*, Ann. of Math. (2) **66** (1957), 395–399. MR **19**, 383.

5. O. Loos, *A structure theory of Jordan pairs* (to appear).

6. K. McCrimmon, *A general theory of Jordan rings*, Proc. Nat. Acad. Sci. U.S.A. **56** (1966), 1072–1079. MR **34** #2643.

7. ———, *Nilpotence and solvability in quadratic Jordan algebras*, Scripta Math. **29** (1973), 467–483.

8. ———, *Quadratic Jordan algebras and cubing operations*, Trans. Amer. Math. Soc. **153** (1971), 265–278. MR **42** #3138.

9. K. McCrimmon and R. D. Schafer, *On a class of noncommutative Jordan rings*, Proc. Nat. Acad. Sci. U.S.A. **56** (1966), 1–4. MR **34** #5888.

10. K. McCrimmon, *Noncommutative Jordan rings*, Trans. Amer. Math. Soc. **158** (1971), 1–33. MR **46** #9127.

11. ———, *Absolute zero divisors and local nilpotence in alternative algebras*, Proc. Amer. Math. Soc. **47** (1975), 293–299.

12. K. Meyberg, *Lectures on algebras and triple systems*, University of Virginia Lecture Notes, Charlottesville, Va., 1972.

13. R. L. Sans Souci, *Right alternative division rings of characteristic two*, Proc. Amer. Math. Soc. **6** (1955), 291–296. MR **16**, 896; 1337.

14. A. I. Širšov, *On some non-associative nil-rings and algebraic algebras*, Mat. Sb. **41** (**83**) (1957) 381–394. (Russian) MR **19**, 727.

15. L. A. Skornjakov, *Right-alternative fields*, Izv. Akad. Nauk SSSR Ser. Mat. **15** (1951), 177–184. (Russian) MR **12**, 669.

16. M. Slater, *Strongly prime and Jordan prime alternative rings*. I (to appear).

17. A. Slin'ko, *The Jacobson radical and absolute divisors of zero of special Jordan rings*, Algebra i Logika **11** (1972), 711–723, 737. MR **47** #5065.

18. T. A. Springer, *Jordan algebras and algebraic groups*, Springer-Verlag, New York, 1973.

19. F. W. Stevenson, *Projective planes*, Freeman, San Francisoco, Calif., 1972.

20. A. Thedy, *Right alternative rings with Peirce decomposition* (to appear).

UNIVERSITY OF VIRGINIA
CHARLOTTESVILLE, VIRGINIA 22093, U.S.A.

Proceedings of the International Congress of Mathematicians
Vancouver, 1974

On Subspaces of Inner Product Spaces

Winfried Scharlau

1. Introduction. Let K be a field and I a partially ordered finite set. An *I-space* $(V, V_i, i \in I)$ over K will be a finite-dimensional K-vector space V together with a family of subspaces V_i such that $i \leqq j$ implies $V_i \subset V_j$. Morphisms, direct sums, decomposable and indecomposable objects are defined in the obvious way in the category of I-spaces. I is of *finite representation type* if there exist up to isomorphisms only finitely many indecomposable I-spaces over any K.

1.1. THEOREM (NAZAROVA-ROITER, KLEINER). *I is of finite representation type if and only if I does not contain a subset which, with the induced ordering, looks like one of the following:*

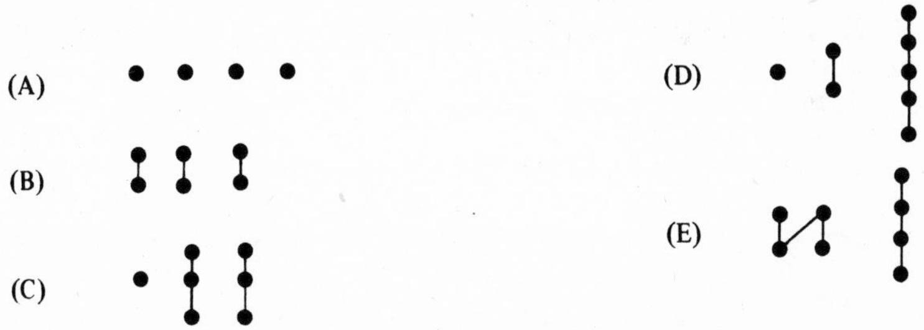

For the proof and related problems see **[6]**, **[5]**, **[2]**, **[3]**, **[1]**.

In this note we are interested in subspaces of inner product spaces (V, b) where b is a nonsingular symmetric bilinear form. (An analogous theory can be developed for b skew-symmetric.) Since every subspace W defines the orthogonal space $W^\perp$ we are led to the following definition.

1.2. DEFINITION. Let K be a field of characteristic $\neq 2$ and let I be a partially ordered finite set with an involution $^\perp: I \to I$, i.e., a map such that $i \leqq j$ implies $j^\perp \leqq i^\perp$, and $i^{\perp\perp} = i$ for all $i, j \in I$. An $(I, ^\perp)$-space $(V, b; V_i, i \in I)$ (over K) will be a nonsingular symmetric bilinear space (V, b) together with a family of subspaces V_i such that $i \leqq j$ implies $V_i \subset V_j$ and $V_{i^\perp} = V_i^\perp$.

Morphisms, orthogonal sums, decomposable and indecomposable objects are defined in the obvious way in the category of $(I, ^\perp)$-spaces. The following questions arise naturally:

Problems. (1) For which $(I, ^\perp)$ do there exist over every field only finitely many indecomposable $(I, ^\perp)$-spaces (up to isometry and multiplication of b by a scalar)? In this case, we say that $(I, ^\perp)$ is of *finite representation type*.

(2) For which $(I, ^\perp)$ can one classify the $(I, ^\perp)$-spaces?

(3) What can be said about the forgetful functor from $(I, ^\perp)$-spaces to I-spaces?

(4) For which $(I, ^\perp)$ does the cancellation law hold?

CONJECTURE. *$(I, ^\perp)$ is of finite representation type if and only if I is of finite representation type.*

This conjecture is proved in the following sections for some $(I, ^\perp)$. We shall also present some examples concerning the classification problem. We shall see that there are interesting relations to other classification problems of linear algebra.

2. Examples of finite representation type. When we describe a partially ordered set with involution $(I, ^\perp)$ graphically we use a dot ● for every $i \neq i^\perp$ and a circle ○ for every $i = i^\perp$. If it is necessary to say which dots correspond under the involution we index them by the same number, e.g.,

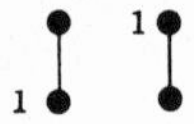

or

2.1. THEOREM. *The following partially ordered sets with involution are of finite representation type:*

(a1)

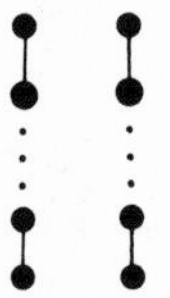

(a2)

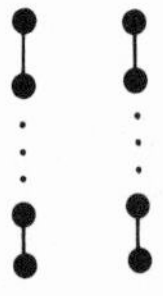

(a3)

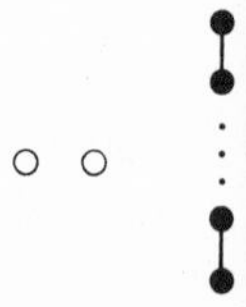

PROOF. (a1) We have to consider a bilinear space (V, b) with a chain $V_1 \subset V_2 \subset \cdots \subset V_r \subset V_{r+1} = V$ of subspaces. (The other chain is given by the orthogonal spaces.) Assume our space is indecomposable. We may assume without loss of generality $V_1 \neq 0$. Then, V_1 must be totally isotropic, since an anisotropic vector e_1 would yield an orthogonal decomposition $V = (e_1K) \perp (e_1K)^\perp$. Let i be the smallest number such that $V_1 \perp V_i$ but $V_1 \not\perp V_{i+1}$. Then there exist $e_1 \in V_1$ and $e_1^* \in V_{i+1}$ such that $b(e_1, e_1^*) = 1$. The nonsingular (hyperbolic) plane $(e_1K + e_1^*K)$ yields a splitting $V = (e_1K + e_1^*K) \perp (e_1K + e_1^*K)^\perp$ which is compatible with the chain $V_1 \subset \cdots \subset V_r$.

(a2) This case is more complicated. Therefore we consider briefly only one special case, namely spaces of the following type: $(V, b; 0 < W_1 < \cdots < W_r = W, 0 < U_1 < \cdots < U_s = U)$ where $V = W \oplus U$ with W, U totally isotropic, and hence in duality under b. (Note that the complete chains are $W_1 \subset \cdots \subset W_r \subset W_{r-1}^{\perp} \subset \cdots \subset W_1^{\perp}$, and similarly for U.) We choose bases $w_1, \cdots, w_n$ and $u_1, \cdots, u_n$ of W and U, compatible with the given filtrations. Let $w_1^*, \cdots, w_n^* \in U$ be the base dual to $w_1, \cdots, w_n$ and let $A = (a_{ij})$ be the matrix of the base change $u_i = \sum a_{ij} w_j^*$. If we choose different bases w_i' and u_i', A will be replaced by BAC with

$$B \in \underbrace{\begin{pmatrix} * & & 0 \\ & \boxed{*} \ddots & \\ * & & \boxed{*} \end{pmatrix}}_{m_1 \; m_2 \; \cdots \; m_s} =: \Gamma_1, \qquad m_i = \dim(U_i/U_{i-1}),$$

$$C \in \underbrace{\begin{pmatrix} * & & * \\ & \boxed{*} \ddots & \\ 0 & & \boxed{*} \end{pmatrix}}_{n_1 \; n_2 \; \cdots \; n_r} =: \Gamma_2, \qquad n_i = \dim(W_i/W_{i-1}).$$

Since $\Gamma_1 \backslash \mathrm{GL}(n, k) / \Gamma_2$ contains only finitely many elements, the assertion is proved in the particular case under consideration.

(a3) Again, we want to consider only one special case, namely $(V, b; V = V_1 \oplus V_2, 0 < W_1 < \cdots < W_k = W)$ where V_1, V_2, W are totally isotropic and pairwise in duality under b. If $\pi_i : V \to V_i$ are the projections corresponding to the direct sum $V = V_1 \oplus V_2$, then $\beta : W \times W \to K$, $\beta(x, y) := b(\pi_1 x, \pi_2 y)$ is a nonsingular skew-symmetric form, which describes $(V, b; V_1, V_2, W)$ completely. Therefore, we have to investigate a skew-symmetric space (W, β) with a chain of subspaces, a problem which is similar to (a1).

Since nonsingular skew-symmetric forms are even dimensional and classified by their dimension, one gets the following well-known result.

2.2. COROLLARY. *If (V, b) is a nonsingular symmetric bilinear space with three totally isotropic subspaces V_1, V_2, V_3 such that $V = V_i \oplus V_j$ for $i \neq j$, then* $\dim(V)$ *is a multiple of* 4. *The orthogonal group $O(V, b)$ operates transitively on the set of triples of subspaces as above.*

3. Relations to other classification problems. This section contains some information concerning the classification problem for the partially ordered sets (A)—(E) of Theorem 1.1 with arbitrary involutions. As a corollary one obtains:

3.1. THEOREM. *The partially ordered sets* (A)—(E) *of* 1.1 *with any involution are of infinite representation type.*

We shall discuss only some typical cases:

(A1) ● ● ● ●

One has to investigate a bilinear space (V, b) with two subspaces V_1 and V_2. (The other two subspaces are the orthogonal spaces.) Assume in addition $V =$

$V_1 \oplus V_2$ and V_1, V_2 in duality. We choose an arbitrary basis of V_1 and the dual basis in V_2. The matrix of b is of the following form

$$\begin{pmatrix} A & E \\ E & B \end{pmatrix}, \qquad A, B \text{ symmetric.}$$

After a basis change X in V_1 and the dual basis change X^{-t} in V_2 one gets the matrix

$$\begin{pmatrix} X^tAX & E \\ E & X^{-1}BX^{-t} \end{pmatrix}.$$

Hence one has to classify the pair $(A, A^{-1}B)$ consisting of the bilinear form A and the selfadjoint transformation $A^{-1}B$. This problem is considered, e.g., in [**4**].

(A2) ● ● ○ ○

As a special case we consider the following situation: $(V, b; V_1, V_2, W)$, $V_i = V_i^{\perp}$, $V = V_1 \oplus V_2 = V_1 \oplus W = V_2 \oplus W$. This leads to the classification problem for the not necessarily symmetric bilinear form $\beta: W \times W \to K$ defined in 2.1(a3). There is much literature concerning this problem; see, e.g., [**7**].

(A3) ○ ○ ○ ○

We have seen in 2.1(a3) that ○ ○ ○ leads to the classification of skew-symmetric bilinear forms. Hence, ○○○○ leads to the classification of a vector space with two skew-symmetric forms. This problem is solved in [**8**, §3].

(A3) ○ ○ ○ ○ (B1)

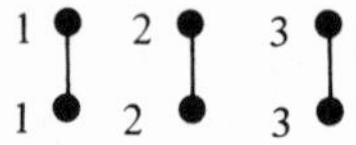

As a special case we consider the following situation $(V, b; V_1, V_2, V_3)$ with $V = V_1 \oplus V_2 \oplus V_3$, V_i totally isotropic and pairwise in duality. Choosing an arbitrary basis in V_1 and dual bases in V_2 and V_3 we obtain for b the matrix

$$\begin{pmatrix} 0 & E & E \\ E & 0 & A \\ E & A^t & 0 \end{pmatrix}$$

and are led to the classification of the bilinear form given by A.

The other cases are handled in a similar fashion.

4. The forgetful functor. It is natural and interesting to study the forgetful functor $(V, b; V_i) \mapsto (V, V_i)$ from $(I, {}^{\perp})$-spaces to I-spaces. Again, we shall consider only one typical example.

Let V be a vector space and $V_1, \cdots, V_4$ four subspaces such that $V = V_i \oplus V_j$ for $i \neq j$.

Questions. (1) When does there exist a symmetric bilinear form b such that $V_3 = V_1^{\perp}$, $V_4 = V_2^{\perp}$ with respect to b?

(2) When does there exist a symmetric bilinear form b such that $V_1, \cdots, V_4$ are totally isotropic?

The answer to Question (1) is "always". Recall that every $(V, V_1, \cdots, V_4)$ as above can be obtained in the following way: Let W be a vector space and α an automorphism of W. Let $V = W \oplus W$, $V_1 = W \oplus 0$, $V_2 = 0 \oplus W$, $V_3 =$ the diagonal, $V_4 =$ the graph of α. Describe b as in (A1) by the matrix

$$\begin{pmatrix} A & E \\ E & B \end{pmatrix}$$

It turns out that the matrix of α is $A^{-1}B$. Hence we get the following question: Is it possible to write an arbitrary invertible matrix as a product of two symmetric matrices? It is left to the reader to show that this is always possible.

Similarly, Question (2) leads to the following problem: Given an arbitrary invertible matrix A, when does there exist a skew-symmetric matrix X such that $X^{-1}AX = -A^t$? It is left to the reader to find necessary and sufficient conditions.

References

1. I. N. Bernšteĭn, I. M. Gel'fand and V. A. Ponomarev, *Coxeter functors and Gabriel quivers*, Uspehi Mat. Nauk **28** (1973), no. 2 (170), 19–33 = Russian Math. Surveys **28** (1973), no. 2, 17–32.
2. P. Gabriel, *Unzerlegbare Darstellungen*, I, Manuscripta Math. **6** (1972), 71–103.
3. ———, *Indecomposable representations*, II, Istituto Nazionale di Alta Matematica, Symposia Mathematica **XI** (1973), 81–104.
4. F. Ischebeck and W. Scharlau, *Hermitesche und orthogonale Operatoren über kommutativen Ringen*, Math. Ann. **200** (1973), 327–334.
5. M. M. Kleiner, *On partially ordered sets with finitely many indecomposable representations*, Zap. Naučn. Sem. Leningrad. Otdel. Mat. Inst. Steklov. (LOMI) **28** (1972).
6. L. A. Nazarova and A. E. Roĭter, *Representations of partially ordered sets*. I, Zap. Naučn. Sem. Leningrad. Otdel. Mat. Inst. Steklov. (LOMI) **28** (1972), 15–31 = J. Soviet Math. (to appear).
7. C. Riehm, *On the equivalence of bilinear forms*, J. Algebra (1974).
8. R. Scharlau, *Paare alternierender Formen* (to appear). Diplomrabeit, Bonn.

MATH. INSTITUT DER UNIVERSITÄT
MÜNSTER, FEDERAL REPUBLIC OF GERMANY

Proceedings of the International Congress of Mathematicians
Vancouver, 1974

Something Like the Brauer Group

Moss Eisenberg Sweedler

Here is a series of ideas and constructions related to the Brauer group and Amitsur cohomology. In alternate sections we indicate what changes to make to achieve a unified generalization of the theory.

I—OLD. The classical theory begins with the matrix ring. We begin a little differently. Let A be a commutative algebra over a ring k. Instead of the general matrix ring focus on $\mathrm{End}_k A$. The k-algebra map $A \xrightarrow{l} \mathrm{End}_k A$, $a \to a^l$ (where a^l is "a" acting as a left translation operator) is important. Identifying A with A^l leads to the picture $\mathrm{End}_k A \supset A = A^l$.

REMARKS. At times additional restrictions are put on A or k. Typical additional restrictions are:

(i) A is a finitely generated projective k-module.
(ii) k is a field.
(iii) A is a field.

I—NEW. Let $\{L_\alpha\}$ with each $L_\alpha \subset A \otimes A$ satisfy:
(i) $\{L_\alpha\}$ is an inductive set; i.e., given L_α and L_β there is L_γ with $L_\alpha \supset L_\gamma \subset L_\beta$.
(ii) Each L_α is an ideal in $A \otimes A$.
(iii) e_1 and mult denote the maps

$$\begin{aligned} e_1 &: A \otimes A \to A \otimes A \otimes A, & a \otimes b &\to a \otimes 1 \otimes b, \\ \mathrm{mult} &: A \otimes A \to A, & a \otimes b &\to ab. \end{aligned}$$

Then given L_α and L_β there is L_γ with $e_1(L_\gamma) \subset L_\alpha \otimes A + A \otimes L_\beta$, and there is an L_ω with $L_\omega \subset \ker \mathrm{mult}$.

$\mathrm{End}_k A$ is an $A \otimes A$-module where $(a \otimes b) \cdot F = a^l F b^l$, for $F \in \mathrm{End}_k A$. Let $E_\alpha = \{F \in \mathrm{End}_k A \mid L_\alpha \cdot F = 0\}$. Let $E = \bigcup E_\alpha$. Conditions (i), (ii) and (iii) insure that E is a subalgebra of $\mathrm{End}_k A$. For example the e_1 condition in (iii) implies

$E_\alpha E_\beta \subset E_\gamma$ and the mult condition in (iii) implies $A^l \subset E_\omega$. So there is the k-algebra map $A \xrightarrow{l} E$, $a \to a^l$.

The E replaces $\mathrm{End}_k A$.

REMARKS. It will be seen in III—NEW that condition (iii) amounts to certain continuity conditions.

As in I—OLD we may wish to impose some additional restrictions. One of these is that $(\underline{A} \otimes A)/L_\alpha$ be a finitely generated projective left A-module for each L_α. (The left action of A on $\underline{A} \otimes A$ and $(\underline{A} \otimes A)/L_\alpha$ arises from the action of A on the underlined tensorands.) This condition corresponds to the condition of "A being a finitely generated projective k-module" in I—OLD.

Another assumption which is sometimes needed, especially in considering questions about simplicity of E as an algebra, is that given L_α there is L_β with twist$(L_\beta) \subset L_\alpha$; where twist: $A \otimes A \to A \otimes A$, $a \otimes b \to b \otimes a$.

If $\{L_\alpha\}$ consists of only the zero ideal then $E = \mathrm{End}_k A$ and all the NEW theory reduces to the OLD. (Note that the "twist" condition just above is automatically satisfied in this case.) Other interesting NEW theories arise when $\{L_\alpha\} = \{(\ker \mathrm{mult})^i\}$ or if $\{A_\alpha\}$ is a suitable collection of subalgebras of A and one takes $\{L_\alpha\} = \{\ker (A \otimes A \to A \otimes_{A_\alpha} A)\}$. In the former case the NEW theory is related to the theory of algebras of differential operators and the cohomology which arises in III—NEW is related to de Rham cohomology when the characteristic is zero.

II—OLD. Consider pairs (U, i) where U is a k-algebra, $i: A \to U$ is an algebra map (giving U an A-bimodule structure), and $U \cong \mathrm{End}_k A$ *as an A-bimodule*. Call two pairs (U, i) and (V, j) equivalent—and write $U \sim V$—if there is an algebra isomorphism $\rho: U \to V$, where $\rho i = j$. Let $[U]$ denote the equivalence class of (U, i) and let $\mathscr{E}_A$ denote the *set* of equivalence classes.

II—NEW. The same as II—OLD except replace $\mathrm{End}_k A$ by E throughout.

III—OLD.

$$A \otimes A \overset{e_0}{\underset{e_2}{\equiv\!\!\Rightarrow}} A \otimes A \otimes A \overset{e_0}{\underset{e_3}{\equiv\!\!\Rightarrow}} A \otimes A \otimes A \otimes A,$$

where e_i inserts "1" in the $(i + 1)$-position. For $x \in A \otimes A \otimes A$, call x a *weak 2-cocycle* if $e_0(x)e_2(x) = e_1(x)e_3(x)$ and both $(\mathrm{mult} \otimes I)(x)$ and $(I \otimes \mathrm{mult})(x)$ are invertible. Call x a *2-cocycle* if in addition x itself is invertible (in which case x is an Amitsur 2-cocycle). For $x, y \in A \otimes A \otimes A$ call x cohomologous to y if there is an invertible $z \in A \otimes A$ with $(e_0(z)e_1(z^{-1})e_2(z))x = y$. If x is cohomologous to y then x is a (weak) 2-cocycle if and only if y is a (weak) 2-cocycle. Lef $\mathscr{F}_A$ denote the set of cohomology classes of weak 2-cocycles and let $H^2(A/k)$ denote the subset of cohomology classes of 2-cocycles. $\mathscr{F}_A$ has a monoid structure induced by product in $A \otimes A \otimes A$; the unit is the cohomology class of $1 \otimes 1 \otimes 1$. $H^2(A/k)$ is the sub*group* of $\mathscr{F}_A$ consisting of elements which are invertible. ($H^2(A/k)$ is the degree two Amitsur cohomology of A over k.)

III—NEW. $A \otimes \cdots \otimes A$ has a topology induced by declaring $L_{\alpha_1} \otimes A \otimes \cdots \otimes A + A \otimes L_{\alpha_2} \otimes A \otimes \cdots \otimes A + \cdots + A \otimes \cdots \otimes A \otimes L_{\alpha_n}$ to be open. (A itself has the discrete topology.) The e_i maps and the maps $I \otimes \cdots \otimes I \otimes \text{mult} \otimes I \otimes \cdots \otimes I$ are continuous by virtue of condition (iii) in I — NEW. Therefore we can complete and have

$$(A \otimes A)^{\wedge} \overset{\hat{e}_0}{\underset{\hat{e}_2}{\Rrightarrow}} (A \otimes A \otimes A)^{\wedge} \overset{\hat{e}_0}{\underset{\hat{e}_3}{\Rrightarrow}} (A \otimes A \otimes A \otimes A)^{\wedge}.$$

Now proceed as in III — OLD except with the (ˆ)'s added.

IV—OLD. If A is a finite projective k-module there is a bijective correspondence $\mathscr{E}_A \leftrightarrow \mathscr{F}_A$, given as follows: Suppose $x = \sum a_i \otimes b_i \otimes c_i \in A \otimes A \otimes A$ is a weak 2-cocycle. Give $\text{End}_k A$ a new multiplication using x. For $F, G \in \text{End}_k A$ the new product is given by

$$(\ast) \qquad F * G = \sum a_i^l F b_i^l G c_i^l.$$

This will be an associative product and the unit will be $((\sum a_i b_i c_i)^{-1})^l$. Let $(\text{End}_k A)^x$ denote $\text{End}_k A$ with the new product. $h: A \to (\text{End}_k A)^x$, $a \to ((a(\sum a_i b_i c_i)^{-1})^l)^x$ is an algebra map making $(\text{End}_k A)^x \cong \text{End}_k A$ as an A-bimodule. Under the bijective correspondence the cohomology class of x corresponds to $[(\text{End}_k A)^x]$.

IV—NEW. This is almost the same as IV—OLD. We must have that $(A \otimes A)/L_\alpha$ is a finitely generated projective left A-module for each L_α. Of course $\text{End}_k A$ is replaced by E and the cohomology in IV—OLD is replaced by the completed cohomology of III—NEW. The only difficulty comes in defining the multiplication alteration. With a little care the formula $(\ast)$ in IV—OLD will still make sense. Suppose $F, G \in E$. Then for some α and β we have $F \in E_\alpha$, $G \in E_\beta$. Since the completion $(A \otimes A \otimes A)^{\wedge}$ is the inverse limit

$$\text{proj lim} \; \frac{A \otimes A \otimes A}{L_{\gamma_1} \otimes A + A \otimes L_{\gamma_2}}$$

we may read x modulo $L_\alpha \otimes A + A \otimes L_\gamma$, i.e.,

$$x \equiv \sum a_i \otimes b_i \otimes c_i \mod (L_\alpha \otimes A + A \otimes L_\beta)^{\wedge},$$

for $\sum a_i \otimes b_i \otimes c_i \in A \otimes A \otimes A$. With this choice of $\sum a_i \otimes b_i \otimes c_i$ the formula $(\ast)$ in IV—OLD makes sense and only depends upon x, F and G.

V—OLD. Given the pairs (U, i) and (V, j) form $U \otimes_A V$, the tensor product with respect to the *left* action of A on both U and V. $U \otimes_A V$ is a right $U \otimes V$-module where for $\sum u_i \otimes v_i \in U \otimes_A V$ and $\sum x_j \otimes y_j \in U \otimes V$ the module action is given by $(\sum u_i \otimes v_i) \cdot (\sum x_j \otimes y_j) = \sum_{i,j} u_i x_j \otimes v_i y_j$. With respect to this right module action form $\text{End}_{U \otimes V}(U \otimes_A V)$. This is the classical description of the product of the pair (U, i) by the pair (V, j). The map $A \to \text{End}_{U \otimes V}(U \otimes_A V)$, $a \to (u \otimes v \mapsto au \otimes v = u \otimes av)$ makes the product again a pair. For some purposes, particularly in the NEW theory, another description of the product is useful. Within $U \otimes_A V$ let

$$U \times_A V = \{\sum u_i \otimes v_i \in U \otimes_A V \mid \sum u_i a \otimes v_i = \sum u_i \otimes v_i a,\ a \in A\}.$$

$U \times_A V$ has a well-defined product determined by $(\sum u_i \otimes v_i)(\sum w_j \otimes z_j) =$

$\sum_{i,j} u_i w_j \otimes v_i z_j$, for $\sum u_i \otimes v_i$, $\sum w_j \otimes z_j \in U \times_A V$. The unit is $1 \otimes 1$, and $i \times j : A \to U \times_A V, a \to i(a) \otimes 1 = 1 \otimes j(a)$, is an algebra map. The product pair $(U \times_A V, i \times j)$ is naturally isomorphic to the product pair given in terms of $\text{End}_{U \otimes V}(U \otimes_A V)$. If A is a finitely generated projective k-module and $U \cong \text{End}_k A \cong V$ as A-bimodules then $U \times_A V \cong \text{End}_k A$ as A-bimodules. $\mathscr{E}_A$ becomes a commutative monoid with unit $[\text{End}_k A]$, the product given by $[U][V] = [U \times_A V]$. Moreover the bijective correspondence given in IV—OLD is an isomorphism of monoids. Thus $H^2(A/k)$ corresponds to $\mathscr{G}_A$, the sub*group* of invertible elements of $\mathscr{E}_A$. If A is a finite degree field extension of k then $\mathscr{G}_A$ consists precisely of equivalence classes of central simple k-algebras which contain A as a maximal commutative subring. This leads to the isomorphisms

$$H^2(A/k) \cong \mathscr{G}_A \cong \text{Br}(A/k)$$

where $\text{Br}(A/k)$ is the subgroup of the Brauer group of k consisting of classes split by A.

V—NEW. The product pair $(U \times_A V, i \times j)$ is the same as in V—OLD. If $(\underset{\sim}{A} \otimes A)/L_\alpha$ is a finitely generated projective left A-module for each L_α then $\mathscr{E}_A$ is a commutative monoid with unit $[E]$. Moreover the correspondence in IV—NEW is a monoid isomorphism. The group $\mathscr{G}_A$ is not in general a relative Brauer group even when A and k are fields. (A and k may be fields and $(\underset{\sim}{A} \otimes A)/L_\alpha$ may be a finite dimensional left A-module for each L_α and yet A need *not* be a finite degree extension of k.) However if A and k are both fields and for each L_α there is an L_β with (twist) $(L_\beta) \subset L_\alpha$, then the group $\mathscr{G}_A$ consists of classes of algebras $[U]$, where U is a simple k-algebra.

VI—OLD. For each pair (U, i) with $[U] \in \mathscr{E}_A$, the image $i(A)$ is a maximal commutative subring of U and the center of U is $i(C)$ where C is the subalgebra of A with C^l the center of $\text{End}_k A$. Often $C = k$.

VI—NEW. This is the same as VI—OLD but with $\text{End}_k A$ replaced by E. A further characterization of C can be given as $\{a \in A \mid 1 \otimes a - a \otimes 1 \in \bigcap L_\alpha\}$.

VII—OLD. Suppose A is a finitely generated projective k-module. If (U, i) is a pair let U° denote the "opposite algebra" to U and $i^\circ : A \to U^\circ, a \to i(a)^\circ$. If A is a Frobenius k-algebra then $\text{End}_k A \cong (\text{End}_k A)^\circ$ as an A-bimodule (and if k is a field the converse holds). So when A is Frobenius if $[U] \in \mathscr{E}_A$ then $[U^\circ] \in \mathscr{E}_A$; moreover if $[U] \in \mathscr{G}_A$ then $[U]^{-1} = [U^\circ]$. This covers the most classical case when A is a finite degree field extension of k, since then A is a Frobenius k-algebra. Without assuming that A is a Frobenius k-algebra if $[U] \in \mathscr{G}_A$ then

$$[U]^{-1} = [((\text{End}_k A)^\circ \times_A U)^\circ].$$

This automatically reduces to U° when $[(\text{End}_k A)^\circ] = [\text{End}_k A]$, which also happens when A is a Frobenius k-algebra.

VII—NEW. Assume $(\underset{\sim}{A} \otimes A)/L_\alpha$ is a finitely generated left A-module for each L_α, and given L_α there is L_β with (twist) $(L_\beta) \subset L_\alpha$. Then for $[U] \in \mathscr{G}_A$, the inverse is given by $[U]^{-1} = [(E^\circ \times_A U)^\circ]$.

VIII—OLD. If k is a field and A a finite dimensional k-algebra then all algebras U with $[U] \in \mathcal{G}_A$ are simple.

VIII—NEW. Assume that $(\underset{\sim}{A} \otimes A)/L_\alpha$ is a finitely generated projective left A-module for each L_α, and given L_α there is L_β with (twist) $(L_\beta) \subset L_\alpha$. The following conditions are equivalent:

(1) A is a simple E-module, recall $E \subset \mathrm{End}_k A$.

(2) E is a simple algebra.

(3) Each algebra U with $[U] \in \mathcal{G}_A$ is simple.

Of course it all depends on properties of $\{L_\alpha\}$ and in terms of $\{L_\alpha\}$ one may add the fourth equivalent condition:

(4) For each ideal $0 \neq J \subsetneq A$ there is an L_α with $A \otimes J \not\subset J \otimes A + L_\alpha$.

IX—OLD. For a pair (U, i) form $\mathrm{End}_A U$ with respect to U as a *left* A-module. The map $\Omega: A \otimes U^\circ \to \mathrm{End}_A U$, $a \otimes u^\circ \to (v \mapsto avu)$ is an algebra map. If A is a finitely generated projective k-module and $[U] \in \mathcal{G}_A$ then Ω is an isomorphism. Using $\mathrm{End}_k A$ in place of U gives the third isomorphism and using the fact that $U \cong \mathrm{End}_k A$ as an A-bimodule (and hence a left A-module) gives the second isomorphism in the series of algebra isomorphisms:

$$A \otimes U^\circ \cong \mathrm{End}_A U \cong \mathrm{End}_A (\mathrm{End}_k A) \cong A \otimes (\mathrm{End}_k A)^\circ.$$

This is one aspect of classical "splitting" theory.

IX—NEW. Assume that $(\underset{\sim}{A} \otimes A)/L_\alpha$ is a finitely generated projective left A-module for each L_α, and given L_α there is L_β with (twist) $(L_\beta) \subset L_\alpha$. The Ω map in IX—OLD is well defined but not in general an isomorphism, not even when $[U] \in \mathcal{G}_A$. Consider U as an $A \otimes A$-module where $(a \otimes b) \cdot u = aub$ $(= i(a)ui(b))$. Let $U_\alpha = \{u \in U \mid L_\alpha \cdot u = 0\}$. $U = \bigcap U_\alpha$ since $U \cong E$ as an A-bimodule. Topologize $\mathrm{End}_A U = \mathrm{Hom}_A(U, U)$ by declaring $\mathrm{Hom}_A(U_\alpha, U)$ to be open. $\mathrm{End}_A U$ is complete since

$$\mathrm{Hom}_A(U,U) = \mathrm{Hom}_A(\text{inj lim } U_\alpha, U) = \text{proj lim } \mathrm{Hom}_A(U_\alpha, U).$$

Topologize $A \otimes U^\circ$ by declaring the left ideals generated by the $(I \otimes i^\circ)(L_\alpha)$ to be open. Let $A \hat{\otimes} U^\circ$ denote the completion, which has a natural algebra structure extending that of $A \otimes U^\circ$. The map Ω is continuous and induces an algebra map $\hat{\Omega}$: $A \hat{\otimes} U^\circ \to \mathrm{End}_A U$ which is an isomorphism if $[U] \in \mathcal{D}_A$. As in IX—OLD this leads to the series of algebra isomorphisms:

$$A \hat{\otimes} U^\circ \cong \mathrm{End}_A U \cong \mathrm{End}_A E \cong A \hat{\otimes} E^\circ.$$

This NEW splitting may be used to show that E and U and $\mathrm{End}_A E$ have the same weak global dimension. And if some additional restrictions hold, this common weak global dimension is equal to the homological dimension of A.

Some of the material in this article will appear in a forthcoming issue of the Inst. Hautes Études Sci. Publ. Math. under the title of *Groups of simple algebras*. Unfortunately the author of that paper only had a glimmer of what was going on.

CORNELL UNIVERSITY
ITHACA, NEW YORK 14850, U.S.A.

Труды Международного Конгресса Математиков
Ванкувер, 1974

Некоторые Вопросы Бирациональной Геометрии Алгебраических Торов*

В. Е. Воскресенский

Ряд результатов арифметики линейных алгебраических групп автор получил, изучая бирациональные характеристики многообразий указанных групп [**1**]. Сразу же было замечено, что эти исследования тесно связаны с результатами Суона о полях инвариантов абелевых групп преобразований [**2**], [**3**] и эта связь оказалась чрезвычайно полезной. Дальнейшие исследования привели к постановке ряда новых интересных задач в теории целочисленных представлений конечных групп, возникших в связи с вопросом бирациональной классификации некоторых многообразий. Изложению имеющихся здесь результатов и проблем и посвящен мой доклад.

Пусть L/k конечное нормальное расширение с группой Галуа Π, $C(L/k)$ категория алгебраических торов, определенных над k и разложимых над L, $C(\Pi)$—двойственная категория Π-модулей без кручения конечного ранга. Двойственность определяется отображением $T \to \hat{T}$, где $\hat{T} = \mathrm{Hom}(T, G_m)$ Π-модуль рациональных характеров тора T. Π-модуль S, обладающий $\mathbf{Z}$-базой, на которой Π действует перестановкой, назовем пермутационным Π-модулем. Модули A и B назовем подобными, если они отличаются только прямыми пермутационными слагаемыми. Через $[A]$ обозначим класс подобия модуля A. Пусть k поле характеристики нуль, тогда существует неособое проективное многообразие V над k, содержащее T в качестве открытого подмножества (проективная модель тора T). Основой для дальнейших расчетов служит

Теорема 1 [**1**]. *Класс* $[\mathrm{Pic}(V \otimes_k L)] = [\mathrm{Pic}\ V_L]$ *есть бирациональный инвариант тора* T.

*Not presented in person.

Впервые этот бирациональный инвариант обнаружили Ю.И. Манин и И.Р. Шафаревич в своих исследованиях по теории поверхностей [4].

Тор T вполне определяется своим Π-модулем характеров $\hat{T}$, полем определения k и полем разложения L, $\mathrm{Gal}(L/k) \cong \Pi$. Запишем это в виде $T = (L/k, \hat{T})$. Можно доказать, что класс $[\mathrm{Pic}\ V_L(T)]$ зависит только от Π-модуля $\hat{T}$, но не от выбора пары L/k. Модули $\mathrm{Pic}\ V_L$ обладают следующим характеристическим свойством.

Теорема 2. $\forall \Pi' \subset \Pi$, $H^{-1}(\Pi', \mathrm{Pic}\ V_L) = 0$.

Пусть $P(\Pi) = \{[N], N \in C(\Pi), H^{-1}(\Pi', N) = 0\ \forall \Pi' \subset \Pi\}$. Нетрудно показать, что каждый элемент из $P(\Pi)$ представлен модулем вида $\mathrm{Pic}\ V_L(T)$, $T \in C(L/k)$.

В статье [5] показывается, что класс $[\mathrm{Pic}\ V_L(T)]$ является бирациональным инвариантом тора T и в случае, когда поле определения имеет характеристику $p > 0$. Здесь уже нельзя прямо использовать теорему Хиронака о разрешении особенностей, в доказательстве используется метод подъема в характеристику нуль. Обозначим класс $[\mathrm{Pic}\ V_L(T)]$ через $[p(T)]$ или $[p(\hat{T})]$, он зависит только от Π-модуля $\hat{T}$. Оператор $[p(\hat{T})]$ перестановочен с операцией взятия прямой суммы. Два тора T_1 и T_2 назовем стабильно эквивалентными над k, если существует бирациональная эквивалентность многообразий над полем k

$$T_1 \times G_m^p \cong T_2 \times G_m^q.$$

Пусть $[T]$ класс стабильной эквивалентности, содержащий тор $T \in C(L/k)$, $Z(L/k)$ полугруппа всех таких классов с операцией прямого произведения.

Теорема 3 [5]. *Отображение* $[T] \to [p(T)]$ *определяет изоморфизм полугруппы* $Z(L/k)$ *на полугруппу* $P(\Pi)$.

Введем в полугруппе $P(\Pi)$ следующую фильтрацию

$$P(\Pi) \supset P^0(\Pi) \supset G(\Pi) \supset I(\Pi),$$

где

$$\begin{aligned} P^0(\Pi) &= \{[N] \in P(\Pi), H^1(\Pi', N) = 0\ \forall \Pi' \subset \Pi\}, \\ G(\Pi) &= \{[N], N + N' = S, [S] = [0]\}, \\ I(\Pi) &= \{[N], [N] = [\mathfrak{A}], \mathfrak{A}\text{—проективный идеал кольца } \mathbf{Z}[\Pi]\}. \end{aligned}$$

$G[\Pi]$ максимальная подгруппа полугруппы $P(\Pi)$ [5]. Отметим следующие результаты

Теорема 4 [5], [6]. *Следующие условия эквивалентны*:
(1) *Всякая силовская подгруппа группы* Π *циклична*;
(2) $P(\Pi) = G(\Pi)$.

Теорема 5 [6]. *Пусть* Π p-*группа. Тогда* $G(\Pi) = I(\Pi)$.

Кажется весьма вероятным, что $P^0(\Pi) = G(\Pi)$ для любой конечной группы Π. Достаточно это доказать для p-групп. Пока неизвестно, имеет ли полугруппа $Z(L/k)$ конечное число образующих, известно только, что ее подгруппа $G(\Pi)$ конечно порождена.

Одной из наиболее интересных задач данной теории является выяснение вопроса о рациональности торов T, для которых $[p(T)] = [0]$. Из этого требования сразу же следует стабильная рациональность тора T над k. Имеются ли стабильно рациональные торы, не являющиеся рациональными, до сих пор неизвестно. Эту задачу мы называем проблемой Зарисского для торов. Очень обстоятельное исследование модулей $\hat{T}$, для которых $[p(\hat{T})] = [0]$ проводят Эндо и Мията [**6**]—[**9**]. Они выяснили, в частности, что проблема Зарисского имеет положительное решение для торов следующих видов:

(1) торы с циклическим полем разложения степени p^m, p простое число;

(2) торы с циклическим полем разложения, модули рациональных характеров которых проективны;

(3) торы, являющиеся моделями полей инвариантов конечных абелевых групп с регулярным действием на образующих.

Кроме этого имеется ряд более частных результатов. Очень интересным с этой точки зрения является вопрос о рациональности торов T с модулем характеров $\hat{T} = \mathbf{Z}[\zeta_n]$. Все эти торы стабильно рациональны, но, насколько мне известно, рациональность их проверена только в случаях $n = p^\alpha$ и $n = 2^\alpha \cdot 3^\beta$. Конечно, достаточно рассматривать только модули с n свободными от квадратов.

В некоторых случаях знание подходящей проективной модели данного тора позволяет решить вопрос о его рациональности. Можно предложить следующий способ построения полных неособых моделей алгебраических торов, сводящий эту задачу к некоторым вопросам геометрии целочисленных представлений конечных групп.

Пусть W конечная подгруппа группы $GL(n, \mathbf{Z})$, f целочисленная положительно определенная W-инвариантная квадратичная форма, M решетка в евклидовом пространстве, соответствующая форме f. Произведем разбиение пространства $\mathbf{R}^n$ на симплициальные углы с вершиной в начале координат, инвариантное относительно группы W и такое, что каждый симплициальный угол натянут на основной репер решетки M. Такое разбиение можно получить, исходя из звезды Делоне решетки M. Пусть $\{B\}$ множество основных реперов данного разбиения. Рассматривая с каждым множеством B и все его части, получим некоторый симплициальный комплекс, который, согласно Демазюру [**10**] определяет $\mathbf{Z}$-схему X конечного типа, собственную и неособую. Группа W действует на X бирегулярно и точно. X содержит тривиальный тор G_m^n в качестве открытого подмножества и действие W на X индуцирует автоморфизм тора G_m^n. Предположим сначала, что X проективная схема, тогда для любого поля k многообразие $X \otimes k$ является неособым проективным. Если L/k нормальное расширение с группой Галуа Π и $h : \Pi \to W$ представление, то h определяет тор T и неособую проективную модель V этого тора как k-формы G_m^n и $X \otimes k$. Неясно, всегда ли можно выбрать W-модель Демазюра тора G_m^n проективной над $\mathbf{Z}$. В случае положительного ответа мы получим метод построения проективных неособых моделей алгебраических торов над полями характеристики $p > 0$. Если X собственная, но не проективная, то в характеристике нуль можно сначала перейти к полному многообразию $X \otimes \boldsymbol{Q}$, а затем посредством конечного числа моноидных преобразований перейти к проективному многообразию Y над $\boldsymbol{Q}$. Важно, что классы W-модулей [Pic X] и [Pic Y] совпадают. В размерности 2 две модели Демазюра: $\boldsymbol{P}^1 \times \boldsymbol{P}^1$ и поверхность дель-Пеццо степени 6. Двумерные торы рациональны. В размерности 3 можно ограничиться 4 моделями Демазюра соответствующими максимальным несопряженным подгруппам группы $GL(3, \boldsymbol{Z})$. Здесь не все торы рациональны над полем определения.

В заключение остановимся на применении данной теории к проблеме рациональности полей инвариантов конечных абелевых групп, о чем уже упоминалось вначале. Пусть $M = k(x_1, \cdots, x_n)$ поле рациональных функций от n переменных. G конечная группа, линейно действующая на векторном пространстве, натянутом на функции $x_1, \cdots, x_n$. В 1969г. Суоном [**2**] были получены первые примеры полей инвариантов конечных групп, не являющихся рациональными. Суон рассматривал группы, циклически переставляющие элементы базиса $x_1, \cdots, x_n$. Первый его контрпример построен для $n = 47$. Этим было дано отрицательное решение старой проблемы Э. Нетер. В то же время, занимаясь проблемой рациональности алгебраических торов, автору удалось построить примеры торов с циклическим полем разложения, которые не являлись рациональными над полем определения. Оказалось, что эти торы очень тесно связаны с полями, которые рассматривал Суон. Более точно поле M^G с абелевой группой G можно реализовать как поле рациональных функций на некотором алгебраическом торе [**11**], [**12**]. Использование торов позволило автору показать, что необходимое условие рациональности, полученное Суоном, является и достаточным. Недавно Эндо и Мията получили более общий результат, относящийся к случаю абелевой группы, действующей регулярно [**7**]. Несколько позже аналогичные результаты получил Ленстра [**13**]. Приведем один из наиболее ярких результатов.

Теорема 6. *Пусть* $(\boldsymbol{Q}, n)$ *поле инвариантов группы, циклически переставляющей элементы базиса* $x_1, \cdots, x_n$ *поля* $\boldsymbol{Q}(x_1, \cdots, x_n)$. *Для того, чтобы* $(\boldsymbol{Q}, n)$ *было рациональным необходимо и достаточно, чтобы выполнялись условия*

(1) $n \not\equiv 0 \pmod 8$,

(2) *для всякого* $q = p^m$, $q \mid n$ *кольцо* $\boldsymbol{Z}[\zeta_{\varphi(q)}]$ *содержит главный идеал* $\mathfrak{p}$, $N\mathfrak{p} = p$.

Известно, что поле $(\boldsymbol{Q}, p)$ не рационально для бесконечного множества простых чисел [**12**], [**13**]. Возможно, что полей $(\boldsymbol{Q}, p)$ с условием рациональности только конечное число.

Литература

1. В.Е. Воскресенский, *О бирациональной эквивалентности линейных алгебраических групп*, Доклады АН СССР **188** (1969), 978–981.

2. R. G. Swan, *Invariant rational functions and a problem of Steenrod,* Invent. Math. **7** (1969), 148–158.

3. В.Е. Воскресенский, *К вопросу о строении подполя инвариантов циклической группы автоморфизмов поля* $\mathbf{Q}(x_1, \cdots, x_n)$, Известия АН СССР, сер. матем. **34** (1970), 366–375.

4. Ю.И. Манин, *Рациональные поверхности над совершенными полями,* I.H.E.S. Publ. Math. **30** (1966), 55–97.

5. В.Е. Воскресенский, *Стабильная эквивалентность алгебраических торов,* Известия АН СССР, сер. матем. **38** (1974), 3–10.

6. S. Endo and T. Miyata, *On a classification of the function fields of algebraic tori* (*preprint*).

7. ———, *Invariants of finite abelian groups*, J. Math. Soc. Japan **25** (1973), 7–26.

8. ———, *Quasi-permutation modules over finite groups*, J. Math. Soc. Japan **25** (1973), 397–421.

9. ———, *Quasi-permutation modules over finite groups.* II (preprint).

10. M. Demazure, *Sous-groupes algébriques de rang maximum du groupe de Cremona,* Ann. Sci. Ecole Norm Sup. 4e, Serie 3 (1970), 507–588.

11. В.Е. Воскресенский, *Геометрия линейных алгебраических групп*, Труды МИАН **132** (1973) 151-161.

12. ———, *Поля инвариантов абелевых групп,* Успехи матем. наук **28** (1973), 77–102.

13. H. W. Lenstra *Rational functions invariant under a finite abelian group* (preprint, 1972).

Саратовский Университет
Саратов, СССР

Section 3

Number Theory

Proceedings of the International Congress of Mathematicians
Vancouver, 1974

Galois Module Structure and Artin L-Functions

A. Fröhlich

1. Normal integral bases. Throughout L and K are number fields of finite degree over the rational field $\boldsymbol{Q}$, with rings of integers $\mathfrak{O}$, and $\mathfrak{o}$, respectively. L is normal over K with Galois group Gal $(L/K) = \Gamma$. We shall be interested in the structure of $\mathfrak{O}$ as a Galois module, i.e., as a module over the group ring $\mathfrak{o}(\Gamma)$. Specifically one can ask whether there exists a NIB ("normal integral basis"), i.e., whether $\mathfrak{O}$ has an $\mathfrak{o}$-basis of form $\{a^\gamma\}$ $(\gamma \in \Gamma)$, or equivalently whether $\mathfrak{O} \cong \mathfrak{o}(\Gamma)$ as Galois module. The local problem was settled by E. Noether (cf. [N]). Namely, $\mathfrak{O}_\mathfrak{p} \cong \mathfrak{o}_\mathfrak{p}(\Gamma)$ if and only if the maximal ideal $\mathfrak{p}$ of $\mathfrak{o}$ is at most tamely ramified in L. Here the subscript $\mathfrak{p}$ denotes localisation. Thus tame ramification of L/K is necessary for the existence of a NIB. For $K = \boldsymbol{Q}$, i. e., $\mathfrak{o} = \boldsymbol{Z}$ this condition is also known to be sufficient in the following cases: (i) Γ Abelian (cf. [H]). (ii) p is an odd prime and Γ is dihedral of order $2p$ (cf. [M1]), or more generally is a subgroup of the group of linear transformation $x \mapsto ax + b$ over the field of p elements. (iii) Γ is dihedral of order 2^n. The first examples for tame extensions L/Q without NIB were given by Martinet (cf. [M2]) for $\Gamma = H_8$, and in fact there are infinitely many of these (cf. [F2]). Here and in the sequel we shall write

(1.1) $$H_{4m} = gp\,[\sigma, \tau | \sigma^m = \tau^2, \tau^4 = 1, \tau\sigma\tau^{-1} = \sigma^{-1}]$$

for the quaternion group of order $4m$, as given by generators and relations.

2. The locally free classgroup (cf. [J], [SE], [RU], [Wa], [F5]). The class group $\mathrm{Cl}(\mathfrak{o}(\Gamma))$ is a finite abelian group, whose elements (M) are classes of locally free rank one $\mathfrak{o}(\Gamma)$-modules M (i.e., finitely generated $\mathfrak{o}(\Gamma)$-modules, with $M_\mathfrak{p} \cong \mathfrak{o}_\mathfrak{p}(\Gamma)$ for all $\mathfrak{p}$). Here $(M) = (N)$, precisely when M and N are stably isomorphic, i.e., $M \oplus \mathfrak{o}(\Gamma) \cong N \oplus \mathfrak{o}(\Gamma)$.

We shall throughout view L as embedded in the complex field $\boldsymbol{C}$. Let ψ run through the "irreducible K-characters", i.e., the characters of Γ corresponding to the simple $K(\Gamma)$-modules. Then

$$K(\Gamma) = \prod_{\psi} A_{\psi} \tag{2.1}$$

where A_{ψ} is the simple K-algebra corresponding to ψ. Let

$$F_{\psi} = \text{centre } (A_{\psi}). \tag{2.2}$$

F_{ψ} is a number field. Denote by I_{ψ} the group of fractional ideals in F_{ψ} prime to card(Γ). Then the reduced norm induces an isomorphism

$$\mathrm{Cl}(\mathfrak{o}(\Gamma)) \cong \left(\prod_{\psi} I_{\psi}\right)\Big/ H \tag{2.3}$$

for a certain subgroup H, which in turn contains a product $\prod_{\psi} H^1_{\psi}$, with H^1_{ψ} an admissible subgroup of I_{ψ}, in the sense of classfield theory. If under this isomorphism (M) maps onto the class of $\{\mathfrak{a}_{\psi}\}$ ($\mathfrak{a}_{\psi} \in I_{\psi}$), we shall call $\{\mathfrak{a}_{\psi}\}$ a *family of invariants* of M.

One knows that $H \subset \prod_{\psi} P_{\psi}$, where P_{ψ} is the subgroup of principal ideals (α) in I_{ψ}, with α positive at all real primes ramified in A_{ψ}. Accordingly we have a surjection

$$\mathrm{Cl}(\mathfrak{o}(\Gamma)) \to \prod_{\psi} (I_{\psi}/P_{\psi}) \tag{2.4}$$

onto a product of classical ideal classgroups. The group on the right may be identified with $\mathrm{Cl}(\mathfrak{M})$, $\mathfrak{M}$ a maximal order in $K(\Gamma)$ containing $\mathfrak{o}(\Gamma)$, and the map (2.4) is then given by extension of scalars. We denote its kernel by $D(\mathfrak{o}(\Gamma))$.

3. Galois module structure and resolvents. We shall generalise the Lagrange resolvent. Let χ be a character of Γ. Choose a matrix representation T of Γ, corresponding to χ with algebraic coefficients. Let a be an element of L generating a normal basis, i.e., so that $aK(\Gamma) = L$. We define the resolvent by

$$(a|\chi) = \det\left(\sum_{\gamma} a^{\gamma} T(\gamma)^{-1}\right). \tag{3.1}$$

This is a nonzero algebraic number, clearly independent of the particular choice of T. The properties of these resolvents (Galois action, reduction mod p, signature in case of real characters) are important for what there is to follow, but we shall not go into these here (cf. **[Fl]**, **[F7]**). We only note that $(a|\chi) \in L(\chi)$, where we shall always write $F(\chi)$ for the extension of a number field by F adjoining the values of χ.

We now impose the condition

(T) *L/K is at most tamely ramified.*

By (T) the $\mathfrak{o}(\Gamma)$-module $\mathfrak{O}$ is locally free, hence defines an element $(\mathfrak{O}) \in \mathrm{Cl}(\mathfrak{o}(\Gamma))$. To describe it, let $(\mathfrak{O}|\chi)$ be the module over the ring $\mathfrak{o}_{K(\chi)}$ of integers in $K(\chi)$, generated by the $(a|\chi)$ with $a \in \mathfrak{O}$. This is finitely generated, rank one over $\mathfrak{o}_{K(\chi)}$.

Choose now $b \in L$ so that $bK(\Gamma) = L$ and in addition $b\mathfrak{o}_\mathfrak{p}(\Gamma) = \mathfrak{O}_\mathfrak{p}$, for all $\mathfrak{p}$ dividing card(Γ). Then

(3.2) $$\mathfrak{b}_\chi = (\mathfrak{O}|\chi)(b|\chi)^{-1}$$

is a fractional ideal in $K(\chi)$, prime to card (Γ), and for all $\sigma \in \mathrm{Gal}(K(\chi)/K)$,

(3.3) $$\mathfrak{b}_\chi^\sigma = \mathfrak{b}_{\chi^\sigma}.$$

Let ϕ be an irreducible K-character, χ an absolutely irreducible character contained in ϕ. Then, with F_ϕ as in (2.2), there is a unique isomorphism $g_\chi : F_\phi \cong K(\chi)$ over K, so that $\chi = g_\chi \circ$ (reduced trace $A_\phi \to F_\phi$). It follows from (3.3) that the fractional ideal $\mathfrak{a}_\phi = g_\chi^{-1}(\mathfrak{b}_\chi)$ solely depends on ϕ. Clearly $\mathfrak{a}_\phi \in I_\phi$. With the fixed choice of $b \in L$, as above, we now have (cf. **[F8]**)

THEOREM 1. *$\{\mathfrak{a}_\phi\}$ is a family of invariants of $\mathfrak{O}$.*

4. Resolvents, conductors and L-functions. Let $\bar{\chi}$ be the complex conjugate of χ. Let $(\mathfrak{O}|\chi)(\mathfrak{O}|\bar{\chi})$ be the module of sums $\sum a_i b_i$, $a_i \in (\mathfrak{O}|\chi)$, $b_i \in (\mathfrak{O}|\bar{\chi})$. Write $\mathfrak{f}(\chi)$ for the Artin conductor of χ. This is an ideal of K. Then we have (cf. **[F8]**)

THEOREM 2. $(\mathfrak{O}|\chi)(\mathfrak{O}|\bar{\chi}) = \mathfrak{o}_{K(\chi)}\mathfrak{f}(\chi)$.

Next let $W(\chi)$ be the Artin root number, i.e., the constant in the functional equation of the Artin L-function. For every real prime ρ of K, denote by $n(\chi, \rho)$ the number of eigenvalues -1, under χ, of a Frobenius element for ρ in Γ. Write $W_\infty(\chi) = i^{-\Sigma n(\chi,\rho)}$ (sum over ρ). Then the "Galois Gauss sum" $\tau(\chi)$ of Hasse is defined by

(4.1) $$\tau(\chi) = W(\chi)W_\infty(\chi)^{-1}N\mathfrak{f}(\chi)^{1/2},$$

where we take the positive square root of the absolute norm $N\mathfrak{f}(\chi)$ of the conductor.

There is a natural extension of the norm map $K \to \boldsymbol{Q}$ to resolvents. Let σ run through the embeddings $K \to \boldsymbol{C}$. Then $\prod_\sigma (a|\chi^{\sigma^{-1}})^\sigma$, with each σ extended to $L(\chi)$, depends on the choice of these extended embeddings only to within a root of unity in $\boldsymbol{Q}(\chi)$. Therefore the $\mathfrak{o}_{\boldsymbol{Q}(\chi)}$-module generated by the $\prod_\sigma(a|\chi^{\sigma^{-1}})^\sigma$, with $a \in \mathfrak{O}$, will not depend on any arbitrary choice. We denote it by $N((\mathfrak{O}|\chi))$ (the norm of $(\mathfrak{O}|\chi)$). We have (cf. **[F8]**)

THEOREM 3. $N((\mathfrak{O}|\chi)) = \mathfrak{o}_{\boldsymbol{Q}(\chi)}\tau(\chi)$.

COROLLARY. *In the case $K = \boldsymbol{Q}$, we have $(\mathfrak{O}|\chi) = \mathfrak{o}_{\boldsymbol{Q}(\chi)}\tau(\chi)$.*

The proofs of Theorems 2 and 3 are based on the theory of "module resolvents" and "module conductors" (cf. **[F6]**). This theory is itself not restricted to the tame case. The procedure is to prove the results for abelian characters χ, and then to establish and to use the functorial properties of the various character functions, in particular under induction of characters.

5. Applications. Let $K = \boldsymbol{Q}$. By the corollary to Theorem 3, the $\mathfrak{a}_\phi$ as defined in § 3 are principal ideals. Using, moreover, the appropriate properties of the $\tau(\chi)$ and the $(a|\chi)$ at infinity one can show that $\mathfrak{a}_\phi \in P_\phi$. Hence

THEOREM 4. *In the case* $K = \boldsymbol{Q}$ *we have* $(\mathfrak{O}) \in D(\boldsymbol{Z}(\Gamma))$.

Thus on extension of operators to a maximal order $\mathfrak{M}$, the module $\mathfrak{O}$ becomes stably free (Martinet's conjecture). The same result was proved by Cougnard (cf. [**C**]) for Γ a p-group or $\Gamma = H_{4p}$, without assuming tame ramification.

If Γ is dihedral of order 2^n then $D(\boldsymbol{Z}(\Gamma)) = 1$ (cf. [**FKW**]). Hence there exists a NIB as asserted in § 1(iii).

Analogous methods, using congruence properties of the $\tau(\chi)$ and the $(a|\chi)$, yield result §1 (ii). Moreover these methods, based on the corollary to Theorem 3, also give a better insight into the relation between root numbers and Galois module structure (see next section).

Another consequence of Theorem 2: If there exists a NIB for L/K then $\mathfrak{f}(\chi)$ becomes a principal ideal in $K(\chi)$.

6. Rootnumbers. Here condition (T) is not required. Let now χ be real valued. Then $W(\chi) = \pm 1$.

THEOREM 5. *If* χ *is the character of a real representation then* $W(\chi) = 1$ (*cf.* [**FQ**]).

This was conjectured by Serre.

In view of the last theorem the problem of the value of $W(\chi)$ for real χ essentially reduces to quaternion characters, i.e., characters χ of a representation of some quaternion group H_{4m} (cf. (1.1)) given by

$$\tau \mapsto \begin{pmatrix} 0 & 1 \\ -1 & 0 \end{pmatrix}, \qquad \sigma \mapsto \begin{pmatrix} \eta & 0 \\ 0 & \eta^{-1} \end{pmatrix},$$

with η a primitive $2d$th root of unity. We shall write $d = d(\chi)$. Note for future reference that two such characters χ and χ^1 are conjugate over $\boldsymbol{Q}$ precisely when $d(\chi) = d(\chi^1)$. For any given basefield K there then exist infinitely many pairs $(L/K, \chi)$, χ a quaternion character of Gal(L/K), with $W(\chi)$ of prescribed sign—even with additional arithmetic "boundary conditions" prescribed (cf. [**F3**]).

The possibility of an arithmetic interpretation of $W(\chi)$ arises in the tame case, in view of

THEOREM 6. *Let* L/K *be at most tamely ramified and let* χ *and* χ^1 *be real valued characters of* Gal(L/K), *which are conjugate over* $\boldsymbol{Q}$. *Then* $W(\chi) = W(\chi^1)$ (*cf.* [**F3**]).

From now on we shall again impose condition (T), and assume that $K = \boldsymbol{Q}$. The first Galois module interpretation was found for H_8 (cf. [**F2**]). Here we describe one for H_{4l^r}, l an odd prime, $r \geqq 1$. (See [**F4**]; the original impetus for this came from [**Q**], where the case $4l^r = 12$ was dealt with, although in different language.) With each $j = 1, \cdots, r$, one can associate a surjective homomorphism θ_j : $D(\boldsymbol{Z}(H_{4l^r})) \to \pm 1$. These θ_j are independent, and as S. Wilson has recently shown (cf. [**Wi**]) they generate the dual of the 2-primary part of $D(\boldsymbol{Z}(H_{4l^r}))$. If Gal$(L/\boldsymbol{Q}) = H_{4l^r}$ we shall write $U_j(L) = \theta_j(\mathfrak{O})$. On the other hand there are exactly r conjugacy classes of quaternion characters χ, according to the value of $d(\chi)$, and accordingly we get r root numbers $W(\chi) = W_j(L)$, where $l^j = d(\chi)$. Then

THEOREM 7. (i) *If* $l \equiv -1 \pmod 4$, *then* $U_j(L) = W_j(L)$.
(ii) *If* $l \equiv 1 \pmod 4$, *then* $U_j(L) = 1$.

As we see, there is no interpretation of $W_j(L)$ in the case $l \equiv 1 \pmod 4$. A similar phenomenon occurs for H_{2^n}, $n > 3$. One is thus led to consider more structure on $\mathfrak{O}$.

7. The Hermitian classgroup. We now consider triplets (M, V, h), where, as before, M is a locally free rank one $\mathfrak{o}(\Gamma)$-module, $V = M \otimes_{\mathfrak{o}} K$, and $h: V \times V \to K(\Gamma)$ is a nonsingular Hermitian form, with respect to the involution of $K(\Gamma)$ over K, given by $\gamma \mapsto \gamma^{-1}$. In this situation (and more generally for orders with involution) one can define a Hermitian classgroup $\mathrm{HCl}(\mathfrak{o}(\Gamma))$, again an abelian group. The language of Hermitian forms over $K(\Gamma)$ is equivalent to that of quadratic forms over K, which are Γ-invariant. In particular we now obtain a triplet $C_L = (\mathfrak{O}, L, h)$, where

$$h(a, b) = \sum_{\gamma} t(a \cdot (b^{\gamma}))\gamma^{-1},$$

with $t : L \to K$ the trace. One can then derive interpretations of (i) the Artin conductor $\mathfrak{f}(\chi)$, (ii) the conductor exponents $n(\chi, \rho)$ mentioned in §4 (cf. **[F7]**) and (iii) the root numbers $W(\chi)$ for $\Gamma = H_{4m}$ and for $K = \boldsymbol{Q}$ all in terms of this element C_L of $\mathrm{HCl}(\boldsymbol{Z}(\Gamma))$. We describe briefly the last of these.

Firstly to each divisor d of m, $d > 1$, there corresponds a $\boldsymbol{Q}$-conjugacy class of quaternion characters χ with $d = d(\chi)$. We shall denote the associated root number by $W(d, L)$, indicating also the field L. For convenience we shall write $W(1, L) = 1$.

On the other hand, using properties both of the $\tau(\chi)$ and the $(a|\chi)$ one can show that C_L belongs to a certain subgroup F of $\mathrm{HCl}(\boldsymbol{Z}(H_{4m}))$. Corresponding to each pair d, s of positive divisors of m, with $d = sl^r$, l a prime and $(s, l) = 1$ one obtains a homomorphism $\mu_{d,s} : \mathrm{HCl}(\boldsymbol{Z}(H_{4m})) \to (\mathfrak{A}_d/\mathfrak{L}_d)^*$, where $\mathfrak{A}_d$ is the ring of integers in the maximal real subfield of the field of dth roots of unity and $\mathfrak{L}_d$ the product of prime ideal divisors of l in $\mathfrak{A}_d$, and * denotes the group of units. Then one has

THEOREM 8. $\mu_{d,s}(C_L) = W(d, L)/W(s, L) \bmod \mathfrak{L}$.

A more detailed examination of these maps can explain the difference between the primes $l \equiv 1$ and $l \equiv -1 \pmod 4$, appearing in Theorem 7. One then gets a commutative diagram

$$\begin{array}{ccc} F & \xrightarrow{\ \mu_{l^r,1}\ } & (\mathfrak{A}_{l^r}/\mathfrak{L}_{l^r})^* = (\boldsymbol{Z}/l\boldsymbol{Z})^* \\ \downarrow & & \Big\downarrow \frac{l-1}{2} \\ D(\boldsymbol{Z}(H_{4l^r})) & \xrightarrow{\ \theta_j\ } & \pm 1 \end{array}$$

(REMARKS ADDED MAY 1975. (i) There are now general theorems, with $\boldsymbol{Q}$ replaced by any number field K and with H_{4l^r} by any Galois groups, of which Theorems

7 and 8 are special cases. (ii) Cougnard's results now extend to certain other metacyclic groups.)

Literature

[C] J. Cougnard, *Proprietes galoisiennes des anneaux d'entiers*, Thèse, Bordeaux University, 1975.

[F1] A. Fröhlich, *Resolvents, discriminants and trace invariants*, J. Algebra **4** (1966), 173–198. MR **34** # 7499.

[F2] ———, *Artin rootnumbers and normal integral bases for quaternion fields*, Invent. Math **17** (1972), 143–166. MR **48** # 2115.

[F3] ———, *Artin root numbers, conductors and representations for generalized quaternion groups*, Proc. London Math. Soc. **28** (1974), 402–438.

[F4] ———, *Module invariants and root numbers for quaternion fields of degree* $4l^r$, Proc. Cambridge Philos. Soc. **76** (1974), 393–399.

[F5] ———, *Locally free modules over arithmetic orders*, J. Reine Angew. Math. (to appear).

[F6] ———, *Module conductors and module resolvents*, Proc. London Math. Sco. (to appear).

[F7] ———, *Resolvents and trace form*, Math. Proc. Cambridge Philos. Soc. (to appear).

[F8] ———, *Arithmetic and Galois module structure for tame extensions* (to appear).

[FQ] A. Fröhlich and J. Queyrut, *On the functional equation of the Artin L-function for character of real representations*, Invent. Math. **20** (1973), 125–138. MR **48** #253

[FKW] A. Fröhlich, M. Keating and S. Wilson, *The classgroups of dihedral and quaternion 2 groups*, Mathematika **21** (1974), 64–71.

[H] D. Hilbert, *Die Theorie der algebraischen Zahlkörper*, Jber. Deutsch. Math. Verein. 1897 *Collected works*. Vol. 1, pp. 63–363.

[J] H. Jacobinski, *Genera and decompositions of lattices over orders*, Acta. Math. **121** (1968), 1–29. MR **40** #4294.

[M1] J. Martinet, *Sur l'arithmétique des extensions galoisiennes à groupe de Galois diédral d'ordr 2p*, Ann. Inst. Fourier (Grenoble) **19** (1969), fasc. 1, 1–80. MR **41** #6820.

[M2] ———, *Modules sur l'algèbre du group quaternionien*, Ann. Sci. École Norm. Sup. **4** (1971), 299–308.

[M3] J. Martinet, *Bases normales et constante de l'équation fonctionelle des fonctions L d'Artin* Séminaire Bourbaki, 1973/74, Exposé 450.

[N] E. Noether, *Normal Basis bei Körpern ohne höhere Verzweigung*, J. Reine Angew. Math **167** (1932), 147–162.

[Q] J. Queyrut, *Extensions quaternioniennes généralisées et constante de l'équation fonctionell des séries L d'Artin*, Publ. Math. Bordeaux (1972/73), 91–119.

[RU] I. Reiner and S. Ullom, *A Mayer-Vietoris sequence for classgroups* J. Algebra **31** (1974) 305–342.

[SE] R. G. Swan, *K-theory of finite groups and orders*, Notes by E. G. Evans, Lecture Notes in Math., vol. 149, Springer-Verlag, Berlin and New York, 1970. MR **46** #7310.

[Wa] C. T. C. Wall, *On the classification of Hermitian forms*, V. *Global rings*, Invent. Math. **2** (1974), 261–288.

[Wi] S. Wilson, *Reduced norms in the K*-theory *of orders*, J. Algebra (to appear).

King's College
London, England WC2

Proceedings of the International Congress of Mathematicians
Vancouver, 1974

The Distribution of Sequences in Arithmetic Progressions

C. Hooley

1. Introduction. The subject of prime numbers in arithmetic progressions has certainly been of interest since Legendre enunciated his celebrated theorem on ternary quadratic forms in 1785, his demonstration having assumed that there exist primes in any arithmetic progression whose terms are coprime to the common difference. Although Gauss subsequently established Legendre's theorem unconditionally by other means, Legendre's method was vindicated by Dirichlet when the latter proved in 1837 the famous theorem to the effect that admissible arithmetical progressions—that is to say, those whose terms are coprime to the common difference—contained infinitely many primes. Subsequently it has been realized that Legendre's theorem is but one of many interesting arithmetical theorems that are related to the theory of primes in arithmetic progressions, there being several important unproved conjectures for whose solution we await further developments in the latter theory. In like manner there are important applications to the theory of numbers of results about the distribution in arithmetic progressions of sequences other than that of the primes.

After briefly summarizing the more important earlier work in the subject in order to put the main substance of our survey in historical perspective, we propose to discuss some recent developments which not only have already had some application but which also seem to be of interest when viewed purely as part of the theory of sequences in arithmetic progressions. To this end it is appropriate to introduce at once the customary notation

$$\pi(x; a, k) = \sum_{p \leqq x;\, p \equiv a \bmod k} 1, \qquad \theta(x; a, k) = \sum_{p \leqq x;\, p \equiv a \bmod k} \log p,$$

where the summations are over positive primes p, it being familiar that it is normally immaterial whether results are expressed in terms of $\pi(x; a, k)$ or $\theta(x; a, k)$.[1] We also always assume that $(a, k) = 1$, and define $E(x; a, k)$ by

$$E(x; a, k) = \theta(x; a, k) - x/\phi(k).$$

Dirichlet's result, which may be expressed in our notation as $\theta(x; a, k) \to \infty$ as $x \to \infty$, was followed by the asymptotic formula

$$\theta(x; a, k) \sim x/\phi(k) \tag{1}$$

obtained by de Vallée Poussin in 1896. Later work centred round the two questions of the degree of accuracy with which (1) represented $\theta(x; a, k)$ and of the uniformity of (1) with respect to k. The Siegel-Walfisz theorem, for example, gave

$$E(x; a, k) = O(x \exp(-c\sqrt{\log x})) \tag{2}$$

for $k < \log^A x$, while a result due to Titchmarsh gave

$$E(x; a, k) = O(x^{1/2} \log^2 x)$$

on the supposition of the extended Riemann hypothesis (to which, for brevity, we hereafter refer as E.R.H.). Here we should remark in passing that it never seems to have been subsequently noticed that Titchmarsh's result can be easily improved to

$$E(x; a, k) = O(x^{1/2} \log x \log \{2x^{1/2}/\phi(k)\}) \qquad (k < x^{1/2}),$$

in which form it leads to the validity of (1) for large values of x whenever k is less than about $x^{1/2}/\log x$. These results were augmented and complemented in the middle of the past decade by the important Bombieri-Vinogradov theorem, which asserted that, for any assigned positive constant A, there exists a positive constant B such that[2]

$$\sum_{k \leqq Q} \overline{\text{bd}}_{0<a\leqq k;\, y \leqq x} |E(y; a, k)| < x \log^{-A} x$$

for $Q < x^{1/2} \log^{-B} x$. It would be superfluous for us to dwell here on the importance of this theorem in view of Professor Chandrasekharan's comments on Professor Bombieri's work in his article in these PROCEEDINGS. Suffice it then to mention that the theorem asserts, roughly speaking, that (1) holds almost always for values of k nearly up to $x^{1/2}$, the consequence being that it has often proved to be an effective unconditional substitute for Titchmarsh's result in applications.

The results so far described lose all significance when $k > x^{1/2}$. If, however, we waive the requirement of asymptotic equality and are content with meaningful upper bounds, then we have the useful Brun-Titchmarsh theorem, which can be proved in the form

$$\pi(x; a, k) < (2 + \varepsilon)x/\{\phi(k) \log (2x/k)\} \tag{3}$$

by an easy application of Selberg's sieve method. Thus, for values of k as large as $x^{1-\eta}$, the sum $\pi(x; a, k)$ is of the expected order of magnitude $x/\{\phi(k)\log x\}$ although the constant implicit in the statement becomes large as η becomes small. The result does not, however, reflect the anticipated size of $\pi(x; a, k)$ for larger values of k such as $x \log^{-r} x$.

[1]Or the associated $\psi(x; a, k)$ whose use here we avoid.

[2]The condition $(a, k) = 1$ remains implicit in all summations involving k.

2. The Brun-Titchmarsh theorem for the larger values of k. We conclude from the above summary that the extension of Bombieri's theorem to cover values of Q as large as $x^{1-\delta}$ is a desideratum in the theory. In the absence of such a generalization, it is therefore of interest to investigate whether (3) can be substantially improved for nearly all values of k up to a limit almost as large as x. Recently, in this direction, the author [2] proved the following

THEOREM 1. *Let a be a fixed nonzero integer. Then almost all numbers k have the property that*

$$\pi(x; a, k) < (4 + \varepsilon)x/\{\phi(k) \log k\}$$

for all values of x exceeding $k \log^{34} k$.

If the exponent 34 in $\log k$ is replaced by a larger number B, then the method used also leads to sharp estimates for the measure of the exceptional set of k in which the inequality fails.

To interpret the result, we should note in particular that when x is large we obtain $\pi(x; a, k) < (8 + \varepsilon)x/\{\phi(k) \log x\}$ for nearly all k between $x^{1/2}$ and $x \log^{-34} x$, an inequality in which 8 can be replaced by 5 by the method given in [2] and an earlier paper [1]. Thus, in a suitable sense, we have achieved an inequality for $\pi(x; a, k)$ of the required order of magnitude for values of k as large as $x \log^{-34} x$.

A few comments on the method are in place. In Selberg's upper bound method we use a nonnegative function of n which is equal to 1 when n is a prime number exceeding ξ and which is of the form $\sum_{d|n} \rho_d$, where $\rho_d = 0$ if $d > \xi^2$. Thus, by the usual reasoning,

$$(4) \qquad \pi(x; a, k) \leqq \frac{\xi}{k} + \sum_{n \leqq x;\ n \equiv a \bmod k} \sum_{d|n} \rho_d = \frac{\xi}{k} + \frac{x}{k} \sum_{(d,k)=1} \frac{\rho_d}{d} + O(\xi^2),$$

in which we are constrained to limit ξ to $(x/k)^{1/2-\varepsilon}$ in order to obtain a meaningful result, there being a consequent diminution in the efficacy of the ensuing inequality when k is large. Yet we would suspect that a better result is true because the estimate $O(\xi^2)$ for the remainder term in (4) is probably too large. We therefore consider, along the lines of Linnik's dispersion method, an expression of the type

$$\sum_{Q<k\leqq 2Q} \left(\sum_{n \leqq x;\ n \equiv a \bmod k} \sum_{d|n} \rho_d - \frac{x}{k} \sum_{(d,k)=1} \frac{\rho_d}{d} \right)^2$$

in order to show that the remainder term is usually smaller and that therefore larger values of ξ can usually be chosen. We should notice here that ρ_d must be independent of k so that the minimal property inherent in Selberg's method cannot be retained. This, however, is not important, and we have here an example of the *enveloping sieve*—a term due to Linnik to express a similar application of the idea by the author to the Hardy-Littlewood problem about numbers as the sum of two squares and a prime.

3. Theorems of the Barban-Davenport-Halberstam type. Results about larger moduli k are also supplied by theorems of the Barban-Davenport-Halberstam type, which are concerned with the adjusted variance

$$G(x, k) = \sum_{0<a\leqq k} E^2(x; a, k)$$

and the sum

$$H(x, Q) = \sum_{k\leqq Q} G(x, k).$$

The fundamental result in this theory is the following theorem, due essentially to the independent work of Barban and of Davenport and Halberstam. This is stated here in the improved form given by Gallagher.

THEOREM 2. *For $Q \leqq x$ and for any positive constant A, we have*

$$H(x, Q) = O(Qx \log x) + O(x^2 \log^{-A} x).$$

The main importance of the theorem of course lies in its assertion that almost all moduli k between $x \log^{-A} x$ and x are such that (1) holds for almost all residue classes a, modulo k.

Previously, apart from earlier large sieve results to prime moduli which were the harbingers of this theorem, the only other known theorem of this type was the conditional estimate

$$\sum_{0<a\leqq k} E^2(x; a, k) = O(x \log^4 x) \tag{5}$$

that was obtained by Turán on E.R.H. Although the latter is weaker in some respects than Theorem 1, the author [3] has noted that it can be utilized in combination with Gallagher's method in order to obtain

THEOREM 3. *For $Q \leqq x$, we have*

$$H(x, Q) = O(Qx \log x) + O(x^{3/2} \log^3 x)$$

on E.R.H.

Thus (5) can certainly be improved on average for $k > x^{1/2}$. Later, however, we shall see that such improvements can be effected in a more precise sense over certain ranges of k.

In 1970 Montgomery [10] obtained a striking improvement in Theorem 2 in which the upper bound was replaced by an asymptotic equality. This work had, however been partially anticipated by Barban, who had enunciated the result for the special case $Q = x$. Montgomery's results, as improved and augmented by his later work are given by

THEOREM 4. *For $Q \leqq x$, we have*

(i) $$H(x, Q) = Qx \log Q + O(Qx) + O(x^2 \log^{-A} x),$$

(ii) $$H(x, Q) = Qx \log Q + O(Qx) + O(x^{7/4+\varepsilon})$$

on E. R. H.

The proof depends intrinsically on the equation

$$G(x, k) = \sum_{0<a\leqq k} \theta^2(x; a, k) - \frac{x^2}{\phi(k)} + O(x^2 \log^{-A} x),$$

in which the first sum on the right-hand side is equal to

$$\sum_{p \leqq x} \log^2 p + 2 \sum_{0<a\leqq k} \sum_{p'<p\leqq x;\, p\equiv p'\equiv a \bmod k} \log p \log p' \tag{6}$$

$$= x \log x + O(x) + 2 \sum_{p-p'=lk\leqq x} \log p \log p', \tag{7}$$

the summation in the final sum being over p, p', and positive integers l. Montgomery then writes this final sum as

$$\sum_{l\leqq x/k} \{J(x, lk) + K(x, lk)\}, \tag{8}$$

where $J(x, m)$ is the usual heuristic estimate for the sum

$$\sum_{p-p'=m;\, p\leqq x} \log p \log p'.$$

The contribution of $J(x, lk)$ to the problem through (7) and subsequent summation over k is then in principle easy to assess, whereas the effect of $K(x, lk)$ is handled by Lavrik's theorem on the mean-square value of $K(x, m)$.

Montgomery's treatment lies deep because Lavrik's theorem is of the same order of sophistication as Vinogradov's theorem. The author [3], however, has developed an alternative proof that depends only on the comparatively simple large sieve inequality and the Siegel-Walfisz theorem (2). In sketching the ideas behind this proof, we note first that Theorem 2 implies that it suffices to estimate the contribution to $H(x, Q)$ due to values of k exceeding a number Q_1 that is not much smaller than Q. Summation of (7) over these values of k then gives rise to a sum of the form

$$\sum_{p-p'=lk\leqq x} \log p \log p'$$

in which the variables of summation are p, p', l, k and in which l in particular is subject to the condition $l < x/Q_1$. Since this sum possesses a certain symmetry in terms of l, k, it is then possible to utilize in reverse the transformation that took (6) into (7) save that l and k exchange rôles. The modulus l in the counterpart of the final sum in (6) being small, the estimations can then be completed by appealing to (2).

Theorem 4 by no means exhausts the potentialities of either method, there being several applications to which we shall presently refer. Since, however, the two methods differ in character, it frequently happens in any given situation that the balance of advantage lies decisively with one of the methods.

The author's method, for example, leads to the following improved version of the second part of Theorem 4 [4].

THEOREM 5. *On E. R. H. we have*

$$H(x, Q) = Qx \log Q + O(Qx) + O(x^{3/2+\varepsilon})$$

for $Q \leqq x$.

It also leads to

THEOREM 6. *We have*

$$\sum_{k\leqq Q} k \sum_{0<a\leqq k} E^3(x; a, k) = o(Q^{3/2}x^{3/2} \log^{3/2} x) + O(x^3 \log^{-A} x)$$

provided that $Q/x \to 0$ *as* $x \to \infty$.

These results when considered together are tantalizing in that they suggest that

$$G(x, k) \sim x \log k \tag{9}$$

and that

$$\frac{E(x; a, k)}{\{(x \log k)/\phi(k)\}^{1/2}}$$

may have a distribution function, subject to any obvious qualifications that may have to be made. Yet the evidence supplied is weakened because in the theorems quoted so far the value of x remains constant with respect to the variables of summation. It is, therefore, of interest that further supporting evidence for such conjectures is supplied by the following theorem, which can be derived by a development of Montgomery's method [**6**]. This is quoted in conditional form for effect, although the same method leads to a much weaker unconditional version.

THEOREM 7. *On E.R.H. we have*

(i)
$$\sum_{k \leq Q} \overline{\mathrm{bd}}_{1 \leq y \leq x}\, G(y, k) \sim Qx \log Q$$

provided that $x^{4/5+\varepsilon} < Q \leqq x$;

(ii) *almost all numbers k have the property that*

$$G(x, k) = x \log k + O(x \log^{1/2} k)$$

for all x such that $k \leqq x \leqq k^{5/4+\varepsilon}$.

This theorem should be compared with Uchiyama's interesting bound [**11**]

$$\sum_{k \leq Q} \sum_{0 < a \leq k} \overline{\mathrm{bd}}_{1 \leq y \leq x}\, E^2(y; a, k) = O(Qx \log^3 x) + O(x^2 \log^{-A} x),$$

an improved form of which is given by the following

THEOREM 8. *We have*

$$\sum_{k \leq Q} \sum_{0 < a \leq k} \overline{\mathrm{bd}}_{1 \leq y \leq x}\, E^2(y; a, k) = \begin{cases} O(Qx \log x), & \text{if } x \log^{-1} x \leqq Q \leqq x, \\ O(Qx \log x (\log \log x))^2, & \text{if } x \log^{-A} x < Q < x \log^{-1} x. \end{cases}$$

Here it would be desirable to discover whether we could dispense with the factor $(\log \log x)^2$ in the second estimate.

Before quitting the subject of the Barban-Davenport-Halberstam theorem, we remark on the apparent anomaly whereby theorems of this type have so far only been obtained for values of k larger than $x^{1/2}$ while the asymptotic formulae described in §1 are only significant for values of k less than $x^{1/2}$. Modest progress for the smaller values of k can, however, be made with theorems of the type considered in this section. We can prove [7], for example, the following theorem, which is consistent with the conjecture (9).

THEOREM 9. *On E.R.H. we have*

$$\int_1^x \frac{G(t, k)}{t^2}\, dt = O(\log x \log k).$$

We can also obtain an extension of Turán's estimate (5) that is related to Theorem 8 [8].

THEOREM 10. *On E.R.H. we have*

$$\sum_{0<a\leqq k} \operatorname*{bd}_{1\leqq y\leqq x} E^2(y; a, k) = O(x \log^4 x)$$

for $k \leqq x$.

4. Other sequences. We end with a brief discussion on the application of these ideas to other sequences.

In considering possible generalizations of the Barban-Davenport-Halberstam theorem to other sequences, we should observe that the original form of the theorem implies a weakish form of the prime number theorem for arithmetic progressions. Likewise a sequence cannot possess a Barban-Davenport-Halberstam property unless it is well distributed among arithmetic progressions with small moduli. However, it can be shown that an analogue of the theorem always holds provided that this obvious necessary condition obtains [5].

The Bombieri-Vinogradov theorem, on the other hand, is not susceptible to an analogous generalization unless additional stringent hypotheses about the sequence are made. Here we confine our remarks to the square-free numbers, which perhaps constitute the case next in interest after the primes.

Let $S(x; a, k)$ be the number of square-free numbers not exceeding x that are congruent to a mod k. Then Prachar has obtained an asymptotic formula for $S(x; a, k)$ that is significant for $k \leqq x^{2/3-\varepsilon}$, while Orr has subsequently derived a Bombieri-Vinogradov type theorem for $S(x; a, k)$ in which, however, the range of significance is still limited to values of k not exceeding about $x^{2/3}$. Although Prachar's formula is almost certainly true for $k \leqq x^{1-\varepsilon}$, the problem of extending the range of validity beyond $k = x^{2/3}$ seems to present considerable difficulty. Partial progress, however, has been made by the author [9] by means of

THEOREM 11. *Let* $Q \leqq x^{3/4-\varepsilon}$. *Then, for a positive proportion of moduli k satisfying* $Q < k < 2Q$, *we have*

$$S(x; a, k) \sim \frac{6x}{\pi^2 k} \prod_{p|k} \left(1 - \frac{1}{p^2}\right)^{-1}$$

for all residue classes a mod *k coprime to k.*

References

1. C. Hooley, *On the Brun-Titchmarsh theorem.* I, J. Reine Angew. Math. **255** (1972), 60–79. MR **46** #3463.

2. ———, *On the Brun-Titchmarsh theorem.* II, Proc. London Math. Soc. (3) **30** (1975), 114–128.

3. ———, *On the Barban-Davenport-Halberstam theorem.* I, J. Reine Angew. Math. (to appear).

4. ———, *On the Barban-Davenport-Halberstam theorem.* II, J. London Math. Soc. (2) **9** (1975), 625–636.

5. ———, *On the Barban-Davenport-Halberstam theorem.* III, J. London Math. Soc. (to appear).

6. ———, *On the Barban-Davenport-Halberstam theorem.* IV, J. London Math. Soc. (to appear).

7. ———, *On the Barban-Davenport-Halberstam theorem.* V, Proc. London Math. Soc. (to appear).

8. ———, *On the Barban-Davenport-Halberstam theorem.* VI, J. London Math. Soc. (to appear).

9. ———, *A note on square-free numbers in arithmetic progressions*, Bull. London Math. Soc. **8** (1975).

10. H. L. Montgomery, *Primes in arithmetic progressions*, Michigan Math. J. **17** (1970), 33–39. MR **41** #1660.

11. S. Uchiyama, *Prime numbers in arithmetic progressions*, Math. J. Okayama Univ. **15** (1971, 72), 187–196. MR **47** #8464.

UNIVERSITY COLLEGE
CARDIFF, WALES CF1 1XL

Труды Международного Конгресса Математиков
Вакнувер, 1974

Тригонометрические Суммы и их Применения*

А. А. Карацуба

Многие проблемы аналитической теории чисел приводят к конечным суммам вида

$$S = S(N; F) = \sum_{n=1}^{N} e^{2\pi i F(n)}, \tag{1}$$

где $F(n)$—действительная функция натурального аргумента n. К таким проблемам относятся проблемы поведения дробных долей различного вида функций, аддитивные проблемы, проблемы асимптотического поведения средних значений арифметических функций и др.

Одним из самых важных вопросов относительно сумм (1) является вопрос о верхней грани модуля S. Тривиально

$$|S| \leqq N.$$

Однако для широкого класса функций $F(n)$ удается получить оценку

$$|S| \leqq \Delta N,$$

где $0 < \Delta < 1$, Δ—понижающий множитель.

К настоящему времени существует два общих подхода к оценке $|S|$: один из них состоит в том, что S заменяется интегралом, который во многих случаях удается достаточно точно оценить; однако этот подход применим к очень узкому классу сумм S; другой подход состоит в том, что S приближается некоторой суммой T того же вида (1), но в которой F—многочлен. Такие суммы T стали называться полиномиальными или суммами Г. Вейля, который первый дал общую оценку модуля этих сумм.

*Delivered by S.A. Stepanov.

В 1934 г. И.М. Виноградов создал новый исключительно точный метод оценок сумм Г. Вейля. Этот метод состоит в том, что оценка суммы T,

$$T = \sum_{n=1}^{N} e^{2\pi i f_k(n)},$$

где $f_k(n) = \alpha_1 n + \cdots + \alpha_k n^k$, сводится к оценке интеграла J,

$$J = \int_0^1 \cdots \int_0^1 \left| \sum_{n=1}^{N} e^{2\pi i f_k(n)} \right|^{2m} d\alpha_1 \cdots d\alpha_k,$$

который является средним значением $2m$-й степени модуля сумм T. Оценка интеграла J является основной в методе И.М. Виноградова и соответствующая теорема называется теоремой о среднем.

В 1961, 1962 гг. мной был предложен p-адический метод оценки величины J. В этом методе оценка J сводится к оценке числа решений некоторой системы сравнений, в которой неизвестные пробегают полную систему вычетов. Следовательно, оценки сумм Г. Вейля, которые, вообще говоря, являются неполными тригонометрическими суммами, через теорему о среднем сводятся к полным тригонометрическим суммам (см. [**1**]—[**3**]).

p-адический метод дает возможность получить ряд новых результатов в тех вопросах, где можно по-существу использовать арифметическую природу изучаемых объектов; это, в частности, относится к диофантовым уравнениям Варинговского типа [**4**]. Например, для числа решений системы неопределенных уравнений вида

$$\begin{aligned} x_1^{k_1} + \cdots + x_m^{k_1} &= y_1^{k_1} + \cdots + y_m^{k_1}, \\ x_1^{k_r} + \cdots + x_m^{k_r} &= y_1^{k_r} + \cdots + y_m^{k_r}, \end{aligned} \qquad 1 \leqq x_i,\ y_i \leqq N,\ i = 1, \cdots, m,$$

в числах x_i, y_i, имеющих "малые" простые делители, удается получить асимптотическую формулу при числе слагаемых m порядка $(k_1 + \cdots + k_r) \cdot \ln(k_1 + \cdots + k_r)$. Отсюда следует также асимптотическая формула для числа решений уравнения Варинга

$$x_1^k + \cdots + x_m^k = N$$

в числах $x_1, \cdots, x_m$ с малыми простыми делителями и числом слагаемых m порядка $k \ln k$.

Применения оценок сумм Г. Вейля в проблемах порядка роста дзета-функции Римана и теории простых чисел, а также в ряде проблем асимптотического поведения средних значений арифметических функций известны давно. На этом пути получены самые точные результаты в названных проблемах. Недавно мне удалось найти новые применения оценок, получаемых методом тригонометрических сумм, к ряду проблем асимптотического поведения средних значений арифметических функций и получить принципиально новые результаты в этих проблемах [**5**], [**6**]. Остановлюсь на одной из них—проблеме делителей Л. Дирихле.

Пусть $\tau_k(n)$—число представлений n в виде произведения k натуральных омножителей

$$n = n_1 \cdots n_k.$$

Рассмотрим сумму

$$T_k(X) = \sum_{n \leqq X} \tau_k(n),$$

оторая равняется числу натуральных $n_1, \cdots, n_k$ таких, что $n_1 \cdots n_k \leqq X$, ругими словами, числу целых положительных точек под k-мерной гиперболической поверхностью $x_1 \cdots x_k = X$. Задачу об асимптотической формуле ля $T_k(X)$ в 1849 г. рассмотрел Л. Дирихле, который доказал, что

$$T_k(X) = XP_{k-1}(\ln X) + O(X^{\alpha_k} \ln^k X),$$

де $P_{k-1}(u)$—многочлен $k-1$-й степени и

$$\alpha_k \leqq 1 - 1/k, \qquad k \geqq 2.$$

Проблема нахождения наилучшего значения α_k в этой формуле стала называться проблемой делителей Дирихле. В 1903 г. Г. Вороной доказал, что

$$\alpha_k \leqq 1 - 2/(k+1), \qquad k \geqq 2;$$

в 1912 г. этот результат повторил аналитическим методом Э. Ландау, а в 1922 г. при $k \geqq 4$ его уточнили Г. Харди и Д. Литтлвуд:

$$\alpha_k \leqq 1 - 3/(k+2), \qquad k \geqq 4.$$

При больших k все приведенные оценки α_k принципиально не отличаются от оценки Л. Дирихле и хуже, чем, например, такая:

$$\alpha_k \leqq 1 - 3/k.$$

В 1971 г. я [**5**] доказал, что

(2) $$\alpha_k \leqq 1 - c/k^{2/3},$$

$c > 0$—абсолютная постоянная.

Существо дела состоит в следующем. Как известно,

$$T_k(X) = \frac{1}{2\pi i} \int_{2-i\infty}^{2+i\infty} \zeta^k(s) \frac{X^s}{s}\, ds.$$

В последнем интеграле контур интегрирования переносят левее прямой $\operatorname{Re} s = 1$, получают главный член $T_k(X)$ и оценивают остаток. Раньше контур интегрирования переносился на "критическую" прямую $\operatorname{Re} s = 1/2$ или левее ее и использовались оценки $\zeta(s)$ на прямой $\operatorname{Re} s = 1/2$. Я заметил, что в этой проблеме можно получить принципиально новые результаты, если контур интегрирования перенести на прямую, достаточно близкую к $\operatorname{Re} s = 1$, и воспользоваться оценкой дзета-функции вида

(3) $$\zeta(\sigma + it) = O(|t|^{\alpha(1-\sigma)^\lambda} \ln^\gamma |t|), \qquad 1/2 \leqq \sigma \leqq 1, \ |t| \geqq 2.$$

Оценки (3), где $\lambda > 1$, $\alpha > 0$, $\gamma > 0$—постоянные, получаются с помощью оценок тригонометрических сумм методом И.М. Виноградова и известны с 1937 г. Сейчас (3) доказано с $\lambda = 3/2$, $\alpha \leqq 20$, $\gamma = 2/3$. Это и дало возможность получить (2).

К настоящему времени появился ряд работ, в которых, с одной стороны, вычисляется постоянная c в (2); например, доказано, что $c \leqq 1/14$, и, с другой стороны, обобщается оценка (2) на более широкий класс арифметических функций, например, на случай мультипликативных функций $f(n)$, $f(p) = k$ для простых p, и $|f(n)| \leqq \tau_k(n)$.

Литература

1. А.А. Карацуба, *Проблема Варинга для сравнения по модулю, равному степени простого числа*, Вестник Московского университета, серия 1, ном. 4 (1962), 28–38.

2. ———, *О системах сравнений*, Известия АН СССР, сер. матем. **29** (1965), 959–968.

3. ———, *Теоремы о среднем и полные тригонометрические суммы*, Известия АН СССР, сер. матем. **30** (1966), 183–206.

4. ———, *Системы сравнений и уравнения Варинговского типа*, Доклады АН СССР **165** (1965), 274–276.

5. ———, *Оценки тригонометрических сумм методом И. М. Виноградова и их применения*, Труды МИАН, т. 112, "Наука", Москва, 1971, стр. 241–255.

6. ———, *Проблема делителей Дирихле в числовых полях*, Доклады АН СССР **204** (1972), 540–541.

Математический Институт им. В.А. Стеклова АН СССР
Москва, СССР

Proceedings of the International Congress of Mathematicians
Vancouver, 1974

p-Adic Analytic Number Theory of Elliptic Curves and Abelian Varieties over $\boldsymbol{Q}$

B. Mazur

The "p-adic analytic number theory" alluded to in the title of my article is in a very beginning state: [**4**], [**6**], [**2**]. In different contexts, and from different points of view, p-adic analytic number theory has been the subject of much recent work: "the p-adic analytic number theory of totally real number fields" has been developed by Serre [**10**], using work of Siegel, and more recently by Katz, and Deligne-Ribet; "of quadratic imaginary number fields": by Katz, and Manin; "of modular forms of weight $k \geqq 2$ for the full modular group": by Manin [**3**]; "of Eichler cohomology classes associated to certain arithmetic groups": being presently worked on by V. Miller.

One exciting aspect of this emerging theory is its sheer difficulty: for example, no matter which elliptic curve $E/\boldsymbol{Q}$ you choose (e.g., $y^2 + y = x^3 + x^2$), its p-adic analytic number theory is hard to get to know intimately for *most* primes p, either conceptually or computationally.

Nevertheless, for the jacobian of the modular curve $X_0(N)/\boldsymbol{Q}$, there are certain special primes[1] where things are under better control, and for which a more precise picture is beginning to come into view.

One obtains a number of by-products of this picture which are of independent diophantine interest. Notably, as we shall discuss below, one can prove Mordell's conjecture for the curves $X_0(N)$ for prime N over $\boldsymbol{Q}$. For general prime numbers N the "Mordell conjecture" is proven in a bleakly indeterminate form; Ogg and I have been working with (and sharpening) the result, however, and have obtained an actu-

[1]These special primes are not *rational* primes, but rather certain prime ideals in the Hecke algebra, called *Eisenstein primes*.

al determination of the $\boldsymbol{Q}$-rational points of $X_0(N)$ in a great number of cases (se §5).

In this article I shall try to describe some results and (terribly briefly) som methods in the theory of these special (*Eisenstein*) primes, emphasizing question of diophantine interest. Full results and details will be given in [**5**].

1. Arthmetic of elliptic curves over $\boldsymbol{Q}$. Let E be an elliptic curve defined over $\boldsymbol{Q}$ The following extremely conjectural formula has been a focal point for researcl concerning the arithmetic of $E/\boldsymbol{Q}$ for about ten years, and will probably continue t be so for some years to come. We shall state this conjectural formula baldly an then we shall recall, rather than define, the terms which intervene:

CONJECTURE OF BIRCH AND SWINNERTON-DYER.

$$|Ш| \cdot R = |M_{\text{tors}}|^2 \cdot \lim_{s \to 1} \frac{L^*(E,s)}{(s-1)^r} \cdot \prod c_l^{-1}, \qquad l\text{: primes of bad reduction for } E,$$

where M is the *Mordell-Weil* group of E: the group $E_{\boldsymbol{Q}}$ of points of E rationa over $\boldsymbol{Q}$. This group is a finitely generated abelian group, as proved by Mordell The finite subgroup M_{tors} of torsion elements in M is easily computed in any give case. The rank r of the torsion-free quotient of M is not at all easily computable even in special cases. One may obtain *upper* bounds for r by a difficult, but mechani cal, procedure.

R is the regulator of $E/\boldsymbol{Q}$: It is the real number (probably transcendental) whic is the discriminant of image$(M) \subset M \otimes \boldsymbol{R}$ computed by means of the inner pro duct structure on $M \otimes \boldsymbol{R}$ coming from the 'canonical height' [**12**]. Intuitively, i is a measure of the size of the rational coordinates of a basis of the torsion-fre part of M.

c_l is the number of components of multiplicity one, rational over $\boldsymbol{F}_l$ on the specia fiber of Néron's minimal model for E at l.

Ш is the *Shafarevitch-Tate group* of $E/\boldsymbol{Q}$: It is often "yoked" to the Mordel Weil group in the sense that when one tries to obtain information about M, it i sometimes the case that one must first deal with Ш, or at least some p-primar component of Ш. The group Ш is known to be a torsion group, and is conjecture to be finite. In no case, however, is Ш known to be finite.

$L^*(E, s)$ is the *Hasse-Weil L* series of $E/\boldsymbol{Q}$. See [**12**] for its appropriate normaliza tion.[2] It is defined as an infinite (Euler) product, and is a Dirichlet series whicl may be seen to be convergent in the half-plane $\text{Re}(s) > 3/2$. This domain of con vergence is totally inadequate for the role played by $L^*(E, s)$ in our above formula It is conjectured that $L^*(E,s)$ extends to an entire function. This conjecture has bee proved in the important (and possibly general) case where $E/\boldsymbol{Q}$ is parametrized b modular forms. We shall make precis ewhat is meant by "parametrized by modula forms", below.

[2]We have allowed *our* normalization to absorb the "real period of the Néron differential", factor about which we have little to say in this article. Compare our formula with the formula (Conjecture 4(b) of [**12**].

Note that the conjectured formula implies:

Weak version of the conjecture. The rank of (the torsion-free part of) M is the order of zero of $L^*(E, s)$ at $s = 1$.

2. p-adic analytic analogues. In a recent paper **[6]** Swinnerton-Dyer and I have defined a p-adic analytic power series $L_p(E, s) \in \boldsymbol{Z}_p[[s]]$ for any $E/\boldsymbol{Q}$ which is, again, parametrized by modular functions, and any prime p of good, nonsupersingular reduction for E.[3] We regard $L_p(E, s)$ as something in the spirit of an *analytic continuation* of $L^*(E, s)$, suitably normalized, *onto the p-adic disc*. In many respects it behaves just like the Hasse-Weil L-series of $E/\boldsymbol{Q}$, and we have computational and some theoretical reasons to expect that

CONJECTURE. $L_p(E, s)$ and $L^*(E, s)$ have the same order of zero at $s = 1$.

All one can show at present **[6]** is that $L_p(E, s)$ (when defined) vanishes at $s = 1$ if and only if $L^*(E, s)$ vanishes at $s = 1$. In fact one has a precise formula relating their values.

The p-adic L-series extends to an analytic function on a disc somewhat larger than the unit disc (call it the *extended* disc) and it is interesting to consider:

(a) the precise power of p which divides $L_p(E, s)$ in $\boldsymbol{Z}_p[[s]]$,

(b) the zeroes (counted with multiplicity) of $L_p(E, s)$ in the extended disc.

Evidence is accumulating which suggests that one may hope for a certain *arithmetical* interpretation of the information contained in (a), (b) which is analogous to the theory of Iwasawa and Kubota-Leopoldt. See **[4]**, **[6]**.

At the moment, nothing is known about p-adic analogues of the regulator R. At first it might be reasonable to try to set up such a theory in the case where $E/\boldsymbol{Q}$ has complex multiplication (especially in the light of some recent results of Katz **[1]**).

3. The modular curves. For any integer $N \geqq 1$, there is a smooth projective curve defined over $\boldsymbol{Q}$ and usually denoted $X_0(N)$ **[11]**. As a Riemann surface, one has $X_0(N)_{\boldsymbol{C}} = U/\Gamma_0(N) \cup$ cusps where U is the upper half-plane, $\Gamma_0(N) \subset \mathrm{Sl}_2(\boldsymbol{Z})$ is the subgroup of matrices $\left(\begin{smallmatrix} a & b \\ c & d \end{smallmatrix}\right)$ where $c \equiv 0 \bmod N$, and $X_0(N)_{\boldsymbol{C}}$ is the compact Riemann surface obtained by adjoining to the quotient $U/\Gamma_0(N) = Y_0(N)$ the *finite* set of cusps.

The structure of $X_0(N)$ *over* $\boldsymbol{Q}$ is related to an important diophantine problem in the theory of elliptic curves over number fields. Namely, if K is a number field in $\boldsymbol{C}$, to any pair $[C_N \subset \underline{E}]$ consisting in an elliptic curve $\underline{E}$ defined over K and a cyclic subgroup C_N of order N, rationally defined over K one may associate a noncuspidal point of $X_0(N)$, defined over K,

$$[C_N \subset \underline{E}] \mapsto e \in Y_0(N)_K.$$

Moreover, any point of $Y_0(N)_K$ may be obtained in this way,[4] and two pairs $[C_N \subset \underline{E}]$, $[C'_N \subset \underline{E}']$ correspond to the same point of $Y_0(N)_K$ if and only if they are isomorphic over $\boldsymbol{C}$.

[3]At this Congress I learned that Amice and Vélu have a generalization of this theory for the supersingular primes p as well.

[4]See **[13]** and a forthcoming book of A. Ogg which will treat these issues thoroughly.

We may now explain the requirement that $E/\mathbf{Q}$ be *parametrized by modular forms*, made twice before, namely: For some N we require that there be a surjective map $X_0(N) \to E$ defined over $\mathbf{Q}$.

For the rest of our constructions, we shall be (implicitly and explicitly) studying *quotients of the jacobian of* $X_0(N)$. Fix N a *prime number*. We make this restriction since our nontrivial results have only been proved for N prime, and it enables us to avoid discussing the technical matter of primitive (or *new*) forms. Let J be the jacobian of $X_0(N)$, regarded as abelian variety over $\mathbf{Q}$.

By the *Hecke algebra* $\underline{T} \subset$ End J we shall mean the ring of endomorphisms of J generated by the Hecke operators T_l for prime numbers $l \neq N$, and by the canonical involution w (which, on U is $z \mapsto -1/Nz$). The Hecke algebra $\underline{T}$ is a free module over $\mathbf{Z}$ of rank equal to dim J, and is a subalgebra of finite index in a finite product of Dedekind domains, each factor being the ring of integers in some totally real number field.

If $P \subset \underline{T}$ is a maximal ideal, let $\underline{T}_P$ denote the completion of $\underline{T}$ at P. Let $\underline{a} \subset \underline{T}$ denote the kernel of $\underline{T} \to \underline{T}_P$. Let $\underline{a} \cdot J \subset J$ denote the subabelian variety generated by the images of J under elements in $\underline{a}$.

Form $J/\underline{a} \cdot J = J^{(P)}$ which may again be regarded as an abelian variety defined over $\mathbf{Q}$, and which we call the *factor associated to* P. The construction of p-adic L-series alluded to above is not restricted to the case of elliptic curves parametrized by modular forms but rather, with a certain twist, makes sense for arbitrary factors of J. For example, let $P \subset \underline{T}$ be any maximal ideal lying over the rational prime p. Suppose that *the Hecke operator* T_p *does not lie in* P. Then the construction of **[6]** provides a (p-adic) analytic power series $L_P(J, s)$. The "twist" consists in that this power series does *not* naturally lie in $\underline{T}_P[[s]]$, but rather in $\underline{T}_P[[s]] \otimes_{\underline{T}_P} H_P^+$ where H_P^+ is the following $\underline{T}_P$-module. Let $H = H_1(J_{\mathbf{C}}, \mathbf{Z})$, the classical 1-dimensional singular homology group of the complex torus $J_{\mathbf{C}}$. Let $\mathfrak{S}$ denote complex conjugation, and $H \to H^+$ the quotient by the minus-eigenspace of $\mathfrak{S}$. Set $H_P^+ = H^+ \otimes_{\underline{T}} \underline{T}_P$.

In *good* cases, H_P^+ is a free $\underline{T}_P$-module of rank one.

4. Eisenstein primes. We are now ready to describe prime ideals in the Hecke algebra which seem to play an effective part in the study of certain arithmetic questions.

We repeat that N is assumed to be prime. By the *Eisenstein ideal* $I \subset \underline{T}$ we mean the ideal generated by the elements $1 + l - T_l$ for all primes $l \neq N$, and by $1 + w$.

Let ν denote the numerator of $(N - 1)/12$. Let p be a prime number *dividing* ν, and let p^α denote the precise power of p which divides ν. By the *Eisenstein prime* $P \subset \underline{T}$ *over* p we mean the ideal $P = (I, p)$. Using the fact that p divides ν one can prove that $\underline{T}/P = \mathbf{Z}/p$, and in particular that $P \neq \underline{T}$.

We can now state our results. The first main result may be loosely paraphrased as follows: "*The Birch Swinnerton-Dyer conjecture is valid locally at an Eisenstein prime*". We actually have something stronger in mind: "locally with respect to an Eisenstein prime" each of the relevant factors of the conjectural (P-adic) Birch

Swinnerton-Dyer formula may be evaluated. Explicitly, we describe the evaluation of the arithmetically interesting factors:

THEOREM A. *Let N be a prime, and suppose p is an odd prime dividing ν. Let P be the Eisenstein prime over p.*

1. (*Nonvanishing of the L-series*) *H_P^+ is free of rank 1 over $\mathbf{T}_P$ and $L_P(J, 1)\cdot \mathbf{T}_P$ is of finite index in H_P^+.*[5]

2. (*Finiteness of Mordell-Weil*) *$J^{(P)}$ has only a finite number of rational points over $\boldsymbol{Q}$. (This result remains valid if $p = 2$, at least in the case where $N \equiv 1 \bmod 16$.)*

3. (*Torsion part of Mordell-Weil*) *The P-primary component of the Mordel-Weil group of $J^{(P)}$ is cyclic of order p^α.*

4. (*Shafarevitch-Tate*) *The P-primary component of the Shafarevitch-Tate group of $J^{(P)}/\boldsymbol{Q}$ is zero.*

REMARKS. 1. *What is the dimension of $J^{(P)}$?* By part 3 of the above theorem, $J^{(P)}$ has a point of order p^α. Using the Riemann hypothesis applied to $J^{(P)}$ over $\boldsymbol{F}_2$ one may conclude that dim $J^{(P)} \geqq \log_6 p^\alpha$. Actual computation ($N < 250$) finds the $J^{(P)}$'s to be of significantly larger dimension than this. Indeed, factors associated to Eisenstein primes usually account for all or almost all of the minus-eigenspace of the involution w on J.

A consequence of some of the theory developed in [5] is the following: If $\alpha = 1$, then $J^{(P)}$ is an absolutely irreducible abelian variety. By appropriate choice of N and p, using the Dirichlet theorem on primes in arithmetic progressions, one may then deduce (using part 2 of Theorem A):

THEOREM B. *There are absolutely irreducible abelian varieties of arbitrarily high dimensions defined over $\boldsymbol{Q}$, with finite Mordell-Well group.*

We state this theorem explicitly because at present we know of no other means of obtaining such examples.

2. *Torsion in the Mordell-Weil group of J.* If N is a prime, then the divisor class of the difference $(0) - (i\infty)$ of the two cusps on $X_0(N)$ is a point of J, rational over $\boldsymbol{Q}$, and of order precisely ν = numerator $(N - 1)/12$, as has been shown by Ogg. Ogg conjectured that this point generates *all* the torsion in the Mordell-Weil group of J over $\boldsymbol{Q}$. In the course of proving part 3 of Theorem A, we have shown the following:

THEOREM C. *The torsion subgroup of the Mordell-Weil group of J is generated by* $(0) - (i\infty)$ *if* $N \equiv -1$ (4) *or* $N \equiv 1$ (16). *In all cases, the quotient of* M_{tors} *by the subgroup generated by* $(0) - (i\infty)$ *is a 2-group.*

3. *Finiteness of Mordell-Weil of $J^{(P)}$ over larger fields?* From the explicit calculation of the P-adic L-series given in part 1 of Theorem A and from general conjec-

[5] A more precise formula, which depends, of course, on the normalization chosen for $L_P(J, 1)$, will be given in [5]. Curiously, the size of this index seems to depend on whether p is a pth power modulo N.

tures (relating the so-called *analytically defined* characteristic polynomials to the *algebraically defined* ones; cf. [6]), one is led to ask a question, which may be attackable, and may have an affirmative answer, at least when p is not a pth power mod N.

Question. Let $\mathbf{Q}^{(p)}/\mathbf{Q}$ be the unique Galois extension with Galois group isomorphic to $\mathbf{Z}_p$. Does $J^{(P)}$ have only a finite number of rational points over $\mathbf{Q}^{(p)}$?[6]

4. *The proper context of Eisenstein primes*. Wherever there are Eisenstein series in the theory of modular forms, there seems to be the analogue of Eisenstein primes in the relevant Hecke algebra. The next task of our theory should be to make a systematic connection between these two notions. Among other things, this should encompass a study of the jacobian of $X_0(N)$ where N is no longer necessarily prime.[7] Especially intriguing, however, is the prospect of studying other quotient curves of the modular curve $X(N)$, and modular forms of weight higher than 2.

5. The Mordell conjecture for $X_0(N)$ over $\mathbf{Q}$. Here N remains a prime number.

THEOREM D. *Let $X_0(N)$ have genus greater than zero. Then $X_0(N)$ has no more than a finite number of rational points over* $\mathbf{Q}$.[8]

One is after something *much finer* than this, though.

PROOF BASED ON THE RESULTS OF §4. One checks, with no trouble, that the genus of $X_0(N)$ is greater than zero if and only if $\nu > 1$. Also, either there is an *odd* prime p dividing ν, or $p = 2$ divides ν and $N \equiv 1 \bmod 16$. Thus, by part 2 of Theorem A applied to such a p, there is always some Eisenstein prime P such that $J^{(P)}$ has a finite number of rational points over $\mathbf{Q}$. Now consider

$$(*)\qquad \begin{array}{ccc} X_0(N) & \longrightarrow & J \\ & {\scriptstyle\beta}\searrow \quad \swarrow & \\ & J^{(P)} & \end{array}$$

and since $X_0(N)$ generates J as a group and the factor $J^{(P)}$ is of positive dimension, it follows that β must be nonconstant, and therefore a finite map of the curve $X_0(N)$ onto its image. Theorem D then follows.

In *actually* determining the rational points of $X_0(N)$ for some value of N, the fun only *begins* with diagram $(*)$. For example, if $N \not\equiv 9 \bmod 16$ or if $p \neq 2$ one can produce a certain set Δ of points in $J^{(P)}$ which is of cardinality 2,3,4, or 5 depending on the congruence class of N modulo 12 ($N \equiv 1, 5, 7$, or $11 \bmod 12$ resp.) such that if x is a rational point of $X_0(N)$, then $\beta(x) \in \Delta$.

Using this, geometric analysis of β (cf. [8], [9]), and work of Brumer and Kramer on certain elliptic curve factors of J which are *not* associated to Eisenstein primes, Ogg and I have calculated the set of rational points of $X_0(N)$ for all primes $N < 250$ *except for* $N = 53, 113, 137, 151, 227$ (in the first three of these unresolved cases the method gives that there are either two noncuspidal rational points on $X_0(N)$

[6]Cf. [4] where the first nontrivial case $N = 11$ is worked out.

[7]There seem to be conceptual as well as technical barriers to this, at present.

[8]We give no upper bound for the number of these rational points in general.

or there are none). Based on this numerical work, Ogg has made a conjecture, which we describe below.

Suppose that N is any positive integer, no longer necessarily prime. The cases where the genus of $X_0(N)$ is zero are well known; so are the 12 cases where $X_0(N)$ is of genus one, and in these cases, all rational points of $X_0(N)$ are known. Therefore let us suppose that the genus of $X_0(N)$ is greater than one. The following curious list of noncuspidal rational points is also known:

$N = 43, 67, 163$: $X_0(N)$ has a (single) noncuspidal rational point "coming from a quadratic imaginary field of class number one".

$N = 37$: $X_0(37)$ has two noncuspidal rational points interchanged by the canonical involution w.

CONJECTURE. The above list gives all noncuspidal rational points on all $X_0(N)$ of genus greater than one.

The case $N = 37$ was studied at great length by Swinnerton-Dyer and myself [**6**]. The extra lever one has in this case is the following: $X_0(37)$ is a hyperelliptic curve whose hyperelliptic involution u is different from w. Ogg has recently proved that among the $X_0(N)$'s, $X_0(37)$ is the *only* curve with the above property. Note that the image under u of the two cusps (0) and $(i\infty)$ are rational points of $X_0(37)$. Swinnerton-Dyer and I were able to show (from general principles) that these two rational points are *different* from the cusps, thereby establishing these points as candidates for the above list.

6. Indications of the method of proof. There are three main stages in the proof of Theorem A.

1. Proof that H_P^+ is free of rank 1 over $\underline{T}_P$. This uses the theory of modular forms in characteristic p.

2. Proof that I_P (the ideal generated by the Eisenstein ideal I in $\underline{T}_P$) is a *principal* ideal in $\underline{T}_P$. One does this by defining a $\underline{T}_P$-homomorphism $I_P \to H_P^+$ and shows, using the theory of the *modular symbol*, that this homomorphism is an isomorphism.

3. The "geometric" descent. One takes an element α in I which is a local generator of I_P, and uses the endomorphism α of J to perform a "descent" as explained in [**4**] and [**7**].

By far the longest and most involved stage is the first. I shall try, in a few brief paragraphs, to convey the flavor of the arguments that enter into it. We keep to $p \neq 2$, as hypothesized in Theorem A. At one point (which we shall gloss over) in the argument, one must do some extra work when $p = 3$.

To prove that H_P^+ is free of rank one over $\underline{T}_P$, it suffices to prove that H_P is free of rank two over $\underline{T}_P$. We identify the $\underline{T}_P$-module H_P with the $\bar{\boldsymbol{Q}}$-rational points of the "P-primary" factor of $\text{Tate}_p J$. By $\text{Tate}_p J$ we mean the pro-p Barsotti-Tate group associated to the abelian scheme J over Spec $\boldsymbol{Z}[1/N]$. Refer to this "P-primary" factor as $\text{Tate}_P J$. Let $\text{Tate}_P J[1]$ denote the cokernel of "multiplication by p". That is, it is the "first truncation" of the pro-p Barsotti-Tate group, and we regard $\text{Tate}_P J[1]$ as a finite flat group scheme killed by p over Spec $\boldsymbol{Z}[1/N]$, which is self-dual under Cartier duality. Let V denote the group of $\bar{\boldsymbol{Q}}$-rational points of this finite flat group scheme. We regard V as a $\mathrm{Gal}(\bar{\mathbf{Q}}/\mathbf{Q})$-module and as $\underline{T}_P$-module. Consider the P-adic filtration on V and form the associated graded $\mathrm{Gal}(\bar{\mathbf{Q}}/\mathbf{Q})$-module $\mathrm{gr}_P V$. Any element x of $\mathrm{gr}_P V$ is killed by P, and therefore

$$(**) \qquad T_l \cdot x = (1 + l)\cdot x, \qquad l \neq N, \qquad w \cdot x = -x.$$

By the Eichler-Shimura relations, and Cartier self-duality of V, one obtains from $(**)$ that the eigenvalues of l-Frobenius ($l \neq N$) acting on $\mathrm{gr}_P V$ are 1 and l with the same multiplicity m. By the Čebotarev density theorem and standard representation theory, one obtains that the semisimplification of the representation of $\mathrm{Gal}(\bar{\mathbf{Q}}/\mathbf{Q})$ on V is isomorphic to $(\mathbf{Z}/p)^m \oplus (\boldsymbol{\mu}_p)^m$, where $\mathbf{Z}/p$ means the $\mathrm{Gal}(\bar{\mathbf{Q}}/\mathbf{Q})$-module with trivial action, and $\boldsymbol{\mu}_p$ means the $\mathrm{Gal}(\bar{\mathbf{Q}}/\mathbf{Q})$-module of pth roots of unity.

Using standard techniques in the theory of finite flat group schemes, and using the Oort-Tate classification theorem of finite flat group schemes of order p, one then learns that there is a filtration of the finite flat group scheme $\mathrm{Tate}_P J[1]$ by subgroup schemes, finite and flat over Spec $\mathbf{Z}[1/N]$ whose associated graded finite flat group scheme over $\mathbf{Z}[1/N]$ is $(\mathbf{Z}/p)^m \oplus (\boldsymbol{\mu}_p)^m$ where $\mathbf{Z}/p$ and $\boldsymbol{\mu}_p$ now refer to the group schemes over Spec $\mathbf{Z}[1/N]$. We are now ready to reduce the Barsotti-Tate group $\mathrm{Tate}_P J$ *to characteristic p*.

One thing we discover from our group scheme filtration of $\mathrm{Tate}_P J[1]$ is that $\mathrm{Tate}_P J$ is an "ordinary" Barsotti-Tate group. Over $\mathbf{F}_p$ we may write it as

$$\mathrm{Tate}_P J/\mathbf{F}_p = \textit{multiplicative part} \times \textit{étale part}$$

where each part is a $\underline{T}_P$-module and is dual to the other part. To establish the assertion of stage 1, it suffices to show that the $\bar{\mathbf{F}}_p$-rational points of the *étale part* form a free $\underline{T}_P$-module of rank one. After much difficult work,[9] one finds that the key to this is to show that the étale part of the kernel of P in $J/\bar{\mathbf{F}}_p$ is a group scheme of order precisely p. Let this étale group scheme be denoted C. There is a *general* geometric construction which gives us an imbedding

$$C(k) \otimes_{\mathbf{F}_p} k \xrightarrow{\ c\ } H^0(X_0(N)/k, \Omega^1_{X_0(N)/k})$$

for any extension field $k/\mathbf{F}_p$. Moreover, by naturality, c maps the domain to the kernel of P in the range. Consider an element f in the kernel of P in the range of the above map. We regard f as a modular form, parabolic, of weight 2 under $\Gamma_0(N)$, which is an eigenvector for the Hecke operators T_l with eigenvalue $(1 + l)$, $l \neq N$, and an eigenvector for w with eigenvalue -1. With some work, one discovers that mod p, up to scalar multiplication, f has the same q-expansion as the Eisenstein series of weight 2 for $\Gamma_0(N)$. By the q-expansion principle f must be (mod p) a scalar multiple of the Eisenstein series. In other words $C(k)$ is an $\mathbf{F}_p$-vector space of dimension ≤ 1; it is seen to be of dimension precisely one by explicit construction.

[9] ADDED IN PROOF. It was only after the Congress that I realized how difficult this point is. In working it out, however, some new things emerge. Firstly, Theorem D may now be proved in a more elementary way. Secondly, some of the results may be significantly sharpened. Cf. **[5]** and the Bourbaki seminar report (*Points rationnels des modulaires $X_0(N)$*, n° 469, Juin 1975) by J.-P. Serre and myself.

References

1. N. Katz, *Letter to S. Lichtenbaum*, June 1974.

2. Ju. I. Manin, *Cyclotomic fields and modular curves*, Uspehi Mat. Nauk **26** (1971), no. 6 (162), 7–71 = Russian Math. Surveys **26** (1971), no. 6, 7–78.

3. ———, *The values of p-adic Hecke series at integer points of the critical strip*, Mat. Sb. **93 (135)** (1974), 621–626 = Math. USSR Sb. **22** (1974) (to appear).

4. B. Mazur, *Rational points of abelian varieties with values in towers of number fields*, Invent. Math. **18** (1972), 183–266.

5. ———, *Modular curves and the Eisenstein ideal* (in preparation).

6. B. Mazur and P. Swinnerton-Dyer, *Arithmetic of Weil curves*, Invent Math. **25** (1974), 1–16.

7. B. Mazur and J. Tate, *Points of order* 13 *on elliptic curves*, Invent. Math. **22** (1973), 41–49.

8. A. Ogg, *Diophantine equations and modular forms*, Bull. Amer. Math. Soc. **81** (1975), 14–27.

9. ———, *Hyperelliptic modular curves* (to appear).

10. J.-P. Serre, *Formes modulaires et fonctions zêta p-adiques*, Modular Functions on one Variable, III, Proc. Internat. Summer School, Univ. of Antwerp, RUCA, Lecture Notes in Math., vol. 350, Springer-Verlag, Berlin and New York, 1973, pp. 191–268. MR **48** #2080.

11. Goro Shimura, *Introduction to the arithmetic theory of automorphic functions*, Kanô Memorial Lectures, no. 1, Publ. Math. Soc. Japan, no. 11, Iwannami Shoten, Tokyo; Princeton Univ. Press, Princeton, N.J., 1971. MR **47** #3318.

12. J. Tate, *Arithmetic of elliptic curves*, Invent. Math. **23** (1974), 179–206.

13. P. Deligne and M. Rapoport, *Les schémas de modules de courbes elliptiques*, Modular Functions on one Variable, II, Proc. Internat. Summer School, Univ. of Antwerp, RUCA, Lecture Notes in Math., vol. 349, Springer-Verlag, Berlin and New York, 1973, pp. 143–317.

HARVARD UNIVERSITY
CAMBRIDGE, MASSACHUSETTS 02138, U.S.A.

Proceedings of the International Congress of Mathematicians
Vancouver, 1974

Distribution of the Zeros of the Riemann Zeta Function

Hugh L. Montgomery

One of the most tantalizing problems of number theory is that of determining effectively all imaginary quadratic fields $\boldsymbol{Q}(\sqrt{-d})$ possessing a given class number h. For $h = 1$ this was settled independently by Heegner, Baker, and Stark, and the latter two also settled the question for $h = 2$. For $h \geqq 3$ the problem remains open, although it is known that of all imaginary quadratic fields $\boldsymbol{Q}(\sqrt{-d})$ with class number h, we have $d < Ch^2 \log^2 h$, except for at most one exceptional field, for which d may be larger. The Generalized Riemann Hypothesis implies that there is no such exceptional field, but the opposing assumption, that there is a field $\boldsymbol{Q}(\sqrt{-d})$ with very large d and small h, has many interesting consequences. For example, Mordell deduced that all nontrivial zeros of the Riemann zeta function lie on the critical line $\operatorname{Re} s = \frac{1}{2}$, at least up to a height $T(d)$ which increases with d. Weinberger and I [3] carried this analysis somewhat further by showing that up to $T(d)$ the zeros of the Riemann zeta function are well spaced on the critical line. Let $0 < \gamma_1 \leqq \gamma_2 \leqq \cdots$ be the ordinates of the nontrivial zeros of $\zeta(s)$. The average of $\gamma_{n+1} - \gamma_n$ is $2\pi/\log \gamma_n$. For γ_n nearly as large as $T(d)$, we found that

$$\gamma_{n+1} - \gamma_n > (\tfrac{1}{4} - \varepsilon)2\pi/\log \gamma_n.$$

Results of this sort, with specifically known close pairs of zeros, enable one to show, for example, that there are no fields $\boldsymbol{Q}(\sqrt{-d})$ with $h = 3$ and $10^{12} \leqq d \leqq 10^{2500}$. To effect a complete solution of these problems by this approach, it would suffice to show that there is a constant $c < \frac{1}{4}$ such that, for all large T,

$$\min_{T \leqq \gamma_n \leqq 2T} (\gamma_{n+1} - \gamma_n)\log T \leqq 2\pi c. \tag{1}$$

From this one can deduce that $h(-d)$ tends to infinity effectively.

In attempting to demonstrate (1), one may seek an estimate for the expression

(2) $$D(\alpha, \beta) = \sum_{\substack{0<\gamma\leqq T;\, 0<\gamma'\leqq T \\ 2\pi\alpha/\log T \leqq \gamma-\gamma' \leqq 2\pi\beta/\log T}} 1;$$

here γ and γ' run independently over ordinates of nontrivial zeros of $\zeta(s)$. Taking Fourier transforms, we see that estimating the density $D(\alpha, \beta)$ is essentially a matter of evaluating the form function

$$F(\alpha) = \left(\frac{T}{2\pi} \log T\right)^{-1} \sum_{0<\gamma\leqq T;\, 0<\gamma'\leqq T} T^{i\alpha(\gamma-\gamma')} w(\gamma - \gamma')$$

for real α, where $w(u) = 4/(4 + u^2)$. Since F is symmetric in γ and γ', we see that F is real and even. Recently I showed **[2]** that if the Riemann Hypothesis is true then F is nearly nonnegative, $F(\alpha) \geqq -\varepsilon$ uniformly in α, for $T > T_0(\varepsilon)$, and that

(3) $$F(\alpha) = (1 + o(1))T^{-2\alpha} \log T + \alpha + o(1)$$

for $0 \leqq \alpha \leqq 1$. For $\alpha > 1$ the behavior changes, and we conjecture that

(4) $$F(\alpha) = 1 + o(1)$$

for $\alpha \geqq 1$. This conjecture is based on number-theoretic heuristics; it implies that

(5) $$D(\alpha, \beta) \sim \left(\int_\alpha^\beta \left(1 - \left(\frac{\sin u}{u}\right)^2\right) du + \delta(\alpha,\beta)\right) \frac{T}{2\pi} \log T$$

for each fixed $\alpha < \beta$. Here $\delta(\alpha, \beta) = 1$ if $0 \in [\alpha, \beta]$, and $\delta(\alpha, \beta) = 0$ otherwise. The occurrence of the Dirac δ-function here is to be expected, for if $\alpha \leqq 0 \leqq \beta$ then the sum (2) includes terms with $\gamma = \gamma'$. We note that our conjecture (5) implies (1) for all $c > 0$.

It is interesting to note that the pair correlation function $1 - ((\sin \pi u)/\pi u)^2$, which occurs in (5), also arises as the limiting pair correlation of eigenvalues of random Hermitian matrices of large order **[1]**. This is in accord with the view, originally propounded by Pólya, that the Riemann Hypothesis might be proved by exhibiting a Hermitian operator whose eigenvalues are related to the zeros of the zeta function. Indeed, it would probably be difficult to interpret (5) in a different framework.

Since (5) remains unproved, it is useful to note that, subject to the Riemann Hypothesis, the estimate (3) enables one to evaluate asymptotically the sum

$$\sum_{0<\gamma\leqq T;\, 0<\gamma'\leqq T} r\left((\gamma - \gamma')\frac{\log T}{2}\right) w(\gamma - \gamma')$$

provided that the spectrum of r is sufficiently small. For example, we find that

$$\sum_{0<\gamma\leqq T;\, 0<\gamma'\leqq T} \left(\frac{\sin \frac{1}{2}(\gamma - \gamma')\log T}{\frac{1}{2}(\gamma - \gamma')\log T}\right)^2 \sim \frac{4}{3} \frac{T}{2\pi} \log T.$$

From this we can show, still assuming RH, that at least 2/3 of the zeros of $\zeta(s)$ are simple, as follows. Let m_ρ be the multiplicity of the zero $\rho = \frac{1}{2} + i\gamma$. In the above sum there are m_ρ^2 paris γ, γ' for which $\gamma = \gamma' = \operatorname{Im} \rho$, so that

$$\sum_{0<\gamma\leqq T} m_\rho^2 \leqq \left(\frac{4}{3} + o(1)\right) \frac{T}{2\pi} \log T.$$

On the other hand, we know classically that

$$\sum_{0<\gamma\leqq T} m_\rho \sim \frac{T}{2\pi}\log T.$$

Thus, combining these estimates,

$$\sum_{0<\gamma\leqq T;\rho \text{ simple}} 1 \geqq \sum_{0<\gamma\leqq T} m_\rho(2-m_\rho) \geqq \left(\frac{2}{3}+o(1)\right)\frac{T}{2\pi}\log T.$$

Upon examination it will be seen that the above argument is not as efficient as it might be. To obtain a sharp result, one is led to an extremal problem in which we seek $r \in L^1(\boldsymbol{R})$ with $r(u) \geqq 0$. We want

$$\hat{r}(\alpha) = \int_{-\infty}^{+\infty} r(u)e^{-2\pi i\alpha u}du$$

to have support contained in $[-1, 1]$, and we want

$$\left(\hat{r}(0) + 2\int_0^1 \alpha\hat{r}(\alpha)\,d\alpha\right)\Big/\int_0^1 \hat{r}(\alpha)\,d\alpha$$

to be minimal. M. E. Taylor and I have recently addressed ourselves to this problem, and under the reasonable assumption that $\hat{r}(\alpha)$ is of the form $\hat{r}(\alpha) = h(\alpha)*h(-\alpha)$, we found that

$$\begin{aligned} h(\alpha) &= \cos 2^{1/2}(\alpha - \tfrac{1}{2}) \quad &&\text{for } |\alpha| \leqq 1,\\ &= 0 &&\text{otherwise,}\end{aligned}$$

yields the extremal function r. This leads to the result that, subject to the Riemann Hypothesis, at least $3/2 - 2^{-1/2}\cot 2^{-1/2} = 0.6725\cdots$ of the zeros of the zeta function are simple.

References

1. M. L. Mehta, *Random matrices and the statistical theory of energy levels*, Academic Press, New York, 1967. MR **36** #3553.

2. H. L. Montgomery, *The pair correlation of zeros of the zeta function*, Proc. Sympos. Pure Math., vol. 24, Amer. Math. Soc., Providence, R.I., 1973, pp. 181–193.

3. H. L. Montgomery and P. J. Weinberger, *Notes on small class numbers*, Acta Arith. **24** (1974), 329–342.

University of Michigan
Ann Arbor, Michigan 48104, U.S.A.

Труды Международного Конгресса Математиков
Ванкувер, 1974

Элементарный Метод в Теории Уравнений над Конечными Полями

С. А. Степанов

1. Пусть p—простое число и $F(x, y)$—многочлен от переменных x, y с целыми рациональными коэффициентами не равный тождественно нулю по mod p. Обозначим через N_p количество решений сравнения

$$F(x, y) \equiv 0 \pmod p. \tag{1}$$

Уже давно были получены отдельные результаты, касающиеся количества N_p решений сравнения (1) в вырожденных случаях. Чтобы доказать теорему о том, что каждое натуральное число представляется суммой четырех квадратов, Лагранжу [1] потребовалось утверждение о том, что сравнение

$$x^2 + y^2 + 1 \equiv 0 \pmod p$$

разрешимо. Обратим внимание на доказательство этого утверждения, предложенное Лагранжем. Предположим, что указанное сравнение не разрешимо. Тогда, по критерию Эйлера, сравнение

$$1 + (-1 - x^2)^{(p-1)/2} \equiv 0 \pmod p$$

должно иметь p решений. Но степень последнего сравнения равна $p - 1$ и оно не может иметь (по теореме Лагранжа) более, чем $p - 1$ решений. Полученное противоречие показывает, что сравнение

$$x^2 + y^2 + 1 \equiv 0 \pmod p$$

имеет по крайней мере одно решение.

Задача о числе решений сравнения

$$y^2 \equiv f(x) \pmod p \tag{2}$$

очевидным образом сводится к оценке сумм символов Лежандра

$$\sum_{x=0}^{p-1}\left(\frac{f(x)}{p}\right). \tag{3}$$

Если $f(x)$—многочлен второй степени, то для суммы (3) известна точная формула. Нетривиальная ситуация возникает в случае, когда степень $f(x)$ больше двух. Артин [**2**] в 1924 году высказал гипотезу, что для количества N_p решений сравнения (2), где $f(x)$—многочлен степени n, не являющийся квадратом другого многочлена по mod p, справедлива оценка

$$|N_p - p| \leqq 2\left[\frac{n-1}{2}\right]p^{1/2}.$$

Гипотеза Артина может быть выражена также в виде

$$\left|\sum_{x=0}^{p-1}\left(\frac{f(x)}{p}\right)\right| \leqq 2\left[\frac{n-1}{2}\right]p^{1/2}.$$

Г. Хопфом [**3**] для оценки сумм вида (3) был использован метод кратных сумм. В этом методе оцениваемая сумма представляется как среднее по некоторому количеству таких же сумм, но с другими параметрами, затем осреднение распространяется на все многочлены данной степени. В дальнейшем этот метод был развит в работах Давенпорта [**4**] и Морделла [**5**]. Однако методом кратных сумм гипотеза Артина не только не была доказана, но даже не был получен истинный порядок оценки по p. По сути дела, метод кратных сумм в задачах о сравнениях по простому модулю—это лишь проявление общего метода аналитической теории чисел, без учета специфики конечного поля, а именно, наличия эндоморфизма Фробениуса. Этим, по-видимому, объясняется тот факт, что методом кратных сумм не были получены результаты оптимальной силы.

В 1934 году Г. Хассе [**6**], основываясь на формуле сложения точек якобиева многообразия кривой $y^2 = x^3 + ax + b$ доказал, что для количества N_p решений эллиптического сравнения

$$y^2 \equiv x^3 + ax + b \pmod p$$

справедлива оценка

$$|N_p - p| < 2p^{1/2}.$$

Элементарное доказательство теоремы Хассе было дано в 1956 году Ю.И. Маниным [**7**]. Однако, его доказательство лишь моделирует доказательство Г. Хассе и поэтому не может быть распространено на сравнения более общего вида.

Сравнение (1) можно трактовать как уравнение над простым конечным полем k_p, состоящим из p элементов, а количество N_p решений этого сравнения как число k_p—рациональных точек кривой, определяемой этим уравнением. Ввиду этого, к изучению алгебраических сравнений (1) по простому модулю, наряду с теоретико-числовыми методами могут применяться методы теории алгебраических функций и алгебраической геометрии.

А. Вейль [8] распространил метод Г. Хассе на широкий класс алгебраических уравнений с двумя неизвестными, определенных над произвольными конечными полями k_q, состоящими из $q = p^r$ элементов. Именно, в случае абсолютно неприводимого многочлена $F(x, y)$, для числа N_q решений уравнения

$$F(x, y) = 0 \tag{4}$$

в конечном поле k_q им была получена оценка

$$\left|N_q - q\right| \leqq 2gq^{1/2}, \tag{5}$$

где g—род кривой (4).

Доказательство А. Вейля оценки (5) требует привлечения современного аппарата алгебраической геометрии и довольно сложно. В 1968 году мною [9], в случае многочлена $f(x)$ нечетной степени n, для количества N_p решений гиперэллиптического сравнения (2) с помощью простых арифметических соображений была получена оценка

$$\left|N_p - p\right| \leqq (3n)^{1/2}\, np^{1/2}. \tag{6}$$

В дальнейшем метод работы [9] был распространен мною [10], [11], [12] на сравнения

$$y^n \equiv f(x) \pmod p$$

и уравнения

$$y^2 = f(x), \qquad y^p - y = R(x)$$

над полями Галуа k_q, состоящими из q элементов. Полученная при этом элементарными средствами асимптотическая формула для числа решений последнего уравнения позволила дать вполне арифметическое доказательство оценок А. Вейля рациональных тригонометрических сумм с простым знаменателем

$$\left|\sum_{x\in k_q;\, Q(x)\neq 0} e^{2\pi i\,(\mathrm{Sp}\, R(x)/p)}\right| \leqq \left(r - 2 + \sum_{i=1}^{r} d_i\right) q^{1/2},$$

где r—число различных полюсов функции $R = P(x)/Q(x)$ в алгебраическом замыкании поля k_p и d_i—кратность полюса x_i, в частности, сумм Г. Вейля

$$\left|\sum_{x=0}^{p-1} e^{2\pi i\,(f(x)/p)}\right| \leqq (n-1)\, p^{1/2}, \qquad n = \deg f(x),$$

и Клостермана

$$\left|\sum_{x=1}^{p-1} e^{2\pi i\,((x+a/x)/p)}\right| \leqq 2p^{1/2}.$$

Кроме того, после работ автора [9] и А.А. Карацубы [13] вполне элементарным стал вывод оценки Берджеса

$$N_{\min} \leqq C(\delta)\, p^{1/4e^{1/2}+\delta}$$

для наименьшего квадратичного невычета $N_{\min}$ по простому модулю p.

Рассмотрение уравнения $y^2 = f(x)$ во всех конечных расширениях k_q поля k_p позволило улучшить результат (6). Именно, в работе автора [**11**] для числа N_q решений уравнения $y^2 = f(x)$ в элементах поля k_q, в случае многочлена $f(x)$ нечетной степени n с коэффициентами из простого подполя k_p поля k_q была получена оценка

$$|N_q - q| \leqq (n-1)\, q^{1/2}, \tag{7}$$

которая эквивалентна гипотезе Римана для Z-функций Артина квадратичных расширений поля рациональных функций $k_p(x)$ с коэффициентами из k_p.

Некоторые уточнения метода моей работы [**9**] позволили Х. Старку [**14**] и Н.М. Коробову [**15**] получить для количества N_p решений сравнения (2) оценку, которая не только не уступает оценке (7), но при растущих вместе с p значениях n, $n = \deg f(x)$, оказывается даже сильнее последней.

В работе [**16**] мною была доказана следующая теорема:

Теорема 1. *Пусть $m, n \geqq 2$—взаимно простые натуральные числа, $p > 196\, m^3 n (n-1)^2$—простое число, $F(x, y) = y^n + a_1(x) y^{n-1} + \cdots + a_n(x)$—неприводимый многочлен от x, y с коэффициентами из k_p, такой что*

$$\deg a_n(x) = m, \qquad n \deg a_i(x) < im, \qquad i = 1, 2, \cdots, n-1. \tag{8}$$

Тогда для количества N_p решений сравнения

$$F(x, y) \equiv 0 \pmod p$$

справедлива оценка

$$|N_p - p| \leqq 14\, (mn)^{1/2}\, m(n-1)\, p^{1/2}. \tag{9}$$

Заметим, что в последнем неравенстве константа при $p^{1/2}$ несколько хуже, нежели константа в неравенства А. Вейля. Получение в теореме такой же константы, как у Вейля не составляет большого труда. Для этого достаточно перенести доказательство на произвольные конечные поля k_q и затем применить теорию Z-функций алгебраических кривых. Однако при этом нужно дополнительно потребовать, чтобы многочлен $F(x, y)$ был абсолютно неприводим. С другой стороны, улучшение константы в неравенстве (9) возможно и без выхода за рамки предложенного в работе [**16**] доказательства, а только за счет некоторого его уточнения.

Доказательство теоремы 1, так же как и доказательство результатов работ автора [**9**]—[**12**] основывается на построении многочлена $R_0(x)$ не слишком высокой степени, имеющего корнями достаточно высокой кратности все те значения переменной x (за исключением $O(1)$ значений), которые являются решениями сравнения $F(x, y) \equiv 0 \pmod p$. Сравнение числа корней многочлена $R_0(x)$, взятых с их кратностями, со степенью $R_0(x)$ дает оценку величины N_p сверху. Аналогичным способом получается и оценка величины N_p снизу. Основным моментом во всех этих построениях является наличие эндоморфизма Фробениуса $x^p \mapsto x$, оставляющего неподвижными элементы поля k_p.

Дополнительное условие (8) связано с трудностями, которые возникают при доказательстве того факта, что построенный многочлен $R_0(x)$ с необходимыми свойствами не является тождественным нулем.

Независимо от работы [16] В. Шмидт [17] аналогичным методом получил общий результат

$$|N_q - q| \leqq 2 \min(m^2n, mn^2)q^{1/2}$$

для числа N_q решений уравнений $F(x, y) = 0$ в полях Галуа k_q, состоящих из q элементов, потребовав от многочлена $F(x, y)$ только его абсолютную неприводимость.

В работе Е. Бомбьери [18] метод работ [9]—[12], [14]—[17] был значительно упрощен за счет отказа от явной конструкции многочленов $R_0(x)$ и выбора их как элементов некоторого непустого множества многочленов с требуемыми свойствами. Следует однако отметить, что явные конструкции обладают тем преимуществом, что с их помощью в некоторых случаях удается получать более сильные оценки (см. [14], [15]), чем те, которые следуют из общих теорий.

2. Доказательство теоремы 1. Сравнение $F(x, y) \equiv 0 \pmod p$ будем трактовать как уравнение $F(x, y) = 0$ над простым конечным полем k_p, состоящим из p элементов, а величину N_p как число k_p-рациональных точек кривой C, определяемой уравнением

$$F(x, y) = 0. \tag{10}$$

Введем следующие обозначения: $k_p\,[x]$—кольцо многочленов от x с коэффициентами из k_p, $k_p(x)$—поле частных кольца $k_p[x]$. Пусть $y_s(x)$, $s = 1, 2, \cdots, n$, —корни многочлена $F(x, y)$. Через $k_p(x, y_s)$ обозначим поле алгебраических функций, полученное из $k_p(x)$ присоединением $y_s(x)$ и через $k_p\,[x, y_s]$—кольцо целых элементов поля $k_p(x, y_s)$. Пусть $D(x)$ дискриминант многочлена $F(x, y)$. Разделим элементы поля k_p на непересекающиеся классы $\mathscr{A}_\tau$, $\tau = 0, 1, \cdots, n$, следующим образом: в класс $\mathscr{A}_\tau$ отнесем те элементы $x \in k_p$, для которых $a_n(x) \neq 0$, $D(x) \neq 0$ и уравнение (10) имеет по y в точности τ решений, а в класс $\mathscr{B}$ отнесем те элементы $x \in k_p$, для которых или $a_n(x) = 0$ или $D(x) = 0$.

Пусть $y_s(x)$—какой-либо корень многочлена $F(x, y)$ и $x \in k_p$. Необходимым и достаточным условием того, чтобы $y_s(x) \in k_p$ является выполнимость равенства $y_s^p(x) = y_s(x)$. Далее, легко показать, что $y_s(x) \notin k_p$ тогда и только тогда, когда

$$\sum_{i=0}^{n-1} b_{s,i}(x)\, y_s^{i(p-1)}(x) = 0,$$

где

$$b_{s,i} = \frac{y_s^{n-i-1} + a_1 y_s^{n-i-2} + \cdots + a_{n-i-1}}{y_s^{n-i-1}}.$$

Введем в поле $k_p(x, y_s)$ оператор дифференцирования $D = d/dx$ и рассмотрим выражение

$$R_0(x, y_s) = \sum_{i=1}^{n-1} (1 - y_s^{i(p-1)}) \sum_{j=1}^{N} r_{s,i,j}^{(0)} (x^p - x)^{j-1} + \sum_{j=1}^{N} t_{s,j}^{(0)} (x^p - x)^j,$$

где $N < p/n$—натуральное число и $r_{s,i,j}^{(0)}, t_{s,j}^{(0)} \in k_p[x, y]$—неопределенные коэффициенты. Ясно, что $R_0(x, y_s) = 0$ при тех значениях $x \in k_p$, для которых $0 \neq y_s(x) \in k_p$. Положим

$$R_k(x, y_s) = D^k R_0(x, y_s), \qquad k = 1, 2, \cdots,$$

и подберем $r_{s,i,j}^{(0)}$ и $t_{s,j}^{(0)}$ таким образом, чтобы $R_k(x, y_s)$, $k = 0, 1, \cdots nN - 1$, имели такой же вид, как и выражение $R_0(x, y_s)$.

Пусть $r_{s,i,j}^{(r)}, t_{s,j}^{(k)}$ задаются рекуррентными соотношениями

(11)
$$r_{s,i,j}^{(k)} = Dr_{s,i,j}^{(k-1)} - jr_{s,i,j+1}^{(k-1)} - i \frac{Dy_s}{y_s} r_{s,i,j}^{(k-1)},$$
$$i = 1, 2, \cdots, n;\ j = 1, 2, \cdots, N;\ k = 1, 2, \cdots$$
$$t_{s,j}^{(k)} = Dt_{s,j}^{(k-1)} - (j + 1)\, t_{s,j+1}^{(k-1)} + \frac{Dy_s}{y_s} \sum_{i=1}^{n-1} i r_{s,i,j+1}^{(k-1)},$$
$$j = 1, 2, \cdots, N;\ k = 1, 2, \cdots$$

с начальными значениями $r_{s,i,j}^{(0)}, t_{s,j}^{(0)}$ такими, что $r_{s,i,j}^{(0)} = 0$, $t_{s,j}^{(0)} = 0$ при $j > N$. Мы скажем, что выражение $R_k(x, y_s)$ имеет "нужный" вид, если оно представляется в форме

$$R_k(x, y_s) = \sum_{i=1}^{n-1} (1 - y_s^{i(p-1)}) \sum_{j=1}^{N} r_{s,i,j}^{(k)} (x^p - x)^{j-1} + \sum_{j=1}^{N} t_{s,j}^{(k)} (x^p - x)^j,$$

где $r_{s,i,j}^{(k)}, t_{s,j}^{(k)}$ определены рекуррентными соотношениями (11).

Выберем теперь коэффициенты $r_{s,i,j}^{(0)}, t_{s,j}^{(0)} \in k_p[x, y_s]$ таким образом, чтобы все выражения $R_k(x, y_s)$, $k = 0, 1, \cdots, nN - 1$, имели "нужный" вид. Для этого достаточно, чтобы выполнялись соотношения

(12)
$$j!\, t_{s,j}^{(0)} = \sum_{i=1}^{n-1} \sum_{k=1}^{j} H_{s,i,k}^{(j)} r_{s,i,k}^{(0)}, \qquad j = 1, 2, \cdots, N,$$

(13)
$$0 = \sum_{i=1}^{n-1} \sum_{k=1}^{N} H_{s,i,k}^{(j)} r_{s,i,k}^{(0)}, \qquad j = N + 1, \cdots, nN - 1,$$

где $H_{s,i,k}^{(j)}$ определяются следующим образом:

(14)
$$H_{s,i,1}^{(1)} = i \frac{Dy_s}{y_s}, \qquad i = 1, 2, \cdots, n - 1,$$
$$H_{s,i,k}^{(j)} = DH_{s,i,k}^{(j-1)} + (k - 1)\, H_{s,i,k-1}^{(j-1)} + i \frac{Dy_s}{y_s} H_{s,i,k}^{(j-1)},$$
$$i = 1, 2, \cdots, n - 1;\ j = 2, 3, \cdots;\ k = 1, 2, \cdots, j - 1$$
$$H_{s,i,j}^{(j)} = (j - 1)\, H_{s,i,j-1}^{(j-1)} + (j - 1)!\, H_{s,i,1}^{(1)},$$
$$i = 1, 2, \cdots, n - 1;\ j = 2, 3, \cdots$$

Из (14) следует, что алгебраические функции $H_{s,i,k}^{(j)}$ представляются в виде

$$H^{(j)}_{s,i,k} = \frac{h^{(j)}_{1,i,k}\, y_s^{n-1} + \cdots + h^{(j)}_{n,i,k}}{y_s^{j-k+1}\left(\dfrac{\partial F}{\partial y_s}\right)^{2(j-k)+1}},$$

где степени многочленов $h^{(j)}_{\rho,i,k}$ не превосходят соответственно величин $\delta^{(j)}_{\rho,i,k} = 5m(j-k) + 2m$. Положим

$$r^{(0)}_{s,i,k} = y_s^{N-k+1}\left(\frac{\partial F}{\partial y_s}\right)^{2(N-k)+1} r_{s,i,k}$$

и будем искать $r_{s,i,k}$ в виде

$$r_{s,i,k} = \sum_{\sigma=1}^{n} R_{\sigma,i,k}\, y_s^{n-\sigma}, \qquad R_{\sigma,i,k} \in k_p[x].$$

Тогда система (13) запишется следующим образом:

$$\sum_{i=1}^{n-1}\sum_{k=1}^{N}\sum_{\sigma=1}^{n} A^{(j,\rho)}_{\sigma,i,k}\, R_{\sigma,i,k} = 0, \qquad \rho = 1, 2, \cdots, n;\ j = N+1, \cdots, nN-1,$$

где степени многочленов $A^{(j,\rho)}_{\sigma,i,k}$ не превосходят соответственно величин $\nu^{(j,\rho)}_{\sigma,i,k} = 5m(j-k+1)$. Последняя же система нетривиальным образом разрешима в многочленах $R_{\sigma,i,k}$, таких что $\deg R_{\sigma,i,k} \leqq 5m((n-1)^2N^2 - N + k)$.

Пусть далее $t^{(0)}_{s,j}$ определяются соотношениями (12). Положим

$$(1 - y_s^{i(p-1)})\, r^{(0)}_{s,i,k}(x^p - x)^{k-1} = \sum_{\rho=1}^{n} B^{(\rho)}_{i,k}\, y_s^{n-\rho}, \qquad B^{(\rho)}_{i,k} \in k_p[x],$$
$$i = 1, 2, \cdots, n-1;\ k = 1, 2, \cdots, N,$$

$$t^{(0)}_{s,j}(x^p - x)^j = \sum_{\nu=1}^{n} C^{(\nu)}_j\, y_s^{n-\nu}, \qquad C^{(\nu)}_j \in k_p[x], \qquad j = 1, 2, \cdots, N.$$

Пусть $N \leqq 1/(n-1)\,(p/6mn)^{1/2}$ и пусть i_0, k_0, j_0 такие из чисел i, j, k соответственно, для которых $r^{(0)}_{s,i,k} \neq 0$, $t^{(0)}_{s,j} \neq 0$ и значения величин $(k-1)p + imp/n$, jp максимальны. Из (8), условий $(m, n) = 1$, $p > 196m^3n(n-1)^2$ и из выбора $r^{(0)}_{s,i,k}$, $t^{(0)}_{s,j}$ следует, что или при некотором ρ_0

$$\deg B^{(\rho_0)}_{i_0,k_0} > \deg B^{(\rho)}_{i,k}, \qquad \deg B^{(\rho_0)}_{i_0,k_0} > \deg C^{(\nu)}_j$$

при всех $i = 1, 2, \cdots, n-1$; $k, j = 1, 2, \cdots, N$; $\rho, \nu = 1, 2, \cdots, n$; $(i, k, \rho) \neq (i_0, k_0, \rho_0)$, или при некотором ν_0

$$\deg C^{(\nu_0)}_{j_0} > \deg C^{(\nu)}_j, \qquad \deg C^{(\nu_0)}_{j_0} > \deg B^{(\rho)}_{i,k}$$

при всех $i = 1, 2, \cdots, n-1$; $k, j = 1, 2, \cdots, N$; $\rho, \nu = 1, 2, \cdots, n$; $(j, \nu) \neq (j_0, \nu_0)$. В таком случае в выражении $R_0(x, y_s)$ члены $(1 - y_s^{i(p-1)})\ r^{(0)}_{s,i,k}\,(x^p - x)^{k-1}$ и $t^{(0)}_{s,j}(x^p - x)^j$ не смогут проинтерферировать и, следовательно, $R_0\,(x, y_s) \neq 0$.

Заметим далее, что $R_0(x, y_s)$, $s = 1, 2, \cdots, n$, сопряжены между собой над полем $k_p(x)$, так что выражение $R_0(x) = \prod_{s=1}^{n} R_0(x, y_s)$ есть многочлен из кольца $k_p[x]$, причем

$$\deg R_0(x) \leqq nNp + mnp + 5mn(n-1)^2N^2 + 11mn.$$

Из конструкции многочлена $R_0(x)$ ясно, что все элементы класса $\mathscr{A}_\tau$, $\tau = 1$,

$2, \cdots, n$, являются его корнями кратности по меньшей мере $\tau(nN-1)$. Сравнивая число корней многочлена $R_0(x)$ с его степенью, мы получаем

$$(nN-1)\sum_{\tau=1}^{n}\tau\left|\mathscr{A}_\tau\right| \leqq nNp+mnp+5mn(n-1)^2N^2+11mn.$$

Положив теперь $N=[1/(n-1)\,(p/6mn)^{1/2}]$, мы получаем отсюда, что

$$N_p=\sum_{\tau=1}^{n}\tau\left|\mathscr{A}_\tau\right|+r\leqq p+14(mn)^{1/2}\ m(n-1)\,p^{1/2},$$

где $0\leqq r\leqq 2mn^2$.

Аналогичным образом при $N\leqq(p/11mn)^{1/2}$ строится не равный нулю в кольце $k_p[x]$ многочлен $R_0^*(x)=\prod_{s=1}^{n}R_0^*(x, y_s)$, где

$$R_0^*(x, y_s)=\sum_{i=0}^{n-1}b_{s,i}\,y_s^{i(p-1)}\sum_{j=1}^{N}r_{s,j}^{(0)}\,(x^p-x)^{j-1}+\sum_{i=0}^{n-2}y_s^{i(p-1)}\sum_{j=1}^{N}t_{s,i,j}^{(0)}\,(x^p-x)^j,$$

степени не выше $nNp+mnp+10mnN^2+12mn$ такой, что все элементы класса $\mathscr{A}_\tau$, $\tau=0, 1, \cdots, n-1$, являются его корнями кратности по меньшей мере $(n-\tau)\,(N+[(N-1)/(n-1)])$. Сравнение числа корней многочлена $R_0^*(x)$ с его степенью дает

$$\left(N+\left[\frac{N-1}{n-1}\right]\right)\sum_{\tau=0}^{n-1}(n-\tau)\left|\mathscr{A}_\tau\right|\leqq nNp+mnp+10mnN^2+12mn.$$

Отсюда при $N=[(p/11mn)]$ мы имеем

$$\sum_{\tau=0}^{n-1}(n-\tau)\left|\mathscr{A}_\tau\right|\leqq(n-1)p+12(mn)^{1/2}\ m(n-1)p^{1/2}$$

и поскольку

$$\sum_{\tau=0}^{n}\left|\mathscr{A}_\tau\right|+\left|\mathscr{B}\right|=p,\qquad\left|\mathscr{B}\right|\leqq 2mn^2,$$

то

$$N_p=\sum_{\tau=0}^{n}\tau\left|\mathscr{A}_\tau\right|+r\geqq p-14(mn)^{1/2}m(n-1)p^{1/2}.$$

Теорема доказана.

Литература

1. I. L. Lagrange, *Démonstration d'un théorème d'arithmétique*, Oevres Lagrange **3** (1896), 189.

2. E. Artin, *Quadratische Körper im Gebiete der höheren Kongruenzen.* II, Math. Z. **19** (1924), 207.

3. H. Hopf, *Über die verteilung quadratischen Reste*, Math. Z. **32** (1930), 222.

4. H. Davenport, *On the distribution of quadratic residues* mod *p*, J. London Math. Soc. **6** (1931), 49.

5. L. J. Mordell, *The number of solutions of some congruences in two variables,* Math. Z. **37** (1933), 193.

6. H. Hasse, *Abstrakte Begründung der komplexen Multiplikation und Riemannsche Vermutung in Funktionen Körper*, Abh. Math. Sem. Univ. Hamburg **10** (1934), 235.

7. Ю.И. Манин, *О сравнениях третьей степени по простому модулю*, Известия АН ССР, сер. матем. **20** (1956), 673.

8. A. Weil, *Sur les courbes algébriques et les variétés qui s'en deduisent,* Actualités Sci. Indust., o. 1041, Paris, 1948.

9. С.А. Степанов, *О числе точек гиперэллиптической кривой над простым конечным олем*, Известия АН СССР, сер. матем. **33** (1969), 1171.

10. ———, *Elementary method in the theory of congruences for a prime modulus*, Acta Arith. **17** 970), 231.

11. ———, *An elementary proof of the Hasse-Weil theorem for hyperelliptic curves*, J. Number heory **4** (1972), 118.

12. ———, *Об оценке рациональных тригонометрических сумм с простым знатенате-ем*, Труды МИАН, т. 112, "Наука", Москва, 1971, стр. 364.

13. А.А. Карацуба,*Суммы характеров и примитивные корни в конечных полях*,Доклады Н СССР **180** (1968), 1287.

14. H. M. Stark, *On the Riemann hypothesis in hyperelliptic function fields*, Proc. Sympos. Pure ath., vol. 24, Amer. Math. Soc., Providence, R. I., 1973, p. 285.

15. Н. М. Коробов, *Оценка суммы символов Лежандра*, Доклады АН СССР **196** (1971),

16. С.А. Степанов, *Сравнения с двумя неизвестными*, Известия АН СССР, сер. матем. 5 (1972), 683.

17. W. M. Schmidt, *Zur Methode von Stepanov*, Acta Arith. **24** (1973), 347.

18. E. Bombieri, *Counting points on curves over finite fields*, Séminaire Bourbaki 1972/73, xposé 25, p. 430.

Математический Институт им. В.А. Стеклова АН СССР
Москва, СССР

Section 4

Algebraic Geometry

Actes du Congrès Internationale des Mathematiciens
Vancouver, 1974

Le Groupe de Monodromie du Déploiement des Singularités Isolées de Courbes Planes. II

Norbert A'Campo

Introduction. Soit f: $(\boldsymbol{C}^{n+1}, 0) \to (\boldsymbol{C}, 0)$ un polynôme ayant une singularité isolée [26] en $0 \in \boldsymbol{C}^{n+1}$. Le déploiement au sens de R. Thom [27] de cette singularité est un polynôme $g(x, \lambda)$: $\boldsymbol{C}^{n+1} \times \boldsymbol{C}^{\mu} \to \boldsymbol{C}$ tel que $f(x) = g(x, 0)$ et que les dérivées partielles $(\partial g/\partial \lambda_i)(x, 0)$, $1 \leqq i \leqq \mu$, forment une base vectorielle de $\boldsymbol{C}\{x_0, \cdots, x_n\}/(\partial f/\partial x_0, \cdots, \partial f/\partial x_n)$.

Soient $B_\varepsilon \subset \boldsymbol{C}^{n+1}$ une boule de Milnor pour la singularité, et $\mathscr{D} \subset \boldsymbol{C}^{\mu}$ une boule centrée en 0, assez petite pour que les hypersurfaces $\{x \in \boldsymbol{C}^{n+1} | g(x, \lambda) = 0\}$, $\lambda \in \mathscr{D}$, rencontrent transversalement le bord de B_ε. On pose $X = \{(x, \lambda) \in B_\varepsilon \times \mathscr{D} | g(x, \lambda) = 0\}$ et soit φ: $X \to \mathscr{D}$ la projection, qui est une application fibrée au dessus du complémentaire du discriminant $\Delta \subset \mathscr{D}$. La fibre $\varphi^{-1}(\lambda_0)$, $\lambda_0 \in \mathscr{D} - \Delta$, est difféomorphe à la fibre de Milnor de f en 0; $H_n(\varphi^{-1}(\lambda_0), \boldsymbol{Z}) \cong \boldsymbol{Z}^{\mu}$. On a donc un homomorphisme de monodromie $\pi_1(\mathscr{D} - \Delta, \lambda_0) \to \mathrm{GL}(\boldsymbol{Z}^{\mu})$, dont l'image est le groupe de monodromie Γ de f en 0.

Au §2 nous donnons un système de générateurs du groupe Γ pour le cas où f est un polynôme à deux variables [2], [18], [19]. Les singularités simples sont caractérisées au §3 par une propriété de confluence.

Les résultats du §2 ont aussi été obtenus par S. M. Gusein-Zade [18], [19], et ont été conjecturés par V. I. Arnol'd [4]. Nos démonstrations détaillées sont dans [2].

1. Rappels, définitions. (1) Soient f, B_ε et μ comme ci-dessus. Une déformation de f est un polynome $f(x, t)$, $(x, t) \in \boldsymbol{C}^{n+1} \times \boldsymbol{C}$, tel que $f(x, 0) = f(x)$. Soit $\eta > 0$, assez petit pour que les hypersurfaces $H_t = \{x \in \boldsymbol{C}^{n+1} | f(x, t) = 0\}$, $|t| \leqq \eta$, rencontrent transversalement le bord de B_ε. Une *confluence de Morse* pour f est un polynôme $\tilde{f}(x) = f(x, t_0)$, $|t_0| \leqq \eta$, tel que $\tilde{f}$ possède μ points critiques dans B_ε (qui sont donc quadratiques non dégénérés). On dit que la confluence de Morse est *réelle* si $\tilde{f}$ est réel et si $\tilde{f}$ possède μ points critiques dans $D_\varepsilon = \boldsymbol{R}^{n+1} \cap B_\varepsilon$.

EXEMPLE 1. Soit f: $\boldsymbol{C} \ni x \to x^a \in \boldsymbol{C}$, $a \geqq 2$, $\mu = a - 1$. Alors le polynôme $\tilde{f}(x) = f(x, t_0)$, $t_0 \in \boldsymbol{R}$ et $t_0 > 0$ (où $f(x, t_0)$ est le polynôme de Tchebycheff de degré a pour l'intervalle $[-t_0, t_0]$) est une confluence de Morse réelle pour f. Si $a \geqq 3$, cette confluence a 2 valeurs critiques. (Voir [**28**].)

Etant donné que tout germe non nul de fonction $(\boldsymbol{C}, 0) \to (\boldsymbol{C}, 0)$ est équivalent à x^a, $a \geqq 1$, on obtient:

"Tout germe non nul f de fonction $(\boldsymbol{C}, 0) \to (\boldsymbol{C}, 0)$ tel que $f'(0) = 0$ possède une confluence de Morse à k valeurs critiques, $1 \leqq k \leqq 2$. ($k = 1$ si $a = 2$, sinon $k = 2$.)"

REMARQUE. Toute singularité isolée admet une confluence de Morse. Alain Chenciner et René Thom posent la question: Quelles sont les singularités isolées, qui admettent une confluence de Morse réelle?

(2) Une confluence de Morse équipée est une donnée $(\tilde{f}, v_0, \gamma_1, \cdots, \gamma_k)$ où

(i) $\tilde{f}$ est une confluence de Morse pour f à k valeurs critiques $(v_l)_{1 \leqq l \leqq k}$,

(ii) v_0 est une valeur régulière de $\tilde{f} \mid B_\varepsilon$,

(iii) $\gamma_1, \cdots, \gamma_k$ forment un système distingué de chemins [**17**]; γ_l: $[0, 1] \to \tilde{f}(B_\varepsilon) \subset \boldsymbol{C}$ tel que $\gamma_l(0) = v_0$, $\gamma_l(1) = v_l$, $1 \leqq l \leqq k$.

Lorsque $\tilde{f}$ est une confluence de Morse réelle, son équipement standard est la donnée $v_0 = -ia$, $a \in \boldsymbol{R}$, $a > 0$ assez petit, et γ_l ([0, 1]) est le segment $[v_0, v_l]$, $1 \leqq l \leqq k$.

Soient $(c_i)_{1 \leqq i \leqq \mu}$ les μ points critiques de $\tilde{f} \mid B_\varepsilon$, ordonnés de telle sorte que $c_i \mapsto \tilde{f}(c_i) = v_{l_i}$ soit croissante sur les indices. Une base distinguée de $H_n(\tilde{f}^{-1}(v_0), \boldsymbol{Z})$ est une base $(\delta_1, \cdots, \delta_\mu)$ telle que le cycle δ_i corresponde via le chemin γ_{l_i} au cycle évanescent du point critique c_i. Lorsque $(\delta_1, \cdots, \delta_\mu)$ est une base distinguée $(\varepsilon_1\delta_1, \cdots, \varepsilon_\mu\delta_\mu)$ est encore une base distinguée, $\varepsilon_i = \pm 1$.

EXEMPLE 1 (SUITE). Le graphe de la fonction $\tilde{f}(x) = f(x, 1)$ (avec $a = 5$) est

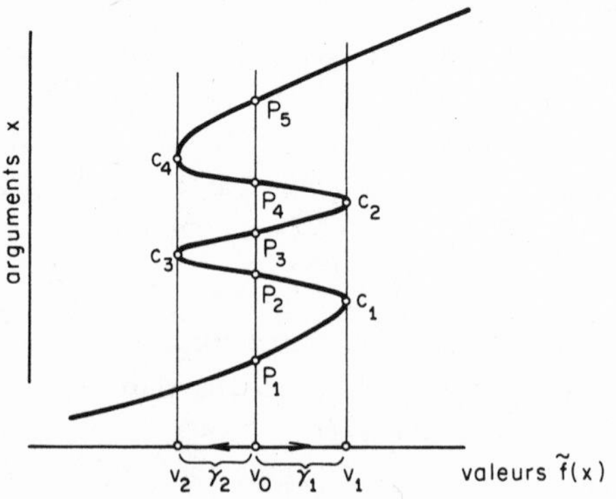

On choisit $v_0 = 0$, $v_1 = \tilde{f}(c_1) = \tilde{f}(c_2)$ et $v_2 = \tilde{f}(c_3) = \tilde{f}(c_4)$. Dans ce cas $\delta_1 = p_1 - p_2$, $\delta_2 = p_3 - p_4$, $\delta_3 = p_2 - p_3$, et $\delta_4 = p_4 - p_5$ forment une base distinguée

de $\tilde{H}_0(\tilde{f}^{-1}(v_0), \boldsymbol{Z})$. La matrice de la forme quadratique des intersections sur la base $(\delta_1, \delta_3, \delta_2, \delta_4)$ est

$$\begin{pmatrix} 2 & -1 & & \\ -1 & 2 & -1 & \\ & -1 & 2 & -1 \\ & & -1 & 2 \end{pmatrix}$$

C'est la forme A_4. En général pour la fonction x^a, $a \geqq 2$, on trouve la forme A_μ, $\mu = a - 1$.

(3) En utilisant un théorème de Lê Dũng Tráng et Hamm [16], et la formule de Picard-Lefschetz [12], [13], on peut calculer un système de générateurs pour le groupe de monodromie de f, si l'on dispose d'une base distinguée pour une confluence de Morse équipée: Soit $(\delta_1, \cdots, \delta_\mu)$ une base distinguée, alors le groupe de monodromie Γ de f est engendré par les transformations

$$T_i\colon \tilde{H}_n(\tilde{f}^{-1}(v_0), \boldsymbol{Z}) \to \tilde{H}_n(\tilde{f}^{-1}(v_0), \boldsymbol{Z})$$
$$x \mapsto x - (-1)^{n(n-1)/2}\,(x, \delta_i)\,\delta_i.$$

Etant donné que les self-intersections (δ_i, δ_i) valent $(-1)^{n(n-1)/2} \cdot 2$ si n est pair, et 0 si n est impair, les transformations T_i sont des réflexions ou des transvections selon la parité de n.

Exemple 1 (Suite). Le groupe de monodromie de la singularité x^a, $a \geqq 2$, est le groupe de Coxeter A_μ, $\mu = a - 1$. Plus précisement, le groupe Γ et les générateurs $T_1, \cdots, T_\mu$ sont le système de Coxeter A_μ.

2. Confluences de Morse pour les courbes planes [2], [18], [19]. Soient $f\colon \boldsymbol{C}^{n+1} \to \boldsymbol{C}$, B_ε et μ comme dans l'introduction. Dans tout ce paragraphe $n = 1$ et on suppose que f vérifie l'hypothèse B. $\boldsymbol{R}$.: "Le polynôme f admet une décomposition en produit $f = f_1 \cdot \cdots \cdot f_r$ de facteurs analytiquement irréductibles en 0 et à coefficients réels. Donc les r branches de f sont réelles."

La confluence de Morse $\tilde{f}$ du théorème suivant est en quelque sorte un polynôme de Tchebycheff associé à f.

Théorème 1. *Soit f comme ci-dessus. Alors f possède une confluence de Morse réelle $\tilde{f}$ à k valeurs critiques,* $1 \leqq k \leqq 3$. *De plus, l'indice d'un point critique $c \in D_\varepsilon = \boldsymbol{R}^2 \cap B_\varepsilon$ de $\tilde{f}\,|D_\varepsilon\colon D_\varepsilon \to \boldsymbol{R}$ est* 0 *si* $\tilde{f}(c) < 0$, 1 *si* $\tilde{f}(c) = 0$, *et* 2 *si* $\tilde{f}(c) > 0$.

Exemple 2. Soit $f(x, y) = xy(x^2 - y^2)$. Alors pour $t \in \boldsymbol{R}$, $t \neq 0$, $\tilde{f}(x, y) = (x - t)(y + 2t)(x^2 - y^2)$ est une confluence de Morse réelle pour f ayant les propriétés du théorème.

Soit $\tilde{f}$ une confluence de Morse réelle pour f satisfaisant au théorème. On pose $C = \tilde{f}^{-1}(0) \cap D_\varepsilon$; C est une courbe qui n'a que des points doubles ordinaires. On appelle region de $D_\varepsilon - C$ les composantes connexes de $D_\varepsilon - C$ disjointes du bord de D_ε. Dans chaque région la fonction $\tilde{f}$ atteint une valeur extrême (un maximum dans une région où $\tilde{f} > 0$, un minimum dans une région où $\tilde{f} < 0$).

Exemple 2 (Suite). La courbe C, les régions $\oplus$ et $\ominus$, les points doubles ● sont indiqués sur la figure.

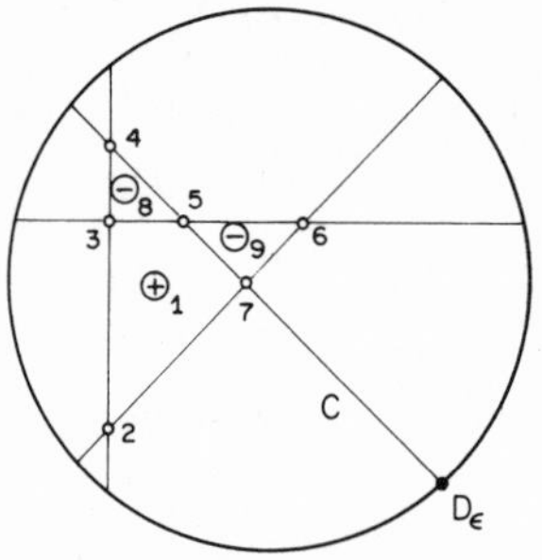

Le Théorème 1 reste encore vrai lorsque l'on exige que deux régions A et B de $C = \tilde{f}^{-1}(0) \cap D_\varepsilon$ vérifient:

(1) $$\bar{A} \cap \bar{B} = \varnothing \quad \text{ou } \bar{A} \cap \bar{B} = \text{un segment de } C.$$

Nous supposons désormais que la confluence de Morse $\tilde{f}$ du théorème vérifie cette propriété.

Soit $(\delta_1, \cdots, \delta_\mu)$ une base distinguée pour la confluence $\tilde{f}$ équipée de façon standard. Alors la configuration de la courbe C détermine les nombres d'intersections (δ_i, δ_j) ([**2**], voir [**18**] pour le cas ou $\tilde{f}$ ne vérifie pas la propriété (1)); Soient $\delta_1^+, \cdots, \delta_p^+$ les cycles correspondants aux régions $\oplus$ $P_1, \cdots, P_p^\bullet$, $\delta_{p+1}, \cdots, \delta_q^\bullet$ les cycles correspondants aux points doubles $D_{p+1}, \cdots, D_q$ de C, et $\delta_{q+1}^-, \cdots, \delta_\mu^-$ les cycles correspondants aux régions $\ominus$ $N_{q+1}, \cdots, N_\mu$; les nombres d'intersections (δ_i, δ_j), $1 \leqq i < j \leqq \mu$, sont donnés (pour une orientation convenable) par

$$(\delta_i, \delta_j) = 1 \quad \text{si } (1)\ \delta_i = \delta_i^+,\ \delta_j = \delta_j^\bullet \text{ et } D_j \in \bar{P}_i,$$
$$(2)\ \delta_i = \delta_i^\bullet,\ \delta_j = \delta_j^- \text{ et } D_i \in \bar{N}_j,$$
$$(3)\ \delta_i = \delta_i^+,\ \delta_j = \delta_j^- \text{ et } \bar{P}_i \cap \bar{N}_j \text{ est un segment de } C;$$
$$= 0 \quad \text{dans les autres cas}$$

Donc (δ_i, δ_j), $1 \leqq i, j \leqq \mu$, ne prend que les valeurs $-1, 0, 1$ et $(\delta_i, \delta_j) \geqq 0$ si $i \leqq j$.

EXEMPLE 2 (SUITE). Le diagramme de Dynkin des intersections est

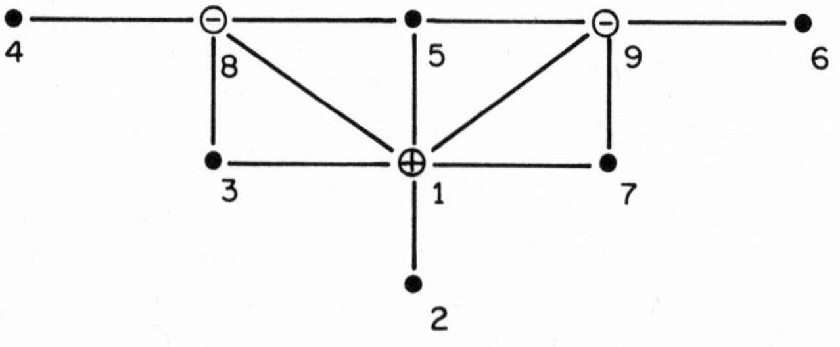

Notations. $\bullet_i = \delta_i^\bullet$, $\oplus_i = \delta_i^+$, $\ominus_i = \delta_i^-$, un traite—représente une intersection $(\delta_i, \delta_j) = 1$, $i < j$.

La démonstration du Théorème 1 utilise la résolution partielle des singularités des courbes planes [**2**]; elle contient une méthode constructive et très efficace pour obtenir la configuration de la courbe C. Nous traitons ici deux exemples.

EXEMPLE 3. Soit $f(x, y) = x^3 + y^5$. Par éclatements de points on peut transformer la courbe plane $H = \{(x, y) \in \mathbf{C}^2 \mid f(x, y) = 0\}$ de la manière suivante:

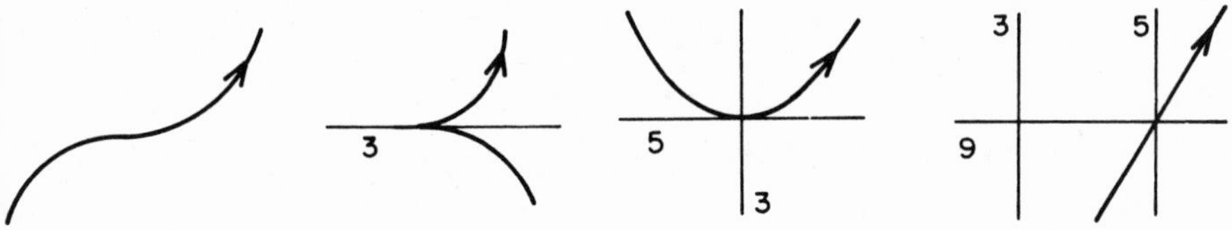

Un éclatement supplémentaire aurait transformé H en un diviseur à croisements normaux. La dernière configuration se déforme par une translation de la composante non exceptionelle en

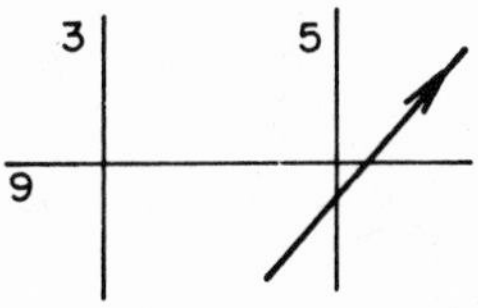

après contraction du brin de multiplicité 9

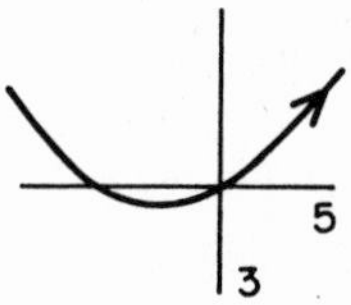

après une déformation

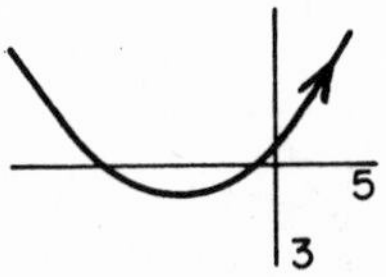

après une contraction du brin de multiplicité 5

après une déformation

après une contraction du brin de multiplicité 3

finalement après une mise en position générale vient la courbe C

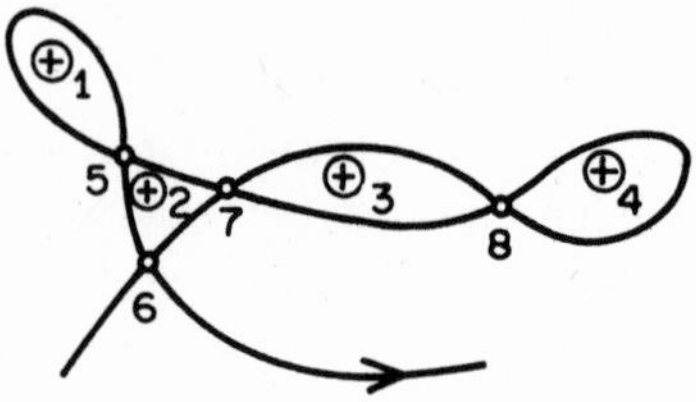

Le diagramme de Dynkin est l'arbre E_8.

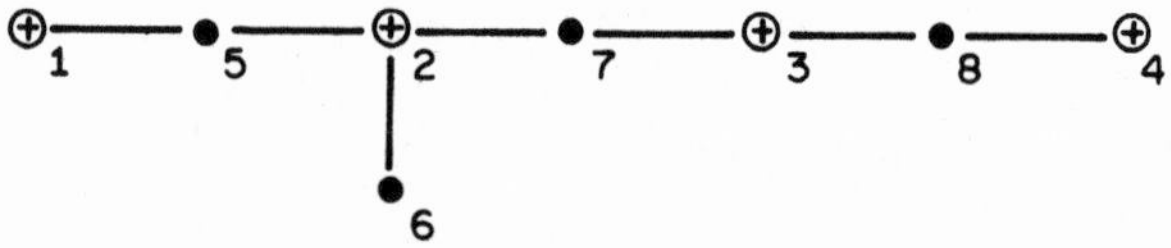

Il existe une déformation réelle $\tilde{f}(x, y)$ de $f(x, y)$ telle que $C = \{(x, y) \in D_\varepsilon \mid \tilde{f}(x, y) = 0\}$. Les points critiques de $\tilde{f}$ sont les 4 points doubles de C et les 4 points extrémaux (tous des maxima) des régions. Donc on peut encore modifier $\tilde{f}$ pour mettre les maxima sur un même niveau. On voit qu'il existe une confluence de Morse réelle pour $f(x, y)$ ayant 2 valeurs critiques.

Exemple 4. $f(x, y) = y^4 - 2y^2x^3 - 4yx^5 + x^6 - x^7$, $\mu = 16$. La résolution est

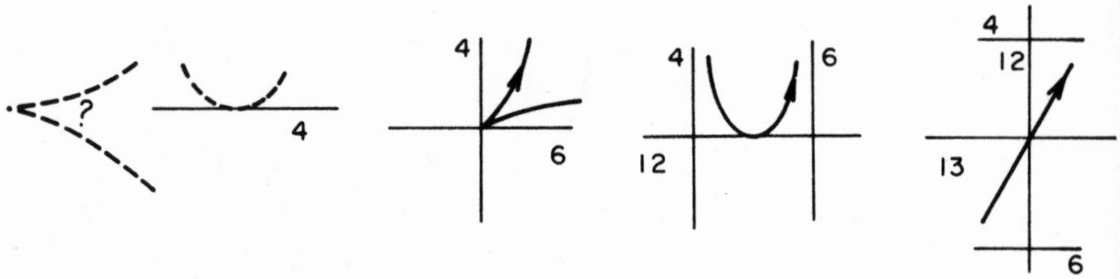

Après les opérations de déformation, contraction, et mise en position générale vient la courbe C

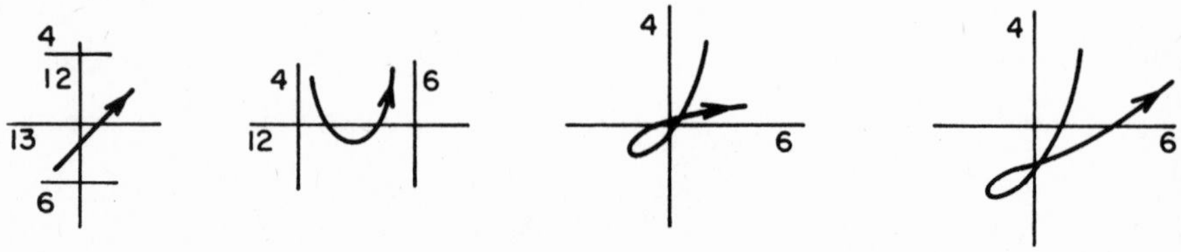

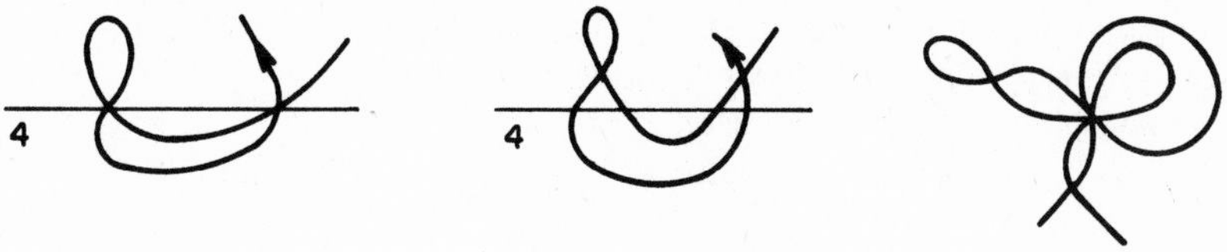

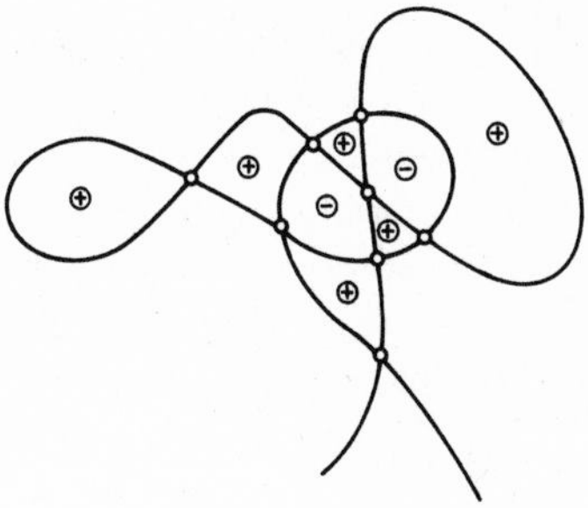

Le diagramme est

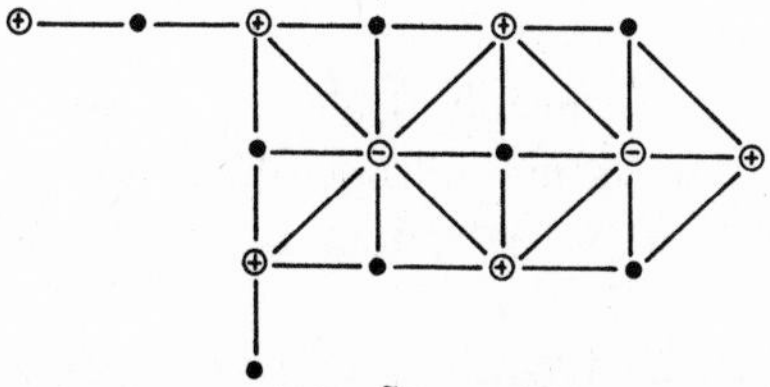

Il existe une confluence de Morse réelle $\tilde{f}$ pour f ayant 3 valeurs critiques $a < 0 < b$; au-dessus de a il y a 2 minima, au-dessus de 0 il y a 8 points selle, au-dessus de b il y a 6 maxima.

3. Une caractérisation des singularités isolées simples d'hypersurfaces. Les singularités isolées simples d'hypersurfaces complexes sont

$$\begin{aligned}
&A_n: 0 \in \{x^{n+1} + z_1^2 + \cdots + z_r^2 = 0\} \subset \mathbf{C}^{r+1}, && \mu = n \geqq 1,\\
&D_n: 0 \in \{x^{n-1} + xy^2 + z_1^2 + \cdots + z_r^2 = 0\} \subset \mathbf{C}^{r+2}, && \mu = n \geqq 4,\\
&E_6: 0 \in \{x^3 + y^4 + z_1^2 + \cdots + z_r^2 = 0\} \subset \mathbf{C}^{r+2}, && \mu = 6,\\
&E_7: 0 \in \{x^3y + y^3 + z_1^2 + \cdots + z_r^2 = 0\} \subset \mathbf{C}^{r+2}, && \mu = 7,\\
&E_8: 0 \in \{x^3 + y^5 + z_1^2 + \cdots + z_r^2 = 0\} \subset \mathbf{C}^{r+2}, && \mu = 8.
\end{aligned}$$

Ces équations ont de nombreuses propriétés (F. Klein [**25**], du Val [**31**], Herzberg [**15**], Artin [**5**], Grothendieck [**20**], Lipman [**23**], Brieskorn [**7**], [**8**], Kas [**32**], Arnol'd [**3**], [**4**], Tjurina [**30**], $\cdots$).

Une singularité isolée d'hypersurface complexe est simple si le déploiement de cette singularité ne contient qu'un nombre fini de singularités isolées analytiquement non isomorphes. Le théorème d'Arnol'd [**3**] dit que la liste ci-dessus est la liste complète des singularités isolées simples d'hypersurfaces complexes.

Le théorème suivant est une autre caractérisation des singularités de la liste ci-dessus.

THÉORÈME 2. *Soit* $f:(\boldsymbol{C}^{n+1}, 0) \to (\boldsymbol{C}, 0)$ *un polynôme ayant une singularité isolée en* 0. *Alors les propriétés suivantes sont équivalentes:*

(i) *f possède une confluence de Morse $\tilde{f}$ à k niveaux critiques,* $1 \leqq k \leqq 2$.

(ii) *Il existe une confluence de Morse équipée pour f telle que le diagramme de Dynkin est un arbre.*

(iii) *La singularité de f est simple.*

PREUVE (i) $\Rightarrow$ (ii). Si $k = 1$, la singularité est la singularité A_1 **[21]** donc on a (ii). Soit $(\tilde{f}, v_0, \gamma_1, \gamma_2)$ un équipement pour la confluence de Morse $\tilde{f}$. Soient $(\delta_1, \cdots, \delta_p)$ les cycles de $H_n(\tilde{f}^{-1}(v_0), \boldsymbol{Z})$ correspondant aux points critiques de la fibre $\tilde{f}^{-1}(v_1)$, $v_1 = \gamma_1(1)$, et $(\delta_{p+1}, \cdots, \delta_\mu)$ ceux correspondants aux points critiques de la fibre $\tilde{f}^{-1}(v_2)$, $v_2 = \gamma_2(1)$. Alors on va montrer que le diagramme de Dynkin est un arbre pour la base distinguée $(\delta_1, \cdots, \delta_p, \delta_{p+1}, \cdots, \delta_\mu)$.

Soit A la matrice $\mu \times \mu$ donnée par

$$\begin{aligned} A(i,j) &= 0, & i \leqq j, \\ &= (\delta_i, \delta_j), & i > j. \end{aligned}$$

On a $A^2 = 0$. Soit S la matrice $\mu \times \mu$

$$S = (-1)^{n(n-1)/2}\,\mathrm{Id} + A,$$

qui est la matrice de Seifert du noeud algébrique $f^{-1}(0) \cap \partial B_\varepsilon \subsetneq \partial B_\varepsilon$ **[13]**, **[14]**. Donc $T = (-1)^{n+1}\,{}^tS^{-1}S$ est la monodromie locale de la singularité de f en 0. On a d'après **[1]** que $\mathrm{Tr}\,(T) = (-1)^{n+1}$, donc $1 = (-1)^{n+1}\,\mathrm{Tr}\,(T) = \mathrm{Tr}({}^tS^{-1}S) = \mu - \mathrm{Tr}\,({}^tAA)$.

Soit b_1 le nombre de traits du diagramme de Dynkin, donc le nombre de couples (i, j), $1 \leqq i < j \leqq \mu$, avec $(\delta_i, \delta_j) \neq 0$. On a $b_1 \geqq \mu - 1$ car le diagramme est connexe **[21]** et on a

$$b_1 \leqq \sum_{1 \leqq i < j \leqq \mu} (\delta_i, \delta_j)^2 = \mathrm{Tr}\,({}^tAA) = \mu - 1.$$

Donc $b_1 = \mu - 1$ et le diagramme est un arbre. De plus on a démontré que $(\delta_i, \delta_j)^2 = 1$, ou $= 0$ pour $1 \leqq i < j \leqq \mu$.

PREUVE (ii) $\Rightarrow$ (iii). Quitte à rajouter à f quelques carrés $f(x) + z_1^2 + \cdots + z_r^2$ on peut supposer que le nombre de variables de f est $4n + 1$. Soit $\boldsymbol{D}$ le diagramme de Dynkin des intersections (δ_i, δ_j) oú $(\delta_1, \cdots, \delta_\mu)$ est une base distinguée. Par hypothèse $\boldsymbol{D}$ est un arbre. Les nombres d'intersections (δ_i, δ_j) valent ± 1 ou 0 car d'aprés **[1]** on a que

$$-1 = \mathrm{Tr}\,(T) = \mathrm{Tr}\,(T_1 T_2 \cdots T_\mu) = \sum_{i,j} (\delta_i, \delta_j)^2 - \mu.$$

Donc en changeant quelques signes $\pm \delta_i$, on peut obtenir que $(\delta_i, \delta_j) = -1$ ou 0. On a asussi $(\delta_i, \delta_i) = 2$. Dans ce cas d'après un théorème de J. Tits **[6]** les réflexions $T_i \in \mathrm{GL}(\mu, \boldsymbol{Z})$ engendrent un sous-groupe Γ de Coxeter présenté par $\{T_i;\ T_i^2 = \mathrm{Id},\ (T_iT_j)^{m_{ij}} = \mathrm{Id},\ m_{ij} = 2 - (\delta_i, \delta_j)\}$. Le graphe de Coxeter **[6]** de ce système de Coxeter $(\Gamma, T_1, \cdots, T_\mu)$ est le diagramme de Dynkin $\boldsymbol{D}$, qui est donc un arbre d'après l'hypothèse.

L'élément de Coxeter $C = T_1 T_2 \cdots T_\mu$ est encore la monodromie locale de f en 0.

Donc les valeurs propres de C sont des racines de l'unité d'après le théorème de la monodromie [**10**], [**25**], [**13**]. Ceci entraîne d'après [**2 bis**] que le groupe de Coxeter est sphérique ou affine. Etant donné le graphe de Coxeter est un arbre et que les nombres m_{ij} valent 2 ou 3, les seules possibilités sont les groupes de Coxeter [**10**] A_n, D_n, $\tilde{D}_n$, E_6, $\tilde{E}_6$, E_7, $\tilde{E}_7$, E_8, $\tilde{E}_8$. Un raisonnement d'Arnol'd [**4**] permet de conclure que les seules singularités qui conviennent sont les singularités A_n, D_n, E_6, E_7, E_8, ce qui prouve (ii) $\Rightarrow$ (iii).

PREUVE (iii) $\Rightarrow$ (i). Dans [**2**] tous les cas sont traités (voir ici Exemple 1 pour la série A_n et Exemple 3 pour E_8).

L'Exemple 1, les Théorèmes 1 et 2 suggèrent les questions:

Question 1. Une singularité isolée $f: \boldsymbol{C}^{n+1} \to \boldsymbol{C}$ admet-elle une confluence de Morse à k valeurs critiques, $1 \leqq k \leqq n + 2$?

Question 2. Les singularités $f(x, y, z) = g(x, y) + z^a$; $\boldsymbol{C}^3 \to \boldsymbol{C}$, où $g: \boldsymbol{C}^2 \to \boldsymbol{C}$ est une singularité simple, admettent une confluence de Morse à k valeurs critiques $1 \leqq k \leqq 3$. La question est de caractériser les singularités isolées $f: \boldsymbol{C}^3 \to \boldsymbol{C}$ qui admettent une confluence de Morse à k valeurs critiques, $1 \leqq k \leqq 3$.

REMARQUE. Lorsque le diagramme de Dynkin d'une confluence de Morse équipée pour une singularité isolée f: $\boldsymbol{C}^{4n\pm1} \to \boldsymbol{C}$ est un arbre, le groupe de monodromie Γ et les reflexions $T_1, \cdots, T_\mu$ forment un système de Coxeter. Ceci découle du théorème de J. Tits, voir ci-dessus.

Le groupe de monodromie Γ de $f(x, y, z) = xy(x^2 - y^2) + z^2$: $\boldsymbol{C}^3 \to \boldsymbol{C}$ et les réflexions $T_1, \cdots, T_9$ de la confluence de Morse réelle de l'Exemple 2 équipée de facon standard ne forment pas un système de Coxeter. En effet pour chaque triangle (α, β, γ) du diagramme de Dynkin on a les relations

$$(T_\alpha T_\beta T_\gamma)^4 = (T_\alpha T_\beta T_\gamma)^2\, T_\beta (T_\alpha T_\beta T_\gamma)^2\, T_\beta = 1.$$

Bibliographie

1. N. A'Campo, *Le nombre de Lefschetz d'une monodromie*, Nederl. Akad. Wetensch. Proc. Ser. A **76** = Indag. Math. **35** (1973), 113–118. MR **47** #8903.

2. ———, *Le groupe de monodromie du déploiement des singularités isolées de courbes planes*. I, Math. Ann. **213** (1975), 1–32.

2bis. ———, *Les valeurs propres de l'élément de Coxeter* (preprint).

3. V. I. Arnol'd, *Normal forms for functions near degenerate critical points, the Weyl groups of A_k, D_k, E_k and Lagrangian singularities*, Funkcional. Anal. i Priložen. **6** (1972), 254–272 = Functional Anal. Appl. **6** (1972), 3–25.

4. ———, *Remarques sur la méthode de la phase stationnaire*, Uspehi Mat. Nauk **28** (1973), no. 5 (1973), 17–44 = Russian Math. Surveys **28** (1973), no. 5, 19–48.

5. M. Artin, *On isolated rational singularities of surfaces*, Amer. J. Math. **88** (1966), 129–136. MR **33** #7340.

6. N. Bourbaki, *Élements de mathématique*. Fasc. XXXIV. *Groupes et algèbres de Lie*. Chaps. 4, 5, 6, Actualités Sci. Indust., no. 1337, Hermann, Paris, 1968. MR **39** #1590.

7. E. Brieskorn, *Über die Auflösung gewisser Singularitäten von holomorphen Abbildungen*, Math. Ann. **166** (1966), 76–102. MR **34** #6789.

8. ———, *Singular elements of semi-simple algebraic groups*, Proc. Internat. Congress Math. (Nice, 1970), vol. 2, Gauthier-Villars, Paris, 1971, pp. 279–284.

9. ———, *Die Monodromie der isolierten Singularitäten von Hyperflächen*, Manuscripta Math. **2** (1970), 103–170. MR **42** #2509.

10. H. S. M. Coxeter and W. O. J. Moser, *Generators and relations for discrete groups*, Ergebnisse der Mathematik und ihrer Grenzgebiete, Springer-Verlag, Berlin, 1957. MR **19**, 527.

11. C. H. Clemens, Jr., *Picard-Lefschetz theorem for families of nonsingular algebraic varieties acquiring ordinary singularities*, Trans. Amer. Math. Soc. **136** (1969), 93–108. MR **38** #2135.

12. P. Deligne and N. Katz, *Groupes de monodromie en géométrie algébrique*, SGA 7, Lecture Notes in Math., vol. 340, Springer-Verlag, Berlin and New York, 1973.

13. M. Demazure, *Séminaire Bourbaki*, Fevr. 74, Travaux d'Arnol'd.

14. A. Durfee, *Fibered knots and algebraic singularities*, Topology **13** (1974), 47–60.

15. J. Herzberg, *Algebraic characterization of types of nodes of surfaces in* S_3, J. London Math. Soc. **32** (1957), 187–198. MR **19**, 457.

16. H. Hamm et Lê Dũng Tráng, *Un théorème de Zariski du type de Lefschetz*, Ann. Sci. École Norm. Sup. (4) **6** (1973), 317–366.

17. A. M. Gabrielov, *Intersection matrices for certain singularities*, Funkcional. Anal. i Priložen. **7** (1973), no. 3, 18–32 = Functional Anal. Appl. **7** (1973), 182–193 (1974). MR **48** #2418.

18. S. M. Gusein-Zade, *Matrices d'intersections pour certaines singularités de fonctions de* 2 *variables*, Funkcional. Anal. i Priložen. **8** (1974), no. 1, 11–15. (Russian)

19. ———, *Diagrammes de Dynkin des singularités des fonctions de* 2 *variables*, Funkcional. Anal. i Priložen. (à paraître); (cette référence nous á été communiquée par V. I. Arnol'd).

20. A. Grothendieck, Exposés faits à Bures-sur Yvette, 1970.

21. F. Lazzeri, *Singularités à Cargèse* 1971, Astérisque n° 8.

22. K. Lamotke, *Die Homologie isolierter Singularitäten*, Math. Z. (à paraître).

23. J. Lipman, *Rational singularities, with applications to algebraic surfaces and unique factorizations*, Inst. Hautes Études Sci. Publ. Math. No. 36 (1969), 195–279, MR **43** #1986.

24. A. Landman, *On the Picard-Lefschetz transformation for algebraic manifolds acquiring general singularities*, Trans. Amer. Math. Soc. **181** (1973), 89–126.

25 F. Klein, *Vorlesungen über das Ikosaeder und die Auflösung der Gleichung vom fünften Grade*, Leibzig, 1884.

26. J. Milnor, *Singular points of complex hypersurfaces*, Ann. of Math. Studies, no. 61, Princeton Univ. Press, Princeton, N. J.; Univ. of Tokyo Press, Tokyo, 1968. MR **39** #969.

27. R. Thom, *Stabilité structurelle et morphogénèse*, Benjamin, New York, 1972.

28. ———, *L'équivalence d'une fonction différentiable et d'un polynôme*, Topology **3** (1965), suppl. 2, 297–307. MR **32** #4702.

29. G. N. Tjurina, *Locally semi-universal flat deformations of isolated singularities of complex spaces*, Izv. Akad. Nauk SSSR Ser. Mat. **33** (1969), 1026–1058 = Math. USSR Izv. **3** (1969), 967–1000. MR **40** #5903.

30. ———, *Resolution of singularities of plane deformations of double rational points*, Funkcional. Anal. i Priložen. **4** (1970), no. 1, 77–83 = Functional Anal. Appl. **4** (1970), 68–73. MR **42** #2031.

31. P. du Val *On isolated singularities of sufaces which do not affect the condition of adjunction.* I, II, III, Proc. Cambridge Philos. Soc. **30** (1934), 453–465, 483–491.

32. A. Kas, *On deformations of a certain type of irregular algebraic surface*, Amer. J. Math. **90** (1968), 789–804. MR **39** #3532.

Université Paris VII
Paris, France

Proceedings of the International Congress of Mathematicians
Vancouver, 1974

Theory of Intersections on the Arithmetic Surface

S. J. Arakelov*

1. Let K be an algebraic number field, $\Lambda \subset K$ be the ring of integers in K, X be a curve of genus g over K and f: $V \to \operatorname{Spec} \Lambda$ be its nonsingular model. Here we shall describe a method which yields a very close analogy between a two-dimensional scheme V and compact algebraic surface.

For the sake of simplicity we shall supopse that the fibration family f: $V \to \operatorname{Spec}\Lambda$ has no degenerate fibres. We shall denote an inclusion of our field K in the complex number field by the symbol ∞. We choose one inclusion from each pair of complex conjugated inclusions. From now on the symbol $\sum_\infty$ means that every real inclusion and one of every pair of complex conjugated inclusions is present in our sum. Let us denote the Riemann surface of an algebraic curve $X \otimes_\infty \boldsymbol{C}$ by X_∞. First of all, we shall define a notion which is analogous to the notion of a divisor on the compact algebraic surface.

DEFINITION. A compactified divisor or c-divisor is a formal linear combination

$$D = \sum_i k_i C_i + \sum_\infty \lambda_\infty X_\infty.$$

Here C_i is an irreducible closed subset in V of codimension 1, $k_i \in \boldsymbol{Z}$, $\lambda_\infty \in \boldsymbol{R}$. To avoid confusion we shall call a usual divisor on our scheme V a finite divisor, or f-divisor, and write accordingly a letter "c" or "f" near the corresponding symbol. We shall often consider a finite divisor as a c-divisor with $\lambda_\infty = 0$. All c-divisors form a group which we denote by $\operatorname{Div}_c(V)$.

To define a principal divisor, it is necessary to fix on each surface X_∞ a hermitian metric ds^2_∞. We shall assume the corresponding volume element to satisfy the following condition: $\int_{X_\infty} d\mu_\infty = 1$.

Let $\varphi \in K(X)$ be a rational function. The divisor of the function φ is defined by the formula

*Not presented in person.

$$(\varphi) = \sum_{C\subset V} \nu_C(\varphi)\cdot C + \sum_{\infty} \nu_\infty(\varphi)\cdot X_\infty.$$

Here $\sum \nu_C(\varphi)\cdot C = (\varphi)_f$ is a usual divisor of the function φ and

$$\nu_\infty(\varphi) = -\int_{X_\infty} \log|\varphi|\, d\mu_\infty.$$

All c-divisors modulo principal divisors form a group which we denote by $\mathrm{Pic}_c(V)$.

2. There exists a theory of intersections for c-divisors. For two c-divisors D_1, D_2 their real intersection index $(D_1, D_2) \in \boldsymbol{R}$ can be defined. It is bilinear, symmetrical and is invariant under c-equivalence: For $\varphi \in K(X)$, $((\varphi)_c, D) = 0$. When written in terms of the finite divisors the invariance property has the following form:

$$(D_f + (\varphi)_f, D'_f) = (D_f, D'_f) + \deg D' \cdot \sum_{\infty} \int_{X_\infty} \log|\varphi|\, d\mu_\infty.$$

Here and below deg D means the degree of D on the general fibre. It follows from this relation that when restricted on the divisors of degree 0 our index is an invariant under usual linear equivalence. In this case such an index is equal to Neron's index.

The intersection index depends on the choice of the metrics ds^2_∞. However, there exists one metric on the curve X_∞ which is the most convenient for the theory of intersections. To define it, let us consider the Jacobian J_∞ of the curve X_∞ and let $ds^2_{J,\infty}$ be the invariant metric on J_∞ defined by its Θ-polarisation.

DEFINITION. The canonical metric ds^2_∞ is a restriction of the metric $ds^2_{J,\infty}$, under the canonical inclusion $X_\infty \to J_\infty$.

From this moment we shall consider every metric ds^2_∞ to be a canonical one. It is interesting to note that there exists a c-divisor class $\mathscr{K} \in \mathrm{Pic}_c(X)$ which is an analogue of the canonical divisor class on the algebraic surface and which has the following property: If $C \subset V$ is an irreducible horizontal curve on V and δ_C is an absolute discriminant of its ring of regular functions, then

$$(*) \qquad (C, C) + (C, \mathscr{K}) = \log|\delta_C|.$$

3. Now we shall formulate an analogue of the Riemann-Roch theorem. First of all we shall describe an interpretation of c-divisor classes which is analogous to the interpretation of usual divisor classes as linear bundles. Let $\mathscr{L}$ be an invertible sheaf on V. Then $\mathscr{L}$ defines for each ∞ a complex linear bundle L_∞ over the surface X_∞. If every bundle L_∞ is provided with a hermitian metric $\|\ \|_\infty$ on it, whose curvature form is proportional to the form $d\mu_\infty$, we shall call $\mathscr{L}$ a c-bundle. The group of c-bundles is isomorphic to the group $\mathrm{Pic}_c(V)$.

Let us denote by $V_\infty(\mathscr{L})$ the complex linear space of sections of the bundle L_∞ for the complex ∞ and the corresponding real space for the real ∞. The metric $\|\ \|_\infty$ defines a positive function F_∞ on the $V_\infty(\mathscr{L})$ by the following formula:

$$\log F_\infty(s) = \int_{X_\infty} \log\|s\|_\infty\, d\mu_\infty \quad \text{for } s \in V_\infty(\mathscr{L}).$$

Let us define on the space $V(\mathscr{L}) = \bigoplus_\infty V_\infty(\mathscr{L})$ a "norm" function $F = \prod_\infty F_\infty^{\alpha_\infty}$. Here α_∞ equals 1 for a real ∞ and 2 for a complex ∞. If $\deg \mathscr{L} > 2g - 2$, then the Λ

module $\Omega_{\mathscr{L}} = \Gamma(V, \mathscr{L})$ is a projective module of rank $m + 1 - g$ and has a natural inclusion as a lattice into the space $V(\mathscr{L})$. We can define the density of $\Omega_{\mathscr{L}}$ with respect to the norm function F by the formula

$$\mathfrak{r}(\Omega_{\mathscr{L}}) = \left(\prod_{\infty} \nu(B_{\infty})\right) \Big/ \nu(\Omega_{\mathscr{L}}).$$

Here B_{∞} is a unit ball of the norm function F_{∞}, $\nu(B_{\infty})$ is its volume measured by any euclidean metric E_{∞} on the space V_{∞} and $\nu(\Omega_{\mathscr{L}})$ is a volume of the fundamental cube of the lattice $\Omega_{\mathscr{L}}$ measured by the metric $E = \bigoplus E_{\infty}$ on the $V(\mathscr{L})$.

CONJECTURE 1.

$$\log \mathfrak{r}(\Omega_{\mathscr{L}}) = \tfrac{1}{2}(\mathscr{L}, \mathscr{L} - \mathscr{K}) + \tfrac{1}{2}\deg \mathscr{L} \cdot \log|\partial| + d.$$

Here ∂ is the discriminant of the field K and $d = d(X)$ is some invariant of the curve X.

CONJECTURE 2. Invariant $d(X)$ has an interpretation as the height of the point which corresponds to X in the moduli variety of curves of genus g.

Let us put $\tilde{d}(\mathscr{L}) = \log \mathfrak{r}(\Omega_{\mathscr{L}}) - \tfrac{1}{2}(\mathscr{L}, \mathscr{L} - \mathscr{K}) - \tfrac{1}{2}\deg \mathscr{L} \cdot \log|\partial|$. Conjecture 1 asserts that $\tilde{d}(\mathscr{L})$ does not depend on $\mathscr{L}$.

It is possible to prove that $\tilde{d}(\mathscr{L})$ is absolutely bounded if $\deg \mathscr{L}$ is fixed. For an elliptic curve X it is possible to prove that $\tilde{d}(\mathscr{L}) = \text{const}$ if $\deg \mathscr{L}$ is fixed.

4. In the last section we shall consider two questions. For the first one let $\xi \in \operatorname{Pic}(X/K)$ be a divisor class of degree $m > 2g - 2$ on X. Suppose, for the sake of simplicity, that the class number of K equals 1. Then ξ corresponds to the single invertible sheaf $\mathscr{L}_{\xi}$ on V, and all effective divisors on V of class ξ are interpreted as classes of equivalent elements of the lattice $\Omega_{\xi} = \Gamma(V, \mathscr{L}_{\xi})$ under the action of the group of units of K.

Let us consider those vectors of the lattice Ω_{ξ} which correspond to irreducible divisors on V. The discriminant δ of a prime divisor is a function which is defined only on such vectors, but it can be extended on the whole lattice Ω_{ξ} by the formula (*). In this way we get a function δ on the lattice Ω_{ξ} which is proportional to the $(m + 2g - 2)$th power of the norm function. Using Conjecture 1 we can compute the density $\mathfrak{r}_{\delta}(\xi)$ of the lattice Ω_{ξ} with respect to the function $\delta^{(m+2g-2)^{-1}}$. Here is the asymptotic behavior of this density when $\deg \xi = m$ is fixed:

$$\log \mathfrak{r}_{\delta}(\xi) = -\text{const} \cdot (g - 1) \cdot B(\xi, \xi) + o(B(\xi, \xi)).$$

Here const is positive and $B(\xi, \xi)$ is the quadratic part of the height of the point on the Jacobian of the curve X with respect to Θ-polarisation. So we can see that if $g > 1$ than $\mathfrak{r}_{\delta}(\xi) \to 0$ when $\xi \to \infty$.

The second question is about the distribution of the divisors of degree $m > 2g - 2$ with regard to height.

Let H be any c-divisor of degree 1 and D be an f-divisor. We shall call the magnitude $N_H(D) = \exp(D \cdot H)$ a height of a divisor D with regard to H. It is possible to prove that the series

$$\sum_{D>0:\ \deg D=m} \frac{1}{N_H(D)^s} = \zeta_H^{(m)}(s)$$

converges if $s > m+1-g$ and that the limit

$$T = \lim_{s\to m+1-g} (s-(m+1-g))\cdot\zeta_H^{(m)}(s)$$

exists and does not equal zero. Using Conjecture 1 we can compute that

$$T = \mathrm{const}(m)\cdot R\cdot\frac{h}{\mu}\cdot|\delta|^{m/2}\exp\alpha(H)\exp d(X)\cdot\sum_{\xi\in\mathrm{Pic}(X/K)}\exp(-F(\xi)).$$

Here $\alpha(H) = \frac{1}{2}m(m+2-2g)(H,H) + \frac{1}{2}m(H,\mathscr{K})$, h is the class number of K, R is its regulator and μ is the number of roots of unity of K. At last $F(\xi)$ is the sum of the quadratic and linear parts of the height on the Jacobian of X in regard to Θ-polarisation.

References

С.Ю. Аракелов, *Теория пересечений на арифметической поверхности*, Известия АН СССР, матем. серия **38** (1974).

University of Moscow
Moscow, U.S.S.R.

Proceedings of the International Congress of Mathematicians
Vancouver, 1974

Submanifolds of Low Codimension in Projective Space

Wolf Barth

0. Let A be a nonsingular, connected, algebraic subvariety of some projective space $\boldsymbol{P}_n$ over $\boldsymbol{C}$. Let a be the *dimension* of A and g its *degree*. To the author's knowledge, Hartshorne was the first to observe that A is a complete intersection if a is much larger than g. To be precise, he shows in [**5**]: *There exists a function* $\mathcal{N}(g)$, *such that A is a complete intersection, if* $a \geqq \mathcal{N}(g)$.

His proof, however, gives no estimate for the function $\mathcal{N}$. At the same time, Van de Ven and the author gave in [**1**] an effective estimate for $\mathcal{N}$ in the case that A has codimension two. In fact, one can choose $\mathcal{N}(g) = 4g - 7$ in this case [**2**, Theorem 5.3]. Here I want to give a short report on joint work with Van de Ven, where we generalize the methods from [**1**] to the case of arbitrary codimension to obtain $\mathcal{N}(g) = 5g(g-1)/2$. The precise function $\mathcal{N}$ is not known at the moment. However the simple examples $A = \boldsymbol{P}_{g-1} \times \boldsymbol{P}_1$, embedded by the Segre map, show that necessarily $\mathcal{N}(g) \geqq g + 1$.

The main idea of our proof is to use the lines contained in A. All other methods are either classical or very formal and will probably be very similar to those used by Hartshorne, as far as the author can judge from [**5**]. Full details will appear elsewhere.

1. Let $A \subset \boldsymbol{P}_n$ be a closed connected algebraic submanifold of dimension a and degree g. We may assume $g \geqq 3$. We need the following facts:

(1) There is a linear subspace of dimension at most $a + g - 1$ containing A.

This is classical and easy to see. It implies that we may assume $n = a + g - 1$ without loss of generality.

(2) Assume $a \geqq 3(g-1)$. Then restriction $H^q(\boldsymbol{P}_n, Z) \to H^q(A, Z)$ is bijective for $0 \leqq q \leqq 2(g-1)$.

This follows from Larsen's version of the generalized Lefschetz theorem [7]. It implies that we may view the Chern classes $c_i(N)$ of the *normal bundle* $N = N_{A/P}$ as integers since they are contained in $H^{2i}(A, Z) \simeq Z$, $0 \leqq i \leqq 2(g-1)$. Another consequence is that $H^1(A, \mathcal{O}_A^*) \simeq Z$ and that this group is generated by $\mathcal{O}_A(1)$. Consequently $\det N = \mathcal{O}_A(k)$ for some $k \in Z$.

(3) For this integer k, $k \leqq 2(g-1)$ holds.

PROOF. The intersection of A with a general $\boldsymbol{P}_g \subset \boldsymbol{P}_{a+g-1}$ is a nonsingular curve C of degree g. By a classical formula the genus π of this curve is at most $\frac{1}{2}(g-1)\cdot(g-2)$. Since $N_{C/\boldsymbol{P}_g} = N|C$, we find $T_C = \mathcal{O}_C(g+1-k)$. Thus $g(g+1-k) = 2-2\pi$, which implies the estimate.

(4) The canonical bundle of A is $\mathcal{O}_A(k-(a+g))$.

This follows from the exact sequence $0 \to T_A \to T_{\boldsymbol{P}}|A \to N \to 0$.

2. The variety C_x of lines in A through a point $x \in A$. Let $x \in A$ be a fixed point and $T_x \subset \boldsymbol{P}_n$ the tangent a-plane of A at x. The lines through x in T_x form a projective space P_x of dimension $a-1$. If $\sigma\colon \tilde{T}_x \to T_x$ is the σ-transform with center x, there is a natural $\boldsymbol{P}_1$-bundle $\tau\colon \tilde{T}_x \to P_x$, the fibres of which are just the proper transforms of the lines through x. If $M \subset P_x$ is a subset, denote $\tau^{-1}M \subset \tilde{T}_x$ by $\tilde{M}$ and $\sigma\tau^{-1}M \subset T_x$ by M'. Let $C_x \subset P_x$ be the subvariety corresponding to lines L through x, which are *completely contained* in A.

(5) In each of its points, $\operatorname{codim}_{P_x} C_x \leqq g-1$.

PROOF. This is well known for the case of a hypersurface A. To prove it in our case, choose a general $\boldsymbol{P}_{g-3} \subset \boldsymbol{P}_n$ and let $p\colon \boldsymbol{P}_n \to \boldsymbol{P}_{a+1}$ be the projection with center $\boldsymbol{P}_{g-3}$. Then $p(A)$ will be a hypersurface in $\boldsymbol{P}_{a+1}$ of degree g. The point $p(x) \in p(A)$ will be nonsingular and $p|A\colon A \to p(A)$ will be injective near x. If L is a line in $p(A)$ through $p(x)$, then $A \cap p^{-1}(L)$ contains a curve C through x. C is contained in $p^{-1}(L) \simeq \boldsymbol{P}_{g-1}$ and the intersections of C with hyperplanes in $\boldsymbol{P}_{g-1}$ of the form $p^{-1}(y)$, $y \in L$ near to $p(x)$, consist of one point. This shows that C is a line. So C_x is projected isomorphically onto the cone of lines in $p(A)$ through $p(x)$.

Let us denote $(g-1)$-tuples $(k_1, \cdots, k_{g-1})$ of integers k_i by $\boldsymbol{k}$. We identify two such $(g-1)$-tuples if they differ only by a permutation. So we can assume $k_1 \geqq k_2 \geqq \cdots \geqq k_{g-1}$. Put $\mathcal{O}(\boldsymbol{k}) := \mathcal{O}(k_1) \oplus \cdots \oplus \mathcal{O}(k_{g-1})$. By Grothendieck's theorem, every rank $(g-1)$ bundle V over $\boldsymbol{P}_1$ is of the form $\mathcal{O}_{\boldsymbol{P}_1}(\boldsymbol{k})$, with $\boldsymbol{k}$ uniquely determined by V.

(6) Let L be a line in A. Then $N|L \simeq \mathcal{O}_L(\boldsymbol{k})$ with $k_i \geqq 1$ for $i = 1, \cdots, g-1$ and $k_1 + \cdots + k_{g-1} \leqq 2(g-1)$.

PROOF. Since $N|L$ is a quotient of $T_{\boldsymbol{P}}|L \simeq \mathcal{O}_L(2, 1, \cdots, 1)$, none of the integers k_i can be smaller than 1. On the other hand, $k_1 + \cdots + k_{g-1} = \boldsymbol{k}$ with $\mathcal{O}_A(\boldsymbol{k}) \simeq \det N$. So the second statement follows from (3).

Using (6), we can easily estimate the dimension of $H^1(L, \operatorname{End} N|L)$ to obtain, for example,

$$h^1(\operatorname{End} N|L) \leqq (g-1)^2. \tag{7}$$

We put next $\tilde{N} := \sigma^* N|\tilde{C}_x$. The projection τ puts on $\tilde{N}$ the structure of a family of $(g-1)$-bundles over $\boldsymbol{P}_1$ with C_x as base space. Each bundle $\mathcal{O}_{\boldsymbol{P}_1}(\boldsymbol{k})$ is the distinguished element in a complete family, the base of which has dimension $h^1(\mathrm{End}\ \mathcal{O}_{P_1}(\boldsymbol{k}))$. Compare [3, Satz 6.2]. From deformation theory follows that each element $L_0 \in C_x$ is contained in a (local analytic) subvariety $S \subset C_x$, such that all bundles $N|\tau^{-1}L$ are isomorphic for $L \in S$. Furthermore, in all of its points, S has codimension at most $(g-1)^2$ in C_x because of (7). Now we use the lexicographic order on the $(g-1)$-tuples $\boldsymbol{k}$. Let $\boldsymbol{k}(x) = (m_1(\mu_1 \text{ times}), \cdots, m_j(\mu_j \text{ times}))$ be the maximal one with respect to this ordering among the $(g-1)$-tuples $\boldsymbol{k}$ appearing with all the bundles $N|L = \mathcal{O}_L(\boldsymbol{k})$, $L \in C_x$. If we apply the semicontinuity theorem to the proper morphism $\tau|\tilde{C}_x$ and the $\mathcal{O}_{C_x}$-flat sheaf $\tilde{N}$, we find

(8) There is a closed algebraic subvariety $M_x \subset C_x$ such that, for all $L \in M_x$, the bundle $N|L$ is isomorphic to $\mathcal{O}_L(\boldsymbol{k}(x))$. In all of its points, M_x has codimension at most $g(g-1)$ in P_x.

(9) There is a chain of subbundles

$$0 = V_0 \subset V_1 \subset \cdots \subset V_j = \tilde{N}|\tilde{M}_x$$

defined by the following property: For each $L \in M_x$, $V_i|\tau^{-1}(L) \subset \tilde{N}|\tau^{-1}(L) \simeq \mathcal{O}_L(\boldsymbol{k}(x))$ is just the uniquely determined subbundle $\mu_1\mathcal{O}_L(m_1) \oplus \cdots \oplus \mu_i\mathcal{O}_L(m_i)$.

In fact, one obtains V_i as the subbundle $(\tau^*\tau_*\tilde{N}(-m_i)|\tilde{M}_x)(m_i)$. From this construction follows

$$(V_{i+1}/V_i)(-m_{i+1}) = \tau^*(\tau|M_x \cap \sigma^{-1}x)_*(V_{i+1}/V_i|\tilde{M}_x \cap \sigma^{-1}x).$$

(10) If $a \geqq 5g(g-1)/2$, then $V_{i+1}/V_i \simeq \mu_{i+1}\sigma^*\mathcal{O}_{P_*}(m_{i+1})|\tilde{M}_x$.

PROOF. We show by induction that $V_{i+1}/V_i|\tilde{M}_x \cap \sigma^{-1}x$ is the trivial bundle of rank μ_{i+1}. Since $V_{i+1}/V_i \subset \tilde{N}/V_i$ and $\tilde{N}|\sigma^{-1}x$ is trivial, it is enough to show the following. Each subbundle V of a trivial bundle $M_x \times \boldsymbol{C}^r$, $r \leqq g-1$, is of the form $M_x \times E$, where $E \subset \boldsymbol{C}^r$ is a linear subspace. But V is determined by a morphism f of M_x into some Grassmann variety of linear subspaces of $\boldsymbol{C}^r$. The dimension of this Grassmannian cannot exceed $\frac{1}{4}r^2$. Then each fibre of f is a subvariety of P_x of codimension at most $g(g-1) + \frac{1}{4}(g-1)^2$. By assumption, two such subspaces must always intersect. This implies that f is constant and $V = M_x \times E$ with E the subspace corresponding to $f(M_x)$.

3. The normal bundle of A. Assume from now on $a \geqq 5g(g-1)/2$. From (9) and (10) it follows that the total Chern class of $\tilde{N}|\tilde{M}_x$ equals the total Chern class of $\sigma^*(\mu_1\mathcal{O}_A(m_1) + \cdots + \mu_j\mathcal{O}_A(m_j))$ restricted to $\tilde{M}_x$. This implies that both the rank $(g-1)$ bundles N and $\mathcal{O}_A(\boldsymbol{k}(x))$ have the same total Chern classes because of

(11) If $a \geqq (g+1)(g-1)$, then $(\sigma|\tilde{M}_x)^*: H^i(A, Z) \to H^i(\tilde{M}_x, Z)$ is injective for $0 \leqq i \leqq 2(g-1)$.

PROOF. In view of (2), it is enough to show that $H^i(\boldsymbol{P}_n, Z) \xrightarrow{\text{restr}} H^i(A, Z) \to H^i(\tilde{M}_x, Z)$ is injective. But this follows as in [1, Proposition 2.3], since $\dim M'_x \geqq a - g(g-1) \geqq g-1$. Since the construction above was done using an arbitrary point $x \in A$, we deduce from (11), in particular, that $\boldsymbol{k}(x)$ is independent of $x \in A$. Let us denote this $\boldsymbol{k}(x)$ by $\boldsymbol{k}$ from now on.

(12) For all $l \geqq -m_1$, we have $h^0(N(l)) = h^0(\mathcal{O}_A(\boldsymbol{k})(l))$.

PROOF. Since the total Chern class of both the bundles in question is the same, this will follow from the Riemann-Roch formula, if we can prove for all these l and all $i \geqq 1$:

$$h^i(N(l)) = h^i(\mathcal{O}_A(\boldsymbol{k})(l)) = 0.$$

Since N is generated by global sections, the statement for this bundle follows from [4, Theorem G], provided that the line bundle $K_A \otimes \det N \otimes \mathcal{O}_A(-l)$ is negative. But because of (3) and (4), this bundle equals $\mathcal{O}_A(2k - (a + g - 1) - l)$ with $k \leqq 2(g - 1)$ and it will be negative if $a > 5(g - 1)$. The other statement follows from Kodaira's vanishing theorem for line bundles, since $\mathcal{O}_A(l) \otimes K_A^*$ is positive if $a > g - l - 1$. Next we define a chain of subsheaves $0 \subset \mathcal{S}_1 \subset \cdots \subset \mathcal{S}_j \subset N$ by defining $\mathcal{S}_i(-m_i) \subset N(-m_i)$, $i = 1, \cdots, j$: Let $\mathcal{S}_i(-m_i)$ be the sheaf generated by global sections in $N(-m_i)$. We show by induction on i: The sheaf $\mathcal{S}_i$ corresponds to a subbundle $V_i \subset N$ of rank $\mu_1 + \cdots + \mu_i$ and $V_i/V_{i-1} \simeq \mu_i\mathcal{O}_A(m_i)$. We shall only describe the first step ($i = 1$), the induction step being very similar: By (12), the sheaf $\mathcal{S}_1(-m_1)$ is generated by μ_1 global sections $s_1, \cdots, s_{\mu_1}$. We claim that these sections must be linearly independent in each point $x \in A$. In fact, assume that there is a linear relation between the values of these sections in some point $x \in A$. Since for each line $L \subset A$ the restriction $N(-m_1)|L$ cannot contain a nontrivial section with a zero, the same relation must hold in each point $x' \in C'_x$. Since by (5) any two sets C'_{x_1} and C'_{x_2}, $x_1, x_2 \in A$, intersect, we may apply the same argument once more to find that this linear relation holds in each point of A, i.e., in the vector space $\Gamma(A, (N - m_1))$, which is impossible.

Using Kodaira's vanishing theorem again for $H^1(\mathcal{O}_A(m_i) \otimes \mathcal{O}_A(-m_j))$, $j = 1, \cdots, i - 1$, we see by induction on i that all extensions $0 \to V_{i-1} \to V_i \to V_i/V_{i-1} \to 0$ split. Then we finally get

(13) If $a \geqq 5g(g - 1)/2$, the normal bundle N is isomorphic to a direct sum $\mu_1\mathcal{O}_A(m_1) \oplus \cdots \oplus \mu_j\mathcal{O}_A(m_j)$, $1 \leqq m_i \leqq 2(g - 1)$.

Therefore N is the restriction to A of a rank $(g - 1)$ bundle $\bar{N}$ on $\boldsymbol{P}_n$, which is the direct sum of line bundles.

(14) For all $\nu \geqq 1$ we have $H^1(I_A^\nu/I_A^{\nu+1} \otimes_{\mathcal{O}_P} \bar{N}) = 0$.

PROOF.

$$I_A^\nu/I_A^{\nu+1} \otimes_{\mathcal{O}_P} \bar{N} \simeq S^\nu(I_A/I_A^2)|A \otimes_{\mathcal{O}_A} N \simeq S^\nu(N^*) \otimes_{\mathcal{O}_A} N$$

is a direct sum of line bundles.

4. The equations defining A. The isomorphism $I_A/I_A^2 \simeq N^*$ corresponds to a section $s_2 \in \Gamma(I_A/I_A^2 \otimes_{\mathcal{O}_P} \bar{N})$ without zeroes on A. Using the exact sequences

$$0 \to (I_A^\nu/I_A^{\nu+1}) \otimes_{\mathcal{O}_P} \bar{N} \to I_A/I_A^{\nu+1} \otimes_{\mathcal{O}_P} \bar{N} \to I_A/I_A^\nu \otimes_{\mathcal{O}_P} \bar{N} \to 0$$

and (14), we get sections $s_{\nu+1} \in \Gamma(I_A/I_A^{\nu+1} \otimes_{\mathcal{O}_P} \bar{N})$, which modulo I_A^ν restrict to s_ν, i.e., a section $\hat{s} \in \Gamma(\hat{N})$, contained in $I_A \otimes_{\mathcal{O}_P} \hat{N}$ but without zeroes modulo I_A^2. (Here $\hat{N}$ is the formal completion of $\bar{N}$ along A.) Since A is connected and has positive dimension, by [6, Theorem 3.3] this section extends to a section $\bar{s}$ in $\bar{N}$ over all of $\boldsymbol{P}$. The zero set of this section has codimension at most $g - 1$ and therefore is connected. So it has to coincide with A. Since N is a direct sum of line bundles, this shows that A is a complete intersection of $g - 1$ hypersurfaces.

References

1. W. Barth and A. Van de Ven, *A decomposability criterion for algebraic 2-bundles in projective spaces*, Invent. Math. **25** (1974), 91–106.

2. ———, *On the geometry in codimension 2 of Grassmann manifolds*, Springer Lecture Notes in Math., No. 412.

3. E. V. Brieskorn, *Über holomorphe P_n-Bündel über P_1*, Math. Ann. **157** (1965), 343–357. MR **37** #5897.

4. P. A. Griffiths, *Hermitian differential geometry, Chern classes, and positive vector bundles*, Global Analysis (Papers in Honor of K. Kodaira), Univ. of Tokyo Press, Tokyo; Princeton Univ. Press, Princeton, N. J., 1969, pp. 185–251. MR **41** #2717.

5. R. Hartshorne, *Varieties of small codimension in projective space*, Bull. Amer. Math. Soc. **80** (1974), 1017–1032.

6. H. Hironaka and H. Matsumura, *Formal functions and formal embeddings*, J. Math. Soc. Japan **20** (1968), 52–82. MR **40** #4274.

7. M. E. Larsen, *On the topology of complex projective manifolds*, Invent. Math. **19** (1973), 251–260. MR **47** #7058.

MATHEMATISCH INSTITUUT DER UNIVERSITEIT
LEIDEN, THE NETHERLANDS

Proceedings of the International Congress of Mathematicians
Vancouver, 1974

Applications of the Theory of Prym Varieties

C. H. Clemens

1. Let C be a complete nonsingular algebraic curve over the complex numbers (i.e., a compact Riemann surface) of genus g. If $H^{1,0}(C)$ denotes the holomorphic one-forms on C and $B \in C$ is a basepoint, there is a multivalued map

$$C \to H^{1,0}(C)^*$$
$$P \mapsto \int_B^P$$

which becomes a well-defined immersion

$$k: C \to \frac{H^{1,0}(C)^*}{H_1(C; \boldsymbol{Z})} = J(C)$$

into the *Jacobian variety* $J(C)$ of C for $g \geqq 1$. k induces a canonical identification of $H_1(C; \boldsymbol{Z})$ with $H_1(J(C); \boldsymbol{Z})$ and therefore transforms the intersection pairing on C to an element

$$\Phi_C \in (\Lambda^2 H_1(J(C); \boldsymbol{Z}))^* = H^2(J(C); \boldsymbol{Z}).$$

Φ_C is the Poincaré dual of the divisor $\Theta_C = k(C^{(g(C)-1)})$ in $J(C)$, and Θ_C is uniquely determined up to translation in $J(C)$ by its homology class. This "rigidity" of Θ_C leads to the recovery of C from the data $(J(C), \Phi_C)$. (See, for example, Andreotti's beautiful proof of the Torelli theorem using the Gauss map on Θ_C [**1**].)

2. More generally, one defines a *principally polarized abelian variety* by giving a complex vector space V of dimension n, a lattice E in V, and a positive definite Hermitian form H on V such that the imaginary part of H is integral-valued and unimodular on E [**8**]. Then again (im H) $\in H^2(V/E; \boldsymbol{Z})$ is dual to a rigid ample divisor Θ on V/E. To see that Jacobians are in fact principally polarized abelian varieties, one identifies $(H^{1,0}(C))^* = H^{0,1}(C)$ and defines

$$H(\eta_1,\eta_2) = -(-1)^{1/2} \int_C \eta_1 \wedge \bar{\eta}_2.$$

The set of (principally polarized) abelian varieties of dimension n depends on $\frac{1}{2}n(n+1)$ parameters whereas the Jacobians depend only on $(3n-3)$ parameters (if $n > 1$) so that for $n > 3$ the general abelian variety is not a Jacobian. This leads to the

Schottky Problem. Give explicit algebraic criteria on (V, E, H) to determine whether or not it is a Jacobian.

To make this problem more precise: Classically the divisor Θ on V/E is given as the set of zeros of an entire holomorphic function (called a "theta function") $\theta(u)$ on $\boldsymbol{C}^n$ ($\approx V$) with certain periodicity properties. In fact if we choose a standard basis for E with respect to (im H) we can denote the points of order two in V/E by

$$\begin{bmatrix}\delta\\ \varepsilon\end{bmatrix} = \begin{bmatrix}\delta_1, \cdots, \delta_n\\ \varepsilon_1, \cdots, \varepsilon_n\end{bmatrix}, \qquad \delta_i, \varepsilon_j \in \{0, 1\},$$

and there is an entire function

$$\theta\begin{bmatrix}\delta\\ \varepsilon\end{bmatrix}(u) = \sum_{m \in Z^n} \exp(\pi(-1)^{1/2}(m+\delta/2)\Omega^t(m+\delta/2) + 2(m+\delta/2)^t(u+\varepsilon/2))$$

associated to each $[{}^{\delta}_{\varepsilon}]$ such that:

(i) the zero set of $\theta[{}^{\delta}_{\varepsilon}]$ (u) is invariant under translation by elements of E and maps onto $\Theta + [{}^{\delta}_{\varepsilon}]$ in V/E;

(ii) $\theta[{}^{\delta}_{\varepsilon}](u)$ is an even or odd function according to whether $\sum \delta_i\varepsilon_i$ is even or odd.

The coefficients of fixed degree in the power series expansions for the $\theta[{}^{\delta}_{\varepsilon}]$ (u) give natural algebraic coordinates for the moduli space of abelian varieties of dimension n. In particular, Schottky **[12]** gave a necessary algebraic condition in the coefficients of degree 0 (the "theta-nulls") such that (V, E, H) is the Jacobian variety of a curve in the case $n = 4$. Farkas and Rauch **[4]**, **[5]** and Andreotti and Mayer **[2]** have given necessary algebraic conditions in terms of the theta coefficients when $n \geqq 5$.

I would like to propose another possible way to attack the Schottky problem in the cases $n = 4$ and $n = 5$. For this we will need a geometric interpretation of a generic principally polarized abelian variety of dimension $n \leqq 5$. This is provided by the notion of the Prym variety developed classically by Wirtinger **[14]** and deepened in modern times by Farkas and Rauch **[4]**, **[5]** and Mumford **[9]**.

3. A Prym variety will be a principally polarized abelian variety of a somewhat more "general" type than a Jacobian. To see what it is, we give ourselves a Riemann surface C of genus $g(C)$ and an unramified two-sheeted covering $\pi: \tilde{C} \to C$. (Such coverings are parametrized by elements of $H_1(C; \boldsymbol{Z}_2)$ or, what is the same thing, by points of order two on $J(C)$.)

The natural involution $i: \tilde{C} \to \tilde{C}$ induces an involution i_* on $(H^{1,0}(C))^*$ and on $H_1(\tilde{C}; \boldsymbol{Z})$. If we let V^- and E^- denote the minus-one eigenspaces of these last two involutions then we can define the Prym variety by $P(C\,\sigma) = V^-/E^-$. The theta divisor Ξ_π arises on $P(C, \sigma)$ via $\frac{1}{2}$(restrition of intersection pairing co E^-)

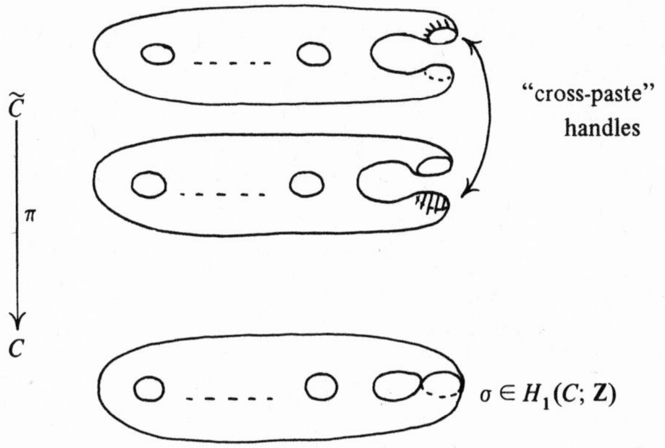

FIGURE 3.1

in a manner completely analogous to the case of Jacobians. Thus $P(C, \sigma)$ becomes a principally polarized abelian variety of dimension $(g(C) - 1)$. It is a classical theorem of Wirtinger [**14**] that the moduli of the set of Prym varieties of dimension n depend on $3n$ parameters rather than $(3n - 3)$, the number of parameters for the moduli space of algebraic curves of genus n. Since principally polarized abelian varieties of dimension n depend on $\frac{1}{2}n(n + 1)$ parameters, this shows that through $n = 5$ the general abelian variety is a Prym variety.

At this point we should mention a trivial lemma which shows that the Prym varieties "include the Jacobians" as special cases: Suppose we are given a flat family of curves C_t such that if $t \neq 0$, C_t is nonsingular, and C_0 has one ordinary double point. Suppose that $\delta_t \in H_1(C_t)$ is the cycle vanishing at $t = 0$.

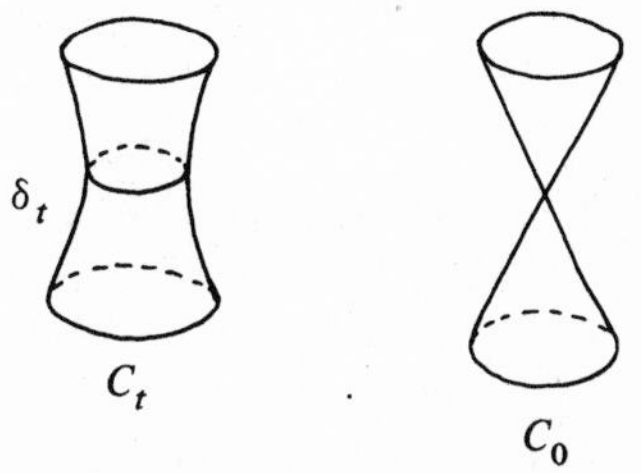

Let $\pi_t\colon \tilde{C}_t \to C_t$ be the two-sheeted covering associated to σ_t as in Figure 3.1, and assume $\delta_t = \sigma_t \bmod 2$. Then

LEMMA 3.2. *The abelian varieties $P(C_t, \sigma_t)$ form a smooth family with fibre above $t = 0$ given by $J(\bar{C}_0)$, where $\bar{C}_0$ is the desingularization of C_0.*

Finally, let us consider what other things can happen to $P(C_t, \sigma_t)$ if we eliminate the requirement that δ_t, the vanishing cycle, be equal modulo 2 to the cycle $\sigma_t \in$

$H_1(C_t; \mathbf{Z}_2)$ used to build the two-sheeted covering $\tilde{C}_t \to C_t$. As Mumford has noted, there are two possible events that occur (besides the one considered in Lemma 3.2).

(3.3) If $\sigma_t \neq \delta_t$ mod 2 but $(\sigma_t \cdot \delta_t) = 0$ mod 2 then $P(C_t, \sigma_t)$ becomes a generalized abelian variety (a C^*-extension of an abelian variety of dimension $(n - 1)$).

(3.4) If $(\sigma_t \cdot \delta_t) = 1$ mod 2, then the $P(C_t, \sigma_t)$ form a flat family with fibre above $t = 0$ equal to the Prym variety associated to a two-sheeted cover of $\bar{C}_0$ ramified at its two-marked points.

(In **[9]**, Mumford extended the theory of principally polarized Prym varieties to the case (3.4) and in his Columbia thesis Masiewicki has further extended the theory to cover the case where C_0 has more than one double point.)

4. Now for $n = 4$ and $n = 5$ one can hope to rephrase the Schottky problem in terms of the theory of Prym varieties. Further evidence in this direction is provided by two theorems, the first of which is due to Tjurin:

THEOREM 4.1. *A principally polarized abelian variety V/E of dimension 5 is a Jacobian if and only if there is a (possibly singular) plane curve C of degree 5 and point σ of order 2 in $J(C)$ such that*

(i) *$\dim H^0(C, \mathfrak{O}(1) \otimes \sigma)$ is even;*

(ii) *$V/E = P(C, \sigma)$ as principally polarized abelian varieties.*

Roughly speaking, V/E is always a Prym variety coming from a curve C of genus 6. V/E becomes a Jacobian when the curve C of genus 6 becomes a plane quintic, that is, when C has a g_5^2 (a linear series of degree 5 and projective dimension 2).

THEOREM 4.2. *A principally polarized abelian variety V/E of dimension 4 is a Jacobian if and only if there exists a curve C of genus 5 with a g_5^2 (or equivalently, with a g_3^1) and $\sigma \in H_1(C; \mathbf{Z}_2)$ such that $V/E = P(C, \sigma)$.*

Roughly V/E is always a Prym variety coming from a curve C of genus 5. V/E becomes a Jacobian when C becomes *trigonal.*

In the case $n = 5$, at least, there is a straightforward way to translate the statement "C has a g_5^2" to a statement about theta-coefficients on $J(C)$. Namely, by the Riemann singularities theorem [7], C has a g_5^2 if and only if there is one odd theta-function *all of whose coefficients of degree* 1 *vanish.* One could make progress on the Schottky problem for $n = 5$, therefore, by translating this information about the theta-coefficients on $J(C)$ to information about the theta-coefficients of $P(C, \sigma)$. Identities relating degree-one theta-coefficients of $J(C)$ and $P(C, \sigma)$ were classically stated by Schottky and Jung **[13]**.

5. There is another setting in which principally polarized abelian varieties arise and which is very closely related, it seems, to the study of Prym varieties. To see what this is let us fix the following class of nonsingular projective varieties over the complex numbers:

We call V of *first Hodge type* if:

(i) $\dim_C V = d$, an odd number;

(ii) the odd Betti numbers of V are all zero, except possibly the dth Betti number;

(iii) if $p + q = d$, then the Hodge components $H^{p,q}(V)$ of $H^d(V; C)$ are all zero unless $|p - q| = 1$.

Examples of such varieties are hypersurfaces of degree $\leqq 4$ in P_4 and the intersection of three quadrics in an even dimensional projective space.

Associated to V is its (intermediate) Jacobian

$$J(V) = \frac{(H^{(d+1)/2,\,(d-1)/2}(V))^*}{H_d(V; \mathbf{Z})}.$$

Just as in the case of curves, the intersection pairing on V induces a principal polarization on $J(V)$. Also, analogous to the case of curves, given an algebraic family $\{Z_s\}_{s\in S}$ of algebraic $((d-1)/2)$-cycles on V, we can pick a basepoint $s_0 \in S$ and define:

$$\begin{aligned} S &\longrightarrow J(V) \\ s &\longrightarrow \int_{Z s_0}^{Z_s} \end{aligned}$$

The *generalized Hodge conjecture* applied to this setting says that there always exists an algebraic family S whose image in $J(V)$ spans $J(V)$.

For example, in the case of the cubic threefold V, the analogy with the theory of algebraic curves is particularly striking. If we take for S the family of lines on V, then S embeds in $J(V)$ and its image carries the homology class of $\Theta_V^2/2$ where Θ_V is the theta-divisor of $J(V)$ [3]. If we take for S the family of twisted cubics on V then the image of S is precisely a translate of Θ itself and the fibers of $S \to \Theta$ are the rational equivalence classes of twisted cubics.

A necessary condition that a threefold of first Hodge type be rational is that its principally polarized intermediate Jacobian be the Jacobian of a curve [3]. In all examples studied so far, this condition has also been sufficient. In higher dimensional examples that have been studied, V being rational corresponds to the fact that $J(V) = J(W)$ where W is of first Hodge type and of dimension less than the dimension of V.

Since the Prym varieties are in some sense "closest" to the Jacobians, one might guess that they often occur as intermediate Jacobians of varieties that are close to being rational. This indeed does happen. Tjurin and Reid, and independently Beauville, have shown that if V is the intersection of three quadrics in $\mathbf{P}_{2n+2}$ then $J(V) = P(C, \sigma)$ where C is a plane curve of degree $2n + 3$ and $\dim H^0(C, \mathfrak{O}(n) \otimes \sigma)$ is even. If V is a cubic hypersurface of $\mathbf{P}_{2n+2}$ containing a linear space of codimension 2 in V, then, if $\bar{V}$ is the desingularization of V, $J(\bar{V}) = P(C, \sigma)$ where C is a plane curve of degree $2n + 3$ and $\dim H^0(C, \mathfrak{O}(n) \otimes \sigma)$ is odd.

6. Thus, for example if V is a nonsingular cubic threefold, then $J(V)$ is a Prym variety associated to a plane quintic. Murre [**11**] shows this in all characteristics $\neq 2$ and thus deduces the irrationality of V (except in characteristic 2) as follows:

(i) It is a theorem of Mumford [**9**] that the codimension of the singular locus of the theta-divisor in a Prym variety $P(C, \sigma)$ is greater than or equal to five except in a finite explicit list of special cases.

(ii) For the cubic threefold V, $J(V) = P(C, \sigma)$ is never on the list.

(iii) Thus $P(C, \sigma)$ is never the Jacobian of a curve. Therefore V is never rational.

In the same way it is shown that if V is a nonsingular intersection of three quadrics in $\boldsymbol{P}_6$, then (at least in characteristic 0) V is never rational.

At this point a natural question arises. If C_t is a family of plane curves of degree 5 (or 7) and as $t \to 0$ we have the family of two-sheeted coverings described in Lemma 3.2, then $P(C_t, \sigma_t)$ becomes the Jacobian of a curve, so should not we expect the corresponding cubics (or the corresponding intersections of three quadrics) to become rational? The answer, in fact, is no. What happens is that the family of two-sheeted coverings of plane curves of degree $(2n + 3)$ is a reducible set, broken up according to the parity of

$$q(\sigma) = \dim H^0(C, \mathfrak{O}(n) \otimes \sigma) + \dim H^0(C, \mathfrak{O}(n)). \tag{6.1}$$

q is a deformation-invariant quadric form on $H_1(C; \boldsymbol{Z}_2)$ whose associated bilinear form is the intersection pairing on C (modulo 2) **[10]**. If σ_t is a vanishing cycle as in Lemma 3.2 then as t goes once around 0, $H_1(C_t; \boldsymbol{Z}_2)$ is transformed by the Picard-Lefschetz formula **[6]**: $\gamma_t \mapsto \gamma_t - (\gamma_t \cdot \sigma_t)\sigma_t$. Thus $q(\gamma_t) = q(\gamma_t) + (\gamma_t \cdot \sigma_t) q(\sigma_t) + (\gamma_t \cdot \sigma_t)^2$ for all $\gamma_t \in H_1(C_t; \boldsymbol{Z}_2)$. Clearly this implies that $q(\sigma_t) = 1$.

What this means is that:

(i) For cubic threefolds V, $J(V) = P(C, \sigma)$ with $q(\sigma) = 0$ so that σ can never be a vanishing cycle in the sense of Lemma 3.2.

(ii) For the intersection Γ of three quadrics in $\boldsymbol{P}_4$, $J(\Gamma) = P(C, \sigma)$ with $q(\sigma) = 1$ and so σ can be a vanishing cycle in Lefschetz pencil. In fact if C_t is a family of plane quintics with two-sheeted coverings given by $\sigma_t \in H_1(C; \boldsymbol{Z}_2)$ and if $P(C_t, \sigma_t) = J(\Gamma_t)$ is the associated family of principally polarized abelian varieties, then the vanishing of σ_t at $t = 0$ is equivalent to the fact that $J(\Gamma_t)$ becomes the Jacobian of a trigonal curve at $t = 0$.

(iii) For the intersection of three quadrics in $\boldsymbol{P}_6$, again we are in the situation of coverings where $q(\sigma) = 0$.

We are thus led to look for a family of threefolds corresponding to the two-sheeted coverings of seventh-degree plane curves for which $q(\sigma) = 1$. Such a family does exist. It is given by the (2, 3)-intersections in $\boldsymbol{P}_5$ such that the quadric and the cubic have a common linear space of dimension 2. (We are assuming that the seven double points of such a (2, 3)-intersection have been resolved.) We ask: What happens to the threefold when the cycle σ vanishes? To be more precise: Let Δ be the unit disc and C_t, $t \in \Delta$, a flat family of seventh-degree plane curves where:

(i) C_t is nonsingular for $t \neq 0$;

(ii) C_0 has one ordinary double point;

(iii) $\sigma_t \in H_1(C_t)$ vanishes at $t = 0$.

Let V_t be a family of (2, 3)-intersections with $P(C_t, \sigma_t) = J(\bar{V}_t)$ for each $t \neq 0$, where $\bar{V}_t$ is the nonsingular variety obtained from V_t by blowing up its seven double points.

Question. Is there a nonsingular rational threefold $\bar{V}_0$ such that:

(i) V_0 is diffeomorphic to $\bar{V}_t$ for $t \neq 0$;

(ii) after perhaps passing to a ramified covering $\tilde{\Delta}$ of Δ we obtain a *smooth* family of threefolds such that the fibre over 0 is $\bar{V}_0$ and the fibres over other points of $\tilde{\Delta}$ are the $\bar{V}_t$. Since, for $t \neq 0$, $P(C_t, \sigma_t)$ does not appear on Mumford's list of exceptional cases this would give a smooth family of threefolds in which one fibre is rational but the general fibre is not.

ADDED IN PROOF. Recillas has recently proved a strong generalization of Theorem 4.2 relating the existence of a g_3^1 on C to the fact that the Prym variety is the Jacobian of a curve with a g_4^1.

Bibliography

1. A. Andreotti, *On a theorem of Torelli*, Amer. J. Math. **80** (1958), 801–828. MR **21** #1309.

2. A. Andreotti and A. Mayer, *On period relations for abelian integrals on algebraic curves*, Ann. Scuola Norm. Sup. Pisa (3) **21** (1967), 189–238. MR **36** #3792.

3. C. H. Clemens and P. A. Griffiths, *The intermediate Jacobian of the cubic threefold*, Ann. of Math. (2) **95** (1972), 281–356. MR **46** #1796.

4. H. Farkas, *On the Schottky relation and its generalization to arbitrary genus*, Ann. of Math. (2) **92** (1970), 56–81. MR **41** #8654.

5. H. M. Farkas and H. E. Rauch, *Period relations of Schottky type on Riemann surfaces*, Ann. of Math. (1) **92** (1970), 434–461. MR **44** #426.

6. S. Lefschetz, *Selected papers* (including *L'analyses situs*), Chelsea, New York, 1971, p. 311. MR **45** #8495.

7. J. Lewittes, *Riemann surfaces and the theta function*, Acta Math. **111** (1964), 37–61. MR **28** #206.

8. D. Mumford, *Abelian varieties*, Tata Institute of Fundamental Research Studies in Math., no. 5, Oxford Univ. Press, London, 1970, Chap. I. MR **44** #219.

9. ———, *Prym varieties.* I, Contributions to Analysis, Academic Press, New York, 1974, pp. 325–350.

10. ———, *Theta characteristics of an algebraic curve*, Ann. Sci. École Norm. Sup. (4) **4** (1971), 181–192. MR **45** #1918.

11. J. Murre, *Reduction of the proof of non-rationality of a non-singular cubic threefold to a result of Mumford*, Compositio Math. **27** (1973), 63–82.

12. F. Schottky, *Zur Theorie der abelschen Funktionen von vier Variabeln*, J. Reine Angew. Math. **102** (1888), 304–352.

13. F. Schottky and H. Jung, *Neue Sätze über symmetral Funktionen und die abel'schen Funktionen der Riemann'schen Theorie*, S.-B. Preuss. Adak. Wiss. Berlin Phys. Math. Kl. **1** (1909), 282–297.

14. W. Wirtinger, *Untersuchungen über Thetafunctionen*, Verlag Teubner, Leipzig, 1895.

COLUMBIA UNIVERSITY
NEW YORK, NEW YORK 10027, U.S.A.

Proceedings of the International Congress of Mathematicians
Vancouver, 1974

New Surfaces with No Meromorphic Functions

Masahisa Inoue

0. Introduction. In his paper [**1**], Kodaira classified (compact complex) surfaces free from exceptional curves into seven classes. In this note, we consider the last class, Class VII_0, which consists of surfaces S satisfying the following condition:

(VII_0) $b_1(S) = 1$ *and* S *is minimal.*

As examples of this class, we have Hopf surfaces and some elliptic surfaces, which satisfy moreover the condition: $b_2(S) = 0$ and S contains at least one curve. Conversely, Kodaira obtained that *if* $b_1(S) = 1$, $b_2(S) = 0$ *and if S contains at least one curve, then S is a Hopf surface or an elliptic surface* (see [**2**, §10]). By this result, to determine all surfaces of Class VII_0, it suffices to consider the following two problems:

Problem 1. *Find all surfaces S satisfying*

(α) $b_1(S) = 1$, $b_2(S) \neq 0$, *and*

(β) S *is minimal.*

Problem 2. *Find all surfaces S satisfying*

(A) $b_1(S) = 1$, $b_2(S) = 0$, *and*

(B) S *contains no curves.*

We note that if a surface satisfies the conditions of Problem 1 or Problem 2, then it has no meromorphic functions other than constants.

In this note, we shall give some examples for these problems and study their properties.

1. Problem 2. As to Problem 2, we have three kinds of examples, S_M, $S^{(+)}_{N,p,q,r;t}$ and $S^{(-)}_{N,p,q,r}$, which are obtained as quotient surfaces of $\boldsymbol{H} \times \boldsymbol{C}$ by automorphism groups G where $\boldsymbol{H}$ is the upper half of the complex plane $\boldsymbol{C}$ and G consists of affine transformations (see [**4**, §§2–4]). For example, S_M is constructed as follows:

Let M be a 3×3 integral matrix with $\det M = 1$ and with eigenvalues $\alpha, \beta, \bar{\beta}$

such that $\alpha > 1$ and $\beta \neq \bar{\beta}$. We choose a *real* eigenvector (a_1, a_2, a_3) and an eigenvector (b_1, b_2, b_3) of M corresponding to α and β, respectively. Let G_M be the group of automorphisms of $\boldsymbol{H} \times \boldsymbol{C}$ generated by

$$g_0 : (w, z) \longrightarrow (\alpha w, \beta z),$$
$$g_i : (w, z) \longrightarrow (w + a_i, z + b_i) \quad \text{for } i = 1, 2, 3.$$

Then G_M acts on $\boldsymbol{H} \times \boldsymbol{C}$ as a properly discontinuous group of analytic automorphisms free from fixed points and has a bounded fundamental domain. We define S_M to be the quotient surface $(\boldsymbol{H} \times \boldsymbol{C})/G_M$. The underlying differentiable manifold of S_M is a 3-torus bundle over a circle.

By definition, it is clear that S_M satisfies the following condition:

(C) *There exists a line bundle F on S such that*

$$\dim H^0(S, \Omega^1 \otimes \mathcal{O}(F)) \neq 0.$$

Other examples, $S^{(+)}_{N,p,q,r;t}$ and $S^{(-)}_{N,p,q,r}$, also satisfy this condition. Conversely, we have the following

THEOREM. *If a surface S satisfies* (A), (B) *and* (C), *then S is complex analytically homeomorphic to* S_M, $S^{(+)}_{N,p,q,r;t}$ *or* $S^{(-)}_{N,p,q,r}$.

We find a proof of this theorem in [**4**].

REMARK. As yet, we have no examples satisfying (A), (B) but not satisfying (C).

2. Problem 1. In this section, we construct an example for Problem 1 and study its properties. Our construction is similar to the construction of the singular fibres of type $_1I_b$ in the theory of elliptic surfaces (see Kodaira [3, §14]).

We take infinitely many copies W_i, $i \in \boldsymbol{Z}$, of $\boldsymbol{C}^2 - 0$ with coordinates (t_i, w_i), and take infinitely many copies V_j, $j \in \boldsymbol{Z}$, of $\boldsymbol{C}^2$ with coordinates (u_j, v_j). We form their union

$$\mathcal{W} = \bigcup_i W_i \bigcup_j V_j$$

by the following indentifications:

Identify $(t_i, w_i) \in W_i$ and $(t_{i-1}, w_{i-1}) \in W_{i-1}$ if and only if

(1) $$w_i = t_{i-1}w_{i-1}, \qquad t_i = t_{i-1}, \qquad t_i \neq 0,\ w_{i-1} \neq 0.$$

Identify $(u_j, v_j) \in V_j$ and $(u_{j-1}, v_{j-1}) \in V_{j-1}$ if and only if

(2) $$v_j = v_{j-1}^2 u_{j-1}, \qquad u_j = 1/v_{j-1}, \qquad u_j \neq 0,\ v_{j-1} \neq 0.$$

Identify $(t_i, w_i) \in W_i$ and $(u_i, v_i) \in V_i$ if and only if

(3) $$w_i = v_i, \qquad t_i = u_i v_i, \qquad w_i \neq 0,\ v_i \neq 0.$$

$\mathcal{W}$ is a Hausdorff space and, hence, an open complex surface with (t_i, w_i) and (u_j, v_j) as its local coordinates. We can easily prove that $\mathcal{W}$ is simply connected. Let $t = t_i$ on W_i and $t = u_j v_j$ on V_j. Then t is a global holomorphic function on $\mathcal{W}$. Let $\tilde{C} = \{P \in \mathcal{W} \mid t(P) = 0\}$. $\tilde{C}$ consists of infinitely many irreducible components C_i, $i \in \boldsymbol{Z}$, where each C_i is a nonsingular rational curve defined locally by $v_{i+1} = 0$ on V_{i+1} and by $u_i = 0$ on V_i. C_i and C_{i+1} intersect in the origin p_{i+1} of

V_{i+1} transversally. C_i and C_j do not intersect when $i - j \neq \pm 1$. The identifications (1), (2), (3) imply that $\mathscr{W} - \tilde{C}$ is analytically equivalent to $\{(t_0, w_0) \in W_0 \mid t_0 \neq 0\} = \boldsymbol{C}^* \times \boldsymbol{C}$. Let $\tilde{E} = \{(t_0, 0) \in W_0\} = \boldsymbol{C}^*$. $\tilde{E}$ is a *closed* submanifold of $\mathscr{W}$ and does not intersect $\tilde{C}$.

Now we introduce an analytic automorphism g of $\mathscr{W}$ as follows:

(4) *g sends (t_i, w_i) of W_i to $(\alpha t_i, \alpha^{i-1} w_i)$ of W_{i-1},*

(5) *g sends (u_j, v_j) of V_j to $(\alpha^{2-j} u_j, \alpha^{j-1} v_j)$ of V_{j-1},*

where α is a fixed complex number such that $0 < |\alpha| < 1$. By definition, it is clear that

(6) *g sends (t_i, w_i) of W_i to $(\alpha t_i, \alpha^i t_i w_i)$ of W_i*

where $t_i \neq 0$, and

(7) $$g(C_i) = C_{i-1},\ g(p_i) = p_{i-1}.$$

We infer from (6) and (7) that g generates a properly discontinuous group $\langle g \rangle$ of analytic automorphisms of $\mathscr{W}$ free from fixed points. We take subsets D' and D'' of W_0 and V_0, respectively, where

$$D' = \{(t_0, w_0) \in W_0 \mid |w_0| \leqq 1, |t_0| \leqq |\alpha|\} - \{(t_0, w_0) \in W_0 \mid |w_0| < |t_0|/|\alpha|, |t_0| < |\alpha|^2\},$$

and

$$D'' = \{(u_0, v_0) \in V_0 \mid |v_0| \leqq 1, |u_0| \leqq |\alpha|\}.$$

The union $D' \cup D''$ of them in $\mathscr{W}$ is a compact subset of $\mathscr{W}$. Let $D = C_0 \cup D' \cup D''$. Then $\mathscr{W} = \bigcup_{n \in \boldsymbol{Z}} g^n(D)$. We define S to be the quotient surface of $\mathscr{W}$ by $\langle g \rangle$. Then S is a compact complex surface free from singularities. The fundamental group of S is clearly an infinite cyclic group. In particular $b_1(S) = 1$.

Since the subvarieties $\tilde{C}$ and $\tilde{E}$ are invariant by g, S contains two curves, $C = \tilde{C}/\langle g \rangle$ and $E = \tilde{E}/\langle g \rangle$. From (6) and (7) we infer that C is a *rational curve with an ordinary double point* and E is an *elliptic curve* $\boldsymbol{C}^*/\langle \alpha \rangle$. Evidently $C \cdot E = 0$. It follows from (6) that $S - C$ is analytically equivalent to $(\boldsymbol{C}^* \times \boldsymbol{C})/\langle g \rangle$ where $g: (t, w) \to (\alpha t, tw)$ for $(t, w) \in \boldsymbol{C}^* \times \boldsymbol{C}$. This implies that $S - C$ is a line bundle over an elliptic curve with E as its zero section. We define R to be a ruled surface $(\boldsymbol{C}^* \times \boldsymbol{P}^1)/\langle g \rangle$ where $g: (t, w) \to (\alpha t, tw)$ for $(t, w) \in \boldsymbol{C}^* \times \boldsymbol{P}^1$. Let $E_\infty = \{(t, \infty) \mid t \in \boldsymbol{C}^*\}/\langle g \rangle$ and let L be a fibre of R. We identify $S - C$ and $R - E_\infty$.

LEMMA (KODAIRA). *$E + L - E_\infty$ is homologous to zero.*

PROOF. Let

$$\phi(t) = \sum_{k=-\infty}^{\infty} \alpha^{k(k-1)/2} t^k.$$

Then $\phi(t)$ is a holomorphic function of t, $0 < |t| < \infty$, and $\phi(\alpha t) = \phi(t)/t$. Hence $\phi(t) \cdot w$ is invariant by g and is a meromorphic function on R. Since $\phi(-1) = 0$ and

$$\oint_{|t|=1} d \log \phi(t) - \oint_{|t|=|\alpha|} d \log \phi(t) = 2\pi(-1)^{1/2},$$

$\phi(t)$ has exactly one zero in $|\alpha| < |t| \leqq 1$. Hence the divisor of $\phi(t)\cdot w$ is homologically equivalent to $E + L - E_\infty$. Q.E.D.

PROPOSITION 1. *$C^2 = 0$ and $E^2 = -1$.*

PROOF. $\tilde{C}$ consists of irreducible components C_i where C_i, C_{i+1} intersect transversally and C_i, C_j do not intersect when $i - j \neq \pm 1$. The formula (2) implies that $C_i^2 = -2$. Thus $C^2 = 0$. By the above lemma, E is homologically equivalent to $E_\infty - L$. Since $E\cdot L = 1$, we obtain that $E^2 = E\cdot E_\infty - E\cdot L = -1$. Q.E.D.

Let K be the canonical bundle of S. If follows from the definitions that

$$\omega = dw_i \wedge dt_i/w_it_i = dv_j \wedge du_j/v_ju_j$$

is a meromorphic 2-form on $\mathscr{W}$ and is invariant by g. Hence $K = [-C - E]$ and $K^2 = -1$ by Proposition 1.

PROPOSITION 2. *$b_2(S) = 1$.*

PROOF. Since $b_1(S) = 1$, we know that $p_g = \dim H^0(S, \mathcal{O}(K)) = 0$ and $q = \dim H^1(S, \mathcal{O}) = 1$ (see Kodaira [**1**]). By Noether's formula, we obtain that $c_2(S) + K^2 = 0$ where $c_2(S)$ is the Euler number of S. Hence $b_2(S) = c_2(S) = -K^2 = 1$. Q.E.D.

By Propositions 1 and 2, C is homologically equivalent to rE for some rational number r. Since $E\cdot C = 0$ and $E^2 = -1$, we obtain that $r = 0$ and C is homologous to zero.

PROPOSITION 3. *S contains no irreducible curves other than C and E. In particular, S is minimal.*

PROOF. Suppose there exists on S an irreducible curve X other than C and E. Since $X\cdot C = 0$, X is contained in $S - C$. Hence, $X\cdot E_\infty = 0$ and $X\cdot L > 0$ on R, while $X\cdot E + X\cdot L = X\cdot E_\infty$ by the above lemma. Thus $X\cdot E < 0$. This contradicts that $X \neq E$. Q.E.D.

By Propositions 2 and 3, S satisfies the conditions (α) and (β) of Problem 1.

REMARK. By similar methods, we can construct some other examples. But, as yet, we have no general results on Problem 1.

References

1. K. Kodaira, *On the structure of compact complex analytic surfaces*. I, Amer. J. Math. **86** (1964), 751–798. MR **32** #4708.

2. ———, *On the structure of compact complex analytic surfaces*. II, Amer. J. Math. **88** (1966), 682–721. MR **34** #5112.

3. ———, *On the structure of compact complex analytic surfaces*. III, Amer. J. Math. **90** (1968), 55–83. MR **37** #3603.

4. M. Inoue, *On surfaces of class* VII_0, Invent. Math. **24** (1974), 269–310.

AOYAMAGAKUIN UNIVERSITY
TOKYO, JAPAN

Proceedings of the International Congress of Mathematicians
Vancouver, 1974

Algebro-Geometrical Equisingularity and Local Topological Classification of Smooth Mappings

A. N. Varchenko

Two subjects are discussed in this report: The first is the relationship between topological and Zariski's algebro-geometrical approaches to classification of singular points of complex-analytic hypersurfaces and the second is local topological classification of smooth mappings. The fundamental results of this report are formulated in Theorems 1, 2 and 3.

1. Classification of singularities of hypersurfaces. Let P be a singular point of a hypersurface V_r: $f(x_1,\cdots,x_{r+1}) = 0$, $P \in V_r \subset \boldsymbol{C}^{r+1}$, where $\boldsymbol{C}^{r+1}$ is a complex affine $(r + 1)$-space, f is a convergent power series and P is the origin. Suppose we have another hypersurface V'_r of the same dimension r, and a singular point P' on it. The singularities V_r and V'_r at P and P' are called *topologically equivalent* if there exists a local homeomorphism h: $\boldsymbol{C}^{r+1} \to \boldsymbol{C}^{r+1\prime}$, of the ambient affine spaces of V_r and V'_r, which sends P into P' and V_r into V'_r.

Now we shall consider analytic families of hypersurfaces V_r, all having a singular point at the origin and depending on a parameter $t = (t_1, t_2, \cdots, t_s)$. Thus a variable member of this family will be a hypersurface $V_r^{(t)}$, defined by an equation

$$V_r^{(t)}: f(x_1, \cdots, x_{r+1}; t_1, \cdots, t_s) = 0, \tag{1}$$

where f is a convergent power series in $(r + s + 1)$ variables (x), (t), in the neighbourhood of $(x) = 0$, $(t) = 0$, and where $f(0, \cdots, 0; t_1, \cdots, t_s) \equiv 0$. Equation (1) can also be interpreted as an equation of the hypersurface $V_n: f((x); (t)) = 0$, $n = r + s$, $V_n \subset \boldsymbol{C}^{n+1}$. This hypersurface carries the nonsingular manifold W: $x_1 = x_2 = \cdots = x_{r+1} = 0$; $r = \operatorname{cod}_{V_n} W$. Our family of r-dimensional hypersurfaces $V_r^{(t)}$ now appears as a family of sections $V_r^{(\bar{t})}$ of V_n, transversal to W: $V_r^{(\bar{t})} = V_n \cap (t_j = \bar{t}_j, j = 1, 2, \cdots, r)$, the singular point of $V_r^{(\bar{t})}$ being the point $P^{(\bar{t})} =$

$(0, 0, \cdots, 0; \bar{t}_1, \cdots, \bar{t}_s)$. We are interested in the initial zero values of the parameter t and therefore in the pair $(V_r^{(0)}, P^{(0)})$.

DEFINITION. V_n is topologically equisingular at $P^{(0)}$ along W if $(V_r^{(\bar{t})}, P^{(\bar{t})})$ and $(V_r^{(0)}, P^{(0)})$ are topologically equivalent for all $(\bar{t})$ sufficiently close to zero.

Now we give the definition of the so-called algebro-geometrical equisingularity introduced by Zariski. The advantage of this definition over the topological one consists in the possibility of more easily establishing algebraic statements on equisingularities.

Let the parameters $t_1, \cdots, t_s$ in (1) be now denoted by $x_{r+2}, \cdots, x_{n+1}$, where $n = r + s$. Then V is defined by $f(x_1, \cdots, x_{n+1}) = 0$, and P still denotes the origin. Consider a set of n convergent power series in the x's — $z_1, \cdots, z_n : z_i = z_i(x_1, \cdots, x_{n+1}) = z_{i,1} + z_{i,2} + \cdots$ $(i = 1, 2, \cdots, n)$, where $z_{i,\alpha}$ is homogeneous of degree α. We shall say that the n power series $z_1, \cdots, z_n$ form *a set of parameters* if the following two conditions are satisfied:

(a) $(x) = 0$ is an isolated solution of the $n + 1$ equations $z_1(x) = z_2(x) = \cdots = z_n(x) = f(x) = 0$.

(b) The n linear forms $z_{i,1}$ are linearly independent.

If condition (b) is satisfied, then the n linear equations $z_{i,1}(x) = 0$ $(i = 1, \cdots, n)$ define a line l_z through P. If the z_i are parameters, then the n equations $z_i(x) = 0$ $(i = 1, \cdots, n)$ define a regular curve Γ through P whose tangent line is l_z. Let m be the intersection multiplicity of Γ and V at P. The n parameters z_i define a projection π_z of a neighbourhood of P in C^{n+1} onto a neighbourhood of the origin of the affine n-space C^n of the n variables z_i — $\pi_z: C^{n+1} \to C^n$, $\pi_z(x_1, \cdots, x_{n+1}) = (z_i(x), \cdots, z_n(x))$. Let $\pi_{z,V}$ be the restriction of π_z on V. The full inverse image $\pi_{z,V}^{-1}(\bar{z})$ of any point $\bar{z}$ near zero consists of at most m points. The set of critical points $\bar{z}$ for which this full inverse image consists of less than m points is a hypersurface in C^n, which will be denoted by Δ_z and called *the discriminant set*.

Now let W be a singular subvariety of V, of codimension r, having a simple point at P. We shall say that the projection π_z is *permissible* if the line l_z does not touch W at P.

Let π_z be a permissible projection. Then $\pi_z(W)$ is a nonsingular variety $\bar{W}$, of the same dimension as W, with a simple point at $\bar{P} = \pi_z(P)$. Since we assumed that W is a singular subvariety of V, we have $\bar{W} \subset \Delta_z$, $\operatorname{cod}_{\Delta_z} \bar{W} = r - 1$, and we are dealing with a triple $(\Delta_z, \bar{W}, \bar{P})$, in codimension $r - 1$.

If $r = 1$, then $\operatorname{cod}_{\Delta_z} \bar{W} = 0$, i.e., $\bar{W}$ is an irreducible component of Δ_z. In that case equisingularity of Δ_z at $\bar{P}$ along $\bar{W}$ means simply that $\bar{P}$ is a simple point of Δ_z.

DEFINITION. V is algebro-geometrically equisingular at P along W if there exists a permissible projection π_z such that Δ_z is algebro-geometrically equisingular at $\bar{P}$ along $\bar{W}$.

The following question was posed by Zariski in [**1**]: Does algebro-geometrical equisingularity imply topological equisingularity? The interest in this question has been heightened by the fact that in his article [**2**] in 1937 Zariski made use of the similar statement without proof. The affirmative answer to the question would give an opportunity to consider the fundamental theorem of the above-mentioned article about the Poincaré group of complement of projective algebraic hypersurface as correct.

The proof of the affirmative answer to Zariski's question was published by the author in [3]. The other proofs of the Poincaré group theorem were published by H.H.Hamm and Le Dung Trang in [4] and by D. Cheniot in [5].

THEOREM 1. *Let V, W, P be the same as considered above, and V is algebro-geometrically equisingular at P along W. Then there exists a family of sections of V, transversal to W, naturally connected with the triple (V, W, P) and V is topologically equisingular at P, along W, relative to this family of sections.*

It should be noted that homeomorphisms existing by Theorem 1 can be chosen having the following special property: They keep the fibers of the projections defining transitions to the successive discriminant sets. This property of homeomorphisms can be used in proving the existence of local topological classification of smooth mappings.

The theorem is proved by induction on $\operatorname{cod}_V W$. The following lemma is the key to the proof.

LEMMA. *Let $V \subset C^{n+1}$ be a hypersurface, P be a singular point on V, (z) be a set of parameters, $\Delta_z \subset C^n$ be a discriminant set. Suppose there exists an isotopy of couples $\phi:(C^n \times I, \Delta_z \times I) \to (C^n, \Delta_z)$ where I is the segment. Then for any point $\bar{z} \in C^n$ the number of different points in $\pi_{z,V}^{-1}\, \phi(\bar{z} \times t)$, $t \in I$, does not change with changing of t.*

The conclusion of the lemma means that in the ramified cover defined by the projection $\pi_{z,V}$ of V on C^n with a ramification along Δ_z the character of the ramification is defined by the topology of the discriminant set.

2. Local topological classification of smooth mappings. Two germs of mappings f_i: $(N_i, x_i) \to (P_i, y_i)$ $(i = 1, 2)$ where N_i, P_i are topological spaces are called topologically equivalent if there exist germs of homeomorphisms $h:(N_1, x_1) \to (N_2, x_2)$, $g: (P_1, y_1) \to (P_2, y_2)$ such that $f_2 h = g f_1$.

R. Thom conjectured [6] that the relation of topological equivalence defines a partition of the space of all germs of smooth mappings in a countable set of semi-algebraic sets and a set of an infinite codimension.

The conjecture of Thom was proved by the author in [7], [8]. To formulate the result the following notations are introduced.

Let $J(n, p)$ be a space of all germs of C^∞-smooth mappings from R^n into R^p sending the origin in the origin, and $J^r(n, p)$ is the space of its r-jets. The spaces J^r have natural coordinates (values of derivatives in the origin).

THEOREM 2. *Let n and p be natural numbers. Then for any natural r there exists a partition of the space $J^r(n, p)$ in disjoint semi-algebraic sets $V_0, V_1, V_2, \cdots$ having the following properties.*

1. *If* $f_1, f_2 \in J(n,p)$ *are such that* $f_1^{(r)}, f_2^{(r)} \in V_i$, $i > 0$, *then the germs* f_1 *and* f_2 *are topologically equivalent.*

2. *Any germ* $f \in J(n,p)$ *such that* $f^{(r)} \in V_i$, $i > 0$, *is a simplicial mapping for a suitable triangulation of* R^n *and* R^p.

3. *The codimension of* V_0 *in* $J^r(n,p)$ *tends to infinity when r tends to infinity.*

Some words about the proof. The homeomorphisms defining topological equivalence of germs of mappings are constructed in the following way. The graph of mappings are embedded into a certain hypersurface. Then it is proved that this hypersurface is algebro-geometrically equisingular along a certain special submanifold. Then Theorem 1 is applied and the homeomorphisms sought for are constructed from the homeomorphisms of Theorem 1.

Making use of similar ideas the author has proved the following results on topological versal deformations which are important objects connected with germs of mappings [**9**].

THEOREM 3. 1. *Almost all germs of* $J(n,p)$, *except a set of an infinite codimension, have finite-dimensional topological versal deformations.*

2. *Sets of germs of* $J(n,p)$ *having the topologically equivalent versal deformation form a countable set of semi-algebraic subsets in* $J(n,p)$.

3. *The set of all germs, the base of any versal deformation of which has the dimension of no less than r, has codimension no less than r.*

(See the discussion by Thom on the existence of topological versal deformation in [**10**].) In conclusion it should be noted that J.N. Mather has announced [**11**] a theorem on the density of topologically stable mappings in the space of all smooth mappings from one compact manifold into another manifold (not necessarily compact). The author does not know whether Theorem 2 implies Mather's density theorem and whether Theorem 2 can be proved by Mather's methods as J. Mather said to me at this Congress that he did not have a proof of this theorem yet.

Bibliography

1. O. Zariski, *Some open questions in the theory of singularities*, Bull. Amer. Math. Soc. **77** (1971) 481–491. MR **43** #3266.

2. ———, *On the Poincaré group of projective hypersurface*, Ann. of Math. **38** (1937), 131–141.

3. A.H. Варченко, *Связь между топологической и алгебро-геометрическойэ квисингулярностями по Зарискому*, Функц. анализ **7** (1973), 1–5.

4. Helmut H. Hamm et Le Dung Trang, *Un théorème de Zariski du type de Lesfchetz*, Ann. Sci. École Norm. Sup. (4) **6** (1973), 317–366.

5. D. Cheniot, *Une démonstration du théorème de Zariski sur les sections hyperplanes d'une hypersurface projective*, École Polytechnique, Centre de mathématiques, Paris (preprint).

6. R. Thom, *Local topological properties of differentiable mappings*, Differential Analysis (Colloq., 1964), Oxford Univ. Press, London, 1964, pp. 191–202. MR **33** #3307.

7. A.H. Варченко, *Локальные топологические свойства аналитических отображений* Известия АН СССР, серия матем. **37** (1973), 883–916.

8. ———, *Локальные топологические свойства гладких отображений*, Известия АН СССР, серия матем. **38** (1974), 1037–1090.

9. А. Н. Варченко, ***Версальные топологические деформации***, Изв. естия АН СССР, серия матем. **39** (1975), 294–314.

10. R. Thom, *The bifurcation subset of a space of maps*, Manifolds—Amsterdam 1970 (Proc. Nuffic Summer School), Lecture Notes in Math., vol. 197, Springer, Berlin, 1971, pp. 202–208. MR 3 #6941.

11. J. Mather, *Stratifications and mappings*, Harvard, 1971, pp. 1–68 (preprint).

Moscow University
Moscow, U.S.S.R.

Section 5

Algebraic Groups and Discrete Subgroups

Proceedings of the International Congress of Mathematicians
Vancouver, 1974

Cohomology of Arithmetic Groups

Armand Borel

This paper is concerned with the Eilenberg-MacLane cohomology groups $H^i(\Gamma; E)$ of an arithmetic or S-arithmetic subgroup Γ of a reductive affine algebraic group G over a number field, with coefficients in a Γ-module E. For the sake of brevity we shall, however, unless otherwise stated, assume G to be connected, semisimple and the groundfield to be $\boldsymbol{Q}$. Then S is a finite set of rational primes. We recall that a subgroup Γ of the group $G(\boldsymbol{Q})$ of $\boldsymbol{Q}$-rational points of G is arithmetic (resp. S-arithmetic) if, given a $\boldsymbol{Q}$-embedding $\rho : G \to \boldsymbol{GL}_n$, the group $\rho(\Gamma)$ is commensurable with $\rho(G) \cap \boldsymbol{GL}_n(\boldsymbol{Z})$ (resp. $\rho(G) \cap \boldsymbol{GL}_n(\boldsymbol{Z}_S)$, where $\boldsymbol{Z}_S$ is the ring of rational numbers whose denominator is a product of elements in S).

I. General Coefficients

1. *In this section S is fixed, Γ is S-arithmetic, torsion-free.* From G and S alone, one can construct a contractible locally compact $G(\boldsymbol{Q})$-space $\bar{X}_S$, whose ith integral cohomology group with compact supports $H^i_c(\bar{X}_S; \boldsymbol{Z})$ is zero except in one dimension $e = e(G, S)$, where it is a free module I_S, on which Γ operates properly and freely, so that the quotient $\bar{X}_S/\Gamma$ is compact, triangulable. It follows that $\boldsymbol{Z}$ admits a $\boldsymbol{Z}[\Gamma]$-free finitely generated resolution (as was shown first by Raghunathan [27] when Γ is arithmetic (i.e., S is empty) and by J.-P. Serre [28] in general); hence $H^*(\Gamma; E)$ is finitely generated if E is (as a $\boldsymbol{Z}$-module), the cohomological dimension $\mathrm{cd}(\Gamma)$ of Γ is finite, equal to $e(G, S)$, Γ is a duality group in the sense of Bieri-Eckmann [1], and we have a canonical isomorphism

$$H^i(\Gamma; E) \xrightarrow{\sim} H_{e-i}(\Gamma; I_S \otimes E) \qquad (i \in \boldsymbol{Z}) \tag{1}$$

[5], [7]. Let $l = \mathrm{rk}_{\boldsymbol{Q}}\, G$ be the $\boldsymbol{Q}$-rank of G (common dimension of its maximal $\boldsymbol{Q}$-split algebraic tori) and l_p the $\boldsymbol{Q}_p$-rank of G, viewed as a group over the field

$\boldsymbol{Q}_p$ of p-adic numbers ($p \in S$). The space $\bar{X}_S$ is the product of the manifold with corners $\bar{X}$ with interior the symmetric space X of maximal compact subgroups of $G(\boldsymbol{R})$, constructed in [6] (which is just X if $l = 0$), by the Bruhat-Tits buildings T_p of the groups $G(\boldsymbol{Q}_p)$. If $S = \emptyset$, then $\bar{X}_S/\Gamma = \bar{X}/\Gamma$ is a compact manifold with corners, hence triangulable. In the general case, triangulability follows from properties of the projection $\bar{X}_S/\Gamma \to T_S/\Gamma$ (where $T_S = \prod_{p \in S} T_p$) and from results of F. E. A. Johnson [**18**].

REMARK. Even if G is not semisimple, any torsion-free arithmetic subgroup of G is a duality group [**5**], [**7**]. For further examples of discrete subgroups of products of reductive groups over local fields (not necessarily of characteristic zero) which have a homological duality, see [**5**], [**7**].

2. In the general case, Γ possesses torsion-free subgroups of finite index. Their common cohomological dimension is, by definition, the virtual cohomological dimension vcd(Γ) of Γ [**28**], which is then finite, equal to $e(G, S)$. The groups $H^i(\Gamma; E)$ are also finitely generated if E is. The group Γ also acts properly on $\bar{X}_S$ with a compact quotient (presumably triangulable, too, but the author is not aware of any proof outside the torsion-free case), which implies that the finite subgroups of Γ form finitely many conjugacy classes. Further cohomological information on Γ can be extracted from those subgroups; we mention some examples.

2.1. The group Γ and its subgroups of finite index Γ' satisfy the conditions under which an Euler characteristic $\chi(\Gamma') \in \boldsymbol{Q}$, in the sense of C. T. C. Wall, can be defined. It is equal to $\bar{\chi}(\Gamma') = \sum(-1)^i \dim H^i(\Gamma'; \boldsymbol{Q})$ if Γ' is torsion-free and satisfies the condition $\chi(\Gamma'') = [\Gamma' : \Gamma'']\, \chi(\Gamma')$ if $\Gamma'' \subset \Gamma' \subset \Gamma$ and $[\Gamma : \Gamma''] < \infty$. This already implies that $[\Gamma:\Gamma'] \cdot \chi(\Gamma) \in \boldsymbol{Z}$ if Γ' is torsion-free. K. Brown [**8**], however, has given an expression for $\chi(\Gamma) - \bar{\chi}(\Gamma)$, involving the lattice of finite subgroups of Γ, which implies in particular that $m \cdot \chi(\Gamma) \in \boldsymbol{Z}$ as soon as the order of any finite subgroup of Γ divides m. Now let k be a totally real number field, n its degree over Q, $\mathfrak{o}_T$ the ring of elements in k which are integral outside a given finite set T of finite primes of k and $\Gamma = \boldsymbol{SL}_2(\mathfrak{o}_T)$. Let further $\zeta_{k,T}$ be the function obtained from Dedekind's zeta-function ζ_k of k by omitting the local factors associated to the primes in T. Then, by a special case of a formula of G. Harder [**14**], if $S \neq \emptyset$, by [**28**, 3.7] in eneral, we have

$$\chi(\boldsymbol{SL}_2(\mathfrak{o}_T)) = \zeta_{k,T}(-1). \tag{1}$$

The results mentioned above then allow one to get estimates of the denominator of the right-hand side using finite subgroups or subgroups of finite index of Γ. (See [**28**, 3.7], [**8**, § 4], where products of values $\zeta_{k,T}(1-2i)$ $(1 \leq i \leq n)$ are also similarly related to the symplectic groups $\boldsymbol{Sp}_{2n}(\mathfrak{o}_T)$.)

2.2. Given a prime p, there is an algebra A_p over $\boldsymbol{Z}/p\boldsymbol{Z}$ constructed from the category of elementary commutative p-subgroups of Γ, and a homomorphism $H^*(\Gamma, \boldsymbol{Z}/p\boldsymbol{Z}) \to A_p$, whose kernel and cokernel are annihilated by some power of the pth power map [**26**, §§ 14, 15]. Thus, asymptotically, the cohomology mod p is to some extent determined by the commutative elementary p-subgroups of Γ.

2.3. Assume now G to be the algebraic group defined by the elements of norm one in a division algebra D over $\boldsymbol{Q}$, and Γ to be arithmetic. Then, via the regular representation, the finite subgroups of Γ (and even $G(\boldsymbol{Q})$) operate on $\boldsymbol{R}^n - 0$ ($n = [D:\boldsymbol{Q}]$) *freely* since D is a division algebra; hence their cohomology is periodic, of period dividing n. From this, using the spectral sequences of equivariant cohomology theory, B.B. Venkov **[29]** has shown the same to hold for Γ, from a certain dimension on. This is also true if Γ is S-arithmetic; the argument is the same, with $X \times T_S$ (notation of § 1) playing the role of X.

2.4. We note finally that an easy spectral sequence argument shows that if d is a common multiple of the orders of the finite subgroups of Γ, then it annihilates $H^i(\Gamma; E)$ for $i > \mathrm{vcd}(\Gamma)$.

II. Real or Complex Cohomology

3. From now on, E is the space of a finite-dimensional real or complex representation of $G(\boldsymbol{R})$, and, unless otherwise stated, Γ is arithmetic. (In fact, the results recalled in this section and their proofs are valid for any discrete subgroup of $G(\boldsymbol{R})$.) The group $G(\boldsymbol{R})$ operates in a natural way on the space $\Omega_X(E)$ of smooth E-valued differential forms on X, and $H^*(\Gamma; E)$ is canonically isomorphic to the cohomology of the complex $\Omega_X(E)^\Gamma$ of Γ-invariant elements in $\Omega_X(E)$. Fix a maximal compact subgroup K of $G(\boldsymbol{R})$. Using the canonical projection of $G(\boldsymbol{R})/\Gamma$ onto X/Γ, one identifies in a well-known way $\Omega_X(E)^\Gamma$ with a space of smooth vector-valued functions on $G(\boldsymbol{R})/\Gamma$, and this yields in fact a natural isomorphism of $\Omega_X(E)^\Gamma$ with the cochain complex $C^*(\mathfrak{g}, \mathfrak{k}; \mathscr{F} \otimes E)$ of relative Lie algebra cohomology, where, if E is real (resp. complex), $\mathscr{F}$ is the space of smooth real (resp. complex) valued functions on $G(\boldsymbol{R})/\Gamma$, $\mathfrak{g}$ and $\mathfrak{k}$ are the Lie algebras (resp. the complexifications of the Lie algebras) of $G(\boldsymbol{R})$ and K, and $\mathscr{F} \otimes E$ is viewed as a $\mathfrak{g}$-module in the obvious way. Thus we get a canonical isomorphism

$$H^*(\mathfrak{g}, \mathfrak{k}; \mathscr{F} \otimes E) \xrightarrow{\sim} H^*(\Gamma; E). \tag{1}$$

(For all this, see **[23]**, **[24]**; the blanket assumption X/Γ compact made there is not used for these general remarks. Actually, (1) is correct as stated if $G(\boldsymbol{R})$ is connected, also a standing assumption in **[23]**, **[24]**, or if Γ is contained in the identity component of $G(\boldsymbol{R})$. Otherwise, the left-hand side has to be replaced by the invariants under a suitable finite group of automorphisms. We shall ignore this technicality.) Let now $\mathscr{V}$ be a subspace of $\mathscr{F}$ stable under K and $\mathfrak{g}$. The inclusion $\mathscr{V} \otimes E \to \mathscr{F} \otimes E$ then induces homomorphisms

$$j^q : H^q(\mathfrak{g}, \mathfrak{k}; \mathscr{V} \otimes E) \to H^q(\Gamma; E) \qquad (q=0, 1, 2, \cdots) \tag{2}$$

which we shall discuss in three cases (in §§ 4, 6, 7).

4. Stable cohomology. Take $E = \mathscr{V} = \boldsymbol{R}$, with the trivial action of $G(\boldsymbol{R})$, where $\mathscr{V}$ is the space of real constant functions on $G(\boldsymbol{R})/\Gamma$. We have then a natural homomorphism $j^q: H^q(\mathfrak{g}, \mathfrak{k}; \boldsymbol{R}) \to H^q(\Gamma; \boldsymbol{R})$. If Γ is cocompact (i.e., $G(\boldsymbol{R})/\Gamma$ is compact), then $\mathscr{F}$ has a $G(\boldsymbol{R})$-invariant supplement to $\mathscr{V}$; hence j^q is injective for all q (as was remarked first, I think, by W. T. van Est [**9**, Theorem 7], from a different point of view) but this is not so in the noncocompact case. Moreover, again in the cocompact case, but without assuming Γ to be arithmetic, Matsushima has shown j^q to be surjective at least up to a constant $m(G)$ computable from $\mathfrak{g}$ [**21**]. Similarly, in the arithmetic case, we have the following:

THEOREM 4.1. *The homomorphism* j^q *is an isomorphism for* $q < (\mathrm{rk}_{\boldsymbol{Q}}G)/4$.

(See [**3**], [**4**]; the surjectivity part had already been proved in substance by H. Garland [**11**, 3.5] or [**4**, 3.5], and used by him to show that $K_2\mathfrak{o}$ is a torsion group.)

Let G_u be a maximal compact subgroup of $G(\boldsymbol{C})$ containing K. Then $X_u = K^\circ\backslash G_u)$, where K° is the identity component of K, is a compact symmetric space, the "dual" space to X. As is well known, and goes back to E. Cartan, $H^*(\mathfrak{g}, \mathfrak{k}; \boldsymbol{R})$ is canonically isomorphic to $H^*(X_u ; \boldsymbol{R})$, whence a homomorphism $\alpha^* : H^q(X_u ; \boldsymbol{R}) \to H^*(\Gamma ; E)$, which is an isomorphism at least in degrees $< (\mathrm{rk}_{\boldsymbol{Q}}G)/\varphi$.

Let now $(G_n, \Gamma_n, X_n, X_{n,u})$ be objects similar to (G, Γ, X, X_u) and $f_n : (G_n, \Gamma_n) \to (G_{n+1}, \Gamma_{n+1})$ an injective $\boldsymbol{Q}$-morphism ($n = 1, 2, \cdots$). Let $\boldsymbol{X}_u = \mathrm{inj\ lim}\ X_{n,u}$. Assume that $\mathrm{rk}_{\boldsymbol{Q}}\, G_n \to \infty$. Then, for many classical sequences of this type, in particular the one of the next section, there exists, given q, an integer $n(q)$ such that

$$(1)\quad H^q(\boldsymbol{X}_u; \boldsymbol{R}) \cong H^q(\mathrm{inj\ lim}\ \Gamma_n ; \boldsymbol{R}) = H^q(X_{n,u} ; \boldsymbol{R}) = H^q(\Gamma_n ; \boldsymbol{R}) \qquad (n \geqq n(q)).$$

(See [**3**], [**4**] for more precise statements, also pertaining to S-arithmetic groups.)

5. The cohomology of $SL(\mathfrak{o})$, higher regulators and values of ζ-functions. We consider the special case where $G_n = R_{k/\boldsymbol{Q}}\boldsymbol{SL}_n$, $\Gamma_n = \boldsymbol{SL}_n\mathfrak{o}$ (where k is a number field, $\mathfrak{o}$ its ring of integers, $R_{k/\boldsymbol{Q}}$ the restriction of scalars [**30**, Chapter 1]) and f_n comes from the natural inclusion $\boldsymbol{SL}_n \to \boldsymbol{SL}_{n+1}$. Passing to homology, we have then an isomorphism $\alpha_* : H_*(\boldsymbol{SL}(\mathfrak{o}); \boldsymbol{R}) \to H_*(\boldsymbol{X}_u; \boldsymbol{R})$, where $\boldsymbol{SL}(\mathfrak{o}) = \mathrm{inj\ lim}\ \boldsymbol{SL}_n(\mathfrak{o})$. For $m = 1, 2, \cdots$, let P_{2m+1} (resp. P'_{2m+1}) be the space of primitive elements in $H_{2m+1}(\boldsymbol{SL}(\mathfrak{o}); \boldsymbol{R})$ (resp. $H_{2m+1}(\boldsymbol{X}_u; \boldsymbol{R})$). Its dimension d_m is equal to r_2 (resp. $r_1 + r_2$) if $m \geqq 1$ is odd (resp. even), where r_1 (resp. r_2) is the number of real (resp. complex) places of k; this also happens to be the order of the zero of $\zeta_k(s)$ at $s = -m$. There is a natural map of $\pi_{2m+1}(\boldsymbol{X}_u)$ (resp. of Quillen's group $K_{2m+1}\mathfrak{o}$) into P'_{2m+1} (resp. P_{2m+1}), whose image is a lattice L'_{2m+1} (resp. L_{2m+1}). The mth *regulator* of k is then, by definition [**20**, § 4], the positive real number R_m such that the map $\Lambda^{d_m} P_{2m+1} \to \Lambda^{d_m} P'_{2m+1}$ defined by α_* sends $\Lambda^{d_m} L_{2m+1}$ onto $R_m \cdot (\Lambda^{d_m} L'_{2m+1})$.

Given two nonzero real numbers, write $a \sim b$ if a/b is rational.

THEOREM 5.1. *Let D_k be the discriminant of k over $\boldsymbol{Q}$. For $m \geqq 1$, we have*

$$R_m \sim D_k^{1/2} \cdot \pi^{-n(m+1)} \cdot \zeta_k(m+1).$$

According to the functional equation for $\zeta_k(s)$, this is equivalent to

$$R_m \sim \pi^{-d_m} \cdot \lim_{s \to -m} \zeta_k(s)/(s+m)^{d_m}.$$

This, however, says nothing about the actual quotient of these two numbers. According to the conjectures in [**20**, § 4], slightly modified to take into account the factor π^{-d_m}, it should be closely related to the orders of $K_{2m}\mathfrak{o}$ and of the torsion subgroup of $K_{2m+1}\mathfrak{o}$.

REMARK. Applied to other sequences of classical groups, the results of § 6 also yield the ranks of Karoubi's groups ${}_{\varepsilon}L_i\mathfrak{o}$ or ${}_{\varepsilon}L_ik$ (see [3], [4]).

6. Cusp cohomology. We come back to the setting of § 3, assume E to be complex, endowed with a hermitian scalar product invariant under K (or more precisely admissible in the sense of [23]), and fix an invariant measure on $G(\boldsymbol{R})/\Gamma$. This allows one to define a scalar product on compactly supported elements of $C^*(\mathfrak{g}, \mathfrak{k}; \mathscr{F} \otimes E)$ (and then on various bigger spaces), an adjoint ∂ to d, and a Laplace operator $\partial d + d\partial$ [23], [24]. Let ${}^0L^2(G(\boldsymbol{R})/\Gamma)$ be the space of cusp forms in the space $L^2(G(\boldsymbol{R})/\Gamma)$ of complex-valued square-integrable functions on $G(\boldsymbol{R})$ [17], [19]. By a well-known result of Gel'fand and Piateckii-Shapiro [13], [17], it is a direct sum of closed irreducible (under $G(\boldsymbol{R})$) subspaces, with finite multiplicities. Take now for $\mathscr{V}$ the space ${}^0\mathscr{F}$ of C^∞-vectors (in the sense of infinite-dimensional representation theory) of ${}^0L^2(G(\boldsymbol{R})/\Gamma)$. Thus, $\mathscr{V}$ consists of the elements $f \in \mathscr{F}$ such that Xf is square-integrable for every $X \in U(\mathfrak{g})$ and

$$\int_{U(\boldsymbol{R})/(U\cap\Gamma)} f(g\cdot u)\, du = 0 \quad \text{for all } g \in G(\boldsymbol{R}),$$

where U is the unipotent radical of an arbitrary proper parabolic $\boldsymbol{Q}$ subgroup of G.

THEOREM 6.1. *The map* ${}^0j^* : H^*(\mathfrak{g}, \mathfrak{k}; {}^0\mathscr{F} \otimes E) \to H^*(\Gamma; E)$ *is injective.*

Its image will be denoted $H^*_{\text{cusp}}(\Gamma; E)$.

Let r be a finite-dimensional representation of K. For $c \in \boldsymbol{R}$, let $A(r, c)$ be the space of elements in $L^2(G(\boldsymbol{R})/\Gamma)$ which transform according to r with respect to left translations by K and are eigenfunctions of the Casimir operator with eigenvalue c. As is well known, these elements are in fact analytic. Let ${}^0A(r, c) = A(r, c) \cap {}^0L^2(G(\boldsymbol{R})/\Gamma)$.

THEOREM 6.2. *The space* ${}^0A(r, c)$ *is finite-dimensional, contained in the sum of finitely many closed irreducible subspaces of* ${}^0L^2(G(\boldsymbol{R})/\Gamma)$; *in particular, its elements are* Z*-finite* (Z *center of* $U(\mathfrak{g})$), *and are automorphic forms in the sense of* [17], [19]. *Given* r, *the set of* c *for which* ${}^0A(r, c)$ *is* $\neq \{0\}$ *is bounded from above and has no finite accumulation point.*

(6.2, the results below, and those of §7 are joint work of H. Garland and the author; they extend theorems proved by H. Garland for $\boldsymbol{Q}$-rank one groups [10].)

In view of Kuga's formula relating the Laplace operator and the Casimir operator [23], it follows immediately from 6.2 that $H^*(\mathfrak{g}, \mathfrak{k}; {}^0\mathscr{F} \otimes E)$ may be identified with the space of harmonic forms in $C^*(\mathfrak{g}, \mathfrak{k}; {}^0\mathscr{F} \otimes E)$. Thus $H^*_{\text{cusp}}(\Gamma; E)$ is isomorphic to the space of harmonic cusp forms. Assume now E to be irreducible. Let c be such that the Casimir operator on E is $c\cdot\text{Id}$. Write further ${}^0L^2(G(\boldsymbol{R})/\Gamma)$ as a Hilbert direct sum of irreducible subspaces H_i and let c_i be the eigenvalue of C in the space of differentiable vectors of H_i. Then we have

(1) $$H^q_{\text{cusp}}(\Gamma; E) = \bigoplus_{i, c_i = c} \text{Hom}_K(\Lambda^q(\mathfrak{g}/\mathfrak{k}) \otimes E, H_i).$$

If E is the trivial representation, then $c = 0$. In the cocompact case (where ${}^0\mathscr{F} = \mathscr{F}$) the formula overlaps with one of Matsushima's [22]. More generally, 6.2 implies that a number of arguments in the cocompact case (such as the generalized Eichler-Shimura isomorphism in [24, § 7]) or the vanishing theorems in [24, § 11] remain valid for cusp forms and cusp cohomology.

7. Square-integrable cohomology. Take now for $\mathscr{V}$ the space of C^∞-vectors in $L^2(G(\boldsymbol{R})/\Gamma)$. The image of j^* is then the space of cohomology classes which can be represented by square-integrable forms (hence also by square-integrable harmonic forms). It contains the image of the cohomology with compact supports, is equal to it if $G = R_{k/\boldsymbol{Q}}\, \boldsymbol{SL}_2$ by [15], but is bigger in general. However, 6.2, induction and the results of § 7 in [19] allow one to prove that 6.2 remains true if ${}^0A(r, c)$ and ${}^0L^2$ are replaced by $A(r, c)$ and L^2 (this was shown to us by Langlands). In particular, a K-finite eigenfunction of C in $L^2(G(\boldsymbol{R})/\Gamma)$ is Z-finite, contained in the sum of finitely many elements of the discrete spectrum. This is the analogue of a result of Okamoto for $L^2(G(\boldsymbol{R}))$ [25]. It also follows that the space of square-integrable E-valued harmonic forms is finite-dimensional, isomorphic to $H^*(\mathfrak{g}, \mathfrak{k}; \mathscr{V} \otimes E)$ and given by a formula similar to (1), but where ${}^0L^2$ is replaced by the discrete spectrum in $L^2(G(\boldsymbol{R})/\Gamma)$, if E is irreducible.

8. The $\boldsymbol{Q}$-rank one case. Assume now $\mathrm{rk}_{\boldsymbol{Q}}\, G = 1$. The manifold with corners $V = \bar{X}/\Gamma$ is then in fact a manifold with boundary, and the connected components of its boundary ∂V correspond bijectively to the Γ-conjugacy classes of minimal parabolic $\boldsymbol{Q}$-subgroups of G [2, § 17]. Let $r: H^*(V; E) \to H^*(\partial V; E)$ be the restriction homomorphism. Using Langlands' theory of Eisenstein series [17], [19], G. Harder has shown the existence of a subspace $H^*_{\mathrm{inf}}(\Gamma; E)$ of $H^*(\Gamma; E) \cong H^*(V; E)$, which restricts isomorphically onto Im r, whose elements are obtained either by taking analytic continuation of suitable Eisenstein series, or residues of such at simple poles [16]. Thus, in this case, every element of $H^*(\Gamma; E)$ has a closed harmonic representative. If $G = R_{k/\boldsymbol{Q}}\boldsymbol{SL}_2$, and $E = \boldsymbol{C}$, G. Harder has given a complete description of Im r; moreover, $H^*(\Gamma; \boldsymbol{C})$ is in this case the direct sum of H^*_{inf}, H^*_{cusp}, and the image of $H^*(\mathfrak{g}, \mathfrak{k}; \boldsymbol{C})$ [15].

9. No such results have yet been obtained in the higher rank case. Still, they point to extremely interesting relations between $H^*(\Gamma; E)$ and the theory of automorphic forms, and lead one to wonder whether (a) all cohomology classes are represented by closed harmonic forms; (b) there is a sum decomposition of $H^*(\Gamma; E)/H^*_{\mathrm{cusp}}(\Gamma; E)$, where each summand is naturally associated to Eisenstein series built from a class $\{P\}$ of associated proper parabolic $\boldsymbol{Q}$-subgroups, starting from harmonic cusp forms on pieces of the boundary of the manifold with corners $\bar{X}/\Gamma$ corresponding to the elements of $\{P\}$.

Finally, I would like to draw attention to two topics left out of this survey: vanishing theorems for subgroups of p-adic groups and related questions, for which we refer to H. Garland's article [12], and the use of cohomology of arithmetic groups in the discussion of zeta-functions or L-functions of certain algebraic varieties

(Eichler, Shimura and, more recently, I. I. Piateckii-Shapiro and R. P. Langlands (in *Modular functions of one variable*. II, Springer Lecture Notes in Mathematics, vol. 349) for modular curves; Shimura, Kuga-Shimura and Langlands for other quotients of bounded symmetric domains).

References

1. R. Bieri and B. Eckmann, *Groups with homological duality generalizing Poincaré duality*, Invent. Math. **20** (1973), 103–124.

2. A. Borel, *Introduction aux groupes arithmétiques*, Publ. Inst. Math. Univ. Strasbourg, 15, Actualités Sci. Indust., no. 1341, Hermann, Paris, 1969. MR **39** #5577.

3. ———, *Cohomologie réelle stable de groupes S-arithmétiques classiques*, C. R. Acad. Sci. Paris Sér. A-B 274 (1972), A1700-A1702. MR **46** #7400.

4. ———, *Stable real cohomology of arithmetic groups*, Ann. Sci. École Norm. Sup. (4) **7** (1974), 235–272.

5. A. Borel and J.-P. Serre, *Cohomologie à supports compacts des immeubles de Bruhat-Tits; applications à la cohomologie des groupes S-arithmétiques*, C. R. Acad Sci. Paris Sér. A-B **272** (1971), A110-A113. MR **43** #221.

6. ———, *Corners and arithmetic groups*, Comment. Math. Helv. **48** (1974), 244–297.

7. ———, *Cohomologie d'immeubles et de groupes S-arithmétiques* (in preparation).

8. K. Brown, *Euler-characteristics of discrete groups and G-spaces*, Invent. Math. **27** (1974), 229–264.

9. W. T. van Est, *A generalization of the Cartan-Leray spectral sequence*. I, II, Nederl. Akad. Wetensch. Proc. Ser. A **61** = Indag. Math. **20** (1958), 399–413. MR **21** #2236.

10. H. Garland, *The spectrum of noncompact G/Γ and the cohomology of arithmetic groups*, Bull. Amer. Math. Soc. **75** (1969), 807–811. MR **40** #269.

11. ———, *A finiteness theorem for K_2 of a number field*, Ann. of Math. (2) **94** (1971), 534–548. MR **45** #6785.

12. ———, *On the cohomology of arithmetic groups*, these PROCEEDINGS.

13. I. M. Gel'fand and I. I. Pjateckiĭ-Šapiro, *Automorphic functions and representation theory*, Trudy Moskov. Mat. Obšč. **12** (1963), 389–412 =Trans. Moscow Math. Soc. **1963**, 438–464. MR **28** #3115.

14. G. Harder, *A Gauss-Bonnet formula for discrete arithmetically defined groups*, Ann. Sci. École Norm. Sup. **4** (1971), 409–455. MR **46** #8255.

15. ———, *On the cohomology of* $\boldsymbol{SL}(2, \mathfrak{o})$ (preprint).

16. ———, *On the cohomology of discrete arithmetically defined groups*, Proc. Internat. Colloquium Bombay 1972 (to appear).

17. Harish-Chandra, *Automorphic forms on semisimple Lie groups*, Lecture Notes in Math., no. 62, Springer-Verlag, Berlin and New York, 1968. MR **38** #1216.

18. F. E. A. Johnson, *On the triangulation of stratified sets and singular varieties* (to appear).

19. R. P. Langlands, *On the functional equations satisfied by Eisenstein series*, Proc. Sympos. Pure Math., vol. 9, Amer. Math. Soc., Providence, R.I., 1965, pp. 235–252. MR **40** #2784.

20. S. Lichtenbaum, *Values of zeta-functions, étale cohomology, and algebraic K-theory*, Algebraic *K*-Theory. II, Lecture Notes in Math., no. 342, Springer-Verlag, New York, 1973, pp. 489–499.

21. Y. Matsushima, *On Betti numbers of compact, locally symmetric Riemannian manifolds*, Osaka Math. J. **14** (1962), 1–20. MR **25** #4549.

22. ———, *A formula for the Betti numbers of compact locally symmetric Riemannian manifolds*, J. Differential Geometry **1** (1967), 99–109. MR **36** #5958.

23. Y. Matsushima and S. Murakami, *On vector bundle valued harmonic forms and automorphic forms on symmetric Riemannian manifolds*, Ann. of Math. (2) **78** (1963), 365–416. MR **27** #2997.

24. ———, *On certain cohomology groups attached to Hermitian symmetric spaces*, Osaka J. Math. **2** (1965), 1–35. MR **32** #1728.

25. K. Okamoto, *On induced representations*, Osaka J. Math. **4** (1967), 85–94. MR **37** #1519.

26. D. G. Quillen, *The spectrum of an equivariant cohomology ring*. I, II, Ann. of Math. (2) **94** (1971), 549–572, 573–602. MR **45** #7743.

27. M. S. Raghunathan, *A note on quotients of real algebraic groups by arithmetic subgroups*, Invent. Math. **4** (1967/68). 318–335. MR **37** #5894.

28. J.-P. Serre, *Cohomologie des groupes discrets*, Prospects in Mathematies, Ann. of Math. Studies, no. 70, Princeton Univ. Press, Princeton, N.J., 1971, pp. 77–169.

29. B. B. Venkov, *On homologies of unit groups in division algebras*, Trudy Mat. Inst. Steklov. **80** (1965), 66–89 = Proc. Steklov Inst. Math. **80** (1965), 73–100. MR **34** #1379.

30. A. Weil, *Adèles and algebraic groups*, Notes by M. Demazure and T. Ono, Institute for Advanced Study, Princeton, N.J., 1961.

INSTITUTE FOR ADVANCED STUDY
PRINCETON, NEW JERSEY 08540, U.S.A.

bhandlungen des Internationalen Kongress der Mathematiker
ancouver, 1974

Singularitäten von Modulmannigfaltigkeiten und Körper Automorpher Funktionen

Eberhard Freitag

Die analytische Theorie der Modulformen mehrerer Veränderlicher erhielt einen eträchtlichen Aufschwung durch die "Kompaktifizierungstheorien", welche von atake begründet wurden. Entscheidend weiterentwickelt wurden sie von Baily nd zur höchsten Allgemeinheit gebracht von Baily und Borel.

Wir erinnern kurz an das Hauptresultat. Sei D ein beschränktes symmetrisches iebiet im $\boldsymbol{C}^N$ und Γ eine diskontinuierliche Gruppe analytischer Automorphismen on D, welche arithmetisch definiert ist. Dann ist D/Γ eine quasiprojektive alebraische Mannigfaltigkeit (i.a. mit Singularitäten) mit einer natürlichen Kom-aktifizierung $\overline{D/\Gamma}$, welche nichts anderes ist, als die projektive algebraische Man-igfaltigkeit, die dem graduierten Ring der Modulformen

$$A(\Gamma) = \sum_{r=0}^{\infty} [\Gamma, r]$$

ugeordnet ist. Hierbei ist $[\Gamma, r]$ der Raum der Modulformen in bezug auf den utomorphiefaktor

$$j(z, \gamma)^r, j(z, \gamma) = \det\left(\frac{\partial \gamma_\nu}{\partial z_\mu}\right).$$

ass obige Algebra endlich erzeugt ist, gehört zu den Hauptresultaten der Kom-aktifizierungstheorie.

Die Mannigfaltigkeit $\overline{D/\Gamma}$ hat i.a. Singularitäten. Insbesondere die Punkte im Jnendlichen $\overline{D/\Gamma} - D/\Gamma$ sind—von einigen Ausnahmen abgesehen—hochkompli-ierte Singularitäten. Es ist ein wichtiges Problem, die Natur dieser Singularitäten ufzuklären. Aufgrund der Desingularisierungstheorie von Hironaka existiert eine Auflösung $\pi : \tilde{X} \to X$, $X = \overline{D/\Gamma}$. Im Falle der Hilbertschen Modulflächen konstruierte Hirzebruch explizit die minimale Auflösung und benutzte sie, um den Typ von $\tilde{X}$ im Sinne von Kodaira (rough classification) zu bestimmen.

Einige der Resultate Hirzebruchs kann man auch ohne Benutzung einer expliziten Desingularisierung beweisen und auf beliebige Dimensionen verallgemeinern. Es gibt in höheren Dimensionen auch interessante Phänomene, welche im Falle der Hilbertschen Modulflächen nicht auftreten.

Wir wollen nun etwas mehr ins Detail gehen. Unter $\Omega^\nu(Y)$ verstehen wir den Raum der holomorphen Differentialformen vom Grade ν auf einer analytischen Mannigfaltigkeit Y.

Im Folgenden machen wir die Voraussetzung

$$\dim(\overline{D/\Gamma} - D/\Gamma) + 2 \leqq \dim D/\Gamma = N.$$

(Dadurch wird im wesentlichen nur der Fall $N = 1$ ausgeschlossen.)

1. Bemerkung: *Man hat einen natürlichen Isomorphismus*

$$\Omega^N(X_{\text{reg}}) \xrightarrow{\sim} [\Gamma, 1]$$

(X_{reg} = *regulärer Ort von* X).

(Durch Restriktion dieses Isomorphismus erhält man eine Einbettung $\Omega^N(\tilde{X}) \hookrightarrow [\Gamma, 1]$.)

2. Satz. *Das Bild von* $\Omega^N(\tilde{X})$ *in* $[\Gamma, 1]$ *stimmt überein mit dem Raum der Spitzenformen* $[\Gamma, 1]_0$.

Die Dimension $g_\nu(\tilde{X}) = \dim \Omega^\nu(\tilde{X})$ hängt nicht ab von der Wahl der Auflösung $\tilde{X}$ und ist daher eine Invariante des Körpers der Modulfunktionen $K(\Gamma)$ (= Körper der rationalen Funktionen auf X).

Ist beispielsweise $K(\Gamma)$ *eine rein transzendente Erweiterung von* $\mathbf{C}$, *so ist* $\dim [\Gamma, 1]_0 = 0$.

Von einigen Spezialfällen abgesehen, konnten die Invarianten g_ν nur für Gruppen berechnet werden, die mit der Hilbertschen Modulgruppe kommensurabel sind.

3. Theorem **[1]**. *Sei* Γ *eine Gruppe von simultan gebrochen linearen Substitutionen*

$$(z_1, \cdots, z_N) \to \left(\frac{a_1 z_1 + b_1}{c_1 z_1 + d_1}, \cdots, \frac{a_N z_N + b_N}{c_N z_N + d_N}\right),$$

welche mit der Hilbertschen Modulgruppe eines total reellen Zahlkörpers kommensurabel ist, Dann gilt:

(a) $g_0(X_{\text{reg}}) = g_0(\tilde{X}) = 1$,

(b) $g_\nu(X_{\text{reg}}) = g_\nu(\tilde{X}) = 0$ *für* $0 < \nu < N$,

(c) $g_N(X_{\text{reg}}) = g_N(\tilde{X}) + h = (-1)^N(P_\Gamma(0) - h - 1)$.

Dabei ist h die Anzahl der *Spitzenklassen* von Γ und $g_\nu(-) = \dim \Omega^\nu(-)$; mit P_Γ wird das *Hilbertpolynom* von $A(\Gamma)$ bezeichnet.

$$P_\Gamma(r) = \dim [\Gamma, r] \quad \textit{für } r \equiv 0 \bmod r_0 \text{ (geeignet)}, \ r \gg 0.$$

Das Polynom P_Γ wurde von Shimizu mit Hilfe der Selbergschen Spurformel berechnet.

BEISPIEL. Sei Γ torsionsfrei und N ungerade. Dann gilt

$$\dim [\Gamma, r]_0 = \dim [\Gamma, r] - h = v(D/\Gamma) \cdot (2r - 1)^N \quad \text{für } r > 1.$$

Es folgt mit Hilfe des Theorems 3 $\dim [\Gamma, 1]_0 > 0$. Der Körper $K(\Gamma)$ kann nicht rein tranzendent sein!

Bevor wir die Hilbertsche Modulgruppe weiter behandeln, wollen wir etwas die allgemeine Situation erläutern.

(1) Es gibt eine Formel, welche das arithmetische Geschlecht $g(K(\Gamma))$ von $K(\Gamma)$ (d.h. eines singularitätenfreien Modells) durch die Werte von Hilbertpolynomen ausdrückt, welche im Prinzip mit Hilfe der Selbergschen Spurformel berechnet werden können.

BEISPIEL. Sei S_n die Siegelsche Halbebene und Γ eine Gruppe, welche mit der Siegelschen Modulgruppe kommensurabel ist, aber keine Torsion hat. Den verschiedenen Randkomponenten $(n - 1)$-ten Grades entsprechen ebensolche Gruppen $\Gamma_1, \cdots, \Gamma_h$ auf S_{n-1}. Bezeichnet man mit P bzw. $P_1, \cdots, P_h$ die Hilbertpolynome der entsprechenden Algebren von Modulformen, so gilt

$$g(K(\Gamma)) := \sum_{\nu=1}^{N} (-1)^\nu g_\nu(\tilde{X}) = P(1) - \sum_{\nu=1}^{h} P_\nu\left(\frac{N+1}{N}\right) \qquad \left(N = \frac{n(n+1)}{2}\right).$$

Unglücklicherweise hat bis jetzt niemand im Falle der Siegelschen Modulgruppe Γ_n, $n > 2$, eine endliche Form der Selbergschen Spurformel für $\dim [\Gamma_n, r]$ ausgearbeitet. Man darf aber hoffen, dass dies eines Tages geschieht.

(2) Die Invarianten $g_\nu(X_0)$, $1 < \nu < N$, verschwinden im allgemeinen nicht.

Ist Γ kommensurabel mit der Siegelschen Modulgruppe, so gilt wohl

$$g_\nu(X_{\text{reg}}) = 0 \quad \text{für } 0 < \nu < n \; (= \text{Rang } S_n).$$

Aber mithilfe der Theorie der Theta-Nullwerte kann man holomorphe alternierende Differentialformen vom Grad $N - 1$ zu gewissen von Igusa definierten Kongruenzuntergruppen der Siegelschen Modulgruppe konstruieren. Es gilt also $\Omega^{N-1}(X_{\text{reg}}) \neq 0$ im allgemeinen.

(3) Im Falle der Hilbertschen Modulgruppe sind die Spitzen isolierte Punkte. Allgemein liegen jedoch auch höherdimensionale Randkomponenten vor.

Ich möchte nun die Spitzen der Hilbertschen Modulgruppe genauer beschreiben.

Sei $\mathfrak{t}$ ein Gitter vom Rang N in einem total reellen Zahlkörper L vom Grad N und Λ eine Untergruppe von endlichem Index in der Gruppe aller total positiven Einheiten, welche auf $\mathfrak{t}$ operiert, $\Lambda \cdot \mathfrak{t} \subset \mathfrak{t}$. Diesen beiden Daten ist eine N-dimensionale analytische Singularität, die Spitze, zugeordnet.

Wir wollen uns hier damit begnügen, die Komplettierung des lokalen Ringes in dieser Spitze zu beschreiben.

Der formale Gruppenring $\boldsymbol{C}[[\mathfrak{t}^+]]$ über der Halbgruppe

$$\mathfrak{t}^+ = \{x \in \mathfrak{t}, x > 0 \text{ (total positiv) oder } x = 0\}$$

besteht aus allen Abbildungen $f : \mathfrak{t}^+ \to \boldsymbol{C}$, wobei die Multiplikation durch

$$f \cdot g(x) = \sum_{x'+x''=x} f(x')\, g(x'')$$

erklärt ist. Diese Summe ist endlich! Die Gruppe Λ operiert auf diesem Ring. Der Fixring wird mit $R = \boldsymbol{C}[[\mathfrak{t}^+]]^\Lambda$ bezeichnet.

4. THEOREM [**2**]. *Der Ring R hat folgende Eigenschaften*:

(1) *Er ist ein noetherscher lokaler vollständiger normaler Ring der Dimension N.*

(2) *Die Tiefe von R (homologische Kodimension) ist zwei.*

(3) *Der kanonische Modul von R ist isomorph zu R.*

(4) *Die Divisorenklassengruppe von R ist* Hom $(\mathfrak{t}^+ \cdot \Lambda,\ \boldsymbol{C}^*)$ (*mit* $\mathfrak{t}^+ \cdot \Lambda$ *wird das semidirekte Produkt bezeichnet*).

(5) *Im Falle* $N \geqq 3$ *ist der Ring R starr.*

In Wirklichkeit wissen wir über den Ring R noch sehr viel genauer Bescheid. Der Raum Spec $R - \{\mathfrak{m}\}$ ist singularitätenfrei; die Elemente der lokalen Divisorenklassengruppe entsprechen also genau den Isomorphieklassen von Geradenbündeln auf diesem Raum. Die Kohomologie all dieser Geradenbündel ist explizit bestimmt.

Obwohl obiges Theorem rein algebraisch formuliert werden konnte, erfordert sein Beweis die analytische Realisierung von R:

$$R = \hat{\mathcal{O}}_{X_{\infty},\infty}; \qquad X_\infty = H^N/\mathfrak{t}^+ \cdot \Lambda \cup \{\infty\}.$$

Wir nehmen nun an, dass der Körper L eine Galoissche Erweiterung von $\boldsymbol{Q}$ ist. Die Galoisgruppe G möge $\mathfrak{t}$ und Λ in sich überführen. Sie operiert dann auch auf R und man kann den Ring R^G betrachten. Auch dessen Tiefe kann berechnet werden.

Im Falle $N \geqq 3$ gilt

$$\begin{aligned} \text{Tiefe } R^G &= 4 \quad \text{falls } G \cong \boldsymbol{Z}/2 \times \cdots \times \boldsymbol{Z}/2, \\ &= 3 \quad \text{sonst.} \end{aligned}$$

Die Divisorenklassengruppe von R^G ist Hom$(\mathfrak{t} \cdot \Lambda \cdot G,\ \boldsymbol{C}^*)$. Dies ist eine endliche Gruppe! Der Ring R^G ist also ein *fastfaktorieller Ring.*

Immer dann, wenn die Gruppe G halbeinfach ist, kann man $\mathfrak{t}$ und Λ so konstruieren, dass R^G ein ZPE-Ring ist. Mithilfe der klassischen Invariantentheorie können total reelle Zahlkörper zur alternierenden Gruppe fünften Grades A_5 konstruiert werden. *Damit erhält man Beispiele* 60-*dimensionaler ZPE-Ringe der Tiefe drei.*

Wir wollen nun noch auf einige globale Eigenschaften der Hilbertschen Modulmannigfaltigkeiten eingehen.

Ist Y ein komplexer Raum, so setzen wir $h^\nu(Y) = \dim H^\nu(Y, \mathcal{O}_Y)$. Sei wiederum $\Gamma \subset \mathrm{SL}(2, \boldsymbol{R})^N$ eine diskrete Untergruppe, welche mit der Hilbertschen Modulgruppe kommensurabel ist.

5. THEOREM [**1**]. *Es gilt*

$$\begin{aligned} h^\nu(X_0) &= 1 \quad \textit{für } \nu = 0, \\ &= \infty \quad \textit{für } \nu = N-1;\ X_0 = H^N/\Gamma, \\ &= 0 \quad \textit{sonst}; \end{aligned}$$

$$\begin{aligned} h^\nu(X) &= 1 && \textit{für } \nu = 0, \\ &= h\cdot\binom{n-1}{\nu-1} && \textit{für } 1 \leqq \nu \leqq N-1, \\ &= \dim[\Gamma, 1] && \textit{für } \nu = N, \\ &= 0 && \textit{sonst}; \end{aligned}$$

$$\begin{aligned} h^\nu(\tilde{X}) &= 1 && \textit{für } \nu = 0, \\ &= \dim\,[\Gamma, 1]_0 && \textit{für } \nu = N, \\ &= 0 && \textit{sonst}. \end{aligned}$$

Die singuläre Kohomologie von X_0 wurde von Harder bestimmt [**4**]. Der Unterraum aller Kohomologieklassen aus $H^\cdot(X_0, \boldsymbol{C})$, welche im de Rham-Komplex durch quadratintegrierbare Differentialformen repräsentiert werden können, wird mit $\tilde{H}^\cdot(X_0, \boldsymbol{C})$ bezeichnet. Seine Kodimension kann man mithilfe der Theorie der Eisensteinreihen berechnen.

6. THEOREM [4].

$$\begin{aligned} \dim H^\nu(X_0, \boldsymbol{C}) - \dim \tilde{H}^\nu(X_0, \boldsymbol{C}) &= 1 && \textit{für } \nu = 0, \\ &= 0 && \textit{für } 1 \leqq \nu \leqq n-1, \\ &= h\cdot\binom{n-1}{\nu-n} && \textit{für } n \leqq \nu \leqq 2n-2, \\ &= h-1 && \textit{für } \nu = 2n-1, \\ &= 0 && \textit{für } \nu \geqq 2n. \end{aligned}$$

Die Differentialformen $(dx_\nu \wedge dy_\nu)/y_\nu^2$, $1 \leqq \nu \leqq N$, sind invariant und definieren Kohomologieklassen ω_ν aus $\tilde{H}^\cdot(X_0, \boldsymbol{C})$. Sie erzeugen einen Unterring $H^\cdot_{\text{univ}}(X_0, \boldsymbol{C})$. Definierende Relation ist $\omega_1 \wedge \cdots \wedge \omega_N = 0$. Man hat eine Zerlegung

$$\tilde{H}^\cdot(X_0, \boldsymbol{C}) = H^\cdot_{\text{univ}}(X_0, \boldsymbol{C}) \oplus H^\cdot_{\text{cusp}}(X_0, \boldsymbol{C}),$$

wobei in $H^\cdot_{\text{cusp}}(X_0, \boldsymbol{C})$ alle Kohomologieklassen zusammengefasst sind, welche sich durch Spitzenformen darstellen lassen. Diese werden wir nun genau beschreiben. Jeder Teilmenge $I \subset \{1, \cdots, N\}$ ordnen wir eine mit Γ kommensurable Gruppe Γ^I zu. Sie entsteht aus Γ durch Konjugation mit dem Automorphismus

$$\sigma(z_1, \cdots, z_N) = (w_1, \cdots, w_N); \quad \begin{aligned} w_\nu &= z_\nu && \textit{für } \nu \in I, \\ &= -\bar{z}_\nu && \textit{für } \nu \notin I. \end{aligned}$$

Die Zuordnung $f \mapsto \sigma^*(f(z_1, \cdots, z_N)dz_1 \wedge \cdots \wedge dz_N)$ induziert eine Einbettung $[\Gamma^I, 1]_0 \subsetneq H^N_{\text{cusp}}(X_0, \boldsymbol{C})$.

7. THEOREM ([**4**], [**5**]).

$$\begin{aligned} H^\nu_{\text{cusp}}(X_0, \boldsymbol{C}) &= 0 \quad \textit{für } \nu \neq N, \\ H^N_{\text{cusp}}(X_0, \boldsymbol{C}) &= \bigoplus_{I \subset \{1, \cdots, N\}} [\Gamma^I, 1]_0. \end{aligned}$$

Die Dimensionen von $[\Gamma^I, 1]_0$ konnen mithilfe Shimizus Formeln ausgedrückt werden (Theorem 3) Sie hängen i.a. von I ab! Die Differenzen lassen sich durch

Werte von L-Reihen ausdrücken. Die Berechnung der Kohomologie von X_0 hat folgende Anwendung.

8. THEOREM [3]. *Im Falle* $N \geqq 3$ *gilt*

(a) Pic $X_0 \cong \boldsymbol{Z}^{N-1} \oplus \Gamma/[\Gamma, \Gamma]$.

Die Kommutatorgruppe $[\Gamma, \Gamma]$ *hat endlichen Index in* Γ (*sogar für* $N \geqq 2$).

(b) Pic $X \cong \boldsymbol{Z}$.

Die Aussage (a) kann man elementarer auch folgendermassen aussprechen. Ist

$$\mathscr{T}(z, M) \in \hat{Z}(\Gamma, \mathcal{O}^*(H^N))$$

ein analytischer *Automorphiefaktor* von Γ, so existiert dine holomorphe nirgends verschwindende Funktion $h\colon H^N \to \boldsymbol{C}$ mit der Eigenschaft

$$\left|\mathscr{T}(z,M)\cdot\frac{h(Mz)}{h(z)}\right| = \prod_{\nu=1}^{N} | c_\nu z_\nu + d_\nu |^{r_\nu}.$$

Die Zahlen r_ν sind rational und ihre Nenner sind beschränkt. Studiert man die Kohomologie der Geradenbündel auf X_0 so stösst man auf interessante Probleme. Aus den bisher bekannten Resultaten lässt sich u.a. folgern, dass die Hilbertschen Modulmannigfaltigkeiten im Falle $N \geqq 3$ starr sind im Sinne der Deformationstheorie komplexer Räume.

Literatur

1. E. Freitag, *Lokale und globale Invarianten der Hilbertschen Modulgruppe*, Invent. Math. **17** (1972) 106–134. MR **47** #6612.

2. E. Freitag und R. Kiehl, *Algebraische Eigenschaften der lokalen Ringe in den Spitzen der Hilbertschen Modulgruppen*, Invent. Math. **24** (1974), 121–148.

3. E. Freitag, *Automorphy-factors of Hilbert's modular group* (preprint).

4. G. Harder, *On the cohomology of* SL(2, σ) (preprint).

5. Y. Matsushima and G. Shimura, *On the cohomology groups attached to certain vector valued differential forms on the product of the upper half planes*, Ann. of Math. (2) **78** (1963), 417–449. MR **27** #5273.

UNIVERSITY OF MAINZ
65 MAINZ, FEDERAL REPUBLIC OF GERMANY

Proceedings of the International Congress of Mathematicians
Vancouver, 1974

On the Cohomology of Discrete Subgroups of p-adic Groups

Howard Garland

0. Introduction. In [1], Borel will give a survey of recent results on the cohomology of arithmetic groups in the real case. In this article we will emphasize the p-adic case. Thus, let k_v be a nondiscrete, locally compact field which is totally disconnected. Let $\boldsymbol{G}$ be a semisimple, linear algebraic group defined over k_v, let l be the k_v-rank of $\boldsymbol{G}$, and let G be the k_v-rational points of $\boldsymbol{G}$. Let $\Gamma \subset G$ be a discrete subgroup, which for the moment we assume to be uniform and torsion-free (where "uniform" means that the quotient G/Γ is compact). In this article we shall discuss three related questions:

(i) For $i \neq l$, what is the dimension of $H^i(\Gamma, \boldsymbol{R})$, the ith Eilenberg-MacLane group of Γ with respect to trivial action on $\boldsymbol{R}$?

(ii) What is the Euler characteristic

$$\chi(\Gamma) = \sum_i (-1)^i \dim H^i(\Gamma, \boldsymbol{R})?$$

(It is known that Γ has finite cohomological dimension equal to l and that each $H^i(\Gamma, \boldsymbol{R})$ is finite dimensional.)

(iii) What is the multiplicity of the special representation in $L^2(G/\Gamma)$?

Also, we shall consider generalizations and extensions of such matters. Thus, in § 2 we shall consider the case when G/Γ is not compact. Also, we shall see that our methods apply to certain (not necessarily discrete) subgroups of real Lie groups (see § 4).

1. First statement of results. Let V be a finite-dimensional, complex vector space with a positive-definite Hermitian inner product, and let $\rho : \Gamma \to \mathrm{Aut}(V)$ be a unitary representation of Γ. Let $H^i(\Gamma, \rho)$ be the ith cohomology group of Γ with respect to ρ. With regard to (i), I proved in [**6**]:

THEOREM 1.1. *There exists an integer $N = N(l)$, depending only on l, so that if G is simply connected, k_v-simple of k_v-rank l, if the residue class field of k_v has at least N elements, and if $\Gamma \subset G$ is a discrete, uniform subgroup, then*

$$H^i(\Gamma, \rho) = 0, \qquad 0 < i < l. \tag{1.2}$$

REMARK. In [**2**], Borel observed that one could drop the restriction that G be simply connected.

The proof of Theorem 1.1 in [**6**] depends on the geometry of the Bruhat-Tits building and a p-adic analogue of Riemannian curvature, which I called "p-adic curvature." It seems likely to me that curvature arguments could be used to eliminate the restriction on the residue class field. For certain i and G, I have been able to do this. Also, Borel and I proved (1.2) when G is semisimple and $\Gamma \subset G$ is irreducible in the sense that Γ has a dense projection off of each factor of G (and again for large residue fields). Recently, using the Bruhat-Tits building, representation theory of p-adic groups, and a different method from mine, W. Casselman has been able to eliminate the restriction on the residue class field, and thus prove (see [**3**]):

THEOREM 1.3. *If G is semisimple of k_v-rank l, if $\Gamma \subset G$ is discrete, uniform and irreducible, then* (1.2) *holds.*

Later on I shall comment briefly on the two methods of proof, and shall indicate a relation between the two approaches which was discovered by Borel. Also, we mention that (1.2) was conjectured by Serre.

With regard to problem (ii), we have Serre's result (see [**8**]):

THEOREM 1.4. *Let G be semisimple of rank l over k_v and let Γ be torsion-free; then $\chi(\Gamma)$ has sign $(-1)^l$.*

The proof of Theorem 1.4 is based on the existence of what Serre calls an Euler-Poincaré measure, where

DEFINITION. A (necessarily bi-invariant) Haar measure μ_G on G is called an Euler-Poincaré measure, in case for every uniform, discrete, torsion-free subgroup $\Gamma \subset G$, we have

$$\chi(\Gamma) = \int_{\Gamma\backslash G} \mu_G.$$

Thus, to prove Theorem 1.4, it suffices to compute the sign of μ_G. This is what Serre did in [**8**]. Also, he observed there that Γ has a free, simplicial action on an acyclic, l-dimensional complex, and hence $H^i(\Gamma, \boldsymbol{R}) = 0$, for $i > l$. Thus Theorem 1.3 and the existence of an Euler-Poincaré measure imply

$$\int_{\Gamma\backslash G} \mu_G = 1 + (-1)^l \dim H^l(\Gamma, \boldsymbol{R}), \tag{1.5}$$

and then from Theorem 1.4, one has

(1.6) Replacing Γ by a suitable subgroup of finite index, one can guarantee that $H^l(\Gamma, \boldsymbol{R})$ is arbitrarily large. If l is odd, then for all torsion-free, discrete, uniform Γ, we have $H^l(\Gamma, \boldsymbol{R}) \neq 0$.

The conclusion of Theorem 1.4 and an earlier vanishing theorem of D. A. Kazhdan led Serre to conjecture the vanishing Theorem 1.3 (see **[5]**, **[7]**). Kazhdan's result states that if G is k_v-simple of k_v-rank at least two, and if $\Gamma \subset G$ is discrete and G/Γ has finite volume, then $H^1(\Gamma, \boldsymbol{R}) = 0$. This of course leads one to ask about the case of noncompact quotients for higher cohomologies, and we shall discuss this matter in § 2. We also mention

THEOREM 1.7. *Let G be semisimple of rank l over k_v and let $\Gamma \subset G$ be a discrete, uniform subgroup of G. Then* dim $H^l(\Gamma, \boldsymbol{R})$ *is equal to the multiplicity of the special representation in* $L^2(\Gamma \backslash G)$.

Thus, from (1.6), we see that if Γ is torsion-free and l odd then the special representation occurs in $L^2(\Gamma\backslash G)$ and for all l we can, by passing to a suitable subgroup of Γ of finite index, guarantee that the special representation occurs in $L^2(\Gamma\backslash G)$ with arbitrarily high multiplicity.

2. A description of methods; square-summable cohomology. To describe the approach in **[6]**, we first consider a simplicial complex $\mathscr{S}$ and assume that to every geometric simplex σ of $\mathscr{S}$ we have assigned a positive number $\lambda(\sigma)$ (the function λ will be called a metric). If Φ, Ψ are two oriented i-cochains on $\mathscr{S}$, with values in $\boldsymbol{R}$, we let

$$(\Phi, \Psi) = \sum_{\sigma} \Phi(\hat{\sigma})\Psi(\hat{\sigma})\lambda(\sigma), \tag{2.1}$$

where the right-hand side is summed over geometric i-simplices σ, and where for each σ we choose some fixed, oriented i-simplex $\hat{\sigma}$ corresponding to σ. We remark that the right side of (2.1) is independent of our choice of $\hat{\sigma}$, and that of course (Φ, Ψ) is defined only when the right side of (2.1) converges absolutely. We say Φ is *square-integrable*, in case $(\Phi, \Phi) < \infty$. We let $\mathscr{L}^i(\mathscr{S})$ be the Hilbert space of square-integrable i-cochains on $\mathscr{S}$, and we assume

(2.2) The simplicial coboundary d maps $\mathscr{L}^i(S)$ into $\mathscr{L}^{i+1}(\mathscr{S})$, and is a bounded operator.

REMARK 2.3. For example, let G be a k_v-simple group over k_v of k_v-rank l and let $\mathscr{T}$ be the Bruhat-Tits building associated with G. Then $\mathscr{T}$ is an acyclic simplicial complex, and if for a simplex σ of $\mathscr{T}$, we let $\lambda(\sigma)$ denote the number of simplices of $\mathscr{T}$ of maximal dimension having σ as a face, then (2.2) is satisfied. Also, G acts simplicially (to the left, say) on $\mathscr{T}$ and if $\Gamma \subset G$ is torsion-free, then we can carry over our methods to $\Gamma\backslash\mathscr{L}$ (even if $\Gamma\backslash\mathscr{L}$ is not simplicial).

Now let $\mathscr{S}$ and λ be given and let $\delta : \mathscr{L}^i(\mathscr{S}) \to \mathscr{L}^{i-1}(\mathscr{S})$ be the adjoint of d and $\Delta = d\delta + \delta d$ be the Laplacian. Let $\boldsymbol{H}_i = (\text{kernel } \Delta) \cap \mathscr{L}^i(\mathscr{S})$; then we have an orthogonal direct sum decomposition (Hodge decomposition):

$$\mathscr{L}^i(\mathscr{S}) = \boldsymbol{H}^i \oplus \overline{\text{Im}}\, d \oplus \overline{\text{Im}}\, \delta, \tag{2.4}$$

where "—" denotes closure. If $\mathscr{S}$ is finite then $\mathscr{L}^i(\mathscr{S})$ is just the space $C^i(\mathscr{S})$ of all

$\boldsymbol{R}$-valued i-cochains and (2.4) is a decomposition of a finite-dimensional vector space. It follows that $\boldsymbol{H}^i = H^i(\mathscr{S}, \boldsymbol{R})$, the ith cohomology of $\mathscr{S}$ with coefficients in $\boldsymbol{R}$. In [6], we proved:

THEOREM 2.5. *Let G be k_v-simple of k_v-rank l and let $\Gamma \subset G$ be discrete and torsion-free. Let $N(l)$ be as in § 1. Then, if k_v has at least $N(l)$ elements in its residue field, $\boldsymbol{H}^i = 0$ for $0 < i < l$ and $d : \mathscr{L}^i(\Gamma\backslash\mathscr{T}) \to \mathscr{L}^{i+1}(\Gamma\backslash\mathscr{T})$ has closed range for $i > 0$.*

Clearly, in view of our above remarks, Theorem 1.1 is a corollary of Theorem 2.5. On the other hand if $\Gamma = \{e\}$ then G acts on $\boldsymbol{H}^l$ and Borel and Serre proved (for $\Gamma = \{e\}$):

THEOREM 2.6. *The action of G on $\boldsymbol{H}^l$ is irreducible and is the special representation of G.*

We mention that though the proof of Theorem 2.5 depends on λ, the statement depends only on the space $\mathscr{L}^i(\Gamma\backslash\mathscr{T})$. Thus $(\mathscr{L}^i(\Gamma\backslash\mathscr{T}), d)$ is a complex and Theorem 2.5 asserts that for $2 \leqq i \leqq l - 1$, and sufficiently large residue fields, the ith cohomology group of this complex is zero.

3. A description of methods (continued). The proof that $\boldsymbol{H}^i = 0$ is analogous to Bochner's method, using curvature to prove that harmonic forms on Riemannian manifolds are zero. Thus, if $\mathscr{S}$, λ are as in § 2, we can, for each simplex σ of $\mathscr{S}$, define a certain operator R_σ (the curvature at σ) on the cochain complex of the link of σ. Thus let ${}_\sigma\lambda$ be the metric on the link of σ which assigns $\lambda(\tau\cdot\sigma)$ to each τ ($\tau\cdot\sigma$ denotes the join of τ and σ). Let ${}_\sigma d$ be the simplicial coboundary on the link of σ, and let ${}_\sigma\delta$ denote the adjoint of ${}_\sigma d$, with respect to ${}_\sigma\lambda$. Then by definition $R_\sigma = {}_\sigma\delta\ {}_\sigma d$. We then prove Theorem 2.5 by showing the positive eigenvalues of the R_σ are sufficiently large.

The approach in [3] depends on the theory of admissible representations of p-adic groups and takes as its starting point Shapiro's lemma (see [4]). For simplicity take ρ to be the trivial representation and assume G to be simply connected. Let I be the space of all $\boldsymbol{C}$-valued, locally constant functions on $\Gamma\backslash G$. The group G acts on I by right translation. The module I is a unitary, admissible representation of G. By Shapiro's lemma as proved in [4]:

$$H^*(\Gamma, \boldsymbol{C}) \cong H^*_{\text{cont.}}(G, I),$$

where $H^*_{\text{cont.}}$ denotes the continuous cohomology of G (where I is given the discrete topology). But I is a direct sum of irreducible, unitary representations and thus we are led to study $H^i_{\text{cont.}}(G, I')$ for an admissible, unitary representation of G on I'. But Casselman proves:

(3.1) If $0 < i < l$, then $H^i_{\text{cont.}}(G, I') = 0$, unless $I' = V_\Theta$, Θ a subset of the simple roots of G of cardinality $l - i$.

Here V_Θ is the following space: Let P_ϕ be a minimal parabolic in G with k_v-split torus A_ϕ. Let Δ be the corresponding set of simple roots of A_ϕ, and for $\Theta \subseteq \Delta$, let $P_\Theta \supseteq P_\phi$ be the corresponding standard parabolic subgroup. We let $U_\Theta = C^\infty(P_\Theta\backslash G)$ be the locally constant $\boldsymbol{C}$-valued functions on $P_\Theta\backslash G$, and

$$V_\Theta = U_\Theta \Big/ \sum_{\Theta \subsetneqq \Omega} U_\Omega,$$

where we note that for $\Theta \subsetneqq \Omega$, we may regard U_Ω as contained in U_Θ. Right translation then induces a G-module structure on V_Θ which is irreducible and admissible. Casselman then proves that unless $\Theta = \phi$ or Δ, one has that V_Θ is *not* unitary. This is his central result. Clearly (1.2) follows from (3.1).

Earlier, using a sheaf-theoretic version of the curvature argument sketched earlier, Borel was able to prove $H^i_{\text{cont.}}(G, V_\Theta) = 0$ for $0 < i < l$, provided V_Θ is unitary (and for large residue fields). Since Casselman had proved

$$H^i_{\text{cont.}}(G, V_\Theta) \cong \boldsymbol{C}, \quad i = |\Delta - \Theta|,$$

this gave the nonunitarity result for large residue fields.

4. An application to the real case. Let $\boldsymbol{G}$ now denote a linear algebraic group which is semisimple and defined over $\boldsymbol{Q}$. Let G denote the $\boldsymbol{R}$-rational points of $\boldsymbol{G}$, and let $G_{\boldsymbol{Q}}$ denote the $\boldsymbol{Q}$-rational points; then Borel and I have proved:

THEOREM 4.1. *If $\boldsymbol{G}$ is $\boldsymbol{Q}$-anisotropic, then the restriction homomorphism*

$$\varphi : H^i_{\text{cont.}}(G, \boldsymbol{R}) \to H^i(G_{\boldsymbol{Q}}, \boldsymbol{R})$$

is an isomorphism (for all i!).[1]

The proof is based on a sheaf-theoretic version of the curvature arguments mentioned earlier. The size of the residue field plays no role since "in the limit" one introduces arbitrarily large primes. In fact, if one only allows sets containing finitely many primes (e.g., one prime) one still gets an analogous result for sets containing a sufficiently large prime and for a certain range of i.

Bibliography

1. A. Borel, *Cohomology of arithmetic groups*, these PROCEEDINGS.

2. ———, *Cohomologie de certains groupes discrets et Laplacian P-adique*, Séminaire Bourbaki 1973–74, Exposé 437.

3. W. Casselman, *On a p-adic vanishing theorem of Garland's*, Bull. Amer. Math. Soc. **68** (1974), 1001–1004.

4. W. Cassleman and D. Wigner, *Continuous cohomology and a conjecture of Serre's*, Invent. Math. **25** (1974), 199–211.

5. G. Delaroche and A. Kirillov, *Sur les relations entre l'espace dual d'un groupe et la structure de ses sous-groupes fermés* (d'aprés D. A. Každan Sém. Bourbaki, 1967–68, Exposé 343, Benjamin, New York, 1969.

6. H. Garland, *p-adic curvature and the cohomology of discrete subgroups of p-adic groups*, Ann. of Math (2) **97** (1973), 375–423. MR **47** #8719.

7. D. A. Každan, *On the connection of the dual space of a group with the structure of its closed subgroups*, Funkcional. Anal. i Priložen. **1** (1967), 71–74 = Functional Anal. Appl. **1** (1967), 63–65. MR **35** #288.

8. J.-P. Serre, *Cohomologie des groupes discrets*, Prospects in Mathematics, Ann. of Math. Studies, no. 70, Princeton Univ. Press, Princeton, N.J., 1970.

YALE UNIVERSITY
NEW HAVEN, CONNECTICUT 06520, U.S.A.

[1]Casselman has informed me that Theorem 4.1 and other results alluded to in §4 also follow from his methods.

Proceedings of the International Congress of Mathematicians
Vancouver, 1974

Representations of p-adic Division Algebras: An Example of the Change of Base Problem in Representation Theory of Algebraic Groups

Roger Howe

We discuss a very special case of the following general problem. Let G be a linear group scheme over a finite or local field F. Let F' be a finite Galois extension of F. Then we have an embedding $G(F) \to G(F')$ of the groups of rational points, and the Galois group Gal (F'/F) acts on $G(F')$ so that its fixed point subgroup is $G(F)$. If $G(F)^\wedge$ and $G(G')^\wedge$ are the unitary dual spaces (spaces of equivalence classes of irreducible unitary representations) of $G(F)$ and $G(F')$, then Gal(F'/F) also acts on $G(F')^\wedge$, and one may consider the problem: What relation is there between $G(F)^\wedge$ and the Gal(F'/F) fixed points in $G(F')^\wedge$?

Here is one example of the kind of relation that can obtain. Let D be a division algebra over the p-adic F, central of degree m. Let F' be a tamely ramified Galois extension of degree l. Assume l is prime to m and to p. Put $D' = D \otimes F'$. Under our assumptions D' is again a division algebra, central of degree m over F'. The multiplicative groups D^X and D'^X are respectively the F and F' rational points of a group scheme over F.

Now let D_1 be a division algebra of degree l, and embed F' in D_1. Then $D_2 = D_1 \otimes D$ is a division algebra, central of degree lm over F, and D' may be thought of as embedded in D_2, as the centralizer of F'. Then $N(F')$, the normalizer of F' in D_2^X, satisfies the exact sequence

$$1 \to D'^X \to N(F') \to \mathrm{Gal}(F'/F) \to 1$$

and the action of Gal(F'/F) on D'^X is what it should be. In this situation we have the following result.

THEOREM. *There is a virtually canonical bijection between $D^{X\wedge}$ and the set of representations of $N(F')$ which are irreducible on D'^{X}.*

Let us explain "virtually" as used above. It means there are characters ε and ε' of D^X and of $N(F')$, of order at most two, so that the pair $\{\sigma, \varepsilon \otimes \sigma\} \subseteq D^{X\wedge}$ is assigned unambiguously and canonically to some pair $\{\tau, \varepsilon' \otimes \tau\} \subseteq N(F')$, but that it is unclear to me at this point how to match up individual elements inside these pairs. This ambiguity arises from the following phenomenon. Let $\mathscr{W}(F'/F)$ be the relative Weil group of F' over F. Then local reciprocity gives a canonical map $r : \mathscr{W}(F'/F) \to F^X$. On the other hand, Shafarevitch's theorem gives an embedding $s : \mathscr{W}(F'/F) \to D_1^X$ for a suitable division algebra D_1. Also we have the reduced norm, $\det : D_1^X \to F^X$. It happens that the triangle

$$\begin{array}{ccc} \mathscr{W}(F'/F) & \xrightarrow{\;r\;} & F^X \\ {\scriptstyle s}\downarrow & \nearrow{\scriptstyle \det} & \\ D_1^X & & \end{array}$$

does not always commute. Indeed if $p \equiv 3 \pmod 4$, and the ramified degree of F' over F is even, the long way around is not even surjective. However, when F' is tamely ramified anyway, the triangle commutes up to a character of order 2, which is what shows up in the theorem.

One may of course ask what happens when one drops the conditions on l. Related results are still valid, and potentially useful, but the situation is more complicated and technical, and especially if l and m are divisible by p, not completely resolved. See [**1**] for a more detailed discussion.

I now will indicate a potential application of such a result. To do so, we must recall the conjectural local reciprocity law for division algebras envisioned by R.P. Langlands. For a group G, let $(\hat{G})_n$ denote the subset of $\hat{G}$ which consists of representations of degree n. Then one expects there to be a canonical bijection

$$\lambda_n : \bigcup_{d/n} (\mathscr{W}(F)^\wedge)_d \to D^{X\wedge},$$

where $\mathscr{W}(F)$ is the absolute Weil group of F, D a division algebra over F of degree n, and d runs over the divisors of n. The map λ_n should satisfy various properties, in particular, some properties related to L-functions specified by Langlands. The existence of λ_n is known when $n = 1$ (this is local class field theory) and when $n = 2$ and $p > 2$ (this is Jacquet-Langlands-Hecke theory). A candidate for λ_n is known in other cases, but for $n = 2$, $p = 2$, no one to my knowledge has come up with any concrete proposals. One reason for this seems to be that the case $n = 2$, $p = 2$, is the first instance where some representations in $(\mathscr{W}(F)^\wedge)_n$ are not monomial. If a representation $\sigma \in (\mathscr{W}(F)^\wedge)_n$ is monomial, then it may be associated by abelian class field theory to a character $\psi \in F'^{X\wedge}$, for some extension F' of F with $\dim(F'/F) = n$. Then if D is a division algebra with $\deg(D/F) = n$, we may embed F' in D, and this provides a physical link of σ with D^X, facilitating the construction of $\lambda_n(\sigma)$. This is how most concrete reciprocity constructions have proceeded so far.

and this method clearly is useless if σ is not monomial.

In this light consider the case $n = 2, p = 2$. There is an easy

LEMMA. *For a 2-adic field F, and $\sigma \in (\mathscr{W}(F)^{\wedge})_2$, there exists F', a tamely ramified Galois extension of degree* 1, 3, *or* 6 *over F, such that $\sigma|_{\mathscr{W}(F')}$ is irreducible and monomial. Moreover, if the residue class field of F has* 4 *or more elements, F' may be taken of degree* 1 *or* 3.

Thus, assume the residue class field has 4 or more elements. Let F'' be the compositum of the cubic extensions of F. Then, using the theorem to make a correspondence of the sort

$$\begin{array}{ccccc} & & \sigma \in \mathscr{W}(F) & \longrightarrow & \sigma|_{\mathscr{W}(F')} \\ & \swarrow & \downarrow & & \downarrow \\ D^{\times\wedge} & \longrightarrow & N(F')^{\wedge} & \longrightarrow & D'^{\times\wedge} \end{array}$$

one may hope to form the broken arrow by pullback and establish a candidate for λ_2. Other similar applications can be envisaged. The details of these constructions however are somewhat involved and not completely worked out. Furthermore, the fact that even these simple cases cause problems does not lead to optimism concerning direct construction of the local reciprocity map.

Reference

1. R. Howe, *On tamely ramified change of base in local Langlands reciprocity* (in preparation).

YALE UNIVERSITY
NEW HAVEN, CONNECTICUT 06520, U.S.A.

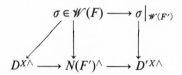

Proceedings of the International Congress of Mathematicians
Vancouver, 1974

Euler Products and Automorphic Forms

Herve Jacquet

This article is largely based upon the ideas and results of Gel'fand, Kajdan, Piateckii-Shapiro, Shalika. Its purpose is to extend the classical correspondence between automorphic forms and Dirichlet series—formulated in terms of group representations—to all linear groups GL(r). Although complete results are, at the present time, available only for $r = 2$ or 3, it is useful to formulate the problem in general terms, keeping in mind that many statements are still conjectural or partially proved—except as noted for $r = 2$ or 3.

1. Fourier expansion of a cusp form. Let F be a commutative field, G (resp. G') the group GL(r) (resp. GL($r-1$)) regarded as an algebraic group defined over F. We regard G' as imbedded into G by the map

$$g \to \begin{pmatrix} g & 0 \\ 0 & 1 \end{pmatrix}.$$

A horicycle of G is the unipotent radical of a proper F-parabolic subgroup of G.

In this section we take F to be a global field whose ring of adeles we denote by A. An automorphic form φ on G is essentially a function on $G(F)\backslash G(A)$ and it is a cusp form if

$$\int_{V(F)\backslash V(A)} \varphi(vg)\, dv = 0, \tag{1.1}$$

for all $g \in G(A)$ and all horicycles V of G.

Let N be the group of upper triangular matrices with diagonal entries equal to one. Choose a basic character ψ of A and define a character θ of $N(A)$ by

$$\theta(n) = \prod_{1 \leqq i \leqq m-1} \psi[n_{i+1,i}]. \tag{1.2}$$

For an automorphic form φ on G set

(1.3) $$W(g) = \int_{N(F)\backslash N(A)} \varphi[ng]\bar{\theta}(n)\,dn.$$

If φ is a cusp form then

(1.4) $$\varphi(g) = \sum_{\gamma\in N'(F)\backslash G'(F)} W(\gamma g),$$

where $N' = N \cap G'$ ([5], [6]).

We sketch a proof. Denote by P the group of matrices of the form

$$\begin{pmatrix} g & u \\ 0 & a \end{pmatrix}, \quad g \in G',\ a \in \mathrm{GL}(1),$$

and by P_1 the subgroup of those for which $a = 1$. In (1.4) the sum may be thought of as being on $N(F)\backslash P_1(F)$. Now it suffices to prove (1.4) for a function φ on $P_1(F)\backslash P_1(A)$ which satisfies (1.1) for all $g \in P_1(A)$ and all horicycles V of G contained in N. This is done by induction on r, the case $r = 1$ being trivial. Let U be the unipotent radical of P and $P_1' \subseteq G'$ the subgroup analogous to P_1. For $\xi \in P_1'(F)\backslash G'(F)$, the characters $u \to \theta(\xi u \xi^{-1})$, $u \in U(A)$, are all the nontrivial characters of the compact abelian group $U(A)/U(F)$. Therefore if we set

$$w(g) = \int_{U(F)\backslash U(A)} \varphi(ug)\bar{\theta}(u)\,du$$

the numbers $w(\xi g)$ are all the Fourier coefficients of the function $u \to \varphi(ug)$—all but the constant Fourier coefficient which vanishes by (1.1) applied to U. Therefore

(1.5) $$\varphi(g) = \sum_{P_1'(F)\backslash G'(F)} w(\xi g).$$

On the other hand applying the induction hypothesis to the function $h \to w(hg)$ on $P_1'(A)$ and noting that

$$W(g) = \int_{N'(F)\backslash N'(A)} w(n'g)\bar{\theta}(n')\,dn'$$

one arrives at

(1.6) $$w(g) \sum_{N'(F)\backslash P_1'(F)} W(\eta g).$$

Combining (1.5) and (1.6) gives (1.4).

Finally denote by g^{ι} the matrix ${}^t(g^{-1})$ and by $\tilde{\varphi}$ the automorphic form $g \to \varphi(g^{\iota})$. Then the function $\tilde{W}$ associated to $\tilde{\varphi}$ by (1.3) is given by

(1.7) $$\tilde{W}(g) = W(wg^{\iota}).$$

where w is the permutation matrix defined by $w_{ij} = 0$ if $i + j \neq p + 1$, $w_{p+1-i,i} = (-1)^{i-1}$.

2. A Mellin transform. Let φ be a cusp form on G and φ' an automorphic form on G'. The integral

(2.1) $$\int_{G'(F)\backslash G'(A)} \varphi(g)\varphi'(g)\,|\det g|^{s-1/2}dg$$

is always convergent. Replace φ by its expansion (1.4). Since φ' is invariant under $G'(F)$, this gives an integration on $N'(F)\backslash G'(A)$ or, what amounts to the same, on $N'(F)\backslash N'(A)$ and $N'(A)\backslash G'(A)$:

$$\int_{N'(A)\backslash G'(A)} W(g)|\det g|^{s-1/2}\, dg \int_{N'(F)\backslash N'(A)} \varphi'(n'g)\theta(n')\, dn'$$

or

$$\Psi'(s,W,W') = \int_{N'(A)\backslash G'(A)} W(g)W'(\varepsilon g)|\det g|^{s-1/2}dg. \tag{2.2}$$

Here W is given by (1.3), W' also by (1.3) with φ replaced by φ', and $\varepsilon \in G'$ is the diagonal matrix defined by $\varepsilon_{ij} = \delta_{ij}(-1)^i$. Replace φ and φ' by $\tilde{\varphi}$ and $\tilde{\varphi}'$. Then the integral

$$\int \tilde{\varphi}(g)\tilde{\varphi}'(g)|\det g|^{s-1/2}dg \tag{2.3}$$

is equal to $\Psi(s, \tilde{W}, \tilde{W}')$ where $\tilde{W}$ is given in terms of W by (1.7) and $\tilde{W}'$ determined in terms of W' in a similar manner.

Change g into g^ι in (2.1). Then we see that (2.1) is equal to (2.3) with s replaced by $1 - s$. Therefore

$$\Psi(s,W,W') = \Psi(1 - s, \tilde{W}, \tilde{W}'). \tag{2.4}$$

Actually and at least for $r = 2$ or 3 one finds that $\Psi(s, W, W')$ is given by a convergent integral for large Re s, can be analytically continued to the whole plane as an entire function of s, and satisfies (2.4).

3. Local functional equation. We let now F be a local field, nonarchimedean of module q to simplify and state some conjectures of Gel'fand and Kajdan.

Fix a character $\psi \neq 1$ of F and let θ be the character of $N(F)$ defined by (1.2). Let π be an admissible irreducible representation of $G(F)$. We say that it is nondegenerate if there is a space $\mathscr{W}$ of functions W on $G(F)$ satisfying

$$W(ng) = \theta(n)W(g),$$

the space being invariant under right shifts and the representation of $G(A)$ on $\mathscr{W}$ equivalent to π. The space $\mathscr{W}$ is then unique and noted $\mathscr{W}(\pi, \psi)$ ([**1**], [**6**]).

If π is nondegenerate so is the representation $\tilde{\pi}$ contragredient to π. More precisely $\tilde{\pi}$ is equivalent to the representation $g \to \pi(g^\iota)$ (cf. [**1**]) and if W is in $\mathscr{W}(\pi, \psi)$ then the function $\tilde{W}$ defined by (1.7) is in $\mathscr{W}(\tilde{\pi}, \psi)$.

If π and π' are nondegenerate representations of $G(F)$ and $G'(F)$ we form for $W \in \mathscr{W}(\pi, \psi)$ and $W' \in \mathscr{W}(\pi', \psi)$ an integral $\Psi(s, W, W')$ analogous to (2.2) with $N'(F)\backslash G'(F)$ replacing $N'(A)\backslash G'(A)$. Then the integrals $\Psi(s, W, W')$ should converge for large Re s and be rational functions of q^{-s}, with a common denominator. Taking this for granted, the subvector space of $\boldsymbol{C}(q^{-s})$ they span is a fractional ideal $\mathscr{W}$ of $\boldsymbol{C}[q^{-s}, q^s]$ with a unique generator of the form

$$L(s, \pi \times \pi') = 1/P(q^{-s}), \qquad P \in \boldsymbol{C}[X],\ P(0) = 1.$$

Replacing the pair (π, π') by the pair $(\tilde{\pi}, \tilde{\pi}')$, similar properties are expected for

$\Psi(s, \tilde{W}, \tilde{W}')$ and there should be a functional equation

$$\Psi(1 - s, \tilde{W}, \tilde{W}')/L(1 - s, \tilde{\pi} \times \tilde{\pi}') = \varepsilon(s, \pi \times \pi', \psi)\Psi(s, W, W')/L(s, \pi, \pi')$$

where ε is a monomial in q^{-s}.

All this is known if π is supercuspidal [**1**], or if $r = 2, 3$ ([**1**], [**4**]).

4. Conclusion. Take F to be global, a function field to simplify. Let π be an irreducible admissible representation of $G(A)$. We assume π preunitary and trivial on the center of $G(F)$. There is, for each place v of F, an irreducible representation π_v of $G(F_v)$, which contains the trivial representation of $K_v = \mathrm{GL}(r, R_v)$ for almost all v, such that $\pi = \bigotimes \pi_v$. We assume each π_v to be nondegenerate and let $\mathscr{W}(\pi, \psi)$ be the space spanned by the functions W of the form $W(g) = \prod_v W_v(g_v)$, where W_v is in $\mathscr{W}(\pi_v, \psi_v)$ for all v and, for almost all v, is the element of that space invariant under K_v and equal to 1 on K_v.

Suppose $\mathscr{U}$ is a space of automorphic forms invariant under $G(A)$, the representation of $G(A)$ on $\mathscr{U}$ being equivalent to π. Then for $\varphi \in \mathscr{U}$ the function W of (1.3) is on $\mathscr{W}(\pi, \psi)$. In particular if $\mathscr{U}$ is a space of cusp forms it is completely determined by π as follows from (1.4) ([**5**], [**6**]).

Let now π' be a representation of $G'(A)$ satisfying the same assumptions as π. Form the products

$$L(s, \pi \times \pi') = \prod_v L(s, \pi_v \times \pi_v'), \quad L(s, \tilde{\pi} \times \tilde{\pi}'),$$
$$\varepsilon(s, \pi \times \pi') = \prod_v \varepsilon(s, \pi_v \times \pi_v', \psi_v).$$

The two first are convergent for large $\mathrm{Re}\, s$; the third has almost all its factors equal to one. Combining global and local results one should arrive at the following statement: π is a component of the space of cusp forms for G if and only if for any component π' of the space of automorphic forms of G' the products $L(s, \pi \times \pi')$ and $L(s, \tilde{\pi} \times \tilde{\pi}')$ are entire and satisfy

$$L(s, \pi \times \pi') = \varepsilon(s, \pi \times \pi')L(1 - s, \tilde{\pi} \times \tilde{\pi}').$$

Actually if π' is a component of the space of automorphic forms but not cusp forms, it may be taken as a component of a space of Eisenstein series and $L(s, \pi \times \pi')$ should be a product of L-functions which remain to be defined. Namely, to each pair (π, π') of a representation of $\mathrm{GL}(n, A)$ and a representation of $\mathrm{GL}(m, A)$ with $m < n$ satisfying the above conditions one would want to attach a function $L(s, \pi \times \pi')$. Then the components π of the space of cusp forms for G would be characterized by the analytic properties of all the products $L(s, \pi \times \pi')$ where π' is a component of the space of *cusp forms* of $\mathrm{GL}(m, A)$ and $1 \leqq m < n$.

This program can be carried out for $r = 2$ [**4**] and also for $r = 3$. Note that for $m = 1$, the product $L(s, \pi \times \pi')$ is the one in [**2**].

Bibliography

1. I. M. Gel'fand and D. A. Každan, *Representations of* GL(n, K) *where K is a local field*, Institute for Applied Mathematics, Moscow, no. 942, 1971.

2. R. Godement and H. Jacquet, *Zeta functions of simple algebras*, Lecture Notes in Math., no. 260, Springer-Verlag, Berlin and New York, 1972.

3. H. Jacquet and R. Langlands, *Automorphic forms on* GL(2), Lecture Notes in Math., no. 114, Springer-Verlag, Berlin and New York, 1970.

4. H. Jacquet and J. Shalika, *Hecke theory for* GL(3), Compositio Math. **29** (1974), 75–87.

5. J. J. Piateckii-Shapiro, *Euler subgroups* (preprint).

6. J. Shalika, *The multiplicity one theorem for* GL_n, Ann. of Math. (2) **100** (1974), 171–193.

The Fourier expansion of §1 is given in [5] and [6], the formal manipulations of §2 in [5]. The uniqueness of the space $\mathscr{W}(\pi, \psi)$ is proved in [1], and also in [6] which treats the archimedean case as well. These ideas should have led to the conjectures of [1] that we have reformulated in §3; however, the conjectures were formulated first and were instrumental in developing the ideas given in §2 (cf. [5]). The case $r = 2$ was treated in [3] and the case $r = 3$ sketched in [4].

City University of New York
New York, New York 10036, U.S.A.

Proceedings of the International Congress of Mathematicians
Vancouver, 1974

On the Discrete Series Representations of the Classical Groups over Finite Fields

G. Lusztig

1. One of the main unsolved problems in the representation theory of the finite Chevalley groups is the determination of the discrete series representations; these are the most basic, but least accessible, representations of such groups. Let me recall that an (ordinary) representation D of a finite Chevalley group G is said to be in the discrete series, or cuspidal, if, for any proper parabolic subgroup $P \subset G$, the restriction of D to the "unipotent radical" of P does not contain the unit representation.

The theme of this section is that we encounter discrete series representations in the process of decomposing the Brauer lifting of some very natural modular representations. The idea of the Brauer lifting was introduced by J. A. Green in 1955 in his well-known work on the characters of $\mathrm{GL}_n(F_q)$, and revived by Quillen in connection with his solution of the Adams conjecture.

Part of the results presented here, namely the ones on GL_n, are proved in my publication *The discrete series of* GL_n *over a finite field*, Annals of Mathematics Studies, No. 81, Princeton University Press, 1974.

Let F be a finite field with q elements, $q = p^e$; let W_F be the ring of Witt vectors associated to F and Q_F its quotient field. The canonical homomorphism $F^* \to Q_F^*$ will be denoted by $\lambda \to \tilde{\lambda}$.

Let V be a vector space of dimension $n \geqq 1$ over F. Define S to be the set of all pairs (d, P) where $d = (V_1 \subset V_2 \subset \cdots \subset V_{n-1})$ is a complete flag in V ($\dim V_i = i$) and $P \in V—V_{n-1}$. The group $\mathrm{GL}(V)$ acts transitively on S. Let V' be a vector space of dimension $2n \geqq 2$ over F endowed with a nondegenerate symplectic form. Define S' to be the set of all pairs (d, P) where $d = (V_1 \subset V_2 \subset \cdots \subset V_n)$ is a complete isotropic flag in V', ($\dim V_i = i$) and $P \in V_{n-1}^{\perp} - V_n$. Let $\mathrm{CSp}(V')$ be the group of all symplectic similitudes of V' (a similitude must transform the given symplectic form in a nonzero multiple of it). The group $\mathrm{CSp}(V')$ acts transitively on S'.

Let $\mathscr{F}$ (resp. $\mathscr{F}'$) be the Q_F-vector space of all functions $f:S \to Q_F$ (resp. $f:S' \to Q_F$) such that $f(d, \lambda P) = \tilde{\lambda}^{-1} f(d, P)$ for all $\lambda \in F^*$ and all $(d, P) \in S$ (resp. $(d, P) \in S'$). Then $\mathrm{GL}(V)$ (resp. $\mathrm{CSp}(V')$) acts linearly on $\mathscr{F}$ (resp. $\mathscr{F}'$). Let ${}^\circ\mathscr{F}$ (resp. ${}^\circ\mathscr{F}'$) be the cuspidal part of $\mathscr{F}$ (resp. $\mathscr{F}'$). It can be shown that ${}^\circ\mathscr{F}$ (resp. ${}^\circ\mathscr{F}'$) is a multiplicity free representation of $\mathrm{GL}(V)$ (resp. $\mathrm{CSp}(V')$).

Define $T \in Q[\mathrm{GL}(V)]$ (resp. $T' \in Q[\mathrm{CSp}(V')]$) as $\sum(\mathrm{St}(g)/\mathrm{St}(1))g^{-1}$, where the sum is over all semisimple elements $g \in \mathrm{GL}(V)$ (resp. $g \in \mathrm{CSp}(V')$) such that the trace of g on V (resp. on V') equals 1. Here St is the character of the Steinberg representation of $\mathrm{GL}(V)$ (resp. $\mathrm{CSp}(V')$). T (resp. T') acts on ${}^\circ\mathscr{F}$ (resp. ${}^\circ\mathscr{F}'$) and is diagonalizable; moreover it is easy to see that all eigenvalues lie in W_F.

THEOREM 1. *There exists a unique $\lambda \in W_F$ (resp. $\lambda' \in W_F$) such that $\lambda \equiv 1 \pmod p$ (resp. $\lambda' \equiv 1 \pmod p$) and λ (resp. λ') is an eigenvalue of T on ${}^\circ\mathscr{F}$ (resp. of T' on ${}^\circ\mathscr{F}'$). If μ (resp. μ^{-1}) is an eigenvalue of T on ${}^\circ\mathscr{F}$ (resp. of T' on ${}^\circ\mathscr{F}'$) such that $\lambda \neq \mu$ (resp. $\lambda' \neq \mu'$), then $\mu \equiv 0 \pmod p$ (resp. $\mu' \equiv 0 \pmod p$).*

Let F' (resp. F'') be an extension of F of degree n (resp. $2n$). It can be proved that

$$\lambda = \sum \tilde{x}^{-1},$$

where the summation is over $x \in F'$, $\mathrm{trace}_{F'/F} x = 1$. It is very likely that λ' is equal to

$$\sum_{x \in F''} \tilde{x}^{-1}, \qquad x^{(q-1)(q^n+1)} = 1, \qquad \operatorname*{trace}_{F''/F} x = 1.$$

DEFINITION. $D(V) = \{f \in {}^\circ\mathscr{F} \mid Tf = \lambda f\}$, $D'(V') = \{f \in {}^\circ\mathscr{F}' \mid T'f = \lambda' f\}$.

THEOREM 2. *$D(V)$ (resp. $D'(V')$ is an absolutely irreducible cuspidal* $\mathrm{GL}(V)$ *(resp.* $\mathrm{CSp}(V')$*) submodule of ${}^\circ\mathscr{F}$ (resp. ${}^\circ\mathscr{F}'$). As a Q_F-vector space, $D(V)$ (resp. $D'(V')$) has dimension equal to $(q-1)(q^2-1)\cdots(q^{n-1}-1)$ (resp. $(q^2-1)(q^4-1)\cdots(q^{2n-2}-1)(q^n-1)$).*

For example if $\dim V' = 4$, we have $\dim D'(V') = (q^2-1)^2$ (compare B. Srinivasan, *The characters of the finite symplectic group* $\mathrm{Sp}(4, q)$, Trans. Amer. Math. Soc. **131** (1968), 488–525).

Next we observe that V (resp. V') can be regarded as a modular representation of $\mathrm{GL}(V)$ (resp. $\mathrm{CSp}(V')$) and hence we can consider the Brauer lifting $\mathrm{Br}(V) \in R_{Q_F}(\mathrm{GL}(V))$ (resp. $\mathrm{Br}(V') \in R_{Q_F}(\mathrm{CSp}(V'))$), where R_{Q_F} denotes the appropriate Grothendieck group.

THEOREM 3. *Let $X_i = \bigoplus D(V_i)$ (sum over all i-dimensional subspaces V_i of V). Then* $\mathrm{Br}(V) = X_1 - X_2 + \cdots + (-1)^{n-1} X_n$.

Note that X_i is a $\mathrm{GL}(V)$-module in a natural way; in fact it is an absolutely irreducible one, provided that $q > 2$ or $i > 1$.

We have

$$\dim X_i = \frac{(q^{n-i+1} - 1) \cdots (q^{n-1} - 1)(q^n - 1)}{q^i - 1}$$

and $X_n = D(V)$. We now wish to find a symplectic analogue of Theorem 3. For any i, $1 \leq i \leq n$, let $X_i' = \bigoplus D(V_i)$ (sum over all i-dimensional isotropic subspaces V_i of V'). X_i' is a $\mathrm{CSp}(V)$-module in a natural way and as such it is absolutely irreducible provided that $q > 2$ or $i > 2$.

We have

$$\dim X_i' = \frac{(q^{2(n-i+1)} - 1) \cdots (q^{2(n-1)} - 1)(q^{2n} - 1)}{q^i - 1}.$$

For any i, $1 \leq i \leq n - 1$, let $E_i = \bigoplus D'(V_{n-i}^{\perp}/V_{n-i})$ (sum over all isotropic flags $V_1 \subset V_2 \subset \cdots \subset V_{n-i}$ in V' (dim $V_j = j$)); note that $V_{n-i}^{\perp}/V_{n-i}$ has a natural symplectic form if V' has one. E_i is a $\mathrm{CSp}(V)$-module in a natural way. Let $\mathcal{H}(E_i)$ be the algebra of endomorphisms of E_i commuting with the action of $\mathrm{CSp}(V)$. For any j, $1 \leq j \leq n - i - 1$, define $T_j \in \mathcal{H}(E_i)$ by the formula

$$(T_j\phi)(V_1 \subset \cdots \subset V_{j-1} \subset V_j \subset V_{j+1} \subset \cdots \subset V_{n-i})$$
$$= \sum \phi(V_1 \subset \cdots \subset V_{j-1} \subset V_j' \subset V_{j+1} \subset \cdots \subset V_{n-i})$$

where the sum is over all V_j' such that $V_{j-1} \subset V_j' \subset V_{j+1}$, $V_j' \neq V_j$ (q terms). Here we regard $\phi \in E_i$ as a function which associates to any $V_1 \subset \cdots \subset V_{n-i}$ an element $\phi(V_1 \subset \cdots \subset V_{n-i}) \in D'(V_{n-i}^{\perp}/V_{n-i})$.

Define an element $T_{n-i} \in \mathcal{H}(E_i)$ by the formula

$$(T_{n-i}\phi)(V_1 \subset \cdots \subset V_{n-i-1} \subset V_{n-i}) = \sum D'(u) \, \phi(V_1 \subset \cdots \subset V_{n-i-1} \subset V_{n-i}')$$

where the sum is over all V_{n-i}' such that $V_{n-i-1} \subset V_{n-i}' \subset V_{n-i-1}^{\perp}$, $V_{n-i} \cap V_{n-i}'^{\perp} = V_{n-i-1}$ (q^{2i+1} terms); here $D'(u) \colon D'(V_{n-i}'^{\perp}/V_{n-i}') \to D'(V_{n-i}^{\perp}/V_{n-i})$ is the isomorphism induced by the isomorphism $u = \alpha \beta^{-1}$ in the diagram:

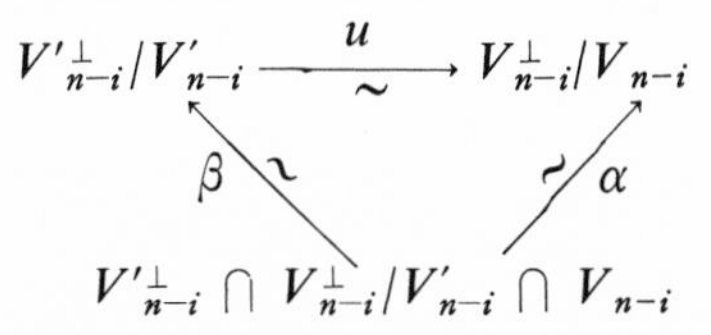

$$
\begin{array}{ccc}
V_{n-i}'^{\perp}/V_{n-i}' & \xrightarrow[\sim]{\ u\ } & V_{n-i}^{\perp}/V_{n-i} \\
& & \\
{\scriptstyle \beta} \nwarrow & & \nearrow {\scriptstyle \alpha} \\
& V_{n-i}'^{\perp} \cap V_{n-i}^{\perp}/V_{n-i}' \cap V_{n-i} &
\end{array}
\qquad (\alpha, \beta \text{ are canonical isomorphisms}).
$$

It can be proved that $T_1, \cdots, T_{n-i}$ generate $\mathcal{H}(E_i)$ as an algebra; they satisfy the relations $(T_j + 1)(T_j - q) = 0$, $1 \leq j \leq n - 1$, $(T_{n-i} - q^i)(T_{n-i} + q^{i+1}) = 0$, and the "braid group relations" corresponding to the Weyl group C_{n-i} (compare C.W. Curtis, N. Iwahori, R. Kilmoyer, *Hecke algebras and characters of parabolic type* $\cdots$, Inst. Hautes Études Sci. Publ. Math. 40, p. 84, formula (1.6)). The only relation which does not admit a straightforward proof is the relation

$$(T_{n-i} - q^i)(T_{n-i} + q^{i+1}) = 0.$$

Its proof involves the following fact which was conjectured by B. Srinivasan:

LEMMA. *Let* $g \in \mathrm{CSp}(V')$ *be a transvection. Then*

$$\operatorname{trace}(g|D'(V')) = -(q^2-1)(q^4-1)\cdots(q^{2n-2}-1).$$

We now define a subspace $Y_i \subset E_i$ by $Y_i = \{\phi \in E_i | T_j\phi = q\phi,\ 1 \leqq j \leqq n-i-1,\ T_{n-i}\phi = -q^{i+1}\phi\}$. Then Y_i is an absolutely irreducible $\mathrm{CSp}(V')$-submodule of E_i.

THEOREM 4.

$$\dim Y_i = \frac{(q^{2(n-i+1)}-1)\cdots(q^{2(n-1)}-1)(q^{2n}-1)}{q^i+1}.$$

If we put $Y_n = D'(V')$, we have

THEOREM 5. $\mathrm{Br}(Y') = X_1' - X_2' + \cdots + (-1)^{n-1}X_n' + (-1)^n Y_n + \cdots + Y_2 - Y_1$.

All results mentioned so far for the symplectic hold with only minor modification for the orthogonal groups in odd characteristics and for the unitary groups. For example we have.

THEOREM 6. *For each of the following groups there exists an ordinary irreducible cuspidal representation of the indicated dimension:*

$SO_{2n+1}(F_q)$, $n \geqq 1: (q^2-1)(q^4-1)\cdots(q^{2n-2}-1)(q^n-1)$.

$SO_{2n}^+(F_q)$, q odd, $n \geqq 2: (q^2-1)(q^4-1)\cdots(q^{2n-2}-1)(q^n-1)(q+1)^{-1} \cdot (q^{n-1}+1)^{-1}$.

$SO_{2n}^-(F_q)$, q odd, $n \geqq 2: (q^2-1)(q^4-1)\cdots(q^{2n-2}-1)$.

$U_{2n+1}(F_{q^2})$, $n \geqq 1: (q+1)(q^2-1)\cdots(q^{2n-1}+1)(q^{2n}-1)$.

$U_{2n}(F_{q^2})$, $n \geqq 1: (q+1)(q^2-1)\cdots(q^{2n-1}+1)(q^{2n}-1)(q+1)^{-1} \cdot (q^{2n-1}+1)^{-1}$.

Here $SO_{2n}^+(F_q)$ (resp. $SO_{2n}^-(F_q)$) denotes the split (resp. twisted) special orthogonal group.

2. In this section I wish to describe briefly some joint work with Deligne in which we use étale cohomology to realize representations of finite Chevalley groups.

Let G be a linear algebraic group (reductive, connected) defined over a finite field F, $|F| = q$. We identify G with the set of its points over $\bar{F}$. Let $\phi: G \to G$ be the Frobenius endomorphism of G. Then G^ϕ, the fixed point set of ϕ, is a finite group, and we are interested in its representations.

Let $T \subset G$ be a maximal torus in G such that $\phi T = T$. According to Macdonald, every character $\pi \in \hat{T}^\phi$ in general position should given rise to an irreducible G^ϕ-module $M_{T,\pi}$ defined over some large field of characteristic zero, and such that $\dim M_{T,\pi} = |G^\phi|_* \cdot |T^\phi|^{-1}$ (here $|G^\phi|_*$ denotes the order of G^ϕ divided by the order of a Sylow p-subgroup). Macdonald also predicts the values of the character of $M_{T,\pi}$ on regular elements in G^ϕ. This conjecture of Macdonald is still unproved except for a few special cases, including GL_n (Green), Sp_4 (Srinivasan) and G_2 (Chang, Ree).

Let $T_0 \subset G$ be a fixed maximal torus and $B_0 \subset G$ a fixed Borel subgroup, $T_0 \subset B_0$; we assume $\phi T_0 = T_0$, $\phi B_0 = B_0$. Let $w \in N(T_0)$; we may write $w = y^{-1}\phi(y)$, $y \in G$. Then yTy^{-1} is a ϕ-invariant maximal torus. If $T_{0,w} = \{t \in T_0 | \phi t = w^{-1}tw\}$, the map $t \to yty^{-1}$ induces an isomorphism of finite groups

$$T_{0,w} \xrightarrow{\sim} (yTy^{-1})^\phi.$$

Hence we also get an isomorphism

$$\hat{T}_{0,w} \xleftarrow{\sim} \widehat{(yTy^{-1})^\phi}.$$

The correspondence $w \to yTy^{-1}$ defines a bijection between the ϕ-conjugacy classes in the Weyl group $W = N(T_0)/T_0$ and the conjugacy classes of maximal tori $T \subset G$, $\phi T = T$ (conjugacy under G^ϕ); we recall that two elements $\bar{w}, \bar{w}' \in W$ are said to be ϕ-conjugate if $\bar{w}' = \bar{w}_1\bar{w}\phi(\bar{w}_1)^{-1}$ for some $\bar{w}_1 \in W$. Thus we may reformulate Macdonald's conjecture by saying that each $\bar{w} \in W$ should give rise to a series of representations parametrized by the characters $\pi \in \hat{T}_{0,w}$, in general position.

We now give the following definition: Two Borel subgroups B_1, B_2 in G are said to be in position $\bar{w}$ ($\bar{w} \in W$) if there exists $g \in G$ such that $gB_1g^{-1} = B_0$, $gB_2g^{-1} = wB_0w^{-1}$ where $w \in N(T_0)$ represents $\bar{w}$. Any ordered pair of Borel subgroups gives rise in this way to a well-defined $\bar{w} \in W$. For any $\bar{w} \in W$, define $X_{\bar{w}}$ to be the set of all Borel subgroups B in G such that B, ϕB are in position $\bar{w}$. Then $X_{\bar{w}}$ is a nonsingular and in general noncomplete algebraic variety of dimension $l(\bar{w})$. The varieties $X_{\bar{w}}$ ($\bar{w} \in W$) cover the set of all Borel subgroups and $X_{\bar{w}} \cap X_{\bar{w}'} = \emptyset$ for $\bar{w} \neq \bar{w}'$. The group G^ϕ acts on each $X_{\bar{w}}$ by conjugation. Thus we get a nonlinear representation of G^ϕ on $X_{\bar{w}}$. In order to get linear ones we must pass to the cohomology of $X_{\bar{w}}$. For this purpose we define some sheaves on $X_{\bar{w}}$.

Let $S_w = \{g \in G | g^{-1}\phi(g) \in wR_0\}$ where $w \in N(T_0)$ and R_0 is the unipotent radical of B_0. Let $R_0^w = R_0 \cap wR_0w^{-1}$. Then S_w is stable under right multiplication by R_0^w and $T_{0,w}$. Let $\tilde{X}_w = S_w/R_0^w$. Then $T_{0,w}$ still acts on $\tilde{X}_w$ (without isotropy) and the orbit space is canonically equal to $X_{\bar{w}}$. Thus we have an étale (Galois) covering $\tilde{X}_w \to X_{\bar{w}}$ with group $T_{0,w}$. Using this covering we see that each character $\pi: T_{0,w} \to \bar{Q}_l^*$ gives rise to an l-adic, locally constant sheaf $\mathscr{F}_\pi$, of rank 1 over $X_{\bar{w}}$. The group G^ϕ acts naturally on $\mathscr{F}_\pi$. Thus we may consider the alternating sum $\Delta(\bar{w},\pi) = \sum_i(-1)^i H^i(X_{\bar{w}};\mathscr{F}_\pi)$ as an element in the representation ring $R_{\bar{Q}_l}(G^\phi)$.

CONJECTURE. *The objects* $(-1)^{l(w)}\Delta(\bar{w}, \pi)$, $\bar{w} \in W$, $\pi \in \hat{T}_{0,w}$, *give a solution to Macdonald's conjecture.*

In particular, for π in general position, $(-1)^{l(\bar{w})}\Delta(\bar{w}, \pi)$ should be irreducible. One may also conjecture that, in case $\bar{w}$ has minimal length in its ϕ-conjugacy class, and π is in general position, we have $H^i(X_{\bar{w}}; \mathscr{F}_\pi) = 0$ for all i, $i \neq l(\bar{w})$. (This vanishing theorem has been verified for GL_n.)

Our conjecture states in particular that the Euler characteristic $\chi(X_{\bar{w}})$ equals $(-1)^{l(\bar{w})}|G^\phi|_* \cdot |T_{0,w}|^{-1}$. We have proved that this is indeed the case for GL_n and Sp_4. We have the following

THEOREM 7. (i) *The character values of* $(-1)^{l(w)}\Delta(\bar{w}, \pi)$ *at any regular semisimple element of* G^ϕ *agree with Macdonald's conjecture.*

(ii) *If* $\bar{w}, \bar{w}' \in W$ *are* ϕ*-conjugate then the two series* $\{\Delta(\bar{w}, \pi), \pi \in \hat{T}_{0,w}\}$, $\{\Delta(\bar{w}', \pi'), \pi' \in \hat{T}_{0,w'}\}$ *coincide.*

We now give some examples.

EXAMPLE 1. Let V be a vector space of dimension n over $\bar{F}$ with an F-structure and let $\phi: V \to V$ be the Frobenius map. We define a decomposition $P(V) = C_1 \cap C_2 \cup \cdots \cup C_n$ by $C_i = \{L \mid L \text{ line in } V, \dim(L + \phi L + \phi^2 L + \cdots) = i\}$. It can be proved that C_i has Euler characteristic equal to

$$((1 - q^{n-i+1}) \cdots (1 - q^{n-1})(1-q^n))/(1 - q^i).$$

(This decomposition of $P(V)$ is closely related to the decomposition of $\mathrm{Br}(V)$ described in Theorem 3.) Moreover C_n is isomorphic to $X_{\bar{w}}$ for a suitable Coxeter element $\bar{w}$.

EXAMPLE 2. Let V be a 4-dimensional vector space over $\bar{F}$ with an F-structure and with a nondegenerate symplectic form $\langle\, ,\rangle$ defined over F. Let $\phi: V \to V$ be, as before, the Frobenius map.

Consider the nonsingular surface $S \subset P(V)$ given by the set of lines $L \subset V$ such that $\langle L, \phi L\rangle = 0$. Then $\phi S = S$; hence ϕ acts on $H^2(S; Q_l)$. It can be proved that the eigenvalues of ϕ on $H^2(S; Q_l)$ are equal to q or $-q$. It can be also proved that the $(-q)$ eigenspace has dimension $\frac{1}{2}q(q-1)^2$ and that, as an $\mathrm{Sp}_4(F)$-module, this is isomorphic to the famous Srinivasan module θ_{10}.

Finally, I would like to mention that in finding the above results we were influenced by the work of Drinfeld in Moscow, an account of which was given to us by Springer. Drinfeld has observed that one can find the discrete series representations of $\mathrm{SL}_2(F)$ by decomposing $H^1(X; Q_l)$ where X is the affine plane curve $xy^q - x^q y = 1$ on which $\mathrm{SL}_2(F)$ acts. Note that X can be identified with our $\tilde{X}_w$ (w the Coxeter element for SL_2).

UNIVERSITY OF WARWICK
COVENTRY, ENGLAND CV4 7AL

Труды Международного Конгресса Математиков
Ванкувер, 1974

Арифметические и Структурные Проблемы в Линейных Алгебраических Группах

В. П. Платонов

Развитие теории алгебраических групп в последние годы характеризуется исследованием таких проблем, в которых арифметика, алгебраическая геометрия и алгебра глубоко и органично связаны между собой. В некоторых, наиболее удивительных случаях чисто арифметические свойства алгебраических групп полностью определяются их абстрактно-групповой структурой. Один из самых впечатляющих и широко известных примеров доставляет проблема сильной аппроксимации.

1. Сильная аппроксимация и гипотезаКнезера-Титса. Пусть G—связная линейная алгебраическая группа, определенная над глобальным полем k. Как обычно, G_A—группа аделей G, S—конечное множество неэквивалентных нормирований k, G_S—подгруппа G_A, у которой все v-компоненты ($v \notin S$) равны 1; π_S: $G_A \to G_S$—каноническая проекция; G_k—подгруппа k-точек G. Проблема сильной аппроксимации состоит в следующем: когда $\overline{G_S G_k} = G_A$, где черта означает замыкание в адельной топологии? Так как основным методом исследования в арифметической теории алгебраических групп является метод редукции к алгебраическим группам над локальными полями, то проблема сильной аппроксимации играет важную роль в большинстве арифметических вопросов (см. [2], [4], [11], [12], [25]).

Первым важным результатом о проблеме сильной аппроксимации была классическая теорема Эйхлера о группе SL(n, D), где D—тело конечного k-ранга [1]. Позднее различные частные случаи этой проблемы над числовым полем k исследовали Эйхлер, Шимура, Вейль [2]. Наиболее существенные результаты были получены Кнезером [3], [4], который решил проблему аппроксимации для классических групп над числовыми полями и указал необходимые условия для ее положительного решения: (а) G_S—некомпактная группа; (б) G — односвязная. Для функционального поля k необходимость этих условий доказана в [**5**].

Наконец, в работах автора [**6**], [**7**] с помощью нового метода проблема сильной аппроксимации была полностью решена не только над числовыми, но и над функциональными полями. В основе метода [**6**], [**7**] лежит редукция арифметической проблемы сильной аппроксимации к известной гипотезе Кнезера-Титса [**8**] о структуре алгебраических групп над локально компактными полями, имеющей абстрактную природу. А именно, гипотеза Кнезера-Титса утверждает: если G—простая односвязная k-изотропная алгебраическая группа над произвольным полем k, то фактор-группа $G_k/Z(G_k)$, где $Z(G_k)$ —центр G_k, является абстрактно простой группой. В [**6**], [**7**] гипотеза Кнезера-Титса доказана для локально компактных полей k и отсюда выводится решение проблемы сильной аппроксимации над числовыми полями. Для функциональных полей редукция оказывается заметно сложнее, так как используемая в числовом случае техника алгебр Ли непосредственно неприменима в этой ситуации. Однако в настоящее время и в функциональном случае можно столь же коротким путем вывести решение проблемы сильной аппроксимации из доказательства гипотезы Кнезера-Титса, если применить теорему о тривиальности одномерных когомологий Галуа $H^1(k,G)$ для односвязной полупростой группы G над функциональным глобальным полем k, анонсированную Хардером в [**9**].[1] Так как ряд специалистов проявил особый интерес к функциональному случаю, то я приведу необходимое дополнительное к [**6**], [**7**] рассуждение. Предположим вначале, что G не есть группа типа A_n. Тогда из $H^1(k, G) = 0$ следует, что группа G является k-изотропной, т.е. $\operatorname{rank}_k G > 0$. Если T—конечное множество неэквивалентных нормирований k и $S \cap T = \varnothing$, то достаточно доказать, что для $W = S \cup T$ группа W-единиц $G_{O(W)}$ плотна в G_T. Рассмотрим в G_k нормальный делитель R, порожденный унипотентными однопараметрическими k-подгруппами. Так как такие подгруппы обладают свойством сильной аппроксимации, то замыкание $\bar{R} \subseteq \bar{G}_{O(W)}$. Далее, по теореме о слабой аппроксимации, доказанной в [**6**], [**7**], $\bar{G}_k = G_T$, значит, $\bar{R}$—нормальный делитель G_T. Из гипотезы Кнезера-Титса теперь уже нетрудно вывести, что замыкание $\bar{R} = \bar{G}_{O(W)} = G_T$. Случай группы G типа A_n рассматривается с помощью некоторой модификации рассуждений из [**7**].

Недавно мне удалось показать, что аналогично [**6**], [**7**] и с учетом результатов [**10**] о группах типа A_n можно доказать гипотезу Кнезера-Титса для функциональных полей.

Теорема 1. *Пусть G—простая k-изотропная односвязная алгебраическая группа над глобальным функциональным полем k, тогда $G_k/Z(G_k)$ является абстрактно простой группой.*

Несомненно, что Теорема 1 справедлива и для поля k алгебраических чисел,

[1]Уже появилось полное доказательство в препринтной форме.

однако это не удается пока доказать для некоторых групп типа E_6 и D_4.

2. Несюрьективность накрытий алгебраических групп на k-точках. Пусть $f: G \to G'$—k-изогения связных k-определенных алгебраических групп над произвольным полем k. Когда $f(G_k) \neq G'_k$? Для некоторых специальных полей эта задача исследовалась в ряде работ (например, для конечного поля —Ленгом [**13**], для поля вещественных чисел—Борелем и Титсом [**14**]).

Автора побудила к исследованию этой задачи следующая гипотеза Дьедонне [**15**]. Пусть D/k—некоммутативное тело конечной размерности m^2 над центром k (char $k \neq 2$) с нетривиальной инволюцией τ; S_τ—подпространство элементов D, симметричных относительно τ; Σ—подгруппа мультипликативной группы D^*, порожденная ненулевыми симметричными элементами. В действительности Σ—нормальный делитель D^* и изучение строения фактор-группы D^*/Σ представляет интерес с разных точек зрения (см. [**10**], [**15**], [**16**]). Предположим, что $k \subseteq S_\tau$, т.е. инволюция первого рода. Тогда $\dim S_\tau = m(m+1)/2$ или $m(m-1)/2$. Это соответствует случаю симплектических или ортогональных форм. Если $\dim S_\tau = m(m+1)/2$, то $D^* = \Sigma$ из размерностных соображений. В связи с этим Дьедонне в [**15**, стр. 379], высказал, как весьма вероятную, гипотезу о совпадении D^* и Σ для более существенного случая, когда $\dim S_\tau = m(m-1)/2$ и $m > 2$ (для $m=2$ очевидно, что $\Sigma = k^*$ и $D^* \neq \Sigma$). Оказывается, гипотеза Дьедонне является весьма частным случаем сформулированной выше общей задачи и почти всегда $D^* \neq \Sigma$. А именно, если Φ—n-мерная ($n > 2$) невырожденная эрмитова форма над D положительного индекса, $U(\Phi)$—унитарная группа, соответствующая Φ, и $TU(\Phi)$—подгруппа, порожденная трансвекциями, то по теореме Уолла [**16**] $D^* = \Sigma \Leftrightarrow U(\Phi) = TU(\Phi)$, т.е. гипотеза Дьедонне эквивалентна тривиальности спинорной нормы (см. [**16**], [**17**]) для унитарной группы $U(\Phi)$. Хорошо известно, что $U(\Phi)$ является группой k-точек G_k некоторой k-формы G обычной ортогональной группы. Пусть $\tilde{G}$—односвязная накрывающая группа G, определенная над k, $\varphi: \tilde{G} \to G$—соответствующая k-изогения. Нетрудно доказать, что

$$\varphi(\tilde{G}_k) \neq G_k \Leftrightarrow D^* \neq \Sigma.$$

Сформулируем теперь основной результат, полученный в [**18**].

Теорема 2. *Пусть k—бесконечное конечнопорожденное поле, f: $G \to G'$ —нетривиальная k-изогения. Тогда $f(G_k) \neq G'_k$.*

Замечание 1. Условие конечнопорожденности поля k существенно и, например, для вещественных или $\mathfrak{p}$-адических полей Теорема 2, вообще говоря, неверна. Вместе с тем следует указать, что ее доказательство проходит в несколько более общей ситуации, когда k—конечное расширение произвольного поля функций над простым подполем.

Замечание 2. Если k—конечное поле, то из [**13**] следует, что

$$f(G_k) \neq G'_k \Leftrightarrow (\operatorname{Ker} f)_k \neq (1).$$

Для доказательства Теоремы 2 автором в [**18**] был разработан новый метод, имеющий, как нам кажется, принципиальное значение и обладающий широкими возможностями для применения в различных арифметических и структурных вопросах теории алгебраических групп. Этот метод базируется на некотором аналоге теоремы плотности Артина-Чеботарева для неархимедовых локально-компактных нормирований произвольных конечнопорожденных полей в сочетании с аппроксимационными соображениями для подобных нормирований. В частности, важную роль играет следующее утверждение.

Теорема 3. *Пусть Δ—конечное сепарабельное расширение поля k. Тогда существует бесконечное множество неархимедовых локально-компактных нормирований v поля k, для которых пополнения $k_v \supset \Delta$.*

Замечание 3. Условие сепарабельности в Теореме 3 существенно и не может быть опущено, как показывает пример уже простейшего чисто несепарабельного расширения.

3. Строение анизотропных групп. Пусть G—k-определенная алгебраическая группа. Напомним, что она называется k-анизотропной, если в ней нет нетривиальных k-разложимых торов, т.е. $\operatorname{rank}_k G = 0$. В настоящее время усилиями главным образом Бореля, Титса и Сатаке классификация полупростых k-определенных алгебраических групп в существенной степени редуцирована к классификации k-анизотропных групп (см. [**19**], [**20**]). Проблема классификации k-анизотропных групп над произвольным полем k представляется в настоящее время нереальной. Поэтому естественно попытаться получить классификацию хотя бы для наиболее употребительных полей. Пока наиболее общий результат принадлежит Брюа и Титсу [**21**], которые доказали, что над полным дискретно нормированным полем k с совершенным полем вычетов k-анизотропная группа G является k-формой группы типа A_n, а если когомологическая размерность поля вычетов $\bar{k}$, $\operatorname{cd}(\bar{k})$ не превосходит единицы, то G является внутренней k-формой типа A_n, т.е. $G_k = \mathrm{SL}(1, D)$, где $\mathrm{SL}(1, D)$ обозначает подгруппу элементов некоммутативного конечномерного тела D с центром k, приведенная норма которых равна единице: $\mathrm{SL}(1, D) = (d \in D \mid \operatorname{Nrd}(d) = 1)$. Это обобщает более ранний результат Кнезера для $\mathfrak{p}$-адического числового поля k.

Следовательно, в проблеме классификации k-анизотропных простых групп имеются определенные успехи. Значительно хуже обстоит дело с изучением структуры k-анизотропных групп. Мы располагаем весьма незначительными сведениями о строении k-анизотропных групп G, в особенности об абстрактном строении группы G_k, что важно как для разнообразных применений, так и с точки зрения классических традиций в теории групп. Даже для k-анизотропной группы G типа A_1 мало что известно о строении группы G_k. Более того, для поля алгебраических чисел k до сих пор не доказана гипотеза Кнезера [**22**] о том, что для односвязной k-анизотропной группы G типа A_1 (т.е. $G_k = \mathrm{SL}(1, D)$, где D—тело кватернионов над k) фактор-группа $G_k/Z(G_k)$ абстрактно проста тогда и только тогда, когда G разложима над всеми $\mathfrak{p}$-адическими пополнениями $k_{\mathfrak{p}}$ поля k. В тоже время заострение внимания на группах типа A_1, по-видимому, не связано с существом дела и целесообразно сформулировать следующую общую *гипотезу*: если G—односвязная k-анизотропная простая алгебраическая группа над полем алгебраических чисел k, то группа $G_k/Z(G_k)$ абстрактно проста тогда и только тогда, когда она $k_{\mathfrak{p}}$-изотропна над всеми $\mathfrak{p}$-адическими пополнениями поля k.

Наиболее естественным классом полей k, для которых выяснение структуры группы G_k имеет важное значение, является класс полных дискретно нормированных полей с совершенным полем вычетов $\bar{k}$. Если к тому же $\mathrm{cd}(\bar{k}) \leqq 1$, то $G_k = \mathrm{SL}(1, D)$. Для таких полей Хардером высказана интересная гипотеза [**23**]: если F—нормальный делитель $\mathrm{SL}(1, D)$, содержащий максимальный тор, соответствующий неразветвленному максимальному подполю D (т.е. для неразветвленного максимального подполя $L \supset k$ в F содержится $T = (x \in L | N_{L/k}(x) = 1)$, где $N_{L/k}$—символ нормы L над k), тогда $F = \mathrm{SL}(1, D)$. Эта гипотеза имеет не только самостоятельное значение—в качестве следствия из нее получаются некоторые результаты о слабой аппроксимации (см. [**23**]).

Автору совместно с Янчевским удалось доказать гипотезу Хардера и попутно установить, что для рассматриваемых полей каждый элемент группы $\mathrm{SL}(1, D)$ есть произведение не более двух коммутаторов мультипликативной группы D^*, в частности, $\mathrm{SL}(1, D) = [D^*, D^*]$. Дадим более точные формулировки.

Пусть O_D—кольцо целых элементов D, $\mathfrak{p}$—простой идеал O_D. Хорошо известно (см. [**24**, гл. 12, § 2]), что D обладает неразветвленными максимальными подполями; пусть L—одно из них и $T = (x \in L | N_{L/k}(x) = 1)$.

Теорема 4. *Если тело $O_D/\mathfrak{p}$ коммутативно, то всякий нормальный делитель F группы* $\mathrm{SL}(1, D)$, *содержащий T, совпадает с* $\mathrm{SL}(1, D)$.

Следствие. *Если* $\mathrm{cd}(\bar{k}) \leqq 1$, *то $O_D/\mathfrak{p}$—коммутативно и гипотеза Хардера справедлива.*

Теорема 5. *В условиях Теоремы* 4 *каждый элемент из* $\mathrm{SL}(1, D)$ *есть произведение не более двух коммутаторов группы D^*, в частности,* $\mathrm{SL}(1, D) = [D^*, D^*]$.

Замечание 4. Нетрудно построить примеры, показывающие, что для максимального тора, связанного с разветвленным максимальным подполем тела D, Теорема 4 не верна.

Замечание 5. Если тело $O_D/\mathfrak{p}$ некоммутативно, то Теорема 4 также, вообще говоря, не верна. Вопрос о справедливости Теоремы 5 в этом случае остается открытым.

По-видимому, мы находимся сейчас в преддверии принципиальных идей, необходимых для исследования строения k-анизотропных групп, что в свою очередь должно привести к новому прогрессу в арифметической теории алгебраических групп.

Литература

1. M. Eichler, *Allgemeine Kongruenzklasseneinteilungen der Ideale einfacher Algebren über algebraischen Zahlkörpern und ihre L-Reihen,* J. Reine Angew. Math. **179** (1938), 227–251.

2. A. Weil, *Sur la formule de Siegel dans la théorie des groupes,* Acta Math. **113** (1965), 1–87.

3. M. Kneser, *Starke approximation in algebraischen Gruppen,* J. Reine Angew. Math. **218** (1965), 190–203.

4. ———, *Strong approximation,* Proc. Sympos. Pure Math., vol. 9, Amer. Math. Soc., Providence, R. I., 1966, pp. 187–197.

5. H. Behr, *Zur starken Approximation in algebraischen Gruppen über globalen Körpern,* J. Reine Angew. Math. **229** (1968), 107–116.

6. В. П. Платонов, *Проблема сильной аппроксимации и гипотеза Кнезера-Титса для алгебраических групп,* Известия АН СССР, сер. матем. **33** (1969), 1211–1220.

7. ———, *Дополнение к работе "Проблема сильной аппроксимации и гипотеза Кнезера-Титса для алгебраических групп",* Известия АН СССР, сер. матем. **34** (1970), 775–777.

8. J. Tits, *Algebraic and abstract simple groups,* Ann. of Math. (2) **80** (1964), 313–329.

9. G. Harder, *Semi-simple group schemes over curves and automorphic functions,* Actes Congr. Inter. Math., vol. 2, 1971, pp. 307–312.

10. В. П. Платонов и В. И. Янчевский, *Коммутант простой алгебры и унитарные группы над глобальными полями,* Доклады АН СССР **208** (1973), 541–544.

11. ———, *Арифметическая теория линейных алгебраических групп и теория чисел,* Труды Матем. ин-та им. Стеклова **132** (1973), 162–168.

12. ———, *Алгебраические группы, "Алгебра. Топология. Геометрия",* Итоги науки, т. II, 1974, 5–37.

13. S. Lang, *Algebraic groups over finite fields,* Amer. J. Math. **78** (1956), 555–563.

14. A. Borel and J. Tits, *Complements a l'article "Groupes reductifs",* I. H. E. S. Publ. Math. **41** (1972), 253–276.

15. J. Dieudonné, *On the structure of unitary groups,* Trans. Amer. Math. Soc. **72** (1952), 367–385.

16. G.E. Wall, *The structure of a unitary factor group,* I.H.E.S. Publ. Math. **1** (1959).

17. J. Dieudonné, *La géometrie des groupes classiques,* Ergebnisse der Mathematik und ihre Grenzgebiete, Band 5, Springer-Verlag, Berlin, 1971.

18. В.П. Платонов, *Гипотеза Дьедонне и несюрьективность накрытий алгебраических групп на k-точках,* Доклады АН СССР **216** (1974), 986–989.

19. A. Borel and J. Tits, *Groupes reductifs,* I.H.E.S. Publ. Math. **27** (1965), 659–755.

20. J. Tits, *Classification of semisimple groups,* Algebraic Groups and Discontinuous Subgroups, Proc. Sympos. Pure Math., vol. 9, Amer. Math. Soc., Providence, R.I., 1966, pp. 33–62,

21. F. Bruhat and J. Tits, *Groupes algébriques simples sur un corps local: cohomologie galoisienne, decompositions d'Iwasawa et de Cartan,* C.R. Acad. Sci. Paris **263** (1966), No. 23A, 867–869.

22. M. Kneser, *Ortogonale Gruppen über algebraischen Zahlkörpern,* J. Reine Angew. Math. **196** (1956), 213–220.

23. G. Harder, *Eine Bemerkung zum schwachen Approximationssatz,* Arch. Math. **19** (1968), 465–472.

24. J.-P. Serre, *Corps locaux,* Hermann, Paris, 1962.

25. T. Ono, *On the relative theory of Tamagawa numbers,* Ann. of Math. (2) **82** (1965), 88–111.

Институт Математики Академии Наук БССР
Минск, СССР

Section 6

Geometry

Proceedings of the International Congress of Mathematicians
Vancouver, 1974

Some Open Questions on Convex Surfaces*

William J. Firey

1. The questions I have in mind concern the determination of a convex surface from a certain amount of local data about the surface. By a convex surface I mean the whole boundary of a compact, convex set with interior points in Euclidean n-space. A convex surface is doubly simple: In the large it is topologically a sphere; in the small it cannot behave too badly near any of its points. The nature of the support function of such a surface Σ reflects these facts. For each point u on the unit sphere Ω there is a support hyperplane

$$\langle x, u \rangle = H(u) \tag{1}$$

with normal direction u which meets Σ and so that Σ lies in the nonpositive half-space determined by (1). The sharp brackets signify inner product; I write $\|x\|$ for $\langle x, x \rangle^{1/2}$ and o for the origin. Extend H by

$$H(o) = 0, \qquad H(x) = \|x\| H(x/\|x\|), \quad \text{for } x \neq o.$$

The resulting support function of Σ is convex, continuous and differentiable almost everywhere. H determines Σ uniquely.

If Σ is strictly convex and H smooth enough then, viewing Σ as the envelope of hyperplanes (1), we find

$$x(u) = (\partial H(u)/\partial x_1, \cdots, \partial H(u)/\partial x_n) \tag{2}$$

is that point of Σ with outer normal direction u. I call (2) the normal representation of Σ. Next

$$dx(u) = du\mathscr{H}(u), \tag{3}$$

*This work was supported in part by a grant from the U.S. National Science Foundation (NSF GP-28291).

where $\mathscr{H}(u)$ is the Hessian matrix $(\partial^2 H(u)/\partial x_i\, \partial x_j)$ of H. The homogeneity of H shows $\mathscr{H}(u)$ is homogeneous of degree (-1) and has rank no more than $n-1$. Indeed, by Euler's theorem

$$u\mathscr{H}(u) = o. \tag{4}$$

The strict convexity of Σ implies $\mathscr{H}(u)$ has $n-1$ positive eigenvalues $R_1(u), \cdots, R_{n-1}(u)$ which, by the formulas of Olinde Rodrigues, are precisely the principal radii of curvature of Σ at $x(u)$. I write $\{R_1 \cdots R_p\}(u)$ for the elementary symmetric function of degree p in these radii at $x(u)$; $\{R_1 \cdots R_p\}(u)$ is the sum of the principal minors of order p in $\mathscr{H}(u)$. Finally, let us generate the measures

$$S_p(\Sigma; \omega) = \int_\omega \{R_1 \cdots R_p\}(u)\, d\omega(u) \Big/ \binom{n-1}{p}$$

over the Borel sets ω of Ω; $d\omega$ is the area element on Ω. S_p is called the pth area function of Σ. In particular $S_{n-1}(\Sigma, \omega)$ is the area of the set σ of points of Σ which lie in (1) for some u in ω; σ is the inverse spherical image of ω on Σ. If $\Sigma(\lambda)$ denotes the outer parallel of Σ in the amount λ, that is the set of points $x(u) + \lambda u$, then the inverse spherical image $\sigma(\lambda)$ of ω on $\Sigma(\lambda)$ has area

$$S_{n-1}(\Sigma(\lambda); \omega) = \sum_{p=0}^{n-1} \binom{n-1}{p} S_p(\Sigma\,; \omega)\lambda^{n-p-1}. \tag{5}$$

where $S_0(\Sigma\,; \omega)$ is just the area of ω.

For a general convex surface Σ the description of $S_{n-1}(\Sigma\,; \omega)$ as the area of the inverse spherical image σ is still valid and $S_{n-1}(\Sigma(\lambda); \omega)$ is a polynomial in λ of degree $n-1$. We may take (5) as defining the measures $S_p(\Sigma; \omega)$ for $p = 0, 1, \cdots, n-2$. Details are in **[3]**. Here is a direct definition of S_p when Σ is a polytope. Let Ω_p be the set of outer normal directions to support hyperplanes which contain a p-dimensional face of Σ; this is a union of $(n-p-1)$-dimensional closed spherical polytopes, one for each p-face of Σ. Over each such spherical polytope distribute mass with constant density equal to the p-dimensional volume of the corresponding p-face. Then $S_p(\Sigma\,; \omega)$ is the mass in $\omega \cap \Omega_p$ divided by $\binom{n-1}{p}$

2. This prepares us for Minkowski-Christoffel problems. Given a measure μ over the Borel sets of Ω, which is positive over open hemispheres, is there a convex surface Σ whose pth area function is this measure? Minkowski treated the case $p = n-1$ for polytopes and smooth figures. W. Fenchel and B. Jessen **[3]** and A. D. Aleksandrov **[1]** found the complete answer for $p = n-1$: A solution exists if and only if

$$\int_\Omega \langle u, v\rangle \mu(d\omega(u)) = 0, \quad \text{for all } v \text{ in } \Omega. \tag{6}$$

The solution is unique up to translations. Indeed this uniqueness result holds for each choice of p.

For $1 \leqq p < n-1$, (5) shows that (6) is still a necessary condition, but (6) suffices for no such p. A. D. Aleksandrov **[1]** showed this for Christoffel's problem, $p = 1$, by two counterexamples. One depended on the fact that $S_1(\Sigma\,; \omega)$ cannot have point concentrations. The other counterexample relates to the smooth form of Christoffel's problem: Find a support function H such that the sum of the eigenvalues of $\mathscr{H}(u)$ is a preassigned function $f(u)$ over Ω. Here the necessary condition (6) takes the form

$$\int_\Omega \langle u, v\rangle f(u)\, d\omega(u) = 0, \quad \text{for all } v \text{ in } \Omega. \tag{7}$$

Aleksandrov produced a nonconvex H for which the positive sum $f(u)$ of the eigenvalues of $\mathscr{H}(u)$ satisfied (7).

Independently C. Berg [**2**] and I [**4**] found two further conditions on μ, needed along with (6), to make up a set necessary and sufficient for the solvability of Christoffel's problem. One is global to guarantee the convexity of H; the other limits the concentrations in the mass distribution on Ω which generates μ.

For all intermediate problems, $1 < p < n - 1$, the existence question is open. There is a solution for smooth surfaces of revolution [**5**]. A. V. Pogorelov [**11**] has sufficient conditions in the smooth general case, but these are not necessary. W. Weil [**13**] has suggestive results about the support of the measure $S_1(\Sigma\,; \omega)$. Finally [**6**] gives necessary restrictions on mass concentrations in distributions generating $S_p(\Sigma\,; \omega)$. I suspect that a single global condition for each p, ensuring the convexity of H, is all we lack for the complete solution of the intermediate Minkowski-Christoffel problems.

I add some related, possibly simpler, questions. Does the support of $S_p(\Sigma\,; \omega)$ contain that of $S_q(\Sigma\,; \omega)$ for $q > p$? W. Weil [**13**] showed this is so for $p = 1$. Are the pth area functions necessarily qth area functions for $q > p$ (for different surfaces)? Yes, if $q = n - 1$ because (6) is always a necessary condition and is also sufficient for μ to be an S_{n-1}. Lastly, is the sum of the two pth area functions another one? Yes for $p = 1$ and $n - 1$.

The foregoing problems have normal data, that is data specified in terms of outer normal directions. Recently H. Gluck [**7**] solved a generalized Minkowski problem—what I call by contrast a problem with free data. The problem is to find an embedding of Ω onto a convex surface which has preassigned positive reciprocal Gauss curvature $R_1 \cdots R_{n-1}$ over Ω, but not necessarily as a function of outer normal directions. The case $n = 2$ has interesting special features which, for brevity, I must omit; but for $n \geqq 3$ the problem has a solution (generally not unique) based on a crucial deformation theorem. A normal vector field on a smooth convex surface Σ assigns a normal vector $g(u)u$ to each point $x(u)$ on Σ; a deformation of this field is a normal field $f(u)u$ with $f = g \circ h$, h being a C^∞ diffeomorphism of Ω onto Ω, diffeotopic to the identity. Gluck showed that a continuous normal field over a smooth convex surface Σ can be deformed so that (7) holds. Now (7) replaces (6) in the Minkowski problem for smooth surfaces, where f is the reciprocal Gauss curvature. Thus (7) ensures that the problem with normal data has a solution; hence so does the generalized Minkowski problem with free data.

As further problems with free data, I ask: Is there an embedding of Ω onto a convex surface with $\{R_1 \cdots R_p\}$ preassigned as free data on Ω? In particular, can we deform a normal vector field $g(u)u$ over Σ, g positive and continuous on Ω, to the field $(R_1(u) + \cdots + R_{n-1}(u))u$ over Σ?

3. Next some questions suggested by a problem of H. Weyl. Again I begin with some background. For each point $y \neq o$, let $\mathscr{B}(y)$ signify an $n \times n$ symmetric matrix-valued C^1 function for which

$$\mathscr{B}(\lambda y) = \lambda^{-p}\mathscr{B}(y), \quad \lambda > 0; \qquad y\mathscr{B}(y) = o.$$

Let $\mathscr{Q}_p$ be the set of quadratic differential forms, one for each function $\mathscr{B}$, $\langle dy\mathscr{B}(y), dy\rangle = B(y, dy)$. The restriction of B to points u on Ω and vectors du tangent to Ω at u specifies a quadratic differential form $B(u, du)$ over Ω. I write $\mathscr{Q}(\Omega)$ for the class of such forms over Ω. In turn, each quadratic differential form $B(u, du)$ in $\mathscr{Q}(\Omega)$ has a unique extension in $\mathscr{Q}_p$:

$$B(y, dy) = \|y\|^{-p}B(u, dy - \langle u, dy\rangle u), \qquad u = y/\|y\|.$$

What follows could all be put in terms of $\mathscr{Q}(\Omega)$, but it is sometimes convenient to use an appropriate $\mathscr{Q}_p$. In this discussion I assume $n \geqq 3$.

Let Σ be a smooth convex surface with normal representation $u \to x(u)$. The forms $\langle du, du\rangle$, $\langle du, dx(u)\rangle$, $\langle dx(u), dx(u)\rangle = ds^2(u)$ in $\mathscr{Q}(\Omega)$ are the three fundamental forms of Σ in the Gaussian theory of surfaces in 3-space. I use (3) and the symmetry of $\mathscr{H}(u)$ to write these forms as

$$\langle du\mathscr{H}^p(u), du\rangle \tag{8}$$

for $p = 0, 1, 2$. This suggests that, for a convex surface Σ in n-space, we allow $p = 0, 1, \cdots, n - 1$ so as to generate $n-1$ fundamental forms (8). The pth fundamental form may be viewed as one in $\mathscr{Q}_p$ because of (4) and the homogeneity of $\mathscr{H}$; in doing this, we must define $\mathscr{H}^0$ by

$$\langle dy\, \mathscr{H}^0(y), dy\rangle = \|dy\|^2 - \langle y, dy\rangle^2/\|y\|^2.$$

The forms (8) are not independent: the Cayley-Hamilton theorem and a small extra argument give

$$\sum_{p=0}^{n-1} (-1)^p\{R_1 \cdots R_{n-p-1}\}(u)\langle du\mathscr{H}^p(u), du\rangle = 0.$$

All this is classical for $n = 3$; for general n, but by different methods, it is due to H. Rund [**12**].

A first question: What is the geometric significance of these forms when $p>2$? Rund [**12**] has suggestive remarks to this,

Weyl's problem is this: With $n = 3$, find a convex surface Σ whose squared line element ds^2 is a prescribed form B in $\mathscr{Q}(\Omega)$. The first comprehensive result is H. Lewy's [**9**]. If B is analytic, positive definite and has positive Gauss curvature, computed from B by the usual formula, then B is realisable as the squared line element of an analytic convex surface Σ which is unique up to a rigid motion. For brevity I must pass over the extensive later work on Weyl's problem.

Weyl's problem has free data: If the map: $v \to z(v)$ over Ω describes a solution Σ with squared line element $B(v, dv)$ at $z(v)$, then v is not necessarily normal to Σ at $z(v)$. As a different question, we may alter Weyl's problem to one with normal data. In effect we ask: Given $\langle du\mathscr{B}(u), du\rangle$ in $\mathscr{Q}_2$, can we find a support function H of a convex surface Σ such that the squared Hessian matrix $\mathscr{H}^2(u)$ of H equals $\mathscr{B}(u)$? As a more general problem with normal data, we seek a convex surface Σ with normal representation: $u \to x(u)$ whose pth fundamental form at $x(u)$, $1 \leqq p \leqq n-1$, is a preassigned form $B(u, du)$ in $\mathscr{Q}_p$.

When $p = 1$, a solution surface Σ exists if and only if the matrix $\mathscr{B}$ of the form B in $\mathscr{Q}_1$ is nonnegative and $dy\,\mathscr{B}(y)$ is a closed differential form in the sense that this is so for each of its components. The necessity is immediate. For the sufficiency, construct $x(u)$ by line integration from $dy\,\mathscr{B}(y)$, define H by (1), with $x(u)$ for x, and verify that H is the support function of a solution Σ. For general p a solution exists if and only if $\mathscr{B}$ in $\mathscr{Q}_p$ is nonnegative and $dy(\mathscr{B}(y))^{1/p}$ is closed, where $(\mathscr{B}(y))^{1/p}$ means the nonnegative pth root. In all cases, Σ is unique to within a translation.

This leaves us with the corresponding open questions with free data: For preassigned $1 \leqq p \leqq n-1$, find a convex surface Σ whose pth fundamental form is a prescribed form B in $\mathscr{Q}(\Omega)$. See also **[8]** for related material. In the case of Weyl's problem, we have solutions to both the free data problem and the normal data problem. This should suggest data deformation theorems which might play the same connecting roles as Gluck's deformation theorem did in the study of the generalized Minkowski problem.

4. My last questions are integral-geometric. Let Σ, Σ' be convex surfaces on which we choose subsets σ, σ' which are inverse spherical images of Borel sets ω, ω' of Ω; let $\mathfrak{g}$ be a rigid motion of n-space. I say $\mathfrak{g}\sigma'$ supports Σ in σ if $\mathfrak{g}\sigma'$ meets σ and $\mathfrak{g}\Sigma'$ and Σ bound disjoint open convex sets. The set $\mathfrak{m}$ of all $\mathfrak{g}$ such that $\mathfrak{g}\sigma'$ supports Σ in σ has a rigid motion invariant measure $\bar{\mu}(\mathfrak{m})$. This is derived from Haar measure in the rigid motion group in much the same way Cantor and Minkowski derived surface area measure from volume. As before, let $\sigma(\lambda)$ be the inverse spherical image of ω on the outer parallel $\Sigma(\lambda)$; form the set $\mathfrak{m}(\varepsilon)$ of $\mathfrak{g}$ such that $\mathfrak{g}\sigma'$ supports $\Sigma(\lambda)$ in $\sigma(\lambda)$ for some positive $\lambda < \varepsilon$. Then $\mathfrak{m}(\varepsilon)$ has positive Haar measure $\mu(\mathfrak{m}(\varepsilon))$ and

$$(9)\qquad \bar{\mu}(\mathfrak{m}) = \lim_{\varepsilon \to 0+} \mu(\mathfrak{m}(\varepsilon))/\varepsilon = \sum_{p=0}^{n-1} \binom{n-1}{p} S_p(\Sigma;\omega) S_{n-p-1}(\Sigma';\omega'),$$

if we suitably normalize μ. I call $\bar{\mu}$ the kinematic measure for the set of positions of σ' which support Σ in σ; it serves to calculate probabilities of collisions of preassigned type between convex bodies in relative random motion. Special cases of (9) were found by R. Schneider and independently by P. McMullen **[10]**.

A number of properties of $\bar{\mu}$ follow from (9): $\bar{\mu}$ is defined for all choices of Σ, Σ' and Borel sets ω, ω' on Ω; it is symmetric in the pairs Σ, ω and Σ', ω'; $\bar{\mu}$ is a measure separately in each argument ω, ω'; $\bar{\mu}$ depends continuously on Σ, Σ' in the sense of convergence of set functions (see **[3]**). Finally, $\bar{\mu}$ is rigid-motion invariant in the sense that, if we replace Σ, σ by $\mathfrak{g}_0\Sigma$, $\mathfrak{g}_0\sigma$ for some fixed motion $\mathfrak{g}_0$ in the definition of $\mathfrak{m}$, we do not change the value of $\bar{\mu}$. Do these properties characterize $\bar{\mu}$ to within a normalization?[2]

[2]Recently R. Schneider has characterized $\bar{\mu}$ by these and several additional properties.

Fix Σ', take ω' to be Ω. Does the resulting measure $\bar{\mu}$, defined over the Borel sets ω of Ω, determine Σ up to a translation? Yes, if $n = 3$ and Σ is smooth. In this case $\bar{\mu}$ has a Radon-Nikodym derivative

$$f(R_1, R_2) = \alpha + \beta(R_1 + R_2) + \gamma R_1 R_2,$$

where α, β, γ are the positive total area functions of Σ; f is strictly increasing in R_1, R_2. The asserted uniqueness follows from a theorem of A. D. Aleksandrov [**11**]: with such an f, if two convex surfaces in 3-space have equal values of $f(R_1, R_2)$ at points with corresponding normals, then one surface is a translate of the other. All other cases of this question are open.

References

1. A. D. Aleksandrov, *Zur Theorie des gemischten Volumina von konvexen Körper*. III. *Die Erweiterung zweier Lehrsätze Minkowskis über die konvexen Polyeder auf beliebige konvexen Flächen*, Mat. Sb. **3** (1938), 24–46. (Russian)

2. C. Berg. *Corps convexes et potentiels sphériques*, Mat.-Fys. Medd. Danske Vid. Selsk. **37** (1969), no. 6. MR **40** #7996.

3. W. Fenchel and B. Jessen, *Mengenfunktionen und konvexe Körper*, Mat.-Fys. Medd. Danske Vid. Selsk. **16** (1938), no. 3.

4. W. J. Firey, *Christoffel's problem for general convex bodies*, Mathematika **15** (1968), 7–21. MR **37** #5822.

5. ———, *Intermediate Christoffel-Minkowski problems for figures of revolution*, Israel J. Math. **8** (1970), 384–390. MR **42** #6719.

6. ———, *Local behaviour of area functions of convex bodies*, Pacific J. Math. **35** (1970), 345–357. MR **44** #4189.

7. H. Gluck, *The generalized Minkowski problem in differential geometry in the large*, Ann. of Math. (2) **96** (1972), 245–276. MR **46** #8132.

8. H. Huck, et al., *Beweismethoden der Differentialgeometrie im Grossen*, Lecture Notes in Math., Vol. 335, Springer-Verlag, Berlin and New York, 1973.

9. H. Lewy, *On the existence of a closed convex surface realizing a given Riemannian metric*, Proc. Nat. Acad. Sci. U.S.A. **24** (1938), 104–106.

10. P. McMullen, *A dice probability problem*, Mathematika **21** (1974), 193–198.

11. A. V. Pogorelov, *The extrinsic geometry of convex surfaces*, "Nauka", Moscow, 1969; English transl., Transl. Math. Monographs, vol. 35, Amer, Math. Soc., Providence, R.I., 1973. MR **39** #6222.

12. H. Rund, *Curvature invariants associated with sets of a fundamental forms of hypersurfaces of n-dimensional Riemannian manifolds*, Tensor **22** (1971), 163–173. MR **44** #5898.

13. W. Weil, *Ein Approximationssatz für konvexe Körper*, Manuscripta Math. **8** (1973), 335–362.

Oregon State University
Corvallis, Oregon 97331, U.S.A.

Proceedings of the International Congress of Mathematicians
Vancouver, 1974

Convex Polyhedra and Mathematical Programming

Victor Klee

Introduction. This article surveys the status of certain questions about the combinatorial structure of (convex) polyhedra, with emphasis on four problems of special relevance to mathematical programming. For earlier discussions of these and related problems, see the book of Grünbaum [**1967**], the monograph of McMullen and Shephard [**1971**], and the survey articles of Klee [**1966a**], Grünbaum and Shephard [**1969**], and Grünbaum [**1970**].

As the terms are used here, a *polyhedron* is the intersection of a finite number of closed half-spaces and a *polytope* is a bounded polyhedron; equivalently, a polytope is the convex hull of a finite set of points. A polyhedron of *class* (d, n) is one that is d-dimensional and has exactly n *facets* ($(d-1)$-faces). From the viewpoint of linear programming it is natural to focus on polyhedra of a given class, for even though the class of a feasible region may be computationally difficult to determine precisely, some useful information about it comes free of charge from the manner in which the region is defined. It is also natural to focus on d-polyhedra that are *simple* (each vertex incident to exactly d edges), for they are the ones that arise from nondegenerate linear programming problems. The family of all simple polytopes of class (d, n) is denoted here by $S(d, n)$.

Two of the special problems mentioned earlier are those of determining the minimum and the maximum of $v(P)$ (number of vertices of P) as P ranges over $S(d, n)$. These extrema are important in estimating the computational complexity of various problems related to polytopes. Not only does the problem of finding all vertices arise in many contexts, but $v(P)$ is of interest in connection with optimization because (a) each convex function on a polytope P attains its maximum at a vertex; (b) P admits a convex function for which each vertex provides a strict local maximum; (c) $\eta(P) < v(P)$, where $\eta(P)$ (the *height* of P) is the length (number of edges) of the longest path in P's 1-skeleton along which some linear function is strictly monotone.

Note that $\eta(P)$ is the maximum number of iterations encountered in applying the simplex algorithm, with a very relaxed pivot rule, to solve nondegenerate linear programs over P. Smaller "heights" are similarly defined using more restrictive pivot rules, the most important being the *simplex height* $\xi(P)$ based on the pivot rule of Dantzig [**1951**]. The third special problem is that of determining the maximum $\Xi(d, n)$ of $\xi(P)$ over $S(d, n)$.

The *diameter* $\delta(P)$ of a polyhedron P is the smallest k such that any pair of P's vertices can be joined by a path of length $\leqq k$. The fourth problem is that of determining the maximum $\Delta(d, n)$ of $\delta(P)$ over $S(d, n)$. The number $\Delta(d, n)$ is in a sense the number of iterations required to solve the "worst" (bounded) linear program in d variables and n inequality constraints, using the "best" edge-following algorithm.

1. Minimum number of vertices. The first special problem has been solved. Indeed,

1.1. *The minimum of* $v(P)$ *over* $S(d, n)$ *is equal to* $(n - d)(d - 1) + 2$.

That is immediate for $d = 3$, was proved for $n \leqq d + 3$ by Grünbaum [**1967**], for $d \leqq 5$ by Walkup [**1970**], and in general by Barnette [**1971**]. Barnette [**1973a**] determined the minimum over $S(d, n)$ of $f_k(P)$, the number of k-faces of P. A dual formulation in terms of simplicial polytopes enabled Barnette [**1973b**] to extend 1.1 to a wide class of simplicial manifolds. See § 3 below for a different extension of 1.1.

2. Maximum number of vertices. The second special problem has been solved. Indeed,

2.1. *The maximum* $\gamma(d, n)$ *of* $v(P)$ *over* $S(d, n)$ *is equal to*

$$\binom{n - [(d + 1)/2]}{n - d} + \binom{n - [(d + 2)/2]}{n - d}.$$

That is immediate for $d \leqq 3$ and was conjectured in general by Motzkin [**1957**]. It was proved for $d \leqq 6$ by Fieldhouse [**1961**], for $n \leqq d + 3$ by Gale [**1964**], and for (roughly) $n > [d/2]^2$ by Klee [**1964a**]. Grünbaum [**1969**] improved Klee's bound and the general problem was settled by McMullen [**1970**]. See Grünbaum [**1967**] and McMullen and Shephard [**1971**] for detailed discussions of 2.1 and analogous results on the maximum of $f_k(P)$, and see § 3 for a different extension of 2.1.

McMullen's proof of 2.1 uses much more of the structure of polytopes than does Klee's partial result. In particular, the former relies on shellability (Bruggesser and Mani [**1972**], Danaraj and Klee [**1974**]) while the latter applies in dual formulation to a wide class of not necessarily shellable simplicial complexes (the so-called *Eulerian manifolds*). A recently established generalization of 2.1 (Stanley [**1975a, b**]) is that each simplicial $(d - 1)$-sphere with n vertices has at most $\gamma(d, n)$ $(d - 1)$-simplices. Such a sphere must be combinatorially equivalent to the boundary complex of a simplicial d-polytope if $d \leqq 3$ (Steinitz and Rademacher [**1934**]) or $n \leqq d + 3$ (Mani [**1972**]) but not in general (Grünbaum and Sreedharan [**1967**], Barnette [**1973c**]).

3. Polytope pairs. Since the feasible region of a linear program is often unbounded, it is of interest to extend 1.1 and 2.1 to unbounded polyhedra. Motivated by the desire to do that and to analyze an algorithm of Mattheiss [**1973**] for finding all vertices of a polytope, Klee [**1974**] defined a *polytope pair of class* (d, n, u) as a pair (P, F) consisting of a simple polytope P of class (d, n) and a facet F intersecting precisely u other facets of P. He studied the minimum and maximum of $v(F)$, $v(P)$, $v(P \sim F)$, and $v(P \sim F)/v(F)$ as (P, F) ranges over all polytope pairs of a given class, and was able to determine those completely except for the maximum of $v(P)$ and the minimum of $v(P \sim F)/v(F)$; the exceptions were determined for the important case $u = n - 1$. A corollary of those results is the following extension of 1.1 and 2.1.

3.1. *As P ranges over all simple polyhedra of class (d, n) having precisely u unbounded facets, the minimum and maximum of $v(P)$ are respectively*

$$(u - n - 2)(d - 1) + 2 \quad \textit{and} \quad \gamma(d, n - 1) + d - u - 1.$$

4. Heights of polytopes. Since the inception of linear programming, it was widely believed that the simplex algorithm was a "good" algorithm in the sense that $\Xi(d, n)$ is bounded by a polynomial in d and n. (See Gale [**1969**] for a general discussion, Dantzig [**1963**] and Kuhn and Quandt [**1963**] for reports of computational experience.) However, by combining 2.1, a method of Klee [**1965a**], and a study of "perturbed products" of polytopes, Klee and Minty [**1972**] were able to show:

4.1. *For each d there are positive constants α_d and β_d such that*

$$\alpha_d n^{[d/2]} < \Xi(d, n) < \beta_d n^{[d/2]}.$$

In particular, $\Xi(d, 2d) \geqq 2^d - 1$. The method was extended by Jeroslow [**1973**] to other pivot rules, and analogous examples were obtained by Zadeh [**1973**] for the simplex algorithm as applied to minimum cost flow problems. Presumably the final explanation (if there ever is one) of the contrast between these results and the practical good behavior of the simplex algorithm will come from the realm of geometric probability. (See, for example, Schmidt [**1968**].)

5. Diameters of polytopes. In my opinion the fourth special problem is from several viewpoints (intuitive appeal, interest for linear programming, potential stimulation of new methods) the most important remaining unsolved problem on the combinatorial structure of high-dimensional polyhedra. There is particular interest in the numbers $\Delta(d, 2d)$ because $\Delta(d + k, 2d + k) = \Delta(d, 2d)$. If $\Delta(d, 2d)$ could be shown to increase exponentially with d it would follow there is no "good" edge-following algorithm for linear programming. However, the well-known conjectures of W. Hirsch (in Dantzig [**1963**]) are that $\Delta(d, 2d) = d$ and $\Delta(d, n) \leqq n - d$; they have become known respectively as the *d-step conjecture* and the *Hirsch conjecture*. The sharpest *proven* bounds are the following, due respectively to Adler [**1974**] and Barnette [**1975**]:

$$\left[(n-d) - \frac{(n-d)}{[5d/4]}\right] + 1 \leqq \Delta(d, n) \leqq \frac{1}{3}\, 2^{d-3}\left(n - d + \frac{5}{2}\right). \tag{5.1}$$

It is not even known whether the increase of $\Delta(d, 2d)$ is linear, polynomial or exponential in terms of d.

Klee [**1964b**] showed $\Delta(3, n) = [2n/3] - 1$, and Klee and Walkup [**1967**] proved

$$\Delta(d, n) \leqq n - d \quad \text{for} \quad n \leqq d + 5. \tag{5.2}$$

They also established the equivalence (though not on a dimension-for-dimension basis) of the d-step conjecture, the Hirsch conjecture, and the W_v *conjecture* asserting that any two vertices of a polytope can be joined a by path not revisiting any facet. At present the d-step conjecture has been proved for all $d \leqq 5$ but the other two only for $d \leqq 3$. They all apply to unbounded polyhedra as well for $d \leqq 3$ (see Klee [**1965b**], [**1966b**], Barnette [**1969**]), but not for $d = 5$ for Klee and Walkup [**1967**] produced a polyhedron of class (4, 8) and diameter 5. Their methods were improved by Larman [**1970**] and Goodey [**1972**] to sharpen the bounds on $\Delta(d, n)$ for small d and n (in particular, $\Delta(6, 12) \leqq 7$), and by Adler and Dantzig [**1974**] to extend (5.2) in dual form to a wide class of simplicial complexes, the so-called *abstract polytopes*. (They may be described as simplicial pseudomanifolds in which the link of each simplex is strongly connected.)

For polytopes arising from certain sorts of linear programs, the Hirsch conjecture or close relatives have been established by Saigal [**1969**], Grinold [**1970**], Balas and Padberg [**1972**], and Balinski and Russakoff [**1972**], [**1974**], Balinski [**1974**], and Padberg and Rao [**1974**].

References

I. Adler (**1974**), *Lower bounds for maximum diameters of polytopes*, Math. Programming Study **1**, 11–19.

I. Adler and G. B. Dantzig (**1974**), *Maximum diameter of abstract polytopes*, Math. Programming Study **1**, 20–40.

E. Balas and M. W. Padberg (**1972**), *On the set-covering problem*, Operations Res. **20**, 1152–1161.

M.L. Balinski (**1974**); *On two special classes of transportation polytopes*, Math. Programming Study **1**, 43–58.

M. L. Balinski and A. Russakoff (**1972**), *Some properties of the assignment polytope*, Math. Programming **3**, 257–258.

——— (**1974**), *On the assignment polytope*, SIAM Review **16**, 516–525.

D. W. Barnette (**1969**), *W_v paths on 3-polytopes*, J. Combinatorial Theory **7**, 62–70. MR **40** #1887.

——— (**1971**), *The minimum number of vertices of a simple polytope*, Israel J. Math. **10**, 121–125. MR **45** #7605.

——— (**1973a**), *A proof of the lower bound conjecture for convex polytopes*, Pacific J. Math. **46**, 349–354.

——— (**1973b**), *Graph theorems for manifolds*, Israel J. Math. **16**, 62–72.

——— (**1973c**), *The triangulations of the 3-sphere with up to 8 vertices*, J. Combinatorial Theory Ser. A **14**, 37–52. MR **47** #1068.

——— (**1974**), *An upper bound for the diameter of a polytope*. Discrete Math. **10**, 9–13.

H. Bruggesser and P. Mani (**1972**), *Shellable decompositions of cells and spheres*, Math. Scand. **17**, 179–184.

G. Danaraj and V. Klee (**1974**), *Shellings of spheres and polytopes*, Duke Math. J. **41**, 443–451.

G. B. Dantzig (**1951**), *Maximization of a linear function of variables subject to linear inequalities. Activity analysis of production and allocation*, Cowles Commission Monograph, no. 13, Wiley, New York; Chapman & Hall, London, pp. 339–347. MR **15**, 47.

——— (**1963**), *Linear programming and extensions*, Princeton Univ. Press, Princeton, N. J. MR **34** #1073.

M. Fieldhouse (**1961**), *Linear programming*, Ph.D. Thesis, Cambridge University.

D. Gale (**1964**), *On the number of faces of a convex polytope*, Canad. J. Math. **16**, 12–17. MR **28** #516.

——— (**1969**), *How to solve linear inequalities*, Amer. Math. Monthly **76**, 589–599. MR **39** #4193.

P. R. Goodey (**1972**), *Some upper bounds for the diameter of convex polytopes*, Israel J. Math. **11**, 380–385. MR **46** #9866.

R. C. Grinold (**1970**), *The Hirsch conjecture in Leontieff substitution systems*, SIAM J. Appl. Math. **21**, 483–485.

B. Grünbaum (**1967**), *Convex polytopes*, Pure and Appl. Math., Vol. 16, Interscience, New York. MR **37** #2085.

——— (**1969**), *Some results on the upper bound conjecture for convex polytopes*, SIAM J. Appl. Math. **17**, 1142–1149. MR **41** #4378.

——— (**1970**), *Polytopes, graphs, and complexes*, Bull. Amer. Math. Soc. **76**, 1131–1201. MR **42** #959.

B. Grünbaum and G. C. Shephard (**1969**), *Convex polytopes*, Bull. London Math. Soc. **1**, 257–300. MR **40** #3428.

B. Grünbaum and V. P. Sreedharan (**1967**), *An enumeration of simplicial* 4-*polytopes with* 8 *vertices*, J. Combinatorial Theory **2**, 437–465. MR **35** #6025.

R. G. Jeroslow (**1973**), *The simplex algorithm with the pivot rule of maximizing criterion improvement*, Discrete Math. **4**, 367–377.

V. L. Klee (**1964a**), *On the number of vertices of a convex polytope*, Canad. J. Math. **16**, 701–720. MR **29** #3955.

——— (**1964b**), *Diameters of polyhedral graphs*, Canad. J. Math. **16**, 620–614. MR **29** #2796.

——— (**1965a**), *A class of linear programming problems requiring a large number of iterations*, Numer. Math. **7**, 313–321. MR **32** #5369.

——— (**1965b**), *Paths on polyhedra*. I, J. Soc. Indust. Appl. Math. **13**, 946–956. MR **33** #635.

——— (**1966a**),*Convex polytopes and linear programming*, Proc. IBM Sci. Comput. Sympos. Combinatorial Problems (Yorktown Heights, N.Y., 1964), IBM Data Process Division, White Plains, N.Y., pp. 123–158. MR **36** #786.

——— (**1966b**), *Paths on polyhedra*. II, Pacific J. Math. **17**, 249–262. MR **33** #3187.

——— (**1974**), *Polytope pairs and their relationship to linear programming*, Acta Math. **133**, 1–25.

V. L. Klee and G. J. Minty (**1972**), *How good is the simplex algorithm?*, Inequalities III, Academic Press, New York, pp. 159–175.

V. L. Klee and D. W. Walkup (**1967**), *The d-step conjecture for polyhedra of dimension* $d < 6$, Acta Math. **117**, 53–78. MR **34** #6639.

H. W. Kuhn and R. E. Quandt (**1963**), *An experimental study of the simplex method*, Proc. Sympos. Appl. Math., vol. 15, Amer. Math. Soc., Providence, R. I., pp. 107–124. MR **28** #4950.

D. G. Larman (**1970**), *Paths on polytopes*, Proc. London Math. Soc. (3) **20**, 161–178. MR **40** #7942.

P. Mani (**1972**), *Spheres with few vertices*, J. Combinatorial Theory Ser. A **13**, 346–352. MR **47** #5723.

T. H. Mattheiss (**1973**), *An algorithm for determining irrelevant constraints and all vertices in systems of linear inequalities*, Operations Res. **21**, 247–260.

P. McMullen (**1970**), *The maximum number of faces of a convex polytope*, Mathematika **17**, 179–184. MR **44** #921.

P. McMullen and G. C. Shephard (**1971**), *Convex polytopes and the upper bound conjecture*,

London Math. Soc. Lecture Note Series, 3, Cambridge Univ. Press, London and New York. MR **46** #791.

T. S. Motzkin (**1957**), *Comonotone curves and polyhedra*, Bull. Amer. Math. Soc. **63**, 35.

M. W. Padberg and M.R. Rao (**1974**), *The travelling salesman problem and a class of polyhedra of diameter two*, Math. Programming **7**, 32–45.

R. Saigal (**1969**), *A proof of the Hirsch conjecture on the polyhedron of the shortest route problem*, SIAM J. Appl. Math. **17,** 1232–1238. MR **41** #1440.

W. M. Schmidt (**1968**), *Some results in probabilistic geometry*, Z. Wahrscheinlichkeitstheorie und Verw. Gebiete **9,** 158–162. MR **37** #4847.

R.P. Stanley (**1975a**), *Cohen-Macauley rings and constructible polytopes*, Bull. Amer. Math. Soc. **81**, 133–135.

——— (**1975b**), *The upper bound conjecture and Cohen-Macauley rings*, Studies in App. Math. (to appear).

E. Steinitz and H. Rademacher (**1934**), *Vorlesungen über die Theorie der Polyeder*, Springer, Berlin.

D. W. Walkup (**1970**), *The lower bound conjecture for* 3- *and* 4-*manifolds*, Acta Math. **125,** 75–107. MR **43** #1038.

N. Zadeh (**1973**), *Theoretical efficiency and partial equivalence of minimum cost flow algorithms. a bad network problem for the simplex method*, Math. Programming **5**, 255–266.

UNIVERSITY OF WASHINGTON
SEATTLE, WASHINGTON 98195, U.S.A.

Proceedings of the International Congress of Mathematicians
Vancouver, 1974

Metrical and Combinatorial Properties of Convex Polytopes

P. McMullen

This article takes as its theme the interaction between metrical and combinatorial properties of convex polytopes. To illustrate this theme, we begin with a few examples. The archetypal combinatorial property of polytopes is Euler's relation:

$$\sum_F (-1)^{\dim F} = 1,$$

where the sum extends over all (nonempty) faces F of a polytope P. A result of a similar type, but involving metrical quantities, is Gram's relation:

$$\sum_F (-1)^{\dim F} \beta(F, P) = 0 \qquad (\dim P > 0),$$

where $\beta(F, P)$ is the internal (solid) angle of P at F, measured intrinsically, and normalized so that the total angle is 1. (For results without specific references, see Bonnesen-Fenchel [**1934**], Hadwiger [**1957**] or Grünbaum [**1967**].)

A general result of Shephard [**1968**] is the following. We write $\varphi(P) = V(P, \cdots, P, K_{r+1}, \cdots, K_d)$ for the mixed volume, with the polytope P taken r times, and $K_{r+1}, \cdots, K_d$ general convex bodies. If we define $\varphi^*(P) = \sum_F (-1)^{\dim F} \varphi(F)$, then $\varphi^*(P) = (-1)^r \varphi(-P)$. In particular, if $K_{r+1} = \cdots = K_d = B$, the unit ball in E^d, $\varphi(P) = W_{d-r}(P)$ is the *Quermassintegral* which measures the $(d-r)$-flats of E^d which meet P. We prefer to normalize, and consider instead the *intrinsic r-volume* $V_r(P)$, which is such that

$$\omega_{d-r} V_r(P) = \binom{d}{r} W_{d-r}(P),$$

where ω_k is the volume of the unit k-ball. Then it can be shown that

$$V_r(P) = \sum_{r\text{-faces } F} \gamma(F, P) V(F),$$

where $\gamma(F, P)$ is the (normalized) external angle of P at F, and V denotes r-dimensional volume. Shephard's relation then implies that $V_r^*(P) = (-1)^r V_r(P)$; since $V_0(P) = 1$, this generalizes (in a sense) Euler's relation.

A result of a new type which we shall now present generalizes (in the same way) Gram's relation:

$$\sum_F (-1)^{\dim F} \beta(F, P) V_r(F) = (-1)^r V_r(P) \quad \text{if } \dim P = r,$$
$$= 0 \quad \text{otherwise.}$$

We shall prove this result as an application of a pair of inversion formulae. However, we may note that direct proofs of it, and the previous result, can be obtained by integrating Gram's or Euler's relation for the sections of P by $(d - r)$-flats.

The inversion formulae are as follows. If ϑ, ψ are two functions on polytopes, then the following are equivalent:

$$\psi(P) = \sum_F (-1)^{\dim P - \dim F} \beta(F, P) \vartheta(F),$$
$$\vartheta(P) = \sum_F \gamma(F, P) \psi(F).$$

Since $V(P) = V_r(P)$ if $\dim P = r$, the application above is clear.

We deduce the formulae from three angle-sum relations for polyhedral cones. These are

$$\sum_J \beta(F, J)\, \gamma(J, G) = \zeta(F, G),$$
$$\sum_J (-1)^{\dim J - \dim F} \beta(F, J) \gamma(J, G) = \delta(F, G),$$
$$\sum_J (-1)^{\dim G - \dim J} \gamma(F, J) \beta(J, G) = \delta(F, G),$$

where F, J, G are faces of a polyhedral cone K, $\zeta(F, G) = 1$ if $F \subseteq G$ and 0 otherwise, $\delta(F, G) = 1$ if $F = G$ and 0 otherwise, and all functions $\xi(F, G) = 0$ if $F \nsubseteq G$. (These relations are connected with the Gauss-Bonnet and Steiner parallel formulae for spherical polytopes.) It is enough to prove these results for a pointed polyhedral cone K with apex o, with $F = o$ and $G = K$. For the first, if $\hat{J}$ denotes the face of the polar cone K^* of K corresponding to J, then the cones $J \times \hat{J}$ cover E^d and have disjoint interiors; the solid angle of $J \times \hat{J}$ is $\beta(o, J)\beta(o, \hat{J}) = \beta(o, J)\gamma(J, K)$. The second follows from the first, using a theorem of Sommerville:

$$\sum_J (-1)^{\dim J} \beta(J, K) = (-1)^{\dim K} \beta(o, K),$$

and the third follows from the second by elementary linear algebra (the square matrices with entries $(-1)^{\dim G - \dim F}\beta(F, G)$ and $\gamma(F, G)$ are inverses of each other).

Closely connected with Euler's relation is the idea of an *Euler-type relation*. If φ is a function defined on polytopes, we set $\varphi^*(P) = \sum_F (-1)^{\dim F} \varphi(F)$, as before. If, for all P, $\varphi^*(P) = \pm \varphi(\pm P)$, we say that φ satisfies an Euler-type relation. (We have already met examples of such functions.) Now φ^{**} ($= (\varphi^*)^*$) $= \varphi$, so of course, if φ is any function and we set $\varphi_+ = \frac{1}{2}(\varphi + \varphi^*)$, $\varphi_- = \frac{1}{2}(\varphi - \varphi^*)$, then φ_+ and φ_- both satisfy Euler-type relations, and $\varphi = \varphi_+ + \varphi_-$. This might seem to make the idea of an Euler-type relation less significant, were it not for the following fact. A function φ is called a *valuation* if $\varphi(P \cup Q) + \varphi(P \cap Q) = \varphi(P) + \varphi(Q)$, whenever $P \cup Q$ is convex. Sallee **[1968]** has shown that if φ is continuous (in the Hausdorff metric) and satisfies an Euler-type relation $\varphi^* = \pm \varphi$, then φ is a valuation.

The mixed and intrinsic volumes introduced above are examples of valuations; as this may indicate, valuations are of great importance in this area. The second half of this article will be devoted to the question of valuations in general. We shall look at some very recent results (of the author), which relate properties of valuations to those of Euler-type relations.

Let Λ be an additive subgroup of E^d. We shall assume that aff $\Lambda = E^d$, and, to avoid certain technical difficulties, that Λ is either a discrete lattice or a d-dimensional vector space over some subfield of the real numbers. (Thus $\Lambda = E^d$ is possible.) We denote by $\mathscr{P}(\Lambda)$ the class of all polytopes with vertices in Λ. We call a valuation φ on $\mathscr{P}(\Lambda)$ a *Λ-valuation* if $\varphi(P + t) = \varphi(P)$ for all $t \in \Lambda$. We say φ is *simple* if $\varphi(P) = 0$ whenever dim $P \leqq d - 1$.

The main results concerning Λ-valuations are the following.

Firstly, if we set $P = n_1P_1 + \cdots + n_kP_k$, where $P_i \in \mathscr{P}(\Lambda)$, n_i is a nonnegative integer, and the sum is in the sense of Minkowski, we obtain a polynomial expression in the n_i of total degree at most d, whose coefficients depend only upon the P_i. In particular, we can write $\varphi(nP) = \sum_{r \geqq 0} \varphi_r(P)n^r$, and, in general, the coefficient of $n_1^{r_1} \cdots n_k^{r_k}$ in the general polynomial is a homogeneous valuation in P_i of degree r_i $(i = 1, \cdots, k)$. These coefficients may be called *mixed valuations*, in analogy to the mixed volumes or Quermassintegrals, whose behaviour is very similar.

We note that if $\Lambda = E^d$ and φ is continuous (in the Hausdorff metric) or monotone, we can replace the polytopes P_i by general convex bodies K_i, and the integers n_i by general nonnegative numbers λ_i.

Secondly, if φ is a homogeneous Λ-valuation of degree r, it satisfies the Euler-type relation $\varphi^*(P) = (-1)^r\varphi(-P)$. The mixed volume relation of Shephard (mentioned at the beginning) is a particular example of this result.

We approach both these results by associating with each Λ-valuation a simple Λ-valuation. Specifically, let ψ be defined by

$$\psi(P) = \sum_F (-1)^{\dim P - \dim F} \beta(F, P)\varphi(F).$$

Then ψ itself is not even a valuation, but if we set $\bar{\psi}(P) = \psi(P)$ if dim $P = d$ and 0 otherwise, then $\bar{\psi}$ is a simple Λ-valuation. The inversion formulae introduced earlier show that

$$\varphi(P) = \sum_F \gamma(F, P)\psi(F).$$

Now, after we observe that $\varphi(P_1 + \cdots + P_k)$ is a Λ-valuation in each P_i, it is clear that the first result follows from the case of a simple Λ-valuation for a single polytope. This can be shown, in turn, by establishing it for simplices, which has been done by Hadwiger [**1957**].

For the second result, we prove that if φ is a homogeneous simple Λ-valuation of degree r, then $\varphi(-P) = (-1)^{d-r}\varphi(P)$. We first show this in case $r = 1$, and prove it generally by observing that the behaviour of φ is determined by its behaviour on the *r-cylinders* in $\mathscr{P}(\Lambda)$, which are the sum of r polytopes of dimension at least one lying in independent linear subspaces of E^d. The technical difficulties we mentioned play their part here.

Let us give some other applications of our results, this time to lattice polytopes. That is, we take Λ to consist of all the points of E^d with integer cartesian coordinates. We denote by $G(P)$ the number of lattice points in the lattice polytope P. Clearly, G is a valuation, so we have a polynomial expression

$$G(nP) = \sum_{r\geqq 0} G_r(P)n^r.$$

(We also have a polynomial expression for $G(n_1P_1 + \cdots + n_kP_k)$.) The number of lattice points in the relative interior of P is

$$G^\circ(P) = \sum_F (-1)^{\dim P - \dim F}\, G(F).$$

Thus $G^\circ(nP) = \sum_{r\geqq 0} G_r^\circ(P)n^r$ is also a polynomial in n, and

$$\begin{aligned} G_r^\circ(P) &= (-1)^{\dim P}\, G_r^*(P) = (-1)^{\dim P - r}\, G_r(-P) \\ &= (-1)^{\dim P - r}\, G_r(P), \end{aligned}$$

since $G(-P) = G(P)$. That is,

$$G^\circ(nP) = (-1)^{\dim P} \sum_{r\geqq 0} G_r(P)(-n)^r.$$

This result, due originally to Ehrhart [**1967**], is called the *reciprocity law*. (See also Macdonald [**1971**].)

The function A considered by Macdonald [**1971**] associates with each lattice point in P that proportion of a sufficiently small ball centred at the point which lies in P. Thus $A(P) = \sum_F \beta(F, P)G^\circ(F)$. It is easily checked that A is a simple valuation, and $A(-P) = A(P)$, and so we conclude that we have a polynomial expression $A(nP) = \sum_{r\geqq 0} A_r(P)n^r$, where $A_r(P) = 0$ if $r \not\equiv \dim P \pmod 2$. (Since A is simple, we also have $A_0(P) = 0$ for all P.) This result was first proved by Macdonald.

We may observe in passing that the relationship between G and A is the same as that between the general valuations φ and ψ.

Hitherto, we have tacitly assumed our functions to be real valued. But they could be vector valued. Many of the results we have been discussing have vector valued analogues. For example, there are the Quermassvectors, corresponding to the Quermassintegrals (see Hadwiger and Schneider [**1971**]). In particular, to the constant 1 (the Euler characteristic) corresponds the *Steiner point* $s(P)$, defined by $s(P) = \sum_v \gamma(v, P)v$, where the sum extends over the vertices v of P. Then we have the vector valued analogue of Gram's relation:

$$\sum_F (-1)^{\dim F} \beta(F, P) s(F) = o \qquad (\dim P > 0).$$

We might also note the Euler-type relation (due to Shephard) $s^*(P) = s(P)$ $(= -s(-P))$; this should not surprise us, when we learn that Sallee has shown that s is a valuation.

In fact, as might be expected, there is a theory of vector valued Λ-valuations. We must replace the condition of invariance under Λ by *equivariance*, by which we mean that, for each vector Λ-valuation v, there is a scalar function φ, such that $v(P + t) = v(P) + \varphi(P)t$. It is easy to show that φ must be a Λ-valuation. The vector theory is more involved than the scalar theory we have been discussing, but we can prove that the results are completely analogous to those mentioned in our article. (See also Schneider **[1972]**.)

We have not had time here to consider the extension of the theory of the first half of our article to spherical polytopes. This whole area has been much less deeply explored, and we are, as yet, still uncertain as to which of the Euclidean results have analogues.

The results discussed in this article are considered in much more detail in the two papers by the author listed in the references.

References

T. Bonnesen and W. Fenchel, *Theorie der konvexen Körper*, Springer, Berlin, 1934; reprint, Chelsea, New York, 1948.

E. Ehrhart, *Démonstration de la loi de réciprocité pour un polyèdre entier*, C. R. Acad. Sci. Paris Sér A-B **265** (1967), A5–A7. MR **39** #6826.

B. Grünbaum, *Convex polytopes*, Pure and Appl. Math., vol. 16, Interscience, New York, 1967. MR **37** #2085.

H. Hadwiger, *Vorlesungen über Inhalt, Oberfläche und Isoperimetrie,* Springer-Verlag, Berlin, 1957. MR **21** #1561.

H. Hadwiger and R. Schneider, *Vektorielle Integralgeometrie*, Elem. Math. **26** (1971), 49–57. MR **44** #967.

I. G. Macdonald, *Polynomials associated with finite cell-complexes*, J. London Math. Soc. (2) **4** (1971), 181–192. MR **45** #7594.

P. McMullen, *Non-linear angle-sum relations for polyhedral cones and polytopes*, Proc. Cambridge Philos. Soc. (to appear).

———, *Valuations and Euler-type relations on certain classes of convex polytopes* (in preparation).

G. T. Sallee, *Polytopes, valuations, and the Euler relation*, Canad. J. Math. **20** (1968), 1412–1424. MR **38** #605.

R. Schneider, *Krümmungsschwerpunkte konvexer Körper*. I, Abh. Math. Sem. Univ. Hamburg **37** (1972), 112–132. MR **46** #6160.

G. C. Shephard, *Euler-type relations for convex polytopes*, Proc. London Math. Soc. (3) **18** (1968), 597–606. MR **38** #606.

University College
London, England WCIE 6BT

Proceedings of the International Congress of Mathematicians
Vancouver, 1974

Probabilistic and Combinatorial Methods in the Study of the Geometry of Euclidean Spaces

C. A. Rogers

There are many problems in the geometry of Euclidean space that can be approached both by a probabilistic or measure theoretic method and also by a combinatorial or constructive method. Sometimes one method is more effective, sometimes the other. To fix ideas consider a very simple example: the covering of space with equal spheres. Consider a large cube C in E^n of volume $V(C)$ and a sphere S of unit radius and of volume $V(S)$. Place the centre of the sphere in the large cube by use of a "random" translation. Ignoring wastage near the faces of the large cube, the volume of the cube that is left uncovered is

$$V(C) - V(S) = V(C)\{1 - v\},$$

with $v = V(S)/V(C)$. Translate a second sphere of radius 1 to a "random" position in the cube. The expected volume left uncovered is now $V(C)\{1 - v\}^2$; a fraction v of the space not previously covered being covered at this stage. After placing r spheres of radius 1 with their centres in the cube, the expected value for the volume $V(E)$ of the region E of the cube left uncovered is

$$\begin{aligned}\mathscr{E}V(E) &= V(C)\{1 - v\}^r = V(C)\exp(r\log(1 - v))\\ &= V(C)\exp(-rv - \tfrac{1}{2}rv^2 \cdots) \leqq V(C)\exp(-rv);\end{aligned}$$

here we suppose that the spheres are placed so that the expectation is realized. Take r to be $[v^{-1}n \log n] + 1$. Then

$$V(E) \leqq V(C)\exp(-n\log n) = V(C)(1/n)^n.$$

This arrangement of spheres will not generally cover the whole cube. Place in the set E that remains uncovered a maximal nonoverlapping system of spheres of radius $1/n$. Let the number of these small spheres be s. Then, comparing volumes,

$$sV(S)(1/n)^n \leqq V(E) \leqq V(C)(1/n)^n,$$

so that $sv \leqq 1$. Now place a sphere of radius $1 + (1/n)$ at each of the $r + s$ centres. It is easy to check that these cover the cube. But the total volume of these spheres is

$$\begin{aligned}(r + s)V(S)(1 + (1/n))^n &< (r + s)V(S)\cdot e \\ &= (rv + sv)eV(C) \leqq \{n \log n + v + 1\}eV(C).\end{aligned}$$

So for very large cubes the density of the covering can be made as close as we please to $\{n \log n + 1\}e$. A bit of extra care leads (see [**1**]) to a covering with density $n \log n + n \log \log n + 5n$. Thus we have a probabilistic method of obtaining a covering of space by equal spheres with density at most $n \log n + n \log \log n + 5n$. Of course the method is not wholly probabilistic, in this case; it has a combinatorial aspect through the addition of the disjoint system of small spheres, but on examination this argument, if it is combinatorial, is certainly nonconstructive.

How can combinatorial or constructive methods be applied to this problem? As far as I know, the best known construction (due to Davenport and Watson, see [**2**]) yields only a covering with density $(1.017\cdots)^n$.

It would be very interesting to have an explicit construction for a good covering of space by spherical balls. Perhaps it would suffice to take the centres to be at the points of the lattice generated by the points $\eta(p, 0, \cdots, 0, 0)$, $\eta(0, p, \cdots, 0, 0)$, $\cdots$, $\eta(0, 0, \cdots, p, 0)$, $\eta(g^{n-1}, g^{n-2}, \cdots, g, 1)$, for some suitable choice of the parameters η, p, g.

The corresponding problem for the packing of spheres in E^n is even more interesting and frustrating. There is a "trivial" existence proof. Place spheres of radius 1 in a large cube without overlapping until no extra sphere can be put in. Replace each sphere of radius 1 by a concentric sphere of radius 2. These enlarged spheres cover the cube (with the possible exception of some points within distance 1 of the boundary). It follows that there will be a nonoverlapping packing of equal spheres of density at least 2^{-n}. This trivial result has only been improved to a trivial extent. Probabilistic methods due to W. Schmidt and C. A. Rogers lead after considerable work to the existence of packings with densities about $(n \log 2)/2^n$; see [**3**]. By a result of Blichfeldt dating from 1914, densities of packings of spheres are necessarily less than $((n + 2)/2)(1/\sqrt{2})^n$. In this problem our factor of ignorance remains close to $(\sqrt{2})^n$, but see the contribution of S. S. Ryskoff to these PROCEEDINGS. Combinatorial methods seem to be of no help for large n, but they have had spectacular success up to 24 dimensions. The success is due to the discovery of the Leech lattice which provides a very good packing in 24 dimensions. This is of course the same lattice that led to the discovery of Conway's group of order 8,315,553,613,086,720,000, containing his new simple groups [**4**]. For large values of n, despite ingenious work [**5**] by experts on coding theory, the constructions do not give good packings.

Now consider a problem where combinatorial methods have been more successful. In 1944–1945 Hadwiger and Hopf discussed results of the following form. Given a spherical surface S^n or a Euclidean space E^n covered by r closed sets, is it possible to assert that:

(a) each distance (not exceeding the diameter in the case of S^n) is realized as the distance between two points of one of the sets; or that

(b) there is one of the sets within which each possible distance is realized.

Hopf used topological methods (à la Borsuk) and proved the type (a) result for $r = n + 1$. Hadwiger used measure theoretic methods and obtained type (b) results with $r = n + 1$ for E^n and also for S^n for distances rather less than the diameter. Larman and Rogers [**6**] returned to the problem for E^n, recently, and were able to show by a purely combinatorial argument that if E^n is partitioned into at most $(n(n - 1))/6 - 1$ sets, then there is one of the sets within which all distances are realized. Better results are obtained for some small values of n; in particular 101 sets may be used for the partition of E^{24}, a result obtained by considering a particular configuration of $(4602)^{101}$ points constructed from the Leech-Conway lattice.

There are many further instances where probabilistic and combinatorial methods are important. Dvoretzky has discussed the k-dimensional central sections of a centrally symmetric convex body in N dimensions with N much larger than k. After some refinement (see a forthcoming paper by D. G. Larman and P. Mani) his result asserts that, if a suitable standardizing linear transformation is first applied to the body, then nearly all the central k-dimensional sections are nearly spherical. This result has had considerable influence on Banach space theory. Other recent results in the geometry of Banach spaces seem to depend on even more sophisticated probabilistic techniques involving stochastic processes and martingale theory. Although Enflo's counterexample to the existence of a basis in a Banach space is purely combinatorial, Davie's simplification [**7**] is probabilistic.

Returning to Euclidean spaces of two and three dimensions, some remarkable constructions have been achieved recently by combinatorial means. Besicovitch's remarkable example of a plane set of Lebesgue measure zero containing a line in every direction was the basis for the construction by Ward [**8**] of a plane set of measure zero containing a congruent copy of every plane polygon. It was also the basis of Larman's construction of his "impossible" set [**9**], which is a compact set in E^3, that is the union of disjoint line segments with the property that, while the set of the relative interior points of the line segments is of measure zero, the set of the endpoints of the line segments is a compact set of positive measure.

Let me end with a problem that I have recently attempted, without success, using both constructive and probabilistic methods. The problem, suggested by Busemann, is to find two convex bodies K_1, K_2 in some E^n, $n \geqq 3$, both with the origin as centre of symmetry, both with the same volume, but with the $(n - 1)$-dimensional area (or volume) of each central section of K_1 strictly less than the area (or volume) of the corresponding section of K_2. I believe that there should be such examples with K_2 a spherical ball. I have tried to construct them by examining the solutions of suitable integral equations. I have tried to prove their existence by taking K_1 to be a "rough" sphere obtained by making "random" modifications to a spherical ball. Neither method has worked so far.

If my article has a moral, perhaps it is this. If one has a geometrical problem, one cannot tell a priori whether it is best tackled by probabilistic or combinatorial methods. Try both! One may work, both may work; if neither works, try them both again.

References

1. C. A. Rogers, *Packing and covering*, Cambridge Tracts in Math. and Math. Phys., no. 54, Cambridge Univ. Press, New York, 1964. MR **30** #2405.

2. G. L. Watson, *The covering of space by spheres*, Rend. Circ. Mat. Palermo (2) **5** (1956), 93–100. MR **17**, 1235.

3. W. M. Schmidt, *On the Minkowski-Hlawka theorem*, Illinois J. Math. **7** (1963), 18–23. MR **26** #3675.

4. J. H. Conway, *A group of order* 8,315,553,613,086,720,000, Bull. London Math. Soc. **1** (1969), 79–88. MR **40** #1470.

5. N. J. A. Sloane, *Sphere packings constructed from BCH and Justesen codes*, Mathematika **19** (1972), 183–190. MR **47** #3321.

6. D. G. Larman and C. A. Rogers, *The realization of distances within sets in Euclidean space*, Mathematika **19** (1972), 1–24. MR **47** #7601.

7. A. M. Davie, *The approximation problem for Banach spaces*, Bull. London Math. Soc. **5** (1973), 261–266.

8. D. J. Ward, *A set of plane measure zero containing all finite polygonal arcs*, Canad. J. Math. **22** (1970), 815–821. MR **41** #8634.

9. D. G. Larman, *A compact set of disjoint line segments in* E^3 *whose end set has positive measure*, Mathematika **18** (1971), 112–125. MR **45** #7006.

UNIVERSITY COLLEGE
LONDON, ENGLAND WCIE 6BT

Труды Международного Конгресса Математиков
Ванкувер, 1974

Геометрия Положительных Квадратичных Форм

С. С. Рышков

Две положительные, т.е. положительно определенные, квадратичные формы (ПКФ) $f = f_1(x_1, x_2, \cdots, x_n)$ и $f_2 = f_2(x_1, x_2, \cdots, x_n)$ будем считать эквивалентными, если существует такая целочисленная унимодулярная подстановка переменных $x_1, x_2, \cdots, x_n$, которая переводит ПКФ f_1 в ПКФ f_2.

Каждой ПКФ вида $f = \sum_{i,j=1}^{n} a_{ij} x_i x_j$ в n-мерном евклидовом пространстве E^n ставится в соответствие n-мерная решетка, т.е. совокупность точек целых относительно репера $\bar{e}_1, \bar{e}_2, \cdots, \bar{e}_n$ удовлетворяющего условию $(\bar{e}_i, \bar{e}_j) = a_{ij}$. Эквивалентным ПКФ соответствуют конгруентные решетки.

Каждой ПКФ указанного вида ставится в соответствие точка $(a_{11}, a_{22}, \cdots, a_{nn}, a_{12}, \cdots, a_{n-1,n})$ в N-мерном, где $N = n(n+1)/2$ пространстве E^N. Эти точки заполняют в пространстве E^N некоторый открытый выпуклый конус K (конус положительности).

Изучение ПКФ с определенной выше эквивалентностью производится через геометрические образы в пространствах E^n и E^N, такое изучение и является предметом геометрии ПКФ.

Основоположниками геометрии ПКФ следует считать Минковского и особенно Вороного; впервые термин “геометрия ПКФ” и выделение этой области из геометрии чисел встречается в большой статье Б. Н. Делоне “Геометрия ПКФ” [**1**]. Из дальнейших работ имеющих и обзорный характер отметим книги Фейеш-Тота [**2**] и Роджерса [**3**], статью Ван-дер-Вардена [**4**], а также чисто обзорные статьи Е.П. Барановского [**5**] и Бамбы [**6**].

Мы здесь не претендуем на полный обзор работ последнего времени принадлежащих геометрии ПКФ, а укажем лишь работы наиболее нам близкие либо по методам исследования, либо по характеру результатов; более подробно мы остановимся на работах докладчика и его коллег. Далее предполагается знакомство читателя с основами геометрии ПКФ.

1°. Вопросы приведения и установления эквивалентности ПКФ. Вопрос установления эквивалентности двух ПКФ, т.е. установления конгруентности соответствующих этим ПКФ решеток сводится к вопросу о целочисленном приведении ПКФ. Здесь после классических работ, в частности работ Эрмита, Минковского и несколько в другом направлении, работы Коркина и Золотарева, нам кажется наиболее значительной работа Б.А. Венкова **[7]**, **[8]**, в которой построены континуальные серии конечногранных областей приведения (в конусе K) для любого $n > 2$. Это приведение можно **[9]** проинтерпретировать в пространстве E^n как выбор такого основного репера решетки, что сумма квадратов длин векторов с заданными координатами минимальна (ранг этой системы векторов предполагается равным n).

В последние годы автору удалось построить **[10]**,**[11]** алгорифм приведения для каждой из областей Венкова. Установлено также, что при $n \leqq 5$, см. **[10]**, **[11]** и при $n = 6$, см. **[12]**, **[13]**, симметризованная группой куба область приведения Минковского есть область приведения Венкова относительно формы $\varphi = x_1^2 + x_2^2 + \cdots + x_n^2$. При $n \geqq 7$ это утверждение оказалось неверным **[14]**. В тех же работах дан ответ на вопрос, поставленный Ван-дер-Варденом **[4]**, а именно, доказано, что при $n \leqq 6$ область приведения по Эрмиту полностью совпадает с областью приведения по Минковскому, а при $n \geqq 7$ нет.

Кроме того, в **[10]**, **[11]** для $n = 5$, а в **[12]**, **[13]** для $n = 6$ доказана тесно связанная с этими вопросами гипотеза Минковского **[4]** о строении его области приведения в пространстве E^N.

Наконец в работах **[9]** и **[15]** построены новые конкретные области приведения при $n = 5$, вторая из этих областей есть прямое обобщение области Зеллинга-Шарва.

2°. Группы целочисленных автоморфизмов ПКФ (группы вращения решеток, типы Бравэ в кристаллографии). Вопрос о разыскании всех попарно неэквивалентных полных групп целочисленных автоморфизмов ПКФ естественно вливается в вопрос о перечислении и классификации всех попарно неэквивалентных конечных групп целочисленных подстановок, т.е. целочисленных $n \times n$ -матриц (КГЦМ)—это следует, в частности, из того, что каждая КГЦМ составляет инвариантной по крайней мере одну ПКФ.

Отчасти в связи с запросами зарождающейся сейчас n-мерной кристаллографии, в последние годы возник большой интерес к упомянутому перечислению при $n > 3$ (для $n \leqq 3$ эти задачи были давно решены кристаллографами). Все попарно неэквивалентные КГЦМ для данного n Дэйд **[16]** предложил разыскивать как подгруппы максимальных КГЦМ и нашел все такие максимальные группы для $n = 4$. Остальную программу Дэйда выполнили с применением ЭЦВМ Нейбюзер, Вондрачек и Бюлов **[17]**. В тех же работах **[17]** даны интересные теоретические соображения о классификации КГЦМ.

Докладчик предложил **[18]**, **[19]**, **[20]** алгорифм разыскания максимальных КГЦМ и полных групп целочисленных автоморфизмов ПКФ. Эти алгорифмы требуют знания, по крайней мере, одного разбиения конуса положительности из довольно широкого класса таких разбиений, например, совершенного разбиения или разбиения приведения по Минковскому. Применив этот алгорифм к совершенному разбиению (полиэдру) Вороного докладчик нашел **[18]**, **[19]** все максимальные КГЦМ при $n = 5$.

3°. Примитивные параллелоэдры (области Вороного-Дирихле общих решеток). До недавнего времени из-за существования алгорифма Вороного **[21]** задача разыскания примитивных n-мерных параллелоэдров считалось полностью решенной, однако, когда потребовалось реальное перечисление всех L-типов (типов Вороного) хотя бы общих решеток, выяснилось, что уже при $n = 5$ алгорифм Вороного приводит к столь большим вычислениям, что приходится говорить о его практической неприменимости. По этому поводу см. **[22]**, **[23]**, кроме того докладчик, усовершенствовав алгорифм Вороного и, потратив около двух лет вычислительной работы, нашел 60 типов примитивных пятимерных параллелоэдров, но остался далек, как увидим из дальнейшего, от завершения работы. Все это заставило искать новые пути исследования n-мерных параллелоэдров. Интересный путь был предложен Е.П. Барановским в работах **[24]** в них исследуются условия необходимые для того, чтобы данный симплекс решетки был L-симплексом. На этой основе им повторен вывод 4-мерных примитивных параллелоэдров и исследованы возможные объемы 5-мерных L-симплексов.

Совсем недавно автор предложил **[25]** классифицировать решетки не по аффинной структуре L-разбиений (L-типы), а по аффинной структуре одномерных остовов L-разбиений (C-типы). Алгорифм такой классификации довольно прост и его применение показало **[25]**, что при $n = 5$ имеется ровно 76 C-типов. Совместная работа докладчика и Е.П. Барановского **[26]** посвящена разделению C-типов на L-типы, в частности было установлено, что при $n = 5$ имеется ровно 221 тип Вороного. Такое неожиданно большое число L-типов при $n = 5$ (против трех для $n = 4$) запутанность взаимного расположения соответствующих им областей в конусе K и повлекли за собой указанные ранее трудности в применении алгорифма Вороного.

4°. Решетчатые упаковки (равных шаров) в пространстве E^n. Здесь нам в первую очередь хотелось бы обратить внимание на предложенный Б.А. Венковым вариант теории Вороного, связанный с полиэдром $\Pi(n)$ (см. **[27]**, **[7]**, **[8]**, **[28]**), этот вариант делает всю теорию гораздо более наглядной. С другой стороны, введенный в рассмотрение автором **[29]**, **[30]** полиэдр $M(m)$ позволил создать общую схему для решения экстремальных задач геометрии ПКФ. Рассмотрением полиэдра $M(1)$ удалось показать, что не только все предельные, но и все совершенные формы находятся среди реберных форм области приведения Минковского, т.е., что класс форм предложенный Минковским для решения задачи отыскания всех предельных форм строго включает в себя класс форм, предложенный для тех же целей Вороным **[30]**.

Мы не будем останавливаться на многих и интересных работах посвященных разысканию отдельных совершенных форм, связи теории упаковок с теорией информации и т.д., так как эти вопросы довольно далеки от докладчика. Отметим только, повидимому, мало известные работы Н.К. Игнатьева [**31**], а также замечательную работу Лича и Слона [**32**]. Наконец, обратим внимание на удивительный результат С.М. Сидельникова [**33**].

5°. Решетчатые покрытия (равными шарами) пространства E^n. После полного решения [**34**]—[**38**] задачи о покрытиях для $n = 4$ которое докладывалось на Конгрессе 1966 года, а также после асимптотических оценок Роджерса[**3**] наибольшим событием в этой области явилась теорема Барнса и Диксона [**39**] о том, что в каждом L-типе n-мерных решеток естьне более одного локального минимума плотности покрытия. Теорема эта получила простое геометрическое доказательство [**40**] и естественно вошла в общую схему решения экстремальных задач геометрии ПКФ [**30**].

Наконец, в самое последнее время докладчику совместно с Е.П. Барановским удалось на основе результатов об L-типах при $n = 5$ показать, что наилучшая плотность решетчатого покрытия при $n = 5$ равна

$$\frac{8}{15}\,\pi^2\cdot[35/72]^{5/2}\cdot\sqrt{6} = \frac{8}{15}\,\pi^2\cdot 0,403\cdots.$$

6°. Вопрос об n-мерной решетке, дающей минимальную ζ-функцию Эпштейна $\zeta(s|f)$ при данном $s > n/2$ (задача Соболева-Ранкина). Напомним, что

$$\zeta(s|f) = \zeta(s|\Gamma) = \sum \frac{1}{r^{2s}} = \sum \frac{1}{f^s},$$

здесь через r обозначено расстояние от начала координат до точки решетки, суммирование распространено на все точки решетки Γ, кроме начала координат, т.е. во второй сумме на все целочисленные системы $(x_1, x_2, \cdots, x_n)$ кроме системы $(0, 0, \cdots, 0)$.

Все работы, посвященные этой задаче, известные докладчику отражены в статье [**41**], в этой статье, в частности показано, что при $n \leqq 8$ и каждом достаточно большом s минимальное значение ζ-функции $\zeta(s|\Gamma)$ достигается на решетке, дающей для данного n наиболее плотную решетчатую упаковку равных шаров, даны также примеры предельных форм, не дающих при больших s локального минимума задачи.

7°. Можно назвать еще достаточно много задач, объединяемых геометрией ПКФ, например, задачу о числе представлений минимума ПКФ [**42**], задачу о детерминанте из представлений минимума ПКФ [**43**]—[**46**], задачу об (r, R) плотности (решетчатой) равномерно дискретной системы [**29**], [**47**], задачу об оценке радиуса цилиндра вложимого во всякую решетчатую упаковку равных мерных шаров [**48**] и т.д., но останавливаться на результатах в этих задачах докладчик уже не имеет возможности.

Цитированная Литература

1. Б.Н. Делоне, Успехи матем. наук, вып. 3 (1937); вып. 4 (1938).

2. L. Fejes Toth, *Lagerungen in der Ebene, auf der Kugel und im Raum*, Springer-Verlag, Berlin-Göttingen-Heidelberg, 1953 (русск. перевод: Ласло Фейеш Тот., *Расположенная на плоскости, на сфере и в пространстве*, Москва, 1958).

3. C.A. Rogers, *Packing and covering*, Cambridge, 1964 (русск. перевод: К. Роджерс, *Укладки и покрытия*, Москва, 1968).

4. B.L. van der Waerden, Acta Math. **96** (1956), 265–309.

5. Е.П. Барановский в сб. "Алгебра, Топология, Геометрия, 1967", Москва, 1969, стр. 189–225.

6. R.P. Bambah, Math. Student **39** (1971), 117.

7. Б.А. Венков, Известия АН СССР, сер. матем. **4** (1940).

8. Б.А. Венков в книге [**49**], т. 3, стр. 235–246.

9. С.С. Рышков, Учен. зап. Ивановск. Гос. Ун-та **89** (1974), 3.

10. ______, Доклады АН СССР **198** (1971), 1028.

11. ______, Записки научных семинаров ЛОМИ **33** (1973), 37.

12. П. П. Таммела, Записки научных семинаров ЛОМИ **33** (1973), 72.

13. ______, Доклады АН СССР **209** (1973), 1299.

14. С.С. Рышков, Доклады АН СССР **207** (1973), 1054.

15. Е.П. Барановский, Учен. зап. Ивановск. Гос. Ун-та **89**, 35.

16. E.C. Dade, Illinois J. Math. **9** (1965), 99.

17. J. Neubüser, H. Wondratschek and R. Bülow, Acta Crystallogr. **A-27** (1971), 517–535.

18. С.С. Рышков, Доклады АН СССР **204** (1972), 561.

19. ______, Труды МИАН, т. 128, стр. 183–211.

20. ______, Доклады АН СССР **206** (1972), 542.

21. Г.Ф. Вороной в книге [**49**], т. 2, стр. 241–368.

22. С.С. Рышков, Доклады АН СССР **162** (1965), 277.

23. D.W. Trenerry, *The covering of space by spheres*, Doctoral Thesis, Adelaide, Australia, 1972.

24. Е.П. Барановский, Мат. заметки **10** (1971), 659; **13** (1973), 605; **13** (1973), 771.

25. С.С. Рышков, Доклады АН СССР **212** (1973).

26. Е.П. Барановский и С.С. Рышков, Доклады АН СССР **212** (1973), 531.

27. Б.А. Венков в книге [**49**], т. 2, стр. 379–385.

28. Б.Н. Делоне и С.С. Рышков, Доклады АН СССР **173** (1967), 991.

29. С.С. Рышков, Доклады АН СССР **194** (1970), 514.

30. Б.Н. Делоне и С.С. Рышков, Труды МИАН, т. 112, стр. 203.

31. Н.К. Игнатьев, Сиб. матем. журн. **5** (1964), 815; **7** (1966), 820.

32. J. Leech and N.J.A. Sloane, Bull. Amer. Math. Soc. **76** (1970), 1006.

33. С.М. Сидельников, Доклады АН СССР **213** (1973), 1029.

34. Б.Н. Делоне и С.С. Рышков, Доклады АН СССР **152** (1963), 523.

35. Е.П. Барановский и С.С. Рышков, Сиб. матем. журн. **7** (1966), 731.

36. Е.П. Барановский, Доклады АН СССР **164** (1965), 13.

37. ______, Сиб. матем. журн. **7** (1966), 974.

38. ______, Тезисы кр. научн. сообщ. Международного конгресса математиков, секция 3, Москва, 1966.

39. E.S. Barnes and T.Y. Dickson, J. Austral. Math. Soc. **7** (1967), 115.

40. Б.Н. Делоне и др., Известия АН СССР, сер. матем. **34** (1970), 289.

41. С.С. Рышков, Сиб. матем. журн. **15** (1973), 1065.

42. G.L. Watson, Dissertationes Math. **84** (1971).

43. H. Davenport and G.L. Watson, Mathematika **1** (1954), 14.

44. R.A. Rankin, Math. Z. **84** (1964), 228.
45. G.L. Watson, Mathematika **16** (1969), 170.
46. С.С. Рышков, Записки научных семинаров ЛОМИ, **33** (1973), 65.
47. G.J. Butler, Proc. London Math. Soc. **25** (1972), 721.
48. J. Horvath, Studia Sci. Math. Hungar. **5** (1970), 421.
49. Г.Ф. Вороной, Собр. соч. в 3-х томах, Киев, 1952.

Математический Институт им. В.А. Стеклова АН СССР
Москва, СССР

Section 7

Algebraic and Differential Topology

Proceedings of the International Congress of Mathematicians
Vancouver, 1974

Topological Classification of Simple Homotopy Equivalences

T. A. Chapman*

1. Introduction. We use Q to denote the Hilbert cube, which is the countable infinite product of closed intervals, and we use definitions and results from [**6**] concerning the PL category and from [**5**] concerning simple homotopy theory. The following is the main result of [**4**].

CLASSIFICATION THEOREM. *If $f: X \to Y$ is a homotopy equivalence (h. e.) of compact PL spaces, then f is a simple homotopy equivalence (s.h.e.) iff $f \times \mathrm{id}: X \times Q \to Y \times Q$ is homotopic to a homeomorphism.*

This implies that every TOP homeomorphism of compact PL spaces is a s.h.e., thus giving an affirmative answer to the problem of the topological invariance of Whitehead torsion [**9**].

The proof of the classification theorem relies heavily upon the handle straightening theorem of [**2**], which uses results from Q-manifold theory along with a version of the main diagram of [**8**]. The purpose of this article is to outline a proof of the handle straightening theorem and then show how it implies the classification theorem. This will not only collect together some results which are scattered throughout several papers, but will also serve as a quick introduction to the techniques of Q-manifold theory.

Because of limitations of space we will not have an opporutnity to discuss the important triangulation theorem of [3]. We have chosen to analyze the classification theorem because of its wider appeal.

2. Preliminaries. R^n denotes Euclidean n-space and for any $r > 0$ let $B_r^n = [-r, r]^n \subset R^n$. The boundary and interior of B_r^n are ∂B_r^n and $\mathring{B}_r^n$, respectively. Bd

*The author is an A. P. Sloan Fellow and is supported in part by NSF grant GP-28374.

and Int will be used to denote topological boundary and interior. We use the representation $Q = [-1, 1] \times [-1, 1] \times \cdots$ and $I^k = [-1, 1]^k$, thus giving a factorization $Q = I^k \times Q_k$, for all $k \geqq 0$. All PL spaces are locally compact, separable, metric polyhedra.

In A—F below we state six technical results which are needed in the proof of the handle straightening theorem. The results A—E are a part of Q-manifold theory and their proofs require no apparatus from algebraic topology. In E we use infinite simple homotopy equivalences in the sense of **[10]**; recall that *proper* means that pre-images of compacta are compact. F uses no Q-manifold theory but instead relies on PL topology and Wall's obstruction to finiteness of homotopy types, along with the computation $\tilde{K}_0 Z[\pi_1 S^n] = 0$.

A **[1]**. *Let M be a Q-manifold, $A \subset M$ be a compactum, and let $h: A \to M$ be an embedding such that h is homotopic ($\simeq$) to the inclusion $A \subsetneq M$. If A and $h(A)$ are collared in M, then h can be extended to a homeomorphism $\tilde{h}: M \to M$ such that $\tilde{h} \simeq$* id. (By a *Q-manifold* we mean a separable metric manifold modeled on Q.)

B **[1]**. *If M is a compact contractible Q-manifold, then M is homeomorphic to Q.*

C **[1]**. *Q is homeomorphic to its own cone.*

D **[2]**. *If M is a Q-manifold, X is a PL space, and $\alpha: M \to X \times Q$ is an immersion, then M is triangulated.* (An *immersion* is a local open embedding and a *triangulated* Q-manifold is one which is homeomorphic to some PL space times Q. It turns out that all Q-manifolds are triangulated, but we do not use that result here.)

Remark. D is not exactly like the corresponding statement in [**2**], but it can be similarly proved.

E **[11]**. *If X and Y are PL spaces and $f: X \to Y$ is a s.h.e., then $f \times$ id$: X \times Q \to Y \times Q$ is proper homotopic to a homeomorphism.*

F **[2]**. *Let X be a PL space and let $h: S^n \times Q \times R \to X \times Q$ be an open embedding, for $n \geqq 1$. Then there exist a $k \geqq 0$ and a compact PL subspace S of $X \times I^k$ such that*

(1) *$S \times Q_k \subset h(S^n \times Q \times R)$ and $S \times Q_k \subsetneq h(S^n \times Q \times R)$ is a h. e.,*

(2) *S is PL bicollared,*

(3) *$S \times Q_k$ separates $h(S^n \times Q \times [1, \infty))$ from $h(S^n \times Q\, (-\infty, -1])$.*

3. Handle straightening. We are now ready to prove the key ingredient in the proof of the classification theorem.

Handle Straightening Theorem. *Let X be a PL space and let $h: R^n \times Q \to X \times Q$ be an open embedding, for $n \geqq 1$. Then there exist a $k \geqq 0$ and a homeomorphism $g: X \times Q \to X \times Q$ such that g is supported on $h(B^n_2 \times Q)$ and $gh(B^n_1 \times Q) = Y \times Q_k$, where Y is a compact PL subspace of $X \times I^k$ such that* Bd *Y is PL bicollared.*

Proof. We will work our way through the accompanying diagram of spaces and maps. f_5 will be a homeomorphism such that $h \circ f_5 \circ h^{-1}$ extends via the identity to our required g. For notation let $e: R \to S^1$ be the covering projection defined by $e(x) = \exp(\pi i x/4)$, $T^n = S^1 \times \cdots \times S^1$ be the n-torus, T^n_0 be the punctured torus, and let $\alpha: T_0^n \to R^n$ be an immersion such that $\alpha \circ e^n | B_2^n : B_2^n \to B_2^n$ is the identity [7, p.48], where $e^n : R^n \to T^n$ is the product covering projection.

$$\begin{array}{ccccccc}
B_2^n \times Q & \xrightarrow{f_5} & B_2^n \times Q & & & & \\
\cup & & \cup & & & & \\
\mathring{B}_2^n \times Q & \xrightarrow{f_4} & \mathring{B}_2^n \times Q & & & & \\
\downarrow{\scriptstyle \beta \times \mathrm{id}} & & \downarrow{\scriptstyle \beta \times \mathrm{id}} & & & & \\
R^n \times Q & \xrightarrow{\tilde{f}_3} & R^n \times Q & & & & \\
\downarrow{\scriptstyle e^n \times \mathrm{id}} & & \downarrow{\scriptstyle e^n \times \mathrm{id}} & & & & \\
T^n \times Q & \xrightarrow{f_3} & T^n \times Q & & & & \\
\cup & & \cup & & & & \\
T_0^n \times Q & \xrightarrow{f_2} & T_0^n \times Q & \xrightarrow{\alpha \times \mathrm{id}} & R^n \times Q & \xrightarrow{h} & X \times Q \\
\cup & & \cup & & & & \\
M & \xrightarrow{f_1} & N & & & &
\end{array}$$

I. *Construction of* Y. Consider the restriction of h to $(\mathring{B}_2^n - B_1^n) \times Q$, which may be viewed as an open embedding of $S^{n-1} \times Q \times R$ into $X \times Q$. We can find a $k \geqq 0$ and a compact PL subspace S of $X \times I^k$ such that $S \times Q_k$ splits $h((\mathring{B}_2^n - B_1^n) \times Q)$ as in F. Then S bounds a compact contractible PL subspace Y of $X \times I^k$ such that $h(B_1^n \times Q) \subset Y \times Q_k \subset h(B_2^n \times Q)$.

II. *Construction of* f_1. Put $M = (T_0^n - e^n(\mathring{B}_1^n)) \times Q$ and $N = T_0^n \times Q - \text{Int } W$, with

$$W = [(\alpha \times \mathrm{id}) | e^n(B_2^n) \times Q]^{-1} \circ h^{-1}(Y \times Q).$$

Then M is clearly triangulated and $h \circ (\alpha \times \mathrm{id})$ restricts to give an immersion of N into $(X \times I^k - \text{Int } Y) \times Q_k$. It follows from D that N is also triangulated. Let $Z = (T_0^n - e^n(\mathring{B}_2^n)) \times Q$ and let $f_1' : M \to N$ be a proper h.e. which makes the following diagram proper homotopy commute:

$$\begin{array}{ccc}
N & \xrightarrow{f_1'} & M \\
\cup & & \cup \\
& Z &
\end{array}$$

To use E all we need to do is note that any proper h.e. of a PL space to $T_0^n - e^n(\mathring{B}_1^n)$ is a *s.h.e.* This fact follows from **[10]** because the appropriate obstruction group $\mathscr{S}(T_0^n - e^n(\mathring{B}_1^n))$ vanishes. Involved in the proof of the vanishing of $\mathscr{S}(T_0^n - e^n(\mathring{B}_1^n))$ are Wall's obstruction theory for finiteness of homotopy types along with $\tilde{K}_0 Z[\pi_1 S^{n-1}] = 0$, and compact Whitehead theory along with the computations $\mathrm{Wh}(\pi_1 S^{n-1}) = 0$, $\mathrm{Wh}(Z * Z) = 0$, and $\mathrm{Wh}(Z \oplus \cdots \oplus Z) = 0$. Thus E implies that f_1' is proper homotopic to a homeomorphism f_1. Using A and E we can require that f_1 take $e^n(\partial B_1^n) \times Q$ onto Bd W.

III. *Construction of* f_2. $e^n(B_1^n) \times Q$ is a Hilbert cube and it follows from E that W is also a Hilbert cube. Then using A we can extend f_1 to a homeomorphism f_2.

IV. *Construction of* f_3. Write $T_0^n = T^n - \{t_0\}$ and let D^n be an n-ball in

T^n containing t_0 in its interior such that $D^n \cap e^n(B_2^n) = \emptyset$. The closure of $f_2((D^n - t_0) \times Q)$ is a compact contractible Q-manifold and by B it must be homeomorphic to Q. Then using A we can find a homeomorphism f_3: $T^n \times Q \to T^n \times Q$ which agrees with f_2 on $(T^n - \mathring{D}^n) \times Q$. Note that $f_3 \simeq$ id.

V. *Construction of* $\tilde{f}_3$. We just let $\tilde{f}_3$: $R^n \times Q \to R^n \times Q$ be the homeomorphism which covers f_3 and which also satisfies $\tilde{f}_3(B_1^n \times Q) = h^{-1}(Y \times Q_k)$. Note that $\tilde{f}_3$ is bounded, i.e., $\{\|x_1 - x_2\| \,|\, f_3(x_1, q_1) = (x_2, q_2)\}$ is bounded above. This follows from the fact that $f_3 \simeq$ id.

VI. *Construction of* f_4. Choose t, $1 < t < 2$, so that $\tilde{f}_3(B_1^n \times Q) \subset \mathring{B}_t^n \times Q$. Let $\beta: \mathring{B}_2^n \to R^n$ be a radially-defined homeomorphism which is the identity on B_t^n. Then let f_4 be defined to make the appropriate rectangle commute.

VII. *Construction of* f_5. Let P be the disjoint union of $\mathring{B}_2^n \times Q$ and ∂B_2^n, with the identification topology determined by p: $B_2^n \times Q \to P$, where $p =$ id on $\mathring{B}_2^n \times Q$ and $p(x, q) = x$, for all $(x, q) \in \partial B_2^n \times Q$. Regarding $\mathring{B}_2^n \times Q$ as a subspace of P it follows from the boundedness of $\tilde{f}_3$ that f_4 extends to a homeomorphism $\tilde{f}_4$: $P \to P$ which is the identity on ∂B_2^n. Using C we can find a homeomorphism Υ: $B_2^n \times Q \to P$ which is the identity on $B_t^n \times Q$. Then let $\tilde{f}_5$: $B_2^n \times Q \to B_2^n \times Q$ be defined by $\tilde{f}_5 = \Upsilon^{-1} \circ \tilde{f}_4 \circ \Upsilon$. To get $\tilde{f}_5 =$ id on $\partial B_2^n \times Q$, and thereby arrive at our required f_5, we just apply A to the collared compactum $(\partial B_2^n \times Q) \cup (\partial B_t^n \times Q)$ in the manifold $(B_2^n - \mathring{B}_t^n) \times Q$.

4. The classification theorem. The "only if" part is given in E, so let X, Y be compact PL spaces and let f:$X \to Y$ be a h.e. such that $f \times$ id is homotopic to a homeomorphism h: $X \times Q \to Y \times Q$. We want to prove that f is a s.h.e. Without loss of generality assume X to be connected. We argue inductively on dim X and note that the assertion is trivially true for dim $X = 0$, since in that case both X and Y are contractible spaces.

Passing to the inductive step assume the result to be true in all cases in which dim $X \leqq n - 1$ and then consider a specific case in which dim $X = n$. Without loss of generality assume $X = X^{n-1} \cup \varphi(R^n)$, where X^{n-1} is the $(n - 1)$-skeleton of X and φ: $R^n \to X$ is a PL open embedding such that $\varphi(R^n) \cap X^{n-1} = \emptyset$. Using the handle straightening theorem there exist a $k \geqq 0$ and a homeomorphism g: $Y \times Q \to Y \times Q$ such that $g \circ h(\varphi(B_1^n) \times Q) = Z \times Q_k$, where $Z \subset Y \times I^k$ is a compact PL subspace such that Bd Z is PL bicollared. Note that $g \simeq$ id because it is supported on $h(\varphi(B_2^n) \times Q)$.

Write $X = X_1 \cup X_2$, where $X_1 = \varphi(B_1^n)$, $X_2 = X -$ Int X_1, and $X_0 = X_1 \cap X_2$; also write $Y \times I^k = Y_1 \cup Y_2$, where $Y_1 = Z$, $Y_2 = Y \times I^k -$ Int Z, and $Y_0 = Y_1 \cap Y_2$. Then $g \circ h(X_i \times Q) = Y_i \times Q_k$, for each i. Let α:$X \to Y \times I^k$ and α_i: $X_i \to Y_i$ be defined to make the following rectangles commute:

$$\begin{array}{ccc} X \times Q & \xrightarrow{g \circ h} & Y \times Q \\ {\scriptstyle \times 0}\uparrow & & \downarrow{\scriptstyle \text{proj}} \\ X & \xrightarrow[\alpha]{} & Y \times I^k \end{array} \qquad \begin{array}{ccc} X_i \times Q & \xrightarrow{g \circ h} & Y_i \times Q_k \\ {\scriptstyle \times 0}\uparrow & & \downarrow{\scriptstyle \text{proj}} \\ X_i & \xrightarrow[\alpha_i]{} & Y_i \end{array}$$

(Define $\times\, o(x) = (x, (0, 0, \cdots))$.) Then α_1 is a s.h.e. because X_1 is contractible and α_0 is a s.h.e. because $\mathrm{Wh}\,(\pi_1 S^{n-1}) = 0$. To see that α_2 is a s.h.e. we use the inductive hypothesis along with E and the fact that $X^{n-1} \subsetneq X_2$ is a s.h.e. By the sum theorem for s.h.e.'s α must also be a s.h.e. To see that f is a s.h.e. we just use the homotopy commuting diagram

$$\begin{array}{ccc} X & \xrightarrow{\alpha} & Y \times I^k \\ & \searrow^{f} & \downarrow \text{proj} \\ & & Y \end{array}$$

along with the fact that $\mathrm{proj}\colon Y \times I^k \to Y$ is a s.h.e.

References

1. T. A. Chapman, *Notes on Hilbert cube manifolds* (preprint).

2. ———, *Surgery and handle straightening in Hilbert cube manifolds*, Pacific J. Math. **45** (1973), 59–79.

3. ———, *Compact Hilbert cube manifolds and the invariance of Whitehead torsion*, Bull. Amer. Math. Soc. **79** (1973), 52–56.

4. ———, *Topological invariance of Whitehead torsion*, Amer. J. Math. (to appear).

5. Marshall M. Cohen, *A course in simple homotopy theory*, Springer-Verlag, New York, 1973.

6. J. F. P. Hudson, *Piecewise linear topology*, Univ. of Chicago Lecture Notes, Benjamin, New York, 1969. MR **40** #2094.

7. R. C. Kirby, *Lectures on triangulations of manifolds*, UCLA Lecture Notes.

8. R. C. Kirby and L. C. Siebenmann, *On the triangulation of manifolds and the Hauptvermutung*, Bull. Amer. Math. Soc. **75** (1969), 742–749. MR **39** #3500.

9. J. Milnor, *Whitehead torsion*, Bull. Amer. Math. Soc. **72** (1966), 358–426. MR **33** #4922.

10. L. C. Siebenmann, *Infinite simple homotopy types*, Nederl. Akad. Wetensch. Proc. Ser. A **73** = Indag. Math. **32** (1970), 479–495. MR **44** #4746.

11. James E. West, *Infinite products which are Hilbert cubes*, Trans. Amer. Math. Soc. **150** (1970), 1–25. MR **42** #1055.

UNIVERSITY OF KENTUCKY
LEXINGTON, KENTUCKY 40506, U.S.A.

Proceedings of the International Congress of Mathematicians
Vancouver, 1974

Multidimensional Plateau Problem on Riemannian Manifolds. On the Problem of the Algorithmical Recognizability of the Standard Three-Dimensional Sphere

A. T. Fomenko

1. The author's results concerning the multidimensional Plateau problem are stated in the first part of this report; the second part is devoted to the common work of I. A. Volodin, V. E. Kuznetzov, A. T. Fomenko on the problem of sphere recognition.

A soap-film X_0 which spans a fixed contour A in the three-dimensional Euclidean space $\boldsymbol{R}^3$ is a local minimal film. And it is the mathematical proof of the existence (and of the regularity almost everywhere) of such a film in more general situations which is the essence of the Plateau problem.

This problem was solved in dimension two by Douglas, Rado, Courant (see [1]); namely, there is a mapping f_0: $D^2 \to \boldsymbol{R}^3$ (where D^2 is a disk); $f_0(\partial D^2) = A$, minimizing the two-dimensional Dirichlet functional. A minimal film $X_0 = f_0(D^2)$ may not be homeomorphic to a disk D^2, but it allows a parametrization by the disk D^2.

The multidimensional Plateau problem was outstanding in all dimensions greater than two: Let $A \subset M^n$ be a closed smooth $(k - 1)$-dimensional submanifold in a Riemannian manifold M^n and let $\{X\}$ be the class of all such films X, having a boundary A, each having a continuous parametrization; that is $X = f(W)$, where W is some k-dimensional smooth manifold with a boundary $\partial W \cong A$, and a mapping f: $W \to M^n$ is continuous and is a homeomorphism between A and ∂W; the question is: Does there exist a film X_0 in M^n which is a minimal film in a reasonable sense?

If we reject the classical notion of the manifold-film W with the boundary $\partial W \cong A$, then the Plateau problem may be formulated in terms of the usual homology theory. The problem was solved in this way by Federer, Almgren, Fleming (see **[2]**, **[3]**), Reifenberg, Morrey (see **[1]**).

We consider and solve the Plateau problem in the class of the films with a parametric representation $X = f(W)$.

Some parts of the film X may contract during the process of minimization of the volume (measure) on the subcomplexes of lesser dimensions, and these subcomplexes may not be removed because the remainder of the film (of a maximal dimension) may not have a continuous parametrization with a given boundary. (See Figure 1.) It is evident that the two-dimensional Plateau problem with a parametric representation does not meet this obstacle. (See Figure 2.) The parametrized

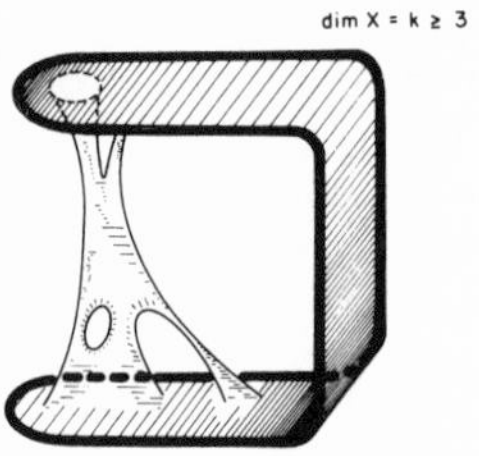

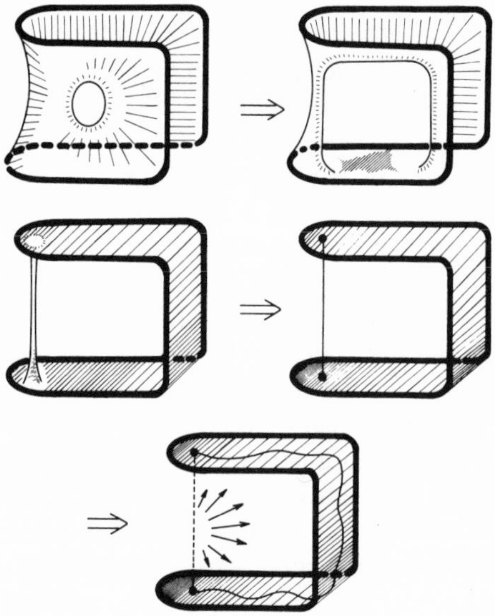

FIGURE 1 FIGURE 2

Plateau problem may be stated in terms of the singular bordism theory: It is required to find a minimal film X_0 which annihilates (by embedding $A \to X_0$) a fixed bordism class σ, where $\sigma = \{A; 1_A\}$ is a class of the manifold A; 1_A is an identity mapping. Let $O(\sigma)$ be the class of all such compacts X which annihilate σ (the singular bordism theory may be transferred to the class of compacts by means of Čech's process). Let the including manifold M^n be complete and $\pi_1(M) = \pi_2(M) = 0$, where π_i are the homotopic groups. Let $O(\sigma) \neq \emptyset$ and let the embedding $A \to M$ be such that even at least one film $X \in O(\sigma)$ has a finite Hausdorff measure Λ^k; $\Lambda^k(X) < \infty$; the sequence of the following statements holds:

THEOREM 1.1. (1) *If* $\{X\}_k$ *is the class of all compacts* X, $A \subset X \subset M^n$, *such that* $X \in O(\sigma)$ *and* $\Lambda^k(X) = d_k = \inf \Lambda^k(Y)$, *where* $Y \in O(\sigma)$, *we assert that* $\{X\}_k \neq \emptyset$, $d_k > 0$, *and that each compact* $X \in \{X\}_k$ *contains a uniquely defined k-dimensional, dimensionally-homogeneous* (*that is having the dimension* k *in each of its points*) *subset* $S^k \subset X \setminus A$ *such that* $A \cup S^k$ *is a compact in* M^n; S^k *contains a subset* Z_k, *where* $\Lambda^k(Z_k) = 0$ *and* $S^k \setminus Z_k$ *is a smooth global minimal k-dimensional submanifold in* M^n, *dense everywhere in* S^k; *and* $\Lambda^k(S^k) = \Lambda^k(X) = d_k > 0$.

(2) *Further, if* $\{X\}_{k-1}$ *is a class of all compacts* X, $A \subset X \subset M^n$, *such that* $X \in O(\sigma)$, $X \in \{X\}_k$ *and* $\Lambda^{k-1}(X \setminus S^k) = d_{k-1} = \inf \Lambda^{k-1}(Y \setminus S^k)$, *where* $Y \in \{X\}_k$, *then we assert that* $\{X\}_{k-1} \neq \emptyset$, *and in the case when* $d_{k-1} > 0$, *each compact* $X \in \{X\}_{k-1}$ *contains a uniquely defined* $(k-1)$*-dimensional, dimensionally-homogenous (that is having the dimension* $(k-1)$ *in each of its points) subset* $S^{k-1} \subset X \setminus A \setminus S^k$ *such that* $A \cup S^k \cup S^{k-1}$ *is a compact in* M^n; S^{k-1} *contains a subset* Z_{k-1}, *where* $\Lambda^{k-1}(Z_{k-1}) = 0$ *and* $S^{k-1} \setminus Z_{k-1}$ *is a smooth global minimal* $(k-1)$*-dimensional submanifold in* M^n, *dense everywhere in* S^{k-1}; *and* $\Lambda^{k-1}(S^{k-1}) = \Lambda^{k-1}(X \setminus A \setminus S^k) = d_{k-1} > 0$. *If* $d_{k-1} = 0$, *then let* $S^{k-1} = \emptyset$.

(3)$\cdots$, (4)$\cdots$, (5)$\cdots$, *and so on, down over all dimensions.*

If we restrict ourselves to item (1) of Theorem 1.1 only, then we obtain the existence theorem of the minimal film X_0, which is minimal in its maximal dimension k ($k = \dim X_0$); the description of the low dimensional zones (items (2), (3), (4),$\cdots$) is additional information which is of a topological significance—namely, no zone of this kind S^α, $\alpha \leqq k-1$, can be removed, because S^k has no parametric representation in the following case: $S^\alpha \neq \emptyset$ by some $\alpha \leqq k-1$. Theorem 1.1 is a very particular case of a general existence theorem of minimal films (see **[4]**, **[6]**), proved for very wide classes of boundary conditions.

It is shown in **[4]**, **[6]** that the multidimensional Plateau problem is formulated most naturally in the classes of films which are defined by the requirement of the groups of extraordinary (co)homology theories. In our statement of the problem the set of all extraordinary (co)homology theories is exactly the set of all different types of the multidimensional Plateau problems. The existence theorem of a minimal solution is proved in **[4]**, **[6]** for all these classes.

Let us demonstrate an example of the contravariant Plateau problem. Let ξ be a stable nontrivial vector bundle on the compact Riemannian manifold M^n, let $O(\xi)$ be the class of all compacts $X \subset M^n$ such that the restriction $\xi|_X$ of the bundle ξ over X is stable nontrivial. (See Figure 3.) Then there exists a compact $X_0 \in O(\xi)$ which is a globally minimal film (in all its dimensions) which is regular almost everywhere. The proof of the general existence theorem is really constructive; see examples below.

Let $e \in M^n$ be a fixed point, $\tilde{Q}(r) = \exp(Q(r))$, where $Q(r) \subset T_e(M_u)$ is an open ball of the radius r. Let r_θ be a maximal r such that $\tilde{Q}(r)$ is diffeomorphic to $Q(r)$. Let $x \in \partial\tilde{Q}(r)$ $(r < r_e)$; then there exists a unique geodesic γ which connects the points e and x in $\tilde{Q}(r)$. Let us consider a tangent vector $\dot{\gamma}$ in $T_x(M^n)$ and let Π_x^{k-1} be an arbitrary plane of dimension $(k-1)$, which is orthogonal to $\dot{\gamma}$ $(2 \leqq k \leqq n-1)$. Let $B^n(x, \varepsilon)$ be a ball of radius ε with the point x as the centre and $A_\varepsilon = B^n(x, \varepsilon) \cap \exp_x(\Pi_x^{k-1})$; let CA be a cone over A_ε with the point e as the vertex; this cone is constituted by all geodesics γ, which connect the point e with all the points of the ball A_ε. Let

$$\mathfrak{r}_k(e, x, \Pi_x^{k-1}) = \lim_{e\to 0} \{\Lambda^k[CA]/\Lambda^{k-1}(A_\varepsilon)\};$$

$$\mathfrak{x}_k(e, r) = \max \mathfrak{x}_k(e, x, \Pi_x^{k-1}),$$

where max is considered over all pairs (x, Π_x^{k-1}) such that $x \in \partial\tilde{Q}(r)$. Further, let

$$\hbar_k(r) = \exp \int 1/\mathfrak{x}_k(e, r)\, dr;$$
$$\Omega_e(k) = \alpha_k \cdot \hbar_k(r_e) \cdot \lim_{r \to 0} [r^k/\hbar_k(1)];$$

where α_k is the volume of the standard ball $B^k(0, 1)$, and $\hbar_k(r_e) = \lim_{r \to r_e} \hbar_k(r)$.

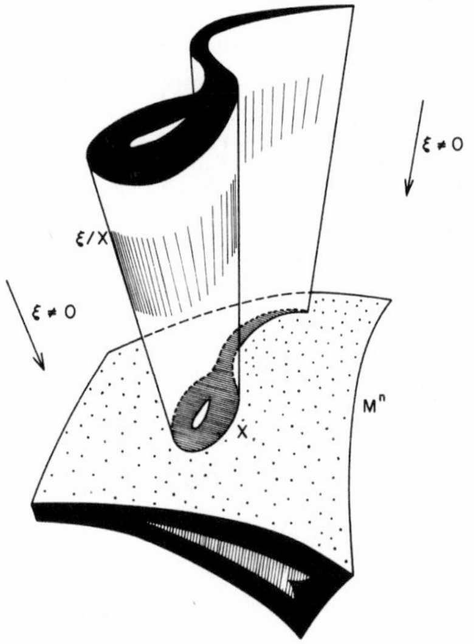

FIGURE 3

THEOREM 1.2 (SEE [5]). *Let $X_0 \subset M^n$ be an arbitrary k-dimensional minimal compact, which realizes an arbitrary nontrivial element (or a subgroup) σ in $H_k^{(k)}(M^n)$, where $H_*^{(*)}$ is a usual (co)homology theory, $e \in X_0$ is an arbitrary point on X_0 and $\psi_k(P)$, $P \in X_0$, is the density function over X_0. Then $\Lambda^k(X_0) \geqq \psi_k(e) \cdot \Omega_e(k) \geqq \Omega_e(k)$.*

If $M = G/H$ is a homogeneous manifold, then $\Omega_e(k) \equiv \Omega(k)$, that is, it does not depend on the point e. The universal function $\Omega_e(k)$ (which can be calculated quite easily) gives a general lower estimation of the volumes of all k-dimensional (co)-cycles in M^n. This estimation is nonimprovable in a general case, that is there exist important series of examples of (co)cycles X_0, for which we have $\Lambda^k(X_0) = \Omega_e(k)$. From Theorem 1.2, there follows that $\psi_k(e) \leqq \Lambda^k(X_0)/\Omega_e(k)$; hence there ensues the solution of the Reifenberg problem (see [5]) on the structure of the singular points of minimal realizing films. If $M = G/H$, then the function $\Omega(k)$ may be calculated in an explicit way, which allows the description of all those minimal (co)cycles in $H_*^{(*)}(M)$ for which $\Lambda^k(X_0) = \Omega(k)$.

If $M = G/H$ is a symmetric space, then all minimal compacts X_0 for which $\Lambda^k(X_0) = \Omega_e(k)$ are the totally geodesic submanifolds of the range 1. For example, the standard filtration in the symmetric spaces of the range 1, the quaternion and complex projective spaces in the Grassmannian manifolds, are such submanifolds.

2. The following problem of the algorithmic topology is well known: Is there an algorithm which allows us to recognize the standard sphere S^n in the class of all manifolds? If $n = 1, 2$, then the question has a trivial solution. If $n \geqq 5$, then such an algorithm does not exist, which was proved by S. P. Novikov in 1962. The problem is quite vague if $n = 4$. An article (see [7]) has recently become available for $n = 3$ proving the algorithmic recognizability of the Heegaard diagrams of the three-dimensional sphere in some subclass of the Heegaard diagrams of manifolds; this subclass contains, in particular, all the diagrams of the genus two. This algorithm is, indeed, Haken's algorithm of the comparison of a knot with a trivial knot, and, hence, is not a real effective algorithm (having some numerical realization for example).

The authors of the present work (I. A. Volodin, V. E. Kuznetzov, A. T. Fomenko), which will be published in Uspehi Mat. Nauk **5** (1974), are absolutely convinced that in the three-dimensional topology there exist not only the algorithms of the Haken type, but also real effective simple and elegant algorithms; for example in the problem of the sphere-recognition. In our work we have found serious reasons to assert our observation that the existence of a necessary and sufficient topological invariant of the standard three-dimensional sphere, which admits an exceedingly simple algorithmic description in the class of *all* Heegaard diagrams, is possible. We understand necessity and sufficiency in the sense that some (co)-representation (that is, a code) of the manifold is a (co)representation of the sphere if and only if our invariant of this (co)representation is trivial. The sufficiency is proved by the authors. The necessity has not been proved yet. But the authors did prove the necessity for some infinite classes of (co)representations of the sphere. In other cases the necessity of this invariant is confirmed by the great computing experiments which were carried on by the authors making use of E. C. M. БЭСМ-6. The authors hope to obtain the complete proof of necessity.

Let us consider the Riemannian surface V_n of the genus n, $n \geqq 1$, and let a system (α) of noncrossing and self-noncrossing smooth circles $S_1, \cdots, S_n$ such that we obtain a two-dimensional manifold, which is diffeomorphic to the sphere S^2 with $2n$ holes, after cutting V_n in accordance with system (α), be fixed on V_n. Let us consider a pair of systems: (α_1, α_2) on V_n, the circles of the systems α_1 and α_2 being thought of as intersecting transversally only. We will call the circles $S_i \in (\alpha_1)$ as having index 1; and circles $\bar{S}_j \in (\alpha_2)$ as having index 2. We will call the two pairs (α_1, α_2) and (α_1', α_2') equivalent, if there exists a diffeomorphism $\Upsilon: V_n \to V_n$ such that $\Upsilon(\alpha_i) = \alpha_i'$, $i = 1, 2$.

DEFINITION 2.1. We call a class of equivalent pairs on V_n a net (β).

A cobordism of a two-dimensional sphere (and, consequently, a closed three-dimensional manifold $M(\beta)$) corresponds uniquely to each net (β). For each closed smooth three-dimensional manifold M there exists a (co)representation $M = M(\beta)$ (for some n). The nets (β) are the analogues of the Heegaard diagrams. There exists an algorithm which enumerates the set K of all oriented nets (the orientation of the circles and of the nets is a list of (co)representations of all manifolds). The sphere recognition problem is: How to recognize in an algorithmic way whether the manifold $M(\beta)$ of an arbitrary net (β) is diffeomorphic to the sphere S^3?

The circles $\{S_i; \bar{S}_j\}$, $1 \leqq i, j \leqq n$, divide V_n into a system of regions U_β.

DEFINITION 2.2. The region $U \in U_\beta$ is called a marked one if among the edges forming its boundary there are two edges φ_1, φ_2, belonging to one circle and having a coinciding orientation with any boundary circuit. (See Figure 4.) We shall call the wave $\tilde{v}$ the segment with the marked region which connects two interior points A_1, A_2 of the edges φ_1, φ_2, respectively.

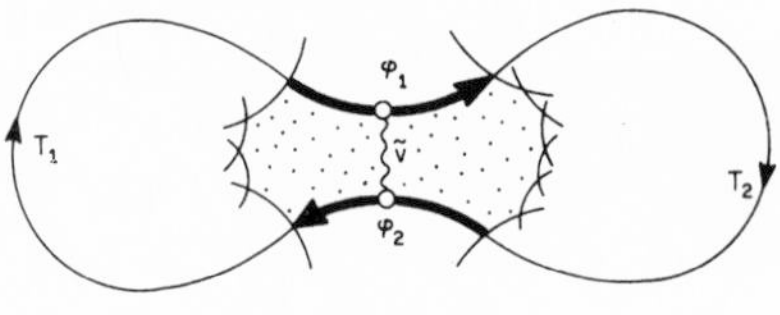

FIGURE 4

Let us consider the standard system (α_1) of the parallels and (α_2) of the meridians on V_n. (See Figure 5.) It is clear that $(\beta) = (\alpha_1, \alpha_2)$ is a net and that $M(\beta)$ is diffeo-

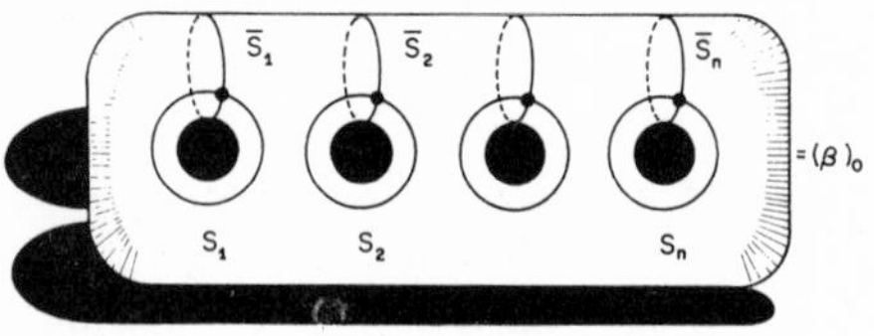

FIGURE 5

morphic to S^3. Let us denote this standard spherical net as $(\beta)_0$. We will construc some algorithm (A), defined on K, and processing this list into itself. Let us give some oriented net (β), which is denoted by (β_1) on the INPUT of the algorithm (A) then we look over the regions U_β and search for the marked region. If such a region is absent, then the net (β_1) is given to the OUTPUT of the algorithm (A). If the marked region has been found, then we choose the edges φ_1, φ_2, after which we connect them by the wave $\tilde{v}$ and proceed to the next step. The net (β) may have several waves; we choose an arbitrary wave. Let the edges φ_1, φ_2 belong to the circle S_1 of index 1, for example (if $\varphi_1, \varphi_2 \in \bar{S}_j$, then all the following consideration are similar). Let us construct an abstract graph $W(\alpha_1)$ using the net (β_1), where $S_i \in (\alpha_1)$. We cut V_n along all the circles of index 1; then we obtain the sphere S with $2n$ holes: $X_1^{+1}, \cdots, X_n^{+1}; X_1^{-1}, \cdots, X_n^{-1}$. The circles of index 2 (after this operation either remain unchanged or tear to pieces—and become a collection of segment connecting (in some order) the holes on the sphere S^2. Let us identify these holes with the vertices $X_1^{+1}, \cdots, X_n^{+1}; X_1^{-1}, \ldots, X_n^{-1}$ of the graph and the segments of the circles with the edges of this graph. We obtain some graph $W(\alpha_1)$ which is flatly realized on S^2 (it may contain circles without vertices). The circle S_i (with the edges φ_1, φ_2) generates two vertices: X_i^{+1}, X_j^{-1}. The wave $\tilde{v}$ turns into a segmen

τ on the sphere S^2 which goes from the vertex X_i^ε (where $\varepsilon = \pm 1$ depending on the orientation of S_i) and returns again to this vertex; τ does not intersect the graph $W(\alpha_1)$ in its other points. The graph $W(\alpha_1)$ disintegrates into two nonintersecting components: g_1 and g_2, after removing the vertex X_i^ε from the graph $W(\alpha_1)$. (See Figure 6.) The vertex $X_i^{-\varepsilon}$ belongs either to g_1 or to g_2. Let $X_i^{-\varepsilon} \in g_2$, for example.

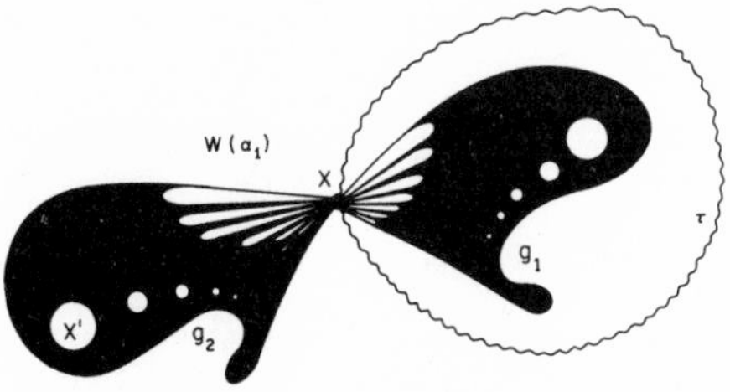

FIGURE 6

The points A_1, A_2 on V_n (see Definition 2.2) break the circle S_i into two segments T_1, T_2. The edges of the graph $W(\alpha_1)$ which are incident with X_i^ε and belong to the component g_1 define uniquely one of two segments T_i ($i = 1, 2$) with which they intersect, for example T_1. The segment T_1 together with the segment τ bounds a region not containing the vertex $X_i^{-\varepsilon}$ and containing the subgraph g_1 on the sphere with $2n$ holes. Let us replace the segment T_1 of the circle $\tilde{S}_i$ in the net (β) by the segment $\tilde{v}$; then S_i will be replaced by the circle $\tilde{S}_i$ consisting of the segments $\tilde{v}$ and T_2. The other circles of the net (β) remain unchanged.

THEOREM 2.1. *The above operation of the stripping of the net* $(\beta) = (\beta_1)$ *using the wave* $\tilde{v}$ *generates some new net* (β_2).

Each step of this algorithm (A) (provided the wave exists) strictly decreases the number of the knots of the net (that is, the number of the intersections of the circles); consequently, if N is the number of the knots of the initial net, the algorithm (A) stops its work after the number s of the steps, where $s \leqq N$, and we obtain some net with no wave at the OUTPUT.

DEFINITION 2.3. The net (β) we call spherical if $M(\beta)$ is diffeomorphic to S_3.

Hypothesis X. The net (β) is spherical if and only if it is presented to the INPUT of the algorithm (A), a standard spherical net $(\beta)_0$ is obtained at the OUTPUT.

The sufficiency of this statement follows from Theorem 2.2.

THEOREM 2.2 *The algorithm* (A) *does not change the topological type of the manifold; that is,* $M(\beta)$ *and* $M(A(\beta))$ *are diffeomorphic.*

The necessity of hypothesis X has not been proved yet. The hypothesis X amounts to the following statement:

Hypothesis X^1. Every spherical net, different from $(\beta)_0$, contains at least one wave.

Let us introduce the notion of the displacement to describe the cases when the truth of this hypothesis is proved by the authors. Let us consider S_i, $S_j \in (\alpha_1)$,

$i \neq j$; then let us choose two points on each of these circles: $y_1 \in S_i$; $y_2 \in S_j$ and connect y_1 with y_2 a smooth segment s on V_n, intersecting with (α_1) in the points y_1, y_2 only. Let us replace (S_i, S_j) by $(\tilde{S}_i, \tilde{S}_j)$, where $\tilde{S}_i = S_i s S_j s^{-1}$; $\tilde{S}_j = S_j$; add to S_i the doubled segment s and one copy of S_j (after it has been doubled). (See Figure 7.) We call these operations (with the operations of birth and destruction of the trivial loops of pp^{-1} type) operations of index 1. The operations of index 2 are defined in a similar way.

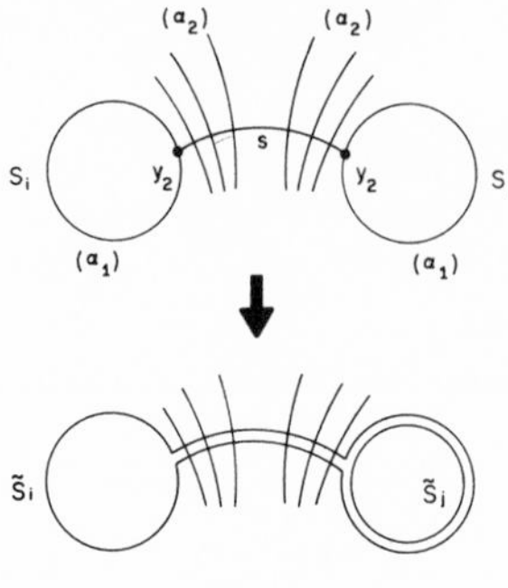

FIGURE 7

THEOREM 2.3. *The net* (β) *is spherical if and only if it may be obtained from the net* $(\beta)_0$ *by some sequence of operations of indices* 1 *and* 2.

Let us denote the set of all the spherical nets as R; then $R_1 \subset R$ is a subset of the nets which are obtained from $(\beta)_0$ by the operations of index 1. The set $R_2 \subset R$ is defined similarly.

THEOREM 2.4. *If* $(\beta) \in R_1 \cup R_2$ *and* $(\beta) \neq (\beta)_0$, *then* (β) *contains one wave at least.*

Let $(\beta) \in R$ and $p(\beta)$ be the number of the knots (points of intersection) in the net (β). We shall call the set of all nets (β) in R with $p(\beta) \leqq l$ as the ball of the radius l. The authors made a programme for E. C. M. БЭСМ-6 which verified the hypothesis X^1 on the set R. Starting from the net $(\beta)_0 \in R$ the programme chanced to form the net $(\beta) \in R$ making use of the operations of both indices (see Theorem 2.3) and realized a random walk along a random trajectory in a ball of radius 16000 in the space R. The genus n of the surface was also defined by chance from the interval $2 \leqq n \leqq 32$. If a net (β) rises in the random walk process on the sphere $p(\beta) = 16000$, the programme started a monotonic stripping by means of waves of the net obtained to the net $(\beta)_0$; that is, the programme employed the algorithm (A); and then again started forming a new random trajectory, and so on. (See Figure 8.)

PROPOSITION 2.1. *Each of* ($\sim 10^6$) *the spherical nets* (β) *which were formed in the process of this computational experiment by the random walk on the ball of the radius* 16000 *in the space R contains at least one wave* (*if* $(\beta) \neq (\beta)_0$).

The computational experiment confirms the truth of the hypothesis X^1. If nevertheless instances of spherical nets with no waves do exist, then our experiment

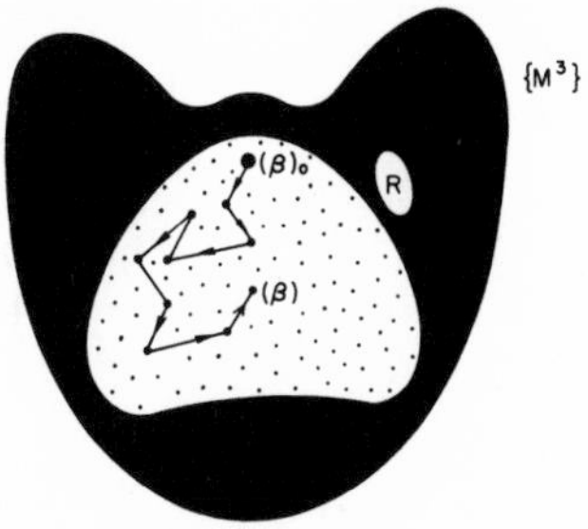

FIGURE 8

shows that these fluctuations will be very rare. The authors hope that there are enough grounds to believe that the problem of the sphere recognition algorithmically is solved positively by using the above constructed effective algorithm (A).

Bibliography

1. Charles B. Morrey, *Multiple integrals in the calculus of variations*, Die Grundlehren der math. Wissenschaften, Band 130, Springer-Verlag, New York, 1966. MR **34** #2380.

2. H. Federer, *Geometric measure theory*, Die Grundlehren der math. Wissenschaften, Band 153, Springer-Verlag, New York, 1969. MR **41** #1976.

3. F. J. Almgren, *Existence and regularity almost everywhere of solutions to elliptic variational problems among surfaces of varying topological type and singularity structure*, Ann. of Math. (2) **87** (1968), 321–391. MR **37** #837.

4. A. T. Fomenko, *The multidimensional Plateau problem in Riemannian manifolds*, Mat. Sb. **89 (131)** (1972), 475–519 = Math. USSR Sb. **18** (1972), 487–528.

5. ———, *Minimal compacta in riemannian manifolds and Reifenberg's conjecture*, Izv. Akad. Nauk SSSR Ser. Mat. **36** (1972), 1049–1079 = Math. USSR Izv. **6** (1972), 1037–1066.

6. ———, *Multidimensional Plateau problems on Riemannian manifolds and extraordinary homology and cohomology theories*. I, Proc. Vector and Tensor Anal. Seminar, vol. 17, Moscow State Univ., Moscow, 1974, pp. 3–176. (Russian)

7. J. S. Birman and H. M. Hilden, *The homeomorphism problem for* S^3, Bull. Amer. Math. Soc. **79** (1973), 1006–1010. MR **47** #7726.

MOSCOW STATE UNIVERSITY
MOSCOW, U.S.S.R.

Proceedings of the International Congress of Mathematicians
Vancouver, 1974

Global and Local Characteristic Class Theory in Topological Transformation Groups

Wu-Yi Hsiang*

1. Cohomology theory of topological transformation groups in the setting of global characteristic class. Historically, applications of algebraic topology to the study of transformation groups were originated in the work of L. E. J. Brouwer on periodic transformations and a little later the beautiful fixed point theorem of P. A. Smith for prime periodic maps on homology spheres. In comparison of the fixed point theorem of Smith with its predecessors, the fixed point theorems of Brouwer and Lefschetz, one finds that it is possible, at least for the case of homology spheres, to upgrade the conclusion of mere existence (or nonexistence) to the actual determination of the cohomology type of the fixed point set, if the map is assumed to be prime periodic. This pioneer result of Smith clearly suggests a fruitful general direction of studying transformation groups in the framework of algebraic topology. A far-reaching generalization of the Smith fixed point theorem can be formulated and proved in the setting of the following equivariant cohomology introduced by A. Borel [2]:

Let G be a compact Lie group and X be a given G-space. Then the equivariant cohomology of X, denoted by $H_G^*(X, k)$, is defined to be the ordinary cohomology of the total space X_G of the universal bundle $X \to X_G \to B_G$ with X as the typical fibre. Intuitively and heuristically, the complexity of the G-space X will be reflected in the complexity of the associated universal bundle; and the usual characteristic class theory (of vector bundles) demonstrates that cohomology theory can then be used to detect such complexity. Technically, the above equivariant cohomology naturally brings together the modern theory of fibre bundles, spectral sequences and sheaves in a nice convienient way. Hence, it not only possesses all convenient formal properties that one may expect, but also is effectively computable. Alge-

*Research partially supported by NSF grant GP-34785X.

braically, $H_G^*(X, k)$ is an algebra over $H_G^*(pt, k) = H^*(B_G, k)$ which has rich ideal theoretical structure. An ideal situation would be that such an algebraic structure can be neatly correlated to the cohomological aspect of the orbit structure of X. One of the most profound as well as fascinating facts in the cohomology theory of transformation groups is the sharp contrast of behaviors between elementary abelian groups, i.e., torus T^r and p-torus Z_p^r, and the rest of compact Lie groups, namely, *there exists a definitive correlation between the algebraic structure of* $H_G^*(X, k)$ *and the cohomological orbit structure of* X *if* G *is an elementary abelian group*, but otherwise, *there are wild counterexamples to show the nonexistence of any such correlation for all other compact Lie groups.*

(A) *Cohomological splitting theorems for actions of elementary p-groups.* In this subsection, we shall always assume that G is an elementary p-group (i.e., Z_p^r or T^r if $p = 0$) and the coefficient field k is Z_p or Q if $p = 0$. Recall that $H^*(B_G, k) \cong k[t_1, \cdots, t_r]$, $\deg(t_i) = 2$ (resp. 1) when $G = T^r$ (resp. Z_2^r) and $k = Q$ (resp. Z_2); and $H^*(B_G, k) \cong k[t_1, \ldots, t_r] \otimes \bigwedge [v_1, \ldots, v_r]$, $\beta_p v_i = t_i$, $\deg(t_i) = 2$ when $G = Z_p^r$ and $k = Z_p$ for odd prime. Let R be the polynomial part of $H^*(B_G)$ and R_0 be the quotient field of R, i.e., $R_0 = k(t_1, \ldots, t_r)$. Then $H_G^*(X) \otimes_{H_G^*(pt)} R_0$ carries the torsion-free part of $H_G^*(X)$, which is an R_0-algebra with mod 2 gradation if $p \neq 2$. The following fundamental fixed point theorem [5] relates the torsion-free part of $H_G^*(X)$ to the cohomology of the fixed point set F.

THEOREM 1. *Suppose* $H_G^*(X) \otimes_{H_G^*(pt)} R_0$ *is given by the following presentation*:

$$\begin{aligned} I &= \operatorname{Ker}(\rho) \subseteq A \\ &= R_0[x_1, \ldots, x_l] \otimes_{R_0} \bigwedge_{R_0} [v_1, \ldots, v_m] \xrightarrow{\rho} H_G^*(X) \otimes_{H_G^*(pt)} R_0. \end{aligned}$$

Then

(i) *the radical of* I, $\sqrt{I}$, *decomposes into the intersection of s maximal ideals* $M_j = M(a_j)$ *whose varieties are respectively the rational points* $a_j = (a_{j1}, \ldots, a_{jl}) \in R_0^l$,

(ii) *there is a* 1-1 *correspondence between* $\{a_j\}$ *and the connected components of the fixed point set* $\{F^j\}$ *such that the restriction homomorphism of* $q_j \in F^j \subseteq X$ *maps* $x_i \in H_G^*(X)$ *to* $a_{ji} \in R$,

(iii) $H^*(F^j; k) \otimes_k R_0 \cong A/I_j$ *where* $I_j = I_{M_j} \cap A$ *and* I_{M_j} *is the localization of* I *at* M_j,

(iv) $I = I_1 \cap \cdots \cap I_s = I_1 \cdot I_2 \cdots I_s$.

The above general theorem is valid for all conceivable finite-dimensional spaces and it provides the key step both in the formulation and in the proof of various fixed point theorems of Smith type. Let us mention a few of its simplest corollaries and refer to [7] for its many specific applications.

COROLLARY 1. *The fixed point set F is nonempty if and only if* $H^*(B_G) \longrightarrow H_G^*(X)$ *is injective, i.e., the unit* $1 \in H_G^*(X)$ *is torsion-free.*

COROLLARY 2. *For each connected component* F^j, *there exists a generator system of the k-algebra* $H^*(F^j, k)$ *with at most l even generators and at most m odd generators* (*cf. Theorem* 1).

COROLLARY 3. *Suppose G is a torus and F is nonempty. If* $\pi_{2i}(X) \otimes Q = 0$ *for all* $i > 0$, *then F must be connected.*

COROLLARY 4. *Suppose* $H^*(X) \cong k[x_0]/(x_0^{n+1})$, $\deg(x_0) = 2, p \neq 2$. *Then*

$$H_G^*(X; k) \cong H_G^*(pt, k)[x]/(f(x)),$$

where $f(x) = (x - a_1)^{m_1} \dots (x - a_s)^{m_s}$ *and correspondingly* $H^*(F^j) = k[x_j]/(x_j^{m_j})$.

Roughly speaking, F carries the torsion-free part of $H_G^*(X)$ and $(X - F)$ carries the torsion part of $H_G^*(X)$. Observe that subgroups (resp. connected subgroups for $p = 0$) of an elementary p-group are again elementary p-groups. Moreover, there is a natural bijection between the set of subgroups (resp. connected subgroups) of a given elementary p-group G and the set of *linear prime ideals* in $H^*(B_G)$, namely,

$$G \supseteq H \longleftrightarrow P_H = \operatorname{Ker}(H^*(B_G, k) \longrightarrow H^*(B_H\ k)) \subseteq H^*(B_G, k).$$

Therefore, it is rather natural to try to correlate annihilating ideals of submodules of $H_G^*(X)$ to *isotropy subgroups* (resp. connected isotropy subgroups) of sub-G-spaces of X. For simplicity, let us look at the case $F =$ empty set.

THEOREM 2. *Let X be a G-space without fixed point, and J be the annihilating ideal of the whole module* $H_G^*(X)$. *Then*

(i) *those prime ideals in the prime decomposition of the radical of J are all linear ideals, i.e., generated by linear polynomials,*

(ii) *the set of prime ideals belonging to* $J, \{P_j\}$, *naturally corresponds to the set of maximal isotropy subgroups (resp. maximal connected isotropy subgroups)* $\{H_j\}$ *such that the variety of* P_j *is exactly the Lie algebra of* H_j,

(iii) *let* $Y^j = F_j(H, X), j = 1, \cdots, m$. *Then*

$$H_G^*(X, k)_{P_j} = H_G^*(Y^j, k)_{P_j} = H^*(Y^j/G, k) \otimes_k H^*(B_{H_j}, k)_{P_j}.$$

REMARKS. (i) In case X is compact, J is simply the annihilator of the unit 1, which is also equal to the kernel of $H^*(B_G, K) \to H_G^*(X, k)$.

(ii) If the fixed point set F is nonempty, then one simply applies the above theorem to $(X - F)$ instead of X.

(iii) Combining Theorem 2 with Theorem 1, one has a firm grip on the structure of $H^*(Y^j/G, k)$. Moreover, one may further apply Theorem 2 to $(X - \bigcup Y^j)$ to obtain the cohomological structure of less singular orbits. However, such an inductive approach is in general too complicated to be practically feasible.

COROLLARY 1. *In the special case of homology sphere X, the fixed point set F is again a homology sphere and it is easy to see that the annihilating ideal J of* $H_G^*(X - F, k)$ *is a principal ideal. Therefore, it follows from Theorem 2 that the generator of J splits into the product of linear polynomials, i.e.,* $J = (w_1^{k_1} \cdot w_2^{k_2} \dots w_m^{k_m})$, $w_i \in H^2(B_G, k)$.

We refer to [7] for a systematic discussion of such relationships between the ideal theoretical invariants of $H_G^*(X)$ and the cohomological orbit structure of X.

(B) *A general class of counterexamples.* Let G be a compact Lie group such that either the identity component G^0 is nonabelian, or G/G^0 is non-p-primary. It is then always possible to find a suitable linear representation of G satisfying the following properties:

(i) the restricted linear action on the unit sphere S^n has no fixed point,

(ii) the G-space S^n admits an equivariant map into itself f: $S^n \to S^n$ with degree of f equal to zero.

Let Y be the inverse limit of the system of iterated maps $\{f^j\}$ generated by f. Then it is easy to verify that Y is a compact, finite-dimensional G-space, without fixed points, and with acyclic cohomology. Let K be an arbitrary finite complex with trivial G-action, and $X = Y \circ K$ be the join of Y and K. Then X is again an acyclic G-space with $F = K$. Observe that the equivariant cohomology of X is the same as that of a single point, but its fixed point set $F = K$ can be any given finite complex. Therefore, there is absolutely no hope of generalizing Theorem 1 beyond elementary p-groups. We refer to [3, Part I], [7] for the construction and significance of such examples.

(C) *F-varieties, geometric weight systems and splitting principle.* To put recent developments in cohomology theory of transformation groups into historical perspective, let us first recall the following two basic theorems which constitute the foundation of linear representation theory of compact Lie groups:

(i) STRUCTURAL SPLITTING THEOREM OF LINEAR ACTIONS OF ELEMENTARY p-GROUPS. *Every complex (resp. real) representation of an elementary p-group (resp. $p = 2$) always splits into the sum of one-dimensional representations.*

(ii) MAXIMAL TORI THEOREM (É. CARTAN). *The set of maximal tori of a given compact connected Lie group G forms a single conjugacy class of subgroups, and any maximal torus T of G intersects every conjugacy class of G.*

The maximal tori theorem enables us to reduce the classification of linear G-actions to that of the restricted T-actions, and the splitting theorem classifies linear actions of elementary p-groups in terms of an extremely simple invariant called "*p-weight system*". In the setting of characteristic class theory of vector bundles, the splitting of *linear* actions of elementary p-groups at the space level obviously implies the splitting at the characteristic class level, if the structural group of the given vector bundles is reducible to elementary p-groups. And moreover, the maximal tori theorem again enables us to reduce the structural group G to one of its maximal tori T via suitable lifting, which is usually called the *splitting principle* in characteristic class theory of vector bundles.

Methodologically, the recent approach to cohomology theory of transformation groups can be characterized as the *geometric characteristic class theory of general fibre bundles*, and one of the central themes in such an approach is that *topological* transformations of compact Lie groups can be studied along the same line as that of the classical *linear* representation theory of compact connected Lie groups. Then, the central results in the theory of *topological* transformation groups are those cohomological splitting theorems which prove that the *splittings at characteristic class level* are still valid even for the vastly more general family of *topological* actions of elementary p-groups. In case the space X is of a given type, such cohomological splitting theorems usually enable us to organize the "*totality of cohomological orbit structure*" of a given action of elementary p-groups on X into a simple invariant that we shall call the "*geometric weight system*" of the given action. Geometrically, a G-space is quite analogous to an algebraic variety, and as an analogy of the Zariski closure, *the F-variety spanned by a point* $x \in X$ is defined to be the *connected* component of x in $\bigcup \{F(H, X);\ H \sim G_x\}$ (resp. $\bigcup \{F(H,X);\ H \sim G_x^0\}$ if G is connected). Then, the totality of cohomological orbit structure of X consists of the cohomological data of the whole network of F-varieties of X.

Finally, as a generalization of the splitting principle in characteristic class theory of vector bundles, one may again study the geometric behavior of a given topological G-action via its *restrictions to its maximal elementary p-subgroups*. We refer to [7] for a systematic discussion of such an approach of cohomology theory of topological transformation groups.

2. Characteristic class and local orbit structure. The characteristic class theory of equivariant bundles over homogeneous spaces provides a powerful tool in the study of local orbit structure, especially in the setting of differentiable compact transformation groups. Let G be a compact Lie group and M be a differentiable G-manifold. Then the equivariant normal bundle of a given orbit $G(x) \subseteq M$ is completely determined by the slice representation ϕ_x of G_x on the space, R^n_x, of normal vectors of $G(x)$ at x, namely, $\nu(G(x)) = \alpha(\phi_x) = \{R^n \to G \times_{G_x} R^n \to G/G_x\}$. Therefore, one has the following simple but rather rigid equation in $(KO)^\sim(G(x))$:

$$i^*\tau(M) = \tau(G(x)) + \nu(G(x)) = \alpha(\mathrm{Ad}_G \big| G_x - \mathrm{Ad}_{G_x} + \phi_x) = \alpha(\phi_x - \mathrm{Ad}_{G_x}).$$

In particular, if $G(x)$ is a principal orbit, then $i^*\tau(M) = \tau(G(x)) = -\alpha(\mathrm{Ad}_{G_x})$ in $(KO)^\sim(G(x))$. For example, if the tangent bundle $\tau(M)$ satisfies certain vanishing conditions such as $P_i(M) = 0$ for $1 \leqq i \leqq b$, then the tangent bundle of the principal orbit type must also satisfy the same vanishing condition. Hence, it is rather natural to apply the usual splitting principle of characteristic class to study the above equation of vector bundles over homogeneous spaces of compact Lie groups. We refer to [3], [6] for systematic discussions of this topic. Let us mention some simple results of [6] to indicate what type of results one may expect in this direction:

THEOREM 3. *Suppose H is a connected subgroup of* $\mathrm{Sp}(m)$ *such that* $P_i(\mathrm{Sp}(m)/H) = 0$ *for* $i = 1, 2, 3$. *Then either H is a torus subgroup, or* $H = \mathrm{Sp}(1)^k \subseteq \mathrm{Sp}(k) \subseteq \mathrm{Sp}(m)$, *or H is a simple Lie group of type* C_k, G_2, E_6, *or* E_7 *with* $\psi\colon H \subseteq \mathrm{Sp}(m)$ *equal to the lowest dimensional irreducible symplectic representation of H modulo trivial ones, namely,* $\dim_H \psi = n$, 7, 27, *or* 56 *resp.*

COROLLARY 1. *Let G be* $\mathrm{Sp}(m)$ *and M be a given connected differentiable G-manifold. If* $P_i(M) = 0$ *for* $i = 1, 2, 3$ *and the connected principal isotropy subgroup type*

(H_M^0) *is nontrivial, then either* H_M^0 *is a torus subgroup of* $\mathrm{Sp}(m)$, *or* $H_M^0 = \mathrm{Sp}(1)^k \subseteq \mathrm{Sp}(k) \subseteq \mathrm{Sp}(m)$, *or* H_M^0 *is a simple Lie group of type* C_k, G_2, E_6, *or* E_7 *with* $\psi: H_M^0 \subseteq \mathrm{Sp}(m)$ *equal to the lowest dimensional irreducible symplectic representation modulo trivial ones.*

THEOREM 4. *Let G be* $\mathrm{Sp}(m)$ *and M be a given connected differentiable G-manifold with nontrivial connected principal isotropy subgroup type* (H^0). *If* $P_i(M) = 0$ *for* $i = 1, 2, 3$, *then the (connected) local orbit structures of M are respectively as follows according to the type of its connected principal orbit type* (H^0):

(i) *if* H^0 *are subtori of rank at least* 2, *then* $\mathrm{rk}(G_x) = \mathrm{rk}(H^0)$ *for all* $x \in M$ *and* $\phi_x = \mathrm{Ad}_{G_x}$ *modulo trivial representations,*

(ii) *if* $H^0 = \mathrm{Sp}(1)^k, k \geqq 2$, *then* $G_x^0 = (\nu_{k_1} \oplus \dots \oplus \nu_{k_a})(\mathrm{Sp}(k_1) \times \dots \times \mathrm{Sp}(k_a))$, $k_1 + \cdots + k_a = k$, *and* $\phi_x = \wedge^2 \nu_{k_1} \oplus \cdots \oplus \wedge^2 \nu_{k_a}$ *modulo trivial ones,*

(ii) *if* $H^0 = \nu_k(\mathrm{Sp}(k))$, *then all connected isotropy subroups* G_x^0 *are also of the type* $\nu(\mathrm{Sp}(n_x))$,

(iv) *if* H_0 *are of the type* G_2, *or* E_6, *or* E_7, *then all connected isotropy subgroups are of the same type, i.e.,* $(G_x^0) = (H^0)$ *for all* $x \in M$.

3. Testing spaces and testing problems. The existence of abundant linear actions and the simplicity of topological structure form an ideal combination that makes Euclidean spaces, disks, spheres, and projective spaces the best testing spaces for the study of transformation groups. So far, most of the deep results in topological transformation groups are still largely concentrated in the case of such testing spaces. We refer to [**3**, Parts I, II, III], [**4**], [**7**] for some of the results in this area. Generally speaking, the ideal combination of topological simplicity and abundant linear actions of those testing spaces is certainly very helpful in obtaining some *basic understanding to begin with.* For example, it is exactly the classical linear representation theory and those specific results such as Corollary 4 of Theorem 1 and Corollary 1 of Theorem 2 that leads us to the basic understanding of the *central importance of elementary p-groups* in the study of transformation groups, as well as to the formulation of those *fundamental cohomological splitting theorems* in the setting of equivariant cohomology theory. In view of the recent developments of global and local characteristic class theory in transformation groups, it is both natural and necessary that we should begin to broaden the domain of testing spaces to include such important spaces as homotopy spheres, homotopy projective spaces and compact homogeneous spaces. Due to the fact that compact homogeneous spaces cover a wide range of topological types but still accommodate a rich variety of natural actions, they are particularly suitable to serve as our testing spaces, at the present stage of transformation group theory. Let us conclude this article by formulating some natural testing problems in the realm of compact transformation groups on compact homogeneous spaces:

(A) *Transitive actions and classification of compact homogeneous spaces in terms of their diffeomorphic (resp. topological, homotopic or rational homotopic) types.* Compact homogeneous spaces are by definition those manifolds with given transitive actions of compact Lie groups. Hence, it is natural to classify such transitive actions on them. A transitive action is called *primitive* if the restriction to any *proper normal* subgroup is no longer transitive.

Problem 1. Suppose $M = G/H$ is a coset space of a *simple* compact Lie group G. Classify all primitive transitive actions on M. For most cases, one would expect that the original G-action is the *only* primitive action on M.

Classification of transitive actions on compact homogeneous spaces essentially amounts to the classification of compact homogeneous spaces in terms of diffeomorphic or topological types. For such a purpose, it is useful to find *explicit* relationships between the "infinitesimal data" of the pair (G, H) and the topological or diffeomorphic invariants of G/H.

Problem 2. Is it true that two homeomorphic compact homogeneous spaces are necessarily diffeomorphic? (In the special case of spheres, the well-known positive answer of the above problem means that only the standard spheres are homogeneous. Moreover, for most cases of classical homogeneous spaces such as Stiefel manifolds, Grassmann manifolds, it is in fact not difficult to show that their homotopic types already uniquely characterize them among homogeneous spaces.)

Problem 3. In the study of compact transformation groups, it is rather natural and useful to define the *torus rank* of a space X to be the *maximal rank* of those tori that act *almost freely* on X. Is it true that the torus rank of G/H is equal to $\mathrm{rk}(G) - \mathrm{rk}(H)$? (The special case $\mathrm{rk}(H) = 0$ was proved by C. Allday in his thesis [**1**].)

(B(*Actions of "large" groups and degree of symmetry*. Roughly speaking, an effective transformation group K on a homogeneous space $M = G/H$ is considered to be large if dim K is not too small as compared to dim G.

Problem 4. Classify all G-actions on $M = G/H$. (For most cases, one of the natural conjectures would be that the given transitive G-action is the only nontrivial G-action on G/H.)

For example, in most cases of Stiefel manifolds $SO(n)/SO(k)$ (resp. $SU(n)/SU(k)$, $Sp(n)/Sp(k)$), it was proved in [**6**] that the only nontrivial $SO(n)$ (resp. $SU(n)$, $Sp(n)$) action on M is the originally given transitive one. However, in the extreme case of $k = 0$, the adjoint action suddenly becomes a new possibility.

CONJECTURE. Let G be a *simple* compact Lie group. Then a nontrivial G-action on G itself is either *transitive* or is of the same cohomological orbit structure as that of the adjoint action.

Problem 5. Let G be a simple compact Lie group, K be a closed subgroup with $\dim K \geqq \frac{1}{4}\cdot\dim G$ and $M = G/K$. Is it true that any K-action on M must have a nonempty fixed point set? In the special case of compact irreducible symmetric spaces such as Grassmann manifolds, is it true that any nontrivial K-action on $M = G/K$ must have the same cohomological orbit structure as the isotropy K-action on G/K?

Problem 6. Suppose $M = G/H$ is a compact homogeneous space and G is one of the *highest dimensional, effective, transitive* transformation groups on M. Is it true that the degree of symmetry of $M = \dim G$? (The degree of symmetry of M is defined to be the maximal dimension of all compact subgroups of Diff (M).)

References

1. C. Allday, *On the rank of a space*, Trans. Amer. Math. Soc. **166** (1972), 173–184. MR **45** #1158.

2. A. Borel, et al., *Seminar on transformation groups*, Ann. of Math. Studies, no. 46, Princeton Univ. Press, Princeton, N. J., 1960. MR **22** #7129.

3. W.-C. Hsiang and W.-Y. Hsiang, *Differentiable actions of compact connected classical groups*. I, Amer. J. Math. **89** (1967), 705–786; II, Ann. of Math. (2) **92** (1970), 189–223; III, Ann. of Math. (2) **99** (1974), 220–256. MR **36** #304; **42** #420.

4. W.-Y. Hsiang, *A survey on regularity theorems in differentiable compact transformation groups*, Proc. Conf. on Transformation Groups (New Orleans, La., 1967), Springer, New York, 1968, pp. 77–124. MR **41** #1072.

5. ———, *On some fundamental theorems in cohomology theory of topological transformation groups*, Taita J. Math. **2** (1970), 61–87. MR **46** #8247. (Some of the results were announced in Bull. Amer. Math. Soc. **77** (1971), 1094–1098. MR **46** #8249.)

6. ———, *Differentiable transformation groups on manifolds with vanishing Pontrjagin classes*, mimeographed at Univ. of California, Berkeley.

7. ———, *Cohomology theory of topological transformation groups*, Ergebnisse der Mathematik und ihrer Grenzgebiete, Springer-Verlag, Berlin and New York, 1975.

University of California
Berkeley, California 94720, U.S.A.

Proceedings of the International Congress of Mathematicians
Vancouver, 1974

The Structure of the Oriented Topological and Piecewise Linear Bordism Rings

R. James Milgram

In this article we describe the oriented cobordism rings for topological and piecewise linear manifolds $\Omega_*^{\mathrm{Top}}(pt)$ and $\Omega_*^{\mathrm{PL}}(pt)$. Full details and proofs will appear in [3], [4].

1. Perhaps the most interesting parts of these rings are the torsion-free pieces, i.e., the quotient rings $\Omega_*^{\mathrm{PL}}(pt)/\mathrm{Tor}$, $\Omega_*^{\mathrm{Top}}(pt)/\mathrm{Tor}$. It is well known that there are rational isomorphisms induced by the natural inclusions

$$\Omega_*^{\mathrm{Diff}}(pt) \otimes \boldsymbol{Q} \cong \Omega_*^{\mathrm{PL}}(pt) \otimes \boldsymbol{Q} \cong \Omega_*^{\mathrm{Top}}(pt) \otimes \boldsymbol{Q}$$

and $\Omega_*^{\mathrm{Diff}}(pt) \otimes \boldsymbol{Q} \cong \boldsymbol{Q}[CP^2, \cdots, CP^4, \cdots, CP^{2n}, \cdots]$. Moreover $\Omega_*^{\mathrm{Diff}}(pt)/\mathrm{Tor} \cong Z[CP^2, \ldots]$, a polynomial algebra on generators x_{4i} where x_{4i} is either a CP^{2i} or a certain hypersurface in a product of CP^n's [6]. Now, for the PL and topological rings we have

THEOREM 1. 1. *The natural inclusion induces an isomorphism* $\Omega_*^{\mathrm{PL}}(pt)/\mathrm{Tor} \cong \Omega_*^{\mathrm{Top}}(pt)/\mathrm{Tor}$. *Moreover either ring is generated by the differential generators above, together with the index* 8 *Milnor manifolds and the exotic complex projective spaces* (*i. e., those PL manifolds homotopy equivalent to* CP^{2n}).

We indicate how to construct a sufficient number of these exotic CP^{2n}'s in §3. Here we make some more precise comments on the rings themselves.

THEOREM 1.2 (BRUMFIEL-SULLIVAN). *Let* $Z_{(p)}$ *be the integers localized at* p; *then* $\Omega_*^{\mathrm{PL}}(pt)/\mathrm{Tor} \otimes Z_{(p)}$ *is a polynomial ring at each odd prime* p.

However the generators are different at different primes. In fact $\Omega_*^{\mathrm{PL}}(pt)/\mathrm{Tor}$ cannot be a polynomial ring since we have recently shown

THEOREM 1.3 [2]. $\Omega_*^{\mathrm{PL}}(pt)/\mathrm{Tor} \otimes Z_{(2)}$ *is not a polynomial ring. In fact*

$$\Omega_*^{\mathrm{PL}}(pt)/\mathrm{Tor} \otimes Z_{(2)} \cong Z_{(2)}\,[CP^{2n} \mid \alpha(n) - 4 < \nu(n)] \otimes \Gamma\,[M^{4n} \mid \alpha(n) - 4 \geqq \nu(n)].$$

Here $\alpha(n)$ is the number of ones in the dyadic expansion of n, $\nu(n)$ is the exponent of the highest power of 2 dividing n and Γ is a divided power algebra. Specifically it has generators M^{4n}, $\gamma^1(M^{4n})$, $\gamma^i(M^{4n}), \cdots$ with relations $M^2 = 2\gamma^1(M)$, $(\gamma^1 M))^2 = 2\gamma^2(M)$, $(\gamma^i(M))^2 = 2\gamma^{i+1}(M)$, etc.

As corollaries we obtain integrality theorems for topological manifolds. For example

THEOREM 1.4. *Let $\mathscr{G}$ be any multiplicative sequence in the rational Pontrjagin classes; then $\langle \mathscr{G}, [M] \rangle$ takes values in the 2-adic integers if and only if the $\mathscr{P}$ series for $\mathscr{G}$*

$$\Sigma\,(-1)^i s_{4i} t^i \qquad (s_{4i} = \textit{coefficient of } p_i \textit{ in } \mathscr{G}_{4i})$$

satisfies

(1) $s_{4i} \in Z_{(2)}$ *all* i,

(2) $s_{2^{i+2}j} \equiv s_{2^{i+1}(j)}\ (2^i)$ *all* $i \geqq 1$,

(3) *if* $\alpha(i) - 4 \geqq \nu(i)$ *then* $2^{\alpha(i)-3}$ *divides* s_{4i}.

Similarly taking into account the odd primes we have

COROLLARY 1.5. *If $\mathscr{G}$ is integral on all topological manifolds, then if $\mathscr{P}(L) = \Sigma(-1)^i l_{4i} t^i$ is the $\mathscr{P}$ series for the Hirzebruch $\mathscr{L}$-genus L then s_{4i} is an integral multiple of $\frac{1}{4} l_{4i}$.*

Unfortunately we do not know exaotly what integral multiples are required.

REMARK 1.6. Sullivan's $B_{O(1/2)}$ orientation shows that away from 2 a basic set of polynomials integral on topological manifolds has the form $L \cup \mathrm{ph}\,(\gamma)$ where ph is a Pontrjagin character.

2. The torsion in $\Omega_*^{\mathrm{PL}}(pt)$ arises in several distinct ways. Here we discuss a few of them.

First there is the homomorphism

$$\eta\colon \Omega_*^{\mathrm{Diff}}(G/\mathrm{PL}) \to \Omega_*^{\mathrm{PL}}(pt) \tag{2.1}$$

defined as follows. Let $\alpha \in \Omega_*^{\mathrm{Diff}}(G/\mathrm{PL})$ be represented by the map $f\colon M \to G/\mathrm{PL}$. Then, corresponding to (f, M) is a degree 1 normal map $\pi_f\colon \tilde{M} \to M$ where $\tilde{M}$ is a PL manifold, and we set $\eta\,\{f, M\} = \{\tilde{M}\}$. It is easily verified that the result does not depend on the particular choices made.

On $G/O \subsetneq G/\mathrm{PL}$ we may again give η as before. But here $\pi_f\colon \tilde{M} \to M$ always can be chosen with $\tilde{M}$ also differentiable so $\eta \mid \Omega_*^{\mathrm{Diff}}(G/O)$ factors through $\Omega_*^{\mathrm{Diff}}(pt)$, and we have the commutative diagram

$$\begin{array}{ccc} \Omega_*^{\mathrm{Diff}}(G/O) & \xrightarrow{\ i_*\ } & \Omega_*^{\mathrm{Diff}}(G/\mathrm{PL}) \\ \downarrow \eta & & \downarrow \eta \\ \Omega_*^{\mathrm{Diff}}(pt) & \xrightarrow{\ i\ } & \Omega_*^{\mathrm{PL}}(pt) \end{array} \tag{2.2}$$

Now suppose $\alpha \in \Omega_*^{\text{Diff}}(G/O)$ is in the kernel of both η and i_* in (2.2). Then we can define the suspension of α, $\sigma(\alpha)$, in $\Omega_*^{\text{PL}}(pt)$ as follows. Let α be represented by (f, M); then $\tilde{M} = \partial W$ with W differentiable and $\tilde{M} \to M$ is (PL) normally bordant to 0. Let $\tilde{W}$ be the normal bordism on $\tilde{M}$. Then

$$\sigma(\alpha) = \{W \cup_M W\} \tag{2.3}$$

and $\sigma(\alpha)$ is well defined up to im $(i) \oplus$ im (η).

LEMMA 2.4. *$\sigma(\alpha)$ is always torsion modulo its indeterminacy.*

Here is a third way of obtaining torsion generators, again using (2.2). Suppose $i_*(\alpha) = m(\beta)$ and $\eta(\alpha) = s(\Upsilon)$ and $k > 1 = \text{g.c.d.}(m, s)$. Then $m|k\,(\eta(\beta)) - s|k\,(i\,(\Upsilon))$ represents k torsion in $\Omega_*^{\text{PL}}(pt)$. In particular

$$A = \{7M^8 - 200(CP^2 \times CP^2) + 144CP^4\},$$
$$\{31M^{12} - 1620CP^6 + 5292\,(CP^4 \times CP^2) - 3920(CP^2 \times CP^2 \times CP^2)\}$$

are obtained this way. They both have order 4 in Ω^{PL}, but the first has order 2 in Ω^{Top} while the second is unchanged. It would be interesting to be able to study the topological bordism in some detail.

There are two further constructions that give torsion generators at the prime 2 but they are quite complex manifold Massey product constructions so we do not go into them here.

At odd primes it would seem likely that only a form of the suspension is necessary to describe the torsion generators though this is not yet verified.

3. We now indicate briefly how to construct the Milnor manifolds and the exotic CP^{2n}'s needed in 1.1. The singularities which we thereby construct are in some sense generic.

Let $\Gamma_{k,\varepsilon}^{4n}$ be the algebraic hypersurface

$$z_0^{6k-1} + z_1^3 + z_2^2 + \cdots + z_{2n}^2 = \varepsilon.$$

For $\varepsilon \neq 0$ but $|\varepsilon|$ sufficiently small $\mathring{M}_k^{4n} = \Gamma_{k,\varepsilon}^{4n} \cap D^{4n+2}$ is a nonsingular manifold with boundary Σ^{4n-1} homeomorphic to S^{4n-1} ([1], [5]). Moreover $\mathring{M}_k^{4n}$ is parallelizable and its index $I(\mathring{M}_k^{4n}) = 8k$.

DEFINITION 3.1. *The index 8k Milnor manifold M_k^{4n} is $\mathring{M}_k^{4n} \cup_{\Sigma^{4n-1}} D^{4n}$.*

To construct the needed exotic projective spaces we modify the construction above. The Brieskorn knot

$$\Sigma_k^{4n-1} \subset S^{4n+1} \tag{3.2}$$

is the intersection of $\Gamma_{k,0}^{4n}$ with S^{4n+1}. It is easily seen that the normal bundle to Σ_k^{4n-1} is trivial so we have an embedding $R\colon D^2 \times S^{4k-1} \subsetneq S^{4k+1}$ after identifying Σ^{4k-1} with S^{4k-1}.

Now, let M^{4n+2} have the homotopy type of CP^{2n+1}. On M there is the canonical line bundle H and let $D(H)$ be its disk bundle and $S(H)$ the associated sphere (circle) bundle. The total space of $S(H)$ has the homotopy type of S^{4k+3}, hence is PL homeomorphic to it for $k \geqq 1$. Now consider the diagram of embeddings

$$\begin{array}{ccc} D(H) & \hookrightarrow & D(2H) \\ \uparrow & & \uparrow \\ S^{4n+3} & \underset{j}{\hookrightarrow} & S(2H) \end{array} \tag{3.3}$$

The normal bundle to $j(S^{4n+3})$ is trivial so we have an embedding $\hat{j}: D^2 \times S^{4n+3} \hookrightarrow S(2H)$ and we construct

$$W^{4n+6} = D^{4n+6} \cup_{R(D^2\times S^{4n+3})=\hat{j}(D^2\times S_{4n+3})} D(2H). \tag{3.4}$$

W is a manifold with boundary having the homotopy type of CP^{2n+2}, and one easily verifies

LEMMA 3.5. $\partial W \simeq S^{4n+5}$.

Hence we can cone off ∂W and obtain an $M^{4n+6} \cong CP^{2n+3}$. To obtain an even dimensional M^{4n} from this we simply take $D(H_M) \cup_{S^{4n+7}} D^{4n+8}$ imitating the construction of CP^{2n+4} using CP^{2n+3}.

To construct all the necessary exotic CP^{2n}'s we simply start with $M = CP^3$ and proceed inductively as above.

Bibliography

1. E. Brieskorn, *Beispiele zur Differentialtopologie von Singularitäten*, Invent. Math. **2** (1966), 1–14. MR **34** #6788.

2. I. Madsen and R. J. Milgram, *The oriented topological and* PL-*cobordism rings*, Bull. Amer. Math. Soc. **80** (1974), 855–860.

3. ———, *The smooth surgery class*, Comment. Math. Helv. (1975) (to appear).

4. ———, *The oriented bordism of topological manifolds and integrality relations*, mimeographed, Aarhus University.

5. J. Milnor, *Singular points of complex hypersurfaces*, Ann. of Math. Studies, no. 61, Princeton Univ. Press, Princeton, N. J.; Univ. of Tokyo Press, Tokyo, 1968. MR **39** #969.

6. R. E. Stong, *Notes on cobordism theory*, Math. Notes, Princeton Univ. Press, Princeton, N. J.; Univ. of Tokyo Press, Tokyo, 1968. MR **40** #2108.

STANFORD UNIVERSITY
STANFORD, CALIFORNIA 94305, U.S.A.

Proceedings of the International Congress of Mathematicians
Vancouver, 1974

Equivariant Quasi-Equivalence, Transversality and Normal Cobordism

Ted Petrie*

0. The setting. Let G be a compact Lie group and Y a (smooth closed) G manifold with underlying manifold $|Y|$. The motivating problem we consider is this:

Question 1. How can we construct all G manifolds X together with G maps f: $X \to Y$ such that $|f|: |X| \to |Y|$ is a homotopy equivalence? Moreover, given such a map f, what restrictions are imposed on the local G invariants of X and Y?

The special case $G = 1$ has seen a vigorous and fruitful history for which there is a complete solution. There are three fundamental concepts involved: fiber-homotopy equivalence of vector bundles, transversality and surgery (cobordism theory). Briefly one starts with a fiber homotopy equivalence ω: $\xi \to \eta$ of vector bundles over Y and via a proper homotopy converts ω to a proper map θ: $\xi \to \eta$ which is transverse to the zero section $Y \subset \eta$ (written $\theta \pitchfork Y$). Then $X = \theta^{-1}(Y)$ is a smooth manifold; $\theta_{|X} = f$: $X \to Y$ is a degree one map (with some additional structure). The technique for converting f to a homotopy equivalence is surgery.

The three concepts mentioned above have important generalizations for general G. The results and problems for each can only be briefly mentioned here. What I shall do is to restrict to a special situation where enough of the problems have been solved so that the full theory can be appreciated. The special situation is that of pseudofree S^1 manifolds as introduced by Montgomery and Yang **[1]**. Here $G = S^1$ and a pseudofree S^1 manifold Y is an S^1 manifold with $Y^{S^1} = \varnothing$ and dim $Y^H = 1$ if $Y^H \neq \varnothing$ for $1 < H < S^1$. We require $|Y|$ to be oriented.The hypothesis implies that the orbit space $\bar{Y} = Y/S^1$ is a manifold except at a finite number of points $\bar{y}_1, \cdots, \bar{y}_n$ corresponding to exceptional orbits in Y, i.e., points $y_1 \cdots y_n \in Y$ whose

*The author is a Guggenheim Fellow. Research partially supported by Rutgers Research Council, N.S.F. (U.S.), S.F.B. (Bonn) and S.R.C. (Oxford).

isotropy groups G_{y_i} are not 1. This is useful from our point of view since the difficulties with equivariant transversality and surgery arise from the fixed point sets Y^H and it helps to have these as simple as possible.

1. The three fundamental concepts.

1.1. *Quasi-equivalence.* Let ξ and η be two G vector bundles (complex) over Y of the same dimension. A G map $\omega: \xi \to \eta$ which is proper, fiber preserving and degree one on fibers is called a quasi-equivalence. Define $\xi \leqq \eta$ to mean there exists a G bundle θ and a quasi-equivalence $\omega: \xi \oplus \theta \to \eta \oplus \theta$.

Problem 1.2. *Give necessary and sufficient conditions that* $\xi \leqq \eta$.

Even for the case Y = point this is interesting and useful. Here the problem is completely solved. I confine discussion to two important cases.

Let G denote the set of irreducible representations of G and $R(G)$ its complex representation ring which is closed under the Adams operations ψ^p. Let $P = \{p_1, \cdots, p_k\}$ be a set of relatively prime positive integers with $k \geqq 2$. Set $\boldsymbol{P} = \prod_{i=1}^{k} (\psi^{p_i} - 1)$. Then $\boldsymbol{P}$ operates on $R(G)$.

THEOREM (MEYERHOFF). *Let T be a torus and N and M two T modules. Then $N \leqq M$ iff*

$$M - N = \sum_{\boldsymbol{P}} \sum_{\chi \in \hat{T}} a_{\boldsymbol{P},\chi}\, \boldsymbol{P}\chi$$

in $R(T)$ where $a_{\boldsymbol{P},\chi}$ are nonnegative integers.

THEOREM 1.3. *Let G be arbitrary and $\chi \in \hat{G}$. Suppose either all $p_i \in P$ are prime to the order of the Weyl group of G or prime to $n!$, $n = \dim \chi$. Then $\boldsymbol{P}\chi = M - N$ in $R(G)$ and $N \leqq M$.*

A trivial but important observation is that if N and M are G modules with $N \leqq M$ then, for any G space Y, $\xi = Y \times N$ and $\eta = Y \times M$ are G bundles over Y and $\xi \leqq \eta$. This has important consequences as seen in §3.

1.4. *G transversality.* Given a quasi-equivalence $\omega: \xi \to \eta$, when is ω properly G homotopic to a map $\theta: \xi \to \eta$ which is transverse to the zero section $Y \subset \eta$?

There is an obstruction theory hinted at in [2] (further results to appear) for solving this problem. Here is the essential point: Suppose G is abelian and that θ exists. Let $X = \theta^{-1}(Y)$ and $f = \theta_{|X}$. Let $H \subset G$ and $\upsilon(X^H, X)$ be the G normal bundle of the fixed set X^H in X. Define a G bundle η_H over Y^H by

$$\eta_{|Y^H} = \eta^H \oplus \eta_H. \tag{1.5}$$

Then in $K_G^0(X^H)$

$$\upsilon(X^H, X) = (f^H)^* \{\upsilon(Y^H, Y) - \eta_H + \xi_H\}. \tag{1.6}$$

1.7. *G normal cobordism.* Let X and Y be closed G manifolds of the same dimension and υ_X the G normal bundle of a G embedding of X in a large G module. A G normal map $f: X \to Y$ consists of a degree one G map f together with a G bundle ξ over Y with $f^*(\xi) = \upsilon_X$ and a G bundle map $F: \upsilon_X \to \xi$ covering f. The definition of G normal cobordism is obvious.

Problem 1.8. *Give necessary and sufficient conditions that a G normal map* (X, f) *be G normally cobordant to* (X', f') *where* $|f'|$ *is a homotopy equivalence.*

Aside from free actions 1.8 is hardly touched. We restrict attention to the case $G = S^1$ and $Y^{S^1} = \emptyset$. Then for any $H \subset S^1$, Y^H is an S^1 manifold and Y^H/S^1 is a rational homology manifold.

Suppose $f: X \to Y$ is an S^1 normal map. If dim $Y = 4k + 3$ and all isotropy groups have odd order, using S^1 transversality, one can define an Arf invariant $A(f) \in Z_2$. If dim $Y = 4k + 1$ one defines $I(f)$ as $I(Y/S^1) - I(X/S^1)$ where $I(Z)$ is the index of the rational homology manifold Z.

If dim $Y^H = 4k + 3$ and S^1/H acts with all isotropy groups of odd order, set $\sigma_H(f) = A(f^H)$. If dim $Y^H = 4k + 1$ set $\sigma_H(f) = I(f^H)$. These invariants should be appropriately interpreted according to the components of Y^H.

THEOREM 1.9. *If* 1.8 *has an affirmative answer,* $\sigma_H(f) = 0$ *for all p groups* $H \subset S^1$.

2. Applications to pseudofree S^1 manifolds. Let X be a pseudofree S^1 manifold. The orbit of $x \in X$ determines a point $\bar{x}$ in the orbit space $\bar{X} = X/S^1$. Set $G_{\bar{x}} = G_x$, the isotropy group of any point x in the orbit $\bar{x}$. The slice representation at x, $\upsilon(X^{G_x}, X)_x$, is abbreviated by υ_x. We can suppose it to be a complex G_x module. Since the complex representation ring of G_x is $R(G_x) = Z[t]/(1-t^m)$, $m = |G_x|$ (the order of G_x), $\upsilon_x = t^{a_1} + \cdots + t^{a_n}$ for integers a_i prime to m and $2n + 1 =$ dim X. Set $|\upsilon_x| = \prod_{i=1}^n a_i \in Z_m$. We say υ_x is a special G_x module if at most one a_i is different from 1 mod m.

THEOREM 2.1. *Suppose Y is a pseudofree* S^1 *manifold and* $f: X \to Y$ *is an* S^1 *normal map with* $|f|$ *a homotopy equivalence. Then*

(i) $G_{\bar{y}}$ *is the direct product of all* $G_{\bar{x}}$ *with* $\bar{x} \in \bar{f}^{-1}(\bar{y})$ *and*

(ii) $|\upsilon_{f(x)}|/|\upsilon_x| \equiv (m_x/m_{f(x)})$ mod m_x *where* $m_x = |G_x|$.

In the spirit of Question 1 this is a relation between the local G invariants of the action imposed by the hypothesis that $|f|$ is a homotopy equivalence. It is a consequence of the three concepts of the preceding section. In particular (1.6) implies that if Y is a pseudofree S^1 manifold and $\omega: \xi \to \eta$ is a quasi-equivalence which is properly S^1 homotopic to θ, $\theta \pitchfork Y$, then

$$\upsilon_x - \upsilon_{f(x)} = \xi_{f(x)} - \eta_{f(x)} \quad \text{in } R(G_x) \tag{2.2}$$

for $x \in X = \theta^{-1}(Y)$ and $\xi_{f(x)}$ denotes ξ restricted to $f(x)$. This and quasi-equivalence imply the second part of 2.1.

The thrust of 2.1 is that the nature of the isotropy groups $\{G_{\bar{x}}, \bar{x} \in \bar{X}\}$ implies a direct product splitting of the *cyclic* groups $G_{\bar{y}}$, $\bar{y} \in \bar{Y}$, and that the slice representations υ_y can only be exchanged in the relation (ii).

Conversely we can fracture exceptional orbits. Set $S_Y = \{\bar{y} \in \bar{Y} \mid G_{\bar{y}} \neq 1\}$.

FRACTURING LEMMA 2.3. *Suppose Y is a pseudofree* S^1 *manifold with* $S_Y = \bigcup_{i=1}^k \bar{y}_i$. *Suppose* $|G_{\bar{y}_1}|$ *is prime to* $|G_{\bar{y}_i}|$, $i > 1$. *Given any splitting* $G_{\bar{y}_1} \cong G_{11} \times G_{12}$ *and any one dimensional* $G_{\bar{y}_1}$ *module* χ *which is a factor of* υ_{y_1}, *there is an* S^1 *manifold*

X with $S_x = \bar{x}_{11} \cup \bar{x}_{12} \cup \bigcup_{i=2}^{k} \bar{x}_i$ and an S^1 normal map $f: X \to Y$ such that

(i) $G_{\bar{x}_{11}} = G_{11}, G_{\bar{x}_{12}} = G_{12}, \bar{f}^{-1}(\bar{y}_1) = \bar{x}_{11} \cup \bar{x}_{12}$,

(ii) $G_{\bar{x}_i} = G_{\bar{y}_i}, i > 1, \bar{f}^{-1}(\bar{y}_i) = \bar{x}_i$,

(iii) $\upsilon_{x_{11}} = \upsilon_{y_1} + \chi^q - \chi, \upsilon_{x_{12}} = \upsilon_{y_1} + \chi^p - \chi$ *where* $p = |G_{11}|$ *and* $q = |G_{12}|$,

(iv) $\upsilon_{x_i} = \upsilon_{y_i}$ *for* $i > 1$.

We can also exchange slice representations subject to 2.1(ii).

EXCHANGE LEMMA 2.4. *Let Y be a pseudofree S^1 manifold with $S_Y = \bigcup_{i=1}^{k} \bar{y}_i$ and $|G_{\bar{y}_1}|$ prime to $|G_{\bar{y}_i}|$ for $i > 1$. Let V be a special $G_{\bar{y}_1}$ module which factors υ_{y_1}. For any $G_{\bar{y}_1}$ module W with* $\dim W = \dim V$ *and $|W| = |V|$, there is an S^1 manifold X and an S^1 normal map $f: X \to Y$ with*

(i) $S_X = \bigcup_{i=1}^{k} \bar{x}_i, \bar{x}_i = \bar{f}^{-1}(\bar{y}_i), G_{\bar{x}_1} = G_{\bar{y}_i}$,

(ii) $\upsilon_{x_1} - \upsilon_{y_1} = W - V$ *in* $R(G_{\bar{x}_1})$,

(iii) $\upsilon_{x_i} - \upsilon_{y_i} = 0, i > 1$.

THEOREM 2.5. *Let Y be a pseudofree S^1 manifold and $f: X \to Y$ an S^1 normal map. If* $\dim Y = 4k + 3$ *assume all $G_{\bar{y}}, y \in Y$, have odd order. Then (X, f) is S^1 normally cobordant to (X^1, f^1) where $|f^1|$ is a homotopy equivalence iff $\sigma_H(f) = 0$ for every p group H in S^1.*

Putting 2.3, 2.4 and 2.5 together gives a converse to 2.1, e.g., let $V = nt + t^q$ be the $(n + 1)$-dimensional S^1 module where $R(S^1) = Z[t, t^{-1}]$ and q and n are odd integers. Compare [**1**].

THEOREM 2.6. *Let $Y = S(V)$ be the unit sphere of V. For any splitting of the unique isotropy group $G_{\bar{y}} \neq 1, y \in Y$,*

(i) $G_{\bar{y}} = Z_{q_1} \times \cdots \times Z_{q_k} = Z_q, \Pi q_i = q$ *and for any set of Z_{q_i} modules V_i, $i = 1, 2, \cdots, k$, satisfying*

(ii) $|\upsilon_y|/|V_i| = (q_i/q) \bmod q_i$,

there is a pseudofree S^1 manifold X with exactly k exceptional orbits $\bigcup_{i=1}^{k} \bar{x}_i$ and isotropy groups Z_{q_i}; moreover, if $G_{\bar{x}_i} = Z_{q_i}, \upsilon_{x_i} = V_i$ and there is an S^1 normal map $f: X \to Y$ with $|f|$ a homotopy equivalence.

REMARKS ON PROOFS. Consider 2.3. Since the order of $G_{\bar{y}_1} = pq$ is prime to $|G_{\bar{y}_i}|$, $i > 1$, there is an S^1 module ρ of dimension 1 which restricts to χ as a $G_{\bar{y}_1}$ module and to 1 as a $G_{\bar{y}_i}$ module $i > 1$. Let $N = \rho^p + \rho^q$, $M = \rho + \rho^{pq}$; then $N \leqq_{S^1} M$ by 1.3. This implies there is an S^1 quasi-equivalence $\omega : \xi = Y \times N \to Y \times M = \eta$. There are no obstructions to making ω equivariantly transverse to $Y \times 0$ yielding an S^1 manifold $X \subset \xi$ with the relevant properties.

The key facts are that (i) $(\eta_{y_1})_{Gy_1} = \chi$ (see (1.5)) which factors υ_{y_1} and (ii) $\xi_{y_i} = \eta_{y_i}$, $i > 1$. The obstructions to S^1 transversality are concentrated at the k exceptional orbits $\bar{y}_i$ and vanish because of (i) and (ii). Since $\eta_{y_1} = \chi + \chi^{pq}$ and $\xi_{y_1} = \chi^p + \chi^q$, 2.3 (iii) and (iv) follow from (2.2).

The proof of 2.6 follows from 2.3, 2.4, 2.5 and a reduction to the case where $q = 1$ so that S^1 acts freely on $S(V)$. In this case we can apply Sullivan's formula [**3**] to compute the Arf invariant obstruction $\sigma_1(f)$ where $f: X \to Y$ is provided (2.3

and 2.4). We can arrange that $\sigma_1(f) = 0$.

In short all the theorems of this section depend on a judicious choice of S^1 modules N and M depending on Y with $N \leqq_{S^1} M$. The S^1 manifold X and map f: $X \to Y$ appear as $\theta^{-1}(Y \times 0)$ where $\theta : X \times N \to Y \times M$ is properly S^1 homotopic to a quasi-equivalence and $\theta \pitchfork Y, f = \theta_{|X}$.

References

1. D. Montgomery and C. T. Yang, *Differentiable pseudo-free circle actions*, Proc. Nat. Acad. Sci. U.S.A. **68** (1971), 894–896. MR **43** #4066.

2. T. Petrie, *Obstructions to transversality for compact Lie groups*, Bull. Amer. Math. Soc. **80** (1974), 1133–1136.

3. D. Sullivan, *Geometric topology*, Mimeographed notes, Princeton, 1967.

University of Bonn
Bonn, Federal Republic of Germany

Rutgers University
New Brunswick, New Jersey 08903, U.S.A.

Proceedings of the International Congress of Mathematicians
Vancouver, 1974

Compact Leaves of Foliations

Paul A. Schweitzer, S. J.*

This paper is a survey of theorems and problems about the existence of compact leaves in foliations of a manifold M with a countable base.

Question 1. For which manifolds M does every C^r codimension q foliation of M have a compact leaf? (Here q and r are given integers, $0 < q < m = \dim M$ and $0 \leqq r \leqq \infty$.)

As an example of a partial answer, Novikov's theorem states that every C^2 codimension one foliation of S^3 has a compact leaf which is a torus [**N**, Theorem 7.1]. On the other hand, the *Seifert conjecture* that every codimension two foliation of S^3 has a compact leaf (i.e., a circle) has been shown to be false in the C^1 case [**S1**], but remains open for C^r foliations when $r \geqq 2$. It is unknown whether Novikov's theorem can be extended to sufficiently smooth codimension one foliations of any higher dimensional manifolds, but it does not extend to C^0 foliations on any manifold of dimension five or more (see Theorem 6, below).

We explore what is known about the above question for codimensions greater than one in §1, and for codimension one in §2.

1. Eliminating closed leaves in codimensions greater than one. A C^r ($0 \leqq r \leqq \infty$) codimension q ($0 < q \leqq m$) *foliation* F of the C^r m-dimensional manifold M is a maximal family of C^r submersions $\alpha: U_\alpha \to \boldsymbol{R}^q$ such that $\{U_\alpha\}_{\alpha \in F}$ is an open cover of M and for every $x \in U_\alpha \cap U_\beta$ there is a local diffeomorphism $g_{\alpha\beta x}$ of $\boldsymbol{R}^q$ such that $\alpha = g_{\alpha\beta x} \circ \beta$ in a neighborhood of x. The sets $\alpha^{-1}(y)$ for all $\alpha \in F$ and $y \in \boldsymbol{R}^q$ form a base of the *leaf topology* on the underlying set of M, and the components relative to this topology are C^r submanifolds of M called the *leaves* of F. A leaf is *closed* if it is a closed subset of M relative to the original topology. The C^r codi-

*Partially supported by CNPq T.C. 17.029, CAPES, and FINEP.

mension q foliations F_0 and F_1 are C^r *homotopic* if they are connected by a one parameter family of foliations F_t of $M \times \{t\}$, $t \in \mathbf{R}$, whose leaves taken together are the leaves of a C^r codimension $q + 1$ foliation of $M \times \mathbf{R}$.

THEOREM 1 [**S1**]. *Let F be a C^r foliation of M of codimension $q < m$. If either*
(i) $q = 2$ *and* $r = 0$ *or* 1, *or*
(ii) $q < 2$ *and* $0 \leqq r \leqq \infty$,
then F is C^r homotopic to a foliation with no closed leaf.

When $q = m - 1 > 2$ this is a theorem of Wilson [**W**]. When $q = 2$, this theorem implies the falsity of the Seifert conjecture for C^1 foliations.

In order to elucidate the content of this theorem, we recall that a set S in a manifold M with a foliation F is *saturated* (relative to F) if S is the union of a set of leaves of F. A closed nonempty saturated set C is *minimal* if it contains no other set with these properties. Thus every closed leaf is a minimal set, and every leaf contained in a minimal set C is dense in C. Since the property of being a compact nonempty saturated set is inductive, the usual argument by Zorn's lemma shows that every such set contains a minimal set. In particular, every compact foliated manifold must contain a minimal set. As a consequence, when in proving Theorem 1 we modify the given foliation to eliminate the closed leaves from among the minimal sets, it will generally be necessary to introduce other minimal sets.

The desired modifications can be made locally, as follows. A small transversal open q-manifold N with a small tubular neighborhood diffeomorphic to $N \times D^q$ is constructed, such that the induced foliation has leaves $\{n\} \times D^q$, $n \in N$. We deform this foliation by pushing the leaves along the trajectories of a smooth flow Z on N with a compact saturated set C in such a way that all closed leaves which meet C are cut open. New minimal sets are created, but it is possible to avoid introducing any new closed leaves by choosing C to be an *exceptional* minimal set of the foliation induced by Z (i.e., a minimal set which is neither a single closed trajectory nor all of N).

In the case $q = 2$, we may choose N to be the torus punctured by removing one point, and Z to be the restriction of Denjoy's toroidal flow with exceptional minimal set C [**D**]. The conclusion in this case is only C^1 since Denjoy's flow is C^1 but not C^2. (See [**S1**] for the complete proof of Theorem 1.)

It seems unlikely that S^3 could be a minimal set of a codimension two foliation, but if it were, that would give a new type of foliation of S^3 without compact leaves. This is a special case of an interesting open question.

Question 2. Which manifolds can be minimal sets of C^r codimension q foliations?

2. The compact leaf property in codimension one. The state of the question whether foliations of M must have compact leaves is different in codimension one, as several affirmative results are known. The following definition will simplify their statements.

DEFINITION. A C^r manifold M has the C^r *compact leaf property* (CLP) if M has a C^r codimension one foliation and every such foliation has a compact leaf.

If we replace "foliation" by "transversely oriented foliation" (i.e., a foliation for which the bundle of vectors orthogonal to the leaves is trivial) in this definition we get the analogous property CLP$^+$.

REMARK. It is now known that a manifold M admits a C^∞ codimension one foliation if and only if it admits a codimension one plane field (equivalently, if either M is open or has Euler characteristic zero). Phillips **[P]** proved this for open manifolds and Thurston **[T2]** recently extended it to closed manifolds.

THEOREM 2 [**K**, P. 153]. *The Klein bottle has the C^0 CLP.*

THEOREM 3 [**N**]. *A closed 3-manifold M has the C^2 CLP if either*
(i) $\pi_1(M)$ *is finite, or*
(ii) $\pi_2(M) \neq 0$.

CONJECTURE. In these cases, M has the C^0 CLP.

THEOREM 4 [**T1**]. *If the closed 3-manifold M is the total space of an oriented circle bundle ξ over an orientable surface N whose Euler numbers satisfy $|\chi(\xi)| > |\chi(N)| > 0$, then M has the C^2 CLP$^+$.*

The above results are proved by detailed geometric arguments. For example, Thurston shows that if the given foliation has no toroidal leaf it must be isotopic to a foliation transversal to the fibers, and then applies a result of John Wood involving the two Euler numbers. On the other hand, J. Plante **[P]** uses a homological argument involving invariant transversal measures (or currents or "asymptotic cycles") to establish the following interesting result. (I thank Dennis Sullivan for informing me of the strengthened version given here. For definitions and an earlier version, see **[P]**. For full details, see [**P3**, 6.4].)

THEOREM 5. *Let M be a smooth closed manifold with first Betti number less than two. If a C^1 transversely orientable foliation F of M has a leaf with nonexponential growth, then F has a compact leaf.*

COROLLARY. *If the fundamental group $\pi_1(M)$ of a closed 3-manifold M has nonexponential growth and the first Betti number of M is less than two, then M has the C^2 CLP$^+$.*

This corollary (Plante [**P2**, 7.4]) follows since a leaf L with exponential growth in a C^2 transversely orientable codimension one foliation F of M will be covered by nonclosed leaves in the induced foliation on the universal cover of M which has nonexponential growth by the hypothesis on $\pi_1(M)$. This implies the existence of a closed null homotopic curve transversal to F, which by Novikov's proof implies the existence of a compact leaf. The corollary gives a new proof of Rosenberg's result that the 3-manifold M has the C^2 CLP$^+$ if M is a torus bundle over S^1 obtained by suspending a linear automorphism $A \in SL(2, \mathbf{Z})$ of $T^2 = \mathbf{R}^2/\mathbf{Z}^2$ such that the eigenvalues of A are on the unit circle and both different from 1.

In contrast to these affirmative results, the result is negative if the smoothness is relaxed and the dimension increased.

THEOREM 6 [**S2**]. *No manifold of dimension five or more has the C^0 CLP.*

To understand this theorem, examine the Reeb foliation R. On one side of the torus leaf T^2 the leaves spiral around one of the generators of $\pi_1(T^2)$, but on the other side they spiral around the complementary generator. This phenomenon of leaves spiraling in toward a closed leaf L along distinct generators of $\pi_1(L)$ is related to the "vanishing cycles" in Novikov's proof, and also occurs in Thurston's general construction [**T2**] and earlier particular constructions of codimension one foliations of closed manifolds (Lawson, Durfee, etc.).

The essence of the proof of Theorem 6 involves the insertion of an exceptional minimal set C which separates the manifold and toward which the leaves spiral in along different directions in distinct complementary components. The exceptional minimal set C is derived from Raymond's construction of a C^∞ codimension one foliation of S^3 containing an exceptional minimal set [**RA**]. (For full details see [**S2**].)

The question remains open when we impose a greater degree of smoothness. For example, does S^5 have the C^2 CLP?

References

[**D**] A. Denjoy, *Sur les courbes définies par les équations différentielles à la surface du tore*, J. Math. Pures Appl. **11** (1932), 333–375.

[**K**] H. Kneser, *Reguläre Kurvenscharen auf den Ringflächen*, Math. Ann. **91** (1924), 135–154.

[**N**] S. P. Novikov, *Topology of foliations*, Trudy Moskov. Mat. Obšč. **14** (1965), 248–278 = Trans. Moscow Math. Soc. **1965**, 268–304. MR **34** #824.

[**P**] J. Plante, *A generalization of the Poincaré-Bendixson theorem for foliations of codimension-one*, Topology **12** (1973), 177–182.

[**P2**] ———, *On the existence of exceptional minimal sets in foliations of codimension one*, J. Differential Equations **15** (1974), 178–194.

[**P3**] ———, *Foliations with measure preserving holonomy*, 1975, preprint.

[**PH**] A. Phillips, *Foliations on open manifolds*. I, Comment. Math. Helv. **43** (1968), 204–211. MR **37** #4829.

[**RA**] B. Raymond, *Cantor sets and foliations* (to appear).

[**R**] G. Reeb, *Sur certaines propriétés topologiques des variétés feuilletées*, Actualités Sci. Indust., no. 1183 = Publ. Inst. Math. Univ. Strasbourg 11, 91–154, 157–158. Hermann, Paris, 1952. MR **14**, 1113.

[**S1**] P. A. Schweitzer, *Counterexamples to the Seifert conjecture and opening closed leaves of foliations*, Ann. of Math. (2) **100** (1974), 386–400.

[**S2**] ———, *Codimension one foliations without compact leaves* (in preparation).

[**T1**] W. Thurston, *Foliations of 3-manifolds which are circle bundles*, Thesis, Univ. of California, Berkeley, Calif., 1972.

[**T2**] ———, *Existence of codimension one foliations* (to appear).

[**W**] F. W. Wilson, Jr., *On the minimal sets of non-singular vector fields*, Ann. of Math. (2) **84** (1966), 529–536. MR **34** #2028.

Pontifícia Universidade Católica do Rio de Janeiro
Rio de Janeiro, Brazil

Proceedings of the International Congress of Mathematicians
Vancouver, 1974

On the Construction and Classification of Foliations

William Thurston

Given a large supply of some sort of fabric, what kinds of manifolds can be made from it, in a way that the patterns match up along the seams? This is a very general question, which has been studied by diverse means in differential topology and differential geometry. For open manifolds, Gromov's theorem gives a good answer for a wide variety of fabrics. The techniques needed to analyze such a question on a closed manifold are usually different, at least to a casual eye.

A foliation is a manifold made out of a striped fabric—with infinitely thin stripes, having no space between them. The complete stripes, or "*leaves*", of the foliation are submanifolds; if the leaves have codimension k, the foliation is called a codimension k foliation.

In order that a manifold admit a codimension k foliation, it must have a plane field of dimension $(n - k)$.

THEOREM 1. *Let M^n be any manifold without boundary. If M^n has an $(n - 1)$-plane field, then every $(n - 1)$-plane field τ^{n-1} on M^n is homotopic to the tangent-plane field of a C^∞ codimension one foliation.*

See [**9**].

COROLLARY. *Every closed connected manifold with zero Euler characteristic has a C^∞ codimension one foliation.*

THEOREM 2. *Every smooth plane field τ^{n-k} on a closed manifold is homotopic to the tangent plane field of a Lipschitz foliation, with C^∞ leaves.*

See [**11**].

The proof makes use of a slightly altered version of a result of John Mather [**4**] which states that the homology of the group of homeomorphisms of $\boldsymbol{R}^n$ with compact support, considered as a discrete group, is trivial.

Bott has shown this to be false if one demands C^2 foliations, for all real characteristic classes of the normal bundle of a C^2 foliation of codimension k must vanish above dimension $2k$ [**1**]. The foliations of Theorem 2 can be found in a category where first derivatives of the transition functions make sense, but Bott's argument depends essentially on the use of second derivatives.

General statements can be made about C^∞ foliations, and foliations on manifolds with boundary, but first some background is required. Reeb gave some counterexamples to the existence of codimension one foliations on manifolds with boundary in his thesis. These depend on the Reeb stability theorem, which I will state in a generalized form:

GENERALIZED REEB STABILITY THEOREM (THEOREM 3). (a) *Let $\mathscr{F}$ be a codimension one C^1, transversely oriented foliation on a compact manifold M. Suppose L^{n-1} is a compact leaf of $\mathscr{F}$ such that $H^1(L; \boldsymbol{R}) \approx 0$. Then, every leaf of $\mathscr{F}$ is diffeomorphic with L^{n-1}, and M^n fibers over S^1 or O^1 with fiber L^{n-1}.*

(b) *Let $\mathscr{F}$ be a C^1 codimension k foliation. If L is a compact leaf of $\mathscr{F}$ such that the linear holonomy around L is trivial, and if $H^1(L; \boldsymbol{R}) \approx 0$, then the holonomy around L is trivial, and L has a tubular neighborhood which fibers over D^k with leaves as fibers.*

See Reeb [7] and Thurston [**10**].

Reeb proved this theorem under the hypothesis that $\pi_1(L)$ is finite, and he allowed C^0 foliations.

As a corollary, many manifolds with boundary do not have codimension one foliations tangent to the boundary. But these are the only counterexamples.

THEOREM 4. *Let M^n be a compact manifold such that each component of ∂M^n has a nontrivial first real cohomology group. Then every $(n - 1)$-plane field tangent to ∂M^n is homotopic, rel ∂M^n, to a C^∞ foliation which is trivial in a neighborhood of ∂M^n.*

For more refined statements, the concept of a Haefliger structure is needed. A Haefliger structure is a foliated microbundle, i.e., a microbundle of dimension k with codimension k foliation transverse to the fiber. Haefliger showed that there is a classifying space $B\Gamma_k^r$ for codimension k, C^∞, Haefliger structures [**3**]. There is a canonical map $B\Gamma_k^r \to BO_k$. The following theorem is due to Haefliger in the case M^n is an open manifold:

THEOREM 5. *Let M^n be a manifold, τ^{n-k} a plane field on M^n, let $\nu^k = T(M^n)/\tau^{n-k}$, and let $\chi: M^n \to BO_k$ be the classifying map for ν_k. Then τ^{n-k} is homotopic to a C^r foliation iff χ factors through a map to $B\Gamma_k^r$, and every such factorization is realized by a foliation with tangent bundle homotopic to τ^{n-k}.*

If $k \geqq 2$, this theorem is true relative to a closed set K such that τ^{n-k} is integrable in a neighborhood of K. If $k = 1$ and if τ^{n-k} is transverse to ∂M^n and integrable in a neighborhood, this is true rel ∂M^n [**9**], [**11**], [**12**].

COROLLARY 1. *If M^n has a k-frame field, or a k-dimensional subbundle which admits a flat connection, then the complementary bundle is homotopic to a C^∞ foliation.*

This was proved by Phillips for open manifolds.

COROLLARY 2. *When $k \leqq n/2$, S^n has a codimension k foliation provided it has a k-plane field.*

Direct, specific, constructions for foliation on spheres are by no means trivial. Reeb first discovered a codimension one foliation of S^3 in his thesis in 1944. There was a long gap until Lawson found codimension one foliations for S^5, S^7, and all spheres of the form S^{2^k+3} in 1970 [**4**]. The next year, Durfee [**2**] and Tamura [**8**] independently generalized this to all odd-dimensional spheres.

COROLLARY 3. *Every 2-plane field is homotopic to a C^∞ foliation.*

This follows from a result on the connectedness of $B\Gamma_k^\infty$ [**6**], [**13**]. This has a close connection to the theorem that the group of C^∞ diffeomorphisms isotopic to the identity is simple, for any closed connected manifold—see the article of Mather in these PROCEEDINGS, or Mather [**6**] and Thurston [**13**].

References

1. R. Bott, *On topological obstruction to integrability*, Proc. Sympos. Pure Math., vol. 16, Amer. Math. Soc., Providence, R.I., 1970, pp. 127–131. MR **42** #1155.

2. A. Durfee, *Foliations of odd-dimensional spheres*, Ann. of Math. (2) **96** (1972), 407–411; erratum, ibid. (2) **97** (1973), 187. MR **47** #7757.

3. A. Haefliger, *Homotopy and integrability*, Manifolds—Amsterdam 1970 (Proc. Nuffic Summer School), Lecture Notes in Math., vol. 197, Springer, Berlin, 1971, pp. 133–163. MR **44** #2251.

4. H. B. Lawson, Jr., *Codimension-one foliations of spheres*, Ann. of Math. (2) **94** (1971), 494–503. MR **44** #4774.

5. J. Mather, *The vanishing of the homology of certain groups of homeomorphisms*, Topology **10** (1971), 297–298. MR **44** #5973.

6. ———, *Integrability in codimension* 1, Comment. Math. Helv. **48** (1973), 195–233.

7. G. Reeb, *Sur certaines propriétés topologiques des variétés feiulletées*, Actualités Sci. Indust., no. 1183 = Publ. Inst. Math. Univ. Strasbourg 11, Hermann, Paris, 1952, pp. 91–154, 157–158. MR **14,** 1113.

8. I. Tamura, *Every odd dimensional homotopy sphere has a foliation of codimension one*, Comment. Math. Helv. **47** (1972), 164–170. MR **47** #5887.

9. W. Thurston, *Existence of codimension one foliations* (to appear).

10. ———, *A generalization of the Reeb stability theorem*, Topology (to appear).

11. ———, *The theory of foliations of codimension greater than one*, Comment. Math. Helv. (2) **49** (1974), 214–231.

12. ———, *A local construction of foliations for three-manifolds*, Proc. Sympos. Pure Math., vol. 27, Part 1, Amer. Math. Soc., Providence, R. I., 1975, pp. 317–324.

13. ———, *Foliations and groups of diffeomorphisms*, Bull. Amer. Math. Soc. **80** (1974), 304–307.

PRINCETON UNIVERSITY
PRINCETON, NEW JERSEY 08540, U.S.A.

Index

Roman numbers refer to pages in Volume 1.
Italic numbers refer to pages in Volume 2.